May 21–23, 2012
Scottsdale, Arizona, USA

**Association for
Computing Machinery**

Advancing Computing as a Science & Profession

PODS'12

Proceedings of the 31st Symposium on
Principles of Database Systems

Editors:
Michael Benedikt, Markus Krötzsch, and Maurizio Lenzerini

Sponsored by:
ACM SIGACT, ACM SIGART, and ACM SIGMOD

Supported by:
**SAP, Greenplum-EMC^2, IO, Microsoft, Oracle, Facebook, Google,
IBM Research, LinkedIn, MarkLogic, Turn, Twitter, Vertica, VMware,
Actian, AT&T, HP, @WalmartLabs, Yahoo!, Arizona State University,
University of Arizona, and National Science Foundation**

Association for Computing Machinery

Advancing Computing as a Science & Profession

The Association for Computing Machinery
2 Penn Plaza, Suite 701
New York, New York 10121-0701

Notice to Past Authors of ACM-Published Articles

ISBN: 978-1-4503-1248-6

Additional copies may be ordered prepaid from:

ACM Order Department
PO Box 30777
New York, NY 10087-0777, USA

Phone: 1-800-342-6626 (USA and Canada)
+1-212-626-0500 (Global)
Fax: +1-212-944-1318
E-mail: acmhelp@acm.org
Hours of Operation: 8:30 am – 4:30 pm ET

Printed in the USA

PODS 2012 General Chair's Welcome Message

It is our great pleasure to welcome you to the *2012 ACM Symposium on Principles of Database Systems – PODS'12*, held in Scottsdale, Arizona, USA, on May 20–23, 2012, in conjunction with the 2012 ACM SIGMOD International Conference on Management of Data.

This year's symposium continues its tradition of being the premier international conference on the theoretical aspects of data management. Since the first edition of the symposium in 1982, the PODS papers are distinguished by a rigorous approach to widely diverse problems in databases, often bringing to bear techniques from a variety of different areas, including computational logic, finite model theory, computational complexity, algorithm design and analysis, programming languages, and artificial intelligence. The interested reader is referred to the PODS web pages at http://www09.sigmod.org/sigmod/pods/ for various information on the history of the conference series.

As usual, putting together *PODS'12* was a team effort. We are particularly grateful to the Program Chair, Michael Benedikt, who did a magnificent job in selecting and coordinating the program committee members, and to the whole program committee, who worked very hard in reviewing papers and providing feedback for authors. We are also grateful to the SIGMOD 2012 General Chairs, K. Selçuk Candan and Yi Chen, for their collaboration in all the issues requiring coordination between SIGMOD and PODS. Finally, we thank Markus Krötzsch, the PODS'12 Proceedings and Publicity Chair; Wim Martens, for maintaining the PODS web pages, and all our sponsors, in particular the ACM Special Interest Groups on Management of Data, for their invaluable support.

We wish you a profitable and enjoyable stay in Arizona, and we hope that you will find the PODS'12 program exciting and thought provoking, in the best tradition of the PODS Symposium.

Maurizio Lenzerini
PODS 2012 General Chair

PODS 2012 Program Chair's Welcome Message

First, a brief overview of the contents of this volume, the proceedings of the thirty-first ACM SIGMOD-SIGACT-SIGART Symposium on Principles of Database Systems (PODS 2012). The proceedings includes an overview of the keynote address by Surajit Chaudhuri along with two papers based on invited tutorials, one by Michael Mahoney and one by Benjamin Pierce. There are 26 research papers that were selected by the Program Committee, out of 101 submissions with authors from over 25 countries across the world. Out of the 26 accepted papers, the program committee selected the paper *Worst Case Optimal Join Algorithms* by Hung Q. Ngo, Ely Porat, Christopher Ré and Atri Rudra for the PODS 2012 Best Paper Award. In addition, the announcement of the 2012 ACM PODS Alberto O. Mendelzon Test-of-Time Award appears in the proceedings, given to *Containment and Equivalence for an XPath Fragment* by Gerome Miklau and Dan Suciu. The latter paper originally appeared in the proceedings of PODS 2002. Congratulations to the authors of these papers.

The review process was grueling, and involved enormous effort from a large group of researchers. This year PODS experimented with the use of an External Review Committee, consisting of distinguished experts in areas of particular interest to PODS, in addition to our core Program Committee. We relied heavily on the Easychair system for management of all aspects of the review process, and we are extremely grateful to Andrei Voronkov for his help in adding and modifying new features to support the External Review Committee. All members of the Program Committee, External Review Committee, and the additional external referees deserve thanks for their work – both for producing the selection of papers that appear here in the proceedings, and for providing high-quality feedback to all authors of submitted papers.

The proceedings would not have been possible without the constant attention and support of Maurizio Lenzerini, the PODS General Chair. The PODS Executive Committee helped select the Program Committee and External Review Committee, and played an important role in advising on issues of policy during the conference. Special thanks are also due to Markus Krötzsch, who served as the PODS Proceedings Chair and as PODS Publicity Chair – both of these jobs were more complicated than usual this year due to the earlier date of the conference. In advising us we leaned heavily on the advice of Thomas Schwentick and Wim Martens, the previous PODS Program Chair and Publicity Chair, who patiently answered questions on every aspect of the conference.

Many people outside of the PODS community also provided critical support. I want to particularly express heartfelt thanks to K. Selçuk Candan and Yi Chen, the SIGMOD General Chairs: great colleagues who supported PODS in every possible way. We also thank Huiping Cao and Yan Qi, the Web/Information Chairs, for their great work in managing the website.

Finally, I thank the SIGMOD Executive Committee for their help in arranging supplemental support from Easychair for the 2012 electronic review process, and the SIGMOD/PODS sponsors for their support.

Michael Benedikt
PODS 2012 Program Chair

Table of Contents

Opening and Keynote Address
Session Chair: Maurizio Lenzerini *(University of Rome La Sapienza)*

Session 1: Streaming
Session Chair: Milan Vojnovic *(Microsoft Research, Cambridge)*

Session 2: Awards Session
Session Chair: Richard Hull *(IBM T.J. Watson Research Center)*

Session 3: Tutorial Session 1
Session Chair: Phokion Kolaitis *(University of California, Santa Cruz and IBM Almaden Research Center)*

Session 4: Privacy and Semantic Web
Session Chair: Pierre Senellart *(Telecom ParisTech)*

Session 10: Streaming and Aggregation

Session Chair: Yufei Tao *(Chinese University of Hong Kong)*

PODS 2012 Symposium Organization

General Chair: Maurizio Lenzerini *(University of Rome La Sapienza, Italy)*

Program Chair: Michael Benedikt *(University of Oxford, UK)*

Proceedings & Publicity Chair: Markus Krötzsch *(University of Oxford, UK)*

Program Committee: Mikhail Atallah *(Purdue University, USA)*
Toon Calders *(Technische Universiteit Eindhoven, Netherlands)*
Diego Calvanese *(Free University of Bozen-Bolzano, Italy)*
James Cheney *(University of Edinburgh, UK)*
Graham Cormode *(AT&T Labs Research, USA)*
Alin Deutsch *(University of California, San Diego, USA)*
Gianluigi Greco *(Universita della Calabria, Italy)*
Todd J. Green *(University of California, Davis, USA)*
Martin Grohe *(Humboldt-Universität zu Berlin, Germany)*
Marc Gyssens *(Hasselt University, Belgium)*
T.S. Jayram *(IBM Research – Almaden, USA & IBM Research – India)*
Daniel Kifer *(Penn State University, USA)*
Phokion Kolaitis *(University of California, Santa Cruz
      & IBM Research – Almaden, USA)*
Rasmus Pagh *(IT University of Copenhagen, Denmark)*
Luc Segoufin *(INRIA Cachan, France)*
Pierre Senellart *(Télécom ParisTech, France)*
Sophie Tison *(Lille University, France)*
Victor Vianu *(University of California, San Diego, USA)*
David Woodruff *(IBM Research – Almaden, USA)*

External Review Committee: **Querying and Mining of Unstructured Data**
AnHai Doan *(University of Wisconsin, USA)*
Aristides Gionis *(Yahoo! Research Barcelona, Spain)*
Djoerd Hiemstra *(University of Twente, Netherlands)*
Stefano Leonardi *(University of Rome La Sapienza, Italy)*
Evimaria Terzi *(Boston University, USA)*

Web Services, Web Programming and Data-Centric Workflow
Wil van der Aalst *(Technische Universiteit Eindhoven, Netherlands)*
Anders Møller *(Aarhus University, Denmark)*
Farouk Toumani *(ISIMA & Blaise Pascal University, France)*
David Walker *(Princeton University, USA)*
Karsten Wolf *(University of Rostock, Germany)*

Learning of Data Models and Queries
Deepak Agarwal *(Yahoo! Research Silicon Valley, USA)*
James Cussens *(York University, USA)*
Amol Deshpande *(University of Maryland, USA)*
Kristian Kersting *(Fraunhofer Institute IAIS & University of Bonn,
      Germany)*

Additional reviewers (continued):

Kobbi Nissim	Slawek Staworko
Dan Olteanu	Francesco Scarcello
Martin Otto	Dan Suciu
Vinayaka Pandit	Yufei Tao
Jean-Marc Petit	Giorgio Terracina
Jeff Phillips	Srikanta Tirthapura
Pawel Parys	Marc Tommasi
Debmalya Panigrahi	Jonathan Ullman
Mihai Patrascu	Gregory Valiant
Vibhor Rastogi	Philippe Vanheeghe
Romain Rouvoy	Stijn Vansummeren
Paolo Romano	Sergei Vassilvitzkii
Riccardo Rosati	Jan Vondrak
Sambuddha Roy	Jef Wijsen
Srinivasa Rao Satti	Ryan Williams
Mukund Sundararajan	Ke Yi
Yogish Sabharwal	Hongbo Zhang
Nicole Schweikardt	Qin Zhang

Alberto O. Mendelzon Test-of-Time Award Committee:

Richard Hull (chair, *IBM T. J. Watson Research Center, USA*)

Phokion Kolaitis *(University of California, Santa Cruz & IBM Research – Almaden, USA)*

Dirk Van Gucht *(Computer Science Department, Indiana University, USA)*

PODS 2012 Sponsors & Supporters

ACM Sponsor:

Diamond:

Platinum:

Gold:

IBM Research

Silver:

Academic:

Student Travel Awards:

What Next? A Half-Dozen Data Management Research Goals for Big Data and the Cloud

Surajit Chaudhuri
Microsoft Research
surajitc@microsoft.com

ABSTRACT

In this short paper, I describe six data management research challenges relevant for Big Data and the Cloud. Although some of these problems are not new, their importance is amplified by Big Data and Cloud Computing.

Categories and Subject Descriptors

H.2.0 [Database Management]: - General.

General Terms

Algorithms, Performance, Theory.

Keywords

Big Data, Data Analytics, Cloud Infrastructure, Research Challenges.

1. INTRODUCTION

Two accelerating trends are beginning to have impact on the landscape of data management. One is *Big Data*. It is a catch phrase that has many different interpretations but in this paper I will use this term primarily in the context of data analytics. In recent years, here has been a very significant expansion of data analytics [5]. This phenomenon has been fueled by decreasing cost of acquisition of data as more and more data is *born digitally* enabling businesses to collect data that is extremely *fine-grained*. Very low cost of data storage has made it attractive to retain such fine-grained data in the hope of obtaining business insight (e.g., understanding customers). Here are a few specific characteristics of the Big Data phenomenon as they relate to analytics:

- Exploring text and semi-structured data to see if these sources could provide additional insight.

- Narrowing the time gap between data acquisition and acting on a business decision based on the data, sometimes referred to as near real-time business analytics.

- Experimenting with deep analytics beyond the functionality offered by the traditional business intelligence (BI) stack.

- Seeking low cost, highly scalable analytics platforms.

A second disruptive trend that is influencing our field, and indeed

the entire computing industry, is the rise of *cloud computing*. The IT infrastructure is gravitating towards a rent model of usage that has the benefit of elasticity (Infrastructure as Service). There is also increasing appetite for web-based services (Software as Service) instead of using packaged on-premise software. The most ambitious aspect of cloud computing is Platform as Service. Unlike Infrastructure as Service, the goal of these platforms is to enable creation of scalable applications without having to think in terms of virtual machines. But, these platforms do impact the model of application development and thus have the danger of lock-in.

These two disruptive trends are shaping our field and it is still not clear what will be the characteristics of the infrastructure and platforms that will emerge from these disruptions. In this paper, instead of speculating on how the industry will evolve, I have tried to identify a few key data management research challenges in the context of big data and the cloud that are hard but where breakthroughs may have significant impact. I will focus on six such problems where I have spent some time working with my colleagues. I have attempted to pick problems with a mix of conceptual, algorithmic, and systems challenges. While not all of these problems are new, the emergence of Big Data and the cloud have amplified the importance of all the six challenges. The rest of the paper consists of brief descriptions of each of these problems, brief remarks on a few other open questions, and the conclusion. The title and the structure of this paper are inspired by Jim Gray's Turing Award lecture.

2. DATA PRIVACY

The term privacy is increasingly being used to refer to all aspects of access to data. With the exploding use of online services and proliferation of mobile devices, the concern about access to and sharing of personal information is growing. Increasing volume and variety of data sets within an enterprise also highlight the need for control of access to such information. While resolution to the policy issues is very important for consumers and enterprises alike, it is also crucial to understand what support for privacy can be provided at the platform level to ease implementation of privacy policies. The three well-known pillars of privacy mechanisms are access control, auditing, and statistical privacy. There are key open questions for each of these facets. For access control, many argue that we should be supporting predicate-based fine-grained control. Such an approach has the potential to provide tighter control on access to information but at the cost of increased complexity of administration as well as performance challenges in providing such support. An example of a mechanism to enable such fine-grained access has been described in [19]. Other experts hold a contrarian view that a rigid access control has been a failure and only coarse-grain access control policies should be implemented [16]. The area of statistical privacy is still at a rather exploratory stage although it has been an active area of research within our field. The initial set of proposals based on data perturbation did not provide the needed combination of high utility along with strong protection from attacks leveraging background knowledge [10]. The model around Differential Privacy [9] provides a sound theoretical foundation. However, whether this framework can be reduced to practice is open to question. Specifically, effective utility of query answers subject to such statistical privacy techniques in real-world SQL applications is unknown. An initial effort to enable such study was the development of PINQ [17]. Probably the most non-controversial area of data privacy and security has been auditing. However, much of today's auditing infrastructure is ad-hoc and unlike statistical privacy and access control, this area has received less attention in research. We also have no conceptual framework to help applications decide how they should deploy a combination of access control and auditing. *Challenge 1: Redefine the abstractions for access control and auditing for data platforms.*

3. APPROXIMATE RESULTS

As the data sets continue to grow larger, the need to do "back of the envelope" calculation to answer queries or progressive refinement of query results is more important than ever. This goal so far has remained unfulfilled except for the simplest of the queries although such functionality is more important for complex business intelligence queries. The difficulty with this problem begins with semantics itself. The simplest semantics could be that of providing a uniform random sample of the result of the query. Yet, such a definition is unsatisfactory. Consider a simple OLAP aggregation query with a measure attribute (e.g., sum of sales by town during winter). The notion of approximation for such a query has two dimensions. One dimension of approximation is how accurate the measure attribute is (e.g., sum of sales for a given town). The other dimension is which of the groups (e.g., towns) are missing in the output. Beyond the semantics, there are significant algorithmic challenges as well. Efficiently obtaining a sample of a simple select-project-join is nontrivial [1][3]. Typically, data is physically organized to serve the access patterns that best match the workload. Not surprisingly, query execution plans are also picked to take advantage of the existing access patterns to reduce cost. The net consequence is execution of even a simple select-project-join query in a database systems often results in the answer stream having ordering properties which prevent using the prefix of the result stream as a random sample of the query. One approach to sidestep this difficulty is to lay out the data randomly and use physical operators for query execution that preserve the randomness of resulting data streams [12][13]. However, the challenge is to ensure that such techniques can be generalized and achieve a significant speed-up over traditional query execution. This remains an open problem and offers opportunities for novel thinking on semantics and alternate execution strategies. *Challenge 2: Devise a querying technique for approximate results that is an order of magnitude faster compared to traditional query execution.*

4. DATA EXPLORATION TO ENABLE DEEP ANALYTICS

One of the big drivers of excitement around Big Data is the expectation that we will be able to identify novel insights in data to drive business decisions. Machine learning is viewed as a key technology that will unlock such insight. Indeed, machine learning has been successfully used for decades in a number of vertical applications (e.g., fraud detection, internet search and advertising). Machine learning toolkits of varying quality and popularity, both commercial and open-source, are widely available. However, effectively leveraging the machine learning toolkits requires understanding of probability and statistics. Even for those who possess that expertise (often called data scientists), the challenge in identifying deep insights from data is quite significant. The critical stage where data scientists lack support in today's infrastructure is in the phase of preparing data for deeper analysis, e.g., in identifying candidate features for machine learning models. Today, for data scientists to be effective they need to be proficient in data querying and use that as the primary means of such exploration. The fundamental difficulties they face to efficiently search for deep insights in data are: (a) How to identify relevant fragments of data easily from a multitude of data sources, (b) How to use data cleaning techniques such as approximate joins across two data sources, (c) How to sample results of a query progressively (see Section 3), and (d) How to obtain rich visualization? While building such a data exploration platform requires systems skills, there are fundamental algorithmic challenges in each of the problems (a)-(d) above as well. *Challenge 3: Build an environment to enable data exploration for deep analytics.*

5. ENTERPRISE DATA ENRICHMENT WITH WEB AND SOCIAL MEDIA

The Big Data phenomenon has provided the opportunity to leverage many diverse sources of data, both structured and unstructured. It is the unique properties of web data such as its vastness, its statistical redundancy and availability of user feedback (via query logs and click information) that has made extraction of structured information (e.g., entities) from web data especially interesting. Such entity extraction techniques have been successfully used for identifying references to specific product names, locations, or people in web pages. For example, the Voice of the Customer class of enterprise applications tries to identify meaningful trends and sentiment information for a given set of products from web pages and blogs. While the rise of these applications represents rich examples of connecting enterprise data to web and social media, building such applications to achieve high precision and good recall is difficult and invariably requires sophisticated custom analytic techniques. Therefore, it would be ideal to identify a set of high precision services that shield the application developers from the above difficulties. For example, given a set of product names and a partial list of their attribute-value pairs, search engine providers and social networking sites could provide a service to identify objects in their respective repositories (web pages, social media posts) that mention one of more of the given entities with high precision and good recall [14][15][23]. Another example of a useful service will be product data conflation based on web information, e.g., discovering common synonyms of products from the web query log and click information [6]. Identifying such high value services, offering a set of derived data assets (e.g., structured contents of infoboxes in Wikipedia), and providing information extraction tools together can help create a platform that has the potential to democratize use of the web and social media data for a much wider class of applications. *Challenge 4: Identify services that given a list of entities and their properties, returns enrichment of entities based on information in web and social media with sufficiently high precision and recall.*

6. QUERY OPTIMIZATION

Query Optimization has been crucial for efficiently answering a large class of complex analytic SQL queries. Even for newer platforms based on MapReduce and its variants, the interest in leveraging higher level query languages (HiveQL [22], PigLatin [18], and SCOPE [2]) is extremely strong. In such highly parallel platforms, the cost of shuffling data across nodes is considerable and thus query optimization and physical design continue to be critical elements of the infrastructure. It is important to take a fresh look at query optimization because Big Data platforms such as MapReduce introduce changes to some of the fundamental assumptions in query optimization, as explained below. Recall that one of the reasons why MapReduce is a popular framework is because it is easy to express data parallel programs where Map and Reduce functions could be user-defined code. For query optimization, the above is a major departure because optimization of user-defined functions in relational databases was not a central issue. As a consequence, traditional techniques for estimation of sizes of intermediate results need to be revisited. Another related issue is that unlike relational databases, there is no opportunity to create pre-defined statistical summaries of the full data set. Together, these two factors compound the already well-known difficulties of cardinality estimation for query sub-expressions [4]. However, unlike relational systems, MapReduce uses materialization extensively. Therefore, it is attractive to revisit the class of optimization techniques originally pioneered by Teradata to do "optimize and execute" iteratively and inform the next stage of query optimization of properties of intermediate results. Yet another difference is the user expectation that MapReduce systems are batch oriented and hence we can relax the traditional approach to query optimization that had an implicit requirement that optimization time for ad-hoc queries be limited. Although I have cast the above discussion primarily in the context of MapReduce platforms, much of the above is also relevant for parallel SQL database systems. *Challenge 5: Rethink query optimization for data parallel platforms.*

7. PERFORMANCE ISOLATION FOR MULTI-TENANCY

The movement to the cloud is inspired by the opportunity to reduce cost and to leverage the elasticity it offers. For a cloud system provider to deliver on these promises requires multiple users (tenants) to share the same server resources. However, in order for enterprises to feel comfortable to use cloud services, they would also like to achieve performance isolation, i.e., avoid interference with other tenants for the same resources. Although today's cloud service providers offer a service level agreement (SLA) for availability, no such SLA for performance isolation exists. Of course, as soon as multi-tenancy is used, perfect performance isolation is not feasible except at a prohibitive cost to the provider. Therefore, what is needed is a specification of the performance SLAs complete with penalty clauses to mitigate violation of SLAs by providers (as is done today with respect to availability). For our research community, this challenge reduces to defining the framework for multi-tenant data systems. The key technical difficulty inherent in this challenge is that of metering violation of performance SLAs. Therefore, the choice of any model for performance SLAs must also be accompanied by a low-overhead implementation for metering.

Another related problem is the classical challenge of resource allocation among multiple tenants. Even without performance SLAs, this problem still does not have well-founded solutions. For example, the problem of allocation of working memory among adaptive query operators (from multiple queries) in classical relational databases has not received the attention it deserves, despite some recent work [7][21]. In a multi-tenant system, taking into account performance SLAs for doing resource allocation is essential and thus the problem becomes harder. *Challenge 6: Define a model of performance SLAs for multi-tenant data systems that can be metered at low overhead. Develop resource allocation techniques to support multi-tenancy.*

8. Remarks on A Few other Challenges

I have described six of the research problems in Big Data and the Cloud above. However, six is not a magic number and there are indeed several other important issues where our community can be influential. I will briefly mention three such open issues:

Scalable Data Platforms: Recently much attention has focused on this topic [8][20] and so I decided not to discuss this problem in details in this short article. For the foreseeable future, analytics based on relational infrastructure remains essential for the enterprises. Although the MapReduce based infrastructure today lacks much of the maturity of the relational world, it is an emerging ecosystem with much momentum. The rise of this infrastructure offers some unique technical challenges (e.g., see Section 6). However, the longer term goal should be to clearly understand the architectural needs of the spectrum of data analysis platforms for online, near online and batch oriented analysis workloads as each one has unique characteristics.

Operational Business Intelligence: As mentioned in the introduction, there is increasing desire to shorten the gap between data acquisition and business action. For example, a retailer would like to decide on promotions for the next week based on the data collected during this week. For online stores, it is desirable to take action based on data even more quickly. Existing solutions are based on log based shipping, streaming as well as other ETL techniques. However, this field is still at an early phase of its development.

Manageability and Auto-Tuning: One attraction for enterprises transitioning to cloud-based infrastructure is sharply reduced overhead of manageability. Although Infrastructure as Service provides some value in this regard, it is Platform as Service where the providers must fully owe the responsibilities for manageability and tuning of the service. Therefore, the cloud provider needs to develop automated solutions for all aspects of manageability including diagnostics, system parameter tuning, and physical design. On the positive side, with appropriate instrumentation, the provider has the ability to monitor the workload and system events and in fact has the opportunity to tweak such instrumentation much more flexibly compared to packaged software. As a consequence, they are also able to experiment with changes in infrastructure in a seamless manner. Developing such monitoring infrastructure and leveraging deep analytics to support auto-tuning of cloud based services is a very exciting opportunity as well as a significant challenge.

9. CONCLUSION

The increasing interest in Big Data to leverage all sources of available data, public as well as private, to create novel consumer and enterprise value is clearly visible. Our research challenge is to develop the infrastructure and tools that can help enterprises identify signal (insight) effectively from their collection of data assets. We are also witnessing strong movement towards cloud infrastructure. These two disruptions have presented great opportunities to rethink our assumptions. Such significant changes happen rarely. Therefore, as a community, we should seize this opportunity to address hard problems whose solution can greatly impact the future course of data platforms and tools.

10. ACKNOWLEDGMENTS

I am indebted to my talented colleagues in Data Management, Exploration, and Mining Group at Microsoft Research for their insights on the problems described in this paper. Vivek Narasayya has been a great sounding board and a partner in wide ranging brainstorming over the years. Arnd Christian König and Vivek Narasayya read many revisions of this short paper.

11. REFERENCES

[1] Acharya, S., Gibbons, P., Poosala, V., Ramaswamy, S.: Join Synopses for Approximate Query Answering. SIGMOD Conference 1999: 275-286.

[2] Chaiken R. et. al.: SCOPE: easy and efficient parallel processing of massive data sets. PVLDB 1(2), 2008.

[3] Chaudhuri, S., Motwani, R., Narasayya, V..: On Random Sampling over Joins. SIGMOD Conference 1999: 263-274.

[4] Chaudhuri, S.: Query optimizers: time to rethink the contract? SIGMOD Conference 2009: 961-968.

[5] Chaudhuri, S., Dayal, U., Narasayya, V. An Overview of Business Intelligence Technology. Communications of the ACM Vol. 54 No. 8, Pages 88-98.

[6] Cheng T., Lauw H.W., Paparizos S.: Entity Synonyms for Structured Web Search, IEEE Trans. Knowledge and Data Eng., 2011.

[7] Dageville, B., Zait, M. SQL Memory Management in Oracle 9i. In Proceedings of VLDB 2002, Hong Kong, China.

[8] Dean, J., Ghemawat, S.: MapReduce: a flexible data processing tool. Communications of the ACM 53(1): 72-77 (2010).

[9] Dwork, C., Differential Privacy. 33rd International Colloquium on Automata, Languages and Programming, part II (ICALP 2006), Springer Verlag, Venice, Italy, July 2006.

[10] Dwork,C., McSherry, F., Nissim,K., Smith, A. Calibrating noise to sensitivity in private data analysis. In Proceedings of the 3rd Theory of Cryptography Conference, pages 265–284, 2006.

[11] Gonzalez, H., Halevy, A.Y., Jensen, C.S., Langen,A., Madhavan, J., Shapley, R., Shen, R., Goldberg-Kidon, J.: Google fusion tables: web-centered data management and collaboration. SIGMOD Conference 2010: 1061-1066

[12] Haas, P.J., Hellerstein, J.M.: Ripple Joins for Online Aggregation. SIGMOD Conference 1999: 287-298

[13] Hellerstein, J.M., Haas, P.J., Wang, H.J.: Online Aggregation. SIGMOD Conference 1997: 171-182

[14] Hoffart J. et.al.: Robust Disambiguation of Named Entities in Text, EMNLP 2011.

[15] Kulkarni K., Singh A., Ramakrishnan G., Chakrabarti, S.: Collective Annotation of Wikipedia Entities in Web Text. KDD 2009.

[16] Lampson, B.: Privacy and security - Usable security: how to get it. Communications of the ACM 52(11): 25-27 (2009).

[17] McSherry, F.: Privacy integrated queries: an extensible platform for privacy-preserving data analysis. SIGMOD Conference 2009: 19-30.

[18] Olston C. et.al. : Pig Latin: a not-so-Foreign Language for Data Processing. SIGMOD'08.

[19] Oracle Virtual Private Database (VPD). http://www.oracle.com.

[20] Stonebraker, M., Abadi, D.A., DeWitt, D.J., Madden, S., Paulson, E., Pavlo, A., Rasin, A.: MapReduce and parallel DBMSs: friends or foes? Communications of the ACM 53(1): 64-71 (2010).

[21] Storm et al. Adaptive Self-Tuning Memory in IBM DB2. In Proceedings of VLDB 2006, Seoul, Korea.

[22] Thusoo, A. et al. Hive: a Warehousing Solution over a Map-Reduce Framework. PVLDB 2(2), 2009.

[23] Wang C., Chakrabarti K, Cheng T., Chaudhuri S.: Targeted Disambiguation of Ad-hoc, Homogeneous Sets of Named Entities, WWW 2012.

Graph Sketches: Sparsification, Spanners, and Subgraphs

Kook Jin Ahn[*]
University of Pennsylvania
kookjin@cis.upenn.edu

Sudipto Guha[*]
University of Pennsylvania
sudipto@cis.upenn.edu

Andrew McGregor[†]
University of Massachusetts
mcgregor@cs.umass.edu

ABSTRACT

When processing massive data sets, a core task is to construct *synopses* of the data. To be useful, a synopsis data structure should be easy to construct while also yielding good approximations of the relevant properties of the data set. A particularly useful class of synopses are *sketches*, i.e., those based on linear projections of the data. These are applicable in many models including various parallel, stream, and compressed sensing settings. A rich body of analytic and empirical work exists for sketching numerical data such as the frequencies of a set of entities. Our work investigates *graph sketching* where the graphs of interest encode the relationships between these entities. The main challenge is to capture this richer structure and build the necessary synopses with only linear measurements.

In this paper we consider properties of graphs including the size of the cuts, the distances between nodes, and the prevalence of dense sub-graphs. Our main result is a sketch-based sparsifier construction: we show that $\tilde{O}(n\epsilon^{-2})$ random linear projections of a graph on n nodes suffice to $(1 + \epsilon)$ approximate *all* cut values. Similarly, we show that $O(\epsilon^{-2})$ linear projections suffice for (additively) approximating the fraction of induced sub-graphs that match a given pattern such as a small clique. Finally, for distance estimation we present sketch-based spanner constructions. In this last result the sketches are adaptive, i.e., the linear projections are performed in a small number of batches where each projection may be chosen dependent on the outcome of earlier sketches. All of the above results immediately give rise to data stream algorithms that also apply to dynamic graph streams where edges are both inserted and deleted. The non-adaptive sketches, such as those for sparsification and subgraphs, give us single-pass algorithms for distributed data streams with insertion and deletions. The adaptive sketches can be used to analyze MapReduce algorithms that use a small number of rounds.

---

[*] Supported by NSF Awards CCF-0644119 and IIS-0713267 and a gift from Google.
[†] Supported by NSF CAREER Award CCF-0953754.

Categories and Subject Descriptors

F.2 [**Analysis of Algorithms & Problem Complexity**]

General Terms

Algorithms, Theory

Keywords

data streams, graph sketching, sparsification, spanners, subgraphs

1. INTRODUCTION

When processing massive data sets, a core task is to construct *synopses* of the data. To be useful, a synopsis data structure should be easy to construct while also yielding good approximations of the relevant properties of the data set. A particularly useful class of synopses are *sketches*, i.e., those based on linear projections of the data. These are applicable in many settings including various parallel, stream, and compressed sensing models. There is a large body of work on sketching numerical data, e.g., finding heavy hitters and quantiles [10, 13]; estimating norms and support sizes [32, 33]; and constructing histograms and low-dimensional approximations [11, 26]. See Cormode [12] for a survey. In this paper, we design and analyze sketches for graph data.

Massive graphs arise in any application where there is data about both basic entities and the relationships between these entities, e.g., web-pages and hyperlinks between web-pages, IP addresses and flows between addresses, people and their friendships. Properties of interest include the distances between nodes of the graph, natural partitions and the size of cuts, and the prevalence of dense sub-graphs. Applicable synopses for these properties include *spanners* and *sparsifiers*. These are sparse (weighted) subgraphs of the original graph from which properties of the original graph can be approximated. Both spanners and sparsifiers have been studied extensively [8, 22, 34]. Our work addresses the problem of constructing these synopses for massive graphs. Specifically, we show how to construct such synopses given only linear projections of the input graph.

Sketching is naturally connected to dimensionality reduction. For example, the classic tug-of-war sketch of Alon, Mattias, and Szegedy [5] is closely related to the Johnson-Lindenstrauss lemma for ℓ_2 metric embedding [29]. Our results can similarly be viewed as a form of linear dimensionality reduction for graphs. For example, a graph on n nodes is essentially an $O(n^2)$ dimensional object. However, our sparsification result shows that it is possible to linearly project the graph into a $O(\epsilon^{-2} \cdot n \cdot \text{polylog } n)$ dimensional sketch space such that the size of every cut in the graph can still be approximated up to a $(1 + \epsilon)$ factor from the sketch of the graph.

1.1 Applications of Sketches

One of the main motivations for our work was to design algorithms for processing *dynamic graph streams*. A dynamic graph stream consists of a sequence of updates to a graph, i.e., edges are added and removed. The goal is to compute properties of this evolving graph without storing the entire graph. Sketches are immediately applicable for this task since the linearity of the sketch ensures that the sketch is updatable with edge deletions canceling out previously insertions. One proviso is that linear measurements required in the sketch can themselves be implicitly stored in small space and constructed when required. The sketches we design have this property.

Our sketches are also applicable in the distributed stream model [15] where the stream is partitioned over multiple locations and communication between the sites should be minimized. Again this follows because the linearity of the sketches ensures that by adding together the sketches of the partial streams, we get the sketch of the entire stream. More generally, sketches can be applied in any situation where the data is partitioned between different locations, e.g., data partitioned between reducer nodes in a MapReduce job or between different data centers.

1.2 Related Work

There exists a growing body on processing graph streams. In this setting, an algorithm is presented with a stream of m edges on n nodes and the goal is to compute properties of the resulting graph given only sequential access to the stream and limited memory. The majority of work considers the *semi-streaming* model in which the algorithm is permitted $O(n \operatorname{polylog} n)$ memory [19, 38]. Recent results include algorithms for constructing graph sparsifiers [1, 35], spanners [16, 20], matchings [2, 3, 18, 36, 41], and counting small subgraphs such as triangles [6, 9, 30]. This includes both single-pass algorithms and algorithms that take multiple pass over the data. See McGregor [37] for an overview.

This paper builds upon our earlier work [4] in which we established the first results for processing dynamic graph in the semi-streaming model. In the previous paper we presented sketch-based algorithms for testing if a graph was connected, k-connected, bipartite, and for finding minimum spanning trees and sparsifiers. We also consider sparsifiers in this paper (in addition to estimating shortest path distances and the frequency of various subgraphs) however our earlier results required sketches that were adaptive and the resulting semi-streaming algorithm used multiple passes. In this paper we present a single-pass sparsification algorithm. No previous work on distance estimation addresses the case of edges being both inserted and deleted. The space/accuracy trade-off of our new algorithm for counting small subgraphs matches that of the state-of-the-art result for counting triangles in the insert-only case [9].

This paper also uses several techniques which are standard in streaming such as hierarchical sampling [23, 28], ℓ_0 sampling [21, 31] and sparse recovery [24].

1.3 Our Results and Roadmap

We start in Section 2 with some preliminary definitions and lemmas. In the following three sections we present our results.

1. *Sparsifiers:* Our main result is a sketch-based sparsifier construction: we show that $O(\epsilon^{-2} n \operatorname{polylog} n)$ random linear projections of a graph on n nodes suffice to $1 + \epsilon$ approximate *all* cut values including the minimum cut. This leads to a one-pass semi-streaming algorithm that constructs a graph sparsifier in the presence of both edge insertions and deletions. This result improves upon the previous algorithm that

required $O(\log n)$ passes [4]. These results are presented in Section 3.

2. *Subgraphs:* We show that $O(\epsilon^{-2})$ linear projections suffice for approximating the fraction of non-empty sub-graphs that match a given pattern up to an ϵ additive term. This leads to a $\tilde{O}(\epsilon^{-2})$-space, single-pass algorithm for dynamic graph streams. In the special case of estimating the number of triangles, the space used by our algorithm matches that required for the state-of-the-art result in the insert-only data stream model [9]. We present this result in Section 4.

3. *Spanners:* In our final section, we consider adaptive sketches. We say that a sketches scheme is r-adaptive if the linear measurements are performed in r batches where measurements performed in a given batch may depend on the outcome of measurements performed in previous batches. We first show that a simple adaptation of an existing non-streaming algorithm gives rise to a k-adaptive sketch that uses $\tilde{O}(n^{1+1/k})$ linear measurements that can be used to approximate every graph distance up to a factor of $2k - 1$. This naturally yields a k-pass, $\tilde{O}(n^{1+1/k})$-space algorithm. The main result of this section is our second algorithm in which we reduce the adaptivity/passes to $\log k$ at the expense of increasing the approximation factor to $k^{\log_2 5} - 1$. We present these results in Section 5.

2. PRELIMINARIES

2.1 Model Definitions

We start with the basic model definitions of a dynamic graph stream, sketches, and linear measurements.

DEFINITION 1 (DYNAMIC GRAPH STREAM). *A stream* $S = \langle a_1, \ldots, a_t \rangle$ *where* $a_k \in [n] \times [n] \times \{-1, 1\}$ *defines a multi-graph graph* $G = (V, E)$ *where* $V = [n]$ *and the multiplicity of an edge* (i, j) *equals*

$$A(i, j) = |\{k : a_k = (i, j, +)\}| - |\{k : a_k = (i, j, -)\}| .$$

We assume that the edge multiplicity is non-negative and that the graph has no self-loops.

DEFINITION 2 (LINEAR MEASUREMENTS AND SKETCHES). *A linear measurement of a graph is defined by a set of coefficients* $c(i, j)$ *for* $1 \leq i < j \leq n$. *Given a multi-graph* $G = (V, E)$ *where edge* (i, j) *has multiplicity* $A(i, j)$, *the evaluation of this measurement is* $\sum_{1 \leq i < j \leq n} c(i, j) A(i, j)$. *A sketch is a collection of linear measurements. An* r-adaptive sketching scheme *is a sequences of* r *sketches where the linear measurements performed in the* rth *sketch may be chosen based on the outcomes of earlier sketches.*

2.2 Graph Definitions and Notation

We denote the shortest path distance between two nodes u, v in graph $G = (V, E)$ by $d_G(u, v)$. We denote the minimum cut of G by $\lambda(G)$. For $u, v \in V$, let $\lambda_{u,v}(G)$ denote the minimum u-v cut in G. Finally, let $\lambda_A(G)$ denote the capacity of the cut $(A, V \setminus A)$.

DEFINITION 3 (SPANNERS). *Given a graph* $G = (V, E)$, *we say that a subgraph* $H = (V, E')$ *is an* α-spanner *for* G *if*

$$\forall u, v \in V, \quad d_G(u, v) \leq d_H(u, v) \leq \alpha \cdot d_G(u, v) .$$

DEFINITION 4 (SPARSIFICATION). *Given a graph* $G = (V, E)$, *we say that a weighted subgraph* $H = (V, E', w)$ *is an* ϵ-sparsification *for* G *if*

$$\forall A \subset V, \quad (1 - \epsilon)\lambda_A(G) \leq \lambda_A(H) \leq (1 + \epsilon)\lambda_A(G) .$$

2.3 Algorithmic Preliminaries

An important technique used throughout this paper is ℓ_0-sampling [14, 21, 31]. Consider a turnstile stream $S = \langle s_1, \ldots, s_t \rangle$ where each $s_i \in (u_i, \Delta_i) \in [n] \times \mathbb{R}$ and the aggregate vector $\mathbf{x} \in \mathbb{R}^n$ defined by this stream, i.e., $x_i = \sum_{j:u_j=i} \Delta_i$. A δ-error ℓ_0-sampler for $\mathbf{x} \neq 0$ returns FAIL with probability at most δ and otherwise returns (i, x_i) where i is drawn uniformly at random from

$$\text{support}(\mathbf{x}) = \{i : x_i \neq 0\} .$$

The next lemma is due to Jowhari et al. [31].

THEOREM 2.1 (ℓ_0-SAMPLING). *There exists a sketch-based algorithm that performs ℓ_0 sampling using $O(\log^2 n \log \delta^{-1})$ space assuming access to a fully independent random hash function.*

While our final results will not make any assumptions about fully independent hash functions, it will be useful to state the previous results under this assumption and only address the assumption once the we have constructed the full algorithm. Another useful result will be that we can efficiently recover $\mathbf{x}$ exactly if $\mathbf{x}$ is sparse.

THEOREM 2.2 (SPARSE RECOVERY). *There exists a sketch-based algorithm, k-RECOVERY, that recovers $\mathbf{x}$ exactly with high probability if $\mathbf{x}$ has at most k non-zero entries and outputs FAIL otherwise. The algorithm uses $O(k \log n)$ space assuming access to a fully independent random hash function.*

In our previous paper [4], we presented an algorithm that tests k-connectivity of a graph. In addition to testing k-connectivity, the algorithm returns a "witness" which will be useful in Section 3.

THEOREM 2.3 (EDGE CONNECTIVITY). *There exists a sketch-based algorithm k-EDGECONNECT that returns a subgraph H with $O(kn)$ edges such that $e \in H$ if e belongs to a cut of size k or less in the input graph. Assuming access to a fully independent random hash function, the algorithm runs in $O(kn \log^2 n)$ space.*

3. SPARSIFICATION

In this section we design a linear sketch for graph sparsification. This yields a single-pass, semi-streaming algorithm for processing dynamic graphs.

Many sparsification algorithms are based on independently sampling edges based on their connectivity properties [8, 22, 34]. In particular, we will make use of the following recent result.

THEOREM 3.1 (FUNG ET AL. [22]). *Given an undirected unweighted graph G, let λ_e be the size of the minimum u-v cut for each edge $e = (u, v)$. If we sample each edge e with probability*

$$p_e \geq \min\{253 \lambda_e^{-1} \epsilon^{-2} \log^2 n, 1\}$$

and assign weight $1/p_e$ to sampled edges, then the resulting graph is an ϵ-sparsification of G with high probability.

The challenges in performing such sampling in a dynamic graph stream are numerous. Even sampling a random edge is non-trivial since the selected edge may be subsequently removed from the graph. We solve this problem using random hash functions to ensure a consistent sampling process. However, there are two major complications that we need to overcome if we want our algorithm to run in a single pass and use small space.

- First, the sampling probability of an edge can be computed only after analyzing the entire graph stream. Unfortunately, at this point it is too late to actually sample the edges. To overcome this we develop an approach that will allow us to simultaneously sample edges and estimate sample properties. We present a basic version of our technique in Section 3.2. We then bootstrap the process to develop a more efficient construction in Section 3.3.

- Second, the random hash function being used for the consistent hashing needs to be stored in $\tilde{O}(n)$ space. However, such a random hash function cannot guarantee the full independence between random variables which is required for Lemma 3.1 and Theorem 3.1. We will use Nisan's pseudorandom generator [39] which produces a random bits that are indistinguishable to an algorithm that uses a small space, along the same lines as Indyk [27]. In the next three sections, we will assume a random oracle that facilitates full independence. In Section 3.4, we remove this assumption and detail the application of Nisan's pseudorandom generator.

3.1 Warm-up: Minimum Cut

To warm up, we start with a one-pass semi-streaming algorithm, MINCUT, for the minimum cut problem. This will introduce some the ideas used in the subsequent sections on sparsification. The algorithm is based on Karger's Uniform Sampling Lemma [34].

LEMMA 3.1 (UNIFORM SAMPLING). *Given an undirected unweighted graph G, let λ be the minimum cut value. If we sample each edge with probability*

$$p \geq \min\{6 \lambda^{-1} \epsilon^{-2} \log n, 1\}$$

and assign weight $1/p$ to sampled edges, then the resulting graph is an ϵ-sparsification of G with high probability.

See Fig. 1 for our Minimum Cut Algorithm. The algorithm generates a sequence of graphs $G = G_0 \supseteq G_1 \supseteq G_2 \supseteq \ldots$ where G_i is formed by independently removing each edge in G_{i-1} with probability $1/2$. Simultaneously we use k-EDGECONNECT to construct a sequence of graphs $H_0, H_1, H_2, \ldots$ where H_i contains all edges in G_i that participate in a cut of size k or less. The idea is that if i is not too large, $\lambda(G)$ can be approximated via $\lambda(G_i)$ and if $\lambda(G_i) \leq k$ then $\lambda(G_i)$ can be calculated from H_i.

THEOREM 3.2. *Assuming access to fully independent random hash functions, there exists a single-pass, $O(\epsilon^{-2} n \log^4 n)$-space algorithm that $(1 + \epsilon)$-approximates the minimum cut in the dynamic graph stream model.*

PROOF. If a cut in G_i has less than k edges that cross the cut, the witness contains all such edges. On the other hand, if a cut value is larger than k, the witness contains at least k edges that cross the cut. Therefore, if G_i is not k-edge-connected, we can correctly find a minimum cut in G_i using the corresponding witness.

Let $\lambda(G)$ be the minimum cut size of G and let

$$i^* = \left\lfloor \log \max\left\{1, \frac{\lambda \epsilon^2}{6 \log n}\right\} \right\rfloor .$$

For $i \leq i^*$, the edge weights in G_i are all 2^i and therefore G_i approximates all the cut values in G w.h.p. by Lemma 3.1. Therefore, if MINCUT returns a minimum cut from G_i with $i \leq i^*$, the returned cut is a $(1 + \epsilon)$-approximation.

By Chernoff bound, the number of edges in G_{i^*} that crosses the minimum cut of G is $O(\epsilon^{-2} \log n) \leq k$ with high probability. Hence, MINCUT terminates at $i \leq i^*$ and returns a $(1 + \epsilon)$-approximation minimum cut with high probability. □

Algorithm MINCUT

1. For $i \in \{1, \ldots, 2 \log n\}$, let $h_i : E \to \{0, 1\}$ be a uniform hash function.

2. For $i \in \{0, 1, \ldots, 2 \log n\}$,

    (a) Let G_i be the subgraph of G containing edges e such that $\prod_{j \leq i} h_j(e) = 1$.

    (b) Let $H_i \leftarrow k\text{-EDGECONNECT}(G_i)$ for $k = O(\epsilon^{-2} \log n)$

3. Return $2^j \lambda(H_j)$ where $j = \min\{i : \lambda(H_i) < k\}$

Figure 1: Minimum Cut Algorithm. Steps 1 and 2 are performed together in a single pass. Step 3 is performed in post-processing.

Algorithm SIMPLE-SPARSIFICATION

1. For $i \in \{1, \ldots, 2 \log n\}$, let $h_i : E \to \{0, 1\}$ be a uniform hash function.

2. For $i \in \{0, 1, \ldots, 2 \log n\}$,

    (a) Let G_i be the subgraph of G containing edges e such that $\prod_{j \leq i} h_j(e) = 1$.

    (b) Let $H_i \leftarrow k\text{-EDGECONNECT}(G_i)$ for $k = O(\epsilon^{-2} \log^2 n)$.

3. For each edge $e = (u, v)$, find $j = \min\{i : \lambda_e(H_i) < k\}$. If $e \in H_j$, add e to the sparsifier with weight 2^j.

Figure 2: Simple Sparsification Algorithm. Steps 1 and 2 are performed in a single pass. Step 3 is performed in post-processing.

3.2 A Simple Sparsification

See Fig. 2 for a simple Sparsification Algorithm. The algorithm extends the Min-Cut Algorithm by taking into account the connectivity of different edges.

LEMMA 3.2. *Assuming access to fully independent random hash functions,* SIMPLE-SPARSIFICATION *uses* $O(\epsilon^{-2} n \log^5 n)$ *space and the number of edges in the sparsification is* $O(\epsilon^{-2} n \log^3 n)$.

PROOF. Each of the $O(\log n)$ instance of k-EDGECONNECT runs in $O(kn \log^2 n)$ space. Hence, the total space used by the algorithm is $O(\epsilon^{-2} n \log^5 n)$. Since the total number of edges returned is $O(kn \log n)$, the number of edges in the sparsification is also bounded by $O(\epsilon^{-2} n \log^3 n)$. $\square$

As mentioned earlier, the analysis of our sparsification result uses a modification of Theorem 3.1 that arises from the fact that we will not be able to independently sample each edge. The proof of Theorem 3.1 is based on the following version of the Chernoff bound.

LEMMA 3.3 (FUNG ET AL. [22]). *Consider any subset C of edges of unweighted edges, where each edge $e \in C$ is sampled independently with probability p_e for some $p_e \in (0, 1]$ and given weight $1/p_e$ if selected in the sample. Let the random variable X_e denote the weight of edges e in the sample; if e is not selected, then $X_e = 0$. Then, for any $p \leq p_e$ for all edges e, any $\epsilon \in (0, 1]$, and any $N \geq |C|$, the following bound holds:*

$$\mathbb{P}\left[\left|\sum_{e \in C} X_e - |C|\right| \geq \epsilon N\right] < 2 \exp(-0.38 \epsilon^2 p N).$$

We will need to prove an analogous lemma for our sampling procedure. Consider the SIMPLE-SPARSIFICATION algorithm as a sampling process that determines the edge weight in the sparsification. Initially, the edge weights are all 1. For each round $i = 1, 2, \ldots$ if an edge e is not k-connected in G_{i-1}, we freeze the

edge weight. For an edges e that is not frozen, we sample the edge with probability $1/2$. If the edge is sampled, we double the edge weight and otherwise, we assign weight 0 to the edge.

DEFINITION 5. *Let $X_{e,i}$ be random variables that represent the edge weight of e at round i and let X_e be the final edge weight of e. Let $p_e = \min\left\{253 \lambda_e^{-1} \epsilon^{-2} \log^2 n, 1\right\}$ where λ_e is the edge-connectivity of e and let $p'_e = \min\{4 p_e, 1\}$. Let B_e be the event that the edge weight of e is not frozen until round $\lfloor \log 1/p'_e \rfloor$ and let $B_C = \cup_{e \in C} B_e$ for a set C of edges.*

In the above process, freezing an edge weight at round i is equivalent to sampling an edge with probability $1/2^{i-1}$. We will use Azuma's inequality, which is an exponentially decaying tail inequality for dependent random process, instead of Lemma 3.3.

LEMMA 3.4 (AZUMA'S INEQUALITY). *A sequence of random variables $X_1, X_2, X_3, \ldots$ is called a martingale if for all $i \geq 1$,*

$$\mathbb{E}[X_{i+1}|X_i] = X_i.$$

If $|X_{i+1} - X_i| \leq c_i$ almost surely for all i, then

$$\mathbb{P}[|X_n - X_1| \geq t] < 2 \exp(-t^2/2 \sum_i c_i^2).$$

We prove the following lemma which is identical to Theorem 3.3 if no bad event B_e occurs.

LEMMA 3.5. *Let C be a set of edges. For any $p \leq p_e$ for all $e \in C$ and any $N \geq |C|$, we have*

$$\mathbb{P}\left[\neg B_C \text{ and } \left|\sum_{e \in C} X_e - |C|\right| \geq \epsilon N\right] < 2 \exp(-0.38 \epsilon^2 p N).$$

PROOF. Suppose that we sample edges one by one and let $Y_{i,j}$ be the total weight of edges in C after j steps at round i. If $Y_{i,0} \geq |C| + \epsilon N$ for any i, we stop the sampling process.

Algorithm SPARSIFICATION

1. Using SIMPLE-SPARSIFICATION, construct a $(1 \pm 1/2)$-sparsification H.

2. For $i \in \{1, \ldots, 2 \log n\}$, let $h_i : E \to \{0, 1\}$ be a uniform hash function.

3. For $i \in \{0, 1, \ldots, 2 \log n\}$,

   (a) Let G_i be the subgraph of G containing edges e such that $\prod_{j \leq i} h_j(e) = 1$.

   (b) For each $u \in V$, compute k-RECOVERY $(\mathbf{x}^{u,i})$ for $k = O(\epsilon^{-2} \log^2 n)$ where $\mathbf{x}^{u,i} \in \{-1, 0, 1\}^{\binom{V}{2}}$ with entries

   $$\mathbf{x}^{u,i}[v, w] = \begin{cases} 1 & \text{if } u = v \text{ and } (v, w) \in G_i \\ -1 & \text{if } u = w \text{ and } (v, w) \in G_i \\ 0 & \text{otherwise} \end{cases} . \tag{1}$$

4. Let $T = (V, E_T, w)$ be the Gomory-Hu tree of H and for each edge $e \in E_T$,

   (a) Let C be the cut induced by e and let $w(e)$ be the weight of the cut.

   (b) Let $j = \lfloor \log(\max\{w(e)\epsilon^2/\log n, 1\}) \rfloor$.

   (c) k-RECOVERY $(\sum_{u \in A} \mathbf{x}^{u,j})$ returns all the edges in G_j that cross C with high probability.

   (d) Let $e = (u, v)$ be a returned edge and f be the minimum weight edge in the u-v path in the Gomory-Hu tree. If f induces C, include e to the graph sparsification with edge weight 2^j.

Figure 3: Better Sparsification Algorithm. Steps 1-3 are performed in a single pass. Step 4 is performed in post-processing.

For each step in round i, we change the edge weight from 2^{i-1} to either 2^i or 0 with equal probability. The expectation of the edge weight is 2^{i-1} and therefore, $\mathbb{E}[Y_{i,j}|Y_{i,j-1}] = Y_{i,j-1}$. In addition, there are at most $\frac{|C|+\epsilon N}{2^{i-1}}$ random variables $Y_{i,j}$ at round i since otherwise, $Y_{i,0}$ has to be greater than $|C| + \epsilon N$ and we would have stopped the sampling process. So

$$\sum_{i' < i} \sum_j |Y_{i',j} - Y_{i',j-1}|^2 \leq \sum_{i' < i} \frac{|C| + \epsilon N}{2^{i'-1}} 2^{2(i'-1)}$$
$$= \sum_{i' < i} 2^{i'-1}(|C| + \epsilon N) \leq 2^{i+1} N .$$

Now the following inequality follows from Azuma's inequality.

$$\mathbb{P}\left[|Y_{i,0} - |C|| \geq \epsilon N\right] < 2 \exp\left(-\frac{\epsilon^2 N}{2^{i+2}}\right)$$

Let $i = \lfloor \log \max\{1/(4p), 1\} \rfloor$. If B_C does not occur, $Y_{i,0} = \sum_{e \in C} X_e$. From the definition of i, $i = 0$ or $2^{-(i+2)} \geq 0.38p$. If $i = 0$, obviously $Y_{i,0} = |C|$. If $2^{-(i+2)} \geq 0.38p$, we get the desired result: $\mathbb{P}[|Y_{i,0} - |C|| \geq \epsilon N] < 2 \exp(-0.38\epsilon^2 pN)$. $\square$

THEOREM 3.3. *Assuming access to fully independent random hash functions, there exists a single-pass, $O(\epsilon^{-2} n \log^5 n)$-space $(1 + \epsilon)$-sparsification algorithm in the dynamic graph stream model.*

PROOF. By replacing Theorem 3.3 by Lemma 3.5, we can conclude that SPARSIFICATION produces a sparse graph that approximates every cut with high probability or for some edge e, B_e occurs. Consider an edge $e = (u, v)$ and some minimum u-v cut of cut value λ_e. For $i = \lfloor \log 1/p'_e \rfloor$, the expected number of edges in this cut is smaller than $k/2$ (assuming that we use a sufficiently large constant to decide k). By the Chernoff bound, e is not k-connected in G_i with high probability. By union bound, B_e do not occur for all e with high probability and we obtain the desired result. $\square$

3.3 A Better Sparsification

In this section we present a more efficient implementation of SIMPLE-SPARSIFICATION. See Fig. 3. The idea is to first construct a less accurate "rough" sparsifier that we can use to estimate the connectivity of an edge. Then, rather than constructing all the H_i graphs via k-EDGECONNECT, we can use the more efficient sparse-recovery algorithm k-RECOVERY in combination with the Gomory-Hu data structure.

1. *Rough-Sparsification:* We construct a $(1\pm1/2)$-sparsification using the algorithm in the previous section. The goal is to compute the sampling probability of edges upto a constant factor.

2. *Final-Sparsification:* For each edge $e = (u, v)$, we find a $O(1)$-approximate minimum u-v cut C_e using the rough sparsification. Based on the cut value of C_e, we compute a sampling probability p_e of e. Let $i_e = \lfloor \log 1/p_e \rfloor$. We find all edges in G_{i_e} that cross C_e. If $e \in G_{i_e}$, assign weight 2^{i_e} to e and otherwise, assign weight 0 to e.

It is important to note that dividing the process into two steps is conceptual and that both steps are performed in a single pass over the stream.

We next discuss finding the cut C_e for each e. Note that the collection of C_e has to be efficiently computable and stored in a small space. Fortunately, Gomory-Hu tree [25] is such a data structure, and it can be computed efficiently [40].

DEFINITION 6. *A tree T is a Gomory-Hu tree of graph G if for every pair of vertices u and v in G, the minimum edge weight along the u-v path in T is equal to the cut value of the minimum u-v cut.*

Each edge in the Gomory-Hu tree induces a cut. It is a well-known fact that the cut value of such a cut is equal to the weight of the corresponding edge.

The method for finding the edges across a cut (line 4c) is based an ideas developed in our previous paper [4]. The definition of $\mathbf{x}^{u,i}$ in Eq. 1 ensures that for any cut $(A, V \setminus A)$,

$$\text{support}\left(\sum_{u \in A} \mathbf{x}^{u,i}\right) = E_{G_i}(A) ,$$

where $E_{G_i}(A)$ is the set of edges in G_i that cross the cut. Because k-RECOVERY is a linear sketch, to find $E_{G_i}(A)$ (on the assumption there are at most k edges crossing the cuts) it suffices to have computed k-RECOVERY $(\mathbf{x}^{u,i})$ because

$$\sum_{u \in A} k\text{-RECOVERY}(\mathbf{x}^{u,i}) = k\text{-RECOVERY}\left(\sum_{u \in A} \mathbf{x}^{u,i}\right) .$$

THEOREM 3.4. *Assuming access to fully independent random hash functions, there exists a single-pass, $O(n(\log^5 n + \epsilon^{-2} \log^4 n))$-space ϵ-sparsification algorithm in the dynamic graph stream model.*

PROOF. The algorithm can be implemented in one pass. The sparse-recovery sketches do not require any knowledge of the Gomory-Hu tree and thus can be constructed in parallel with the rough sparsification. The rest of the algorithm is performed in post-processing.

The space required to construct a $(1 \pm 1/2)$-sparsification is $O(n \log^5 n)$. The space required for each sampler is $O(k \log n)$ which is $O(\epsilon^{-2} \log^3 n)$. Since there are n such samplers per G_i, the total space required for the samplers is $O(\epsilon^{-2} n \log^4 n)$. We obtain the desired space bound by summing up both terms. $\square$

3.4 Derandomization

In this section, we prove that we can replace the uniform random hash function with Nisan's pseudorandom generator [39]. This can be viewed as a limited independence style analysis, however this construction yields the basic result cleanly. Nisan's pseudorandom generator has the following property.

THEOREM 3.5 (NISAN [39]). *Any randomized algorithm that runs in S space and using one way access to R random bits may be converted to an algorithm that uses $O(S \log R)$ random bits and runs in $O(S \log R)$ space using a pseudorandom generator.*

A pseudorandom generator is different from a hash function that only one-way read is allowed. If a random bit has been read, it cannot be read again. So Theorem 3.5 does not apply to the graph sparsification algorithm as it is. Instead, we rearrange the input data so that the algorithm read each random bit only once. The argument was used first in Indyk [27].

Assume that the data stream is sorted, i.e., insertion and deletion operations of the same edge appear consecutively. For each edge, we generate necessary random bits (which are $O(\text{polylog } n)$ in number) and remember them until all the operations on the edge are read. In this way, we read each random bit only once and the algorithm still runs in $S = \tilde{O}(n)$ space and R is at most polynomial in n. We apply Theorem 3.5 to the algorithm with the sorted input stream. The graph sparsification algorithm (with the pseudorandom generator) succeeds with high probability.

Now note that because the algorithm is sketch-based, the algorithm's behavior does not change even if we change the order of the data stream. Therefore, the algorithm succeeds with high probability. The same argument also applies to the minimum cut algorithm. We have the following theorems.

THEOREM 3.6 (VARIANT OF THEOREM 3.2). *There exists a single-pass, $O(\epsilon^{-2} n \log^5 n)$-space algorithm that $(1+\epsilon)$-approximates the minimum cut in the dynamic graph stream model.*

THEOREM 3.7 (VARIANT OF THEOREM 3.4). *There exists a single-pass, $O(n(\log^6 n + \epsilon^{-2} \log^5 n))$-space ϵ-sparsification algorithm in the dynamic graph stream model.*

3.5 Sparsifying a Weighted Graph

LEMMA 3.6. *Let C be a set of edges such that edge weights are in $[1, L]$. For any $p \leq p_e$ for all $e \in C$ and any $N \geq |C|$, we have*

$$\mathbb{P}\left[\neg B_C \text{ and } \left|\sum_{e \in C} X_e - \sum_{e \in C} w_e\right| \geq \epsilon N L\right] < 2\exp(-0.38\epsilon^2 pN)$$

Lemma 3.6 is a variant of Lemma 3.5 where we have a weighted graph with edge weights in $[1, L]$ rather than an unweighted graph. The proof of Lemma 3.6 is identical to Lemma 3.5. Lemma 3.6 implies that by increasing sampling probability of edges by factor L (or equivalently, increasing k by factor L), we have a sparsification algorithm for a weighted graph with edge weights in $[1, L]$. This increases the space requirement and the number of edges in the graph sparsification.

LEMMA 3.7. *There is a semi-streaming sparsification algorithm that runs in a single pass, $O(nL(\log^6 n + \epsilon^{-2} \log^5 n))$ space, and polynomial time in the dynamic graph stream model where edge weights are in $[1, L]$.*

For graphs with polynomial edge weights, we will partition the input graph into $O(\log n)$ subgraphs where edge weights are in range $[1, 2), [2, 4), \ldots$. We construct a graph sparsification for each subgraph and merge the graph sparsifications. The merged graph is a graph sparsification for the input graph. Summarizing, we have the following theorem:

THEOREM 3.8. *There is a semi-streaming sparsification algorithm that runs in a single pass, $O(n(\log^7 n + \epsilon^{-2} \log^6 n))$ space, and polynomial time in the dynamic graph stream model where edge weights are $O(\text{poly } n)$.*

4. SMALL SUBGRAPHS

In this section, we present sketches for estimating the number of subgraphs of a graph G that are isomorphic to a given pattern graph H with k nodes. Specifically we are interested in estimating the fraction of non-empty induced subgraphs that match H. We denote this quantity by

$$\gamma_H(G) := \frac{\text{Number of induced subgraphs in } G \text{ isomorphic to } H}{\text{Number of non-empty subgraphs in } G \text{ of order } |H|} .$$

Our result is as follows:

THEOREM 4.1. *For a given order-k graph H and an order-n graph G determined by a dynamic graph stream, it is possible to approximate $\gamma_H(G)$ up to an additive ϵ term with probability $1 - \delta$ using $\tilde{O}(\epsilon^{-2} \log \delta^{-1})$ space.*

We assume k is a small constant. In the case when H is a triangle, i.e., a size-3 clique, the above result matches the parameters of the best known[1] algorithm for the insert-only case [9].

The algorithm uses a simple extension of ℓ_0 sampling. Given a vector $\mathbf{x} = (x_1, x_2, \ldots, x_n)$, the goal of ℓ_0 sampling is to return a pair (i, x_i) for an i that is chosen uniformly from $\{i : x_i \neq 0\}$,

---

[1]Note that Buriol et al. [9] state their result in terms of approximating the number of triangles T_3 up to a $(1 + \epsilon)$ factor with $\tilde{O}(\epsilon^{-2}(T_1 + T_2 + T_3)/T_3)$ space but the result can equivalently be stated as an additive ϵ approximation to $T_3/(nm)$ using the fact that $T_1 + T_2 + T_3 = \Theta(mn)$. Note that nm is an upper bound on the number of non-empty induced subgraphs of size 3.

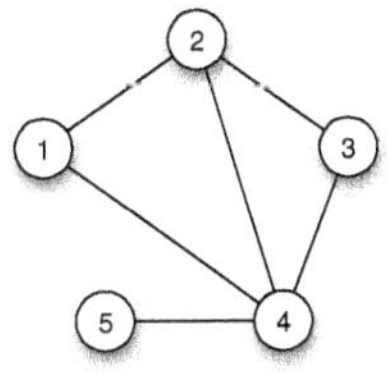

$$\rightarrow X = \begin{pmatrix} 1 & 1 & 1 & 0 & 0 & 1 & 1 & 1 & 1 & 1 \\ 0 & 1 & 0 & 1 & 0 & 0 & 1 & 0 & 0 & 0 \\ 1 & 1 & 0 & 1 & 0 & 1 & 1 & 0 & 1 & 1 \end{pmatrix} \rightarrow \text{Squash}(X) = \begin{pmatrix} 5 & 7 & 1 & 6 & 0 & 5 & 7 & 1 & 5 & 5 \end{pmatrix}$$

Figure 4: Linearly Encoding Small Subgraphs. See text for description.

i.e., the support set of **x**. For our application we will consider a $a \times b$ binary matrix X with columns $x^1, \ldots, x^b$ and the goal is to return (i, x^i) where i is chosen uniformly from $\{i : x^i \neq 0\}$, i.e., we're picking a column of X uniformly from the set of non-zero columns.

This can easily be achieved with the machinery of ℓ_0 sampling. To do this, we encode the binary matrix X as a vector

$$\text{squash}(X) \in \{0, 1, 2, \ldots, 2^{a-1}\}^b .$$

Specifically, adding 1 to the (i, j)th entry of X corresponds to adding 2^i to the j entry of squash(X). Then performing ℓ_0 sampling of squash(X) returns the encoding of a column picked uniformly from the set of all non-zero columns.

The application to finding small subgraphs is as follows. For a graph G, define the matrix $X_G \in \{0, 1\}^{a \times b}$ where $a = \binom{k}{2}$ and $b = \binom{n}{k}$. The columns of X_G correspond to size-k subsets of the nodes of G and the entries in the column encode the set of edges in the induced subgraph on the size-k subset.

See Fig. 4 for an example where $n = 5$ and $k = 3$. The first column of X corresponds to the subset of nodes $\{1, 2, 3\}$ and the top entry is 1 because the graph G has an edge between node 1 and 2. The non-zero entries in squash(X_G) correspond to the number to the number non-empty induced subgraphs of G. In the case of triangles, the entries equal to 7 correspond to the induced subgraphs which are triangles. More generally, the pattern graph H will correspond to multiple values A_H since each we are interested in induced subgraphs that are isomorphic to H are there may be multiple isomorphisms. Therefore, estimating $\gamma_H(G)$ is equivalent to estimating the fraction of non-zero entries that are in A_H. By an application of the Chernoff bound, this can be estimated up to an additive ϵ using $O(\epsilon^{-2} \log \delta^{-1})$ samples from the non-zero entries, i.e., ℓ_0-samples from squash(X_G).

5. SPANNERS

In this section, we consider the problem of approximating graph distances via the construction of graph spanners. Several papers have investigated spanner construction in an insertion-only graph stream [7, 17, 20]. The best result constructs a $(2k - 1)$-spanner using $O(n^{1+1/k})$ space in a single pass and it is known that this accuracy/space tradeoff is optimal. All these algorithms are based on growing shallow trees from a set of randomly-selected nodes. Unfortunately, this emulating this process is hard in the dynamic graph setting if we only are permitted one pass over the data.

However, if we may take multiple passes over the stream, it is straight-forward to emulate these algorithms via the ℓ_0-sampling and sparse-recovery primitives from Section 2. For example, the Baswana-Sen construction [7] leads to an $O(k)$-pass $(2k - 1)$-spanner construction using $O(n^{1+1/k})$ space in a dynamic graph streams. Their construction operates as follows:

- **Part 1: Growing Trees.** This part consists of $k - 1$ phases

where at the end of phase i we have constructed a set of rooted vertex-disjoint trees $T_i[v]$ where v is the root of the tree and the set of roots is going to be denoted by S_i. Each $T_i[v]$ will have the property that the distance between a leaf and v is at most i. At the end of phase i there may be many vertices that are not in a tree.

- *First phase:* Pick each vertex with probability $n^{-1/k}$. Call the selected vertices S_1. We will start growing trees around the selected vertices where the selected vertices will be the roots of their respective trees. Specifically, if vertex u is adjacent to a selected vertex v add (u, v) to the tree $T_1[v]$. If u is adjacent to multiple selected vertex, add (u, v) to one of the trees arbitrarily. If a vertex u is not adjacent to any selected vertex, we remember the set of incident edges $L(u)$.

- *i-th phase:* Construct S_i from S_{i-1} by sampling each vertex with probability $n^{-1/k}$. For each $v \in S_i$ initialize $T_i[v] = T_{i-1}[v]$. If u is adjacent to a vertex w in some tree $T_i[v]$ add (u, w) to $T_i[v]$. If u is adjacent to multiple trees, just add u to one of the trees (doesn't matter which). Again if a vertex is not adjacent to any selected tree, then remember the set of incident edges $L(u)$ where you only store one edge to vertices in the same T_{i-1} tree.

- **Part 2: Final Clean Up.** Once we have defined $T_{k-1}[v]$ for $v \in S_{k-1}$ (and deleted all vertices not in these trees) let V' be the set of vertices in the T_{k-1} trees. For each $u \in V'$ add a single edge to a vertex in some $T_{k-1}[v]$ if such an edge exists.

See [7] for a proof of correctness. Note that each phase requires selecting $O(n^{1/k})$ edges incident on each node and this can be performed via either sparse recovery of ℓ_0 sampling.

5.1 Pass-Efficient Recursive Contraction

The above application of the Baswana-Sen construction gave an optimum trade-off between space $\tilde{O}(n^{1+1/k})$ and approximation $2k - 1$, but used $O(k)$ passes which is less desirable. For example, to achieve a semi-streaming space bound, the number of passes will need to be $\Omega(\log n / \log \log n)$. While this is interesting, it is natural to ask whether we can produce a spanner in fewer passes. In what follows, we answer the question in the affirmative and provide an algorithm that uses $\log k$ passes at the expense of a worse approximation factor.

The idea behind the pass reduction is as follows. In the Baswana-Sen algorithm we were growing regions of small diameter (at various granularities) and in each pass we are growing the radius at most one. Thus the growth of the regions is slow. Moreover in each of these steps we are using $O(n)$ space (if the graph is dense).

Yet the space allowed for the vertex is $\tilde{O}(n^{1/k})$ and we expect the extra space to matter precisely when the graphs are dense! But if we are growing BFS trees, the extra edges are simply not useful. We will therefore relax the BFS constraint — this will allow us to grow the regions faster. The algorithm RECURSECONNECT is as follows.

1. The algorithm proceeds in phases which correspond to passes over the stream. In pass i, we construct a graph $\tilde{G}_i$ which corresponds to a contraction of the graph $G = \tilde{G}_0$; that is, subsets of vertices of the G have been merged into super-vertices. This process will proceed recursively and we will maintain the invariant
$$|\tilde{G}_i| \le n^{1-(2^i-1)/k} \ .$$
After $\log k$ passes we have a graph of size $\sqrt{n}$ and we can remember the connectivity between every pair of vertices in $O(n)$ space. We next describe how to construct $\tilde{G}_{i+1}$ from $\tilde{G}_i$.

2. For each vertex in $\tilde{G}_i$ we sample $n^{2^i/k}$ distinct neighbors.[2] To do this, for each vertex in $\tilde{G}_i$, we independently partition the vertex set of $\tilde{G}_i$ into $\tilde{O}(n^{2^i/k})$ subsets, and use an ℓ_0-sampler for each partition. This can be achieved in $\tilde{O}(n^{1/k})$ space per vertex and in total $\tilde{O}(n^{1+1/k})$ space, using the hypotheses $|\tilde{G}_i| \le n^{1-(2^i-1)/k}$. Using sparse recovery we can also find all vertices in $\tilde{G}_i$ whose degree is at most $n^{2^i/k}$.

3. The set of sampled edges in $\tilde{G}_i$ gives us a graph H_i. We now choose a clustering of H_i where the centers of the clusters are denoted by C_i. Consider the subset S_i of vertices of H_i which have degree at least $n^{2^i/k}$. We will ensure that C_i is a maximal subset of S_i which is independent in H_i^2. This is a standard construction used for the approximate k-center problem: We start from the set C_i^0 being an arbitrary vertex in H_i. We repeatedly augment C_i^j to C_i^{j+1} by adding vertices which are (i) at distance at least 3 (as measured in number of hops in H_i) from each vertex in C_i^j. and (ii) have degree at least $n^{2^i/k}$. Denote the final C_i^j, when we cannot add any more vertices, as C_i. Observe that
$$|C_i| \le |\tilde{G}_i|/n^{2^i/k} \le n^{1-(2^{(i+1)}-1)/k} \ .$$

4. For each vertex $p \in C_i$ all neighbors of p in H_i are assigned to p. For each vertex q with degree at least $n^{2^i/k}$ in $\tilde{G}_i$, if it is not chosen in C_i, we have a center p in C_i within 2 hops of q in H_i; then q is assigned to p as well.

5. We now collapse all the vertices assigned to $p \in C_i$ into a single vertex and these $|C_i|$ vertices define $\tilde{G}_{i+1}$.

We now analyze the approximation guarantee of the above algorithm.

LEMMA 5.1. *The distance between any pair of adjacent nodes* $u, v \in G$ *is at most* $k^{\log_2 5} - 1$.

PROOF. Define the maximum distance between any u, v which are in the same collapsed set in $\tilde{G}_i$ as a_i. Note that $a_1 \le 4$ since the clustering C_1 has radius 2, and therefore any collapsed pair are at a distance at most 4. For $i > 1$ observe that $a_{i+1} \le 5a_i + 4$ and the result follows. □

---

[2]Note that nodes in $\tilde{G}_i$ are subsets of the original vertex set. Vertices p, q in $\tilde{G}_i$ are neighbors in $\tilde{G}_i$ if there exists an edge $(u, v) \in G$ such that $u \in p$ and $v \in q$.

THEOREM 5.1. RECURSECONNECT *constructs a* $(k^{\log_2 5} - 1)$-*spanner in* $\log k$ *passes and* $\tilde{O}(n^{1+1/k})$ *space.*

Acknowledgments

We thank Graham Cormode, Atri Rudra, and David Woodruff for helpful discussions.

6. REFERENCES

[1] K. J. Ahn and S. Guha. Graph sparsification in the semi-streaming model. In *ICALP (2)*, pages 328–338, 2009.

[2] K. J. Ahn and S. Guha. Laminar families and metric embeddings: Non-bipartite maximum matching problem in the semi-streaming model. *Manuscript, available at http://arxiv.org/abs/1104.4058*, 2011.

[3] K. J. Ahn and S. Guha. Linear programming in the semi-streaming model with application to the maximum matching problem. In *ICALP (2)*, pages 526–538, 2011.

[4] K. J. Ahn, S. Guha, and A. McGregor. Analyzing graph structure via linear measurements. In *SODA*, 2012.

[5] N. Alon, Y. Matias, and M. Szegedy. The space complexity of approximating the frequency moments. *Journal of Computer and System Sciences*, 58:137–147, 1999.

[6] Z. Bar-Yossef, R. Kumar, and D. Sivakumar. Reductions in streaming algorithms, with an application to counting triangles in graphs. In *Proc. of SODA*, pages 623–632, 2002.

[7] S. Baswana and S. Sen. A simple and linear time randomized algorithm for computing sparse spanners in weighted graphs. *Random Struct. Algorithms*, 30(4):532–563, 2007.

[8] A. A. Benczúr and D. R. Karger. Approximating s-t minimum cuts in $\tilde{O}(n^2)$ time. In *STOC*, pages 47–55, 1996.

[9] L. S. Buriol, G. Frahling, S. Leonardi, A. Marchetti-Spaccamela, and C. Sohler. Counting triangles in data streams. In *PODS*, pages 253–262, 2006.

[10] M. Charikar, K. Chen, and M. Farach-Colton. Finding frequent items in data streams. *Theor. Comput. Sci.*, 312(1):3–15, 2004.

[11] K. L. Clarkson and D. P. Woodruff. Numerical linear algebra in the streaming model. In *STOC*, pages 205–214, 2009.

[12] G. Cormode. Sketch techniques for approximate query processing. In G. Cormode, M. Garofalakis, P. Haas, and C. Jermaine, editors, *Synposes for Approximate Query Processing: Samples, Histograms, Wavelets and Sketches*, Foundations and Trends in Databases. NOW publishers, 2011.

[13] G. Cormode and S. Muthukrishnan. An improved data stream summary: the count-min sketch and its applications. *J. Algorithms*, 55(1):58–75, 2005.

[14] G. Cormode, S. Muthukrishnan, and I. Rozenbaum. Summarizing and mining inverse distributions on data streams via dynamic inverse sampling. In *VLDB*, pages 25–36, 2005.

[15] G. Cormode, S. Muthukrishnan, K. Yi, and Q. Zhang. Optimal sampling from distributed streams. In *PODS*, pages 77–86, 2010.

[16] M. Elkin. A near-optimal fully dynamic distributed algorithm for maintaining sparse spanners, 2006.

[17] M. Elkin. Streaming and fully dynamic centralized algorithms for constructing and maintaining sparse spanners. *ACM Transactions on Algorithms*, 7(2):20, 2011.

[18] L. Epstein, A. Levin, J. Mestre, and D. Segev. Improved approximation guarantees for weighted matching in the semi-streaming model. *CoRR*, abs/00907.0305, 2000.

[19] J. Feigenbaum, S. Kannan, A. McGregor, S. Suri, and J. Zhang. On graph problems in a semi-streaming model. *Theor. Comput. Sci.*, 348(2):207–216, 2005.

[20] J. Feigenbaum, S. Kannan, A. McGregor, S. Suri, and J. Zhang. Graph distances in the data-stream model. *SIAM Journal on Computing*, 38(5):1709–1727, 2008.

[21] G. Frahling, P. Indyk, and C. Sohler. Sampling in dynamic data streams and applications. In *Symposium on Computational Geometry*, pages 142–149, 2005.

[22] W. S. Fung, R. Hariharan, N. J. A. Harvey, and D. Panigrahi. A general framework for graph sparsification. In *STOC*, pages 71–80, 2011.

[23] S. Ganguly and L. Bhuvanagiri. Hierarchical sampling from sketches: Estimating functions over data streams. *Algorithmica*, 53(4):549–582, 2009.

[24] A. Gilbert and P. Indyk. Sparse recovery using sparse matrices. *Proceedings of the IEEE*, 98(6):937 –947, june 2010.

[25] R. E. Gomory and T. C. Hu. Multi-Terminal Network Flows. *Journal of the Society for Industrial and Applied Mathematics*, 9(4):551–570, 1961.

[26] S. Guha, N. Koudas, and K. Shim. Approximation and streaming algorithms for histogram construction problems. *ACM Trans. Database Syst.*, 31(1):396–438, 2006.

[27] P. Indyk. Stable distributions, pseudorandom generators, embeddings and data stream computation. *J. ACM*, 53(3):307–323, 2006.

[28] P. Indyk and D. Woodruff. Optimal approximations of the frequency moments of data streams. In *Proceedings of the thirty-seventh annual ACM symposium on Theory of computing*, pages 202–208. ACM New York, NY, USA, 2005.

[29] W. B. Johnson and J. Lindenstrauss. Extensions of Lipshitz mapping into Hilbert Space. *Contemporary Mathematics, Vol 26*, pages 189–206, May 1984.

[30] H. Jowhari and M. Ghodsi. New streaming algorithms for counting triangles in graphs. In *COCOON*, pages 710–716, 2005.

[31] H. Jowhari, M. Saglam, and G. Tardos. Tight bounds for lp samplers, finding duplicates in streams, and related problems. In *PODS*, pages 49–58, 2011.

[32] D. M. Kane, J. Nelson, E. Porat, and D. P. Woodruff. Fast moment estimation in data streams in optimal space. In *STOC*, pages 745–754, 2011.

[33] D. M. Kane, J. Nelson, and D. P. Woodruff. An optimal algorithm for the distinct elements problem. In *PODS*, pages 41–52, 2010.

[34] D. R. Karger. Random sampling in cut, flow, and network design problems. In *STOC*, pages 648–657, 1994.

[35] J. A. Kelner and A. Levin. Spectral sparsification in the semi-streaming setting. In *STACS*, pages 440–451, 2011.

[36] A. McGregor. Finding graph matchings in data streams. *APPROX-RANDOM*, pages 170–181, 2005.

[37] A. McGregor. Graph mining on streams. In *Encyclopedia of Database Systems*, pages 1271–1275, 2009.

[38] S. Muthukrishnan. *Data Streams: Algorithms and Applications*. Now Publishers, 2006.

[39] N. Nisan. Pseudorandom generators for space-bounded computation. *Combinatorica*, 12(4):449–461, 1992.

[40] A. Schrijver. *Combinatorial Optimization - Polyhedra and Efficiency*, volume 24 of *Algorithms and Combinatorics*. Springer, 2003.

[41] M. Zelke. Weighted matching in the semi-streaming model. *Algorithmica DOI: 10.1007/s00453-010-9438-5*, 2010.

Approximating and Testing k-Histogram Distributions in Sub-linear Time

Piotr Indyk[*]
CSAIL, MIT, Cambridge MA 02139
indyk@theory.lcs.mit.edu

Reut Levi[†]
School of Computer Science, Tel Aviv University
reuti.levi@gmail.com

Ronitt Rubinfeld[‡]
CSAIL, MIT, Cambridge MA 02139 and the Blavatnik School of Computer Science, Tel Aviv University
ronitt@csail.mit.edu

ABSTRACT

A discrete distribution p, over $[n]$, is a k-histogram if its probability distribution function can be represented as a piece-wise constant function with k pieces. Such a function is represented by a list of k intervals and k corresponding values. We consider the following problem: given a collection of samples from a distribution p, find a k-histogram that (approximately) minimizes the ℓ_2 distance to the distribution p. We give time and sample efficient algorithms for this problem.

We further provide algorithms that distinguish distributions that have the property of being a k-histogram from distributions that are ϵ-far from any k-histogram in the ℓ_1 distance and ℓ_2 distance respectively.

Categories and Subject Descriptors

F.2 [**Theory of Computation**]: ANALYSIS OF ALGO-RITHMS AND PROBLEM COMPLEXITY

General Terms

Algorithms

Keywords

distribution, histogram, property testing

[*]This material is based upon work supported by David and Lucille Packard Fellowship, MADALGO (Center for Massive Data Algorithmics, funded by the Danish National Research Association) and NSF grant CCF-0728645

[†]Research supported by the Israel Science Foundation grant nos. 1147/09 and 246/08

[‡]Research supported by NSF grants 0732334 and 0728645, Marie Curie Reintegration grant PIRG03-GA-2008-231077 and the Israel Science Foundation grant nos. 1147/09 and 1675/09.

1. INTRODUCTION

The ubiquity of massive data sets is a phenomenon that began over a decade ago, and is becoming more and more pervasive. As a result, there has been recently a significant interests in constructing *succinct representations* of the data. Ideally, such representations should take little space and computation time to operate on, while (approximately) preserving the desired properties of the data.

One of the most natural and useful succinct representations of the data are *histograms*. For a data set D whose elements come from the universe $[n]$, a k-histogram H is a piecewise constant function defined over $[n]$ consisting of k pieces. Note that a k-histogram can be described using $O(k)$ numbers. A "good" k-histogram is such that (a) the value $H(i)$ is a "good" approximation of the total number of times an element i occurs in the data set (denoted by $P(i)$) and (b) the value of k is small. Histograms are a popular and flexible way to approximate the distribution of data attributes (e.g., employees age or salary) in databases. They can be used for data visualization, analysis and approximate query answering. As a result, computing and maintaining histograms of the data has attracted a substantial amount of interests in databases and beyond, see e.g., [GMP97, JPK+98, GKS06, CMN98, TGIK02, GGI+02], or the survey [Ioa03].

A popular criterion for fitting a histogram to a distribution P is the "least-squares" criterion. Specifically, the goal is to find H that minimizes the ℓ_2 norm $\|P - H\|_2^2$. Such histograms are often called *v-optimal histograms*, with "v" standing for "variance". There has been a substantial amount of work on algorithms, approximate or exact, that compute the optimal k-histogram H given P and k by taking the dynamic programming approach [JPK+98, GKS06]. However, since these algorithms need to read the whole input to compute H, their running times are at least linear in n.

A more efficient way to construct data histograms is to use random samples from data set D. There have been some results on this front as well [CMN98, GMP97]. However, they have been restricted to so-called *equi-depth histograms* (which are essentially approximate quantiles of the data distribution) or *compressed histograms*. Although the name by which they are referred to sounds similar, both of these representations are quite different from the representations considered in this paper. We are not aware of any work on constructing v-optimal histograms from random samples with provable guarantees.

The problem of constructing an approximate histogram from random samples can be formulated in the framework of distribution property testing and estimation (see surveys [Rub06, Ron08]). In this framework, an algorithm is given access to i.i.d. samples from an unknown probability distribution p, and its goal is to to characterize or estimate various properties of p. In our case we define $p = P/\|p\|_1$. Then choosing a random element from the data set D corresponds to choosing $i \in [n]$ according the distribution p.

In this paper we propose several algorithms for constructing and testing for the existence of good histograms approximating a given distribution p.

1.1 Histogram taxonomy

Formally a histogram is a function $H : [n] \to [0,1]$ that is defined by a sequence of intervals $I_1, \ldots, I_k$ and a corresponding sequence of values $v_1, \ldots, v_k$. For $t \in [n]$, $H(t)$ represents an estimate to $p(t)$. We consider the following classes of histograms (see [TGIK02] for a full list of classes):

1. *Tiling histograms:* the intervals form a tiling of $[n]$ (i.e., they are disjoint and cover the whole domain). For any t we have $H(t) = v_i$, where $t \in I_i$. In practice we represent a tiling k-histogram as a sequence $\{(I_1, v_1) \ldots (I_k, v_k)\}$.

2. *Priority histograms:* the intervals can overlap. For any t we have $H(t) = v_i$, where i is the largest index such that $t \in I_i$; if none exists $H(t) = 0$. In practice we represent a priority k-histogram as $\{(I_1, v_1, r_1) \ldots (I_k, v_k, r_k)\}$ where $r_1, \ldots, r_k$ correspond to the priority of the intervals.

Note that if a function has a tiling k-histogram representation then it has a priority k-histogram representation. Conversely if it has a priority k-histogram representation then it has a tiling $2k$-histogram representation.

1.2 Results

The following algorithms receive as input a distribution over $[n]$, p, an accuracy parameter ϵ and an integer k.

In Section 3, we describe an algorithm which outputs a priority $k \ln(1/\epsilon)$-histogram that is closest to p in the ℓ_2 distance up to ϵ-additive error. The algorithm is a greedy algorithm, at each step it enumerates over all possible intervals and adds the interval which minimizes the approximated ℓ_2 distance. The sample complexity of the algorithm is $\tilde{O}((k/\epsilon)^2 \ln n)$ and the running time is $\tilde{O}((k/\epsilon)^2 n^2)$. We then improve the running time substantially to $\tilde{O}((k/\epsilon)^2 \ln n)$ by enumerating on a partial set of intervals.

In Section 4, we provide a testing algorithm for the property of being a tiling k-histogram with respect to the ℓ_1 norm. The sample complexity of the algorithm is $\tilde{O}(\epsilon^{-5}\sqrt{kn})$. We provide a similar test for the ℓ_2 norm that has sample complexity of $O(\epsilon^{-4} \ln^2 n)$. We prove that testing if a distribution is a tiling k-histogram in the ℓ_1-norm requires $\Omega(\sqrt{kn})$ samples for every $k \le 1/\epsilon$.

1.3 Related Work

Our formulation of the problem falls within the framework of property testing [RS96, GGR98, BFR+00]. Properties of single and pairs of distributions has been studied quite extensively in the past (see [BFR+10, BFF+01, AAK+07, BDKR05, GMP97, BKR04, RRSS09, Val08, VV11]). One

question that has received much attention in property testing is to determine whether or not two distributions are similar. A problem referred to as *Identity testing* assumes that the algorithm is given access to samples of distribution $\mathbf{p}$ and an explicit description of distribution $\mathbf{q}$. The goal is to distinguish a pair of distributions that are identical from a pair of distributions that are far from each other. A special case of Identity testing is Uniformity Testing, where the fixed distribution, $\mathbf{q}$, is the uniform distribution. A uniform distribution can be represented by a tiling 1-histogram and therefore the study of uniformity testing is closely related to our study. Goldreich and Ron [GR00] study Uniformity Testing in the context of approximating graph expansion. They show that counting pairwise collisions in a sample can be used to approximate the ℓ_2-norm of the probability distribution from which the sample was drawn from. Several more recent works, including this one, make use of this technical tool. Batu et al. [BFR+10] note that running the [GR00] algorithm with $\tilde{O}(\sqrt{n})$ samples yields an algorithms for uniformity testing in the ℓ_1-norm. Paninski [Pan08] gives an optimal algorithm in this setting that takes a sample of size $O(\sqrt{n})$ and proves a matching lower bound of $\Omega(\sqrt{n})$. Valiant [Val08] shows that a tolerant tester for uniformity (for constant precision) would require $n^{1-o(1)}$ samples. Several works in property testing of distributions approximate the distribution by a small histogram distribution and use this representation as an essential way in their algorithm [BKR04], [BFF+01].

Histograms were subject of extensive research in data stream literature, see [TGIK02, GGI+02] and the references therein. Our algorithm in Section 3 is inspired by streaming algorithm in [TGIK02].

2. PRELIMINARIES

Denote by $\mathcal{D}_n$ the set of all discrete distributions over $[n]$. A *property* of a discrete distributions is a subset $\mathcal{P} \subseteq \mathcal{D}_n$. We say that a distribution $p \in \mathcal{D}_n$ is ϵ-far from $p' \in \mathcal{D}_n$ in the ℓ_1 distance (ℓ_2 distance) if $\|p - p'\|_1 > \epsilon$ ($\|p - p'\|_2 > \epsilon$).

We say that an algorithm, $\mathcal{A}$, is a *testing algorithm* for the property $\mathcal{P}$ if given an accuracy parameter ϵ and a distribution p:

1. if $p \in \mathcal{P}$, $\mathcal{A}$ accepts p with probability at least $2/3$

2. if p is ϵ-far (according to any specified distance measure) from every distribution in $\mathcal{P}$, $\mathcal{A}$ rejects p with probability at least $2/3$.

Let $p \in \mathcal{D}_n$, then for every $\ell \in [n]$, denote by p_ℓ the probability of the ℓ-th element. For every $I \subseteq [n]$, let $p(I)$ denote the weight of I, i.e. $\sum_{\ell \in I} p_\ell$. For every $I \subseteq [n]$ such that $p(I) \ne 0$, let p_I denote the distribution of p restricted to I i.e. $p_I(\ell) = \frac{p_\ell}{p(I)}$. Call an interval I *flat* if p_I is uniform or $p(I) = 0$.

Given a set of m samples from p, S, denote by S_I the samples that fall in the interval I. For interval I such that $|S_I| > 0$, define the *observed collision probability* of I as $\frac{coll(S_I)}{\binom{|S_I|}{2}}$ where $coll(S_I) \stackrel{\text{def}}{=} \sum_{i \in I} \binom{occ(i, S_I)}{2}$ and $occ(i, S_I)$ is the number of occurrences of i in S_I. In [GR00], in the proof of Lemma 1, it was shown that $\mathrm{E}\left[\frac{coll(S_I)}{\binom{|S_I|}{2}}\right] = \|p_I\|_2^2$

and that

$$\Pr\left[\left|\frac{coll(S_I)}{\binom{|S_I|}{2}} - \|p_I\|_2^2\right| > \delta \|p_I\|_2^2\right] < \frac{2}{\delta^2 \cdot \left(\binom{|S_I|}{2} \cdot \|p_I\|_2^2\right)^{1/2}}$$

$$< \frac{4}{\delta^2 |S_I| \|p_I\|_2} . \qquad (1)$$

In particular, since $\|p_I\|_2 \leq 1$, we also have that

$$\Pr\left[\left|\frac{coll(S_I)}{\binom{|S_I|}{2}} - \|p_I\|_2^2\right| > \epsilon\right] < \left(\frac{1}{\epsilon}\right)^2 \cdot \frac{1}{|S_I|} . \qquad (2)$$

In a similar fashion we prove the following lemma.

LEMMA 1 (BASED ON [GR00]). *If we take $m \geq \frac{24}{\epsilon^2}$ samples, S, then, for every interval I,*

$$\Pr\left[\left|\frac{coll(S_I)}{\binom{|S|}{2}} - \sum_{\ell \in I} p_\ell^2\right| \leq \epsilon p(I)\right] > \frac{3}{4} \qquad (3)$$

PROOF. For every $i < j$ define an indicator variable $C_{i,j}$ so that $C_{i,j} = 1$ if the ith sample is equal to the jth sample and is in the interval I. For every $i < j$, $\mu \stackrel{\text{def}}{=} \mathrm{E}[C_{i,j}] = \sum_{\ell \in I} p_\ell^2$. Let $P \stackrel{\text{def}}{=} \{(i,j) : 1 \leq i < j \leq m\}$. By Chebyshev's inequality:

$$\Pr\left[\left|\frac{\sum_{(i,j) \in P} C_{i,j}}{|P|} - \sum_{\ell \in I} p_\ell^2\right| > \epsilon p(I)\right] \leq \frac{\mathbf{Var}[\sum_{(i,j) \in P} C_{i,j}]}{(\epsilon \cdot p(I) \cdot |P|)^2}$$

From [GR00] we know that

$$\mathbf{Var}\left[\sum_{(i,j) \in P} C_{i,j}\right] \leq |P| \cdot \mu + |P|^{3/2} \cdot \mu^{3/2} \qquad (4)$$

and since $\mu \leq p^2(I)$ we have $\mathbf{Var}\left[\sum_{(i,j) \in P} C_{i,j}\right] \leq p(I)^2 \cdot (|P| + |P|^{3/2} \cdot \mu^{1/2})$, thus

$$\Pr\left[\left|\frac{\sum_{(i,j) \in P} C_{i,j}}{|P|} - \sum_{\ell \in I} p_\ell^2\right| > \epsilon p(I)\right] < \frac{|P| + |P|^{3/2} \cdot \mu^{1/2}}{\epsilon^2 |P|^2}$$

$$\leq \frac{2}{\epsilon^2 |P|^{1/2}} \qquad (5)$$

$$\leq \frac{6}{\epsilon^2 m} \leq \frac{1}{4} \qquad (6)$$

$\square$

3. NEAR-OPTIMAL PRIORITY k-HISTOGRAM

In this section we give an algorithm that given $p \in \mathcal{D}_n$, outputs a priority $k\ln(1/\epsilon)$-histogram which is close in the ℓ_2 distance to an optimal tiling k-histogram that describes p. The algorithm, based on a sketching algorithm in [TGIK02], takes a greedy strategy. Initially the algorithm starts with an empty priority histogram. It then proceed by doing $k\ln(1/eps)$ iterations, where in each iteration it goes over all $\binom{n}{2}$ possible intervals and adds the best one, i.e the interval $I \subseteq [n]$ which minimizes the distance between p and H when added to the currently constructed priority histogram H. The algorithm has an efficient sample complexity of only logarithmic dependence on n but the running time has polynomial dependence on n. This polynomial dependency

is due to the exhaustive search for the interval which minimizes the distance between p and H. We note that it is not clear that a logarithmic dependence, or any dependence at all, on the domain size, n, is needed. Furthermore, we suspect that a linear dependence on k, and not quadratic, is sufficient.

THEOREM 1. *Let $p \in \mathcal{D}_n$ be the distribution and let H^* be the tiling k-histogram which minimizes $\|p - H^*\|_2^2$. The priority histogram H reported by Algorithm 1 satisfies $\|p - H\|_2^2 \leq \|p - H^*\|_2^2 + 5\epsilon$. The sample complexity of Algorithm 1 is $\tilde{O}((k/\epsilon)^2 \ln n)$. The running time complexity of Algorithm 1 is $\tilde{O}((k/\epsilon)^2 n^2)$.*

Algorithm 1: Greedy algorithm for priority k-histogram

1 Obtain $\ell = \frac{\ln(12n^2)}{2\xi^2}$ samples, S, from p, where $\xi = \epsilon/(k\ln(1/\epsilon))$;

2 For each interval $I \subseteq [n]$ set $y_I := \frac{|S_I|}{\ell}$;

3 Obtain $r = \ln(6n^2)$ sets of samples, $S^1, \ldots, S^r$, each of size $m = \frac{24}{\epsilon^2}$ from p;

4 For each interval $I \subseteq [n]$ let z_I be the median of $\frac{coll(S_I^1)}{\binom{|S_I^1|}{2}}, \ldots, \frac{coll(S_I^r)}{\binom{|S_I^r|}{2}}$;

5 Initialize the priority histogram H to empty;

6 for $i := 1$ to $k\ln(1/\epsilon)$ **do**

7   **foreach** *interval* $J \subseteq [n]$ **do**

8   Create H_{J,y_J} obtained by:

- Adding (J, y_J, r) to H, where $r = r_{\max} + 1$ and $r_{\max}$ is the maximal priority in H;
- Recomputing the interval to the left (resp. right) of J, I_L (resp. I_R) so it would not intersect with J;
- Adding (I_L, y_{I_L}, r) and (I_R, y_{I_R}, r) to H;

         $c_J := \sum_{I \in H_{J,y_J}} \left(z_I - \frac{y_I^2}{|I|}\right)$;

9   Let $J_{\min}$ be the interval with the smallest value of c_J;

10   Update H to be $H_{J_{\min}, y_{J_{\min}}}$;

11 return H

PROOF. By Chernoff's bound and union bound over the intervals in $[n]$, with high constant probability, for every I,

$$|y_I - p(I)| \leq \xi . \qquad (7)$$

By Lemma 1 and Chernoff's bound, with high constant probability, for every I,

$$|z_I - \sum_{i \in I} p_i^2| \leq \xi p(I) . \qquad (8)$$

Henceforth, we assume that the estimations obtained by the algorithm are good, namely, Equations (7) and (8) hold for every interval. It is clear that any function f that has a representation as a tiling k-histogram, H^*, has a representation as a priority histogram H. Moreover, we can transform H to represent f in k steps, simply by adding the k intervals of

H^*, $(I_1, v_1), \ldots, (I_k, v_k)$, to H, as $(I_1, v_1, r), \ldots, (I_k, v_k, r)$, where $r = r_{\max} + 1$ and $r_{\max}$ is the maximal priority over all intervals in H. This implies that there exists an interval J and a value y_J such that adding them to H (as described in Algorithm 1) decreases the error in the following way

$$\|p - H_{J, y_J}\|_2^2 - \|p - H^*\|_2^2 \leq \tag{9}$$

$$\left(1 - \frac{1}{k}\right) \cdot \left(\|p - H\|_2^2 - \|p - H^*\|_2^2\right) . \tag{10}$$

where H_{J, y_J} is defined in Algorithm 1 in Step (8). Next, we would like to write the distance between H_{J, y_J} and p as a function of $\sum_{i \in I} p_i^2$ and $p(I)$, for $I \in H_{J, y_J}$. We note that the value of x that minimizes the sum $\sum_{i \in I}(p_i - x)^2$ is $x = \frac{p(I)}{|I|}$, therefore

$$\|p - H_{J, y_J}\|_2^2 \geq \sum_{I \in H_{J, y_J}} \sum_{i \in I} \left(p_i - \frac{p(I)}{|I|}\right)^2 \tag{11}$$

$$= \sum_{I \in H_{J, y_J}} \sum_{i \in I} \left(p_i^2 - 2p_i \frac{p(I)}{|I|} + \left(\frac{p(I)}{|I|}\right)^2\right) \tag{}$$

$$= \sum_{I \in H_{J, y_J}} \left(\left(\sum_{i \in I} p_i^2\right) - \frac{p(I)^2}{|I|}\right) . \tag{12}$$

Since $c_J = \sum_{I \in H_{J, y_J}} \left(z_I - \frac{y_I^2}{|I|}\right)$, by applying the triangle inequality twice we get that

$$c_J \leq \sum_{I \in H_{J, y_J}} \left(|z_I - \sum_{i \in I} p_i^2| + |\sum_{i \in I} p_i^2 - \frac{y_I^2}{|I|}|\right) \tag{13}$$

$$\leq \sum_{I \in H_{J, y_J}} |z_I - \sum_{i \in I} p_i^2| \tag{14}$$

$$+ \sum_{I \in H_{J, y_J}} \left(|\left(\sum_{i \in I} p_i^2\right) - \frac{p(I)^2}{|I|}| + |\frac{p(I)^2}{|I|} - \frac{y_I^2}{|I|}|\right) ,$$

After reordering, we obtain that

$$c_J \leq \sum_{I \in H_{J, y_J}} \left(\left(\sum_{i \in I} p_i^2\right) - \frac{p(I)^2}{|I|}\right) \tag{15}$$

$$+ \sum_{I \in H_{J, y_J}} \left(|z_I - \sum_{i \in I} p_i^2| + \frac{|y_I^2 - p(I)^2|}{|I|}\right) . \tag{16}$$

From the fact that $|y_I^2 - p(I)^2| = |y_I - p(I)| \cdot (y_I + p(I))$ and Equation (7) it follows that

$$|y_I^2 - p(I)^2| \leq \xi(\xi + 2p(I)) . \tag{17}$$

Therefore we obtain from Equations (8), (12), (16) and (17) that

$$c_J \leq \|p - H_{J, y_J}\|_2^2 + \sum_{I \in H_{J, y_J}} \left(\xi p(I) + \frac{\xi(\xi + 2p(I))}{|I|}\right)$$

$$\leq \|p - H_{J, y_J}\|_2^2 + 3\xi + |\{I \in H_{J, y_J}\}|\xi^2 . \tag{18}$$

Since the algorithm calculates c_J for every interval J, we derive from Equations (10) and (18) that at the q-th step

$$\left\|p - H_{J_{\min}, y_{J_{\min}}}\right\|_2^2 - \|p - H^*\|_2^2 \leq \tag{19}$$

$$\left(1 - \frac{1}{k}\right) \cdot \left(\|p - H\|_2^2 - \|p - H^*\|_2^2\right) + 3\xi + q\xi^2 \tag{20}$$

So for H obtained by the algorithm after q steps we have $\|p - H\|_2^2 - \|p - H^*\|_2^2 \leq \left(1 - \frac{1}{k}\right)^q + q(3\xi + q\xi^2)$. Setting $q = k \ln \frac{1}{\epsilon}$ we obtain that $\|p - H\|_2^2 \leq \|p - H^*\|_2^2 + 5\epsilon$ as desired. $\square$

3.1 Improving the Running Time

We now turn to improving the running time complexity to match the sample complexity. Instead of going over all possible intervals in $[n]$ in search for an interval $I \subseteq [n]$ to add to the constructed priority histogram H. We search for I over a much smaller subset of intervals, in particular, only those intervals whose endpoints are samples or neighbors of samples. In Lemma 2 we prove that if we decrease the value a histogram H assigns to an interval I, then the square of the distance between H and p in the ℓ_2-norm can grow by at most $2p(I)$. The lemma implies that we can treat light weight intervals as atomic components in our search because they do not affect the distance between H and p by much. While the running time is reduced significantly, we prove that the histogram this algorithm outputs is still close to being optimal.

LEMMA 2. *Let $p \in \mathcal{D}_n$ and let I be an interval in $[n]$. For $0 \leq \beta_1 < \beta_2 \leq 1$,*

$$\sum_{i \in I}(p_i - \beta_1)^2 - \sum_{i \in I}(p_i - \beta_2)^2 \leq 2p(I) \tag{21}$$

THEOREM 2. *Let p and H^* be as in Theorem 1. There is an algorithm that outputs a priority histogram H that satisfies $\|p - H\|_2^2 \leq \|p - H^*\|_2^2 + 8\epsilon$. The sample complexity of the algorithm and the running time complexity of the algorithm is $\tilde{O}((k/\epsilon)^2 \ln n)$.*

PROOF. In the improved algorithm, as in Algorithm 1, we take $\ell = \frac{\ln(12n^2)}{2\xi^2}$ samples, T. Instead of going over all $J \subseteq [n]$ in Step (7) we consider only a small subset of intervals as candidates. We denote this subset of intervals by $\mathcal{T}$. Let T' be the set of all elements in T and those that are distance one away, i.e. $T' = \{\min\{i + 1, n\}, i, \max\{i - 1, 0\} | i \in T\}$. Then $\mathcal{T}$ is the set of all intervals between pairs of elements in T', i.e. $[a, b] \in \mathcal{T}$ if and only if $a \leq b$ and $a, b \in T'$. Thus, the size of $\mathcal{T}$ is bounded above by $\binom{3\ell+1}{2}$. Therefore we decrease the number of iterations in Step (7) from $\binom{n}{2}$ to at most $\binom{3\ell+1}{2}$.

It is easy to see that intervals which are not in $\mathcal{T}$ have small weight. Formally, let I be an intervals such that $p(I) > \xi$. The probability that I has no hits after taking ℓ samples is at most $(1 - \xi)^\ell < 1/(2n^2)$. Therefore by union bound over all the intervals $I \subseteq [n]$, with high constant probability, for every interval which has no hits after taking ℓ samples, the weight of the interval is at most ξ.

Next we see why in Step (7) we can ignore intervals which have small weight. Consider a single run of the loop in Step (7) in Algorithm 1. Let H be the histogram constructed by the algorithm so far and let $J_{\min}$ be the interval added to H at the end of the run. We shall see that there is an interval $J \in \mathcal{T}$ such that

$$\left\|p - H_{J, \frac{p(J)}{|J|}}\right\|_2^2 - \left\|p - H_{J_{\min}, y_{J_{\min}}}\right\|_2^2 \leq 4\xi . \tag{22}$$

Denote the endpoints of $J_{\min}$ by a and b where $a < b$. Let $I_1 = [a_1, b_1]$ be the largest interval in $\mathcal{T}$ such that $I_1 \subseteq J_{\min}$ and let $I_2 = [a_2, b_2]$ be the smallest interval in $\mathcal{T}$ such that

$J_{\min} \subseteq I_2$. Therefore for every interval $J = [x, y]$ where $x \in \{a_1, a_2\}$ and $y \in \{b_1, b_2\}$ we have that $\sum_{i \subset J \Delta J_{\min}} p_i \leq 2\xi$ where $J \Delta J_{\min}$ is the symmetric difference of J and $J_{\min}$. Let β_1, β_2 the value assigned to $i \in [a_2, a_1]$, $i \in [a_2, a_1]$ by $H_{J_{\min}}, y_{J_{\min}}$, respectively. Notice that the algorithm only assigns values to intervals in $\mathcal{T}$, therefore β_1 and β_2 are well defined. Take J to be as follows. If $\beta_1 > y_J$ then take the start-point of J to be a_1 otherwise take it to be a_2. If $\beta_2 > y_J$ then take the end-point of J to be b_1 otherwise take it to be b_2. By lemma 2 it follows that

$$\left\| p - H_{J, y_{J_{\min}}} \right\|_2^2 - \left\| p - H_{J_{\min}, y_{J_{\min}}} \right\|_2^2 \leq 2 \sum_{i \in J \Delta J_{\min}} p_i \leq 4\xi .$$
(23)

Thus, we obtain Equation (22) from the fact that

$$\left\| p - H_{J, \frac{p(J)}{|J|}} \right\|_2^2 = \min_\delta \| p - H_{J, \delta} \|_2^2$$
(24)

Thus, by similar calculations as in the proof of theorem 1, after q steps, $\| p - H \|_2^2 - \| p - H^* \|_2^2 \leq \left(1 - \frac{1}{k}\right)^q + q(3\xi + q\xi^2 + 4\xi)$; Setting $q = k \ln \frac{1}{\epsilon}$ we obtain that $\| p - H \|_2^2 - \| p - H^* \|_2^2 \leq 8\epsilon$. $\square$

Proof of Lemma 2:

$$\sum_{i \in I} (p_i - \beta_1)^2 - \sum_{i \in I} (p_i - \beta_2)^2 = $$
(25)

$$\sum_{i \in I} (p_i^2 - 2\beta_1 p_i + \beta_1^2) - \sum_{i \in I} (p_i^2 - 2\beta_2 p_i + \beta_2^2) \leq$$
(26)

$$2p(I)(\beta_2 - \beta_1) + |I|(\beta_1^2 - \beta_2^2) \leq 2p(I)$$
(27)

$\square$

4. TESTING WHETHER A DISTRIBUTION IS A TILING k-HISTOGRAM

In this section we provide testing algorithms for the property of being a tiling k-histogram. The testing algorithms attempt to partition $[n]$ into k intervals which are flat according to p (recall that an interval is flat if it has uniform conditional distribution or it has no weight). If it fails to do so then it rejects p. Intervals that are close to being flat can be detected because either they have light weight, in which case they can be found via sampling, or they are not light weight, in which case they have small ℓ_2-norm. Small ℓ_2-norm can in turn be detected via estimations of the collision probability. Thus an interval that has overall small number of samples or alternatively small number of pairwise collisions is considered by the algorithm to be a flat interval. The search of the flat intervals' boundaries is performed in a similar manner to a search of a value in a binary search. The efficiency of our testing algorithm is stated in the following theorems:

THEOREM 3. *Algorithm 2 is a testing algorithm for the property of being a tiling k-histogram for the ℓ_2 distance measure. The sample complexity of the algorithm is $O(\epsilon^{-4} \ln^2 n)$. The running time complexity of the algorithm is $O(\epsilon^{-4} k \ln^3 n)$.*

THEOREM 4. *There exists a testing algorithm for the property of being a tiling k-histogram for the ℓ_1 distance measure. The sample complexity of the algorithm is $\tilde{O}(\epsilon^{-5}\sqrt{kn})$. The running time complexity of the algorithm is $\tilde{O}(\epsilon^{-5}k\sqrt{kn})$.*

Algorithm 2: Test Tiling k-histogram

1 Obtain $r = 16 \ln(6n^2)$ sets of samples, $S^1, \ldots, S^r$, each of size $m = 64 \ln n \cdot \epsilon^{-4}$ from p;
2 Set previous := 1, low := 1, high := n;
3 **for** $i := 1$ *to* k **do**
4   **while** *high $\geq$ low* **do**
5   mid := low + (high - low) /2;
6   **if** *testFlatness-ℓ_2 ([previous,mid], $S^1, \ldots, S^r, \epsilon$)* **then**
7   low := mid+1;
8   **else**
9   high := mid−1;
10   previous := low;
11   high := n;
12   If (previous = n) then **return** ACCEPT;
13 **return** REJECT

Algorithm 3: testFlatness-$\ell_2(I, S^1, \ldots, S^r, \epsilon)$

1 For each $i \in [r]$ set $\hat{p}^i(I) := \frac{2|S_I^i|}{m}$;
2 If there exists $i \in [r]$ such that $\frac{|S_I^i|}{m} < \frac{\epsilon^2}{2}$ then **return** ACCEPT ;
3 Let z_I be the median of $\frac{coll(S_I^1)}{\binom{|S_I^1|}{2}}, \ldots, \frac{coll(S_I^r)}{\binom{|S_I^r|}{2}}$;
4 If $z_I \leq \frac{1}{|I|} + \max_i\{\frac{\epsilon^2}{2\hat{p}^i(I)}\}$ then **return** ACCEPT ;
5 **return** REJECT;

Proof of Theorem 3: Let I be an interval in $[n]$ we first show that

$$\Pr\left[\left| z_I - \| p_I \|_2^2 \right| \leq \max_i\{\frac{\epsilon^2}{2\hat{p}^i(I)}\} \right] > 1 - \frac{1}{6n^2} .$$
(28)

where z_I is the median of $\frac{coll(S_I^1)}{\binom{|S_I^1|}{2}}, \ldots, \frac{coll(S_I^r)}{\binom{|S_I^r|}{2}}$. Recall that $\hat{p}^i(I) = \frac{2|S_I^i|}{m}$, hence, due to the facts that $m \geq \frac{64}{\epsilon^4}$ and $m \geq |S_I^i|$ we get that $|S_I^i| \geq |S_I^i| \cdot \frac{64}{\epsilon^4 m} \cdot \frac{|S_I^i|}{m} \geq \frac{16\hat{p}^i(I)^2}{\epsilon^4}$. By Equation 2, for each $i \in [r]$,

$$\Pr\left[\left| \frac{coll(S_I^i)}{\binom{|S_I^i|}{2}} - \| p_I \|_2^2 \right| \leq \frac{\epsilon^2}{2\hat{p}^i(I)} \right] > \frac{3}{4}.$$
(29)

Since each estimate $\frac{coll(S_I^i)}{\binom{|S_I^i|}{2}}$ is close to $\| p_I \|_2^2$ with high constant probability, we get from Chernoff's bound that for $r = 16\ln(6n^2)$ the median of r results is close to $\| p_I \|_2^2$ with very high probability as stated in Equation (28). By union bound over all the intervals in $[n]$, with high constant probability, the following holds for everyone of the at most n^2 intervals in $[n]$, I,

$$\left| z_I - \| p_I \|_2^2 \right| \leq \max_i\{\frac{\epsilon^2}{2\hat{p}^i(I)}\} .$$
(30)

So henceforth we assume that this is the case.

Assume the algorithm rejects. When this occurs it implies that there are at least k distinct intervals such that for each interval the test testFlatness-ℓ_2 returned REJECT. For each of these intervals I we have $p(I) \neq 0$ and $z_I >$

$\frac{1}{|I|} + \max_i\{\frac{\epsilon^2}{2\hat{p}^i(I)}\}$. In this case $\|p_I\|_2^2 \geq \frac{1}{|I|}$, and so I is not flat and contains at least one bucket boundary. Thus, there are at least k internal bucket boundaries. Therefore p is not a tiling k-histogram.

Assume the algorithm accepts p. When this occurs there is a partition of $[n]$ to k intervals, $\mathcal{I}$, such that for each interval $I \in \mathcal{I}$, testFlatness-ℓ_2 returned ACCEPT. Define p' to be $\frac{p(I)}{|I|}$ on the intervals obtained by the algorithm. For every $I \in \mathcal{I}$, If is the case that there exists $i \in [r]$, such that $\frac{|S_I^i|}{m} < \frac{\epsilon^2}{2}$, then by fact 1 (below), $p(I) < \epsilon^2$. Therefore, from the fact that $\sum_{i \in I}(p_i - x)^2$ is minimized by $x = \frac{p(I)}{|I|}$ and the Cauchy-Schwarz inequality we get that

$$\sum_{i \in I}\left(p_i - \frac{p(I)}{|I|}\right)^2 \leq \sum_{i \in I} p_i^2 \tag{31}$$

$$\leq p(I)^2 \leq \epsilon^2 p(I) . \tag{32}$$

Otherwise, if $\frac{|S_I^i|}{m} \geq \frac{\epsilon^2}{2}$ for every $i \in [r]$ then by the second item in fact 1, $p(I) \geq \frac{\epsilon^2}{4}$. By the first item in fact 1, it follows that $\hat{p}^i(I) = \frac{2|S_I^i|}{m} \geq p(I)$ and therefore

$$z_I \leq \frac{1}{|I|} + \frac{\epsilon^2}{2p(I)} . \tag{33}$$

where z_I is the median of $\frac{coll(S_I^1)}{\binom{|S_I^1|}{2}}, \ldots, \frac{coll(S_I^r)}{\binom{|S_I^r|}{2}}$. This implies that $\|p_I\|_2^2 \leq \frac{1}{|I|} + \frac{\epsilon^2}{p(I)}$. Thus, $\|p_I - u\|_2^2 \leq \frac{\epsilon^2}{p(I)}$ and since $\|p_I - u\|_2^2 = \sum_{i \in I}\left(\frac{p_i}{p(I)} - \frac{1}{|I|}\right)^2$ we get that $\sum_{i \in I}\left(p_i - \frac{p(I)}{|I|}\right)^2 \leq \epsilon^2 p(I)$. Hence $\sum_{I \in \mathcal{I}}\sum_{i \in I}\left(p_i - \frac{p(I)}{|I|}\right)^2 \leq \epsilon^2$, thus, p is ϵ-close to p' in the ℓ_2-norm. $\square$

FACT 1. *If we take $m \geq \frac{48\ln(2n^2\gamma)}{\epsilon^2}$ samples, S, then with probability greater than $1 - \frac{1}{\gamma}$:*

1. *For any I such that $p(I) \geq \frac{\epsilon^2}{4}$, $\frac{p(I)}{2} \leq \frac{|S_I|}{m} \leq \frac{3p(I)}{2}$*

2. *For any I such that $\frac{|S_I|}{m} \geq \frac{\epsilon^2}{2}$, $p(I) > \frac{\epsilon^2}{4}$*

3. *For any I such that $\frac{|S_I|}{m} < \frac{\epsilon^2}{2}$, $p(I) < \epsilon^2$*

PROOF. Fix I, if $p(I) \geq \frac{\epsilon^2}{4}$, by Chernoff's bound with probability greater than $1 - 2e^{-\frac{m\epsilon^2}{48}}$,

$$\frac{p(I)}{2} \leq \frac{|S_I|}{m} \leq \frac{3p(I)}{2} . \tag{34}$$

In particular, if $p(I) = \frac{\epsilon^2}{4}$, then $\frac{|S_I^i|}{m} \leq \frac{3\epsilon^2}{8}$, thus if $\frac{|S_I|}{m} \geq \frac{\epsilon^2}{2} > \frac{3\epsilon^2}{8}$ then $p(I) > \frac{\epsilon^2}{4}$. If $\frac{|S_I|}{m} < \frac{\epsilon^2}{2}$ then either $p(I) \leq \frac{\epsilon^2}{4}$ or $p(I) > \frac{\epsilon^2}{4}$ but then $p(I) \leq \frac{2|S_I|}{m} < \epsilon^2$. By the union bound, with probability greater than $1 - n^2 \cdot 2e^{-\frac{m\epsilon^2}{48}} > 1 - \frac{1}{\gamma}$, the above is true for every I. $\square$

Proof of Theorem 4: Apply Algorithm 2 with the following changes: take each set of samples S^i to be of size $m = 2^{13}\sqrt{kn}\epsilon^{-5}$ and replace testFlatness-ℓ_2 with testFlatness-ℓ_1. By Equation 1

$$\Pr\left[\left|\frac{coll(S_I)}{\binom{|S_I|}{2}} - \|p_I\|_2^2\right| > \delta\|p_I\|_2^2\right] < \frac{4}{\delta^2|S_I|\|p_I\|_2} . \tag{35}$$

Algorithm 4: testFlatness-$\ell_1(I, S^1, \ldots, S^r, \epsilon)$

1 If there exists $i \in [r]$ such that $|S_I^i| < \frac{16^3\sqrt{|I|}}{\epsilon^4}$ then
   return ACCEPT;

2 Let z_I be the median of $\frac{coll(S_I^1)}{\binom{|S_I^1|}{2}}, \ldots, \frac{coll(S_I^r)}{\binom{|S_I^r|}{2}}$;

3 If $z_I \leq \frac{1}{|I|}(1 + \frac{\epsilon^2}{4})$ then **return** ACCEPT ;

4 return REJECT;

Thus, if S_I is such that $|S_I| \geq \frac{16\sqrt{|I|}}{\delta^2} \geq \frac{16}{\delta^2\|p_I\|_2}$, then

$$\Pr\left[\left|\frac{coll(S_I)}{\binom{|S_I|}{2}} - \|p_I\|_2^2\right| > \delta\|p_I\|_2^2\right] > \frac{3}{4} . \tag{36}$$

By additive Chernoff's bound and the union bound for $r = 16\ln(6n^2)$ and $\delta = \frac{\epsilon^2}{16}$, with high constant probability for every interval I that passes Step 1 in Algorithm 4 it holds that $\left|\frac{coll(S_I)}{\binom{|S_I|}{2}} - \|p_I\|_2^2\right| \leq \delta\|p_I\|_2^2$ (the total number of intervals in $[n]$ is less than n^2). So from from this point on we assume that the algorithm obtains a δ-multiplicative approximation of $\|p_I\|_2^2$ for every I that passes Step 1.

Assume the algorithm rejects p, then there are at least k distinct intervals such that for each interval the test testFlatness-ℓ_1 returned REJECT. By our assumption each of these intervals is not flat and thus contains at least one bucket boundary. Thus, there are at least k internal buckets boundaries, therefore p is not a tiling k-histogram.

Assume the algorithm accepts p, then there is a partition of $[n]$ to k intervals, $\mathcal{I}$, such that for each interval $I \in \mathcal{I}$, testFlatness-ℓ_1 returned ACCEPT. Define p' to be $\frac{p(I)}{|I|}$ on the intervals obtained by the algorithm. For any interval I for which testFlatness-ℓ_1 returned ACCEPT and passes Step 1 it holds that $\|p_I - u\|_2 < \frac{\epsilon}{2\sqrt{|I|}}$ thus $\sum_{i \in I}\left|p_i - \frac{p(I)}{|I|}\right| \leq \frac{\epsilon}{2}p(I)$. Denote by $\mathcal{L}$ the set of intervals for which testFlatness-ℓ_1 returned ACCEPT on Step 1. By Chernoff's bound, for every $I \in \mathcal{L}$, with probability greater than $1 - e^{-\frac{me}{32k}}$, either $p(I) \leq \frac{\epsilon}{4k}$ or $p(I) \leq \frac{2 \cdot 16^3\sqrt{|I|}}{m\epsilon^4}$. Hence, with probability greater than $1 - n^2 \cdot r \cdot e^{-\frac{me}{32k}} > 1 - \frac{1}{6}$, the total weight of the intervals in $\mathcal{L}$:

$$\sum_{I \in \mathcal{L}}\max\{\frac{2 \cdot 16^3\sqrt{|I|}}{m\epsilon^4}, \frac{\epsilon}{4k}\} \leq \frac{\epsilon}{4} + \sum_{I \in \mathcal{L}}\frac{2 \cdot 16^3\sqrt{|I|}}{m\epsilon^4} \tag{37}$$

$$= \frac{\epsilon}{4}\left(1 + \sum_{I \in \mathcal{L}}\frac{\sqrt{|I|}}{\sqrt{kn}}\right) \leq \frac{\epsilon}{2} ,$$

where the last inequality follows from the fact that $|\mathcal{L}| \leq k$ which implies that $\sum_{I \in \mathcal{L}}\sqrt{|I|/n} \leq \sqrt{k}$. Therefore, p is ϵ-close to p' in ℓ_1-norm. $\square$

4.1 Lower Bound

We prove that for every $k \leq 1/\epsilon$, the upper bound in Theorem 4 is tight in term of the dependence in k and n. We note that for $k = n$, testing tiling k-histogram is trivial, i.e. every distribution is a tiling n-histogram. Hence, we can not expect to have a lower bound for any k. We also note that the testing lower bound is also an approximation lower bound.

THEOREM 5. *Given a distribution D testing if D is a tiling k-histogram in the ℓ_1-norm requires $\Omega(\sqrt{kn})$ samples for every $k \leq 1/\epsilon$.*

PROOF. Divide $[n]$ into k intervals of equal size (up to ± 1). In the YES instance the total probability of each interval alternates between 0 and $\lfloor 2/k \rfloor$ and within each interval the elements have equal probability. The NO instance is defined similarly with one exception, randomly pick one of the intervals that have total probability $\lfloor 2/k \rfloor$, I, and within I randomly pick half of the elements to have probability 0 and the other half of the elements to have twice the probability of the corresponding elements in the YES instance. In the proof of the lower bound for testing uniformity it is shown that distinguishing a uniform distribution from a distribution that is uniform on a random half of the elements (and has 0 weight on the other half) requires $\Omega(\sqrt{n})$. Since the number of elements in I is $\Theta(n/k)$, by a similar argument we know that at least $\Omega(\sqrt{n/k})$ samples are required from I in order to distinguish the YES instance from the NO instance. From the fact that the total probability of I is $\Theta(1/k)$ we know that in order to obtain $\Theta(\sqrt{n/k})$ hits in I we are required to take a total number of samples which is of order $\sqrt{nk}$, thus we obtain a lower bound of $\Omega(\sqrt{nk})$. $\square$

5. REFERENCES

[AAK+07] N. Alon, A. Andoni, T. Kaufman, K. Matulef, R. Rubinfeld, and N. Xie. Testing k-wise and almost k-wise independence. In *Proceedings of the Thirty-Ninth Annual ACM Symposium on the Theory of Computing (STOC)*, pages 496–505, 2007.

[BDKR05] T. Batu, S. Dasgupta, R. Kumar, and R. Rubinfeld. The complexity of approximating the entropy. *SIAM Journal on Computing*, 35(1):132–150, 2005.

[BFF+01] T. Batu, L. Fortnow, E. Fischer, R. Kumar, R. Rubinfeld, and P. White. Testing random variables for independence and identity. In *Proceedings of the Forty-Second Annual Symposium on Foundations of Computer Science (FOCS)*, pages 442–451, 2001.

[BFR+00] T. Batu, L. Fortnow, R. Rubinfeld, W.D. Smith, and P. White. Testing that distributions are close. In *Proceedings of the Forty-First Annual Symposium on Foundations of Computer Science (FOCS)*, pages 259–269, Los Alamitos, CA, USA, 2000. IEEE Computer Society.

[BFR+10] T. Batu, L. Fortnow, R. Rubinfeld, W. D. Smith, and P. White. Testing closeness of discrete distributions. *CoRR*, abs/1009.5397, 2010. This is a long version of [BFR+00].

[BKR04] T. Batu, R. Kumar, and R. Rubinfeld. Sublinear algorithms for testing monotone and unimodal distributions. In *Proceedings of the Thirty-Sixth Annual ACM Symposium on the Theory of Computing (STOC)*, pages 381–390, 2004.

[CMN98] S. Chaudhuri, R. Motwani, and V. Narasayya. Random sampling for histogram construction: how much is enough? *SIGMOD*, 1998.

[GGI+02] A. Gilbert, S. Guha, P. Indyk, Y. Kotidis, M. Muthukrishnan, and M. Strauss. Fast, small-space algorithms for approximate histogram maintenance. *STOC*, 2002.

[GGR98] O. Goldreich, S. Goldwasser, and D. Ron. Property testing and its connection to learning and approximation. *Journal of the ACM*, 45(4):653–750, 1998.

[GKS06] S. Guha, N. Koudas, and K. Shim. Approximation and streaming algorithms for histogram construction problems. *ACM Transactions on Database Systems (TODS)*, 31(1), 2006.

[GMP97] P.B. Gibbons, Y Matias, and V. Poosala. Fast incremental maintenance of approximate histograms. *VLDB*, 1997.

[GR00] O. Goldreich and D. Ron. On testing expansion in bounded-degree graphs. *Electronic Colloqium on Computational Complexity*, 7(20), 2000.

[Ioa03] Y. Ioannidis. The history of histograms (abridged). *VLDB*, 2003.

[JPK+98] H. V. Jagadish, V. Poosala, N. Koudas, K. Sevcik, S. Muthukrishnan, and T. Suel. Optimal histograms with quality guarantees. *VLDB*, 1998.

[Pan08] L. Paninski. Testing for uniformity given very sparsely-sampled discrete data. *IEEE Transactions on Information Theory*, 54(10):4750–4755, 2008.

[Ron08] D. Ron. Property testing: A learning theory perspective. *Foundations and Trends in Machine Learning*, 3:307–402, 2008.

[RRSS09] S. Raskhodnikova, D. Ron, A. Shpilka, and A. Smith. Strong lower bonds for approximating distributions support size and the distinct elements problem. *SIAM Journal on Computing*, 39(3):813–842, 2009.

[RS96] R. Rubinfeld and M. Sudan. Robust characterization of polynomials with applications to program testing. *SIAM Journal on Computing*, 25(2):252–271, 1996.

[Rub06] R. Rubinfeld. Sublinear time algorithms. In *Proc. International Congress of Mathematicians*, volume 3, pages 1095–1111, 2006.

[TGIK02] Nitin Thaper, Sudipto Guha, Piotr Indyk, and Nick Koudas. Dynamic multidimensional histograms. In *SIGMOD Conference*, pages 428–439, 2002.

[Val08] P. Valiant. Testing symmetric properties of distributions. In *Proceedings of the Fourtieth Annual ACM Symposium on the Theory of Computing (STOC)*, pages 383–392, 2008.

[VV11] G. Valiant and P. Valiant. Estimating the unseen: an $n/\log(n)$-sample estimator for entropy and support size, shown optimal via new CLTs. In *Proceedings of the Fourty-Third Annual ACM Symposium on the Theory of Computing*, pages 685–694, 2011. See also ECCC TR10-179 and TR10-180.

Mergeable Summaries

Pankaj K. Agarwal[*]
Duke University
pankaj@cs.duke.edu

Graham Cormode
AT&T Labs–Research
graham@research.att.com

Zengfeng Huang
HKUST
huangzf@cse.ust.hk

Jeff M. Phillips
University of Utah
jeffp@cs.utah.edu

Zhewei Wei
HKUST
wzxac@cse.ust.hk

Ke Yi[†]
HKUST
yike@cse.ust.hk

ABSTRACT

We study the *mergeability* of data summaries. Informally speaking, mergeability requires that, given two summaries on two data sets, there is a way to merge the two summaries into a single summary on the union of the two data sets, while preserving the error and size guarantees. This property means that the summaries can be merged in a way like other algebraic operators such as sum and max, which is especially useful for computing summaries on massive distributed data. Several data summaries are trivially mergeable by construction, most notably all the *sketches* that are linear functions of the data sets. But some other fundamental ones like those for heavy hitters and quantiles, are not (known to be) mergeable. In this paper, we demonstrate that these summaries are indeed mergeable or can be made mergeable after appropriate modifications. Specifically, we show that for ε-approximate heavy hitters, there is a deterministic mergeable summary of size $O(1/\varepsilon)$; for ε-approximate quantiles, there is a deterministic summary of size $O(\frac{1}{\varepsilon} \log(\varepsilon n))$ that has a restricted form of mergeability, and a randomized one of size $O(\frac{1}{\varepsilon} \log^{3/2} \frac{1}{\varepsilon})$ with full mergeability. We also extend our results to geometric summaries such as ε-approximations and ε-kernels.

We also achieve two results of independent interest: (1) we provide the best known randomized streaming bound for ε-approximate quantiles that depends only on ε, of size $O(\frac{1}{\varepsilon} \log^{3/2} \frac{1}{\varepsilon})$, and (2) we demonstrate that the MG and the SpaceSaving summaries for heavy hitters are isomorphic.

Categories and Subject Descriptors

F.2.2 [**Analysis of algorithms and problem complexity**]: Nonnumerical algorithms and problems

General Terms

Algorithms, theory

Keywords

Summaries, streaming algorithms

1. INTRODUCTION

Data summarization is an important tool for answering queries on massive data sets, especially when they are distributed over a network or change dynamically, as working with the full data is computationally infeasible. In such situations, it is desirable to compute a compact summary S of the data D that preserves its important properties, and to use the summary for answering queries, hence occupying considerably less resources. Since summaries have much smaller size, they answer queries approximately, and there is a trade-off between the size of the summary and the approximation error. A variety of data summaries have been proposed in the past, starting with statistical summaries like heavy hitters, quantile summaries, histograms, various sketches and synopses, to geometric summaries like ε-approximations and ε-kernels, and to graph summaries like distance oracles. Note that the error parameter ε has different interpretations for different types of summaries.

Algorithms for constructing summaries have been developed under several models. At the most basic level, we have the data set D accessible in its entirety, and the summary S is constructed offline. More generally, we often want the summary to be maintained in the presence of updates, i.e., when a new element is added to D, S can be updated to reflect the new arrival without recourse to the underlying D. Much progress has been made on incrementally maintainable summaries in the past years, mostly driven by the study of data stream algorithms. Some applications, especially when data is distributed over a network, call for a stronger requirement on summaries, namely, one should be able to *merge* the ε-summaries of two (separate) data sets to obtain an ε-summary of the union of the two data sets, without increasing the size of the summary or its approximation error. This merge operation can be viewed as a simple algebraic operator like sum and max; it is commuta-

[*]Supported by NSF under grants CNS-05-40347, IIS-07-13498, CCF-09-40671, and CCF-1012254, by ARO grants W911NF-07-1-0376 and W911NF-08-1-0452, by an NIH grant 1P50-GM-08183-01, and by a grant from the U.S.–Israel Binational Science Foundation.
[†]Supported by an RPC grant from HKUST and a Google Faculty Research Award.

tive and associative. We motivate the need for such a merge operation by giving two specific applications.

Motivating Scenario 1: Distributed Computation. The need for a merging operation arises in the MUD (Massive Unordered Distributed) model of computation [18], which describes large-scale distributed programming paradigms like MapReduce and Sawzall. In this model, the input data is broken into an arbitrary number of pieces, each of which is potentially handled by a different machine. Each piece of data is first processed by a *local* function, which outputs a message. All the messages are then pairwise combined using an *aggregation* function in an arbitrary fashion, eventually producing an overall message. Finally, a post-processing step is applied. This exactly corresponds to our notion of mergeability, where each machine builds a summary of its share of the input, the aggregation function is the merging operation, and the post-processing step corresponds to posing queries on the summary. The main result of [18] is that any deterministic streaming algorithm that computes a symmetric function defined on all inputs can be simulated (in small space but with very high time cost) by a MUD algorithm, but this result does not hold for indeterminate functions, i.e., functions that may have many correct outputs. Many popular algorithms for computing summaries are indeterminate, so the result in [18] does not apply in these cases.

Motivating Scenario 2: In-network aggregation. Nodes in a sensor network organize themselves into a routing tree rooted at the base station. Each sensor holds some data and the goal of *data aggregation* is to compute a summary of all the data. Nearly all data aggregation algorithms follow a bottom-up approach [29]: Starting from the leaves, the aggregation propagates upwards to the root. When a node receives the summaries from its children, it *merges* these with its own summary, and forwards the result to its parent. Depending on the physical distribution of the sensors, the routing tree can take arbitrary shapes. If the size of the summary is independent of $|D|$, then this performs load-balancing: the communication along each branch is equal, rather than placing more load on edges closer to the root.

These motivating scenarios are by no means new. However, results to this date have yielded rather weak results. Specifically, in many cases, the error increases as more merges are done [13, 22, 30, 31]. To obtain any overall guarantee, it is necessary to bound the number of rounds of merging operations so that the error parameter ε can be scaled accordingly. Consequently, this weaker form of mergeability fails when the number of merges is not pre-specified, generates larger summaries (due to the scaled down ε), and is not mathematically elegant.

1.1 Problem statement

Motivated by these and other applications, we study the mergeability property of various widely used summarization methods and develop efficient merging algorithms. We use $S()$ to denote a summarization method. Given D and an error parameter ε, $S()$ may have many valid outputs (e.g., depending on the order in which it processes D, it may return different valid ε-summaries), i.e., $S()$ could be a one-to-many mapping. We use $S(D, \varepsilon)$ to denote any valid summary for data set D with error ε produced by this method, and use

$k(n, \varepsilon)$ to denote the maximum size of any $S(D, \varepsilon)$ for any D of n items.

We say that $S()$ is *mergeable* if there exists an algorithm $\mathcal{A}$ that produces a summary $S(D_1 \uplus D_2, \varepsilon)^1$ from any two input summaries $S(D_1, \varepsilon)$ and $S(D_2, \varepsilon)$. Note that, by definition, the size of the merged summary produced by $\mathcal{A}$ is at most $k(|D_1| + |D_2|, \varepsilon)$. If $k(n, \varepsilon)$ is independent of n, which we can denote by $k(\varepsilon)$, then the size of each of $S(D_1, \varepsilon), S(D_2, \varepsilon)$, and the summary produced by $\mathcal{A}$ is at most $k(\varepsilon)$. The merge algorithm $\mathcal{A}$ may represent a summary $S(D, \varepsilon)$ in a certain way or may store some additional information (e.g., a data structure to expedite the merge procedure). With a slight abuse of notation, we will also use $S(D, \varepsilon)$ to denote this representation of the summary and to include the additional information maintained.

Note that if we restrict the input so that $|D_2| = 1$, i.e., we always merge a single item at a time, then we recover a streaming model: $S(D, \varepsilon)$ is the summary (and the data structure) maintained by a streaming algorithm, and $\mathcal{A}$ is the algorithm to update the summary with every new arrival. Thus mergeability is a strictly stronger requirement than streaming, and the summary size should be at least as large.

Some summaries are known to be mergeable. For example, all *sketches* that are linear functions of D are trivially mergeable. These include the F_2 AMS sketch [4], the Count-Min sketch [15], the ℓ_1 sketch [17, 37], among many others. Summaries that maintain the maximum or top-k values can also be easily merged, most notably summaries for estimating the number of distinct elements [6, 26]. However, several fundamental problems have summaries that are based on other techniques, and are not known to be mergeable (or have unsatisfactory bounds). This paper focuses on summaries for several key problems, which are widely applicable. We develop both randomized and deterministic algorithms. For randomized algorithms, we require that the produced summary is valid with constant probability after any number of merging operations; the success probability can always be boosted to $1 - \delta$ by building $O(\log \frac{1}{\delta})$ independent summaries.

Finally, we note that our algorithms operate in a comparison model, in which only comparisons are used on elements in the data sets. In this model we assume each element, as well as any integer no more than n, can be stored in one unit of storage. Some prior work on building summaries has more strongly assumed that elements are drawn from a bounded universe $[u] = \{0, \ldots, u-1\}$ for some $u \geq n$, and one unit of storage has $\log u$ bits. Note that any result in the comparison model also holds in the bounded-universe model, but not vice-versa.

1.2 Previous results

In this subsection we briefly review the previous results on specific summaries that we study in this paper.

Frequency estimation and heavy hitters. For a multiset D, let $f(x)$ be the frequency of x in D. A ε-approximate frequency estimation summary of D can be used to estimate $f(x)$ for any x within an additive error of εn. A heavy hitters summary allows one to extract all frequent items approximately, i.e., for a user-specified ϕ, it returns all items x with

---
$^1 \uplus$ denotes multiset addition.

$f(x) > \phi n$, no items with $f(x) < (\phi - \varepsilon)n$, while an item x with $(\phi - \varepsilon)n < f(x) < \phi n$ may or may not be returned.

In the bounded-universe model, the frequency estimation problem can be solved by the Count-Min sketch [15] of size $O(\frac{1}{\varepsilon} \log u)$, which is a linear sketch, and is thus trivially mergeable. Since the Count-Min sketch only allows querying for specific frequencies, in order to report all the heavy hitters efficiently, we need a hierarchy of sketches and the space increases to $O(\frac{1}{\varepsilon} \log u \log(\frac{\log u}{\varepsilon}))$ from the extra sketches with adjusted parameters. The Count-Min sketch is randomized; while there is also a deterministic linear sketch for the problem [19], its size is $O(\frac{1}{\varepsilon^2} \log^2 u \log n)$. In some cases $\log u$ is large, for example when the elements are strings or user-defined types, so we seek to avoid such factors.

The counter-based summaries, most notably the MG summary [36] and the SpaceSaving summary [35], have been reported [14] to give the best results for both the frequency estimation and the heavy hitters problem (in the streaming model). They are deterministic, simple, and have the optimal size $O(\frac{1}{\varepsilon})$. They also work in the comparison model. However, only recently were they shown to support a weaker model of mergeability, where the error is bounded provided the merge is always "into" a single summary [8]. Some merging algorithms for these summaries have been previously proposed, but the error increases after each merging step [30, 31].

Quantile summaries. For the quantile problem we assume that the elements are drawn from a totally ordered universe and D is a set (i.e., no duplicates); this assumption can be removed by using any tie breaking method. For any $0 < \phi < 1$, the ϕ-quantile of D is the item x with rank $r(x) = \lfloor \phi n \rfloor$ in D, where the *rank* of x is the number of elements in D smaller than x. An ε-approximate ϕ-quantile is an element with rank between $(\phi - \varepsilon)n$ and $(\phi + \varepsilon)n$, and a quantile summary allows us to extract an ε-approximate ϕ-quantile for any $0 < \phi < 1$. It is well known [14] that the frequency estimation problem can be reduced to an ε'-approximate quantile problem for some $\varepsilon' = \Theta(\varepsilon)$, by identifying elements that are quantiles for multiples of ε' after tie breaking. Therefore, a quantile summary is automatically a frequency estimation summary (ignoring a constant-factor difference in ε), but not vice versa.

Quite a number of quantile summaries have been designed [15, 20–22, 32, 39], but all the mergeable ones work only in the bounded-universe model and have dependency on $\log u$. The Count-Min sketch (more generally, any frequency estimation summary) can be organized into a hierarchy to solve the quantile problem, yielding a linear sketch of size $O(\frac{1}{\varepsilon} \log^2 u \log(\frac{\log n}{\varepsilon}))$ after adjusting parameters [15]. The q-digest [39] has size $O(\frac{1}{\varepsilon} \log u)$; although not a linear sketch, it is still mergeable. Neither approach scales well when $\log u$ is large. The most popular quantile summary technique is the GK summary [21], which guarantees a size of $O(\frac{1}{\varepsilon} \log(\varepsilon n))$. A merging algorithm has been previously designed, but the error could increase to 2ε when two ε-summaries are merged [22].

ε-approximations. Let $(D, \mathcal{R})$ be a *range space*, where D is a finite set of objects and $\mathcal{R} \subseteq 2^D$ is a set of *ranges*. In geometric settings, D is typically a set of points in $\mathbb{R}^d$ and the ranges are induced by a set of geometric regions, e.g., points of D lying inside axis-aligned rectangles, half-spaces, or balls. A subset $S \subseteq D$ is called an ε-approximation of

$(D, \mathcal{R})$ if

$$\max_{R \in \mathcal{R}} \mathsf{abs}\left(\frac{|R \cap D|}{|D|} - \frac{|R \cap S|}{|S|}\right) \leq \varepsilon,$$

where $\mathsf{abs}(x)$ denotes the absolute value of x. Over the last two decades, ε-approximations have been used to answer several types of queries, including range queries, on multidimensional data.

For a range space $(D, \mathcal{R})$ of VC-dimension[2] ν, a random sample of $O(1/\varepsilon^2(\nu + \log(1/\delta)))$ points from D is an ε-approximation with probability at least $1 - \delta$ [28, 42]. Random samples are easily mergeable, but they are far from optimal. It is known that, if $\mathcal{R}$ is the set of ranges induced by d-dimensional axis-aligned rectangles, there is an ε-approximation of size $O((1/\varepsilon) \log^{d+1/2}(1/\varepsilon))$ [27], and an ε-approximation of size $O((1/\varepsilon) \log^{2d}(1/\varepsilon))$ [38] can be computed efficiently. More generally, an ε-approximation of size $O(1/\varepsilon^{2\nu/(\nu+1)})$ exists for a range space of VC-dimension ν [34]. Furthermore, such an ε-approximation can be constructed using Bansal's algorithm [5]; see also [11, 34].

These algorithms for constructing ε-approximations are not known to be mergeable. Although they proceed by partitioning D into small subsets, constructing ε-approximations of each subset, and then repeatedly combining pairs and reducing them to maintain a fixed size, the error accumulates during each reduction step of the process. In particular, the reduction step is handled by a low-discrepancy coloring, and an intense line of work (see books of Matousek [34] and Chazelle [12]) has gone into bounding the discrepancy, which governs the increase in error at each step. We are unaware of any mergeable ε-approximations of $o(1/\varepsilon^2)$ size.

ε-kernels. Finally, we consider ε-kernels [1] which are summaries for approximating the convex shape of a point set P. Specifically, they are a specific type of coreset that approximates the width of P within a relative $(1 + \varepsilon)$-factor in any direction. These summaries have been extensively studied in computational geometry [2, 9, 10, 43] as they can be used to approximate many other geometric properties of a point set having to do with its convex shape, including diameter, minimum enclosing annulus, and minimum enclosing cylinder. In the static setting in $\mathbb{R}^d$, ε-kernels of size $O(1/\varepsilon^{(d-1)/2})$ [9, 43] can always be constructed, which is optimal. In the streaming setting, several algorithms have been developed [1, 3, 9] ultimately yielding an algorithm using $O((1/\varepsilon^{(d-1)/2}) \log(1/\varepsilon))$ space [44].

However, ε-kernels, including those maintained by streaming algorithms, are not mergeable. Combining two ε-kernels will in general double the error or double the size.

1.3 Our results

In this paper we provide the best known mergeability results for the problems defined above.

- We warm-up by showing that the (deterministic) MG and SpaceSaving summaries are mergeable (Section 2): we present a merging algorithm that preserves the size $O(1/\varepsilon)$ and the error parameter ε. Along the way we make the surprising observation that the two summaries are isomorphic, namely, an MG summary can be mapped to a SpaceSaving summary and vice versa.

---

[2] The VC-dimension of (X, R) is the size of the largest subset $N \subset D$ such that $\{N \cap R \mid R \in \mathcal{R}\} = 2^N$.

problem	offline	streaming	mergeable
heavy hitters	$1/\varepsilon$	$1/\varepsilon$ [35, 36]	$1/\varepsilon$ (§2)
quantiles (deterministic)	$1/\varepsilon$	$(1/\varepsilon)\log(\varepsilon n)$ [21]	$(1/\varepsilon)\log u$ [39] $(1/\varepsilon)\log(\varepsilon n)$ (§3.1, restricted merging)
quantiles (randomized)	$1/\varepsilon$	$1/\varepsilon \cdot \log^{3/2}(1/\varepsilon)$ (§3.3)	
ε-approximations (rectangles)	$(1/\varepsilon)\log^{2d}(1/\varepsilon)$	$(1/\varepsilon)\log^{2d+1}(1/\varepsilon)$ [40]	$(1/\varepsilon)\log^{2d+3/2}(1/\varepsilon)$ (§4)
ε-approximations (range spaces) (VC-dim ν)	$1/\varepsilon^{\frac{2\nu}{\nu+1}}$	$1/\varepsilon^{\frac{2\nu}{\nu+1}}\log^{\nu+1}(1/\varepsilon)$ [40]	$1/\varepsilon^{\frac{2\nu}{\nu+1}}\log^{3/2}(1/\varepsilon)$ (§4)
ε-kernels	$1/\varepsilon^{\frac{d-1}{2}}$	$1/\varepsilon^{\frac{d-1}{2}}\log(1/\varepsilon)$ [44]	$1/\varepsilon^{\frac{d-1}{2}}$ (§5, w/assumptions on data)

Table 1: **Best constructive summary size upper bounds under different models; the generality of model increases from left to right.**

- In Section 3 we first show a limited result, that the (deterministic) GK summary for ε-approximate quantiles satisfies a weaker mergeability property with no increase in size. Then using different techniques, we achieve our main result of a randomized quantile summary of size $O(\frac{1}{\varepsilon}\log^{3/2}\frac{1}{\varepsilon})$ that is mergeable. This in fact even improves on the previous best randomized streaming algorithm for quantiles, which had size $O(\frac{1}{\varepsilon}\log^{3}\frac{1}{\varepsilon})$ [40].

- In Section 4 we present mergeable ε-approximations of range spaces of near-optimal sizes. This generalizes quantile summaries (for intervals) to more general range spaces. Specifically, for d-dimensional axis-aligned rectangles, our mergeable ε-approximation has size $O((1/\varepsilon)\log^{2d+3/2}(1/\varepsilon))$; for range spaces of VC-dimension ν (e.g., ranges induced by halfspaces in $\mathbb{R}^\nu$), the size is $O(1/\varepsilon^{2\nu/(\nu+1)} \cdot \log^{3/2}(1/\varepsilon))$.

- In Section 5 we provide a mergeable ε-kernel for a restricted, but reasonable variant. We assume that we are given a constant factor approximation of the width in every direction ahead of time. This allows us to specify a fixed reference frame, and we can maintain a mergeable ε-kernel of optimal size $O(1/\varepsilon^{(d-1)/2})$ with respect to this fixed reference frame. We leave the unrestricted case as an open question.

We summarize the current best summary sizes for these problems under various models in Table 1. The running times of our merging algorithms are polynomial (in many cases near-linear) in the summary size.

2. HEAVY HITTERS

The MG summary [36] and the SpaceSaving summary [35] are two popular counter-based summaries for the frequency estimation and the heavy hitters problem. We first recall how they work on a stream of items. For a parameter k, an MG summary maintains up to k items with their associated counters. There are three cases when processing an item x in the stream: (1) If x is already maintained in the summary, its counter is increased by 1. (2) If x is not maintained and the summary currently maintains fewer than k items, we add x into the summary with its counter set to 1. (3) If the summary maintains k items and x is not one of them, we decrement all counters by 1 and remove all items with counters being 0. The SpaceSaving summary is the same as the MG summary except for case (3). In SpaceSaving, if the

summary is full and the new item x is not currently maintained, we find any item y with the minimum counter value, replace y with x, and increase the counter by 1. Previous analysis shows that the MG and the SpaceSaving summaries estimate the frequency of any item x with error at most $n/(k+1)$ and n/k, respectively, where n is the number of items processed. Thus they solve the frequency estimation problem with additive error εn with space $O(1/\varepsilon)$, which is optimal. They can also be used to report the heavy hitters in $O(1/\varepsilon)$ time by going through all counters; any item not maintained cannot have frequency higher than εn.

We show that both MG and SpaceSaving summaries are mergeable. We first prove the mergeability of MG summaries by presenting a merging algorithm that preserves the size and error. Then we show that SpaceSaving and MG summaries are fundamentally the same, which immediately leads to the mergeability of the SpaceSaving summary.

We start our proof by observing that the MG summary provides a stronger error bound. Let $f(x)$ be the true frequency of item x and let $\hat{f}(x)$ be the counter of x in MG (set $\hat{f}(x) = 0$ if x is not maintained).

Lemma 1 *For any item x, $\hat{f}(x) \le f(x) \le \hat{f}(x) + (n - \hat{n})/(k+1)$, where $\hat{n}$ is the sum of all counters in MG.*

PROOF. It is clear that $\hat{f}(x) \le f(x)$. To see that $\hat{f}(x)$ underestimates $f(x)$ by at most $(n - \hat{n})/(k+1)$, observe that every time the counter for a particular item x is decremented, we decrement all k counters by 1 and ignore the new item. All these $k + 1$ items are different. This corresponds to deleting $k + 1$ items from the stream, and exactly $(n - \hat{n})/(k+1)$ such operations must have been done when the sum of counters is $\hat{n}$. □

This is related to the result that the MG error is at most $F_1^{res(k)}/k$, where $F_1^{res(k)}$ is the sum of the counts of all items except the k largest [8]. Since each counter stored by the algorithm corresponds to (a subset of) actual arrivals of the corresponding item, we have that $\hat{n} \le n - F_1^{res(k)}$. But we need the error bound in the lemma above in order to show mergeability.

We present an algorithm that, given two MG summaries with the property stated in Lemma 1, produces a merged summary with the same property. More precisely, let S_1 and S_2 be two MG summaries on data sets of sizes n_1 and n_2, respectively. Let $\hat{n}_1$ (resp. $\hat{n}_2$) be the sum of all counters in S_1 (resp. S_2). We know that S_1 (resp. S_2) has error at most $(n_1 - \hat{n}_1)/(k+1)$ (resp. $(n_2 - \hat{n}_2)/(k+1)$). Our merging algorithm is very simple. We first combine the two summaries by adding up the corresponding counters. This could result in up to $2k$ counters. We then perform a prune operation: Take the $(k+1)$-th largest counter, say C_{k+1}, and subtract it from all counters, and then remove all non-positive ones. Clearly this is an efficient procedure: it can be completed with a constant number of sorts and scans of summaries of size $O(k)$.

Theorem 1 *The MG summaries are mergeable with the above merging algorithm. They have size $O(1/\varepsilon)$.*

PROOF. Setting $k+1 = \lceil 1/\varepsilon \rceil$, the size is $O(1/\varepsilon)$ and the claimed error is $(n-\hat{n})/(k+1) \leq n\varepsilon$. That the size remains the same on a merge follows trivially from the algorithm. If we store the (items, counter) pairs in a hash table, the merging algorithm can be implemented to run in time linear in the total number of counters. So it only remains to argue that the error is preserved, i.e., the merged summary has error at most $(n_1 + n_2 - \hat{n}_{12})/(k+1)$ where $\hat{n}_{12}$ is the sum of counters in the merged summary.

The combine step clearly does not introduce additional error, so the error after the combine step is the sum of the errors from S_1 and S_2, that is, at most $(n_1 - \hat{n}_1 + n_2 - \hat{n}_2)/(k+1)$.

The prune operation incurs an additional error of C_{k+1}, so if we can show that

$$C_{k+1} \leq (\hat{n}_1 + \hat{n}_2 - \hat{n}_{12})/(k+1), \qquad (1)$$

we will arrive at the desired error in the merged summary. If after the combine step, there are no more than k counters, $C_{k+1} = 0$. Otherwise, the prune operation reduces the sum of counters by at least $(k+1)C_{k+1}$: the $k+1$ counters greater than or equal to C_{k+1} get reduced by C_{k+1} and they remain non-negative. So we have $\hat{n}_{12} \leq \hat{n}_1 + \hat{n}_2 - (k+1)C_{k+1}$ and the inequality (1) follows. $\square$

Next we show that MG and SpaceSaving are isomorphic. Specifically, consider an MG summary with k counters and a SpaceSaving summary of $k+1$ counters, processing the same stream. Let min^{SS} be the minimum counter of the Space-Saving summary (set $min^{SS} = 0$ when the summary is not full), and $\hat{n}^{MG}$ be the sum of all counters in the MG summary. Let $\hat{f}^{MG}(x)$ (resp. $\hat{f}^{SS}(x)$) be the counter of item x in the MG (resp. SpaceSaving) summary, and set $\hat{f}^{MG}(x) = 0$ (resp. $\hat{f}^{SS}(x) = min^{SS}$) if x is not maintained.

Lemma 2 *After processing n items, $\hat{f}^{SS}(x) - \hat{f}^{MG}(x) = min^{SS} = (n - \hat{n}^{MG})/(k+1)$ for all x.*

PROOF. We prove $\hat{f}^{SS}(x) - \hat{f}^{MG}(x) = min^{SS}$ for all x by induction on n. For the base case $n = 1$, both summaries store the first item with counter 1, and we have $min^{SS} = 0$ and the claim trivially holds. Now suppose the claim holds after processing n items. We analyze the MG summary case by case when inserting the $(n+1)$-th item, and see how SpaceSaving behaves correspondingly. Suppose the $(n+1)$-th item is y.

(1) y is currently maintained in MG with counter $\hat{f}^{MG}(y) > 0$. In this case MG will increase $\hat{f}^{MG}(y)$ by 1. By the induction hypothesis we have $\hat{f}^{SS}(y) = \hat{f}^{MG}(y) + min^{SS} > min^{SS}$ so y must be maintained by Space-Saving, too. Thus SpaceSaving will also increase $\hat{f}^{SS}(y)$

by 1. Meanwhile min^{SS} remains the same and so do all $\hat{f}^{SS}(x), \hat{f}^{MG}(x)$ for $x \neq y$, so the claim follows.

(2) y is not maintained by the MG summary, but it is not full, so it will create a new counter set to 1 for y. By the induction hypothesis $\hat{f}^{SS}(y) = min^{SS}$, which means that y either is not present in SpaceSaving or has the minimum counter. We also note that $\hat{f}^{SS}(y)$ cannot be a unique minimum counter in SpaceSaving with $k+1$ counters; otherwise by the induction hypothesis there would be k items x with $\hat{f}^{MG}(x) > 0$ and the MG summary with k counters would be full. Thus, min^{SS} remains the same and $\hat{f}^{SS}(y)$ will become $min^{SS} + 1$. All other $\hat{f}^{SS}(x), \hat{f}^{MG}(x), x \neq y$ remain the same so the claim still holds.

(3) y is not maintained by the MG summary and it is full. MG will then decrease all current counters by 1 and remove all zero counters. By the induction hypothesis $\hat{f}^{SS}(y) = min^{SS}$, which means that y either is not present in SpaceSaving or has the minimum counter. We also note that in this case there is a unique minimum counter (which is equal to $\hat{f}^{SS}(y)$), because the induction hypothesis ensures that there are k items x with $\hat{f}^{SS}(x) = \hat{f}^{MG}(x) + min^{SS} > min^{SS}$. SpaceSaving will then increase $\hat{f}^{SS}(y)$, as well as min^{SS}, by 1. It can then be verified that we still have $\hat{f}^{SS}(x) - \hat{f}^{MG}(x) = min^{SS}$ for all x after inserting y.

To see that we always have $min^{SS} = (n - \hat{n}^{MG})/(k+1)$, just recall that the sum of all counters in the SpaceSaving summary is always n. If we decrease all its $k+1$ counters by min^{SS}, it becomes MG, so $min^{SS}(k+1) = n - \hat{n}^{MG}$ and the lemma follows. $\square$

Due to this correspondence, we can immediately state:

Corollary 1 *The SpaceSaving summaries are mergeable.*

3. QUANTILES

We first describe a result of a weaker form of mergeability for a deterministic summary, the GK algorithm [21]. We say a summary is "one-way" mergeable if the summary meets the criteria of mergeability under the restriction that one of the inputs to a merge is not itself the output of a prior merge operation. One-way mergeability is essentially a "batched streaming" model where there is a main summary S_1, into which we every time insert a batch of elements, summarized by a summary S_2. As noted in Section 1.2, prior work [8] showed similar one-way mergeability of heavy hitter algorithms.

The bulk of our work in this section is to show a randomized construction which achieves (full) mergeability by analyzing quantiles through the lens of ε-approximations of the range space of intervals. Let D be a set of n points in one dimension. Let $\mathcal{I}$ be the set of all half-closed intervals $I = (-\infty, x]$. Recall that an ε-approximation S of D (w.r.t. $\mathcal{I}$) is a subset of points of D such that for any $I \in \mathcal{I}$, $n|S \cap I|/|S|$ estimates $|D \cap I|$ with error at most εn. In some cases we may use a weighted version, i.e., each point p in S is associated with a weight $w(p)$. A point p with weight $w(p)$ represents $w(p)$ points in D, and we require that the weighted sum $\sum_{p \in S \cap I} w(p)$ estimates $|D \cap I|$ with error at most εn. Since $|D \cap I|$ is the rank of x in D, we can then do a binary search[3] to find an ε-approximate ϕ-quantile for any given ϕ. We will first develop a randomized mergeable ε-approximation of size $O((1/\varepsilon)\log(\varepsilon n)\sqrt{\log(1/\varepsilon)})$ inspired by low-discrepancy halving. Then after we review some classical results about random sampling, we combine the random-sample-based and low-discrepancy-based algorithms to produce a hybrid mergeable ε-approximation whose size is independent of n.

3.1 One-way mergeability

We define a restricted form of mergeability where the merging is always "one-way".

Definition 1 (One-way mergeability) A summary $S(D, \varepsilon)$ is *one-way mergeable* if there exist two algorithms $\mathcal{A}_1$ and $\mathcal{A}_2$ such that, (1) given any D, $\mathcal{A}_2$ creates a summary of D, as $S(D, \varepsilon)$; (2) given any $S(D_2, \varepsilon)$ produced by $\mathcal{A}_2$ and any $S(D_1, \varepsilon)$ produced by $\mathcal{A}_1$ or $\mathcal{A}_2$, $\mathcal{A}_1$ builds a merged summary $S(D_1 \uplus D_2, \varepsilon)$.

Note that one-way mergeability degenerates to the standard streaming model when we further restrict to $|D_2| = 1$ and assume wlog that $S(D_2, \varepsilon) = D_2$ in this case. One-way mergeability is essentially a "batched streaming" model where there is a main summary, into which we every time insert a batch of elements, summarized by a summary in S_2. As noted in Section 1.2, prior work showed one-way mergeability of heavy hitter algorithms.

Theorem 2 *Any quantile summary algorithm which is incrementally maintainable is one-way mergeable.*

PROOF. Given a quantile summary S, it promises to approximate the rank of any element by εn. Equivalently, since D defines an empirical frequency distribution f (where, as in the previous section, $f(x)$ gives the count of item x) we can think of S as defining an approximate cumulative frequency function $\hat{F}$, that is, $\hat{F}(i)$ gives the (approximate) number of items in the input which are dominated by i. The approximation guarantees mean that $\|F - \hat{F}\|_\infty \leq \varepsilon n$, where F is the (true) cumulative frequency function (CFF) of f, and the ∞-norm, $\|\cdot\|_\infty$, takes the maximal value. Further, from $\hat{F}$ and n, we can derive $\hat{f}$, the distribution whose cumulative frequency function is $\hat{F}$.

Given summaries S_1 and S_2, which summarize n_1 and n_2 items respectively with error ε_1 and ε_2, we can perform a one-way merge of S_2 into S_1 by extracting the distribution $\hat{f}_2$, and interpreting this as n_2 updates to S_2. The resulting summary is a summary of $f' = f_1 + \hat{f}_2$, that is, $f'(x) = f_1(x) + \hat{f}_2(x)$. This summary implies a cumulative frequency function $\hat{F}'$, whose error relative to the original data is

$$\|\hat{F}' - (F_1 + F_2)\|_\infty$$
$$\leq \|\hat{F}' - (\hat{F}_2 + F_1)\|_\infty + \|(\hat{F}_2 + F_1) - (F_1 + F_2)\|_\infty$$
$$\leq \varepsilon_1(n_1 + n_2) + \|\hat{F}_2 - F_2\|_\infty$$
$$= \varepsilon_1(n_1 + n_2) + \varepsilon_2 n_2.$$

By the same argument, if we merge in a third summary S_3 of n_3 items with error ε_3, the resulting error is at most $\varepsilon_1(n_1 + n_2 + n_3) + \varepsilon_2 n_2 + \varepsilon_3 n_3$. So if this (one-way) merging is done over a large number of summaries $S_1, S_2, S_3 \ldots S_s$, then the resulting summary has error at most

$$\epsilon_1 \left(\sum_{i=1}^{s} n_i \right) + \sum_{i=2}^{s} \varepsilon_i n_i \leq (\epsilon_1 + \max_{1 < i \leq s} \varepsilon_i) N$$

Setting $\varepsilon_1 = \varepsilon_2 = \ldots \varepsilon_i = \varepsilon/2$ is sufficient to meet the requirements on this error. $\square$

An immediate observation is that the GK algorithm [21] (along with other deterministic techniques for streaming computation of quantiles which require more space [32]) meets these requirements, and is therefore one-way mergeable. The merging is fast, since it takes time linear in the summary size to extract an approximate distribution, and near-linear to insert into a second summary.

Corollary 2 *The GK algorithm is one-way mergeable, with a summary size of $O(\frac{1}{\varepsilon}\log(\varepsilon n))$.*

3.2 Low-discrepancy-based summaries

Unfortunately, we cannot show that the GK summary is (fully) mergeable, nor can we give a negative proof. We conjecture it is not, and in fact we conjecture that any deterministic mergeable quantile summary must have size linear in n in the comparison model. On the hand, in this section we give a randomized mergeable quantile summary of size $O(1/\varepsilon \log^{1.5}(1/\varepsilon))$. The idea is to the merge-reduce algorithm [13, 33] for constructing deterministic ε-approximations of range spaces, but randomize it in a way so that error is preserved.

Same-weight merges. We first consider a restricted merging model where each merge is applied only to two summaries (ε-approximations) representing data sets of the same size. Let S_1 and S_2 be the two summaries to be merged. The algorithm is very simple: Set $S' = S_1 \cup S_2$, and sort S'. Then let S_e be all even points in the sorted order and S_o be all odd points in the sorted order. We retain either S_e or S_o with equal probability as our merged summary S. We call this a *same-weight merge*. We note essentially the same algorithm was used by Suri *et. al.* [40], but their analysis shows that the error increases gradually after a series of merges. Below we give our analysis which shows that the error is actually preserved. We first consider a single merge.

Lemma 3 *For any interval $I \in \mathcal{I}$, $2|I \cap S|$ is an unbiased estimator of $|I \cap S'|$ with error at most 1.*

PROOF. If $|I \cap S'|$ is even, then $I \cap S'$ contains the same number of even and odd points. Thus $2|I \cap S| = |I \cap S'|$ no matter whether we choose the even or odd points.

If $|I \cap S'|$ is odd, it must contain exactly one more odd point than even points. Thus if we choose the odd points, we overestimate $|I \cap S'|$ by 1; if we choose the even points, we underestimate by 1. Either happens with probability $1/2$. $\square$

Below we generalize the above lemma to multiple merges, but each merge is a *same-weight* merge. We set the summary size to be k_ε, and note that each merge operation takes time $O(k_\varepsilon)$ to merge the sorted lists and pick every other

---

[3]We will need all $O(\log\frac{1}{\varepsilon})$ comparisons in the binary search to succeed, so there is actually an $O(\log\log\frac{1}{\varepsilon})$ difference between the two problems, which we omit to keep the expressions simple.

point. Let D be the entire data set of size n. We assume that n/k_ε is a power of 2 (this assumption will be removed later). Thus, the whole merging process corresponds to a complete binary tree with $m = \log(n/k_\varepsilon)$ levels. Each internal node in the tree corresponds to the (same-weight) merge of its children. Let S be the final merged summary, corresponding to the root of the tree. Note that each point in S represents 2^m points in D. Recall that (randomized) mergeability requires that S is a valid ε-summary after any number of merges, so it important that the merging algorithm is oblivious to m (hence n). In fact, our algorithm only has one parameter k_ε. We first analyze the correctness of S for any *one* query.

Lemma 4 *If we set $k_\varepsilon = O((1/\varepsilon)\sqrt{\log(1/\delta)})$, then for any interval $I \in \mathcal{I}$ with probability at least $1 - \delta$,*

$$\mathsf{abs}(|I \cap D| - 2^m|I \cap S|) \le \varepsilon n.$$

PROOF. Fix any I. We prove this lemma by considering the over-count error $X_{i,j}$ (which could be positive or negative) produced by a single merge of two sets S_1 and S_2 to get a set $S^{(j)}$ in level i. Then we consider the error $M_i = \sum_{j=1}^{r_i} X_{i,j}$ of all $r_i = 2^{m-i}$ merges in level i, and sum them over all m levels using a single Chernoff-Hoeffding bound. We will show that the errors for all levels form a geometric series that sums to at most εn with probability at least $1 - \delta$.

Start the induction at level 1, before any sets are merged. Merging two sets S_1 and S_2 into $S^{(j)}$ causes the estimate $2|S^{(j)} \cap I|$ to have over-count error

$$X_{1,j} = 2|S^{(j)} \cap I| - |(S_1 \cup S_2) \cap I|.$$

Now $\mathsf{abs}(X_{1,j}) \le 1 = \Delta_1$, by Lemma 3. There are $r_1 = 2^{m-1}$ such merges in this level, and since each choice of even/odd is made independently, this produces r_1 independent random variables $\{X_{1,1}, \ldots, X_{1,r_1}\}$. Let their total over-count error be denoted $M_1 = \sum_{j=1}^{r_1} X_{1,j}$. So, now except for error M_1, the set of r_1 sets $S^{(j)}$, each the result of an independent merge of two sets, can be used to represent $|D \cap I|$ by $2|(\bigcup_j S^{(j)}) \cap I|$.

So inductively, up to level i, we have accumulated at most $\sum_{s=1}^{i-1} M_s$ error, and have $2r_i$ point sets of size k_ε, where $r_i = 2^{m-i}$. We can again consider the merging of two sets S_1 and S_2 into $S^{(j)}$ by a same-weight merge. This causes the estimate $2^i|S^{(j)} \cap I|$ to have error

$$X_{i,j} = 2^i|S^{(j)} \cap I| - 2^{i-1}|(S_1 \cup S_2) \cap I|,$$

where $\mathsf{abs}(X_{i,j}) \le 2^{i-1} = \Delta_i$, by Lemma 3. Again we have r_i such merges in this level, and r_i independent random variables $\{X_{i,1}, \ldots, X_{i,r_i}\}$. The total error in this level is $M_i = \sum_{j=1}^{r_i} X_{i,j}$, and except for this error M_i and $M_{i-1}, \ldots, M_1$, we can accurately estimate $|D \cap I|$ as $2^i|(\bigcup_j S^{(j)}) \cap I|$ using the r_i sets $S^{(j)}$.

We now analyze $M = \sum_{i=1}^m M_i$ using the following Chernoff-Hoeffding bound. Given a set $\{Y_1, \ldots, Y_t\}$ of independent random variables such that $\mathsf{abs}(Y_j - E[Y_j]) \le \Upsilon_j$, then for $T = \sum_{j=1}^t Y_j$ we can bound $\Pr[\mathsf{abs}(T - \sum_{j=1}^t E[Y_j]) > \alpha] \le 2e^{-2\alpha^2/(\sum_{j=1}^t (2\Upsilon_j)^2)}$. In our case, the random variables are m sets of r_i variables $\{X_{i,j}\}_j$, each with $E[X_{i,j}] = 0$ and $\mathsf{abs}(X_{i,j} - E[X_{i,j}]) = \mathsf{abs}(X_{i,j}) \le \Delta_i = 2^{i-1}$. There are m such sets for $i \in \{1, \ldots, m\}$. Setting $\alpha = h2^m$ for some

parameter h, we can write

$$\Pr[\mathsf{abs}(M) > h2^m] \le 2\exp\left(-\frac{2(h2^m)^2}{\sum_{i=1}^m \sum_{j=1}^{r_i}(2\Delta_i)^2}\right)$$

$$= 2\exp\left(-\frac{2(h2^m)^2}{\sum_{i=1}^m (r_i)(2^{2i})}\right)$$

$$= 2\exp\left(-\frac{2h^2(2^{2m})}{\sum_{i=1}^m (2^{m-i})(2^{2i})}\right)$$

$$= 2\exp\left(-\frac{2h^2(2^{2m})}{\sum_{i=1}^m 2^{m+i}}\right)$$

$$= 2\exp\left(-\frac{2h^2}{\sum_{i=1}^m 2^{i-m}}\right)$$

$$= 2\exp\left(-\frac{2h^2}{\sum_{i=1}^m 2^{-i}}\right) < 2\exp\left(-2h^2\right).$$

Thus if we set $h = \sqrt{(1/2)\ln(2/\delta)}$, with probability at least $1 - \delta$ we have $\mathsf{abs}(M) < h2^m = hn/k_\varepsilon$. Thus for $k_\varepsilon = O(h/\varepsilon)$ the error will be smaller than εn, as desired. $\square$

An ε-approximation is required to be correct for *all* intervals $I \in \mathcal{I}$, but this can be easily achieved by increasing k_ε appropriately. There is a set of $1/\varepsilon$ evenly spaced intervals $\mathcal{I}_\varepsilon$ such that any interval $I \in \mathcal{I}$ has

$$\mathsf{abs}(|D \cap I| - |D \cap I'|) \le \varepsilon n/2$$

for some $I' \in \mathcal{I}_\varepsilon$. We can then apply the union bound by setting $\delta' = \delta\varepsilon$ and run the above scheme with $k_\varepsilon = O((1/\varepsilon)\sqrt{\log(1/\delta')})$. Then with probability at least $1 - \delta$, no interval in $\mathcal{I}_\varepsilon$ has more than $\varepsilon n/2$ error, which means that no interval in $\mathcal{I}$ has more than εn error.

Theorem 3 *There is a same-weight merging algorithm that maintains a summary of size $O((1/\varepsilon)\sqrt{\log(1/\varepsilon\delta)})$ which is a one-dimensional ε-approximation with probability at least $1 - \delta$.*

Uneven-weight merges. We next reduce uneven-weight merges to $O(\log(n/k_\varepsilon))$ weighted instances of the same-weight ones. This follows the so-called *logarithmic technique* used in many similar situations [22].

Set $k_\varepsilon = O((1/\varepsilon)\sqrt{\log(1/\varepsilon\delta)})$ as previously. Let n be the size of data set currently being summarized. We maintain $\log(n/k_\varepsilon)$ layers, each of which summarizes a disjoint subset of data points. Each layer is either empty or maintains a summary with exactly k_ε points. In the 0th layer, each summary point has weight 1, and in the ith layer, each summary point has weight 2^i. We assume n/k_ε is an integer; otherwise we can always store the extra $\le k_\varepsilon$ points exactly without introducing any error.

We merge two such summaries S_1 and S_2 via same-weight merging, starting from the bottom layer, and promoting retained points to the next layer. At layer i, we may have $0, 1, 2$, or 3 sets of k_ε points each. If there are 0 or 1 such sets, we skip this layer and proceed to layer $i+1$; if there are 2 or 3 such sets we merge any two of them using a same-weight merge, and promote the merged set of k_ε points to layer $i+1$. Consequently, each merge takes time $O(k_\varepsilon \log \varepsilon n)$, linear in the total size of both summaries.

The analysis of this logarithmic scheme is straightforward because our same-weight merging algorithm preserves the error parameter ε across layers: Since each layer is produced by only same-weight merges, it is an ε-approximation of the set of points represented by this layer, namely the error is εn_i for layer i where n_i is the number of points being represented. Summing over all layers yields a total error of εn. Again it should be clear that this algorithm works without the *a priori* knowledge of the number of merges.

Theorem 4 *There is a mergeable summary of size $O((1/\varepsilon)\cdot \sqrt{\log(1/\varepsilon\delta)}\log(\varepsilon n))$ which is a one-dimensional ε-approximation with probability at least $1 - \delta$.*

3.3 Hybrid quantile summaries

In this section, we build on the above ideas to remove the dependence on n in the size of the summary.

Random sampling. A classic result [41, 42] shows that a random sample of $k_\varepsilon = O((1/\varepsilon^2)\log(1/\delta))$ points from D is an ε-approximation with probability $1 - \delta$. So an ε-approximation can also be obtained by just retaining a random sample of D. Random samples are easily mergeable: A standard way of doing so is to assign a random value $u_i \in [0, 1]$ for each point $p_i \in D$, and we retain in $S \subset D$ the k_ε elements with the smallest u_i values. On a merge of two summaries S_1 and S_2, we retain the set $S \subset S_1 \cup S_2$ that has the k_ε smallest u_i values from the $2k_\varepsilon$ points in $S_1 \cup S_2$. It is also easy to show that finite precision ($O(\log n)$ bits with high probability) is enough to break all ties.

Fact 1 *A random sample of size $k_\varepsilon = O((1/\varepsilon^2)\log(1/\delta))$ is mergeable and is an ε-approximation with probability at least $1 - \delta$.*

We next show how to combine the approaches of random sampling and the low-discrepancy-based method to achieve a summary size independent of n. At an intuitive level, for a subset of points, we maintain a random sample of size about $(1/\varepsilon)\log(1/\varepsilon)$. The sample guarantees an error of $\sqrt{\varepsilon}$ for any range, so we make sure that we only use this on a small fraction of the points (at most εn points). The rest of the points are processed using the logarithmic method. That is, we maintain $O(\log(1/\varepsilon))$ levels of the hierarchy, and only in the bottom level use a random sample. This leads to a summary of size $(1/\varepsilon)$ poly $\log(1/\varepsilon)$.

Hybrid structure. We now describe the summary structure in more detail for n points, where $2^{j-1}k_\varepsilon \le n < 2^j k_\varepsilon$ for some integer j, and $k_\varepsilon = (4/\varepsilon)\sqrt{\ln(4/\varepsilon)}$. Let $g_\varepsilon = (64/\varepsilon^2)\ln(16/\varepsilon)$. For each level l between $i = j - \log_2(g_\varepsilon)$ and $j - 1$ we either maintain k_ε points, or no points. Each point at the lth level has weight 2^l. The remaining $m \le 2^i k_\varepsilon$ points are in a *random buffer* at level i, represented by a random sample of k_ε points (or only m if $m < k_\varepsilon$). Each point in the sample has weight m/k_ε (or 1 if $m < k_\varepsilon$). Note the total size is $O(k_\varepsilon \log(g_\varepsilon)) = O((1/\varepsilon)\log^{1.5}(1/\varepsilon))$.

Merging. Two hybrid summaries S_1 and S_2 are merged as follows. Let n_1 and n_2 be the sizes of the data sets represented by S_1 and S_2, and w.l.o.g. we assume $n_1 \ge n_2$. Let $n = n_1 + n_2$. Let j be an integer such that $2^{j-1}k_\varepsilon \le n < 2^j k_\varepsilon$, and let $i = j - \log_2(g_\varepsilon)$.

First consider the random buffer in the merged summary; it now contains both random buffers in S_1 and S_2, as well as all points represented at level $i - 1$ or below in either S_1 or S_2. Note that if $n_1 \ge 2^{j-1}k_\varepsilon$, then S_1 cannot have points at level $l \le i - 1$. Points from the random buffers of S_1 and S_2 already have u_i values. For every p of weight $w(p) = 2^l$ that was in a level $l \le i - 1$, we insert $w(p)$ copies of p into the buffer and assign a new u_i value to each copy. Then the k_ε points with the largest u_i values are retained.

When the random buffer is full, i.e., represents $2^i k_\varepsilon$ points, then it performs an "output" operation, and outputs the sample of k_ε points of weight 2^i each, which is then merged into the hierarchy at level i. It is difficult to ensure that the random buffer represents exactly $m = 2^i k_\varepsilon$ points when it outputs points, but it is sufficient if this occurs when the buffer has this size in expectation. There are two ways the random buffer may reach this threshold of representing m points:

1. On insertion of a point from the hierarchy of level $l \le i - 1$. Since copies of these points are inserted one at a time, representing 1 point each, it reaches the threshold exactly. The random buffer outputs and then inserts the remaining points in a new random buffer.

2. On the merge of two random buffers B_1 and B_2, which represent b_1 and b_2 points, respectively. Let $b_1 \ge b_2$, and let B be the union of the two buffers and represent $b = b_1 + b_2$ points. If $b < m$ we do not output; otherwise we have $m/2 \le b_1 < m \le b < 2m$. To ensure the output from the random buffer represents m points in expectation we either:

   (i) With probability $\rho = (b-m)/(b-b_1)$, we do not merge, but just output the sample of B_1 and let B_2 be the new random buffer.
   (ii) With probability $1 - \rho = (m-b_1)/(b-b_1)$, output the sample of B after the merge, and let the new random buffer be empty.

   Note that the expected number of points represented by the output from the random buffer is $\rho b_1 + (1-\rho)b = \frac{b-m}{b-b_1}b_1 + \frac{m-b_1}{b-b_1}b = m$.

Next, the levels of the hierarchy of both summaries are merged as before, starting from level i. For each level if there are 2 or 3 sets of k_ε points, two of them are merged using a same-weight merge, and the merged set is promoted to the next level. See Figure 1 for illustration of hybrid structure.

Analysis. First we formalize the upward movement of points.

Lemma 5 *Over time, a point only moves up in the hierarchy (or is dropped): it never decreases in level.*

PROOF. For this analysis, the random buffer is considered to reside at level i at the end of every action. There are five cases we need to consider.

1. A point is involved in a same weight merge at level l. After the merge, it either disappears, or is promoted to level $l + 1$.

2. A point is merged into a random buffer from the hierarchy. The point must have been at level $l \le i - 1$, and the random buffer resides at level i, so the point moves up the hierarchy. If its u_i value is too small, it may disappear.

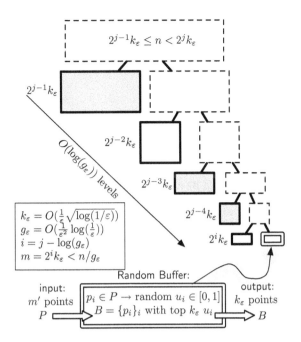

$2^{j-1}k_\varepsilon \le n < 2^j k_\varepsilon$

$2^{j-1}k_\varepsilon$

$O(\log(g_\varepsilon))$ levels

$2^{j-2}k_\varepsilon$

$2^{j-3}k_\varepsilon$

$2^{j-4}k_\varepsilon$

$2^i k_\varepsilon$

$k_\varepsilon = O(\frac{1}{\varepsilon}\sqrt{\log(1/\varepsilon)})$
$g_\varepsilon = O(\frac{1}{\varepsilon^2}\log(\frac{1}{\varepsilon}))$
$i = j - \log(g_\varepsilon)$
$m = 2^i k_\varepsilon < n/g_\varepsilon$

Random Buffer:

input:
m' points
P

$p_i \in P \to$ random $u_i \in [0,1]$
$B = \{p_i\}_i$ with top k_ε u_i

output:
k_ε points
B

Figure 1: Illustration of the hybrid summary. The labels at each level of the hierarchy shows the number of points represented at that layer. Each filled box contains only k_ε summary points.

3. A point is in a random buffer B that is merged with another random buffer B'. The random buffer B could not be at level greater than i before the merge, by definition, but the random buffer afterward is at level i. So the point's level does not decrease (it may stay the same). If the u_i value is too small, it may disappear.

4. A point is in a random buffer when it performs an output operation. The random buffer was at level i, and the point is now at level i in the hierarchy.

5. Both j and i increase. If the point remains in the hierarchy, it remains so at the same level. If it is now at level $i-1$, it gets put in the random buffer at level i, and it may be dropped. If the point is in the random buffer, it remains there but the random buffer is now at level i where before it was at level $i-1$. Again the point may disappear if too many points moved to the random buffer have larger u_i values. □

Now we analyze the error in this hybrid summary. We will focus on a single interval $I \in \mathcal{I}$ and show the over-count error X on I has $\mathsf{abs}(X) \le \varepsilon n/2$ with probability $1 - \varepsilon/4$. Then applying a union bound will ensure the summary is correct for all $1/\varepsilon$ intervals in $\mathcal{I}_\varepsilon$ with probability at least $3/4$. This will imply that for all intervals $I \in \mathcal{I}$ the summary has error at most εn.

The total over-count error can be decomposed into two parts. First, we invoke Theorem 4 to show that the effect of all same-weight merges has error at most $\varepsilon n/4$ with probability at least $1 - \varepsilon/8$. This step assumes that *all* of the data that ever comes out of the random buffer has no error, it is accounted for in the second step. Note that the total number of merge steps at each level is at most as many as in Theorem 4, even those merges that are later absorbed into the random buffer. Second, (the focus of our analysis)

we show the total error from all points that pass through the random buffer is at most $\varepsilon n/4$ with probability at least $1 - \varepsilon/8$. This step assumes that all of the weighted points put into the random buffer have no error, this is accounted for in the first step. So there are two types of random events that affect X: same-weight merges and random buffer outputs. We bound the effect of each event, independent of the result of any other event. Thus after analyzing the two types separately, we can apply the union bound to show the total error is at most $\varepsilon n/2$ with probability at least $1 - \varepsilon/4$.

It remains to analyze the effect on I of the random buffer outputs. First we bound the number of times a random buffer can output to level l, i.e., output a set of k_ε points of weight 2^l each. Then we quantify the total error attributed to the random buffer output at level l.

Lemma 6 *A summary of size n, for $2^{j-1}k_\varepsilon \le n < 2^j k_\varepsilon$, has experienced $h_l \le 2^{j-l} = 2^{i-l}g_\varepsilon$ random buffer promotions to level l within its entire merge history.*

PROOF. By Lemma 5, if a point is promoted from a random buffer to the hierarchy at level l, then it can only be put back into a random buffer at a level $l' > l$. Thus the random buffer can only promote, at a fixed level l, points with total weight $n < 2^j k_\varepsilon$. Since each promotion outputs points with a total weight of $2^l k_\varepsilon$, this can happen at most $h_l < 2^j k_\varepsilon / 2^l k_\varepsilon = 2^{j-l}$ times. The proof concludes using $g_\varepsilon = 2^{j-i}$. □

Lemma 7 *When the random buffer promotes a set B of k_ε points representing a set P of m' points (where $m/2 < m' < 2m$), for any interval $I \in \mathcal{I}$ the over-count*

$$X = (m/k_\varepsilon)|I \cap B| - |I \cap P|$$

has expectation 0 and $\mathsf{abs}(X) \le 2m$.

PROOF. The expectation of over-count X has two independent components. B is a random sample from P, so in expectation is has the correct proportion of points in any interval. Also, since $E[|P|] = m$, and $|B| = k_\varepsilon$, then m/k_ε is the correct scaling constant in expectation.

To bound $\mathsf{abs}(X)$, we know that $|P| < 2m$ by construction, so the maximum error an interval I could have is to return 0 when it should have returned $2m$, or vice-versa. So $\mathsf{abs}(X) < 2m$. □

Since $m \le n/g_\varepsilon$ at level i, then $m \le 2^{l-i}n/g_\varepsilon$ at level l, and we can bound the over-count error as $\Delta_l = \mathsf{abs}(X) \le 2m \le 2^{l-i+1}n/g_\varepsilon$. Now we consider a random buffer promotion that causes an over-count $X_{l,s}$ where $l \in [0,i]$ and $s \in [1,h_l]$. The expected value of $X_{l,s}$ is 0, and $\mathsf{abs}(X_{l,s}) \le \Delta_l$. These events are independent so we can apply another Chernoff-Hoeffding bound on these $\sum_{l=0}^i h_l$ events. Recall that $g_\varepsilon = (64/\varepsilon^2)\ln(16/\varepsilon)$ and let $\hat{T} = \sum_{i=0}^i \sum_{s=1}^{h_l} X_{l,s}$, which has expected value 0. Then

$$\Pr[\mathsf{abs}(\hat{T}) \ge \varepsilon n/4] = 2\exp\left(-2\frac{(\varepsilon n/4)^2}{\sum_{l=0}^i h_l \Delta_l^2}\right)$$

$$\le 2\exp\left(-2\frac{(\varepsilon n/4)^2}{\sum_{l=0}^i (2^{i-l}g_\varepsilon)(2^{l-i+1}n/g_\varepsilon)^2}\right)$$

$$\le 2\exp\left(-g_\varepsilon \frac{\varepsilon^2}{8}\frac{1}{\sum_{l=0}^i 2^{i-l}2^{2(l-i)+2}}\right)$$

$$= 2 \exp\left(-g_\varepsilon \frac{\varepsilon^2}{32} \frac{1}{\sum_{l=0}^{i} 2^{l-i}}\right)$$

$$= 2 \exp\left(-2\ln(16/\varepsilon) \frac{1}{\sum_{l=0}^{i} 2^{-l}}\right)$$

$$\leq 2 \exp(-\ln(16/\varepsilon))$$

$$= 2(\varepsilon/16) = \varepsilon/8.$$

Theorem 5 *The above scheme maintains a fully mergeable one-dimensional ε-approximation of size $O(\frac{1}{\varepsilon}\log^{1.5}(1/\varepsilon))$, with probability at least $3/4$.*

4. ε-APPROXIMATIONS OF RANGE SPACES

In this section, we generalize the approach of the previous section to ε-approximations of higher dimensional range spaces. Let D be a set of points in $\mathbb{R}^d$, and let $(D, \mathcal{R})$ be a range space of VC-dimension ν (see Section 1.2 for the definition). We will use $\mathcal{R}_d$ to denote the set of ranges induced by a set of d-dimensional axis-aligned rectangles, i.e., $\mathcal{R}_d = \{D \cap \rho \mid \rho \text{ is a rectangle}\}$.

The overall merge algorithm is the same as in Section 3, except that we use a more intricate procedure for each same-weight merge operation of two summaries S_1 and S_2. Suppose $|S_1| = |S_2| = k$, and let $S' = S_1 \cup S_2$. Using the algorithm in [5], we compute a low-discrepancy coloring $\chi : S' \to \{-1, +1\}$ such that for any $R \in \mathcal{R}$, $\sum_{a \in S' \cap R} \chi(a) = O(k^{1/2-1/2\nu})$. Let $S^+ = \{a \in S' \mid \chi(a) = +1\}$ and $S^- = \{a \in S' \mid \chi(a) = -1\}$. Then we choose to retain either S^+ or S^- at random as the merged summary S. We can then generalize Lemma 3 as follows.

Lemma 8 *Given any range $R \in \mathcal{R}$, $2|S \cap R|$ is an unbiased estimator of $|S' \cap R|$ with error at most $\Lambda_\nu = O(k^{1/2-1/2\nu})$.*

For the range space $(P, \mathcal{R}_d)$, we can reduce the discrepancy of the coloring to $O(\log^{2d} k)$ using [38]. Hence the generalization of Lemma 3 is as follows.

Lemma 9 *Given any range $R \in \mathcal{R}_d$, $2|S \cap R|$ is an unbiased estimator of $|S' \cap R|$ with error at most $\Lambda_d = O(\log^{2d} k)$.*

Lemma 4 and its proof generalize in a straightforward way, the only change being that now $\Delta_i = 2^{i-1}\Lambda_\nu$, hence implying $h > O(\Lambda_v \log^{1/2}(1/\varepsilon\delta))$ and

$$\varepsilon' = \varepsilon/h = \Omega(\varepsilon/\Lambda_v \log^{1/2}(1/\varepsilon\delta)).$$

Solving $n/k_\varepsilon = n\varepsilon'$ for k_ε yields

$$k_\varepsilon = \frac{1}{\varepsilon} O\left(\Lambda_v \sqrt{\log \frac{1}{\varepsilon\delta}}\right)$$

$$= O\left(\frac{1}{\varepsilon}\left(k_\varepsilon^{1/2-1/(2\nu)} \log^{1/2} k_\varepsilon\right) \sqrt{\log \frac{1}{\varepsilon\delta}}\right)$$

$$= O\left(\left(\frac{1}{\varepsilon}\right)^{2\nu/(\nu+1)} \log^{\nu/(\nu+1)}\left(\frac{1}{\varepsilon\delta}\right)\right).$$

For $(P, \mathcal{R}_d)$ we get

$$k_\varepsilon = O((1/\varepsilon)\Lambda_d \sqrt{\log(1/\varepsilon\delta)})$$

$$= O\left(\frac{1}{\varepsilon} \log^{2d}\left(\frac{\log(1/\delta)}{\varepsilon}\right) \sqrt{\log \frac{1}{\varepsilon\delta}}\right).$$

Applying the rest of the machinery as before we can achieve ε-approximations of size k_ε under same-weight merges, with probability at least $1 - \delta$.

Lemma 10 *Using the above framework, on same-weight merges, we can maintain an ε-approximation of $(P, \mathcal{A})$ with constant VC-dimension ν of size $O((1/\varepsilon)^{2\nu/(\nu+1)} \log^{\nu/(\nu+1)}(1/\varepsilon\delta))$, with probability at least $1 - \delta$. For the range space $(P, \mathcal{R}_d)$, the size is $O((1/\varepsilon) \log^{2d}(\log(1/\delta)/\varepsilon) \cdot \sqrt{\log(1/\varepsilon\delta)})$.*

Then this extends to different-weight merges with an extra $\log(n\varepsilon)$ factor, as with intervals. Also, the random buffer can maintain a random sample of the same asymptotic size $O((1/\varepsilon^2)\log(1/\delta))$ and 0 expected over-count error. Substituting the increased k_ε value, the generalizations of Lemma 6 and Lemma 7 follow. We can also move the $\log(1/\delta)$ term to the outside, by setting $\delta = 1/2$ in these expressions, and then repeating the processes $O(\log(1/\delta')$ times independently to drive the probability of failure down to δ'.

Theorem 6 *A mergeable ε-approximation of a range space $(D, \mathcal{R})$ of VC-dimension ν of size $O(1/\varepsilon^{\frac{2\nu}{\nu+1}} \log^{\frac{2\nu+1}{\nu+1}} \frac{1}{\varepsilon} \log \frac{1}{\delta})$ can be maintained with probability at least $1 - \delta$. If $\mathcal{R} = \mathcal{R}_d$, then the size is $O\left(\frac{1}{\varepsilon} \log^{2d+3/2}\left(\frac{1}{\varepsilon}\right) \log \frac{1}{\delta}\right)$.*

5. ε-KERNELS

A unit vector u in $\mathbb{R}^d$ defines a direction, and a point $p \in \mathbb{R}^d$ is projected to the line through u using the inner product $\langle u, p \rangle$. Given a point set $P \subset \mathbb{R}^d$, the *extent* in direction u is $E[P, u] = \max_{p \in P} \langle u, p \rangle$, and the width $\text{wid}[P, u] = E[P, u] + E[P, -u]$. An *$\varepsilon$-kernel* is a subset $K \subset P$ such that over all directions u,

$$\max_u E[P, u] - E[K, u] \leq \varepsilon \text{wid}[P, u]$$

and

$$\max_u \frac{\text{wid}[P, u] - \text{wid}[K, u]}{\text{wid}[P, u]} \leq 2\varepsilon.$$

An ε-kernel of size $O(1/\varepsilon^{(d-1)/2})$ can be computed in time $O(|P| + 1/\varepsilon^{d-3/2})$ [9, 43]. It is also known that the union of two ε-kernels is an ε-kernel [9], but this observation alone is not sufficient to have mergeable ε-kernels of size $1/\varepsilon^{O(1)}$ since the size of the kernel doubles after taking the union. We therefore need a merge procedure that reduces $K_1 \cup K_2$ to an appropriate size without increasing the error.

Reference frames and ε-kernel basics. We say a point set P is *β-fat* if over all directions u, v we can bound the width ratio $\max_{u,v}(\text{wid}(P, u)/\text{wid}(P, v)) \leq \beta$. Given a box $B \supset P$, P is *β-fat with respect to B* if

$$\max_{u,v}(\text{wid}(B, u)/\text{wid}(P, v)) \leq \beta.$$

If β is less than some fixed constant (that depends only on d) we say that P is just *fat* (with respect to B). B represents a *reference frame* in that it fixes a set of axis, as well as a relative scale along those axis. That is, the d orthogonal directions the of box's face normals $\{b_1, \ldots, b_d\}$ define coordinate axis, and the width of the box in each of these directions provides a relative scale of the contained point sets. Given P and B, we will use this reference frame to construct/merge kernels.

Most standard techniques to create ε-kernels use the following observations.

- Let A be an affine transform. If K is an ε-kernel of P, then $A(K)$ is an ε-kernel of $A(P)$ [1].

- Let $I = [-1, 1]^d$ and $\beta_d = 2^d d^{5/2} d!$. There exists an $O(d^2|P|)$ size algorithm to construct an affine transform A such that $A(P) \subset I$ and $A(P)$ is β_d-fat with respect to I [7, 25].

- Place a grid G_ε on I so that each grid cell has width ε/β_d. For each grid cell $g \in G_\varepsilon$, place one point (if it exists) from $g \cap A(P)$ in K. Then K is an ε-kernel of $A(P)$. Clearly the same holds if for each column in the grid, you only retain the most extreme such points, reducing the size to $O(1/\varepsilon^{d-1})$ [1].

Because of the first two observations, for static ε-kernel algorithms it is convenient to simply assume that $P \subset I$ and P is fat with respect to I. The main difficulty in incremental ε-kernel algorithms is maintaining such a reference frame I.

The size of ε-kernels can be reduced to $O(1/\varepsilon^{(d-1)/2})$ using an additional trick [1], given that we have an $(\varepsilon/3)$-kernel K_1 of P that is β-fat with respect to I. Consider a sphere S of radius $\sqrt{d} + 1$ centered at the origin, and place a set Q_ε of $O(1/(\varepsilon\beta)^{(d-1)/2})$ evenly spaced points on S. For each point $q \in Q_\varepsilon$ place the closest point to q from K_1 into K. Then K is an ε-kernel of P (of size $O(1/\varepsilon^{(d-1)/2})$).

Mergeable ε-kernels in a common reference frame.
Let B be a d-dimensional box, and let $P_1, P_2 \subset I$ be two point sets that are fat with respect to B. A result in [1] implies that we can assume $B = [-1, +1]^d$. We can now create mergeable ε-kernels for P_1 and P_2. More precisely, we create ε-kernels K_1, K_2 of P_1, P_2, respectively, such that (1) $|K_1|, |K_2| \leq b_{\varepsilon,d} = c(1/\varepsilon)^{(d-1)/2}$ for some constant c, and (2) from K_1 and K_2 we can create an ε-kernel K of $P = P_1 \cup P_2$ such that $|K| \leq b_{\varepsilon,d}$.

First we create K_1 and K_2 using the three observations above and the additional trick to reduce the size. For each point $q \in Q_\varepsilon$, we retain in K, the merged ε-kernel of $P_1 \cup P_2$, the closest point to q in $K_1 \cup K_2$. This approach can be used to merge as many ε-kernels as desired, without increasing the ε error factor or the size beyond $b_{\varepsilon,d}$, provided each of the input point sets is fat with respect to the same box B.

Theorem 7 *A mergeable ε-kernels of size $O(1/\varepsilon^{(d-1)/2})$ can be maintained, assuming all input point sets are fat with respect to a fixed box.*

Although the requirement of being fat with respect to the same box may seem too restrictive, it is a reasonable assumption for most data sets in practice. Given a distributed data set, we probably have upper bounds and rough lower bounds on the total extent of point sets. This is enough to provide a bounding box for which the point sets are fat with respect to. Even if one partition of the data set is not fat with respect to the full bounding box (it may be a small localized subset), the full result will be fat.

We leave open the question of maintaining a mergeable ε-kernel that does not restrict the points to a fixed reference frame.

6. CONCLUDING REMARKS

We have formalized the notion of mergeable summaries, and demonstrated fully mergeable summaries for the central problems of heavy hitters, quantiles, ε-approximations and ε-kernels. The obvious open question is for what other problems do there exist fully mergeable summaries. In some cases, it may be possible to adapt existing solutions from the streaming literature to this setting. For example, consider the problem of k-median clustering. Guha *et al.* [24] show that clustering the union of cluster centers from disjoint parts of the input gives a guaranteed approximation to the overall clustering. In our terminology, this means that clusterings can be merged, although since the accuracy degrades by a constant amount each time, we may think of this as a one-way merge algorithm. Similarly, results on k-center clustering on the stream can generate a mergeable summary of size $O(\frac{k}{\varepsilon} \log 1/\varepsilon)$ that provides a $2 + \varepsilon$ guarantee [23].

In the graph setting, a simple technique for finding a t-spanner is to eject any edges which complete a cycle of length t. Given two such spanners, we can merge by simply applying the same rule as we add one graph to the other, edge by edge. This results in a mergeable summary of size $\tilde{O}(n^{1+2/(t+1)})$ [16]. However, there are many other problems in the domain of high-dimensional data, geometric data and graph data for which no mergeable summary is known or for which bounds are not tight.

7. REFERENCES

[1] P. K. Agarwal, S. Har-Peled, and K. R. Varadarajan. Approximating extent measure of points. *Journal of the ACM*, 51(4):660–635, 2004.

[2] P. K. Agarwal, J. M. Phillips, and H. Yu. Stability of ε-kernels. In *Proc. European Symposium on Algorithms*, 2010.

[3] P. K. Agarwal and H. Yu. A space-optimal data-stream algorithm for coresets in the plane. In *Proc. Annual Symposium on Computational Geometry*, 2007.

[4] N. Alon, Y. Matias, and M. Szegedy. The space complexity of approximating the frequency moments. *Journal of Computer and System Sciences*, 58(1):137–147, 1999.

[5] N. Bansal. Constructive algorithms for discrepancy minimization. In *Proc. IEEE Symposium on Foundations of Computer Science*, pages 407–414, 2010.

[6] Z. Bar-Yossef, T. S. Jayram, R. Kumar, D. Sivakumar, and L. Trevisan. Counting distinct elements in a data stream. In *RANDOM*, 2002.

[7] G. Barequet and S. Har-Peled. Efficiently approximating the minimum-volume bounding box of a point set in three dimensions. *Journal of Algorithms*, 38:91–109, 2001.

[8] R. Berinde, G. Cormode, P. Indyk, and M. Strauss. Space-optimal heavy hitters with strong error bounds. *ACM Transactions on Database Systems*, 35(4), 2010.

[9] T. Chan. Faster core-set constructions and data-stream algorithms in fixed dimensions. *Computational Geometry: Theory and Applications*, 35:20–35, 2006.

[10] T. Chan. Dynamic coresets. In *Proc. Annual Symposium on Computational Geometry*, 2008.

[11] M. Charikar, A. Newman, and A. Nikolov. Tight

hardness results for minimizing discrepancy. In *Proc. ACM-SIAM Symposium on Discrete Algorithms*, 2011.

[12] B. Chazelle. *The Discrepancy Method*. Cambridge, 2000.

[13] B. Chazelle and J. Matousek. On linear-time deterministic algorithms for optimization problems in fixed dimensions. *Journal of Algorithms*, 21:579–597, 1996.

[14] G. Cormode and M. Hadjieleftheriou. Finding frequent items in data streams. *Proc. VLDB Endowment*, 1(2):1530–1541, 2008.

[15] G. Cormode and S. Muthukrishnan. An improved data stream summary: The count-min sketch and its applications. *Journal of Algorithms*, 55(1):58–75, 2005.

[16] J. Feigenbaum, S. Kannan, A. McGregor, S. Suri, and J. Zhang. Graph distances in the streaming model: The value of space. In *ACM-SIAM Symposium on Discrete Algorithms*, 2005.

[17] J. Feigenbaum, S. Kannan, M. J. Strauss, and M. Viswanathan. An approximate L1-difference algorithm for massive data streams. *SIAM Journal on Computing*, 32(1):131–151, 2003.

[18] J. Feldman, S. Muthukrishnan, A. Sidiropoulos, C. Stein, and Z. Svitkina. On distributing symmetric streaming computations. In *Proc. ACM-SIAM Symposium on Discrete Algorithms*, 2008.

[19] S. Ganguly and A. Majumder. CR-precis: A deterministic summary structure for update data streams. In *ESCAPE*, 2007.

[20] A. C. Gilbert, Y. Kotidis, S. Muthukrishnan, and M. J. Strauss. How to summarize the universe: Dynamic maintenance of quantiles. In *Proc. International Conference on Very Large Data Bases*, 2002.

[21] M. Greenwald and S. Khanna. Space-efficient online computation of quantile summaries. In *Proc. ACM SIGMOD International Conference on Management of Data*, 2001.

[22] M. Greenwald and S. Khanna. Power conserving computation of order-statistics over sensor networks. In *Proc. ACM Symposium on Principles of Database Systems*, 2004.

[23] S. Guha. Tight results for clustering and summarizing data streams. In *Proc. International Conference on Database Theory*, 2009.

[24] S. Guha, N. Mishra, R. Motwani, and L. O'Callaghan. Clustering data streams. In *Proc. IEEE Conference on Foundations of Computer Science*, 2000.

[25] S. Har-Peled. *Approximation Algorithm in Geometry (Chapter 21)*. http://valis.cs.uiuc.edu/~sariel/teach/notes/aprx/, 2010.

[26] D. M. Kane, J. Nelson, and D. P. Woodruff. An optimal algorithm for the distinct elements problem. In *Proc. ACM Symposium on Principles of Database Systems*, 2010.

[27] K. G. Larsen. On range searching in the group model and combinatorial discrepancy. under submission, 2011.

[28] Y. Li, P. M. Long, and A. Srinivasan. Improved bounds on the sample complexity of learning. *Journal of Computer and System Sciences*, 62:516–527, 2001.

[29] S. Madden, M. J. Franklin, J. M. Hellerstein, and W. Hong. TAG: a tiny aggregation service for ad-hoc sensor networks. In *Proc. Symposium on Operating Systems Design and Implementation*, 2002.

[30] A. Manjhi, S. Nath, and P. B. Gibbons. Tributaries and deltas: efficient and robust aggregation in sensor network streams. In *Proc. ACM SIGMOD International Conference on Management of Data*, 2005.

[31] A. Manjhi, V. Shkapenyuk, K. Dhamdhere, and C. Olston. Finding (recently) frequent items in distributed data streams. In *Proc. IEEE International Conference on Data Engineering*, 2005.

[32] G. S. Manku, S. Rajagopalan, and B. G. Lindsay. Approximate medians and other quantiles in one pass and with limited memory. In *Proc. ACM SIGMOD International Conference on Management of Data*, 1998.

[33] J. Matousek. Approximations and optimal geometric divide-and-conquer. In *Proc. ACM Symposium on Theory of Computing*, 1991.

[34] J. Matousek. *Geometric Discrepancy; An Illustrated Guide*. Springer, 1999.

[35] A. Metwally, D. Agrawal, and A. Abbadi. An integrated efficient solution for computing frequent and top-k elements in data streams. *ACM Transactions on Database Systems*, 31(3):1095–1133, 2006.

[36] J. Misra and D. Gries. Finding repeated elements. *Science of Computer Programming*, 2:143–152, 1982.

[37] J. Nelson and D. P. Woodruff. Fast manhattan sketches in data streams. In *Proc. ACM Symposium on Principles of Database Systems*, 2010.

[38] J. M. Phillips. Algorithms for ε-approximations of terrains. In *Proc. ICALP*, 2008.

[39] N. Shrivastava, C. Buragohain, D. Agrawal, and S. Suri. Medians and beyond: New aggregation techniques for sensor networks. In *Proc. ACM SenSys*, 2004.

[40] S. Suri, C. Toth, and Y. Zhou. Range counting over multidimensional data streams. *Discrete and Computational Geometry*, 36(4):633–655, 2006.

[41] M. Talagrand. Sharper bounds for Gaussian and emperical processes. *Annals of Probability*, 22:76, 1994.

[42] V. Vapnik and A. Chervonenkis. On the uniform convergence of relative frequencies of events to their probabilities. *Theory of Probability and its Applications*, 16:264–280, 1971.

[43] H. Yu, P. K. Agarwal, R. Poreddy, and K. R. Varadarajan. Practical methods for shape fitting and kinetic data structures using coresets. In *Proc. Annual Symposium on Computational Geometry*, 2004.

[44] H. Zarrabi-Zadeh. An almost space-optimal streaming algorithm for coresets in fixed dimensions. In *Proc. European Symposium on Algorithms*, 2008.

The ACM PODS Alberto O. Mendelzon Test-of-Time Award 2012

In 2007, the PODS Executive Committee decided to establish a Test-of-Time Award, named after the late Alberto O. Mendelzon, in recognition of his scientific legacy, and his service and dedication to the database community. Mendelzon was an international leader in database theory, whose pioneering and fundamental work has inspired and influenced both database theoreticians and practitioners, and continues to be applied in a variety of advanced settings. He served the database community in many ways; in particular, he served as the General Chair of the PODS conference, and was instrumental in bringing together the PODS and SIGMOD conferences. He also was an outstanding educator, who guided the research of numerous doctoral students and postdoctoral fellows. The Award is to be awarded each year to a paper or a small number of papers published in the PODS proceedings ten years prior, that had the most impact (in terms of research, methodology, or transfer to practice) over the intervening decade. The decision was approved by SIGMOD and the ACM. The funds for the Award were contributed by IBM Toronto.

The PODS Executive Chair has appointed us to serve as the Award Committee for 2012. After careful consideration, we have decided to select the following paper as the award winner for 2012:

Containment and Equivalence for an XPath Fragment
by Gerome Miklau and Dan Suciu

The paper studied static analysis problems for XPath, a query language at the core of processing XML documents and XML document databases. XPath, an important paradigm of a query language for semi-structured data, is designed with tree-navigation in mind and supports such navigation along three axes: ancestor-descendant, branching, and wildcards.

In this paper, Miklau and Suciu established that if all three axes are allowed, then the query-containment problem for XPath queries is coNP-complete. Furthermore, this intractability persists even when certain tight bounds on the number of wildcards and the number of branches are imposed. These results shed light on the boundary between tractability and intractability for XPath query containment, since it was previously known that the containment problem was solvable in polynomial time for XPath queries in which any two of the three axes are allowed.

Both the paper in the PODS 2002 proceedings and its subsequent full version in the Journal of the Association for Computing Machinery have received hundreds of citations each. Moreover, this work initiated a fruitful line of research on the static analysis of XML query languages that brought together researchers from database theory and automata theory.

Richard Hull (chair)
IBM T. J. Watson Research Center, USA

Phokion G. Kolaitis
University of California at Santa Cruz &
IBM Research-Almaden, USA

Dirk Van Gucht
Computer Science Department, Indiana University, USA

The Alberto O. Mendelzon Test-of-Time Award Committee for 2012

Worst-case Optimal Join Algorithms

Hung Q. Ngo
University at Buffalo, SUNY
hungngo@buffalo.edu

Ely Porat
Bar-Ilan University
porately@cs.biu.ac.il

Christopher Ré
University of
Wisconsin–Madison
chrisre@cs.wisc.edu

Atri Rudra
University at Buffalo, SUNY
atri@buffalo.edu

ABSTRACT

Efficient join processing is one of the most fundamental and well-studied tasks in database research. In this work, we examine algorithms for natural join queries over many relations and describe a novel algorithm to process these queries optimally in terms of worst-case data complexity. Our result builds on recent work by Atserias, Grohe, and Marx, who gave bounds on the size of a full conjunctive query in terms of the sizes of the individual relations in the body of the query. These bounds, however, are not constructive: they rely on Shearer's entropy inequality which is information-theoretic. Thus, the previous results leave open the question of whether there exist algorithms whose running time achieve these optimal bounds. An answer to this question may be interesting to database practice, as we show in this paper that any project-join plan is polynomially slower than the optimal bound for some queries. We construct an algorithm whose running time is worst-case optimal for all natural join queries. Our result may be of independent interest, as our algorithm also yields a constructive proof of the general fractional cover bound by Atserias, Grohe, and Marx without using Shearer's inequality. In addition, we show that this bound is equivalent to a geometric inequality by Bollobás and Thomason, one of whose special cases is the famous Loomis-Whitney inequality. Hence, our results algorithmically prove these inequalities as well. Finally, we discuss how our algorithm can be used to compute a relaxed notion of joins.

Categories and Subject Descriptors

H.2.4 [**Database Management**]: Systems—*Relational databases*

General Terms

Algorithms, Theory

Keywords

Join Algorithms, fractional cover bound, Loomis-Whitney inequality, Bollobás-Thomason inequality

1. INTRODUCTION

Recently, Grohe and Marx [17] and Atserias, Grohe, and Marx [5] (AGM's results henceforth) derived tight bounds on the number of output tuples of a *full conjunctive query*[1] in terms of the sizes of the relations mentioned in the query's body. As query output size estimation is fundamentally important for efficient query processing, these results have generated a great deal of excitement.

To understand the spirit of AGM's results, consider the following example where we have a schema with three attributes, A, B, and C, and three relations, $R(A, B)$, $S(B, C)$ and $T(A, C)$, defined over those attributes. Consider the following natural join query:

$$q = R \bowtie S \bowtie T \qquad (1)$$

Let $q(I)$ denote the set of tuples that is output from applying q to a database instance I, i.e. $q(I)$ is the set of triples of constants (a, b, c) such that $R(ab)$, $S(bc)$, and $T(ac)$ are in I. Our goal is to bound the number of tuples returned by q on I, denoted by $|q(I)|$, in terms of $|R|$, $|S|$, and $|T|$. For simplicity, let us consider the case when $|R| = |S| = |T| = N$. A trivial bound is $|q(I)| \le N^3$. One can obtain a better bound by noticing that the output of any pair-wise join (say $R \bowtie S$) will be a superset of $q(I)$, since the union of the attributes in R and S together contain (or "cover") all attributes. This leads to the bound $|q(I)| \le N^2$. AGM showed that one can get a better upper bound of $|q(I)| \le N^{3/2}$ by generalizing the notion of cover to a so-called "fractional cover" (see Section 2). Moreover, this estimate is tight in the sense that for infinitely many values of N, one can find a database instance I for which $|R| = |S| = |T| = N$ and $|q(I)| = N^{3/2}$. These non-trivial estimates are exciting to database researchers as they offer previously unknown, nontrivial methods to estimate the cardinality of a query result – a fundamental problem to support efficient query processing.

More generally, given an arbitrary natural-join query q and given the sizes of input relations, the AGM method can generate an upper bound U such that $|q(I)| \le U$, where U depends on the "best" fractional cover of the attributes. This "best" fractional cover can be computed by a linear program (see Section 2 for more details). Henceforth, we refer to this inequality as the *AGM's fractional cover inequality*, and the bound U as the *AGM's fractional cover bound*. They also show that the bound is essentially optimal in the sense that for infinitely many sizes of input relations, there exists an instance I such that each relation in I is of the prescribed size and $|q(I)| = U$.

AGM's results leave open whether one can compute the actual set $q(I)$ in time $O(U)$. In fact, AGM observed this issue and presented an algorithm that computes $q(I)$ with a running time of $O(|q|^2 \cdot$

---

[1] A full conjunctive query is a conjunctive query where every variable in the body appears in the head.

$U \cdot N$) where N is the cardinality of the largest input relation and $|q|$ denotes the size of the query q. AGM established that their join-project plan can in some cases be super-polynomially better than any join-only plan. However, AGM's join algorithm is not optimal. Even on query (1), we can construct a family of database instances $I_1, I_2, \ldots, I_N, \ldots$, such that in the Nth instance I_N we have $|R| = |S| = |T| = N$ and any join-project plan (which includes AGM's algorithm) takes $\Omega(N^2)$-time even though from AGM's bound we know that $|q(I)| \leq U = N^{3/2}$, which is the best worst-case run-time that one can hope for.

The $\sqrt{N}$-gap on a small example motivates our central question. In what follows, *natural join queries* are defined as the join of a set of relations $R_1, \ldots, R_m$.

> **Optimal Worst-case Join Evaluation Problem** (Optimal Join Problem). *Given a fixed database schema $\bar{R} = \left\{ R_i(\bar{A}_i) \right\}_{i=1}^{m}$ and an m-tuple of integers $\bar{N} = (N_1, \ldots, N_m)$. Let q be the natural join query joining the relations in $\bar{R}$ and let $I(\bar{N})$ be the set of all instances such that $|R_i^I| = N_i$ for $i = 1, \ldots, m$. Define $U = \sup_{I \in I(\bar{N})} |q(I)|$. Then, the optimal worst-case join evaluation problem is to evaluate q in time $O(U + \sum_{i=1}^{m} N_i)$.*

Since any algorithm to produce $q(I)$ requires time at least $|q(I)|$, an algorithm that solves the above problem would have an optimal worst-case data-complexity.[2] (Note that we are mainly concerned with data complexity and thus the $O(U)$ bound above ignores the dependence on $|q|$. Our results have a small $O(|q|)$ factor.)

Implicitly, this problem has been studied for over three decades: a modern RDBMS uses decades of highly tuned algorithms to efficiently produce query results. Nevertheless, as we described above, such systems are asymptotically suboptimal – even for query (1). Our main result is an algorithm that achieves asymptotically optimal worst-case running times for all join queries.

We begin by describing connections between AGM's inequality and a family of inequalities in geometry. In particular, we show that the AGM's inequality is *equivalent* to the discrete version of a geometric inequality proved by Bollobás and Thomason [8, Theorem 2]. This equivalence is shown in Section 2.2.

Our ideas for an algorithm solving the optimal join problem begin by examining a special case of the Bollobás-Thomason (BT) inequality: the classic Loomis-Whitney (LW) inequality [26]. The LW inequality bounds the measure of an n-dimensional set in terms of the measures of its $(n-1)$-dimensional projections onto the co-ordinate hyperplanes. The bound $|q(I)| \leq \sqrt{|R||S||T|}$ for query (1) is *exactly* the LW inequality with $n = 3$ applied to the discrete measure. Our algorithmic development begins with a slight generalization of query (1). We describe an algorithm for join queries which have the same format as in the LW inequality setup with $n \geq 3$. In particular, we consider "LW instances" of the optimal join problem, where the query is to join n relations whose attribute sets are all the distinct $(n-1)$-subsets of a universe of n attributes. Since the LW inequality is tight, and our join algorithm has running time that is asymptotically data-optimal for this class of queries (e.g., $O(N^{3/2})$ in our motivating example), our algorithm is worst-case data-complexity optimal for LW instances.

Our algorithm for LW instances exhibits a key twist compared to a conventional join algorithm. The twist is that our algorithm partitions the values of the join key on each side of the join into two sets: those values that are *heavy* and those that are *light*. Intuitively, a value of a join key is heavy if its fanout is high enough so that joining all such join keys could violate the size bound (e.g., $N^{3/2}$ above). The art is selecting the precise fanout threshold for when a join key is heavy. This per-tuple choice of join strategy is not typically done in standard RDBMS join processing.

Building on the algorithm for LW instances, we next describe our main result: an algorithm to solve the optimal join problem for all join queries. In particular, we design an algorithm for evaluating join queries which not only *proves* AGM's fractional cover inequality *without* using the information-theoretic Shearer's inequality, but also has a running time that is linear in the bound (modulo pre-processing time). As AGM's inequality is equivalent to BT inequality and thus implies LW inequality, our result is the first algorithmic proof of these geometric inequalities as well. To do this, we must carefully select which projections of relations to join and in which order our algorithm joins relations on a "per tuple" basis as in the LW-instance case. Our algorithm computes these orderings, and then at each stage it performs a heavy/light tuple check that is similar to the strategy used for the LW instances earlier.

It is easy to show that any join-only plan is suboptimal for some queries. A natural question is, *when do classical RDBMS algorithms have higher worst-case run-time than our proposed approach?* AGM's analysis of their join-project algorithm leads to a worst case run-time complexity that is a factor of the largest relation worse than the AGM's bound. To investigate whether AGM's analysis is tight, we ask a sharper variant of this question: *Given a query q does there exist a family of instances I such that our algorithm runs asymptotically faster than a standard binary-join-based plan or AGM's join-project plan?* We give a partial answer to this question by describing a sufficient syntactic condition for the query q such that for each $k \geq 2$, we can construct a family of instances where each relation is of size N such that any project-join plan (which as a special case includes AGM's algorithm) will need time $\Omega(N^2/k^2)$, while the fractional cover bound is $O(N^{1+1/(k-1)})$ – an asymptotic gap. We then show through a more detailed analysis that our algorithm on these instances takes $O(k^2 N)$-time.

We consider several extensions and improvements of our main result. In terms of the dependence on query size, our algorithms are also efficient (at most linear in $|q|$, which is better than the quadratic dependence in AGM) for full queries, but they are not necessarily optimal. In particular, if each relation in the schema has arity 2, we are able to give an algorithm with better query complexity than our general algorithm. This shows that in general our algorithm's dependence on the factors of the query is not the best possible. We also consider computing a relaxed notion of joins and give worst-case optimal algorithms for this problem as well.

Outline. The remainder of the paper is organized as follows: in the rest of this section, we describe related work. In Section 2 we describe our notation, formulate the main problem, and prove the connection between AGM's inequality and BT inequality. Our main results are in Section 3. We first present a data-optimal join algorithm for LW instances, and then present the optimal algorithm for arbitrary join queries. We also discuss the limits of performance of prior approaches and our approach in more detail. In Section 4, we describe several extensions. We conclude in Section 5. Due to space constraints some proofs are deferred to the full version [30].

Related Work

Grohe and Marx [17] made the first (implicit) connection between fractional edge cover and the output size of a conjunctive query. (Their results were stated for constraint satisfaction problems.) At-

---

[2]In an RDBMS, one computes information, e.g., indexes, offline that may obviate the need to read the entire input relations to produce the output. In a similar spirit, we can extend our results to evaluate any query q in time $O(U)$, removing the term $\sum_i N_i$ by precomputing some indices.

serias, Grohe, and Marx [5] extended Grohe and Marx's results in the database setting.

The first relevant result of AGM is the following inequality. Consider a join query over relations R_e, $e \in E$, where E is a collection of subsets of an attribute "universe" V, and relation R_e is on attribute set e. Then, the number of output tuples is bounded above by $\prod_{e \in E} |R_e|^{x_e}$, where $\mathbf{x} = (x_e)_{e \in E}$ is an *arbitrary* fractional cover of the hypergraph $H = (V, E)$.

They also showed that this bound is tight. In particular, for infinitely many positive integers N there is a database instance with $|R_e| = N$, $\forall e \in E$, and the upper bound gives the actual number of output tuples. When the sizes $|R_e|$ were given as inputs to the (output size estimation) problem, obviously the best upper bound is obtained by picking the fractional cover $\mathbf{x}$ which minimizes the linear objective function $\sum_{e \in E} (\log |R_e|) \cdot x_e$. In this "size constrained" case, however, their lower bound is off from the upper bound by a factor of 2^n, where n is the total number of attributes. AGM also presented an inapproximability result which justifies this gap. Note, however, that the gap is only dependent on the query size and the bound is still asymptotically optimal in the data-complexity sense.

The second relevant result from AGM is a join-project plan with running time $O\left(|q|^2 N_{\max}^{1 + \sum x_e}\right)$, where $N_{\max}$ is the maximum size of input relations and $|q| = |V| \cdot |E|$ is the query size.

The AGM's inequality contains as a special case the discrete versions of two well-known inequalities in geometry: the *Loomis-Whitney* (LW) inequality [26] and its generalization the *Bollobás-Thomason* (BT) inequality [8]. There are two typical proofs of the discrete LW and BT inequalities. The first proof is by induction using Hölder's inequality [8]. The second proof (see Lyons and Peres [27]) essentially uses "equivalent" entropy inequalities by Han [19] and its generalization by Shearer [9], which was also the route Grohe and Marx [17] took to prove AGM's bound. All of these proofs are non-constructive.

There are many applications of the discrete LW and BT inequalities. The $n = 3$ case of the LW inequality was used to prove communication lower bounds for matrix multiplication on distributed memory parallel computers [22]. The inequality was used to prove submultiplicativity inequalities regarding sums of sets of integers [18]. In [25], a special case of BT inequality was used to prove a network-coding bound. Recently, some of the authors of this paper have used our *algorithmic* version of the LW inequality to design a new sub-linear time decodable compressed sensing matrices [12] and efficient pattern matching algorithms [31].

Inspired by AGM's results, Gottlob, Lee, and Valiant [13] generalized AGM's results to conjunctive queries with functional dependencies. Their key idea was a new notion, *the "coloring number"*, which is derived from the dual linear program of the fractional cover linear program.

Join processing is one of the most studied problems in database research. On the theoretical side, that acyclic queries can be computed in polynomial time is one of the classic results in database theory [1, Ch. 6.4]. When the join graph is acyclic, there are several known results which achieve (near) optimal run time with respect to the output size [32, 38]. One direction to extend the reach of these positive results is using *hypertree decompositions* that capture the idea that many queries are nearly acyclic [14, 15]; This work has culminated in efficient algorithms for broad classes of conjunctive queries – a more general class of queries than we consider here. The algorithms in this work are complementary: our algorithms are most interesting when the queries are cyclic. In practice, a staggering number of variants have been considered, we list a few: Block-Nested loop join, Hash-Join, Grace, Sort-merge (see Grafe [16] for a survey). Conceptually, it is interesting that none of the classical

algorithms consider performing a per-tuple cardinality estimation as our algorithm does. It is interesting future work to implement our algorithm to better understand its performance.

Related to the problem of estimating the size of an output is cardinality estimation. A large number of structures have been proposed for cardinality estimation [2, 10, 20, 23, 24, 33]. Often, deriving estimates for arbitrary query expressions involves making statistical assumptions, such as the independence or containment assumptions, which may result in large estimation errors [21]. Follow-up work has considered sophisticated probability models, entropy-based models [28, 35] and graphical models [36]. In contrast, in this work we examine the *worst case behavior* of algorithms in terms of its cardinality estimates.

On a technical level, the work *adaptive query processing* is related, e.g., Eddies [6] and RIO [7]. The main idea is that to compensate for erroneous statistics, the query plan may adaptively be changed (as it better understands the properties of the data). While both our method and the methods proposed here are adaptive in some sense, our focus is different: this body of work focuses on heuristic optimization methods, while our focus is on provable worst-case running time bounds. A related idea has been considered in practice: heuristics that split tuples based on their fanout have been deployed in modern parallel databases to handle skew [39]. This idea was not used to theoretically improve the running time of join algorithms. We are excited that a key mechanism used by our algorithm is implemented in a modern commercial system.

2. PRELIMINARIES

We first describe our notation and formal problem statement. Then, we describe the connection between AGM's result and the BT inequality.

2.1 Notation and Formal Problem Statement

We assume the existence of a set of attribute names $\mathcal{A} = A_1, \ldots, A_n$ with associated domains $\mathbf{D}_1, \ldots, \mathbf{D}_n$ and infinite set of relational symbols $R_1, R_2, \ldots$. A relational schema for the symbol R_i of arity k is a tuple $\bar{A}_i = (A_{i_1}, \ldots, A_{i_k})$ of distinct attributes that defines the attributes of the relation. A relational database schema is a set of relational symbols and associated schemas denoted by $R_1(\bar{A}_1), \ldots, R_m(\bar{A}_m)$. A relational instance for $R(A_{i_1}, \ldots, A_{i_k})$ is a subset of $\mathbf{D}_{i_1} \times \cdots \times \mathbf{D}_{i_k}$. A relational database I is an instance for each relational symbol in schema, denoted by R_i^I. A *natural join* query (or simply query) q is specified by a finite subset of relational symbols $q \subseteq \mathbb{N}$, denoted by $\bowtie_{i \in q} R_i$. Let $\bar{A}(q)$ denote the set of all attributes that appear in some relation in q, that is $\bar{A}(q) = \{A \mid A \in \bar{A}_i \text{ for some } i \in q\}$. Given a tuple $\mathbf{t}$ we will write $\mathbf{t}_{\bar{A}}$ to emphasize that its support is the attribute set $\bar{A}$. Further, for any $\bar{S} \subset \bar{A}$ we let $\mathbf{t}_{\bar{S}}$ denote $\mathbf{t}$ restricted to $\bar{S}$. Given a database instance I, the output of the query q on I is denoted $q(I)$ and is defined as

$$q(I) \overset{\text{def}}{=} \left\{ \mathbf{t} \in \mathbf{D}^{\bar{A}(q)} \mid \mathbf{t}_{\bar{A}_i} \in R_i^I \text{ for each } i \in q \right\}$$

where $\mathbf{D}^{\bar{A}(q)}$ is a shorthand for $\times_{i : A_i \in \bar{A}(q)} \mathbf{D}_i$.

We also use the notion of a *semijoin*: Given two relations $R(\bar{A})$ and $S(\bar{B})$ their semijoin $R \ltimes S$ is defined by

$$R \ltimes S \overset{\text{def}}{=} \{\mathbf{t} \in R : \exists \mathbf{u} \in S \text{ s.t. } \mathbf{t}_{\bar{A} \cap \bar{B}} = \mathbf{u}_{\bar{A} \cap \bar{B}} \}.$$

For any relation $R(\bar{A})$, and any subset $\bar{S} \subseteq \bar{A}$ of its attributes, let $\pi_{\bar{S}}(R)$ denote the *projection* of R onto $\bar{S}$, i.e.

$$\pi_{\bar{S}}(R) = \left\{ \mathbf{t}_{\bar{S}} \mid \exists \mathbf{t}_{\bar{A} \setminus \bar{S}}, (\mathbf{t}_{\bar{S}}, \mathbf{t}_{\bar{A} \setminus \bar{S}}) \in R \right\}.$$

For any tuple $\mathbf{t}_{\bar{S}}$, define the $\mathbf{t}_{\bar{S}}$-*section* of R as

$$R[\mathbf{t}_{\bar{S}}] = \pi_{\bar{A} \setminus \bar{S}}(R \bowtie \{\mathbf{t}_{\bar{S}}\}).$$

From Join Queries to Hypergraphs. A query $q = \bowtie_{i \in q} R_i$ on attributes $\bar{A}(q)$ can be viewed as a hypergraph $H = (V, E)$ where $V = \bar{A}(q)$ and there is an edge $e_i = \bar{A}_i$ for each $i \in q$. Let $N_e = |R_e|$ be the number of tuples in R_e. *From now on we use the hypergraph and the original notation for the query interchangeably.*

We use this hypergraph to introduce the *fractional edge cover polytope* that plays a central role in our technical developments. The fractional edge cover polytope defined by H is the set of all points $\mathbf{x} = (x_e)_{e \in E} \in \mathbb{R}^E$ such that

$$\sum_{e: v \in e} x_e \geq 1, \text{ for any } v \in V$$

$$x_e \geq 0, \text{ for any } e \in E$$

Note that the solution $x_e = 1$ for $e \in E$ is always a feasible solution for hypergraphs representing join queries (since each vertex appears in some edge, $\sum_{e: v \in e} x_e \geq 1$). A point $\mathbf{x}$ in the polytope is also called a *fractional (edge) cover solution* of the hypergraph H.

Atserias, Grohe, and Marx [5] establish that for *any* point $\mathbf{x} = (x_e)_{e \in E}$ in the fractional edge cover polytope

$$|\bowtie_{e \in E} R_e| \leq \prod_{e \in E} N_e^{x_e}. \tag{2}$$

The bound is proved nonconstructively using Shearer's entropy inequality [9]. However, AGM provide an algorithm based on join-project plans that runs in time $O(|q|^2 \cdot N_{\max}^{1 + \sum_e x_e})$ where $N_{\max} = \max_{e \in E} N_e$. They observed that for a fixed hypergraph H and given sizes N_e the bound (2) can be minimized by solving the linear program which minimizes the linear objective $\sum_e (\log N_e) \cdot x_e$ over fractional edge cover solutions $\mathbf{x}$. (Since in linear time we can determine if we have an empty relation, and hence an empty output, for the rest of the paper we are always going to assume that $N_e \geq 1$.) We recast our problem using the above language.

DEFINITION 2.1 (OJ PROBLEM – OPTIMAL JOIN PROBLEM). *With the notation above, design an algorithm to compute $\bowtie_{e \in E} R_e$ with running time*

$$O\left(f(|V|, |E|) \cdot \prod_{e \in E} N_e^{x_e} + g(|V|, |E|) \sum_{e \in E} N_e \right).$$

Here $f(|V|, |E|)$ and $g(|V|, |E|)$ are ideally polynomials with (small) constant degrees, which only depend on the query size. The linear term $\sum_{e \in E} N_e$ is to read and index the input (in a specific way). Such an algorithm would be data-optimal in the worst case.[3]

We recast our motivating example from the introduction in our notation. Recall that we are given as input, $R(A, B), S(B, C), T(A, C)$. The resulting hypergraph (V, E) is such that $V = \{A, B, C\}$ and E contains three edges corresponding to each of R, S, and T. More explicitly, we have $E = \{\{A, B\}, \{B, C\}, \{A, C\}\}$. Thus, $|V| = 3$ and $|E| = 3$. If $N_e = N$, one can check that the optimal solution to the LP is $x_e = \frac{1}{2}$ for $e \in E$ which has the objective value $\frac{3}{2} \log N$;

---

[3] As shall be seen later, the worst-case preprocessing time is linear in the RAM model using the *"lazy array"* technique of Lemma A.3 of Flum, Frick, and Grohe [11], at the expense of potentially huge space overhead. To remove this excess space, we can build a set of hash indices in expected linear time using any perfect hashing scheme with worst-case constant time, e.g., *Cuckoo hashing*. Also, one can build a search tree for each relation to ensure a worst-case guarantee but with an extra log factor in the running time.

in turn, this gives $\sup_{I \in I(\bar{N})} |q(I)| \leq N^{3/2}$ (recall $I(\bar{N}) = \{I : |R_e^I| = N_e$ for $e \in E\}$).

Example 1. Given an odd integer N, we construct an instance I_N such that (1) $|R^{I_N}| = |S^{I_N}| = |T^{I_N}| = N$, (2) $|R \bowtie S| = |R \bowtie T| = |S \bowtie T| = (N+1)^2/4 + (N-1)/2$, and (3) $|R \bowtie S \bowtie T| = (3N-1)/2$. The following instance satisfies all three properties:

$$R^{I_N} = S^{I_N} = T^{I_N} = \{(0, j)\}_{j=0}^{(N-1)/2} \cup \{(j, 0)\}_{j=0}^{(N-1)/2}.$$

For example,

$$R \bowtie S = \{(i, 0, j)\}_{i,j=0}^{(N-1)/2} \cup \{(0, i, 0)\}_{i=1,...,(N-1)/2}$$

and $R \bowtie S \bowtie T = \{(0, 0, j)\}_{j=0}^{(N-1)/2} \cup \{(0, j, 0)\}_{j=1}^{(N-1)/2} \cup \{(j, 0, 0)\}_{j=1}^{(N-1)/2}$. Thus, any standard join-based algorithm takes time $\Omega(N^2)$. We show later that any project-join plan (which includes AGM's algorithm) takes $\Omega(N^2)$-time too. Recall that the AGM bound for this instance is $O(N^{3/2})$, and our algorithm thus takes time $O(N^{3/2})$. In fact, as shall be shown later, on this particular family of instances our algorithm takes only $O(N)$ time.

2.2 Connections to Geometric Inequalities

We describe the Bollobás-Thomason (BT) inequality from discrete geometry and prove that the BT inequality is equivalent to the AGM inequality. We then look at a special case of the BT inequality called the Loomis-Whitney (LW) inequality, from which our algorithmic development starts in the next section. The BT inequality can be stated as follows.

THEOREM 2.2 (DISCRETE BOLLOBÁS-THOMASON (BT) INEQUALITY). *Let $S \subset \mathbb{Z}^n$ be a finite set of n-dimensional grid points. Let $\mathcal{F}$ be a collection of subsets of $[n]$ in which every $i \in [n]$ occurs in exactly d members of $\mathcal{F}$. Let S_F be the set of projections $\mathbb{Z}^n \to \mathbb{Z}^F$ of points in S onto the coordinates in F. Then, $|S|^d \leq \prod_{F \in \mathcal{F}} |S_F|$.*

To prove the equivalence between BT inequality and the AGM bound, we first need a simple observation, whose proof can be found in the full version [30].

LEMMA 2.3. *Consider an instance of the OJ problem consisting of a hypergraph $H = (V, E)$, a fractional cover $\mathbf{x} = (x_e)_{e \in E}$ of H, and relations R_e for $e \in E$. Then, in linear time we can transform the instance into another instance $H' = (V, E')$, $\mathbf{x}' = (x'_e)_{e \in E'}$, $(R'_e)_{e \in E'}$, such that the following properties hold:*

(a) *$\mathbf{x}'$ is a "tight" fractional edge cover of the hypergraph H', namely $\mathbf{x}' \geq 0$ and*

$$\sum_{e \in E': v \in e} x'_e = 1, \quad \text{for every } v \in V.$$

(b) *The two problems have the same answer:*

$$\bowtie_{e \in E} R_e = \bowtie_{e \in E'} R'_e.$$

(c) *AGM's bound on the transformed instance is at least as good as that of the original instance:*

$$\prod_{e \in E'} |R'_e|^{x'_e} \leq \prod_{e \in E} |R_e|^{x_e}.$$

With this technical observation, we can now connect the two families of inequalities:

PROPOSITION 2.4. *BT inequality and AGM's fractional cover bound are equivalent.*

PROOF. To see that AGM's inequality implies BT inequality, we think of each coordinate as an attribute, and the projections S_F as the input relations. Set $x_F = 1/d$ for each $F \in \mathcal{F}$. It follows that $\mathbf{x} = (x_F)_{F \in \mathcal{F}}$ is a fractional cover for the hypergraph $H = ([n], \mathcal{F})$. AGM's bound then implies that $|S| \leq \prod_{F \in \mathcal{F}} |S_F|^{1/d}$.

Conversely, consider an instance of the OJ problem with hypergraph $H = (V, E)$ and a rational fractional cover $\mathbf{x} = (x_e)_{e \in E}$ of H. First, by Lemma 2.3, we can assume that all cover constraints are tight, i.e., $\sum_{e:v \in e} x_e = 1$, for any $v \in V$. Second, when all variables x_e are rational we can write x_e as d_e/d for a positive common denominator d. Consequently,

$$\sum_{e:v \in e} d_e = d, \quad \text{for any } v \in V.$$

Now, create d_e copies of each relation R_e. Call the new relations R'_e. We obtain a new hypergraph $H' = (V, E')$ where every attribute v occurs in exactly d hyperedges. This is precisely the Bollóbas-Thomason's setting of Theorem 2.2. Hence, the size of the join is bounded above by $\prod_{e \in E'} |R'_e|^{1/d} = \prod_{e \in E} |R_e|^{d_e/d} = \prod_{e \in E} |R_e|^{x_e}$. When some of the x_e are not rational, we can replace each irrational x_e by a rational $x'_e > x_e$ with a sufficiently small difference and apply the above analysis. □

Loomis-Whitney. We now consider a special case of the BT inequality, the discrete version of a classic geometric inequality called the *Loomis-Whitney inequality* [26]. The setting is that for $n \geq 2$, $V = [n]$ and $E = \binom{V}{|V|-1}$,[4] where in this case $x_e = 1/(|V| - 1)$, $\forall e \in E$ is a fractional cover solution for (V, E). LW showed the following:

THEOREM 2.5 (DISCRETE LOOMIS-WHITNEY (LW) INEQUALITY). *Let $S \subset \mathbb{Z}^n$ be a finite set of n-dimensional grid points. For each dimension $i \in [n]$, let $S_{[n]\setminus\{i\}}$ denote the $(n-1)$-dimensional projection of S onto the coordinates $[n] \setminus \{i\}$. Then, $|S|^{n-1} \leq \prod_{i=1}^n |S_{[n]\setminus\{i\}}|$.*

The LW inequality is a special case of the BT inequality (and so the AGM inequality), and it is with this special case that we begin our algorithmic development in the next section.

3. MAIN RESULTS

We first describe our algorithm for the LW inequality. We then describe our main algorithmic result, which is an algorithm that proves the AGM bound and whose running time matches the bound. Finally, we observe some limitations of project-join plans, which include as special cases both standard binary join-based algorithms and AGM's join algorithm.

3.1 Algorithm for Loomis-Whitney Instances

We first consider queries whose forms are slightly more general than that in our motivating example (1). This class of queries has the same setup as in LW inequality of Theorem 2.5. In this spirit, we define a *Loomis-Whitney (LW) instance* of the OJ problem to be a hypergraph $H = (V, E)$ such that E is the collection of all subsets of V of size $|V| - 1$. When the LW inequality is applied to this setting, it guarantees that $|\bowtie_{e \in E} R_e| \leq (\prod_{e \in E} N_e)^{1/(n-1)}$, and the bound is tight in the worst case. The main result of this section is the following:

THEOREM 3.1 (LOOMIS-WHITNEY INSTANCE). *Let $n \geq 2$ be an integer. Consider a Loomis-Whitney instance $H = (V = [n], E)$ of*

---

[4]We use $E = \binom{V}{k}$ to denote the set of all undirected hyperedges (subsets of nodes) of size exactly k.

the OJ problem with input relations R_e, where $|R_e| = N_e$ for $e \in E$. Then the join $\bowtie_{e \in E} R_e$ can be computed in time

$$O\left(n^2 \cdot \left(\prod_{e \in E} N_e\right)^{1/(n-1)} + n^2 \sum_{e \in E} N_e\right).$$

Before describing our algorithm, we give an example that illustrates the intuition behind our algorithm and solves the motivating example (1) from the introduction.

Example 2. Recall that our input has three relations $R(A, B)$, $S(B, C)$, $T(A, C)$ and an instance I such that $|R^I| = |S^I| = |T^I| = N$. Let $J = R \bowtie S \bowtie T$. Our goal is to construct J in time $O(N^{3/2})$. For exposition, define a parameter $\tau \geq 0$ that we will choose below. We use τ to define two sets that effectively partition the tuples in R^I.

$$D = \{t_B \in \pi_B(R) : |R^I[t_B]| > \tau\} \text{ and } G = \{(t_A, t_B) \in R^I : t_B \notin D\}$$

Intuitively, D contains the heavy join keys in R. Note that $|D| < N/\tau$. Observe that $J \subseteq (D \times T) \cup (G \bowtie S)$ (also note that this union is disjoint). Our algorithm will construct $D \times T$ (resp. $G \bowtie S$) in time $O(N^{3/2})$, then it will filter out those tuples in both S and R (resp. T) using the hash tables on S and R (resp. T); this process produces exactly J. Since our running time is linear in the above sets, the key question is how big are these two sets?

Observe that $|D \times T| \leq (N/\tau)N = N^2/\tau$ while $|G \bowtie S| = \sum_{t_B \in \pi_B(G)} |R[t_B]||S[t_B]| \leq \tau N$. Setting $\tau = \sqrt{N}$ makes both terms at most $N^{3/2}$, establishing the running time of our algorithm. One can check that if the relations are of different cardinalities, then we can still use the same algorithm; moreover, by setting $\tau = \sqrt{\frac{|R||T|}{|S|}}$, we achieve a running time of $O(\sqrt{|R||S||T|} + |R| + |S| + |T|)$.

To describe the general algorithm underlying Theorem 3.1, we need to introduce some data structures and notation.

Data Structures and Notation. Let $H = (V, E)$ be an LW instance. Algorithm 1 begins by constructing a labeled, binary tree $\mathcal{T}$ whose set of leaves is exactly V and each internal node has exactly two children. Any binary tree over this leaf set can be used. We denote the left child of any internal node x as $LC(x)$ and its right child as $RC(x)$. Each node $x \in \mathcal{T}$ is labeled by a function LABEL, where $LABEL(x) \subseteq V$ are defined inductively as follows: $LABEL(x) = V \setminus \{x\}$ for a leaf node $x \in V$, and $LABEL(x) = LABEL(LC(x)) \cap LABEL(RC(x))$ if x is an internal node of the tree. It is immediate that for any internal node x we have $LABEL(LC(x)) \cup LABEL(RC(x)) = V$ and that $LABEL(x) = \emptyset$ if and only if x is the root of the tree. Let J denote the output set of tuples of the join, i.e. $J = \bowtie_{e \in E} R_e$. For any node $x \in \mathcal{T}$, let $\mathcal{T}(x)$ denote the subtree of $\mathcal{T}$ rooted at x, and $\mathcal{L}(\mathcal{T}(x))$ denote the set of leaves under this subtree. For any three relations R, S, and T, define $R \bowtie_S T = (R \bowtie T) \ltimes S$.

Algorithm for LW instances. Algorithm 1 works in two stages. Let u be the root of the tree $\mathcal{T}$. First we compute a tuple set $C(u)$ containing the output J such that $C(u)$ has a relatively small size (at most the size bound times n). Second, we prune those tuples that cannot participate in the join (which takes only linear time in the size of $C(u)$). The interesting part is how we compute $C(u)$. Inductively, we compute a set $C(x)$ that at each stage contains candidate tuples and an auxiliary set $D(x)$, which is a superset of the projection $\pi_{LABEL(x)}(J \setminus C(x))$. The set $D(x)$ intuitively allows us to deal with those tuples that would blow up the size of an intermediate relation. The key novelty in Algorithm 1 is the construction of the set G that contains all those tuples (join keys) that are in some

---

Algorithm 1 Algorithm for Loomis-Whitney Instances

1: An LW instance: R_e for $e \in \binom{V}{|V|-1}$ and $N_e = |R_e|$.
2: $P = \prod_{e \in E} N_e^{1/(n-1)}$ (the size bound from LW inequality)
3: $u \leftarrow \text{root}(\mathcal{T})$; $(C(u), D(u)) \leftarrow \text{LW}(u)$
4: "Prune" $C(u)$ and return

$\text{LW}(x) : x \in \mathcal{T}$ returns (C, D)

1: **if** x is a leaf **then**
2:     **return** $(\emptyset, R_{\text{LABEL}(x)})$
3: $(C_L, D_L) \leftarrow \text{LW}(\text{LC}(x))$ and $(C_R, D_R) \leftarrow \text{LW}(\text{RC}(x))$
4: $F \leftarrow \pi_{\text{LABEL}(x)}(D_L) \cap \pi_{\text{LABEL}(x)}(D_R)$
5: $G \leftarrow \{\mathbf{t} \in F : |D_L[\mathbf{t}]| + 1 \leq \lceil P/|D_R| \rceil\}$ // $F = G = \emptyset$ if $|D_R| = 0$
6: **if** x is the root of $\mathcal{T}$ **then**
7:     $C \leftarrow (D_L \bowtie D_R) \cup C_L \cup C_R$
8:     $D \leftarrow \emptyset$
9: **else**
10:     $C \leftarrow (D_L \bowtie_G D_R) \cup C_L \cup C_R$
11:     $D \leftarrow F \setminus G$.
12: **return** (C, D)

---

sense *light*, i.e., joining over them would not exceed the size/time bound P by much. The elements that are not light are postponed to be processed later by pushing them to the set $D(x)$. This is in full analogy to the sets G and D defined in Example 2.

By induction on each step of the algorithm, we establish in the full version of this paper that the following three properties hold for every node $x \in \mathcal{T}$: (1) $\pi_{\text{LABEL}(x)}(J \setminus C(x)) \subseteq D(x)$; (2) $|C(x)| \leq (|\mathcal{L}(\mathcal{T}(x))| - 1) \cdot P$; and (3)

$$|D(x)| \leq \min \left\{ \min_{l \in \mathcal{L}(\mathcal{T}(x))} \{N_{[n] \setminus \{l\}}\}, \frac{\prod_{l \in \mathcal{L}(\mathcal{T}(x))} N_{[n] \setminus \{l\}}}{P^{|\mathcal{L}(\mathcal{T}(x))|-1}} \right\}.$$

Assuming the above three properties, we next prove that our algorithm correctly computes the join J. Let u denote the root of the tree $\mathcal{T}$. By property (1),

$$\pi_{\text{LABEL}(\text{LC}(u))}(J \setminus C(\text{LC}(u))) \subseteq D(\text{LC}(u))$$
$$\pi_{\text{LABEL}(\text{RC}(u))}(J \setminus C(\text{RC}(u))) \subseteq D(\text{RC}(u))$$

Hence,

$$J \setminus (C(\text{LC}(u)) \cup C(\text{RC}(u))) \subseteq D(\text{LC}(u)) \times D(\text{RC}(u)) = D(\text{LC}(u)) \bowtie D(\text{RC}(u)).$$

This implies $J \subseteq C(u)$. Thus, from $C(u)$ we can compute J by keeping only tuples in $C(u)$ whose projection on any attribute set $e \in E = \binom{[n]}{n-1}$ is contained in R_e (the "pruning" step).

Running Time. For the run time complexity of the above algorithm, we claim that for every node x, we need time $O(n|C(x)| + n|D(x)|)$. To see this note that for each node x, the lines 4, 5, 7, 10, and 11 of Algorithm 1 can be computed within the time bound using hashing. Using property (3) above, we have a (loose) upper bound of $O(nP + n \min_{l \in \mathcal{L}(\mathcal{T}(x))} N_{[n] \setminus \{l\}})$ on the run time for node x. Summing the run time over all the nodes in the tree gives the claimed run time.

3.2 An Algorithm for All Join Queries

This section presents our algorithm for proving the AGM inequality that has a running time that matches the bound.

THEOREM 3.2. *Let $H = (V, E)$ be a hypergraph representing a natural join query. Let $n = |V|$ and $m = |E|$. Let $\mathbf{x} = (x_e)_{e \in E}$ be an*

arbitrary point in the fractional cover polytope

$$\sum_{e: v \in e} x_e \geq 1, \quad \text{for any } v \in V$$
$$x_e \geq 0, \quad \text{for any } e \in E$$

For each $e \in E$, let R_e be a relation of size $N_e = |R_e|$ (number of tuples in the relation). Then,

(a) The join $\bowtie_{e \in E} R_e$ has size (number of tuples) bounded by

$$|\bowtie_{e \in E} R_e| \leq \prod_{e \in E} N_e^{x_e}.$$

(b) Furthermore, the join $\bowtie_{e \in E} R_e$ can be computed in time

$$O\left(mn \prod_{e \in E} N_e^{x_e} + n^2 \sum_{e \in E} N_e + m^2 n \right)$$

REMARK 3.3. *In the running time above, $m^2 n$ is the query pre-processing time, $n^2 \sum_{e \in E} N_e$ is the data preprocessing time, and $mn \prod_{e \in E} N_e^{x_e}$ is the query evaluation time. If all relations in the database are indexed in advance to satisfy three conditions (HT1), (HT2), and (HT3) from Section 3.2.3, then we can remove the term $n^2 \sum_{e \in E} N_e$ from the running time. To make the bound tight, the fractional cover solution $\mathbf{x}$ should be the best fractional cover in terms of the linear objective $\sum_e (\log N_e) \cdot x_e$. The data-preprocessing time of $O(n^2 \sum_e N_e)$ is for a single known query. If we were to index all relations in advance without knowing which queries to be evaluated, then the advance-indexing takes $O(n \cdot n! \sum_e N_e)$-time. This price is paid once, up-front, for an arbitrary number of future queries.*

Before turning to our algorithm and proof of this theorem, we observe that a consequence of this theorem is the following algorithmic version of the discrete version of BT inequality.

COROLLARY 3.4. *Let $S \subset \mathbb{Z}^n$ be a finite set of n-dimensional grid points. Let $\mathcal{F}$ be a collection of subsets of $[n]$ in which every $i \in [n]$ occurs in exactly d members of $\mathcal{F}$. Let S_F be the set of projections $\mathbb{Z}^n \to \mathbb{Z}^F$ of points in S onto the coordinates in F. Then,*

$$|S|^d \leq \prod_{F \in \mathcal{F}} |S_F|. \tag{3}$$

Furthermore, given the projections S_F we can compute S in time

$$O\left(|\mathcal{F}| n \left(\prod_{F \in \mathcal{F}} |S_F| \right)^{1/d} + n^2 \sum_{F \in \mathcal{F}} |S_F| + |\mathcal{F}|^2 n \right)$$

Recall that the LW inequality is a special case of the BT inequality. Hence, our algorithm proves the LW inequality as well.

3.2.1 The Algorithm and Terminology

Algorithm 2 has three main phases: (1) We first construct a labeled binary tree that we call a *query plan tree* or QP tree. Then, we construct a total order of attributes to be used in the next step. (2) Using the total order from phase (1), we construct a set of hash indices for various probing operations in the next step. In step (3), we give a recursive algorithm to compute the required join (whose recursion is based on the QP tree). The algorithm in (3) is similar to our LW algorithm: it uses a notion of heavy and light join keys, it computes a superset of the join and uses hash tables to filter this set. It does have some key technical differences: the structure of the recursion is different and the handling of heavy/light join keys is more general.

Algorithm 2 Computing the join $\bowtie_{e \in E} R_e$

Input: Hypergraph $H = (V, E)$, $|V| = n$, $|E| = m$
Input: Fractional cover solution $\mathbf{x} = (x_e)_{e \in E}$
Input: Relations $R_e, e \in E$
1: Compute the query plan tree $\mathcal{T}$, let u be $\mathcal{T}$'s root node
2: Compute a total order of attributes
3: Compute a collection of hash indices for all relations
4: **return** RECURSIVE-JOIN$(u, \mathbf{x}, \text{NIL})$

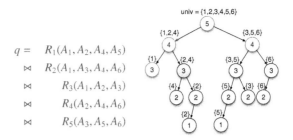

$$q = \quad R_1(A_1, A_2, A_4, A_5)$$
$$\bowtie \quad R_2(A_1, A_3, A_4, A_6)$$
$$\bowtie \quad R_3(A_1, A_2, A_3)$$
$$\bowtie \quad R_4(A_2, A_4, A_6)$$
$$\bowtie \quad R_5(A_3, A_5, A_6)$$

Figure 1: (a) A query q and (b) a sample QP tree for q.

To make this section self-contained, we repeat some terminology and notation. For each tuple $\mathbf{t}$ on attribute set A, we will write $\mathbf{t}$ as $\mathbf{t}_A$ to emphasize the support of $\mathbf{t}$: $\mathbf{t}_A = (t_a)_{a \in A}$. Consider any relation R with attribute set S. Let $A \subset S$ and $\mathbf{t}_A$ be a fixed tuple. Then, $\pi_A(R)$ denotes the projection of R on to attributes in A and,

$$R[\mathbf{t}_A] := \pi_{S \setminus A}(R \bowtie \{\mathbf{t}_A\}) = \{\mathbf{t}_{S \setminus A} \mid (\mathbf{t}_A, \mathbf{t}_{S \setminus A}) \in R\}.$$

In particular, $R[\mathbf{t}_\emptyset] = R$. There is a complete worked example of our algorithm in the full version of this paper.

3.2.2 Step (1): Build a query plan tree

Given a query $H = (V, E)$, fix an arbitrary order $e_1, e_2, \ldots, e_m$ of *all* the hyperedges in E. We construct a labeled binary tree $(\mathcal{T}, \text{LC}, \text{RC})$ where LC (resp. RC) maps an internal node to their left child (resp. right child) and to a special constant NIL if no such child exists. Each node $x \in \mathcal{T}$ is equipped with a pair of functions LABEL$(x) \in [m]$ and UNIV$(x) \subseteq V$. Very roughly, each node x and the sub-tree below it forms the "skeleton" of a sub-problem. There will be many sub-problems that correspond to each skeleton. The value LABEL(x) points to an "anchor" relation for the sub-problem and UNIV(x) is the set of attributes that the sub-problem is joining on. The anchor relation divides the universe UNIV(x) into two parts to further sub-divide the recursion structure.

Algorithm 3 Constructing the query plan tree $\mathcal{T}$

1: Fix an arbitrary order $e_1, e_2, \ldots, e_m$ of all the hyperedges in E.
2: $\mathcal{T} \leftarrow$ BUILD-TREE(V, m)

BUILD-TREE(U, k)

1: **if** $e_i \cap U = \emptyset, \forall i \in [k]$ **then**
2:      **return** NIL
3: Create a node u with LABEL$(u) \leftarrow k$ and UNIV$(u) = U$
4: **if** $k > 1$ and $\exists i \in [k]$ such that $U \not\subseteq e_i$ **then**
5:      LC$(u) \leftarrow$ BUILD-TREE$(U \setminus e_k, k - 1)$
6:      RC$(u) \leftarrow$ BUILD-TREE$(U \cap e_k, k - 1)$
7: **return** u

Algorithm 3 builds the query plan tree $\mathcal{T}$. Note that line 5 and 6 will not be executed if $U \subseteq e_i, \forall i \in [k]$, in which case u is a leaf node. When u is not a leaf node, if $U \subseteq e_k$ then u will not have a left child (LC$(u) = $ NIL). If $e_i \cap U \cap e_k = \emptyset$ for all $i \in [k - 1]$ then u will not have a right child (RC$(u) = $ NIL). The running time for this pre-processing step is $O(m^2 n)$. Figure 1 shows a query plan tree produced by Algorithm 3 on an example query.

From $\mathcal{T}$, we compute a total order on V in two steps. First, we define a partial order of all attributes by traversing the tree $\mathcal{T}$ in post-order. If a node u is visited before a node v, then all elements of UNIV(u) precede elements UNIV$(v) \setminus$ UNIV(u) in this partial order. Second, we take an arbitrary linear extension of this partial order and call it *the total order*. A complete pseudocode listing of this routine can be found in the full version of this paper, along with a few properties of the total order. In the example of Figure 1, the total order is $1, 4, 2, 5, 3, 6$.

3.2.3 Step (2): Build a Family of Indexes

We describe the form of the hash tables constructed by our algorithm. Each hash table is described by a triple $(i, \bar{K}, \bar{A})$ where $i \in [m]$, $\bar{K} \subseteq e_i$ is the search key, and $\bar{A} \subseteq e_i \setminus \bar{K}$ are the value attributes. For each such triple, our algorithm builds three hash tables that map hash keys $\mathbf{t} \in D^{\bar{K}}$ to one of three data types below.

(HT1) A hash table that maps $\mathbf{t}$ to a Boolean that is true if $\mathbf{t} \in \pi_{\bar{K}}(R_e)$. Thus, we can decide for any fixed tuple $\mathbf{t} \in D^{\bar{K}}$ whether $\mathbf{t} \in \pi_{\bar{K}}(R_e)$ in time $O(|\bar{K}|)$.

(HT2) A hash table that maps each $\mathbf{t}$ to $|\pi_{\bar{A}}(R_e[\mathbf{t}])|$, i.e., the number of tuples $\mathbf{u} \in \pi_{\bar{K} \cup \bar{A}}(R_e)$ such that $\mathbf{t}_{\bar{K}} = \mathbf{u}_{\bar{K}}$. For a fixed $\mathbf{t} \in D^{\bar{K}}$, this can be queried in time $O(|\bar{K}|)$.

(HT3) A hash table that returns all tuples $\mathbf{u} \in \pi_{\bar{A}}(R_e[\mathbf{t}])$ in time linear in the output size (if the output is not empty).

The hash tables for relation R_e can be built in total time $O(N_e)$. We denote this hash table by HTw$(i, \bar{K}, \bar{A})$ for $w \in \{1, 2, 3\}$. We abuse notation slightly and write HTw$(i, U, \bar{A})$ for $w \in \{1, 2, 3\}$ when $U \setminus e_i \neq \emptyset$ by defining HTw$(i, U, \bar{A}) = $ HTw$(i, U \cap e_i, (\bar{A} \setminus U) \cap e_i)$.

We will describe later how the total order allows us to reduce the total number hash indices down to $O(n^2 m)$. We will only need to build 3 hash tables for every triple $(i, \bar{K}, \bar{A})$ such that $\bar{K}$ precede $\bar{A}$ in the total order. Thus, for R_4 in Figure 1 we need to build at most 21 indices, i.e., three indexes for each of the following nine different key pairs: $[(), (A_4)], [(), (A_4, A_2)], [(), (A_4, A_2, A_6)], [(A_4), (A_2)], [(A_4), (A_2, A_6)], [(A_4, A_2), (A_6)],$ and $[(A_4, A_2, A_6), ()]$. (It is less than 21 because some indices are trivial or not defined, e.g. HT1 when $\mathbf{t} = ()$.) We group the pairs by brackets to make them easier to visually parse.

3.2.4 Step (3): Compute the Join Recursively

We are ready to present the heart of Algorithm 2 which computes the join recursively in a nested-loop-like fashion. The input to the algorithm consists of the hypergraph $H = (V, E)$ with $|V| = n$, $|E| = m$, and a point $\mathbf{x} = (x_e)_{e \in E}$ in the fractional cover polytope

$$\sum_{e : i \in e} x_e \geq 1, \quad \text{for any } i \in V$$
$$x_e \geq 0, \quad \text{for any } e \in E$$

Throughout this section, we denote the final output by J which is defined to be $J = \bowtie_{e \in E} R_e$.

The crux of Algorithm 2 is a procedure called RECURSIVE-JOIN (Procedure 4) that takes as inputs three arguments: (1) a node u from the QP-tree $\mathcal{T}$ whose label is k for some $k \in [m]$. (2) A tuple $\mathbf{t}_S \in \mathbf{D}^S$ where S is the set of *all* attributes preceding UNIV(u) in the total order, and (3) a fractional cover solution $\mathbf{y}_{E_k} = (y_{e_1}, \ldots, y_{e_k})$ of the hypergraph instance (UNIV$(u), E_k$). (Here, $E_k = \{e_1, \ldots, e_k\}$ and

Procedure 4 RECURSIVE-JOIN($u, \mathbf{y}, \mathbf{t}_S$)

1: Let $U = \text{UNIV}(u)$, $k = \text{LABEL}(u)$
2: Ret $\leftarrow \emptyset$ // *Ret is the returned tuple set*
3: **if** u is a leaf node of $\mathcal{T}$ **then** // *note that $U \subseteq e_i, \forall i \le k$*
4:     $j \leftarrow \text{argmin}_{i \in [k]} \left\{ |\pi_U(R_{e_i}[\mathbf{t}_{S \cap e_i}])| \right\}$
5:     // *By convention, $R_e[\text{NIL}] = R_e$ and $R_e[\mathbf{t}_\emptyset] = R_e$*
6:     **for** each tuple $\mathbf{t}_U \in \pi_U(R_{e_j}[\mathbf{t}_{S \cap e_j}])$ **do**
7:         **if** $\mathbf{t}_U \in \pi_U(R_{e_i}[\mathbf{t}_{S \cap e_i}])$, for all $i \in [k] \setminus \{j\}$ **then**
8:             Ret $\leftarrow$ Ret $\cup \{(\mathbf{t}_S, \mathbf{t}_U)\}$
9:     **return** Ret
10: **if** $\text{LC}(u) = \text{NIL}$ **then** // *u is not a leaf node of $\mathcal{T}$*
11:     $L \leftarrow \{\mathbf{t}_S\}$
12:     // *note that $L \ne \emptyset$ and $\mathbf{t}_S$ could be NIL (when $S = \emptyset$)*
13: **else**
14:     $L \leftarrow \text{RECURSIVE-JOIN}(\text{LC}(u), (y_1, \ldots, y_{k-1}), \mathbf{t}_S)$
15: $W \leftarrow U \setminus e_k$, $W^- \leftarrow e_k \cap U$
16: **if** $W^- = \emptyset$ **then**
17:     **return** L
18: **for** each tuple $\mathbf{t}_{S \cup W} = (\mathbf{t}_S, \mathbf{t}_W) \in L$ **do**
19:     **if** $y_{e_k} \ge 1$ **then**
20:         **go to** line 27
21:     **if** $\left(\prod_{i=1}^{k-1} |\pi_{e_i \cap W^-}(R_{e_i}[\mathbf{t}_{(S \cup W) \cap e_i}])| \right)^{\frac{y_{e_j}}{1-y_{e_k}}} < |\pi_{W^-}(R_{e_k}[\mathbf{t}_{S \cap e_k}])|$
    then
22:         $Z \leftarrow \text{RECURSIVE-JOIN}\left(\text{RC}(u), \left(\frac{y_{e_i}}{1 - y_{e_k}} \right)_{i=1}^{k-1}, \mathbf{t}_{S \cup W} \right)$
23:         **for** each tuple $(\mathbf{t}_S, \mathbf{t}_W, \mathbf{t}_{W^-}) \in Z$ **do**
24:             **if** $\mathbf{t}_{W^-} \in \pi_{W^-}(R_{e_k}[\mathbf{t}_{S \cap e_k}])$ **then**
25:                 Ret $\leftarrow$ Ret $\cup \{(\mathbf{t}_S, \mathbf{t}_W, \mathbf{t}_{W^-})\}$
26:     **else**
27:         **for** each tuple $\mathbf{t}_{W^-} \in \pi_{W^-}(R_{e_k}[\mathbf{t}_{S \cap e_k}])$ **do**
28:             **if** $\mathbf{t}_{e_i \cap W^-} \in \pi_{e_i \cap W^-}(R_{e_i}[\mathbf{t}_{(S \cup W) \cap e_i}])$ for all e_i such
            that $i < k$ and $e_i \cap W^- \ne \emptyset$ **then**
29:                 Ret $\leftarrow$ Ret $\cup \{(\mathbf{t}_S, \mathbf{t}_W, \mathbf{t}_{W^-})\}$
30: **return** Ret

---

we only take the restrictions of hyperedges in E_k onto the universe $\text{UNIV}(u)$). More precisely, $\mathbf{y}_{E_k}$ is a point in the following polytope:

$$\sum_{e \in E_k : i \in e} y_e \ge 1, \text{ for any } i \in \text{UNIV}(u)$$

$$y_e \ge 0, \text{ for any } e \in E_k$$

The goal of RECURSIVE-JOIN is to compute a superset of the relation $\{\mathbf{t}_S\} \times \pi_{\text{UNIV}(u)}(J[\mathbf{t}_S])$, i.e., a superset of the output tuples that start with $\mathbf{t}_S$ on the attributes $S \cup \text{UNIV}(u)$. This intermediate output is analogous to the set C in Algorithm 1 for LW instances. A second similarity to Algorithm 1 is that our algorithm makes a choice per tuple based on the output's estimated size.

Theorem 3.2 is a special case of the following lemma where we set u to be the root of the QP-tree $\mathcal{T}$, $\mathbf{y} = \mathbf{x}$, and $S = \emptyset$ ($\mathbf{t}_S = \text{NIL}$). Finally, we observe that we need only $O(n^2)$ number of hash indices per input relation, which completes the proof.

LEMMA 3.5. *Consider a call* RECURSIVE-JOIN($u, \mathbf{y}, \mathbf{t}_S$) *to Procedure 4. Let $k = \text{LABEL}(u)$ and $U = \text{UNIV}(u)$. Then,*

(a) The procedure outputs a relation Ret on attributes $S \cup U$ with at most the following number of tuples

$$B(u, \mathbf{y}, \mathbf{t}_S) := \prod_{i=1}^{k} |\pi_{U \cap e_i}(R_{e_i}[\mathbf{t}_{S \cap e_i}])|^{y_i}.$$

(For the sake of presentation, we use the convention that when $U \cap e_i = \emptyset$ we set $|\pi_{U \cap e_i}(R_{e_i}[\mathbf{t}_{S \cap e_i}])| = 1$ so that the factor does not contribute anything to the product.)

(b) Furthermore, the procedure runs in time $O(mn \cdot B(u, \mathbf{y}, \mathbf{t}_S))$.

The lemma is proved by induction on the height of the sub-tree of $\mathcal{T}$ rooted at u. We include a full formal proof in the full version of this paper, but give the main ideas here.

Base Case. In the base case, the node u is a leaf, and $\text{UNIV}(u) \subseteq e_i, \forall i \in [\text{LABEL}(u)]$. Observe that

$$\min_{i=1,\ldots,k} |\pi_U(R_{e_i}[\mathbf{t}_S])| \le \prod_{i=1}^{k} |\pi_U(R_{e_i}[\mathbf{t}_S])|^{y_i} = B(u, \mathbf{y}, \mathbf{t}_S).$$

since $\sum_{i=1}^{k} y_i \ge 1$ (**y** is a fractional cover solution). Because the left-hand-side of the above inequality is clearly an upper bound on the number of output tuples, so is the right-hand-side. Hence, (a) holds. To control the running time and prove (b), a nested-loop strategy works: we first find the j that achieves the left-hand side of the inequality, i.e., for which $\pi_U(R_{e_j}[\mathbf{t}_S])$ is smallest among $j \in [k]$. To find this minimum, we probe HT2(i, S, U) with search key $\mathbf{t}_S$ for $i \in [k]$ (i.e., once for each relation). Since u is a leaf node, $\text{UNIV}(u) \subseteq e_i$ for each $i \in [k]$ and hence $U = U \cap e_i$. Thus, we can query HT3(j, S, U) to find all tuples in relation $\pi_U(R_{e_j}[\mathbf{t}_S])$ in time $O(|\pi_U(R_{e_j}[\mathbf{t}])|)$. Then, for each such tuple $\mathbf{v} \in \pi_U(R_{e_j}[\mathbf{t}])$, and for each relation R_{e_i} with $i \in [k] \setminus \{j\}$ we probe into R_{e_i} with HT1(i, S, U); the tuple $\mathbf{v}$ is returned iff this probe returns true for all $i \in [k] \setminus \{j\}$. This procedure takes $O(kn + kn|\pi_U(R_{e_j}[\mathbf{t}_S])|)$ where j is the minimum as above.

Induction Step. In this case, u is an internal node. The key challenge is that we have to make a cost-based decision about which lower subproblems to solve. The interesting case is when there are both a left- and a right-child problem. We recursively solve the left subproblem, from which we get back a relation on $S \cup U \setminus e_k$ (each of whose tuples has values $\mathbf{t}_S$ on attributes S), which we then store in a variable L (formally, $L \supseteq \{\mathbf{t}_S\} \times \pi_{U \setminus e_k}(J[\mathbf{t}_S])$). For example, consider the highlighted node in Figure 1(b). We will refer to this node throughout this section as our example. Here, $S = \{1\}$ and so we have a fixed tuple $\mathbf{t}_S$ as input. The left-subproblem is the leaf that computes the tuples in $\{\mathbf{t}_S\} \times \pi_{\{4\}}(J[\mathbf{t}_S])$, which have support $\{1, 4\}$.

Next, for each tuple $\mathbf{t} = \mathbf{t}_{S \cup (U \setminus e_k)} \in L$, we will make a decision on whether to solve an associated "right subproblem." There are $|L|$ such subproblems and thus $|L|$ decisions to make. Each decision is based on our estimation of the running time if we were to solve the subproblem. The run-time estimation is the AGM's bound on the output size of the sub-problem. To obtain the estimation, we define for each right subproblem a fractional cover solution. The relation R_{e_k} is used as an "anchor" for the entire process.

Specifically, we construct a hypergraph ($\text{UNIV}(\text{RC}(u)), E_{k-1}$) with an associated fractional cover $\mathbf{y}'_{E_{k-1}}$ where $y'_{e_i} = y_{e_i}/(1 - y_{e_k})$ for $i \in [k-1]$. (When $y_{e_k} \ge 1$ we will not solve this subproblem and directly take option (1) below.) For each $\mathbf{t} \in L$, the input relation sizes for this sub-problem are $|\pi_{e_i \cap U \setminus e_k}(R_{e_i}[\mathbf{t}])|$ for $i \in [k-1]$.

For each $\mathbf{t}_{S \cup W} = (\mathbf{t}_S, \mathbf{t}_W) \in L$, where $W = U \setminus e_k$, our algorithm considers two options, and we use the estimated run-time of the projected subproblem to choose between these options.

Option (1) Our algorithm loops over each tuple in $\pi_{U \cap e_k}(R_{e_k}[\mathbf{t}_{S \cap e_k}])$ and filters it against all projections that are below it (lines 27–29). In this case our running time is $O(|\pi_{U \cap e_k}(R_{e_k})[\mathbf{t}_{S \cap e_k}]|)$. In our running example, given the tuple $\mathbf{t}_{\{1,4\}} = (t_1, t_4) \in L$, we would loop over each tuple $\mathbf{t}_{\{2\}} = (t_2) \in \pi_{\{2\}}(R_3[t_1])$.

For each such tuple, we add (t_1, t_4, t_2) to the output Ret if $t_2 \in \pi_{\{2\}}(R_1[(t_1, t_4)])$. This check can be done by probing R_1 using $\mathrm{HT1}(1, (A_1, A_4, A_2), ())$.

Option (2) Our algorithm solves the right subproblem recursively and filters the result with $\pi_{U \cap e_k}(R_{e_k}[\mathbf{t}_{S \cap e_k}])$ (lines 22–25). In our running example, given $(t_1, t_4) \in L$ the right subproblem will compute those tuples (t_2) in $\pi_{\{2\}}(R_1[\mathbf{t}_{\{1,4\}}])$ and then filter them with $\mathrm{HT1}(3, (A_1, A_2), ())$. The important property of option (2) is that its running time does *not* depend on $|\pi_{U \cap e_k}(R_{e_k}[\mathbf{t}_{S \cap e_k}])|$. In particular, option (2)'s running time only depends on the output size of the right subproblem.

To decide between these two options, we compare the following two quantities:

$$\mathrm{LHS} = |\pi_{U \cap e_k}(R_{e_k}[\mathbf{t}_{S \cap e_k}])| \text{ versus } \mathrm{RHS} = \prod_{i=1}^{k-1} \left| \pi_{e_i \cap U \cap e_k}(R_{e_i}[\mathbf{t}_{(S \cup W) \cap e_i}]) \right|^{y'_{e_i}}$$

We choose option (1) if either $y_{e_k} \geq 1$ or the LHS is less than the RHS and option (2) otherwise. Observe that we can compute both quantities given our indices in time proportional to $O(kn)$. Our overall running time is proportional to the minimum of these two quantities (plus the inconsequential term $O(kn)$). Summing over all tuples $\mathbf{t} \in L$ the minimum of the above two quantities and "unroll" the sum by applying a generalized Hölder's inequality many times we can then prove both the output size and the running time.

Used Search Keys. Finally, we need to understand which search keys are used in the hash table. Observe that whenever an attribute v is used in a search key (e.g., $\mathrm{HTw}(i, S, U)$ for $w \in \{1, 2, 3\}$), all attributes that come before v in the total order and are in e_i are *bound*. Thus, if $e_i = (v_{i_1}, \ldots, v_{i_{|e_i|}})$ and the attributes are ordered as above, then the search key and the returned keys is always a *prefix* of $v_{i_1}, \ldots, v_{i_k}$. Hence, we only need to have $3n \sum_{e \in E} |e|$ indices. In the full version of this paper, we describe a slightly more complex data structure that combines all hash tables for one relation into a single "search tree" structure. The search trees have the advantage that their building time is deterministic (unlike a typically perfect hashing scheme which has a constant worst-case lookup time but only expected linear building time). However, the search trees necessitate a log-factor blow up in the total run time of our algorithm.

3.3 Limits of Standard Approaches

For a given join query q, we describe a sufficient syntactic condition for q so that when computed by any join-project plan is asymptotically slower than the worst-case bound. Our algorithm runs within this bound, and so for such q there is an asymptotic running-time gap.

Recall that an *LW instance* of the OJ problem is a join query q represented by the hypergraph (V, E), where $V = [n]$, and $E = \binom{[n]}{n-1}$ for some integer $n \geq 2$. Our main result in this section is the following lemma.[5]

LEMMA 3.6. *Let* $n \geq 2$ *be an arbitrary integer. Given any LW-query* q *represented by a hypergraph* $([n], \binom{[n]}{n-1})$, *and any positive integer* $N \geq 2$, *there exist relations* R_i, $i \in [n]$, *such that* $|R_i| = N, \forall i \in [n]$, *the attribute set for* R_i *is* $[n] \setminus \{i\}$, *and that any join-project plan for* q *on these relations runs in time* $\Omega(N^2 / n^2)$.

Before proving the lemma, we note that both the traditional join-tree algorithm and AGM's algorithm are join-project plans, and

[5]We thank an anonymous PODS'12 referee for showing us that our example works for all join-project plans rather than just the AGM algorithm and arbitrary join-only algorithms.

thus their running times are asymptotically worse than the best AGM bound for this instance which is $| \bowtie_{i=1}^{n} R_i | \leq \prod_{i=1}^{n} |R_i|^{1/(n-1)} = N^{1+1/(n-1)}$. On the other hand, both Algorithm 1 and Algorithm 2 take $O(N^{1+1/(n-1)})$-time as we have analyzed. In fact, for Algorithm 2, we are able to demonstrate a stronger result: its run-time on this instance is $O(n^2 N)$ which is better than what we can analyze for a general instance of this type. In particular, the run-time gap between Algorithm 2 and AGM's algorithm is $\Omega(N)$ for constant n.

PROOF OF LEMMA 3.6. In the instances below the domain of any attribute will be $\mathbf{D} = \{0, 1, \ldots, (N - 1)/(n - 1)\}$ For the sake of clarity, we ignore the integrality issue. For any $i \in [n]$, let R_i be the set of *all* tuples in $\mathbf{D}^{[n]-\{i\}}$ each of which has at most one non-zero value. Then, it is not hard to see that $|R_i| = (n - 1)[(N - 1)/(n - 1) + 1] - (n - 2) = N$, for all $i \in [n]$; and, $| \bowtie_{i=1}^{n} R_i | = n[(N - 1)/(n - 1) + 1] - (n - 1) = N + (N - 1)/(n - 1)$.

A relation R on attribute set $\bar{A} \subseteq [n]$ is called *simple* if R is the set of *all* tuples in $\mathbf{D}^{\bar{A}}$ each of which has at most one non-zero value. Then, we observe the following properties. (a) The input relations R_i are simple. (b) An arbitrary projection of a simple relation is simple. (c) Let S and T be any two simple relations on attribute sets $\bar{A}_S$ and $\bar{A}_T$, respectively. If $\bar{A}_S$ is contained in $\bar{A}_T$ or vice versa, then $S \bowtie T$ is simple. If neither $\bar{A}_S$ nor $\bar{A}_T$ is contained in the other, then $|S \bowtie T| \geq (1 + (N - 1)/(n - 1))^2 = \Omega(N^2/n^2)$.

For an arbitrary join-project plan starting from the simple relations R_i, we eventually must join two relations whose attribute sets are not contained in one another and this step alone requires $\Omega(N^2/n^2)$ run time. $\square$

Finally, we analyze the run-time of Algorithm 2 directly on this instance without resorting to Theorem 3.2.

LEMMA 3.7. *On the collection of instances from the previous lemma, Algorithm 2 runs in time* $O(n^2 N)$.

PROOF. Without loss of generality, assume the hyperedge order Algorithm 2 considers is $[n] - \{1\}, \ldots, [n] - \{n\}$. In this case, the universe of the left-child of the root of the QP-tree is $\{n\}$, and the universe of the right-child of the root is $[n - 1]$.

The first thing Algorithm 2 does is that it computes the join $L_n = \bowtie_{i=1}^{n-1} \pi_{\{n\}}(R_i)$, in time $O(nN)$. Note that $L_n = \mathbf{D}$, the domain. Next, Algorithm 2 goes through each value $a \in L_n$ and decides whether to solve a subproblem or not. First, consider the case $a > 0$. Here Algorithm 2 estimates a bound for the join $\bowtie_{j=1}^{n-1} \pi_{[n-1]}(R_j[a])$. The estimate is 1 because $|\pi_{[n-1]}(R_j[a])| = 1$ for all $a > 0$. Hence, the algorithm will recursively compute this join which takes time $O(n^2)$ and filter the result against R_n. Overall, solving the sub problems for $a > 0$ takes $O(n^2 N)$ time. Second, consider the case when $a = 0$. In this case $|\pi_{[n-1]}(R_j[0])| = \frac{(n-2)N-1}{(n-1)}$. The subproblem's estimated size bound is

$$\prod_{i=1}^{n-1} |\pi_{[n-1]}(R_j[0])|^{\frac{1/(n-1)}{1-1/(n-1)}} = \left[\frac{(n-2)N-1}{(n-1)} \right]^{(n-1)/(n-2)} > N$$

if $N \geq 4$ and $n \geq 4$. Hence, in this case R_n will be filtered against the $\pi_{[n-1]}(R_j[0])$, which takes $O(n^2 N)$ time. $\square$

Extending beyond LW instances. Using the above results, we give a sufficient condition for when there exist a family of instances $\mathcal{I} = I_1, \ldots, I_N, \ldots$, such that on instance I_N every binary join strategy takes time at least $\Omega(N^2)$, but our algorithm takes $o(N^2)$. Given a hypergraph $H = (V, E)$. We first define some notation. Fix $U \subseteq V$ then call an attribute $v \in V \setminus U$ *U-relevant* if for all e such that $v \in e$ then $e \cap U \neq \emptyset$; call v *U-troublesome* if for all $e \in E$, if $v \in e$ then $U \subseteq e$. Now we can state our result:

LEMMA 3.8. *Given a join query $H = (V, E)$ and some $U \subseteq V$ where $|U| \geq 2$, then if there exists $F \subseteq E$ such that $|F| = |U|$ that satisfies the following three properties: (1) each $u \in U$ occurs in exactly $|U| - 1$ elements in F, (2) each $v \in V$ that is U-relevant appears in at least $|U| - 1$ edges in F, (3) there are no U-troublesome attributes. Then, there is some family of instances $\mathcal{I}$ such that (a) computing the join query represented by H with a join tree takes time $\Omega(N^2/|U|^2)$ while (b) the algorithm from Section 3.2 takes time $O(N^{1+1/(|U|-1)})$.*

Given a (U, F) as in the lemma, the idea is to simply to set all those edges in $f \in F$ to be the instances from Lemma 3.6 and extend all attributes with a single value, say c_0. Since there are no U-troublesome attributes, to construct the result set at least one of the relations in F must be joined. Since any pair F must take time $\Omega(N^2/|U|^2)$ by the above construction, this establishes (a). To establish (b), we need to describe a particular feasible solution to the cover LP whose objective value is $N^{1+1/(|U|-1)}$, implying that the running time of our proposed algorithm is upper bounded by this value. To do this, we first observe that any attribute not in U takes the value only c_0. Then, we observe that any node $v \in V$ that is not U-relevant is covered by some edge e whose size is exactly 1 (and so we can set $x_e = 1$). Thus, we may assume that all nodes are U-relevant. Then, observe that all relevant attributes can be set by the cover $x_e = 1/(|U| - 1)$ for $e \in F$. This is a feasible solution to the LP and establishes our claim.

4. EXTENSIONS

4.1 Combined Complexity

Given that our algorithms are data optimal for worst-case inputs it is tempting to wonder if one can obtain an join algorithm whose run time is both query and data optimal in the worst-case. We show that in the special case when each input relation has arity at most 2 we can attain a data-optimal algorithm that is simpler than Algorithm 2 with an asymptotically better query complexity.

Further, given promising results in the worst case, it is natural to wonder whether or not one can obtain a join algorithm whose run time is polynomial in both the size of the query *as well as* the size of the output. More precisely, given a join query q and an instance I, can one compute the result of query q on instance I in time $\text{poly}(|q|, |q(I)|, |I|)$. Unfortunately, this is not possible unless NP = RP. We briefly present a proof of this fact below.

Each relation has at most 2 attributes. As is mentioned in the introduction, our algorithm in Theorem 3.2 not only has better data complexity than AGM's algorithm (in fact we showed our algorithm has optimal worst-case data complexity), it has better query complexity. In this section, we show that for the special case when the join query q is on relations with at most two attributes (i.e., the corresponding hypergraph H is a graph), we can obtain better query complexity compared to the algorithm in Theorem 3.2 (while retaining the same (optimal) data complexity).

Without loss of generality, we can assume that each relation contains exactly 2 attributes because a 1-attribute relation R_e needs to have $x_e = 1$ in the corresponding LP and thus, contributes a separate factor N_e to the final product. Thus, R_e can be joined with the rest of the query with any join algorithm (including the naive Cartesian product based algorithm). In this case, the hypergraph H is a graph which can be assumed to be simple. We assume that all relations are indexed in advanced, which takes $O(\sum_e N_e)$ time. In what follows we will not include this preprocessing time in the analysis.

We first state a lemma for the case when H is a cycle.

LEMMA 4.1 (CYCLE LEMMA). *If H is a cycle, then $\bowtie_{e \in E} R_e$ can be computed in time $O(m \sqrt{\prod_{e \in H} N_e})$.*

The proof of the lemma shows that we can reduce the computation of the case when H is a cycle to our previous algorithm for Loomis-Whitney instances with $n = 3$.

With the help of Lemma 4.1, we can now derive a solution for the case when H is an arbitrary graph. Consider any *basic feasible solution* $\mathbf{x} = (x_e)_{e \in E}$ of the fractional cover polyhedron

$$\sum_{e:v \in e} x_e \geq 1, \text{ for any } v \in V$$
$$x_e \geq 0, \text{ for any } e \in E.$$

It is known that $\mathbf{x}$ is *half-integral*, i.e., $x_e \in \{0, 1/2, 1\}$ for all $e \in E$ (see Schrijver's book [34], Theorem 30.10). However, we will also need a graph structure associated with the half-integral solution; hence, we adapt a known proof of the half-integrality property with a slightly more specific analysis [34].

LEMMA 4.2. *For any basic feasible solution $\mathbf{x} = (x_e)_{e \in E}$ of the fractional cover polyhedron above, $x_e \in \{0, 1/2, 1\}$ for all $e \in E$. Furthermore, the collection of edges e for which $x_e = 1$ is a union S of stars. And, the collection of edges e for which $x_e = 1/2$ form a set C of vertex-disjoint odd-length cycles that are also vertex disjoint from the union S of stars.*

Now, let $\mathbf{x}^*$ be an *optimal* basic feasible solution to the following linear program.

$$\min \quad \sum_e (\log N_e) \cdot x_e$$
$$s.t. \quad \sum_{e:v \in e} x_e \geq 1, \text{ for any } v \in V$$
$$x_e \geq 0, \text{ for any } e \in E.$$

Then $\prod_{e \in E} N_e^{x_e^*} \leq \prod_{e \in E} N_e^{x_e}$ for any feasible fractional cover $\mathbf{x}$. Let S be the set of edges on the stars and C be the collection of disjoint cycles as shown in the above lemma, applied to $\mathbf{x}^*$. Then,

$$\prod_{e \in E} N_e^{x_e^*} = \left(\prod_{e \in S} N_e\right) \prod_{C \in C} \sqrt{\prod_{e \in C} N_e}.$$

Consequently, we can apply Lemma 4.1 to each cycle $C \in C$ and take a cross product of all the resulting relations with the relations R_e for $e \in S$. We summarize the above discussion in the following theorem.

THEOREM 4.3. *When each relation has at most two attributes, we can compute the join $\bowtie_{e \in E} R_e$ in time $O(m \prod_{e \in E} N_e^{x_e})$.*

Impossibility of Instance Optimality. We use the standard reduction of 3SAT to conjunctive queries but with two simple specializations: (i) We reduce from the 3UniqueSAT, where the input formula is either unsatisfiable or has *exactly* one satisfying assignment, and (ii) q is a full join query instead of a general conjunctive query. It is known that 3UniqueSAT cannot be solved in deterministic polynomial time unless NP = RP [37].

We sketch the reduction here. Let $\phi = C_1 \wedge C_2 \wedge \ldots C_m$ be a 3UniqueSAT CNF formula on n variables $a_1, \ldots, a_n$. (W.l.o.g. assume that a clause does not contain both a variable and its negation.) For each clause C_j for $j \in [m]$, create a relation R_j on the variables that occur in C_j. The query q is $\bowtie_{j \in [m]} R_j$. Now define the database I as follows: for each $j \in [m]$, R_j^I contains the seven assignments to the variables in C_j that makes it true. Note that $q(I)$ contains all the satisfying assignments for ϕ: in other words, $q(I)$ has one element if ϕ is satisfiable otherwise $q(I) = \emptyset$. In other words, we have $|q(I)| \leq 1$, $|q| = O(m + n)$ and $|I| = O(m)$. Thus an instance optimal algorithm with time complexity $\text{poly}(|q|, |q(I)|, |I|)$ for q would be able to determine if ϕ is satisfiable or not in time $\text{poly}(n, m)$, which would imply $\mathsf{NP} = \mathsf{RP}$.

4.2 Relaxed Joins

We observe that our algorithm can actually evaluate a relaxed notion of join queries. Say we are given a query q represented by a hypergraph $H = (V, E)$ where $V = [n]$ and $|E| = m$. The m input relations are R_e, $e \in E$. We are also given a "relaxation" number $0 \leq r \leq m$. Our goal is to output all tuples that agree with at least $m - r$ input relations. In other words, we want to compute $\cup_{S \subseteq E, |S| \geq m-r} \bowtie_{e \in S} R_e$. However, we need to modify the problem to avoid the case that the set of attributes of relations indexed by S does not cover all the attributes in the universe V. Towards this end, define the set

$$C(q, r) = \left\{ S \subseteq E \mid |S| \geq m - r \text{ and } \bigcup_{e \in S} e = V \right\}.$$

With the notations established above, we are now ready to define the relaxed join problem.

DEFINITION 4.4 (RELAXED JOIN PROBLEM). *Given a query q represented by the hypergraph $H = (V = [n], E)$, and an integer $0 \leq r \leq m$, evaluate*

$$q_r \overset{def}{=} \bigcup_{S \in C(q,r)} \left(\bowtie_{e \in S} R_e \right).$$

Before we proceed, we first make the following simple observation: given any two sets $S, T \in C(q, r)$ such that $S \subseteq T$, we have $\bowtie_{e \in T} R_e \subseteq \bowtie_{e \in S} R_e$. This means in the relaxed join problem we only need to consider subsets of relations that are not contained in any other subset. In particular, define $\hat{C}(q, r) \subseteq C(q, r)$ to be the largest subset of $C(q, r)$ such that for any $S \neq T \in \hat{C}(q, r)$ neither $S \subset T$ nor $T \subset S$. We only need to evaluate $q_r = \bigcup_{S \in \hat{C}(q,r)} (\bowtie_{e \in S} R_e)$.

Given an $S \in \hat{C}(q, r)$, let $\mathsf{LPOpt}(S)$ denote the size bound given by the AGM fractional cover inequality (2) on the join query represented by the hypergraph (V, S), so that $\mathsf{LPOpt}(S) = \prod_{e \in S} |R_e|^{x_e^*}$ where $\mathbf{x}_S^* = (x_e^*)_{e \in S}$ is an optimal solution to the following linear program called $\mathsf{LP}(S)$:

$$
\begin{aligned}
\min \quad & \sum_{e \in S} (\log |R_e|) \cdot x_e \\
\text{subject to} \quad & \sum_{e \in S : v \in e} x_e \geq 1 \quad \text{for any } v \in V \quad\quad (4) \\
& x_e \geq 0 \quad\quad \text{for any } e \in S.
\end{aligned}
$$

Upper bounds. We start with a straightforward upper bound.

PROPOSITION 4.5. *Let q be a join query on m relations and let $0 \leq r \leq m$ be an integer. Then given sizes of the input relations, the number of output tuples for query q_r is upper bounded by*

$$\sum_{S \in \hat{C}(q,r)} \mathsf{LPOpt}(S).$$

Further, Algorithm 2 evaluates q_r with data complexity linear in the bound above. The next natural question is to determine how good the upper bound is. Before we answer the question, we prove a stronger upper bound.

Given a subset of hyperedges $S \subseteq E$ that "covers" V, i.e. $\cup_{e \in S} e = V$, let $\mathsf{BFS}(S) \subseteq S$ be the subset of hyperedges in S that gets a *positive* x_e^* value in an *optimal* basic feasible solution to the linear program $\mathsf{LP}(S)$ defined in (4). (If there are multiple such solutions, pick any one in a consistent manner.) Call two subsets $S, T \subseteq E$ bfs-*equivalent* if $\mathsf{BFS}(S) = \mathsf{BFS}(T)$. Finally, define $C^*(q, r) \subseteq \hat{C}(q, r)$ as the collection of sets from $\hat{C}(q, r)$ which contains exactly one arbitrary representative from each bfs-equivalence class.

THEOREM 4.6. *Let q be a join query represented by $H = (V, E)$, and let $0 \leq r \leq m$ be an integer. The number of output tuples of q_r is upper bounded by $\sum_{S \in C^*(q,r)} \mathsf{LPOpt}(S)$. Further, the query q_r can be evaluated in time*

$$O\left(\sum_{S \in C^*(q,r)} (mn \cdot \mathsf{LPOpt}(S) + \text{poly}(n, m)) \right)$$

plus the time needed to compute $C^*(q, r)$ from q.

Note that since $C^*(q, r) \subseteq \hat{C}(q, r)$, the bound in Theorem 4.6 is no worse than that in Proposition 4.5. We will show later that the bound in Theorem 4.6 is indeed tight.

We defer the proof of Theorem 4.6 to the full version and mention the main idea here. Let $S \neq S' \in \hat{C}(q, r)$ be two different sets of hyperedges with the following property. Define $T \overset{def}{=} \mathsf{BFS}(S) = \mathsf{BFS}(S')$ and let $\mathbf{x}_T^* = (x_i^*)_{i \in T}$ be the projection of the corresponding optimal basic feasible solution to the (V, S) and the (V, S') problems projected down to T. (The two projections result in the same vector $\mathbf{x}_T^*$.) The outputs of the joins on S and on S' are both subsets of the output of the join on T. We can simply run Algorithm 2 on inputs (V, T) and $\mathbf{x}_T^*$, then prune the output against relations R_e with $e \in S \setminus T$ or $S' \setminus T$. In particular, we only need to compute $\bowtie_{e \in T} R_e$ once for both S and S'.

Lower bound. We now show that the bound in Theorem 4.6 is (almost) tight for some query and some database instance I.

We first define the query q. The hypergraph is $H = (V = [n], E)$ where $m = |E| = n + 1$. The hyperedges are $E = \{e_1, \ldots, e_{n+1}\}$ where $e_i = \{i\}$ for $i \in [n]$ and $e_{n+1} = [n]$. The database instance I consists of relations R_e, $e \in E$, all of which are of size N. For each $i \in [n]$, $R_{e_i} = [N]$. And, $R_{e_{n+1}} = \bigcup_{i=1}^{N} \{N + i\}^n$.

It is easy to check that for any $r \geq n$, $q_r(I)$ is the set $R_{e_{n+1}} \cup [N]^n$, i.e. $|q_r(I)| = N + N^n$. (For $0 < r < n$, we have $|q_r(I)| = N^n$.) Next, we claim that for this query instance for any $r > 0$, $C^*(q, r) = \{\{n + 1\}, [n]\}$. Note that $\mathsf{BFS}(\{n + 1\}) = \{n + 1\}$ and $\mathsf{BFS}([n]) = [n]$, which implies that $\mathsf{LPOpt}(\{n + 1\}) = N$ and $\mathsf{LPOpt}([n]) = N^n$. This along with Theorem 4.6 implies that $|q_r(I)| \leq N + N^n$, which proves the tightness of the size bound in Theorem 4.6 for ($r \geq n$), as desired. (For $0 < r < n$, the bound is almost tight.)

Finally, we argue that $C^*(q, r) = \{\{n + 1\}, [n]\}$. Towards this end, consider any $T \in \hat{C}(q, r)$. Note that if $(n + 1) \notin T$, we have $T = [n]$ and since $\mathsf{BFS}(T) = T$ (and we will see soon that for any other $T \in \hat{C}(q, r)$, we have $\mathsf{BFS}(T) \neq [n]$), which implies that $[n] \in C^*(q, r)$. Now consider the case when $(n + 1) \in T$. Note that in this case $T = \{n+1\} \cup T'$ for some $T' \subset [n]$ such that $|T'| \geq n - r$. Now note that all the relations in T cannot cover the n attributes but R_{n+1} by itself does include all the n attributes. This implies that $\mathsf{BFS}(T) = \{n + 1\}$ in this case. This proves that $\{n + 1\}$ is the other element in $C^*(q, r)$, as desired.

5. CONCLUSION AND FUTURE WORK

We establish optimal algorithms for the worst-case behavior of join algorithms. We also demonstrate that the join algorithms employed in RDBMSs do not achieve these optimal bounds. Moreover, we demonstrate families of instances where join-project algorithms are asymptotically worse by factors close to the size of the largest relation. It is interesting to ask similar questions for average case complexity. Our work offers a different way to approach join optimization rather than the traditional binary-join/dynamic-programming-based approach. Thus, our immediate future work is to implement these ideas to see how they compare in real RDBMS settings to the algorithms in a modern RDBMS.

Another interesting direction is to extend these results to a larger classes of queries and to database schemata that have constraints. We include in the full version some preliminary results on full conjunctive queries and simple functional dependencies (FDs). Not surprisingly, using dependency information one can obtain tighter bounds compared to the (FD-unaware) fractional cover technique.

There are potentially interesting connections between our work and several inter-related topics. We algorithmically prove that the AGM inequality is equivalent to the BT inequality; in turn both inequalities are essentially equivalent to Shearer's entropy inequality. There are known combinatorial interpretations of entropy inequalities (which include Shearer's as a special case); for example, Alon et al. [3] derived some such connections using a notion of "sections" similar to what we used in this paper. An analogous partitioning procedure is used by Marx [29] to compute joins by relating the number of solutions to submodular functions. Query (1) is essentially equivalent to the problem of enumerating all triangles in a tri-partite graph, which can be solved in time $O(N^{3/2})$ [4].

6. ACKNOWLEDGMENTS

We thank Georg Gottlob for sending us a full version of his work [13] and XuanLong Nguyen for introducing us to the Loomis-Whitney inequality. We thank the anonymous referees for many helpful comments that greatly improved the presentation of the paper. In particular, we thank a reviewer for pointing out the current proof (and statement) of Lemma 3.6 and an error in previous lower bound argument in Section 4.2. AR's work on this project is supported the NSF CAREER Award under CCF-0844796. CR's work on this project is generously supported by the NSF CAREER Award under IIS-1054009, the ONR under N000141210041, and gifts from Google, Greenplum, LogicBlox, and Oracle.

7. REFERENCES

[1] S. Abiteboul, R. Hull, and V. Vianu. *Foundations of Databases*. Addison-Wesley, 1995.

[2] N. Alon, P. B. Gibbons, Y. Matias, and M. Szegedy. Tracking join and self-join sizes in limited storage. In *PODS*, pages 10–20, 1999.

[3] N. Alon, I. Newman, A. Shen, G. Tardos, and N. K. Vereshchagin. Partitioning multi-dimensional sets in a small number of "uniform" parts. *Eur. J. Comb.*, 28(1):134–144, 2007.

[4] N. Alon, R. Yuster, and U. Zwick. Finding and counting given length cycles. *Algorithmica*, 17(3):209–223, 1997.

[5] A. Atserias, M. Grohe, and D. Marx. Size bounds and query plans for relational joins. In *FOCS*, pages 739–748. IEEE, 2008.

[6] R. Avnur and J. M. Hellerstein. Eddies: Continuously adaptive query processing. In *SIGMOD Conference*, pages 261–272, 2000.

[7] S. Babu, P. Bizarro, and D. J. DeWitt. Proactive re-optimization. In *SIGMOD Conference*, pages 107–118, 2005.

[8] B. Bollobás and A. Thomason. Projections of bodies and hereditary properties of hypergraphs. *Bull. London Math. Soc.*, 27(5), 1995.

[9] F. R. K. Chung, R. L. Graham, P. Frankl, and J. B. Shearer. Some intersection theorems for ordered sets and graphs. *J. Combin. Theory Ser. A*, 43(1):23–37, 1986.

[10] A. Deligiannakis, M. N. Garofalakis, and N. Roussopoulos. Extended wavelets for multiple measures. *TODS*, 32(2):10, 2007.

[11] J. Flum, M. Frick, and M. Grohe. Query evaluation via tree-decompositions. *J. ACM*, 49(6):716–752, 2002.

[12] A. C. Gilbert, H. Q. Ngo, E. Porat, A. Rudra, and M. J. Strauss. Efficiently decodable ℓ_2/ℓ_2 for each compressed sensing with tiny failure probability, November 2011. Manuscript.

[13] G. Gottlob, S. T. Lee, and G. Valiant. Size and treewidth bounds for conjunctive queries. In *PODS*, pages 45–54, 2009.

[14] G. Gottlob, N. Leone, and F. Scarcello. Hypertree decompositions: A survey. In *MFCS*, 2001.

[15] G. Gottlob, Z. Miklós, and T. Schwentick. Generalized hypertree decompositions: np-hardness and tractable variants. In *PODS*, 2007.

[16] G. Graefe. Query evaluation techniques for large databases. *ACM Computing Surveys*, 25(2):73–170, June 1993.

[17] M. Grohe and D. Marx. Constraint solving via fractional edge covers. In *SODA*, pages 289–298, 2006.

[18] K. Gyarmati, M. Matolcsi, and I. Z. Ruzsa. A superadditivity and submultiplicativity property for cardinalities of sumsets. *Combinatorica*, 30(2):163–174, 2010.

[19] T. S. Han. Nonnegative entropy measures of multivariate symmetric correlations. *Information and Control*, 36(2):133–156, 1978.

[20] Y. E. Ioannidis. The history of histograms (abridged). In *VLDB*, 2003.

[21] Y. E. Ioannidis and S. Christodoulakis. On the propagation of errors in the size of join results. In *SIGMOD Conference*, 1991.

[22] D. Irony, S. Toledo, and A. Tiskin. Communication lower bounds for distributed-memory matrix multiplication. *J. Parallel Distrib. Comput.*, 64(9):1017–1026, 2004.

[23] H. V. Jagadish, N. Koudas, S. Muthukrishnan, V. Poosala, K. C. Sevcik, and T. Suel. Optimal Histograms with Quality Guarantees. In *VLDB*, 1998.

[24] A. C. König and G. Weikum. Combining Histograms and Parametric Curve Fitting for Feedback-Driven Query Result-size Estimation. In *VLDB*, 1999.

[25] A. R. Lehman and E. Lehman. Network coding: does the model need tuning? In *SODA*, pages 499–504, 2005.

[26] L. H. Loomis and H. Whitney. An inequality related to the isoperimetric inequality. *Bull. Amer. Math. Soc*, 55:961–962, 1949.

[27] R. Lyons. Probability on trees and networks, jun 2011. with Yuval Peres url: http://php.indiana.edu/ rdlyons/prbtree/prbtree.html.

[28] V. Markl, N. Megiddo, M. Kutsch, T. M. Tran, P. J. Haas, and U. Srivastava. Consistently estimating the selectivity of conjuncts of predicates. In *VLDB*, pages 373–384, 2005.

[29] D. Marx. Tractable hypergraph properties for constraint satisfaction and conjunctive queries. In *STOC*, pages 735–744, 2010.

[30] H. Q. Ngo, E. Porat, C. Ré, and A. Rudra. Worst-case optimal join algorithms, 2012. arXiv:1203.1952 [cs.DB].

[31] H. Q. Ngo, E. Porat, and A. Rudra. Personal Communciation.

[32] A. Pagh and R. Pagh. Scalable computation of acyclic joins. In *PODS*, pages 225–232, 2006.

[33] V. Poosala, Y. Ioannidis, P. Haas, and E. J. Shekita. Improved histograms for selectivity estimation of range predicates. In *SIGMOD*, pages 294–305, 1996.

[34] A. Schrijver. *Combinatorial optimization. Polyhedra and efficiency. Vol. A*, volume 24 of *Algorithms and Combinatorics*. Springer-Verlag, Berlin, 2003.

[35] U. Srivastava, P. J. Haas, V. Markl, M. Kutsch, and T. M. Tran. Isomer: Consistent histogram construction using query feedback. In *ICDE*, page 39, 2006.

[36] K. Tzoumas, A. Deshpande, and C. S. Jensen. Lightweight graphical models for selectivity estimation without independence assumptions. *PVLDB*, 4(11):852–863, 2011.

[37] L. G. Valiant and V. V. Vazirani. NP is as easy as detecting unique solutions. *Theor. Comput. Sci.*, 47(3):85–93, 1986.

[38] D. E. Willard. Applications of range query theory to relational data base join and selection operations. *J. Comput. Syst. Sci.*, 52(1), 1996.

[39] Y. Xu, P. Kostamaa, X. Zhou, and L. Chen. Handling data skew in parallel joins in shared-nothing systems. In *SIGMOD*, 2008.

Deterministic Regular Expressions in Linear Time

Benoît Groz
Mostrare, INRIA
University of Lille, France

Sebastian Maneth
NICTA and UNSW
Sydney, Australia

Sławek Staworko
Mostrare, INRIA
University of Lille, France

ABSTRACT

Deterministic regular expressions are widely used in XML processing. For instance, all regular expressions in DTDs and XML Schemas are required to be deterministic. In this paper we show that determinism of a regular expression e can be tested in linear time. The best known algorithms, based on the Glushkov automaton, require $O(\sigma|e|)$ time, where σ is the number of distinct symbols in e. We further show that matching a word w against an expression e can be achieved in combined linear time $O(|e| + |w|)$, for a wide range of deterministic regular expressions: (i) star-free (for multiple input words), (ii) bounded-occurrence, i.e., expressions in which each symbol appears a bounded number of times, and (iii) bounded plus-depth, i.e., expressions in which the nesting depth of alternating plus (union) and concatenation symbols is bounded. Our algorithms use a new structural decomposition of the parse tree of e. For matching arbitrary deterministic regular expressions we present an $O(|e| + |w| \log \log |e|)$ time algorithm.

Categories and Subject Descriptors: F.2.2, I.1.1

General Terms: Algorithms

Keywords: DTD, XML Schema, Deterministic Regular Expression, Glushkov Automaton, Linear Time.

1. INTRODUCTION

Deterministic regular expressions are widely used in XML processing. For instance, all regular expressions in DTDs and in XML Schemas are required to be deterministic. The idea stems from the earlier SGML standard where right-hand sides of context-free productions ("content models") are deterministic regular expressions. Such expressions can be parsed more efficiently than unrestricted ones.

Within XML databases and XML processing, the two main tasks performed over regular expressions are (1) testing determinism and (2) matching (= parsing) against (child sequences of) the given input document.

PODS '12, May 21–23, 2012, Scottsdale, Arizona, USA.

Testing Determinism. The original terminology used in SGML was to restrict content models to be "unambiguous"; it means that at any position in the regular expression (positions are labeled by symbols, such as a or b, but not by operators such as $*$) and for each symbol there may be *at most* one position that follows. For instance, the expression ab^*b is ambiguous because the a-position is followed by two b-positions. Intuitively, the parser upon reading ab has to choose against which b to parse. There exist many translations from regular expressions to finite automata, see e.g. [16]. The particular translation due to Glushkov [12] (see also [2]) associates to each position a state of the automaton. As Brüggemann-Klein shows [8], a regular expression is unambiguous if and only if its Glushkov automaton is deterministic. We therefore use the term "deterministic regular expression." Brüggemann-Klein's result allows to test determinism of an expression e as follows: (i) build the Glushkov automaton A of e and (ii) test determinism of A. The worst-case size of A is $O(\sigma|e|)$, where σ is the number of distinct symbols in e, and A can be built and checked for determinism in this time bound. Thus, this test has *quadratic* time complexity in the size of e. It is a general misconception in the literature that testing determinism of regular expressions can be performed in linear time (cf. e.g., the abstract of [8]). The known algorithms build the Glushkov automaton in quadratic worst-case time. Note that large alphabets appear in practice, and that the quadratic behavior of building the Glushkov automaton is experienced even for very simple expressions such as $E = (a_1 + a_2 + \cdots + a_m)^*$.

For the expression E, determinism can easily be checked in linear time (by checking distinctness of the a_i). The "mixed content" of XML, for instance, is similar to E and some XML validators such as Xerces [11] use specialized linear time procedures for this case. For more complicated expressions, however, it has remained open whether linear time determinism testing is possible. Here we close the problem affirmatively and show that all regular expressions can be tested for determinism in time $O(|e|)$. Our idea is a new decomposition of e's parse tree. For each distinct symbol a of e we build its "skeleton"; roughly speaking, it is a tree consisting of all positions labeled a, plus their iterated LCAs (lowest common ancestors) in e's parse tree; skeleton trees can be obtained in linear time [7] using preprocessing and constant time LCA [1] queries. By adding more nodes and pointers into the skeleton trees, we are able to test determinism in linear time.

Matching. Consider now matching a deterministic regular expression e against an input word w. What makes it difficult to match e against w? We identify several "easy" cases: (i) Star-free: in this case, $|w| \leq |e|$, and we can match easily during one traversal over the parse tree of e. (ii) Bounded number of distinct symbols in e: we simply build the Glushkov automaton. (iii) Bounded number of occurrences of each symbol in e (k-occurrence): Here we use our first technical lemma. It says that testing if two positions follow each other in e (this means the Glushkov automaton has a transition between the positions) can be realized in constant time. This is achieved by preprocessing e's parse tree for LCA [1] and by using LCA queries to realize a structural relationship of follow positions known from [9, 25]. Hence, we do *not* build the Glushkov automaton. Since at most k positions need to be checked for the follow relationship when matching against a k-occurrence expression, the lemma implies linear time $O(|e|+k|w|)$. Note that for real world DTDs it has been reported that a large percentage of regular expressions is k-occurrence for small k [3, 21].

One finding is that plus-symbols (union) play an essential role in the combined complexity of matching. For instance, if no plus-symbols in e are nested, then we show that matching can be done in time $O(|e| + |w|)$. The idea is to annotate particular nodes in e's parse tree with candidates of follow-positions in e. The determinism requirement of e then allows to *amortize* the number of annotated nodes that have to be visited in order to go from one symbol in w to the next.

Our amortization argument fails when the *depth of alternation* of plus and concatenation symbols is not bounded. Such expressions seem the hardest to match, and finding a time $O(|e| + |w|)$ algorithm remains an open problem. Note that the alternation depth is small in practice: Grijzenhout's large collection of real-world DTDs [13] does not contain a single expression with alternation depth larger than 4. We present an algorithm with time $O(|e| + |w| \log \log |e|)$ complexity that works for arbitrary deterministic expressions. It is derived from our linear time determinism test which assigns colors (i.e., labels in Σ) to nodes of e's parse tree. At a position p, the next position labeled a is obtained by a lookup at the lowest ancestor of p with color a. The expression e is preprocessed for lowest colored ancestor queries, using [23] (based on van Emde Boas trees). Note that for arbitrary (nondeterministic) regular expressions, the best known time complexities are time $O(nm/\log n + (n+m)\log n)$ [24] which was improved recently to $O(nm(\log \log n)/(\log n)^{3/2} + n + m)$ [6], where $m = |e|$ and $n = |w|$.

Our results are summarized as follows:

(1) Determinism of a regular expression e can be tested in time $O(|e|)$. This improves previous algorithms requiring quadratic time. Besides a direct proof, we present an alternative one which uses a fixed XPath query, and then applies the result of Bojańczyk and Parys [7].

(2) Deterministic regular expression can be matched in time $O(|e| + |w|)$ against an input word w, if

    (a) each symbol occurs only a bounded number of times in e ("k-occurrence"), or

    (b) the maximal depth of alternating union and concatenation operations in e is bounded.

(3) Star-free deterministic regular expression can be matched against several input words $w_1, \ldots, w_n$, in time $O(|e| + |w_1| + \cdots + |w_n|)$.

(4) Arbitrary deterministic regular expression can be matched in time $O(|e| + |w| \log \log |e|)$.

Recently it was proved that even in the presence of numeric occurrence indicators (as used in XML Schema), determinism of expressions can be tested in time $O(\sigma|e|)$ [18]. We show that our result extends to this case: even in the presence of numeric occurrence indicators we can decide determinism in time $O(|e|)$. We note that all our matching algorithms are *streamable*, i.e., they do not need to store w in memory, but read w in one sequential pass, symbol by symbol. We have implemented all our algorithms and made them available at http://gforge.inria.fr/projects/lire/.

Related Work

The idea of our algorithm (3), and also to a lesser extent of our determinism check (1), is similar to that of Hagenah and Muscholl [14] in their algorithm that computes for any regular expression an ε-free NFA in time $\Omega(|e| \log^2 |e|)$. They decompose the transitions leaving each state into a few sets and group states sharing such sets of outgoing transitions. This decomposition is based on a *heavy path* decomposition of the parse tree of e. We use another decomposition of this parse tree in order to amortize the evaluation cost.

An orthogonal direction of research involves algorithms for the efficient validation of huge documents against a small DTD. Several works [27, 28] focused on obtaining space efficient algorithms in a streaming framework. This is challenging when document trees are deep. Konrad and Magniez [20] provide streaming algorithms in sublinear space for the validation against DTDs. They consider a framework where the algorithm has access to a read-only input stream and several auxiliary read/write streams. The algorithm is allowed to perform read or write passes on the streams. At the beginning of each pass on a stream, the algorithm decides in which direction the stream is processed, and also decides if the pass is a write or a read pass. The authors propose an algorithm that validates a tree t against a constant-size DTD in $O(\log^2 |t|)$ passes, using space $O(\log |t|)$ and 3 auxiliary streams, with $O(\log |t|)$ processing time per symbol. Note that the validator checks the sibling sequences of t against the corresponding deterministic regular expression.

In the context of DTD inference, Bex et al. identify two classes of regular expressions which account for most of the regular expressions in real schemas: the single occurrence regular expressions (1-ORE) and the chain regular expressions (CHARE). An expression is an 1-ORE iff no symbol appears more than once in e, therefore 1-ORE are always deterministic. CHARE are a subclass of 1-ORE, and contain the 1-ORE that consist of a sequence of factors of the form $(a_1 + a_2 + \cdots + a_n)$ where every a_i is a symbol, each factor being possibly extended with a star or a question mark. 1-ORE account for 98% of the regular expressions in real schemas, while CHARE account for 90% of them. Bex, Neven, and van den Bussche [4] also define *simple regular expressions*, which generalize CHARE in that symbols a_i in factors can appear with a star or question mark, and the number of occurrences of a symbol is not restricted.

The class of expressions for which our algorithm (2b) performs in linear time properly contains deterministic simple regular expressions. Moreover although stars are allowed in simple regular expressions, which makes them unfit for algorithm (3), those stars can occur only above a single symbol, or above a union of strings (with possibly a star or question mark above the strings). Therefore, an easy extension of algorithm (3) handles simple deterministic regular expressions.

2. REGULAR EXPRESSIONS

Let Σ be a finite set of symbols. *Regular expressions over* Σ are defined by the following grammar, where $\odot$ represents concatenation, $+$ union, ? choice, and $*$ the Kleene star: $e :=$ $a(a \in \Sigma) \mid (e) \odot (e) \mid (e) + (e) \mid (e)? \mid (e)^*$. The language $L(e)$ of e is defined as usual [16]. Note that $L((e)?) = L(e) \cup \{\varepsilon\}$, where ε denotes the empty word. We say that e is *nullable* if $\varepsilon \in L(e)$. In expressions, we do not write parentheses around words over Σ and often omit $\odot$ symbols. We require of our regular expressions e that:

(R1) $e = (\#e')\$$ and $\#$ and $\$$ do not appear in e'

(R2) $((e')^*)^*$ does not appear in e

(R3) if $(e')?$ appears in e, then $\varepsilon \notin L(e')$

An arbitrary regular expression can be changed easily (in linear time) into an equivalent one of the required form. Note that $\#$ and $\$$ are tacitly present and required, but, for better readability, are omitted in most examples.

We identify a regular expression with its parse tree (as illustrated in Figure 1), and define the *positions* $Pos(e)$ of e as the leaves of e whereas N_e denotes the set of all nodes from e. For a node $n \in N_e$ we denote by e/n the subexpression of e rooted at n. Every tree t is implemented as a pointer structure, where $Lchild_t(n)$ (resp. $Rchild_t(n)$) returns the left (resp. right) child of node n in t and $parent_t(n)$ returns the parent of n in t. The pointers return $Null$ if the respective node does not exist. For unary nodes $Rchild_t(n)$ returns $Null$. We denote by $lab_t(n)$ the label of n in t, and by $\preccurlyeq_t$ the (reflexive) ancestor relationship in t. If $m \preccurlyeq_t n$ then we also say that n is a descendant of m. Thus, each node is ancestor and descendant of itself.

The *size* of a tree t, denoted $|t|$, is the number of nodes in t, whereas the *depth* of t $depth(t)$ is the length of path from the root to the deepest node in t. Our restrictions (R2) and (R3) guarantee that $|e|$ is linear in $|Pos(e)|$. We denote by $\overline{e}$ the regular expression obtained from e by marking the i-th position (from left to right) with subscript i. We denote by $\overline{\Sigma}$ the set of symbols obtained from Σ by adding subscripts below symbols. In particular, $Pos(\overline{e}) = Pos(e)$.

Given a position p of e, $Follow_e(p)$ is the set of positions that may follow p in e:

$$Follow_e(p) = \{q \mid \exists u, v \in \overline{\Sigma}^*, u \cdot lab_{\overline{e}}(p) \cdot lab_{\overline{e}}(q) \cdot v \in L(\overline{e})\}.$$

The expression e is *deterministic* if for all $p, q, q' \in Pos(e)$ with $q, q' \in Follow_e(p)$: $q \neq q'$ implies that $lab_e(q) \neq lab_e(q')$. Whenever the regular expression or the tree is clear from context, we drop the subscript and write $Follow$, lab, and $\preccurlyeq$.

EXAMPLE 2.1. *Let $e_1 = (ab + b(b?)a)^*$ and $e_2 = (a^*ba + bb)^*$. Denote by $p_1, \ldots, p_5$ the positions of e_1 in left-to-right order, and by $q_1, \ldots, q_5$ those of e_2. Then $\overline{e_1} = (a_1b_2 + b_3(b_4?)a_5)^*$ and $Follow_{e_1}(p_3) = \{p_4, p_5\}$. Similarly, $\overline{e_2} = (a_1^*b_2a_3 + b_4b_5)^*$, and $Follow_{e_2}(q_3) = \{q_1, q_2, q_4\}$. Expression e_1 is deterministic, while e_2 is non-deterministic because $lab_{e_2}(q_2) = lab_{e_2}(q_4) = b$.*

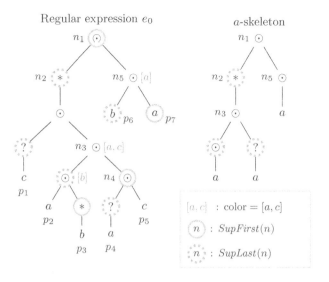

Figure 1: Expression $e_0 = (c?((ab^*)(a?c)))^*(ba)$.

Structure of Regular Expressions

The *First* and *Last*-positions of a regular expression e are

$$
\begin{aligned}
First(e) &= \{p \mid \exists u \in \overline{\Sigma}^*, lab_{\overline{e}}(p) \cdot u \in L(\overline{e})\} \\
Last(e) &= \{p \mid \exists u \in \overline{\Sigma}^*, u \cdot lab_{\overline{e}}(p) \in L(\overline{e})\}.
\end{aligned}
$$

We also define, for a node n of e, $First(n)$ and $Last(n)$ as $First(e/n)$ and $Last(e/n)$, respectively. Note that $First(n)$ and $Last(n)$ are non-empty for every node n of e. For instance, for the expression e_0 in Figure 1 $First(n_2) = \{p_1, p_2\}$ and $Last(n_2) = \{p_5\}$.

Given two nodes u, v of e, let $LCA(u, v)$ denote the lowest common ancestor of u and v in e. The next lemma was stated before, e.g., in [9, 25], but not in terms of LCA.

LEMMA 2.2. *Let $p, q \in Pos(e)$ and $n = LCA(p, q)$. Then $q \in Follow(p)$ iff*

(1) *$lab(n) = \odot$, $q \in First(Rchild(n))$, $p \in Last(Lchild(n))$, or*

(2) *$q \in First(s)$ and $p \in Last(s)$ where s is the lowest $*$-labeled ancestor of n.*

Lemma 2.2 says that there are only two ways in which positions follow each other: (1) through a concatenation, or (2) through a star. We write $q \in Follow_e^{\odot}(p)$ if (1) is satisfied, and $q \in Follow_e^*(p)$ if (2) is satisfied. For instance, in e_0 (Figure 1), we have $p_4 \in Follow_{e_0}^{\odot}(p_3)$ and $p_1 \in Follow_{e_0}^*(p_5)$. Note, however, that there may exist some positions p and q that satisfy simultaneously (1) and (2).

It was also observed earlier, e.g., [9, 25, 14], that First and Last-sets (and nullability) can be defined in a syntax-directed way over the parse tree of e. For instance, if $lab(n) = \odot$ and $Lchild(n)$, $Rchild(n)$ are non-nullable then $First(n) = First(Lchild(n))$ and $Last(n) = Last(Rchild(n))$. We define now the Boolean properties $SupFirst$ and $SupLast$ for every node n, where n' denotes $parent(n)$:

$SupFirst(n)$ iff $lab(n') = \odot, n = Rchild(n')$, and

$$Lchild(n') \text{ is non-nullable}$$

$SupLast(n)$ iff $lab(n') = \odot, n = Lchild(n')$, and

$$Rchild(n') \text{ is non-nullable.}$$

If $SupFirst(n)$ then the First-set changes at n's parent: $First(parent(n)) \cap First(n) = \varnothing$, and otherwise is a super-set: $First(parent(n)) \supseteq First(n)$. For instance, in e_0 (Figure 1), n_4 is a $SupFirst$-node since $First(n_3) = \{p_2\}$ and $First(n_4) = \{p_4, p_5\}$. This explains the name "$SupFirst$": a node with this property is "maximal" with respect the First-sets of its direct descendants (without the property). The same holds for $SupLast$ and $Last$. We define for any node n, the pointers $pSupFirst(n)$ and $pSupLast(n)$ as the lowest ancestors x of n such that $SupFirst(x)$ and $SupLast(x)$, respectively. Recall that by (R1), $e = (\#e')\$$; this implies that for every node of e', both $pSupFirst(n)$ and $pSupLast(n)$ are defined. These definitions will never be applied to the "help nodes" of e that are not in e' (such as the root node of e); note however, that the root n_1 in Figure 1 is a $SupFirst$-node (because of the phantom position $\#$ not shown in the figure). We can check membership in First and Last, using $pSupFirst$ and $pSupLast$.

LEMMA 2.3. *Let* $p \in Pos(e)$ *and* $n \in N_e$.

(1) $p \in First(n)$ *iff* $pSupFirst(p) \preccurlyeq n \preccurlyeq p$, *and*

(2) $p \in Last(n)$ *iff* $pSupLast(p) \preccurlyeq n \preccurlyeq p$.

It is well-known, see [15, 1], that arbitrary LCA queries on a tree t can be answered in constant time, after preprocessing of t in linear time. For positions p and q, define the Boolean $checkIfFollow(p, q)$ as true iff $q \in Follow(p)$.

THEOREM 2.4. *After preprocessing of* e *in* $O(|e|)$ *time,* $checkIfFollow(p, q)$ *can be answered in constant time for every* $p, q \in Pos(e)$.

PROOF. First preprocess e for LCA queries. Next, add to each node n of e the pointers $pSupLast(n)$, $pSupFirst(n)$, and $pStar(n)$. The latter points to the lowest $*$-labeled ancestor of n. Clearly, this preprocessing can be carried out in time $O(|e|)$. We are ready to compute $checkIfFollow(p, q)$ in constant time: first obtain $n = LCA(p, q)$. By Lemmas 2.2 and 2.3 we return *true* (1) if $lab(n) = \odot$, $pSupFirst(q) \preccurlyeq Rchild(n)$, and $pSupLast(p) \preccurlyeq Lchild(n)$. These conditions can be checked in constant time ($n \preccurlyeq n'$ can be realized, e.g., by testing if $LCA(n, n') = n$). If case (1) fails then we compute $n' = pStar(n)$ and check in constant time if $pSupFirst(q) \preccurlyeq n'$ and $pSupLast(p) \preccurlyeq n'$. We return *true* if the checks succeed and *false* otherwise. $\square$

The following technical lemmas state relationships between positions and their $pSupFirst$ and $pSupLast$ nodes.

LEMMA 2.5. *Let* $p, q \in Pos(e)$ *and* $q \in Follow_e(p)$. *Then*

(1) $parent(pSupFirst(q)) \preccurlyeq p$ *and*

(2) $parent(pSupLast(p)) \preccurlyeq q$.

PROOF. To show (1), assume that $parent(pSupFirst(q))$ is not an ancestor of p. Then $n = LCA(p, q)$ is an ancestor of $parent(pSupFirst(q))$, hence $pSupFirst(q) \npreccurlyeq n$. By Lemma 2.3(1) we obtain $q \notin First(n)$ and therefore, by Lemma 2.2, q does not follow p. Point (2) can be proved similarly. $\square$

LEMMA 2.6. *Let* p *and* q *be two positions of* e *such that* q *follows* p. *If* $pSupLast(p) \preccurlyeq parent(pSupFirst(q))$ *then* $pSupFirst(q)$ *is nullable.*

PROOF. Let $p, q \in Pos(e)$ such that $q \in Follow(p)$ and $pSupLast(p) \preccurlyeq parent(pSupFirst(q))$, and let $x = LCA(p, q)$. Assume first that $q \in Follow^{\odot}(p)$. Then $lab(x) = \odot$ and there are no $SupLast$ nodes between p and $pSupLast(p)$ except $pSupLast(p)$. It means that in particular $Rchild(x)$ is nullable. Hence $pSupFirst(q)$ is nullable if it is the right-child of x. Otherwise $pSupFirst(q)$ is an ancestor of x. In that case, there are no $SupFirst$ nodes between q and $pSupFirst(q)$, except $pSupFirst(q)$, so that $Lchild(x)$ is nullable. Consequently, x is nullable, and there are no $SupFirst$ nor $SupLast$ nodes between x and $pSupFirst(q)$, except the node $pSupFirst(q)$. Therefore, $pSupFirst(q)$ is nullable. The case $q \in Follow^*(p)$ is handled similarly: $pStar(x)$ is nullable and satisfies $pSupFirst(q) \preccurlyeq pStar(x) \preccurlyeq x$. Moreover there are no $SupFirst$ nor $SupLast$ nodes between x and $pSupFirst(q)$, except $pSupFirst(q)$. Thus, $pSupFirst(q)$ is nullable. $\square$

3. TESTING DETERMINISM

To test determinism we need to check for every $a \in \Sigma$ and positions $q \neq q'$ labeled a whether there exists a p such that q and q' follow p. The challenge of a linear time algorithm is to deal with the quadratically many candidate pairs (q, q').

3.1 Candidate Pair Reduction

We define the following condition:

(P1) for all $q \neq q'$ in $Pos(e)$, $pSupFirst(q) = pSupFirst(q')$ implies $lab(q) \neq lab(q')$.

Clearly, if (P1) is false then e is non-deterministic. To see this, let $q \neq q'$ and $n = pSupFirst(q) = pSupFirst(q')$. Since the First and Last sets of any node are non-empty, there exists a p in $Last(Lchild(parent(n)))$. Note that $parent(n) = LCA(p, q) = LCA(p, q')$. By Lemma 2.2, $q, q' \in Follow_e(p)$, and hence by definition of determinism, $lab(q) \neq lab(q')$. Testing (P1) in linear time is straightforward: during one traversal of e we group the positions with same $pSupFirst$-pointer; for each group we check that all contained positions have distinct labels. This can easily be achieved in linear time, using an adapted bucket sorting algorithm. Therefore we assume from now on that (P1) is true.

According to Lemma 2.5(1) we store information about p in the parent of $pSupFirst(p)$. For each position p labeled a, we

- assign *color* a to the node $parent(pSupFirst(p))$

- say that position p is a *witness* for color a in the node $parent(pSupFirst(p))$.

Observe that each node may be assigned several colors, but, since (P1) holds, each node has at most one witness per color. In Figure 1, node n_3 has colors a and c. The witness for color a (resp. c) in n_3 is p_4 (resp. p_5). Lemma 2.5 states that a position q labeled a that follows p is a witnesses for color a in *some ancestor* of p. Thus, if two positions labeled a follow p, then each of them is witness for color a in ancestors of p.

We say that a node $n \in N_e$ has *class* a if n has color a, or n is a position labeled a, or n is the lowest common ancestor of two nodes of class a. The a-skeleton t_a of e consists of all nodes n of class a plus their $pSupLast$ and $pStar$ nodes (as defined in Section 2). The node labels in t_a are taken over from e, and the tree structure is inherited from e: n' is the left (resp. right) child of n in t_a if (1) n' is in the subtree of the left (resp. right) child of n in e, (2) $n \preccurlyeq n'$, and (3) there is no n'' in t_a with $n \preccurlyeq n'' \preccurlyeq n'$. If a node has no left (resp. right) child defined in this way, then the corresponding pointer is set to $Null$. Note that a node in t_a can be labeled $\odot$ or $+$ and have its left (or right) child point to $Null$. Figure 1 presents a regular expression and its a-skeleton.

LEMMA 3.1. *The collection of a-skeleta for all $a \in \Sigma$ can be computed in time $O(|e|)$.*

PROOF. The size of the a-skeleton is linear in the number of positions labeled a in e. Hence the size of the collection of a-skeleta is linear in $|e|$. The skeleta can be constructed in linear time by simply applying LCA repeatedly, inserting each position from e in left-to-right order using the linear preprocessing so that the LCA of two nodes of e is obtained in constant time. This construction is detailed in Proposition 4.4 of [7]. □

In the a-skeleton t_a, we equip each node n with three pointers: $Witness(n, a)$, $FirstPos(n, a)$, and $Next(n, a)$. For every node n in t_a,

- if n has color a then $Witness(n, a)$ is the witness for color a in n (and is undefined otherwise)

- $FirstPos(n, a)$ is the position p labeled a such that $p \in First(n)$ if it exists (and is undefined otherwise); note that property (P1) guarantees that there is at most one such position p

- $Next(n, a)$ is the set of all positions in $FollowAfter_e(n)$ labeled a.

The set $FollowAfter_e(n)$ is the extension of $Follow$ to internal nodes n of e,

$$FollowAfter_e(n) = \{q \not\preccurlyeq n \mid \exists p \in Last(n), q \in Follow_e(p)\}.$$

Constructing the data structures $FirstPos$ and $Witness$ is straightforward: $Witness$ is built simultaneously with the a-skeleton; $FirstPos$ can for instance be computed in a single bottom-up traversal of each a-skeleton, using pointers $pSupFirst$ from e and ancestor queries in e. Let n be the root node of the a-skeleton. Then $BuildNext(a, n, \varnothing)$ in Algorithm 1 builds the data structure $Next(n', a)$ for all nodes n' of the a-skeleton.

LEMMA 3.2. *Calling $BuildNext(n, a, \varnothing)$ for each $a \in \Sigma$ and root node n of t_a takes in total time $O(|e|)$. If any call returns false then e is non-deterministic. Otherwise, the set $Next(n, a)$ defined during the execution consists of all positions in $FollowAfter_e(n)$ labeled a, for $n \in N_{t_a}$ and $a \in \Sigma$.*

PROOF. The $O(|e|)$ time is achieved because (1) $Build$-$Next$ is called at most m-times, where m is the number of nodes of all skeleta, and $m \in O(|e|)$ by Lemma 3.1, and (2) each line of the algorithm runs in constant time because $|Y| \leq 2$ at each call, due to Line 10. To see the correctness consider the execution along a path in t_a. If at Line 7

Algorithm 1 Computing $Next(n, a)$, if e is deterministic.

procedure $BuildNext(a : \Sigma, n : \mathrm{Node}, Y : \mathrm{Set(Node)}) : \mathrm{Bool}$
1   **if** $SupLast(n)$
2   **then** $Y \leftarrow \varnothing$
3   **if** n is the left child in t_a of a $\odot$-node **and**
4   n has a right sibling n' in t_a **and**
5     $(\neg SupLast(n)$ **or** $parent_{t_a}(n) = parent_e(n))$
6   **then** $Y \leftarrow Y \cup \{FirstPos(n', a)\}$
7   $Next(n, a) \leftarrow \{p \in Y \mid n \not\preccurlyeq p\}$
8   **if** $lab(n) = *$
9   **then** $Y \leftarrow Y \cup \{FirstPos(n, a)\}$
10 **if** $|Y| > 2$
11   **then return** $false$
12 **if** $Lchild_{t_a}(n) = Null$
13   **then return** $true$
14   **else** $B \leftarrow BuildNext(a, Lchild_{t_a}(n), Y)$
15 **if** $Rchild_{t_a}(n) = Null$
16   **then return** B
17   **else return** $B \wedge BuildNext(a, Rchild_{t_a}(n), Y)$
end procedure

---

the current node n has an ancestor u labeled $*$ with no $SupLast$-node on their path, then Y contains $FirstPos(u, a)$; if n is in the left subtree of an ancestor u labeled $\odot$ with no $SupLast$-node on their path, and n has a right sibling n' in t_a, then Y contains $FirstPos(n', a)$. These conditions imply that the set defined in Line 7 holds all a-labeled positions in $FollowAfter_e(n)$. Clearly, e is non-deterministic if $|Y| > 2$ in Line 10. □

We define another condition:

(P2) for every $a \in \Sigma$ and $n \in N_{t_a}$, $Next(n, a)$ contains at most one element.

Clearly, (P2) can be tested in linear time (for instance by incorporating it into Algorithm 1). If (P2) is false, then e is non-deterministic. Thus, from now on we assume that both (P2) and (P1) are true. We identify $Next(n, a)$ with q if $Next(n, a) = \{q\}$, and let it be undefined otherwise.

LEMMA 3.3. *Let $p, q \in Pos(e)$ with $lab_e(q) = a$. If $q \in Follow_e(p)$ then the lowest ancestor n of p having color a exists and satisfies $q = Witness(n, a)$ or $q = FirstPos(n, a)$ or $q \in Next(n, a)$.*

PROOF. By Lemma 2.2, Lemma 2.5 (1), and Lemma 3.2: $q = Witness(n, a)$ if $Rchild(n) \preccurlyeq_e q$, $q = FirstPos(n, a)$ if $Lchild(n) \preccurlyeq_e q$, and $q = Next(n, a)$ if $n \not\preccurlyeq_e q$. □

From Lemma 3.3 and the definition of (P1) and (P2) we obtain the following result.

LEMMA 3.4. *The expression e is non-deterministic iff (P1) or (P2) is false, or there exist $a \in \Sigma$, $n \in N_{t_a}$ of color a, and $q, q' \in \{FirstPos(n, a), Witness(n, a), Next(n, a)\}$ such that $q \neq q'$ and $Follow_e^{-1}(q) \cap Follow_e^{-1}(q') \neq \varnothing$.*

3.2 Determinism Testing Algorithm

To check determinism using Lemma 3.4 we need to check for $a \in \Sigma$ and $n \in N_{t_a}$ of color a, and for every pair of distinct positions q and q' in $\{FirstPos(n, a), Witness(n, a), Next(n, a)\}$ whether or not

$$Follow_e^{-1}(q) \cap Follow_e^{-1}(q') \neq \varnothing.$$

Three combinations can occur for a position p:

53

(1) $Witness(n,a)$ and $Next(n,a)$ follow p, or

(2) $Witness(n,a)$ and $FirstPos(n,a)$ follow p, or

(3) $FirstPos(n,a)$ and $Next(n,a)$ follow p.

The third combination, however, reduces to the other two and therefore needs not be considered: let F and N denote the nodes $Next(n,a)$ and $FirstPos(n,a)$, and let n_F and n_N denote the parent of their $SupFirst$-node. We can prove that either $n_F \preccurlyeq n_N \preccurlyeq n$, in which case $F = FirstPos(n_N,a)$ (and $N = Witness(n_N,a)$), or $n_N \preccurlyeq n_F \preccurlyeq n$, in which case N is one of $FirstPos(n_F,a)$ or $Next(n_N,a)$ (and $F = Witness(n_F,a)$).

To understand the first combination, consider the expression $e = (c(b?a?))a$, and let n be the parent of the c node in e. Thus, n is of color a, with the left a in e as witness. Clearly e is non-deterministic: take p as the c position, then both $Witness(n,a)$ and $Next(n,a)$ follow p. The same holds for the expressions $e' = (c(a?b?))a$ and $e'' = (c(b?a)^*)a$. However, expression $e''' = (c(b?a))a$ is deterministic; this is because n's right subtree is non-nullable, which prevents that $Next(n,a)$ and $Witness(n,a)$ both follow a same position p. It is not hard to see, and is formally shown in the proof of Theorem 3.5, that the first combination occurs if and only if the right-child of n is nullable.

Let us now consider combination (2). This combination can only occur if there is a $*$-node $S = pStar(n)$ above n, and $pSupLast(n)$ is above this node S. Let $e = (a(b?a))^*$ and let n be the parent of the first a-position. As we can see, this expression is deterministic. This is for a similar reason as before: because the right child of n is non-nullable. If we consider $e' = (a(b?a?))^*$ then this expression is indeed non-deterministic and it holds that both $FirstPos(n,a)$ and $Witness(n,a)$ follow position p, where p is for instance the b-position. Thus, combination (2) requires that the right child of n is nullable, and also that $FirstPos(S,a) = FirstPos(n,a)$. The latter guarantees that on the path from S to $FirstPos(n,a)$ there is nothing non-nullable "to the left", and hence, that $FirstPos(n,a)$ follows the same position p that $Witness(n,a)$ follows.

To check determinism of e we check (P1), (P2), and then we execute for every $a \in \Sigma$ and every node n with color a, $CheckNode(n,a)$ of Algorithm 2; if any call returns $false$, then e is non-deterministic.

THEOREM 3.5. *Determinism of a regular expression e can be decided in time $O(|e|)$.*

PROOF. Let S, W, N, and F denote the nodes $pStar(n)$, $Witness(n,a)$, $Next(n,a)$, and $FirstPos(n,a)$ respectively. Since (P1) and (P2) can be tested in $O(|e|)$ time, it suffices, by Lemma 3.4, to prove the following two statements.

(i) $Follow_e^{-1}(W) \cap Follow_e^{-1}(N) \neq \varnothing$ iff $Rchild_e(n)$ is nullable and $N \neq Null$,

(ii) $Follow_e^{-1}(W) \cap Follow_e^{-1}(F) \neq \varnothing$ iff $F \neq Null$, $S \neq Null$, $Rchild_e(n)$ is nullable, $FirstPos(S,a) = F$, and $pSupLast(n) \preccurlyeq S$.

Let us prove statement (i) first. If $N \neq Null$ and $Rchild_e(n)$ is nullable then $Lchild_e(n)$ is not a $SupLast$-node. Therefore any position in $Last(Lchild_e(n))$ belongs to $Follow_e^{-1}(W) \cap Follow_e^{-1}(N)$. For the only-if direction, let q be a position in $Follow_e^{-1}(W) \cap Follow_e^{-1}(N)$. Then in particular

$N \neq Null$. Node n is a strict ancestor of q since $q \in Follow_e^{-1}(W)$ and $n = parent_e(pSupFirst(W))$. As q belongs to $Follow_e^{-1}(N)$, $pSupLast(q)$ is an ancestor of n. This implies that $Rchild(n)$ is nullable according to Lemma 2.6, since $Rchild(n) = pSupFirst(W)$ and W follows q.

Proof of (ii): If $F \neq Null$, $S \neq Null$, $Rchild_e(n)$ is nullable, $FirstPos(S,a) = F$, and $pSupLast(n) \preccurlyeq S$, then any q in $Last(Lchild(n))$ is in $(Follow_e^{\circlearrowright})(W) \cap (Follow_e^{*})^{-1}(F)$. Conversely, let q be a position in $Follow_e^{-1}(W) \cap Follow_e^{-1}(F)$. As q belongs to $Follow_e^{-1}(W)$, node n is a strict ancestor of q. If $Rchild_e(n) \preccurlyeq_e q$ then $q \in (Follow_e^{*})^{-1}(F)$, hence $FirstPos(S,a) = F$ and $pSupLast(n) \preccurlyeq S$, and furthermore $pSupLast(q) \preccurlyeq S$, so that $Rchild_e(n)$ is nullable according to Lemma 2.6. Assume now that $Lchild_e(n)$ is an ancestor of q, and let $x = LCA(q,F)$. As an ancestor of both q and F, $Lchild_e(n)$ is an ancestor of x. Furthermore, there is no $SupLast$-node between q and $Lchild_e(n)$, except possibly $Lchild_e(n)$, and there is no $SupFirst$-node between F and $Lchild_e(n)$. Consequently, x is non-nullable because $Lchild_e(n)$ is, and, there is no $*$-labeled node between x and $Lchild_e(n)$. Hence $q \notin (Follow_e^{\circlearrowright})^{-1}(F)$, and, more generally, $Follow_e^{-1}(W) \cap (Follow_e^{\circlearrowright})^{-1}(F)$ is empty. This means that $q \in (Follow_e^{*})^{-1}(F)$. Thus $S = pStar(x)$ is not $Null$, satisfies $FirstPos(S,a) = F$, and is an ancestor of n since there is no $*$-labeled nodes between x and $Lchild_e(n)$. Accordingly, $pSupLast(q) \preccurlyeq S$ and hence $Rchild_e(n)$ is non-nullable. $\square$

Algorithm 2 Checking determinism.

procedure $CheckNode(n : \text{Node}, a : \Sigma) : \text{Bool}$
1 $F \leftarrow FirstPos(n,a)$
2 $S \leftarrow pStar(n)$
3 **if** $Rchild_e(n)$ is nullable **and**
4    $(Next(n,a) \neq Null$ **or**
5    $(FirstPos(S,a) = F$ **and** $pSupLast(n) \preccurlyeq S))$
6   **then return** $false$
7 **return** $true$
end procedure

3.3 Testing Numeric Occurrences

Regular expression occurring in XML Schema may contain numeric occurrence indicators. Following the definitions in [19], regular expressions with numeric occurrence indicators extend regular expressions with $e^{i..j}$ where $i \in \mathbb{N}$, $j \in \mathbb{N} \cup \{\infty\}$, and $i \leq j$. The expression $e^{i..j}$ denotes the union of $L(\underbrace{e \odot e \cdots \odot e}_{k\text{-times}})$ for $i \leq k \leq j$. Also e^i denotes $e^{i..i}$. The definition of determinism in presence of numeric occurrence indicators must take into accounts the iterations. Informally, e is deterministic if for every word w there exists at most one position that can be reached after reading w. For instance, $e = (ab)^{2..2}a(b+d)$ is deterministic, but $e' = (ab)^{1..2}a$ is not, because $w = aba$ can lead to two a-labeled positions in e'. We refer the reader to [19] for the notion of determinism in regular expressions with numeric occurrence indicators. Note that nested iterations can interact with each other: consider the expression $e_5 = ((a^{2..3}+b)^2)^2 b$ from [19]. This expression is non-deterministic because word $w = a^8 b$ can lead to the two b-labeled positions: to the first one if we decompose it into $(a^3)^2 a^2 b$, and to the second one with decomposition $((a^2)^2)^2 b$.

In order to deal with those interactions between iterations, Kilpeläinen and Tukhanen [19] define the *flexibility* of f in e, for every subexpression f of e. They explain how to annotate, in time $O(|e|)$, every node n of e with a Boolean value indicating the flexibility of n. Essentially, flexible iterations are the only ones we have to consider when assessing determinism (in particular $*$ expressions are flexible). The authors give a (more accurate) characterization for determinism of numeric occurrences as Theorem 5.5 in [19]. This characterization can be verified in linear time using a case study similar to the one above (but with flexible iterations instead of $*$ expressions). Therefore, given a regular expression e with numeric occurrence indicators we can decide in time $O(|e|)$ whether or not e is deterministic.

This improves upon the complexity $O(\sigma|e|)$ from [18], where $\sigma = |\Sigma|$. Actually, in Theorem 3.3 from [18], the complexity is stated as $n^2/(\log(n))$, with n representing the size of the binary representation of the regular expression. But with our notations, this translates into a quadratic $O(\sigma|e|)$. Kilpeläinen obtains this complexity by a merging-based examination of *First* and *Follow* sets, similar to the approach in [19], but relying on a more careful analysis of the *Follow* sets. Interestingly, he observes after his Theorem 3.3 that it seems difficult to go below $O(\sigma n)$ using his approach. We believe that our skeleton-based algorithm offers a good solution to the limitations of the merging-based approach.

3.4 Alternative Determinism Test

Determinism of e can be formulated as follows:

$$\neg(\exists p, p_1, p_2 \in Pos(e).\ lab_e(p_1) = lab_e(p_2) \wedge$$
$$p_1 \in Follow_e(p) \wedge p_2 \in Follow_e(p)).$$

A natural question arises: Is there a logic that allows to capture determinism, and at the same time, has efficient model checking that yields a procedure for checking determinism in linear time? The answer is positive: It is possible with $\mathcal{X}_{reg}^=$, the language of Regular XPath expressions with data equality tests for binary trees with data values as defined in [7].

Trees with data values allow to store with every node its label, drawn form a finite set, and additionally, a data value, drawn form an infinite set. Regular XPath allows to navigate the nodes of the tree using regular expressions of simple steps (e.g., parent to the left child) and filter expressions. Filter expressions with data equality allow essentially to test whether two nodes have the same data value. In [7] Bojańczyk and Parys show that an $\mathcal{X}_{reg}^=$-expression φ can be evaluated over a tree t in time $2^{O(|\varphi|)}|t|$.

We wish to construct an $\mathcal{X}_{reg}^=$-expression φ_{det} that captures determinism and whose size is constant i.e., does not depend on the regular expression e. The main challenge is to handle position labels of e that can be drawn from an alphabet of arbitrary size. This is accomplished by: 1) storing the labels of positions of e as data values and 2) using data equality to check whether two positions have the same label.

THEOREM 3.6. *There exists an $\mathcal{X}_{reg}^=$-expression φ_{det} such that for any regular expression e, φ_{det} is satisfied in e if and only if e is deterministic.*

PROOF. We present only the construction of φ_{det}. Let *SupFirst* and *SupLast* denote $\mathcal{X}_{reg}^=$-expressions that are sat-

isfied only in *SupFirst*- and *SupLast*-nodes, respectively.

$$D - (\text{child}/[\text{not } SupFirst])^*/P \qquad\qquad P = [\text{not child}]$$
$$U = ([\text{not } SupLast]/\text{parent})^* \qquad F = ([\text{lab}() = \odot])/\text{to-right}/D$$
$$\varphi_{\odot\odot} = \text{child}^*/[\text{not } SupLast]/\text{from-left}/[F = (U/\text{from-left}/F)]$$
$$\varphi_{**} = \text{child}^*/[\text{lab}() = *]/$$
$$[D = (U/[SupFirst]/\text{parent}/U/[\text{lab}() = *]/D)]$$
$$\varphi_{\odot*} = \text{child}^*/[\text{not } SupLast]/\text{from-left}/$$
$$[(\text{to-right}/[SupFirst]/D) = (\text{parent}/U/[\text{lab}() = *]/D)]$$
$$\cup \text{child}^*/[\text{lab}() = *]/[D = (U/\text{from-left}/F)]$$
$$\varphi_{P_1} = \text{child}^*/[(\text{to-left}/[\text{not } SupFirst]/D) =$$
$$(\text{to-right}/[\text{not } SupFirst]/D)]$$

$$\varphi_{det} = [\text{not } (\varphi_{P_1} \text{ or } \varphi_{\odot\odot} \text{ or } \varphi_{\odot*} \text{ or } \varphi_{*\odot} \text{ or } \varphi_{**})].$$

Basically, φ_{P_1} checks if (P1) is violated in e and the expression $\varphi_{\ell\ell'}$ for $\{\ell, \ell'\} \subseteq \{*, \odot\}$ checks whether there exist two distinct positions p_1 and p_2 of e such that $lab(p_1) = lab(p_2)$ and $(Follow_e^\ell)^{-1}(p_1) \cap (Follow_e^{\ell'})^{-1}(p_2) \neq \varnothing$. $\square$

4. MATCHING

In this section we present a collection of algorithms matching a word w against e. First, we present an algorithm for arbitrary deterministic regular expressions that uses the constructions from Section 3 and lowest color ancestor queries to achieve expected time complexity $O(|e| + |w| \log \log |e|)$. Next, we present a matching algorithm for k-occurrence regular expressions in time $O(|e| + k|w|)$, which is linear if k is a constant. The most intricate matching algorithm that we present in this paper is the path-decomposition algorithm. It works in time $O(|e| + c_e|w|)$, where c_e is the maximal depth of alternating union and concatenation operators in e. The three algorithms above perform matching by providing a *transition simulation procedure*: given a position p and a symbol a return the position q labeled a that follows p, or *Null* if no such position exists. If $e = (\#e')\$$, matching a word w against e' is straightforward: begin with position $\#$, use the transition simulation procedure iteratively on subsequent symbols of w, and finally test if the position obtained after processing the last symbol of w is followed by $\$$.

The algorithms above allow to match multiple input words $w_1, \ldots, w_N$ against one regular expression e: the corresponding running times are obtained by replacing the factor $|w|$ by $|w_1| + \ldots + |w_N|$. We also present an algorithm that runs in time $O(|e| + |w_1| + \ldots + |w_N|)$ for star-free deterministic regular expressions e, a setting in which none of the previously mentioned algorithms guarantee linear complexity.

In the reminder of this section, we fix a deterministic regular expression e, and when talking about positions and nodes, we implicitly mean positions and nodes of e.

4.1 Lowest Colored Ancestor Algorithm

Our previous construction that tests determinism in linear time, provides an efficient procedure for transition simulation. Recall that we color the parent of any *SupFirst*-node n with the labels of the positions that belong to $First(n)$. By Lemma 3.3, given a position p and a symbol a the a-labeled position q that follows p is one of: $Witness(n, a)$, $FirstPos(n, a)$, and $Next(n, a)$, where n is the lowest ancestor of p with color a. We use the *checkIfFollow* test (Theorem 2.4) to select the correct following position q among the three candidates.

EXAMPLE 4.1. *Consider the expression in Figure 1, position p_3, and the symbol c. The lowest ancestor of p_3 with color c is n_3. Here, $Witness(n_3, c) = p_5$, $Next(n_3, c) = p_1$, and $FirstPos(n_3, c) = Null$. Using checkIfFollow we find that it is p_5 that follows p_3. This ends the transition simulation procedure. Now, at position p_5 we read the next symbol a. The lowest ancestor of p_5 with color a is again n_3. This time it is $FirstPos(n_3, a) = p_2$ that follows p_5.*

The basic ingredient of this procedure is an efficient algorithm for answering lowest colored ancestor queries. Recall from [23, 10], that given a tree t with colors assigned to its nodes (some nodes possibly having multiple colors), we can preprocess t in expected time $O(|t| + C)$, where C is the total number of color assignments, so that any lowest colored ancestor query is answered in time $O(\log \log |t|)$. In this way, the transition simulation is accomplished in time $O(\log \log |e|)$, which gives us the following result.

THEOREM 4.2. *For any deterministic regular expression e, after preprocessing in expected time $O(|e|)$, we can decide for any word w whether $w \in L(e)$ in time $O(|w| \log \log |e|)$.*

4.2 Bounded Occurrence Algorithm

A regular expressions e is called *k-occurrence* (*k-ORE* for short) if each symbol $a \in \Sigma$ occurs at most k times in e. While every regular expression is k-ORE for a sufficiently large k, Bex et al. [5] report that the majority of regular expressions in real-life XML schemas are in fact 1-OREs. Given a position p and a symbol a, to find the following a-labeled position q we only need to perform the *checkIfFollow* test (Theorem 2.4) on all a-labeled positions in e, which are gathered into a designated list during preprocessing of e. Thus, transition simulation is performed in time $O(k)$.

THEOREM 4.3. *For any deterministic k-ORE e, after preprocessing in time $O(|e|)$, we can decide for any word w whether $w \in L(e)$ in time $O(k|w|)$.*

We note that an analogous technique can be used to match a word w against a nondeterministic k-ORE e: we maintain a set P of at most k positions and when reading symbol a we identify among the a-labeled positions those that follow any of the positions in P. Here, reading one symbol requires $O(k^2)$ time, and thus, the matching can be done in time $O(k^2|w|)$ after $O(|e|)$ preprocessing.

4.3 Path Decomposition Algorithm

Next, we describe an algorithm for matching a word w against a regular expression e in time $O(|e| + c_e|w|)$, where c_e is the maximal depth of alternating union and concatenation operators in e (as mentioned at the end of the Introduction, c_e is bounded by 4 in real-life DTDs [13]).

First, we define the function $h_{First}(n, a)$ that for a node n and a symbol a returns the unique a-labeled position in $First(n)$ and $Null$ if it does not exist. Queries of the form $h_{First}(n, a)$ can be answered in constant time after preprocessing in time $O(|e|)$, but since h_{First} is not used in the final algorithm, we omit the implementation details.

Climbing algorithm. We first present a simple transition simulation procedure that uses h_{First}, and later improve it to obtain the desired evaluation algorithm. Given a position p and a symbol a, it suffices to find an ancestor n of p such that $q = h_{First}(Rchild(n), a)$ follows p (tested with

checkIfFollow). If such ancestor does not exists, then p has no a-labeled following position. The soundness of this procedure follows from that of *checkIfFollow* and the completeness from Lemma 2.5. A naïve implementation seeks the ancestor in question by climbing up the parse tree starting from p, which yields $O(depth(e))$ time per transition simulation and overall $O(|e| + depth(e) \cdot |w|)$ time for matching.

Path decomposition. Our algorithm speeds up climbing the path using jumps that follow precomputed pointers. The precomputed pointers lead to nodes where we store an aggregation of the values of h_{First} for several nodes skipped during the jump. The pointers are defined using the notion of path decomposition of the parse tree.

Recall that a *path decomposition* of a tree is a set of pairwise disjoint paths covering all nodes of the tree, and here, a path means a sequence of nodes $n_1, \ldots, n_k$ such that n_i is the parent of n_{i+1}. Note that a path decomposition of a tree can be specified by the set of the top-most nodes of the paths, which is how we define the path decomposition of e. A node y of e is the *top-most node* of a path if it is the root of e, or satisfies one of the following conditions:

(i) $SupLast(y)$

(ii) $SupFirst(y)$

(iii) y is the nullable right child of its parent, or

(iv) y is the right child of a +-labeled node.

For a position p we define $top(p)$ as the top-most node of the path of the left sibling of $pSupFirst(p)$.

EXAMPLE 4.4. *Consider the regular expression presented in Figure 2 together with its path decomposition. For this expression $c_e = 4$ because there are at most 4 alternations of union and concatenation operators on any path of the expression, and in particular, it is 4 on the path from p_1 to the root node. Note that $top(p_1) = n_3$ and $top(p_2) = n_1$.*

We now define the function h which is similar to h_{First} but defined for top-most nodes only: $h(n, a)$ points to the a-labeled position p such that $n = top(p)$, i.e., we assign $h(top(p), lab(p)) = p$ for every position p. For instance, in the expression in Figure 2, $h(n_3, a) = p_1$ and $h(n_1, d) = p_2$.

There exists a subtle connection between h and h_{First}. If we consider a top-most node n, then the values of h assigned to n can be viewed as an aggregation of values of h_{First} of several nodes $n_1, \ldots, n_k$, which are gathered from around the path (but not from the path). The decomposition of e ensures that the aggregation is collision-free, i.e., if $h_{First}(n_i, a) \neq Null$ for some i, then $h_{First}(n_j, a) = Null$ for all $j \neq i$. Formally, we state this property as follows.

LEMMA 4.5. *For any two different positions p and p', if $top(p) = top(p')$, then p and p' have different labels.*

PROOF. Let y denote the lowest node in the path of $top(p)$ and let p_0 denote some position in $Last(y)$. We show that p follows p_0. By definition of $top(p)$, the left sibling of $pSupFirst(p)$ is on the path between y and $top(p)$. Therefore, $pSupLast(p_0) = pSupLast(y)$ is an ancestor of the left sibling of $pSupFirst(p)$ because there is no $SupLast$-node on a path except for the top-most node of the path. Moreover, we observe that the parent of $pSupFirst(p)$ is labeled with $\odot$. Thus, by Lemma 2.2 we get $p \in Follow(p_0)$. Similarly,

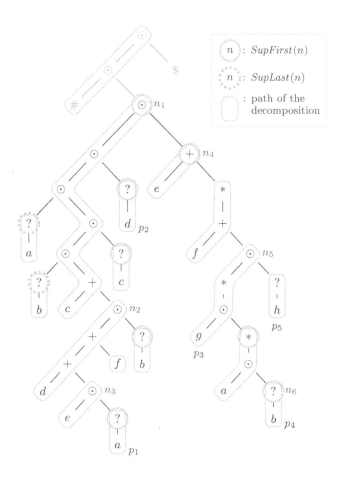

n : $SupFirst(n)$

n : $SupLast(n)$

: path of the
decomposition

Figure 2: Path decomposition.

we show that $p' \in Follow(p_0)$. Because e is deterministic, there cannot be two different positions with the same label in $Follow(p_0)$. $\square$

Lazy arrays. To store the values of h we use *lazy arrays*, which we describe in detail next. This interesting data structure, known in programmer's circles [17, 22], provides the functionality of an associative array with constant time initialization, assignment, and lookup operations. The finite set of keys K needs to be known prior to initialization of the data structure. Furthermore, every key needs to be associated with a unique element from a continuous fragment of natural numbers, and here for simplicity, we assume that $K = \{1, \ldots, N\}$ for some $N \geq 1$.

A lazy array consists of an array A that stores the values associated with the keys, a counter C of active keys having a value assigned, and additionally two arrays B and F that store the set of active keys. At initialization, C is set to 0 and uninitialized memory of length N is allocated for each of the arrays A, F, and B (an operation assumed to work in $O(1)$ time). To *assign* value v to key k, we add k to the set of active keys (if k is not in that set already), and assign $A[k] = v$. To *lookup* key k, we return $A[k]$ if k is active and return *Null* otherwise. To add a key k to the set of active keys, we increment C, set $F[C] = k$, and set $B[k] = C$. In this way a key k is active if and only if $1 \leq B[k] \leq C$ and $F[B[k]] = k$. Note that the first condition alone is

insufficient to check if a key k is active because B has been allocated with uninitialized memory.

We found out that in practice, hash arrays offer compatible functionality with superior performance while theoretically providing only expected $O(1)$ time for the assignment and lookup operations. As a side note, we point out that lazy arrays stand on their own merit because they allow a constant time reset operation (by simply setting $C = 0$), unmatched by hash arrays (but not needed by our algorithm).

Preprocessing. We construct and fill the lazy-array h in one bottom-up traversal of e. In the same traversal we also compute an additional pointer *nexttop* for every position and every top-most node of a path, defined as follows. We set $nexttop(n)$ to the lowest top-most node y of a path above $parent(n)$ that is either the root of e, or satisfies one of the following conditions:

(1) $SupLast(y)$

(2) $SupFirst(y)$

(3) there exists a non-nullable $\odot$-labeled ancestor of n in the path of y.

For instance, in the expression in Figure 2, $nexttop(p_3) = n_5$, $nexttop(p_4) = n_6$, and $nexttop(p_5) = n_4$. We point out that $nexttop(n)$ is always the top-most node of some path, and furthermore, $nexttop(n)$ is a strict ancestor of n.

Transition simulation. *FindNext* in Algorithm 3 follows *nexttop* pointers on the path from p to the node $pSupLast(p)$ while attempting to find a-labeled follow positions stored in h at the visited nodes. If this does not succeed, then

---

Algorithm 3 Transition simulation.

procedure $FindNext(p : \text{Position}, a : \Sigma) : \text{Position}$
1   $x \leftarrow p$
2   **while** $pSupLast(p) \neq x$
3   **if** $checkIfFollow(h(x, a), p)$
4   **then return** $h(x, a)$
5      $x \leftarrow nexttop(x)$
6   **if** $checkIfFollow(h(x, a), p)$
7   **then return** $h(x, a)$
8   $y \leftarrow pSupFirst(parent(x))$
9   **if** y is nullable
10   **then** $q \leftarrow h(nexttop(y), a)$
11   **else** $q \leftarrow h(Lchild(parent(y)), a)$
12 **if** $checkIfFollow(q, p)$
13   **then return** q
14   **else return** *Null*
end procedure

FindNext checks in $First(parent(pSupLast(p)))$ (Lines 8–14) to find follow positions. This task would be easy to accomplish with h_{First} through $h_{First}(parent(pSupLast(p)), a)$. Since we wish to use h instead, we need to locate the node n such that $h(n, a)$ returns the position we look for. The location of this node depends on whether or not the node $y = parent(pSupLast(p))$ is nullable. If y is nullable, we perform a single *nexttop* jump from y to reach n. Otherwise, n is the left sibling of y. Finally, we remark that if $h_{First}(parent(pSupLast(p)), a)$ is not *Null*, then $h(n, a)$ returns the same node but the converse needs not be true: even if $q = h(n, a)$ is not *Null*, $h_{First}(parent(pSupLast(p)), a)$

might be *Null*. Consequently, we verify in Line 12 that the node q indeed follows p.

EXAMPLE 4.6. *Consider expression in Figure 2, position p_1, and symbol d. The computation of $FindNext(p_1, d)$ follows the jump sequence: $p_1, parent(p_1), n_3, n_2, n_1$. At node n_1, $h(n_1, d)$ yields position p_2, and since p_2 follows p_1, the procedure returns p_2.*

Correctness. To reason about iterations of the main loop of *FindNext*, we introduce this notation: $nexttop^0(n) = n$, and $nexttop^{i+1}(n) = nexttop(nexttop^i(n))$ for $i \geq 0$. Also, the *jump sequence* of p is the sequence

$$nexttop^0(p), nexttop^1(p), \ldots, nexttop^K(p),$$

where K is such that $nexttop^K(p) = pSupLast(p)$. We call K the *length* of the jump sequence of p. We first show that the main loop performs a sufficient number of *nexttop* jumps.

LEMMA 4.7. *Let p be a position and K the length of the jump sequence of p. For every position q that follows p, either $top(q) = nexttop^i(p)$ for some $0 \leq i \leq K$ or q belongs to $First(parent(pSupLast(p)))$.*

PROOF. By Lemma 2.5 $top(q)$ is an ancestor of p or the left sibling of a non-nullable *SupFirst*-ancestor of p. Furthermore, if $pSupFirst(q)$ is nullable then $top(q)$ is the top of the path containing $parent(pSupFirst(q))$. From the definition of *top* and *nexttop*, the jump sequence of p visits every *SupFirst*- and *SupLast*-ancestor of p, as well as every ancestor y of p such that y is top-most node of a path and there exists some non-nullable $\odot$-labeled ancestor of p on that path.

We assume that $q \notin First(parent(pSupLast(p)))$, and show that in this case no other ancestor of q needs to be visited. Under that assumption, a case analysis for Lemma 2.2 shows that $pSupFirst(q)$ is the right sibling of $pSupLast(p)$, or satisfies $pSupLast(p) \preccurlyeq parent(pSupFirst(q)) \preccurlyeq p$. If $pSupFirst(q)$ is the right sibling of $pSupLast(p)$, then $top(q)$ is equal to $pSupLast(p)$ and is therefore visited by the jump sequence. Otherwise, $pSupLast(p) \preccurlyeq parent(pSupFirst(q))$. By Lemma 2.6, $pSupFirst(q)$ is nullable. Consequently, its parent belongs to the path of $top(q)$. Furthermore, the left sibling of $pSupFirst(q)$, and therefore its parent, are non-nullable. It follows that the parent of $pSupFirst(q)$ is a non-nullable $\odot$-labeled ancestor of p that belongs to the path of $top(q)$ which is thus visited. $\square$

We now show the correctness of *FindNext*.

LEMMA 4.8. *For any position p and any symbol a, the procedure $FindNext(p, a)$ returns q iff $q \in Follow(p)$ and $lab(q) = a$.*

PROOF. The soundness of *FindNext* follows from the use of *checkIfFollow* prior to returning a position. If a position q is labeled with a and follows p, then *FindNext* returns q by Lemma 4.7 and because the algorithm returns q at Line 13 if q belongs to $First(parent(pSupLast(p)))$. $\square$

Complexity. We show that the amortized running time of the transition simulation procedure in Algorihtm 3, when matching a word w against the deterministic regular expression e, is proportional to c_e, the maximal depth of alternating union and concatenation operators in e.

LEMMA 4.9. *Procedure $FindNext(p, a)$ works in amortized time $O(c_e)$, when matching a word against a deterministic regular expression e.*

PROOF. We use the potential *pot* of the data structure defined as a function of the current position:

$$pot(p) = |\{v \preccurlyeq p \mid SupFirst(v)\}|.$$

At the phantom position #, the initial potential is set to zero. The potential is decreased by one with every other jump through *nexttop* and is increased by at most one each time the transition simulation procedure is executed.

Now, let q be the position returned by $FindNext(p, q)$, i.e., the a-labeled position that follows p in e. We prove that $FindNext(p, a)$ executes at most $2(pot(q) - pot(p)) + c_e + O(1)$ iterations of the loop (*nexttop* jumps) before returning q.

By definition of *top*, there are no *SupFirst*-nodes between $pSupFirst(q)$ and $top(q)$, hence

$$pot(q) \leq pot(top(q)) + 1. \tag{1}$$

Let K be the length of the jump sequence of p and let $n_i = nexttop^i(p)$ for $0 \leq i \leq K$. Now, from the sequence $n_0, \ldots, n_K$ we remove every node that is the non-nullable right child of a +-labeled node and obtain a subsequence $n_{i_0}, n_{i_1}, \ldots, n_{i_{K'}}$. For every $0 \leq j < K' - 1$, if n_{i_j} is the nullable right child of its parent, then $n_{i_{j+1}}$ is a *SupFirst*-node by definition of *nexttop*. Hence, for every $0 \leq j \leq K'$,

$$j \leq 2(pot(n_{i_0}) - pot(n_{i_j})) + 2.$$

Thus, for every $0 \leq j \leq K$,

$$j \leq 2(pot(p) - pot(n_j)) + 2 + K - K'. \tag{2}$$

Let ℓ be the natural number such that $n_\ell = top(q)$. Combining equations (1) and (2), as c_e is an upper bound for $K - K'$, we obtain the result claimed before:

$$\ell \leq 2(pot(p) - pot(q)) + 4 + c_e. \tag{3}$$

From this result, establishing the amortized complexity is straightforward. Given a word $w = a_1 \cdots a_n$, let $p_1, \ldots, p_n$ be the sequence of positions with $p_i = FindNext(p_{i-1}, a_i)$ for $1 \leq i \leq n$ and $p_0 = \#$. Then, the number of iterations through the loop of *FindNext* while matching w against e is at most:

$$n(4 + c_e) + 2 \sum_{i=1}^{n} (pot(p_{i-1}) - pot(p_i))$$
$$= n(4 + c_e) + 2(pot(p_0) - pot(p_n))$$
$$\leq n(4 + c_e).$$

This implies the amortized cost of $O(c_e)$, because each line of *FindNext* runs in constant time. $\square$

Note that in the previous proof it suffices to take a smaller value of c_e, the maximum number of ancestors of a position of e that are labeled with +, are non-nullable, and have a parent labeled with $\odot$.

Finally, we formally state the result.

THEOREM 4.10. *For any deterministic regular expression e, after preprocessing in time $O(|e|)$, we can decide for any word w whether $w \in L(e)$ in time $O(c_e|w|)$, where c_e is the maximal depth of alternating union and concatenation operators in e.*

4.4 Star-Free Algorithm

Finally, we present an algorithm that matches simultaneously several words $w_1, \ldots, w_N$ against a star-free deterministic regular expression e. For a single word this is trivial: in a star-free regular expression, $q \in Follow(p)$ implies that position q is after p in the preorder traversal of e, and therefore, to simulate a transition it suffices to run the *checkIfFollow* test on subsequent positions until a match is found. In fact, the *checkIfFollow* tests can be hard-coded into the traversal to avoid lowest common ancestor queries.

The result is non-trivial when matching several words $w_1, \ldots, w_N$. Also this time, the expression is traversed only once and for every word w_i we maintain the current index d_i, indicating the prefix of w_i matched so far. The matching is driven by the preorder traversal of e: with every position visited in the traversal we update the indices $d_1, \ldots, d_N$ accordingly. The update process is, however, not straightforward and to perform it efficiently we use a variant of the *a*-skeleta, constructed dynamically.

First, we define some terminology. We say that the word w_i at index d_i *expects* the symbol a if the symbol of w_i at index $d_i + 1$ is a. We also say that w_i at d_i *reaches* position p if after simulating transitions on the corresponding prefix of w_i we arrive at p (or more precisely, the Glushkov automaton of e reaches p after reading the prefix of w_i). A *dynamic a-skeleton* t_a is essentially a structure containing a subset of positions closed under lowest common ancestors. Additionally, with each position p in t_a we associate a list of (pointers to) words such that if word w_i is associated with p, then the word w_i at index d_i reaches the position p and expects the symbol a.

When processing a position p labeled a, we remove from the dynamic *a*-skeleton t_a every position q that is followed by p, update indices of the words on the list associated with q, and insert p to some dynamic *a*-skeleta accordingly. We illustrate the procedure in the following example.

EXAMPLE 4.11. *We consider the deterministic regular expression $e = (\#(((a + ba)(c?))(d?b)))\$$, where $\#$ and $\$$ are two phantom positions that do not need to be matched. The expression e has 8 positions: $\#, p_1, \ldots, p_6, \$$. We match against e the words $w_1 = bcdb$, $w_2 = acdba$, $w_3 = acb$, and $w_4 = bada$.*

Initially, all indices are $d_1 = d_2 = d_3 = d_4 = 0$. When describing dynamic a-skeleta, we write $\langle p, W \rangle$ to indicate that a position p has an associated list of words W. Initially, $t_a = \langle \#, [w_2, w_3] \rangle$, $t_b = \langle \#, [w_1, w_4] \rangle$, and all other dynamic a-skeleta are empty.

In the first step, we read the a-labeled position p_1. Because p_1 follows $\#$, we remove from t_a the position $\langle \#, [w_2, w_3] \rangle$, increment d_2 and d_3, and insert $\langle p_1, [w_2, w_3] \rangle$ to t_c.

Next, we read the b-labeled position p_2. Because p_2 follows $\#$, we remove from t_b the position $\langle \#, [w_1, w_4] \rangle$, increment d_1 and d_4, and insert $\langle p_2, [w_4] \rangle$ to t_a and $\langle p_2, [w_1] \rangle$ to t_c. Because we keep the dynamic a-skeleta closed under lowest common ancestors, t_c becomes $\langle p_1, [w_2, w_3] \rangle + \langle p_2, [w_1] \rangle$, where $+$ is a binary node whose children are p_1 and p_2.

At the position p_3 labeled with a, because p_3 follows p_2, we remove $\langle p_2, [w_4] \rangle$ from t_a, increment d_4 and add $\langle p_3, [w_4] \rangle$ to t_d. At the position p_4 labeled with c, because p_4 follows p_1, we remove from t_c the position $\langle p_1, [w_2, w_3] \rangle$, increment d_2 and d_3, and insert $\langle p_4, [w_2] \rangle$ to t_d and $\langle p_4, [w_3] \rangle$ to t_b. Although p_2 is not followed by p_4, we also remove $\langle p_2, [w_1] \rangle$

from t_c and discard it because we observe that p_2 will not be followed by any of the subsequent positions. After this step, $t_b = \langle p_4, [w_3] \rangle$, t_c is empty, and $t_d = \langle p_3, [w_4] \rangle \odot \langle p_4, [w_2] \rangle$.

The next position p_5 is labeled with d and follows both p_3 and p_4. Therefore, we remove from t_d both $\langle p_3, [w_4] \rangle$ and $\langle p_4, [w_2] \rangle$, increment d_2 and d_4, and insert $\langle p_5, [w_4] \rangle$ to t_a and $\langle p_5, [w_2] \rangle$ to t_b. This way, t_b is $\langle p_4, [w_3] \rangle \odot \langle p_5, [w_2] \rangle$.

In the last step we move to the position p_6 labeled with b. Because p_6 follows both p_4 and p_5, we remove $\langle p_5, [w_2] \rangle$ and $\langle p_4, [w_3] \rangle$ from t_b and increment d_2 and d_3. We insert $\langle p_6, [w_2] \rangle$ to t_a. Because $d_3 = |w_3|$ and $\$$ follows p_6, w_3 matches e. Since there are no further positions to process, the words w_1, w_2, and w_4 do not match d.

Details on how to efficiently handle *a*-skeleta follow. We assume that the positions $p_1, \ldots, p_m$ of e are given in the traversal order of e and that e has been preprocessed for LCA and *Last* queries. Every time we process a position $\langle p, W \rangle$, the list W is nonempty and we increment the index of every word in W, which corresponds to consuming one symbol of every word in W. By $|t_a|$ we denote the number of all nodes that are inserted to t_a throughout the execution of the matching algorithm. Note that for every consumed symbol we add to *a*-skeleton at most one position and at most one additional LCA node. Therefore, the sum of $|t_a|$ over $a \in \Sigma$ is in $O(|w_1| + \cdots + |w_N|)$. We shall use this observation when characterizing the total time necessary to identify, remove, and insert positions in the dynamic *a*-skeleta.

With every dynamic *a*-skeleton t_a we maintain the right-most position p_a, i.e., the position most recently added to t_a. We also provide a procedure $findLCA(t_a, p_i)$ for localizing in t_a the possible position of the lowest common ancestor n_{LCA} of p_a and a new position p_i which follows p_a in the traversal of e. Note that n_{LCA} needs not be present in t_a and $findLCA(t_a, p_i)$ returns the top-most descendant of n_{LCA} present in t_a (which may possibly be n_{LCA} itself if t_a contains it). The procedure simply climbs the right-most path in t_a until the desired node is found. Furthermore, our algorithm performs calls to $findLCA$ with subsequent positions in the traversal order, i.e., if a call $findLCA(t_a, p_i)$ is followed by a call $findLCA(t_a, p_j)$, then $i < j$. The procedure $findLCA$ takes advantage of this assumption by saving the result of the previous call and beginning to climb the right-most path of t_a from the saved node (if no new nodes have been added in between). This way the cumulative execution time of all $findLCA$ calls with t_a is $O(|t_a|)$, which sums over $a \in \Sigma$ to $O(|w_1| + \cdots + |w_N|)$.

The $findLCA$ procedure is used to insert new positions as well as to identify and to remove relevant positions from the dynamic *a*-skeleton. Inserting p_i into t_a is straightforward: we find the lowest common ancestor n_{LCA} of n_a and p_i in e, use $findLCA(t_a, p_i))$ to find if and where to insert n_{LCA} to t_a, and then insert p_i. Identifying and retrieving positions in t_a that are followed by p_i is based on Lemma 2.2. We climb the path from $findLCA(t_a, p_i)$ to $n_i = parent(pSupFirst(p_i))$ and at every $\odot$-labeled node n we pick the subtree t' rooted at the left child of n. In one traversal of t' we retrieve all of its Last-positions, because they are followed by p_i, and remove all remaining nodes, because none of the remaining positions is followed by any of the subsequent positions $p_{j \geq i}$. Again, because the number of nodes traversed by the procedure in t_a is proportional to $|t_a|$, the overall time necessary to insert and remove positions in all *a*-skeleta is $O(|w_1| + \cdots + |w_N|)$.

THEOREM 4.12. *For any star-free deterministic regular expression e and words $w_1, \ldots, w_N$, we can decide which words belong to $L(e)$ in time $O(|e| + |w_1| + \cdots + |w_N|)$.*

5. CONCLUSIONS

We have presented a linear time algorithm for testing if a regular expression is deterministic, an efficient algorithm for matching words against deterministic regular expressions, and linear time algorithms for matching against k-occurrence, $*$-free (multiple words), and bounded $+$-depth expressions.

It was our original motivation for this work, but remains an open theoretical problem, whether matching for deterministic regular expressions can be carried out in time $O(|e| + |w|)$. We note that our $O(|e| + |w| \log \log |e|)$ matching algorithm is not optimal because of the $O(\log \log |e|)$ cost of lowest color ancestor queries. We plan to find out if the cost of those lowest colored ancestor queries can be amortized and if the particular order of the queries can be used to devise better data structures. Can other approaches solve the problem in $O(|e| + |w|)$ time, e.g., by giving up the the streaming aspect of using transition simulation? Which larger classes of regular expressions, exceeding the deterministic ones, can be matched efficiently? An example of such class is mentioned after Theorem 4.3, the k-OREs. Another interesting and largely open problem is the one of matching under linear time preprocessing of w. Very simple matching problems such as substring search have time $O(|e|)$ solutions; can those be extended to more general regular expressions? Finally, can lower bounds matching the upper bounds be shown? Note that for general regular expressions and NFAs, it is known that no approach relying on constructing an equivalent epsilon-free NFA can achieve linear complexity. This follows from the fact that all epsilon-free NFAs equivalent to $a_1?a_2? \ldots a_m?$ have at least $m \log^2 m$ transitions [26].

Acknowledgments

We are grateful to the PODS reviewers. Their careful reading of the earlier draft and their plentiful comments allowed to largely improve the presentation of the paper. This research has been partially supported by International Initiatives INRIA Associate Teams TRANSDUCE.

6. REFERENCES

[1] M. A. Bender, M. Farach-Colton, G. Pemmasani, S. Skiena, and P. Sumazin. Lowest common ancestors in trees and directed acyclic graphs. *J. Algorithms*, 57(2):75–94, 2005.

[2] G. Berry and R. Sethi. From regular expressions to deterministic automata. *Theor. Comput. Sci.*, 48(3):117–126, 1986.

[3] G. J. Bex, W. Gelade, F. Neven, and S. Vansummeren. Learning deterministic regular expressions for the inference of schemas from XML data. *TWEB*, 4(4), 2010.

[4] G. J. Bex, F. Neven, and J. Van den Bussche. DTDs versus XML Schema: A practical study. In *WEBDB*, pages 79–84, 2004.

[5] G. J. Bex, F. Neven, T. Schwentick, and S. Vansummeren. Inference of concise regular expressions and DTDs. *TODS*, 35(2), 2010.

[6] P. Bille and M. Thorup. Faster regular expression matching. In *ICALP*, pages 171–182, 2009.

[7] M. Bojanczyk and P. Parys. XPath evaluation in linear time. *J. ACM*, 58(4):17, 2011.

[8] A. Brüggemann-Klein. Regular expressions into finite automata. *TCS*, 120(2):197–213, 1993.

[9] C.-H. Chang and R. Paige. From regular expressions to DFA's using compressed NFA's. *TCS*, 178(1–2):1–36, 1997.

[10] M. Farach and S. Muthukrishnan. Optimal parallel dictionary matching and compression. In *SPAA*, pages 244–253, 1995.

[11] Apache Software Foundation. Xerces-C++ ver. 3.1.1. http://xerces.apache.org/xerces-c/. File MixedContentModel.cpp.

[12] V. M. Glushkov. The abstract theory of automata. *Russ. Math. Surveys*, 16(5):1–53, 1961.

[13] S. Grijzenhout. Quality of the XML web. Master's thesis, University of Amsterdam, July 2010. Draft, see also http://data.politicalmashup.nl/xmlweb/.

[14] C. Hagenah and A. Muscholl. Computing epsilon-free NFA from regular expressions in $O(n \log^2(n))$ time. In *MFCS*, pages 277–285, 1998.

[15] D. Harel and R. E. Tarjan. Fast algorithms for finding nearest common ancestors. *SIAM J. Comput.*, 13(2):338–355, 1984.

[16] J. E. Hopcroft and J. D. Ullman. *Introduction to Automata Theory, Languages and Computation, Second Edition*. Addison-Wesley, 2000.

[17] R. Kecher. Reset an array in constant time. Blog entry cplusplus.co.il, May 2009.

[18] P. Kilpeläinen. Checking determinism of XML schema content models in optimal time. *Inf. Syst.*, 36(3):596–617, 2011.

[19] P. Kilpeläinen and R. Tuhkanen. One-unambiguity of regular expressions with numeric occurrence indicators. *Inf. Comput.*, 205(6):890–916, 2007.

[20] C. Konrad and F. Magniez. Validating XML documents in the streaming model with external memory. In *ICDT*, 2012.

[21] W. Martens, F. Neven, T. Schwentick, and G. J. Bex. Expressiveness and complexity of XML Schema. *TODS*, 31(3):770–813, 2006.

[22] B. Moret and H. Shapiro. *Algorithms from P to NP*. Benjamin/Cummings, 1990.

[23] S. Muthukrishnan and Müller M. Time and space efficient method-lookup for object-oriented programs. In *SODA*, pages 42–51, 1996.

[24] E. W. Myers. A four russians algorithm for regular expression pattern matching. *J. ACM*, 39(2):430–448, 1992.

[25] J.-L. Ponty, D. Ziadi, and J.-M. Champarnaud. A new quadratic algorithm to convert a regular expression into an automaton. In *WIA*, pages 109–119, 1996.

[26] G. Schnitger. Regular expressions and NFAs without *epsilon*-transitions. In *STACS*, pages 432–443, 2006.

[27] L. Segoufin and C. Sirangelo. Constant-memory validation of streaming XML documents against DTDs. In *ICDT*, pages 299–313, 2007.

[28] L. Segoufin and V. Vianu. Validating streaming XML documents. In *PODS*, pages 53–64, 2002.

Linguistic Foundations for Bidirectional Transformations (Invited Tutorial)

Benjamin C. Pierce
University of Pennsylvania

ABSTRACT

Computing is full of situations where two different structures must be "connected" in such a way that updates to each can be propagated to the other. This is a generalization of the classical *view update problem*, which has been studied for decades in the database community [11, 2, 22]; more recently, related problems have attracted considerable interest in other areas, including programming languages [42, 28, 34, 39, 4, 7, 33, 16, 1, 37, 35, 47, 49] software model transformation [43, 50, 44, 45, 12, 13, 14, 24, 25, 10, 51], user interfaces [38] and system configuration [36]. See [18, 17, 10, 30] for recent surveys.

Among the fruits of this cross-pollination has been the development of a *linguistic* perspective on the problem. Rather than taking some view definition language as fixed (e.g., choosing some subset of relational algebra) and looking for tractable ways of "inverting" view definitions to propagate updates from view to source [9], we can directly design new *bidirectional programming languages* in which every expression defines a *pair* of functions mapping updates on one structure to updates on the other. Such structures are often called *lenses* [18].

The foundational theory of lenses has been studied extensively [20, 47, 26, 32, 48, 40, 15, 31, 46, 41, 21, 27], and lens-based language designs have been developed in several domains, including strings [5, 19, 3, 36], trees [18, 28, 39, 35, 29], relations [6], graphs [23], and software models [43, 50, 44, 12, 13, 14, 24, 25, 8]. These languages share some common elements with modern functional languages—in particular, they come with very expressive type systems. In other respects, they are rather novel and surprising.

This tutorial surveys recent developments in the theory of lenses and the practice of bidirectional programming languages.

Categories and Subject Descriptors

D.3.2 [**Programming Languages**]: Language Classifications—*Specialized application languages*

General Terms

Design, Languages, Theory

Keywords

lens, bidirectional programming, view update

1. REFERENCES

[1] A. Alimarine, S. Smetsers, A. van Weelden, M. van Eekelen, and R. Plasmeijer. There and back again: Arrows for invertible programming. In *ACM SIGPLAN Workshop on Haskell*, pages 86–97, 2005.

[2] F. Bancilhon and N. Spyratos. Update semantics of relational views. *ACM Transactions on Database Systems*, 6(4):557–575, Dec. 1981.

[3] D. M. J. Barbosa, J. Cretin, N. Foster, M. Greenberg, and B. C. Pierce. Matching lenses: Alignment and view update. In *ACM SIGPLAN International Conference on Functional Programming (ICFP), Baltimore, Maryland*, Sept. 2010.

[4] N. Benton. Embedded interpreters. *Journal of Functional Programming*, 15(4):503–542, 2005.

[5] A. Bohannon, J. N. Foster, B. C. Pierce, A. Pilkiewicz, and A. Schmitt. Boomerang: Resourceful lenses for string data. In *ACM SIGPLAN-SIGACT Symposium on Principles of Programming Languages (POPL), San Francisco, California*, Jan. 2008.

[6] A. Bohannon, J. A. Vaughan, and B. C. Pierce. Relational lenses: A language for updateable views. In *Principles of Database Systems (PODS)*, 2006. Extended version available as University of Pennsylvania technical report MS-CIS-05-27.

[7] C. Brabrand, A. Møller, and M. I. Schwartzbach. Dual syntax for XML languages. *Information Systems*, 2007. To appear. Extended abstract in *Database Programming Languages (DBPL)* 2005.

[8] J. Bradfield and P. Stevens. Recursive checkonly QVT-R transformations with general when and where clauses via the modal mu calculus. In *15th International Conference on Fundamental Approaches to Software Engineering (FASE)*, 2012.

[9] P. Buneman, S. Khanna, and W.-C. Tan. On propagation of deletions and annotations through views. In *ACM SIGACT-SIGMOD-SIGART Symposium on Principles of Database Systems, Madison, Wisconsin*, pages 150–158, 2002.

[10] K. Czarnecki, J. N. Foster, Z. Hu, R. Lämmel, A. Schürr, and J. F. Terwilliger. Bidirectional transformations: A cross-discipline perspective. In R. F. Paige, editor, *ICMT*, volume 5563 of *Lecture*

Notes in Computer Science, pages 260–283. Springer, 2009.

[11] U. Dayal and P. A. Bernstein. On the correct translation of update operations on relational views. *TODS*, 7(3):381–416, September 1982.

[12] Z. Diskin. Algebraic models for bidirectional model synchronization. In K. Czarnecki, I. Ober, J.-M. Bruel, A. Uhl, and M. Völter, editors, *MoDELS*, volume 5301 of *Lecture Notes in Computer Science*, pages 21–36. Springer, 2008.

[13] Z. Diskin. Algebraic models for bidirectional model synchronization. In *Model Driven Engineering Languages and Systems, 11th International Conference, MoDELS*, pages 21–36. Springer, 2008.

[14] Z. Diskin, K. Czarnecki, and M. Antkiewicz. Model-versioning-in-the-large: algebraic foundations and the tile notation. In *Proceedings of the 2009 ICSE Workshop on Comparison and Versioning of Software Models*, pages 7–12. IEEE Computer Society, 2009.

[15] Z. Diskin, Y. Xiong, K. Czarnecki, H. Ehrig, F. Hermann, and F. Orejas. From state- to delta-based bidirectional model transformations: The symmetric case. Technical Report GSDLAB-TR 2011-05-03, University of Waterloo, May 2011.

[16] K. Fisher and R. Gruber. PADS: a domain-specific language for processing ad hoc data. In *ACM SIGPLAN Conference on Programming Language Design and Implementation (PLDI), Chicago, IL*, pages 295–304, 2005.

[17] J. N. Foster. *Bidirectional Programming Languages.* PhD thesis, University of Pennsylvania, Dec. 2009.

[18] J. N. Foster, M. B. Greenwald, J. T. Moore, B. C. Pierce, and A. Schmitt. Combinators for bi-directional tree transformations: A linguistic approach to the view update problem. *ACM Transactions on Programming Languages and Systems*, 29(3):17, May 2007. Extended abstract in *Principles of Programming Languages* (POPL), 2005.

[19] J. N. Foster, B. C. Pierce, and S. Zdancewic. Updatable security views. In *IEEE Computer Security Foundations Symposium (CSF), Port Jefferson, NY*, July 2009.

[20] J. N. Foster, A. Pilkiewicz, and B. C. Pierce. Quotient lenses. In *ACM SIGPLAN International Conference on Functional Programming (ICFP), Victoria, Canada*, Sept. 2008.

[21] J. Gibbons and M. Johnson. Relating algebraic and coalgebraic descriptions of lenses. In *First International Workshop on Bidirectional Transformations (BX 2012)*, March 2012.

[22] G. Gottlob, P. Paolini, and R. Zicari. Properties and update semantics of consistent views. *ACM Transactions on Database Systems (TODS)*, 13(4):486–524, 1988.

[23] S. Hidaka, Z. Hu, K. Inaba, H. Kato, K. Matsuda, and K. Nakano. Bidirectionalizing graph transformations. In *ACM SIGPLAN International Conference on Functional Programming (ICFP), Baltimore, Maryland*, Sept. 2010.

[24] S. Hidaka, Z. Hu, H. Kato, and K. Nakano. A compositional approach to bidirectional model transformation. In *New Ideas and Emerging Results Track of 31st International Conference on Software Engineering (ICSE 2009, NIER Track)*, 2009.

[25] S. Hidaka, Z. Hu, H. Kato, and K. Nakano. Towards a compositional approach to model transformation for software development. In *Proceedings of the 2009 ACM symposium on Applied Computing*, pages 468–475. ACM New York, NY, USA, 2009.

[26] M. Hofmann, B. C. Pierce, and D. Wagner. Symmetric lenses. In *ACM SIGPLAN–SIGACT Symposium on Principles of Programming Languages (POPL), Austin, Texas*, Jan. 2011.

[27] M. Hofmann, B. C. Pierce, and D. Wagner. Edit lenses. In *ACM SIGPLAN–SIGACT Symposium on Principles of Programming Languages (POPL), Philadelphia, Pennsylvania*, Jan. 2012.

[28] Z. Hu, S.-C. Mu, and M. Takeichi. A programmable editor for developing structured documents based on bi-directional transformations. In *Partial Evaluation and Program Manipulation (PEPM)*, pages 178–189, 2004. Extended version in *Higher Order and Symbolic Computation*, Volume 21, Issue 1-2, June 2008.

[29] Z. Hu, S.-C. Mu, and M. Takeichi. A programmable editor for developing structured documents based on bidirectional transformations. *Higher-Order and Symbolic Computation*, 21(1–2), June 2008. Short version in PEPM '04.

[30] Z. Hu, A. Schürr, P. Stevens, and J. F. Terwilliger. Dagstuhl seminar on bidirectional transformations (bx). *SIGMOD Record*, 40(1):35–39, 2011.

[31] M. Johnson, R. Rosebrugh, and R. Wood. Lenses, fibrations, and universal translations. *Mathematical Structures in Computer Science*, 22:25–42, 2012.

[32] M. Johnson, R. D. Rosebrugh, and R. Wood. Algebras and Update Strategies. *Journal of Universal Computer Science*, 16:729–748, 2010.

[33] S. Kawanaka and H. Hosoya. bixid: a bidirectional transformation language for XML. In *ACM SIGPLAN International Conference on Functional Programming (ICFP), Portland, Oregon*, pages 201–214, 2006.

[34] A. J. Kennedy. Functional pearl: Pickler combinators. *Journal of Functional Programming*, 14(6):727–739, 2004.

[35] D. Liu, Z. Hu, and M. Takeichi. Bidirectional interpretation of xquery. In *ACM SIGPLAN Symposium on Partial Evaluation and Semantics-based Program Manipulation (PEPM), Nice, France*, pages 21–30, New York, NY, USA, 2007.

[36] D. Lutterkort. Augeas: A Linux configuration API, Feb. 2007. Available from `http://augeas.net/`.

[37] K. Matsuda, Z. Hu, K. Nakano, M. Hamana, and M. Takeichi. Bidirectionalization transformation based on automatic derivation of view complement functions. In *ACM SIGPLAN International Conference on Functional Programming (ICFP)*, pages 47–58. ACM Press New York, NY, USA, 2007.

[38] L. Meertens. Designing constraint maintainers for user interaction, 1998. Manuscript.

[39] S.-C. Mu, Z. Hu, and M. Takeichi. An algebraic approach to bi-directional updating. In *ASIAN Symposium on Programming Languages and Systems (APLAS)*, pages 2–20, Nov. 2004.

[40] R. O'Connor. Functor is to lens as applicative is to biplate: Introducing multiplate. *CoRR*, abs/1103.2841, 2011.

[41] H. Pacheco, A. Cunha, and Z. Hu. Delta lenses over inductive types. In *First International Workshop on Bidirectional Transformations (BX)*, 2012.

[42] N. Ramsey. Embedding an interpreted language using higher-order functions and types. In *ACM SIGPLAN Workshop on Interpreters, Virtual Machines and Emulators (IVME), San Diego, CA*, pages 6–14, 2003.

[43] P. Stevens. Bidirectional model transformations in QVT: Semantic issues and open questions. In *International Conference on Model Driven Engineering Languages and Systems (MoDELS), Nashville, TN*, volume 4735 of *Lecture Notes in Computer Science*, pages 1–15. Springer-Verlag, 2007.

[44] P. Stevens. A landscape of bidirectional model transformations. *Postproceedings of GTTSE*, 7, 2008.

[45] P. Stevens. Towards an algebraic theory of bidirectional transformations. In *Graph Transformations: 4th International Conference, Icgt 2008, Leicester, United Kingdom, September 7-13, 2008, Proceedings*, page 1. Springer, 2008.

[46] P. Stevens. Observations relating to the equivalences induced on model sets by bidirectional transformations. In F. Hermann and J. Voigtländer, editors, *Proceedings of the First International Workshop on Bidirectional Transformations (BX 2012)*, 2012. Electronic Communications of the EASST, Volume X.

[47] J. Voigtländer. Bidirectionalization for free! (Pearl). In *ACM SIGPLAN–SIGACT Symposium on Principles of Programming Languages (POPL), Savannah, Georgia*, 2009.

[48] J. Voigtländer, Z. Hu, K. Matsuda, and M. Wang. Combining syntactic and semantic bidirectionalization. In P. Hudak and S. Weirich, editors, *ICFP*, pages 181–192. ACM, 2010.

[49] M. Wang, J. Gibbons, and N. Wu. Incremental updates for efficient bidirectional transformations. In M. M. T. Chakravarty, Z. Hu, and O. Danvy, editors, *ICFP*, pages 392–403. ACM, 2011.

[50] Y. Xiong, D. Liu, Z. Hu, H. Zhao, M. Takeichi, and H. Mei. Towards automatic model synchronization from model transformations. In *IEEE/ACM International Conference on Automated Software Engineering (ASE), Atlanta, GA*, pages 164–173, 2007.

[51] Y. Yu, Y. Lin, Z. Hu, S. Hidaka, H. Kato, and L. Montrieux. blinkit: Maintaining invariant traceability through bidirectional transformations. In *34th International Conference on Software Engineering (ICSE)*, 2012.

The Power of the Dinur-Nissim Algorithm:
Breaking Privacy of Statistical and Graph Databases

Krzysztof Choromanski
Department of Industrial Engineering and
Operations Research,
Columbia University
New York, USA
kmc2178@columbia.edu

Tal Malkin
Department of Computer Science,
Columbia University
New York, USA
tal@cs.columbia.edu

ABSTRACT

A few years ago, Dinur and Nissim (PODS, 2003) proposed an algorithm for breaking database privacy when statistical queries are answered with a perturbation error of magnitude $o(\sqrt{n})$ for a database of size n. This negative result is very strong in the sense that it completely reconstructs $\Omega(n)$ data bits with an algorithm that is simple, uses random queries, and does not put any restriction on the perturbation other than its magnitude. Their algorithm works for a model where the database consists of *bits*, and the statistical queries asked by the adversary are *sum queries* for a subset of locations.

In this paper we extend the attack to work for much more general settings in terms of the type of statistical query allowed, the database domain, and the general tradeoff between perturbation and privacy. Specifically, we prove:

- For queries of the type $\sum_{i=1}^{n} \phi_i x_i$ where ϕ_i are i.i.d. and with a finite third moment and positive variance (this includes as a special case the sum queries of Dinur-Nissim and several subsequent extensions), we prove that the quadratic relation between the perturbation and what the adversary can reconstruct holds even for smaller perturbations, and even for a larger data domain. If ϕ_i is Gaussian, Poissonian, or bounded and of positive variance, this holds for arbitrary data domains and perturbation; for other ϕ_i this holds as long as the domain is not too large and the perturbation is not too small.

- A positive result showing that for a sum query the negative result mentioned above is tight. Specifically, we build a distribution on bit databases and an answering algorithm such that any adversary who wants to recover a little more than the negative result above allows, will not succeed except with negligible probability.

- We consider a richer class of summation queries, fo-

cusing on databases representing graphs, where each entry is an edge, and the query is a structural function of a subgraph. We show an attack that recovers a big portion of the graph edges, as long as the graph and the function satisfy certain properties.

The attacking algorithms in both our negative results are straight-forward extensions of the Dinur-Nissim attack, based on asking ϕ-weighted queries or queries choosing a subgraph uniformly at random. The novelty of our work is in the analysis, showing that this simple attack is much more powerful than was previously known, as well as pointing to possible limits of this approach and putting forth new application domains such as graph problems (which may occur in social networks, Internet graphs, etc). These results may find applications not only for breaking privacy, but also in the positive direction, for recovering complicated structure information using inaccurate estimates about its substructures.

Categories and Subject Descriptors

E.4 [**Coding and Information Theory**]: Error Control Codes; H.2.8 [**Database Applications**]: Statistical Databases; G.3 [**Probability and Statistics**]: Probabilistic Algorithms

General Terms

Algorithms, Theory

Keywords

Data Privacy, Graph Privacy, Statistical Databases, Statistical Attacks, Blatant non-privacy

1. INTRODUCTION

Private data analysis aims to provide statistical information about the database while maintaining privacy of the records. Motivating applications abound, including settings where each database record contains medical, financial, or other private information of an individual. An emerging application domain that has received far less attention, is one where the database corresponds to a graph (say a social, wireless, or wired network graph) that one would like to compute statistics on, while maintaining some privacy of the topology. Typical examples of statistical information that may be provided include approximate sums (e.g., for counting or averaging), distribution parameters, histograms, etc.

A seminal paper by Dinur and Nissim [DN03] initiated a theoretically sound study of reasonable notions supporting both privacy and utility, followed by a large body of work (cf., [DMNS06, Dwo06, DKM+06a, Dwo07, Dwo09, Dwo10, DNPR10, Yek10, DNP+10, NST10, BN10, MM10, GLM+10, GLM+09, MM09, HT10]) addressing definitions, possibility, and impossibility results in different settings. The typical model (and the one that we use here), is one where the database is represented by a string $d = d_1, \ldots, d_n$ held by a curator, who answers user queries using a mechanism A which first computes the correct answer, and then adds a perturbation according to some distribution (such a mechanism is indeed often used in practice).

The community has converged on the notion of differential privacy [DMNS06] as the right privacy notion for designing mechanisms balancing privacy and utility. However, in this paper we focus on attacks that violate privacy in a very strong way (beyond just violating differential privacy), following the approach introduced by [DN03] and described below. In this model, the attacker uses perturbated answers to queries on a database d to come up with another database x, such that with overwhelming probability, x is the same as the original d for a huge fraction of the entries. This is clearly not private for any reasonable notion of privacy, and is commonly referred to as "blatantly non-private". For the rest of the paper, this is what we will mean when we refer to breaking privacy (or "reconstructing all but a small fraction of entries").

The Dinur-Nissim Attack.

Dinur and Nissim [DN03] considered a database $d \in \{0, 1\}^n$ consisting of *bits*, and *sum queries*, where the query is given in the form of a subset of indices, and the answer is the (perturbed) sum of data bits in those locations. They proved that if a mechanism A uses a perturbation whose magnitude is bounded by $o(\sqrt{n})$), then there is an efficient adversary that for every given $\sigma > 0$ can ask a polynomial number of queries and then reconstruct all but σn bits of the database with overwhelming probability. Specifically, the adversary's queries are simply uniformly chosen random subsets, which we will denote $\sum_{i=1}^{n} \phi_i d_i$ ("ϕ-weighted sums"), where each ϕ_i is chosen independently and uniformly from $\{0, 1\}$. The output x is computed by solving the resulting linear program, and rounding each entry to $\{0, 1\}$. We will refer to this as the *DN attack*. The proof relies on a "disqualifying lemma" that shows that this solution, with overwhelming probability, must agree with the original data d on all but an arbitrarily small linear fraction of entries. We discuss various extensions of the DN attack and other related work in Section 1.3.

1.1 Motivation and Goals

The main goal of our paper is to extend the DN attack to work for a wider variety of settings, focusing on the following aspects.

Queries: We want to extend the attack to other queries beyond the ones considered before, since in different application domains different statistical information about the data may be obtainable. It is arguably not reasonable to assume that the adversary has complete control over exactly which queries he may obtain answers to; in fact, in some cases the adversary may have no control whatsoever, and the information is just published by the curator using some

distribution. The more flexibility there is regarding what type and distribution of queries are needed in order for the attack to succeed, the stronger the attack is.

Data domain: The DN attack and its extensions were analyzed for binary databases, where each entry is a bit. It is not hard to extend the attack to work for databases where each entry is taken from some constant size domain. We want to support larger domains (ideally, exponential size domains such as arbitrary polynomial-size strings, but it is not even clear how to extend the analysis of previous work for a polynomial size domain).

Tradeoff between perturbation and privacy compromise: The quadratic relation between the magnitude of the perturbation $\epsilon(n) = o(h(n))$ and what the attack can reconstruct (all but $O(h^2(n))$ entries) was proven in [DN03] for $h(n) = o(\sqrt{n})$. For a larger perturbation $\Omega(\sqrt{n})$ this relation is vacuously true, and in fact [DN03] show that in this case a reasonable notion of privacy can be achieved (as further developed in subsequent work to differential privacy). However, it is interesting to consider what happens if we allow *smaller* perturbations – can the attack be extended to reveal *even more than a linear fraction* of elements in the database? This question is especially relevant if one views this not as an attack, but as a way to recover data from noisy information, where a very small perturbation may be likely. This quadratic relation is indeed proved to hold for a specific type of queries in [DMT07] (see Section 1.3), but it is not clear how to extend their analysis (or the analysis of [DN03]) to handle random sum queries or other ϕ-weighted sum queries for smaller perturbations.

1.2 Our Results

We significantly extend the applicability of the DN attack along the fronts discussed above, in two settings. First, we consider more general ϕ-weighted sum queries, with a wider range of possible domains and perturbations. Second, we consider more complex summation queries, motivated by graph privacy applications. We prove both our attacks, as well as proving a positive result indicating the tightness of our first result. We provide more detail on each of these results below. The attacking algorithms in both our negative results are straight-forward extensions of the DN attack, asking simple randomized queries; we view this as a virtue of the attacks. The technical novelty of our work is in the analysis, showing that this simple attack is much more powerful than was previously known.

Our proof follows the same structure as [DN03], relying on a "disqualifying lemma" to prove that the rounded solution to the linear program agrees with the original database in many entries. However, [DN03] uses the Azuma inequality to prove their disqualifying lemma for random sums, while we have more general queries (including unbounded and non-i.i.d. summations), for which their techniques do not go through. Thus, we use (for different results) the Central Limit Theorem, utilizing a non-uniform version of the Berry-Esseen inequality [NT07] and a martingale version of Azuma's inequality.

We note that, although we present our results from the perspective of a privacy-breaking attack, they may also find applications in the positive direction, for recovering data from noisy information. This direction seems particularly promising in the context of structural databases such as graphs, where inaccurate information about substructures may be locally obtained, and used to deduce global information.

1.2.1 ϕ-weighted Sum Queries for Statistical Databases

A Negative Result. Consider the setting where each data element is taken from the domain $\{0, 1, \ldots, g(n)\}$ and queries are of the form $\sum_{i=1}^{n} \phi_i d_i$. Further consider any mechanism that adds a perturbation bounded by some $\epsilon(n) = o(h(n))$ for some $h(n)$. We prove that in this setting there is an efficient algorithm that can recover all but $O(h^2(n))$ entries, as long as either:

- ϕ_i are i.i.d. with a positive variance and a finite third moment, and $g(n) = o(n^{-\frac{1}{3}} h(n))$; or

- ϕ_i are i.i.d. random variables that are Gaussian, Poissonian, or bounded and with a positive variance.

Note that the second result holds for arbitrary size domains (even exponential) and a more limited class of ϕ, while the first result has more general ϕ, but holds only as long as the domain is not too large and the perturbation is not too small.[1]

We can use the first result to obtain separate generalizations of the DN attack to a larger domain or a smaller perturbation: Taking a binary $\{0, 1\}$ database gives the quadratic tradeoff as long as the perturbation satisfies $h(n) = \omega(n^{\frac{1}{3}})$. Taking $h(n) = \sqrt{n}$ gives the quadratic tradeoff as long as the domain satisfies $g(n) = o(n^{\frac{1}{6}})$. We can also use the first result to simultaneously improve both, recovering all but a sublinear number of entries, each taken from a sublinear size domain.

A Positive Result for Sums. We provide a positive result for sum queries showing that, roughly, for any given perturbation $o(h(n))$, the attacker cannot recover $n - o(\frac{h^2(n)}{\log n})$ bits, except with negligible probability. This matches the negative result above (recovering $n - O(h^2(n))$ bits) up to a logarithmic factor. Specifically, we build a distribution on bit databases and an answering mechanism for which we prove that no non-adaptive adversary can break the bound except with negligible probability. This holds for any non-adaptive adversary (even a computationally unbounded one) who asks polynomially many queries.

We emphasize that this positive result serves to show our negative result is tight, and not as a claim of privacy. Indeed, showing that blatant-non-privacy doesn't hold does not preclude other (possibly weaker) types of privacy violations.

Note that this result is in a different direction from the tightness result shown in [DN03]. They show that increasing the perturbation to $\Omega(\sqrt{n})$ will no longer let the attacker recover information as in their original attack. We show that for any perturbation in our range ($o(\sqrt{n})$ or lower) the adversary cannot recover any more than what our attack recovers.

1.2.2 Graph Databases

For the ϕ-weighted query setting considered so far, each element was selected according to some distribution ϕ_i independently of other elements. We now turn our attention to more complex queries, that may depend on structural properties and connections among the data elements. A particular motivation for us are graph databases, where the detailed topology of the graph should remain private, but some information about the graph may be released.

We consider a setting where the query is a subset of indices, and the answer is (a perturbation of) some function h on the collection of all these entries together. In the most general form, our results can be presented as some conditions on this answer function h and the underlying data, such that an adaptation of the DN attack recovers most of the original data. However, we will present our results in a more narrow form, for reasons of readability and motivation (we mention several generalizations later in the paper). In particular, we will focus on databases representing graphs, and consider summation queries, where the entries included in the sum depend on the global structure of the graph. It is interesting to explore additional instantiations (for graphs and maybe also for other types of databases) where privacy is important and our conditions hold.

Let G_b (the "base graph") be an undirected public graph with m edges. We will consider a database of size m, where each entry is a (secret) weight of the corresponding edge. We will discuss only binary databases (weights of 0 or 1), but all our results can be readily extended for constant weights. We will denote by G_a the subgraph[2] of G_b obtained by considering only edges of weight 1. The graph G_a is the private information the adversary is trying to reconstruct. Intuitively, G_b represents what the adversary knows about the underlying graph (if he knows nothing, we can take G_b to be the complete graph), while which edge weights are non-zero (G_a) is what he is trying to find out.

The answer to a query consisting of a subset S is computed as follows. First, take the corresponding subgraph G_S and apply to it some (public) selection function Λ which selects which edges from G_S will participate in the sum. Importantly, Λ may select edges based on the structural properties of the graph (e.g., select only edges that are part of a 4-clique in the subgraph). Now, the (exact) answer is a function h which sums up, for all edges selected by Λ, some function f of their weights. That is, $h(G_S) = \sum f(w(e_i))$ where e_i are the edges selected by Λ and $w(e_i)$ are their weights. The mechanism then adds a perturbation bounded by $o(\sqrt{m})$ and outputs.

For this setting we prove that there is an efficient attack that asks uniformly random subgraph queries, and reconstruct a big portion of the data (weights), if the following conditions on h and the graph hold. (See later in the paper for more accurate statements).

- h is "not too sensitive": for any two data vectors v_1, v_2 that are close, $|h(v_1) - h(v_2)|$ is not too big. We have two such requirements for different notions of closeness, and an h that satisfies both of them is called *gradual*.

- h is "sensitive enough": recall that h is defined as the sum of a function f applied to the weight of each in-

---

[1] We do not know whether this lower bound on the size of the perturbation is inherent, or just a technical obstacle that can be overcome with a better analysis.

[2] All subgraphs in this paper are weak-subgraphs generated by the given edges, as opposed to (node-) induced subgraphs.

cluded edge. We require f to be *sensitive*, defined as having a slope that is bounded away from zero.

- Most edges in the graph are "not too sensitive" with respect to G, Λ, and h. This is a technical condition which very roughly says that, for most edges e, we want there to be a positive probability η that for a *random* subgraph G_S containing e, e is what we call (G_S, Λ)-active, which means: (1) Λ selects e to count towards the sum in h; and (2) removing e from G_S will not change which of the remaining edges are selected by Λ. Finally, this positive probability η should satisfy some equation in relation to sensitivity parameters of h.

Depending on the underlying structure of G_b and the functions h we are interested in, these conditions may or may not be satisfied, and may or may not be easy to check. We note that even when the conditions are hard to check, the attack can be applied, and the resulting reconstructed data has the guarantee that if the conditions happen to hold, then it agrees with the original graph database for a linear fraction of the entries. Our work is just a first step in this domain, and gives rise to several interesting open problems; in particular, identifying graph related problems where our conditions can be satisfied and that arise naturally (either in privacy-related settings, or in settings where we try to learn information about a graph).

To give a flavor of the scenarios where our attack can be mounted, consider the following example. Recall that an edge e in a graph is called a *bridge* if its removal increases the number of connected components in the graph. Consider a model where the answer to a query (subgraph) is the (perturbed) sum of weights for all the bridges in that subgraph. Let m be the length of the shortest cycle of the database graph G, let M be the length of the longest cycle in this graph, and assume that $m \geq 3$. Then as long as each edge in the graph is in no more than $\frac{2^{\frac{m}{2}-2}}{\sqrt{M}}$ cycles, all our conditions hold, and the adversary can reveal almost all weights of the edges in G. (See Section 3 for further details and other examples).

1.3 Related Work

The problem of releasing database statistics while preserving privacy has received much attention due to its fast-growing applicability and importance. Work on this topic dates back at least to the 80's (e.g., [DD82]), as well as more recent work such as [AS00, KMN05, NMK$^+$06, DKM$^+$06b, AFK$^+$10] and many others.

Not many models where graph queries are considered were analyzed so far, and to our knowledge, our paper is the first one providing an attack (blatant non-privacy) in this setting. Among privacy papers with "graph-database" model we should mention the very recent work of Gupta, Roth, and Ullman [GRU11], which addresses differential privacy of graph cuts. Roughly, each query can be identified with some subset of the vertices of the graph and an exact answer to that query is the cut induced by this subset; [GRU11] provide new algorithms solving the problem of approximately releasing the cut function of a graph while preserving differential privacy. It would be interesting to investigate how (and weather) our techniques can be applied to show a match-

ing lower bound in the form of blatant non-privacy for this cut problem.[3]

There were several works extending the DN attack [DMNS06, DMT07, DY08, HT10, KRSU10], showing lower bounds on the perturbation necessary for certain databases, query functions and certain notions of privacy. Of most relevance for us is the attack of Dwork, McSherry and Talwar [DMT07], who show (among other things) that the quadratic relation between the perturbation and the number of entries that can be reconstructed holds in general for three types of attack queries of the form $\sum_{i=1}^{n} \phi_i d_i$ where ϕ_i are i.i.d.: either chosen uniformly at random from $\{-1, 0, 1\}$, from $\{-1, 1\}$, or chosen according to a Gaussian distribution with mean 0. (Recall that the DN attack can also be cast using these "ϕ-weighted sum" queries, where each ϕ_i is chosen uniformly at random from $\{0, 1\}$, corresponding to sums over random subsets). It is not clear how to extend the analysis of [DMT07] to apply to the setting of [DN03] or more general ϕ-hiding queries for smaller perturbations or polynomial size domains (which is one of our results).

Dwork and Yekhanin [DY08] use Fourier analysis to extend the DN attack to use fewer sum queries ($O(n)$ instead of $O(n \log^2(n))$) which are deterministic. Kasiviswanathan, Rudelson, Smith and Ullman [KRSU10] consider a database where each entry consists of several attributes (rather than a bit), and where each query is related to the so-called contingency table for a subset of attributes. They provide several types of lower bounds for this setting. The model in which a perturbated contingency table is released is very natural and has lots of applications. However, trying to compare to our results, it is not clear whether this model can be parameterized by some function ϕ fitting our conditions (i.e., finite third moment and positive variance) to obtain similar results for smaller perturbation error regimes. We also note that our approach uses much less advanced mathematical machinery than [KRSU10]. While [KRSU10] motivates models with queries of non-independent coefficients, they do not consider a graph database model and graph queries.

We note that while the original [DN03] attack is strictly a special case of ours, this is not so for follow up works such as [DMT07, DY08], who extend the DN attack on other fronts (e.g., allowing a small fraction of answers with unbounded perturbation, or optimizing the number of queries needed for the attack). On the other hand, our proofs do not require the heavy mathematical machinery utilized by [DMT07, DY08].

Finally, in a recent work (and independent of our own), Merener [Mer10] used similar mathematical tools (Berry-Esseen inequalities) to extend the DN attack. However, he focused on the analysis of the relation between the perturbation error added and the complexity of the adversary. He gave a formula for the number of queries used by the adversary as a function of the perturbation error. He considered databases with binary and real values from some bounded set. The database-access scheme he considered is similar to the one described in Dinur-Nissim paper. In contrast, we do not focus much on the complexity of the adversary. Our main goal is to prove that if the perturbation error is small enough the adversary can reveal much more than a linear

---

[3]We have not considered this yet, as we just found out about this work very recently. However, it seems that our theorems will not apply as-is, but that our techniques can potentially be used to directly attack this setting.

number of entries. Moreover, we consider database-access schemes using more complex functions defined on graphs.

2. RESULTS FOR ϕ-WEIGHTED QUERIES

In this section we describe our results for general ϕ-weighted sum queries, extended data domains and perturbations.

2.1 A Negative Result for Larger Domains and Smaller Perturbation Errors

Consider database vector d of length n, having entries from the set $\{0, 1, 2, ..., g(n)\}$. The database mechanism, given any query of the form $q = \{\phi_1, \phi_2, ..., \phi_n\}$, calculates $\sum_{i=1}^{n} \phi_i d_i$ and adds some perturbation error of magnitude $o(h(n))$ for some $h(n)$ (we often require $h(n)$ to be bounded from above by $O(\sqrt{n})$, because for a larger $h(n)$ the attack holds vacuously in a meaningless way, recovering all but n of the bits). Here ϕ_i's are independent copies of some random variable ϕ of positive variance and finite third moment. We give an efficient attack algorithm that allows to reveal all but $h^2(n)$ entries of a database with overwhelming probability $(1 - neg(n))$.

DEFINITION 1. *We say that a random variable ϕ is primal if it is Gaussian, Poissonian or bounded and of positive variance.*

THEOREM 1. *Let ϕ be a random variable of positive variance and finite third moment. If the database domain is of the form $\{0, 1, 2, ..., g(n)\}$, perturbation error $\epsilon = o(h(n))$ for some $h(n) = O(\sqrt{n})$ and $g(n) = o(n^{-\frac{1}{3}} h(n))$, then there is an efficient algorithm using $O(n \log^2(n))$ ϕ-weighted sum queries and revealing all but $h^2(n)$ entries of a database with probability (1-neg(n)). Moreover, if ϕ is primal the above holds for arbitrary $g(n)$.*

Plugging in $g(n) = 1$ for the first, and $h(n) = \sqrt{n}$ for the second, we obtain the following corollaries.

COROLLARY 1. *For a random variable ϕ of positive variance and finite third moment and a perturbation error $\epsilon = o(h(n))$ for $h(n) = O(\sqrt{n})$ such that: $h(n) = \omega(n^{\frac{1}{3}})$ there exists an efficient algorithm using ϕ-weighted sum queries and revealing all but $h^2(n)$ bits with probability (1-neg(n)), where neg(n) is some negligible function of n. Moreover, if ϕ is primal this holds for arbitrary $h(n)$.*

COROLLARY 2. *For a random variable ϕ of positive variance and finite third moment, any fixed $\sigma > 0$, perturbation error $\epsilon = o(\sqrt{n})$ and $g(n) = o(n^{\frac{1}{6}})$ there exists an efficient algorithm using ϕ-weighted sum queries and revealing all but σn entries with probability (1-neg(n)), where neg(n) is some negligible function of n. Moreover, if ϕ is primal this holds for arbitrary $g(n)$.*

Note that the original DN attack is a special case of both these corollaries.

The proof of Theorem 1 rests on the following "disqualifying lemma", which generalizes the [DN03] disqualifying lemma for sum functions.

LEMMA 1 (DISQUALIFYING LEMMA). *Let ϕ be a random variable of finite third moment and positive variance. Let $x, d \in [0, 1]^n$ and $\epsilon = o(\frac{h(n)}{g(n)})$, where $g(n) = o(n^{-\frac{1}{3}} h(n))$. If*

$|\{i : |x_i - d_i| \geq \frac{1}{3g(n)}\}| > \frac{h^2(n)}{n}$, *then $\exists \delta > 0$ such that for sufficiently large n we have:*

$$Pr_{q = \{\phi_1, \phi_2, ..., \phi_n\}}[|\sum_{i=1}^{n} \phi_i(x_i - d_i)| > 2\epsilon + 1] > \delta$$

Moreover, if ϕ is primal the inequality above holds for arbitrary $g(n)$ (without assuming $g(n) = o(n^{-\frac{1}{3}} h(n))$).

The proof appears in Appendix A.2. The high level idea is to prove that any vector x with many entries that are far from the corresponding entries in the database vector d, will with high probability be "disqualified" by one of the randomly chosen queries (namely, the answers on d and on x will be farther than the perturbation bound). Thus, any solution that "survives" all the queries and answers is with overwhelming probability very close to d on a large fraction of entries, and thus will be equal to d on those entries when rounded.

[DN03] proved their sum-function disqualifying lemma by using Azuma's inequality. For our ϕ-weighted queries where ϕ is bounded and of positive variance, we need to use a stronger version of Azuma's inequality to prove the lemma. However, for unbounded variables ϕ it is not clear how to use Azuma's inequality. In our proof we show that as long as we can prove that some sequence of random variables we define is uniformly-integrable then our proof goes through. The sequence is easily uniformly-integrable when ϕ is Gaussian or Poissonian, which completes the proof of those special cases. In the general case, we replace the use of Azuma's inequality with the use of the Central Limit Theorem, where the idea is to approximate the sum of random variables by a Gaussian. However, we need a good approximation, which we achieve by using a non-uniform version of the Berry-Esseen inequality [NT07] instead of the uniform one.

2.2 Positive results

Here we consider only bit databases and sum queries. From the last section we know that it is possible to extend the DN attack to smaller perturbation errors. A natural question is whether the parameters achieved can be improved, and in particular, whether for any fixed perturbation magnitude we may recover more bits than guaranteed by our proof. Dinur and Nissim [DN03] obtained some tightness result in their work, from a somewhat different direction. They considered perturbation error of order $o(\sqrt{n})$ (for which they reconstruct an arbitrarily large linear fraction of the database). They then show that if the perturbation order increases a little, it is no longer possible to reveal those data bits. On the other hand, we do not change the magnitude of the perturbation error. We consider perturbation error of magnitude $E = o(h(n))$ for some $h(n)$. If $h(n)$ is not too small then from Theorem 1 we know that there is an efficient adversary that reveals all but $O(h^2(n))$ bits. This adversary is *non-adaptive*, namely chooses the queries independently from the answers he already received. (In fact, the queries are simply random subsets of $\{1, 2, 3, ..., n\}$.) We ask whether, for the same perturbation magnitude, there is an attack algorithm that can reconstruct even more bits. Our next result shows that if the adversary is non-adaptive, he cannot reconstruct all but $o(\frac{h^2(n)}{\log(n)})$ bits (namely, our negative result was tight up to a logarithmic factor).

THEOREM 2. *Assume that perturbation error ϵ of a database algorithm is of the order $o(h(n))$, where $h(n) = O(\sqrt{n})$. Assume that the non-adaptive adversary chose polynomially many sum queries to ask. Then there is a probability distribution and an efficient database algorithm A such that the following holds: if database d was chosen from this distribution, $f(n) = o(\frac{h^2(n)}{\log(n)})$, algorithm A was used to add the perturbation error and $f(n) = \omega(1)$ then the adversary cannot guess all but $f(n)$ bits with probability greater than negligible.*

This result is especially interesting because it does not bound the adversary to run in a polynomial time. The only bound put on him is that he can ask only polynomially many queries. The proof uses some tricky distribution over databases. We prove that if we choose database using such a distribution then with probability almost 1 the adversary won't be able to reveal sufficiently many bits. To construct such a distribution we create a special combinatorial pattern – a family of subsets satisfying some conditions on their intersections. To prove that such a pattern exists we use the probabilistic method, namely randomly construct such a family and prove that with non-zero probability it satisfies all necessary conditions. The details of the construction can be found in the full version of the paper.

3. RESULTS FOR GRAPH FUNCTIONS

We now turn to consider more complex query functions. Although our results can also apply to other functions, we focus on databases representing graphs, as explained in Section 1.2.2.

3.1 Graph model and basic definitions

We consider here an undirected weighted graph G. The adversary works with a graph with edge weights from the discrete set $\{0, 1\}$ (this can be generalized to constant size domains). The query-function is defined for every weighted graph G with weights from the interval $[0, 1]$. We emphasize here that nonedges are not equivalent to edges with weight 0. We associate with a weighted graph G the "base graph" G_b which is the underlying unweighted graph, and the "active graph" G_a, which is the graph formed by edges of positive weight. G_b is public, while G_a is not (and this is what the adversary is trying to recover). We will think of the database as consisting of m entries, where m is the number of edges in G_b. Each entry will contain the 0/1 weight of the corresponding edge. A query is a subset of edges of G_b, and the exact answer is the value of some function h on the weighted graph created by this subset of edges. As usual, a perturbation is added to the output before it is released (here we will use a perturbation of magnitude $o(\sqrt{m})$)

We consider an output function h that is defined by summing up $\sum f(w_e)$ for *some* of the edges in the query subset, where w_e is the weight of the edge e (the value in the database), and f is some function (e.g., the identity, in which case we are just summing weights). To determine which edges e will participate in the sum, we use some selection function Λ that may depend on the structure of the graph. Our rigorous results and proof that our attack works efficiently, apply to what we call *the basic setting*, where Λ is only allowed to rely on the structure of query subgraph (which is public, as it is a subgraph of G_b), but is *not* allowed to depend on the weights. For example, Λ may be

select edges that are bridges in the subgraph (namely edges whose removal will disconnect the subgraph). The *complex setting* is one where Λ is also allowed to depend on the structure of the hidden G_a. We discuss this setting later.

Notations. The set of all edges of a weighted graph G will be denoted by E. For a weighted graph G and an edge e we will denote by $G-e$ the graph obtained by deleting e from G. For a weighted edge e and a graph G we will denote by $G+e$ the graph obtained by adding edge e to G. In the analogous way we define operations: $G + E$ and $G - E$, where G is a graph and E is a set of edges. While deleting or adding an edge we always delete/add weight associated with this edge. The weight of an edge e will be denoted as w_e. For the set of edges $q \subseteq E$ we denote by $G_{|q}$ the subgraph of G obtained by considering only edges from q. The output of the function h on a graph G will be denoted as $h(G)$. For $E_s \subseteq E$ we denote by $h(E_s)$ the output of h on a graph determined by the set E_s. Let S be a subset of indices of a vector d representing some graph G. We denote by $h^d(S)$ the value of the function h on the subgraph of a graph represented by vector d, obtained by choosing edges of G related to the indices from S. Sometimes we will get rid of d and use shorter denotation: $h(S)$. Having some fixed graph G for which we enumerated all m edges we consider values of the function h on subgraphs of G. Every such subgraph will be denoted by a vector of length m where we put special symbol · for every index related to the edge that wasn't chosen to the subgraph. We need to extend arithmetical operations on real numbers to take into account also this new symbol. We assume that subtracting · from · gives 0. We extend linear order on real numbers such that · is less than every real number. Denote $R_e = R \bigcup \{\cdot\}$.

DEFINITION 2. *We say that 2 vectors v_1 and v_2 of length m are* similar *if they have special symbol · on the same entries. Intuitively, they represent subgraphs of the same structure but possibly different weights on edges.*

DEFINITION 3. *Function $h : R_e^m \to R$ is called* gradual *if it satisfies the following conditions:*

- $\exists_{w>0} |h(v_1) - h(v_2)| \leq w$ *for every two vectors v_1, v_2 that differ on at most one coordinate*

- *for every pair of two similar vectors: $a = (a_1, a_2, ..., a_m)$, $b = (b_1, b_2, ..., b_m)$ such that $\forall_{i \in \{1,2,...,m\}} |a_i - b_i| \leq \frac{1}{m}$ we have $|h(a) - h(b)| = o(\sqrt{m})$*

DEFINITION 4. *A function $f : R \to R^+ \bigcup \{0\}$ is* sensitive *if $\inf_{\Delta > 0, x} \frac{f(x+\Delta) - f(x)}{\Delta} \geq c_f$ for some $c_f > 0$.*

DEFINITION 5. *An edge e of a graph G is (G,h,A,B)-gradual for $A, B > 0$ if for any subgraph H of the graph $G-e$ we have:*

- $h(H + e) - h(H) \leq B$

- $h(H + e) - h(H) \geq -A$

Intuitively this definition says that function h is not too sensitive on the edge e. So the absence of an edge e does not change much the value of function h.

DEFINITION 6. *We say that a graph is* labelled *if its vertices have labels (say, $1, \ldots, n$ for an n-vertex graph). We say two labelled graphs g_1, g_2 are* isomorphic *if they are isomorphic as unlabeled graphs, and there is an isomorphic embedding that maps vertices of g_1 to vertices of g_2 with the same labels (that is, if the isomorphic mapping maintains both node labels and edge structure).*

We say that a labelled graph g is isomorphic to some subgraph of labelled graph G if there is a (labelled) subgraph G_S of G such that g and G_S are isomorphic (as labelled graphs).

We now define when an edge e is (G_S, Λ)-active for a (public) selection function Λ in the general setting of labelled graphs (we may view unlabeled graphs as a special case).

DEFINITION 7. *Take a labelled weighted graph G. Consider unweighted labelled graph G_b. Denote by G_b^S the set of all subgraphs of G_b. Consider the function $\Lambda : G_b^S \to E^S \to \{0, 1\}$ that for every subgraph G_S of G_b outputs a function that maps the set of edges of G_S into the binary set $\{0, 1\}$. We call Λ the selecting function because for every edge e of the subgraph G_S it determines whether e is selected (i.e $\Lambda(G_S)(e) = 1$) or not.*

Whenever $\Lambda(G_S)(e) = 1$ we say that e is (G_S, Λ)-acceptable. Denote by $A(G_S, \Lambda)$ the set of all (G_S, Λ)-acceptable edges. Whenever we have: $A(G_S, \Lambda) = A(G_S - \{e\}, \Lambda) + \{e\}$ for $e \in G_S$ we say that an edge e is (G_S, Λ)-active.

In other words, an edge e is (G_S, Λ)-active if it is selected by Λ (i.e., it is (G_S, Λ)-acceptable), and removing it from G_S will not change which other edges in G_S are selected by Λ.

3.2 Negative Results for Graph Models

We are ready to state our main result of this section (defined for the *basic setting* which we already explained informally above). The intuitive meaning of this theorem was given in the Introduction (Section 1.2.2).

THEOREM 3. *Let G be some weighted undirected database graph of m edges with weights taken from the discrete set $\{0, 1\}$. Fix some public sensitive function f and selecting function Λ. Let h be a gradual function defined such that the output of h on a subgraph G_S is the sum of outputs of f on the weights of (G_S, Λ)-acceptable edges. Assume each edge of G is (G, h, A, B)-gradual for some positive constants A, B. Denote by P_e the conditional probability that e is not (G_S, Λ)-active in a random subgraph G_S of G given that e is in G_S. If for every edge e of a graph G we have: $P_e \le 1 - \eta$ for some $\eta > 0$ such that $\frac{\eta}{1-\eta} > \frac{2(A+B)}{c_f}$ then for every fixed $\sigma > 0$ there exists a linear program of polynomial size that when solved enables the adversary to reveal all but σm weights of edges of a graph G with probability $1\text{-}neg(m)$ as long as the perturbation error added by database algorithm is of the order $o(\sqrt{m})$. Furthermore, this program can be constructed by the adversary by asking queries choosing uniformly at random subgraphs of a given graph.*

We discuss applications of the theorem below. We note that the theorem can be generalized, e.g., by relaxing the condition that all edges e have a positive probability to be active, to require this for almost all edges (the price is the quality of the attack – a slightly smaller, though still linear, fraction of the entries is revealed). This follows from the

proof of Theorem 3, which is given in the full version of the paper.

The proof uses an attack similar to the DN attack in that it consists of polynomially many random subset queries, and then the resulting program is solved, and the solution rounded. We prove this by establishing a disqualifying lemma for a graph model, using a Martingale based version of Azuma's inequality. While that proof pertains to the basic setting, the mathematical machinery that we develop may be useful for the complex setting as well.

The challenges when moving to the complex setting are the following. First, once we ask random queries and obtain perturbated answers, the resulting program may not be solvable in polynomial time. Next, even if we manage to find a solution (or assume we have access to a solution oracle), it may be that the solution will in fact not let us reconstruct the original data. However, if a solution (in the complex setting) is found, and if it satisfies certain conditions, then it can be rounded and outputted; if it doesn't satisfy the conditions, we can iterate again, asking another set of random queries. If at any point we have a solution to the program, and the solution satisfies some conditions, then we can reconstruct most of the original database. This may be useful for applications where we can prove that a solution can be found, the condition can be checked, and a good solution will be arrived after a reasonable number of iterations. We leave it as an open problem to provide provable solutions for problems in the complex setting (general classes of such problems, or specific useful instantiations). For example, it would be interesting to find useful applications in the complex scenario where the program can be efficiently solved.

Applications.

Clearly, the sum function (as in the DN attack) is a special case where Λ always selects every edge (in particular, the edge selection does not rely on any structural properties). Of course, the power of this theorem is in allowing structure dependent queries.

Examples include scenarios in which an entry can contribute to the query result only when it is selected with edges creating a special configuration. Maybe it is the case that the publisher of database statistics does not want to give in the same time information of some special subset of entries that are crucial from his point of view so he creates for such a subset a forbidden pattern. It seems that it makes the goal of the adversary much more difficult. Our result gives sufficient conditions for a structure of the database graph that allows to completely break privacy. Moreover, under those conditions privacy is broken by solving a simple linear program that is completely analogous to the one used in the DN attack. Below we give two example application domains of our result.

Labelled-Graph model.

Consider a setting where the database answering mechanism stores a public finite set of labelled forbidden graphs F, each of at least one edge. For each forbidden graph $f \in F$ one of the edges of f is fixed, denote it by $e(f)$. The information which edge is fixed is also public. The function h on input G_S outputs the sum of weights of edges that satisfy the following property:

There is no isomorphic embedding that maps a forbidden graph f from F into some subgraph of G_S and $e(f)$ into this edge.

A perturbation error of order $o(\sqrt{m})$ is added (where m is the number of edges of G, namely the size of the database). Assume furthermore that each edge of the database graph is contained in at most A subgraphs of G that are isomorphic to some graph from F. We need one more condition for each edge e, namely:

$$\sum_{g \in F^e} \frac{1}{2^{e_g - 1}} \leq 1 - \eta, \qquad (1)$$

where F^e is the set of all subgraphs of G, isomorphic to some graph from F and containing e, e_g is the number of edges of g and η is chosen such that $\frac{\eta}{1-\eta} > 2(A+1)$.

In such a scenario for every given $\sigma > 0$ there exists efficient algorithm that reveals all but σm edges (weights) of G with probability $1 - neg(m)$.

Bridge-counter model.

We define h as a function that for a subgraph G_S outputs the sum of weights of all its bridges. We may think about h as a sum function that takes into consideration only 'important edges' where important are edges that are bridges. As in the previous case, in order to break the privacy we need to assume few more things. For each edge e define by L_e the set of all edges e_1 such that e and e_1 are both edges of some cycle. We assume that: $\forall_e |L_e| \leq A$ for some fixed A.

The last condition that each edge of the graph should satisfy, analogous to the one from the previous example, is now of the form:

$$\sum_{c \in C_e} \frac{1}{2^{|c|-1}} \leq 1 - \eta, \qquad (2)$$

where C_e is the set of all cycles of G containing e and once more η is satisfying: $\frac{\eta}{1-\eta} > 2(A+1)$.

For such a model, as before, for every given $\sigma > 0$ there exists efficient algorithm that reveals all but σm edges of G with probability 1-neg(m).

REMARK 1. *If we denote a girth of a hidden graph by g then the inequality 2 may be replaced by a stronger one, namely: $\sum_{c \in C_e} \frac{1}{2^{g-1}} \leq 1 - \eta$. So we require each edge e to be in no more than $2^{g-1}(1 - \eta)$ cycles of G.*

REMARK 2. *Denote by g the girth of a hidden database graph and by M the length of the longest cycle. Assume that $g \geq 3$. Then the conditions above may be easily replaced by a stronger one, namely: each edge of G is in no more than $\frac{2^{\frac{g}{2}-2}}{\sqrt{M}}$ cycles of G. If this condition is satisfied, then the privacy of a database can be broken.*

Acknowledgments

We thank Sharon Goldberg, Moritz Hardt, Kobbi Nissim, and Adam Smith for several illuminating discussions and pointers.

4. REFERENCES

[AFK+10] Gagan Aggarwal, Tomas Feder, Krishnaram Kenthapadi, Samir Khuller, Rina Panigrahy, Dilys Thomas, and An Zhu. Achieving anonymity via clustering. *ACM Transactions on Algorithms (TALG)*, 6, 2010.

[AS00] Rakesh Agrawal and Ramakrishnan Srikant. Privacy-preserving data mining. 2000.

[BN10] Hai Brenner and Kobbi Nissim. Impossibility of differentially private universally optimal mechanisms. *CoRR*, abs/1008.0256, 2010.

[Cha10] Moses Charikar, editor. *Proceedings of the Twenty-First Annual ACM-SIAM Symposium on Discrete Algorithms, SODA 2010, Austin, Texas, USA, January 17-19, 2010*. SIAM, 2010.

[DD82] Dorothy E. Denning and Peter J. Denning. *Cryptography and Data Security*. 1982.

[DKM+06a] Cynthia Dwork, Krishnaram Kenthapadi, Frank McSherry, Ilya Mironov, and Moni Naor. Our data, ourselves: Privacy via distributed noise generation. In Serge Vaudenay, editor, *EUROCRYPT*, volume 4004 of *Lecture Notes in Computer Science*, pages 486–503. Springer, 2006.

[DKM+06b] Cynthia Dwork, Krishnaram Kenthapadi, Frank McSherry, Ilya Mironov, and Moni Naor. Our data, ourselves: Privacy via distributed noise generation. In *Advances in Cryptology - EUROCRYPT 2006, 25th Annual International Conference on the Theory and Applications of Cryptographic Techniques*, pages 486–503, 2006.

[DMNS06] Cynthia Dwork, Frank McSherry, Kobbi Nissim, and Adam Smith. Calibrating noise to sensitivity in private data analysis. In Shai Halevi and Tal Rabin, editors, *TCC*, volume 3876 of *Lecture Notes in Computer Science*, pages 265–284. Springer, 2006.

[DMT07] Cynthia Dwork, Frank McSherry, and Kunal Talwar. The price of privacy and the limits of LP decoding. In David S. Johnson and Uriel Feige, editors, *STOC*, pages 85–94. ACM, 2007.

[DN03] Irit Dinur and Kobbi Nissim. Revealing information while preserving privacy. In *Proceedings of the Twenty-Second ACM SIGACT-SIGMOD-SIGART Symposium on Principles of Database Systems (PODS)*, pages 202–210. ACM, 2003.

[DNP+10] Cynthia Dwork, Moni Naor, Toniann Pitassi, Guy N. Rothblum, and Sergey Yekhanin. Pan-private streaming algorithms. In Andrew Chi-Chih Yao, editor, *ICS*, pages 66–80. Tsinghua University Press, 2010.

[DNPR10] Cynthia Dwork, Moni Naor, Toniann Pitassi, and Guy N. Rothblum. Differential privacy under continual observation. In Schulman [Sch10], pages 715–724.

[Dwo06] Cynthia Dwork. Differential privacy. In Michele Bugliesi, Bart Preneel, Vladimiro Sassone, and Ingo Wegener, editors, *ICALP (2)*, volume 4052 of *Lecture Notes in Computer Science*, pages 1–12. Springer, 2006.

[Dwo07] Cynthia Dwork. Ask a better question, get a

better answer a new approach to private data analysis. In Thomas Schwentick and Dan Suciu, editors, *ICDT*, volume 4353 of *Lecture Notes in Computer Science*, pages 18–27. Springer, 2007.

[Dwo09] Cynthia Dwork. The differential privacy frontier (extended abstract). In Omer Reingold, editor, *TCC*, volume 5444 of *Lecture Notes in Computer Science*, pages 496–502. Springer, 2009.

[Dwo10] Cynthia Dwork. Differential privacy in new settings. In Charikar [Cha10], pages 174–183.

[DY08] Cynthia Dwork and Sergey Yekhanin. New efficient attacks on statistical disclosure control mechanisms. In David Wagner, editor, *CRYPTO*, volume 5157 of *Lecture Notes in Computer Science*, pages 469–480. Springer, 2008.

[GLM+09] Anupam Gupta, Katrina Ligett, Frank McSherry, Aaron Roth, and Kunal Talwar. Differentially private approximation algorithms. *CoRR*, abs/0903.4510, 2009.

[GLM+10] Anupam Gupta, Katrina Ligett, Frank McSherry, Aaron Roth, and Kunal Talwar. Differentially private combinatorial optimization. In Charikar [Cha10], pages 1106–1125.

[GRU11] Anupam Gupta, Aaron Roth, and Jonathan Ullman. Iterative constructions and private data release. *CoRR*, abs/1107.3731, 2011.

[HT10] Moritz Hardt and Kunal Talwar. On the geometry of differential privacy. In Schulman [Sch10], pages 705–714.

[KMN05] Krishnaram Kenthapadi, Nina Mishra, and Kobbi Nissim. Simulatable auditing. *Proceedings of the twenty-fourth ACM SIGMOD-SIGACT-SIGART symposium on Principles of database systems (PODS)*, 2005.

[KRSU10] Shiva Prasad Kasiviswanathan, Mark Rudelson, Adam Smith, and Jonathan Ullman. The price of privately releasing contingency tables and the spectra of random matrices with correlated rows. In Schulman [Sch10], pages 775–784.

[Mer10] Martin Merener. Polynomial-time attack on output perturbation sanitizers for real-valued datasets. *Journal of Privacy and Confidentiality*, 2(2):65–81, 2010.

[MM09] Frank McSherry and Ilya Mironov. Differentially private recommender systems: Building privacy into the netflix prize contenders. In John F. Elder IV, Françoise Fogelman-Soulié, Peter A. Flach, and Mohammed Javeed Zaki, editors, *KDD*, pages 627–636. ACM, 2009.

[MM10] Frank McSherry and Ratul Mahajan. Differentially-private network trace analysis. In Shivkumar Kalyanaraman, Venkata N. Padmanabhan, K. K. Ramakrishnan, Rajeev Shorey, and Geoffrey M. Voelker, editors, *SIGCOMM*, pages 123–134. ACM, 2010.

[NMK+06] Shubha U. Nabar, Bhaskara Marthi,

Krishnaram Kenthapadi, Nina Mishra, and Rajeev Motwani. Towards robustness in query auditing. *VLDB '06 Proceedings of the 32nd international conference on Very large data bases*, 2006.

[NST10] Kobbi Nissim, Rann Smorodinsky, and Moshe Tennenholtz. Approximately optimal mechanism design via differential privacy. *CoRR*, abs/1004.2888, 2010.

[NT07] K. Neammanee and P. Thongtha. Improvement of the non-uniform version of berry-esseen inequality via paditz-siganov theorems. *Journal of Inequalities in Pure and Applied Mathematics (JIPM)*, 8(4), 2007.

[Sch10] Leonard J. Schulman, editor. *Proceedings of the 42nd ACM Symposium on Theory of Computing, STOC 2010, Cambridge, Massachusetts, USA, 5-8 June 2010*. ACM, 2010.

[She96] Ross M. Sheldon. *Stochastic Processes*. Wiley, 1996.

[Yek10] Sergey Yekhanin. Private information retrieval. *Commun. ACM*, 53(4):68–73, 2010.

APPENDIX

A. RESULTS FOR ϕ-WEIGHTED QUERIES: RIGOROUS EXPOSITION AND PROOFS

In this section we consider *ϕ-weighted sum queries*, where the query is defined by a random string $\{\phi_1, ..., \phi_n\}$, where ϕ_i's are independent copies of some random variable ϕ. The exact answer to the query is of the form: $\sum_{i=1}^n \phi_i d_i$ (which as usual will be perturbed by the mechanism). When ϕ takes values from the discrete set $\{v_1, ..., v_k\}$, each with the same probability $\frac{1}{k}$, we call the corresponding query a $\{v_1, ..., v_k\}$-query. The $\{0, 1\}$-query is a *sum query*. The Gaussian query is a ϕ-weighted sum query with ϕ being a Gaussian random variable. We assume that ϕ has finite third moment and positive variance.

For these queries, we will consider an extension on the DN attack, showing the quadratic relation holds even for small perturbations and all but sublinear entries revealed, as well as for larger domains, where each database entry is taken from the set $\{0, 1, 2, ..., g(n)\}$, where $g(n)$ is some function of n. The key part of the proof is a modified version of the so-called disqualifying lemma proposed by Dinur and Nissim in [DN03]. Before stating it we will describe the algorithm proposed by Dinur and Nissim and introduce some useful notation.

A.1 Database model and algorithms breaking privacy

DEFINITION 8. *Let ϕ be a random variable of finite third moment and positive variance. Each query is of the form $\{\phi_1, ..., \phi_n\}$, where ϕ_i's are independent copies of ϕ and n is the size of a database. By a database $D(d, A, \epsilon, g(n))$ we mean vector d of n entries from a discrete set $\{0, 1, 2, ...g(n)\}$ together with the algorithm A, possibly randomized, that given any query $q = \{\phi_1, ..., \phi_n\}$ returns number $\hat{a}_q$ such that:*

$$|\hat{a}_q - \sum_{i=1}^n \phi_i d_i| \leq \epsilon$$

Fix some $\sigma > 0$. The aim of the adversary is to reveal all but σn entries of a database. In the following algorithm we assume that each entry of a database is either 0 or 1 so this is a special case of our model for g(n)=1. The following algorithm was proposed by Dinur and Nissim to achieve this goal for sum queries:

- Let $t = cn \log^2 n$ for some constant c that depends on chosen σ. For $1 \leq j \leq t$ choose uniformly at random $q_j \subseteq \{1, 2, ...n\}$ and get answer $\hat{a}_{q_j}$ from the database algorithm.

- Solve the following linear program with unknown $c_1, ..., c_n$:

$$\hat{a}_{q_j} - \epsilon \leq \sum_{i \in q_j} c_i \leq \hat{a}_{q_j} + \epsilon$$

$$0 \leq c_i \leq 1$$

for $1 \leq j \leq t$ and $1 \leq i \leq n$

- Let $x_i = 1$ if $c_i > \frac{1}{2}$ and $x_i = 0$ otherwise. Output vector x.

It turns out that as long as $\epsilon = o(\sqrt{n})$ the output vector x is exactly the same as d on all but σn bits with probability (1-neg(n)), where neg(n) is some negligible function of n.

Below we give a version of the algorithm for general ϕ-weighted sum queries (where ϕ satisfies the above conditions), a database with domain $\{0, 1, 2, ...g(n)\}$, where $g(n)$ is not necessarily 1, and perturbation error of the magnitude $o(h(n))$ for some $h(n) = O(\sqrt{n})$. We call this algorithm - the extended Dinur-Nissim algorithm:

- Let $t = cn \log^2 n$ for some big enough constant c appropriately chosen. For $1 \leq j \leq t$ take a query $q_j = \{\phi_1^j, \phi_2^j, ...\phi_n^j\}$ and get answer $\hat{a}_{q_j}$ from the database algorithm.

- Solve the following linear program with unknown $c_1, ..., c_n$:

$$\hat{a}_{q_j} - \epsilon \leq \sum_{i=1}^{n} \phi_i^j c_i \leq \hat{a}_{q_j} + \epsilon$$

$$0 \leq c_i \leq g(n)$$

for $1 \leq j \leq t$ and $1 \leq i \leq n$

- $\forall_i$ let x_i be obtained by rounding c_i to the nearest integer from $\{0, 1, 2, ...g(n)\}$. Output vector x.

The proof of the correctness of the first algorithm is based on the fact that for every vector that differs too much from d with some probability bounded from below by some constant greater than 0 the randomly chosen query will disqualify it. The precise analysis is contained in the so-called disqualifying lemma proposed and proved by Dinur and Nissim in the same paper. Later we will give our version of the disqualifying lemma that suites the situation when we want to reveal all but sublinear number of bits, we have larger domains for database entries and more general queries. As an immediate corollary we get:

THEOREM 1. Let ϕ be a random variable of positive variance and finite third moment. If the database domain is of the form $\{0, 1, 2, ..., g(n)\}$, perturbation error $\epsilon = o(h(n))$ for some $h(n) = O(\sqrt{n})$ and $g(n) = o(n^{-\frac{1}{3}}h(n))$, then there

is an efficient algorithm using ϕ-weighted sum queries and revealing all but $h^2(n)$ entries of a database with probability (1-neg(n)). Moreover, if ϕ is primal the above holds for arbitrary $g(n)$.

Plugging in $g(n) = 1$ gives Corollary 1, generalizing the DN attack on binary databases to work also for a smaller perturbation, as long as $h(n) = \omega(n^{\frac{1}{3}})$. Plugging in $h(n) = \sqrt{n}$ gives Corollary 2, generalizing the DN attack with $o(\sqrt{n})$ perturbation to work also for a larger domain, as long as $g(n) = o(n^{\frac{1}{6}})$.

The reason why Theorem 1 follows from our version of Disqualifying Lemma lies in the same analysis that was done by Dinur and Nissim in [DN03] so we skip it.

A.2 Disqualifying lemma for small perturbation errors

In this section we prove the so-called disqualifying lemma for the case when perturbation error for unscaled vectors is of the order $o(h(n))$ for some $h(n)$. We do not assume that $h(n) = \sqrt{n}$ as Dinur and Nissim did. Our result can be applied for h(n) of order $o(\sqrt{n})$ as long as h(n) is not of 'too small' order. In this case the lemma enables us to reveal much more than all but θn entries for some fixed small θ. We will use the notation introduced before. Especially, by ϵ we denote the perturbation error. By $g(n)$ we denote the maximal value that database entry can take.

LEMMA 1 (DISQUALIFYING LEMMA). Let ϕ be a random variable of finite third moment and positive variance. Let $x, d \in [0, 1]^n$ and $\epsilon = o(\frac{h(n)}{g(n)})$, where $g(n) = o(n^{-\frac{1}{3}}h(n))$. If $|\{i : |x_i - d_i| \geq \frac{1}{3g(n)}\}| > \frac{h^2(n)}{n}$, then $\exists \delta > 0$ such that for sufficiently large n we have:

$$Pr_{q=\{\phi_1, \phi_2, ...\phi_n\}}[|\sum_{i=1}^{n} \phi_i(x_i - d_i)| > 2\epsilon + 1] > \delta$$

Moreover, if ϕ is primal the inequality above holds even if we do not assume that $g(n) = o(n^{-\frac{1}{3}}h(n))$.

PROOF. We use the following denotation:

- Let $X_i = \phi_i(x_i - d_i)$. Random variables X_i for $i = 1, 2, ...n$ are independent because ϕ_i's are independent.

- Let $Z_i = X_i - E(X_i)$ for i=1,2,...n. So we have: $E(Z_i) = 0$ and $Var(Z_i) = Var(X_i)$

- Let $X = \sum_{i=1}^{n} X_i$

- Let $Y = (X - EX)^2$. In particular: $EY = Var(X) = \sum_{i=1}^{n} Var(X_i)$, because X_i are independent r.v

So to prove lemma we only need to prove that: $Pr[|X| > 2\epsilon + 1] > c$ for some positive constant c. We introduce constant T. Its exact numerical value will be determined later. Having it, we will consider two cases.

A.2.1 Case 1: $|E(X)| \leq T\sqrt{\sum_{i=1}^{n} Var(Z_i)}$

In this case we prove that:

$$Pr[|X - EX| > 2T\sqrt{\sum_{i=1}^{n} Var(Z_i)}] > C$$

for some positive constant C. This proves lemma because: $\sum_{i=1}^{n} Var(Z_i) \geq \sigma \frac{h^2(n)}{g^2(n)}$ for some $\sigma > 0$ and $\epsilon = o(\frac{h(n)}{g(n)})$.

The lower bound on $\sum_{i=1}^{n} Var(Z_i)$ is a direct implication of the fact that $Var(\phi) > 0$.

We partition the probability space into three regions:

- $A = \{Y < \alpha \sum_{i=1}^{n} Var(Z_i)\}$
- $B = \{\alpha \sum_{i=1}^{n} Var(Z_i) \leq Y \leq \beta \sum_{i=1}^{n} Var(Z_i)\}$
- $C = \{Y > \beta \sum_{i=1}^{n} Var(Z_i)\}$,

where constants $0 < \alpha < \beta$ will be determined later. Note that $E(Y) = \sum_{i=1}^{n} Var(Z_i)$.

We have:

$$E(Y) = Pr[A]E(Y|A) + Pr[B]E(Y|B) + Pr[C]E(Y|C) \quad (3)$$

So we obtain:

$$E(Y) \leq \alpha \sum_{i=1}^{n} Var(Z_i) + Pr[B]\beta \sum_{i=1}^{n} Var(Z_i) + Pr[C]E(Y|C) \quad (4)$$

Later we will prove that for fixed α and β sufficiently large we have:

$$Pr[C]E(Y|C) < \alpha \sum_{i=1}^{n} Var(Z_i) \quad (5)$$

Knowing that, we can obtain: $Pr[B] \geq \frac{1-2\alpha}{\beta} > 0$ for $\alpha < \frac{1}{2}$. Now, taking: $T = \sqrt{\frac{\alpha}{4}}$ we have:

$$Pr[|X - EX| > 2T\sqrt{\sum_{i=1}^{n} Var(Z_i)}] = Pr[Y > 4T^2 \sum_{i=1}^{n} Var(Z_i)] \quad (6)$$

Therefore

$$Pr[|X - EX| > 2T\sqrt{\sum_{i=1}^{n} Var(Z_i)}] \geq Pr[B] \geq \frac{1-2\alpha}{\beta} \quad (7)$$

So we obtain the inequality we were looking for to complete the proof in this case. The crucial thing now is to appropriately bound expression: $Pr[C]E(Y|C)$ for sufficiently large β. We need to show that for β large enough we have:

$$E(YI\{Y > \beta \sum_{i=1}^{n} Var(Z_i)\}) < \alpha \sum_{i=1}^{n} Var(Z_i) \quad (8)$$

which is equivalent to:

$$E\left(\frac{Y}{\sum_{i=1}^{n} Var(Z_i)} I\{\frac{Y}{\sum_{i=1}^{n} Var(Z_i)} > \beta\}\right) < \alpha \quad (9)$$

We introduce the following denotation:

$$D_n = \frac{\sum_{i=1}^{n} Z_i}{\sqrt{\sum_{i=1}^{n} Var(Z_i)}}$$

We would like to prove that: $E(D_n^2 I\{D_n^2 > \beta\}) < \alpha$ for β large enough.

REMARK 3. *For ϕ being Gaussian or Poissonian each D_n is also Gaussian or Poissonian. Besides, each has variance equal to 1 and mean 0. So trivially, for ϕ being Gaussian or Poissonian the inequality above is satisfied for β large enough and we are done.*

Assume now that ϕ is bounded. We will bound the probability: $Pr(|D_n| > c)$ for some fixed $c > 0$. We will use the following version of Azuma's inequality (see: [Shc96]):

LEMMA 2. *Let M_i, $i \geq 1$ be a martingale with mean $\mu = E[M_i]$. Let $M_0 = \mu$ and suppose that for nonnegative constants α_i, β_i, $i \geq 1$,*

$$-\alpha_i \leq M_i - M_{i-1} \leq \beta_i$$

. Then for any $n \geq 0, a \geq 0$:

$$Pr(M_n - \mu \geq a) \leq exp(-\frac{2a^2}{\sum_{i=1}^{n}(\alpha_i + \beta_i)^2})$$

and

$$Pr(M_n - \mu \leq -a) \leq exp(-\frac{2a^2}{\sum_{i=1}^{n}(\alpha_i + \beta_i)^2})$$

We apply lemma 2 to the sequence defined as follows:

- $M_0 = 0$
- $M_i = \sum_{i=1}^{n} Z_i$, $i = 1, 2, ..., n$

It is easy to check that $\{M_i\}$ is a martingale of mean 0. We have:

$$Pr(|D_n| > c) = Pr(|M_n| > c\sqrt{\sum_{i=1}^{n} Var(Z_i)}) \quad (10)$$

Therefore from the definition of Z_i:

$$Pr(|D_n| > c) = Pr(|M_n| > c\sqrt{Var(\phi)}\sqrt{\sum_{i=1}^{n}(x_i - d_i)^2}) \quad (11)$$

So we can apply lemma 2 to obtain:

$$Pr(|D_n| > c) \leq 2exp(-\frac{2c^2 Var(\phi)\sum_{i=1}^{n}(x_i - d_i)^2}{\sum_{i=1}^{n}(\alpha_i + \beta_i)^2}), \quad (12)$$

where $\alpha_i = \beta_i = m_\phi |x_i - d_i|$ and m_ϕ is an upper bound on $|\phi|$.

So we have:

$$Pr(|D_n| > c) \leq 2exp(-\frac{c^2 Var(\phi)}{2m_\phi^2}) \quad (13)$$

We have:

$$E(D_n^2 I\{D_n^2 > \beta\}) = \beta Pr[D_n^2 > \beta] + \int_{\beta}^{\infty} Pr[D_n^2 > y]\, dy. \quad (14)$$

So using 13, we obtain:

$$E(D_n^2 I\{D_n^2 > \beta\}) \leq 2\beta e^{-\frac{\beta Var(\phi)}{2m_\phi^2}} + 2\int_{\beta}^{\infty} e^{-\frac{Var(\phi)}{2m_\phi^2}y}\, dy \quad (15)$$

And this last upper bound on $E(D_n^2 I\{D_n^2 > \beta\})$ that we obtained obviously converges to 0 when $\beta \to \infty$. So we proved that for a bounded ϕ we have: $E(D_n^2 I\{D_n^2 > \beta\}) < \alpha$ for β large enough.

From what we said so far we know that if ϕ is primal then indeed: $E(D_n^2 I\{D_n^2 > \beta\}) < \alpha$ for β large enough. However for a general setting we need a little bit different approach.

From the equation 14 we see that it suffices to prove that: $\beta Pr[D_n > \sqrt{\beta}], \beta Pr[D_n < -\sqrt{\beta}], \int_\beta^\infty Pr[D_n > \sqrt{y}]\,dy$, $\int_\beta^\infty Pr[D_n < -\sqrt{y}]\,dy$ are all arbitrarily close to 0 when β is large enough.

To do that, we use Central Limit Theorem, and more precisely: some version of Berry-Esseen inequality, that will enable us to make some approximations using Gaussian distribution.

We use the following lemma (see: [NT07]):

LEMMA 3. *Let $\{S_1, S_2, ...S_n\}$ be a sequence of independent random variables with 0 mean, not necessarily identically distributed, with finite third moment. Assume that $\sum_{i=1}^n E(S_i^2) = 1$. Define: $W_n = \sum_{i=1}^n S_i$. Then:*

$$|Pr[W_n \le x] - \phi(x)| \le \frac{C_1}{1 + |x|^3} \sum_{i=1}^n E(|S_i|^3),$$

for some constant C_1 (we can take $C_1 = 30.84$), where $\phi(x) = Pr(g \le x)$ and g is a normal distribution with variance 1 and mean 0.

We can use this lemma taking: $S_i = \frac{Z_i}{\sqrt{\sum_{i=1}^n Var(Z_i)}}$. Then we have: $W_n = D_n$. It is easy to check that all the conditions that are required to use lemma 3 are satisfied under such a choice. In particular, S_i chosen in such a way has finite third moment because ϕ has finite third moment.

Denote: $\bar{\phi}(x) = 1 - \phi(x)$. From lemma 3 we know that:

$$|Pr[D_n > x] - \bar{\phi}(x)| \le \frac{C_1}{1 + |x|^3} \sum_{i=1}^n E\left(\frac{|Z_i|^3}{\sqrt{\sum_{i=1}^n Var(Z_i)}^3}\right) \quad (16)$$

We also know that:

$$E\left(\frac{|Z_i|^3}{\sqrt{\sum_{i=1}^n Var(Z_i)}^3}\right) \le \frac{\rho}{\sqrt{\frac{h^6(n)}{g^6(n)}}} \quad (17)$$

for some constant ρ.
That is true because $\sup_{i\in\{1,2,...n\}} E(|Z_i|^3)$ is finite and

$$\sum_{i=1}^n Var(Z_i) \ge \sigma \frac{h^2(n)}{g^2(n)}$$

for some constant σ.
As an immediate corollary we have:

$$\sum_{i=1}^n E|S_i^3| = O\left(\frac{n}{\sqrt{\frac{h^6(n)}{g^6(n)}}}\right) = o(1) \quad (18)$$

because of the assumption that we put on g in the statement of the disqualifying lemma. So we have:

$$\beta Pr[D_n > \sqrt{\beta}] \le \beta\left(\bar{\phi}(\sqrt{\beta}) + \frac{C}{1 + \beta^{\frac{3}{2}}}\right) \quad (19)$$

for some positive constant C.
But it is easy to check that expression on the right, bounding $\beta Pr[D_n > \sqrt{\beta}]$, tends to 0 as $\beta \to \infty$.
So we have:

$$\lim_{\beta\to\infty} \sup_n \beta Pr[D_n > \sqrt{\beta}] = 0 \quad (20)$$

Similarly:

$$\lim_{\beta\to\infty} \sup_n \beta Pr[D_n < -\sqrt{\beta}] = 0 \quad (21)$$

This inequality can be obtained by taking $S_i = -\frac{Z_i}{\sqrt{\sum_{i=1}^n Var(Z_i)}}$ in Berry-Esseen inequality and using the same trick as before.
We also have:

$$\int_\beta^\infty Pr[D_n > \sqrt{y}]\,dy \le \int_\beta^\infty \left(\bar{\phi}(\sqrt{y}) + \frac{C}{1 + y^{\frac{3}{2}}}\right) dy \quad (22)$$

And again it is easy to check that expression on the right above converges to 0 as $\beta \to \infty$.
So we also have:

$$\lim_{\beta\to\infty} \sup_n \int_\beta^\infty Pr[D_n > \sqrt{y}]\,dy = 0 \quad (23)$$

And by the same analysis we also get:

$$\lim_{\beta\to\infty} \sup_n \int_\beta^\infty Pr[D_n < -\sqrt{y}]\,dy = 0 \quad (24)$$

Therefore we showed that:

$$\lim_{\beta\to\infty} \sup_n E(D_n^2 I\{D_n^2 > \beta\}) = 0 \quad (25)$$

This is all that we need to prove disqualifying lemma for the first case. Remember that we haven't chosen parameter α yet. So far we only needed: $0 < \alpha < \frac{1}{2}$. When α is fixed, parameter T is determined and we have in fact: $T = \sqrt{\frac{\alpha}{4}}$. We will now consider second case when $|E(X)| > T\sqrt{\sum_{i=1}^n Var(Z_i)}$. We will finally determine α and, as a consequence, T.

A.2.2 Case 2: $|E(X)| > T\sqrt{\sum_{i=1}^n Var(Z_i)}$

We assume that $E(X) > 0$. For $E(X) < 0$ the proof is analogous. Observe that it is enough to prove that: $Pr[(X - EX) < -\gamma\sqrt{\sum_{i=1}^n Var(Z_i)}] < \delta$ for some $\delta < 1$ and $0 < \gamma < T$. This follows from the fact that $\epsilon = o(\sqrt{\sum_{i=1}^n Var(Z_i)})$. So in fact we'd like to bound: $Pr[D_n < -\gamma]$. For ϕ being Gaussian or Poissonian, from what we have said so far, each D_n is also Gaussian or Poissonian with mean 0 and variance equal to 1. So we are done in this case. For ϕ being bounded, using the same analysis as in Case 1, we can easily obtain for any $\gamma > 0$: $Pr[D_n < -\gamma] \le exp(-\frac{\gamma^2 Var(\phi)}{2m_\phi^2}) < 1$. So we are also done in this case. For the general setting, with our additional condition on $g(n)$, finding an upper bound for $Pr[D_n < -\gamma]$ is easy too. The latter probability is equal to $Pr[-D_n > \gamma]$ so we can use Berry-Esseen inequality, taking: $S_i = -\frac{Z_i}{\sum_{i=1}^n Var(Z_i)}$. Thus we obtain:

$$Pr[D_n < -\gamma] \le \bar{\phi}(\gamma) + \frac{C_2}{1 + \gamma^3} \sum_{i=1}^n E(|S_i|^3) \quad (26)$$

for some constant C_2. For $g(n) = o(n^{-\frac{1}{3}} h(n))$ and n sufficiently large, the expression $\frac{C_2}{1+\gamma^3} \sum_{i=1}^n E(|S_i|^3)$ is arbitrarily small. So taking for example $\alpha = \frac{1}{3}$ and $\gamma = \sqrt{\frac{1}{13}}$ we can find n_0 such that

$$\forall_{n > n_0} \frac{C_2}{1 + \gamma^3} \sum_{i=1}^n E(|S_i|^3) < \phi(\gamma)$$

$\square$

A Rigorous and Customizable Framework for Privacy

Daniel Kifer
Penn State University

Ashwin Machanavajjhala
Yahoo! Research

ABSTRACT

In this paper we introduce a new and general privacy framework called Pufferfish. The Pufferfish framework can be used to create new privacy definitions that are customized to the needs of a given application. The goal of Pufferfish is to allow experts in an application domain, who frequently do not have expertise in privacy, to develop rigorous privacy definitions for their data sharing needs. In addition to this, the Pufferfish framework can also be used to study existing privacy definitions.

We illustrate the benefits with several applications of this privacy framework: we use it to formalize and prove the statement that differential privacy assumes independence between records, we use it to define and study the notion of *composition* in a broader context than before, we show how to apply it to protect unbounded continuous attributes and aggregate information, and we show how to use it to rigorously account for prior data releases.

Categories and Subject Descriptors

H.2.8 [**Database Applications**]: Statistical Databases; K.4.1 [**Computers and Society**]: Privacy

General Terms

Theory

Keywords

privacy, differential privacy

1. INTRODUCTION

With improvements in data collection technologies, increased emphasis on data analytics, and the increasing need for different parties to share datasets, the field of statistical privacy is seeing an unprecedented growth in importance and diversity of applications. These applications include protecting privacy and confidentiality in (computer)

network data collections [32], protecting privacy and identifiability in genome-wide association studies (GWAS) [19], protecting confidentiality in Census data products [25, 15], etc. In each case, the goal is to release useful information (i.e. privacy-preserving query answers or a sanitized version of the dataset) while protecting confidential information.

These applications have diverse characteristics: some data sets are more sensitive in nature than others; some applications must protect aggregate secrets while others must protect secrets about individuals; in some cases, only certain attributes (or attribute values) need to be protected, etc.

Furthermore, properties of the data-generating process, such as correlations between records, play an important role. Assumptionless privacy definitions are a myth: if one wants to publish useful, privacy-preserving sanitized data then one *must* make assumptions about the original data and data-generating process [22, 14].

Thus application domain experts, who are frequently not experts in privacy, cannot simply use a single generic privacy definition – they must develop a new privacy definition or customize an existing one. Without guidance this has resulted in ad-hoc solutions and endless cycles of attacks on privacy, followed by proposed fixes, followed by new attacks.

At the same time, privacy experts need new methods for analyzing new and existing privacy definitions in order to evolve the state of the art. Many of the newer definitions are based on "indistinguishability" – making it difficult for attackers to distinguish between certain pairs of datasets; we show how these approaches frequently obscure the semantics of the privacy guarantees that are provided.

In this paper we present a new privacy framework, called Pufferfish. This framework can be used to study existing privacy definitions like differential privacy [12], to study important concepts like *composition* [17], and to generate privacy definitions that are customized for different application domains. The Pufferfish framework follows modern design guidelines such as adherence to privacy axioms [21, 20] and making assumptions as explicit as possible.

The contributions of this paper are:

- A new privacy framework which provides rigorous statistical semantic privacy guarantees.
- An application of the framework to differential privacy which formalizes and then proves the statement that differential privacy "assumes" independence between records.
- Another application to differential privacy showing how to modify it in response to prior release of non-differentially private information (naive applications of differential privacy can lead to a privacy breach [22]).

- An application of the framework that allows us to expand the notion of composition between privacy definitions and to provide conditions under which certain types of composition hold.
- A general application to datasets with unbounded continuous variables; in particular, we show how to prevent an attacker from accurately inferring the value of an unbounded continuous attribute (both in terms of relative and absolute error). We further show how this is related to the protection of aggregate secrets.

The outline of the paper is as follows. In Section 2 we introduce basic concepts and notation. In Section 3 we present the Pufferfish framework. We discuss related work in Section 4. We show that Pufferfish satisfies fundamental privacy axioms in Section 5. Subsequent sections present a variety of applications of this framework. We use Pufferfish to analyze differential privacy and prove its record-independence assumption in Section 6. We show how to deal with continuous attributes and aggregate secrets in Section 7. We use Pufferfish to study composition in Section 8. We show how to provide privacy while accounting for prior data releases in Section 9. Proofs can be found in the full version of this paper.

2. NOTATION AND TERMINOLOGY

Let $\mathcal{I}$ be the set database instances that are possible for a given application. For datasets that are collections of records, we let $\mathcal{T}$ represent the domain of tuples, we use the symbol t to represent a value in the domain $\mathcal{T}$, and we use the variable r to represent a record.[1] For ease of explanation and to simplify notation, we will assume each individual is associated with at most one record; we note that the Pufferfish framework does not need this assumption.

In the setting we consider, a *data curator* has a dataset $\mathfrak{Data}$. Let records($\mathfrak{Data}$) denote the set of records in $\mathfrak{Data}$. To an *attacker* (who does not know what the dataset is), $\mathfrak{Data}$ represents a *random variable*. The data curator will choose a *privacy definition* and an *privacy mechanism* (algorithm) $\mathfrak{M}$ that satisfies that privacy definition. The data curator will then apply $\mathfrak{M}$ to the data to obtain a *sanitized output* $\omega \equiv \mathfrak{M}(\mathfrak{Data})$.

The attacker considers the true dataset $\mathfrak{Data}$ to be a random variable. We use the letter θ to represent a probability distribution and, for $D \in \mathcal{I}$, we will use the notation $P(\mathfrak{Data} = D \mid \theta)$ to represent the probability, under θ, that the true dataset is D. For convenience, we summarize the notation used in this paper in Table 1.

3. THE PUFFERFISH FRAMEWORK

The Pufferfish framework requires a domain expert to specify three crucial components: a set of *potential secrets* $\mathbb{S}$, a set of *discriminative pairs* $\mathbb{S}_{\text{pairs}} \subseteq \mathbb{S} \times \mathbb{S}$, and a collection of *data evolution scenarios* $\mathbb{D}$. We now describe these components in detail.

The set of potential secrets $\mathbb{S}$, is an explicit specification of what we would like to protect.[2] Examples include statements such as *"the record for individual h_i is in the*

$\mathcal{I}$	The set of possible database instances.
D	A dataset belonging to $\mathcal{I}$.
$\mathfrak{Data}$	A random variable representing the true dataset (which is unknown to the attacker).
$\mathcal{T}$	The domain of tuples.
t	A value in $\mathcal{T}$.
r_i	The ith record in a dataset.
$\mathcal{H}$	The set of all individuals. $\mathcal{H} = \{h_1, h_2, \dots\}$
$\mathbb{S}$	Set of potential secrets. Revealing s or $\neg s$ may be harmful if $s \in \mathbb{S}$.
σ_i	$r_i \in$ records($\mathfrak{Data}$): The statement that the record r_i belonging to individual h_i is in the data.
$\sigma_{(i,t)}$	$r_i \in$ records($\mathfrak{Data}$) $\wedge r_i = t$: The statement that the record r_i belonging to individual h_i has value $t \in \mathcal{T}$ and is in the data.
$\mathbb{S}_{\text{pairs}}$	Discriminative pairs. $\mathbb{S}_{\text{pairs}} \subset \mathbb{S} \times \mathbb{S}$.
$\mathbb{D}$	The set of evolution scenarios: a conservative collection of plausible data generating distributions.
θ	A probability distribution. The probability, under θ, that the data equals D_i is $P(\mathfrak{Data} = D_i \mid \theta)$.
$\mathfrak{M}$	A privacy mechanism: a deterministic or randomized algorithm (often used in the context of a privacy definition)

Table 1: Table of Notation

data", "the record for individual h_i is <u>not</u> in the data", "the query volume is $1 - 5$ million queries", etc. Additional examples can be found in Sections 3.2, 6, 7, and 9. A statement $s \in \mathbb{S}$ need not be true for the actual dataset – an attacker will form his own opinions about which statements are likely to be true or not. In general, a domain expert should add a statement s to the potential secrets $\mathbb{S}$ if either the claim that s is true or the claim that s is false can be harmful. The role of $\mathbb{S}$ is to provide a domain for the *discriminative pairs*, a subset of $\mathbb{S} \times \mathbb{S}$ which we discuss next.

The set of discriminative pairs $\mathbb{S}_{\text{pairs}}$ is a subset of $\mathbb{S} \times \mathbb{S}$. The role of $\mathbb{S}_{\text{pairs}}$ is to tell us *how* to protect the potential secrets $\mathbb{S}$. The main intuition is that for any discriminative pair (s_i, s_j), where $s_i \in \mathbb{S}$ and $s_j \in \mathbb{S}$, we would like to guarantee that attackers are unable to distinguish between the case where s_i is true of the actual data and the case where s_j is true of the actual data.[3] For this reason, s_i and s_j must be **mutually exclusive** but not necessarily exhaustive (it could be the case that neither is true). One example of a discriminative pair is ("Bob is in the table", "Bob is not in the table").

The discriminative pairs allow highly customizable privacy guarantees. For example, we can specify discriminative pairs such ("Bob has Cancer", "Bob has AIDS") to prevent inference about what disease Bob has (assuming only one disease is recorded). If, additionally we **avoid** specifying ("Bob is not healthy", "Bob is healthy"), then overall we are

---

[1] We treat records as random variables and tuples are the values they can take.

[2] After all, we cannot provide semantic guarantees if we do not know what the guarantees should be about.

[3] In general, this cannot be simulated by specifying all pairs of databases (D_k, D_ℓ) where s_i is true of D_k and s_j is true of D_ℓ – the resulting privacy definition (instantiated by Definition 3.1) will often be too strong because such D_k, D_ℓ pairs can differ almost arbitrarily.

allowing disclosure of whether Bob is sick or healthy, but if he is sick we are not allowing inference about the disease. For continuous attributes we can specify discriminative pairs of the form ("Bob's salary is $x \pm 10,000$", "Bob's salary is $[x + 20,000] \pm 10,000$") for all x to say that it is not ok to allow inference about Bob's salary to within an absolute error of $10,000$. We can similarly use this trick for aggregates to specify that it is not ok to allow inference about total number of sales to within $20,000$ units. Additional examples are given throughout the paper. We illustrate the particular importance of using discriminative pairs when we discuss continuous attributes in Section 7.

The evolution scenarios $\mathbb{D}$ can be viewed as a set of conservative assumptions about how the data evolved (or were generated) and about knowledge of potential attackers. Note that assumptions are absolutely necessary – privacy definitions that can provide privacy guarantees without making any assumptions provide little utility beyond the default approach of releasing nothing at all [22, 14]. Since the data curator wants to release useful information, the role of the domain expert will be to identify a reasonable set of assumptions; in many cases, they already do this informally [35]. More specifically, $\mathbb{D}$ is a set of probability distributions over $\mathcal{I}$ (the possible database instances). Each probability distribution $\theta \in \mathbb{D}$ corresponds to an attacker that we want to protect against and represents that attacker's belief in how the data were generated (incorporating any background knowledge and side information). We illustrate the importance of specifying these distributions in Section 6 where we analyze differential privacy. Below we give some examples of possible choices of $\mathbb{D}$ and their interpretations.

EXAMPLE 3.1 (NO ASSUMPTIONS). *$\mathbb{D}$ can consist of all possible probability distributions over database instances (i.e. including those with arbitrary correlations between records). This corresponds to making no assumptions. We explore this choice in Section 3.2.*

EXAMPLE 3.2 (I.I.D. DATA). *$\mathbb{D}$ can consist of all probability distributions over tables that generate records i.i.d. That is, for every f that is a distribution over $\mathcal{T}$ (domain of tuples), we have $\theta_f \in \mathbb{D}$ where the distribution θ_f is defined as: $P(\mathfrak{Data} = \{r_1, \ldots, r_n\} \mid \theta_f) = f(r_1) \times \cdots \times f(r_n)$. Thus each attacker can have a widely different opinion about the probability a random individual has cancer, etc. These attackers, however, do not have knowledge about specific individuals (for this, see Example 3.3).*

EXAMPLE 3.3 (INDEPENDENT BUT NOT I.I.D.). *$\mathbb{D}$ can consist of all probability distributions over tables where records are independent but may have different distributions. That is, $\mathbb{D}$ consists of all θ for which $P(\mathfrak{Data} = \{r_1, \ldots, r_n\} \mid \theta)$ equals $f_1(r_1) \times f_2(r_2) \times \cdots \times f_n(r_n)$ for arbitrary $f_1, f_2, \ldots, f_n$. That is, an attacker may know that the first individual is a smoker and so the corresponding record r_1 will have a different distribution than record r_2 which corresponds to an individual who is known to be a non-smoker. This is an extension of Example 3.2 where now attackers may have additional information about all individuals. Many additional variations are possible (i.e. attackers only have information about k individuals, etc.). We shall see in Section 6 the close connection between this example and differential privacy. Note that records here are still independent, so this choice of $\mathbb{D}$ may not be appropriate to social networks where correlations between records exist.*

Role of the domain expert. The goal of our framework is to make assumptions explicit. Thus the domain expert needs to specify the potential secrets $\mathbb{S}$ and discriminative pairs $\mathbb{S}_{pairs}$ (i.e. what should be protected) and evolution scenarios (data assumptions) $\mathbb{D}$ – are data records independent, what correlation structures exist, are attributes independent, etc. Thus to use the Pufferfish framework, the domain expert simply does what he or she does best. Most importantly, the domain expert is no longer required to be a privacy expert.

DEFINITION 3.1 (PUFFERFISH PRIVACY). *Given set of potential secrets $\mathbb{S}$, a set of discriminative pairs $\mathbb{S}_{pairs}$, a set of data evolution scenarios $\mathbb{D}$, and a privacy parameter $\epsilon > 0$, a (potentially randomized) algorithm $\mathfrak{M}$ satisfies ϵ-$\mathcal{P}$uffer$\mathcal{F}$ish$(\mathbb{S}, \mathbb{S}_{pairs}, \mathbb{D})$ privacy if*

- *for all possible outputs $\omega \in \text{range}(\mathfrak{M})$,*
- *for all pairs $(s_i, s_j) \in \mathbb{S}_{pairs}$ of potential secrets,*
- *for all distributions $\theta \in \mathbb{D}$ for which $P(s_i \mid \theta) \neq 0$ and $P(s_j \mid \theta) \neq 0$*

the following holds[4]:

$$P(\mathfrak{M}(\mathfrak{Data}) = \omega \mid s_i, \theta) \leq e^{\epsilon} P(\mathfrak{M}(\mathfrak{Data}) = \omega \mid s_j, \theta) \quad (1)$$

$$P(\mathfrak{M}(\mathfrak{Data}) = \omega \mid s_j, \theta) \leq e^{\epsilon} P(\mathfrak{M}(\mathfrak{Data}) = \omega \mid s_i, \theta) \quad (2)$$

The probabilities in Equations 1 and 2 depend on possible randomness in $\mathfrak{M}$ and as well as the randomness in the data. Note that $P(s_i \mid \theta) \neq 0$ is a technical condition which ensures that the conditional probability $P(\cdot \mid s_i, \theta)$ is defined. Operationally, it means we should focus on attackers (and their associated θ) who still have uncertainty about s_i and s_j (i.e. $P(s_i \mid \theta) \neq 0$ and $P(s_j \mid \theta) \neq 0$).

The Pufferfish framework differs from differential privacy [12] and its variants [11, 30, 5, 3, 22, 21, 25, 27, 18, 41, 33] in that it can provide precise guarantees about precisely what is being protected and under what conditions the protections hold. This enables a wide range of applications, such as those described in Sections 6, 7, 8, and 9. Other distinctions are discussed with related work in Section 4.1.

3.1 Semantic Guarantees

The semantic guarantees of the Pufferfish framework are best interpreted in terms of *odds* and *odds ratios*. If E_1 and E_2 are mutually exclusive events, then the *prior odds* of E_1 and E_2 is the fraction $\frac{P(E_1)}{P(E_2)}$. When the odds are equal to α, this simply means that E_1 is α times as likely as E_2. If we are given a piece of information A, it may alter the beliefs in the probabilities that E_1 or E_2 are true. For this reason we call $\frac{P(E_1 \mid A)}{P(E_2 \mid A)}$ the *posterior odds* of E_1 and E_2. If the prior odds and posterior odds are approximately equal, $\frac{P(E_1 \mid A)}{P(E_2 \mid A)} / \frac{P(E_1)}{P(E_2)} \approx 1$, then the event A did not provide information that was useful in discriminating between the case where E_1 was true or E_2 was true. The quantity $\frac{P(E_1 \mid A)}{P(E_2 \mid A)} / \frac{P(E_1)}{P(E_2)}$ is known as the *odds ratio* and reflects how much more likely event E_1 has become relative to E_2 after observing A.

---

[4]In the case of continuous outputs, these conditions are interpreted in terms of the density function or the Radon-Nikodym derivative and are required to hold *almost everywhere* - the ω for which the conditions are violated must have probability 0.

In the Pufferfish framework, each probability distribution $\theta \in \mathbb{D}$ corresponds to an attacker and reflects the attacker's probabilistic beliefs and background knowledge. For all $(s_i, s_j) \in \mathbb{S}_{\text{pairs}}$, all $\theta \in \mathbb{D}$ for which $P(s_i \mid \theta) \neq 0$ and $P(s_j \mid \theta) \neq 0$, and all $\omega \in \text{range}(\mathfrak{M})$, a simple calculation shows that Equations 1 and 2 in Definition 3.1 are equivalent to the condition:

$$e^{-\epsilon} \leq \frac{P(s_i \mid \mathfrak{M}(\boldsymbol{Data}) = \omega, \theta)}{P(s_j \mid \mathfrak{M}(\boldsymbol{Data}) = \omega, \theta)} \Big/ \frac{P(s_i \mid \theta)}{P(s_j \mid \theta)} \leq e^{\epsilon}$$

This is the odds ratio of s_i to s_j and has the following interpretation: **if an attacker thinks s_i is α times as likely as s_j then after seeing the sanitized output the attacker will believe s_i is at most $e^{\epsilon}\alpha$ times and at least $e^{-\epsilon}\alpha$ times as likely as s_j.** In other words, for small values of ϵ, seeing the sanitized output ω provides nearly no information gain to attackers who are trying to distinguish between whether s_i or s_j is true.

3.2 Example: Privacy with no Assumptions

As a warmup, we use Pufferfish to create a privacy definition with no assumptions (a re-interpretation of no-free-lunch privacy [22]). Let $\mathcal{T}$ be the domain of tuples and let $\mathcal{H} = \{h_1, \dots, h_N\}$ be the set of all individuals. Define σ_i to be the statement *"the record belonging to individual h_i is in the data"* and define $\sigma_{(i,t)}$ to be the statement *"the record belonging to individual h_i is in the data and has value t"*. Define the set of potential secrets $\mathbb{S}$ and discriminative pairs $\mathbb{S}_{\text{pairs}}$ to be:

$$\mathbb{S} = \{\sigma_1, \dots, \sigma_N\} \cup \{\sigma_{i,t} \ : \ i = 1, \dots, N \wedge t \in \mathcal{T}\} \quad (3)$$

$$\mathbb{S}_{\text{pairs}} = \big\{ (\sigma_{(i,t_a)}, \sigma_{(i,t_b)}) \ : \ i = 1, \dots, N \wedge t_a, t_b \in \mathcal{T} \big\}$$
$$\cup \{(\sigma_i, \neg\sigma_i) \ : \ i = 1, \dots, N\} \quad (4)$$

with the interpretation that for every individual h_i we want to avoid leaking information about whether or not the record of h_i is in the data (this is specified by the discriminative pair $(\sigma_i, \neg\sigma_i)$), and if an attacker already believes h_i is in the data, we want to avoid leaking information about the value of the corresponding record (this is specified by the discriminative pairs $(\sigma_{(i,t_a)}, \sigma_{(i,t_b)})$ where t_a and t_b range over all possible tuple values).

To get privacy with no assumptions, we must make the set of distributional assumptions $\mathbb{D}$ as large as possible. That is, we set $\mathbb{D}$ to be the collection of all probability distributions over database instances (i.e. records in a database need not be independent), as in Example 3.1.

THEOREM 3.1. *Let $\epsilon > 0$, let $\mathbb{S}$ and $\mathbb{S}_{pairs}$ be specified as in Equations 3 and 4 and let $\mathbb{D}$ be the set of all possible distributions over database instances. Then an algorithm $\mathfrak{M}$ satisfies ϵ-$\mathcal{P}$uffer$\mathcal{F}$ish$(\mathbb{S}, \mathbb{S}_{pairs}, \mathbb{D})$ if and only if for **every** pair of databases D_1 and D_2 and every $\omega \in \text{range}(\mathfrak{M})$,*

$$e^{-\epsilon} P(\mathfrak{M}(D_2) = \omega) \leq P(\mathfrak{M}(D_1) = \omega) \leq e^{\epsilon} P(\mathfrak{M}(D_2) = \omega)$$

Note that the randomness here only depends on $\mathfrak{M}$ because each of the D_1 and D_2 are given databases (and hence not random). From this warmup example, we see that if we make no assumptions then the goal is to prevent an attacker from distinguishing between any possible input datasets; the result is a total lack of utility. Note that this warmup shows a formal equivalence between Pufferfish with no assumptions and a strawman privacy definition called no-free-lunch privacy that was used in [22] as an example of a privacy definition without utility.

4. RELATED WORK

4.1 Relation to Differential Privacy Variants

One can view the Pufferfish framework as a substantial generalization of differential privacy. Thus we explain the differences between Pufferfish and differential privacy [12] and its variants [11, 30, 5, 3, 22, 21, 25, 27, 18, 41, 33].

A related framework, known as adversarial privacy [33] allows domain experts to plug in various data generating distributions. While there is no known equivalence between adversarial privacy and differential privacy, Rastogi et al. [33] have proved an equivalence between a certain instantiation of adversarial privacy and a variant of differential privacy known as ϵ-indistinguishability (the main difference with differential privacy is the requirement that neighboring databases have the same size) [13]. Adversarial privacy also only seeks to protect the presence/absence of a tuple in the dataset. In contrast, Pufferfish is more flexible. We can prove equivalences between instantiations of Pufferfish and differential privacy as well as ϵ-indistinguishability. Pufferfish also allows more fine-grained protection of a tuple (such as preventing inference of continuous attributes to within a certain absolute error) and can handle aggregate secrets as well. As a result, Pufferfish supports a wide variety of applications such as those in Sections 6, 7, 8, and 9.

Zhou et al. [41] present two variants of differential privacy (δ-constrained and ZLW distributional) whose privacy semantics are unclear. We show approximate equivalences to instantiations of the Pufferfish framework in Section 7.3, thereby providing approximate semantics for those definitions as well.

In general, the difference between Pufferfish and related work is the wide variety of applications it can support, such as those discussed in this paper. This flexibility is the result of a different philosophy about how to phrase privacy definitions. Differential privacy uses concepts like neighboring databases (i.e. those that differ on only one tuple) and tries to avoid making any statements about data probabilities. As we show in Sections 6, 7.3, and 9, that approach can obscure what semantic guarantees are provided and the conditions under which they are provided. Pufferfish takes the opposite approach by focusing directly on what an attacker can infer.

As with [11, 3, 41, 33], Pufferfish explicitly uses data-generating probabilities. Furthermore, like adversarial privacy [33], Pufferfish allows more general probability distributions (records do not have to be independent). This allows us to compare Pufferfish to differential privacy and to show that differential privacy is an instantiation of the Pufferfish framework under an assumption of independence between records (Section 6). The difference with those pieces of work is the following.

The concept of neighboring databases arose in differential privacy from the desire to protect individual records; thus two databases are neighbors if they differ on one record. In subsequent variations, the concept of neighbors (or some generalization) plays a key role [11, 30, 5, 22, 21, 25, 27, 41, 18]. Of the remaining work, adversarial privacy [33] only seeks to protect inference about the presence of a tuple, while BLR distributional privacy [3] does not indicate what secrets it protects. One of the distinguishing approaches of the Pufferfish framework is that it does not search for "the right notion of neighbors" (which can obscure what it is we are trying to protect). Instead, it focuses on the actual secrets to be protected $\mathbb{S}$ and how they are to be protected via the discriminative pairs $\mathbb{S}_{\text{pairs}}$.

The combination of distributional assumptions and allowing explicit (and arbitrary) choices of what to protect give Pufferfish its flexibility and allow the applications described in this paper.

4.2 Relationship to Other Work

Other privacy frameworks also exist. A large class, of which k-anonymity [34] is perhaps the most well known, are known as *syntactic methods* because they are mainly concerned with the syntactic form of the outputs $\omega \in \text{range}(\mathfrak{M})$ rather than the probabilities that govern the relationship between inputs to outputs: $P(\mathfrak{M}(D_i) = \omega)$. Because of this, the resulting privacy definitions tend to be less secure and are often subject to new kinds of attacks (see the surveys [6, 16, 1] for more details). It is also often not clear what data assumptions those definitions are making.

The protection of aggregate information gets less attention than the problem of protecting individual records. The protection of aggregates is most relevant to business data where aggregates reflect different kinds of business secrets. Much of the work in this area is called *knowledge hiding* and focuses on hiding association rules, frequent itemsets, and classification rules (e.g., [9, 7, 31, 38, 37, 28, 8, 2, 39, 10, 36, 29]) that are deemed to be sensitive. Work in this area generally follows the syntactic paradigm and it is often unclear what rigorous privacy guarantees can be provided or what data assumptions are needed for ensuring privacy.

5. PUFFERFISH AND PRIVACY AXIOMS

Research in statistical privacy has been moving away from ad-hoc privacy definitions and towards formal and rigorous privacy definitions. The reason is that rigorous privacy definitions offer the promise of ending the endless cycle of discovering a vulnerability in a privacy definition, proposing a fix, finding a vulnerability in the "fixed" version, etc. (see [6] for some examples).

To this end, recent research has started examining the properties that privacy definitions need to have [21, 20]. Modern design guidelines for privacy definitions include 2 fundamental axioms known as *transformation invariance* and *convexity* [20]. While the ideas contained in the axioms have been accepted by the privacy community for a long time, only recently has there been an insistence that privacy definitions actually satisfy them (in fact, many of the vulnerabilities associated with definitions such as k-anonymity are a direct result of not satisfying those axioms [24]).

In this section we show that every privacy definition in the Pufferfish framework satisfies both fundamental axioms, thus ensuring that it satisfies modern design guidelines.

The axioms are:

AXIOM 5.1. (Transformation Invariance [20]). *If an algorithm $\mathfrak{M}$ satisfies a privacy definition and $\mathcal{A}$ is any algorithm such that (1) its domain contains the range of $\mathfrak{M}$ and (2) its random bits (if any) are statistically independent from the random bits (if any) of $\mathfrak{M}$, then the algorithm $\mathcal{A} \circ \mathfrak{M}$, which first runs $\mathfrak{M}$ on the data and then runs $\mathcal{A}$ on the output should also satisfy the same privacy definition.*

The justification for the transformation invariance axiom is that $\mathcal{A}$ is an algorithm whose only input is the output of $\mathfrak{M}$ and so it simulates a data analyst who is performing a statistical analysis using the output of $\mathfrak{M}$; thus it would be strange if a privacy definition implied the output ω of $\mathfrak{M}$ was safe to release, but the results of the statistical analysis on this output ω were not (many existing privacy definitions fail to satisfy this property [20]).

AXIOM 5.2 (CONVEXITY [20]). *If $\mathfrak{M}_1$ and $\mathfrak{M}_2$ satisfy a privacy definition, and $p \in [0, 1]$, then the algorithm $\mathfrak{M}^p$ which runs $\mathfrak{M}_1$ with probability p and $\mathfrak{M}_2$ with probability $1 - p$ should also satisfy the privacy definition.*

The convexity axiom says that a data curator is allowed to choose any algorithm $\mathfrak{M}$ that satisfies the curator's chosen privacy definition and that this choice can be randomized (thus adding further uncertainty into the creation of sanitized data). Again, most proposed existing privacy definitions fail to satisfy this property.

The following theorem confirms that the Pufferfish framework satisfies modern privacy design guidelines.

THEOREM 5.1. *For every $\mathbb{S}$, $\mathbb{S}_{\text{pairs}}$, $\mathbb{D}$, and $\epsilon > 0$, the privacy definition ϵ-$\mathcal{P}$uffer$\mathcal{F}$ish$(\mathbb{S}, \mathbb{S}_{\text{pairs}}, \mathbb{D})$ satisfies the axioms of convexity and transformation invariance.*

6. PUFFERFISH ANALYSIS OF DIFFERENTIAL PRIVACY

Differential privacy [12] is a state of the art privacy definition which has been very influential in modern privacy research. It is formally defined as:

DEFINITION 6.1 (DIFFERENTIAL PRIVACY [12]). *Given a privacy parameter $\epsilon > 0$, an algorithm $\mathfrak{M}$ satisfies ϵ-differential privacy if for all $\omega \in \text{range}(\mathfrak{M})$ and all pairs of datasets D_i and D_j that differ on the presence of one tuple (i.e. D_i can be derived from D_j by either adding or deleting exactly one tuple), the following holds:*

$$P(\mathfrak{M}(D_i) = \omega) \le e^\epsilon P(\mathfrak{M}(D_j) = \omega)$$

where the probability only depends on the randomness in $\mathfrak{M}$.

This definition has several interpretations: (1) for small ϵ, changing the value of any tuple is unlikely to change the output of $\mathfrak{M}$; (2) an attacker who knows all but one tuples will not learn much about the remaining tuple.

Because neither the definition of differential privacy nor its interpretations mentioned any data-generating distributions, many believed that it was applicable to any setting and that it made no assumptions about the data. These misconceptions were challenged in recent work [18, 22].

With the Pufferfish framework, we can address these claims in a more precise manner. We can answer questions such as: *for what data evolution scenarios $\mathbb{D}$ is ϵ-differential privacy equal to the privacy definition ϵ-$\mathcal{P}$uffer$\mathcal{F}$ish$(\mathbb{S}, \mathbb{S}_{\text{pairs}}, \mathbb{D})$?*. We will see that the appropriate $\mathbb{D}$ requires independence between records[5], thus formalizing the claim that differential privacy assumes tuple independence.

We will do this by formulating a probabilistic model of record independence to define the data evolution scenarios $\mathbb{D}$. With this choice of $\mathbb{D}$ we show that ϵ-differential privacy is an instantiation of the Pufferfish framework (Theorem 6.1). We also show that if $\mathbb{D}$ contains distributions

---

[5] i.e. the assumption (depending on the application) of independence between medical records, edges in a social network, queries in a search log, etc.

with correlated records then the resulting Pufferfish instantiation is strictly stronger than ϵ-differential privacy (Theorem 6.2); alternatively, under correlations between records, ϵ-differential privacy is not strong enough to guarantee that the changes in attacker's beliefs (*viz.* the semantic guarantees represented by the odds ratio in Section 3.1) are bounded by a factor of e^ϵ (hence the bounds on an attacker's inference that result from uses of ϵ-differential privacy degrade under correlations).

To proceed, we must first specify the potential secrets $\mathbb{S}$ and discriminative pairs $\mathbb{S}_{\text{pairs}}$. Let $\mathcal{T}$ be the domain of tuples. Let $\mathcal{H} = \{h_1, h_2, \ldots, h_N\}$ be the set of all individuals in a population of size N. Define σ_i to be the statement $r_i \in \text{records}(\mathbf{Data})$ (i.e. *"record r_i belonging to individual h_i is in the data"*) and let $\sigma_{(i,t)}$ be the statement $r_i \in \text{records}(\mathbf{Data}) \wedge r_i = t$ (i.e. *"record r_i belonging to individual h_i has value t and is in the data"*). Let

$$\mathbb{S} = \left\{ \sigma_{(i,t)} \ : \ h_i \in \mathcal{H}, \ t \in \mathcal{T} \right\} \cup \left\{ \neg\sigma_i \ : \ h_i \in \mathcal{H} \right\} \quad (5)$$

$$\mathbb{S}_{\text{pairs}} = \left\{ (\sigma_{(i,t)}, \neg\sigma_i) \ : \ h_i \in \mathcal{H}, t \in \mathcal{T} \right\} \quad (6)$$

Thus for any individual h_i in the population $\mathcal{H}$ and any possible tuple value $t \in \mathcal{T}$, the goal is to prevent an attacker from distinguishing whether the record r_i belonging to h_i is in the data and has value t vs. the data has no record about individual h_i (this is our mathematical translation of the goals in [12]).

For the probabilistic model, suppose each individual h_i is associated with distributions π_i and f_i in the following roles:

- The probability that record r_i belonging to individual h_i is in the data is $P(r_i \in \text{records}(\mathbf{Data})) \equiv P(\sigma_i) = \pi_i$.

- $P(r_i = t \mid r_i \in \text{records}(\mathbf{Data})) \equiv P(\sigma_{(i,t)} \mid \sigma_i) = f_i(t)$

With this notation, the model is:

$$\theta \equiv \{\pi_1, \ldots, \pi_N, f_1, \ldots, f_N\} \quad (7)$$

$$P(\mathbf{Data} \mid \theta) = \prod_{r_i \in \text{records}(\mathbf{Data})} f_i(r_i)\pi_i \prod_{r_j \notin \text{records}(\mathbf{Data})} (1 - \pi_j)$$

In other words, the presence/absence/record-value of each individual is independent of the presence/absence/record-values of other individuals. We set $\mathbb{D}$ to be the set of all possible probability distributions of the form given in Equation 7 (i.e. for all possible choices of the π_i and f_i).

The following theorem says that under this probabilistic model, ϵ-differential privacy becomes an instantiation of the Pufferfish framework.

THEOREM 6.1. *Let $\mathbb{S}$ and $\mathbb{S}_{pairs}$ be defined as in Equations 5 and 6. Let $\mathbb{D}^*$ be the set of all distributions of the form specified in Equation 7. With these choices, ϵ-differential privacy is equivalent to ϵ-$\mathcal{P}uffer\mathcal{F}ish(\mathbb{S}, \mathbb{S}_{pairs}, \mathbb{D}^*)$.*

The following theorem says that if we have any correlations between records, then some differentially private algorithms leak more information than is allowable (under the odds ratio semantics in Section 3.1), in which case an attacker's posterior beliefs may differ significantly from the prior beliefs depending on the strength of the correlation.

THEOREM 6.2. *Let $\mathbb{S}$ and $\mathbb{S}_{pairs}$ be defined as in Equations 5 and 6. Let $\mathbb{D}^*$ be the set of all distributions of the form specified in Equation 7. If we choose the data evolution scenarios $\mathbb{D}_{other}$ such that $\mathbb{D}_{other} \not\subseteq \mathbb{D}^*$ then ϵ-differential privacy is not equivalent to ϵ-$\mathcal{P}uffer\mathcal{F}ish(\mathbb{S}, \mathbb{S}_{pairs}, \mathbb{D}_{other})$ (i.e.*

with the same ϵ-parameter) and hence does not bound the odds-ratio to the interval $[e^{-\epsilon}, e^\epsilon]$.

Similar results can be shown for ϵ-indistinguishability (defined in [13]).

7. CONTINUOUS ATTRIBUTES AND AGGREGATE SECRETS

One of the difficult problems in privacy-preserving data publishing is protecting the values of continuous variables that are not a priori bounded or which are bounded but can take very large values (such as income). For example, many algorithms for differential privacy do not work in the first case (i.e. no a priori bound) [13] and provide poor utility in the second case.

In this section we use the Pufferfish framework to provide a solution to this problem (Section 7.1). This application shows the importance of specifying discriminative pairs $\mathbb{S}_{\text{pairs}}$. We then show how this solution can be used to protect aggregate secrets (Section 7.2). Finally, we use Pufferfish to provide approximate privacy semantics for δ-constrained α-differential privacy [41] and ZLW distributional privacy [41] (Section 7.3); those two definitions were also designed for continuous attributes but their semantic guarantees and conditions under which those guarantees hold were not clear.

7.1 Protecting Continuous Attributes

As we saw in Section 6, differential privacy is designed to make it difficult to distinguish between the case when an individual's record was included in the data with value t or whether it was not in the data at all. This has to be true whether $t = 1$ or $t = 1,000,000$ (e.g., in the case where the tuple domain $\mathcal{T} = [0, 10^6]$). To account for the possibility that the record of one individual could dominate an aggregate statistic such as $SUM(t)$, an algorithm such as the Laplace mechanism [12] needs to add noise with standard deviation proportional to 10^6 in order to satisfy differential privacy (thus potentially masking out the signal in the data).

If this loss of utility is unacceptable, the data curator may want to relax privacy by stating requirements such as (1) an attacker should not be able to infer any individual's salary to within an absolute error of less than 1,000, or (2) an attacker should not be able to infer any individual's salary to within a relative error of 10%. Both of these requirements can be handled in the Pufferfish framework.

7.1.1 Privacy via Absolute Error

For ease of explanation, suppose that records belonging to individuals $h_1, \ldots, h_n$ are known to be in the data and suppose the data curator only collects an individual's income so that the domain of tuples is $\mathbb{R}^+$, the set of nonnegative real numbers (hence the domain is an unbounded set). If we are interested in preventing inference about income that is within absolute error k, then we can proceed as follows. Let $\sigma_{i,[x-k,x+k]}$ be the statement "the income of individual h_i is in the range $[x - k, x + k]$". Define

$$\mathbb{S} = \left\{ \sigma_{i,[x-k,x+k]} \ : \ i = 1, \ldots, n, \ x \in [0, \infty) \right\} \quad (8)$$

We set discriminative pairs to be neighboring intervals (note that the intervals are half-open so that each discriminative pair consists of mutually exclusive statements). With this setting, we are requiring that the attackers should have difficulty in distinguishing between whether someone's income is between $y-k$ and $y+k$ or a neighboring interval $[y+k, y+3k)$ or $[y-3k, y-k)$ thus ensuring that inference to within $\pm k$ is not possible. Formally,

$$\mathbb{S}_{\text{pairs}} = \left\{ (\sigma_{i,[x-k,x+k)}, \sigma_{i,[x+k,x+3k)}) \ : \ \begin{smallmatrix} i=1,\ldots,n \\ x \in [0,\infty) \end{smallmatrix} \right\} \quad (9)$$

We can set the evolution scenarios $\mathbb{D}$ to be the set of all probability distributions that assign incomes to individuals $h_1, \ldots, h_n$ independently. Thus the model is:

$$\theta \equiv [f_1, \ldots, f_n] \quad (10)$$
$$P(\mathfrak{Data} \mid \theta) = \prod_{r_i \in \text{records}(\mathfrak{Data})} f_i(r_i)$$

where the interpretation of the probability (as a probability mass function or density function) depends on whether the f_i are continuous or not. We set $\mathbb{D}$ to be all probability distributions of the form given in Equation 10 (i.e. for all choices of $f_1, \ldots, f_n$).

With the resulting instantiation $\epsilon\text{-}\mathcal{P}\text{uffer}\mathcal{F}\text{ish}(\mathbb{S}, \mathbb{S}_{\text{pairs}}, \mathbb{D})$, the following lemma shows that we can answer the query "what is the sum of the salaries" as follows. Let $t_1, \ldots, t_n$ be the tuple values. Compute $X + \sum_{i=1}^{n} t_i$ where X is a random variable drawn from the Laplace$(4k/\epsilon)$ distribution with density function $\frac{\epsilon}{8k} e^{-\epsilon|x|/4k}$. Note that when the data set size n is large, the true average salary $\frac{\sum_{i=1}^{n} t_i}{n}$ and the noisy average (i.e. this noisy sum divided by n) are very close to each other with high probability. In contrast, satisfying differential privacy by adding noise to the sum would require a distribution with infinite variance (i.e. not possible) since there is no upper bound on tuple values; thus the relaxation created using Pufferfish allows more utility while clearly describing the privacy lost (i.e. income is inferable to an absolute error of $\geq k$ but to no smaller range).

LEMMA 7.1. *With $\mathbb{S}$ and $\mathbb{S}_{pairs}$ defined in Equations 8 and 9 let $\mathbb{D}$ be the set of all probability distributions having the form specified in Equation 10. The algorithm $\mathfrak{M}$ which returns $X + \sum_{i=1}^{n} t_i$ where X has density $\frac{\epsilon}{8k} e^{-\epsilon|x|/4k}$ satisfies $\epsilon\text{-}\mathcal{P}\text{uffer}\mathcal{F}\text{ish}(\mathbb{S}, \mathbb{S}_{pairs}, \mathbb{D})$.*

7.1.2 Privacy via Relative Error

We can extend these ideas to protect against inference to within a prespecified *relative error* as well. One way to approach this problem is to choose $c \in (0, 1)$ and define $\sigma_{i,[cy,y/c)}$ to be the statement that "the income of individual h_i is in the range $[cy, y/c)$". Thus, for example, to express inference to within 10% we set $c = 0.1$. We define the set of potential secrets to be:

$$\mathbb{S} = \left\{ \sigma_{i,[cy,y/c)} \ : \ i = 1, \ldots, n, \ y > 0 \right\}$$

The discriminative pairs are again neighboring intervals. With this setting, we are requiring that the attackers should have difficulty in distinguishing between whether someone's income is in the interval $[cy, y/c)$ – whose center in terms of geometric mean is y – or a neighboring interval $[y/c, y/c^3)$ or $[cy, c^3 y)$, thus limiting the attacker's ability to infer the income to within a factor of c. Formally,

$$\mathbb{S}_{\text{pairs}} = \left\{ (\sigma_{i,[cy,y/c)}, \sigma_{i,[y/c,y/c^3)}) \ : \ i = 1, \ldots, n, \ y > 0 \right\}$$

As in the case of absolute error, we can set the evolution scenarios $\mathbb{D}$ to be the set of all data-generating distribu-

tions that generate records independently (but not necessarily i.i.d.):

$$\theta \equiv [f_1, \ldots, f_n] \quad (11)$$
$$P(\mathfrak{Data} \mid \theta) = \prod_{r_i \in \text{records}(\mathfrak{Data})} f_i(r_i)$$

Now note that $t \in [cy, y/c)$ if and only if $\log t \in [y + \log c, y - \log c)$ and so protecting y for relative error becomes the same as protecting $\log y$ for absolute error $\pm \log c$. Thus this version of relative error is reduced to the case of absolute error, and so we can protect tuples by applying additive noise to the logarithm, or, equivalently by using multiplicative noise.

7.2 Aggregate Secrets

In this section we discuss how Pufferfish can be used to protect aggregate information (as in business data). The discussion is brief because this is a simple extension of the ideas in Sections 7.1.1 and 7.1.2; yet the discussion is necessary because there is little focus in the literature on rigorous and formal privacy guarantees for business data.[6]

In some cases a business may have a large dataset $\mathfrak{Data} = \{r_1, \ldots, r_n\}$ that can be considered to be an i.i.d. sample from some distribution. The business may decide that letting the public learn about this distribution is acceptable. The business may reason as follows: if an attacker had a large dataset generated independently from that distribution, the attacker may learn that distribution and use it to make inferences about the business's own data. For example, the attacker may use the gained knowledge about the true distribution to infer $\sum_{i=1}^{n} r_i$ up to an additive error of $O(\sqrt{n})$ with high probability (i.e. sampling error). Thus the business may consider it acceptable to create a data release as long as one cannot infer certain sums to within $\pm\sqrt{n}$.

Let μ be a metric over datasets. We define $\sigma_{[\mu,D,\delta]}$ to be the statement that $\mu(\mathfrak{Data}, D) \leq \delta$ and $\sigma^*_{[\mu,D,\delta]}$ to be the statement that $2\delta \geq \mu(\mathfrak{Data}, D) > \delta$. The set of potential secrets and discriminative pairs could then be defined as:

$$\mathbb{S}_\delta = \left\{ \sigma_{[\mu,D,\delta]} \ : \ D \in \mathcal{I} \right\} \cup \left\{ \sigma^*_{[\mu,D,\delta]} \ : \ D \in \mathcal{I} \right\} \quad (12)$$
$$\mathbb{S}_{\text{pairs}_\delta} = \left\{ (\sigma_{[\mu,D,\delta]}, \sigma^*_{[\mu,D,\delta]}) \mid D \in \mathcal{I} \right\} \quad (13)$$

where δ could be set to $\sqrt{n}$ and the data evolution scenarios can be the set of all distributions over $\mathcal{I}$ in which records are generated i.i.d. or just independently.

Note that one can union the potential secrets in Equations 12 and 8 and union the discriminative pairs in Equations 13 and 9 to protect both aggregate information and secrets about individuals.

7.3 δ-Constrained and Distributional Privacy

Zhou et al. [41] also proposed two privacy definitions that can be used with continuous variables. Those definitions were introduced solely for the study of utility and their precise privacy semantics (i.e. what inferences do they protect against) were not explained nor explored. As with differential privacy, they are phrased in terms of databases that should be indistinguishable. As a result the privacy guarantees and conditions under which they hold are not clear. We show an approximate equivalence between those privacy definitions and instantiations of Pufferfish, so that the Pufferfish framework (approximately) subsumes those definitions

_____
[6]Even nonrigorous approaches are rare for business data.

and gives them clearer privacy semantics. We start with those definitions:

DEFINITION 7.1. (Constrained and ZLW-Distributional Privacy [41]) *Let μ be a metric and let $\delta > 0$ and $\epsilon > 0$ be constants. Let $\mathfrak{M}$ be an algorithm. For all $\omega \in \text{range}(\mathfrak{M})$, if the following constraints hold*

$$e^{-\epsilon} P(\mathfrak{M}(D_2) = \omega) \leq P(\mathfrak{M}(D_1) = \omega) \leq e^{\epsilon} P(\mathfrak{M}(D_2) = \omega)$$

- *whenever D_1 and D_2 differ on the value of 1 tuple and $\mu(D_1, D_2) \leq \delta$ then algorithm $\mathfrak{M}$ satisfies $\underline{\delta\text{-constrained}}$ $\underline{\epsilon\text{-differential privacy}}$.*
- *If those conditions hold when (1) D_1 and D_2 belong to a prespecified countable subset $S \subset \mathcal{I}$ and (2) $\mu(D_1, D_2) < \delta$ and (3) $D_1 \cap D_2 \neq 0$ then algorithm $\mathfrak{M}$ satisfies $\underline{ZLW}$ $\underline{(\epsilon, \delta)\text{-distributional privacy}}$[7].*

First, note that δ-constrained ϵ-differential privacy with metric μ is equal to ZLW (ϵ, δ^*)-distributional privacy with a properly chosen metric μ^* that combines Hamming distance with the metric μ, an appropriate choice of δ^*, and setting $S = \mathcal{I}$. Thus, we can focus only on ZLW distributional privacy. Second, the condition $D_1 \cap D_2 = \emptyset$ is also not necessary since it can also be achieved by proper choice of metric (we therefore drop this condition to increase generality). Third, it is not clear what (if any) privacy semantics are produced by the condition $D_1, D_2 \in S$. Thus we remove this condition (i.e. set $S = \mathcal{I}$) and use Pufferfish to provide approximate semantics to the resulting definition:

DEFINITION 7.2. (Modified ZLW-Privacy). *Let μ be a metric and let $\delta > 0$ and $\epsilon > 0$ be constants. An algorithm $\mathfrak{M}$ satisfies (ϵ, δ)-modified ZLW privacy if for every $\omega \in \text{range}(\mathfrak{M})$ and every pair of databases D_1, D_2 such that $\mu(D_1, D_2) \leq \delta$, the following conditions hold:*

$$e^{-\epsilon} P(\mathfrak{M}(D_2) = \omega) \leq P(\mathfrak{M}(D_1) = \omega) \leq e^{\epsilon} P(\mathfrak{M}(D_2) = \omega)$$

The approximate equivalence (subject to a mild condition on μ) to a Pufferfish instantiation is the following:

THEOREM 7.1. *Let μ be a metric over database instances such that whenever $\mu(D_1, D_2) \leq \delta$ there exists[8] a $D^* \in \mathcal{I}$ with $\mu(D_1, D^*) \leq \delta$ and $\mu(D_2, D^*) > \delta$. Let $\epsilon > 0$ and $\delta > 0$. Set $\mathbb{S}_\delta$ as in Equation 12 and $\mathbb{S}_{pairs_\delta}$ as in Equation 13. Define $\mathbb{D}$ to be the set of distributions over dataset instances with n records where record values are independent (e.g., all distributions of the form given in Equation 11). If $\mathfrak{M}$ satisfies ϵ-$\mathcal{P}uffer\mathcal{F}ish(\mathbb{S}_\delta, \mathbb{S}_{pairs_\delta}, \mathbb{D})$ then it also satisfies (ϵ, δ)-modified ZLW privacy; conversely, if $\mathfrak{M}$ satisfies (ϵ, δ)-modified ZLW privacy then it satisfies the definition 4ϵ-$\mathcal{P}uffer\mathcal{F}ish(\mathbb{S}_\delta, \mathbb{S}_{pairs_\delta}, \mathbb{D})$ (i.e. up to a four-fold degradation of semantic guarantees in terms of odds-ratio).*

Thus although the precise privacy semantics of the ZLW privacy definitions [41] are unknown, the ideas discussed in Sections 7.1.1, 7.1.2, and 7.2 combined with Theorem 7.1 show that the Pufferfish framework can give the ZLW privacy definitions some approximate semantics in terms of an odds-ratio bound of $4e^\epsilon$ when protecting secrets about a database to within absolute error (as defined by the metric μ) of $\pm \delta$.

---

[7]We use the prefix ZLW to distinguish it from the distributional privacy definition introduced in [3].

[8]This condition is achieved, for example, by the L_1 norm, L_2 norm, etc. as long as δ is less than the radius of $\mathcal{I}$.

8. COMPOSITION

Given a privacy definition, the notion of *composition* [17] refers to the degradation of privacy due to two independent data releases. For example, Alice may choose two algorithms $\mathfrak{M}_1$ and $\mathfrak{M}_2$ (whose random bits are independent of each other), run both on the same data and publish both results. Alternatively, Alice and Bob may have overlapping datasets; they can each run an algorithm $\mathfrak{M}_{Alice}$ and $\mathfrak{M}_{Bob}$ (possibly satisfying different privacy definitions) on their own dataset and output the result. It is known that privacy can degrade in those instances. For example, two independent releases of k-anonymous tables can lead to a privacy breach [17]. Also, a differentially private release combined with a release of deterministic statistics can also lead to a breach [22]. On the other hand, differential privacy composes well with itself: if Alice uses an ϵ_1-differentially private algorithm and Bob uses an ϵ_2-differentially private algorithm, the result (from an attacker's perspective) is the same as if Alice and Bob pooled their data and used an $(\epsilon_1 + \epsilon_2)$-differentially private algorithm.

Properly handling multiple data releases requires a mixture of policy and technological solutions. If Alice is planning multiple data releases, Alice needs to account for information leaked by her prior data releases. If Alice and Bob are planning to release sanitized data, they need to coordinate their efforts if their raw data are correlated. That is, they need to agree on a technological solution that guarantees that the combination of their data releases will not breach privacy.

8.1 Pufferfish View of Composition

Since the Pufferfish framework provides a wide variety of privacy definitions, it allows us to study composition more generally. The key point is that, as before, we need to specify probabilistic assumptions about how datasets are related.

Suppose Alice has a dataset $\mathfrak{Data}_{Alice}$ and Bob has a dataset $\mathfrak{Data}_{Bob}$. Alice announces that she will use a privacy definition $\mathcal{P}uffer\mathcal{F}ish(\mathbb{S}, \mathbb{S}_{pairs}, \mathbb{D})$ to publish a sanitized version of her data and Bob announces that he will use a privacy definition $\mathfrak{Priv}$ (which need not belong to the Pufferfish framework). Alice would like to examine the consequences to privacy that can occur when they both release sanitized data using their chosen privacy definitions.

In order for Alice to study how her privacy definition composes with possible data releases from Bob, she needs to consider *all* the different plausible relationships between her dataset and Bob's dataset. Thus she also needs to specify a $\underline{set}$ $\mathcal{C}ond$ of conditional probability distributions of Bob's data given her own.[9] Each $\phi \in \mathcal{C}ond$ specifies a conditional probability distribution $P(\mathfrak{Data}_{Bob} = D' \mid \mathfrak{Data}_{Alice} = D, \phi)$. The distributions $\phi \in \mathcal{C}ond$ and $\theta \in \mathbb{D}$ combine to form a joint distribution:

$$P(\mathfrak{Data}_{Bob} \wedge \mathfrak{Data}_{Alice} \mid \phi, \theta)$$
$$= P(\mathfrak{Data}_{Bob} \mid \mathfrak{Data}_{Alice}, \phi) P(\mathfrak{Data}_{Alice} \mid \theta)$$

Alice can then reason as follows. For the moment, suppose Bob has already chosen to apply an algorithm $\mathcal{A}$ to his data. Alice can study the effect of releasing the output of $\mathfrak{M}(\mathfrak{Data}_{Alice})$ by considering the distributions in $\theta \in \mathbb{D}$ and

---

[9]Thus we decompose the joint distribution of $\mathfrak{Data}_{Alice}$ and $\mathfrak{Data}_{Bob}$ into the marginal distribution of $\mathfrak{Data}_{Alice}$ and the conditional distribution of $\mathfrak{Data}_{Bob}$ given $\mathfrak{Data}_{Alice}$.

$\phi \in \mathcal{C}ond$. Simulating an adversary's reasoning, for each $(s_i, s_j) \in \mathbb{S}_{\text{pairs}}$, $\omega \in \text{range}(\mathfrak{M})$, $\omega^* \in \text{range}(\mathcal{A})$, she derives:

$$P(\mathcal{A}(\mathfrak{Data}_{\text{Bob}}) = \omega^* \wedge \mathfrak{M}(\mathfrak{Data}_{\text{Alice}}) = \omega \mid s_i, \phi, \theta)$$

$$= \int \left(\begin{array}{c} P(\mathfrak{M}(D)=\omega)P(\mathfrak{Data}_{\text{Alice}}=D) \mid s_i, \theta) \\ \times E[P(\mathcal{A}(\mathfrak{Data}_{\text{Bob}})=\omega^*) \mid \mathfrak{Data}_{\text{Alice}}=D, \phi] \end{array} \right) \, dD \quad (14)$$

where, $E\left[P(\mathcal{A}(\mathfrak{Data}_{\text{Bob}}) = \omega^*) \mid \mathfrak{Data}_{\text{Alice}} = D, \phi\right]$

$$= \int P(\mathcal{A}(D') = \omega^*) P(\mathfrak{Data}_{\text{Bob}} = D' \mid \mathfrak{Data}_{\text{Alice}} = D, \phi) \, dD'$$

is the averaged conditional probability (using distribution $\phi \in \mathcal{C}ond$) of seeing Bob's sanitized output ω^* given that Alice's dataset is D.

The significance of Equation 14 is that an attacker who uses the distributions $\theta \in \mathbb{D}$ and $\phi \in \mathcal{C}ond$ to reason about the joint data release would reason in the exact same way in an alternate universe in which Bob releases nothing and Alice releases information about her dataset using an algorithm $\mathfrak{M}^*_{\phi,\mathcal{A},\mathfrak{M}}$ with range($\mathfrak{M}$) × range($\mathcal{A}$) and which outputs the pair (ω, ω^*) with probability $P[\mathfrak{M}^*_{\phi,\mathcal{A},\mathfrak{M}}(D) = (\omega, \omega^*)] = P(\mathfrak{M}(D) = \omega)E\left[P(\mathcal{A}(\mathfrak{Data}_{\text{Bob}}) = \omega^*) \mid \mathfrak{Data}_{\text{Alice}} = D, \phi\right]$. Thus to study the privacy properties of this joint data release, Alice only needs to study the algorithms of the form $\mathfrak{M}^*_{\phi,\mathcal{A},\mathfrak{M}}$ (for all choices of $\phi \in \mathcal{C}ond$, all $\mathfrak{M}$ satisfying her privacy definition, and all $\mathcal{A}$ satisfying Bob's privacy definition). In particular, she can ask when $\mathfrak{M}^*_{\phi,\mathcal{A},\mathfrak{M}}$ (for all choices of $\phi, \mathfrak{M}, \mathcal{A}$) satisfies ϵ'-$\mathcal{P}uffer\mathcal{F}ish(\mathbb{S}, \mathbb{S}_{\text{pairs}}, \mathbb{D})$ (i.e. her privacy definition with a different privacy parameter ϵ').

8.2 Self-composition

In this section, we study a special case of the discussion in the previous section. We call this special case *self-composition*. This is a helpful property for privacy definitions to have since it is useful in the design of algorithms. In self-composition, Alice plans multiple independent releases of her own data (i.e. the Alice and Bob from the previous section are the same person, and $\mathcal{C}ond$ consists of the trivial conditional probability where $P(\mathfrak{Data}_{\text{Bob}} = D \mid \mathfrak{Data}_{\text{Alice}} = D) = 1$).

Thus, Alice has a dataset $\mathfrak{Data}$, announces a privacy definition ϵ-$\mathcal{P}uffer\mathcal{F}ish(\mathbb{S}, \mathbb{S}_{\text{pairs}}, \mathbb{D})$ and chooses two algorithms $\mathfrak{M}_1$ and $\mathfrak{M}_2$ (with independent sources of randomness) that satisfy this definition. Alice computes $\omega_1 = \mathfrak{M}_1(\mathfrak{Data})$ and $\omega_2 = \mathfrak{M}_2(\mathfrak{Data})$ and releases the sanitized output (ω_1, ω_2) to the public.

From the previous section, we see that this is the same as if Alice had used an algorithm $\mathfrak{M}^*_{\mathfrak{M}_1,\mathfrak{M}_2}$ whose range equals range($\mathfrak{M}_1$) × range($\mathfrak{M}_2$) and with the probabilistic behavior $P\left[\mathfrak{M}^*_{\mathfrak{M}_1,\mathfrak{M}_2}(D) = (\omega_1, \omega_2)\right] = P(\mathfrak{M}_1(D) = \omega_1)P(\mathfrak{M}_2(D) = \omega_2)$. Ideally, $\mathfrak{M}^*_{\mathfrak{M}_1,\mathfrak{M}_2}$ still satisfies Alice's chosen instantiation of the Pufferfish framework with some privacy parameter ϵ'. This brings up the notion of *linear self-composition*:

DEFINITION 8.1. (Linear Self-composition). *We say that $\mathcal{P}uffer\mathcal{F}ish(\mathbb{S}, \mathbb{S}_{pairs}, \mathbb{D})$ self-composes linearly if $\forall \epsilon_1, \epsilon_2 > 0$, all $\mathfrak{M}_1$ satisfying ϵ_1-$\mathcal{P}uffer\mathcal{F}ish(\mathbb{S}, \mathbb{S}_{pairs}, \mathbb{D})$ and all $\mathfrak{M}_2$ satisfying ϵ_2-$\mathcal{P}uffer\mathcal{F}ish(\mathbb{S}, \mathbb{S}_{pairs}, \mathbb{D})$, the algorithm $\mathfrak{M}^*_{\mathfrak{M}_1,\mathfrak{M}_2}$ satisfies $(\epsilon_1 + \epsilon_2)$-$\mathcal{P}uffer\mathcal{F}ish(\mathbb{S}, \mathbb{S}_{pairs}, \mathbb{D})$, where $\mathfrak{M}^*_{\mathfrak{M}_1,\mathfrak{M}_2}$ is the algorithm with range($\mathfrak{M}^*_{\mathfrak{M}_1,\mathfrak{M}_2}$) = range($\mathfrak{M}_1$) × range($\mathfrak{M}_2$) such that for all $D \in \mathcal{I}$, $P\left[\mathfrak{M}^*_{\mathfrak{M}_1,\mathfrak{M}_2}(D) = (\omega_1, \omega_2)\right] = P[\mathfrak{M}_1(D) = \omega_1]P[\mathfrak{M}_2(D) = \omega_2]$*

Linear self-composition is useful for algorithm design because it allows Alice to split a complicated algorithm $\mathfrak{M}$ into a collection of simpler algorithms $\mathfrak{M}_1, \ldots, \mathfrak{M}_k$ and allocate her overall privacy budget ϵ among them [26].

8.2.1 Sufficient conditions for self-composition

In general, not all instantiations of the Pufferfish framework will self-compose linearly. Furthermore, it is not always easy to tell if a particular instantiation will self-compose linearly. However, we provide an important class of sufficient conditions called *universally composable evolution scenarios*.

When domain experts create instantiations of the Pufferfish framework, they add more and more probability distributions θ into the evolution scenarios $\mathbb{D}$ to create a reasonable (yet conservative) set of data-generating distributions. Each evolution scenario θ adds an additional constraint that an algorithm $\mathfrak{M}$ must satisfy.

If we have a privacy definition $\mathcal{P}uffer\mathcal{F}ish(\mathbb{S}, \mathbb{S}_{\text{pairs}}, \mathbb{D})$ that self-composes linearly, it can happen that adding more evolution scenarios (i.e. replacing $\mathbb{D}$ with a strict superset $\mathbb{D}'$) will break the composition property. However, there are some θ that we can always add without worrying about breaking composition. We refer to these special θ as *universally composable evolution scenarios*.

DEFINITION 8.2. (Universally composable evolution scenarios). *Given $\mathbb{S}$ and $\mathbb{S}_{pairs}$, we say that θ is a universally composable evolution scenario for $\mathbb{S}_{pairs}$ if the privacy definition $\mathcal{P}uffer\mathcal{F}ish(\mathbb{S}, \mathbb{S}_{pairs}, \mathbb{D} \cup \{\theta\})$ self-composes linearly whenever $\mathcal{P}uffer\mathcal{F}ish(\mathbb{S}, \mathbb{S}_{pairs}, \mathbb{D})$ self-composes linearly.*

Universally composable evolution scenarios have a very special form.

THEOREM 8.1. *Given $\mathbb{S}$ and $\mathbb{S}_{pairs}$, the probability distribution θ is a universally composable evolution scenario for $\mathbb{S}_{pairs}$ if and only if for all $(s_i, s_j) \in \mathbb{S}_{pairs}$ having $P(s_i \mid \theta) \neq 0$ and $P(s_j \mid \theta) \neq 0$ there exist datasets $D_i, D_j \in \mathcal{I}$ such that $P(\mathfrak{Data} = D_i \mid s_i, \theta) = 1$ and $P(\mathfrak{Data} = D_j \mid s_j, \theta) = 1$*

The interesting aspect of Theorem 8.1 is that when the set of evolution scenarios $\mathbb{D}$ consists solely of universally composable evolution scenarios, then the resulting instantiation of the Pufferfish framework is a neighbor-based definition similar to differential privacy.

That is, let $\theta \in \mathbb{D}$ be a universally composable evolution scenario and let $(s_i, s_j) \in \mathbb{S}$ be a discriminative pair with nonzero probability under θ and $D_i, D_j \in \mathcal{I}$ be the datasets associated with θ by Theorem 8.1. Then D_i and D_j can be considered "neighbors" and the Pufferfish constraints (Equations 1 and 2 in Definition 3.1) become:

$$P(\mathfrak{M}(D_i) = \omega) \leq e^\epsilon P(\mathfrak{M}(D_j) = \omega)$$
$$P(\mathfrak{M}(D_j) = \omega) \leq e^\epsilon P(\mathfrak{M}(D_i) = \omega)$$

with randomness only depending on $\mathfrak{M}$.

In the case of differential privacy, those universally composable evolution scenarios θ are those for which there exist databases D_1 and D_2 that differ only on one tuple and have $P(\mathfrak{Data} = D_1 \mid \theta) + P(\mathfrak{Data} = D_2 \mid \theta) = 1$. Note that Theorem 6.1 says that we can further increase $\mathbb{D}$ to include all of the other distributions that generate records independently without change to the privacy guarantees, and Theorem 6.2 says that differentially private algorithms may leak too much information if we include any other distributions (i.e. those with correlated records).

9. DIFFERENTIAL PRIVACY WITH DETERMINISTIC CONSTRAINTS

It was shown in [22] that differential privacy does not compose well with deterministic data constraints such as those caused by previous deterministic releases of information. That is, when a data curator provides exact query answers about the data and subsequently publishes additional information using ϵ-differential privacy, the combined data releases can leak much more information than each of the 2 releases in isolation. Constraints caused by deterministic releases of information are often the result of legal or contractual obligations (e.g., the U.S. Decennial Census).

Prior work [22] proposed a modification of differential privacy, called *induced neighbors privacy* [22] to account for prior deterministic data releases. As with many variants of differential privacy, it was a "neighbors-based" based definition that tried to make certain pairs of databases (i.e. neighbors) indistinguishable from each other. As we have shown in Sections 6 and 7, this can obscure privacy guarantees and the conditions under which the guarantees hold. Viewed through the Pufferfish lens, induced neighbors privacy does not properly bound the attacker's odds ratio (the main reason being that neighbor-based privacy definitions often cannot explicitly mention what secrets to protect).

In this section we extend the discussion of composition from Section 8 to show how to use Pufferfish to modify differential privacy in a way that takes into account arbitrary deterministic constraints (not just those caused by prior deterministic releases of data). The result is a privacy definition with precise semantic guarantees and clearly specified assumptions under which they hold. We also show some conditions under which induced neighbors privacy [22] is actually equivalent to an instantiation of the Pufferfish framework, thus providing induced neighbors privacy with precise semantic guarantees in those situations.

9.1 Preliminaries

Several types of constraints are common (some of them result from deterministic releases of data):

- **Counts**: The number of tuples in the dataset or the number of AIDS patients with age less than 25 are pieces of knowledge that impose count constraints. These constraints are often called *marginal constraints*, and can be represented as a constraint like $\sum_{r \in \text{records}(\mathfrak{Data})} g(r) = C$, where g is a function from the tuple domain $\mathcal{T}$ to $\{0, 1\}$, and C is an integer. For instance, to encode a constraint about the number of AIDS patients with age less than 25, one can choose g such that $g(t) = 1$ only when t is a tuple with AIDS and age less than 25, and $g(t) = 0$ otherwise.

- **Univariate Histograms**: These are a special kind of count constraints $\sum_{r \in \text{records}(\mathfrak{Data})} g_i(r) = C_i$ (for $i = 1, \dots, k$) where the g_i have disjoint supports (i.e. if for some $t \in \mathcal{T}$ we have $g_i(t) = 1$ then $g_j(t) = 0$ for all other j). Such constraints capture a variety of statistics that might be known about a database, including the total number of rows, number of tuples satisfying a set of mutually exclusive properties, as well as the results of bucketization algorithms that are common in the k-anonymization and ℓ-diversity literature.

- **General Deterministic Constraints**: In general, deterministic constraints eliminate some of the databases from the domain of database instances $\mathcal{I}$. Such a general constraint $\mathcal{Q}$ can be formally described as a function $\mathcal{Q} : \mathcal{I} \to \{0, 1\}$ such that $\mathcal{Q}(D) = 0$ means D is not possible (i.e. does not satisfy the constraint) and $\mathcal{Q}(D) = 1$ means D is a possible.

EXAMPLE 9.1. *Let us give an example of a general constraint that will help illustrate the benefits of Pufferfish and distinguish it from neighbor-based privacy definitions. Suppose there are n students with ID numbers ranging from 1 to n. They are scheduled take an oral exam in the order determined by their id numbers. The dataset $\mathfrak{Data}$ tracks whether or not a student has taken the exam. Initially $\mathfrak{Data}$ consists of n records with value 0. After student i takes the exam, the ith record is set to 1. At any point in time, the database $\mathfrak{Data}$ can be in only one of the $n+1$ states defined by the constraint $\mathcal{Q}$: $\exists k \forall i \leq k, r_i = 1 \bigwedge \forall i > k, r_i = 0$, as shown below.*

D_0	D_1	D_2	$\dots$	D_{n-2}	D_{n-1}	D_n
0	1	1	$\dots$	1	1	1
0	0	1	$\dots$	1	1	1
$\dots$	$\dots$	$\dots$	$\dots$	$\dots$	$\dots$	$\dots$
0	0	0	$\dots$	0	1	1
0	0	0	$\dots$	0	0	1

Suppose at some time point, the data curator wants to release the current number of students who have taken the exam without revealing who has or has not taken the test. The Laplace mechanism, which satisfies ϵ-differential privacy, would add noise with density $f(x) = \frac{1}{2\epsilon} e^{-|x|/\epsilon}$ to the current number of students who have taken the exam. When n, the number of total students, is large, this strategy leaks too much information. For example, if the noisy answer is close to 0, the true value was probably not n and so the nth student probably has not yet taken the exam. As we shall see, it is not possible to release meaningful information in this situation, but differential privacy does not warn us about it (neither will induced-neighbors privacy, Definition 9.2).

Induced neighbors privacy [22] uses the following definitions:

DEFINITION 9.1. (Move [22]). *Given a database D, a move m is a process that adds or deletes a tuple from D, resulting in a database $m(D)$.*

DEFINITION 9.2. (Induced Neighbors $\mathcal{N}_{\mathcal{Q}}$ [22]). *Given a general constraint $\mathcal{Q}$, let $\mathcal{I}_{\mathcal{Q}}$ be the set of databases satisfying those constraints. Let D_a and D_b be two databases. Let n_{ab} be the smallest number of moves necessary to transform D_a into D_b and let $\{m_1, \dots, m_{n_{ab}}\}$ be the set of those moves. We say that D_a and D_b are neighbors induced by $\mathcal{Q}$, denoted as $\mathcal{N}_{\mathcal{Q}}(D_a, D_b) = true$, if the following holds.*

- *$D_a \in \mathcal{I}_{\mathcal{Q}}$ and $D_b \in \mathcal{I}_{\mathcal{Q}}$.*
- *No subset of $\{m_1, \dots, m_{n_{ab}}\}$ can transform D_a into some $D_c \in \mathcal{I}_{\mathcal{Q}}$.*

DEFINITION 9.3. (Induced Neighbors Privacy). *An algorithm $\mathfrak{M}$ satisfies induced neighbor privacy with constraint $\mathcal{Q}$, if for each output $\omega \in \text{range}(\mathfrak{M})$ and for every pair D_1, D_2 of neighbors induced by Q, the following holds:*

$$P(\mathfrak{M}(D_1) = \omega) \leq e^{\epsilon} P(\mathfrak{M}(D_2) = \omega)$$

It is easy to see that the Laplace mechanism from Example 9.1 also satisfies induced neighbor privacy for this particular scenario since all induced neighbors are pairs (D_i, D_{i+1}). We compute the amount of information leakage (Example 9.2) after considering the Pufferfish view.

9.2 Pufferfish with Deterministic Constraints

Following the notation from Section 6 (also see Table 1 containing our notation), define:

$$\mathbb{S} = \left\{ \sigma_{(i,t)} \, : \, h_i \in \mathcal{H}, \, t \in \mathcal{T} \right\} \cup \left\{ \neg\sigma_i \, : \, h_i \in \mathcal{H} \right\} \quad (15)$$

$$\mathbb{S}_{\text{pairs}} = \left\{ (\sigma_{(i,t)}, \neg\sigma_i) \, : \, h_i \in \mathcal{H}, t \in \mathcal{T} \right\} \quad (16)$$
$$\cup \left\{ (\sigma_{(i,t)}, (\sigma_{t,t'})) \, : \, h_i \in \mathcal{H}, t, t' \in \mathcal{T} \right\}$$

Thus, the goal is to prevent an attacker from (a) learning whether the record of individual h_i is in the data, and (b) distinguishing between two possible values of r_i (in case h_i is known to be in the data). The data evolution scenarios $\mathbb{D}_\mathcal{Q}^*$ is the set of all probability distributions with the following form (i.e., they generate records independently conditioned on $\mathcal{Q}$):

$$\theta \equiv \{\pi_1, \ldots, \pi_N, f_1, \ldots, f_N, \mathcal{Q}\} \quad (17)$$
$$P(\mathbf{Data} \mid \theta) = 0, \text{ if } \mathcal{Q}(\mathbf{Data}) = 0$$
$$= \frac{1}{Z_\mathcal{Q}} \prod_{r_i \in \text{records}(\mathbf{Data})} f_i(r_i)\pi_i \prod_{r_j \notin \text{records}(\mathbf{Data})} (1 - \pi_j), \text{ otherwise}$$

where the normalization constant $Z_\mathcal{Q} = P(\mathcal{Q}(\mathbf{Data}) = 1)$.

We show that ϵ-induced neighbors privacy is a necessary condition for guaranteeing ϵ-$\mathcal{P}$uffer$\mathcal{F}$ish$(\mathbb{S}, \mathbb{S}_{\text{pairs}}, \mathbb{D}_\mathcal{Q}^*)$, for any general constraint $\mathcal{Q}$.

THEOREM 9.1. (Necessary Condition). *Given a general constraint $\mathcal{Q}$, if $\mathfrak{M}$ satisfies ϵ-$\mathcal{P}$uffer$\mathcal{F}$ish$(\mathbb{S}, \mathbb{S}_{\text{pairs}}, \mathbb{D}_\mathcal{Q}^*)$ then $\mathfrak{M}$ satisfies ϵ-induced neighbors privacy with respect to $\mathcal{Q}$.*

However, the next example shows ϵ-induced neighbors privacy is not sufficient, hence does guarantee an attacker's odds ratio is bounded within $[e^{-\epsilon}, e^\epsilon]$.

EXAMPLE 9.2. *Continuing Example 9.1, we show that the Laplace mechanism, which satisfies both ϵ-differential privacy and ϵ-induced neighbors privacy, does not satisfy ϵ-$\mathcal{P}$uffer$\mathcal{F}$ish$(\mathbb{S}, \mathbb{S}_{pairs}, \mathbb{D}_\mathcal{Q}^*)$.*

Consider a θ of the form given in Equation 17 such that for all i, $f_i(0) = f_i(1) = 0.5$, $\pi_i = 1$. Thus all the allowable datasets $D_0, \ldots, D_n$ from Example 9.1 are equally likely under θ. Consider the discriminative pair $(\sigma_{(1,0)}, \sigma_{(1,1)})$ and note that if record 1 has value 0 then, according to our constraints, so do all records r_ℓ for $\ell > 1$, so D_0 is the only dataset for which $\sigma_{(1,0)}$ can be true.

$$P(\mathfrak{M}(\mathbf{Data}) = n \mid \sigma_{(1,1)}, \theta)$$
$$= \sum_{j=1}^{n} \frac{P(\mathfrak{M}(D_j) = n)}{n} = \sum_{j=1}^{n} \frac{\epsilon}{2n} e^{-\epsilon(n-j)}$$
$$> e^\epsilon \cdot \frac{\epsilon}{2} e^{-\epsilon n} = e^\epsilon \cdot P(\mathfrak{M}(\mathbf{Data}) = n \mid \sigma_{(1,0)}, \theta)$$

Therefore satisfying ϵ-differential privacy or induced neighbors privacy in this situation does not bound an attacker's odds-ratio to the range $[e^{-\epsilon}, e^\epsilon]$.

In this situation, ϵ-$\mathcal{P}$uffer$\mathcal{F}$ish$(\mathbb{S}, \mathbb{S}_{pairs}, \mathbb{D}_\mathcal{Q}^*)$ requires

$$\forall D_i, D_j, \; P(\mathfrak{M}(D_i) = \omega) \leq e^\epsilon \cdot P(\mathfrak{M}(D_j) = \omega) \quad (18)$$

The condition is clearly sufficient. Necessity can be shown by considering the output $\omega = n$, and different priors θ_i that assign $f_j(1) = 1 - \delta$ for $j \leq i$, and $f_j(1) = \delta$ otherwise, where δ tends to zero. These priors capture different adversaries who believe strongly (with high prior probability) that i students have taken the exam.

Pufferfish tells us (via Equation 18) that we cannot release meaningful data in this situation because it reduces to the condition that attackers should not be able to distinguish between any pair of valid datasets. However, we next show that it is possible to release meaningful data for a broad class of typical constraints.

9.3 Pufferfish with Univariate Histograms

Univariate histograms, as defined in Section 9.1, form an important subclass of constraints. For instance, the Census Bureau is legally obliged to publish the exact number of people living in each state [4]. A search engine is contractually bound to report to an advertiser the number of users who have clicked on ads using mutually exclusive predefined ranges (e.g., $100 - 200$ clicks). Another interesting use case occurs when there has been a prior release of data using a mechanism $\mathfrak{M}_{uni}$ based on statistical disclosure limitation techniques like partitioning and microaggregation [1], or bucketization algorithms based on syntactic privacy notions like k-anonymity (with say $k = 10,000$), ℓ-diversity, etc. [6, 23, 40]. The output of $\mathfrak{M}_{uni}$ in all the above cases is a univariate histogram. In all these cases, we can provide additional releases of information by using Pufferfish to limit any further inference an attacker could make.

In fact, for those cases, ϵ-induced neighbor privacy becomes an instantiation of the Pufferfish framework (Theorems 9.1 and 9.2).

THEOREM 9.2. (SUFFICIENT CONDITION FOR UNIVARIATE HISTOGRAMS). *Given a univariate histogram constraint $\mathcal{Q}_{uni} : \{\sum_{t \in \mathbf{Data}} g_i(t) = C\}$, define $\mathbb{S}$ and $\mathbb{S}_{pairs}$ as in Equations 15 and 16 and let $\mathbb{D}_\mathcal{Q}^*$ be the set of all distributions with form specified in Equation 17. Then $\mathfrak{M}$ satisfies ϵ-$\mathcal{P}$uffer$\mathcal{F}$ish$(\mathbb{S}, \mathbb{S}_{pairs}, \mathbb{D}_{\mathcal{Q}_{uni}}^*)$ if $\mathfrak{M}$ satisfies ϵ-induced neighbors privacy with respect to $\mathcal{Q}_{uni}$.*

Thus the algorithms proposed in [22] can be used in this case to bound an attacker's inference.

An important question that was left open in [22] is whether induced neighbor privacy is linear self composable. Theorems 9.1 and 9.2 allow us to answer this question. Since ϵ-$\mathcal{P}$uffer$\mathcal{F}$ish$(\mathbb{S}, \mathbb{S}_{pairs}, \mathbb{D}_{\mathcal{Q}_{uni}}^*)$ and induced neighbor privacy (for univariate histograms) are equivalent definitions, it is easy to see that the former can be written solely in terms of universally composable evolution scenarios, proving that ϵ-$\mathcal{P}$uffer$\mathcal{F}$ish$(\mathbb{S}, \mathbb{S}_{pairs}, \mathbb{D}_{\mathcal{Q}_{uni}}^*)$ composes with itself linearly. This means that, for a database with a prior univariate histogram release $\mathcal{Q}_{uni}$, and further releases using $\mathfrak{M}_1$ and $\mathfrak{M}_2$ that satisfy $\mathcal{P}$uffer$\mathcal{F}$ish$(\mathbb{S}, \mathbb{S}_{pairs}, \mathbb{D}_{\mathcal{Q}_{uni}}^*)$ with parameters ϵ_1 and ϵ_2, respectively, the combined mechanism $\mathfrak{M}_{\mathfrak{M}_1, \mathfrak{M}_2}$ guarantees $(\epsilon_1 + \epsilon_2)$-$\mathcal{P}$uffer$\mathcal{F}ish(\mathbb{S}, \mathbb{S}_{pairs}, \mathbb{D}_{\mathcal{Q}_{uni}}^*)$.

10. CONCLUSIONS

We presented the Pufferfish framework, a new and general framework that allows application domain experts to develop rigorous privacy definitions for their data sharing needs. The framework allows the domain experts to customize privacy to the specific set of secrets and data evolution scenarios that are typical in that domain. We used our general framework to prove the statement that differential privacy assumed independence between records, and define and study notions of composition in a broader context than before. We also applied the framework to derive rigorous definitions for handling unbounded continuous attributes, protecting aggregate information, and prior deterministic data releases.

11. ACKNOWLEDGMENTS

This material is based upon work supported by the National Science Foundation under Grant No. 1054389 and a gift from Yahoo!

12. REFERENCES

[1] N. Adam and J. Worthmann. Security-control methods for statistical databases. *ACM Computing Surveys*, 21(4):515–556, 1989.

[2] C. C. Aggarwal, J. Pei, and B. Zhang. On privacy preservation against adversarial data mining. In *KDD*, 2006.

[3] A. Blum, K. Ligett, and A. Roth. A learning theory approach to non-interactive database privacy. In *STOC*, pages 609–618, 2008.

[4] P. J. Cantwell, H. Hogan, and K. M. Styles. The use of statistical methods in the u.s. census: Utah v. evans. *The American Statistician*, 58(3):203–212, 2004.

[5] K. Chaudhuri and N. Mishra. When random sampling preserves privacy. In *CRYPTO*, 2006.

[6] B.-C. Chen, D. Kifer, K. LeFevre, and A. Machanavajjhala. Privacy-preserving data publishing. *Foundations and Trends in Databases*, 2(1-2):1–167, 2009.

[7] C. Clifton. Using sample size to limit exposure to data mining. *Journal of Computer Security*, 8(4), 2000.

[8] C. Clifton, M. Kantarcioglu, and J. Vaidya. Defining privacy for data mining. In *Proc. of the NSF Workshop on Next Generation Data Mining*, 2002.

[9] C. Clifton and D. Marks. Security and privacy implications of data mining. In *Proceedings of the ACM SIGMOD Workshop on Data Mining and Knowledge Discovery*, 1996.

[10] A. Delis, V. S. Verykios, and A. A. Tsitsonis. A data perturbation approach to sensitive classification rule hiding. In *SAC*, 2010.

[11] Y. Duan. Privacy without noise. In *CIKM*, 2009.

[12] C. Dwork. Differential privacy. In *ICALP*, 2006.

[13] C. Dwork, F. McSherry, K. Nissim, and A. Smith. Calibrating noise to sensitivity in private data analysis. In *TCC*, 2006.

[14] C. Dwork and M. Naor. On the difficulties of disclosure prevention in statistical databases or the case for differential privacy. *JPC*, 2(1), 2010.

[15] S. E. Fienberg. Confidentiality and disclosure limitation methodology: Challenges for national statistics and statistical research. Technical Report 668, CMU, 1997.

[16] B. C. M. Fung, K. Wang, R. Chen, and P. S. Yu. Privacy-preserving data publishing: A survey on recent developments. *ACM Computing Surveys*, 42(4), 2010.

[17] S. R. Ganta, S. P. Kasiviswanathan, and A. Smith. Composition attacks and auxiliary information in data privacy. In *KDD*, 2008.

[18] J. Gehrke, E. Lui, and R. Pass. Towards privacy for social networks: A zero-knowledge based definition of privacy. In *TCC*, 2011.

[19] N. Homer, S. Szelinger, M. Redman, D. Duggan, W. Tembe, J. Muehling, J. V. Pearson, D. A. Stephan, S. F. Nelson, and D. W. Craig. Resolving individuals contributing trace amounts of dna to highly complex mixtures using high-density snp genotyping microarrays. *PLoS Genet*, 4(8), 08 2008.

[20] D. Kifer and B.-R. Lin. An axiomatic view of statistical privacy and utility. To appear in Journal of Privacy and Confidentiality.

[21] D. Kifer and B.-R. Lin. Towards an axiomatization of statistical privacy and utility. In *PODS*, 2010.

[22] D. Kifer and A. Machanavajjhala. No free lunch in data privacy. In *SIGMOD*, 2011.

[23] K. LeFevre, D. DeWitt, and R. Ramakrishnan. Mondrian multidimensional k-anonymity. In *ICDE*, 2006.

[24] B.-R. Lin and D. Kifer. A framework for extracting semantic guarantees from privacy definitions. Technical report, Penn State University, 2012.

[25] A. Machanavajjhala, D. Kifer, J. Abowd, J. Gehrke, and L. Vilhuber. Privacy: From theory to practice on the map. In *ICDE*, 2008.

[26] F. D. McSherry. Privacy integrated queries: An extensible platform for privacy-preserving data analysis. In *SIGMOD*, pages 19–30, 2009.

[27] I. Mironov, O. Pandey, O. Reingold, and S. Vadhan. Computational differential privacy. In *CRYPTO*, 2009.

[28] G. V. Moustakides and V. S. Verykios. A maxmin approach for hiding frequent itemsets. *Data Knowl. Eng.*, 65(1), 2008.

[29] J. Natwichai, X. Li, and M. E. Orlowska. A reconstruction-based algorithm for classification rules hiding. In *ADC*, 2006.

[30] K. Nissim, S. Raskhodnikova, and A. Smith. Smooth sensitivity and sampling in private data analysis. In *STOC*, pages 75–84, 2007.

[31] S. R. M. Oliveira and O. R. Zaiane. Algorithms for balancing privacy and knowledge discovery in association rule mining. In *International Database Engineering and Applications Symposium*, 2003.

[32] PREDICT (protected repository for the defense of infrastructure against cyber threats). http://www.cyber.st.dhs.gov/predict/.

[33] V. Rastogi, M. Hay, G. Miklau, and D. Suciu. Relationship privacy: Output perturbation for queries with joins. In *PODS*, pages 107–116, 2009.

[34] P. Samarati. Protecting respondents' identities in microdata release. *TKDE*, 13(6), 2001.

[35] S. Sankararaman, G. Obozinski, M. I. Jordan, and E. Halperin. Genomic privacy and limits of individual detection in a pool. *Nature genetics*, 41(9):965–967, September 2009.

[36] V. S. Verykios, E. Bertino, I. N. Fovino, L. P. Provenza, Y. Saygin, and Y. Theodoridis. State-of-the-art in privacy preserving data mining. *SIGMOD Rec.*, 33(1), 2004.

[37] V. S. Verykios, A. K. Elmagarmid, E. Bertino, Y. Saygin, and E. Dasseni. Association rule hiding. *IEEE Trans. Knowl. Data Eng.*, 16(4), 2004.

[38] E. T. Wang and G. Lee. An efficient sanitization algorithm for balancing information privacy and knowledge discovery in association patterns mining. *Data & Knowledge Engineering*, 65(3), 2008.

[39] K. Wang, B. Fung, and P. Yu. Template-based privacy preservation in classification problems. In *ICDM*, 2005.

[40] X. Xiao and Y. Tao. Anatomy: Simple and effective privacy preservation. In *VLDB*, 2006.

[41] S. Zhou, K. Ligett, and L. Wasserman. Differential privacy with compression. In *ISIT*, 2009.

Static Analysis and Optimization of Semantic Web Queries

Andrés Letelier
Dept. of Computer Science
PUC Chile
aileteli@uc.cl

Jorge Pérez
Dept. of Computer Science
Universidad de Chile
jperez@dcc.uchile.cl

Reinhard Pichler   Sebastian Skritek
Faculty of Informatics
Technische Universität Wien
[pichler,skritek]@dbai.tuwien.ac.at

ABSTRACT

Static analysis is a fundamental task in query optimization. In this paper we study static analysis and optimization techniques for SPARQL, which is the standard language for querying Semantic Web data. Of particular interest for us is the *optionality* feature in SPARQL. It is crucial in Semantic Web data management, where data sources are inherently incomplete and the user is usually interested in partial answers to queries. This feature is one of the most complicated constructors in SPARQL and also the one that makes this language depart from classical query languages such as relational conjunctive queries. We focus on the class of well-designed SPARQL queries, which has been proposed in the literature as a fragment of the language with good properties regarding query evaluation. We first propose a tree representation for SPARQL queries, called pattern trees, which captures the class of well-designed SPARQL graph patterns and which can be considered as a query execution plan. Among other results, we propose several transformation rules for pattern trees, a simple normal form, and study equivalence and containment. We also study the enumeration and counting problems for this class of queries.

Categories and Subject Descriptors

H.2.3 [**Database Management**]: Query languages

Keywords

SPARQL, RDF, Semantic Web, optimization, query containment

1. INTRODUCTION

The Semantic Web is the initiative of the World Wide Web Consortium (W3C) to make information on the Web readable not only by humans but also by machines. The *Resource Description Framework* (RDF) is the standard data model for the Semantic Web, and since its release as a W3C Recommendation in 1999 [23], the problem of managing RDF data has been in the focus of the Semantic Web community. As a result, the language SPARQL was proposed as a query language for RDF, and became a W3C Recommendation in 2008 [31]. Since the appearance of these standards, the Web has witnessed a constant growth in the amount of RDF data published on-line. Moreover, the advent of huge initiatives

like Open Linked Data [6, 7] and Open Government Data [42, 43] that use RDF as a core technology, and the use of RDF in several diverse areas such as bio-informatics, social networks, and data integration, have increased the attention of the research community to study RDF and SPARQL from a database perspective.

Several particular issues of RDF and SPARQL pose new and interesting challenges for the database community [3]. In fact, several research efforts have been pursued towards understanding their fundamental properties and developing specific techniques to efficiently deal with these technologies [25, 1, 30, 40, 36, 2, 32, 27, 24, 34, 3]. Nevertheless, and despite the importance of static query analysis, and in particular of query containment and equivalence for optimization purposes, research on the static analysis of SPARQL queries has received little attention so far (notable exceptions are [35, 9]). The study of static analysis considering the peculiarities of SPARQL and, in particular, query optimization, containment and equivalence, constitute the main focus of this paper.

Let us briefly recall that the data model underlying RDF data is a (directed, arc-labeled) graph. An RDF graph is composed of RDF triples of the form (s, p, o). Regarding SPARQL, its basic constructor is the *triple pattern*, which is essentially an RDF triple that can have variables. The most basic fragment of the language are conjunctions of triple patterns, realized in SPARQL by using the AND operator (see Section 2 for a formal introduction of the language). Thus, if one thinks of RDF graphs as sets of tuples, a triple pattern is essentially a ternary relational atom, and basic SPARQL queries are essentially relational conjunctive queries (CQs). In view of this connection, the rich body of work on static analysis and query optimization on relational CQs including the study of equivalence and containment can be immediately carried over to the conjunctive fragment of SPARQL. Moreover, most of the research focused on statistics, indices, and storage optimization has been concentrated on this fragment [1, 37, 40, 36, 24].

However, when one goes beyond the SPARQL conjunctive fragment, the whole picture changes and the language becomes considerably more complicated. Of particular interest is the *optional matching* feature, which has been the focus of most of the theoretical work regarding this language [2, 27, 34, 3]. The idea behind optional matching, realized in SPARQL by the OPT operator, is to allow information to be added if the information is available in the data source instead of just failing to give an answer whenever some part of the query does not match. This feature is crucial in Semantic Web data management, where data sources are inherently incomplete and have only partial knowledge about the resources that they are modeling. Recent experimental works [15, 28] show that the use of the OPT operator in practice is substantial. For instance, in a query log obtained from the DBPedia SPARQL endpoint [44], after duplicate query elimination, more than 45% of the analyzed queries use the OPT operator [28].

The importance of the OPT operator has also been recognized from a database theory point of view. It has been shown that the combined complexity of SPARQL query evaluation (i.e., checking if some set of variable bindings is a solution) raises from PTIME-membership for the conjunctive fragment to PSPACE-completeness when OPT is considered [27, 34]. In [27], the class of *well-designed* SPARQL *graph patterns* was introduced as a fundamental fragment of OPT queries with good behavior for query evaluation (for a formal definition, see Section 2). In particular, it was shown that the complexity of the evaluation problem for the well-designed fragment is coNP-complete [27].

In this paper we embark on the static analysis of SPARQL queries containing the OPT operator. We focus on the class of *well-designed* SPARQL *graph patterns* mentioned above. As our first contribution we introduce a tree representation of SPARQL queries called SPARQL *pattern trees*. We also introduce a particular class of pattern trees that we call *quasi well-designed* pattern trees (QWDPTs, for short), capturing the class of well-designed SPARQL graph patterns. We further introduce a procedure to evaluate QWDPTs in a top-down way that resembles a top-down evaluation of graph patterns proposed in [25]. Our pattern trees are reminiscent of relational query plans and thus, can be considered as a first step towards an algebra for logical optimization of queries in the SPARQL context, very much like the relational algebra used in relational database systems to construct and manipulate query plans. Notice that previous works on optimization of SPARQL have mainly focused on rewriting queries based on properties of particular operators [27, 34]. We propose transformation rules for QWDPTs that work at the level of the structure of the trees (and thus, the structure of queries). These rules are, for example, capable of eliminating several sources of redundancy in queries, and thus, can be used for query optimization purposes.

Based on our work on the structure of pattern trees, we study the fundamental problems of checking equivalence and containment of SPARQL queries. It is known that full-SPARQL and First-Order Logic have the same expressive power [2]. From this result it is not difficult to prove that equivalence and containment for SPARQL in general are undecidable problems. We show that the equivalence problem for QWDPTs (and therefore, for well-designed SPARQL graph patterns) is NP-complete. The difficult part of the proof is the NP-membership. Recall from the relational world that equivalence and containment are closely related to the search for homomorphisms. The key to our NP-membership result is an appropriate extension of homomorphisms to QWDPTs – leading to the notion of *strong homomorphisms* (for details, see Section 4) and a normal form via the transformation rules for QWDPTs mentioned above.

For the *containment* of queries we consider the *subsumption* relation [3]. As detailed above, solutions for queries containing the OPT operator are essentially incomplete and may possibly bind only a subset of the variables in the query [31, 27]. This naturally leads to the notion of subsumption between solutions: a solution μ_1 subsumes another solution μ_2, if μ_1 extends μ_2 with more variable bindings. More generally, a SPARQL query T_1 subsumes another SPARQL query T_2 if, for every RDF graph G, every solution of T_2 is subsumed by some solution of T_1. It has been argued that subsumption is a meaningful way of comparing the result of SPARQL queries containing the OPT operator [3]. Moreover, subsumption has also been used in the past as a meaningful way of testing containment of queries with incomplete answers over semistructured data [21]. In principle, subsumption can also be used to test equivalence. However, it is not advisable to do so since we prove that

subsumption is presumably harder than equivalence by showing the Π_2^P-completeness of subsumption.

As our final contribution, we study the relationship between tractable fragments of CQ answering and tractable fragments of well-designed SPARQL queries containing the OPT operator. For the classical evaluation problem mentioned above, results on tractable fragments of CQs smoothly carry over to well-designed SPARQL graph patterns. The analysis becomes more intricate when we study the enumeration problem (that is, actually computing the set of solutions) and the counting problem (i.e., determining the number of solutions) of well-designed SPARQL graph patterns. Our main result in this respect states that, for a SPARQL query in which all its conjunctive parts (sequences of AND operators) belong to a tractable class of conjunctive queries, the enumeration of solutions is feasible with *polynomial delay*. In contrast, the counting problem remains intractable (more specifically, #P-complete) also in the restricted case where all conjunctions of triple patterns in a SPARQL query are acyclic CQs.

Summary of results and structure of the paper. In Section 2, we formally introduce RDF and SPARQL. A conclusion and an outlook to future work are given in Section 6. The main results of the paper are detailed in the Sections 3 – 5, namely:

- *Algebra of query plans.* In Section 3, we present an algebra of query plans for well-designed SPARQL graph patterns. To this end, we introduce the data structure of quasi well-designed pattern trees (QWDPTs). We show that they allow for a natural evaluation in a top-down fashion of the tree. Moreover, we introduce transformation rules to modify these QWDPTs. In particular, these rules allow us to eliminate redundancies and to define a useful normal form.

- *Containment and equivalence.* In Section 4, we study the fundamental problems of containment (in the form of subsumption) and equivalence of well-designed SPARQL graph patterns. We establish the relationship between subsumption and equivalence and pinpoint their complexity, namely NP-completeness for equivalence, vs. Π_2^P-completeness for subsumption.

- *Enumeration and counting.* In Section 5, we study both, the enumeration and counting problem of SPARQL queries. In particular, we investigate how tractable fragments of CQ evaluation can be carried over to well-designed SPARQL graph patterns. We show that tractable fragments of CQ evaluation indeed give rise to tractable fragments of the SPARQL enumeration problem. In contrast, the counting problem remains intractable even if all sets of triple patterns in the SPARQL query are restricted to acyclic CQs.

We have implemented a prototype tool based on the theoretical results presented in this paper, which is freely available on-line from http://db.ing.puc.cl/sparql-algebra. In particular, we have implemented the containment and equivalence tests, and the top down evaluation of SPARQL tree patterns, with some encouraging initial results. We report on them in Section 6.

Related work. As we have described, our work is heavily based on the formalization of SPARQL presented in [25, 27] and in particular on the notion of well-designed SPARQL patterns introduced in these papers. In [27] the authors also study the complexity of query evaluation. Schmidt et al. [34] considered several aspects of SPARQL query optimization focused on rewriting queries based on properties of operators [34]. Neither of these works [27, 34] considered the complexity of equivalence and containment, nor the search for tractable fragments for query evaluation, enumeration and counting which are the main problems touched in this paper. The OPT operator in SPARQL resembles a *left-outer join* in SQL. Compared with the huge amount of research on static analysis of

CQs, fragments of SQL containing left-outer join have almost been disregarded with respect to these problems with [??] being one notable exception. Nevertheless, to the best of our knowledge, research on fundamental questions such as the complexity of query equivalence and tractable fragments for query evaluation, has not been carried out to date for queries containing left-outer joins.

Outside the SPARQL context, Kanza et al. [21] studied containment and equivalence for queries over a general semistructured data model. The query language considered in [21] allows for partial answers, nevertheless, as opposed to SPARQL, it does not allow to explicitly state optional parts in a query, and partial answers are generated by considering different semantics for query evaluation. This makes our approach to partial answers, equivalence and containment, orthogonal to [21]. Gutierrez et al. [19] studied similar problems for an abstract RDF query language. The difficulties in [19] arise from considering *blank nodes* and RDFS (features that we do not consider here) but they only consider conjunctive queries without optional parts, thus making their approach also orthogonal to ours. Cohen et al. [11] define a polynomial delay iterator for computing full disjunctions. Full disjunctions are designed to obtain partial answers from relational sources but, in contrast to the OPT operator in SPARQL, full disjunctions are associative and commutative. Thus, the source of difficulties in devising an enumerator for full disjunctions departs from the difficulties that one encounters when enumerating SPARQL queries. Regarding counting partial answers, to the best of our knowledge, this paper is the first one considering the complexity of this problem.

2. BASICS OF RDF AND SPARQL

In this paper we focus on ground RDF graphs, that is, RDF graphs that do not contain blank nodes. Moreover, we do not make an explicit distinction between URIs (uniform resource identifiers) and Literals when defining RDF graphs, and thus we assume that RDF graphs are composed only of URIs. Thus, let $\mathbf{U}$ be an infinite set of URIs. An RDF triple is a tuple in $\mathbf{U} \times \mathbf{U} \times \mathbf{U}$, and an RDF graph (graph for short) is a finite set of RDF triples. The active domain of an RDF graph G, denoted by $\mathrm{dom}(G)$ with $\mathrm{dom}(G) \subseteq \mathbf{U}$ is the set of URIs actually appearing in G.

SPARQL [31] is the standard query language for RDF. We next formalize its *graph pattern matching facility* which forms the core of the language. Assume the existence of an infinite set $\mathbf{V}$ of variables (disjoint from $\mathbf{U}$). We denote variables in $\mathbf{V}$ by using a question mark, as with $?X$. Then a SPARQL triple pattern is a tuple $t \in (\mathbf{U} \cup \mathbf{V}) \times (\mathbf{U} \cup \mathbf{V}) \times (\mathbf{U} \cup \mathbf{V})$. Complex graph patterns are constructed from triple patterns by using operators AND, OPT, UNION, and FILTER. In this paper we focus on the SPARQL fragment composed of the operators AND and OPT. Formally, SPARQL graph patterns are recursively defined as follows. (1) a triple pattern is a graph pattern, and (2) if P_1 and P_2 are graph patterns, then $(P_1 \text{ AND } P_2)$ and $(P_1 \text{ OPT } P_2)$ are graph patterns.

For a triple pattern t, we write $\mathrm{vars}(t)$ to denote the set of variables occurring in t, and for a graph pattern P we write $\mathrm{vars}(P)$ for the set of variables that occur in the triples that compose P.

To define the semantics of SPARQL graph patterns, we follow closely the definitions proposed in [27]. A mapping μ is a partial function $\mu : \mathbf{V} \to \mathbf{U}$. The domain of μ, denoted by $\mathrm{dom}(\mu)$, is the set of all variables from $\mathbf{V}$ for which μ is defined. Given a triple pattern t and a mapping μ such that $\mathrm{vars}(t) \subseteq \mathrm{dom}(\mu)$, we denote by $\mu(t)$ the RDF triple obtained by replacing the variables in t according to μ. Given two mappings μ_1 and μ_2, we say that μ_1 and μ_2 are *compatible*, denoted by $\mu_1 \sim \mu_2$, if for every $?X \in \mathrm{dom}(\mu_1) \cap \mathrm{dom}(\mu_2)$ it holds that $\mu_1(?X) = \mu_2(?X)$. Notice that, for compatible mappings μ_1 and μ_2, we have that $\mu_1 \cup \mu_2$

is also a mapping and is such that $(\mu_1 \cup \mu_2)(?X)$ is $\mu_1(?X)$ if $?X \in \mathrm{dom}(\mu_1)$, or $\mu_2(?X)$ otherwise. Also notice that the mapping with empty domain, denoted by $\mu_\emptyset$ is compatible with any mapping. Before defining the semantics of SPARQL graph patterns, we define some operations between sets of mappings that resemble relational operators over sets of tuples. Let M_1 and M_2 be sets of mappings. We define the *join* and the *left-outer join* between M_1 and M_2 as follows:

$$M_1 \bowtie M_2 = \{\mu_1 \cup \mu_2 \mid \mu_1 \in M_1, \mu_2 \in M_2 \text{ and } \mu_1 \sim \mu_2\}$$
$$M_1 \boxtimes M_2 = (M_1 \bowtie M_2) \cup \{\mu \in M_1 \mid \forall \mu' \in M_2 : \mu \not\sim \mu'\}$$

We now have all the necessary prerequisites to formalize the evaluation of a SPARQL graph pattern over an RDF graph G as a function $[\![\cdot]\!]_G$ that given a pattern returns a set of mappings. Formally, $[\![P]\!]_G$ is defined recursively as follows [27]:

1. If P is a triple pattern t, then $[\![P]\!]_G = \{\mu \mid \mathrm{dom}(\mu) = \mathrm{vars}(t) \text{ and } \mu(t) \in G\}$.

2. If $P = (P_1 \text{ AND } P_2)$, then $[\![P]\!]_G = [\![P_1]\!]_G \bowtie [\![P_2]\!]_G$.

3. If $P = (P_1 \text{ OPT } P_2)$, then $[\![P]\!]_G = [\![P_1]\!]_G \boxtimes [\![P_2]\!]_G$.

We say that two patterns P_1 and P_2 are equivalent, denoted by $P_1 \equiv P_2$, if for every RDF graph G, it holds that $[\![P_1]\!]_G = [\![P_2]\!]_G$. Notice that mappings explicitly refer to the variable names. Hence, unlike for conjunctive queries (CQs), the actual names of the variables matter, since two graph patterns containing different sets of variables can never be equivalent. In [27] the authors show several algebraic properties for graph patterns. In particular they show that AND is commutative and associative which allows us to drop parentheses from sequences of AND operators.

Note that we described the set-semantics of SPARQL, while the W3C Recommendation defines a bag-semantics for query answering [31]. Nevertheless, for the fragment considered in this paper (allowing only for AND and OPT) both semantics coincide [26]. We thus have only formalized the set-semantics of the language.

Example 2.1 (From [27]) *Consider an RDF graph G storing information about professors in a university with the following triples, and the pattern P_1:*

> *(R_1, name, paul), (R_1, phone, 777-3426),*
> *(R_2, name, john), (R_2, email, john@acd.edu),*
> *(R_3, name, george), (R_3, webPage, www.george.edu),*
> *(R_4, name, ringo), (R_4, email, ringo@acd.edu),*
> *(R_4, webPage, www.starr.edu), (R_4, phone, 888-4537)*

$P_1 = \big(\big((?A, name, ?N) \text{ OPT } (?A, email, ?E) \big)$
$\qquad\qquad\qquad\qquad \text{OPT } (?A, webPage, ?W) \big)$

If we evaluate P_1 over G, then intuitively we are retrieving the name of the resources in G and, optionally, for the resources that have an email we retrieve the email, and, optionally, for the resources that have a Web page we retrieve the Web page. When evaluating P_1 over G we obtain the set of mappings $[\![P_1]\!]_G = \{\mu_1, \mu_2, \mu_3, \mu_4\}$ where

> $\mu_1 = \{?A \to R_1, ?N \to paul\}$,
> $\mu_2 = \{?A \to R_2, ?N \to john, ?E \to john@acd.edu\}$,
> $\mu_3 = \{?A \to R_3, ?N \to george, ?W \to www.george.edu\}$,
> $\mu_4 = \{?A \to R_4, ?N \to ringo, ?E \to ringo@acd.edu,$
> $\qquad ?W \to www.starr.edu\}$.

Also, consider now pattern P_2 given by the following expression:
$P_2 = \big((?A, name, ?N) \text{ OPT }$
$\qquad\qquad \big((?A, email, ?E) \text{ OPT } (?A, webPage, ?W) \big) \big)$
In this case the evaluation of P_2 over G is the set of mappings $[\![P_2]\!]_G = \{\mu_1, \mu_2, \mu_3, \mu_4\}$ where

> $\mu_1 = \{?A \to R_1, ?N \to paul\}$,

$\mu_2 = \{?A \to R_2, ?N \to john, ?E \to john@acd.edu\}$,
$\mu_3 = \{?A \to R_3, ?N \to george\}$,
$\mu_4 = \{?A \to R_4, ?N \to ringo, ?E \to ringo@acd.edu,$
$\quad\quad ?W \to www.starr.edu\}$.

Notice that we obtain no information for the Web page of george, since in P_2 that information is retrieved only for the resources that have an email (and george does not have an email address in G).

Well-designed graph patterns. An important class of SPARQL graph patterns identified in [27], that also plays a central role in this paper, is the class of *well-designed* graph patterns. A pattern P is well-designed if for every subpattern $P' = (P_1 \text{ OPT } P_2)$ of P and every variable $?X$ occurring in P, it holds that: if $?X$ occurs inside P_2 and outside P', then $?X$ also occurs inside P_1.

Notice that patterns P_1 and P_2 in Example 2.1 are well-designed. In [27] the authors studied several properties of well-designed patterns. Among others, they showed that the complexity of the evaluation problem is lower for well-designed patterns compared with the general language. Moreover, they suggested that well-designed patterns are suitable for optimization procedures, proposing a set of rewriting rules. In this paper we go an important step further in this direction by proposing an algebra of query plans for well-designed SPARQL graph patterns by introducing an appropriate data structure (so-called pattern trees) and equivalence-preserving transformation rules.

3. PATTERN TREES AND QUERY PLANS

In this section we propose a novel representation of SPARQL graph patterns based on trees, together with an evaluation method for these trees. This tree representation of patterns plays a central role when we study optimization, query equivalence and containment, and also tractable fragments of SPARQL queries.

As usual, we define a *rooted tree* as a tuple $T = (V, E, r)$. We further assume trees to be undirected and unordered. Using this terminology, we can now define our tree representation of SPARQL graph patterns.

Definition 3.1 (Pattern Tree) *A pattern tree $\mathcal{T}$ is a pair $\mathcal{T} = (T, \mathcal{P})$, where $T = (V, E, r)$ is a rooted tree, and $\mathcal{P} = (P_n)_{n \in V}$ is a labeling of the nodes of T such that P_n is a nonempty set of triple patterns, for every $n \in V$.*

Given a pattern tree $\mathcal{T} = ((V, E, r), (P_n)_{n \in V})$ and a node $n \in V$, a *subtree of $\mathcal{T}$ rooted at n* is a pattern tree composed of n and a connected subset of its descendants. Moreover, *the complete subtree of $\mathcal{T}$ rooted at n*, that we usually denote by $\mathcal{T}_n$, is the pattern tree composed of n and *all* its descendants. We further denote by $\text{vars}(P_n)$ the set of variables that occur in the triples of P_n, and by $\text{vars}(\mathcal{T})$ the set $\bigcup_{n \in V} \text{vars}(P_n)$. For pattern trees, we usually depict the tree structure with the corresponding labels in every node, as in the following example.

Example 3.2 *The following are pattern trees that intuitively correspond to the queries introduced in Example 2.1.*

$\mathcal{T}_1$: $\{(?A, name, ?N)\}$
$\{(?A, email, ?E)\}$ $\{(?A, webPage, ?W)\}$

$\mathcal{T}_2$: $\{(?A, name, ?N)\}$
$\{(?A, email, ?E)\}$
$\{(?A, webPage, ?W)\}$

Next, we give a meaning to pattern trees by transforming pattern trees into SPARQL graph patterns. Towards this goal, we need the

following definition of a transformation function $\text{TR}(\cdot, \cdot, \cdot)$. Consider a pattern tree $\mathcal{T} = ((V, E, r), \mathcal{P})$ and a set Σ of functions $\{\sigma_n \mid n \in V\}$ such that for every $n \in V$, function σ_n defines an ordering on the children of n. That is, if n has k children, then σ_n is a function from $\{1, \ldots, k\}$ to the set of children of n, such that $\sigma_n(1)$ is the first child in the order, $\sigma_n(2)$ is the second one, and so on. We need a last definition before presenting the transformation. Given a set $P = \{t_1, \ldots, t_\ell\}$ of triple patterns, we denote by $and(P)$ the graph pattern $(t_1 \text{ AND } t_2 \text{ AND } \cdots \text{ AND } t_\ell)$. For $\mathcal{T}$ and $n \in V$, we are now ready to define the transformation $\text{TR}(\mathcal{T}, n, \Sigma)$ of $\mathcal{T}_n$, the complete subtree of $\mathcal{T}$ rooted at n, given the order Σ. Assume that n has k children in $\mathcal{T}$, then $\text{TR}(\mathcal{T}, n, \Sigma)$ is defined as the graph pattern expression

$$\big(\cdots \big(\big(and(P_n) \text{ OPT } \text{TR}(\mathcal{T}, \sigma_n(1), \Sigma) \big)$$
$$\text{OPT } \text{TR}(\mathcal{T}, \sigma_n(2), \Sigma) \big)$$
$$\cdots \text{ OPT } \text{TR}(\mathcal{T}, \sigma_n(k), \Sigma) \big),$$

and if n has no children, then $\text{TR}(\mathcal{T}, n, \Sigma) = and(P_n)$. Finally, given a pattern tree $\mathcal{T} = ((V, E, r), \mathcal{P})$ and an ordering Σ for $\mathcal{T}$, we define $\text{TR}(\mathcal{T}, \Sigma)$ as $\text{TR}(\mathcal{T}, r, \Sigma)$.

Example 3.3 *Consider the tree $\mathcal{T}_1$ in Example 3.2, and let Σ be the order induced by the picture in the example. Then $\text{TR}(\mathcal{T}_1, \Sigma)$ is pattern P_1 in Example 2.1.*

3.1 Semantics of well-designed pattern trees

We have established a syntactic relationship between pattern trees and SPARQL graph patterns. We now want to establish a semantic relationship between these representations. In particular, we are interested in defining the evaluation of a pattern tree over an RDF graph. Notice that several (different) SPARQL patterns can be obtained from a pattern tree depending on the ordering functions used in the transformation. Thus, we cannot directly define the evaluation of a pattern tree $\mathcal{T}$ by using the evaluation of an arbitrary transformation of $\mathcal{T}$. In this section we introduce a well-designedness condition for pattern trees that will be crucial in defining a semantics for pattern trees. In particular it will allow us to choose an arbitrary transformation of a pattern tree in order to evaluate it. We begin with the definition of the the well-designedness condition for pattern trees.

Definition 3.4 *A pattern tree $\mathcal{T} = ((V, E, r), \mathcal{P})$ is well-designed if for every variable $?X$ occurring in $\mathcal{T}$, the set $\{n \in V \mid ?X \in \text{vars}(P_n)\}$ induces a connected subgraph of T.*

Example 3.5 *The pattern trees in Example 3.2 are well-designed, while the following pattern trees are not:*

$\{(?A, name, ?N)\}$
$\{(?A, email, ?I)\}$ $\{(?A, webPage, ?I)\}$

$\{(?A, name, ?N)\}$
$\{(?B, email, ?E)\}$
$\{(?A, webPage, ?W)\}$

Variable $?I$ in the tree on the left, and variable $?A$ in the tree on the right, induce disconnected subgraphs.

As expected, this well-designedness condition over trees is tightly connected to the well-designedness condition for graph patterns. In particular, the following holds.

Proposition 3.6 *Let $\mathcal{T}$ be a well-designed pattern tree, and Σ an arbitrary set of ordering functions for $\mathcal{T}$. Then $\text{TR}(\mathcal{T}, \Sigma)$ is a well-designed graph pattern.*

Before defining the semantics, we introduce a relaxation of well-designedness that plays a fundamental role in our study.

Definition 3.7 *A pattern tree $\mathcal{T} = ((V, E, r), (P_n)_{n \in V})$ is a quasi well-designed pattern tree (QWDPT for short) if for every pair of nodes $u, v \in V$ and each variable $?X \in \text{vars}(P_u) \cap \text{vars}(P_v)$ there exists a node n that is a common ancestor of u and v in $\mathcal{T}$, such that $?X \in \text{vars}(P_n)$.*

The pattern tree on the right in Example 3.5 is a QWDPT, while the pattern on the left is not (notice that the common ancestor of u and v in Definition 3.7 may be u or v, as in Example 3.5). Another notion that we need to introduce is that of *duplicating triples to children*. Formally, we say that a pattern tree $\mathcal{T}' = ((V', E', r'), (P'_n)_{n \in V'})$ was derived from a pattern tree $\mathcal{T} = ((V, E, r), (P_n)_{n \in V})$ by duplicating a triple to a child, denoted by $\mathcal{T} \hookrightarrow \mathcal{T}'$, if $(V', E', r') = (V, E, r)$ (that is, the underlying trees are the same), and there exist a node $u \in V$, a triple $t \in P_u$, and a child v of u, such that $P'_v = P_v \cup \{t\}$, and $P_n = P'_n$ for all $n \neq v$. We denote by $\hookrightarrow^*$ the reflexive and transitive closure of $\hookrightarrow$, that is, $\mathcal{T} \hookrightarrow^* \mathcal{T}'$ if $\mathcal{T} = \mathcal{T}'$ or there exists a sequence $\mathcal{T}_1 \hookrightarrow \mathcal{T}_2 \hookrightarrow \ldots \hookrightarrow \mathcal{T}_m$ with $\mathcal{T}_1 = \mathcal{T}$ and $\mathcal{T}_m = \mathcal{T}'$. It is easy to observe that every QWDPT can be converted into a well-designed pattern tree by duplicating triples along branches. Formally, for every QWDPT $\mathcal{T}$, there exists a well-designed pattern tree $\mathcal{T}'$ such that $\mathcal{T} \hookrightarrow^* \mathcal{T}'$. It is also easy to observe that the (quasi) well-designed property is invariant under $\hookrightarrow^*$. We now have all the necessary ingredients to define a semantics of pattern trees. We first define the set of SPARQL graph patterns defined by a QWDPT.

Definition 3.8 *Let $\mathcal{T}$ be a QWDPT. The set of SPARQL graph patterns defined by $\mathcal{T}$ is*

$$\text{SEM}(\mathcal{T}) = \{\text{TR}(\mathcal{T}', \Sigma) \mid \Sigma \text{ is an ordering for } \mathcal{T}',$$
$$\mathcal{T} \hookrightarrow^* \mathcal{T}' \text{ and } \mathcal{T}' \text{ is well-designed}\}.$$

To define the result of evaluating a QWDPT $\mathcal{T}$ over an RDF graph G, we first show that all queries in $\text{SEM}(\mathcal{T})$ are equivalent. Using this property, we then define the evaluation of $\mathcal{T}$ to be exactly the same as that of an arbitrarily chosen query from $\text{SEM}(\mathcal{T})$.

Lemma 3.9 *Let $\mathcal{T}$ be a well-designed pattern tree, let Σ_1, Σ_2 be two arbitrary orderings for $\mathcal{T}$, and let $P_1 = \text{TR}(\mathcal{T}, \Sigma_1)$ and $P_2 = \text{TR}(\mathcal{T}, \Sigma_2)$ be the graph patterns obtained by transforming $\mathcal{T}$ with Σ_1 and Σ_2, respectively. Then $P_1 \equiv P_2$.*

Lemma 3.10 *Let $\mathcal{T}$ be a QWDPT, let Σ be an ordering for $\mathcal{T}$, and let $\mathcal{T}_1$ and $\mathcal{T}_2$ be well-designed pattern trees such that $\mathcal{T} \hookrightarrow^* \mathcal{T}_1$ and $\mathcal{T} \hookrightarrow^* \mathcal{T}_2$. If $P_1 = \text{TR}(\mathcal{T}_1, \Sigma)$ and $P_2 = \text{TR}(\mathcal{T}_2, \Sigma)$, then $P_1 \equiv P_2$.*

Putting these two lemmas together, we get the following result.

Theorem 3.11 *Let $\mathcal{T}$ be a QWDPT. Then all graph patterns in $\text{SEM}(\mathcal{T})$ are equivalent, i.e., for any two graph patterns $P_1, P_2 \in \text{SEM}(\mathcal{T})$, it holds that $P_1 \equiv P_2$.*

Definition 3.12 *Let $\mathcal{T}$ be a QWDPT and G an RDF graph. Then the evaluation of $\mathcal{T}$ over G, denoted by $[\![\mathcal{T}]\!]_G$, is defined as the set of mappings $[\![P]\!]_G$ for an arbitrary $P \in \text{SEM}(\mathcal{T})$.*

By Theorem 3.11, the semantics of a QWDPT according to Definition 3.12 is well defined. This means that, for QWDPT $\mathcal{T}$, we may choose any representative from $\text{SEM}(\mathcal{T})$ for evaluation. In particular, if $\mathcal{T}$ is already well-designed, we may simply fix the order of the child nodes of each node and evaluate this SPARQL pattern.

Given two QWDPTs $\mathcal{T}_1$ and $\mathcal{T}_2$, we say that $\mathcal{T}_1$ and $\mathcal{T}_2$ are equivalent, denoted by $\mathcal{T}_1 \equiv \mathcal{T}_2$, if for every RDF graph G it holds

that $[\![\mathcal{T}_1]\!]_G = [\![\mathcal{T}_2]\!]_G$. Similarly, a QWDPT $\mathcal{T}$ is equivalent to a SPARQL graph pattern P, denoted by $\mathcal{T} \equiv P$, if for every RDF graph G it holds that $[\![\mathcal{T}]\!]_G = [\![P]\!]_G$. Notice that Definition 3.12 plus Proposition 3.6 imply that for every QWDPT $\mathcal{T}$ there exists a well-designed graph pattern P such that $\mathcal{T} \equiv P$. The last result of this section states that the opposite also holds, and thus, QWDPTs can represent the entire class of well-designed SPARQL graph patterns.

Proposition 3.13 *For every well-designed graph pattern P, there exists a QWDPT $\mathcal{T}$ such that $P \equiv \mathcal{T}$. Moreover, given a well-designed graph pattern, an equivalent QWDPT can be constructed in polynomial time.*

3.2 Evaluating pattern trees

In this section we introduce a procedural semantics for QWDPTs that takes advantage of our tree representation. In [25] the authors proposed a top-down evaluation method for SPARQL graph patterns and they showed that given a graph G, it is equivalent to the evaluation given by $[\![\cdot]\!]_G$. Our proposal is similar to the approach in [25], but it is based on an alternative characterization of the evaluation of well-designed graph patterns proposed in [27]. We reformulate here this characterization for the case of pattern trees. It will later play an important role when we study transformations of pattern trees as well as containment and equivalence testing. We first introduce the necessary terminology.

We say that a mapping μ_1 is *subsumed by* μ_2, denoted by $\mu_1 \sqsubseteq \mu_2$, if $\text{dom}(\mu_1) \cap \text{dom}(\mu_2) = \text{dom}(\mu_1)$ and for every $?X \in \text{dom}(\mu_1)$ it holds that $\mu_1(?X) = \mu_2(?X)$ (implying that $\mu_1 \sim \mu_2$). We write $\mu_1 \sqsubset \mu_2$ whenever $\mu_1 \sqsubseteq \mu_2$ and $\mu_1 \neq \mu_2$. Further, recall that given a set $P = \{t_1, \ldots, t_\ell\}$ of triple patterns, we denote by $and(P)$ the graph pattern $(t_1 \text{ AND } t_2 \text{ AND } \cdots \text{ AND } t_\ell)$. Now given a pattern tree $\mathcal{T} = ((V, E, r), (P_n)_{n \in V})$, we use $and(\mathcal{T})$ to denote the SPARQL pattern constructed by taking the conjunction (AND) of all the triples that occur in $\mathcal{T}$. That is, if $V = \{n_1, \ldots, n_\ell\}$, then

$$and(\mathcal{T}) = \big(and(P_{n_1}) \text{ AND } \cdots \text{ AND } and(P_{n_\ell})\big).$$

We next characterize the evaluation of a QWDPT. It follows directly from the results in [27] for well-designed graph patterns, and the relationship with QWDPTs shown in the previous section.

Lemma 3.14 *Let $\mathcal{T}$ be a QWDPT with root r, and G an RDF graph. A mapping μ is in $[\![\mathcal{T}]\!]_G$ if and only if*

1. *$\mu \in [\![and(\mathcal{T}')]\!]_G$ for a subtree $\mathcal{T}'$ of $\mathcal{T}$ rooted at r, and*

2. *there are no mapping ν and subtree $\mathcal{T}''$ of $\mathcal{T}$ rooted at r, such that $\mu \sqsubset \nu$ and $\nu \in [\![and(\mathcal{T}'')]\!]_G$.*

Lemma 3.14 essentially states that the mappings in the evaluation of a QWDPT over some graph G are exactly those that map all triples in some subtree $\mathcal{T}'$ of $\mathcal{T}$ (hence $and(\mathcal{T}')$) into G, and that cannot be further extended by considering another subtree $\mathcal{T}''$ of $\mathcal{T}$. This characterization inspires the following procedural semantics that is obtained by evaluating the pattern tree by a top-down traversal. For simplicity, given a label P_n of node n and a graph G, we denote by $[\![P_n]\!]_G$ the set $[\![and(P_n)]\!]_G$.

Definition 3.15 *Consider an RDF graph G, a QWDPT $\mathcal{T} = ((V, E, r), (P_n)_{n \in V})$, and a set M of mappings. For $n \in V$, we define the evaluation of $\mathcal{T}_n$ (the complete subtree of $\mathcal{T}$ rooted at n) given M over G, denoted by $\text{ext}(M, n, G)$ as follows. If n is a leaf, then*

$$\text{ext}(M, n, G) = M \bowtie [\![P_n]\!]_G,$$

and, otherwise, if $n_1, \ldots, n_k$ are the child nodes of n, then

$$\mathrm{ext}(M, n, G) = M_1 \bowtie M_2 \bowtie \cdots \bowtie M_k,$$

where $M_i = (M \bowtie [\![P_n]\!]_G) \bowtie \mathrm{ext}(M \bowtie [\![P_n]\!]_G, n_i, G)$. We define the top-down evaluation *of $\mathcal{T}$ over G, denoted by $[\![\mathcal{T}]\!]_G^{td}$, as*

$$[\![\mathcal{T}]\!]_G^{td} = \mathrm{ext}(\{\mu_\emptyset\}, r, G),$$

where $\mu_\emptyset$ is the mapping with the empty domain.

The following theorem shows that the top-down evaluation defined above coincides with the semantics of pattern trees introduced in the previous section.

Theorem 3.16 *Let $\mathcal{T}$ be a QWDPT and G an RDF graph. Then $[\![\mathcal{T}]\!]_G = [\![\mathcal{T}]\!]_G^{td}$.*

Recall that in Definition 3.12 we defined the semantics of QWDPTs by their extensions to well-designed SPARQL patterns. Theorem 3.16 now allows us to define the semantics of QWDPTs directly via their tree representation. This nicely supports the idea of using QWDPTs as query execution plans for well-designed SPARQL query patterns: they provide a syntactical representation of a query together with an operational semantics working on this representation. In these terms, the relaxation from well-designed pattern trees to QWDPTs provides additional potential for optimization and redundancy elimination for those query plans.

3.3 Transformation of QWDPTs

One advantage of QWDPTs is that they allow us to define several equivalence-preserving transformations on the structure of the pattern trees. Previous works [27, 34] on transformation rules for SPARQL patterns have been based on the properties of the SPARQL operators. In contrast, the transformations that we introduce in this section are based on the tree structure of QWDPTs (i.e. the *operator structure*) and the structure of the sets of triple patterns composing the pattern tree. These structural transformations provide further evidence that pattern trees are a suitable query-plan representation for SPARQL in the spirit of classical relational-algebra query plans.

Before presenting our rules, we need to introduce some additional notation. Let $\mathcal{T} = ((V, E, r), \mathcal{P})$ be a pattern tree, and n a node in V. We define the *branch of n in $\mathcal{T}$*, denoted by $\mathrm{branch}(n, \mathcal{T})$, as the unique path from r to n, given as the sequence of nodes $n_1, \ldots, n_k$ with $n_1 = r$ and $n_k = n$. If it is clear from the context, we may drop the name of the pattern tree and simply write $\mathrm{branch}(n)$. We denote by $P_{\mathrm{branch}(n, \mathcal{T})}$ the set of triple patterns $\bigcup_{i=1}^k P_{n_i}$. Given two sets P_1 and P_2 of triple patterns, a *homomorphism h from P_1 into P_2*, written $h \colon P_1 \to P_2$, is a mapping $h \colon \mathrm{vars}(P_1) \to \mathbf{U} \times \mathbf{V}$ s.t. for all triple patterns $t \in P_1$ it holds that $h(t) \in P_2$, where $h(t)$ denotes the triple obtained from t by replacing all variables $?X \in \mathrm{vars}(t)$ by $h(?X)$ and leaving URIs unchanged. It is further convenient to introduce the following notation to speak about variables occurring in some P_n.

Definition 3.17 *Let $\mathcal{T} = ((V, E, r), \mathcal{P})$ be a pattern tree and $n, \hat{n} \in V$ s.t. $\hat{n}$ is the parent node of n. Then the* new variables *at n are defined as $\mathrm{newvars}(n) = \mathrm{vars}(P_n) \setminus \mathrm{vars}(P_{\mathrm{branch}(\hat{n})})$. For the case of the root r, we define $\mathrm{newvars}(r)$ as $\mathrm{vars}(P_r)$.*

We are now ready to state a set of transformation rules for QWDPTs. In the formulation of the rules we assume that whenever we remove a node n from a pattern tree, then all edges incident to n are removed as well. We further assume a fixed QWDPT $\mathcal{T} = ((V, E, r), (P_n)_{n \in V})$ to be the pattern tree before the application, and we consider $\mathcal{T}' = ((V', E', r'), (P'_n)_{n \in V'})$ as the result-

ing QWDPT after applying the rule. If P'_n is not defined explicitly for some $n \in V'$, we always consider $P'_n = P_n$ by "default".

Rule R1 (*deletion of redundant triples*): Let $n \in V$. If there exists a triple $t \in P_n$ s.t. $t \in P_{n'}$ for some ancestor n' of n, then delete t from P_n, i.e. $P'_n = P_n \setminus \{t\}$. If $P'_n = \emptyset$, delete n and turn its child nodes into children of the parent of n.

Rule R2 (*deletion of unproductive nodes*): Let $n, \hat{n} \in V$ s.t. $\hat{n}$ is the parent of n, and let $n_1, \ldots, n_k \in V$ be the children of n. If $\mathrm{newvars}(n) = \emptyset$, then merge n into each of its children and make each n_i a child of $\hat{n}$. I.e. let $P'_{n_i} = P_{n_i} \cup P_n$ for $i = \{1, \ldots, k\}$, $V' = V \setminus \{n\}$, and $E' = (E \setminus \{(\hat{n}, n), (n, n_1), \ldots, (n, n_k)\}) \cup \{(\hat{n}, n_1), \ldots, (\hat{n}, n_k)\}$. If n has no child node, then applying this rule is equivalent to deleting n.

Rule R3 (*homomorphism upwards*): Let $n, \hat{n} \in V$ be nodes s.t. $\hat{n}$ is the parent of n, and let $n_1, \ldots, n_k \in V$ be the children of n. If there exists a homomorphism $h \colon P_n \to P_{\mathrm{branch}(\hat{n})}$ with $h(?X) = ?X$ for all variables $?X \in \mathrm{vars}(P_n) \cap \mathrm{vars}(P_{\mathrm{branch}(\hat{n})})$, then *merge n into $\hat{n}$*, i.e. let $P'_{\hat{n}} = P_{\hat{n}} \cup P_n$, $V' = V \setminus \{n\}$ (remove n) and $E' = (E \setminus \{(\hat{n}, n), (n, n_1), \ldots, (n, n_k)\}) \cup \{(\hat{n}, n_1), \ldots, (\hat{n}, n_k)\}$ (turn n's child nodes into children of $\hat{n}$).

Rule R4 (*parallelization*): Consider nodes $\hat{n}, n, n' \in V$ s.t. $\hat{n}$ is the parent of n, and n is the parent of n'. If there exists a homomorphism $h \colon P_n \to P_{n'} \cup P_{\mathrm{branch}(\hat{n})}$ with $h(?X) = ?X$ for all variables $?X \in \mathrm{vars}(P_n) \cap \mathrm{vars}(P_{\mathrm{branch}(\hat{n})})$, then turn n' from a child of n into a child of $\hat{n}$, if the resulting pattern tree is quasi well-designed. I.e. $V' = V$, $E = (E \setminus \{(n, n')\}) \cup \{(\hat{n}, n')\}$, if $\mathcal{T}'$ is still quasi well-designed.

The following result shows the correctness of the rules.

Theorem 3.18 *Let $\mathcal{T}$ be a QWDPT and $\mathcal{T}'$ the pattern tree that results from applying either rule R1, or R2, or R3, or R4, to $\mathcal{T}$. Then $\mathcal{T}'$ is a QWDPT such that $\mathcal{T} \equiv \mathcal{T}'$.*

We say that a QWDPT $\mathcal{T}$ is *reduced* w.r.t. to some rule R, if R cannot be applied to $\mathcal{T}$. While checking if some QWDPT $\mathcal{T}$ is reduced w.r.t. R3 or R4 is an expensive task (it requires to decide the existence of some homomorphisms), it is rather easy to determine if $\mathcal{T}$ is reduced w.r.t. R1 or R2. Moreover, already if $\mathcal{T}$ is reduced only w.r.t. R1 and R2, it possesses some useful properties that make it easier to work with – and reason about – $\mathcal{T}$. We thus introduce a first normal form for QWDPTs based on these two rules.

Definition 3.19 *We say that a QWDPT $\mathcal{T}$ is in* non-redundant normal form *(NR normal form) if $\mathcal{T}$ is reduced w.r.t. rules R1 and R2.*

Next, we discuss some properties of the NR normal form.

Proposition 3.20 *Let $\mathcal{T}$ be a QWDPT. Then the following hold:*

1. *Iteratively applying rules R1 and R2 (in arbitrary order) to $\mathcal{T}$ leads to a unique pattern tree $\mathcal{T}^*$ in NR normal form.*

2. *If $\mathcal{T}$ is in NR normal form then it remains in NR normal form when applying rules R3 or R4 to $\mathcal{T}$.*

The crucial property of the NR normal form is the following. Let $\mathcal{T} = ((V, E, r), \mathcal{P})$ be a QWDPT in NR normal form. Then for every $n \in V$ s.t. $n \neq r$, it holds that $\mathrm{newvars}(n) \neq \emptyset$. This simple property, which follows directly from the definition of rule R2, allows us to define an alternative characterization of the solutions of QWDPTs in terms of maximal subtrees. In the characterization we use the following notation. Given a mapping μ and a set of mappings M, we say that M subsumes μ, denoted by $\mu \sqsubseteq M$ if there exists a mapping $\nu \in M$ such that $\mu \sqsubseteq \nu$.

Lemma 3.21 *Let $\mathcal{T}$ be a QWDPT in NR normal form with root r, and G an RDF graph. Then $\mu \in [\![\mathcal{T}]\!]_G$ if and only if there exists a subtree $\mathcal{T}'$ of $\mathcal{T}$ rooted at r such that*

1. $\mathrm{dom}(\mu) = \mathrm{vars}(\mathcal{T}')$, *and*

2. $\mathcal{T}'$ *is the maximal subtree of $\mathcal{T}$ such that $\mu \sqsubseteq [\![and(\mathcal{T}')]\!]_G$.*

Notice that as opposed to Lemma 3.14 that characterizes the mappings in the evaluation of a QWDPT as the maximal (w.r.t. $\sqsubseteq$) mappings satisfying some property, Lemma 3.21 takes advantage of the NR normal form to characterize mappings in terms of the structure of a QWDPT, in particular, in terms of maximal subtrees.

The NR normal form provides a "cheap" elimination of some redundancies. As such it will be an integral part of the equivalence test for QWDPTs in Section 4.2. But also rule R3, which can reduce some more complex sources of redundancy in the structure of trees, will play an important role in the equivalence test. We thus introduce another normal form.

Definition 3.22 *Let $\mathcal{T}$ be a QWDPT. We say that $\mathcal{T}$ is in R3 normal form if $\mathcal{T}$ is reduced w.r.t. rules R1, R2, and R3.*

One intuition of the R3 normal form is that given some QWDPT $((V, E, r), \mathcal{P})$ in this normal form, for every $n \in V$ with parent $\hat{n}$, there exists at least one RDF graph G and mapping μ with $\mu(P_{\mathrm{branch}(\hat{n})}) \subseteq G$ that cannot be extended to a mapping μ' s.t. $\mu'(P_n) \subseteq G$. I.e. from the fact that some variable assignment maps $P_{\mathrm{branch}(\hat{n})}$ into G, we cannot derive any statement about P_n. This intuitively implies that every node in the tree carries some information which is non-redundant with respect to its ancestors. We next discuss some basic properties of the R3 normal form.

Proposition 3.23 *Let $\mathcal{T}$ be a QWDPT. Then the following hold:*

1. *Iteratively applying R1, R2, and R3 to $\mathcal{T}$ eventually leads to a (not necessarily unique) pattern $\mathcal{T}^*$ that is in R3 normal form. Moreover, if $\mathcal{T}$ is in NR-normal form, then iteratively applying R3 leads to a unique pattern $\mathcal{T}^*$ in R3 normal form.*

2. *The number of rule applications of R1, R2, and R3 needed to arrive at a pattern in R3 normal form is linear in the size of $\mathcal{T}$.*

We have proposed a tree representation of SPARQL queries and a set of rules that can be used to restructure these trees. We can consider these trees as query plans for SPARQL queries. The results presented in this section therefore describe a starting point for the study of an algebra of query plans, which forms the basis of query optimization for this language. QWDPTs together with rules R1 – R3 will also be crucial for studying classical static analysis problems for SPARQL in the next section. Rule R4 has been mainly presented so as to give a flavor of what further transformation rules in this algebra could look like. It may be beneficial in particular in an environment where parallel processing is supported.

4. CONTAINMENT AND EQUIVALENCE

In this section we study the fundamental problems of containment and equivalence of well-designed SPARQL queries. Similarly to query languages on relational databases, these problems are crucial for query optimization. For containment we consider the *subsumption relation* ($\sqsubseteq$) introduced in Section 3.2 rather than the classical subset relation ($\subseteq$). Clearly, for CQs, the two notions coincide. However, in the presence of partial query answers, subsumption is the more natural notion of containment [21, 3], and has also been considered in recent work to compare the evaluation of two patterns containing OPT operators [27, 3]. This is illustrated in the following example (taken from [3]).

Example 4.1 (From [3]) *Consider two SPARQL graph patterns $P_1 = (?X, n, ?Y)$ and $P_2 = (?X, n, ?Y)$ OPT $(?X, e, ?Z)$, and an RDF graph $G = \{(a, n, b), (a, e, c)\}$. Then $[\![P_1]\!]_G = \{\mu = \{?X \to a, ?Y \to b\}\}$, while $[\![P_2]\!]_G = \{\mu' = \{?X \to a, ?Y \to b, ?Z \to c\}\}$. Hence $P_1 \not\subseteq P_2$. This is, however, unintuitive, since the answer to P_2 contains strictly more information than that to P_1, and it is easy to see that for no graph G, pattern P_2 returns fewer bindings than P_1.*

For CQs without existentially quantified variables, both equivalence and containment are tractable. In the presence of existential quantifiers, they are classical NP-complete problems [8]. In this paper, we study equivalence and containment for well-designed SPARQL queries, or, equivalently, for our representation by quasi well-designed pattern trees (QWDPTs). In contrast to CQs, the complexities of containment (in the form of subsumption) and equivalence diverge in this case. Indeed, we prove that subsumption between QWDPTs is Π_2^P-complete while the equivalence problem is NP-complete. The NP-membership will be the most difficult part to prove. The key to this NP-membership result is the R3-normal form introduced in the previous section and an appropriate extension of homomorphisms, which we shall refer to as "strong homomorphisms".

4.1 Complexity of subsumption

We extend the definition of subsumption of mappings introduced in Section 3.2, to subsumption of sets of mappings. Given sets of mappings M_1 and M_2 we say that M_1 is subsumed by M_2, denoted by $M_1 \sqsubseteq M_2$, if for every $\mu_1 \in M_1$ there exists a $\mu_2 \in M_2$ such that $\mu_1 \sqsubseteq \mu_2$. Further, for two QWDPTs $\mathcal{T}_1$ and $\mathcal{T}_2$, we say that $\mathcal{T}_1$ is subsumed by $\mathcal{T}_2$, denoted by $\mathcal{T}_1 \sqsubseteq \mathcal{T}_2$, if $[\![\mathcal{T}_1]\!]_G \sqsubseteq [\![\mathcal{T}_2]\!]_G$ holds for every graph G. We are now ready to provide a necessary and sufficient condition to test whether $\mathcal{T}_1 \sqsubseteq \mathcal{T}_2$.

Lemma 4.2 *Consider QWDPTs $\mathcal{T}_1$ and $\mathcal{T}_2$ with roots r_1 and r_2, respectively. Then $\mathcal{T}_1 \sqsubseteq \mathcal{T}_2$ if and only if for every subtree $\mathcal{T}_1'$ of $\mathcal{T}_1$ rooted at r_1, there exists a subtree $\mathcal{T}_2'$ of $\mathcal{T}_2$ rooted at r_2 s.t.:*

1. $\mathrm{vars}(\mathcal{T}_1') \subseteq \mathrm{vars}(\mathcal{T}_2')$, *and*

2. *there exists a homomorphism from the triples in $\mathcal{T}_2'$ to the triples in $\mathcal{T}_1'$ that is the identity over $\mathrm{vars}(\mathcal{T}_1')$.*

Lemma 4.2 yields a straightforward Π_2^P procedure to check whether $\mathcal{T}_1 \sqsubseteq \mathcal{T}_2$ holds: check for every subtree $\mathcal{T}_1'$ of $\mathcal{T}_1$ that there exists a subtree $\mathcal{T}_2'$ of $\mathcal{T}_2$ and a homomorphism satisfying properties (1) and (2). Below, we also show the matching lower bound.

Theorem 4.3 *The subsumption problem of QWDPTs (and, therefore, of well-designed SPARQL graph patterns) is Π_2^P-complete.*

PROOF IDEA. The membership was argued above. The hardness is shown by reduction from the well-known Π_2^P-hard problem 3-QSAT$_{\forall, 2}$. Given an arbitrary instance of this problem by a quantified Boolean formula $\Psi = \forall \vec{x} \exists \vec{y} \phi(\vec{x}, \vec{y})$ where ϕ is in 3-CNF, we define two QWDPTs $\mathcal{T}_1$ and $\mathcal{T}_2$, s.t. $\mathcal{T}_1 \sqsubseteq \mathcal{T}_2$ iff Ψ is valid. The QWDPT $\mathcal{T}_2$ consists of the root only and contains a variable $?X_i$ and $?Y_j$ for every variable x_i in $\vec{x}$ resp. y_j in $\vec{y}$. Moreover, $\mathcal{T}_2$ contains triple patterns which "encode" the clauses in ϕ. The QWDPT $\mathcal{T}_1$ consists of the root plus one child node n_i for every variable x_i in $\vec{x}$. Recall from Lemma 3.14 the correspondence between mappings μ_1 in $[\![\mathcal{T}_1]\!]_G$ (for a some RDF graph G) and subtrees of $\mathcal{T}_1$. Now every $\mu_1 \in [\![\mathcal{T}_1]\!]_G$ corresponds to some subtree $\mathcal{T}_1'$ of $\mathcal{T}_1$ containing a particular subset of the child nodes n_i of the root of $\mathcal{T}_1$. Moreover, every such μ_1 requires a particular binding of the variables $?X_i$ in $\mathcal{T}_2$ and thus defines a particular truth assignment I on $\vec{x}$ (with $I(x_i) = true$ iff $\mu_1(P_{n_i}) \subseteq G$). Then μ_1 can be extended to a mapping μ_2 in $[\![\mathcal{T}_1]\!]_G$ if all triple patterns in $\mathcal{T}_2$ can be sent to G by an appropriate instantiation of the variables $?Y_j$. Again the variable bindings of the variables $?Y_j$ are in 1-to-1 correspondence with truth value assignments to the variables y_j in $\vec{y}$. Moreover, sending the triple patterns in $\mathcal{T}_2$ (which encode the clauses of ϕ) into G comes down to satisfying the clauses in ϕ. $\square$

Our next result establishes the close connection between subsumption and equivalence of well-designed SPARQL queries.

Lemma 4.4 *Let* $\mathcal{T}_1$ *and* $\mathcal{T}_2$ *be two QWDPTs. Then* $\mathcal{T}_1 \equiv \mathcal{T}_2$ *if and only if* $\mathcal{T}_1 \sqsubseteq \mathcal{T}_2$ *and* $\mathcal{T}_2 \sqsubseteq \mathcal{T}_1$.

From Theorem 4.3 and Lemma 4.4 we obtain that equivalence of well-designed SPARQL queries can be tested in Π_2^P. However, in the next section we provide a better upper-bound, namely NP.

4.2 Complexity of equivalence

We now prove that testing the equivalence of two QWDPTs (and, thus of two well-designed SPARQL queries) is NP-complete. The difficult part is the NP-membership. A key concept for this proof is the notion of a *strong homomorphism* between two branches of one or two pattern trees. Based on this concept, we introduce the notion of *strongly homomorphically equivalent* branches.

Definition 4.5 (strong homomorphism) *Consider two QWDPTs* $\mathcal{T}_1 = ((V_1, E_1, r_1), \mathcal{P}_1)$ *and* $\mathcal{T}_2 = ((V_2, E_2, r_2), \mathcal{P}_2)$. *Moreover, let* $n_1 \in V_1$, $n_2 \in V_2$, *and let* $\mathrm{branch}(n_1, \mathcal{T}_1)$ *be the sequence of nodes* $r_1 = n^1, \dots, n^k = n_1$.

We say that there exists a strong homomorphism $\mathcal{H}\colon \mathrm{branch}(n_1, \mathcal{T}_1) \to \mathrm{branch}(n_2, \mathcal{T}_2)$ *if* $\mathcal{H}$ *is a set* $\mathcal{H} = \{h_i \mid 1 \le i \le k\}$ *of homomorphisms* $h_i\colon P_{n^i} \to P_{\mathrm{branch}(n_2, \mathcal{T}_2)} \cup P_{\mathrm{branch}(n^{i-1}, \mathcal{T}_1)}$ *s.t.* $h_i(?X) = ?X$ *for all* $?X \in \mathrm{vars}(P_{n^i}) \cap \mathrm{vars}(P_{\mathrm{branch}(n_2, \mathcal{T}_2)} \cup P_{\mathrm{branch}(n^{i-1}, \mathcal{T}_1)})$ *(where for* $i = 1$ *let* $P_{\mathrm{branch}(n^{i-1}, \mathcal{T}_1)} = \emptyset$).

We further say that $\mathrm{branch}(n_1, \mathcal{T}_1)$ *and* $\mathrm{branch}(n_2, \mathcal{T}_2)$ *are strongly homomorphically equivalent if there exist strong homomorphisms* $\mathcal{H}_1\colon \mathrm{branch}(n_1, \mathcal{T}_1) \to \mathrm{branch}(n_2, \mathcal{T}_2)$ *and* $\mathcal{H}_2\colon \mathrm{branch}(n_2, \mathcal{T}_2) \to \mathrm{branch}(n_1, \mathcal{T}_1)$.

The basic intuition of a strong homomorphism $\mathcal{H}\colon \mathrm{branch}(n_1) \to \mathrm{branch}(n_2)$ is that every variable assignment μ that maps $P_{\mathrm{branch}(n_2)}$ into some RDF graph G can be extended to a variable assignment μ' that also maps $P_{\mathrm{branch}(n_1)}$ into G. Note that a simple homomorphism $h\colon P_{\mathrm{branch}(n_1)} \to P_{\mathrm{branch}(n_2)}$ is not enough to guarantee this, as can be seen in the following example.

Example 4.6 *Consider the following QWDPTs* $\mathcal{T}_1$ *and* $\mathcal{T}_2$:

$n_1\colon \{(?V, c, ?V)\}$
|
$n_2\colon \{(?Y_1, a, ?Y_2), (?X_1, a, ?Z)\}$
|
$n_3\colon \{(?Y_3, a, ?Y_4), (?X_1, b, ?X_1)\}$

$n_1'\colon \{(?V, c, ?V)\}$
/ \
$n_2'\colon \{(?Y_1, a, ?Y_2)\}$ $n_4'\colon \{(?X_1, a, ?Z)\}$
|
$n_3'\colon \{(?Y_3, a, ?Y_4), (?Y_1, b, ?Y_1)\}$

Consider the branches $\mathrm{branch}(n_3, \mathcal{T}_1)$ *and* $\mathrm{branch}(n_3', \mathcal{T}_2)$. *It is easy to see that there exists a homomorphism* $h\colon P_{\mathrm{branch}(n_3, \mathcal{T}_1)} \to P_{\mathrm{branch}(n_3', \mathcal{T}_2)}$, *that is the identity on all shared variables* $?Y_1$, $?Y_2$, $?Y_3$, $?Y_4$, $?V$, *and with* $h(?X_1) = ?Y_1$ *and* $h(?Z) = ?Y_2$. *However, there does not exist a strong homomorphism* $\mathcal{H}\colon P_{\mathrm{branch}(n_3, \mathcal{T}_1)} \to P_{\mathrm{branch}(n_3', \mathcal{T}_2)}$ *because a homomorphism* $h_3\colon P_{n_3} \to P_{\mathrm{branch}(n_3', \mathcal{T}_2)} \cup P_{\mathrm{branch}(n_2, \mathcal{T}_1)}$ *with the desired properties according to Definition 4.5 is missing.*

Now consider the RDF graph $G = \{(v, c, v), (y_1, a, y_2), (x_1, a, z), (y_3, a, y_4), (y_1, b, y_1)\}$, *and some variable assignment* τ *that is defined only on variables in* $\mathrm{branch}(n_3', \mathcal{T}_2)$. *If* τ *maps* $\mathrm{branch}(n_3', \mathcal{T}_2)$ *into* G, *then because of the homomorphism* h *there exists and extension* τ' *of* τ *that also maps* $\mathrm{branch}(n_3, \mathcal{T}_1)$ *into* G.

However, if we consider variable mappings that assign a value to variables not occurring in $\mathrm{branch}(n_3', \mathcal{T}_2)$ *(which will be necessary in order to test equivalence), then simple homomorphisms are not enough. This is especially true if the additional variables occur somewhere in the branch of* n_3. *Consider* $\mu\colon \{?V \to v, ?Z \to z\} \cup \{?Y_i \to y_i \mid 1 \le i \le 4\} \cup \{?X_1 \to x_1\}$, *for which* $\mu(P_{\mathrm{branch}(n_3', \mathcal{T}_2)}) \subseteq G$ *holds. But* $\mu(P_{\mathrm{branch}(n_3, \mathcal{T}_1)}) \not\subseteq G$: *because of* $\mu(?X_1) = x_1$, *the triple* $(?X_1, b, ?X_1)$ *is mapped to* (x_1, b, x_1) *by* μ, *but* $(x_1, b, x_1) \notin G$. *Hence, despite the existence of* h *and* $\mu(\mathrm{branch}(n_3', \mathcal{T}_2)) \subseteq G$, μ *is not a solution to* $\mathcal{T}_1$.

Note that if we replace the pattern $(?X_1, b, ?X_1)$ *in* n_3 *by* $(?Y_1, b, ?Y_1)$, *then there exists a strong homomorphism* $\mathcal{H}\colon P_{\mathrm{branch}(n_3, \mathcal{T}_1)} \to P_{\mathrm{branch}(n_3', \mathcal{T}_2)}$. *Actually,* $\mathcal{T}_1$ *and* $\mathcal{T}_2$ *can then be shown to be equivalent.*

Consider nodes n_1 and n_2 as in Definition 4.5. Intuitively, the reason why a simple homomorphism is not enough is that there may be RDF graphs G and variable assignments μ that not only map all triple patterns in $\mathrm{branch}(n_2)$ into G, but also the triple patterns contained in some "prefix" of $\mathrm{branch}(n_1)$. Hence to extend such variable assignments to the complete branch $\mathrm{branch}(n_1)$, the existing variable assignments on the variables in this "prefix" of $\mathrm{branch}(n_1)$ must not be altered. This idea, which will be crucial for our NP equivalence test, is formalized in the following lemma.

Lemma 4.7 *Consider two QWDPTs* $\mathcal{T}_1 = ((V_1, E_1, r_1), \mathcal{P}_1)$ *and* $\mathcal{T}_2 = ((V_2, E_2, r_2), \mathcal{P}_2)$, *and let* $n_1 \in V_1$ *and* $n_2 \in V_2$ *with* $\mathrm{branch}(n_1, \mathcal{T}_1) = n^1, \dots, n^k$. *Then the following statements are equivalent:*

1. *There exists a strong homomorphism* $\mathcal{H}\colon \mathrm{branch}(n_1, \mathcal{T}_1) \to \mathrm{branch}(n_2, \mathcal{T}_2)$.

2. *For every* $i \in \{1, \dots, k\}$, *for every RDF graph* G *and every mapping* $\mu\colon \mathrm{vars}(P_{\mathrm{branch}(n_2, \mathcal{T}_2)} \cup P_{\mathrm{branch}(n^{i-1}, \mathcal{T}_1)}) \to \mathrm{dom}(G)$ *the following holds:*
   If $\mu(P_{\mathrm{branch}(n_2, \mathcal{T}_2)} \cup P_{\mathrm{branch}(n^{i-1}, \mathcal{T}_1)}) \subseteq G$, *then there exists a mapping* $\mu'\colon \mathrm{vars}(P_{\mathrm{branch}(n_1, \mathcal{T}_1)}) \to \mathrm{dom}(G)$ *s.t.* $\mu'(P_{\mathrm{branch}(n_1, \mathcal{T}_1)}) \subseteq G$ *and* $\mu(?X) = \mu'(?X)$ *for all* $?X \in \mathrm{dom}(\mu) \cap \mathrm{dom}(\mu')$ *(where for* $i = 1$, *let* $P_{\mathrm{branch}(n^{i-1})} = \emptyset$).

If n_1 and n_2 are from the same pattern tree, we can show a slightly stronger result below, namely: for every solution that maps the triple patterns at the branch to n_2 into an RDF graph G, the same solution also maps the triple patterns at the branch to n_1 into G, provided that a strong homomorphism $\mathrm{branch}(n_1) \to \mathrm{branch}(n_2)$ exists.

Proposition 4.8 *Consider a QWDPT* $\mathcal{T} = ((V, E, r), \mathcal{P})$ *and nodes* $n_1, n_2 \in V$. *Then the following statements are equivalent:*

1. *There exists a strong homomorphism* $\mathcal{H}\colon \mathrm{branch}(n_1, \mathcal{T}) \to \mathrm{branch}(n_2, \mathcal{T})$.

2. *For every RDF graph* G *and* $\mu \in [\![\mathcal{T}]\!]_G$ *it holds that* $\mu(P_{\mathrm{branch}(n_1)}) \subseteq G$ *whenever* $\mu(P_{\mathrm{branch}(n_2)}) \subseteq G$.

For convenience, we introduce some more notation. Let $\mathcal{T}_1 = ((V_1, E_1, r_1), \mathcal{P}_1)$ and $\mathcal{T}_2 = ((V_2, E_2, r_2), \mathcal{P}_2)$ be two QWDPTs. For $n_1 \in V_1$, we denote with $\mathrm{cor}(n_1, V_2)$ the set of *corresponding nodes* in V_2, i.e., $\mathrm{cor}(n_1, V_2) = \{n_2 \mid n_2 \in V_2, \mathrm{newvars}(n_1) \cap \mathrm{newvars}(n_2) \ne \emptyset\}$. If clear from the context, we may drop the V_2 and just write $\mathrm{cor}(n_1)$ to increase readability.

Before showing the NP-membership of testing the equivalence between two QWDPTs (and, hence, of two well-designed SPARQL queries), we still need some further results. The following lemma gives 3 necessary conditions for the equivalence of two QWDPTs in R3-normal form: the two QWDPTs must have identical roots, the same set of variables and the same set of triples. Note that the R3-normal form is crucial for the first and the last condition.

Lemma 4.9 *Consider two QWDPTs $\mathcal{T}_1 = ((V_1, E_1, r_1), \mathcal{P}_1)$ and $\mathcal{T}_2 = ((V_2, E_2, r_2), \mathcal{P}_2)$ in R3-normal form. If $\mathcal{T}_1 \equiv \mathcal{T}_2$ then the following properties hold:*

1. $P_{r_1} = P_{r_2}$
2. $\mathrm{vars}(\mathcal{T}_1) = \mathrm{vars}(\mathcal{T}_2)$
3. $\bigcup_{n \in V_1} P_n = \bigcup_{n \in V_2} P_n$

Lemma 4.10 *Consider two QWDPTs $\mathcal{T}_1 = ((V_1, E_1, r_1), \mathcal{P}_1)$ and $\mathcal{T}_2 = ((V_2, E_2, r_2), \mathcal{P}_2)$ in R3-normal form. Let $n_1, n_3 \in V_1$ and $n_2 \in V_2$.*

If there exist strong homomorphisms $\mathcal{H}\colon \mathrm{branch}(n_3, \mathcal{T}_1) \to \mathrm{branch}(n_2, \mathcal{T}_2)$ and $\mathcal{H}'\colon \mathrm{branch}(n_2, \mathcal{T}_2) \to \mathrm{branch}(n_1, \mathcal{T}_1)$, then n_1 is not an ancestor of n_3.

We are now ready to formulate necessary *and* sufficient conditions for the equivalence of two QWDPTs in R3-normal form.

Theorem 4.11 *Let $\mathcal{T}_1 = ((V_1, E_1, r_1), \mathcal{P}_1)$ and $\mathcal{T}_2 = ((V_2, E_2, r_2), \mathcal{P}_2)$ be two QWDPTs in R3-normal form. Then $\mathcal{T}_1 \equiv \mathcal{T}_2$ iff (1) $\bigcup_{n \in V_1} P_n = \bigcup_{n \in V_2} P_n$, (2) $P_{r_1} = P_{r_2}$, and (3) for all pairs (n_1, n_2) of nodes $n_1 \in V_1$ and $n_2 \in V_2$ with $\mathrm{newvars}(n_1) \cap \mathrm{newvars}(n_2) \neq \emptyset$ it holds that $\mathrm{branch}(n_1, \mathcal{T}_1)$ and $\mathrm{branch}(n_2, \mathcal{T}_2)$ are strongly homomorphically equivalent.*

We want to point out that the requirement that both queries contain the same set of atoms is necessary, and does not follow from the strong homomorphical equivalence of all nodes that share "new" variables, as can be seen in the following example.

Example 4.12 *Consider the following two QWDPTs.*

$$\{(?X, a, ?X)\} \qquad\qquad \{(?X, a, ?X)\}$$
$$\mid \qquad\qquad\qquad\qquad \mid$$
$$\{(?X_1, b, ?Y_1)\} \qquad \{(?X_1, b, ?Y_1), (?X_2, b, ?Y_2)\}$$

Obviously these two QWDPTs are not equivalent, as they do not even contain the same set of variables. However it can be easily checked that all required strong homomorphisms exist.

Theorem 4.11 immediately yields an equivalence test for well-designed SPARQL queries $\mathcal{T}_1$ and $\mathcal{T}_2$: just consider the SPARQL queries as QWDPTs, transform them into R3-normal form, and check if the conditions from Theorem 4.11 are fulfilled. However, there is a serious problem with such an algorithm. Indeed, we cannot afford to transform $\mathcal{T}_1$ and $\mathcal{T}_2$ into R3-normal form in an NP-algorithm, since this includes a coNP-test for checking that no further application of rule R3 is possible. The following theorem provides a way to overcome this problem. Intuitively it states that we do not need to transform $\mathcal{T}_1$ and $\mathcal{T}_2$ into R3-normal form. Instead, it suffices to apply rule R3 "often enough" so that the conditions from Theorem 4.11 are fulfilled. Theorem 4.13 guarantees that these conditions still hold for the R3 normal form, which we never explicitly need to compute.

Theorem 4.13 *Consider two QWDPTs $\mathcal{T}_1 = ((V_1, E_1, r_1), \mathcal{P}_1)$ and $\mathcal{T}_2 = ((V_2, E_2, r_2), \mathcal{P}_2)$ in NR normal form such that (1) $\bigcup_{n \in V_1} P_n = \bigcup_{n \in V_2} P_n$, (2) $P_{r_1} = P_{r_2}$, and (3) for*

all pairs (n_1, n_2) of nodes $n_1 \in V_1$ and $n_2 \in V_2$ with $\mathrm{newvars}(n_1) \cap \mathrm{newvars}(n_2) \neq \emptyset$ it holds that $\mathrm{branch}(n_1, \mathcal{T}_1)$ and $\mathrm{branch}(n_2, \mathcal{T}_2)$ are strongly homomorphically equivalent. Further, let $\mathcal{T}_1^* = ((V_1^*, E_1^*, r_1^*), \mathcal{P}_1^*)$ and $\mathcal{T}_2^* = ((V_2^*, E_2^*, r_2^*), \mathcal{P}_2^*)$ be R3 normal forms of $\mathcal{T}_1$ and $\mathcal{T}_2$ respectively.

Then the following conditions still hold for $\mathcal{T}_1^*$ and $\mathcal{T}_2^*$: (1) $\bigcup_{n \in V_1^*} P_n = \bigcup_{n \in V_2^*} P_n$, (2) $P_{r_1^*} = P_{r_2^*}$, and (3) for all pairs (n_1^*, n_2^*) of nodes $n_1^* \in V_1^*$ and $n_2^* \in V_2^*$ with $\mathrm{newvars}(n_1^*) \cap \mathrm{newvars}(n_2^*) \neq \emptyset$, it holds that $\mathrm{branch}(n_1^*, \mathcal{T}_1^*)$ and $\mathrm{branch}(n_2^*, \mathcal{T}_2^*)$ are strongly homomorphically equivalent.

Now we have all ingredients to prove the main result of this section.

Theorem 4.14 *The equivalence problem of QWDPTs (and, therefore, of well-designed SPARQL graph patterns) is NP-complete.*

PROOF. The NP-hardness is shown by a straightforward reduction from 3-Colorability. The NP-membership can be seen by the following algorithm, which takes two QWDPTs $\mathcal{T}_1$ and $\mathcal{T}_2$ as input.

1. Transform $\mathcal{T}_1$ and $\mathcal{T}_2$ into NR normal forms $\mathcal{T}_1^*$ and $\mathcal{T}_2^*$, resp.

2. Guess two application sequences of rule R3 (i.e., nodes where to apply rule R3 and the corresponding homomorphisms).

3. Check that the homomorphisms from step 2 fulfill the conditions of rules R3. Denote the QWDPTs resulting from these R3 applications with $\mathcal{T}_1'$ and $\mathcal{T}_2'$.

4. For any two nodes n_1 in $\mathcal{T}_1'$ and n_2 in $\mathcal{T}_2'$ with $\mathrm{newvars}(n_1) \cap \mathrm{newvars}(n_2) \neq \emptyset$, guess strong homomorphisms (i.e., collections of homomorphisms according to Definition 4.5) in both directions between $\mathrm{branch}(n_1, \mathcal{T}_1')$ and $\mathrm{branch}(n_2, \mathcal{T}_2')$.

5. Check that $\mathcal{T}_1'$ and $\mathcal{T}_2'$ fulfill conditions (1) – (3) of Theorem 4.13.

Step 1 is feasible in polynomial time since rules R1 and R2 are "cheap". The certificate guessed in steps 2 and 4 is polynomially bounded. Finally, the computation and checks in step 3 and the checks in step 5 fit into polynomial time. □

5. ENUMERATION AND COUNTING

Conjunctive query (CQ) evaluation[1] is a classical NP-complete problem [8]. A lot of effort has thus been invested into the search for tractable fragments of CQs [41, 10, 13, 17, 18, 16]. This search for tractable fragments of CQs has also been extended to the enumeration problem (i.e., given a CQ Q and a database D, output all tuples in the result of Q over D) and the counting problem of CQs (i.e., given a CQ Q and a database D, compute the number of tuples in the result of Q over D) [13, 14, 4, 29]. Sets of triple patterns are essentially CQs over a relational schema with a single ternary predicate. We now want to extend the study of tractable fragments of CQ evaluation to tractable fragments of evaluating well-designed SPARQL graph patterns. For the decision problem (i.e., given an RDF graph G, a well-designed SPARQL graph pattern P and a variable binding μ, check if μ is a solution), tractable fragments of CQ evaluation immediately carry over to tractable fragments of SPARQL evaluation. For the enumeration problem (i.e., given an

---

[1]There are several strongly related problems like asking if a given tuple is contained in the result of a given CQ over a given database, or asking if a given Boolean CQ evaluates to true over a given database, or query containment, etc. All these problems have straightforward reductions between each other. By slight abuse of notation we thus simply speak of "CQ evaluation" to refer to any of these problems.

RDF graph G and a well-designed SPARQL graph pattern P, compute all solutions μ) and the counting problem (i.e., given an RDF graph G and a well-designed SPARQL graph pattern P, compute the number of solutions μ), a much more detailed analysis is required. This is the main topic of this section.

But let us first look at the decision problem of evaluating well-designed SPARQL graph patterns. In [27], this problem was shown to be coNP-complete. For our representation of SPARQL graph patterns as QWDPT, a coNP test can work as follows. Let $\mathcal{T} = ((V, E, r), \mathcal{P})$ be a QWDPT and assume that it is in NR normal form (which can be computed in polynomial time). By using the characterization of the evaluation of QWDPTs provided in Lemma 3.21, in order to check if μ is a solution of $\mathcal{T}$ over G, the coNP-algorithm can first find a subtree $\mathcal{T}'$ of $\mathcal{T}$ rooted at r s.t. $\mathrm{dom}(\mu) = \mathrm{vars}(\mathcal{T}')$. Notice that if this subtree exists, then it is unique (since $\mathcal{T}$ is in NR normal form), and thus, this step can be done in polynomial time. Then the algorithm checks that $\mathcal{T}'$ is a maximal subtree such that $\mu \sqsubseteq [\![and(\mathcal{T}')]\!]_G$. The latter test requires coNP-power since we have to check that μ cannot be extended to match any of the sets of triple patterns at nodes "below" the leaf nodes of $\mathcal{T}'$. Note that this simple coNP-algorithm heavily relies on the NR normal form from Section 3.3 (the coNP-algorithm provided in [27] is considerably more complex).

Clearly, if all sets of triple patterns are from tractable fragments of CQ evaluation, the problem of checking if μ is a solution of $\mathcal{T}$ over G becomes tractable:

Corollary 5.1 *Suppose that we only consider QWDPTs (and thus well-designed SPARQL graph patterns), where for each node t the set P_t of triple patterns is from tractable fragments of CQ evaluation. Then the decision problem of such QWDPTs is also tractable.*

Note that tractability is required for each set P_t individually, hence for different nodes t and t', the sets P_t and $P_{t'}$ may belong to different tractable fragments.

5.1 Enumeration of well-designed SPARQL

Recall that an appropriate notion of *tractable* enumeration has to take the size of the output into account. Indeed, even for a single set of triple patterns, the set of solutions can be exponentially big. Hence, our goal is to identify conditions under which the enumeration of the solutions is feasible with *polynomial delay*, i.e., the time to either compute the next solution or to detect that no further solution exists must be polynomially bounded in the input size. For instance, acyclic CQs and CQs of bounded treewidth or hypertreewidth [41, 10, 13, 17] have this property.

Polynomial delay algorithms are usually implemented in the form of *iterators*. I.e., they are implemented in terms of functions **next**() and **hasNext**(), where **next**() returns the next solution, while **hasNext**() returns if there exists yet another solution. For polynomial delay algorithms, both functions run in polynomial time.

Following the presentation in [11], in order to increase readability we do not define the functions **next**() and **hasNext**() explicitly. Instead, the enumeration algorithm is described as an ordinary algorithm, and we consider iterators as constructs that take an enumeration algorithm as argument and provide the **next**() and **hasNext**() functions. I.e., consider an iterator $I := \textbf{new Iterator}(E(x))$ for an enumeration algorithm E with input x. In response to $I.\textbf{next}()$ being called, the iterator executes $E(x)$ until it encounters **output**(A) for the first time. Then the execution of E is interrupted, and A is returned as the result of $I.\textbf{next}()$. At the next call of $I.\textbf{next}()$, the execution of E is continued at the position where it was last interrupted, i.e. right after the last **output**(.) command executed (and the last state of E is restored). Once E terminates (in-

```
Enumerate(t,μ)
 1: cqit := new Iterator(EnumerateCQ(P_t, μ));
 2: while( cqit.hasNext() ){
      // let t_1, …, t_k be the children of t
 3:    maxi := 0;
 4:    μ_curr := cqit.next();
 5:    for( i = 1 to k ){
 6:      it_i := new Iterator(Enumerate(t_i, μ_curr));
 7:      flag_i := it_i.hasNext();
 8:      if(flag_i){
 9:        μ_i := it_i.next();
10:        maxi := i;
11:      }
12:    }
13:    if( ⋀_{i=1}^{k} ¬flag_i ){
14:      output(μ_curr);
15:      continue;
16:    }
17:    repeat{
18:      output( μ_curr ∪ ⋃_{1≤i≤k∧flag_i=true} μ_i );
19:      continueflag := false;
20:      for( i = maxi downto 1 ){
21:        if(it_i.hasNext()){
22:          μ_i := it_i.next();
23:          continueflag := true;
24:          for( j = i+1 to maxi ){
25:            if( flag_j ) {
26:              it_j := new Iterator(Enumerate(t_j, μ_curr));
27:              μ_j := it_j.next();
28:            }
29:          }
30:          i := 0; // leave the for-loop
31:        }
32:      }
33:    } until( ¬continueflag)
34: }
```

Figure 1: Iterator for SPARQL tree patterns.

stead of being interrupted), no further answer exists. The function **hasNext**() can be either implemented by continuing the execution of E and checking if another result is generated or not, or (like in our case) it is implemented by checking the current state of E.

In the following, assume a QWDPT $\mathcal{T} = ((V, E, r), \mathcal{P})$ to be evaluated over some RDF graph G. The algorithm in Figure 1 assumes the existence of some enumeration algorithm EnumerateCQ(P_t, μ) that, given a set P_t of triple patterns and a partial variable assignment μ returns all extensions of μ to P_t over G. We consider EnumerateCQ(P_t, μ) as a black box. The idea of our (recursive) enumeration algorithm Enumerate(t, μ) is as follows. For $t \in V$ and a partial assignment μ, the algorithm first checks if μ can be extended to P_t (lines 1–2). For each such extension μ_{curr}, it checks recursively for each child node t_i if there exists an extension of μ_{curr} to P_{t_i} (lines 5–7). Next, for each t_i that has such an extension the first solution is stored, together with the biggest index i s.t. t_i provides a solution (lines 8–10). If μ_{curr} cannot be extended to any child node, then the algorithm just returns μ_{curr} as one extension of μ to the complete subtree rooted at t (line 14; recall that the execution of the **output**(.) statement ends the execution of the call to **next**(), and the control flow is returned to the caller), and then considers the next extension of μ on t (line

15 jumps to the next iteration of the while loop in line 2). If on the other hand μ_{curr} can be extended to some children of t (lines 17 – 33), the algorithm enumerates all these extensions as follows. (For the sake of simplicity, in the following we only consider the ℓ children to which μ_{curr} can be extended.) In lines 17–33, all possible solutions are created that can be built from combining the extensions of μ_{curr} to $t_1, \ldots, t_\ell$. Note that the first possible extension for each t_i was saved in μ_i in line 9. After returning this solution (line 18), the solutions are enumerated by iterating over the solutions for $t_1, \ldots, t_\ell$ as follows. First, the child node t_i with the highest index i is identified that has yet another solution (lines 20–21). This extension is saved in μ_i (line 22), and for all children t_j with $i < j \leq \ell$ the iterators are reset to the first extension of μ_{curr}, which is stored in μ_j (lines 24–27). If such an index i exists, the new solution is returned in the next iteration of the repeat loop (line 18), otherwise all extensions of μ_{curr} have already been returned, and the algorithm terminates.

Theorem 5.2 *The problem of enumerating all solutions of a QWDPT (and hence, of a well-designed SPARQL graph pattern) can be reduced in polynomial time (by a Turing reduction) to the problem of enumerating all solutions of CQs.*

PROOF IDEA. The iterator described in Figure 1 reduces the problem of enumerating all solutions of a QWDPT to the problem of enumerating all solutions of CQs. Moreover, neglecting the cost of the calls to the iterator for CQs, the algorithm in Figure 1 clearly works in polynomial time. □

We may thus conclude that any tractability results for CQs immediately carry over to well-designed SPARQL graph patterns.

Theorem 5.3 *Suppose that we only consider QWDPTs where the sets of triple patterns at each node are from tractable fragments of CQ evaluation. Then the enumeration problem of such QWDPTs can be solved with polynomial-time delay.*

An inspection of our iterator for QWDPTs reveals that Theorem 5.3 could be further strengthened: for the tractability of the enumeration problem, it is sufficient that the sets of triple patterns are from tractable fragments of CQ evaluation *after considering all "old variables" at each node as constants.* In general, such an elimination of variables from a CQ may yield a significantly bigger tractable class.

5.2 Counting of well-designed SPARQL

Before studying the counting problem of well-designed SPARQL graph patterns, we recall some basic notions and results from counting complexity. The most intensively studied counting complexity class is #P. It contains those problems which consist in counting the number of accepting computation paths of a non-deterministic polynomial-time Turing machine. In other words, #P captures the counting problems corresponding to decision problems in NP. Alternatively, *counting problems* can be presented using a *witness* function R which for every input x returns a set $R(x)$ of *witnesses* for x. Every witness function gives rise to the *counting problem* $\# \cdot R$ defined as follows: given a string $x \in \Sigma^*$, find the cardinality $|R(x)|$ of the *witness* set $R(x)$. According to [20], if $\mathcal{C}$ is a complexity class of decision problems, we define $\# \cdot \mathcal{C}$ as the class of all counting problems whose witness function R satisfies the following conditions.

1. There is a polynomial $p(n)$ such that for every $x \in \Sigma^*$ and every $y \in R(x)$ we have $|y| \leq p(|x|)$;

2. The problem "given x and y, is $y \in R(x)$?" is in $\mathcal{C}$.

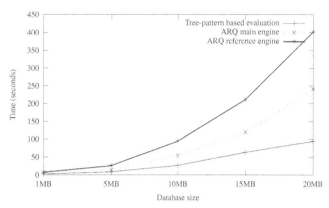

Figure 2: Performance of the QWDPT-based evaluation compared with non-optimized and optimized ARQ, for a modified version of Query 7 of SP^{2}Bench benchmark [33].

It is easy to verify that $\#P = \# \cdot P$. Moreover, the following inclusions hold [20]: $\#P \subseteq \# \cdot NP \subseteq \# \cdot coNP$.

Counting the number of answer tuples of a CQ is #P-complete for CQs with free variables only and $\# \cdot NP$-complete for CQs which may contain existential quantifiers [5]. Recently, it has been shown that the counting problem of CQs where not all variables are free, remains #P-complete even if we restrict ourselves to acyclic CQs. In contrast, the counting problem of CQs without existential quantifiers becomes tractable for CQs of bounded hypertree-width [29]. In this section, we extend the study of the counting problem from CQs to well-designed SPARQL patterns showing that, as opposed to the enumeration problem, tractability does not carry over. More specifically, we prove the following theorems.

Theorem 5.4 *The problem of counting all solutions of a QWDPT (and hence, of a well-designed SPARQL graph pattern) is $\# \cdot coNP$-complete.*

PROOF IDEA. We only discuss the $\# \cdot coNP$-*membership*. Consider the following witness function R: it takes as argument a pair $(\mathcal{T}, G)$ consisting of a QWDPT $\mathcal{T}$ and a graph G. Then R maps each pair $(\mathcal{T}, G)$ to the set of solutions of $\mathcal{T}$ over G. The problem of counting all solutions of a QWDPT $\mathcal{T}$ over a graph G corresponds to the counting problem $\# \cdot R$. The $\# \cdot coNP$-membership follows from the fact that it can be tested in coNP if a given mapping μ is a solution of $\mathcal{T}$ over G [27]. □

Theorem 5.5 *The problem of counting all solutions of a QWDPT (and hence, of a well-designed SPARQL graph pattern) is in #P if the sets of triple patterns at each node are from tractable fragments of CQ evaluation. The problem remains #P-complete even if all sets of triple patterns correspond to acyclic CQs.*

PROOF IDEA. The #P-*hardness* is shown by reduction from the problem of counting the number of perfect matchings in a bipartite graph, which is a classical #P-complete problem [39].

For the #P-*membership*, we consider the same witness function R as in the proof of Theorem 5.4. If all sets of triple patterns are from tractable fragments of CQ evaluation, then we can test in PTIME if a given mapping μ is a solution of $\mathcal{T}$ over G. □

6. CONCLUDING REMARKS

Static analysis is a fundamental task in query optimization. In this paper we have studied this problem for SPARQL queries. One of our main contributions is the introduction of an abstract representation of well-designed queries as trees that resemble relational query plans. This representation allowed us to provide transformation rules and normal forms that proved to be useful when studying equivalence, containment, and tractable query enumeration. An interesting line for future work is the inclusion of more SPARQL operators to our study, in particular, projection and filtering.

On the practical side, we are currently developing a prototype based on the results presented in this paper, by modifying the non-optimized version of the ARQ SPARQL engine [45]. Our preliminary results are encouraging. In particular, the top-down evaluation of QWDPTs performs very well whenever a node in some branch of the tree provides a small set of results. We created examples of queries along with data which represent this case, by using the SP^{2}Bench benchmark [33], in particular modifying *Query 7* of the benchmark (that uses various levels of OPT nesting). In this scenario, our prototype even outperforms ARQ's optimized engine (Figure 2). An extension of these experiments to a systematic comparison of our approach with previous ones is left for future work. We have also implemented some transformation rules, the normal forms, and equivalence test. An on-line interface for our prototype is available from `http://db.ing.puc.cl/sparql-algebra`.

Acknowledgements

This work was funded in part by Marie Curie action IRSES under Grant No. 24761 (Net2), and by the Vienna Science and Technology Fund (WWTF) through project ICT08-032. Jorge Pérez was supported by Fondecyt grant 11110404 and by VID grant U-Inicia 11/04 Universidad de Chile.

7. REFERENCES

[1] D. J. Abadi, A. Marcus, S. Madden, and K. J. Hollenbach. Scalable semantic web data management using vertical partitioning. In *VLDB*, pages 411–422. ACM, 2007.

[2] R. Angles and C. Gutierrez. The expressive power of SPARQL. In *ISWC*, pages 114–129. Springer, 2008.

[3] M. Arenas and J. Pérez. Querying Semantic Web data with SPARQL. In *PODS*, pages 305–316. ACM, 2011.

[4] G. Bagan, A. Durand, and E. Grandjean. On acyclic conjunctive queries and constant delay enumeration. In *CSL*, pages 208–222. Springer, 2007.

[5] M. Bauland, P. Chapdelaine, N. Creignou, M. Hermann, and H. Vollmer. An algebraic approach to the complexity of generalized conjunctive queries. In *SAT 2004 - Revised Selected Papers*, pages 30–45. Springer, 2005.

[6] T. Berners-Lee. Linked data – design issues. http://www.w3.org/DesignIssues/LinkedData.html, 2006.

[7] C. Bizer, T. Heath, and T. Berners-Lee. Linked data - the story so far. *Int. J. Semantic Web Inf. Syst.*, 5(3):1–22, 2009.

[8] A. K. Chandra and P. M. Merlin. Optimal implementation of conjunctive queries in relational data bases. In *STOC*, pages 77–90. ACM, 1977.

[9] M. Chekol, J. Euzenat, P. Genevès, and N. Layaïda. PSPARQL query containment. In *DBPL*, 2011.

[10] C. Chekuri and A. Rajaraman. Conjunctive query containment revisited. *Theor. Comput. Sci.*, 239(2):211–229, 2000.

[11] S. Cohen and I. Fadida and Y. Kanza and B. Kimelfeld and Y. Sagiv. Full Disjunctions: Polynomial-Delay Iterators in Action. In *VLDB*, pages 739–750. ACM, 2006.

[12] A. Durand, M. Hermann, and P. G. Kolaitis. Subtractive reductions and complete problems for counting complexity classes. *Theor. Comput. Sci.*, 340(3):496–513, 2005.

[13] J. Flum, M. Frick, and M. Grohe. Query evaluation via tree-decompositions. *J. ACM*, 49(6):716–752, 2002.

[14] J. Flum and M. Grohe. The parameterized complexity of counting problems. *SIAM J. Comput.*, 33(4):892–922, 2004.

[15] M. A. Gallego, J. D. Fernández, M. A. Martínez-Prieto, and P. de la Fuente. An empirical study of real-world SPARQL queries. In *USEWOD*, 2011.

[16] G. Gottlob, N. Leone, and F. Scarcello. A comparison of structural CSP decomposition methods. *Artif. Intell.*, 124(2):243–282, 2000.

[17] G. Gottlob, N. Leone, and F. Scarcello. Hypertree decompositions and tractable queries. *J. Comput. Syst. Sci.*, 64(3):579–627, 2002.

[18] G. Greco and F. Scarcello. The power of tree projections: local consistency, greedy algorithms, and larger islands of tractability. In *PODS 2010*, pages 327–338. ACM, 2010.

[19] C. Gutierrez, C. A. Hurtado, A. O. Mendelzon, and J. Pérez. Foundations of semantic web databases. *J. Comput. Syst. Sci.*, 77(3):520–541, 2011.

[20] L. A. Hemaspaandra and H. Vollmer. The satanic notations: Counting classes beyond #P and other definitional adventures. *SIGACT News, Complexity Theory Column 8*, 26(1):2–13, 1995.

[21] Y. Kanza and W. Nutt and Y. Sagiv. Querying Incomplete Information in Semistructured Data. *J. Comput. Syst. Sci.*, 64(3):655–693, 2002.

[22] P.-Å. Larson and J. Zhou. View matching for outer-join views. In *VLDB*, pages 445–456. ACM, 2005.

[23] O. Lassila and R. Swick. Resource description framework (RDF) model and syntax. *W3C Recommnedation*, January 1999.

[24] T. Neumann and G. Weikum. The rdf-3x engine for scalable management of rdf data. *VLDB J.*, 19(1):91–113, 2010.

[25] J. Pérez, M. Arenas, and C. Gutierrez. Semantics and complexity of SPARQL. In *ISWC*, pages 30–43. Springer, 2006.

[26] J. Pérez, M. Arenas, and C. Gutierrez. Semantics of SPARQL. Technical Report, Universidad de Chile TR/DCC-2006-17, October 2006.

[27] J. Pérez, M. Arenas, and C. Gutierrez. Semantics and complexity of SPARQL. *ACM Trans. Database Syst.*, 34(3), 2009.

[28] F. Picalausa and S. Vansummeren. What are real SPARQL queries like? In *SWIM*, pages 7:1–7:6. ACM, 2011.

[29] R. Pichler and S. Skritek. Tractable counting of the answers to conjunctive queries. In *AMW*. CEUR-WS.org, 2011.

[30] A. Polleres. From SPARQL to rules (and back). In *WWW*, pages 787–796. ACM, 2007.

[31] E. Prud'Hommeaux and A. Seaborne. SPARQL query language for RDF. *W3C Recommnedation*, January 2008.

[32] M. Schmidt, T. Hornung, N. Küchlin, G. Lausen, and C. Pinkel. An experimental comparison of RDF data management approaches in a SPARQL benchmark scenario. In *ISWC*, pages 82–97. Springer, 2008.

[33] M. Schmidt, T. Hornung, G. Lausen, and C. Pinkel. SP^{2}Bench: A SPARQL performance benchmark. In *ICDE*, pages 222–233. IEEE, 2009.

[34] M. Schmidt, M. Meier, and G. Lausen. Foundations of SPARQL query optimization. In *ICDT*, pages 4–33. ACM, 2010.

[35] G. Serfiotis, I. Koffina, V. Christophides, and V. Tannen. Containment and minimization of RDF/S query patterns. In *ISWC*, pages 607–623. Springer, 2005.

[36] L. Sidirourgos, R. Goncalves, M. L. Kersten, N. Nes, and S. Manegold. Column-store support for RDF data management: not all swans are white. *PVLDB*, 1(2):1553–1563, 2008.

[37] M. Stocker, A. Seaborne, A. Bernstein, C. Kiefer, and D. Reynolds. Sparql basic graph pattern optimization using selectivity estimation. In *WWW*, pages 595–604. ACM, 2008.

[38] J. D. Ullman. Information integration using logical views. In *ICDT*, pages 19–40. Springer, 1997.

[39] L. G. Valiant. The complexity of enumeration and reliability problems. *SIAM J. Comput.*, 8(3):410–421, 1979.

[40] C. Weiss, P. Karras, and A. Bernstein. Hexastore: sextuple indexing for semantic web data management. *PVLDB*, 1(1):1008–1019, 2008.

[41] M. Yannakakis. Algorithms for acyclic database schemes. In *VLDB*, pages 82–94. IEEE, 1981.

[42] http://data.gov.uk.

[43] http://www.data.gov.

[44] http://DBpedia.org/sparql.

[45] ARQ. http://sourceforge.net/projects/jena/files/ARQ/.

The Complexity of Evaluating Path Expressions in SPARQL

Katja Losemann[*]
Universität Bayreuth

Wim Martens
Universität Bayreuth

ABSTRACT

The World Wide Web Consortium (W3C) recently introduced property paths in SPARQL 1.1, a query language for RDF data. Property paths allow SPARQL queries to evaluate regular expressions over graph data. However, they differ from standard regular expressions in several notable aspects. For example, they have a limited form of negation, they have numerical occurrence indicators as syntactic sugar, and their semantics on graphs is defined in a non-standard manner.

We formalize the W3C semantics of property paths and investigate various query evaluation problems on graphs. More specifically, let x and y be two nodes in an edge-labeled graph and r be an expression. We study the complexities of (1) deciding whether there exists a path from x to y that matches r and (2) counting how many paths from x to y match r. Our main results show that, compared to an alternative semantics of regular expressions on graphs, the complexity of (1) and (2) under W3C semantics is significantly higher. Whereas the alternative semantics remains in polynomial time for large fragments of expressions, the W3C semantics makes problems (1) and (2) intractable almost immediately.

As a side-result, we prove that the membership problem for regular expressions with numerical occurrence indicators and negation is in polynomial time.

Categories and Subject Descriptors

F.2 [**Analysis of Algorithms and Problem Complexity**]: General; H.2.3 [**Database Management**]: Languages—*query languages*

Keywords

Graph data, regular expression, query evaluation

[*]Supported by grant number MA 4938/2–1 from the Deutsche Forschungsgemeinschaft (Emmy Noether Nachwuchsgruppe).

1. INTRODUCTION

The Resource Description Framework (RDF) is a data model developed by the World Wide Web Consortium (W3C) to represent linked data on the Web. The underlying idea is to improve the way in which data on the Web is readable by computers and to enable new ways of querying Web data. In its core, RDF represents linked data as an edge-labeled graph. The de facto language developed by the W3C for querying RDF data is the SPARQL Protocol and RDF Query Language (SPARQL).

Recently, the W3C decided to boost SPARQL 1.1 with extensive navigational capabilities by the introduction of *property paths* [25]. Property paths closely correspond to regular expressions and are a crucial tool in SPARQL if one wants to perform non-trivial navigation through RDF data. In the current working draft, property paths are not defined as standard regular expressions, but some syntactic sugar is added. Notably, property paths can use numerical occurrence indicators (making them exponentially more succinct than standard regular expressions) and a limited form of negation. Furthermore, their semantics is different from usual definitions of regular expressions on graphs. In particular, when evaluating a regular expression, the W3C semantics requires some subexpressions to be matched onto *simple walks*,[1] whereas other subexpressions can be matched onto arbitrary paths.

Property paths are very fundamental in SPARQL. For example, the SPARQL query of the form `SELECT ?x,?y WHERE {?x r ?y}` asks for pairs of nodes (x,y) such that there is a path from x to y that matches the property path r. In fact, according to the SPARQL definition, the output of such a query is a multiset in which each pair of nodes (x,y) of the graph occurs as often as the number of paths from x to y that match r under W3C semantics. By only allowing certain subexpressions to match simple walks, the W3C therefore ensures that the number of paths that match a property path is always finite.

The amount of available RDF data on the Web has grown steadily over the last decade [6]. Since it is highly likely to become more and more important in the future, we are convinced that investigating foundational aspects of evaluating regular expressions and property paths over graphs is a very relevant research topic. We therefore make the following contributions.

We investigate the complexity of two problems which we believe to be central for query processing on graph data. In

---

[1] A simple walk is a path that does not visit the same node twice, but is allowed to return to its first node.

the EVALUATION problem, one is given a graph, two nodes x and y, and a regular expression r, and one is asked whether there exists a path from x to y that matches r. In the COUNTING problem, one is asked *how many* paths from x to y match r. Notice that, according to the W3C definition, the answer to the above SELECT query needs to contain the answer to the COUNTING problem in unary notation.

Our theoretical investigation is motivated by an experimental analysis on several popular SPARQL processors that reveals that they deal with property paths very inefficiently. Already for solving the EVALUATION problem, all systems we found require time double exponential in the size of the queries in the worst case. We show that it is, in principle, possible to solve EVALUATION much more quickly: For a graph G and an expression with numerical occurrence indicators r, we can test whether there is a path from x to y that matches r in polynomial time combined complexity.

We then investigate deeper reasons why evaluation of property paths is so inefficient in practice. In particular, we perform an in-depth study on the influence of some W3C design decisions on the computational complexity of property path evaluation. Our study reveals that the high processing times can be partly attributed already to the SPARQL 1.1 definition from the W3C. We formally define two kinds of semantics for property paths: *regular path semantics* and *simple walk semantics*. Here, *simple walk semantics* is our formalization of the W3C's semantics for property paths. Under *regular path semantics*, a path in an edge-labeled graph matches a regular expression if the concatenation of the labels on the edges is in the language defined by the expression.

We prove that, under regular path semantics, EVALUATION remains tractable under combined query evaluation complexity, even when numerical occurrence indicators are added to regular expressions. In contrast, under simple walk semantics, EVALUATION is already NP-complete for the regular expression $(aa)^*$. (So, it is NP-complete under data complexity.) We also identify a fragment of expressions for which EVALUATION under simple walk semantics is in PTIME but, we prove that EVALUATION under simple walk semantics for this fragment is the same problem than EVALUATION under regular path semantics.

The picture becomes perhaps even more striking for the COUNTING problem. Under regular path semantics, we provide a detailed chart of the tractability frontier. When the expressions are *deterministic*, then COUNTING can be solved in polynomial time. However, even for expressions with a very limited amount of non-determinism, COUNTING becomes #P-complete. Under simple walk semantics, COUNTING is already #P-complete for the regular expression a^*. Essentially, this shows that, as soon as the Kleene star operator is used, COUNTING is #P-complete under simple walk semantics. All fragments we found for which COUNTING is tractable under simple walk semantics are tractable because, for these fragments, simple walk semantics equals regular path semantics.

Our complexity results are summarized in Table 2. One result that is not in the table but may be of independent interest is the word membership problem for regular expressions with numerical occurrence indicators and negation. We prove this problem to be in PTIME in Theorem 3.3.

Since the W3C's specification for SPARQL 1.1 is still under development, we want to send a strong message to the W3C that informs them of the computational complexity repercussions of their design decisions; and what could be possible if the semantics of property paths were to be changed. Based on our observations, a semantics for property paths that is based on regular path semantics seems to be recommendable from a computational complexity point of view. We propose some concrete ideas in Section 6.

Related Work and Further Literature.

This paper studies evaluation problems of regular expressions on graphs. Regular expressions as a language for querying graphs have been studied in the database literature for more than a decade, sometimes under the name of regular path queries or general path queries [1, 10, 16, 17, 19, 41]. Various problems for regular path queries have been investigated in the database community, such as optimization [2], query rewriting and query answering using views [13, 12], and containment [11, 18, 20]. Recently, there has been a renewed interest in path expressions on graphs, for example, on expressions with data value comparisons [31].

Regular path queries have also been studied in the context of program analysis. For example, evaluation of path queries on graphs has been studied by Liu et al. [32]. However, their setting is different in the sense that they are interested in a universal semantics of the queries. That is, they are searching for pairs of nodes in the graph such that *all* paths between them match the given expression.

On a technical level, the most closely related work is on regular expressions with numerical occurrence indicators and on the complexity of SPARQL. Regular expressions with numerical occurrence indicators have been investigated in the context of XML schema languages [15, 14, 22, 23, 29, 28] since they are a part of the W3C XML Schema Language [21]. One of our PTIME upper bounds builds directly on Kilpeläinen and Tuhkonen's algorithm for membership testing of a regular expression with numerical occurrence indicators [28].

To the best of our knowledge, the present paper is the first one that studies the complexity of full property paths (i.e., regular expressions with numerical occurrence indicators) in SPARQL. Property paths without numerical occurrence indicators have been studied in [37, 3, 5]. Most closely related to us is Arenas et al. [5], which is conducted independently from us and which complements our work in several respects. The authors study the complexity of computing the answer to SPARQL SELECT queries using property paths without numerical occurrence indicators. They focus their study on the ALP procedure in [25], which defines the semantics of property paths on a very detailed level. Instead, we focus on a more high-level semantics of property paths, namely the definition of the operators ZeroOrMorePath and OneOrMorePath in the SPARQL Algebra in [25]. Further work on the complexity of SPARQL query evaluation can be found in [36, 38]. We refer to [6] for further references on research on RDF databases and query languages.

2. PRELIMINARIES

For the rest of the paper, Δ always denotes a countably infinite set. We use Δ to model the set of IRIs and prefixed names from the SPARQL specification. We assume that we can test for equality between elements of Δ in constant time.

A Δ-*symbol* (or simply *symbol*) is an element of Δ, and a Δ-*string* (or simply string) is a finite sequence $w = a_1 \cdots a_n$

of Δ-symbols. We define the length of w, denoted by $|w|$, to be n. We denote the empty string by ε. The set of *positions of w* is $\{1, \ldots, n\}$ and the *symbol of w at position i* is a_i. By $w_1 \cdot w_2$ we denote the *concatenation* of two strings w_1 and w_2. For readability, we usually denote the concatenation of w_1 and w_2 by $w_1 w_2$. The set of all strings is denoted by Δ^*. A *string language* is a subset of Δ^*. For two string languages $L, L' \subseteq \Delta^*$, we define their concatenation $L \cdot L'$ to be the set $\{ww' \mid w \in L, w' \in L'\}$. We abbreviate $L \cdot L \cdots L$ (i times) by L^i. The set of *regular expressions* over Δ, denoted by RE, is defined as follows: ε and every Δ-symbol is a regular expression; and when r and s are regular expressions, then (rs), $(r+s)$, $(r?)$, (r^*), and (r^+) are also regular expressions. (Usually we omit braces to improve readability.) We consider the following additional operators for regular expressions:

Numerical Occurrence Indicators: If $k \in \mathbb{N}$ and $\ell \in \mathbb{N}^+ \cup \infty$ with $k \leq \ell$, then $(r^{k,\ell})$ is a regular expression.

Negation: If r is a regular expression, then so is $(\neg r)$.

Negated label test: If $\{a_1, \ldots, a_n\}$ is a non-empty, finite subset of Δ, then $!\{a_1, \ldots, a_n\}$ is a regular expression.

Wildcard: The symbol $\bullet$ ($\notin \Delta$) is a regular expression.

By $\mathrm{RE}(\mathcal{X})$ we denote the set of regular expressions with additional features $\mathcal{X} \subseteq \{\#, \neg, \bullet, !\}$ where "$\#$" stands for numerical occurrence indicators, "$\neg$" for negation, "$!$" for the negated label test, and "$\bullet$" for the single-symbol wildcard. For example, $\mathrm{RE}(\#)$ denotes the set of regular expressions with numerical occurrence indicators and $\mathrm{RE}(\#, \neg, \bullet)$ is the set of regular expressions with numerical occurrence indicators, negation, and wildcard. We are particularly interested in the following class of expressions.

DEFINITION 2.1. The set of *SPARQL Regular Expressions* or *SPARQL Property Paths* is the set $\mathrm{RE}(\#, !, \bullet)$.[2]

We consider edge-labeled graphs. A graph G will be denoted as $G = (V, E)$, where V is the set of nodes of G and $E \subseteq V \times \Delta \times V$ is the set of edges. An edge e is therefore of the form (u, a, v) if it goes from node u to node v and bears the label a. When we don't care about the label of an edge, we sometimes also write an edge as a pair (u, v) in order to simplify notation. We assume familiarity with basic terminology on graphs. A *path* from node x to node y in G is a sequence $p = v_0[a_1]v_1[a_2]v_2 \cdots v_{n-1}[a_n]v_n$ such that $v_0 = x$, $v_n = y$, and (v_{i-1}, a_i, v_i) is an edge for each $i = 1, \ldots, n$. When we are not interested in the labels on the edges, we sometimes also write $p = v_0 v_1 \ldots v_n$. We say that path p has *length* n. Notice that a path of length zero does not follow any edges. The *labeled string* induced by the path p in G is $a_1 \cdots a_n$ and is denoted by $\mathrm{lab}^G(p)$. If G is clear from the context, we sometimes also simply write $\mathrm{lab}(p)$. We define the *concatenation* of paths $p_1 = v_0[a_1]v_1 \cdots v_{n-1}[a_n]v_n$ and $p_2 = v_n[a_{n+1}]v_{n_1} \cdots v_{n+m-1}[a_{n+m}]v_{n+m}$ to be the path $p_1 p_2 := v_0[a_1]v_1 \cdots v_{n-1}[a_n]v_n[a_{n+1}]v_{n_1} \cdots v_{n+m-1}[a_{n+m}]v_{n+m}$.

Regular Path Semantics.

The language defined by an expression r, denoted by $L(r)$, is inductively defined as follows: $L(\varepsilon) = \{\varepsilon\}$; $L(a) = \{a\}$; $L(!\{a_1, \ldots, a_n\}) = \Delta - \{a_1, \ldots, a_n\}$; $L(\bullet) = \Delta$; $L(rs) =$

$L(r) \cdot L(s)$; $L(r+s) = L(r) \cup L(s)$; $L(r^*) = \{\varepsilon\} \cup \bigcup_{i=1}^{\infty} L(r)^i$, $L(r^{k,\ell}) = \bigcup_{i=k}^{\ell} L(r)^i$; and, $L(\neg r) = \Delta^* - L(r)$. Furthermore, $L(r?) = \varepsilon + L(r)$ and $L(r^+) = L(r)L(r^*)$.[3] The *size* of a regular expression r over Δ, denoted by $|r|$, is the number of occurrences of Δ-symbols, $\bullet$-symbols, and operators occurring in r, plus the sizes of the binary representations of the numerical occurrence indicators. We say that a path p *matches a regular expression r under regular path semantics* if $\mathrm{lab}(p) \in L(r)$.

Simple Walk Semantics (Semantics in SPARQL).

A *simple path* is a path $v_0 v_1 \cdots v_{n-1} v_n$, where each node v_i occurs exactly once. A *simple cycle* is a path $v_0 v_1 \cdots v_{n-1} v_n$ such that $v_0 = v_n$ and every v_i for $i = 1, \ldots, n-1$ occurs exactly once. We say that a *simple walk* is either a simple path or a simple cycle. In the SPARQL 1.1 definition, the W3C specifies the following constraint, which we call "simple walk requirement":

Simple Walk Requirement: Subexpressions of the form r^* and r^+ should be matched to simple walks.

The W3C SPARQL algebra (Section 18.4 of [25]) defines the semantics of r^* and r^+ through its operators *ZeroOrMorePath* and *OneOrMorePath*. It is not clear to us whether the currently stated definition only allows *simple paths* or *simple walks* to match. Our complexity results hold for both options.

Let $p = v_0[a_1]v_1[a_2]v_2 \cdots v_{n-1}[a_n]v_n$ be a path and r be a SPARQL regular expression. Then *p matches r under simple walk semantics* if one of the following holds:

- If $r = \varepsilon$, $r = a \in \Delta$, $r = \bullet$, or $r = !\{a_1, \ldots, a_n\}$ then $\mathrm{lab}(p) \in L(r)$.
- If $r = s^*$ or $r = s^+$, then $\mathrm{lab}(p) \in L(r)$ and p is a simple walk.
- If $r = s?$, then either $p = v_0$ or p matches s under simple walk semantics.
- If $r = s_1 \cdot s_2$, then there exist paths p_1 and p_2 such that $p = p_1 p_2$ and p_i matches s_i under simple walk semantics for all $i = 1, 2$.
- If $r = s_1 + s_2$, then there exists an $i = 1, 2$ such that p matches s_i under simple walk semantics.
- If $r = s^{k,\ell}$ with $\ell \neq \infty$, then there exists paths $p_1, \ldots, p_m$ with $k \leq m \leq \ell$ such that $p = p_1 \cdots p_m$ and p_i matches s under simple walk semantics for each $i = 1, \ldots, m$.
- If $r = s^{k,\infty}$, then there exist paths p_1 and p_2 such that $p = p_1 p_2$, p_1 matches $s^{k,k}$ under simple walk semantics, and p_2 matches s^* under simple walk semantics.

Notice that, under simple walk semantics, we no longer have that a^* is equivalent to $a^* a^*$, that $a^{1,\infty}$ is equivalent to a^+, or that aa^* is equivalent to a^+. However, aa^* is equivalent to $a^{1,\infty}$. For the expression $(a+b)^{50,60}$ regular path semantics and simple walk semantics coincide.

Problems of Interest.

We will often consider a graph $G = (V, E)$ together with a *source node* x and a *target node* y, for example, when considering paths from x to y. We say that (V, E, x, y) is the *s-t graph* of G w.r.t. x and y. Sometimes we leave the

---

[2]In this paper, we mostly refer to these expressions as "SPARQL regular expressions" to avoid confusion between expressions and paths.

[3]We do not define r^+ as an abbreviation of rr^* since r^+ and rr^* have different semantics in SPARQL.

facts that x and y are source and target implicit and just refer to (V, E, x, y) as a graph.

We consider two paths $p_1 = v_0^1[a_1^1]v_1^1 \cdots [a_n^1]v_n^1$ and $p_2 = v_0^2[a_1^2]v_1^2 \cdots [a_m^2]v_m^2$ in a graph to be *different*, if either the sequences of nodes or the sequences of labels are different, i.e., $v_0^1 v_1^1 \cdots v_n^1 \neq v_0^2 v_1^2 \cdots v_m^2$ or $\mathrm{lab}(p_1) \neq \mathrm{lab}(p_2)$. Notice that this implies that we consider two paths going through the same sequence of nodes but using different edge labels to be different.

We are mainly interested in the following problems, which we consider under regular path semantics and under simple walk semantics:

EVALUATION: Given a graph (V, E, x, y) and a regular expression r, is there a path from x to y that matches r?

FINITENESS: Given a graph (V, E, x, y) and a regular expression r, are there only finitely many different paths from x to y that match r?

COUNTING: Given a graph (V, E, x, y), a regular expression r and a natural number max in unary, how many different paths of length at most max between x and y match r?

The COUNTING problem is closely related to two problems studied in the literature: (1) counting the number of words of a given length in the language of a regular expression and (2) counting the number of paths in a graph that match certain constraints. We chose to have the number max in unary because this was also the case in several highly relevant papers on (1) and (2) (e.g., [27, 4, 40]). Furthermore, it strengthens our hardness results. However, our polynomial-time results for COUNTING still hold when the number max is given in binary (Theorems 4.4 and 3.11).

We will often parameterize the problems with the kind of regular expressions or automata we consider. For example, when we talk about EVALUATION for $\mathrm{RE}(\#, \neg)$, then we mean the EVALUATION problem where the input is a graph (V, E, x, y) and an expression r in $\mathrm{RE}(\#, \neg)$.

3. THE EVALUATION PROBLEM

We conducted a practical study on the efficiency in which SPARQL engines evaluate property paths. We evaluated the most prevalent SPARQL query engines which support property paths, namely the Jena Semantic Web Framework (which is used in, e.g., ARQ), Sesame, RDF::Query, and Corese 3.0.[4] We asked the four frameworks to answer the query `ASK WHERE { x (a|b){1,k} y }` for increasing values of k on the graph

consisting of two nodes and four labeled edges. Formally, this corresponds to answering the EVALUATION problem on the above graph for the expression $(a + b)^{1,k}$. Notice that the answer is always "true". Furthermore, notice that this query has the same semantics under regular path semantics as under simple walk semantics.

The performance of three of the four systems is depicted in Figure 1. The results are obtained from evaluation on a

---

[4] RDF3X was also recommended to us as a benchmark system but, as far as we could see, it does not support property paths.

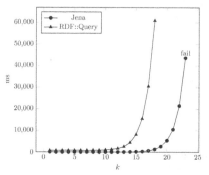

(a) Evaluation time for Jena and RDF::Query.

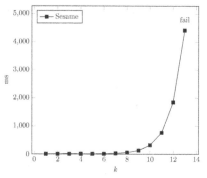

(b) Evaluation time for Sesame.

Figure 1: Time taken by Jena, Sesame and RDF::Query for evaluating the expression $(a + b)^{1,k}$ for increasing values of k on a graph with two nodes and four edges.

desktop PC with 2 GB of RAM. For the Jena and Sesame framework the points in the graph depict all the points we could obtain data on. When we increased the number k by one more as shown on the graphic, the systems ran out of memory. Our conclusion from our measurements is that all three systems seem to exhibit a double exponential behavior: from a certain point, whenever we increase the number k by one (which does not mean that one more bit is needed to represent it), the processing time doubles. Corese 3.0 evaluated queries of the above form very quickly. However, when we asked the query `ASK WHERE {x ((a|b)/(a|b)){1,k} y}`, which asks for the existence of even length paths, its time consumption was the same than the other three systems. In contrast to the other three systems, Corese did not run out of memory so quickly. We note that Arenas, Conca, and Pérez [5] observed double exponential behavior for `SELECT` queries in an independent study. However, `ASK` queries are easier to evaluate since they only ask for a Boolean answer.

3.1 An Efficient Algorithm for Regular Path Semantics

We show that the double exponential behavior we observed in practice can be improved to polynomial-time combined complexity. In particular, we present a polynomial-time algorithm for EVALUATION of SPARQL regular expressions.

We briefly discuss some basic results on evaluating regular expressions on graphs. EVALUATION is in PTIME for standard regular expressions.[5] In this case, the problem basically boils down to testing intersection emptiness of two finite automata: one converts the graph G with the given nodes x and y into a finite automaton A_G by taking the nodes of G as states, the edges as transitions, x as its initial state and y as its accepting state. The expression r is converted into a finite automaton A_r by using standard methods. Then, there is a path from x to y in G that matches r if and only if the intersection of the languages of A_G and A_r is not empty, which can easily be tested in polynomial time. Pérez et al. have shown that the product construction of automata can even be used for a linear-time algorithm for evaluating *nested regular path expressions*, which are regular expressions that have the power to branch out in the graph [37].

The polynomial time algorithm for EVALUATION of RE($\#, !, \bullet$)-expressions follows a dynamic programming approach. We first discuss the main idea of the algorithm and then discuss its complexity. Let r be an RE($\#, !, \bullet$)-expression and let $G = (V, E)$ be a graph. Our algorithm traverses the syntax tree of r in a bottom-up fashion. To simplify notation in the following discussion, we identify nodes from the parse tree of r to their corresponding subexpressions. We store, for each node in the syntax tree with associated subexpression s, a binary relation $R_s \subseteq V \times V$ such that

$(u, v) \in R_s$ if and only if
     there exists a path from u to v in G that matches s.

The manner in which we join relations while going bottom-up in the parse tree depends on the type of the node. We discuss all possible cases next.

If s is a Δ-symbol, then $R_s := \{(u, v) \mid (u, s, v) \in E\}$.

If $s = \varepsilon$, then $R_s := \{(u, u) \mid u \in V\}$.

If $s = !\{a_1, \ldots, a_n\}$, then $R_s := \{(u, v) \mid \exists a \in \Delta - \{a_1, \ldots, a_n\}$ with $(u, a, v) \in E\}$.

If $s = \bullet$, then $R_s := \{(u, v) \mid \exists a \in \Delta$ with $(u, a, v) \in E\}$.

If $s = s_1 + s_2$, then $R_s = R_{s_1} \cup R_{s_2}$.

If $s = s_1 \cdot s_2$, then $R_s := \pi_{1,3}(R_{s_1} \underset{R_{s_1}.2 = R_{s_2}.1}{\bowtie} R_{s_2})$, where

$\underset{R_{s_1}.2 = R_{s_2}.1}{\bowtie}$ denotes the ternary relation obtained by joining R_{s_1} and R_{s_2} by pairing tuples that agree on the right column of R_{s_1} and the left column on R_{s_2}. Furthermore, $\pi_{1,3}$ denotes the projection of these triples onto the leftmost and rightmost column.

If $s = s_1^*$, then R_s is the reflexive and transitive closure of R_{s_1}.

If $s = s_1^+$, then R_s is the transitive closure of R_{s_1}.

If $s = s_1^k$, then consider the connectivity matrix M_{s_1} of pairs that match s_1 in G. That is, for each pair of nodes (u, v) in G, we have that $M_{s_1}[u, v] = 1$ if and only if $(u, v) \in R_{s_1}$ and $M_{s_1}[u, v] = 0$ otherwise. Notice that M_{s_1} is a $|V| \times |V|$ matrix. Then $R_s := \{(u, v) \mid M_{s_1}^k[u, v] \neq 0\}$, where $M_{s_1}^k$ denotes the matrix M_{s_1} to the power of k.

If $s = s_1^{k, \infty}$, then R_s is the relation for the expression $s_1^k \cdot s_1^*$.

If $s = s_1^{k, \ell}$ and $\ell \neq \infty$, then let M_{s_1} be the same matrix as we used in the s_1^k case. Let M'_{s_1} be the matrix obtained from M_{s_1} by setting $M'_{s_1}[u, v] := 1$ if $u = v$. Therefore we have that $M'_{s_1}[u, v] := 1$ if and only if v is reachable from

---

[5]This has already been observed in the literature several times, e.g., as Lemma 1 in [35], on p.7 in [2], and in [3].

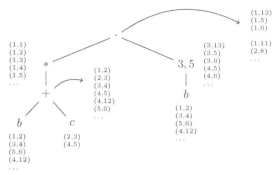

(a) Part of a run on the expression $(b + c)^* b^{3,5}$ and the graph in Fig. 2(b).

$$1 \xrightarrow{b} 2 \xrightarrow{c} 3 \xrightarrow{b} 4 \xrightarrow{c} 5 \xrightarrow{b} 6 \xrightarrow{b} 7 \xrightarrow{b} 8 \xrightarrow{b} 9 \xrightarrow{b} 10 \xrightarrow{b} 11$$
$$\qquad\qquad \searrow^{b} \qquad \searrow^{b}$$
$$12 \xrightarrow{b} 13$$

(b) An edge-labeled graph.

Figure 2: Illustration of the polynomial-time dynamic programming algorithm.

---

u by a path that matches s_1 zero or one times. Let $M_s := (M_{s_1})^k \cdot (M'_{s_1})^{\ell - k}$. Then, $R_s := \{(u, v) \mid M_s[u, v] \neq 0\}$.

Finally, if the input for EVALUATION is G, nodes x and y, and RE($\#, !, \bullet$)-expression r, we return the answer "true" if and only if R_r contains the pair (x, y).

EXAMPLE 3.1. *Figure 2 illustrates part of a run of the evaluation algorithm on the graph in Figure 2(b) and the regular expression $r = (b + c)^* b^{3,5}$. Each node of the parse tree of the expression (Fig. 2(a)) is annotated with the binary relation that we compute for it. Finally, the relation for the root node contains all pairs (x, y) such that there is a path from x to y that matches r.*

We show that EVALUATION is correct and can be implemented to run in polynomial time.

THEOREM 3.2. EVALUATION *for SPARQL regular expressions under regular path semantics is in polynomial time.*

PROOF SKETCH. We prove that the dynamic programming algorithm can be implemented to decide EVALUATION for RE($\#, !, \bullet$) in polynomial time. That is, given a graph $G = (V, E, x, y)$ and RE($\#, !, \bullet$)-expression r, it decides in polynomial time whether there is a path in G from x to y that matches r.

First, we argue correctness. The following invariant holds for every relation R_s that is calculated: For each subexpression s of r, we have $(u, v) \in R_s \Leftrightarrow \exists$ path p in G from u to v : $\text{lab}(p) \in L(s)$.

Next, we argue that the algorithm can be implemented to run in polynomial time. Notice that the parse tree of the input expression s has linear size and that each relation R_s has at most quadratic size in G. We therefore only need to prove that we can implement each separate case in the algorithm in polynomial time.

The cases where $s \in \Delta$, $s = \varepsilon$, $s = \bullet$, $s = s_1^*$, $s = s_1^+$, and $s = s_1 \cdot s_2$ are trivial. For the case $s = s_1^k$, we need to argue that, for a given $|V| \times |V|$ matrix M and a number k given in binary, we can compute M^k in polynomial time. However, this is well-known to be possible in $\lceil \log k \rceil$ iterated squarings (sometimes also called successive squaring) ([7], page 74). In the case $s = s_1^{k,\infty}$, we only need to compute the relation for s_1 once, copy it, compute $M_{s_1}^k$ as before, compute the transitive and reflexive closure of R_{s_1} and join the results. All of this can be performed in polynomial time. Finally, also the case of $s = s_1^{k,\ell}$ can be computed in polynomial time by using the same methods. This concludes our proof. $\square$

We are not the first to think of dynamic programming in the context of regular expressions. The connection between dynamic programming and regular expressions goes back at least to Kleene's recursive formulas for extracting a regular expression from a DFA [30]. Dynamic programming for testing whether a string belongs to a language of a regular expression has been demonstrated in [26] (p.75–76). Kilpeläinen and Tuhkonen adapted this approach for evaluating RE(#) on strings [28]. However, the algorithm from [28] does not naïvely work on graphs: it would need time exponential in the expression.[6]

We conclude this section with a few observations on the dynamic programming algorithm. Most notably: if we want to evaluate expressions on strings instead of graphs, we can also incorporate negation into the algorithm. By MEMBERSHIP we denote the following decision problem: Given a string w and a regular expression r, is $w \in L(r)$?

THEOREM 3.3. MEMBERSHIP for $RE(\#,!,\neg,\bullet)$ is in polynomial time.

However, as we illustrate in the next section, allowing unrestricted negation in expressions does not allow for an efficient algorithm for EVALUATION anymore.

3.2 Negation Makes Evaluation Hard

The negated label test seems to be harmless for the efficiency of evaluating SPARQL regular expressions. On strings, even the full-fledged negation operator "$\neg$" can be evaluated efficiently. However, allowing full-fledged negation for evaluation on graphs makes the complexity of EVALUATION non-elementary. The reason is that EVALUATION is at least as hard as satisfiability of the given regular expression.

LEMMA 3.4. Let C be a class of regular expressions over a finite alphabet Σ. Then there exists a polynomial-time reduction from the non-emptiness problem for C-expressions to the EVALUATION problem with C-expressions.

PROOF. The proof is immediate from the observation that non-emptiness of an expression r over an alphabet Σ is the same decision problem as EVALUATION for r and the graph $G = (V, E)$ with $V = \{x\}$ and $E = \{(x, a, x) \mid a \in \Sigma\}$. $\square$

Since the emptiness problem of *star-free generalized regular expressions*[7] is non-elementary [39], we therefore also immediately have that EVALUATION is non-elementary for RE($\neg$)-expressions, by Lemma 3.4.

---

[6]It uses the fact that the length of the *longest match* of the expression on the string cannot exceed the length of the string. For example, the regular expression a^{42} can only match a string if it contains 42 a's. So the fact that 42 is represented in binary notation does not matter for the combined complexity the problem. This assumption no longer holds in graphs.

[7]A star-free generalized regular expression is a regular expression with concatenation, disjunction, and negation.

THEOREM 3.5. EVALUATION *under regular path semantics is non-elementary for* $RE(\neg)$.

For completeness, since RE($\#,!,\neg,\bullet$)-expressions can be converted into RE($\#,!,\bullet$)-expressions with a non-elementary blow-up, we also mention a general upper bound for EVALUATION.

THEOREM 3.6. EVALUATION *under regular path semantics is decidable but non-elementary for* $RE(\#,!,\neg,\bullet)$

3.3 SPARQL Semantics

We study how the complexity of EVALUATION changes when SPARQL's simple walk semantics rather than regular path semantics is applied.

NP-Complete Fragments.

THEOREM 3.7 ([35]). EVALUATION *under simple walk semantics is NP-complete for the expression* $(aa)^*$ *and for the expression* $(aa)^+$.

The lower bound immediately follows from Theorem 1 in [35], where it is shown that it is NP-hard to decide whether there exists a simple path of even length between two given nodes x and y in a graph G. The upper bound is trivial.

On the other hand, EVALUATION remains in NP even when numerical occurrence indicators are allowed.

THEOREM 3.8. EVALUATION *under simple walk semantics is NP-complete for* $RE(\#,!,\bullet)$-*expressions.*

PROOF SKETCH. The NP lower bound is immediate from Theorem 3.7. The NP upper bound follows from an adaptation of the dynamic programming algorithm of Section 3 where, in the cases for $s = s_1^*$ and $s = s_1^+$, simple walks are guessed between nodes to see if they belong to R_s. $\square$

It follows that EVALUATION under simple walk semantics is also NP-complete for standard regular expressions.

COROLLARY 3.9. EVALUATION *under simple walk semantics is NP-complete for* RE.

Polynomial Time Fragments.

Theorem 3.7 restrains the possibilities for finding polynomial time fragments rather severely. In order to find such fragments and in order to trace a tractability frontier, we will look at syntactically constrained classes of regular expressions that have been used to trace the tractability frontier for the regular expression containment problem [33, 34]. We will also use these expressions in Section 4.

DEFINITION 3.10 (CHAIN REGULAR EXPRESSION [34]). A *base symbol* is a regular expression w, w^*, w^+, or $w?$, where w is a non-empty string; a *factor* is of the form e, e^*, e^+, or $e?$ where e is a disjunction of base symbols of the same kind. That is, e is of the form $(w_1 + \cdots + w_n)$, $(w_1^* + \cdots + w_n^*)$, $(w_1^+ + \cdots + w_n^+)$, or $(w_1? + \cdots + w_n?)$, where $n \geq 0$ and $w_1, \ldots, w_n$ are non-empty strings. An *(extended) chain regular expression (CHARE)* is $\emptyset$, ε, or a concatenation of factors.

We use the same shorthand notation for CHAREs as in [34]. The shorthands we use for the different kind of factors is illustrated in Table 1. For example, the regular expression

Factor	Abbr.
u	a
a^*	a^*
a^+	a^+
$a?$	$a?$
w^*	w^*
w^+	w^+
$w?$	$w?$

Factor	Abbr.	Factor	Abbr.
$(a_1 + \cdots + a_n)$	$(+a)$	$(w_1 + \cdots + w_n)$	$(+w)$
$(a_1 + \cdots + a_n)^*$	$(+a)^*$	$(w_1 + \cdots + w_n)^*$	$(+w)^*$
$(a_1 + \cdots + a_n)^+$	$(+a)^+$	$(w_1 + \cdots + w_n)^+$	$(+w)^+$
$(a_1 + \cdots + a_n)?$	$(+a)?$	$(w_1 + \cdots + w_n)?$	$(+w)?$
$(a_1^* + \cdots + a_n^*)$	$(+a^*)$	$(w_1^* + \cdots + w_n^*)$	$(+w^*)$
$(a_1^+ + \cdots + a_n^+)$	$(+a^+)$	$(w_1^+ + \cdots + w_n^+)$	$(+w^+)$

Table 1: **Possible factors in extended chain regular expressions and how they are denoted. We denote by a and a_i arbitrary symbols in Δ and by w, w_i non-empty strings in Δ^+.**

$((abc)^* + b^*)(a+b)?(ab)^+(ac+b)^*$ is an extended chain regular expression with factors of the form $(+w^*)$, $(+a)?$, w^+, and $(+w)^*$, from left to right. The expression $(a+b)+(a^*b^*)$, however, is not even a CHARE, due to the nested disjunction and the nesting of Kleene star with concatenation. Notice that each kind of factor that is *not* listed in Table 1 can be simulated through one of other ones. For example, a factor of the form $(a_1^+ + \cdots + a_n^+)?$ is equivalent to $(a_1^* + \cdots + a_n^*)$. For a similar reason, no factor of the form w is listed. Our interest in these expressions is that CHAREs often occur in practical settings [8] and that they are convenient to model classes that allow only a limited amount of non-determinism, which becomes pivotal in Section 4. We denote fragments of the class of CHAREs by enumerating the kinds of factors that are allowed. For example, the above mentioned expression is a CHARE($(+w^*)$, $(+a)?$, w^+, $(+w)^*$).

The following theorem shows that it is possible to use the *- and $^+$-operators and have a fragment for which evaluation is in polynomial time. However, below it, one is only allowed to use a disjunction of single symbols.

THEOREM 3.11. EVALUATION *under simple walk semantics for CHARE($(+a)^*$, $(+a)^+$, $(+w)$, $(+w)?$) is in PTIME.*

PROOF SKETCH. This theorem follows from the observation that, for each regular expression r from this class, there exists a path p from a node x to y that matches r under simple walk semantics if and only if there exists a path p' from x to y that matches r under regular path semantics. $\square$

Notice that the range of possibilities between the expressions in CHARE($(+a)^*$, $(+a)^+$, $(+w)$, $(+w)?$) and the expressions in Theorem 3.7 is quite limited. Furthermore, notice the relationship between Theorem 3.11 and Theorem 1 in [35]: Whereas testing the existence of a simple path that matches the expression a^*ba^* is NP-complete [35], testing the existence of a path that matches the expression a^*ba^* under simple walk semantics is in PTIME (Theorem 3.11).

A limitation of Theorem 3.11 is that CHAREs do not allow arbitrary nesting of disjunctions. However, since simple walk semantics and regular path semantics are equal for RE-expressions that do not use the Kleene star or the $^+$-operator, EVALUATION for those expressions under simple walk semantics is tractable as well.

OBSERVATION 3.12. EVALUATION *under simple walk semantics is in PTIME for RE-expressions that do not use the *- or $^+$-operators.*

Theorem 3.11 and Observation 3.12 seem to make one central point apparent: unless P = NP, simple walk semantics is tractable as long as it is essentially the same than regular path semantics.

4. THE COUNTING PROBLEM

In this section we study the complexity of COUNTING and FINITENESS. Our motivation for COUNTING comes from the SPARQL definition that requires that, for simple SPARQL queries of the form SELECT ?x, ?y WHERE {?x r ?y} for a path expression r, the result is a multiset that has n copies of a pair $(x,y) \in V \times V$, when n is the number of paths between x and y that match r. We informally refer to this requirement as the path counting requirement.

Path Counting Requirement: The number of paths from x to y that match r needs to be counted.

First, we investigate COUNTING under regular path semantics and then under simple walk semantics.

4.1 Regular Path Semantics

We first show that it is possible to count paths for deterministic patterns and then that allowing even the slightest amount of non-determinism makes the counting problem #P-complete.

Counting for Deterministic Patterns.

We consider finite automata that read Δ-strings. The automata behave very similarly to standard finite automata (see, e.g., [26]), but they can make use of a wildcard symbol "$\circ$" to deal with the infinite set of labels. More formally, an NFA N over Δ is a tuple $(Q, \Sigma, \Delta, \delta, q_0, Q_f)$, where Q is a finite set of states, $\Sigma \subseteq \Delta$ is a finite alphabet, Δ is the set of input symbols, $\delta : Q \times (\Sigma \uplus \{\circ\}) \times Q$ is the transition relation, q_0 is the initial state, and Q_f is the set of final states. The *size* of an NFA is $|Q|$, i.e., its number of states.

When the NFA is in a state q and reads a symbol $a \in \Delta$, we may be able to follow several transitions. The transitions labeled with Σ-symbols can be followed if $a \in \Sigma$. The $\circ$-label in outgoing transitions is used to deal with everything else, i.e., the $\circ$-transitions can be followed when reading $a \notin \Sigma$. Notice that the semantics of the $\bullet$-symbol in regular expressions is therefore different from $\circ$ in automata. The reason for the difference is twofold: first, we want to define a natural notion of determinism for automata and second, our definition of $\circ$ makes it easy to represent subexpressions of the form $!\{a_1, \ldots, a_n\}$ in automata.[8] Nevertheless, an expression from RE can still be translated into an equivalent NFA in polynomial time. More formally, a *run r of N on*

---

[8] One could also achieve these goals by defining the semantics of $\circ$ to be "all symbols for which the current state has no other outgoing transition". We thought that our definition would be clearer since it defines the semantics of every $\circ$-transition the same across the whole automaton.

a Δ-word $w = a_1 \cdots a_n$ is a string $q_0 q_1 \cdots q_n$ in Q^* such that, for every $i = 1, \ldots, n$, if $a_i \in \Sigma$, then $(q_{i-1}, a_i, q_i) \in \delta$; otherwise, $(q_{i-1}, \circ, q_i) \in \delta$. Notice that, when $i = 1$, the condition states that we can follow a transition from the initial state q_0 to q_1. A run is *accepting* when $q_n \in Q_f$. A word w is accepted by N if there exists an accepting run of N on w. The *language* $L(N)$ of N is the set of words accepted by N. A *path p matches N* if $\mathrm{lab}(p) \in L(N)$.

We say that an NFA is *deterministic*, or a DFA, when the relation δ is a function from $Q \times (\Sigma \uplus \{\circ\})$ to Q. That is, for every $q_1 \in Q$ and $a \in \Sigma \uplus \{\circ\}$, there is at most one q_2 such that $(q_1, a, q_2) \in \delta$. In this case, we will also slightly abuse notation and write $\delta(q_1, a) = q_2$.

We discuss the relationship between SPARQL regular expressions and DFAs by (informally) revisiting the *Glushkov-automaton* of a regular expression (see also [9, 24]). Let r be a SPARQL regular expression and let Σ_r be the set of Δ-symbols occurring in r. By $\mathrm{num}(r)$ we denote the *numbered regular expression* obtained from r by replacing each subexpression of the form $!S$, $\bullet$, or $a \in \Sigma_r$ (that is not in the scope of an !-operator) with a unique number, increasing from left to right. For example, for $r = a \ !\{a\} \bullet (a + bc)^* \bullet !\{a, b\}$ we have $\mathrm{num}(r) = 1\ 2\ 3\ (4\ +5\ 6)^*7\ 8$. Formally, $\mathrm{num}(r)$ can be obtained by traversing the parse tree of r depth-first left-to-right and making the appropriate replacements. By denum_r we denote the mapping that maps each number i to the subexpression it replaced in r. In the above example, $\mathrm{denum}_r(1) = a$, $\mathrm{denum}_r(2) = !\{a\}$, $\mathrm{denum}_r(3) = \bullet$, and so on.

Fix an expression r and its numbered expression r_m. Notice that r_m can be seen as a regular expression over a finite alphabet $\Sigma' \subseteq \mathbb{N}$. Let $\mathrm{first}(r_m)$ be the set of all symbols $i \in \Sigma'$ such that $L(r_m)$ contains a word iz, where $z \in (\Sigma')^*$. Furthermore, let $\mathrm{follow}(r_m, i)$ be the set of symbols $j \in \Sigma'$ such that there exists Σ'-strings v, w with $vijw \in L(r_m)$, and let $\mathrm{last}(r_m)$ be the set of symbols $i \in \Sigma'$ such that there exists a word vi in $L(r_m)$. The *Glushkov-automaton* G_r of r is the tuple $(Q_r, \Sigma_r, \Delta, \delta_r, q_0, Q_f)$ where $Q_r = \{q_0\} \uplus \Sigma'$ is its finite set of states. That is, Q_r contains an initial state and one state for each Σ'-symbol i in the numbered expression r_m. If $\varepsilon \in L(r)$, then the set of accepting states is $Q_f = \mathrm{last}(r_m) \uplus \{q_0\}$. Otherwise, $Q_f = \mathrm{last}(r_m)$. For each $a \in \Sigma_r$ and $i \in Q_r$, the transition function δ_r is defined as follows: (1) $\delta_r(q_0, a) = \{i \in \mathrm{first}(r_m) \mid \mathrm{denum}(i) = a,$ $\mathrm{denum}(i) = \bullet$, or $\mathrm{denum}(i) = !S$ with $a \notin S\}$ and (2) $\delta_r(i, a) = \{j \in \mathrm{follow}(r_m, i) \mid \mathrm{denum}(j) = a, \mathrm{denum}(j) = \bullet,$ or $\mathrm{denum}(j) = !S$ with $a \notin S\}$. Furthermore, (3) $\delta_r(q_0, \circ) = \{i \in \mathrm{first}(r_m) \mid \mathrm{denum}(i) = \bullet$ or $\mathrm{denum}(i) = !S$ for some $S\}$ and (4) $\delta_r(i, \circ) = \{j \in \mathrm{follow}(r_m, i) \mid \mathrm{denum}(j) = \bullet$ or $\mathrm{denum}(j) = !S$ for some $S\}$.

PROPOSITION 4.1. *For each SPARQL regular expression r, the Glushkov automaton of r can be constructed in polynomial time. Furthermore, $L(r) = L(G_r)$.*

We say that a SPARQL regular expression r is *deterministic*, or a *Det-RE*, if G_r is a DFA.

In the following, we slightly generalize the definition of s-t graphs and overload their notation. For an edge-labeled graph $G = (V, E)$, $x \in V$, and $Y \subseteq V$, the *s-t graph of G w.r.t. x and Y* is the quadruple (V, E, x, Y). As before, we refer to x as the source node and to Y as the (set of) target nodes. Let $G = (V, E, x, y)$ be an s-t graph and $A = (Q, \Sigma, \Delta, \delta, q_0, Q_F)$ be a DFA. We define a *product of*

(V, E, x, y) and A, denoted by $G^{x,y} \times A$, similar to the standard product of finite automata. More formally, $G^{x,y} \times A$ is an s-t graph $(V_{G,A}, E_{G,A}, x_{G,A}, Y_{G,A})$, where all of the following hold.

- The set of nodes $V_{G,A}$ is $V \times Q$.
- The source node $x_{G,A}$ is (x, q_0).
- The set of target nodes $Y_{G,A}$ is $\{(y, q_f) \mid q_f \in Q_f\}$.
- For each $a \in \Delta$, there is an edge $((v_1, q_1), a, (v_2, q_2)) \in E_{G,A}$ if and only if there is an edge (v_1, a, v_2) in G and either $a \in \Sigma$ and there is a transition $(q_1, a, q_2) \in \delta$ or $a \notin \Sigma$ and there is a transition $(q_1, \circ, q_2) \in \delta$ in A.

If A is a DFA, then there is a strong correspondence between paths from x to y in G and paths from $q_0^{G,A}$ to $Q_f^{G,A}$ in $G^{x,y} \times A$. We formalize this correspondence by a mapping φ_{PATHS}, which we define inductively as follows:

- $\varphi_{\mathrm{PATHS}}(x) := (x, q_0)$;
- for each v_1 such that $\varphi_{\mathrm{PATHS}}(v_1) = (v_1, q_1)$ and for each edge $e = (v_1, a, v_2)$ in G, we define
  - $\varphi_{\mathrm{PATHS}}(v_2) := (v_2, q_2)$, where q_2 is the unique state such that $\delta_A(q_1, a) = q_2$ or $\delta_A(q_1, \circ) = q_2$; and
  - $\varphi_{\mathrm{PATHS}}(e) := ((v_1, q_1), a, (v_2, q_2))$.

We extend the mapping φ_{PATHS} in the canonical manner to paths in G starting from x. Notice that φ_{PATHS} is only well-defined if A is a DFA.

LEMMA 4.2. *If A is a DFA, then φ_{PATHS} is a bijection between paths from x to y in G that match A and paths from $x_{G,A}$ to some node in $Y_{G,A}$ in $G^{x,y} \times A$. Furthermore, φ_{PATHS} preserves the length of paths.*

We recall the following graph-theoretical result that states that the number of arbitrary paths between two nodes in a graph can be counted quickly (see, e.g., [7], page 74):

THEOREM 4.3. *Let G be a graph, let x and y be two nodes of G, and let max be a number given in binary. Then, the number of paths from x to y of length at most max can be computed in time polynomial in G and the number of bits of max.*

Again, the reason why the number of paths can be counted so quickly is due to the fast squaring method that can compute, for a given (square) matrix M, the matrix M^k in $O(\log k)$ matrix multiplications.

THEOREM 4.4. COUNTING *for DFAs is in polynomial time, even if the number max in the input is given in binary.*

PROOF. We reduce COUNTING for DFAs to the problem of counting the number of paths in a graph, which is in polynomial time even when max is in binary, due to Theorem 4.3.

Let $G = (V, E, x, y)$ be a graph and $A = (Q, \Sigma, \Delta, \delta, q_0, Q_f)$ be a DFA. The algorithms works as follows:

- Let $G^{x,y} \times A$ be the product of (V, E, x, y) and A.
- Return $\sum_{q_f \in Q_f} \mathrm{PATHS}((x, q_0), (y, q_f))$ in $G^{x,y} \times A$.

Here, $\mathrm{PATHS}((x, q_0), (y, q_f))$ denotes the number of paths of length at most max in $G^{x,y} \times A$ from node (x, q_0) to (y, q_f). By Lemma 4.2, this algorithm is correct. Indeed, the lemma shows that the number of paths of length at most max in G between x and y and that are matched by A equals the number of paths of length at most max from (x, q_0) to some node in $\{y\} \times Q_f$ in $G^{x,y} \times A$. $\square$

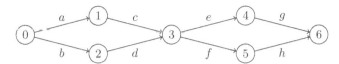

Figure 3: An edge-labeled graph $(V, E, 0, 6)$.

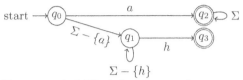

Figure 4: A DFA A for the regular expression $(a\Sigma^* + \Sigma^+ h)$, with $\Sigma = \{a, b, c, d, e, f, g, h\}$.

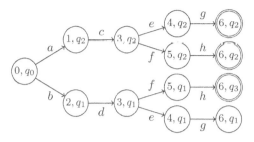

Figure 5: Fragment of the product $G^{0,6} \times A$ of $(V, E, 0, 6)$ from Figure 3 and DFA A from Figure 4. The nodes in $Y_{G,A}$ are in double circles.

Actually, Theorem 4.4 even holds for automata that are *unambiguous*, i.e., automata that only allow exactly one accepting run for each word in the language.

We illustrate the algorithm of Theorem 4.4 on an example. Consider the DFA A in Figure 4. The product of A and the s-t graph $(V, E, 0, 6)$ from Figure 3 is depicted in Figure 5. We see that the number of paths in G from node 0 to 6 that match A is precisely the number of paths from the start state to an accepting state in P.

Counting for Non-Deterministic Patterns.

We start by observing that COUNTING is in #P for standard regular expressions.

THEOREM 4.5. COUNTING *is in #P for all REs.*

PROOF. Let $G = (V, E, x, y)$ be a graph, r be an RE, and $\mathsf{max} \in \mathbb{N}$ be a number given in unary notation. The nondeterministic Turing machine for the #P procedure simply guesses a path of length at most max and tests whether it matches $L(r)$. □

We now prove that COUNTING becomes #P-hard for a wide array of restricted REs that allow for a very limited amount of non-determinism. We consider the chain regular expressions introduced in Section 3.3. For example, the class of CHARE(a,a?) seems, at first sight, to be very limited. However, such expressions cannot be translated to polynomial-size DFAs in general. We show that COUNTING is #P-complete for all classes of CHAREs that allow a single label (i.e., "a") as a factor and can not be trivially converted to polynomial-size DFAs.

THEOREM 4.6. COUNTING *is #P-complete for all of the following classes: (1) CHARE(a, a^*), (2) CHARE(a, a?), (3) CHARE(a, w^+), (4) CHARE($a, (+a^+)$), (5) CHARE($a, (+a)^+$), and (6) CHARE($(+a), a^+$). Moreover, #P-hardness already holds if the graph G is acyclic.*

PROOF SKETCH. The upper bound for all cases is immediate from Theorem 4.5. The lower bounds can be proved by reductions from #DNF. We show the reduction for case (1). Our technique is inspired by a proof in [34], where it is shown that language inclusion for various classes of CHAREs is coNP-hard. Let $\Phi = C_1 \vee \cdots \vee C_k$ be a propositional formula in 3DNF using variables $\{x_1, \ldots, x_n\}$. We encode truth assignments for Φ by paths in the graph. In particular, we construct a graph (V, E, x, y), an expression r, and a number max such that each path of length at most

max in G from x to y that matches r corresponds to a unique satisfying truth assignment for Φ and vice versa. Formally, we will have that the number of paths of length at most max in G from x to y that match r is equal to the number of truth assignments that satisfy Φ.

The graph G has the structure as depicted in Figure 6, where *(i)* B is a path labeled $\#a\$a\$ \cdots \$a\#$ (with n copies of a) and *(ii)* A is a subgraph as depicted in Figure 6, with n copies of the gadget labeled ab/ba. Notice that all paths from x to y will enter A through the node x_A and leave A through y_A. Notice that G is acyclic.

Each path from x_A to y_A in A corresponds to exactly one truth assignment for the variables $\{x_1, \ldots, x_n\}$: if the path chooses the i-th subpath labeled ab, this means that x_k is "true". If it chooses ba, it means that x_k is "false". This concludes the description of the graph.

The expression r has the form $r = (\#^* a^* \$^* \cdots \$^* a^* \#^*)^k$ $F(C_1) \cdots F(C_k)(\#^* a^* \$^* \cdots \$^* a^* \#^*)^k$, where for each $i = 1, \ldots, k$, we define $F(C_i)$ as $\#e_1\$ \cdots \$e_n\#$ with, for each $j = 1, \ldots, n$,

$$e_j := \begin{cases} b^* a^*, & \text{if } x_j \text{ occurs negated in } C_i, \\ aa^* b^* a^*, & \text{if } x_j \text{ occurs positively in } C_i, \text{ and} \\ a^* b^* a^*, & \text{otherwise.} \end{cases}$$

This concludes the reduction for case (1). □

We conclude this section by stating the general #P upper bound on the counting problem.

THEOREM 4.7. COUNTING *for RE($\#, \neg, \bullet$) is #P-complete.*

4.2 SPARQL Semantics

We investigate how the complexity of COUNTING changes when we apply SPARQL's simple walk semantics. The picture is even more drastic than in Section 3.3. COUNTING already turns #P-complete as soon as the Kleene star or plus are used. We start by mentioning a polynomial-time result.

THEOREM 4.8. COUNTING *under simple walk semantics for CHARE($a, (+a)$) is in PTIME*

This result trivially holds since, for this fragment, simple walk semantics is the same as regular path semantics, and expressions from this fragment can be translated into DFAs in polynomial time.

THEOREM 4.9. COUNTING *under simple walk semantics is #P-complete for the expressions a^* and a^+.*

109

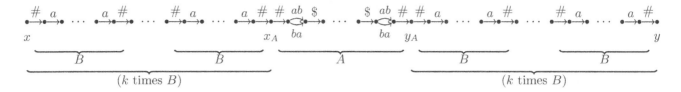

Figure 6: The graph G from the proof of Theorem 4.6.

PROOF. We reduce from the problem of counting the number of simple s-t paths in a graph, which was shown to be #P-complete by Valiant [40]. □

Theorem 4.9 immediately implies that COUNTING under simple walk semantics is #P-complete for CHARE(a, a^*), CHARE(a, w^+), CHARE$(a, (+a^+))$, CHARE$(a, (+a)^+)$, and CHARE$(a^+, (+a))$ as well. The result for CHARE$(a,a?)$ is not immediate from Theorem 4.9, but it is immediate from the observation that the reduction for regular path semantics applies here as well.

THEOREM 4.10. COUNTING *under simple walk semantics for CHARE(a, a?) is #P-complete.*

Finally, we mention that COUNTING is in #P for the full fragment of expressions in RE$(\#, !, \bullet)$.

THEOREM 4.11. COUNTING *under simple walk semantics for RE(#, !, •) is #P-complete.*

5. THE FINITENESS PROBLEM

Under simple walk semantics, there can never be an infinite number of paths that match a certain regular expression. Under regular path semantics, however, this can be the case. Therefore we complete the picture of our complexity analysis by looking at the FINITENESS problem.

Using the product construction (Section 4.1), we can test in polynomial time whether there is a path from x to y that is labelled uvw, such that v labels a loop and such that $uv^k w$ matches r for every $k \in \mathbb{N}$. If there is such a loop, then we return that there are infinitely many paths.

OBSERVATION 5.1. FINITENESS *is in PTIME for RE.*

By adapting the dynamic programming algorithm to also annotate the length of the longest paths associated to a pair in each relation, we can even decide FINITENESS for RE$(\#, !, \bullet)$ in PTIME.

THEOREM 5.2. FINITENESS *for RE(#, !, •) is in PTIME.*

Similar to EVALUATION, the complexity of FINITENESS becomes non-elementary once unrestricted negation is allowed in regular expressions. Analogously to EVALUATION we show that FINITENESS is at least as hard as satisfiability of a given regular expression.

LEMMA 5.3. *Let C be a class of regular expressions over a finite alphabet Σ, such that membership testing of ε for expressions in C is in polynomial time. Then there exists a polynomial reduction from the emptiness problem for C-expressions to the FINITENESS problem with C-expressions.*

For $r \in \text{RE}(\neg)$, one can test whether $\varepsilon \in L(r)$ in linear time traversing the syntax tree of r. If $\varepsilon \notin L(r)$, then testing emptiness for r is equivalent to FINITENESS on the expression r^* and the graph $G = (V, E, x, x)$ with $V = \{x\}$ and $E = \{(x, a, x) \mid a \in \Sigma\}$. Therefore, by [39] and Lemma 5.3 we have the following.

THEOREM 5.4. FINITENESS *is decidable but non-elementary for RE(¬).*

6. DISCUSSION

An overview of our results is presented in Table 2. CHAREs are defined in Section 3.3. By "star-free RE", we denote standard regular expressions that do not use the operators "*" and "+". The SPARQL-negation operator "!" is defined in Section 3.3. Det-RE stands for the class of deterministic SPARQL expressions that we defined in Section 4.

The table presents complexity results under combined query evaluation complexity. However, for simple walk semantics, all the NP-hardness or #P-hardness results hold under data complexity as well, except for the result on CHARE$(a, a?)$. Indeed, if the CHARE$(a, a?)$ is fixed, we can translate it to a DFA and perform the algorithm for COUNTING under regular path semantics. (For this fragment, simple walk semantics equals regular path semantics.) For regular path semantics, all #P-hardness results become tractable under data complexity: when the query is fixed, we can always translate it to a DFA and perform the algorithm for DFAs. When considering data complexity, the difference between regular path semantics and simple walk semantics therefore becomes even more striking.

Possible alternatives for the W3C.

The NP-complete and #P-complete data complexities make the current semantics of W3C property paths highly problematic from a computational complexity perspective, especially on a Web scale. There are two orthogonal requirements in the current W3C proposal that render the evaluation of simple queries of the form SELECT ?x, ?y WHERE {?x r ?y} computationally difficult:

Simple Walk Requirement: Subexpressions of the form r^* and r^+ should be matched to *simple walks*.

Path Counting Requirement: The number of paths from x to y that match r need to be counted.

By removing the simple walk requirement and the path counting requirement, the answer to the above SELECT query would be the set of pairs (x, y) in the graph such that there exists a path from x to y that matches r under regular path semantics. As such, each pair is returned at most once. Similar to [5], which is work conducted independently from ours, we believe that the W3C should use this semantics as a default semantics for property paths in SELECT queries. Our results show that SPARQL property

Problem	Fragment	Regular path semantics	Simple walk semantics
EVALUATION	CHARE$((+u)^*,(+a)^+,(+w),(+w)?)$	in PTIME	**in PTIME** (3.11)
	star-free RE	in PTIME	**in PTIME** (3.12)
	$(aa)^*$	in PTIME	NP-complete [35]
	RE	in PTIME	**NP-complete**
	RE$(\#,!,\bullet)$	**in PTIME** (3.2)	**NP-complete** (3.8)
	RE$(\neg)$	**non-elementary** (3.5)	—
	RE$(\#,!,\neg,\bullet)$	**non-elementary** (3.6)	—
COUNTING	DFA	**in FPTIME** (4.4)	—
	CHARE$(a,(+a))$	**in FPTIME**	**in FPTIME** (4.8)
	a^+	**in FPTIME**	#P-complete (4.9,[40])
	a^*	**in FPTIME**	#P-complete (4.9,[40])
	Det-RE	**in FPTIME**	**#P-complete**
	CHARE(a,a^*)	**#P-complete** (4.5,4.6)	**#P-complete**
	CHARE$(a,a?)$	**#P-complete** (4.5,4.6)	**#P-complete**(4.10)
	CHARE$(a,(+a^+))$	**#P-complete** (4.5,4.6)	**#P-complete**
	CHARE$(a,(+a)^+)$	**#P-complete** (4.5,4.6)	**#P-complete**
	CHARE(a,w^+)	**#P-complete** (4.5,4.6)	**#P-complete**
	CHARE$((+a),a^+)$	**#P-complete** (4.5,4.6)	**#P-complete**
	RE	**#P-complete** (4.5,4.6)	**#P-complete**
	RE$(\#,!,\bullet)$	**#P-complete** (4.7)	**#P-complete** (4.11)
	RE$(\#,!,\neg,\bullet)$	**#P-complete** (4.7)	—
FINITENESS	RE	**in PTIME** (5.1)	—
	RE$(\#,!,\bullet)$	**in PTIME** (5.2)	—
	RE$(\neg)$	**non-elementary** (5.4)	—
	RE$(\#,!,\neg,\bullet)$	**non-elementary** (5.4)	—

Table 2: An overview of most of our complexity results. The results printed in bold are new, to the best of our knowledge. The entries marked by "—" signify that the question is either trivial or not defined. We annotated new results with the relevant theorem numbers. If no such number is provided, it means that the result directly follows from other entries in the table. These results concern combined complexity. In data complexity, the entire column "Regular path semantics" drops to PTIME/FPTIME. For simple walk semantics, only the complexity of CHARE(a,a?) drops to FPTIME under data complexity.

paths (cfr. Def. 2.1), which can be exponentially more succinct than standard regular expressions, can then be evaluated in polynomial time combined complexity by a simple dynamic programming algorithm. Preliminary results indicate that we can even leverage this technique to evaluate *nested regular expressions* [37] with numerical occurrence indicators in polynomial time combined complexity.

However, it is possible that in some scenarios one would like to have a bag semantics for property paths and, therefore, paths would need to be counted. We think that removing the simple walk requirement would be wise here as well. As we showed, doing so would drop the data complexity of COUNTING from #P-complete to polynomial time for almost all non-trivial queries. However, in this case, it is still less clear *how* one would like to count paths. At the moment, the W3C has a procedural definition for counting paths which is studied in depth in [5], where it is proved that it leads to massive computational problems. Furthermore, we believe that this definition is rather opaque and that it should be much more transparent to end-users and researchers.

So, what could we do? When one would naïvely adopt regular path semantics for counting paths, one would need to find a way to deal with the case where there are infinitely many paths between two nodes that match an expression. In principle, it is possible to deal with this case efficiently. We proved that deciding whether this case applies, i.e., solving the FINITENESS problem, is possible for SPARQL regular expressions in polynomial time. One could also avoid the need

to decide this case entirely. An ad-hoc solution could be to simply not count paths anymore beyond a certain number. Such a solution may be sufficient for many practical purposes but is theoretically not very elegant. Perhaps more elegant would be to only count paths that are, in some sense, *shortest paths*.[9] Again, various options are possible. One could, e.g., first compute the length of the shortest path and then count all paths that have this length. Another option is to count all the paths p from x to y such that there does not exist a sub-path of p from x to y that also matches the expression r. We do not think that the last word has been said on this topic and that further research is needed. Essentially, we need to find a semantics that is intuitive, easy to understand, and efficient to compute. Unfortunately, the present semantics fulfills neither condition.

We strongly believe that a feasible solution for property paths in SPARQL should avoid the simple walk requirement due to complexity reasons: from our perspective, the choice between NP-complete data complexity already for the query $(aa)^*$; or polynomial time combined complexity for the full fragment of SPARQL property paths seems to be a rather easy one to make.

---

[9] This idea was pitched by Serge Abiteboul during a Dagstuhl seminar on foundations of distributed data management.

Acknowledgments

Several people contributed to this work through inspiring discussions. We thank Marcelo Arenas for sending us a draft of [5] and for his comments on a draft of this paper; Thomas Schwentick for pointing out that emptiness testing of star-free regular expressions with negation is non-elementary (i.e, Theorem 3.5); and Pekka Kilpeläinen for giving us the 1979 reference for dynamic programming for evaluating regular expressions on strings. We thank the anonymous reviewers of PODS 2012 for their insightful comments that helped to improve the presentation of the paper.

7. REFERENCES

[1] S. Abiteboul, D. Quass, J. McHugh, J. Widom, and J. L. Wiener. The Lorel query language for semistructured data. *Int. J. on Digital Libraries*, 1(1):68–88, 1997.

[2] S. Abiteboul and V. Vianu. Regular path queries with constraints. *J. Comput. Syst. Sci.*, 58(3):428–452, 1999.

[3] F. Alkhateeb, J.-F. Baget, and J. Euzenat. Extending SPARQL with regular expression patterns (for querying RDF). *J. Web Sem.*, 7(2):57–73, 2009.

[4] C. Álvarez and B. Jenner. A very hard log-space counting class. *Theor. Comput. Sci.*, 107:3–30, 1993.

[5] M. Arenas, S. Conca, and J. Pérez. Counting beyond a yottabyte, or how SPARQL 1.1 property paths will prevent the adoption of the standard. In *World Wide Web Conference (WWW)*, 2012. To appear.

[6] M. Arenas and J. Pérez. Querying semantic web data with SPARQL. In *Principles of Database Systems (PODS)*, p. 305–316, 2011.

[7] C. Berge. *Graphs and Hypergraphs*. North-Holland Publishing Company, 1973.

[8] G. J. Bex, F. Neven, T. Schwentick, and S. Vansummeren. Inference of concise regular expressions and DTDs. *ACM Trans. Database Syst.*, 2010.

[9] R. Book, S. Even, S. Greibach, and G. Ott. Ambiguity in graphs and expressions. *IEEE Trans. Comput.*, 20:149–153, 1971.

[10] P. Buneman, S. B. Davidson, G. G. Hillebrand, and D. Suciu. A query language and optimization techniques for unstructured data. In *SIGMOD Conference*, p. 505–516, 1996.

[11] D. Calvanese, G. De Giacomo, M. Lenzerini, and M. Y. Vardi. Containment of conjunctive regular path queries with inverse. In *Principles of Knowledge Representation and Reasoning (KR)*, p. 176–185, 2000.

[12] D. Calvanese, G. De Giacomo, M. Lenzerini, and M. Y. Vardi. View-based query processing for regular path queries with inverse. In *Principles of Database Systems (PODS)*, pages 58–66, 2000.

[13] D. Calvanese, G. De Giacomo, M. Lenzerini, and M.Y. Vardi. Rewriting of regular expressions and regular path queries. *J. Comput. Syst. Sci.*, 64(3):443–465, 2002.

[14] D. Colazzo, G. Ghelli, and C. Sartiani. Efficient asymmetric inclusion between regular expression types. In *International Conference on Database Theory (ICDT)*, pages 174–182, 2009.

[15] D. Colazzo, G. Ghelli, and C. Sartiani. Efficient inclusion for a class of XML types with interleaving and counting. *Information Systems*, 34(7):643–656, 2009.

[16] M. P. Consens and A. O. Mendelzon. GraphLog: a visual formalism for real life recursion. In *Principles of Database Systems (PODS)*, p. 404–416, 1990.

[17] I. F. Cruz, A. O. Mendelzon, and P. T. Wood. A graphical query language supporting recursion. In *SIGMOD Conference*, p. 323–330, 1987.

[18] A. Deutsch and V. Tannen. Optimization properties for classes of conjunctive regular path queries. In *Database Programming Languages (DBPL)*, p. 21–39, 2001.

[19] M. F. Fernández, D. Florescu, A. Y. Levy, and D. Suciu. Declarative specification of web sites with strudel. *VLDB J.*, 9(1):38–55, 2000.

[20] D. Florescu, A. Y. Levy, and D. Suciu. Query containment for conjunctive queries with regular expressions. In *Principles of Database Systems (PODS)*, p. 139–148, 1998.

[21] S. Gao, C. M. Sperberg-McQueen, H.S. Thompson, N. Mendelsohn, D. Beech, and M. Maloney. W3C XML Schema Definition Language (XSD) 1.1 part 1: Structures. Tech. report, World Wide Web Consortium, April 2009.

[22] W. Gelade, M. Gyssens, and W. Martens. Regular expressions with counting: Weak versus strong determinism. *SIAM J. Comput.*, 41(1):160–190, 2012.

[23] W. Gelade, W. Martens, and F. Neven. Optimizing schema languages for XML: Numerical constraints and interleaving. *SIAM J. Comput.*, 38(5), 2009.

[24] V. M. Glushkov. The abstract theory of automata. *Russian Math. Surveys*, 16(5(101)):1–53, 1961.

[25] S. Harris and A. Seaborne. SPARQL 1.1 query language. Tech. report, World Wide Web Consortium (W3C), January 2012.

[26] J.E. Hopcroft and J.D. Ullman. *Introduction to Automata Theory, Languages, and Computation*. Addison-Wesley, 1979.

[27] S. Kannan, Z. Sweedyk, and S. R. Mahaney. Counting and random generation of strings in regular languages. In *Symp. on Discrete Algorithms (SODA)*, p. 551–557, 1995.

[28] P. Kilpeläinen and R. Tuhkanen. Regular expressions with numerical occurrence indicators — preliminary results. In *Symp. on ProgLang. and Software Tools (SPLST)*, p. 163–173, 2003.

[29] P. Kilpeläinen and R. Tuhkanen. One-unambiguity of regular expressions with numeric occurrence indicators. *Information and Computation*, 205(6):890–916, 2007.

[30] S. C. Kleene. *Automata Studies*, chapter Representations of events in nerve sets and finite automata, p. 3–42. Princeton Univ. Press, 1956.

[31] L. Libkin and D. Vrgoč. Regular path queries on graphs with data. In *International Conference on Database Theory (ICDT)*, 2012. To appear.

[32] Y. A. Liu and F. Yu. Solving regular path queries. In *Intl. Conf. on Mathematics of Program Construction (MPC)*, p. 195–208, 2002.

[33] W. Martens, F. Neven, and T. Schwentick. Complexity of decision problems for simple regular expressions. In *Mathematical Foundations of Computer Science (MFCS)*, p. 889–900, 2004.

[34] W. Martens, F. Neven, and T. Schwentick. Complexity of decision problems for XML schemas and chain regular expressions. *SIAM J. Comput.*, 39(4):1486–1530, 2009.

[35] A. O. Mendelzon and P. T. Wood. Finding regular simple paths in graph databases. *SIAM J. Comput.*, 24(6):1235–1258, 1995.

[36] J. Pérez, M. Arenas, and C. Gutierrez. Semantics and complexity of SPARQL. *ACM Trans. Database Syst.*, 34(3), 2009.

[37] J. Pérez, M. Arenas, and C. Gutierrez. nSPARQL: A navigational language for RDF. *J. Web Sem.*, 8(4):255–270, 2010.

[38] M. Schmidt, M. Meier, and G. Lausen. Foundations of SPARQL query optimization. In *International Conference on Database Theory (ICDT)*, pages 4–33, 2010.

[39] L. Stockmeyer. *The complexity of decision problems in automata theory and logic*. PhD thesis, Massachusetts Institute of Technology, 1974.

[40] L. G. Valiant. The complexity of enumeration and reliability problems. *SIAM J. Comput.*, 8(3):410–421, 1979.

[41] M. Yannakakis. Graph-theoretic methods in database theory. In *Principles of Database Systems (PODS)*, p. 230–242, 1990.

Space-Efficient Range Reporting for Categorical Data

Yakov Nekrich *
Department of Computer Science
University of Chile
yakov.nekrich@googlemail.com

ABSTRACT

In the colored (or categorical) range reporting problem the set of input points is partitioned into categories and stored in a data structure; a query asks for categories of points that belong to the query range. In this paper we study two-dimensional colored range reporting in the external memory model and present I/O-efficient data structures for this problem.

In particular, we describe data structures that answer three-sided colored reporting queries in $O(K/B)$ I/Os and two-dimensional colored reporting queries in $O(\log_2 \log_B N + K/B)$ I/Os when points lie on an $N \times N$ grid, K is the number of reported colors, and B is the block size. The space usage of both data structures is close to optimal.

Categories and Subject Descriptors

F2.2 [**Analysis of Algorithms and Problem Complexity**]: Nonnumerical Algorithms and Problems—*Geometrical problems and computations*; H.3.1 [**Information Storage and Retrieval**]: Content Analysis and Indexing—*Indexing methods*

Keywords

Data Structures, Orthogonal Range Reporting, Colored Range Reporting

1. INTRODUCTION

The problem of reporting all tuples that belong to a specified query range is a fundamental problem in the database theory. This task can be also formulated as the orthogonal range reporting problem extensively studied in the data structures and computational geometry communities: a set of points S is stored in a data structure; for any query rectangle Q we should report all points $p \in S$ that are in Q. In many situations input objects are classified into categories,

and we may be interested in listing only categories of objects that occur in the query range. Such scenarios can be modeled by the colored (or categorical) range reporting problem: each point p in a set S is assigned a color $col(p)$; for a query rectangle Q we must report the colors of all points that occur in Q. Data structures for regular range reporting queries can obviously answer colored reporting queries by listing all points in the query range and finding distinct colors of those points. However, the efficiency of such solution can be arbitrarily bad because the number of object categories can be significantly smaller than the total number of objects in the query range. Output-sensitive solutions of the colored reporting problem were considered in a number of papers, e.g., [14, 6, 12, 13, 7, 20, 22, 17].

In this paper we present for the first time I/O-efficient data structures for two-dimensional colored range reporting with guaranteed worst-case performance. Our solutions achieve optimal query costs and almost the same space usage as the corresponding data structures for regular range reporting queries.

Applications. A typical application of colored range reporting is a database that stores a set of locations on a plane and the type of soil for each location; given a two-dimensional rectangular area, we want to find the types of soil that occur in this area. Colored range reporting queries are also important in the context of text databases and databases that contain non-text strings, such as DNA sequences. Frequently we need to find documents that contain a certain string P, but documents that contain multiple occurrences of P must be reported only once. Moreover, we may ask for documents that contain P and satisfy some additional requirements. Such queries can be reduced to colored reporting queries and their variants, see e.g., [20, 11, 17, 18].

Previous work. Colored range reporting queries and their variants were extensively studied in the main memory model, see e.g., [14, 12, 6, 7, 2, 20, 16]. For instance, the data structures described in [12, 14] support two-dimensional colored range reporting queries in $O(\log N + K)$ time[1] and use $O(N \log^2 N)$ words of space. In [14] the authors also described another structure that uses $O(N \log N)$ words, but needs $O(\log^2 N + K)$ time to answer a query. Henceforth K denotes the number of elements in the answer and N is the total number of points in the data structure. Agarwal *et al.* [2] considered the two-dimensional colored reporting problem in the case when points lie on a $U \times U$ grid, i.e. all point coordinates are positive integers bounded by pa-

*Partially funded by Fondecyt Grant 1-110066.

---

[1]In this paper $\log N$ denotes the binary logarithm of N if the logarithm base is not specified.

rameter U. In [2], the authors described a data structure that uses $O(N \log^2 N)$ words of space and supports queries in $O(\log \log U + K)$ time. Three-sided queries are a special case of two-dimensional queries when the query range $Q = [a, b] \times [0, c]$ is bounded on three sides. The data structure of [2] supports three-sided queries in $O(\log \log U + K)$ time and uses $O(N \log N)$ space.

Even in the main memory, there are significant complexity gaps between the data structures that report points and data structures that report colors. For instance, there are data structures for three-sided and two-dimensional point reporting that use $O(N)$ and $O(N \log^\varepsilon N)$ words for any $\varepsilon > 0$ respectively [21, 8]. Moreover, three-sided queries can be answered in $O(K)$ time and linear space when points lie on an $N \times N$ grid. We observe that the case of reporting on a grid is important for database applications because in most cases properties of objects stored in a database are specified by integers bounded by a parameter U (frequently $U = N^{O(1)}$ or even $U = O(N)$).

In the external memory model [1], the main memory consists of M words. Every I/O operation reads a *block* of B contiguous words from disk into the main memory (respectively, writes a block into external disk). The time complexity is measured in the number of I/O operations; the space usage is measured in the number of blocks occupied by the data structure on disk.

External memory data structures for reporting two-dimensional points were studied in a number of papers, see e.g., [26, 27, 3, 24]. The structure of Arge *et al.* [3] uses $O((N/B) \log_2 N / \log_2 \log_B N)$ blocks of space space and answers range reporting queries in $O(\log_B N + K/B)$ I/Os; the space usage can be reduced to $O(N/B)$ blocks in case of three-sided queries. In the case when all points lie on a $U \times U$ grid, the data structure of Nekrich [23] answers point reporting queries in $O(\log \log_B U + K/B)$ I/Os. In [23] the author also described data structures for three-sided queries that use $O(N/B)$ blocks of space and answer queries in $O(\log \log_B U + K/B)$ I/Os on a $U \times U$ grid and $O(\log_B^{(h)} N)$ I/Os on an $N \times N$ grid[2] for any constant $h > 0$. Very recently, Larsen and Pagh [19] showed that three-sided point reporting queries can be answered in $O(K/B)$ I/Os using $O(N/B)$ blocks of space.

Using the approach of [12], we can answer one-dimensional color reporting queries using a data structure for three-sided point reporting queries. Hence, all results for three-sided reporting can be transformed into structures for color reporting in one dimension. Heuristic solutions for colored range reporting in $d > 1$ dimensions are described in [22]. We are not aware of any previously described external memory structures for colored reporting in $d > 1$ dimensions with worst-case performance guarantees.

Our Results. In this paper we present several efficient data structures for three-sided and two-dimensional colored reporting problem. We describe a $O(N/B)$ space data structure that answers three-sided reporting queries in $O((N/B)^\delta + K/B)$ I/Os for any constant $\delta > 0$. This is the first linear space data structure for this problem. Furthermore we address the problem of reporting colors in the case when all points lie on an $N \times N$ grid. We describe a data structure that answers

---
[2]Here $\log_B^{(h)} N = \log_B(\log_B^{(h-1)} N)$ for $h > 1$ and $\log_B^{(1)} N = \log_B N$.

three-sided queries in optimal $O(K/B)$ I/O operations ans uses $O((N/B) \log \log N \log^{(3)} N)$ blocks of space, where $\log^{(3)} N = \log \log \log N$. We also describe another data structure that uses $O((N/B) \log \log N)$ blocks of space, but answers three-sided queries in $O((\log \log N)^\delta + K/B)$ I/Os for any constant $\delta > 0$. Our results can be extended to queries on a $U \times U$ grid. We show that there is a data structure that answers three-sided colored reporting queries on a $U \times U$ grid in $O(\log \log_B U + K/B)$ I/Os and uses $O((N/B) \log \log N \log^{(3)} N)$ blocks of space. We also show that there is a data structure that answers general two-dimensional queries in $O(\log \log_B U + K/B)$ I/Os and uses $O((N/B) \log N \log \log N \log^{(3)} N)$ blocks of space. By the predecessor lower bound [25], any data structure stored in $O((N/B) \log^{O(1)} N)$ blocks of space needs $O(\log \log_B U + K/B)$ I/Os to answer an orthogonal range reporting query. All our results are listed in Table 1. We observe that our results for colored range reporting on a grid can be extended to the case of arbitrary point coordinates using a standard technique [10]; the space usage of all data structures remains unchanged and the query cost increases by an additive $O(\log_B N)$ factor.

Thus we achieve optimal query cost for three-sided colored reporting on an $N \times N$ grid and for two-dimensional colored range reporting on a $U \times U$ grid. Even in the main memory, the best previous structure [2] needs $O(\log \log N)$ time and $O(N \log N)$ words of space to answer three-sided queries on an $N \times N$ grid. The space usage of our structure for three-sided queries is close to optimal $O(N/B)$ blocks. It was shown in [3] that any data structure for regular range reporting which answers queries in $\log_B^{O(1)} N + O(K/B)$ I/O operations uses $\Omega((N/B) \log N / \log \log_B N)$ blocks of space. Hence, the space usage of our two-dimensional data structure is almost optimal (i.e., differs from optimal by a very small $O(\log \log N \cdot \log \log_B N \log^{(3)} N)$ factor). Even in comparison with the previous fastest main memory structures, we improve the space usage almost by a logarithmic factor.

Overview. We describe a linear space data structure that supports three-sided color reporting queries in section 2. In section 3 we describe a novel data structure, called path-range tree, and show how it can be used to answer colored three-sided queries . In section 4 we describe data structures that answer colored queries in the case when the set of points is small. We sum up the results for three-sided colored queries on an $N \times N$ grid and show how they can be extended to more general two-dimensional queries in section 5. Throughout this paper $p.x$ and $p.y$ denote the x- and y-coordinates of a point p and $col(p)$ denotes the color of p.

2. THREE-SIDED COLOR REPORTING IN LINEAR SPACE

In this section we show that three-sided color reporting queries on an $N \times N$ grid can be answered in $O((N/B)^\delta + (K/B))$ I/Os using a $O(N/B)$ space data structure for any $\delta > 0$. Our data structure combines the sweepline approach with a reduction of one-dimensional color queries to three-sided point reporting queries.

A data structure is called partially persistent if every update operation creates a new version of the data structure and queries on any version can be answered. That is, the t-th update operation on a (partially) persistent variant of a data structure D creates the t-th version $D(t)$. The an-

Ref.	Query Type	Space Usage	Query Cost	Grid	Memory Model
[12, 14]	Two-Dimensional	$O((N/B)\log^2 N)$	$O(\log N + K)$		Main
[14]	Two-Dimensional	$O((N/B)\log N)$	$O(\log^2 N + K)$		Main
[2]	Three-Sided	$O((N/B)\log N)$	$O(\log\log U + K)$	$U \times U$	Main
[2]	Two-Dimensional	$O((N/B)\log^2 N)$	$O(\log\log U + K)$	$U \times U$	Main
New	Three-Sided	$O(N/B)$	$O((N/B)^\delta + K/B)$		External
New	Three-Sided†	$O((N/B)\log\log N \log^{(3)} N)$	$O(K/B)$	$N \times N$	External
New	Three-Sided†	$O((N/B)\log\log N)$	$O((\log\log N)^\delta + K/B)$	$N \times N$	External
New	Three-Sided†	$O((N/B)\log\log N \log^{(3)} N)$	$O(\log\log_B U + K/B)$	$U \times U$	External
New	Two-Dimensional†	$O((N/B)\log N \log\log N \log^{(3)} N)$	$O(\log\log_B U + K/B)$	$U \times U$	External

Table 1: **Our results and selected previous results for three-sided and two-dimensional colored reporting. For convenience, the space usage of main memory data structures is measured in blocks of size B. Data structures marked with † produce a list of colors that may contain duplicates; see a remark after Lemma 4.**

swer to a query Q at time t is the same as the answer to Q asked to $D(t)$. A data structure is called offline partially persistent if the sequence of update operations is known in advance. We refer to the seminal paper of Driscoll et al. [9] and to a survey of Kaplan [15] for an extensive description of persistent data structures.

We start by describing a partially persistent data structure that supports three-sided point reporting queries. Then we show how this result can be transformed into a one-dimensional persistent structure that supports color reporting queries. Finally, in Lemma 3 we use persistence to transform a one-dimensional structure into a structure that supports three-sided color queries. Lemma 3 is based on the sweepline technique, i.e., we convert the insertion times of one-dimensional points in a persistent data structure into the y-coordinates of two-dimensional points. In this and the following sections we will assume w. l. o. g. that all points have different x-coordinates.

LEMMA 1. *There exists an offline partially persistent data structure D that stores two-dimensional points and uses $O(N/B)$ space for a sequence of N insert and delete operations; for every version $D(t)$ and any three-sided range $Q = [a,b] \times [0,c]$ we can report all points from $Q \cap D(t)$ in $O((N/B)^\delta + (K/B))$ I/Os for any $\delta > 0$.*

Proof: We maintain a range tree with node degree $(N/B)^\delta$ on the set of x-coordinates. Each leaf of T contains the x-coordinates of B points. If leaves are counted in the left-to-right order, the i-th leaf v_l contains all points p with $p.x \in rng(v_l)$ where $rng(v_l) = [(i-1)B+1, iB]$. The i-th internal node v on level ℓ contains all points p with $p.x \in rng(v)$ where $rng(v) = [(i-1)(N/B)^{\ell\delta}B + 1, i(N/B)^{\ell\delta}B]$. Every point is stored in exactly one node on each tree level. Since the height of the tree is $1/\delta$, the structure uses $O(N/B)$ blocks of space.

All points stored in a node v are maintained in a persistent tree L_v [4, 28]. The points of L_v are sorted by their y-coordinates. L_v uses $O(N_v/B)$ space for a sequence of N_v updates and supports range reporting queries on any version $L_v(t)$ in $O(\log_B N_v + K/B)$ I/Os. Hence, we can report all points $p \in L_v(t)$ such that $p.y \le c$ in $O(\log_B N + K/B)$ I/Os.

When a new point p is inserted, we identify the nodes v such that $p.x \in rng(v)$ and insert $p.y$ into persistent trees L_v. Deletions are handled in a symmetric way.

Consider a query $Q = [a,b] \times [0,c]$ at time t. We use a standard representation of the interval $[a,b]$ in a range tree. On every level ℓ we can identify $O((N/B)^\delta)$ nodes $v_{i,\ell}$ with $rng(v_{i,\ell}) \subset [a,b]$ and $rng(parent(v_{i,\ell})) \not\subset [a,b]$. There are also at most two leaves u_1 and u_2 such that $rng(u_i) \cap [a,b] \ne \emptyset$ but $rng(u_i) \not\subset [a,b]$, $i = 1,2$. We can report all points $p \in L_{v_{i,\ell}}(t), p.y \le c$, in $O(\log_B N + K/B)$ I/Os. Each $L_{u_i}(t)$, $i = 1,2$, contains $O(B)$ points at any time t because u_i is a leaf. We can construct the list L_i' that contains all points $p \in L_{u_i}(t)$, in $O(\log_B N + 1)$ I/Os. Then, we can traverse L_i' and identify all $p \in L_i' \cap Q$ in $O(1)$ I/Os. The total cost of answering a query is $O((N/B)^\delta \log_B N + (K/B))$. If $B = N^{\Theta(1)}$, $\log_B N = O(1)$. Otherwise $(N/B)^\delta \log_B N = (N/B)^{\delta'}$ for an appropriately chosen $\delta' < \delta$. Hence, we can obtain the result of this Lemma by substituting δ' instead of δ in the above construction. □

LEMMA 2. *There exists an offline partially persistent data structure D that contains colored one-dimensional points and uses $O(N/B)$ space for a sequence of N insertions; for every version $D(t)$ and any one-dimensional range $Q = [a,b]$ we can report all distinct colors of points from $Q \cap D(t)$ in $O((N/B)^\delta + (K/B))$ I/Os.*

Proof: Using the technique described in [12], we can answer one-dimensional colored range reporting queries by a data structure for three-sided point reporting queries. Suppose that S is a set of one-dimensional points. We denote by $prev(p)$ the rightmost point p_1 such that $p_1.x < p.x$ and p_1 has the same color as p. If p is the leftmost point of color ν, we assume that $prev(p) = p_d$ for a dummy point p_d with $p_d.x = 0$. We denote by $succ(p)$ the leftmost point p_2 such that $p_2.x > p.x$ and p_2 has the same color as p. For every one-dimensional point $p \in S$, the set S' contains a two-dimensional point p' such that $p'.x = p.x$, $p.y = prev(p).x$, and $col(p') = col(p)$. If an interval $[a,b]$ contains one or more points $p \in S$ of color $\nu \in \mathcal{C}$, then the range $Q = [a,b] \times [0,a]$ contains exactly one point $p' \in S'$ such that $col(p') = \nu$.

Using Lemma 1 and the approach of [12] described above, we can obtain a partially persistent data structure for one-dimensional color reporting queries that uses $O(N/B)$ space for a sequence of N insertions. Let S' be the set defined above. When a new point p is inserted into S, the set S' is updated as follows. We insert the point $p_1 = (p.x, prev(p).x)$ into S'. If $succ(p)$ exists, we delete $p_2 = (succ(p).x, prev(p).x)$ from S' and insert a new point

$p_3 = (succ(p).x, p.x)$. We maintain the set S' in the data structure E implemented as in Lemma 1. □

LEMMA 3. *There exists a $O(N/B)$ space data structure that answers three-sided color range reporting queries for points on an $N \times N$ grid in $O((N/B)^\delta + (K/B))$ I/Os.*

Proof: Our construction is based on the combination of the sweepline technique and the result of Lemma 2. To construct our data structure, we sweep a horizontal line h in the $+y$ direction. Initially the y-coordinate of h is 0; when h hits a point p, we add p to the partially persistent data structure E that supports colored reporting queries in one dimension. E is implemented as in Lemma 2.

Let t_c denote the version of E after the point with y-coordinate c was inserted. Since points lie on an $N \times N$ grid, we can store t_c for all c in an array with N entries. $E(t_c)$ contains all points $p \in S$ with $p.y \leq c$. Hence, we can answer a three-sided query $Q = [a, b] \times [0, c]$ by asking the query $Q_1 = [a, b]$ to the t_c-th version $E(t_c)$ of the data structure E. □

3. PATH-RANGE TREES

In this section we describe data structures for three-sided colored reporting with optimal or almost optimal query cost. After giving some preliminary definitions we define a new data structure, called path-range tree. Then, we show how path-range trees can be used to answer three-sided colored queries.

We associate x-coordinates of points with the leaves of a full binary tree T. The i-th leaf of T is associated with the i-th smallest x-coordinate x_i of a point from S. The *range* of the i-th leaf is an interval $[x_i, x_{i+1} - 1]$. The range of an internal node v is the union of ranges of its children. The set $S(v)$ contains all points p such that $p.x$ belongs to the range of v.

Range trees [5] and priority trees [21] are two handbook data structures used in numerous geometric applications. In the range tree, we store a set $S(v)$ in each node v. Since each point belongs to $O(\log N)$ nodes, a range tree contains $O(N \log N)$ points. In the priority tree, each node v contains only one point $p(v) \in S(v)$. We select $p(v)$ to be the lowest point from $S(v)$ such that $p(v)) \neq p(w)$ for any ancestor w of v. Since each point is stored only once, a priority tree contains $O(N)$ points.

Structure. A path-range tree, combines some properties of range trees and priority trees with a new approach. While in the range tree and priority tree points are associated with tree nodes, the path-range tree is based on sets $Y(\pi)$ for selected node-to-leaf paths π; points of $Y(\pi)$ belong to nodes that hang off a path π. For every $Y(\pi)$, only a subset $L(\pi) \subset Y(\pi)$ is stored in the data structure. Points of $L(\pi)$ are chosen in such way that each color from $Y(\pi)$ occurs at most once in $L(\pi)$; points in $L(\pi)$ are stored in ascending order of their y-coordinates. A detailed description of the path-range tree is given below.

We denote by $\pi(u, v)$ (the set of nodes on) the path from the node u to its descendant v (excluding u). Sets $\pi_l(u, v)$ and $\pi_r(u, v)$ contain all nodes that satisfy the following condition: If a node $w \in \pi(u, v)$ is the right child of its parent $w' \in \pi(u, v)$, then the sibling of w belongs to $\pi_l(u, v)$; if a node $w \in \pi(u, v)$ is the left child of its parent $w' \in \pi(u, v)$, then the sibling of w belongs to $\pi_r(u, v)$. See Fig. 1 for an example. We define $\Pi_l(u, v) = \cup_{w \in \pi_l(u,v)} S(w)$ and $\Pi_r(u, v) =$

$\cup_{w \in \pi_r(u,v)} S(w)$. Let $\text{ymin}(\nu, F)$ for a color ν and a set of points F denote the point with the smallest y-coordinate among all points $p \in F$ with $col(p) = \nu$. The set $Y_l(u, v)$ ($Y_r(u, v)$) contains the point $\text{ymin}(c, \Pi_l(u, v))$ (respectively, $\text{ymin}(c, \Pi_r(u, v))$ for any color c that occurs in $\Pi_l(u, v)$ ($\Pi_r(u, v)$)). Thus $Y_l(u, v)$ contains exactly one point for each color that occurs in $\Pi_l(u, v)$. The list $Y_l(u, v)[1..i]$ contains i points from $Y_l(u, v)$ with the smallest y-coordinates; we assume that the points of $Y_l(u, v)[1..i]$ are sorted by their y-coordinates. $Y_r(u, v)[1..i]$ is defined in the same way with respect to $Y_r(u, v)$.

We say that a node v is on level ℓ if the shortest path from v to a leaf node consists of ℓ edges. Let $\mathcal{N}_i$ denote the set of nodes on level[3] $\log B + f(i) \log \log N$ for $f(i) = 2^i$ and $i = 1, \ldots, \log \log_{\log N}(N/B)$. A set $S(v)$, $v \in \mathcal{N}_i$ contains $O(B \log^{f(i)} N)$ points. For each $v \in \mathcal{N}_i$ and each ancestor u of v we store the lists $L_l(u, v) = Y_l(u, v)[1..m_i]$ and $L_r(u, v) = Y_r(u, v)[1..m_i]$ where $m_i = B \log^{f(i)-1} N$. We also store all points from $S(v)$ for a node $v \in \mathcal{N}_i$ and $i \geq 2$ in a $O(|S_v|/B)$ space data structure $D(v)$ that answers three-sided color reporting queries in $O((|S(v)|/B)^{1/4} + K/B)$ I/Os. This data structure is implemented as in Lemma 3. All points from $S(v)$ for each $v \in \mathcal{N}_1$ are stored in a structure $D'(v)$ that will be described in section 4. $D'(v)$ supports three-sided color reporting queries in $O(q(N) + K/B)$ I/Os and uses space $O((|S(v)|/B)s(N))$ for functions $s(N)$ and $q(N)$ that will be defined in section 4.

Queries. Let $Q = [a, b] \times [0, c]$ be the query range; let l_a and l_b be the the leaves that contain the largest value smaller than a and the smallest value larger than b. We denote by w the lowest common ancestor of l_a and l_b. For any point p, $p.x \in [a, b]$ if and only if p belongs to some set $S(u)$ for $u \in \pi_r(w, l_a) \cup \pi_l(w, l_b)$; see Fig. 1. Therefore our goal is to examine the points from $\Pi_r(w, l_a) \cup \Pi_l(w, l_b)$ and report the distinct colors of points p with $p.y \leq c$. Our structure does not store sets $\Pi_r(w, l_a)$ and $\Pi_l(w, l_b)$ (this would take at least $\Theta(n^2)$ space). However, we will show that the information contained in sets $L_l(u, v)$, $L_r(u, v)$, and structures $D(v)$ for nodes $v \in \mathcal{N}_i$ is sufficient to examine relevant parts of the set $\Pi_r(w, l_a) \cup \Pi_l(w, l_b)$.

We show how relevant colors from the set $\Pi_l(w, l_b) = \cup_{u \in \pi_l(w,l_b)} S(u)$ can be reported. The set $\Pi_r(w, l_a)$ can be processed symmetrically. Let v_i denote the ancestor of l_b that belongs to $\mathcal{N}_i$. For $i = 1, \ldots$ we traverse the lists $L_l(w, v_i)$ until a point p_i, $p_i.y > c$, is encountered or the node v_i is not a descendant of w. In each visited node v_i, $i \geq 1$, our procedure works as follows. If $v_i = w$ or v_i is an ancestor of w, we answer the query $Q = [a, b] \times [0, c]$ to data structure $D(v_i)$ (respectively $D'(v_i)$ if $i = 1$) and stop. If v_i is a descendant of w, the list $L_l(w, v_i)$ is traversed until a point p with $p.y > c$ is found. If we reach the end of $L_l(w, v_i)$ and $p.y \leq c$ for all $p \in L_l(w, v_i)$, we increment i and proceed in the next node v_i. Otherwise we traverse $L_l(w, v_i)$ once again and report colors of all points $p \in L_l(w, v_i)$, $p.y \leq c$. Then, we answer the query $Q = [a, b] \times [0, c]$ to data structure $D(v_i)$ (respectively $D'(v_i)$ if $i = 1$) and stop.

Let t be the index of the last visited node v_t. Suppose that there is at least one point $p \in \Pi_l(w, v_t)$ of color ν, such that $p.y \leq c$. Then $\text{ymin}(\nu, \Pi_l(w, v_t)) \leq c$ and $L_l(w, v_t)$ contains exactly one point p' such that $col(p') = \nu$ and $p.y \leq$

---

[3] To avoid tedious details, we assume throughout this paper that B, N, and $\log N$ are powers of 2.

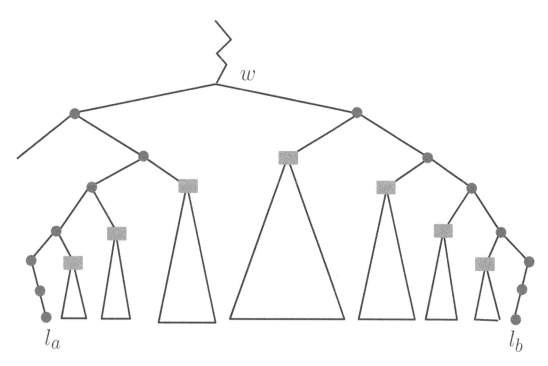

Figure 1: Paths in a path-range tree. Node w is the lowest common ancestor of l_a and l_b. Nodes in $\Pi(w, l_a)$ and $\Pi(w, l_b)$ are marked with circles. Nodes in $\Pi_r(w, l_a)$ and $\Pi_l(w, l_b)$ are marked with rectangles. Only relevant parts of the tree are shown.

c. Colors of all such points are reported when $L_l(w, v_t)$ is traversed for the second time. If a point p belongs to $\Pi_l(w, l_b) \setminus \Pi_l(w, v_t)$, then p belongs to $S(v_t)$. Hence, colors of all points $p \in \Pi_l(w, l_b) \setminus \Pi_l(w, v_t)$ are found by a query to $D(v_t)$.

Let K be the total number of distinct colors in $\Pi_l(w, l_b)$. As follows from the description of our search procedure, $K \geq |L_l(w, v_{t-1})| = \Theta(B \log^{f(t-1)-1} N)$. Since $|L_l(w, v_{t-1})| \geq \sum_{i=1}^{t-2} |L_l(w, v_i)|$, $K = \Omega(\sum_{i=1}^{t-1} |L_l(w, v_i)|)$. Hence, the total cost of traversing $L_l(w, v_i)$, $1 \leq i < t$, is $O(K/B)$. Every point in the traversed prefix of $L_l(w, v_t)$ corresponds to a distinct color in $\Pi_l(w, v_t)$. Therefore $L(w, v_t)$ is also traversed in $O(K/B)$ I/Os. The cost of a query to the data structure $D(v_t)$ is $O(((B \log^{f(t)} N)/B)^{1/4} + K'/B)$ where $K' \leq K$ is the number of distinct colors in $S(v_t) \cap Q$. Since $(\log^{f(t)} N)^{1/4} = O(\log^{f(t-1)-1} N) = O(|L(w, v_{t-1})|/B) = O(K/B)$ for $t > 1$, the query to $D(v_t)$ is answered in $O(K/B)$ I/Os. If $t = 1$, the query to $D'(v_1)$ takes $O(q(N) + K'/B)$ I/Os.

Space Usage. There are $O(N/(B \log^{f(i)} N))$ nodes in $\mathcal{N}_i$. Since $S(v)$, $v \in \mathcal{N}_i$, contains $O(B \log^{f(i)} N)$ points, all data structures $D(v)$ for $v \in \mathcal{N}_i$ and $2 \leq i \leq \log \log_{\log N}(N/B)$ use $O((N/B) \log \log(N/B))$ blocks of space. Each list $L_l(u, v)$ and $L_r(u, v)$ for $v \in \mathcal{N}_i$ contains $O(B \log^{f(i)-1} N)$ points. There are $O(\log N)$ lists for each $v \in \mathcal{N}_i$. Hence, all $L_l(u, v)$, $L_r(u, v)$ also use $O((N/B) \log \log(N/B))$ blocks of space. Finally, all structures $D'(v)$ for $v \in \mathcal{N}_1$ use $O((N/B)s(N))$ blocks of space.

The result of this section can be summed up as follows

LEMMA 4. *Suppose that there exists a data structure that answers three-sided colored reporting queries on a set of $r = O(B \log^2 N)$ points in $O(q(N) + K/B)$ I/Os and uses $O(\frac{r}{B}s(r))$ space. Then there exists a $O(\frac{N}{B}(\log \log N + s(N)))$*

space data structure that answers three-sided color reporting queries on a set of N points in $O(q(N) + K/B)$ I/Os.

Remark The data structure of Lemma 4 produces a list of size $O(K)$ that contains all K colors occurring in a three-sided range and no other colors. However, the list of colors may contain duplicates. That is, the same color may appear in the list more than once, but no more than a constant number of times. If necessary, we can remove duplicates from the list in $O(\frac{K}{B} \log_{M/B} \frac{K}{B})$ additional I/Os, where M is the size of the main memory. For instance if $K = B^{O(1)}$ and $M = B^{1+\varepsilon}$ for any constant $\varepsilon > 0$, duplicates are deleted in $O(K/B)$ I/Os. The same remark also applies to results in sections 4 and 5.

4. THREE-SIDED COLOR REPORTING FOR $O(B \log^2 N)$ POINTS

Using the same idea as in section 3, we can obtain two efficient data structures for a set that contains $r = O(B \log^2 N)$ points. We construct a path-range tree on the set of r points and use the same notation as in section 3. Again a three-sided query $Q = [a, b] \times [0, c]$ is answered by reporting all distinct colors in $Q \cap \Pi_r(w, l_a)$ and $Q \cap \Pi_l(w, l_b)$. We assume in this section that the position of leaves l_a and l_b is known. To avoid repetitions, we will describe only the differences between the new structures and the path-range tree presented in section 3.

LEMMA 5. *Let S be a set of $r = O(B \log^2 N)$ points on an $N \times N$ grid. There exists a $O((|S|/B) \log \log N)$ space data structure that supports three-sided colored queries on S in $O((\log \log N)^\delta + K/B)$ I/Os for any $\delta > 0$.*

Proof: The set $\mathcal{N}_i$, $i \geq 1$, contains all nodes on level $\log B + f(i) \log^{(3)} N$. The data structures $D(v)$ for $v \in \mathcal{N}_1$ are implemented using Lemma 3 with parameter $\delta' = \delta/2$. A set $S(v)$, $v \in \mathcal{N}_1$, contains $O(B(\log \log N)^2)$ points. Hence, $D(v)$ answers three-sided color queries in $O((|S(v)|/B)^{\delta'} + K/B) = O((\log \log N)^\delta + K/B)$ I/Os.

The procedure that reports all distinct colors in $\Pi_l(w, l_b) \cap Q$ visits ancestors $v_i \in \mathcal{N}_i$ of l_b for $i = 1, 2, \ldots$ and traverses lists $L_l(w, v_i)$ as in the proof of Lemma 4. Suppose that v_t is the last visited node. We can report all distinct colors from $L_l(w, v_t)$ in $O(K/B)$ I/Os. If $t = 1$, the query to $S(v_t)$ is answered in $O((\log \log N)^\delta + K/B)$ I/Os; otherwise the query to $S(v_t)$ is answered in $O(K/B)$ I/Os. Colors that occur in $\Pi_r(w, l_a) \cap Q$ can be found by a symmetric procedure. $\square$

We can improve the query cost by slightly increasing the space usage.

LEMMA 6. *Let S be a set of $r = O(B \log^2 N)$ points on an $N \times N$ grid. There exists a $O((|S|/B) \log \log N \log^{(3)} N)$ space data structure that supports three-sided colored queries on S in $O(K/B)$ I/Os.*

Proof: The only important difference from the structure in section 3 is in the choice of parameters. The set $\mathcal{N}_1$ consists of all nodes on level $\log B$. For $2 \leq i \leq \log^{(3)}(N/B)$ the set $\mathcal{N}_i$ contains all nodes on the level $\log B + f(i)$. Since $|S(v)| = O(B)$ for $v \in \mathcal{N}_1$, we can store $S(v)$ in one block of space and answer colored queries on $S(v)$ in $O(1)$ I/Os. A query is answered in the same way as in section 3 or in the proof of Lemma 5. Since a query to a data structure $D(v)$ for $v \in \mathcal{N}_1$ can be answered in $O(1)$ I/Os, the total query cost is $O(K/B)$.

All sets $S(v)$ contain $O(r \cdot \log \log r)$ points. All lists $L_l(u, v)$ and $L_r(u, v)$ for $v \in \mathcal{N}_i$ and a fixed i contain $O(r \log r)$ points. Hence, the total space usage is $O((r/B) \log r \log \log r) = O((|S|/B) \log \log N \log^{(3)} N)$ $\square$

5. COLORED RANGE REPORTING IN TWO DIMENSIONS

Combining Lemma 4 and Lemma 6, we obtain the data structure with optimal query cost.

THEOREM 1. *There exists a $O((N/B) \log \log N \log^{(3)} N)$ space data structure that answers three-sided color reporting queries on an $N \times N$ grid in $O(K/B)$ I/Os.*

Combining Lemma 4 and Lemma 5, we obtain the data structure with a slightly better space usage and slightly worse query cost.

THEOREM 2. *There exists a $O((N/B) \log \log N)$ space data structure that answers three-sided color reporting queries on an $N \times N$ grid in $O((\log \log N)^\delta + K/B)$ I/Os for any $\delta > 0$.*

We can extend the result of Theorem 1 to a more general scenario.

THEOREM 3. *There exists a $O((N/B) \log \log N \log^{(3)} N)$ space data structure that answers three-sided color reporting queries on a $U \times U$ grid in $O(\log \log_B U + K/B)$ I/Os. There exists a $O((N/B) \log N \log \log N \log^{(3)} N)$ space data structure that answers two-dimensional color reporting queries on a $U \times U$ grid in $O(\log \log_B U + K/B)$ I/Os.*

Proof: Orthogonal queries on a $U \times U$ grid can be reduced to queries on an $N \times N$ grid using the rank space technique [10]. The query cost increases by the time necessary to search in an ordered set of N elements and the space usage remains unchanged. We can search in a one-dimensional set in $O(\log_2 \log_B U)$ I/Os [25].

We can answer a general orthogonal colored reporting queries in two dimensions by answering two three-sided colored reporting queries. This reduction is standard in range reporting structures; it was also applied to colored range reporting in [2]. For completeness, we sketch this method below.

We construct a range tree T_y on the y-coordinates of points. In each node v of T_y, we define the set $S(v)$ as in section 3. All points of $S(v)$ are stored in two data structures, $P_1(v)$ and $P_2(v)$ that support three-sided queries. $P_1(v)$ answers queries of the form $[a, b] \times [0, c]$; it can be implemented using Theorem 1. $P_2(v)$ supports queries of the form $[a, b] \times [c, +\infty]$; it can be implemented in a symmetric way.

To answer a query $[a, b] \times [c, d]$, we identify the lowest common ancestor w of leaves l_c and l_d; l_c and l_d are the leaves that contain c and d respectively. Let w_1 and w_2 be the left and right children of w. All points in $S \cap Q$ belong to either $S(w_1) \cap ([a, b] \times [c, +\infty])$ or $S(w_2) \cap ([a, b] \times [0, d])$. Hence, we can find all colors in $S \cap Q$ by answering two three-sided color queries on $P_2(w_1)$ and $P_1(w_2)$. Thus the query cost is the same as the cost of three-sided queries. The space usage increases by $O(\log N)$ factor. Again, we can extend the result for an $N \times N$ grid to the result on a $U \times U$ grid by applying the reduction to rank space [10] $\square$

Using the same methods, we can also extend the result of Theorem 2.

THEOREM 4. *There exists a $O((N/B) \log \log N)$ space data structure that answers three-sided color reporting queries on a $U \times U$ grid in $O((\log \log N)^\delta + \log \log_B U + K/B)$ I/Os. There exists a $O((N/B) \log N \log \log N)$ space data structure that answers two-dimensional color reporting queries on a $U \times U$ grid in $O((\log \log N)^\delta + \log \log_B U + K/B)$ I/Os.*

We can also use the rank space technique [10] to apply all results described in Theorems 1-4 and Lemma 3 to the situation when point coordinates are arbitrary reals. The space usage of all data structures does not change and the query cost increases by an additive factor $O(\log_B N)$.

6. CONCLUSIONS

In this paper we presented efficient data structures for colored range reporting in external memory. All presented data structures are static; existence of a dynamic data structure that efficiently supports two-dimensional color queries, insertions, and deletions is an interesting open question. The main memory data structure of [12] uses $O(N \log^2 N)$ words of space and supports color reporting queries and insertions in $O(\log^2 N + K)$ and $O(\log^3 N)$ time respectively. But even in the main memory, no data structure that supports both insertions and deletions in $\log^{O(1)} N$ and answers queries in $\log^{O(1)} N + O(K)$ time is currently known.

We observed at the end of section 3 that our data structures (with exception of the structure in section 2) generate a list of colors in which the same color may occur a constant number of times. The problem of duplicate colors can be easily solved in the main memory: we can remove duplicates from a list of K colors in $O(K)$ time. In the external memory we need $O((K/B)\log_{M/B}\frac{K}{B})$ I/Os to get rid of duplicates. Since in many situations $K = B^{O(1)}$ and usually $M = B^{1+\Omega(1)}$, we can often remove duplicates without increasing the query cost. It would also be interesting to design an external memory data structure that produces a list colors in a query range, so that each relevant color occurs exactly once and a query is answered in $\log_B^{O(1)} N + O(K/B)$ I/Os for any K and B.

7. REFERENCES

[1] A. Aggarwal and J. S. Vitter, *The Input/Output Complexity of Sorting and Related Problems*, Communications of the ACM (CACM), 31(9), 1116-1127, 1988.

[2] P. Agarwal, S. Govindarajan, S. Muthukrishnan, *Range Searching in Categorical Data: Colored Range Searching on Grid*, Proc. 10th European Symp. on Algorithms (ESA) 2002, 17-28.

[3] L. Arge, V. Samoladas, J. S. Vitter, *On Two-Dimensional Indexability and Optimal Range Search Indexing*, Proc. 18th ACM Symp. on Principles of Database Systems (PODS) 1999, 346-357.

[4] B. Becker, S. Gschwind, T. Ohler, B. Seeger, and P. Widmayer, *An Asymptotically Optimal Multiversion B-Tree*, VLDB Journal, 5(4), 264-275, 1996.

[5] J. L. Bentley, *Multidimensional Divide-and-Conquer*, Commun. ACM 23, 214-229, 1980.

[6] P. Bozanis, N. Kitsios, C. Makris, A.-K. Tsakalidis, *New Upper Bounds for Generalized Intersection Searching Problems*, Proc. 22nd Int. Colloquium on Automata, Languages and Programming (ICALP), 1995, 464-474.

[7] P. Bozanis, N. Kitsios, C. Makris, A.-K. Tsakalidis, *New Results on Intersection Query Problems*, Computer Journal 40(1), 22-29 (1997).

[8] B. Chazelle, *A Functional Approach to Data Structures and Its Use in Multidimensional Searching*, SIAM Journal on Computing 17(3), 427-462, 1988.

[9] J. R. Driscoll, N. Sarnak, D. D. Sleator, R. E. Tarjan, *Making Data Structures Persistent*, J. Comput. Syst. Sci. 38(1), 86-124 (1989).

[10] H. N. Gabow, J. L. Bentley, R. E. Tarjan, *Scaling and Related Techniques for Geometry Problems*, Proc. 16th ACM Symp. on Theory of Computing (STOC) 1984, 135-143.

[11] T. Gagie, G. Navarro, and S. J. Puglisi, *Colored Range Queries and Document Retrieval*, Proc. 17th Int. Symp. on String Processing and Information Retrieval (SPIRE) 2010, 67-81.

[12] P. Gupta, R. Janardan, M. Smid, *Further Results on Generalized Intersection Searching Problems: Counting, Reporting, and Dynamization*, Journal of Algorithms 19(2), 282-317, 1995.

[13] P. Gupta, R. Janardan, and M. Smid, *Efficient Algorithms for Generalized Intersection Searching on Non-Iso-oriented Objects*, Computational Geometry: Theory & Applications 6(1), 1-19, 1996.

[14] R. Janardan, M. Lopez, *Generalized Intersection Searching Problems*, Internat. J. Comput. Geom. Appl. 3, 39-69, 1993.

[15] H. Kaplan, *Persistent Data Structures*, In Handbook on Data Structures and Applications, D. Mehta and S. Sahni, editors, CRC Press, 2005.

[16] M. Karpinski and Y. Nekrich, *Searching for Frequent Colors in Rectangles*, Proc. Canadian Conf. on Computational Geometry (CCCG) 2008.

[17] M. Karpinski and Y. Nekrich, *Top-K Color Queries for Document Retrieval*, Proc. 22nd ACM-SIAM Symp. on Discrete Algorithms (SODA) 2011, 401-411.

[18] G. Navarro, Y. Nekrich, *Top-k Document Retrieval in Optimal Time and Linear Space*, Proc. 23rd ACM-SIAM Symp. on Discrete Algorithms (SODA) 2012, 1066-1077.

[19] K. G. Larsen, R. Pagh, *I/O-Efficient Data Structures for Colored Range and Prefix Reporting*, Proc. 23rd ACM-SIAM Symp. on Discrete Algorithms (SODA) 2012, to appear.

[20] S. Muthukrishnan, *Efficient Algorithms for Document Retrieval Problems*, Proc. 13th ACM-SIAM Symp. on Discrete Algorithms (SODA) 2002, 657-666.

[21] E. M. McCreight, *Priority Search Trees*, SIAM Journal on Computing 14(2), 257-276, 1985.

[22] A. Nanopoulos, P. Bozanis, *Categorical Range Queires in Large Databases*, Proc. 8th Int. Symp. on Advances in Spatial and Temporal Databases (SSTD) 2003, 122-139.

[23] Y. Nekrich, *External Memory Range Reporting on a Grid*, Proc. 18th Int. Symp. on Algorithms and Computation (ISAAC) 2007, 525-535.

[24] Y. Nekrich, *External Memory Orthogonal Range Reporting with Fast Updates*, Proc. 22nd Int. Symp. on Algorithms and Computation (ISAAC) 2011, 395-404.

[25] M. Pătraşcu, M. Thorup, *Time-space Trade-offs for Predecessor Search*, Proc. 38th ACM Symp. on Theory of Computing (STOC) 2006, 232-240.

[26] S. Ramaswamy, S. Subramanian, *Path Caching: A Technique for Optimal External Searching*, Proc. 13th ACM Symp. on Principles of Database Systems (PODS) 1994, 25-35.

[27] S. Subramanian, S. Ramaswamy, *The P-range Tree: A New Data Structure for Range Searching in Secondary Memory*, Proc. 6th ACM-SIAM Symp. on Discrete Algorithms (SODA) 1995, 378-387.

[28] P. J. Varman, R. M. Verma, *An Efficient Multiversion Access Structure*, IEEE Transactions on Knowledge and Data Engineering, 9(3), 391-409, 1997.

Dynamic Top-K Range Reporting in External Memory

Cheng Sheng[†]   Yufei Tao[‡]

[†]Department of CSE, CUHK, Hong Kong
[‡]Division of WebST, KAIST, Republic of Korea

ABSTRACT

In the *top-K range reporting* problem, the dataset contains N points in the real domain $\mathbb{R}$, each of which is associated with a real-valued *score*. Given an interval $[x_1, x_2]$ in $\mathbb{R}$ and an integer $K \leq N$, a query returns the K points in $[x_1, x_2]$ having the smallest scores. We want to store the dataset in a structure so that queries can be answered efficiently. In the external memory model, the state of the art is a static structure that consumes $O(N/B)$ space, answers a query in $O(\log_B N + K/B)$ time, and can be constructed in $O(N + (N \log N/B) \log_{M/B}(N/B))$ time, where B is the size of a disk block, and M the size of memory. We present a fully-dynamic structure that retains the same space and query bounds, and can be updated in $O(\log_B^2 N)$ amortized time per insertion and deletion. Our structure can be constructed in $O((N/B) \log_{M/B}(N/B))$ time.

Categories and Subject Descriptors

F.2.2 [**Analysis of algorithms and problem complexity**]: Nonnumerical Algorithms and Problems—*computations on discrete structures*; H.3.1 [**Information storage and retrieval**]: Content analysis and indexing—*indexing methods*

General Terms

Theory

Keywords

Range top-k, data structure, external memory, logarithmic sketch

1. INTRODUCTION

In the *top-K range reporting* problem, the dataset is a set P of N points in the real domain $\mathbb{R}$, where each point x is associated with a distinct *score*, denoted as $score(x)$, in $\mathbb{R}$. Given an interval $[x_1, x_2]$ in $\mathbb{R}$ and an integer $K \leq N$, a

query reports, among all the points of P in $[x_1, x_2]$, the K points with the lowest scores. As a special case, if $P \cap [x_1, x_2]$ contains less than K points, the query returns all of them. The objective is to maintain P in a structure such that every query can be answered efficiently. In this paper, we study the problem in a *dynamic* setting, i.e., points can be inserted into and deleted from P. The top-K range reporting problem can also be defined in a symmetric manner, so that a query returns the K points with the *highest* scores.

We consider the *external memory* (EM) model [2], where a machine has a disk of an unlimited capacity, and memory of M words. The disk is formatted into disjoint blocks of B words. The value of M is at least $2B$. We further require that $B \geq 64$. Time is measured by the number of I/Os performed, and space is measured by the number of blocks occupied. On an input of size N, a *linear* complexity is $O(N/B)$, whereas a *poly-logarithmic* complexity is $O(\log_B^c N)$ for some positive constant c.

1.1 Applications

The top-K range reporting problem has been studied in a variety of areas, e.g., information retrieval [1, 5], OLAP [9], data streams [8], etc. It finds use in applications where people would like to identify the best few objects, among only a *subset* of the dataset satisfying a range predicate. For example, a user of a hotel database may be interested in discovering the K best rated hotels whose prices are in a designated range. Likewise, for promotion purposes, the manager of a company may want to find the K salesmen with the best performance, among those salesmen whose salaries are in a certain range. In fact, one can easily notice that the top-K range reporting problem generalizes conventional SQL construct of the form

`SELECT MIN(A₁) FROM ... WHERE A₂ ∈ [x₁, x₂].`

That is, instead of retrieving simply the min (a.k.a. top-1) of A_1, a top-K range query aims at returning the K objects with the best A_1 values. Therefore, an efficient structure for this problem augments a relational database with the power to support the top-K version of `MIN` aggregation (and hence, also `MAX` aggregation) in the presence of a range predicate.

1.2 Related work

We will focus on only structures with non-trivial worst-case query cost, as they are the subject of this paper. Afshani, Brodal and Zeh [1] developed a static structure that occupies $O(N/B)$ space, answers a query in

$O(\log_B N + K/B)$ I/Os, and can be built in $O(N + (N \log N/B) \log_{M/B}(N/B))$ time. They also considered a variant of the problem called *ordered top-K range reporting* where the points in the query result must be sorted by their scores. For this variant, they show that, for any parameter $\alpha \in [1, \log_{M/B}(N/B)]$, a data structure that achieves $\log^{O(1)} N + O(\alpha K/B)$ query time must consume

$$\Omega\left(\frac{N}{B} \cdot \frac{\alpha^{-1} \log_M(N/B)}{\log(\alpha^{-1} \log_M(N/B))}\right)$$

space. In other words, if only linear space is allowed, α has to be

$$\Omega\left(\frac{\log_M(N/B)}{\log\log_M(N/B)}\right).$$

Interestingly, this provides motivation to focus on the *unordered* version (i.e., the target problem of this paper) because, as long as an unordered query can be solved in $O(\log_B N + K/B)$ time, we can trivially produce the ordered output by sorting. The total cost $O(\log_B N + (K/B) \log_{M/B}(K/B))$ is already optimal up to a small factor, which is $\log\log_M(N/B)$ for $M = \Omega(B^{1+\epsilon})$ where ϵ is any positive constant.

In RAM, by combining the priority search tree of Mc-Creight [10] with the algorithm of Frederickson [6] for selecting the K smallest items from a priority queue, one can obtain a structure for solving the unordered top-K range reporting problem that consumes $O(N)$ space, answers a query in $O(\log N + K)$ time, and supports an update in $O(\log N)$ time. Brodal, Fagerberg, Greve and Lopez-Ortiz [5] considered a special version of the problem where the points of P take distinct values from the integer set $\{1, \ldots, N\}$. In this case, they gave a static structure that uses $O(N)$ space and answers a query in $O(K)$ time. Their solution also works for the ordered variant.

1.3 Our results

We give the first dynamic structure for the top-K range reporting problem in external memory:

THEOREM 1. *For the top-K range reporting problem, there is a data structure that consumes linear space, answers a query in $O(\log_B N + K/B)$ time, and can be updated in $O(\log_B^2 N)$ amortized time per insertion and deletion. The structure can be constructed in $O((N/B) \log_{M/B}(N/B))$ I/Os.*

Our construction time improves the result of [1] by a factor of nearly B (also recall that the structure of [1] is static). The starting point of our techniques is an obvious connection between the top-K range reporting problem and *3-sided range searching*. In the latter problem, we want to index a set of 2d points such that, given a 3-sided rectangle $q = [x_1, x_2] \times (-\infty, y]$, all the points in q can be reported efficiently. To see the connection, let us map each point x in the input dataset P (of the top-K range reporting problem) to a 2d point $(x, score(x))$. Denote by S the set of resulting 2d points. Given a top-K range query with search range $[x_1, x_2]$, we can answer it by finding all the points in S that fall in the rectangle $q = [x_1, x_2] \times (-\infty, \tau]$ for some properly chosen τ.

3-sided range searching has been well solved [3]. The challenge, however, lies in finding a good τ. Ideally, we would like q to cover exactly K points of S, but as remarked by Afshani, Brodal and Zeh [1], this "does not seem to be any easier" than the original problem. They circumvented the issue by resorting to an interesting method called *shallow cutting*. Unfortunately, a shallow cutting is costly to compute, which explains why the structure of [1] is expensive to construct and update.

Motivated by this, we turned our attention back to the problem of finding τ. The key to our eventual success is that, we do not need an ideal τ, but any τ that makes q cover cK (for some $c \geq 1$) points in S is good enough. After retrieving those $O(K)$ points, we can run an external version of the K-selection algorithm (e.g., the one by Aggarwal and Vitter [2]) to find the point having the K-th smallest score among them. This algorithm requires only linear time, or in our case, $O(K/B)$ I/Os.

We therefore introduce a new problem:

PROBLEM 1 (APPROXIMATE K-THRESHOLD PROBLEM). *Let P be as defined in the top-K range reporting problem. Given an interval $[x_1, x_2]$ in $\mathbb{R}$ and an integer $K \leq N$, a query reports a value $\tau \in \mathbb{R}$ such that at least K but at most $O(K)$ points $x \in P$ satisfy the condition that $x \in [x_1, x_2]$ and $score(x) \leq \tau$. If $[x_1, x_2]$ covers less than K points in P, the query returns ∞.*

As a side product that is of independent interest, we prove:

LEMMA 1. *For the approximate K-threshold problem, there is a structure that consumes $O(N/B)$ space, answers a query in $O(\log_B N)$ time, and can be updated in $O(\log_B^2 N)$ amortized time per insertion and deletion. The structure can be constructed in $O((N/B) \log_{M/B}(N/B))$ I/Os.*

The above lemma, combined with the *external priority search tree* of Arge, Samoladas and Vitter [3], leads directly to Theorem 1. An external priority search tree on N points uses $O(N/B)$ space, answers a 3-sided range query in $O(\log_B N + K/B)$ time (where K is the number of points reported), supports an update in $O(\log_B N)$ time, and can be built in $O((N/B) \log_{M/B}(N/B))$ time. The rest of the paper will therefore focus on the approximate K-threshold problem.

From now on, we will consider only that the query range $[x_1, x_2]$ contains at least K points in P. Otherwise (i.e., $P \cap [x_1, x_2]$ has less than K points), there is a simple solution to answer the query in $O(\log_B N)$ time. For this purpose, we only need to create a slightly augmented B-tree (see, for example, [11]) on the points of P such that, the number of data points covered by any interval can be retrieved in $O(\log_B N)$ I/Os. If this number for $[x_1, x_2]$ is below K, we simply return ∞.

1.4 Techniques

It would be natural to index P with a B-tree. Searching the B-tree with query range $[x_1, x_2]$ in a standard way yields $h = O(\log_B N)$ canonical subsets $P_1, \ldots, P_h$ that partition the points of $P \cap [x_1, x_2]$. In the approximate K-threshold problem, one source of difficulty is the lack of a clear decomposability property that allows us to deal with each P_i

individually. We overcome this by precomputing a *logarithmic sketch* for each P_i, which is a subset of P_i containing the points with the lowest score, the 2nd lowest, the 4th lowest, and so on. As it probably has become clearer, by adapting the algorithm of Frederickson and Johnson [7] for finding the K smallest elements from multiple sorted lists, we manage to find a good τ by using just the sketches of $P_1, \ldots, P_h$.

Some other technical challenges then arise. First, unlike RAM, an EM structure typically has a large, non-constant, node fanout. In this case, care must be exercised in deciding which sketches to store, so that not many sketches will be needed by a query, and yet, the overall space can still be kept linear. Second, updating a sketch is problematic because, as can be imagined, a single insertion/deletion in a set could destroy its sketch completely. We managed to achieve the result in Lemma 1 by (i) replacing a sketch with an approximate version where the i-th point does not have exactly the 2^i-th lowest score, but has instead the $\Theta(2^i)$-th lowest, and (ii) creating several sets of structures, with each set designed to update the i-th point of a sketch for a different range of i.

1.5 Top-K range reporting without the distinct-score condition

Points have distinct scores in the standard top-K range reporting problem as defined in [1]. If two points are allowed to have an identical score, the query semantics can be adapted in two natural ways, depending on how ties are treated. The first one is to break ties arbitrarily, namely, if multiple points have the K-th lowest score c (among the points satisfying the range condition), return $K - z$ of them arbitrarily, where z is the number of points with scores less than c. The second adaptation is not to break ties at all, that is, all the points with scores at most c are reported.

As long as the original top-K range reporting problem (i.e., with distinct scores) has been solved, both of the above semantics can be supported easily. In fact, this is trivial for the first semantics, in which case we can break ties by letting an object with a smaller id have a lower score, and apply our distinct-score structure directly. For the second semantics, we can maintain a separate B-tree where the data points are sorted first by their scores, and then by their values. In this way, after we have found score c using our distinct-score structure, all the points (covered by the query range) with score c can be retrieved in $O(\log_B N)$ I/Os, plus the linear output time. Therefore, for each semantics, we obtain a linear-size structure that answers a query in $O(\log_B N)$ time plus the linear output time, and can be updated with the same cost as in Theorem 1.

2. A STATIC STRUCTURE

This section will present a static structure, which explains some ingredients of our dynamic structure in the next section. Henceforth, we use the term *point* to refer to a real value x associated with a score (which is denoted with $score(x)$, as before). From now on, B would be interpreted as the number of points that can be stored in a block. Furthermore, we say that two point sets D_1, D_2 are *score-disjoint* if no point in D_1 has the same score as a point in D_2. All logarithms have base 2 by default.

Figure 1: Original array and conceptual array in the proof of Lemma 3 (gray cells represent points in $\Sigma(D_i)$)

Let us start by reviewing a classic result:

LEMMA 2 ([7]). *Let $A_1, \ldots, A_h$ be arrays of values from a totally ordered set such that (i) each array is sorted, (ii) the values in each array are distinct, and (iii) the arrays are mutually disjoint. All arrays are in internal memory. Given an integer $K \le \sum_{i=1}^{h} |A_i|$, there is a comparison-based algorithm that finds in $O(h)$ CPU time a value τ that is greater than at least K but at most $O(K)$ values in $A_1 \cup \cdots \cup A_h$.*

As an immediate corollary, when $A_1, \ldots, A_h$ are stored in the disk, there is an algorithm that solves the same problem in $O(h)$ I/Os – just a trivial simulation of the in-memory algorithm suffices. Furthermore, this algorithm accesses only $O(h)$ elements of the arrays (otherwise, the CPU time of the algorithm in internal memory would not be $O(h)$).

Given a value $\tau \in \mathbb{R}$, define its *rank* in a point set D, denoted as $\text{rank}_D(\tau)$, to be the number of points in D whose scores are at most τ.

DEFINITION 1. *The **logarithmic sketch** $\Sigma(D)$ of a point set D is a sequence $(x_0, \ldots, x_{\lfloor \log |D| \rfloor})$, where x_k ($0 \le k \le \lfloor \log |D| \rfloor$) is the point in D whose score has rank 2^k.*

For a point set D, we use $D[k]$ ($1 \le k \le |D|$) to denote the point with the k-th lowest score in D. The next lemma shows that in order to compute a suitable τ, much less information is needed than is required by Lemma 2.

LEMMA 3. *Let $D_1, \ldots, D_h$ be point sets that are mutually score-disjoint. Given their logarithmic sketches and an integer $K \le \sum_{i=1}^{h} |D_i|$, we can find in $O(h)$ I/Os a value τ whose rank in $D_1 \cup \cdots \cup D_h$ is at least K and at most $O(K)$.*

PROOF. For each $i \in [1, h]$, we construct a conceptual array A_i of size $|D_i|$, based on the logarithmic sketch $\Sigma(D_i)$. Suppose $\Sigma(D_i) = (x_0, \ldots, x_{|\Sigma(D_i)|-1})$. The k-th entry of A_i equals[1] $x_{\lceil \log k \rceil}$. Figure 1 illustrates an example. It holds that

$$score(A_i[\lceil k/2 \rceil]) \le score(D_i[k]) \le score(A_i[k]) \quad (1)$$

for all $k = 1, \ldots, |D_i|$. Specifically, $score(D_i[k]) \le score(A_i[k])$ is because the score of $x_{\lceil \log k \rceil}$ has rank $2^{\lceil \log k \rceil} \ge k$ in D_i, whereas $score(A_i[\lceil k/2 \rceil]) \le score(D_i[k])$ is because the score of $x_{\lceil \log \lceil k/2 \rceil \rceil}$ has rank $2^{\lceil \log \lceil k/2 \rceil \rceil} \le k$ in D_i.

Next, given K, we apply Lemma 2 to $A_1, \ldots, A_h$. Recall that, in Lemma 2, each input array should be stored in the

---
[1] In case $\lceil \log k \rceil \ge |\Sigma(D_i)|$, define $x_{\lceil \log k \rceil}$ to be a dummy point with score ∞.

123

disk. Apparently, we cannot afford to materialize $A_1, \ldots,$ A_h into the disk because their sizes are large. Interestingly, we can apply Lemma 2 *without* disk materialization as follows. Every time the algorithm asks for a cell in the array, say $A_i[k]$ for some i, k satisfying $1 \leq i \leq h, 1 \leq k \leq |A_i|$, we probe $\Sigma(D_i)$ to return the score of its $\lceil \log k \rceil$-th point. As mentioned earlier, the algorithm finishes in $O(h)$ time in internal memory, implying that we only need to probe $\Sigma(D_1)$, $\ldots, \Sigma(D_h)$ for $O(h)$ times in total. Furthermore, Lemma 2 requires that no two numbers, from either the same array or different arrays, should be identical. To fulfill this requirement, when the scores of two entries $A_i[k]$ and $A_{i'}[k']$ are identical, we break the tie by comparing i and i'; if there is still a tie, we compare k and k'. Therefore, when the algorithm of Lemma 2 finishes, we have obtained a τ whose rank in $A_1 \cup \cdots \cup A_h$ falls in $[K, cK]$ for some constant c.

In the sequel, we will show that

$$\text{rank}_{A_i}(\tau) \leq \text{rank}_{D_i}(\tau) \leq 2\,\text{rank}_{A_i}(\tau)$$

for every $i \in [1, h]$. This will conclude the proof since it implies that the rank of τ in $D_1 \cup \cdots \cup D_h$ is covered by $[K, 2cK]$.

Set $\alpha = \text{rank}_{A_i}(\tau)$. To prove $\text{rank}_{A_i}(\tau) \leq \text{rank}_{D_i}(\tau)$, we point out: (i) $score(A_i[\alpha]) \leq \tau$, by the definition of α, and (ii) $score(D_i[\alpha]) \leq score(A_i[\alpha])$, by (1). Therefore, for all $k \leq \alpha$, $score(D_i[k]) \leq score(D_i[\alpha]) \leq \tau$. Hence, $\text{rank}_{D_i}(\tau) \geq \alpha = \text{rank}_{A_i}(\tau)$.

To prove $\text{rank}_{D_i}(\tau) \leq 2\,\text{rank}_{A_i}(\tau)$, suppose that $2\alpha + 1 \leq |D_i|$; otherwise, the statement is trivially true. Observe: (i) $score(A_i[\alpha + 1]) > \tau$, by the definition of α, and (ii) $score(D_i[2\alpha + 1]) \geq score(A_i[\alpha + 1])$, by (1). Therefore, for all $k > 2\alpha$, $score(D_i[k]) \geq score(D_i[2\alpha + 1]) > \tau$. This implies that $\text{rank}_{D_i}(\tau) \leq 2\alpha = 2\,\text{rank}_{A_i}(\tau)$. $\square$

Structure. We are ready to describe our structure for the approximate K-threshold problem. The base tree is a B-tree on the points of P, where each leaf node contains at least (most) $B/2$ (B) points, and each internal node has at least (most) $f/2$ (f) children [2]. All the points are stored at the leaf level. Set $f = B^{1/5}$. For every node u of the B-tree, denote by $S(u)$ the set of points in the subtree rooted at u. If u is an internal node, define its *multi-slabs* as follows. Assuming that the children of u are $u_1, \ldots, u_f$ ordered from left to right, define a multi-slab $u[i, j]$ ($1 \leq i \leq j \leq f$) as the union of the subtrees of $u_i, \ldots, u_j$. Use $S(u[i, j])$ to denote the set of points in $u[i, j]$, i.e., $S(u[i, j]) = S(u_i) \cup \cdots \cup S(u_j)$. We store sketches $\Sigma(S(u[i, j]))$ at each internal node u, for all i, j satisfying $1 \leq i \leq j \leq f$.

Query. Given an approximate K-threshold query with search range $[x_1, x_2]$, first identify, in a standard way, $h = O(\log_B N)$ canonical sets $D_1, \ldots, D_h$ of $P \cap [x_1, x_2]$. For each D_i, its logarithmic sketch is either available in the form of $\Sigma(S(u[i, j]))$ for some multi-slab $u[i, j]$, or can be computed in $O(1)$ I/Os from a leaf node. Then, apply Lemma 3 to find the result.

Analysis. The query time is $O(\log_B N)$, noticing that the canonical sets can be identified in $O(\log_B N)$ I/Os, while applying Lemma 3 takes another $O(\log_B N)$ time. We now

---

[2] Except the root. We ignore such standard details.

bound the space consumption of the structure. The base tree obviously uses $O(N/B)$ blocks. Next, we analyze the space occupied by the sketches. Define the level of leaf nodes to be 0, and in general, the parent of a level-l node is at level $l+1$. Since there are at most $\frac{N}{(B/2)(f/2)^l}$ nodes at level l, each node stores f^2 sketches, and each sketch uses $O(\frac{1}{B} \log(Bf^l))$ space, the total space occupied by level-l sketches is

$$\frac{N}{(B/2)(f/2)^l} \cdot f^2 \cdot O\left(\frac{1}{B} \log(Bf^l)\right)$$

$$(\text{as } f = B^{1/5}) = O\left(\frac{N \cdot f^2 \cdot l \log B}{B^2 (f/2)^l}\right)$$

$$= O(N/B) \cdot \frac{\log B}{B^{3/5}} \cdot \frac{l}{(f/2)^l} = O(N/B)\frac{l}{(f/2)^l}.$$

Summing up all levels, overall, the sketches require space:

$$O(N/B) \cdot \sum_{l=1}^{O(\log_B N)} \frac{l}{(f/2)^l} = O(N/B),$$

since $B \geq 64$ implies $f/2 > 1$.

3. MAKING THE STRUCTURE DYNAMIC

This section extends our structure to support an update in $O(\log_B^2 N)$ amortized time, while retaining the space and query bounds. We will also show that the new index can be constructed in $O((N/B) \log_{M/B}(N/B))$ time.

3.1 Approximate sketch

It is obvious that a single insertion in a point set can invalidate its entire logarithmic sketch, thus making the sketch expensive to maintain. Motivated by this, we resort to a looser version of the sketch:

DEFINITION 2. *An* **approximate logarithmic sketch** $\Pi(D)$ *of point set* D *is a sequence* $(y_0, y_1, y_2, \ldots)$ *whose length is at least* $\lfloor \log |D| \rfloor$ *but at most* $1 + \lfloor \log |D| \rfloor$. *The rank of* y_k $(0 \leq k \leq |\Pi(D)| - 1)$ *in* D *is in the range* $[2^k, 2^{k+1} - 1]$.

Here is a more intuitive interpretation of the definition. First, imagine that the real domain $\mathbb{R}$ is partitioned into intervals by the scores of the points in the *static* sketch $\Sigma(D) = (D[1], D[2], \ldots, D[2^k], \ldots)$ of D. We call these intervals the *fragments* induced by D. Specifically,

- the first fragment is the interval $(-\infty, score(D[1]))$;

- for k between 0 and $\lfloor \log |D| \rfloor - 1$, the $(k+2)$-nd fragment is $[score(D[2^k]), score(D[2^{k+1}]))$; and

- the last fragment is $[score(D[2^{\lfloor \log |D| \rfloor}]), +\infty)$.

Notice that each score in $\Sigma(D)$ belongs to the fragment on its right. Then, except the first fragment and possibly the last one, every other fragment contributes one number to the approximate sketch $\Pi(D)$. The last fragment can contribute either one or *no* number. More precisely, the $(k+2)$-nd fragment $(0 \leq k \leq \lfloor \log |D| \rfloor)$ contributes, if it does, the y_k of $\Pi(D)$. The value of y_k can be chosen *arbitrarily* from the fragment, i.e., it does not even need to be the score of a point in D. The first two arrays and the axis in Figure 2 illustrate the computation of an approximate sketch $\Pi(D_i)$

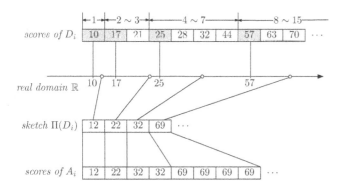

Figure 2: Original array, induced fragments, approximate logarithmic sketch and conceptual array in the proof of Lemma 4 (gray cells represent scores that partition the real domain)

for a point set D_i. For example, y_1 of $\Pi(D_i)$, which equals 22, comes from the third fragment $[17, 25)$.

The following lemma indicates that an approximate sketch serves the purpose of Lemma 3 equally well.

LEMMA 4. *Let $D_1, \ldots, D_h$ be point sets that are mutually score-disjoint. Given their approximate logarithmic sketches and an integer $K \leq \sum_{i=1}^{h} |D_i|$, we can find in $O(h)$ I/Os a value τ whose rank in $D_1 \cup \cdots \cup D_h$ is at least K and at most $O(K)$.*

PROOF. For each $i \in [1, h]$, we construct a conceptual array A_i of size $|D_i|$, based on the approximate logarithmic sketch $\Pi(D_i)$. Let $\Pi(D_i)$ be a sequence $(y_0, \ldots, y_{|\Pi(D_i)|-1})$, as in Definition 2. The k-th entry of A_i is a dummy point with score[3] $y_{\lceil \log k \rceil}$. Figure 2 illustrates an example. In general, it holds that $score(D_i[k]) \leq score(A_i[k])$ for all $k \in [1, |D_i|]$, since the rank of $y_{\lceil \log k \rceil}$ in D_i is at least $2^{\lceil \log k \rceil} \geq k$.

As in the proof of Lemma 3, with the same tie-breaking policy, we can apply Lemma 2 on input K and $A_1, \ldots, A_h$, without materializing the arrays. The algorithm of Lemma 2 returns, in $O(h)$ time, a value τ whose rank in $A_1 \cup \cdots \cup A_h$ falls in $[K, cK]$ for some constant c. Next, we will show that

$$\text{rank}_{A_i}(\tau) \leq \text{rank}_{D_i}(\tau) \leq 4\,\text{rank}_{A_i}(\tau)$$

for every $i \in [1, h]$, which will conclude the proof since it implies that the rank of τ in $D_1 \cup \cdots \cup D_h$ is covered by $[K, 4cK]$.

The fact $\text{rank}_{A_i}(\tau) \leq \text{rank}_{D_i}(\tau)$ can be established in exactly the same way as in the proof of Lemma 3. Next, we will focus on proving $\text{rank}_{D_i}(\tau) \leq 4\,\text{rank}_{A_i}(\tau)$. Set $\alpha = \text{rank}_{A_i}(\tau)$. If $|D_i| < 4\alpha$, $\text{rank}_{D_i}(\tau) \leq 4\,\text{rank}_{A_i}(\tau)$ is trivially true. If $\alpha = 0$, $\tau < score(A_i[1]) = score(D_i[1])$, leading to $\text{rank}_{D_i}(\tau) = 0 \leq 4\,\text{rank}_{A_i}(\tau)$. Next, we consider $|D_i| \geq 4\alpha$ and $\alpha \geq 1$. In this case, $\lceil \log(\alpha + 1) \rceil < |\Pi(D_i)|$ since

$$\lceil \log(\alpha + 1) \rceil \leq \log(2\alpha) \leq \log(|D_i|/2) \leq \lfloor \log |D_i| \rfloor.$$

Therefore, the rank of $score(A_i[\alpha + 1]) = y_{\lceil \log(\alpha+1) \rceil}$ in D_i, by Definition 2, is at most

$$2^{\lceil \log(\alpha+1) \rceil + 1} - 1 \leq 2^{\log(2\alpha)+1} - 1 = 4\alpha - 1.$$

---

[3] In case $\lceil \log k \rceil \geq |\Pi(D_i)|$, define $y_{\lceil \log k \rceil}$ to be ∞.

This implies $score(D_i[4\alpha]) > score(A_i[\alpha + 1]) > \tau$. As a result, $\text{rank}_{D_i}(\tau) < 4\alpha = 4\,\text{rank}_{A_i}(\tau)$. □

Henceforth, all *sketches* will refer to approximate logarithmic sketches.

3.2 Preliminary: weight-balanced B-tree

We will adopt the *weight-balanced B-tree* (WBB-tree) of Arge and Vitter [4] as the base tree of our dynamic structure. This subsection reviews the part of the WBB-tree that is sufficient for our discussion.

While an ordinary B-tree determines the balance of a node by its number of children, a WBB-tree determines the balance by its *weight*, namely, the number of points stored in the subtree rooted at the node. Formally, in a WBB-tree with *leaf capacity* b and *branching factor* f, the weight $w(u)$ of a level-l node u satisfies

$$bf^l/4 \leq w(u) \leq bf^l$$

if it is not the root node (recall that leaf nodes are at level 0). If, on the other hand, u is the root, it requires that u has at least two children and $w(u) \leq bf^l$. A node is *unbalanced* if it violates any of these constraints. By definition, the height of a WBB-tree with N points is $O(\log_f(N/b))$; an internal node has at least $f/4$ and at most $4f$ children; and a leaf node stores $b/4$ to b points.

A crucial property of the WBB-tree is that to make a level-l node u unbalanced, $\Omega(bf^l)$ updates must have been performed in its subtree since it was created, if u is not the root; or $\Omega(bf^{l-1})$ if it is the root. This provides considerable convenience in handling the unbalancing of a node u. We adopt the following simple rebalancing strategy: if u is not the root, we rebuild the whole subtree rooted at *its parent*, whose weight is at most bf^{l+1}; if u is the root, we rebuild the whole tree, which contains $N = O(bf^l)$ points in total. Either way, the strategy guarantees that the cost to reconstruct a subtree of Z points can be amortized on $\Omega(Z/f)$ updates; and an update bears at most one such cost at each level. It will be clear later that this suffices to establish the desired bound on the update cost.

3.3 Structure

We are now ready to make our structure dynamic. For simplicity, let us assume that $\log_B N$ does not change; the assumption can be removed by globally rebuilding the whole structure every time N has been doubled or halved from its value at the moment when the structure was last rebuilt. We also assume that the tree has at least two levels. Given a point set D and an integer $k \in [1, |D|]$, define the *top-k points* of D as the k points in D with the lowest scores.

The base tree is a WBB-tree with leaf capacity $b = B \log_B N$ and branching factor $f = B^{1/5}$. Its height is thus $O(\log_f(N/B)) = O(\log_B N)$. In each internal node u, we store the following secondary structures:

- $O(f^2)$ sketches. As before, for each multi-slab $u[i, j]$, we store a sketch of all points in $S(u[i, j])$.

- a *multi-way list*. It contains the top-$(B^{4/5}/4)$ points from every child of u. Note that a multi-way list can be stored in a single block since $4f \cdot B^{4/5}/4 = B$.

- a *one-way list*. It contains the top-$(B^{3/5} \log_B N)$ points of $S(u)$, in ascending order of scores.

For each leaf node v, store the points of $S(v)$ in ascending order of scores. For convenience, sometimes we will refer to the first $B^{3/5} \log_B N$ points of this ordering as the one-way list of v.

Furthermore, we maintain an external priority search tree [3] on the 2d point set converted from P in the way as explained in Section 1.3. That is, each point $x \in S$ is mapped to a 2d point $(x, score(x))$. We refer to the 2d point as the *image* of x.

Space. The WBB-tree and the external priority search tree use $O(N/B)$ space. For sketches, we follow a similar argument as in the static case: since (i) each internal node carries $O(f^2)$ sketches, (ii) each level-l sketch occupies $O((1/B) \log(bf^l))$ space, and (iii) the number of level-l nodes is at most $\frac{N}{bf^l/4}$, the space consumption of all sketches is

$$\sum_{l=1}^{O(\log_B N)} \frac{N}{bf^l/4} \cdot O(f^2) \cdot O\left(\frac{1}{B} \log(bf^l)\right)$$

$$= O(N/B) \cdot \sum_{l=1}^{O(\log_B N)} \left(\frac{f^2 \log b}{b} \cdot \frac{1}{f^l} + \frac{f^2 \log f}{b} \cdot \frac{l}{f^l}\right)$$

$$= O(N/B) \cdot O\left(\frac{f^2 \log b}{b} + \frac{f^2 \log f}{b}\right) = o(N/B)$$

(as $f = B^{1/5} > 1$ and $b = B \log_B N$).

As the multi-way and one-way lists of an internal node together consume $O(1 + (1/B) \cdot B^{3/5} \log_B N)$ space, and the number of internal nodes is $O(N/(bf))$, all the lists occupy

$$O(1 + (1/B) \cdot B^{3/5} \log_B N) \cdot O(N/(bf))$$

$$= O\left(\frac{N}{bf}\right) + O\left(\frac{NB^{3/5} \log_B N}{Bbf}\right)$$

$$(\text{as } b = B \log_B N) = O\left(\frac{N}{Bf \log_B N}\right) + O\left(\frac{N}{B^{7/5}f}\right)$$

$$= O(N/B)$$

space. Therefore, our structure consumes linear space overall.

Query. An approximate K-threshold query with search range $[x_1, x_2]$ can be answered by the same procedure as in Section 2. First, identify $O(\log_B N)$ canonical sets of $P \cap [x_1, x_2]$. Sketches are available for all but at most two of the canonical sets at the leaf level. Hence in the second step, for these two canonical sets, we compute their sketches in $O(\log_B N)$ time by scanning the corresponding leaf nodes once. Finally, apply Lemma 4 to obtain the query result. As each step takes $O(\log_B N)$ time, the query cost is $O(\log_B N)$.

3.4 Update

This subsection explains how to support insertions and deletions in our structure. We will first discuss how to modify sketches before elaborating the entire update algorithm.

Updating sketches. For each number in sketch $\Pi(D)$, we store a *counter* to indicate its real rank in D. Next,

we describe how to update a sketch $\Pi(S(u[i,j]))$ if a point x is inserted in or deleted from a multi-slab $u[i,j]$. First, scan the whole sketch to update the counters. Recall that $\Pi(S(u[i,j]))$ is a sequence $(y_0, y_1, y_2, \ldots)$ of numbers, where y_k comes from the $(k+2)$-nd fragment induced by $S(u[i,j])$. For each y_k in the sequence, increase or decrease its counter by one if $score(x) \leq y_k$. Then, if its rank constraint is violated (i.e., the counter is no longer in the range $[2^k, 2^{k+1}-1]$), check if the $(k+2)$-nd fragment is the last fragment, i.e., $k = \lfloor \log |S(u[i,j])| \rfloor$. If yes, fix the violation by simply discarding y_k, since the last fragment is allowed to contribute no number to the sketch. Otherwise, recompute y_k by retrieving a super-set of the top-(1.5×2^k) points[4] of the multi-slab. The super-set has size $O(2^k)$, with its points fetched in an *arbitrary* order. After that, select the point with the (1.5×2^k)-th lowest score in the super-set, which can be done in $O(2^k/B)$ time using the algorithm of [2]. The score of this point becomes the new y_k. Assuming that the multi-way list of node u is already in memory, the aforementioned super-set can be produced in $O(2^k/B^{3/5})$ I/Os as follows.

1. If $1.5 \times 2^k \leq B^{4/5}/4$, obtain the super-set via accessing the multi-way list of u with *no cost*, since the multi-way list is in memory.

2. If $B^{4/5}/4 < 1.5 \times 2^k \leq B^{3/5} \log_B N$, fetch the super-set from the one-way lists of the children of u whose subtrees compose multi-slab $u[i,j]$: First, apply Lemma 2 on those one-way lists to obtain a value τ whose rank in $S(u[i,j])$ is at least 1.5×2^k and at most $O(2^k)$. This can be done in $O(f)$ I/Os. Then, generate the super-set by collecting all the points of each one-way list whose scores are at most τ. This costs $O(f + 1.5 \times 2^k/B) = O(2^k/B^{3/5})$ time, since $1.5 \times 2^k/B^{3/5} > (B^{4/5}/4)/B^{3/5} = \Omega(f)$.

3. If $1.5 \times 2^k > \max\{B^{4/5}/4, B^{3/5} \log_B N\}$, issue a 3-sided range query on the external priority search tree. This query retrieves all the points in P whose images fall in $[x_1, x_2] \times (-\infty, y_{k+1}]$, where $[x_1, x_2]$ is the x-range of multi-slab $u[i,j]$. Here, y_{k+1} is the number that succeeds y_k in $\Pi(S(u[i,j]))$; in case y_k is the last number of the sketch, set $y_{k+1} = \infty$. The 3-sided query returns a super-set as needed because the rank of y_{k+1} in $S(u[i,j])$ is (i) at least $2^{k+1} - 1$ (if $y_{k+1} \neq \infty$) or at least 1.5×2^k (if $y_{k+1} = \infty$), and (ii) at most $2^{k+2} - 1$. The cost is $O(\log_B N + 2^{k+2}/B) = O(2^k/B^{3/5})$.

We have finished explaining how to recompute existing numbers in the sketch. Finally, check if we need to add a new number to $\Pi(S(u[i,j]))$. Specifically, let y_k be the last number in $\Pi(S(u[i,j]))$. If the $(k+3)$-rd fragment is no longer the last fragment induced by $S(u[i,j])$, i.e., $k + 1 < \lfloor \log |S(u[i,j])| \rfloor$, add a y_{k+1} to the sketch. The value of y_{k+1} can also be computed with the above procedure.

Now, we analyze the cost of updating sketches. As will be clear shortly, inserting/deleting a point can affect the sketches of $O(\log_B N)$ nodes, such that $O(f^2)$ sketches at each node can be modified. There are two types of sketch updates: counter update and number recomputation. At

---

[4] As a special case, when $k = 0$, we replace 1.5×2^k with 1. The same convention is adopted in the sequel.

each node, the counters of the affected sketches can be updated in $O((f^2 \log N)/B) = O(\log_B N)$ time by scanning the $O(f^2)$ sketches once.

Next, we bound the cost of number recomputation. Recall, once again, that a sketch is a sequence $(y_0, y_1, \ldots)$ of numbers. Let us focus on one specific number, say y_k. Since the last recomputation of y_k, at least 0.5×2^k updates must have happened before we need to recompute it again. As mentioned earlier, each recomputation requires $O(2^k/B^{3/5})$ I/Os. We amortize this cost over those 0.5×2^k updates, so that each update accounts for only $O(1/B^{3/5})$ I/Os. As a sketch has $O(\log N)$ numbers, each update can be charged $O(\log N)$ times with respect to one sketch. Hence, the update can be charged $O(f^2 \log N)$ times with respect to a node. Finally, an update needs to bear cost for $O(\log_B N)$ nodes. Therefore, overall, the amortized cost of an update is

$$O(f^2 \log N) \cdot O(1/B^{3/5}) \cdot O(\log_B N)$$
$$= O\left(\frac{\log N}{B^{1/5}}\right) \cdot O(\log_B N) = O(\log_B^2 N).$$

Full update steps. We now give the complete update algorithm. An insertion/deletion of a point x is carried out in five steps:

1. Insert/delete x in the WBB-tree. We use the term *update path* to refer to the path from the root to the leaf node containing x.

2. Only nodes on the update path may have become unbalanced. Find the highest unbalanced node u^*, and follow the rebalancing strategy as in Section 3.2: if u^* is the root, reconstruct the whole tree; otherwise, reconstruct the subtree rooted at the parent of u^*. We defer the construction algorithm to Section 3.5.

   If u^* or its parent is the root, the update is complete because the whole tree has been reconstructed. Otherwise, let U be the set of nodes on the update path that have not been reconstructed. Specifically, if u^* does not exist, U includes all the nodes on the update path. If u^* exists, U includes all the proper ancestors of the parent of u^*. Perform the following steps on the nodes u of U in the bottom-up order.

3. Recompute the one-way list of u by merging the one-way lists of its children.

4. Let v be the child of u on the update path. In the multi-way list of u, only the $B^{4/5}/4$ points from the subtree of v can be affected by the update. Replace them with the top-$(B^{4/5}/4)$ points in the multi-way list of v.

5. Load the multi-way list of u into memory. Then, update the sketches of u as described previously.

Analysis. To analyze the update cost, we will use in advance the fact that we can construct a subtree in $O((Z/B) \log_{M/B}(Z/B))$ time if the subtree contains Z points (the fact will be proved in the next subsection). Steps 1 and 5 consume $O(\log_B N)$ and $O(\log_B^2 N)$ amortized time, respectively. Next, we will show that Steps 2 to 4 incur $O(\log_B N)$ amortized cost per level. This will establish that the overall update time is $O(\log_B^2 N)$ amortized.

- As mentioned in Section 3.2, if the reconstruction of Step 2 involves Z points, we can amortize the cost over $\Omega(Z/f)$ updates, so that each update bears cost

$$\frac{O((Z/B) \log_{M/B}(Z/B))}{\Omega(Z/f)} = O\left(\frac{\log_{M/B}(Z/B)}{B^{4/5}}\right)$$
$$= O\left(\frac{\log(N/B)}{B^{4/5}}\right) = O(\log_B N).$$

- As each one-way list contains $B^{3/5} \log_B N$ points, the f-way merge of Step 3 can be performed in time

$$O\left(\frac{fB^{3/5} \log_B N}{B} \log_{M/B} f\right)$$
$$= O\left(\frac{\log_B N}{B^{1/5}} \log B\right) = O(\log_B N).$$

- Finally, Step 4 takes one I/O.

3.5 Construction

This subsection describes an $O((Z/B) \log_{M/B}(Z/B))$-time algorithm to reconstruct the subtree of a node, where Z is the number of points in the subtree. Given those Z points, the algorithm outputs a new subtree $\mathcal{T}$ in which all the secondary structures have been properly constructed. As $\mathcal{T}$ is itself a WBB-tree, its nodes can be built in $O((Z/B) \log_{M/B}(Z/B))$ I/Os [4]. In the sequel, we focus on building the secondary structures.

For a node u in $\mathcal{T}$, define the *ranked list* of u, denoted as $rlist(u)$, to be the list of points from $S(u)$ in ascending order of their scores (recall that $S(u)$ is the set of points in the subtree of u). We first explain the computation of sketches, which will be used as a building block of the full construction algorithm.

Computing sketches. Consider u to be an internal node in $\mathcal{T}$. Given $rlist(u)$, we next show how to compute the $O(f^2)$ sketches of u in two steps. The first one scans $rlist(u)$ to generate all the sketch entries of u. At this point, those entries are not necessarily grouped by the sketches they belong to. Then, the second step achieves the grouping by sorting. Here are the details:

- For the first step, allocate one block of memory as the output buffer, and another block to keep track of $O(f^2)$ counters, one for each multi-slab $u[i,j]$ ($1 \le i \le j \le 4f$). The counter of $u[i,j]$ indicates how many points in the multi-slab have already been scanned in $rlist(u)$. Every time the counter reaches 1.5×2^k for some $k \ge 0$, a tuple $((i,j),k,y)$ is output, where y is the score of the last point scanned. Reading the ranked list obviously takes $O(|rlist(u)|/B)$ I/Os. In addition, we have to write in total $O(f^2 \log Z)$ tuples to the disk, whose overhead is

$$O(1 + (f^2 \log Z)/B) = O\left(1 + \frac{1}{B^{2/5}} \cdot \frac{\log Z}{B^{1/5}}\right) \quad (2)$$
$$= O(1 + (1/B^{2/5}) \log_B Z).$$

- Given a tuple $((i,j),k,y)$, refer to (i,j) as its *key*. The second step groups the $O(f^2 \log Z)$ tuples by their keys. Since the number of the distinct keys is $O(f^2)$, this can be done using the distribution sort algorithm of [2] in time

$$O\left(1 + \frac{f^2 \log Z}{B} \log_{M/B}(f^2)\right)$$
$$= O(1 + (1/B^{2/5}) \log_B Z). \tag{3}$$

The algorithm is stable, i.e., at its termination, the tuples with the same key are still in ascending order of their values of k. The sketches can then be created by reading the sorted list once more.

Therefore, the sketches of u can be computed in $O(|rlist(u)/B|) + O((1/B^{2/5}) \log_B Z)$ I/Os. In the sequel, we will refer to the above algorithm as *sketch-build*.

Full construction algorithm. We are now ready to explain the details of building the secondary structures for a subtree containing Z points. Let us first consider $M = O(B^2)$. In this case, we generate the ranked lists of all the internal nodes of $\mathcal{T}$ in a bottom-up manner, where the ranked list of a node is obtained by an f-way merge which combines the ranked lists of its children. All the f-way merges that take place at the same level perform $O((Z/B) \log_{M/B} f)$ I/Os. As there are $O(\log_f Z)$ levels, all the ranked lists can be produced in $O((Z/B) \log_{M/B}(Z/B))$ time. Then, for each internal node u, compute its sketches with *sketch-build*. Since $|rlist(u)|/B = \Omega(bf)/B = \Omega(\log_B N)$, the computation of those sketches requires

$$O(|rlist(u)/B|) + O((1/B^{2/5}) \log_B Z)$$
$$= O(|rlist(u)/B|) + O(\log_B N) = O(|rlist(u)|/B) \tag{4}$$

I/Os. The multi-way list of u can be obtained by reading $rlist(u)$ once – recall that a multi-way list occupies only one block. The one-way list of u can be generated by another scan of $rlist(u)$, as it is just a prefix of $rlist(u)$. Thus, the construction of all the secondary structures is no more expensive than the generation of all the ranked lists. Therefore, the algorithm entails in total $O((Z/B) \log_{M/B}(Z/B))$ I/Os.

Now, consider $M = \Omega(B^2)$. In this case, we cannot afford to generate the ranked lists of all the internal nodes. This is because, the height of the subtree, which is $\Omega(\log_f Z)$, can be much greater than $\log_{M/B}(Z/B)$, such that we can no longer spend $O(Z/B)$ I/Os at each level. We circumvent this obstacle by computing the ranked lists for the nodes at only $O(\log_{M/B}(Z/B))$ levels, and deploying each ranked list to build secondary structures for multiple nodes of different levels. In general, suppose that we have obtained all the ranked lists at some level l. We will proceed to compute the ranked lists for the nodes at level $l + \lambda$, where λ is the maximum integer satisfying

$$4f^\lambda < \frac{M}{2B} \cdot \min\{1, f - 1\}. \tag{5}$$

As $B \geq 64$, $f - 1 = \Omega(1)$, meaning that the right hand side of the above inequality is $\Omega(M/B) = \Omega(B)$. This guarantees the existence of a valid λ. For each level-$(l + \lambda)$ node u, its ranked list $rlist(u)$ can be obtained by merging the ranked lists of the descendants of u at level l. Node u has at most $4f^\lambda$ descendants at level l because, a node at level l has at least $bf^l/4$ points in its subtree, whereas u has at most $bf^{l+\lambda}$ points in its subtree. As a result, the merge can be

completed in $O(|rlist(u)|/B)$ I/Os by assigning a memory block to each of the $4f^\lambda < M/(2B)$ descendants. After that, the secondary structures of u can be created as discussed before with $O(|rlist(u)|/B)$ I/Os, as shown in (4).

Next, we will explain how to build, simultaneously, the secondary structures for all the descendants of u at levels from $l + 1$ to $l + \lambda - 1$. Let t be the number of such descendants, denoted as $v_1, \ldots, v_t$. Since each level-$(l + i)$ node has at least $bf^{l+i}/4$ points in its subtree, the number of level-$(l + i)$ descendants of u is at most $4f^{\lambda - i}$, meaning that

$$t \leq \sum_{i=1}^{\lambda - 1} 4f^{\lambda - i} < 4f^\lambda/(f - 1) < M/(2B).$$

Let us first elaborate how to compute the sketches of v_1, $\ldots$, v_t at the same time. For any v_i, if we *had* the ranked list of v_i, then we could simply invoke the *sketch-build* algorithm on v_i. Recall that *sketch-build* involves two steps. A crucial observation is that, the first step can still be performed with $rlist(u)$, in replacement of the ranked list of v_i. This is because, as $rlist(u)$ is scanned, we can ignore those points that do not belong to the subtree of v_i, whereas those that do belong are encountered in ascending order of their scores. Hence, using only 2 blocks of memory (excluding the input buffer for $rlist(u)$), we can carry out the first step on v_i by reading $rlist(u)$ only once. Recall that $2t$ is smaller than M/B. Thus, we can dedicate 2 blocks of memory for each of $v_1, \ldots, v_t$, so that we can perform the first step for all of them simultaneously with a single scan of $rlist(u)$. Summing up the time of reading $rlist(u)$ and that of outputting the $O(f^2 \log Z)$ tuples for each v_i, we know from (2) that the total cost is

$$O(|rlist(u)|/B) + t \cdot O\left(1 + (1/B^{2/5}) \log_B Z\right). \tag{6}$$

Now, we can carry out the second step of *sketch-build* for each v_i *individually*. By (3), doing so for all v_i requires

$$t \cdot O\left(1 + (1/B^{2/5}) \log_B Z\right)$$

I/Os in total. Therefore, the overall cost of computing the sketches of $v_1, \ldots, v_t$ is dominated by (6). Since $v_1, \ldots, v_t$ are internal nodes in the subtree of u and the subtree contains $|rlist(u)|$ points, t is bounded by $O(|rlist(u)|/(bf))$, meaning that

$$t \cdot O\left(1 + (1/B^{2/5}) \log_B Z\right) = t \cdot O(\log_B N)$$
$$= O(|rlist(u)|/(bf)) \cdot O(\log_B N)$$
$$(\text{as } b = B \log_B N) = O(|rlist(u)|/(Bf)).$$

Therefore, (6) $= O(|rlist(u)|/B)$.

Finally, by allocating one block of memory for each node v_i, the one-way lists of all $v_1, \ldots, v_t$ can be computed with one scan of $rlist(u)$. Similarly, the multi-way lists of all $v_1, \ldots, v_t$ can be computed with another scan (recall that each multi-way list can be stored in one block). At this point, we have finished constructing the secondary structures of $v_1, \ldots, v_t$ in totally $O(|rlist(u)|/B)$ time.

The above analysis shows that, in $O(|rlist(u)|/B)$ I/Os, we can build the secondary structures for u and all of its descendants at level $l + 1$ or above. This implies that the secondary structures of all the nodes from levels $l + 1$ to

$l + \lambda$ can be computed in $O(Z/B)$ time. As the height of the subtree $\mathcal{T}$ we are reconstructing is $O(\log_B Z)$, we need to pay the $O(Z/B)$ cost for $O(\log_B Z)/\lambda$ times. Since λ is the maximum integer satisfying (5), $4f^{\lambda+1} = \Omega(M/B)$. This means that $\lambda = \Omega(\log_f(M/B)) = \Omega(\log_B(M/B))$, indicating $O(\log_B Z)/\lambda = O(\log_{M/B}(Z/B))$. Therefore, the total reconstruction cost of $\mathcal{T}$ is $O((Z/B)\log_{M/B}(Z/B))$ for the case $M = \Omega(B^2)$.

Remark. As a direct corollary, our structure can be built from scratch in $O((N/B)\log_{M/B}(N/B))$ time. We thus have completed the proof of Lemma 1, and hence, Theorem 1.

4. ACKNOWLEDGEMENTS

This work was supported in part by (i) projects GRF 4169/09, 4166/10, 4165/11 from HKRGC, and (ii) the WCU (World Class University) program under the National Research Foundation of Korea, and funded by the Ministry of Education, Science and Technology of Korea (Project No: R31-30007).

5. REFERENCES

[1] P. Afshani, G. S. Brodal, and N. Zeh. Ordered and unordered top-k range reporting in large data sets. In *Proceedings of the Annual ACM-SIAM Symposium on Discrete Algorithms (SODA)*, pages 390–400, 2011.

[2] A. Aggarwal and J. S. Vitter. The input/output complexity of sorting and related problems. *Communications of the ACM (CACM)*, 31(9):1116–1127, 1988.

[3] L. Arge, V. Samoladas, and J. S. Vitter. On two-dimensional indexability and optimal range search indexing. In *Proceedings of ACM Symposium on Principles of Database Systems (PODS)*, pages 346–357, 1999.

[4] L. Arge and J. S. Vitter. Optimal dynamic interval management in external memory (extended abstract). In *Proceedings of Annual IEEE Symposium on Foundations of Computer Science (FOCS)*, pages 560–569, 1996.

[5] G. S. Brodal, R. Fagerberg, M. Greve, and A. Lopez-Ortiz. Online sorted range reporting. In *International Symposium on Algorithms and Computation (ISAAC)*, pages 173–182, 2009.

[6] G. N. Frederickson. An optimal algorithm for selection in a min-heap. *Information and Computation*, 104(2):197–214, 1993.

[7] G. N. Frederickson and D. B. Johnson. The complexity of selection and ranking in x+y and matrices with sorted columns. *Journal of Computer and System Sciences (JCSS)*, 24(2):197–208, 1982.

[8] H.-P. Hung, K.-T. Chuang, and M.-S. Chen. Efficient process of top-k range-sum queries over multiple streams with minimized global error. *IEEE Transactions on Knowledge and Data Engineering (TKDE)*, 19(10):1404–1419, 2007.

[9] Z. W. Luo, T. W. Ling, C.-H. Ang, S. Y. Lee, and B. Cui. Range top/bottom k queries in olap sparse data cubes. In *Proceedings of International Conference on Database and Expert Systems Applications (DEXA)*, pages 678–687, 2001.

[10] E. M. McCreight. Priority search trees. *SIAM Journal of Computing*, 14(2):257–276, 1985.

[11] J. Yang and J. Widom. Incremental computation and maintenance of temporal aggregates. *The VLDB Journal*, 12(3):262–283, 2003.

Indexability of 2D Range Search Revisited: Constant Redundancy and Weak Indivisibility

Yufei Tao[*]

ABSTRACT

In the 2D *orthogonal range search* problem, we want to pre-process a set of 2D points so that, given any axis-parallel query rectangle, we can report all the data points in the rectangle efficiently. This paper presents a lower bound on the query time that can be achieved by any external memory structure that stores a point at most r times, where r is a constant integer. Previous research has resolved the bound at two extremes: $r = 1$, and r being arbitrarily large. We, on the other hand, derive the explicit tradeoff at every specific r. A premise that lingers in existing studies is the so-called *indivisibility assumption*: all the information bits of a point are treated as an atom, i.e., they are always stored together in the same block. We partially remove this assumption by allowing a data structure to freely divide a point into individual bits stored in different blocks. The only assumption is that, those bits must be *retrieved* for reporting, as opposed to being *computed* – we refer to this requirement as the *weak indivisibility assumption*. We also describe structures to show that our lower bound is tight up to only a small factor.

Categories and Subject Descriptors

F.2.3 [**Analysis of Algorithms and Problem Complexity**]: Tradeoffs among Complexity Measures; H.3.1 [**Information Storage and Retrieval**]: Content Analysis and Indexing—*indexing methods*

General Terms

Theory

[*]Affiliation 1: Department of Computer Science and Engineering, Chinese University of Hong Kong, Sha Tin, Hong Kong (*taoyf@cse.cuhk.edu.hk*); Affiliation 2: Division of Web Science and Technology, Korea Advanced Institute of Science and Technology, Daejeon, Republic of Korea (*taoyf@kaist.ac.kr*).

Keywords

Indexibility, range search, lower bound, indivisibility

1. INTRODUCTION

This paper revisits *orthogonal range search* (henceforce, *range search*) in 2D space, addressing an aspect termed *r-redundant indexing*. Let us start by defining this notion, and explain the reasons motivating its study.

1.1 *r*-redundant indexing

Let P be a set of N points in the data space $\mathbb{R}^2$, where $\mathbb{R}$ represents the domain of real values. We will refer to each point $p \in P$ interchangeably as an *object*. Object p is associated with an *information field*, denoted as $info(p)$. Given an axis-parallel rectangle, a *range query* returns the information fields of all the points in P that are covered by q, namely:

$$\{info(p) \mid p \in P \cap q\}.$$

See Figure 1. The objective is to index P with a structure so that range queries can be answered efficiently in the worst case.

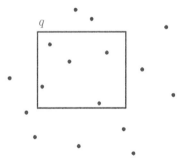

Figure 1: A range query. The information fields of the points inside the rectangle are reported.

The computation model we assume is the standard *external memory* (EM) model [1] that prevails in research of I/O-oriented algorithms. In this model, a computer has M words of memory, and a disk of unbounded capacity that has been formatted into *blocks* of size B words. The value of M is at least $2B$, i.e., the memory can accommodate at least two blocks. An *I/O operation* reads a block of data from the disk into memory, or conversely, writes a block of data from the memory into disk. The time of an algorithm is measured as the number of I/Os performed, whereas the space of a structure is measured as the number of disk blocks occupied.

We consider that an information field is $L = o(B)$ words in length (as will be explained shortly, $L = \Omega(B)$ is not interesting). The dataset therefore needs at least NL/B blocks to store. Hence, a *linear complexity* refers to $O(NL/B)$. Likewise, if a query retrieves K objects, $\Omega(1 + KL/B)$ I/Os are compulsory to read their information fields.

We now clarify the definition of an r-redundant structure.

DEFINITION 1. *A structure on P is **r-redundant** if it stores the information field of each object in P at most r times.*

Apparently, every object must have its information field stored at least once in order to answer all range queries correctly. A 1-redundant index is known as a *non-replicating* structure [12] because no information field can be duplicated. Such structures have played an important role in the database field, where most well-known indexes are non-replicating: the *kd-tree* [5, 15], the *R-tree* [4, 8], the *O-tree* [12], to mention just a few. The main reason (see [12]) is that, the dataset cardinality N in practice can be so huge that each information field should be stored only once in order to meet a tight space budget. Today, while linear-size structures are still mandatory to cope with the vast data scale in many applications, constraining each information field to be stored *exactly once* appears excessively stringent. After all, the dollar-per-byte price of hard disks has been dropping continuously, making it realistic to replicate an information field a small number of times.

Motivated by this, we are interested in r-redundant structures where r is a constant. But does duplication of information fields bring any benefit to query efficiency? The answer is yes, and as a matter of fact, very much so. Previous findings have revealed that query time can be reduced by *polynomial* factors, when space is increased only constant times. To be specific, when $L = O(1)$, any 1-redundant structure must entail $\Omega(\sqrt{N/B} + K/B)$ I/Os in answering a query [9, 12] (under certain assumptions, as will be detailed in the next subsection). However, when constant r is *sufficiently* large, there is a linear-size r-redundant structure that guarantees query cost $O((N/B)^\epsilon + K/B)$ for any, arbitrarily small, constant $\epsilon > 0$ [18] (again, for $L = O(1)$).

What the previous research has *not* shown is precisely *how much* benefit can be gained by investing additional space. This leaves open several intriguing questions. For example, if we can store every object twice (i.e., $r = 2$), what is the best query time possible? Conversely, if we aim at achieving query cost, say, $O((N/B)^{1/10} + K/B)$, how many times must each object be stored? At a higher level, if one looks at the query complexity as a function of r, the previous research has resolved the function at two extremes: $r = 1$, and r being arbitrarily big, respectively. In other words, the tradeoff between redundancy and query time within the intermediate range (i.e., from $r = 2$ and onwards) still remains elusive.

This work aims to understand the entire tradeoff at every integer r. On the lower-bound side, we will prove the best query time achievable by any r-redundant structure occupying linear space (for each specific r). On the upper-bound side, we will present r-redundant structures whose query time matches our lower bounds, up to only a small factor.

Why information field anyway? No previous lower-bound study of range search explicitly mentioned any information field. *Storing* an object was implicitly understood as storing its *coordinates*. However, as each coordinate takes up only constant words, demanding each object to be stored constant times appears somewhat unjustified when a hidden constant is permitted in the linear space complexity. This is most obvious for non-replicating structures: what point does it make to force $r = 1$ while allowing the structure to use up to cN/B space for some constant c potentially far greater than 1? One can harvest *polynomial* improvement in query time by setting $r = 2$ and in the meantime, perhaps with some clever tricks, still maintain the space to be at most cN/B.

The introduction of information fields makes certain r-redundant structures especially appealing: those consuming $O(N/B) + rNL/B$ blocks – note that the second term is outside the big-O. Intuitively, they are the most space economical r-redundant structures because other than the storage of information fields, they are allowed to use only $O(N/B)$ extra blocks, thus preventing tricks that "cheat" by keeping $O(NL/B)$ blocks of *search-guiding* data that have nothing to do with information fields. Even though structures with such tricks still consume linear space $O(NL/B)$, one has every right to wonder: why not use the space of those guiding data instead for storing information fields more often? It should be clear that the separation of good r-redundant structures from cheating ones owes to the fact that L can be $\omega(1)$. Conventionally, with $L = O(1)$, $O(N/B) + rNL/B$ is hardly any more meaningful than simply $O(N/B)$.

Indeed, the structures in our contributions all consume $O(N/B) + rNL/B$ space. On the other hand, our lower bounds are proved for structures with $O(NL/B)$ blocks, namely, covering also the cheating structures.

Indulgence in theoretical discussion should not allow us to forget that information fields *do* make sense in practice. In many applications, a user is seldom interested in the coordinates of a point p retrieved; usually, it is the details of the entity represented by p that have triggered the query in the first place. Let the entity be a hotel, for example; then $info(p)$ can include its concrete description (e.g., rating, prices, amenities, etc.). The size of $info(p)$ may not be treated as a constant.

Why $L = o(B)$? It turns out that for $L = B$, there is a trivial 1-redundant structure that occupies $NL/B + O(N/B)$ space, and answers a range query in $O((N/B)^\epsilon + KL/B)$ I/Os for any constant $\epsilon > 0$. We will prove later that such efficiency is impossible for many $L = o(B)$.

The peculiarity at $L = B$ arises from the fact that, the cost of reporting $K \geq 1$ objects is $\Omega(KL/B) = \Omega(K)$, namely, the query algorithm can afford to spend one I/O on each qualifying object. Imagine that we store the information fields of all objects in an array, indexed by object ids. The array uses $NL/B + O(1)$ blocks. Then, create on P an $O(N/B)$-space structure designed for range search with $L = 1$, treating each id as an information field (which is why $L = 1$ suffices). This structure allows us to report the ids of the objects satisfying a query in $O((N/B)^\epsilon + K/B)$ I/Os, after which their information fields can be extracted from the array in $O(K + KL/B) = O(KL/B)$ I/Os. We thus have obtained a 1-redundant index with space $NL/B + O(N/B)$ and query time $O((N/B)^\epsilon + KL/B)$.

The space and query complexities of the above solution remain the same as long as $L = \Omega(B)$. The problem, nonetheless, becomes much more interesting for $L = o(B)$, as we will see shortly.

Average redundancy. In Definition 1, the redundancy of a structure is measured in the maximum number of times an object is stored. In general, an index may choose to store more copies of certain objects than others. Thus, even though the structure may duplicate some objects many times, the total number of information fields stored can be small. The redundancy of such a structure is low in an average sense:

DEFINITION 2. *The **average redundancy** of a structure is the total number of information fields stored, divided by the size N of the dataset.*

Clearly, an r-redundant structure has average redundancy at most r, whereas all structures must have average redundancy at least 1. We will discuss lower bounds with respect to average redundancy.

1.2 Previous results

We now proceed with a review of existing results on range search in the EM model. Focus will be placed on worst-case efficient structures using linear space $O(NL/B)$, as they are the main subject of this paper.

Query upper bounds with linear space. Linear-size 1-redundant indexes have been well studied. The best query time possible is $O(\sqrt{NL/B} + KL/B)$ (as will be clear in Section 1.4). This can be achieved by a slightly modified version [15, 16] of Bentley's kd-tree [5], by ensuring that each leaf node should contain the information fields of $\Theta(B/L)$ objects. The O-tree of Kanth and Singh [12] also guarantees the optimal query time, and has the advantage of being fully dynamic: each insertion and deletion can be supported in $O(\log_B N)$ I/Os amortized (as would be difficult for the kd-tree). Similar performance can also be achieved by the *cross-tree* of Grossi and Italiano [7].

We are not aware of any specific study on r-redundant indexes with $r > 1$. Somewhat related is a result due to Hellerstein et al. [9]. For $L = O(1)$, they showed that when the data points are aligned as a $B \times B$ grid (i.e., $N = B^2$), there is an r-redundant structure that solves a query in $O((N/B)^{1/(2r)} + K/B)$ I/Os. No structure was given in [9] for general datasets.

Query lower bounds and indivisibility assumption. Establishing a lower bound on query time is usually carried out on a certain model of data structures (as well as their accompanying query algorithms), namely, the bound is guaranteed to hold on all the indexes captured by the model, but no guarantee exists for the other structures. For example, under the *comparison-based model*, it is easy to show that the query cost must be $\Omega(\log_B N + KL/B)$. This bound is excessively loose because all linear-size structures incur

polynomial query time in the worst case. Progress has been made in the past decade towards proving polynomial lower bounds. Our discussion below concentrates on $L = O(1)$ which was assumed in the derivation of those bounds.

The model of Kanth and Singh [12] can be thought of as the EM-equivalent of a *pointer machine* in internal memory. It represents a data structure as a tree such that, to visit a node of the tree, a query algorithm must first access all its ancestors, and follow their pointers leading to the node. Kanth and Singh showed that any 1-redundant structure in this model must incur $\Omega(\sqrt{N/B} + K/B)$ I/Os solving a query in the worst case. Due to the model's limitations, their proof does not work for structures that cannot be viewed as a tree, or query algorithms that can jump directly to a node without fetching its ancestors.

To date, the most general modeling of EM structures (for analyzing lower bounds on range search) is due to Hellerstein et al. [9]. Their model imposes no constraint on how a query algorithm may choose the next disk block to access – it can be any block regardless of the I/Os that have already been performed. They developed the *redundancy theorem* which is a powerful tool for analyzing the tradeoff between space and query efficiency for external memory structures, and generalizes earlier results [10, 13, 17] under the same model. For 2D range search, they utilized the theorem to prove the following fact. When $N = B^2$, the average redundancy r (see Definition 2) of an index must satisfy

$$r = \Omega\left(\frac{\log B}{\log A}\right) \tag{1}$$

if the time of processing a query with $K = B$ has to be $O(A)$ where A can be any positive value at most $\sqrt{B}/4$. The fact implies that any linear-size structure must incur query cost $\Omega((N/B)^c + K/B)$ in the worst case for some constant $c > 0$. To see this, notice that when $N = B^2$, $K = B$, and r is at most a constant, (1) indicates $\frac{\log B}{\log A} = O(1)$. This, in turn, means that when B is large enough, $\log A \geq c \cdot \log B$, leading to $A \geq B^c$, where c is some positive constant. Given the choice of N, this translates to $A \geq (N/B)^c$.

Underlying the analysis of [9] is the so-called *indivisibility assumption*, that is, every information field, say $info(p)$ for some object p, must be stored as a *whole* (i.e., with all its bits) in a block. In other words, a structure is not allowed to, for instance, cut $info(p)$ into individual bits, and stores each bit in a different block (at query time, these bits are assembled back into $info(p)$ for reporting). More specifically, the indivisibility assumption lingers in the notion of *flake* (see Definition 5.2 in [9]), which is a subset of objects whose information fields are stored in a common block. This notion is central to proving the redundancy theorem.

Others. There is a rich literature of designing heuristic structures (like the R-tree [4, 8]) that do not have attractive worst-case bounds but are empirically shown to work well on many real datasets. They are not relevant to our work which aims at good worst-case performance.

The preceding survey focused on linear-size structures. Better query time is possible if super-linear space can be afforded. For $L = O(1)$, the *external range search tree* of Arge, Samoladas and Vitter [2] uses $O((N/B)\log_B N/\log_B \log_B N)$ space, and answers a range query in $O(\log_B N + K/B)$ I/Os. The lower bounds of [2, 9, 19] show that this is already optimal under some weak assumptions. It is worth mentioning that, if the query is a *3-sided* rectangle, namely, having the form $(-\infty, x] \times [y_1, y_2]$, it can be solved in $O(\log_B N + K/B)$ I/Os (for constant L) using the *external priority search tree* of [2], which consumes only linear space.

1.3 Weak indivisibility

We mentioned earlier that previous lower bounds were established under the indivisibility assumption that the information field $info(p)$ of an object p is always stored together in the same block (but multiple copies can exist in different blocks). Although this is true in most of the existing indexes (especially the practical ones), it is quite unnecessary from the perspective of designing data structures. This fact already arises even in the traditional scenario where $info(p)$ contains just the coordinates of p. For instance, why can't a structure store the x- and y-coordinates of p in different blocks, as long as the query algorithm can put them together before they are output? This "mild" violation of the indivisibility assumption already escapes the scope of the existing lower bounds.

In this paper, we allow a structure to violate the assumption in a more aggressive manner. First, the bits in the information field $info(p)$ of an object p can be freely divided, and stored across different blocks. Furthermore, the structure is even allowed to store *some* bits of $info(p)$ more often than others. The only constraint is that, when $info(p)$ is reported, each of its bits must have been retrieved from a block, rather than being computed. We refer to this requirement as the *weak indivisibility assumption*. Accordingly, we call the original atomic treatment of information fields as *strong indivisibility assumption*.

An immediate remark concerns the definition of average redundancy – Definition 2 is no longer well defined if some bits of $info(p)$ exist more frequently in the structure than others. However, a straightforward extension to the bit level will eliminate this issue. Denote by w the number of bits in a word. We now redefine the *average redundancy* of a structure as the ratio between

- the total number of stored bits from object's information fields, and

- NwL, i.e., the total number of bits in the information fields of all objects.

Another remark concerns why our requirement is a *weak* form of the indivisibility assumption. Subtle as it may be, our requirement still falls within the grand indivisibility assumption, whose removal would even allow the bits of information fields (of the objects qualifying a query) to be *computed*! As mentioned earlier, we do not allow a data structure to be this powerful. Nonetheless, weak indivisibility appears to be a meaningful concept to coin, given that it enables us to capture a wider class of structures than was previously possible under the strong indivisibility assumption. It is worth mentioning that efforts towards removing the ultimate indivisibility assumption have been reported in [11, 20], but those efforts do not concern range search.

Finally, let us point out that the notion of redundancy in our model applies only to bits taken *directly* from information fields. A pointer to an information field or a hash value computed from any portion of the information field is not counted as redundancy. A structure is permitted to store as much such information as needed, as long as the total space is $O(NL/B)$.

1.4 Our results

The first main theorem of this paper is:

THEOREM 1. *Let τ be an integer at least 2, and $L = B^\mu$, where μ can be any constant satisfying $0 \le \mu < 1$. For any constant ϵ satisfying $0 < \epsilon \le 1/\tau$, to achieve query cost*

$$O((NL/B)^{(1/\tau)-\epsilon} + KL/B)$$

under the weak indivisibility assumption, in the worst case a structure using $O(NL/B)$ space must store at least

$$\tau NwL(1 - o(1))$$

bits from the information fields of the underlying objects (recall that w is the word length).

The theorem implies:

COROLLARY 1. *For $L = B^\mu$ where $0 \le \mu < 1$, under the weak indivisibility assumption, if a linear-space index has average redundancy no more than an integer $r \ge 1$, it is impossible to guarantee query cost $O((NL/B)^{\frac{1}{r+1}-\epsilon} + KL/B)$, no matter how small the positive constant ϵ is.*

To understand the corollary, notice that, as shown in Theorem 1, a structure must store $(r + 1)NwL(1 - o(1))$ bits from objects' information fields to achieve query time $O((NL/B)^{\frac{1}{r+1}-\epsilon} + KL/B)$. However, a structure with average redundancy at most r stores no more than $rNwL$ such bits, i.e., $NwL(1 - o(1))$ bits less than needed.

As mentioned in Section 1.1, when $L = B$, there is a linear-size 1-redundant structure with query cost $O((N/B)^\epsilon + KL/B)$ for any constant $\epsilon > 0$. Hence, Theorem 1 shows that the problem becomes much harder as soon as L drops by a polynomial factor B^δ for an arbitrarily small $\delta > 0$.

To obtain our result, we applied the analytical framework of the redundancy theorem [9] with, however, several new ideas. The necessity of those ideas is due to two reasons. First, apparently, as the original framework makes the strong indivisibility assumption, it needs to be extended in a non-conventional way so that the assumption can be relaxed. Second, while the framework is good for establishing *asymptotic* lower bounds of average redundancy, it is not powerful enough to argue for actual, *constant-revealed*, lower bounds. More specifically, the hidden constant in (1) is $1/12$ according to the proof in [9]. Intuitively, in our context, this says that a structure must consume at least $\frac{r}{12}NL/B$ blocks which, however, is far smaller than the target rNL/B as required to prove Theorem 1.

As mentioned in Section 1.2, when $L = O(1)$ and the data points form a $B \times B$ grid, there is an r-redundant structure [9] with query complexity $O((N/B)^{1/(2r)} + K/B)$. Theorem 1 reveals that this tradeoff is impossible for general data (even if L remains a constant). Instead, as our second main result, we prove:

THEOREM 2. *For any integer $r \geq 1$, there is an r-redundant structure that consumes $rNL/B + O(N/B)$ space, and answers a query in $KL/B + O((NL/B)^{1/(r+1)})$ I/Os.*

The query time of our structure is optimal up to only a small factor (according to Corollary 1). We remind the reader that the term rNL/B in the space cost is outside the big-O.

2. INDEXABILITY THEOREM FOR 2-REDUNDANCY

In this section, we will prove Theorem 1 in the special case of $\tau = 3$. This allows us to explain the core of our technique without being distracted by the extra mathematical subtleties in the proof for arbitrary τ (as will be presented in the next section). Derivation of our lower bound theorems considers that the word length is $w = \Theta(\log N)$ bits.

Let p be an object in the dataset P. We refer to each bit of $info(p)$ as an *information bit*, that is, $info(p)$ has wL information bits. In general, an information bit is uniquely characterized by two factors: (i) the object p that it belongs to, and (ii) the position in $info(p)$ that it is at. With this notion, we slightly rephrase Theorem 1 under $\tau = 3$ for easy referencing.

THEOREM 3. *Let $L = B^\mu$, where μ can be any constant satisfying $0 \leq \mu < 1$. For any constant ϵ satisfying $0 < \epsilon \leq 1/3$, to achieve query cost $O((NL/B)^{(1/3)-\epsilon} + KL/B)$ under the weak indivisibility assumption, in the worst case a structure using $O(NL/B)$ space must store at least*

$$3NwL(1 - o(1))$$

information bits.

The theorem indicates that no 2-redundant structure can ensure query time $O((NL/B)^{(1/3)-\epsilon} + KL/B)$; see Corollary 1.

Our discussion concentrates on a set P of points forming an $n \times n$ grid, namely, $N = n^2$. We choose n such that the query cost is $O(nL/B)$ when $K = n$ points are reported. Towards this purpose, we solve n from:

$$\left(\frac{n^2 L}{B}\right)^{\frac{1}{3}-\epsilon} = \frac{nL}{B}$$

$$\Leftrightarrow n = \left(\frac{B}{L}\right)^{\frac{\epsilon+2/3}{2\epsilon+1/3}} = B^{\frac{(\epsilon+2/3)(1-\mu)}{2\epsilon+1/3}} \quad (2)$$

Since $\mu < 1$, n is always greater 1. Furthermore, as $\epsilon \leq 1/3$, $nL/B = (n^2L/B)^{(1/3)-\epsilon} \geq 1$. For simplicity, let us assume that $\sqrt{n}$ is an integer. This assumption will be removed at the end of the section.

From now on, we will consider only queries with output size $K = n$. Note that each such query must report nwL information bits. Given the choice of n in (2), the query is answered in

$$O((n^2L/B)^{(1/3)-\epsilon} + nL/B) = O(nL/B)$$

I/Os (remember $nL/B \geq 1$, that is, the query must perform at least one I/O). Hence, we can assume that its cost is at most $\alpha nL/B$ for some constant $\alpha > 0$.

Next, we define a notion called *bit-flake* to replace the concept of *flake* in [9].

DEFINITION 3. *Let q be a query with output size n. A **bit-flake of q** is a non-empty set f of bits satisfying two conditions:*

- *All the bits in f are stored in an identical block that is accessed by q.*
- *Each bit in f is an information bit of an object qualifying q.*

To illustrate the definition in an alternative manner, consider a block b accessed by q. Let X be the set of all information bits in b that belong to qualifying objects. Then, any non-empty subset of X is a bit-flake.

LEMMA 1. *A query with output size n has at least*

$$\frac{nwL}{s} - \frac{\alpha nL}{B}$$

pair-wise disjoint bit-flakes of size $s > 0$.

PROOF. We use the following algorithm to collect a number of bit-flakes needed to prove the lemma. Assume that the query accessed $z \leq \alpha nL/B$ blocks, denoted as $b_1, ..., b_z$, respectively (ordering does not matter). For each $i \in [1, z]$, let X_i be the set of information bits in b_i that (i) belong to objects qualifying q, and (ii) are absent from the preceding blocks $b_1, ..., b_{i-1}$. Clearly, $X_1, ..., X_z$ are pair-wise disjoint. Furthermore, $\sum_{i=1}^{z} |X_i| = nwL$ because each information bit of every qualifying object is in exactly one X_i.

From X_i, we form $\lfloor |X_i|/s \rfloor$ pair-wise disjoint bit-flakes, by dividing arbitrarily the bits of X_i into groups of size s, leaving out at most $s - 1$ bits. The bit-flakes thus created from $X_1, ..., X_z$ are mutually disjoint. The number of those bit-flakes equals

$$\sum_{i=1}^{z} \left\lfloor \frac{|X_i|}{s} \right\rfloor > \sum_{i=1}^{z} \left(\frac{|X_i|}{s} - 1\right) = \frac{nwL}{s} - z \geq \frac{nwL}{s} - \frac{\alpha nL}{B}$$

as claimed. $\square$

We construct $3n$ queries as follows. Recall that the points of P form an $n \times n$ grid. Each row or column of the grid is taken as a query, referred to as a *row query* or *column query*, respectively. This has defined $2n$ queries. Each of the remaining n queries is a $\sqrt{n} \times \sqrt{n}$ square, and is therefore called a *square query*. Specifically, the square touches $\sqrt{n}$ consecutive rows and columns of the grid, respectively. All the n square queries are mutually disjoint, and together cover the entire P. Figure 2 illustrates these queries for $n = 16$.

By Lemma 1, the $3n$ queries define in total at least $3n(\frac{nwL}{s} - \frac{\alpha nL}{B})$ bit-flakes of size s (we will decide the value of s later), such that the bit-flakes from the same query are pair-wise disjoint. Refer to all these bit-flakes as *canonical bit-flakes*. Recall that the bits of a bit-flake f are in a common block b. We say that b *contains* f.

LEMMA 2. *Let b be a block, and t the number of information bits in b that appear in at least one canonical bit-flake. Then, b can contain at most*

$$\frac{t}{s} + \frac{3L\sqrt{n} \cdot B^2 w^3}{s^3}$$

canonical bit-flakes.

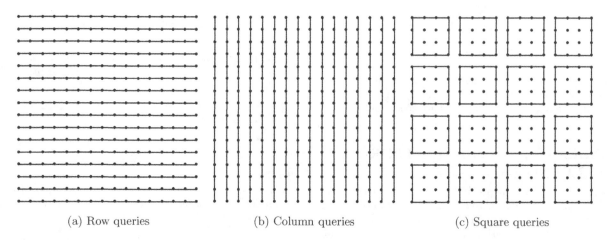

(a) Row queries   (b) Column queries   (c) Square queries

Figure 2: Hard dataset and queries on a 16×16 grid

PROOF. Let F_{row} be the set of canonical bit-flakes that are contained in b, and are defined from row queries. Define F_{col} and F_{sqr} similarly with respect to column and square queries. The total number of information bits covered by at least one bit-flake in $F_{row} \cup F_{col} \cup F_{sqr}$ is t. Note that the bit-flakes in F_{row} are mutually disjoint because no two row queries retrieve a common object. The same is true for F_{col} and F_{sqr}, respectively. Hence, it holds from the set inclusion-exclusion principle that:

$$
\begin{aligned}
\sum_{f \in F_{row} \cup F_{col} \cup F_{sqr}} |f| \;\; & - \\
\sum_{\forall f_{row} \in F_{row}, f_{col} \in F_{col}} |f_{row} \cap f_{col}| \;\; & - \\
\sum_{\forall f_{row} \in F_{row}, f_{sqr} \in F_{sqr}} |f_{row} \cap f_{sqr}| \;\; & - \\
\sum_{\forall f_{col} \in F_{col}, f_{sqr} \in F_{sqr}} |f_{col} \cap f_{sqr}| \;\; \leq & \; \left| \bigcup_{f \in F_{row} \cup F_{col} \cup F_{sqr}} f \right| \\
= & \; t. \qquad (3)
\end{aligned}
$$

Consider any bit-flakes f_{row}, f_{col} and f_{sqr} that are from F_{row}, F_{col} and F_{sqr}, respectively. There are at most wL bits in $f_{row} \cap f_{col}$ since a row query and a column query share exactly 1 object in their results (notice that the bits in $f_{row} \cap f_{col}$ must belong to the information field of that object). On the other hand, a row query and a square query share at most $\sqrt{n}$ objects in their results. It follows that $|f_{row} \cap f_{sqr}| \leq wL\sqrt{n}$. Similarly, it holds that $|f_{col} \cap f_{sqr}| \leq wL\sqrt{n}$.

As the bit-flakes in F_{row} are pair-wise disjoint, we have $|F_{row}| \leq t/s$, which is at most Bw/s because a block has Bw bits. Likewise, the sizes of F_{col} and F_{sqr} are both at most Bw/s. Hence:

$$
\begin{aligned}
\sum_{f_{row} \in F_{row}, f_{col} \in F_{col}} |f_{row} \cap f_{col}| \;\; & \leq \;\; wL \left(\frac{Bw}{s} \right)^2 \\
\sum_{f_{row} \in F_{row}, f_{sqr} \in F_{sqr}} |f_{row} \cap f_{sqr}| \;\; & \leq \;\; wL\sqrt{n} \left(\frac{Bw}{s} \right)^2 \\
\sum_{f_{col} \in F_{col}, f_{sqr} \in F_{sqr}} |f_{col} \cap f_{sqr}| \;\; & \leq \;\; wL\sqrt{n} \left(\frac{Bw}{s} \right)^2 .
\end{aligned}
$$

Plugging the above inequalities into (3) gives:

$$
\begin{aligned}
\sum_{f \in F_{row} \cup F_{col} \cup F_{sqr}} |f| \;\; & \leq \;\; t + wL \left(\frac{Bw}{s} \right)^2 + 2wL\sqrt{n} \left(\frac{Bw}{s} \right)^2 \\
& \leq \;\; t + \frac{3L\sqrt{n} \cdot B^2 w^3}{s^2}
\end{aligned}
$$

As $|f| = s$ for each f on the left hand side, we obtain:

$$
|F_{row} \cup F_{col} \cup F_{sqr}| \leq \frac{t}{s} + \frac{3L\sqrt{n} \cdot B^2 w^3}{s^3}
$$

thus completing the proof. $\square$

We are now ready to prove a lower bound on the total number of information bits that must be stored. Let λ be the number of blocks occupied by the underlying structure. As the structure consumes $O(NL/B)$ space, we know:

$$
\lambda \leq \beta NL/B = \beta n^2 L/B
$$

for some constant $\beta > 0$. Denote by t_i $(1 \leq i \leq \lambda)$ the number of information bits in the i-th block that appear in at least one canonical bit-flake. Combining Lemma 2 and the fact that there are at least $3n(\frac{nwL}{s} - \frac{\alpha nL}{B})$ canonical bit-flakes, it holds that:

$$
\sum_{i=1}^{\lambda} \left(\frac{t_i}{s} + \frac{3L\sqrt{n} \cdot B^2 w^3}{s^3} \right) \;\; \geq \;\; 3n \left(\frac{nwL}{s} - \frac{\alpha nL}{B} \right)
$$

136

Hence:

$$\sum_{i=1}^{\lambda} t_i \geq 3ns\left(\frac{nwL}{s} - \frac{\alpha nL}{B}\right) - s\sum_{i=1}^{\lambda} \frac{3L\sqrt{n} \cdot B^2 w^3}{s^3}$$

$$= 3ns\left(\frac{nwL}{s} - \frac{\alpha nL}{B}\right) - \lambda \cdot \frac{3L\sqrt{n} \cdot B^2 w^3}{s^2}$$

$$\geq 3n^2 wL - \frac{3\alpha n^2 sL}{B} - \frac{\beta n^2 L}{B} \cdot \frac{3L\sqrt{n} \cdot B^2 w^3}{s^2}$$

$$= 3n^2 wL\left(1 - \frac{\alpha s}{Bw} - \frac{\beta BLw^2\sqrt{n}}{s^2}\right) \qquad (4)$$

LEMMA 3. *We can set $s = B^c$ for some $c > 0$ such that both $\alpha s/(Bw)$ and $\beta BLw^2\sqrt{n}/s^2$ are $o(1)$ when B is large enough.*

PROOF. First, note that $w = \Theta(\log N) = \Theta(\log n) = \Theta(\log B)$ because the term $\frac{(\epsilon+2/3)(1-\mu)}{2\epsilon+1/3}$ in (2) is a constant. Hence

$$\frac{\alpha s}{Bw} = O\left(\frac{B^c}{B\log B}\right)$$

which is $o(1)$ when:

$$c \leq 1. \qquad (5)$$

Recall that $L = B^\mu$ where $0 \leq \mu < 1$. This together with (2) gives:

$$\frac{\beta BLw^2\sqrt{n}}{s^2} = O\left(\frac{B \cdot B^\mu \cdot B^{\frac{(\epsilon+2/3)(1-\mu)}{4\epsilon+2/3}}\log^2 B}{B^{2c}}\right)$$

$$= O\left(\frac{B^{1+\mu+\frac{(\epsilon+2/3)(1-\mu)}{4\epsilon+2/3}}\log^2 B}{B^{2c}}\right)$$

which is $o(1)$ when:

$$1 + \mu + \frac{(\epsilon+2/3)(1-\mu)}{4\epsilon+2/3} < 2c. \qquad (6)$$

A value of c satisfying (5) and (6) exists when:

$$1 + \mu + \frac{(\epsilon+2/3)(1-\mu)}{4\epsilon+2/3} < 2$$

$$\Leftrightarrow \frac{(\epsilon+2/3)(1-\mu)}{4\epsilon+2/3} < 1-\mu$$

$$\Leftrightarrow \epsilon + 2/3 < 4\epsilon + 2/3$$

which is always true for $\epsilon > 0$. $\square$

Therefore, by fixing s as stated in the lemma, we can rewrite (4) into

$$\sum_{i=1}^{\lambda} t_i \geq 3n^2 wL(1 - o(1)) = 3NwL(1 - o(1)).$$

We thus conclude the proof of Theorem 3.

It is worth pointing out that the proof does not work for $\mu = 1$, because in this case (6) requires $c > 1$ which conflicts (5). This is consistent with the discussion in Section 1.1 that better query time is possible for $L = B$.

Recall that on a $B \times B$ grid (i.e., $n = B$), a 2-redundant structure can achieve query time $O((N/B)^{1/4} + K/B)$ when

$L = O(1)$ (see Section 1.2). The query complexity in Theorem 3 is exactly $O((N/B)^{1/4} + K/B)$ by setting $\epsilon = 1/12$ and $\mu = 0$. To show that no structure can guarantee such cost, our proof used a $B^{1.5} \times B^{1.5}$ grid (the exponent in (2) equals 1.5). In other words, the problem in fact becomes harder than when n increases from B to $B^{1.5}$.

How is our technique different from [9]? Our proof was inspired by the analysis in [9]. In particular, we owe the method of flake counting to [9], which is the central ingredient for obtaining a tradeoff between space and query time. Nevertheless, some new ideas were deployed to obtain Theorem 3, as summarized below.

The first one is to construct flakes at the bit level, which led to the introduction of bit-flakes (Definition 3). This proved to be a crucial step towards eliminating the strong indivisibility assumption. Naturally, it also demands redesigning several components in flaking counting, most notably (i) the approach described in the proof of Lemma 1 for collecting sufficiently many disjoint bit-flakes from a query, and (ii) in Lemma 2 bounding the number of canonical bit-flakes per block with respect to the number t of bits participating in at least one canonical bit-flake.

The second idea is to decide n in such a way that every query with output size n incurs in $O(nL/B)$ I/Os (see Equation 2). In retrospect, the idea sounds fairly reasonable. It forces the n objects retrieved by each query to be stored in a compact manner. That is, they must be covered by asymptotically the minimum of blocks, noticing that nL/B blocks are compulsory for their storage. As a result, these blocks do not contain much information useful for answering other queries. Intuitively, the effect is that, the data structure must pack all the N objects in $O(NL/B)$ blocks just to answer row queries, pack them again in another $O(NL/B)$ blocks for column queries, and yet again for square queries. Hence, the redundancy needs to be roughly 3. Of course, for the above idea to work, queries should have small overlaps in their results. It turned out that an overlap of no more than $\sqrt{n}$ objects suffices.

The third idea was applied in Lemma 2, which replaced *Johnson's bound* in [9] (see Theorem 5.3 there). In fact, applying Johnson's bound in Lemma 2 would tell us that the number of canonical bit-flakes in b is at most $s/(wL\sqrt{n})$. This is quite different from what we have in Lemma 2, and does not seem to be tight enough for establishing our final result. At a higher level, the cause of the ineffectiveness behind Johnson's bound here is that, in general, the bound can be loose when there are only a small number of canonical bit-flakes. This indeed happens in our proof, because the size s of a canonical bit-flake can be large (the value of c in (12) is close to 1 for small ϵ and μ).

Finally, Lemma 3 is what really turns the flake-counting method into a working argument. The way that s is decided is specific to our context, and does not have a counterpart in [9].

Non-integer $\sqrt{n}$. In this case, set $n' = (\lceil\sqrt{n}\rceil)^2$. Clearly, $n' = \Theta(n)$. It is easy to adapt our proof to work instead with $N = (n')^2$ points forming an $n' \times n'$ grid. We will do so explicitly in the next section.

3. GENERAL INDEXABILITY THEOREM

This section serves as the proof of Theorem 1. Our argument is analogous to the one in the previous section, but includes extra details for handling general τ. Remember that τ is a constant integer at least 2.

As before, we consider a set P of points forming an $n \times n$ grid (i.e., $N = n^2$), where the value of n makes the query cost bounded by $O(nL/B)$ when the output size is $K = n$. Recall that the structure under our analysis has query cost $O((NL/B)^{(1/\tau)-\epsilon} + KL/B)$. We choose:

$$n = \left\lceil (n_0)^{1/(\tau-1)} \right\rceil^{\tau-1} \qquad (7)$$

where

$$n_0 = B^{\frac{\epsilon+(\tau-1)/\tau}{2\epsilon+(\tau-2)/\tau}(1-\mu)}.$$

Our choice ensures that $n^{1/(\tau-1)}$ is an integer. The next lemma is rudimentary:

LEMMA 4. *The following are true:*

$$n = \Theta(n_0)$$
$$(n^2 L/B)^{(1/\tau)-\epsilon} = \Theta(nL/B)$$
$$nL/B \geq 1$$

PROOF. Set $x = \lceil (n_0)^{1/(\tau-1)} \rceil$. Hence, $n_0 > (x-1)^{\tau-1}$, and $n = x^{\tau-1}$. Consider sufficiently large B so that $x \geq 2$. In this case:

$$n \leq (2(x-1))^{\tau-1} < 2^{\tau-1} n_0 = O(n_0).$$

Then, $n = \Theta(n_0)$ follows from the obvious fact that $n \geq n_0$. It can be easily verified that n_0 satisfies $((n_0)^2 L/B)^{(1/\tau)-\epsilon} = n_0 L/B$. Hence:

$$(n^2 L/B)^{(1/\tau)-\epsilon} = \Theta\left(((n_0)^2 L/B)^{(1/\tau)-\epsilon}\right)$$
$$= \Theta(n_0 L/B) = \Theta(nL/B).$$

Finally, $nL/B \geq n_0 L/B = ((n_0)^2 L/B)^{(1/\tau)-\epsilon} \geq 1$ because $\epsilon \leq 1/\tau$. $\square$

It follows that $\log n = \Theta(\log n_0) = \Theta(\log B)$ (recall that ϵ, τ and μ are constants). The subsequent analysis concentrates on queries with output size n. Every such query can be answered in time

$$O((n^2 L/B)^{(1/\tau)-\epsilon} + nL/B)$$

which is $O(nL/B)$ by Lemma 4. Hence, we can assume that its cost is no more than $\alpha nL/B$ for some constant $\alpha > 0$.

An axis-parallel rectangle is said to have *size* $l_x \times l_y$ if it covers exactly $l_x \cdot l_y$ points of P which come from l_x (l_y) columns (rows) in the grid underlying P. Equivalently, this rectangle intersects with l_x (l_y) consecutive columns (rows) of the grid.

We consider τ query sets, referred to as *set 0, ..., set $\tau-1$* respectively, each of which consists of n queries. Specifically, the queries in set i ($0 \leq i \leq \tau-1$) have the same size

$$n^{i/(\tau-1)} \times n^{(\tau-1-i)/(\tau-1)},$$

are pair-wise disjoint, and together cover the entire grid. The total number of queries from all τ sets is τn.

We still use Definition 3 to define *bit-flake*. Lemma 1 still holds in our current context. Furthermore, define a *canonical flake* in the same way as in Section 2. Hence, the $n\tau$ queries constructed earlier give rise to at least

$$n\tau \left(\frac{nwL}{s} - \frac{\alpha nL}{B} \right)$$

canonical bit-flakes. Lemma 2, however, no longer holds, so we provide its counterpart:

LEMMA 5. *Let b be a block, and t the number of information bits in b that appear in at least one canonical bit-flake. Then, b can contain at most*

$$\frac{t}{s} + \frac{n^{(\tau-2)/(\tau-1)} \cdot \tau(\tau-1) \cdot LB^2 w^3}{2s^3}$$

canonical bit-flakes.

PROOF. Recall that our queries are divided into set 0, ..., set $\tau-1$, each of which contains queries with the same size. Let F_i ($i \in [0, \tau-1]$) be the set of canonical bit-flakes that are contained in b, and defined from queries of set i. The bit-flakes in each F_i are mutually disjoint. The total number of information bits that appear in at least one bit-flake in $F_0 \cup ... \cup F_{\tau-1}$ is t. By the set exclusion-inclusion principle, we have:

$$\sum_{f \in (F_0 \cup ... \cup F_{\tau-1})} |f| \; -$$
$$\sum_{\forall i, j \text{ s.t. } i \neq j} \; \sum_{\forall f_1 \in F_i, f_2 \in F_j} |f_1 \cap f_2| \leq$$
$$\left| \bigcup_{f \in (F_0 \cup ... \cup F_{\tau-1})} f \right| = t. \qquad (8)$$

We now show that

$$|f_1 \cap f_2| \leq wL \cdot n^{(\tau-2)/(\tau-1)} \qquad (9)$$

for any $f_1 \in F_i$ and $f_2 \in F_j$ with $i \neq j$. Without loss of generality, suppose $i < j$. Let q_1 (q_2) be the query from which f_1 (f_2) was defined. In other words, q_1 and q_2 have sizes $n^{i/(\tau-1)} \times n^{(\tau-1-i)/(\tau-1)}$ and $n^{j/(\tau-1)} \times n^{(\tau-1-j)/(\tau-1)}$, respectively. Let $l_x \times l_y$ be the size of $q_1 \cap q_2$. It holds that

$$l_x \leq n^{i/(\tau-1)}$$
$$l_y \leq n^{(\tau-1-j)/(\tau-1)}.$$

Therefore, $q_1 \cap q_2$ covers at most

$$l_x \cdot l_y \leq n^{(\tau-1-j+i)/(\tau-1)} \leq n^{(\tau-2)/(\tau-1)}$$

points of P. As $f_1 \cap f_2$ is a subset of the information bits belonging those points, (9) follows from the fact that a point's information field has wL bits.

Hence, (8) leads to:

$$\sum_{f \in (F_0 \cup ... \cup F_{\tau-1})} |f| \; -$$
$$\sum_{\forall i, j \text{ s.t. } i \neq j} \; \sum_{\forall f_1 \in F_i, f_2 \in F_j} \left(wL \cdot n^{(\tau-2)/(\tau-1)} \right) \leq t$$

The disjointness of the bit-flakes in F_i implies that $|F_i| \leq t/s \leq Bw/s$, with which the above inequality gives

$$\sum_{f \in (F_0 \cup \ldots \cup F_{\tau-1})} |f| \ -$$

$$\sum_{\forall i,\, j \text{ s.t. } i \neq j} \left(wL \cdot n^{(\tau-2)/(\tau-1)} \cdot \frac{B^2 w^2}{s^2} \right) \ \leq \ t$$

$$\Rightarrow \sum_{f \in (F_0 \cup \ldots \cup F_{\tau-1})} |f| \ -$$

$$n^{(\tau-2)/(\tau-1)} \cdot \frac{\tau(\tau-1)}{2} \cdot \frac{LB^2 w^3}{s^2} \ \leq \ t.$$

As $|f| = s$ for every $f \in F_0 \cup \ldots \cup F_{\tau-1}$, we arrive at:

$$|F_0 \cup \ldots \cup F_{\tau-1}| \leq \frac{t}{s} + n^{(\tau-2)/(\tau-1)} \cdot \frac{\tau(\tau-1)}{2} \cdot \frac{LB^2 w^3}{s^3}$$

completing the proof. $\square$

As the underlying structure uses $O(n^2 L/B)$ space, we can assume that it occupies $\lambda \leq \beta n^2 L/B$ blocks for some constant $\beta > 0$. Define t_i ($1 \leq i \leq \lambda$) as the number of bits that are stored in the i-th block, and appear in at least one canonical bit-flake. The previous lemma, combined with the fact that there are at least $n\tau(\frac{nwL}{s} - \frac{\alpha nL}{B})$ canonical flakes, shows:

$$\sum_{i=1}^{\lambda} \left(\frac{t_i}{s} + \frac{n^{(\tau-2)/(\tau-1)} \cdot \tau(\tau-1) \cdot LB^2 w^3}{2s^3} \right) \geq$$

$$n\tau \left(\frac{nwL}{s} - \frac{\alpha nL}{B} \right)$$

Hence:

$$\sum_{i=1}^{\lambda} t_i \ \geq \ ns\tau \left(\frac{nwL}{s} - \frac{\alpha nL}{B} \right) -$$

$$\lambda \cdot \frac{n^{(\tau-2)/(\tau-1)} \cdot \tau(\tau-1) \cdot LB^2 w^3}{2s^2}$$

$$\geq \ n^2 \tau wL - \frac{\alpha n^2 \tau s L}{B} -$$

$$\frac{\beta n^2 L}{B} \cdot \frac{n^{(\tau-2)/(\tau-1)} \cdot \tau(\tau-1) \cdot LB^2 w^3}{2s^2}$$

$$= \ n^2 \tau wL \left(1 - \frac{\alpha s}{Bw} - \right.$$

$$\left. \frac{(\tau-1)\beta \cdot BLw^2 \cdot n^{(\tau-2)/(\tau-1)}}{2s^2} \right). \quad (10)$$

LEMMA 6. *We can set $s = B^c$ for some $c > 0$ such that both $\frac{\alpha s}{Bw}$ and $\frac{(\tau-1)\beta \cdot BLw^2 \cdot n^{(\tau-2)/(\tau-1)}}{2s^2}$ are $o(1)$ when B is large enough.*

PROOF. First, note that $w = \Theta(\log N) = \Theta(\log n) = \Theta(\log B)$. With $s = B^c$, we have

$$\frac{\alpha s}{Bw} = O\left(\frac{B^c}{B \log B} \right)$$

which is $o(1)$ when:

$$c \leq 1. \quad (11)$$

Applying $L = B^\mu$, (7) and Lemma 4, we know:

$$\frac{(\tau-1)\beta \cdot BLw^2 \cdot n^{(\tau-2)/(\tau-1)}}{2s^2}$$

$$= O\left(\frac{B^{1+\mu+\frac{\epsilon+(\tau-1)/\tau}{2\epsilon+(\tau-2)/\tau} \cdot \frac{\tau-2}{\tau-1}(1-\mu)} \cdot \log^2 B}{B^{2c}} \right)$$

which is $o(1)$ when:

$$1 + \mu + \frac{\epsilon+(\tau-1)/\tau}{2\epsilon+(\tau-2)/\tau} \cdot \frac{\tau-2}{\tau-1} \cdot (1-\mu) \ < \ 2c. \quad (12)$$

A value of c satisfying (11) and (12) exists when:

$$1 + \mu + \frac{\epsilon+(\tau-1)/\tau}{2\epsilon+(\tau-2)/\tau} \cdot \frac{\tau-2}{\tau-1} \cdot (1-\mu) \ < \ 2$$

$$\Leftrightarrow \frac{\epsilon\tau + (\tau-1)}{2\epsilon\tau + (\tau-2)} \cdot \frac{\tau-2}{\tau-1} \ < \ 1$$

$$\Leftrightarrow \epsilon\tau(\tau-2) \ < \ 2\epsilon\tau(\tau-1)$$

$$\Leftrightarrow \tau - 2 \ < \ 2\tau - 2$$

which is always true (recall that $\tau \geq 2$). $\square$

Therefore, setting s as in the above lemma, (10) becomes

$$\sum_{i=1}^{\lambda} t_i \geq n^2 \tau wL(1 - o(1)) = \tau NwL(1 - o(1))$$

concluding the proof of Theorem 1.

4. r-REDUNDANT STRUCTURES

Next, we present r-redundant structures achieving the performance in Theorem 2, and thereby, nearly matching the lower bound of Theorem 1. For simplicity, we assume that the points in the dataset P are in general position, such that no two points in P share the same x- or y-coordinate. This assumption can be removed by standard tie-breaking techniques.

Preliminary: *external interval tree.* This structure, due to Arge and Vitter [3], settles the following *stabbing problem*. The dataset consists of N intervals in the real domain. Given a real value q, a *stabbing query* reports all the data intervals enclosing q. The external interval tree consumes $O(N/B)$ space, and answers a stabbing query in $O(\log_B N + K/B)$ I/Os, where K is the number of reported intervals.

The first 1-redundant structure. Let us start by giving a 1-redundant structure occupying $NL/B + \sqrt{NL/B} + O(N/B)$ space, and solving a query in $KL/B + O(\sqrt{NL/B})$ I/Os. Note that the space cost is worse than required in Theorem 2. The structure in fact has been used as a component in the *range search tree* of Chazelle [6] and its external counterpart [2]. Our version here differs only in parameterization (as will be pointed out shortly). Nevertheless, we describe it in full anyway because the details are useful in clarifying general r-redundant indexes later.

We introduce a parameter $\rho = \sqrt{NL/B}$. Also, define a *slab* as the part of data space $\mathbb{R}^2$ between and including two vertical lines $x = c_1$ and $x = c_2$. To explain our structure, let us sort the points of P in ascending order of their x-coordinates. Partition the sorted list into ρ segments with the same number of points, except possibly the last segment.

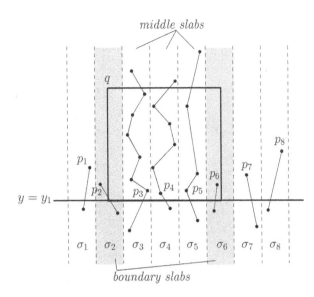

Figure 3: Answering a range query ($\rho = 8$)

Denote by P_i ($1 \leq i \leq \rho$) the set of points in the i-th segment. Hence, for any i_1, i_2 such that $1 \leq i_1 < i_2 \leq \rho$, each point in P_{i_1} has an x-coordinate smaller than the x-coordinates of all the points in P_{i_2}. Denote by σ_i the slab determined by the smallest and largest x-coordinates in P_i.

For each P_i, sort the points there in ascending order of their y-coordinates. From now on, we will treat P_i as a sorted list, abusing the notation slightly. Naturally, *the j-th point of P_i* refers to the j-th point in the sorted list. If $2 \leq j \leq |P_i|$, the *predecessor* of the j-th point is the $(j-1)$-st point. As a special case, the predecessor of the first point in P_i is defined as a dummy point whose y-coordinate is $-\infty$. The x-coordinate of the dummy point is unimportant.

We store the information fields of the points of P_i in an array A_i (respecting the ordering of those points). The array occupies at most $1 + L|P_i|/B$ blocks, i.e., all but the last block contains B words of data. Hence, arrays $A_1, ..., A_\rho$ require in total at most $\rho + NL/B = NL/B + \sqrt{NL/B}$ blocks. Since every object's information field is already in an array, no more information field can be stored in the rest of the index. However, we are still allowed $O(N/B)$ extra space, which is sufficient to store the *coordinates* of each object constant times. As discussed below, we use that space to create an external interval tree $\mathcal{T}$.

$\mathcal{T}$ is built on N one-dimensional intervals obtained as follows. From each P_i, we generate a set I_i of $|P_i|$ intervals. Each point $p \in P_i$ *determines* an interval in I_i having the form (y_{pred}, y_p), where y_p is the y-coordinate of p, and y_{pred} is that of its predecessor. We associate this interval with a pointer to the block of array A_i where $info(p)$ is stored, so that when the interval is fetched, we can jump to that block in one I/O. $\mathcal{T}$ indexes the union of $I_1, ..., I_\rho$. As $\mathcal{T}$ uses $O(N/B)$ blocks, the overall space of our structure is $NL/B + \sqrt{NL/B} + O(N/B)$.

To answer a range query with search region $q = [x_1, x_2] \times [y_1, y_2]$, we first identify the (at most) two *boundary slabs* that contain the left and right edges of q, respectively (this takes $O(\log_B N)$ I/Os with another B-tree on the slabs'

x-ranges; we omit this B-tree in the sequel because it is straightforward). Denote them respectively as σ_{i_1} and σ_{i_2} with $i_1 \leq i_2$. Scan arrays A_{i_1} and A_{i_2} completely to report the qualifying objects there. Since each array has at most N/ρ objects, the cost of the scan is

$$O\left(\frac{NL}{\rho B}\right) = O(\sqrt{NL/B}).$$

In the example of Figure 3 (where $\rho = 8$), the boundary slabs are σ_2 and σ_6, in which all the objects are examined.

The other qualifying objects can lie only in slabs σ_i where i ranges from $i_1 + 1$ to $i_2 - 1$. Refer to those slabs as the *middle slabs*. For each such slab σ_i, we find the lowest point p_i in σ_i on or above the horizontal line $y = y_1$. After this, jump to the block in A_i where $info(p_i)$ is stored, and start scanning A_i from p_i to retrieve the other points above line $y = y_1$. We do so in ascending order of those points' y-coordinates, so that the scan can terminate as soon as encountering a point falling out of q. All the points already scanned prior to this moment are the only objects in σ_i satisfying q. If the number of them is K_i, the scan performs at most $1 + K_i L/B$ I/Os. Hence, carrying out the scan in all slabs σ_i ($i \in [i_1 + 1, i_2 - 1]$) takes at most $\rho + K_{mid} L/B$ I/Os, where K_{mid} is the number of qualifying objects from the middle slabs. In Figure 3, the middle slabs are σ_3, σ_4 and σ_5. The scan in σ_3, for instance, starts from p_3, and ends at the lowest point in σ_3 above the query rectangle.

It remains to explain how to find all the p_i for each $i \in [i_1 + 1, i_2 - 1]$. This can be settled with the external interval tree $\mathcal{T}$. Recall that p_i determines an interval in I_i. The definition of p_i makes that interval the only one from I_i that contains the value y_1. Hence, it can be found by a stabbing query on $\mathcal{T}$ with y_1 as the search value. Note that this stabbing query may retrieve an interval for every slab, including those that are not a middle-slab. In Figure 3, for example, the stabbing query returns (the intervals determined by) 8 points: $p_1, ..., p_8$. Nevertheless, as there are only ρ slabs, the stabbing query finishes in $O(\log_B N + \rho/B)$ I/Os, after which we can keep only the points in the middle-slabs and discard the others. Therefore, overall the time of reporting the qualifying points in the middle slabs is bounded by

$$K_{mid} L/B + \rho + O(\log_B N + \rho/B)$$
$$= K_{mid} L/B + O(\sqrt{NL/B}). \qquad (13)$$

As analyzed earlier, the qualifying objects from the boundary slabs can be found in $O(\sqrt{NL/B})$ I/Os. Hence, the total query time is $O(KL/B + \sqrt{NL/B})$.

As mentioned, this structure has been used in [2, 6]. The only nuance in our scenario is the choice of ρ (which was logarithmic in [2, 6]). The techniques in the rest of the section, on the other hand, are newly developed in this paper.

Reducing the space. The previous index incurs more space than our target in Theorem 2 by an additive term of $\sqrt{NL/B}$ (i.e., ρ). This term can be eliminated with a trick we call *tail collection*, as explained next.

A close look at our earlier description reveals that the extra term ρ exists because each A_i ($1 \leq i \leq \rho$) may have an *under-full* block, which does not have B words of data, and thus, wastes space. This under-full block, if present, must be the last block in A_i. We remove it from A_i, after which all the blocks in A_i are fully utilized. We concatenate the data of all the non-full blocks (from different arrays) into a separate *tail file* G. All blocks in G store B words of data, except possibly one. Therefore, the total space used by G and the arrays is now at most $1 + NL/B$, i.e., ρ blocks less than before.

Note that G itself has no more than ρ blocks. Therefore, we can afford to scan it completely in answering a query, which will add only ρ I/Os to the query cost, and hence, does not change the query complexity $KL/B + O(\sqrt{NL/B})$. The query algorithm is still the same as before, except that in scanning an array, if we have come to its end and see that some information has been moved to G, we should continue scanning the relevant portion in G.

r-redundant structure. Assuming that there is an $(r-1)$-redundant structure with space $(r-1)NL/B + O(N/B)$ and query time $KL/B + O((NL/B)^{1/r})$, we can obtain an r-redundant index with space $rNL/B + O(N/B)$ and query time $KL/B + O((NL/B)^{1/(r+1)})$. This can be done by modifying the earlier 1-redundant structure, as elaborated below.

The first change is the value of ρ, which is now set to $(NL/B)^{1/(r+1)}$. Then, in the same manner as in the 1-redundant case, we divide P into $P_1, ..., P_\rho$, and create arrays $A_1, ..., A_\rho$, the tail file G, and the external interval tree $\mathcal{T}$. Currently, the information field of each object has been stored once, such that the space consumption is $NL/B + O(N/B)$. On each P_i ($1 \le i \le \rho$), we build an $(r-1)$-redundant structure T_i, which occupies $(r-1)|P_i|L/B + O(|P_i|/B)$ space. Hence, $T_1, ..., T_\rho$ together use

$$\sum_{i=1}^{\rho} \frac{(r-1)|P_i|L}{B} + O\left(\frac{|P_i|}{B}\right) = \frac{(r-1)NL}{B} + O(N/B)$$

space. This explains why the overall space is $rNL/B + O(N/B)$. Note that the final structure is r-redundant.

To answer a range query $q = [x_1, x_2] \times [y_1, y_2]$, as in the 1-redundant case, we start by identifying the boundary slabs σ_{i_1} and σ_{i_2} ($i_1 \le i_2$). Recall that they define middle slabs σ_i for each $i \in [i_1+1, i_2-1]$. The qualifying objects in the middle slabs are retrieved in the same way as in the 1-redundant case, i.e., utilizing $\mathcal{T}$, the arrays of the middle slabs, and perhaps also the tail file. If K_{mid} objects from the middle slabs satisfy the query, as shown in (13), they can be extracted in $K_{mid}L/B + O(\rho) = K_{mid}L/B + O((NL/B)^{1/(r+1)})$ I/Os.

Finally, to report the qualifying objects in the boundary slabs, we query the $(r-1)$-redundant structures T_{i_1} and T_{i_2}. Notice that each of these structures indexes at most N/ρ objects. Hence, if K_1 and K_2 objects are found from T_{i_1} and T_{i_2} respectively, searching the two structures entails

$$(K_1 + K_2)L/B + O\left(\left(\frac{NL}{\rho B}\right)^{1/r}\right)$$

$$= (K_1 + K_2)L/B + O\left((NL/B)^{\frac{r}{r+1} \cdot \frac{1}{r}}\right)$$

$$= (K_1 + K_2)L/B + O\left((NL/B)^{1/(r+1)}\right)$$

I/Os. As $K_{mid} + K_1 + K_2 = K$, the overall query time is $KL/B + O((NL/B)^{1/(r+1)})$.

Combining the above inductive construction with our earlier 1-redundant structure, we have established the correctness of Theorem 2.

5. CONCLUDING REMARKS

After explaining why (linear-size) r-redundant structures matter for range search in practice, this paper presented new lower bound results revealing the tradeoff between query efficiency and the number r of times an object can be stored, for every constant integer r. In particular, we showed that those results hold under a weaker form of the indivisibility assumption, and thereby demonstrated (for the first time to our knowledge) how the strong indivisibility assumption can be eliminated from the analytical framework underlying the indexability theorem. We also proved the tightness of our lower bounds by describing indexes realizing the optimal tradeoff up to only a small factor.

Closing the gap between our lower and upper bounds would be an interesting problem for future work. Our current results do not rule out, for example, a 2-redundant structure with query time $O((NL/B)^{1/3}/\text{polylog}_B N)$ plus the linear output cost. It is unknown whether such a structure exists.

The proposed r-redundant structure can be made fully dynamic with standard global-rebuilding techniques [14], however, at the cost of increasing the space and query time. The resulting index answers a query in $O((NL/B)^{1/(r+1)} + KL/B)$ I/Os, supports an insertion and a deletion in $O(\log_B N)$ I/Os amortized, and occupies

$$(1 + \epsilon)rNL/B + O(N/B)$$

space, where $\epsilon > 0$ can be an arbitrarily small constant. How to remove the $(1 + \epsilon)$ factor or prove its impossibility remains open.

6. ACKNOWLEDGEMENTS

This work was supported in part by (i) projects GRF 4169/09, 4166/10, 4165/11 from HKRGC, and (ii) the WCU (World Class University) program under the National Research Foundation of Korea, and funded by the Ministry of Education, Science and Technology of Korea (Project No: R31-30007).

7. REFERENCES

[1] A. Aggarwal and J. S. Vitter. The input/output complexity of sorting and related problems. *Communications of the ACM (CACM)*, 31(9):1116–1127, 1988.

[2] L. Arge, V. Samoladas, and J. S. Vitter. On two-dimensional indexability and optimal range search indexing. In *Proceedings of ACM Symposium on Principles of Database Systems (PODS)*, pages 346–357, 1999.

[3] L. Arge and J. S. Vitter. Optimal external memory interval management. *SIAM Journal of Computing*, 32(6):1488–1508, 2003.

[4] N. Beckmann, H. Kriegel, R. Schneider, and B. Seeger. The R*-tree: An efficient and robust access method for points and rectangles. In *Proceedings of*

ACM Management of Data (SIGMOD), pages 322–331, 1990.

[5] J. L. Bentley. Multidimensional binary search trees used for associative searching. *Communications of the ACM (CACM)*, 18(9):509–517, 1975.

[6] B. Chazelle. Filtering search: A new approach to query-answering. *SIAM Journal of Computing*, 15(3):703–724, 1986.

[7] R. Grossi and G. F. Italiano. Efficient splitting and merging algorithms for order decomposable problems. *Information and Computation*, 154(1):1–33, 1999.

[8] A. Guttman. R-trees: a dynamic index structure for spatial searching. In *Proceedings of ACM Management of Data (SIGMOD)*, pages 47–57, 1984.

[9] J. M. Hellerstein, E. Koutsoupias, D. P. Miranker, C. H. Papadimitriou, and V. Samoladas. On a model of indexability and its bounds for range queries. *Journal of the ACM (JACM)*, 49(1):35–55, 2002.

[10] J. M. Hellerstein, E. Koutsoupias, and C. H. Papadimitriou. On the analysis of indexing schemes. In *Proceedings of ACM Symposium on Principles of Database Systems (PODS)*, pages 249–256, 1997.

[11] J. Iacono and M. Patrascu. Using hashing to solve the dictionary problem (in external memory). To appear in *Proceedings of the Annual ACM-SIAM Symposium on Discrete Algorithms (SODA)*, 2012.

[12] K. V. R. Kanth and A. K. Singh. Optimal dynamic range searching in non-replicating index structures. In *Proceedings of International Conference on Database Theory (ICDT)*, pages 257–276, 1999.

[13] E. Koutsoupias and D. S. Taylor. Tight bounds for 2-dimensional indexing schemes. In *Proceedings of ACM Symposium on Principles of Database Systems (PODS)*, pages 52–58, 1998.

[14] M. H. Overmars. *The Design of Dynamic Data Structures*. Springer-Verlag, 1987.

[15] O. Procopiuc, P. K. Agarwal, L. Arge, and J. S. Vitter. Bkd-tree: A dynamic scalable kd-tree. In *Proceedings of Symposium on Advances in Spatial and Temporal Databases (SSTD)*, pages 46–65, 2003.

[16] J. T. Robinson. The K-D-B-tree: A search structure for large multidimensional dynamic indexes. In *Proceedings of ACM Management of Data (SIGMOD)*, pages 10–18, 1981.

[17] V. Samoladas and D. P. Miranker. A lower bound theorem for indexing schemes and its application to multidimensional range queries. In *Proceedings of ACM Symposium on Principles of Database Systems (PODS)*, pages 44–51, 1998.

[18] M. Streppel and K. Yi. Approximate range searching in external memory. *Algorithmica*, 59(2):115–128, 2011.

[19] S. Subramanian and S. Ramaswamy. The p-range tree: A new data structure for range searching in secondary memory. In *Proceedings of the Annual ACM-SIAM Symposium on Discrete Algorithms (SODA)*, pages 378–387, 1995.

[20] E. Verbin and Q. Zhang. The limits of buffering: a tight lower bound for dynamic membership in the external memory model. In *Proceedings of ACM Symposium on Theory of Computing (STOC)*, pages 447–456, 2010.

Approximate Computation and Implicit Regularization for Very Large-scale Data Analysis

Michael W. Mahoney
Department of Mathematics
Stanford University
Stanford, CA 94305
mmahoney@cs.stanford.edu

ABSTRACT

Database theory and database practice are typically the domain of computer scientists who adopt what may be termed an algorithmic perspective on their data. This perspective is very different than the more statistical perspective adopted by statisticians, scientific computers, machine learners, and other who work on what may be broadly termed statistical data analysis. In this article, I will address fundamental aspects of this algorithmic-statistical disconnect, with an eye to bridging the gap between these two very different approaches. A concept that lies at the heart of this disconnect is that of statistical regularization, a notion that has to do with how robust is the output of an algorithm to the noise properties of the input data. Although it is nearly completely absent from computer science, which historically has taken the input data as given and modeled algorithms discretely, regularization in one form or another is central to nearly every application domain that applies algorithms to noisy data. By using several case studies, I will illustrate, both theoretically and empirically, the nonobvious fact that approximate computation, in and of itself, can implicitly lead to statistical regularization. This and other recent work suggests that, by exploiting in a more principled way the statistical properties implicit in worst-case algorithms, one can in many cases satisfy the bicriteria of having algorithms that are scalable to very large-scale databases and that also have good inferential or predictive properties.

Categories and Subject Descriptors

F.0 [**Theory of Computation**]: General

Keywords

Approximate Computation, Implicit Regularization, Data

1. INTRODUCTION

Several years ago, I had the opportunity to give in several venues a keynote talk and to write an associated overview article on the general topic of "Algorithmic and Statistical Perspectives on Large-Scale Data Analysis" [31]. By the *algorithmic perspective*, I meant roughly the approach that someone trained in computer science might adopt;[1] and by the *statistical perspective*, I meant roughly the approach that someone trained in statistics, or in some area such as scientific computing where strong domain-specific assumptions about the data are routinely made, might adopt.[2] My main thesis was twofold. First, motivated by problems drawn from a wide range of application domains that share the common feature that they generate very large quantities of data, we are being forced to engineer a union between these two extremely different perspectives or worldviews on what the data are and what are interesting or fruitful ways to view the data. Second, rather than *first* making statistical modeling decisions, independent of algorithmic considerations, and *then* applying a computational procedure as a black box—which is quite typical in small-scale and medium-scale applications and which is more natural if one adopts one perspective or the other—in many large-scale applications it will be more fruitful to understand and exploit what may be termed the statistical properties *implicit* in worst-case algorithms. I illustrated these claims with two examples from genetic and Internet applications; and I noted that this approach of more closely coupling the computational procedures used with a statistical understanding of the data seems particularly appropriate more generally for very large-scale data analysis problems.

Here, I would like to revisit these questions, with an emphasis on describing in more detail particularly fruitful directions to consider in order to "bridge the gap" between the theory and practice of Modern Massive Data Set (MMDS)

---

[1]From this perspective, primary concerns include database issues, algorithmic questions such as models of data access, and the worst-case running time of algorithms for a given objective function; but there can be a lack of appreciation, and thus associated cavalierness, when it comes to understanding how the data can be messy and noisy and poorly-structured in ways that adversely affect how confident one can be in the conclusions that one draws about the world as a result of the output of one's fast algorithms.

[2]From this perspective, primary concerns include questions such as how well the objective functions being considered conform to the phenomenon under study, how best to model the noise properties in the data, and whether one can make reliable predictions about the world from the data at hand; but there tends to be very little interest in understanding either computation *per se* or the downstream effects that constraints on computation can have on the reliability of statistical inference.

analysis. On the one hand, very large-scale data are typically stored in some sort of database, either a variant of a traditional relational database or a filesystem associated with a supercomputer or a distributed cluster of relatively-inexpensive commodity machines. On the other hand, it is often noted that, in large part because they are typically generated in automated and thus relatively-unstructured ways, data are becoming increasingly ubiquitous and cheap; and also that the scarce resource complementary to large-scale data is the ability of the analyst to understand, analyze, and extract insight from those data. As anyone who has "rolled up the sleeves" and worked with real data can attest, real data are messy and noisy and poorly-structured in ways that can be hard to imagine before (and even sometimes after) one sees them. Indeed, there is often quite a bit of very practical "heavy lifting," *e.g.*, cleaning and preparing the data, to be done before starting to work on the "real" problem—to such an extent that many would say that big data or massive data applications are basically those for which the preliminary heavy lifting *is* the main problem. This clearly places a premium on algorithmic methods that permit the analyst to "play with" the data and to work with the data interactively, as initial ideas are being tested and statistical hypotheses are being formed. Unfortunately, this is not the sort of thing that is easy to do with traditional databases.

To address these issues, I will discuss a notion that lies at the heart of the disconnect between the algorithmic perspective and the statistical perspective on data and data analysis. This notion, often called *regularization* or *statistical regularization*, is a traditional and very intuitive idea. Described in more detail in Section 2.3, regularization basically has to do with how robust is the output of an algorithm to the noise properties of the input data. It is usually formulated as a tradeoff between "solution quality" (as measured, *e.g.*, by the value of the objective function being optimized) and "solution niceness" (as measured, *e.g.*, by a vector space norm constraint, a smoothness condition, or some other related measure of interest to a downstream analyst). For this reason, when applied to noisy data, regularized objectives and regularized algorithms can lead to output that is "better" for downstream applications, *e.g.*, for clustering or classification or other things of interest to the domain scientist, than is the output of the corresponding unregularized algorithms. Thus, although it is nearly completely absent from computer science, which historically has taken the input data as given and modeled algorithms discretely, regularization in one form or another is central to nearly every application domain that applies algorithms to noisy data.[3]

I will also discuss how, by adopting a very non-traditional perspective on approximation algorithms (or, equivalently, a non-traditional perspective on statistical regularization), one can in many cases satisfy the bicriteria of having algorithms that are scalable to very large data sets and that also have good statistical or inferential or predictive properties. Basically, the non-traditional perspective is that approximate computation—either in the sense of approximation algorithms in theoretical computer science or in the sense of heuristic design decisions (such as binning, pruning, and early stopping) that practitioners must make in order to implement their algorithms in real systems—often *implicitly* leads to some sort of regularization. That is, approximate computation, *in and of itself*, can implicitly lead to statistical regularization. This is very different than the usual perspective in approximation algorithms, where one is interested in solving a given problem, but since the problem is intractable one "settles for" the output of an approximation. In particular, this means that, depending on the details of the situation, approximate computation can lead to algorithms that are both faster *and* better than are algorithms that solve the same problem exactly.

While particular examples of this phenomenon are well-known, typically heuristically and amongst practitioners, in my experience the general observation is quite surprising to both practitioners and theorists of both the algorithmic perspective and the statistical perspective on data. Thus, I will use three "case studies" from recent MMDS analysis to illustrate this phenomenon of *implicit regularization via approximate computation* in three somewhat different ways. The first involves computing an approximation to the leading nontrivial eigenvector of the Laplacian matrix of a graph; the second involves computing, with two very different approximation algorithms, an approximate solution to a popular version of the graph partitioning problem; and the third involves computing an approximation to a locally-biased version of this graph partitioning problem. In each case, we will see that approximation algorithms that are run in practice implicitly compute smoother or more regular answers than do algorithms that solve the same problems exactly.

Characterizing and exploiting the implicit regularization properties underlying approximation algorithms for large-scale data analysis problems is not the sort of analysis that is currently performed if one adopts a purely algorithmic perspective or a purely statistical perspective on the data. It is, however, clearly of interest in many MMDS applications, where anything but scalable algorithms is out of the question, and where ignoring the noise properties of the data will likely lead to meaningless output. As such, it represents a challenging interdisciplinary research front, both for theoretical computer science—and for database theory in particular—as well as for theorists and practitioners of statistical data analysis more generally.

2. SOME GENERAL OBSERVATIONS ...

Before proceeding further, I would like to present in this section some general thoughts. Most of these observations will be "obvious" to at least some readers, depending on their background or perspective, and most are an oversimplified version of a much richer story. Nevertheless, putting them together and looking at the "forest" instead of the "trees" should help to set the stage for the subsequent discussion.

2.1 ... on models of data

It helps to remember that data are whatever data are—records of banking and other financial transactions, hyperspectral medical and astronomical images, measurements of electromagnetic signals in remote sensing applications,

---

[3]Clearly, there will be a problem if the output of a computer scientist's algorithm is manifestly meaningless in terms of the motivating application or if the statistician's objective function takes the age of the universe to optimize. The point is that, depending on one's perspective, data are treated as a black box with respect to the algorithm, or vice versa; and this leads one to formulate problems in very different ways. From an algorithmic perspective, questions about the reliability and robustness of the output to noise in the input are very much secondary; and from a statistical perspective, the same is true regarding the details of the computation and the consequences of resource constraints on the computation.

DNA microarray and single-nucleotide polymorphism measurements, term-document data from the Web, query and click logs at a search engine, interaction properties of users in social and information networks, corpora of images, sounds, videos, etc. To do something useful with the data, one must first model them (either explicitly or implicitly[4]) in some way. At root, a *data model* is a mathematical structure such that—given hardware, communication, input-output, data-generation, sparsity, noise, etc. considerations—one can perform computations of interest to yield useful insight on the data and processes generating the data. As such, choosing an appropriate data model has algorithmic, statistical, and implementational aspects that are typically intertwined in complicated ways. Two criteria to keep in mind in choosing a data model are the following.

- First, on the *data acquisition or data generation side*, one would like a structure that is "close enough" to the data, *e.g.*, to the processes generating the data or to the noise properties of the data or to natural operations on the data or to the way the data are stored or accessed, that modeling the data with that structure does not do too much "damage" to the data.

- Second, on the *downstream or analysis side*, one would like a structure that is at a "sweet spot" between descriptive flexibility and algorithmic tractability. That is, it should be flexible enough that it can describe a range of types of data, but it should not be so flexible that it can do "anything," in which case computations of interest will likely be intractable and inference will be problematic.

Depending on the data and applications to be considered, the data may be modeled in one or more of several ways.

- *Flat tables and the relational model.* Particularly common in database theory and practice, this model views the data as one or more two-dimensional arrays of data elements. All members of a given column are assumed to be similar values; all members of a given row are assumed to be related to one another; and different arrays can be related to one another in terms of predicate logic and set theory, which allows one to query, *e.g.*, with SQL or a variant, the data.

- *Graphs, including special cases like trees and expanders.* This model is particularly common in computer science theory and practice; but it is also used in statistics and machine learning, as well as in scientific computation, where it is often viewed as a discretization of an underlying continuous problem. A graph $G = (V, E)$ consists of a set of vertices V, that can represent some sort of "entities," and a set of edges E, that can be used to represent pairwise "interactions" between two entities. There is a natural geodesic distance between pairs of vertices, which permits the use

of ideas from metric space theory to develop algorithms; and from this perspective natural operations include breadth-first search and depth-first search. Alternatively, in spectral graph theory, eigenvectors and eigenvalues of matrices associated with the graph are of interest; and from this perspective, one can consider resistance-based or diffusion-based notions of distance between pairs of vertices.

- *Matrices, including special cases like symmetric positive semidefinite matrices.* An $m \times n$ real-valued matrix A provides a natural structure for encoding information about m objects, each of which is described by n features; or, if $m = n$, information about the correlations between all m objects. As such, this model is ubiquitous in areas of applied mathematics such as scientific computing, statistics, and machine learning, and it is of increasing interest in theoretical computer science. Rather than viewing a matrix simply as an $m \times n$ array of numbers, one should think of it as representing a linear transformation between two Euclidean spaces, $\mathbb{R}^n$ and $\mathbb{R}^m$; and thus vector space concepts like dot products, orthogonal matrices, eigenvectors, and eigenvalues are natural. In particular, matrices have a very different semantics than tables in the relational model, and Euclidean spaces are much more structured objects than arbitrary metric spaces.

Of course, there are other ways to model data—*e.g.*, DNA sequences are often fruitfully modeled by strings—but matrices and graphs are most relevant to our discussion below.

Database researchers are probably most familiar with the basic flat table and the relational model and its various extensions; and there are many well-known advantages to working with them. As a general rule, these models and their associated logical operations provide a powerful way to process the data at hand; but they are much less well-suited for understanding and dealing with imprecision and the noise properties in that data. (See [18, 16] and references therein.) For example, historically, the focus in database theory and practice has been on business applications, *e.g.*, automated banking, corporate record keeping, airline reservation systems, etc., where requirements such as performance, correctness, maintainability, and reliability (as opposed to prediction or inference) are crucial.

The reason for considering more sophisticated or richer data models is that much of the ever-increasing volume of data that is currently being generated is either relatively-unstructured or large and internally complex in its original form; and many of these noisy unstructured data are better-described by (typically sparse and poorly-structured) graphs or matrices than as dense flat tables. While this may be obvious to some, the graphs and matrices that arise in MMDS applications are very different than those arising in classical graph theory and traditional numerical linear algebra; and thus modeling large-scale[5] data by graphs and matrices poses very substantial challenges, given the way that

---

[4]By implicitly, I mean that, while computations always return answers (yes, modulo issues associated with the Halting Problem, infinite loops, etc.), in many cases one can say that a given computation is the "right" thing to do for a certain class of data. For example, performing matrix-based computations with ℓ_2-based objectives often has an interpretation in terms of underlying Gaussian processes. Thus, performing that computation in some sense implicitly amounts to assuming that that is what the data "look like."

[5]Clearly, large or big or massive means different things to different people in different applications. Perhaps the most intuitive description is that one can call the size of a data set: *small* if one can look at the data, fairly obviously see a good solution to problems of interest, and find that solution fairly easily with almost any "reasonable" algorithmic tool; *medium* if the data fit in the RAM on a reasonably-priced laptop or desktop machine and if one can run computations

databases (in computer science) have historically been constructed, the way that supercomputers (in scientific computing) have historically been designed, the tradeoffs that are typically made between faster CPU time and better IO and network communication, etc.

2.2 ... on the relationship between algorithms and data

Before the advent of the digital computer, the natural sciences (and to a lesser extent areas such as social and economic sciences) provided a rich source of problems; and statistical methods were developed in order to solve those problems. Although these statistical methods typically involved computing something, there was less interest in questions about the nature of computation *per se*. That is, although computation was often crucial, it was in some sense secondary to the motivating downstream application. Indeed, an important notion was (and still is) that of a *well-posed problem*—roughly, a problem is well-posed if: a solution exists; that solution is unique; and that solution depends continuously on the input data in some reasonable topology. Especially in numerical applications, such problems are sometimes called *well-conditioned problems*.[6] From this perspective, it simply doesn't make much sense to consider algorithms for problems that are not well-posed—after all, any possible algorithm for such an ill-posed problem will return answers that are not be meaningful in terms of the domain from which the input data are drawn.

With the advent of the digital computer, there occurred a split in the yet-to-be-formed field of computer science. The split was loosely based on the application domain (scientific computing and numerical computation versus business and consumer applications), but relatedly based on the type of tools used (continuous mathematics like matrix analysis and probability versus discrete mathematics like combinatorics and logic); and it led to two very different perspectives (basically the statistical and algorithmic perspectives) on the relationship between algorithms and data.

On the one hand, for many numerical problems that arose in applications of continuous mathematics, a two-step approach was used. It turned out that, even when working with a given well-conditioned problem,[7] certain algorithms that solved that problem "exactly" in some idealized sense performed very poorly in the presence of "noise" introduced by the peculiarities of roundoff and truncation errors. Roundoff errors have to do with representing real numbers with only finitely-many bits; and truncation errors arise since only a finite number of iterations of an iterative algorithm can actually be performed. The latter are important even in "exact arithmetic," since most problems of continuous mathemat-

ics cannot even in principle be solved by a finite sequence of elementary operations; and thus, from this perspective, fast algorithms are those that converge quickly to approximate answers that are accurate to, *e.g*, 2 or 10 or 100 digits of precision.

This led to the notion of the *numerical stability* of an algorithm. Let us view a numerical algorithm as a function f attempting to map the input data x to the "true" solution y; but due to roundoff and truncation errors, the output of the algorithm is actually some other y^*. In this case, the *forward error* of the algorithm is $\Delta y = y^* - y$; and the *backward error* of the algorithm is the smallest Δx such that $f(x+\Delta x) = y^*$. Thus, the forward error tells us the difference between the exact or true answer and what was output by the algorithm; and the backward error tells us what input data the algorithm we ran actually solved exactly. Moreover, the forward error and backward error for an algorithm are related by the condition number of the problem—the magnitude of the forward error is bounded above by the condition number multiplied by the magnitude of the backward error.[8] In general, a backward stable algorithm can be expected to provide an accurate solution to a well-conditioned problem; and much of the work in numerical analysis, continuous optimization, and scientific computing can be seen as an attempt to develop algorithms for well-posed problems that have better stability properties than the "obvious" unstable algorithm.

On the other hand, it turned out to be much easier to study computation *per se* in discrete settings (see [38, 9] for a partial history), and in this case a simpler but coarser one-step approach prevailed. First, several seemingly-different approaches (recursion theory, the λ-calculus, and Turing machines) defined the same class of functions. This led to the belief that the concept of computability is formally captured in a qualitative and robust way by these three equivalent processes, independent of the input data; and this highlighted the central role of logic in this approach to the study of computation. Then, it turned out that the class of computable functions has a rich structure—while many problems are solvable by algorithms that run in low-degree polynomial time, some problems seemed not to be solvable by anything short of a trivial brute force algorithm. This led to the notion of the complexity classes P and NP, the concepts of NP-hardness and NP-completeness, etc., the success of which led to the belief that the these classes formally capture in a qualitative and robust way the concept of computational tractability and intractability, independent of any posedness questions or any assumptions on the input data.

Then, it turned out that many problems of practical interest are intractable—either in the sense of being NP-hard or NP-complete or, of more recent interest, in the sense of requiring $O(n^2)$ or $O(n^3)$ time when only $O(n)$ or $O(n \log n)$ time is available. In these cases, computing some sort of approximation is typically of interest. The modern theory of approximation algorithms, as formulated in theoretical computer science, provides forward error bounds for such problems for "worst-case" input. These bounds are worst-case in two senses: first, they hold uniformly for all possible input; and second, they are typically stated in terms of a relatively-simple complexity measure such as problem size,

---

of interest on the data in a reasonable length of time; and *large* if the data doesn't fit in RAM or if one can't relatively-easily run computations of interest in a reasonable length of time. The point is that, as one goes from medium-sized data to large-scale data sets, the main issue is that one doesn't have random access to the data, and so details of communication, memory access, etc., become paramount concerns.

[6] In this case, the *condition number* of a problem, which measures the worst-case amount that the solution to the problem changes when there is a small change in the input data, is small for well-conditioned problems.

[7] Thus, the first step is to make sure the problem being considered is well-posed. Replacing an ill-posed problem with a related well-posed problem is common and is, as I will describe in Section 2.3, a form of regularization.

---

[8] My apologies to those readers who went into computer science, and into database theory in particular, to avoid these sorts of numerical issues, but these distinctions really do matter for what I will be describing below.

independent of any other structural parameter of the input data.[9] While there are several ways to prove worst-case bounds for approximation algorithms, a common procedure is to take advantage of relaxations—e.g., solve a relaxed linear program, rather than an integer program formulation of the combinatorial problem [41, 23]. This essentially involves "filtering" the input data through some other "nicer," often convex, metric or geometric space. Embedding theorems and duality then bound how much the input data are distorted by this filtering and provide worst-case quality-of-approximation guarantees [41, 23].

2.3 ... on explicit and implicit regularization

The term *regularization* refers to a general class of methods [34, 13, 8] to ensure that the output of an algorithm is meaningful in some sense—e.g., to the domain scientist who is interested in using that output for some downstream application of interest in the domain from which the data are drawn; to someone who wants to avoid "pathological" solutions; or to a machine learner interested in prediction accuracy or some other form of inference. It typically manifests itself by requiring that the output of an algorithm is not overly sensitive to the noise properties of the input data; and, as a general rule, it provides a tradeoff between the quality and the niceness of the solution.

Regularization arose in integral equation theory where there was interest in providing meaningful solutions to ill-posed problems [40]. A common approach was to assume a smoothness condition on the solution or to require that the solution satisfy a vector space norm constraint. This approach is followed much more generally in modern statistical data analysis [22], where the posedness question has to do with how meaningful it is to run a given algorithm, given the noise properties of the data, if the goal is to predict well on unseen data. One typically considers a loss function $f(x)$ that specifies an "empirical penalty" depending on both the data and a parameter vector x; and a regularization function $g(x)$ that provides "geometric capacity control" on the vector x. Then, rather than minimizing $f(x)$ exactly, one exactly solves an optimization problem of the form:

$$\hat{x} = \operatorname{argmin}_x f(x) + \lambda g(x), \qquad (1)$$

where the parameter λ intermediates between solution quality and solution niceness. Implementing regularization explicitly in this manner leads to a natural interpretation in terms of a trade-off between optimizing the objective and avoiding over-fitting the data; and it can often be given a Bayesian statistical interpretation.[10] By optimizing exactly a combination of two functions, though, regularizing in this way often leads to optimization problems that are harder (think of ℓ_1-regularized ℓ_2-regression) or at least no easier (think of ℓ_2-regularized ℓ_2-regression) than the original problem, a situation that is clearly unacceptable in many MMDS applications.

On the other hand, regularization is often observed as a side-effect or by-product of other design decisions.[11] For example, "binning" is often used to aggregate the data into bins, upon which computations are performed; "pruning" is often used to remove sections of a decision tree that provide little classification power; taking measures to improve numerical properties can also penalize large weights (in the solution vector) that exploit correlations beyond the level of precision in the data generation process; and "adding noise" to the input data before running a training algorithm can be equivalent to Tikhonov regularization. More generally, it is well-known amongst practitioners that certain heuristic approximations that are used to speed up computations can also have the empirical side-effect of performing smoothing or regularization. For example, working with a truncated singular value decomposition in latent factor models can lead to better precision and recall; "truncating" to zero small entries or "shrinking" all entries of a solution vector is common in iterative algorithms; and "early stopping" is often used when a learning model such as a neural network is trained by an iterative gradient descent algorithm.

Note that in addition to its use in making ill-posed problems well-posed—a distinction that is not of interest in the study of computation *per se*, where a sharp dividing line is drawn between algorithms and input data, thereby effectively assuming away the posedness problem—the use of regularization blurs the rigid lines between algorithms and input data in other ways.[12] For example, in addition to simply modifying the objective function to be optimized, regularization can involve adding to it various smoothness constraints—some of which involve modifying the objective and then calling a black box algorithm, but some of which are more simply enforced by modifying the steps of the original algorithm. Similarly, binning and pruning can be viewed as preprocessing the data, but they can also be implemented inside the algorithm; and adding noise to the input before running a training algorithm is clearly a form of preprocessing, but empirically similar regularization effects are observed when randomization is included inside the algorithm, e.g., as with randomized algorithms for matrix problems such as low-rank matrix approximation and least-squares approximation [30]. Finally, truncating small entries of a solution vector to zero in an iterative algorithm and performing early stopping in an iterative algorithm are clearly heuristic approximations that lead an algorithm to compute some sort of approximation to the solution that would have been computed had the truncation and early stopping not been performed.

3. THREE EXAMPLES OF IMPLICIT REGULARIZATION

In this section, I will discuss three case studies that il-

---

[9]The reason for not parameterizing running time and approximation quality in terms of structural parameters is that one can encode all sorts of pathological things in combinatorial parameters, thereby obtaining trivial results.

[10]Roughly, such an interpretation says that if the data are generated according to a particular noise model, then $g(\cdot)$ encodes "prior assumptions" about the input data, and regularizing with this $g(\cdot)$ is the "right" thing to do [22].

[11]See [34, 13, 8, 22, 32] and references therein for more details on these examples.

[12]In my experience, researchers who adopt the algorithmic perspective are most comfortable when given a well-defined problem, in which case they develop algorithms for that problem and ask how those algorithms behave on the worst-case input they can imagine. Researchers who adopt the statistical perspective will note that formulating the problem is typically the hard part; and that, if a problem is meaningful and well-posed, then often several related formulations will behave similarly for downstream applications, in a manner quite unrelated to their worst-case behavior.

lustrate the phenomenon of implicit regularization via approximate computation in three somewhat different ways. For each of these problems, there exists strong underlying theory; and there exists the practice, which typically involves approximating the exact solution in one way or another. Our goal will be to understand the differences between the theory and the practice in light of the discussion from Section 2. In particular, rather than being interested in the output of the approximation procedure insofar as it provides an approximation to the exact answer, we will be more interested in what the approximation algorithm actually computes, whether that approximation can be viewed as a smoother or more regular version of the exact answer, and how much more generally in database theory and practice similar ideas can be applied.

3.1 Computing the leading nontrivial eigenvector of a Laplacian matrix

The problem of computing eigenvectors of the Laplacian matrix of a graph arises in many data analysis applications, including (literally) for Web-scale data matrices. For example, the leading nontrivial eigenvector, *i.e.*, the eigenvector, v_2, associated with the smallest non-zero eigenvalue, λ_2, is often of interest: it defines the slowest mixing direction for the natural random walk on the graph, and thus it can be used in applications such as viral marketing, rumor spreading, and graph partitioning; it can be used for classification and other common machine learning tasks; and variants of it provide "importance," "betweenness," and "ranking" measures for the nodes in a graph. Moreover, computing this eigenvector is a problem for which there exists a very clean theoretical characterization of how approximate computation can implicitly lead to statistical regularization.

Let A be the adjacency matrix of a connected, weighted, undirected graph $G = (V, E)$, and let D be its diagonal degree matrix. That is, A_{ij} is the weight of the edge between the ith node and the jth node, and $D_{ii} = \sum_{j:(ij)\in E} A_{ij}$. The *combinatorial Laplacian* of G is the matrix $L = D - A$. Although this matrix is defined for any graph, it has strong connections with the Laplace-Beltrami operator on Riemannian manifolds in Euclidean spaces. Indeed, if the graph is a discretization of the manifold, then the former approaches the latter, under appropriate sampling and regularity assumptions. In addition, the *normalized Laplacian* of G is $\mathcal{L} = D^{-1/2}LD^{-1/2} = I - D^{-1/2}AD^{-1/2}$. This degree-weighted Laplacian is more appropriate for graphs with significant degree variability, in large part due to its connection with random walks and other diffusion-based processes. For an n node graph, $\mathcal{L}$ is an $n \times n$ positive semidefinite matrix, *i.e.*, all its eigenvalues $\lambda_1 \leq \lambda_2 \leq \cdots \leq \lambda_n$ are nonnegative, and for a connected graph, $\lambda_1 = 0$ and $\lambda_2 > 0$. In this case, the degree-weighted all-ones vector, *i.e.*, the vector whose i^{th} element equals (up to a possible normalization) D_{ii} and which is often denoted v_1, is an eigenvector of $\mathcal{L}$ with eigenvalue zero, *i.e.*, $\mathcal{L}v_1 = 0v_1$. For this reason, v_1 is often called trivial eigenvector of $\mathcal{L}$, and it is the next eigenvector that is of interest. This leading nontrivial eigenvector, v_2, is that vector that optimizes the Rayleigh quotient, defined to be $x^T \mathcal{L} x$ for a unit-length vector x, over all vectors perpendicular to the trivial eigenvector.[13]

In most applications where this leading nontrivial eigenvector is of interest, other vectors can also be used. For example, if λ_2 is not unique then v_2 is not uniquely-defined and thus the problem of computing it is not even well-posed; if λ_3 is very close to λ_2, then any vector in the subspace spanned by v_2 and v_3 is nearly as good (in the sense of forward error or objective function value) as v_2; and, more generally, *any* vector can be used with a quality-of-approximation loss that depends on how far it's Rayleigh quotient is from the Rayleigh quotient of v_2. For most small-scale and medium-scale applications, this vector v_2 is computed "exactly" by calling a black-box solver.[14] It could, however, be approximated with an iterative method such as the Power Method[15] or by running a random walk-based or diffusion-based procedure; and in many larger-scale applications this is preferable.

Perhaps the most well-known example of this is the computation of the so-called PageRank of the Web graph [35]. As an example of a spectral ranking method [42], PageRank provides a ranking or measure of importance for a Web page; and the Power Method has been used extensively to perform very large-scale PageRank computations [7]. Although it was initially surprising to many, the Power Method has several well-known advantages for such Web-scale computations: it can be implemented with simple matrix-vector multiplications, thus not damaging the sparsity of the (adjacency or Laplacian) matrix; those matrix-vector multiplications are strongly parallel, permitting one to take advantage of parallel and distributed environments (indeed, MapReduce was originally developed to perform related Web-scale computations [17]); and the algorithm is simple enough that it can be "adjusted" and "tweaked" as necessary, based on systems considerations and other design constraints. Much more generally, other spectral ranking procedures compute vectors that can be used instead of the second eigenvector v_2 to perform ranking, classification, clustering, etc. [42].

At root, these random walk or diffusion-based methods assign positive and/or negative "charge" (or relatedly probability mass) to the nodes, and then they let the distribution evolve according to dynamics derived from the graph structure. Three canonical evolution dynamics are the following.

- **Heat Kernel.** Here, the charge evolves according to the heat equation $\frac{\partial H_t}{\partial t} = -\mathcal{L}H_t$. That is, the vector of charges evolves as $H_t = \exp(-t\mathcal{L}) = \sum_{k=0}^{\infty} \frac{(-t)^k}{k!}\mathcal{L}^k$, where $t \geq 0$ is a time parameter, times an input seed distribution vector.

- **PageRank.** Here, the charge evolves by either moving to a neighbor of the current node or teleporting to a

---

[13]Eigenvectors of $\mathcal{L}$ can be related to generalized eigenvectors of L: if $\mathcal{L}x = \lambda x$, then $Ly = \lambda Dy$, where $y = D^{-1/2}x$.

[14]To the extent, as described in Section 2.2, that any numerical computation can be performed "exactly."

[15]The Power Method takes as input any $n \times n$ symmetric matrix A and returns as output a number λ and a vector v such that $Av = \lambda v$. It starts with an initial vector, ν_0, and it iteratively computes $\nu_{t+1} = A\nu_t/||A\nu_t||_2$. Under weak assumptions, it converges to v_{max}, the dominant eigenvector of A. The reason is clear: if we expand $\nu_0 = \sum_{i=1}^{n} \gamma_i v_i$ in the basis provided by the eigenfunctions $\{v_i\}_{i=1}^{n}$ of A, then $\nu_t = \sum_{i=1}^{n} \gamma_i^t v_i \rightarrow v_{max}$. Vanilla versions of the Power Method can easily be improved (at least when the entire matrix A is available in RAM) to obtain better stability and convergence properties; but these more sophisticated eigenvalue algorithms can often be viewed as variations of it. For instance, Lanczos algorithms look at a subspace of vectors generated during the iteration.

random node. That is, the vector of charges evolves as

$$R_\gamma = \gamma \left(I - (1-\gamma) M \right)^{-1},\qquad(2)$$

where $M = AD^{-1}$ is the natural random walk transition matrix associated with the graph and where $\gamma \in (0,1)$ is the so-called teleportation parameter, times an input seed vector.

- **Lazy Random Walk.** Here, the charge either stays at the current node or moves to a neighbor. That is, if M is the natural random walk transition matrix, then the vector of charges evolves as some power of $W_\alpha = \alpha I + (1-\alpha)M$, where $\alpha \in (0,1)$ represents the "holding probability," times an input seed vector.

In each of these cases, there is an input "seed" distribution vector, and there is a parameter (t, γ, and the number of steps of the Lazy Random Walk) that controls the "aggressiveness" of the dynamics and thus how quickly the diffusive process equilibrates. In many applications, one chooses the initial seed distribution carefully[16] and/or prevents the diffusive process from equilibrating to the asymptotic state. (That is, if one runs any of these diffusive dynamics to a limiting value of the aggressiveness parameter, then under weak assumptions an exact answer is computed, independent of the initial seed vector; but if one truncates this process early, then some sort of approximation, which in general depends strongly on the initial seed set, is computed.) The justification for doing this is typically that it is too expensive or not possible to solve the problem exactly; that the resulting approximate answer has good forward error bounds on it's Rayleigh quotient; and that, for many downstream applications, the resulting vector is even better (typically in some sense that is not precisely described) than the exact answer.

To formalize this last idea in the context of classical regularization theory, let's ask what these approximation procedures actually compute. In particular, do these diffusion-based approximation methods exactly optimize a regularized objective of the form of Problem (1), where $g(\cdot)$ is nontrivial, $e.g.$, some well-recognizable function or at least something that is "little-o" of the length of the source code, and where $f(\cdot)$ is the Rayleigh quotient?

To answer this question, recall that v_2 exactly solves the following optimization problem.

$$\begin{aligned}
\underset{x}{\text{minimize}} \quad & x^T \mathcal{L} x \\
\text{subject to} \quad & x^T x = 1, \\
& x^T D^{1/2} 1 = 0.
\end{aligned}\qquad(3)$$

The solution to Problem (3) can also be characterized as the solution to the following SDP (semidefinite program).

$$\begin{aligned}
\underset{X}{\text{minimize}} \quad & \text{Tr}(\mathcal{L} X) \\
\text{subject to} \quad & X \succeq 0, \\
& \text{Tr}(X) = 1, \\
& X D^{1/2} 1 = 0,
\end{aligned}\qquad(4)$$

where $\text{Tr}(\cdot)$ stands for the matrix Trace operation. Problem (4) is a relaxation of Problem (3) from an optimization over unit vectors to an optimization over distributions over unit vectors, represented by the density matrix X. These two programs are equivalent, however, in that the solution to Problem (4), call it X^*, is a rank-one matrix, where the vector into which that matrix decomposes, call it x^*, is the solution to Problem (3); and vice versa.

Viewing v_2 as the solution to an SDP makes it easier to address the question of what is the objective that approximation algorithms for Problem (3) are solving exactly. In particular, it can be shown that these three diffusion-based dynamics arise as solutions to the following regularized SDP.

$$\begin{aligned}
\underset{X}{\text{minimize}} \quad & \text{Tr}(\mathcal{L} X) + \tfrac{1}{\eta} G(X) \\
\text{subject to} \quad & X \succeq 0, \\
& \text{Tr}(X) = 1, \\
& X D^{1/2} 1 = 0,
\end{aligned}\qquad(5)$$

where $G(\cdot)$ is a regularization function, which is the generalized entropy, the log-determinant, and a certain matrix-p-norm, respectively [32]; and where η is a parameter related to the aggressiveness of the diffusive process [32]. Conversely, solutions to the regularized SDP of Problem (5) for appropriate values of η can be computed *exactly* by running one of the above three diffusion-based approximation algorithms. Intuitively, $G(\cdot)$ is acting as a penalty function, in a manner analogous to the ℓ_2 or ℓ_1 penalty in Ridge regression or Lasso regression, respectively; and by running one of these three dynamics one is *implicitly* making assumptions about the functional form of $G(\cdot)$.[17] More formally, this result provides a very clean theoretical characterization of how each of these three approximation algorithms for computing an approximation to the leading nontrivial eigenvector of a graph Laplacian can be seen as exactly optimizing a regularized version of the same problem.

3.2 Graph partitioning

Graph partitioning refers to a family of objective functions and associated approximation algorithms that involve cutting or partitioning the nodes of a graph into two sets with the goal that the cut has good quality (*i.e.*, not much edge weight crosses the cut) as well as good balance (*i.e.*, each of the two sets has a lot of the node weight).[18] As such, it has been studied from a wide range of perspectives and in a wide range of applications. For example, it has been studied for years in scientific computation (where one is interested in load balancing in parallel computing applications), machine learning and computer vision (where one is interested in segmenting images and clustering data), and theoretical computer science (where one is interested in it

---

[16]In particular, if one is interested in global spectral graph partitioning, as in Section 3.2, then this seed vector could have randomly positive entries or could be a vector with entries drawn from $\{-1, +1\}$ uniformly at random; while if one is interested in local spectral graph partitioning [39, 1, 15, 33], as in Section 3.3, then this vector could be the indicator vector of a small "seed set" of nodes.

[17]For readers interested in statistical issues, I should note that one can give a statistical framework to provide a Bayesian interpretation that makes this intuition precise [36]. Readers not interested in statistical issues should at least know that these assumptions are implicitly being made when one runs such an approximation algorithm.

[18]There are several standard formalizations of this bi-criterion, *e.g.*, the graph bisection problem, the β-balanced cut problem, and quotient cut formulations. In this article, I will be interested in conductance, which is a quotient cut formulation, but variants of most of what I say will hold for the other formulations.

as a primitive in divide-and-conquer algorithms); and more recently it has been studied in the analysis of large social and information networks (where one is interested in finding "communities" that are meaningful in a domain-specific context or in certifying that no such communities exist).

Given an undirected, possibly weighted, graph $G = (V, E)$, the *conductance* $\phi(S)$ *of a set of nodes* $S \subset V$ is:

$$\phi(S) = \frac{|E(S, \overline{S})|}{\min\{A(S), A(\overline{S})\}}, \qquad (6)$$

where $E(S, \overline{S})$ denotes the set of edges having one end in S and one end in the complement $\overline{S}$; where $|\cdot|$ denotes cardinality (or weight); where $A(S) = \sum_{i \in S} \sum_{j \in V} A_{ij}$; and where A is the adjacency matrix of a graph.[19] In this case, the *conductance of the graph* G is:

$$\phi(G) = \min_{S \subseteq V} \phi(S). \qquad (7)$$

Although exactly solving the combinatorial Problem (7) is intractable, there are a wide range of heuristics and approximation algorithms, the respective strengths and weaknesses of which are well-understood in theory and/or practice, for approximately optimizing conductance. Of particular interest here are *spectral methods* and *flow-based methods*.[20]

Spectral algorithms compute an approximation to Problem (7) by solving Problem (3), either exactly or approximately, and then performing a "sweep cut" over the resulting vector. Several things are worth noting.

- First, Problem (3) is a relaxation of Problem (7), as can be seen by replacing the $x \in \{-1, 1\}^n$ constraint in the corresponding integer program with the constraint $x \in \mathbb{R}^n$ subject to $x^T x = 1$, *i.e.*, by satisfying the combinatorial constraint "on average".

- Second, this relaxation effectively embeds the data on the one-dimensional[21] span of v_2—although, since the distortion is minimized only on average, there may be some pairs of points that are distorted a lot.

- Third, one can prove that the resulting partition is "quadratically good," in the sense that the cut returned by the algorithm has conductance value no bigger than ϕ if the graph actually contains a cut with conductance $O(\phi^2)$ [12, 14]. This bound comes from a discrete

version of Cheeger's inequality, which was originally proved in a continuous setting for compact Riemannian manifolds; and it is parameterized in terms of a structural parameter of the input, but it is independent of the number n of nodes in the graph.

- Finally, note that the worst-case quadratic approximation factor is *not* an artifact of the analysis—it is obtained for spectral methods on graphs with "long stringy" pieces [21], basically since spectral methods confuse "long paths" with "deep cuts"—and that it is a very "local" property, in that it is a consequence of the connections with diffusion and thus it is seen in locally-biased versions of the spectral method [39, 1, 15, 33].

Flow-based algorithms compute an approximation to Problem (7) by solving an all-pairs multicommodity flow problem. Several things are worth noting.

- First, this multicommodity flow problem is a relaxation of Problem (7), as can be seen by replacing the $x \in \{-1, 1\}^n$ constraint (which provides a particular semi-metric) in the corresponding integer program with a general semi-metric constraint.

- Second, this procedure effectively embeds the data into an ℓ_1 metric space, *i.e.*, a real vector space $\mathbb{R}^n$, where distances are measured with the ℓ_1 norm.

- Third, one can prove that the resulting partition is within an $O(\log n)$ factor of optimal, in the sense that the cut returned by the algorithm has conductance no bigger than $O(\log n)$, where n is the number of nodes in the graph, times the conductance value of the optimal conductance set in the graph [29, 26, 23]. This bound comes from Bourgain's result which states that any n-point metric space can be embedded into Euclidean space with only logarithmic distortion, a result which clearly depends on the number n of nodes in the graph but which is independent of any structural parameters of the graph.

- Finally, note that the worst-case $O(\log n)$ approximation factor is *not* an artifact of the analysis—it is obtained for flow-based methods on constant-degree expander graphs [29, 26, 23]—and that it is a very "global" property, in that it is a consequence of the fact that for constant-degree expanders the average distance between all pairs of nodes is $O(\log n)$.

Thus, spectral methods and flow-based methods are complementary in that they relax the combinatorial problem of optimizing conductance in very different ways;[22] they succeed and fail for complementary input (*e.g.*, flow-based methods do not confuse "long paths" with "deep cuts," and spectral methods do not have problems with constant-degree expanders); and they come with quality-of-approximation

---

[19] For readers more familiar with the concept of expansion, where the *expansion* $\alpha(S)$ *of a set of nodes* $S \subseteq V$ is $\alpha(S) = |E(S, \overline{S})| / \min\{|S|, |\overline{S}|\}$, the conductance is simply a degree-weighted version of the expansion.

[20] Other methods include local improvement methods, which can be used to clean up partitions found with other methods, and multi-resolution methods, which can view graphs at multiple size scales. Both of these are important in practice, as vanilla versions of spectral algorithms and flow-based algorithms can easily be improved with them.

[21] One can also view this as "embedding" a scaled version of the complete graph into the input graph. This follows from the SDP formulation of Problem (4); and this is of interest since a complete graph is like a constant-degree expander—namely, a metric space that is "most unlike" low-dimensional Euclidean spaces such as one-dimensional lines—in terms of its cut structure [29, 26]. This provides tighter duality results, and the reason for this connection is that the identity on the space perpendicular to the degree-weighted all-ones vector is the Laplacian matrix of a complete graph [33].

[22] For readers familiar with recent algorithms based on semidefinite programming [4], note that these methods may be viewed as combining spectral and flow in a particular way that, in addition to providing improved worst-case guarantees, also has strong connections with boosting [22], a statistical method which in many cases is known to avoid overfitting. The connections with what I am discussing in this article remain to be explored.

guarantees that are structurally very different.[23] For these and other reasons, spectral and flow-based approximation algorithms for the intractable graph partitioning problem provide a good "hydrogen atom" for understanding more generally the disconnect between the algorithmic and statistical perspectives on data.

Providing a precise statement of how spectral and flow-based approximation algorithms implicitly compute regularized solutions to the intractable graph partitioning problem (in a manner, *e.g.*, analogous to how truncated diffusion-based procedures for approximating the leading nontrivial eigenvector of a graph Laplacian exactly solve a regularized version of the problem) has *not*, to my knowledge, been accomplished. Nevertheless, this theoretical evidence—*i.e.*, that spectral and flow-based methods are effectively "filtering" the input data through very different metric and geometric places[24]—suggests that this phenomenon exists.

To observe this phenomenon empirically, one should work with a class of data that highlights the peculiar features of spectral and flow-based methods, *e.g.*, that has properties similar to graphs that "saturate" spectral's and flow's worst-case approximation guarantees. Empirical evidence [27, 28] clearly demonstrates that large social and information networks have these properties—they are strongly expander-like when viewed at large size scales; their sparsity and noise properties are such that they have structures analogous to stringy pieces that are cut off or regularized away by spectral methods; and they often have structural regions that at least locally are meaningfully low-dimensional. Thus, this class of data provides a good "hydrogen atom" for understanding more generally the regularization properties implicit in graph approximation algorithms.

In light of this, let's say that we are interested in finding reasonably good clusters of size 10^3 or 10^4 nodes in a large social or information network. (See [31] for why this might be interesting.) In that case, Figure 1 presents very typical results. Figure 1(a) presents a scatter plot of the size-resolved conductance of clusters found with a flow-based approximation algorithm (in red) and a spectral-based approximation algorithm (in blue).[25] In this plot, lower values on the Y-axis correspond to better values of the objective

(a) Objective function value (b) One "niceness" measure (c) Another "niceness" measure

Figure 1: **Scatter plot (on log-log scales) of size-resolved conductance (in Fig. 1(a)) and two "niceness" measures (Fig. 1(b) shows average shortest path length and Fig. 1(c) shows the ratio of external conductance to the internal conductance) for clusters found in the AtP-DBLP (AuthToPap-dblp) network with a spectral algorithm (blue) and a flow-based algorithm (red). See [27, 28] for details. For all plots, lower values of the Y-axis are "better." In this and other examples, the flow-based algorithm (red, Metis+MQI) generally yields clusters with better conductance scores, while the spectral algorithm (blue, LocalSpectral) generally yields clusters that are nicer.**

function; and thus the flow-based procedure is unambiguously better than the spectral procedure at finding good-conductance clusters. On the other hand, how useful these clusters are for downstream applications is also of interest. Since we are not explicitly performing any regularization, we do not have any explicit "niceness" function, but we can examine empirical niceness properties of the clusters found by the two approximation procedures. Figures 1(b) and 1(c) presents these results for two different niceness measures. Here, lower values on the Y-axis correspond to "nicer" clusters, and again we are interested in clusters with lower Y-axis values. Thus, in many cases, the spectral procedure is clearly better than the flow-based procedure at finding nice clusters with reasonably good conductance values.

Formalizations aside, this empirical tradeoff between solution quality and solution niceness is basically the defining feature of statistical regularization—except that we are observing it here as a function of two different approximation algorithms for the same intractable combinatorial objective function. That is, although we have not explicitly put any regularization term anywhere, the fact that these two different approximation algorithms essentially filter the data through different metric and geometric spaces leaves easily-observed empirical artifacts on the output of those approximation algorithms.[26] One possible response to these empirical results is is to say that conductance is not the "right"

---

[23]These differences highlight a rather egregious theory-practice disconnect (that parallels the algorithmic-statistical disconnect). In my experience, if you ask nearly anyone within theoretical computer science what is a good algorithm for partitioning a graph, they would say flow-based methods—after all flow-based methods run in low-degree polynomial time, they achieve $O(\log n)$ worst-case approximation guarantees, etc.—although they would note that spectral methods are better for expanders, basically since the quadratic of a constant is a constant. On the other hand, nearly everyone outside of computer science would say spectral methods do pretty well for the data in which they are interested, and they would wonder why anyone would be interested in partitioning a graph without any good partitions.

[24]That is, whereas traditional regularization takes place by solving a problem with an *explicitly-imposed geometry*, where an explicit norm constraint is added to ensure that the resulting solution is "small," one can view the steps of an approximation algorithm as providing an *implicitly-imposed geometry*. The details of how and where that implicitly-imposed geometry is "nice" will determine the running time and quality-of-approximation guarantees, as well as what input data are particularly challenging or well-suited for the approximation algorithm.

[25]Ignore the "size-resolved" aspect of these plots, since by

---

assumption we are interested in clusters of roughly 10^3 or 10^4 nodes (but [27, 28] provides details on this); and don't worry about the details of the flow-based and spectral-based procedures, except to say that there is a nontrivial theory-practice gap (again, [27, 28] provides details).

[26]For other data—in particular, constant-degree expanders—the situation should be reversed. That is, theory clearly predicts that locally-biased flow-based algorithms [3] will have better niceness properties than locally-biased spectral-based algorithms [1]. Observing this empirically on real data is difficult since data that are sufficiently unstructured to be expanders, in the sense of having no good partitions, tend to have very substantial degree heterogeneity.

objective function and that we should come up with some other objective to formalize our intuition;[27] but of course that other objective function will likely be intractable, and thus we will have to approximate it with a different spectral-based or flow-based (or some other) procedure, in which case the same implicit regularization issues will arise [27, 28].

3.3 Computing locally-biased graph partitions

In many applications, one would like to identify locally-biased graph partitions, *i.e.*, clusters in a data graph that are "near" a prespecified set of nodes. For example, in nearly every reasonably large social or information network, there do not exist large good-conductance clusters, but there are often smaller clusters that are meaningful to the domain scientist [2, 27, 28]; in other cases, one might have domain knowledge about certain nodes, and one might want to use that to find locally-biased clusters in a semi-supervised manner [33]; while in other cases, one might want to perform algorithmic primitives such as solving linear equations in time that is nearly linear in the size of the graph [39, 1, 15].

One general approach to problems of this sort is to modify the usual objective function and then show that the solution to the modified problem inherits some or all of the nice properties of the original objective. For example, a natural way to formalize the idea of a locally-biased version of the leading nontrivial eigenvector of $\mathcal{L}$ that can then be used in a locally-biased version of the graph partitioning problem is to modify Problem (3) with a locality constraint as follows.

$$
\begin{aligned}
\underset{x}{\text{minimize}} \quad & x^T \mathcal{L} x \\
\text{subject to} \quad & x^T x = 1, \\
& x^T D^{1/2} 1 = 0 \\
& (x^T D^{1/2} s)^2 \geq \kappa,
\end{aligned}
\tag{8}
$$

where s is a vector representing the "seed set," and where κ is a locality parameter. This *locally-biased* version of the usual spectral graph partitioning problem was introduced in [33], where it was shown that solution inherits many of the nice properties of the solution to the usual global spectral partitioning problem. In particular, the exact solution can be found relatively-quickly by running a so-called Personalized PageRank computation; if one performs a sweep cut on this solution vector in order to obtain a locally-biased partition, then one obtains Cheeger-like quality-of-approximation guarantees on the resulting cluster; and if the seed set consists of a single node, then this is a relaxation of the following *locally-biased graph partitioning problem*: given as input a graph $G = (V, E)$, an input node u, and a positive integer k, find a set of nodes $S \subseteq V$ achieving

$$
\phi(u, k, G) = \min_{S \subseteq V: u \in S, \text{vol}(S) \leq k} \phi(S), \tag{9}
$$

i.e., find the best conductance set of nodes of volume no greater than k that contains the input node v [33]. This "optimization-based approach" has the advantage that it is explicitly solving a well-defined objective function, and as such it is useful in many small-scale to medium-scale applications [33]. But this approach has the disadvantage, at least

for Web-scale graphs, that the computation of the locally-biased eigenvector "touches" all of the nodes in the graph—and this is very expensive, especially when one wants to find small clusters.

An alternative more "operational approach" is to do the following: run some sort of procedure, the steps of which are similar to the steps of an algorithm that would solve the problem exactly; and then either use the output of that procedure in a downstream application in a manner similar to how the exact answer would have been used, or prove a theorem about that output that is similar to what can be proved for the exact answer. As an example of this approach, [39, 1, 15] take as input some seed nodes and a locality parameter and then run a diffusion-based procedure to return as output a "good" cluster that is "nearby" the seed nodes. In each of these cases, the procedure is similar to the usual procedure,[28] except that at each step of the algorithm various "small" quantities are truncated to zero (or simply maintained at zero), thereby minimizing the number of nodes that need to be touched at each step of the algorithm. For example, [39] sets to zero very small probabilities, and [1] uses the so-called *push algorithm* [24, 10] to concentrate computational effort on that part of the vector where most of the nonnegligible changes will take place.

The outputs of these *strongly local spectral methods* obtain Cheeger-like quality-of-approximation guarantees, and by design these procedures are extremely fast—the running time depends on the size of the output and is independent even of the number of nodes in the graph. Thus, an advantage of this approach is that it opens up the possibility of performing more sophisticated eigenvector-based analytics on Web-scale data matrices; and these methods have already proven crucial in characterizing the clustering and community structure of social and information networks with up to millions of nodes [2, 27, 28]. At present, though, this approach has the disadvantage that it is very difficult to use: the exact statement of the theoretical results is extremely complicated, thereby limiting its interpretability; it is extremely difficult to characterize and interpret for downstream applications what actually is being computed by these procedures, *i.e.*, it is not clear what optimization problem these approximation algorithms are solving exactly; and counterintuitive things like a seed node not being part of "its own cluster" can easily happen. At root, the reason for these difficulties is that the truncation and zeroing-out steps implicitly regularize—but they are done based on computational considerations, and it is not known what are the implicit statistical side-effects of these design decisions.

The precise relationship between these two approaches has not, to my knowledge, been characterized. Informally, though, the truncating-to-zero provides a "bias" that is analogous to the early-stopping of iterative methods, such as those described in Section 3.1, and that has strong structural similarities with thresholding and truncation methods, as commonly used in ℓ_1-regularization methods and optimization more generally [19]. For example, the update step of the push algorithm, as used in [1], is a form of stochastic gradient descent [20], a method particularly well-suited for large-scale environments due to its connections with regular-

---

[27]Conductance probably is the combinatorial quantity that most closely captures the intuitive bi-criterial notion of what it means for a set of nodes to be a good "community," but it is still very far from perfect on many real data.

[28]Namely, the three diffusion-based procedures that were described in Section 3.1: [39] performs truncated random walks; [1] approximates Personalized PageRank vectors; and [15] runs a modified heat kernel procedure.

ization and boosting [11]; and the algorithm terminates after a small number of iterations when a truncated residual vector equals zero [20], in a manner similar to other truncated gradient methods [25].

Perhaps more immediately-relevant to database theory and practice as well as to implementing these ideas in large-scale statistical data analysis applications is simply to note that this operational and interactive approach to database algorithms is *already* being adopted in practice. For example, in addition to empirical work that uses these methods to characterize the clustering and community structure of large networks [2, 27, 28], the body of work that uses diffusion-based primitives in database environments includes an algorithm to estimate PageRank on graph streams [37], the approximation of PageRank on large-scale dynamically-evolving social networks [6], and a MapReduce algorithm for the approximation of Personalized PageRank vectors of all the nodes in a graph [5].

4. DISCUSSION AND CONCLUSION

Before concluding, I would like to share a few more general thoughts on approximation algorithm theory, in light of the above discussion. As a precursor, I should point out the obvious fact that the modern theory of NP-completeness is an extremely useful theory. It is a theory, and so it is an imperfect guide to practice; but it is a useful theory in the sense that it provides a qualitative notion of fast computation, a robust guide as to when algorithms will or will not perform well, etc. The theory achieved this by considering computation *per se*, as a one-step process that divorced the computation from the input and the output except insofar as the computation depended on relatively-simple complexity measures like the size of the input. Thus, the success is due to the empirical fact that many natural problems of interest are solvable in low-degree polynomial time, that the tractability status of many of the "hardest" problems in NP is in some sense equivalent, and that neither of these facts depends on the input data or the posedness of the problem.

I think it is also fair to say that, at least in a very wide range of MMDS applications, the modern theory of approximation algorithms is nowhere near as analogously useful. The bounds the theory provides are often very weak; the theory often doesn't provide constants which are of interest in practice; the dependence of the bounds on various parameters is often not even qualitatively right; and in general it doesn't provide analogously qualitative insight as to when approximation algorithms will and will not be useful in practice for realistic noisy data. One can speculate on the reasons—technically, the combinatorial gadgets used to establish approximability and nonapproximability results might not be sufficiently robust to the noise properties of the input data; many embedding methods, and thus their associated bounds, tend to emphasize the properties of "far apart" data points, while in most data applications "nearby" information is more reliable and more useful for downstream analysis; the geometry associated with matrices and spectral graph theory is much more structured than the geometry associated with general metric spaces; structural parameters like conductance and the isoperimetric constant are robust and meaningful and not brittle combinatorial constructions that encode pathologies; and ignoring posedness questions and viewing the analysis of approximate computation as a one-step process might simply be too coarse.

The approach I have described involves going "beyond worst-case analysis" to addressing questions that lie at the heart of the disconnect between what I have called the algorithmic perspective and the statistical perspective on large-scale data analysis. At the heart of this disconnect is the concept of regularization, a notion that is almost entirely absent from computer science, but which is central to nearly every application domain that applies algorithms to noisy data. Both theoretical and empirical evidence demonstrates that approximate computation, in and of itself, can implicitly lead to statistical regularization, in the sense that approximate computation—either approximation algorithms in theoretical computer science or heuristic design decisions that practitioners must make in order to implement their algorithms in real systems—often implicitly leads to some sort of regularization. This suggests treating statistical modeling questions and computational considerations on a more equal footing, rather than viewing either one as very much secondary to the other.

The benefit of this perspective for database theory and the theory and practice of large-scale data analysis is that one can hope to achieve bicriteria of having algorithms that are scalable to very large-scale data sets and that also have well-understood inferential or predictive properties. Of course, this is not a panacea—some problems are simply hard; some data are simply too noisy; and running an approximation algorithm may implicitly be making assumptions that are manifestly violated by the data. All that being said, understanding and exploiting in a more principled manner the statistical properties that are implicit in scalable worst-case algorithms should be of interest in many very practical MMDS applications.

5. REFERENCES

[1] R. Andersen, F.R.K. Chung, and K. Lang. Local graph partitioning using PageRank vectors. In *FOCS '06: Proceedings of the 47th Annual IEEE Symposium on Foundations of Computer Science*, pages 475–486, 2006.

[2] R. Andersen and K. Lang. Communities from seed sets. In *WWW '06: Proceedings of the 15th International Conference on World Wide Web*, pages 223–232, 2006.

[3] R. Andersen and K. Lang. An algorithm for improving graph partitions. In *SODA '08: Proceedings of the 19th ACM-SIAM Symposium on Discrete algorithms*, pages 651–660, 2008.

[4] S. Arora, S. Rao, and U. Vazirani. Geometry, flows, and graph-partitioning algorithms. *Communications of the ACM*, 51(10):96–105, 2008.

[5] B. Bahmani, K. Chakrabarti, and D. Xin. Fast personalized PageRank on MapReduce. In *Proceedings of the 37th SIGMOD international conference on Management of data*, pages 973–984, 2011.

[6] B. Bahmani, A. Chowdhury, and A. Goel. Fast incremental and personalized pagerank. *Proceedings of the VLDB Endowment*, 4(3):173–184, 2010.

[7] P. Berkhin. A survey on PageRank computing. *Internet Mathematics*, 2(1):73–120, 2005.

[8] P. Bickel and B. Li. Regularization in statistics. *TEST*, 15(2):271–344, 2006.

[9] L. Blum, F. Cucker, M. Shub, and S. Smale.

Complexity and real computation: A manifesto. *International Journal of Bifurcation and Chaos*, 6(1):3–26, 1996.

[10] P. Boldi and S. Vigna. The push algorithm for spectral ranking. Technical report. Preprint: arXiv:1109.4680 (2011).

[11] L. Bottou. Large-scale machine learning with stochastic gradient descent. In *Proceedings of the 19th International Conference on Computational Statistics (COMPSTAT'2010)*, pages 177–187, 2010.

[12] J. Cheeger. A lower bound for the smallest eigenvalue of the Laplacian. In *Problems in Analysis, Papers dedicated to Salomon Bochner*, pages 195–199. Princeton University Press, 1969.

[13] Z. Chen and S. Haykin. On different facets of regularization theory. *Neural Computation*, 14(12):2791–2846, 2002.

[14] F.R.K. Chung. *Spectral graph theory*, volume 92 of *CBMS Regional Conference Series in Mathematics*. American Mathematical Society, 1997.

[15] F.R.K. Chung. The heat kernel as the pagerank of a graph. *Proceedings of the National Academy of Sciences of the United States of America*, 104(50):19735–19740, 2007.

[16] J. Cohen, B. Dolan, M. Dunlap, J. M. Hellerstein, and C. Welton. MAD skills: new analysis practices for big data. *Proceedings of the VLDB Endowment*, 2(2):1481–1492, 2009.

[17] J. Dean and S. Ghemawat. MapReduce: Simplified data processing on large clusters. In *Proceedings of the 6th conference on Symposium on Operating Systems Design and Implementation*, pages 10–10, 2004.

[18] R. Agrawal *et al.* The Claremont report on database research. *ACM SIGMOD Record*, 37(3):9–19, 2008.

[19] J. Friedman, T. Hastie, and R. Tibshirani. Additive logistic regression: a statistical view of boosting. *Annals of Statistics*, 28(2):337–407, 2000.

[20] D.F. Gleich and M.W. Mahoney. Unpublished results, 2012.

[21] S. Guattery and G.L. Miller. On the quality of spectral separators. *SIAM Journal on Matrix Analysis and Applications*, 19:701–719, 1998.

[22] T. Hastie, R. Tibshirani, and J. Friedman. *The Elements of Statistical Learning*. Springer-Verlag, New York, 2003.

[23] S. Hoory, N. Linial, and A. Wigderson. Expander graphs and their applications. *Bulletin of the American Mathematical Society*, 43:439–561, 2006.

[24] G. Jeh and J. Widom. Scaling personalized web search. In *WWW '03: Proceedings of the 12th International Conference on World Wide Web*, pages 271–279, 2003.

[25] J. Langford, L. Li, and T. Zhang. Sparse online learning via truncated gradient. *Journal of Machine Learning Research*, 10:777–801, 2009.

[26] T. Leighton and S. Rao. Multicommodity max-flow min-cut theorems and their use in designing approximation algorithms. *Journal of the ACM*, 46(6):787–832, 1999.

[27] J. Leskovec, K.J. Lang, A. Dasgupta, and M.W. Mahoney. Statistical properties of community structure in large social and information networks. In *WWW '08: Proceedings of the 17th International Conference on World Wide Web*, pages 695–704, 2008.

[28] J. Leskovec, K.J. Lang, and M.W. Mahoney. Empirical comparison of algorithms for network community detection. In *WWW '10: Proceedings of the 19th International Conference on World Wide Web*, pages 631–640, 2010.

[29] N. Linial, E. London, and Y. Rabinovich. The geometry of graphs and some of its algorithmic applications. *Combinatorica*, 15(2):215–245, 1995.

[30] M. W. Mahoney. *Randomized algorithms for matrices and data*. Foundations and Trends in Machine Learning. NOW Publishers, Boston, 2011. Also available at: arXiv:1104.5557.

[31] M. W. Mahoney. Algorithmic and statistical perspectives on large-scale data analysis. In U. Naumann and O. Schenk, editors, *Combinatorial Scientific Computing*, Chapman & Hall/CRC Computational Science. CRC Press, 2012.

[32] M. W. Mahoney and L. Orecchia. Implementing regularization implicitly via approximate eigenvector computation. In *Proceedings of the 28th International Conference on Machine Learning*, pages 121–128, 2011.

[33] M. W. Mahoney, L. Orecchia, and N. K. Vishnoi. A local spectral method for graphs: with applications to improving graph partitions and exploring data graphs locally. Technical report. Preprint: arXiv:0912.0681 (2009).

[34] A. Neumaier. Solving ill-conditioned and singular linear systems: A tutorial on regularization. *SIAM Review*, 40:636–666, 1998.

[35] L. Page, S. Brin, R. Motwani, and T. Winograd. The PageRank citation ranking: Bringing order to the web. Technical report, Stanford InfoLab, 1999.

[36] P. O. Perry and M. W. Mahoney. Regularized Laplacian estimation and fast eigenvector approximation. In *Annual Advances in Neural Information Processing Systems 25: Proceedings of the 2011 Conference*, 2011.

[37] A. Das Sarma, S. Gollapudi, and R. Panigrahy. Estimating PageRank on graph streams. In *Proceedings of the 27th ACM Symposium on Principles of Database Systems*, pages 69–78, 2008.

[38] S. Smale. Some remarks on the foundations of numerical analysis. *SIAM Review*, 32(2):211–220, 1990.

[39] D.A. Spielman and S.-H. Teng. Nearly-linear time algorithms for graph partitioning, graph sparsification, and solving linear systems. In *STOC '04: Proceedings of the 36th annual ACM Symposium on Theory of Computing*, pages 81–90, 2004.

[40] A.N. Tikhonov and V.Y. Arsenin. *Solutions of Ill-Posed Problems*. W.H. Winston, Washington, D.C., 1977.

[41] V.V. Vazirani. *Approximation Algorithms*. Springer-Verlag, New York, 2001.

[42] S. Vigna. Spectral ranking. Technical report. Preprint: arXiv:0912.0238 (2009).

Max-Sum Diversification, Monotone Submodular Functions and Dynamic Updates

[Extended Abstract] [*]

Allan Borodin
Department of Computer
Science
University of Toronto
Toronto, Ontario, Canada
M5S 3G4
bor@cs.toronto.edu

Hyun Chul Lee
Linkedin Corporation
2025 Stierlin Court
Mountain View, CA 94043
culee@linkedin.com

Yuli Ye
Department of Computer
Science
University of Toronto
Toronto, Ontario, Canada
M5S 3G4
y3ye@cs.toronto.edu

ABSTRACT

Result diversification has many important applications in databases, operations research, information retrieval, and finance. In this paper, we study and extend a particular version of result diversification, known as max-sum diversification. More specifically, we consider the setting where we are given a set of elements in a metric space and a set valuation function f defined on every subset. For any given subset S, the overall objective is a linear combination of $f(S)$ and the sum of the distances induced by S. The goal is to find a subset S satisfying some constraints that maximizes the overall objective.

This problem is first studied by Gollapudi and Sharma in [17] for modular set functions and for sets satisfying a cardinality constraint (uniform matroids). In their paper, they give a 2-approximation algorithm by reducing to an earlier result in [20]. The first part of this paper considers an extension of the modular case to the monotone submodular case, for which the algorithm in [17] no longer applies. Interestingly, we are able to maintain the same 2-approximation using a natural, but different greedy algorithm. We then further extend the problem by considering any matroid constraint and show that a natural single swap local search algorithm provides a 2-approximation in this more general setting. This extends the Nemhauser, Wolsey and Fisher approximation result [29] for the problem of submodular function maximization subject to a matroid constraint (without the distance function component).

The second part of the paper focuses on dynamic updates for the modular case. Suppose we have a good initial approximate solution and then there is a single weight-perturbation either on the valuation of an element or on the distance between two elements. Given that users expect some stability in the results they see, we ask how easy is it to maintain a good approximation without significantly changing the initial set. We measure this by the number of updates, where each update is a swap of a single element in the current solution with a single element outside the current solution. We show that we can maintain an approximation ratio of 3 by just a single update if the perturbation is not too large.

Categories and Subject Descriptors

H.3.3 [**Information Storage and Retrieval**]: Information Search and Retrieval—*Selection process*

General Terms

Algorithm, Design, Performance, Theory

Keywords

Diversification, information retrieval, ranking, submodular functions, matroids, greedy algorithm, local search, approximation algorithm, dynamic update

1. INTRODUCTION

The objective in many optimization problems is to find the "best" subset amongst a set of given items. While the definition of "best" is often vague, one common approach is to quantify the desired property for each element in the set and then select a subset of elements accordingly. Although this is a viable approach for many problems, for some applications, this does not yield good results. For example, in portfolio management, allocating equities only according to their expected returns might lead to a large potential risk as the portfolio is not diversified. A similar situation occurs in databases, for example, query result handling. When knowledge of the user's intent is not fully available, it is actually better for a database system to diversify its displayed query results to improve user satisfaction. In many such scenarios, *diversity* is a necessary criterion.

We focus on a particular form of result diversification: max-sum diversification. We design algorithms for computing a "quality" subset, while also taking into account diver-

[*]This research is supported by MITACS Accelerate program, Thoora Inc., Natural Sciences and Engineering Research Council of Canada and University of Toronto, Department of Computer Science.

sity which is defined as the sum of pairwise distances between elements of the set being returned. We also show how to gradually change such a set in a dynamically changing environment.

We consider the case where quality is measured by a monotone submodular function $f(S)$ of the returned set S. In this way, we are extending beyond the linear (i.e., modular) case considered in [17]. Submodular functions have been extensively considered since they model many natural phenomena. For example, in terms of keyword based search in database systems, it is well understood that users begin to gradually (or sometimes abruptly) lose interest the more results they have to consider [37, 38]. But on the other hand, as long as a user continues to gain some benefit, additional query results can improve the overall quality but at a decreasing rate. As in [17], we consider the case of maximizing a linear combination of the quality $f(S)$ and the (distance based) diversity subject to a cardinality constraint (i.e., $|S| \leq p$ for some given p). We present a greedy algorithm that is somewhat unusual in that it does not try to optimize the objective in each iteration but rather optimizes a closely related potential function. We show that our greedy approach matches the 2-approximation [17] obtained for the modular case.

Our next result continues with the submodular case but now we go beyond a cardinality constraint (i.e., the uniform matroid) on S and allow the constraint to be that S is independent in a given matroid. This allows a substantial increase in generality. For example, while diversity might represent the distance between retrieved database tuples under a given criterion (for instance, a kernel based diversity measure called *answer tree kernel* is used in [43]), we could use a partition matroid to insure that (for example) the retrieved database tuples come from a variety of different sources. That is, we may wish to have n_i tuples from a specific database field i. This is, of course, another form of diversity but one orthogonal to diversity based on the given criterion. Similarly in the stock portfolio example, we might wish to have a balance of stocks in terms of say risk and profit margins (using some statistical measure of distances) while using a partition matroid to insure that different sectors of the economy are well represented. Another important class of matroids (relevant to our application) is that of transversal matroids. Suppose we have a collection $\{C_1, C_2, \ldots, C_m\}$ of (possibly) *overlapping* sets (i.e., the collection is not a partition) of database tuples (or stocks). Our goal might be to derive a set S such that the database tuples in S form a set of representatives for the collection; that is, every database tuple in S represents (and is in) a unique set C_i in the collection. The set S is then an independent set in the transversal matroid induced by the collection. We also note [35] that the intersection of any matroid with a uniform matroid is still a matroid so that in the above examples, we could further impose the constraint that the set S has at most p elements.

Our final theoretical result concerns dynamic updates. Here we restrict attention to a modular set function $f(S)$; that is, we now have weights on the elements and $f(S) = \sum_{u \in S} w(u)$ where $w(u)$ is the weight of element u. This allows us to consider changes to the weight of a single element as well as changes to the distance function. We also mention some preliminary experiments on synthetic data that in the modular set function case suggest that our greedy and

local search algorithms may perform significantly better in practice than the proven worst case bounds.

The rest of the paper is organized as follows. In Section 2, we discuss related work in result diversification. We formulate the problem into a combinatorial optimization problem and show its connection to the dispersion problem in location theory in Section 3. In Section 4, we discuss max-sum diversification with monotone submodular set functions and give a simple greedy algorithm that achieves a 2-approximation when the set is of bounded cardinality. We extend the problem to the matroid case in Section 5 and discuss dynamic updates in Section 6. Section 7 carries out two preliminary experiments and Section 8 concludes the paper.

2. RELATED WORK

With the proliferation of today's social media, database and web content, ranking becomes an important problem as it decides what gets selected and what does not, and what to be displayed first and what to be displayed last. Many early ranking algorithms, for example in web search, are based on the notion of "relevance", i.e., the closeness of the object to the search query. However, there has been a rising interest to incorporate some notion of "diversity" into measures of quality.

One early work in this direction is the notion of "Maximal Marginal Relevance" (MMR) introduced by Carbonell and Goldstein in [6]. More specifically, MMR is defined as follows:

$$\text{MMR} = \max_{D_i \in R \setminus S} [\lambda \cdot sim_1(D_i, Q) - (1 - \lambda) \max_{D_j \in S} sim_2(D_i, D_j)],$$

where Q is a query; R is the ranked list of documents retrieved; S is the subset of documents in R already selected; sim_1 is the similarity measure between a document and a query, and sim_2 is the similarity measure between two documents. The parameter λ controls the trade-off between novelty (a notion of diversity) and relevance. The MMR algorithm iteratively selects the next document with respect to the MMR objective function until a given cardinality condition is met. The MMR heuristic has been widely used, but to the best of our knowledge, it has not been theoretically justified. Our paper provides some theoretical evidence why MMR is a legitimate approach for diversification. The greedy algorithm we propose in this paper can be viewed as a natural extension of MMR.

There is extensive research on how to diversify returned ranking results to satisfy multiple users. Namely, the result diversity issue occurs when many facets of queries are discovered and a set of multiple users expect to find their desired facets in the first page of the results. Thus, the challenge is to find the best strategy for ordering the results such that many users would find their relevant pages in the top few slots.

Rafiei et al. [32] modeled this as a continuous optimization problem. They introduce a weight vector W for the search results, where the total weight sums to one. They define the portfolio variance to be $W^T C W$, where C is the covariance matrix of the result set. The goal then is to minimize the portfolio variance while the expected relevance is fixed at a certain level. They report that their proposed algorithm can improve upon Google in terms of the diversity on random queries, retrieving 14% to 38% more aspects of queries in top five, while maintaining a precision very close to Google.

Bansal et al. [2] considered the setting in which various types of users exist and each is interested in a subset of the search results. They use a performance measure based on *discounted cumulative gain*, which defines the usefulness (gain) of a document as its position in the resulting list. Based on this measure, they suggest a general approach to develop approximation algorithms for ranking search results that captures different aspects of users' intents. They also take into account that the relevance of one document cannot be treated independent of the relevance of other documents in a collection returned by a search engine. They consider both the scenario where users are interested in only a single search result (e.g., navigational queries) and the scenario where users have different requirements on the number of search results, and develop good approximation solutions for them.

The database community has recently studied the query diversification problem, which is mainly for keyword search in databases [27, 40, 12, 38, 43, 37, 10]. Given a very large database, an exploratory query can easily lead to a vast answer set. Typically, an answer's relevance to the user query is based on *top-k* or *tf-idf*. As a way of increasing user satisfaction, different query diversification techniques have been proposed including some system based ones taking into account query parameters, evaluation algorithms, and dataset properties. For many of these, a max-sum type objective function is usually used.

Other than those discussed above, there are many recent papers studying result diversification in different settings, via different approaches and through different perspectives, for example [42, 9, 44, 41, 30, 1, 3, 34, 11, 36]. The reader is referred to [1, 13] for a good summary of the field. Most relevant to our work is the paper by Gollapudi and Sharma [17], where they develop an axiomatic approach to characterize and design diversification systems. Furthermore, they consider three different diversification objectives and using earlier results in facility dispersion, they are able to give algorithms with good approximation guarantees. This paper is a continuation of research along this line.

Recently, Minack et al. [28] have studied the problem of incremental diversification for very large data sets. Instead of viewing the input of the problem as a set, they consider the input as a stream, and use a simple online algorithm to process each element in an incremental fashion, maintaining a near-optimal diverse set at any point in the stream. Although their results are largely experimental, this approach significantly reduces CPU and memory consumption, and hence is applicable to large data sets. Our dynamic update algorithm deals with a problem of a similar nature, but instead of relying on experimental results, we prove theoretical guarantees. To the best of our knowledge, our work is the first of its kind to obtain a near-optimality condition for result diversification in a dynamically changing environment.

3. PROBLEM FORMULATION

Although the notion of "diversity" naturally arises in the context of databases, social media and web search, the underlying mathematical object is not new. As presented in [17], there is a rich and long line of research in location theory dealing with a similar concept; in particular, one objective is the placement of facilities on a network to maximize some

function of the distances between facilities. The situation arises when proximity of facilities is undesirable, for example, the distribution of business franchises in a city. Such location problems are often referred to as *dispersion* problems; for more motivation and early work, see [15, 16, 23].

Analytical models for the dispersion problem assume that the given network is represented by a set $V = \{v_1, v_2, \ldots, v_n\}$ of n vertices with metric distance between every pair of vertices. The objective is to locate p facilities ($p \leq n$) among the n vertices, with at most one facility per vertex, such that some function of distances between facilities is maximized. Different objective functions are considered for the dispersion problems in the literature including: the max-sum criterion (maximize the total distances between all pairs of facilities) in [39, 15, 33], the max-min criterion (maximize the minimum distance between a pair of facilities) in [23, 15, 33], the max-mst (maximize the minimum spanning tree among all facilities) and many other related criteria in [18, 8]. The general problem (even in the metric case) for most of these criteria is NP-hard, and approximation algorithms have been developed and studied; see [8] for a summary of known results. Most relevant to this paper is the max-sum dispersion problem. The problem is known to be NP-hard [19], but it is not known whether or not it admits a PTAS. In [33], Ravi, Rosenkrantz and Tayi give a greedy algorithm and show it has an approximation ratio within a factor of 4. This is later improved by Hassin, Rubinstein and Tamir [20], who show a different algorithm with an approximation ratio of 2. This is the best known ratio today.

The dispersion problem is related to the diversification problem as both are trying to select a subset of elements which are element-wise far apart. The difference is that the diversification problem also considers vertex weight, so it is a bi-criteria optimization problem.

PROBLEM 1. `Max-Sum Diversification`

Let U be the underlying ground set, and let $d(\cdot, \cdot)$ be a metric distance function on U. For any subset of U, let $f(\cdot)$ be a non-negative set function measuring the value of a subset. Given a fixed integer p, the goal of the problem is to find a subset $S \subseteq U$ that:

$$\text{maximizes} \quad f(S) + \lambda \sum_{\{u,v\}:u,v \in S} d(u,v)$$

$$\text{subject to} \quad |S| = p,$$

where λ is a parameter specifying a desired trade-off between the two objectives.

The max-sum diversification problem is first proposed and studied in the context of result diversification in [17] [1], where the function $f(\cdot)$ is modular. In their paper, the value of $f(S)$ measures the relevance of a given subset to a search query, and the value $\sum_{\{u,v\}:u,v \in S} d(u,v)$ gives a diversity measure on S. The parameter λ specifies a desired trade-off between diversity and relevance. They reduce the problem to the max-sum dispersion problem, and using an algorithm in [20], they obtain an approximation ratio of 2.

In this paper, we first study the problem with more general valuation functions: normalized, monotone submodular set functions. For notational convenience, for any two sets S, T and an element e, we write $S \cup \{e\}$ as $S + e$, $S \setminus \{e\}$ as

---

[1]In fact, they have a slightly different but equivalent formulation.

$S - e$, $S \cup T$ as $S + T$, and $S \setminus T$ as $S - T$. A set function f is *normalized* if $f(\emptyset) = 0$. The function is *monotone* if for any $S, T \subseteq U$ and $S \subseteq T$,

$$f(S) \leq f(T).$$

It is *submodular* if for any $S, T \subseteq U$, $S \subseteq T$ with $u \in U$,

$$f(T + u) - f(T) \leq f(S + u) - f(S).$$

In the remainder of paper, all functions considered are normalized.

We proceed to our first contribution, a greedy algorithm (different than the one in [17]) that obtains a 2-approximation for monotone submodular set functions.

4. SUBMODULAR FUNCTIONS

Submodular set functions can be characterized by the property of a decreasing marginal gain as the size of the set increases. As such, submodular functions are well-studied objects in economics, game theory and combinatorial optimization. More recently, submodular functions have attracted attention in many practical fields of computer science. For example, Kempe et al. [21] study the problem of selecting a set of most influential nodes to maximize the total information spread in a social network. They have shown that under two basic diffusion models, the amount of influence of a set is submodular, hence the problem admits a good approximation algorithm. In natural language processing, Lin and Bilmes [26, 24, 25] have studied a class of submodular functions for document summarization. These functions each combine two terms, one which encourages the summary to be representative of the corpus, and the other which positively rewards diversity. Their experimental results show that a greedy algorithm with the objective of maximizing these submodular functions outperforms the existing state-of-art results in both generic and query-focused document summarization.

Both of the above mentioned results are based on the fundamental work of Nemhauser, Wolsey and Fisher [29], which has shown an $\frac{e}{e-1}$-approximation for maximizing monotone submodular set functions over a uniform matroid; and this bound is known to be tight even for a general matroid [5]. Our max-sum diversification problem with monotone submodular set functions can be viewed as an extension of that problem: the objective function now not only contains a submodular part, but also has a supermodular part: the sum of distances.

Since the max-sum diversification problem with modular set functions studied in [17] admits a 2-approximation algorithm, it is natural to ask what approximation ratio is obtainable for the same problem with monotone submodular set functions. Note that the algorithm in [17] does not apply to the submodular case. In what follows we assume (as is standard when considering submodular function) access to an oracle for finding an element $u \in U - S$ that maximizes $f(S + u) - f(S)$. When f is modular, this simply means accessing the element $u \in U - S$ having maximum weight.

THEOREM 1. *There is a simple linear time greedy algorithm that achieves a 2-approximation for the max-sum diversification problem with monotone submodular set functions satisfying a cardinality constraint.*

Before giving the proof of Theorem 1, we first introduce our notation. We extend the notion of distance function to sets. For disjoint subsets $S, T \subseteq U$, we let $d(S) = \sum_{\{u,v\}: u, v \in S} d(u, v)$, and $d(S, T) = \sum_{\{u,v\}: u \in S, v \in T} d(u, v)$.

Now we define various types of marginal gain. For any given subset $S \subseteq U$ and an element $u \in U - S$: let $\phi(S)$ be the value of the objective function, $d_u(S) = \sum_{v \in S} d(u, v)$ be the marginal gain on the distance, $f_u(S) = f(S + u) - f(S)$ be the marginal gain on the weight, and $\phi_u(S) = f_u(S) + \lambda d_u(S)$ be the total marginal gain on the objective function. Let $f'_u(S) = \frac{1}{2} f_u(S)$, and $\phi'_u(S) = f'_u(S) + \lambda d_u(S)$. We consider the following simple greedy algorithm:

GREEDY ALGORITHM
$S = \emptyset$
while $|S| < p$
    find $u \in U - S$ maximizing $\phi'_u(S)$
    $S = S + u$
end while
return S

Note that the above greedy algorithm is "non-oblivious" (in the sense of [22]) as it is not selecting the next element with respect to the objective function $\phi(\cdot)$. This might be of an independent interest. We utilize the following lemma in [33].

LEMMA 1. *Given a metric distance function $d(\cdot, \cdot)$, and two disjoint sets X and Y, we have the following inequality:*

$$(|X| - 1)d(X, Y) \geq |Y| d(X).$$

Now we are ready to prove Theorem 1.

PROOF. Let O be the optimal solution, and G, the greedy solution at the end of the algorithm. Let G_i be the greedy solution at the end of step i, $i < p$; and let $A = O \cap G_i$, $B = G_i - A$ and $C = O - A$. By lemma 1, we have the following three inequalities:

$$(|C| - 1)d(B, C) \geq |B| d(C) \tag{1}$$
$$(|C| - 1)d(A, C) \geq |A| d(C) \tag{2}$$
$$(|A| - 1)d(A, C) \geq |C| d(A) \tag{3}$$

Furthermore, we have

$$d(A, C) + d(A) + d(C) = d(O) \tag{4}$$

Note that the algorithm clearly achieves the optimal solution if $p = 1$. If $|C| = 1$, then $i = p - 1$ and $G_i \subset O$. Let v be the element in C, and let u be the element taken by the greedy algorithm in the next step, then $\phi'_u(G_i) \geq \phi'_v(G_i)$. Therefore,

$$\frac{1}{2} f_u(G_i) + \lambda d_u(G_i) \geq \frac{1}{2} f_v(G_i) + \lambda d_v(G_i),$$

which implies

$$
\begin{aligned}
\phi_u(G_i) &= f_u(G_i) + \lambda d_u(G_i) \\
&\geq \frac{1}{2} f_u(G_i) + \lambda d_u(G_i) \\
&\geq \frac{1}{2} f_v(G_i) + \lambda d_v(G_i) \\
&\geq \frac{1}{2} \phi_v(G_i);
\end{aligned}
$$

and hence $\phi(G) \geq \frac{1}{2} \phi(O)$.

Now we can assume that $p > 1$ and $|C| > 1$. We apply the following non-negative multipliers to equations (1), (2), (3), (4) and add them: $(1) * \frac{1}{|C|-1} + (2) * \frac{|C|-|B|}{p(|C|-1)} + (3) * \frac{i}{p(p-1)} + (4) * \frac{i|C|}{p(p-1)}$; we then have

$$d(A,C) + d(B,C) - \frac{i|C|(p-|C|)}{p(p-1)(|C|-1)}d(C) \geq \frac{i|C|}{p(p-1)}d(O).$$

Since $p > |C|$,

$$d(C,G_i) \geq \frac{i|C|}{p(p-1)}d(O).$$

By submodularity and monotonicity of $f'(\cdot)$, we have

$$\sum_{v \in C} f'_v(G_i) \geq f'(C \cup G_i) - f'(G_i) \geq f'(O) - f'(G).$$

Therefore,

$$\begin{aligned}
\sum_{v \in C} \phi'_v(G_i) &= \sum_{v \in C}[f'_v(G_i) + \lambda d(\{v\}, G_i)] \\
&= \sum_{v \in C} f'_v(G_i) + \lambda d(C, G_i) \\
&\geq [f'(O) - f'(G)] + \frac{\lambda i|C|}{p(p-1)}d(O).
\end{aligned}$$

Let u_{i+1} be the element taken at step $(i+1)$, then we have

$$\phi'_{u_{i+1}}(G_i) \geq \frac{1}{p}[f'(O) - f'(G)] + \frac{\lambda i}{p(p-1)}d(O).$$

Summing over all i from 0 to $p-1$, we have

$$\phi'(G) = \sum_{i=0}^{p-1} \phi'_{u_{i+1}}(G_i) \geq [f'(O) - f'(G)] + \frac{\lambda}{2}d(O).$$

Hence,

$$f'(G) + \lambda d(G) \geq f'(O) - f'(G) + \frac{\lambda}{2}d(O),$$

and

$$\phi(G) = f(G) + \lambda d(G) \geq \frac{1}{2}[f(O) + \lambda d(O)] = \frac{1}{2}\phi(O).$$

This completes the proof. $\square$

The greedy algorithm runs in linear time when p is a fixed constant. It is also not hard to see the approximation ratio of two is tight for this particular greedy algorithm.

5. MATROIDS AND LOCAL SEARCH

Theorem 1 provides a 2-approximation for max-sum diversification when the set function is submodular and the set constraint is a cardinality constraint, i.e., a uniform matroid. It is natural to ask if the same approximation guarantee can be obtained for an arbitrary matroid. In this section, we show that the max-sum diversification problem with monotone submodular function admits a 2-approximation subject to a general matroid constraint.

Matroids are well studied objects in combinatorial optimization. A matroid $\mathcal{M}$ is a pair $< U, \mathcal{F} >$, where U is a set of ground elements and $\mathcal{F}$ is a collection of subsets of U, called *independent sets*, with the following properties :

- **Hereditary:** The empty set is independent and if $S \in \mathcal{F}$ and $S' \subset S$, then $S' \in \mathcal{F}$.

- **Augmentation:** If $A, B \in \mathcal{F}$ and $|A| > |B|$, then $\exists e \in A - B$ such that $B \cup \{e\} \in \mathcal{F}$.

The maximal independent sets of a matroid are called *bases* of $\mathcal{M}$. Note that all bases have the same number of elements, and this number is called the *rank* of $\mathcal{M}$. The definition of a matroid captures the key notion of independence from linear algebra and extends that notion so as to apply to many combinatorial objects. We have already mentioned two classes of matroids relevant to our results, namely partition matroids and transversal matroids. In a partition matroid, the universe U is partitioned into sets $C_1, \ldots, C_m$ and the independent sets S satisfy $S = \cup_{1 \leq i \leq m} S_i$ with $|S_i| \leq k_i$ for some given bounds k_i on each part of the partition. A uniform matroid is a special case of a partition matroid with $m = 1$. In a transversal matroid, the universe U is a collection of (possibly) non-intersecting sets $\mathcal{C} = C_1, \ldots, C_m$ and a set S is independent if there is an injective function ϕ from S into $\mathcal{C}$ with say $\phi(s_i) = S_i$ and $\phi(s) \in C_i$. That is, S forms a set of representatives for each set C_i. (Note that a given s_i could occur in other sets C_j.)

PROBLEM 2. Max-Sum Diversification for Matroids

Let U be the underlying ground set, and $\mathcal{F}$ be the set of independent subsets of U such that $\mathcal{M} = < U, \mathcal{F} >$ is a matroid. Let $d(\cdot, \cdot)$ be a (non-negative) metric distance function measuring the distance on every pair of elements. For any subset of U, let $f(\cdot)$ be a non-negative monotone submodular set function measuring the weight of the subset. The goal of the problem is to find a subset $S \in \mathcal{F}$ that:

$$\text{maximizes} \quad f(S) + \lambda \sum_{\{u,v\}: u,v \in S} d(u, v)$$

where λ is a parameter specifying a desired trade-off between the two objectives. As before, we let $\phi(S)$ be the value of the objective function. Note that since the function $\phi(\cdot)$ is monotone, S is essentially a basis of the matroid $\mathcal{M}$. The greedy algorithm in Section 4 still applies, but it fails to achieve any constant approximation ratio. This is in contrast to the greedy algorithm of Nemhauser, Wolsey and Fisher, which achieves 2-approximation for general matroids.

Note that the problem is trivial if the rank of the matroid is less than two. Therefore, without loss of generality, we assume the rank is greater or equal to two. Let

$$\{x, y\} = \arg\max_{\{x,y\} \in \mathcal{F}}[f(\{x, y\}) + \lambda d(x, y)].$$

We now consider the following oblivious local search algorithm:

LOCAL SEARCH ALGORITHM
let S be a basis of $\mathcal{M}$ containing both x and y
while there is an $u \in U - S$ and $v \in S$ such that $S + u - v \in \mathcal{F}$
and $\phi(S + u - v) > \phi(S)$
    $S = S + u - v$
end while
return S

THEOREM 2. *The local search algorithm achieves an approximation ratio of 2 for max-sum diversification with a matroid constraint.*

Note that if the rank of the matroid is two, then the algorithm is clearly optimal. From now on, we assume the rank of the matroid is greater than two. Before we prove the theorem, we first give several lemmas. All the lemmas assume the problem and the underlying matroid without explicitly mentioning it. Let O be the optimal solution, and S, the solution at the end of the local search algorithm. Let $A = O \cap S$, $B = S - A$ and $C = O - A$.

LEMMA 2. *For any two sets $X, Y \in \mathcal{F}$ with $|X| = |Y|$, there is a bijective mapping $g : X \to Y$ such that $X - x + g(x) \in \mathcal{F}$ for any $x \in X$.*

This is a known property of a matroid and its proof can be found in [4]. Since both S and O are bases of the matroid, they have the same cardinality. Therefore, B and C have the same cardinality. By Lemma 2, there is a bijective mapping $g : B \to C$ such that $S - b + g(b) \in \mathcal{F}$ for any $b \in B$. Let $B = \{b_1, b_2, \ldots, b_t\}$, and let $c_i = g(b_i)$ for all i. Without loss of generality, we assume $t \geq 2$, for otherwise, the algorithm is optimal by the local optimality condition.

LEMMA 3. $f(S) + \sum_{i=1}^{t} f(S - b_i + c_i) \geq f(S - \sum_{i=1}^{t} b_i) + \sum_{i=1}^{t} f(S + c_i)$.

PROOF. Since f is submodular,

$$f(S) - f(S - b_1) \geq f(S + c_1) - f(S + c_1 - b_1)$$

$$f(S - b_1) - f(S - b_1 - b_2) \geq f(S + c_2) - f(S + c_2 - b_2)$$

$$\vdots$$

$$f\left(S - \sum_{i=1}^{t-1} b_i\right) - f\left(S - \sum_{i=1}^{t} b_i\right) \geq f(S + c_t) - f(S + c_t - b_t).$$

Summing up these inequalities, we have

$$f(S) - f\left(S - \sum_{i=1}^{t} b_i\right) \geq \sum_{i=1}^{t} f(S + c_i) - \sum_{i=1}^{t} f(S - b_i + c_i),$$

and the lemma follows. $\square$

LEMMA 4. $\sum_{i=1}^{t} f(S + c_i) \geq (t-1)f(S) + f(S + \sum_{i=1}^{t} c_i)$.

PROOF. Since f is submodular,

$$f(S + c_t) - f(S) = f(S + c_t) - f(S)$$

$$f(S + c_{t-1}) - f(S) \geq f(S + c_t + c_{t-1}) - f(S + c_t)$$

$$f(S + c_{t-2}) - f(S) \geq f(S + c_t + c_{t-1} + c_{t-2}) - f(S + c_t + c_{t-1})$$

$$\vdots$$

$$f(S + c_1) - f(S) \geq f\left(S + \sum_{i=1}^{t} c_i\right) - f\left(S + \sum_{i=2}^{t} c_i\right)$$

Summing up these inequalities, we have

$$\sum_{i=1}^{t} f(S + c_i) - tf(S) \geq f\left(S + \sum_{i=1}^{t} c_i\right) - f(S),$$

and the lemma follows. $\square$

LEMMA 5. $\sum_{i=1}^{t} f(S - b_i + c_i) \geq (t-2)f(S) + f(O)$.

PROOF. Combining Lemma 3 and Lemma 4, we have

$$f(S) + \sum_{i=1}^{t} f(S - b_i + c_i)$$

$$\geq f\left(S - \sum_{i=1}^{t} b_i\right) + \sum_{i=1}^{t} f(S + c_i)$$

$$\geq (t-1)f(S) + f\left(S + \sum_{i=1}^{t} c_i\right)$$

$$= (t-1)f(S) + f(S + C)$$

$$\geq (t-1)f(S) + f(O).$$

Therefore, the lemma follows. $\square$

LEMMA 6. *If $t > 2$, $d(B, C) - \sum_{i=1}^{t} d(b_i, c_i) \geq d(C)$.*

PROOF. For any b_i, c_j, c_k, we have

$$d(b_i, c_j) + d(b_i, c_k) \geq d(c_j, c_k).$$

Summing up these inequalities over all i, j, k with $i \neq j$, $i \neq k$, $j \neq k$, we have each $d(b_i, c_j)$ with $i \neq j$ is counted $(t-2)$ times; and each $d(c_i, c_j)$ with $i \neq j$ is counted $(t-2)$ times. Therefore

$$(t-2)\left[d(B, C) - \sum_{i=1}^{t} d(b_i, c_i)\right] \geq (t-2)d(C),$$

and the lemma follows. $\square$

LEMMA 7. $\sum_{i=1}^{t} d(S - b_i + c_i) \geq (t-2)d(S) + d(O)$.

PROOF.

$$\sum_{i=1}^{t} d(S - b_i + c_i)$$

$$= \sum_{i=1}^{t} [d(S) + d(c_i, S - b_i) - d(b_i, S - b_i)]$$

$$= td(S) + \sum_{i=1}^{t} d(c_i, S - b_i) - \sum_{i=1}^{t} d(b_i, S - b_i)$$

$$= td(S) + \sum_{i=1}^{t} d(c_i, S) - \sum_{i=1}^{t} d(c_i, b_i) - \sum_{i=1}^{t} d(b_i, S - b_i)$$

$$= td(S) + d(C, S) - \sum_{i=1}^{t} d(c_i, b_i) - d(A, B) - 2d(B).$$

There are two cases. If $t > 2$ then by Lemma 7, we have

$$d(C, S) - \sum_{i=1}^{t} d(c_i, b_i)$$

$$= d(A, C) + d(B, C) - \sum_{i=1}^{t} d(c_i, b_i)$$

$$\geq d(A, C) + d(C).$$

Furthermore, since $d(S) = d(A) + d(B) + d(A, B)$, we have

$2d(S) - d(A, B) - 2d(B) \geq d(A)$. Therefore

$$\sum_{i=1}^{t} d(S - b_i + c_i)$$

$$= td(S) + d(C, S) - \sum_{i=1}^{t} d(c_i, b_i) - d(A, B) - 2d(B)$$

$$\geq (t-2)d(S) + d(A, C) + d(C) + d(A)$$

$$\geq (t-2)d(S) + d(O).$$

If $t = 2$, then since the rank of the matroid is greater than two, $A \neq \emptyset$. Let z be an element in A, then we have

$$2d(S) + d(C, S) - \sum_{i=1}^{t} d(c_i, b_i) - d(A, B) - 2d(B)$$

$$= d(A, C) + d(B, C) - \sum_{i=1}^{t} d(c_i, b_i) + 2d(A) + d(A, B)$$

$$\geq d(A, C) + d(c_1, b_2) + d(c_2, b_1) + d(A) + d(z, b_1) + d(z, b_2)$$

$$\geq d(A, C) + d(A) + d(c_1, c_2)$$

$$\geq d(A, C) + d(A) + d(C)$$

$$= d(O).$$

Therefore

$$\sum_{i=1}^{t} d(S - b_i + c_i)$$

$$= td(S) + d(C, S) - \sum_{i=1}^{t} d(c_i, b_i) - d(A, B) - 2d(B)$$

$$\geq (t-2)d(S) + d(O).$$

This completes the proof. $\square$

Now with the proofs of Lemma 5 and Lemma 7, we are ready to complete the proof of Theorem 2.

PROOF. Since S is a locally optimal solution, we have $\phi(S) \geq \phi(S - b_i + c_i)$ for all i. Therefore, for all i we have

$$f(S) + \lambda d(S) \geq f(S - b_i + c_i) + \lambda d(S - b_i + c_i).$$

Summing up over all i, we have

$$tf(S) + \lambda td(S) \geq \sum_{i=1}^{t} f(S - b_i + c_i) + \lambda \sum_{i=1}^{t} d(S - b_i + c_i).$$

By Lemma 5, we have

$$tf(S) + \lambda td(S) \geq (t-2)f(S) + f(O) + \lambda \sum_{i=1}^{t} d(S - b_i + c_i).$$

By Lemma 7, we have

$$tf(S) + \lambda td(S) \geq (t-2)f(S) + f(O) + \lambda[(t-2)d(S) + d(O)].$$

Therefore,

$$2f(S) + 2\lambda d(S)) \geq f(O) + \lambda d(O).$$

$$\phi(S) \geq \frac{1}{2}\phi(O),$$

this completes the proof. $\square$

Theorem 2 shows that even in the more general case of a matroid constraint, we can still achieve the approximation ratio of 2. As is standard in such local search algorithms,

with a small sacrifice on the approximation ratio, the algorithm can be modified to run in polynomial time by requiring at least an ϵ-improvement at each iteration rather than just any improvement.

6. DYNAMIC UPDATE

In this section, we discuss dynamic updates for the max-sum diversification problem with modular set functions. The setting is that we have initially computed a good solution with some approximation guarantee. The weights are changing over time, and upon seeing a change of weight, we want to maintain the quality (the same approximation ratio) of the solution by modifying the current solution without completely recomputing it. We use the number of updates to quantify the amount of modification needed to maintain the desired approximation. An *update* is a single swap of an element in S with an element outside S, where S is the current solution. We ask the following question:

> Can we maintain a good approximation ratio with a limited number of updates?

Since the best known approximation algorithm achieves approximation ratio of 2, it is natural to ask whether it is possible to maintain that ratio through local updates. And if it is possible, how many such updates it requires. To simplify the analysis, we restrict to the following oblivious update rule. Let S be the current solution, and let u be an element in S and v be an element outside S. The marginal gain v has over u with respect to S is defined to be

$$\phi_{v \to u}(S) = \phi(S \setminus \{u\} \cup \{v\}) - \phi(S).$$

OBLIVIOUS (SINGLE ELEMENT SWAP) UPDATE RULE
Find a pair of elements (u, v) with $u \in S$ and $v \notin S$ maximizing $\phi_{v \to u}(S)$. If $\phi_{v \to u}(S) \leq 0$, do nothing; otherwise swap u with v.

Since the oblivious local search in Theorem 2 uses the same single element swap update rule, it is not hard to see that we can maintain the approximation ratio of 2. However, it is not clear how many updates are needed to maintain that ratio. We conjecture that the number of updates can be made relatively small (i.e., constant) by a non-oblivious update rule and carefully maintaining some desired configuration of the solution set. We leave this as an open question.

However, we are able to show that if we relax the requirement slightly, i.e., aiming for an approximation ratio of 3 instead of 2, and restrict slightly the magnitude of the weight-perturbation, we are able to maintain the desired ratio with a single update. Note that the weight restriction is only used for the case of a weight decrease (Theorem 4).

We divide weight-perturbations into four types: a weight increase (decrease) which occurs on an element, and a distance increase (decrease) which occurs between two elements. We denote these four types: (I), (II), (III), (IV); and we have a corresponding theorem for each case.

Before getting to the theorems, we first prove the following two lemmas. After a weight-perturbation, let S be the current solution set, and O be the optimal solution. Let S^* be the solution set after a single update using the oblivious update rule, and let $\Delta = \phi(S^*) - \phi(S)$. We again let $Z = O \cap S$, $X = O \setminus S$ and $Y = S \setminus O$.

LEMMA 8. *There exists $z \in Y$ such that*

$$\phi_z(S \setminus \{z\}) \leq \frac{1}{|Y|}[f(Y) + 2\lambda d(Y) + \lambda d(Z, Y)].$$

PROOF. If we sum up all marginal gain $\phi_y(S \setminus \{y\})$ for all $y \in Y$, we have

$$\sum_{y \in Y} \phi_y(S \setminus \{y\}) = f(Y) + 2\lambda d(Y) + \lambda d(Z, Y).$$

By an averaging argument, there must exist $z \in Y$ such that

$$\phi_z(S \setminus \{z\}) \leq \frac{1}{|Y|}[f(Y) + 2\lambda d(Y) + \lambda d(Z, Y)].$$

□

Lemma 8 ensures the existence of an element in S such that after removing it from S, the objective function value does not decrease much. The following lemma ensures that there always exists an element outside S which can increase the objective function value substantially if we bring it in.

LEMMA 9. If $\phi(S^*) < \frac{1}{3}\phi(O)$, then for all $y \in Y$, there exists $x \in X$ such that

$$\phi_x(S \setminus \{y\}) > \frac{1}{|X|}[2\phi(Z) + 3\phi(Y) + 3\lambda d(Z, Y) + 3\Delta].$$

PROOF. For any $y \in Y$, and by Lemma 1, we have

$$\begin{aligned} & f(X) + \lambda d(S \setminus \{y\}, X) \\ = \; & f(X) + \lambda d(Z, X) + \lambda d(Y \setminus \{y\}, X) \\ \geq \; & f(X) + \lambda d(Z, X) + \lambda d(X). \end{aligned}$$

Note that since $\phi(S^*) = \phi(S) + \Delta < \frac{1}{3}\phi(O)$, we have

$$\begin{aligned} \phi(O) \; = \; & \phi(Z) + f(X) + \lambda d(X) + \lambda d(Z, X) \\ > \; & 3\phi(Z) + 3\phi(Y) + 3\lambda d(Z, Y) + 3\Delta. \end{aligned}$$

Therefore,

$$\begin{aligned} & f(X) + \lambda d(S \setminus \{y\}, X) \\ \geq \; & f(X) + \lambda d(Z, X) + \lambda d(X) \\ > \; & 2\phi(Z) + 3\phi(Y) + 3\lambda d(Z, Y) + 3\Delta. \end{aligned}$$

This implies there must exist $x \in X$ such that

$$\phi_x(S \setminus \{y\}) > \frac{1}{|X|}[2\phi(Z) + 3\phi(Y) + 3\lambda d(Z, Y) + 3\Delta].$$

□

Combining Lemma 8 and 9, we can give a lower bound for Δ. We have the following corollary.

COROLLARY 1. If $\phi(S^*) < \frac{1}{3}\phi(O)$, then we have $|Y| > 3$ and furthermore

$$\Delta > \frac{1}{|Y| - 3}[2\phi(Z) + 2f(Y) + \lambda d(Y) + 2\lambda d(Z, Y)].$$

PROOF. By Lemma 8, there exists $y \in Y$ such that

$$\phi_y(S \setminus \{y\}) \leq \frac{1}{|Y|}[f(Y) + 2\lambda d(Y) + \lambda d(Z, Y)].$$

Since $\phi(S^*) < \frac{1}{3}\phi(O)$, by Lemma 9, for this particular y, there exists $x \in X$ such that

$$\phi_x(S \setminus \{y\}) > \frac{1}{|X|}[2\phi(Z) + 3\phi(Y) + 3\lambda d(Z, Y) + 3\Delta].$$

Since $|X| = |Y|$, we have

$$\Delta > \frac{1}{|Y|}[2\phi(Z) + 2f(Y) + \lambda d(Y) + 2\lambda d(Z, Y) + 3\Delta].$$

If $|Y| \leq 3$, then it is a contradiction. Therefore $|Y| > 3$. Rearranging the inequality, we have

$$\Delta > \frac{1}{|Y| - 3}[2\phi(Z) + 2f(Y) + \lambda d(Y) + 2\lambda d(Z, Y)].$$

□

COROLLARY 2. If $p \leq 3$, then for any weight or distance perturbation, we can maintain an approximation ratio of 3 with a single update.

PROOF. This is an immediate consequence of Corollary 1 since $p \geq |Y|$. □

Given Corollary 2, we will assume $p > 3$ for all the remaining results in this section. We first discuss weight-perturbations on elements.

THEOREM 3. [TYPE (I)] For any weight increase, we can maintain an approximation ratio of 3 with a single update.

PROOF. Suppose we increase the weight of s by δ. Since the optimal solution can increase by at most δ, if $\Delta \geq \frac{1}{3}\delta$, then we have maintained a ratio of 3. Hence we assume $\Delta < \frac{1}{3}\delta$. If $s \in S$ or $s \notin O$, then it is clear the ratio of 3 is maintained. The only interesting case is when $s \in O \setminus S$. Suppose, for the sake of contradiction, that $\phi(S^*) < \frac{1}{3}\phi(O)$, then by Corollary 1, we have $|Y| > 3$ and

$$\Delta > \frac{1}{|Y| - 3}[2\phi(Z) + 2f(Y) + \lambda d(Y) + 2\lambda d(Z, Y)].$$

Since $\Delta < \frac{1}{3}\delta$, we have

$$\delta > \frac{1}{|Y| - 3}[6\phi(Z) + 6f(Y) + 3\lambda d(Y) + 6\lambda d(Z, Y)].$$

On the other hand, by Lemma 8, there exists $y \in Y$ such that

$$\phi_y(S \setminus \{y\}) \leq \frac{1}{|Y|}[f(Y) + 2\lambda d(Y) + \lambda d(Z, Y)].$$

Now considering a swap of s with y, the loss by removing y from S is $\phi_y(S \setminus \{y\})$, while the increase that s brings to the set $S \setminus \{y\}$ is at least δ (as s is increased by δ, and the original weight of s is non-negative). Therefore the marginal gain of the swap of s with y is $\phi_{s \to y} \geq \delta - \phi_y(S \setminus \{y\})$ and hence

$$\phi_{s \to y}(S) \geq \delta - \frac{1}{|Y|}[f(Y) + 2\lambda d(Y) + \lambda d(Z, Y)].$$

However, $\phi_{s \to y}(S) \leq \Delta < \frac{1}{3}\delta$. Therefore, we have

$$\frac{1}{3}\delta > \delta - \frac{1}{|Y|}[f(Y) + 2\lambda d(Y) + \lambda d(Z, Y)].$$

This implies

$$\delta < \frac{1}{|Y|}[\frac{3}{2}f(Y) + 3\lambda d(Y) + \frac{3\lambda}{2}d(Z, Y)],$$

which is a contradiction. □

THEOREM 4. [TYPE (II)] For a weight decrease of magnitude δ, we can maintain an approximation ratio of 3 with

$$\lceil \log_{\frac{p-2}{p-3}} \frac{w}{w - \delta} \rceil$$

updates, where w is the weight of the solution before the weight decrease. In particular, if $\delta \leq \frac{w}{p-2}$, we only need a single update.

162

PROOF. Suppose we decrease the weight of s by δ. Without loss of generality, we can assume $s \in S$. Suppose, for the sake of contradiction, that $\phi(S^*) < \frac{1}{3}\phi(O)$, then by Corollary 1, we have $|Y| > 3$ and

$$\Delta > \frac{1}{|Y|-3}[2\phi(Z) + 2f(Y) + \lambda d(Y) + 2\lambda d(Z,Y)]$$
$$\geq \frac{1}{p-3}\phi(S).$$

Therefore

$$\phi(S^*) > \frac{p-2}{p-3}\phi(S).$$

This implies that we can maintain the approximation ratio with

$$\lceil \log_{\frac{p-2}{p-3}} \frac{w}{w-\delta} \rceil$$

number of updates. In particular, if $\delta \leq \frac{w}{p-2}$, we only need a single update. □

We now discuss the weight-perturbations between two elements. We assume that such perturbations preserve the metric condition. Furthermore, we assume $p > 3$ for otherwise, by Corollary 1, the ratio of 3 is maintained.

THEOREM 5. [TYPE (III)] *For any distance increase, we can maintain an approximation ratio of 3 with a single update.*

PROOF. Suppose we increase the distance of (x,y) by δ, and for the sake of contradiction, we assume that $\phi(S^*) < \frac{1}{3}\phi(O)$, then by Corollary 1, we have $|Y| > 3$ and

$$\Delta > \frac{1}{|Y|-3}[2\phi(Z) + 2f(Y) + \lambda d(Y) + 2\lambda d(Z,Y)].$$

Since $\Delta < \frac{1}{3}\delta$, we have

$$\delta > \frac{3}{|Y|-3}[2\phi(Z) + 2f(Y) + \lambda d(Y) + 2\lambda d(Z,Y)]$$
$$\geq \frac{3}{p-3}\phi(S).$$

If both x and y are in S, then it is not hard to see that the ratio of 3 is maintained. Otherwise, there are two cases:

1. Exactly one of x and y is in S, without loss of generality, we assume $y \in S$. Considering that we swap x with any vertex $z \in S$ other than y. Since after the swap, both x and y are now in S, by the triangle inequality of the metric condition, we have

$$\Delta \geq (p-1)\delta - \phi(S) > (\frac{2}{3}p - 2)\delta.$$

Since $p > 3$, we have

$$\Delta > (\frac{2}{3}p - 2)\delta \geq \frac{2}{3}\delta > 2\Delta,$$

which is a contradiction.

2. Both x and y are outside in S. By Lemma 8, there exists $z \in Y$ such that

$$\phi_z(S \setminus \{z\}) \leq \frac{1}{|Y|}[f(Y) + 2\lambda d(Y) + \lambda d(Z,Y)].$$

Consider the set $T = \{x,y\}$ with $S \setminus \{z\}$, by the triangle inequality of the metric condition, we have

$d(T, S \setminus \{z\}) \geq (p-1)\delta$. Therefore, at least one of x and y, without loss of generality, assuming x, has the following property:

$$d(x, S \setminus \{z\}) \geq \frac{(p-1)\delta}{2}.$$

Considering that we swap x with z, we have:

$$\Delta \geq \frac{(p-1)}{2}\delta - \frac{1}{|Y|}[f(Y) + 2\lambda d(Y) + \lambda d(Z,Y)].$$

Since $\Delta < \frac{1}{3}\delta$, we have

$$\frac{1}{3}\delta > \frac{(p-1)}{2}\delta - \frac{1}{|Y|}[f(Y) + 2\lambda d(Y) + \lambda d(Z,Y)].$$

This implies that

$$\delta < \frac{6}{3p-5} \cdot \frac{1}{|Y|}[f(Y) + 2\lambda d(Y) + \lambda d(Z,Y)].$$

Since $p > 3$, we have

$$\delta < \frac{1}{|Y|}[\frac{6}{7}f(Y) + \frac{12\lambda}{7}d(Y) + \frac{6\lambda}{7}d(Z,Y)],$$

which is a contradiction.

Therefore, $\phi(S^*) \geq \frac{1}{3}\phi(O)$; this completes the proof. □

THEOREM 6. [TYPE (IV)] *For any distance decrease, we can maintain an approximation ratio of 3 with a single update.*

PROOF. Suppose we decrease the distance of (x,y) by δ. Without loss of generality, we assume both x and y are in S, for otherwise, it is not hard to see the ratio of 3 is maintained. Suppose, for the sake of contradiction, that $\phi(S^*) < \frac{1}{3}\phi(O)$, then by Corollary 1, we have $|Y| > 3$ and

$$\Delta > \frac{1}{|Y|-3}[2\phi(Z) + 2f(Y) + \lambda d(Y) + 2\lambda d(Z,Y)]$$
$$\geq \frac{1}{p-3}\phi(S).$$

If $\Delta \geq \delta$, then the ratio of 3 is maintained. Otherwise,

$$\delta > \Delta \geq \frac{1}{p-3}\phi(S).$$

By the triangle inequality of the metric condition, we have

$$\phi(S) \geq (p-2)\delta > \frac{p-2}{p-3}\phi(S) > \phi(S),$$

which is a contradiction. □

Combining Theorem 3, 4, 5, 6, we have the following corollary.

COROLLARY 3. *If the initial solution achieves approximation ratio of 3, then for any weight-perturbation of* TYPE (I), (III), (IV); *and any weight-perturbation of* TYPE (II) *that is no more than $\frac{1}{p-2}$ of the current solution for $p > 3$ and arbitrary for $p \leq 3$, we can maintain the ratio of 3 with a single update.*

7. EXPERIMENTS

In this section, we present the results of some preliminary experiments. Note that all our results in this paper are of theoretical nature, and the purpose of the experiments in this section are to provide additional insights about our algorithms. They shall not be treated as experimental evidences for the performance of our algorithms.

We consider the max-sum diversification problem with modular set functions. In order to have gradual control of the parameters, we use the following different, but equivalent form of the objective function:

$$\alpha f(S) + (1 - \alpha) \sum_{u,v \in S} d(u,v),$$

where α is a real number in $[0, 1]$. We conduct two sets of experiments:

1. We compare the performance (the approximation ratio) of the greedy algorithm proposed in [17] with the greedy algorithm that we propose in this paper.

2. We simulate three different dynamically changing environments, and record the worst approximation ratio occurring with a single application of the oblivious update rule.

Note that both experiments use synthetic data which is generated uniformly at random within a given range, and in order to compute the optimal solution (to evaluate the approximation ratio), we restrict the size of the input data. Therefore, our experiments are not representative for real data sets and large input cases, but nevertheless, they shed some light on the behavior of the proposed algorithm and the dynamic update rule.

7.1 Comparing Two Greedy Algorithms

The first experiment is designed to compare the greedy algorithm proposed in [17] with the greedy algorithm that we propose in this paper. We generate input instances of 50 vertices, with vertex weights chosen uniformly at random from $[0, 1]$ and distances chosen uniformly at random from $[1, 2]$ to ensure the triangle inequality. The target set size is chosen to be five. These instances are small enough that we can determine the optimal solution. We run both the greedy algorithm of [17], denoted as Greedy A, and our greedy algorithm, denoted as Greedy B, on the same instance for different values of α. This is repeated 100 times for each value of α and both approximation ratios are recorded for every instance. These approximation ratios are then averaged to represent the performance of the algorithm for each α value. The results are shown in Fig. 1; the horizontal axis measures α values, and the vertical axis measures the approximation ratio (the smaller the bar height, the better the ratio).

Although both algorithms have the same provable theoretical approximation ratio of 2, we observe the following phenomena:

1. Greedy B significantly outperforms Greedy A for every value of α. The worst case for each algorithm occurs at $\alpha = 0$ (i.e., no element weight), where Greedy A has an approximation ratio of 1.26 while Greedy B is still well below 1.05.

2. Both algorithms performs well below the theoretical approximation bound of 2.

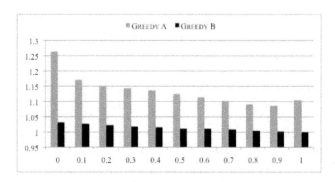

Figure 1: A Comparison of Two Greedy Algorithms

3. As α increase, both algorithms tend to perform better. Note that Greedy B achieves the optimum when $\alpha = 1$ as it then becomes the "standard" greedy algorithm [31, 14]; however, this is not the case for Greedy A.

Despite the fact that the experiment is only conducted for very limited cases, it gives some evidence that our greedy algorithm outperforms the one proposed in [17].

7.2 Approximation Ratio in Dynamic Updates

For dynamic update, we use the same type of random instance in the previous experiment. We have three different dynamically changing environments:

1. VPERTURBATION: each perturbation is a weight change on an element.

2. EPERTURBATION: each perturbation is a weight change between two elements.

3. MPERTURBATION: each perturbation is one of the above two with equal probability.

For each of the environments above and every value of α, we start with a greedy solution (a 2-approximation) and run 20 steps of simulation, where each step consists of a weight change of the stated type, followed by a single application of the oblivious update rule. We repeat this 100 times and record the worst approximation ratio occurring during these 100 updates. The results are shown in Fig. 2; again the hori-

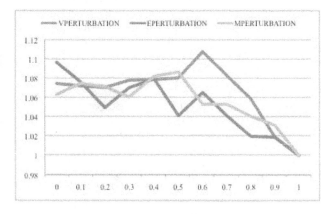

Figure 2: Approximation Ratio in Dynamic Updates

zontal axis measures α values, and the vertical axis measures the approximation ratio.

We have the following observations:

1. In any dynamic changing environment, the maintained ratio is well below the provable ratio of 3. The worst observed ratio is about 1.11.

2. The maintained ratios are decreasing to 1 for increasing $\alpha \geq 0.6$ approximately.

From the experiment, we see that oblivious update rule seems effective for maintaining a good approximation ratio in a dynamically changing environment.

8. CONCLUSION

We study the max-sum diversification with monotone submodular set functions and give a natural 2-approximation greedy algorithm for the problem. We further extend the problem to matroids and give a 2-approximation local search algorithm for the problem. We examine the dynamic update setting for modular set functions, where the weights and distances are constantly changing over time and the goal is to maintain a solution with good quality with a limited number of updates. We propose a simple update rule: the oblivious (single swap) update rule, and show that if the weight-perturbation is not too large, we can maintain an approximation ratio of 3 with a single update.

The diversification problem has many important applications and there are many interesting future directions. Although in this paper we restricted ourselves to the max-sum objective, there are many other well-defined notion of diversity that can be considered, see for example [7]. The max-sum case can be also viewed as the ℓ_1-norm; what about other norms?

Another important open question is to find the tight approximation ratio for max-sum diversification with monotone submodular set functions (for both the uniform matroid case and the general matroid case). We know the ratio cannot be better than $\frac{e}{e-1}$ assuming P is not equal to NP [29] and an approximation ratio of 2 is obtained in this paper. Is it possible to beat 2? In the general matroid case, the greedy algorithm given in Section 4 fails to achieve any constant approximation ratio, but how about other greedy algorithms? What if we start with the best pair?

In a dynamic update setting, we only considered the oblivious single swap update rule. It is interesting to see if it is possible to maintain a better ratio than 3 with a limited number of updates, by larger cardinality swaps, and/or by a non-oblivious update rule. We leave this as an interesting open question of the paper.

Finally, a crucial property used throughout our results is the triangle inequality. For a relaxed version of the triangle inequality can we relate the approximation ratio to the parameter of a relaxed triangle inequality?

9. ACKNOWLEDGMENTS

We thank MITACS and Thoora Inc. for its generous support and Justin Ward for many helpful discussions. We also thank anonymous referees for pointing out several small mistakes in the primary version of the paper and references to some early work in diversification.

10. REFERENCES

[1] R. Agrawal, S. Gollapudi, A. Halverson, and S. Ieong. Diversifying search results. In *WSDM*, pages 5–14, 2009.

[2] N. Bansal, K. Jain, A. Kazeykina, and J. Naor. Approximation algorithms for diversified search ranking. In *ICALP (2)*, pages 273–284, 2010.

[3] C. Brandt, T. Joachims, Y. Yue, and J. Bank. Dynamic ranked retrieval. In *WSDM*, pages 247–256, 2011.

[4] R. A. Brualdi. Comments on bases in dependence structures. *Bulletin of the Australian Mathematical Society*, 1(02):161–167, 1969.

[5] G. Călinescu, C. Chekuri, M. Pál, and J. Vondrák. Maximizing a monotone submodular function subject to a matroid constraint. *SIAM J. Comput.*, 40(6):1740–1766, 2011.

[6] J. Carbonell and J. Goldstein. The use of mmr, diversity-based reranking for reordering documents and producing summaries. In *Proceedings of the 21st annual international ACM SIGIR conference on Research and development in information retrieval*, SIGIR '98, pages 335–336, New York, NY, USA, 1998. ACM.

[7] B. Chandra and M. M. Halldórsson. Facility dispersion and remote subgraphs. In *Proceedings of the 5th Scandinavian Workshop on Algorithm Theory*, pages 53–65, London, UK, 1996. Springer-Verlag.

[8] B. Chandra and M. M. Halldórsson. Approximation algorithms for dispersion problems. *J. Algorithms*, 38(2):438–465, 2001.

[9] H. Chen and D. R. Karger. Less is more: probabilistic models for retrieving fewer relevant documents. In *SIGIR*, pages 429–436, 2006.

[10] E. Demidova, P. Fankhauser, X. Zhou, and W. Nejdl. Divq: diversification for keyword search over structured databases. In *Proceeding of the 33rd international ACM SIGIR conference on Research and development in information retrieval*, SIGIR '10, pages 331–338. ACM, 2010.

[11] Z. Dou, S. Hu, K. Chen, R. Song, and J.-R. Wen. Multi-dimensional search result diversification. In *WSDM*, pages 475–484, 2011.

[12] M. Drosou and E. Pitoura. Diversity over continuous data. *IEEE Data Eng. Bull.*, 32(4):49–56, 2009.

[13] M. Drosou and E. Pitoura. Search result diversification. *SIGMOD Record*, 39(1):41–47, 2010.

[14] J. Edmonds. Matroids and the greedy algorithm. *Mathematical Programming*, 1:127–136, 1971.

[15] E. Erkut. The discrete p-dispersion problem. *European Journal of Operational Research*, 46(1):48–60, May 1990.

[16] E. Erkut and S. Neuman. Analytical models for locating undesirable facilities. *European Journal of Operational Research*, 40(3):275–291, June 1989.

[17] S. Gollapudi and A. Sharma. An axiomatic approach for result diversification. In *World Wide Web Conference Series*, pages 381–390, 2009.

[18] M. M. Halldórsson, K. Iwano, N. Katoh, and T. Tokuyama. Finding subsets maximizing minimum structures. In *Symposium on Discrete Algorithms*, pages 150–159, 1995.

[19] P. Hansen and I. D. Moon. Dispersion facilities on a network. *Presentation at the TIMS/ORSA Joint National Meeting, Washington, D.C.*, 1988.

[20] R. Hassin, S. Rubinstein, and A. Tamir. Approximation algorithms for maximum dispersion. *Oper. Res. Lett.*, 21(3):133–137, 1997.

[21] D. Kempe, J. Kleinberg, and E. Tardos. Maximizing the spread of influence through a social network. In *Proceedings of the ninth ACM SIGKDD international conference on Knowledge discovery and data mining*, KDD '03, pages 137–146, 2003.

[22] S. Khanna, R. Motwani, M. Sudan, and U. V. Vazirani. On syntactic versus computational views of approximability. *Electronic Colloquium on Computational Complexity (ECCC)*, 2(23), 1995.

[23] M. J. Kuby. Programming models for facility dispersion: The p-dispersion and maxisum dispersion problems. *Geographical Analysis*, 19(4):315–329, 1987.

[24] H. Lin and J. Bilmes. Multi-document summarization via budgeted maximization of submodular functions. In *HLT-NAACL*, pages 912–920, 2010.

[25] H. Lin and J. Bilmes. A class of submodular functions for document summarization. In *North American chapter of the Association for Computational Linguistics/Human Language Technology Conference (NAACL/HLT-2011)*, Portland, OR, June 2011. (long paper).

[26] H. Lin, J. Bilmes, and S. Xie. Graph-based submodular selection for extractive summarization. In *Proc. IEEE Automatic Speech Recognition and Understanding (ASRU)*, Merano, Italy, December 2009.

[27] Z. Liu, P. Sun, and Y. Chen. Structured search result differentiation. *PVLDB*, 2(1):313–324, 2009.

[28] E. Minack, W. Siberski, and W. Nejdl. Incremental diversification for very large sets: a streaming-based approach. In *SIGIR*, pages 585–594, 2011.

[29] G. Nemhauser, L. Wolsey, and M. Fisher. An analysis of the approximations for maximizing submodular set functions. *Mathematical Programming*, 1978.

[30] F. Radlinski, R. Kleinberg, and T. Joachims. Learning diverse rankings with multi-armed bandits. In *ICML*, pages 784–791, 2008.

[31] R. Rado. A note on independence functios. *Proceedings of the London Mathematical Society*, 7:300–320, 1957.

[32] D. Rafiei, K. Bharat, and A. Shukla. Diversifying web search results. In *WWW*, pages 781–790, 2010.

[33] S. S. Ravi, D. J. Rosenkrantz, and G. K. Tayi. Heuristic and special case algorithms for dispersion problems. *Operations Research*, 42(2):299–310, March-April 1994.

[34] R. L. T. Santos, C. Macdonald, and I. Ounis. Intent-aware search result diversification. In *SIGIR*, pages 595–604, 2011.

[35] A. Schrijver. *Combinatorial Optimization: Polyhedra and Efficiency*. Springer, 2003.

[36] A. Slivkins, F. Radlinski, and S. Gollapudi. Learning optimally diverse rankings over large document collections. In *ICML*, pages 983–990, 2010.

[37] M. R. Vieira, H. L. Razente, M. C. N. Barioni, M. Hadjieleftheriou, D. Srivastava, C. T. Jr., and V. J. Tsotras. Divdb: A system for diversifying query results. *PVLDB*, 4(12):1395–1398, 2011.

[38] M. R. Vieira, H. L. Razente, M. C. N. Barioni, M. Hadjieleftheriou, D. Srivastava, C. T. Jr., and V. J. Tsotras. On query result diversification. In *ICDE*, pages 1163–1174, 2011.

[39] D. W. Wang and Y.-S. Kuo. A study on two geometric location problems. *Inf. Process. Lett.*, 28:281–286, August 1988.

[40] C. Yu, L. Lakshmanan, and S. Amer-Yahia. It takes variety to make a world: diversification in recommender systems. In *Proceedings of the 12th International Conference on Extending Database Technology: Advances in Database Technology*, EDBT '09, pages 368–378, 2009.

[41] Y. Yue and T. Joachims. Predicting diverse subsets using structural svms. In *ICML*, pages 1224–1231, 2008.

[42] C. Zhai, W. W. Cohen, and J. D. Lafferty. Beyond independent relevance: methods and evaluation metrics for subtopic retrieval. In *SIGIR*, pages 10–17, 2003.

[43] F. Zhao, X. Zhang, A. K. H. Tung, and G. Chen. Broad: Diversified keyword search in databases. *PVLDB*, 4(12):1355–1358, 2011.

[44] X. Zhu, A. B. Goldberg, J. V. Gael, and D. Andrzejewski. Improving diversity in ranking using absorbing random walks. In *HLT-NAACL*, pages 97–104, 2007.

Query-Based Data Pricing

Paraschos Koutris, Prasang Upadhyaya,
Magdalena Balazinska, Bill Howe, and Dan Suciu
University of Washington, Seattle, WA
{pkoutris,prasang,magda,billhowe,suciu}@cs.washington.edu

ABSTRACT

Data is increasingly being bought and sold online, and Web-based marketplace services have emerged to facilitate these activities. However, current mechanisms for pricing data are very simple: buyers can choose only from a set of explicit views, each with a specific price. In this paper, we propose a framework for pricing data on the Internet that, given the price of a few views, allows the price of any query to be derived automatically. We call this capability "query-based pricing." We first identify two important properties that the pricing function must satisfy, called *arbitrage-free* and *discount-free*. Then, we prove that there exists a unique function that satisfies these properties and extends the seller's explicit prices to all queries. When both the views and the query are Unions of Conjunctive Queries, the complexity of computing the price is high. To ensure tractability, we restrict the explicit prices to be defined only on selection views (which is the common practice today). We give an algorithm with polynomial time data complexity for computing the price of any chain query by reducing the problem to network flow. Furthermore, we completely characterize the class of Conjunctive Queries without self-joins that have PTIME data complexity (this class is slightly larger than chain queries), and prove that pricing all other queries is NP-complete, thus establishing a dichotomy on the complexity of the pricing problem when all views are selection queries.

Categories and Subject Descriptors

H.2.4 [**Systems**]: Relational Databases

General Terms

Algorithms, Economics, Theory

Keywords

Data Pricing, Arbitrage, Query Determinacy

1. INTRODUCTION

Whether for market research, targeted product advertisement, or other business decisions, companies commonly purchase data. Increasingly, such data is being bought and sold online. For example, Xignite [31] sells financial data, Gnip [1] provides data from social media, PatientsLikeMe [2] sells anonymized, self-reported patient statistics to pharmaceutical companies, and AggData [6] aggregates various types of data available on the Web. To support and facilitate this online *data market*, Web-based marketplace services have recently emerged: the Windows Azure Marketplace [9] offers over 100 data sources from 42 publishers in 16 categories, and Infochimps [17] offers over 15,000 data sets also from multiple vendors.

Current marketplace services do not support complex ad hoc queries, in part because it is not clear how to assign a price to the result. Instead, sellers are asked to define a fixed set of (possibly parameterized) views and assign each a specific price. This simplistic approach not only forces the seller to try and anticipate every view in which a buyer might be interested, but also forces the buyer to browse a large catalog of views (with possibly unknown redundancies and relationships), then often purchase some superset of the data they actually need. Worse, this pricing model can expose non-obvious arbitrage situations that can allow a cunning buyer to obtain data for less than the advertised price. A better approach, which we explore in this paper, is to allow the seller to assign prices to a manageable number of views, then automatically derive the correct price for *any query*.

Consider an example. CustomLists [13] sells the American Business Database for $399; a customer can also buy the subset of companies that have an e-mail address for $299 or only information about businesses in Washington State for $199. A customer interested in only a set of specific counties in various states may not be willing to pay $399 for data she does not need, and so refuses to buy. In response, the seller might provide a view for each county in every state. However, the relationship between state-based pricing and county-based pricing is difficult for either the seller or the buyer to reason about, and inconsistencies or arbitrage situations may result. For example, if the database does not contain any business information for some fraction of counties in a state, then purchasing the data for the remaining counties could be cheaper, yet could yield the same information content as purchasing the data for the entire state.

Query-based Pricing. To address the above challenge, in this paper, we propose a framework for pricing data on the Internet that allows the seller to assign explicit prices to only a few views (or sets of views), yet allows the buyer to issue and purchase any query. The price of the query is derived *automatically* from the explicit prices of the views. Thus, buyers have full freedom to choose which query to buy, without requiring the seller to explicitly set prices on an exhaustive catalog of all possible queries. We call this pricing mechanism *query-based pricing*. Our mechanism is based on the economic theory of pricing information products using *versions* [27] (reviewed in Section 5), in the sense that each query corresponds to a version of the original data. Since every query (in a given query language) is a version, our framework allows a large number of versions, and, consequently, appeals to large variety of buyers with a large variety of needs.

Formally, query-based pricing consists of a *pricing function*, which takes as input a database instance and a query (or set of queries) and returns a non-negative real number representing the price. We argue that a reasonable pricing function should satisfy two axioms.

First, the pricing function should be *arbitrage-free*. Consider the USA business dataset: if p is the price for the entire dataset and $p_1, \ldots p_{50}$ the prices for the data in each of the 50 states, then a rational seller would ensure that $p_1 + \ldots + p_{50} \geq p$. Otherwise, no buyer would pay for the entire dataset, but would instead buy all 50 states separately. In general, we say that a pricing function is arbitrage-free if whenever a query q is "determined" by the queries $q_1, \ldots, q_n$, then their prices satisfy $p \leq p_1 + \ldots + p_n$. Determinacy means that the first query can be answered from the latter queries. It should not be confused with query containment: if q is contained in q', it does not mean that the price of q' is related to that of q. For example, q' may return the list of all Fortune 500 companies, while q returns a small subset of companies whose stocks have a "strong buy" recommendation. The seller computes q by semi-joining with a proprietary database, and the buyer cannot answer it only from q'. In this example, while q is contained in q', we expect the price of q to be much higher than the price of q', even though q returns less data.

Second, the pricing function should be *discount-free*. This axiom concerns the way the pricing function is derived from the explicit views and prices set by the seller. When she specifies an explicit price p_i for view V_i, the sellers' intent is to sell the view at a discount over the entire data set: the latter is normally sold at a premium price, $p \gg p_i$. The discount-free axiom requires that the pricing function will not introduce any new discounts additional to those explicitly defined by the seller.

In addition to these two axioms, we argue that the pricing function should also be *monotone* with respect to database updates: when new data items are inserted into the database, the price of a query should not decrease. We show that, in general, the pricing function is not necessarily monotone, but give sufficient conditions under which it is.

In today's data markets, the price of the data reflects only its information value, and does not include any computational costs associated with user queries. We make the same assumption in this paper. We also ignore the computational cost in the definition of arbitrage, assuming the worst-case scenario that a buyer has the capability to determine any query given apropriate views, assuming the task is computationally feasible.

Contributions. In this paper, we present several results on query-based pricing.

Our first result is a simple but fundamental formula for computing an arbitrage-free, discount-free pricing function that agrees with the seller's explicit price points, and for testing whether one exists; if it exists, we call the set of price points *consistent*. To check consistency, it suffices to check that no arbitrage is possible between the explicit price points defined by the seller: there are only finitely many arbitrage combinations, as opposed to the infinitely many arbitrage combinations on all possible queries; hence, consistency is decidable. When the set is consistent, the pricing function is unique, and is given by the *arbitrage-price* formula (Equation 2). This implies an explicit, yet inefficient method for computing the price, which is presented in Section 2.

Second, we turn to the tractability question. We show that even when the seller's explicit price points are restricted to selection queries (which is the common case for data sold online today), computing the price of certain conjunctive queries is NP-hard in the size of the input database. For this reason, we propose a restriction of conjunctive queries, which we call *Generalized Chain Queries*, or GCHQ. These are full conjunctive queries whose atoms can be ordered in a sequence such that for any partition into a prefix and a suffix, the two sets of atoms share at most one variable. GCHQ includes all path joins, like $R(x,y), S(y,z), T(z,u), P(u,v)$, star joins, like $R(x,y), S(x,z,u), T(x,v), P(x,w)$, and combinations. We prove that, when all explicit price points are selection queries, one can compute the price of every GCHQ query in PTIME data complexity. This is the main result of our paper, and provides a practical framework for query-based pricing. The algorithm is based on a non-trivial reduction to the MIN-CUT problem in weighted graphs, which is the dual of the MAX-FLOW problem [12], Subsection 3.1.

Third, we study the complexity of all conjunctive queries without self-joins. We prove that cycle queries (which are *not* generalized chain queries) can also be computed in polynomial time: this is the most difficult result in our paper, and the algorithm is quite different from the algorithm for GCHQ. With this result, we can prove a dichotomy of the data complexity of all conjunctive queries without self-joins, in PTIME or NP-complete, Subsection 3.2.

Our pricing framework is based on a notion of query determinacy. Informally, we say that a set of views V *determines* some query Q if we can compute the answer of Q only from the answers of the views without having access to the underlying database. *Information-theoretic* determinacy, denoted $V \twoheadrightarrow Q$, is discussed by Segoufin and Vianu [26] and by Nash, Segoufin, and Vianu [23, 24], and is a notion that is independent of the database instance; their motivation comes from *local-as-view* data integration and *semantic caching*, where an instance independent rewriting is needed. For query-based pricing, however, the database instance cannot be ignored when checking determinacy, since the price normally depends on the state of the database. For example, consider a query Q_1 that asks for the businesses that are located in both Oregon and Washington State and a query Q_2 that asks for the restaurants located in Oregon, Washington and Idaho. In general, we cannot answer Q_2 if we know the answer of Q_1. But suppose we examine the answer for Q_1 and note that it includes no restaurants: then we can safely determine that Q_2 is empty. We define *instance-*

based determinacy, $D \vdash V \twoheadrightarrow Q$, to mean that, for all D' if $V(D') = V(D)$, then $Q(D) = Q(D')$. Information-theoretic determinacy is equivalent to instance-based determinacy *for every instance D*. We prove several results on the complexity of checking instance-based determinacy: for unions of conjunctive queries, it is Π_2^p, and the data complexity (when V, Q are fixed and the input is only D) is co-NP complete (Theorem 2.3). When the views are restricted to selection queries (which is a case of special interest in query-based pricing), then for any monotone query Q, instance-based determinacy has polynomial time data complexity, assuming Q itself has PTIME data complexity (Theorem 3.3).

The paper is organized as follows. We introduce the query-based pricing framework and give the fundamental formula for checking consistency and computing the pricing function in Section 2. We turn to the tractability questions in Section 3, where we describe our main result consisting of the polynomial time algorithm for Generalized Chain Queries in Subsection 3.1, and give the dichotomy theorem in Subsection 3.2. We discuss some loose ends in Section 2 and related work in Section 5, then conclude in Section 6.

2. THE QUERY PRICING FRAMEWORK

2.1 Notations

Fix a relational schema $\mathbf{R} = (R_1, \ldots, R_k)$; we denote a database instance with $D = (R_1^D, \ldots, R_k^D)$, and the set of all database instances with $Inst_{\mathbf{R}}$ [20]. In this paper we only consider monotone queries, and we denote $\mathcal{L}$ a fixed query language; in particular, CQ, UCQ are Conjunctive Queries, and Unions of Conjunctive Queries respectively. $Q(D)$ denotes the answer of a query Q on a database D. A *query bundle* is a finite set of queries; we use the term "bundle" rather than "set" to avoid confusion between a set of queries and a set of answers. We denote by $B(\mathcal{L})$ the set of query bundles over $\mathcal{L}$, and write a bundle as $\mathbf{Q} = (Q_1, \ldots, Q_m)$. The *output schema* of a query bundle is $\mathbf{R}_{\mathbf{Q}} = (R_{Q_1}, \ldots, R_{Q_m})$, and consists of one relation name for each query. Thus, a bundle defines a function $\mathbf{Q} : Inst_{\mathbf{R}} \to Inst_{\mathbf{R}_{\mathbf{Q}}}$.

The *identity bundle*, $\mathbf{ID}$, is the bundle that returns the entire dataset, $\mathbf{ID}(D) = (R_1^D, \ldots, R_k^D)$. The *empty bundle* is denoted (): it is the empty set of queries, not to be confused with the emptyset query. Given two bundles, $\mathbf{Q}_1$ and $\mathbf{Q}_2$, we denote their union as $\mathbf{Q} = \mathbf{Q}_1, \mathbf{Q}_2$: this is the query bundle consisting of all queries in $\mathbf{Q}_1$ and $\mathbf{Q}_2$, not to be confused with the union $Q_1 \cup Q_2$ of two queries of the same arity.

2.2 The Pricing Function

DEFINITION 2.1 (PRICING FUNCTION). *Fix a database instance $D \in Inst_{\mathbf{R}}$. A static pricing function is a function $p_D : B(\mathcal{L}) \to \mathbb{R}$.*

A dynamic pricing function is a partial function $p : Inst_{\mathbf{R}} \to (B(\mathcal{L}) \to \mathbb{R})$, s.t. for each D where p is defined, $p(D)$ is a static pricing function. We write p_D for $p(D)$.

For now, we allow prices to be negative, but we show in Proposition 2.8 that they are always non-negative under reasonable assumptions. The intuition is as follows. If the user asks for the bundle $\mathbf{Q}$, then she has to pay the price $p_D(\mathbf{Q})$, where D is the current database instance. The static pricing function is defined only for the current state of the database D. A dynamic pricing function p allows

the database to be updated, and associates a different pricing function p_D to each database; notice that it need not be defined for all instances $D \in Inst_{\mathbf{R}}$. We start with static pricing in this section, and call a static pricing function simply a pricing function; we discuss dynamic pricing in Subsection 2.7.

The price is for an entire query bundle, not just for one query. For example, if a user needs to compute queries Q_1, Q_2, and Q_3, then she could issue them separately, and pay $p_D(Q_1) + p_D(Q_2) + p_D(Q_3)$, but she also has the option of issuing them together, as a bundle, and pay $p_D(Q_1, Q_2, Q_3)$. We will show that, in general, the pricing function is subadditive: the price of a bundle is always lower than the sum of the individual prices.

In the query pricing framework, the seller does not specify the pricing function directly, but gives only a finite set of explicit price points. The system then computes the pricing function on all queries; this function must, furthermore, satisfy two axioms, arbitrage-free and discount-free. In the rest of this section we discuss the details of this framework.

2.3 Axiom 1: Arbitrage-Free

The first axiom that a pricing function must satisfy is defined in terms of a notion of determinacy. Intuitively, a bundle $\mathbf{V}$ determines a bundle $\mathbf{Q}$ given a database D, denoted $D \vdash \mathbf{V} \twoheadrightarrow \mathbf{Q}$, if one can answer $\mathbf{Q}$ from the answer of $\mathbf{V}$ by applying a function f such that $\mathbf{Q}(D) = f(\mathbf{V}(D))$. The impact on pricing is that if the user needs to answer $\mathbf{Q}$, she also has the option of purchasing $\mathbf{V}$, and then applying f. The arbitrage-free axiom requires that $p_D(\mathbf{Q}) \le p_D(\mathbf{V})$, meaning that the user never has the incentive to compute $\mathbf{Q}$ indirectly by purchasing $\mathbf{V}$. Thus, the notion of arbitrage depends on the notion of determinacy, which we define here:

DEFINITION 2.2 (INSTANCE-BASED DETERMINACY). *We say $\mathbf{V}$ determines $\mathbf{Q}$ given a database D, denoted $D \vdash \mathbf{V} \twoheadrightarrow \mathbf{Q}$, if for any D', $\mathbf{V}(D) = \mathbf{V}(D')$ implies $\mathbf{Q}(D) = \mathbf{Q}(D')$.*

The connection to answerability is the following. Let $f : Inst_{\mathbf{R}_{\mathbf{V}}} \to Inst_{\mathbf{R}_{\mathbf{Q}}}$ be Q composed with any left inverse of $\mathbf{V}$: that is, for every $E \in Inst_{\mathbf{R}_{\mathbf{V}}}$, if there exists D s.t. $\mathbf{V}(D) = E$, then choose any such D and define $f(E) = \mathbf{Q}(D)$; otherwise, $f(E)$ is undefined. One can check that $D \vdash \mathbf{V} \twoheadrightarrow \mathbf{Q}$ iff $\forall D'.\mathbf{V}(D) = \mathbf{V}(D') \Rightarrow f(\mathbf{V}(D')) = \mathbf{Q}(D')$. Thus, if the user knows $\mathbf{V}(D)$ and $D \vdash \mathbf{V} \twoheadrightarrow \mathbf{Q}$ holds, then she can compute $\mathbf{Q}(D)$ as $f(\mathbf{V}(D))$. The proof of the following theorem is in the full version of the paper [19].

THEOREM 2.3. *The combined complexity of instance-based determinacy, $D \vdash \mathbf{V} \twoheadrightarrow \mathbf{Q}$, when $\mathbf{V}, \mathbf{Q}$ are in $B(UCQ)$ is in Π_2^p; the data complexity (where $\mathbf{V}, \mathbf{Q}$ are fixed) is co-NP-complete, and remains co-NP complete even for $B(CQ)$.*

We leave open the question whether the bound on the combined complexity is tight. Instance-based determinacy is different from *information-theoretic determinacy*, defined in [23] as follows: $\mathbf{V} \twoheadrightarrow \mathbf{Q}$ if $\forall D : D \vdash \mathbf{V} \twoheadrightarrow \mathbf{Q}$. Information-theoretic determinacy, $\mathbf{V} \twoheadrightarrow \mathbf{Q}$, is undecidable for $B(UCQ)$ and its status is unknown for $B(CQ)$ [23].

EXAMPLE 2.4. *Let $Q_1(x, y, z) = R(x, y), S(y, z)$, $Q_2(y, z, u) = S(y, z), T(z, u)$ and $Q(x, y, z, u) = R(x, y), S(y, z), T(z, u)$. Then $(Q_1, Q_2) \twoheadrightarrow Q$, since it suffices to define f as the function that joins $Q_1(D)$ and $Q_2(D)$. Then, we have that*

$Q(D) = f(Q_1(D), Q_2(D))$ for all D. On the other hand, $Q_1 \not\twoheadrightarrow Q$. However, let D be a database instance s.t. $Q_1(D) = \emptyset$. Then $D \vdash Q_1 \twoheadrightarrow Q$, because we know that $Q(D) = \emptyset$. For example, let f always return the emptyset: then, for any D' s.t. $Q_1(D) = Q_1(D')(= \emptyset)$ we have $Q(D') = f(Q_1(D'))$.

In this paper we use instance-based determinacy to study pricing. However, other options are possible: for example one may use information-theoretic determinacy, or one may use its restriction that we discuss in Subsection 2.7. To keep the framework general, we base our discussion on an abstract notion of determinacy, defined below. Our results in this section apply to any determinacy relation that satisfies this definition, except for complexity results, which are specific to instance-based determinacy. Our results in the next section are specific to instance-based determinacy.

DEFINITION 2.5. *A determinacy relation is a ternary relation* $D \vdash \mathbf{V} \twoheadrightarrow \mathbf{Q}$ *that satisfies the following properties:*

Reflexivity: $D \vdash \mathbf{V}_1, \mathbf{V}_2 \twoheadrightarrow \mathbf{V}_1$.
Transitivity: *if* $D \vdash \mathbf{V}_1 \twoheadrightarrow \mathbf{V}_2$ *and* $D \vdash \mathbf{V}_2 \twoheadrightarrow \mathbf{V}_3$, *then* $D \vdash \mathbf{V}_1 \twoheadrightarrow \mathbf{V}_3$.
Augmentation: *if* $D \vdash \mathbf{V}_1 \twoheadrightarrow \mathbf{V}_2$, *then* $D \vdash \mathbf{V}_1, \mathbf{V}' \twoheadrightarrow \mathbf{V}_2, \mathbf{V}'$.
Boundedness: $D \vdash \mathbf{ID} \twoheadrightarrow \mathbf{V}$

We prove in [19] that both instance-based and information-theoretic determinacy satisfy this definition. We also have:

LEMMA 2.6. *If* $\twoheadrightarrow$ *is a determinacy relation, then (a)* $D \vdash \mathbf{V} \twoheadrightarrow ()$ *for every bundle* $\mathbf{V}$, *and (b) if* $D \vdash \mathbf{V} \twoheadrightarrow \mathbf{V}_1$ *and* $D \vdash \mathbf{V} \twoheadrightarrow \mathbf{V}_2$, *then* $D \vdash \mathbf{V} \twoheadrightarrow \mathbf{V}_1, \mathbf{V}_2$.

PROOF. The reflexivity axiom $D \vdash \mathbf{V}, () \twoheadrightarrow ()$ proves the first claim, since $\mathbf{V}, () = \mathbf{V}$. For the second, we apply augmentation to $D \vdash \mathbf{V} \twoheadrightarrow \mathbf{V}_1$ and obtain $D \vdash \mathbf{V}, \mathbf{V} \twoheadrightarrow \mathbf{V}, \mathbf{V}_1$; next apply augmentation to $D \vdash \mathbf{V} \twoheadrightarrow \mathbf{V}_2$ and obtain $D \vdash \mathbf{V}, \mathbf{V}_1 \twoheadrightarrow \mathbf{V}_1, \mathbf{V}_2$; transitivity gives us $D \vdash \mathbf{V}, \mathbf{V} \twoheadrightarrow \mathbf{V}_1, \mathbf{V}_2$, which proves the claim because $\mathbf{V}, \mathbf{V} = \mathbf{V}$. $\square$

The Arbitrage-Free Axiom. We can now state the first axiom that a pricing function must satisfy:

DEFINITION 2.7. (ARBITRAGE-FREE). *A pricing function* p_D *is* arbitrage-free *if, whenever* $D \vdash \mathbf{Q}_1, \ldots, \mathbf{Q}_k \twoheadrightarrow \mathbf{Q}$, *then* $p_D(\mathbf{Q}) \leq \sum_i p_D(\mathbf{Q}_i)$.

Of course, even if $\mathbf{Q}_1, \ldots, \mathbf{Q}_k$ determine $\mathbf{Q}$, it may be non-trivial for the buyer to compute the answer of $\mathbf{Q}$ from the answers of $\mathbf{Q}_1, \ldots, \mathbf{Q}_k$, for two reasons: she first needs to find the function f for which $f(\mathbf{Q}_1(D), \ldots, \mathbf{Q}_k(D)) = \mathbf{Q}(D)$, and, second, it may be computationally expensive to evaluate f. In this paper, however, we do not address the economic cost of the computation, focusing only on the information-theoretic aspect; i.e. we assume that the only cost that matters is that of the data itself. Thus, if an arbitrage condition exists, then the buyer will exploit it, by avoiding to pay $p_D(\mathbf{Q})$ and purchasing $\mathbf{Q}_1, \ldots, \mathbf{Q}_k$ instead, then computing $\mathbf{Q}$ (at no extra cost).

Arbitrage-free pricing functions exists: the trivial function $p_D(\mathbf{Q}) = 0$, for all $\mathbf{Q}$, is arbitrage-free; we will show non-trivial functions below. First, we prove some properties.

PROPOSITION 2.8. *Any arbitrage-free pricing function* p_D *has the following properties:*

1. *Subadditive:* $p_D(\mathbf{Q}_1, \mathbf{Q}_2) \leq p_D(\mathbf{Q}_1) + p_D(\mathbf{Q}_2)$.
2. *Non-negative:* $p_D(\mathbf{Q}) \geq 0$.
3. *Not asking[1] is free:* $p_D() = 0$.
4. *Upper-bounded:* $p_D(\mathbf{Q}) \leq p_D(\mathbf{ID})$.

PROOF. We apply arbitrage-freeness to two instances of the reflexivity property. First to $D \vdash \mathbf{Q}_1, \mathbf{Q}_2 \twoheadrightarrow \mathbf{Q}_1, \mathbf{Q}_2$, and derive $p_D(\mathbf{Q}_1, \mathbf{Q}_2) \leq p_D(\mathbf{Q}_1) + p_D(\mathbf{Q}_2)$, which proves item 1. Next to $D \vdash \mathbf{Q}, \mathbf{Q}' \twoheadrightarrow \mathbf{Q}'$, and derive $p_D(\mathbf{Q}') \leq p_D(\mathbf{Q}) + p_D(\mathbf{Q}')$, which implies $p_D(\mathbf{Q}) \geq 0$, proving item 2. For item 3, take $\mathbf{Q} = ()$ and $k = 0$ in Definition 2.7: then $D \vdash \mathbf{Q}_1, \ldots, \mathbf{Q}_k \twoheadrightarrow \mathbf{Q}$ holds by reflexivity ($D \vdash () \twoheadrightarrow ()$) and $p_D(\mathbf{Q}) \leq \sum_i p_D(\mathbf{Q}_i)$ implies $p_D() \leq 0$. Also, arbitrage-freeness applied to the boundedness axiom $D \vdash \mathbf{ID} \twoheadrightarrow \mathbf{Q}$ proves item 4. $\square$

2.4 Explicit Price Points

It is difficult to specify a non-trivial arbitrage-free pricing function, and we do not expect the seller to define such a function herself. Instead, the data seller specifies a set of explicit price points, and the system extrapolates them to a pricing function on all query bundles. A *price point* is a pair consisting of a *view* (query bundle) and a *price* (positive real number).

DEFINITION 2.9 (PRICE POINTS). *A price point is a pair* $(\mathbf{V}, p)$, *where* $\mathbf{V} \in B(\mathcal{L})$ *and* $p \in \mathbb{R}^+$. *We denote a finite set of price points* $\mathcal{S}$ *as* $\{(\mathbf{V}_1, p_1), \ldots, (\mathbf{V}_m, p_m)\}$.

We will assume that $D \vdash (\mathbf{V}_1, \ldots, \mathbf{V}_m) \twoheadrightarrow \mathbf{ID}$; i.e., the seller is always willing to sell the entire dataset, perhaps indirectly through other views. This is a reasonable assumption: if the seller does not wish to sell certain parts of the data, we can simply not model those parts by removing relation names from the schema or removing tuples from the instance. To simplify the discussion, in this section we assume that $(\mathbf{ID}, B) \in \mathcal{S}$; i.e., $\mathbf{ID}$ is sold explicitly at a (high) premium price B. We relax this assumption in Section 3.

DEFINITION 2.10 (VALIDITY). *A pricing function* p_D *is* valid *w.r.t. a set* $\mathcal{S}$ *of price points if:*

1. p_D *is arbitrage-free.*
2. $\forall (\mathbf{V}_i, p_i) \in \mathcal{S}, p_D(\mathbf{V}_i) = p_i$.

Our goal is to compute a valid pricing function for a set $\mathcal{S}$. In general, such a function may not exist; if it exists, then we call $\mathcal{S}$ consistent.

DEFINITION 2.11 (CONSISTENCY). *A set of price points* $\mathcal{S}$ *is* consistent *if it admits a valid pricing function.*

2.5 Axiom 2: Discount-Free

To see the intuition behind the second axiom, recall that B is the price set by the seller for the entire dataset. Any arbitrage-free pricing function will be $\leq B$, by Proposition 2.8 (item 4). The explicit price points in $\mathcal{S}$ can be viewed as *discounts* offered by the seller relative to the price that would be normally charged if that price point were not included in $\mathcal{S}$. The second axiom requires that a pricing function makes no additional implicit discounts.

DEFINITION 2.12 (DISCOUNT-FREE). *A valid pricing function* p_D *for* $\mathcal{S}$ *is called* discount-free *if for every valid pricing function* p'_D *for* $\mathcal{S}$ *we have:* $\forall \mathbf{Q} \in B(\mathcal{L}), p'_D(\mathbf{Q}) \leq p_D(\mathbf{Q})$.

---

[1] $p_D()$ means $p_D(())$, the price of the empty bundle.

A discount-free pricing function is unique, because if both p_D and p'_D are discount-free, then we have both $p_D \leq p'_D$ and $p'_D \leq p_D$, hence $p_D = p'_D$. We will show that, if $\mathcal{S}$ is consistent, then it admits a discount-free pricing function.

2.6 The Fundamental Query Pricing Formula

The fundamental formula gives an explicit means for checking consistency and for computing the discount-free price. The formula associates with any $\mathcal{S}$ (not necessarily consistent) a pricing function, called *arbitrage-price*; if $\mathcal{S}$ is consistent, then the arbitrage-price is the unique valid, discount-free pricing function, and if $\mathcal{S}$ is inconsistent, we can use arbitrage-price to detect it.

If $\mathbf{Q}_i$, $i = 1, 2 \ldots, k$, are query bundles, then denote their union as $\bigodot_i \mathbf{Q}_i = \mathbf{Q}_1, \ldots, \mathbf{Q}_k$. If $\mathcal{C} \subseteq \mathcal{S}$ is a set of price points, then we denote its total price as $p(\mathcal{C}) = \sum_{(\mathbf{V}_i, p_i) \in \mathcal{C}} p_i$.

Fix a price points set $\mathcal{S}$ and an instance D. The *support* of a query bundle $\mathbf{Q}$ is:

$$supp_D^{\mathcal{S}}(\mathbf{Q}) = \{\mathcal{C} \subseteq \mathcal{S} \mid D \vdash \bigodot_{(\mathbf{V}, p) \in \mathcal{C}} \mathbf{V} \twoheadrightarrow \mathbf{Q}\} \quad (1)$$

The support is non-empty, because we assumed that $\mathcal{S}$ contains **ID**. This allows us to define:

DEFINITION 2.13 (ARBITRAGE-PRICE). *The arbitrage-price of a query bundle $\mathbf{Q}$ is:*

$$p_D^{\mathcal{S}}(\mathbf{Q}) = \min_{\mathcal{C} \in supp_D^{\mathcal{S}}(\mathbf{Q})} p(\mathcal{C}) \quad (2)$$

The arbitrage-price represents the strategy of a savvy buyer: to purchase $\mathbf{Q}$, buy the cheapest support $\mathcal{C}$ for $\mathbf{Q}$, meaning the cheapest set of views that determine $\mathbf{Q}$. We prove:

LEMMA 2.14. *(a) For all $(\mathbf{V}_i, p_i) \in \mathcal{S}$, $p_D^{\mathcal{S}}(\mathbf{V}_i) \leq p_i$. In other words, the arbitrage-price is never larger than the explicit price. (b) The arbitrage-price $p_D^{\mathcal{S}}$ is arbitrage-free.*

PROOF. The first claim follows from the fact that $\{(\mathbf{V}_i, p_i)\} \in supp_D^{\mathcal{S}}(\mathbf{V}_i)$, because of the reflexivity axiom $D \vdash \mathbf{V}_i \twoheadrightarrow \mathbf{V}_i$. For the second claim, consider $D \vdash \mathbf{Q}_1, \ldots, \mathbf{Q}_k \twoheadrightarrow \mathbf{Q}$; we will prove that $p_D^{\mathcal{S}}(\mathbf{Q}) \leq \sum_i p_D^{\mathcal{S}}(\mathbf{Q}_i)$. For $i = 1, \ldots, k$, let $\mathcal{C}_i^m = \arg\min_{\mathcal{C} \in supp_D^{\mathcal{S}}(\mathbf{Q}_i)} p(\mathcal{C})$. By definition, $D \vdash \bigodot_{(\mathbf{V}_j, p_j) \in \mathcal{C}_i^m} \mathbf{V}_j \twoheadrightarrow \mathbf{Q}_i$ and $p_D^{\mathcal{S}}(\mathbf{Q}_i) = p(\mathcal{C}_i^m)$. Let $\mathcal{C} = \bigcup_i \mathcal{C}_i^m \subseteq \mathcal{S}$. Let $\mathbf{V}^m = \bigodot_{(\mathbf{V}_j, p_j) \in \mathcal{C}} \mathbf{V}_j$. Since $\mathcal{C}_i^m \in supp_D^{\mathcal{S}}(\mathbf{Q}_i)$, it follows that $\mathcal{C} \in supp_D^{\mathcal{S}}(\mathbf{Q}_i)$ because the set $supp_D^{\mathcal{S}}(\mathbf{Q}_i)$ is upwards closed[2]. It follows that $D \vdash \mathbf{V}^m \twoheadrightarrow \mathbf{Q}_i$, for every $i = 1, k$. By inductively applying Lemma 2.6 (b), we derive $D \vdash \mathbf{V}^m \twoheadrightarrow \mathbf{Q}_1, \ldots, \mathbf{Q}_k$ and, by transitivity, we further derive $D \vdash \mathbf{V}^m \twoheadrightarrow \mathbf{Q}$. This implies $\mathcal{C} \in supp_D^{\mathcal{S}}(\mathbf{Q})$, and therefore:

$$p_D^{\mathcal{S}}(\mathbf{Q}) \leq p(\mathcal{C}) = \sum_{(\mathbf{V}_j, p_j) \in \mathcal{C}} p_j \leq \sum_i \sum_{(\mathbf{V}_j, p_j) \in \mathcal{C}_i^m} p_j = \sum_i p_D^{\mathcal{S}}(\mathbf{Q}_i)$$

The second inequality holds because the p_i's are non-negative (Proposition 2.8). This proves that $p_D^{\mathcal{S}}$ is arbitrage-free. $\square$

The arbitrage-price is our fundamental formula because it allows us to check consistency, and, in that case, it gives the discount-free price.

THEOREM 2.15. *Consider a set of price points $\mathcal{S}$. Let $p_D^{\mathcal{S}}$ denote the arbitrage-price function (Equation 2). Then:*

---
[2] For any query bundle $\mathbf{Q}$, if $\mathcal{C}_1 \in supp_D^{\mathcal{S}}(\mathbf{Q})$ and $\mathcal{C}_1 \subseteq \mathcal{C}_2$ then $\mathcal{C}_2 \in supp_D^{\mathcal{S}}(\mathbf{Q})$, by the reflexivity axiom.

1. *$\mathcal{S}$ is consistent iff $\forall(\mathbf{V}_i, p_i) \in \mathcal{S}$, $p_i \leq p_D^{\mathcal{S}}(\mathbf{V}_i)$.*
2. *If $\mathcal{S}$ is consistent, then $p_D^{\mathcal{S}}$ is the unique discount-free pricing function for $\mathcal{S}$.*

PROOF. We claim that, for any pricing function p_D valid for $\mathcal{S}$ and every query bundle $\mathbf{Q}$, we have that $p_D(\mathbf{Q}) \leq p_D^{\mathcal{S}}(\mathbf{Q})$. The claim proves the theorem. Indeed, the "if" direction of item 1 follows from two facts. First, $p_D^{\mathcal{S}}$ is arbitrage-free by Lemma 2.14(b). Second, if $p_i \leq p_D^{\mathcal{S}}(\mathbf{V}_i)$ holds for all price points $(\mathbf{V}_i, p_i) \in \mathcal{S}$, then by Lemma 2.14(a) $p_D^{\mathcal{S}}(\mathbf{V}_i) = p_i$. Hence, $p_D^{\mathcal{S}}$ is valid, proving that $\mathcal{S}$ is consistent. The "only if" direction follows from the claim: if p_D is any valid pricing function for $\mathcal{S}$ then $p_i = p_D(\mathbf{V}_i) \leq p_D^{\mathcal{S}}(\mathbf{V}_i)$. The claim also implies item 2 immediately.

To prove the claim, let p_D be a valid pricing function (thus $p_D(\mathbf{V}_i) = p_i$ for all $(\mathbf{V}_i, p_i) \in \mathcal{S}$), and let $\mathbf{Q}$ be a bundle. Let $\mathcal{C} \in supp_D^{\mathcal{S}}(\mathbf{Q})$, and $\mathbf{V} = \bigodot_{(\mathbf{V}_i, p_i) \in \mathcal{C}} \mathbf{V}_i$. By definition we have $D \vdash \mathbf{V} \twoheadrightarrow \mathbf{Q}$. Since p_D is arbitrage-free, we have:

$$p_D(\mathbf{Q}) \leq \sum_{(\mathbf{V}_i, p_i) \in \mathcal{C}} p_D(\mathbf{V}_i) = \sum_{(\mathbf{V}_i, p_i) \in \mathcal{C}} p_i = p(\mathcal{C})$$

It follows that $p_D(\mathbf{Q}) \leq \min_{\mathcal{C} \in supp_D^{\mathcal{S}}(\mathbf{Q})} p(\mathcal{C}) = p_D^{\mathcal{S}}(\mathbf{Q})$ $\square$

The theorem says that, in order to check consistency, it suffices to rule out arbitrage situations among the views in $\mathcal{S}$. There are infinitely many possible arbitrage situations in Definition 2.7, but the theorem reduces this to a finite set.

Next, we examine the complexity of checking consistency and computing the price. For this discussion, we will assume that $\twoheadrightarrow$ is the instance-based determinacy given by Definition 2.2. Denote by PRICE$(\mathcal{S}, \mathbf{Q})$ the decision version of the price computation problem: "given a database D and k, is the price $p_D^{\mathcal{S}}(\mathbf{Q})$ less than or equal to k"? Let us also denote by PRICE$(\mathbf{Q})$ the decision version of the same problem, but where the set of price points $\mathcal{S}$ is now part of the input.

COROLLARY 2.16. *Suppose $\mathcal{S}, \mathbf{Q}$ consist of UCQs. Then, (a) the complexity of PRICE$(\mathbf{Q})$ is in Σ_2^p and (b) the complexity of PRICE$(\mathcal{S}, \mathbf{Q})$ is coNP-complete.*

PROOF. For (a), to check whether $p_D^{\mathcal{S}}(\mathbf{Q}) \leq k$, guess a subset of price points $(\mathbf{V}_1, p_1), \ldots, (\mathbf{V}_m, p_m)$ in $\mathcal{S}$, then check that both $D \vdash \mathbf{V}_1, \ldots, \mathbf{V}_m \twoheadrightarrow \mathbf{Q}$ (this is in coNP by Theorem 2.3) and that $\sum_i p_i \leq k$. For (b), instead of guessing, we can iterate over all subset of price points, since there is only a fixed number of them. $\square$

Thus, computing the price is expensive. This expense is unacceptable in practice, since prices are computed as frequently as queries, perhaps even more frequently (for example, users may just inquire about the price, then decide not to buy). We have an extensive discussion of tractability in Section 3, and will describe an important restriction under which pricing is tractable. For now, we restrict our discussion of the complexity to showing that pricing is at least as complex as computing the determinacy relation.

Let PRICE-CONSISTENCY$(\mathcal{S})$ be the problem of deciding whether a set of price points $\mathcal{S}$ is consistent for a database D, and DETERMINACY$(\mathbf{V}, Q)$ the problem of checking determinacy $D \vdash \mathbf{V} \twoheadrightarrow Q$. The proof of Corollary 2.16 shows that the former problem is no more than exponentially worse than the latter. We prove in the full paper [19] a weak converse:

PROPOSITION 2.17. *There is a polynomial time reduction from* DETERMINACY$(\mathbf{V}, Q)$ *to*[3] PRICE-CONSISTENCY$(\mathcal{S})$.

We end this section with a brief discussion of the case when **ID** is not determined by $\mathcal{S} = \{(\mathbf{V}_1, p_1), \ldots, (\mathbf{V}_k, p_k)\}$, that is, $D \vdash (\mathbf{V}_1, \ldots, \mathbf{V}_k) \not\twoheadrightarrow \mathbf{ID}$; in other words, the seller does not sell the entire dataset. In this case, $\mathcal{S}$ admits no discount-free pricing function. Indeed, consider any B such that $B \geq \sum_i p_i$, and denote $\mathcal{S}+B = \mathcal{S} \cup \{(\mathbf{ID}, B)\}$. One can check that, if $\mathcal{S}$ is consistent, then so is $\mathcal{S}+B$, and that $p_D^{\mathcal{S}+B}$ is a valid pricing function for $\mathcal{S}$. If p_D were any discount-free pricing function for $\mathcal{S}$, we fix some database instance D and choose $B > p_D(\mathbf{ID})$. Then, $p_D^{\mathcal{S}+B}(\mathbf{ID}) = B > p_D(\mathbf{ID})$, contradicting the fact that p is discount-free. In the rest of the paper, we will always assume that **ID** is included in the set of price points.

2.7 Dynamic Pricing

So far we assumed that the database instance was static. We now consider the pricing function in a dynamic setting, i.e. when the database D is updated; in this paper, we consider only insertions. Note that the set of price points $\mathcal{S}$ remains unchanged, even when the database gets updated. For example, the seller has decided to sell the entire dataset for the price B, $(\mathbf{ID}, B) \in \mathcal{S}$, and this price remains unchanged even when new items are inserted in the database. This is the most common case encountered today: explicit prices remain fixed over long periods of time, even when the underlying data set is updated.

When the database is updated, we can simply recompute the pricing function on the new data instance. However, we face two issues. The first is that the price points $\mathcal{S}$ may become inconsistent: $\mathcal{S}$ was consistent at D_1, but after inserting some items, $\mathcal{S}$ becomes inconsistent at D_2. This must be avoided in practice. Second, as more data items are added, in most cases the seller does not want any price to drop. As an example, adding more businesses to the USA business database should not remove value from any query. However, there are cases where more data adds noise and hence decreases the value of the dataset: we do not explore this scenario in this paper.

EXAMPLE 2.18. *Let* $V(x, y) = R(x), S(x, y)$ *and* $Q() = R(x)$ *(a boolean query checking whether R is non-empty). Let* $D_1 = \emptyset$, $D_2 = \{R(a), S(a, b)\}$. *Then* $D_1 \vdash V \not\twoheadrightarrow Q$ *and* $D_2 \vdash V \twoheadrightarrow Q$. *The second claim is obvious: since* $V(D_2) = \{(a, b)\}$ *we know for certain that* $R^{D_2} \neq \emptyset$. *To see the first claim consider* $D_1' = \{R(a)\}$. *Then* $V(D_1) = V(D_1') = \emptyset$ *but* $Q(D_1) = false \neq Q(D_1') = true$, *proving that* $D_1 \vdash V \not\twoheadrightarrow Q$.

This example implies two undesired consequences. First, let $\mathcal{S}_1 = \{(V, \$1), (Q, \$10), (\mathbf{ID}, \$100)\}$: *the entire dataset costs $100, the query Q $10, and the view V $1. $\mathcal{S}_1$ is consistent when the database instance is D_1, but when tuples are inserted and the database instance becomes D_2, $\mathcal{S}_1$ is no longer consistent (because a buyer can avoid paying $10 for Q by asking V instead, for just $1). Alternatively, consider the set of price points* $\mathcal{S}_2 = \{(V, \$1), (\mathbf{ID}, \$100)\}$. *The reader may check that $\mathcal{S}_2$ is consistent for any database instance D. However, the price of Q decreases when the database is updated:* $p_{D_1}^{\mathcal{S}_2}(Q) = \$100$, *while* $p_{D_2}^{\mathcal{S}_2}(Q) = \$1$.

Next, we describe two ways to fix both issues.

DEFINITION 2.19. *Fix the bundles* $\mathbf{V}, \mathbf{Q}$. *We say that a determinacy relation* $\twoheadrightarrow$ *is monotone for* $\mathbf{V}, \mathbf{Q}$ *if, whenever* $D_1 \subseteq D_2$ *and* $D_2 \vdash \mathbf{V} \twoheadrightarrow \mathbf{Q}$, *then* $D_1 \vdash \mathbf{V} \twoheadrightarrow \mathbf{Q}$.

Information-theoretic determinacy is vacuously monotone, since it does not depend on the instance. But, as we saw in Example 2.18, instance-based determinacy is not monotone in general. We prove in [19]:

PROPOSITION 2.20. *If* $\mathbf{V}$ *is a bundle consisting only of selection queries and* $\mathbf{Q}$ *is a bundle of full conjunctive queries, then instance-based determinacy is monotone for* $\mathbf{V}, \mathbf{Q}$.

A conjunctive query is full if it has no projections; in particular, a selection query is full. We show in the full version [19] that the property fails for CQs with projections.

As we mentioned earlier, we would like that a dynamic pricing function be *monotone*: when data is added to the database, the price should never decrease:

DEFINITION 2.21 (MONOTONICITY). *Let p be a totally defined, dynamic pricing function. We say that p is monotone on* $\mathbf{Q}$ *if, for any* $D_1 \subseteq D_2$, $p_{D_1}(\mathbf{Q}) \leq p_{D_2}(\mathbf{Q})$.

Fix a set of price points $\mathcal{S}$. The arbitrage-price given by Equation 2 is a totally defined function $p^{\mathcal{S}}$, since $p_D^{\mathcal{S}}$ is well defined for every database instance D. We prove:

PROPOSITION 2.22. *Fix $\mathcal{S}$ and $\mathbf{Q}$, and suppose that $\twoheadrightarrow$ is monotone for every subset* $\mathbf{V}_1, \ldots, \mathbf{V}_m$ *of $\mathcal{S}$, and $\mathbf{Q}$. Then, the dynamic arbitrage-price $p^{\mathcal{S}}$ is monotone on $\mathbf{Q}$.*

PROOF. By Equation 1: $supp_{D_1}^{\mathcal{S}}(\mathbf{Q}) \supseteq supp_{D_2}^{\mathcal{S}}(\mathbf{Q})$. By Equation 2: $p_{D_1}^{\mathcal{S}}(\mathbf{Q}) \leq p_{D_2}^{\mathcal{S}}(\mathbf{Q})$. □

PROPOSITION 2.23. *If $p^{\mathcal{S}}$ is monotone on every $\mathbf{V}_i$, $\mathcal{S}$ is consistent on D_1, and $D_1 \subseteq D_2$, then $\mathcal{S}$ is consistent on D_2.*

PROOF. To check consistency on D_2 it suffices to check that $p_i \leq p_{D_2}^{\mathcal{S}}(\mathbf{V}_i)$, for all $i = 1, \ldots, m$. We have $p_i \leq p_{D_1}^{\mathcal{S}}(\mathbf{V}_i)$ since $\mathcal{S}$ is consistent on D_1, and $p_{D_1}^{\mathcal{S}}(\mathbf{V}_i) \leq p_{D_2}^{\mathcal{S}}(\mathbf{V}_i)$ because $p^{\mathcal{S}}$ is monotone. □

The goal in the dynamic setting is to ensure that $p^{\mathcal{S}}$ is monotone on every query (Definition 2.21). There are two ways to achieve this. One is to restrict all views to selection queries and all queries to full conjunctive queries: we pursue this in Section 3. However, if one needs more general views and queries, then we propose a second alternative: to consider a different determinacy relation along with monotone views. Let $\twoheadrightarrow$ be any determinacy relation (Definition 2.5). Its *restriction* $D \vdash \mathbf{V} \twoheadrightarrow^* \mathbf{Q}$ is: $\forall D_0, \mathbf{V}(D_0) \subseteq \mathbf{V}(D)$, $D_0 \vdash \mathbf{V} \twoheadrightarrow \mathbf{Q}$. We prove in detail in [19]:

PROPOSITION 2.24. *For the restriction $\twoheadrightarrow^*$: (a) $\twoheadrightarrow^*$ is a determinacy relation (Definition 2.5), (b) $\twoheadrightarrow^*$ is monotone (Definition 2.19) for any monotone $\mathbf{V}$ and any $\mathbf{Q}$, (c) if $p_D^{\mathcal{S}}$ and $q_D^{\mathcal{S}}$ are the arbitrage-prices for $\twoheadrightarrow$ and $\twoheadrightarrow^*$, respectively, then $p_D^{\mathcal{S}}(\mathbf{Q}) \leq q_D^{\mathcal{S}}(\mathbf{Q})$ for all $\mathbf{Q}$, and (d) if $\twoheadrightarrow$ is instance-based determinacy, then the data complexity of $\twoheadrightarrow^*$ is in coNP.*

Thus, by replacing instance-based determinacy $\twoheadrightarrow$ with its restriction $\twoheadrightarrow^*$, we obtain a monotone pricing function $q^{\mathcal{S}}$. In particular, if $\mathcal{S}$ is consistent in a database D, then it will remain consistent after insertions. To illustrate, recall that in Example 2.18 $\mathcal{S}_1$ became inconsistent when D_1 was updated to D_2: this is because $D_1 \vdash V \not\twoheadrightarrow Q$ and $D_2 \vdash V \twoheadrightarrow Q$. Now we have both $D_1 \vdash V \not\twoheadrightarrow^* Q$ and $D_2 \vdash V \not\twoheadrightarrow^* Q$, hence $\mathcal{S}_1$ is consistent in both states of the database.

---

[3]$\mathcal{S}$ has one price point for each $V \in \mathbf{V}$ and one for Q; the database instance D is part of the input in both cases.

3. TRACTABLE QUERY-BASED PRICING

The combined complexity for computing the price when the views and queries are UCQs is high: it is coNP-hard and in Σ_2^P. This is unacceptable in practice. In this section, we restrict both the views on which the seller can set explicit prices and the queries that the buyer can ask, and present a polynomial time algorithm for computing the price. This is the main result in the paper, since it represents a quite practical framework for query-based pricing. For the case of conjunctive queries without self-joins, we prove a dichotomy of their complexity into polynomial time and NP-complete, which is our most technically difficult result.

The Views. We restrict the views to *selection queries*. We denote a selection query by $\sigma_{R.X=a}$, where R is a relation name, X an attribute, and a a constant. For example, given a ternary relation $R(X, Y, Z)$, the selection query $\sigma_{R.X=a}$ is $Q(x, y, z) = R(x, y, z) \wedge x = a$. Throughout this section, the seller can set explicit prices only on selection views. We argue that this restriction is quite reasonable in practice. Many concrete instances of online data pricing that we have encountered set prices only on selection queries[4]. For example, CustomLists [13] sells the set of all businesses in any given state for $199, thus it sells 50 selection views. Infochimps [17] sells the following selection queries, in the form of API calls. The Domains API: *given IP address, retrieve the domain, company name and NAICS Code*. The MLB Baseball API: *given an MLB team name, retrieve the wins, losses, current team colors, seasons played, final regular season standings, home stadium, and team_ids.* The Team API: *given the team_ids, get the team statistics, records, and game_ids.* And, the Game API: *given game_id, get the attendance, box scores, and statistics.* Thus, we argue, restricting the explicit price points to selection queries is quite reasonable for practical purposes.

An important assumption made by sellers today is that the set of values on which to select is known. For example, the set of valid MLB team names is known to the buyers, or can be obtained for free from somewhere else. In general, for each attribute $R.X$ we assume a finite set $Col_{R.X} = \{a_1, \ldots, a_n\}$, called the *column*. This set is known both to the seller and the buyer. Furthermore, the database D satisfies the inclusion constraint $R^D.X \subseteq Col_{R.X}$. The input to the pricing algorithm consists of both the database instance D, and all the columns $Col_{R.X}$: thus, the latter are part of the input in data complexity. A column should not be confused with a domain: while a domain may be infinite, a column has finitely many values. It should not be confused with the active domain either, since the database need not have all values in a column. We also assume that columns always remain fixed when the database is updated.

We call the set of all selections on column $R.X$, $\Sigma_{R.X} = \{\sigma_{R.X=a} \mid a \in Col_{R.X}\}$, the *full cover* of $R.X$. Note that $D \vdash \Sigma_{R.X} \twoheadrightarrow R$. We denote Σ the set of all selections on all columns. Given $\mathbf{V} \subseteq \Sigma$, we say that it *fully covers* $R.X$ if $\Sigma_{R.X} \subseteq \mathbf{V}$. Thus, the explicit price points $\mathcal{S} = \{(V_1, p_1), (V_2, p_2), \ldots\}$ are such that each $V_i \in \Sigma$. We denote $p : \Sigma \to \mathbb{R}^+$ the partial function defined as: $p(V_i) = p_i$ if $(V_i, p_i) \in \mathcal{S}$.

Recall that $\text{PRICE}(\mathcal{S}, \mathbf{Q})$ denotes the data complexity of

the pricing problem in Section 2. Since now $\mathcal{S}$ can be as large as Σ, we treat it as part of the input. Thus, we denote the pricing problem as $\text{PRICE}(\mathbf{Q})$, where the input consists of the database instance D, all columns $Col_{R.X}$, and the function p. We start with a lemma (which we prove in [19]):

LEMMA 3.1. *Let* $\mathbf{V} \subseteq \Sigma$. *Then* $D \vdash \mathbf{V} \twoheadrightarrow \sigma_{R.X=a}$ *iff (a) it is trivial (i.e. $\sigma_{R.X=a} \in \mathbf{V}$), or (b) $\mathbf{V}$ fully covers some attribute Y of R.*

The lemma has two consequences. First, recall that in Subsection 2.4 we required that the views in $\mathcal{S}$ determine **ID**. By the lemma, this requirement becomes equivalent to requiring that, for any relation R, $\mathcal{S}$ fully covers some attribute X. Second, the lemma gives us a simple criterion for checking whether $\mathcal{S}$ is consistent. By Theorem 2.15, this holds iff there is no arbitrage between the views in $\mathcal{S}$. The lemma implies that the only risk of arbitrage is between a full cover $\Sigma_{R.Y}$ and a selection view $\sigma_{R.X=a}$, hence:

PROPOSITION 3.2. $\mathcal{S}$ *is consistent iff for every relation* R, *any two attributes* X, Y *of* R *and any constant* $a \in Col_{R.X}$:

$$p(\sigma_{R.X=a}) \leq \sum_{b \in Col_{R.Y}} p(\sigma_{R.Y=b})$$

Note that now consistency is independent of the database instance; this is unlike Subsection 2.7, where we showed that consistency may change with the database.

The Queries. We would like to support a rich query language that buyers can use, while ensuring tractability for the price computation. We start with an upper bound on the data complexity of pricing. We say that a query Q has PTIME data complexity if $Q(D)$ can be computed in polynomial time in the size of D. UCQ queries, datalog queries, and extensions of datalog with negation and inequalities have PTIME data complexity[4].

THEOREM 3.3. *Assume* $\mathbf{V} \subseteq \Sigma$. *Let* Q *be any monotone query that has PTIME data complexity. Then,* $D \vdash \mathbf{V} \twoheadrightarrow Q$ *for* $\mathbf{V} \subseteq \Sigma$ *can be decided in PTIME data complexity.*

We give the proof in the full version of this paper [19].

COROLLARY 3.4. *Let* $\mathbf{Q}$ *be a bundle of monotone queries that have polynomial time data complexity. Then* $\text{PRICE}(\mathbf{Q})$ *is in NP.*

PROOF. To check if $p_D^{\mathcal{S}}(\mathbf{Q}) \leq k$, guess a subset of selection views $\mathbf{V} \subseteq \Sigma$, then check that both $D \vdash \mathbf{V} \twoheadrightarrow \mathbf{Q}$ (which is equivalent to $D \vdash \mathbf{V} \twoheadrightarrow Q_i$, for all $Q_i \in \mathbf{Q}$, by Lemma 2.6) and that $\sum_{V \in \mathbf{V}} p(V) \leq k$. $\square$

Thus, the restriction to selection queries has lowered the complexity of price computation from Σ_2^p (Corollary 2.16) to NP. However, for some Conjunctive Queries, computing the price is still NP-hard (the detailed proof is in [19]):

THEOREM 3.5 (NP-COMPLETE QUERIES). $\text{PRICE}(Q)$ *is NP-complete (data complexity) when Q is any of the following queries:*

$$H_1(x, y, z) = R(x, y, z), S(x), T(y), U(z) \quad (3)$$

$$H_2(x, y) = R(x), S(x, y), T(x, y) \quad (4)$$

$$H_3(x, y) = R(x), S(x, y), R(y) \quad (5)$$

$$H_4(x) = R(x, y) \quad (6)$$

---

[4]The only exception are sites that sell data by the number of tuples; for example, Azure allows the seller to set a price on a "transaction", which means any 100 tuples.

If Q is one of H_1, H_2, H_3 then the pricing complexity remains NP-complete even when the database instance D is restricted s.t. $Q(D) = \emptyset$.

Thus, we cannot afford to price every conjunctive query. In Subsection 3.1, we introduce a class of conjunctive queries whose prices can be computed in PTIME. In Subsection 3.2, we study the complexity of *all* conjunctive queries without self-joins, and establish a dichotomy for pricing into PTIME and NP-complete.

3.1 A PTIME Algorithm

We define a class of conjunctive queries, called *Generalized Chain Queries*, denoted GCHQ, and we provide a non-trivial algorithm that computes their prices in polynomial time.

We consider conjunctive queries with interpreted unary predicates $C(x)$ that can be computed in PTIME: that is, we allow predicates like $x > 10$ or USER-DEFINED-PREDICATE(x), but not $x < y$. A conjunctive query is *without self-joins* if each relation R_i occurs at most once in Q; e.g. query H_3 in Theorem 3.5 has a self-join (since R occurs twice), the other three queries are without self-joins. A conjunctive query is *full* if all variables in the body appear in the head; e.g. queries H_1, H_2, H_3 are full, while H_4 is not. We restrict our discussion to full, conjunctive queries without self-joins. We abbreviate such a query with $Q = R_0, R_1, \ldots, R_k, C_1, \ldots, C_p$, where each R_i is an atomic relational predicate, and each C_j is an interpreted unary predicate; we assume the order $R_1, \ldots, R_k$ to be fixed. For $0 \le i \le j \le k$, we denote $Q_{[i,j]}$ the full conjunctive $Q_{[i,j]} = R_i, R_{i+1}, \ldots, R_j$ (ignoring the unary predicates). For example, if $Q(x,y,z) = R(x), S(x,y), T(y), U(y,z), V(z)$, then $Q_{[1:2]}(x,y) = S(x,y), T(y)$ If k is the index of the last relational predicate, then we abbreviate $Q_{[j,k]}$ with $Q_{[j:*]}$. Denote $Var(Q)$ the set of variables in Q.

DEFINITION 3.6. *A generalized chain query, GCHQ, is a full conjunctive query without self-joins, Q, such that, for all i, $|Var(Q_{[0:i-1]}) \cap Var(Q_{[i:*]})| = 1$. We denote x_i the unique variable shared by $Q_{[0:i-1]}$ and $Q_{[i:*]}$. The (not necessarily distinct) variables $x_1, \ldots, x_k$ are called* join variables. *All other variables are called* hanging variables.

In other words, a GCHQ query is one in which every join consists of only one shared variable. Note that the definition ignores the interpreted unary predicates occurring in Q. The following are some examples of GCHQ queries:

$$Q_1(x,y) = R(x), S(x,y), T(y)$$
$$Q_2(x,y,z,w) = R(x,y), S(y,z), T(z), U(z), V(z,w)$$
$$Q_3(x,y,z,u,v,w) = R(x,y), S(y,u,v,z), T(z,w), U(w)$$

On the other hand, none of the queries in Theorem 3.5 are GCHQ: the atoms in queries H_1 and H_2 cannot be ordered to satisfy Definition 3.6, H_3 has a self-join, and H_4 is not a full query.

We can now state our main result in this paper:

THEOREM 3.7 (MAIN THEOREM). *Assume that all explicit price points in $\mathcal{S}$ are selection queries. Then, for any GCHQ query, one can compute its price in PTIME (data complexity).*

Before we give the algorithm, we illustrate pricing with an example.

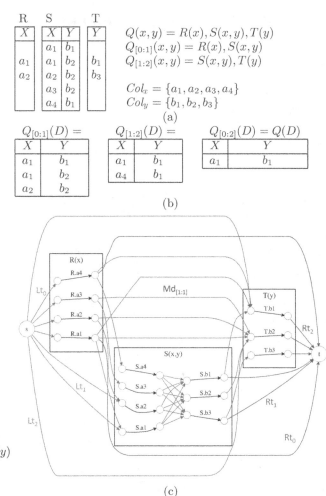

$$Q(x,y) = R(x), S(x,y), T(y)$$
$$Q_{[0:1]}(x,y) = R(x), S(x,y)$$
$$Q_{[1:2]}(x,y) = S(x,y), T(y)$$

$$Col_x = \{a_1, a_2, a_3, a_4\}$$
$$Col_y = \{b_1, b_2, b_3\}$$
(a)

(b)

(c)

Figure 1: (a) The database D and query Q for Example 3.8 (b) The answers to the partial queries $Q_{[0:1]}, Q_{[1:2]}, Q_{[0:2]}$ (c) The flow graph for computing the price of the example (see Theorem 3.13).

EXAMPLE 3.8. *Consider $Q = R(x), S(x,y), T(y)$ over the database D in Figure 1(a). We have $Q(D) = \{(a_1, b_1)\}$. There are 14 possible selection queries that are priced: $\Sigma_{R.X} = \{\sigma_{R.X=a_1}, \sigma_{R.X=a_2}, \sigma_{R.X=a_3}, \sigma_{R.X=a_4}\}$, as well as $\Sigma_{S.X} = \{\sigma_{S.X=a_1}, \sigma_{S.X=a_2}, \sigma_{S.X=a_3}, \sigma_{S.X=a_4}\}$, and similarly for $S.Y$ and $T.Y$. Suppose $\mathcal{S}$ assigns the price \$1 to each selection query.*

To compute the price of Q, we need to find the smallest set $\mathbf{V} \subseteq \Sigma$ that "determines" Q: that is, forall D' s.t. $\mathbf{V}(D) = \mathbf{V}(D')$, the query must return the same answer $\{(a_1, b_1)\}$ on D', as on D. First, $\mathbf{V}$ must guarantee that (a_1, b_1) is an answer, and for that it must ensure that all three tuples $R(a_1), S(a_1, b_1), T(b_1)$ are in D'; for example, it suffices to include in $\mathbf{V}$ the views $\mathbf{V}_0 = \{\sigma_{R.X=a_1}, \sigma_{S.Y=b_1}, \sigma_{T.Y=b_1}\}$ (we could have chosen $\sigma_{S.X=a_1}$ instead of $\sigma_{S.Y=b_1}$). Second, $\mathbf{V}$ must also ensure that none of the other 11 tuples (a_i, b_j) are in the answer to Q. $\mathbf{V}_0$ is not sufficient yet. For example, consider the tuple (a_3, b_2), which is not in the answer. Let $D' = D \cup \{R(a_3), T(b_2)\}$; then $\mathbf{V}_0(D) = \mathbf{V}_0(D')$, since $\mathbf{V}_0$ does not inquire about either $R(a_3)$ or $T(b_2)$, yet $Q(D')$ contains (a_3, b_2). Thus, $\mathbf{V}$ must ensure that either $R(a_3)$ is not in D', or that $T(b_2)$ is not in D'. Continuing this reasoning, leads us to the following set of views $\mathbf{V} = \{\sigma_{R.X=a_1}, \sigma_{R.X=a_4}, \sigma_{S.Y=b_1}, \sigma_{S.Y=b_3}, \sigma_{T.Y=b_1}, \sigma_{T.Y=b_2}\}$. The reader may check that this is a minimal set that determines Q, hence the price of Q is $p_D^S(Q) = 6$.

We can also generalize the algorithm to GCHQ query bundles, which are defined as follows.

DEFINITION 3.9. *A GCHQ query bundle is a set $\mathbf{Q}$ of GCHQ queries without interpreted predicates, such that any two queries $Q, Q' \in \mathbf{Q}$ only share in common a prefix and/or a suffix: $\exists i, j, m : Q_{[0:i-1]} = Q'_{[0:i-1]}, Q_{[j:*]} = Q'_{[m:*]}$, and $Q_{[i:j-1]}, Q'_{[i:m-1]}$ have no common relation names.*

For example, the bundle $\{Q_1 = S(x, y), R(y, z), U(z), Q_2 = S(x, y), T(y, z), Q_3 = S(x, y), T(y, z), U(z)\}$ is a GCHQ bundle. To simplify the presentation, we discuss only single queries and defer query bundles to [19]. We now describe the algorithm, which consists of the four steps below.

STEP 1: Remove Atomic Predicates. Suppose Q has a variable x with an atomic predicate $C(x)$: here we simply shrink the column[5] of x to $Col'_x = \{a \in Col_x \mid C(a) = true\}$, thus removing all constants that do not satisfy C. Let $\mathcal{S}' \subseteq \mathcal{S}$ be obtained by removing all selection views that refer to these constants, and similarly $D' \subseteq D$ be the database obtained by filtering on the predicate C. Finally, let Q' be the query obtained from Q by removing the predicate $C(x)$. We prove in [19] that $p_{D'}^{S'}(Q') = p_D^S(Q)$.

To illustrate this step, consider the query $Q(y, w, z) = R(y), S(y, w, z), T(z), w = a_1$ and $Col_w = \{a_1, a_2, a_3\}$. Then, we restrict the column of w to $\{a_1\}$, next remove the views $\sigma_{S.W=a_2}, \sigma_{S.W=a_3}$ from $\mathcal{S}$ to obtain $\mathcal{S}'$, filter D on $w = a_1$ to obtain D', and then compute the price of $Q'(x, y, z) = R(y), S(y, w, z), T(z)$.

STEP 2: Remove Multiple Variable Occurrences from Each Atom. We only sketch this step, and defer the details to the full version [19]. Suppose a variable x occurs twice in the atom $R(x, x, z)$, where R has schema $R(X, Y, Z)$. Let $R'(X, Z)$ be a new relation name s.t. $Col_{R'.X} = Col_x$, and let us set the prices on $R'.X$ as follows: $p(\sigma_{R'.X=a}) = \min\{p(\sigma_{R.X=a}), p(\sigma_{R.Y=a})\}$. We prove that the price of the new query (obtained by replacing the atom $R(x, x, z)$ with $R'(x, z)$) is the same as the price of Q.

STEP 3: Removing Hanging Variables. Recall that a *hanging* variable is one that occurs in only one atom of Q; by the previous step, it only occurs in one position $R.X$. We prove in the full paper the following:

LEMMA 3.10. *Let x be a hanging variable in Q, occurring in the attribute position $R.X$. Let $\mathbf{V} \subseteq \Sigma$. If $D \vdash \mathbf{V} \twoheadrightarrow Q$ then either (a) $\mathbf{V}$ fully covers $R.X$ or (b) $D \vdash (\mathbf{V} \setminus \Sigma_{R.X}) \twoheadrightarrow \mathbf{Q}$ (in other words, every view in $\mathbf{V}$ referring to $R.X$ is redundant).*

Thus, when computing the price of Q, for each hanging variable we need to consider two cases: either fully cover it, or not cover it at all. We claim that each of these cases becomes another price computation problem, namely for the query Q', obtained from Q by replacing R with R' (obtained from R by removing the attribute $R.X$), on the database D' obtained from D by projecting out $R.X$:

---

[5] If x occurs on several attribute positions $R.X$, $S.Y$, etc, then we may assume w.l.o.g. that $Col_{R.X} = Col_{S.Y} = \ldots$ and denote it with Col_x.

LEMMA 3.11. *Let $R.X$ be an attribute containing a hanging variable in Q, $\mathbf{V} \subseteq \Sigma$, and $\mathbf{V}' = \mathbf{V} \setminus \Sigma_{R.X}$.*

- *If $\mathbf{V}$ fully covers $R.X$, let Y be any attribute $Y \neq X$ of R. Then $D \vdash \mathbf{V} \twoheadrightarrow Q$ iff $D' \vdash \mathbf{V}', \Sigma_{R'.Y} \twoheadrightarrow Q'$.*
- *If $\mathbf{V}$ does not fully cover $R.X$, then $D \vdash \mathbf{V} \twoheadrightarrow Q$ iff $D' \vdash \mathbf{V}' \twoheadrightarrow Q'$.*

We prove this as part of a more general lemma in the full version [19]. The lemma gives us an algorithm for removing hanging variables: compute two prices for Q', and take the minimum. The first price corresponds to the case when $R.X$ is fully covered: in that case, we give out R' for free (by setting all prices $\sigma_{R'.Y=a}$ to 0, for some other attribute Y) and compute the price of Q': then, add to that the true cost of the full cover $\Sigma_{R.X}$, i.e. $\sum_a p(\sigma_{R.X=a})$. The second price corresponds to the case when $R.X$ is not covered at all, and is equal to the price of Q'. For a simple example, if $Q(x, y, z) = R(x, y), S(y, z), T(z)$, then $Q'(y, z) = R'(y), S(y, z), T(z)$. Let p_1 be the price of Q' where we set all prices of $\sigma_{R'.Y=b}$ to 0; let p_2 be the regular price of Q' (where all prices are unchanged, but the views $\sigma_{R.X=a}$ are removed); return $\min(p_1 + p(\Sigma_{R.X}), p_2)$. In general, we need to repeat this process once for every hanging variable; thus, we end up computing 2^k prices, if there are k attributes with hanging variables.

STEP 4: Reduction to Maximum Flow. Finally, we have reached the core of the algorithm. At this point, the query is a *Chain Query*:

DEFINITION 3.12. *A Chain Query is a full conjunctive query without self-joins, $Q = R_0, R_1, \ldots, R_k$ s.t.: (a) every atom R_i is either binary or unary, (b) any two consecutive atoms R_i, R_{i+1} share exactly one variable, denoted x_i, (c) the first and the last atoms are unary, $R_0(x_0), R_k(x_k)$. Denote CHQ the set of chain queries.*

We show that pricing a chain query can be reduced to the MIN-CUT problem, which is the dual of the MAX-FLOW graph problem and can be solved in polynomial time [12].

Given a chain query Q, denote x_i, x_{i+1} the variables occurring in R_i: if R_i is unary, then $x_i = x_{i+1}$. In particular, $x_0 = x_1$ and $x_k = x_{k+1}$, since the first and last atoms are unary. Thus, each query $Q_{[i:j]} = R_i, \ldots, R_j$ has variables $x_i, \ldots, x_{j+1}$. Also, let us define $Q_{[i:i-1]} = Col_{x_i} = Col_{R_{i-1}.Y} \cap Col_{R_i.X}$. Define the *left-, middle-,* and *right-partial-answers*:

$$Lt_i = \Pi_{x_i}(Q_{[0:i-1]}(D)), \qquad\qquad 0 \leq i \leq k$$
$$Md_{[i:j]} = \Pi_{x_i, x_{j+1}}(Q_{[i:j]}(D)), \quad 1 \leq i \leq k, i-1 \leq j \leq k-1$$
$$Rt_j = \Pi_{x_{j+1}}(Q_{[j+1:k]}(D)), \qquad\quad 0 \leq j \leq k$$

We construct the following graph G. The graph has a source node s and a target (sink) node t. Moreover, for each attribute $R.X$ and constant $a \in Col_{R.X}$, we introduce two nodes: $v_{R.X=a}$ and $w_{R.X=a}$. The edges of G are:

View edges: For each attribute $R.X$ and constant $a \in Col_{R.X}$ we create the edge: $v_{R.X=a} \xrightarrow{view} w_{R.X=a}$, where the capacity equals the price[6] $p(\sigma_{R.X=a})$ in $\mathcal{S}$.

Tuple edges: For each binary atom $R(X, Y)$ and constants $a \in Col_{R.X}$, $b \in Col_{R.Y}$, we create the following edge: $w_{R.X=a} \xrightarrow{tuple} v_{R.Y=b}$, where capacity $= \infty$.

---

[6] If the query has no explicit price in $\mathcal{S}$ then capacity $= \infty$.

Skip edges: For all partial answers we create the edges:

$$s \xrightarrow{skip} v_{R_i.X=a} \qquad \text{if } a \in Lt_i$$

$$w_{R_{j-1}.Y=b} \xrightarrow{skip} v_{R_{i+1}.X=a} \qquad \text{if } (b,a) \in Md_{[j:i]}$$

$$w_{R_j.Y=b} \xrightarrow{skip} t \qquad \text{if } a \in Rt_j$$

In all cases, capacity $= \infty$.

In particular, since $Lt_0 = Col_{x_0}$, $Md_{[i:i-1]} = Col_{x_i}$, $Rt_k = Col_{x_k}$ we also have the following skip edges:

$$s \xrightarrow{skip} v_{R_0.X=a}, \quad w_{R_{i-1}.Y=a} \xrightarrow{skip} v_{R_i.X=a}, \quad w_{R_k.Y=a} \xrightarrow{skip} t$$

We explain now the intuition behind the graph construction, and will also refer to Figure 1 (b) and (c), which illustrates the graph for Example 3.8. Notice that the edges of finite capacity in G are in one-to-one correspondence with the views in $\mathcal{S}$. The main invariant (which we prove in the full paper) is: *for every set of edges C of finite capacity, C is a "cut" (it separates s and t) if and only if the corresponding set of views $\mathbf{V}$ determines the query.* Before justifying this invariant, note that the core of the graph consists of sequences of three edges:

$$v_{R_i.X=a} \xrightarrow{view} w_{R_i.X=a} \xrightarrow{tuple} w_{R_i.Y=b} \xrightarrow{view} w_{R_i.Y=b}$$

for all binary relations $R_i(X,Y)$ and constants $a \in Col_{R_i.X}, b \in Col_{R_i.Y}$ (unary relations have just one *view* edge.) Consider a possible answer to Q, $t = (u_1, u_2, \ldots, u_k)$, where $u_1 \in Col_{x_1}, \ldots, u_k \in Col_{x_2}$. If $D \vdash \mathbf{V} \twoheadrightarrow Q$, then, for all D' s.t. $\mathbf{V}(D) = \mathbf{V}(D')$, $\mathbf{V}$ must ensure two things: if $t \in Q(D)$ then it must ensure that $t \in Q(D')$, and if $t \notin Q(D)$ then it must ensure that $t \notin Q(D')$. Take the first case, $t \in Q(D)$. For each $i = 0, \ldots, k$, denoting $a = u_i$ and[7] $b = u_{i+1}$, we have: $a \in Lt_i$ (is a left partial answer), $R_i(a,b) \in D$, and $b \in Rt_i$ (is a right partial answer). Hence there are two skip edges:

$$s \xrightarrow{skip} v_{R_i.X=a} \qquad\qquad w_{R_i.Y=b} \xrightarrow{skip} t$$

Combined with the three edges above, they form an $s - t$ path: thus, any cut of finite capacity must include one of the two *view* edges, hence, the corresponding set of views $\mathbf{V}$ includes either $\sigma_{R_i.X=a}$ or $\sigma_{R_i.Y=b}$, ensuring $R_i(a,b) \in D'$. Since this holds for any i, it follows that D' has all the tuples needed to ensure $t \in Q(D')$. For example, in Figure 1 the answer $(a_1, b_1) \in Q(D)$ leads to three $s - t$ paths:

$$s \xrightarrow{skip} v_{R.X=a_1} \xrightarrow{view} w_{R.X=a_1} \xrightarrow{skip} t$$

$$s \xrightarrow{skip} v_{S.X=a_1} \xrightarrow{view} w_{S.X=a_1} \xrightarrow{tuple} v_{S.Y=b_1} \xrightarrow{view} w_{S.Y=a_1} \xrightarrow{skip} t$$

$$s \xrightarrow{skip} v_{T.Y=b_1} \xrightarrow{view} w_{T.Y=b_1} \xrightarrow{skip} t$$

Any cut ensures that $R(a_1), S(a_1, b_1), T(b_1)$ are present.

Take the second case, $t \notin Q(D)$. Then some of the tuples $R_i(u_i, u_{i+1})$ are missing from D, and $\mathbf{V}$ must ensure that *at least one* is missing. The sequence $u_1, \ldots, u_k$ consists of partial answers, alternating with missing tuples. We are interested only in the latter and the skip edges help by skipping over the partial answers. Thus the missing tuples are on a path from s to t. For an illustration, assume that exactly two tuples are missing, $R_i(u_i, u_{i+1})$ and $R_j(u_j, u_{j+1})$;

---

[7]When $i = k$ then $u_i = u_{i+1}$, hence $a = b$.

denoting $a = u_i, b = u_{i+1}, c = u_j, d = u_{j+1}$ we have:

$$a \in Lt_i, (a,b) \notin Md_{[i:i]}, (b,c) \in Md_{[i+1:j-1]}, (c,d) \notin Md_{[j:j]}, d \in Rt_j$$

leading to the following $s - t$ path:

$$s \xrightarrow{skip} v_{R_i.X=a} \xrightarrow{view} w_{R_i.X=a} \xrightarrow{tuple} w_{R_i.Y=b} \xrightarrow{view} w_{R_i.Y=b}$$
$$\xrightarrow{skip} v_{R_j.X=c} \xrightarrow{view} w_{R_j.X=c} \xrightarrow{tuple} w_{R_j.Y=d} \xrightarrow{view} w_{R_j.Y=d} \xrightarrow{skip} t$$

To summarize, we prove the following in the full paper [19]:

Theorem 3.13. *The cost of the minimum cut in G is equal to the price of Q. Therefore, the price of Q can be computed in polynomial time, by reduction to MIN-CUT.*

3.2 A Dichotomy Theorem

Are there any other queries besides GCHQ whose data complexity is in PTIME? The answer is *yes*. We study them here, and give a full characterization of the complexity of all conjunctive queries without self-joins, showing that for each query its complexity is either PTIME or NP-complete. Note that our characterization applies to *all* queries without self-joins, not just full queries. However, it only applies to single queries, not to query bundles: we leave open whether query bundles admit a similar dichotomy as single queries.

We start by characterizing the PTIME class. Clearly, all GCHQ queries are in PTIME. By definition, every GCHQ query is connected: it is easy to check that PTIME queries are closed under cartesian products:

Proposition 3.14. *Assume that Q is disconnected, and partitioned into $Q(\bar{x}_1, \bar{x}_2) : -Q_1(\bar{x}_1), Q_2(\bar{x}_2)$, where $\bar{x}_1, \bar{x}_2$ are disjoint sets of variables. Then,*

$$p_D^{\mathcal{S}}(Q) = \begin{cases} \min\{p_D^{\mathcal{S}}(Q_1), p_D^{\mathcal{S}}(Q_2)\} & \text{if } Q_1(D) = Q_2(D) = \emptyset, \\ p_D^{\mathcal{S}}(Q_1) & \text{if } Q_1(D) = \emptyset, Q_2(D) \neq \emptyset, \\ p_D^{\mathcal{S}}(Q_2) & \text{if } Q_2(D) = \emptyset, Q_1(D) \neq \emptyset, \\ p_D^{\mathcal{S}}(Q_1) + p_D^{\mathcal{S}}(Q_2) & \text{else} \end{cases}$$

We prove this proposition, along with the converse reduction, in [19]. As a consequence, the complexity of any disconnected query is no larger than that of any of its connected components.

A more surprising class of queries that admits a PTIME algorithm is the the class of *cycle queries*:

Theorem 3.15. *For any integer k, PRICE(C_k) is in PTIME, where $C_k(x_1, \ldots, x_k) = R_1(x_1, x_2), \ldots, R_k(x_k, x_1)$.*

The algorithm for computing C_k is described in the full version. It is technically the most difficult result in this paper, and is quite different from the reduction to MIN-CUT that we used for GCHQ, suggesting that these two classes cannot be unified in a natural way. The class of queries C_k is also much more brittle than GCHQ: adding a single unary predicate makes the query NP-hard. For example, see the query H_2 in Theorem 3.5: it is obtained by adding one unary predicate to C_2, and is NP-hard. By contrast, we can add freely unary predicates to GCHQ.

We conclude our analysis with the following theorem, whose proof can be found in the full version of this paper [19]:

Theorem 3.16 (DICHOTOMY THEOREM). *Let $\mathcal{S}$ contain only selection views (in Σ) and Q be a CQ w/o self-joins. The data complexity for PRICE(Q) is the following:*

- If Q has connected components $Q_1, \ldots, Q_k$, then: if all components Q_i are in PTIME, it is in PTIME, and if one component Q_i is NP-complete, Q is NP-complete.

- Else if Q is neither full nor boolean, it is NP-complete.

- Else if Q is a boolean query, then let Q^f be the corresponding full query (add all variables to the head); then the complexity of Q is the same as that of Q^f.

- Else if Q is a full CQ, let Q' be obtained from Q by removing all hanging variables, constants and multiple occurrences of a variable in the same atom: (a) if Q' is a GCHQ then it is PTIME, (b) if $Q' = C_k$ for some k, then it is also PTIME, (c) otherwise, Q is NP-complete.

4. DISCUSSION

We end this this paper with a brief discussion on loose ends and design choices.

Step v.s. smooth pricing function. The pricing function p^S can take only finitely many values, because the arbitrage-price is always the sum of a subset of prices from S. For some applications, this may be too limiting. One such example is selling private data, where the price should be proportional to the degree of privacy breached by the query: since privacy mechanisms add a noise that can be tuned continuously (e.g. the ε parameter in differential privacy [15]), one expects the pricing function to also vary continuously. Studying such "smooth" pricing functions is part of future work.

Pricing and query containment. The price should *not* be required to be monotone w.r.t. query containment. Recall that two queries (of the same arity) are said to be contained if $Q_1(D) \subseteq Q_2(D)$ for any database D. If Q_2 always returns at least as much data as Q_1, one might insist that $p_D(Q_1) \leq p_D(Q_2)$. We argue against this.

EXAMPLE 4.1. *Let $Q_1(x,y) = R(x), S(x,y)$ and $Q_2(x,y) = S(x,y)$. Then, $Q_1 \subseteq Q_2$, but the information in Q_1 may be more valuable than that in Q_2. For example, $S(x,y)$ may be the list of the top 500 companies and their stock price, while $R(x)$ may be an analyst's confidential list of 5 companies with very high potential for growth. Clearly, the seller wants to set $p_D(Q_1) \gg p_D(Q_2)$.*

There is also a theoretical argument: if p_D is arbitrage-free *and* monotone w.r.t. query containment, then all Boolean queries have the same price! Indeed, let T be the Boolean query that is always true, i.e. $T(D) = true$ for any database D, and let Q be any Boolean query. We have $Q \subseteq T$, hence $p_D(Q) \leq p_D(T)$; on the other hand, $D \vdash Q \twoheadrightarrow T$, which implies $p_D(T) \leq p_D(Q)$.

Price updates. What happens if the seller adds price points to S? We prove in the full paper [19] that, as long the price points remain consistent, the prices never increase; in other words, the seller can only add more discounts, but cannot raise the prices (of course, one can modify S to raise prices, but prices do not increase through additions to S.)

Selections on Multiple Attributes. The PTIME algorithm in Subsection 3.1 allows explicit prices only on selection queries on single attributes, e.g. $\sigma_{R.X=a}$. A natural question is whether one can extend it to prices for selections on two or more attributes, e.g. $\sigma_{R.X=a,R.Y=b}$. The answer to this question varies. For Chain Queries (Definition 3.12) this is possible: simply modify the flow graph by setting the capacity of the TUPLE-EDGE $(w_{R.X=a}, v_{R.Y=b})$ to $p(\sigma_{R.X=a,R.Y=b})$

instead of ∞. For Generalized Chain Queries, however, this is not possible in general. In fact, even for a very simple query, $Q(x,y,z) = R(x,y,z)$, if S has prices on all these types of selection queries: $\sigma_{R.X=a}$, $\sigma_{R.Y=b}$, $\sigma_{R.Z=c}$, $\sigma_{R.X=a,R.Y=b,R.Z=c}$, then we prove in the full paper [19] that computing the price of Q is NP-hard.

5. RELATED WORK

There exist many independent vendors selling data online [1, 2, 6, 13, 31] and Amazon cloud users can sell their S3 data for a profit [7]. In addition, digital market services for data have recently emerged in the cloud [9, 17, 29], which enable content providers to upload their data and make it available either freely or for a fee, and support some limited forms of views. In the case of Infochimps [17], the seller can set prices on APIs (modeled as selection queries) or entire datasets. The Azure Marketplace [9] uses data subscriptions with query limits on transactions, *i.e.* a group of records returned by a query that can fit on a page (currently 100). WebScaled is a pre-launch startup providing a marketplace for datasets from ongoing Web crawls: social graphs, lists of sites using particular advertising platforms, frequency of specific doctypes and other HTML elements, etc. [29, 30]. Apollo Mapping sells access to satellite imagery [8]. The approach that we develop in this paper extends these pricing methods with the ability to interpolate prices for *arbitrary queries* over a seller's database.

While the interaction between data management and economics has been studied in the database research community before [14, 28], to the best of our knowledge, this paper is the first to study the problem of data pricing, with the exception of a short vision paper that we recently published [10].

There is a rich literature on pricing information products (*e.g.*, [18, 27]). We were mostly influenced by Shapiro and Varian [27], who argue that the price of *information products* is quite different from that of *physical goods*, and propose a new theory for pricing information products, based on the notion of versions. The difference is that information products have very high fixed costs, while the marginal costs are tiny. For example, the cost of conducting a detailed consumer survey in several countries is very high, while the cost of distributing the resulting data tiny (copying a file). As a consequence, the price of information products cannot be determined by traditional means (production costs and competition), but must be linked to the value that the buyers place on the data. Different buyers may use the data in different ways, and should be charged different prices. For example, a retailer may be willing to pay a high price for the entire consumer survey, while a journalist may only be willing to pay a small amount for a few interesting statistics from the consumer survey. In order to leverage these differences in willingness to pay, Shapiro and Varian conclude that information products should be offered in different *versions*, at different prices. Our approach extends version-based pricing to relational data, by associating a version of the product to each query that a user may ask.

The classic notion of determinacy was extensively studied by Nash, Segoufin and Vianu [26, 23, 24], who have investigated both the decidability question, and the subtle relationship between determinacy and rewritability. We have reviewed information-theoretic determinacy earlier ($\mathbf{V} \twoheadrightarrow Q$ if forall D, D', $\mathbf{V}(D) = \mathbf{V}(D')$ implies $Q(D) = Q(D')$). Rewritability is specific to a query language $\mathcal{L}$: Q can be rewritten using **V** in the language $\mathcal{L}$ if there exists a query $R \in \mathcal{L}$ s.t. $Q(D) = R(\mathbf{V}(D))$ for all D. One goal of this line of research was to establish tight bounds on the language $\mathcal{L}$; a surprising result is an example where both **V** and Q are conjunctive queries, yet R is non-monotone, proving that no monotone language is sufficient for CQ to CQ rewriting. In our query pricing framework we do not impose any restriction on the language used for rewriting; in other words, we assume that the buyer has unrestricted computational power, and as a consequence the two notions become equal. A second goal of the research [26, 23, 24] is to study the decision problem for determinacy: it is shown to be undecidable even for Unions of Conjunctive Queries, and its status is open for Conjunctive Queries. However, several classes of CQ queries where determinacy is well-behaved have been found: path queries [5], syntactic restrictions of FO and UCQ (packed FO and UCQ [21]) and monadic views [24]. Determinacy has also been examined in the restricted setting of aggregate queries [16].

A key difference in our paper is that we consider instance-based determinacy, where determinacy is defined with respect to a view extension. While applications like data integration or semantic caching require instance-independent determinacy, in query pricing the current state of the database cannot be ignored. Instance-based determinacy is identical to the notion of *lossless views* [11] under the exact view assumption. The definition is further based on the notion of *certain answers* [3]. We note that instance-specific reasoning also arises in data security and authorization views: in that context, Zhang and Mendelzon study *conditional query containment*, where containment is conditioned on a particular view output [32].

Finally, we should mention that, on the surface, our complexity results for pricing seem related to complexity results for computing *responsibility* [22]. The PTIME algorithm for responsibility is also based on network flow, but the reduction for pricing is harder to establish. Furthermore, even though some queries have the same complexity for both pricing and responsibility, the connection is superficial: the price of H_2 (Theorem 3.5) is NP-complete, while its responsibility is in PTIME; and the price of C_3 (Theorem 3.15) is in PTIME while its responsibility is NP-complete.

6. CONCLUSION

We have presented a framework for pricing relational data based on queries. The seller sets explicit prices on some views, while the buyer may ask arbitrary queries; their prices are determined automatically. We gave several results: an explicit formula for the price, a polynomial time algorithm for pricing Generalized Chain Queries, and a dichotomy theorem for conjunctive queries without self-joins. We also presented several results on instance-based determinacy.

Interesting future work includes considering competition: when a seller sets prices for her data, she needs to consider other data instances on the market that offer "related" data, to avoid arbitrage. This requires reasoning about mappings between the different data sources, and these mappings are often approximate in practice. Another is the interaction between pricing and privacy. Most of the literature on data privacy [15] focuses on restricting access to private information. Privacy, however, has a broader definition, and usually means the ability of the data owner to control how her private information is used [25]. Setting a price for private data is one form of such control that we plan to investigate.

Acknowledgments. This work is supported in part by the NSF and Microsoft through NSF grant CCF-1047815 and also grant IIS-0915054. We also thank the anonymous reviewer for pointing out an inconsistency in the early version of Corollary 2.16.

7. REFERENCES

[1] http://gnip.com.

[2] http://www.patientslikeme.com.

[3] S. Abiteboul and O. M. Duschka. Complexity of answering queries using materialized views. In *PODS*, pages 254–263. ACM Press, 1998.

[4] S. Abiteboul, R. Hull, and V. Vianu. *Foundations of Databases*. Addison-Wesley, 1995.

[5] F. N. Afrati. Rewriting conjunctive queries determined by views. In *MFCS*, pages 78–89, 2007.

[6] http://www.aggdata.com/.

[7] Using Amazon S3 Requester Pays with DevPay. http://docs.amazonwebservices.com/AmazonDevPay/latest/DevPayDeveloperGuide/index.html?S3RequesterPays.html.

[8] http://www.apollomapping.com/.

[9] https://datamarket.azure.com/.

[10] M. Balazinska, B. Howe, and D. Suciu. Data markets in the cloud: An opportunity for the database community. *Proc. of the VLDB Endowment*, 4(12), 2011.

[11] D. Calvanese, G. D. Giacomo, M. Lenzerini, and M. Y. Vardi. Lossless regular views. In L. Popa, editor, *PODS*, pages 247–258. ACM, 2002.

[12] T. H. Cormen, C. E. Leiserson, R. L. Rivest, and C. Stein. *Introduction to Algorithms, Second Edition*. The MIT Press and McGraw-Hill Book Company, 2001.

[13] http://www.customlists.net/.

[14] D. Dash, V. Kantere, and A. Ailamaki. An economic model for self-tuned cloud caching. In *Proc. of the 25th ICDE Conf.*, pages 1687–1693, 2009.

[15] C. Dwork. A firm foundation for private data analysis. *Commun. ACM*, 54(1):86–95, 2011.

[16] S. Grumbach and L. Tininini. On the content of materialized aggregate views. *J. Comput. Syst. Sci.*, 66(1):133–168, 2003.

[17] http://www.infochimps.com/.

[18] S. Jain and P. K. Kannan. Pricing of information products on online servers: Issues, models, and analysis. *Management Science*, 48(9):1123–1142, 2002.

[19] P. Koutris, P. Upadhyaya, M. Balazinska, B. Howe, and D. Suciu. Query-based data pricing. Research Report UW-CSE-12-03-02, University of Washington, 2012.

[20] L. Libkin. *Elements of Finite Model Theory*. Springer, 2004.

[21] M. Marx. Queries determined by views: pack your views. In L. Libkin, editor, *PODS*, pages 23–30. ACM, 2007.

[22] A. Meliou, W. Gatterbauer, K. F. Moore, and D. Suciu. The complexity of causality and responsibility for query answers and non-answers. *PVLDB*, 4(1):34–45, 2010.

[23] A. Nash, L. Segoufin, and V. Vianu. Determinacy and rewriting of conjunctive queries using views: A progress report. In *ICDT*, pages 59–73, 2007.

[24] A. Nash, L. Segoufin, and V. Vianu. Views and queries: Determinacy and rewriting. *ACM Trans. Database Syst.*, 35(3), 2010.

[25] B. Schneier. *Secrets & Lies, Digital Security in a Networked World*. John Wiley & Sons, 2000.

[26] L. Segoufin and V. Vianu. Views and queries: determinacy and rewriting. In C. Li, editor, *PODS*, pages 49–60. ACM, 2005.

[27] C. Shapiro and H. R. Varian. Versioning: The smart way to sell information. *Harvard Business Review*, 76:106–114, November-December 1998.

[28] Stonebraker et al. Mariposa: a wide-area distributed database system. *VLDB Journal*, 5(1):048–063, 1996.

[29] http://webscaled.com/.

[30] Web marketing. Google group forum post, http://groups.google.com/group/webmarketing/msg/c6643da409802f85.

[31] http://www.xignite.com/.

[32] Z. Zhang and A. O. Mendelzon. Authorization views and conditional query containment. In *ICDT*, pages 259–273, 2005.

Local Transformations and Conjunctive-Query Equivalence

Ronald Fagin
IBM Research – Almaden
fagin@us.ibm.com

Phokion G. Kolaitis
UC Santa Cruz & IBM Research – Almaden
kolaitis@cs.ucsc.edu

ABSTRACT

Over the past several decades, the study of conjunctive queries has occupied a central place in the theory and practice of database systems. In recent years, conjunctive queries have played a prominent role in the design and use of schema mappings for data integration and data exchange tasks. In this paper, we investigate several different aspects of conjunctive-query equivalence in the context of schema mappings and data exchange.

In the first part of the paper, we introduce and study a notion of a local transformation between database instances that is based on conjunctive-query equivalence. We show that the chase procedure for GLAV mappings (that is, schema mappings specified by source-to-target tuple-generating dependencies) is a local transformation with respect to conjunctive-query equivalence. This means that the chase procedure preserves bounded conjunctive-query equivalence, that is, if two source instances are indistinguishable using conjunctive queries of a sufficiently large size, then the target instances obtained by chasing these two source instances are also indistinguishable using conjunctive queries of a given size. Moreover, we obtain polynomial bounds on the level of indistinguishability between source instances needed to guarantee indistinguishability between the target instances produced by the chase. The locality of the chase extends to schema mappings specified by a second-order tuple-generating dependency (SO tgd), but does not hold for schema mappings whose specification includes target constraints.

In the second part of the paper, we take a closer look at the composition of two GLAV mappings. In particular, we break GLAV mappings into a small number of well-studied classes (including LAV and GAV), and complete the picture as to when the composition of schema mappings from these various classes can be guaranteed to be a GLAV mapping, and when they can be guaranteed to be conjunctive-query equivalent to a GLAV mapping.

We also show that the following problem is decidable: given a schema mapping specified by an SO tgd and a GLAV mapping, are they conjunctive-query equivalent? In contrast, the following problem is known to be undecidable: given a schema mapping specified by an SO tgd and a GLAV mapping, are they logically equivalent?

Categories and Subject Descriptors

H.2.5 [**Database Management**]: Heterogeneous Databases—*data translation*; H.2.4 [**Database Management**]: Systems—*relational databases*

General Terms

Algorithms, Theory

Keywords

local transformations, continuity, conjunctive queries, schema mappings, chase, composition

1. Introduction

Conjunctive queries have played a major role in both the theory and practice of relational database systems since the early days of the relational data model. They are now ubiquitous in the study of data inter-operability tasks, such as data exchange and data integration (see the overviews [Len02, Kol05, ABLM10]). In particular, conjunctive queries play a key role in the design of schema-mapping languages, that is, high-level, declarative languages whose formulas are used to describe the relationship between two database schemas, often referred to as the source schema and the target (or global) schema. For example, GLAV mappings, the most widely used and extensively studied schema mappings, are specified by a finite set of source-to-target tuple-generating dependencies (s-t tgds) each of which, intuitively, asserts that some conjunctive query over the source schema is contained in some conjunctive query over the target schema. Furthermore, much of the study of query answering in data exchange and data integration has focused on the problem of computing the certain answers of conjunctive queries over the target schema in the case of data exchange (or over the global schema in the case of data integration).

In a different yet related direction of research, conjunctive queries have been also used to formulate a notion of equivalence between schema mappings that is a relaxation of the classical notion of logical equivalence. Specifically, schema mappings $\mathbf{M_1}$ and $\mathbf{M_2}$ are said to be *conjunctive-query equivalent* (or, in short, *CQ-equivalent*) if for every conjunctive query q over the target schema and for every source instance I, the certain answers of q on I w.r.t. $\mathbf{M_1}$ coincide with the certain answers of q on I w.r.t. $\mathbf{M_2}$. In [FKNP08], CQ-equivalence was studied in the context of schema-mapping optimization. In particular, CQ-equivalence was shown to coincide with logical equivalence for GLAV mappings, but to be a strict relaxation of logical equivalence for schema mappings involving target constraints, as well as for schema mappings specified by second-order tuple-generating dependencies (SO tgds). Subsequent investigations of CQ-equivalence in the context of schema-mapping optimization include [PSS11] and [FPSS11]. Prior to all these investigations, however, a notion of composition of two schema mappings based on CQ-equivalence was introduced and studied in [MH03]. More recently, a notion of an inverse of schema mapping based on CQ-equivalence was introduced and studied in [APRR09].

Our goal in this paper is to investigate several different aspects of conjunctive-query equivalence in the context of data exchange, as well as in the context of composing schema mappings. We begin by introducing and studying the notion of a CQ-*local* transformation between database instances, a notion that is based on *bounded conjunctive-query equivalence*. Intuitively, a CQ-local transformation has the property that if two instances are indistinguishable using conjunctive queries of a sufficiently large size, then their images under the transformation are also indistinguishable using conjunctive queries of a given size. Formally, a transformation $\mathcal{F}$ between database instances is CQ-*local* if for every positive integer n, there is a positive integer N such that if I_1 and I_2 are instances that satisfy the same Boolean conjunctive queries with at most N variables, then their images $\mathcal{F}(I_1)$ and $\mathcal{F}(I_2)$ satisfy the same Boolean conjunctive queries with at most n variables.

We show that if $\mathbf{M}$ is a GLAV mapping, then the chase procedure w.r.t. $\mathbf{M}$ is a CQ-local transformation. As a matter of fact, we give two different proofs of this result. The first proof entails combining the main technical result in Rossman's proof of the preservation-under-homomorphisms theorem in the finite [Ros08] with a result from the full, unpublished version of [ABFL04] to the effect that the chase transformation for GLAV mappings is local in a sense of first-order equivalence. This proof yields an N that is a stack of exponentials in n, because this type of blow-up already occurs in Rossman's proof [Ros08], and no smaller bounds are presently known. We therefore give a different and direct proof of the CQ-locality of the chase procedure for a GLAV mapping that also yields an N that is bounded by a polynomial in the size of n. In fact, the degree of the polynomial is equal to the maximum arity of the relation symbols of the target schema. We also point out that the CQ-locality of the chase procedure extends to schema mappings specified by SO tgds, but does not hold for schema mappings whose specification includes target constraints.

In the second part of the paper, we take a closer look at the composition of two GLAV mappings. In [FKPT05], it was shown that the composition of two GLAV mappings is guaranteed to be logically equivalent to a schema mapping specified by an SO tgd, but may not be logically equivalent to any GLAV mapping. In fact, as also shown in [FKPT05], the composition of two GLAV mappings may not even be CQ-equivalent to any GLAV mapping. It is also known, however, that the state of affairs is different for the important cases of GAV and LAV mappings. A GAV (global-as-view) mapping is a schema mapping specified by a finite set of s-t tgds whose right-hand side is a single atom, while a LAV (local-as-view) mapping is a schema mapping specified by a finite set of s-t tgds whose left-hand side is a single atom in which no variable occurs more than once. As regards GAV mappings, it was shown in [FKPT05] that the composition of two GAV mappings is guaranteed to be logically equivalent to a GAV mapping; furthermore, the composition of a GAV mapping with a GLAV mapping is guaranteed to be logically equivalent to a GLAV mapping. As regards LAV mappings, it was shown in [AFM10] that the composition of two LAV mappings is guaranteed to be logically equivalent to a GLAV mapping (in fact, to a LAV mapping). Here, we generalize this result by showing that the composition of a GLAV mapping with a LAV mapping is guaranteed to be logically equivalent to a

GLAV mapping. After this, we consider the class of *extended* LAV mappings, which are schema mappings specified by a finite set of s-t tgds whose left-hand side is a single atom in which a variable may occur more than once. Clearly, extended LAV mappings form a proper extension of the class of LAV mappings. We show that the composition of a GLAV mapping with an extended LAV mapping is guaranteed to be CQ-equivalent to a GLAV mapping (such a composition may not be logically equivalent to any GLAV mapping [FKPT05]). With the aid of these two results, we complete the picture as to when the composition of schema mappings taken from the classes of GAV, LAV, extended LAV, and arbitrary GLAV mappings can be guaranteed to be a GLAV mapping, and when it can be guaranteed to be CQ-equivalent to a GLAV mapping.

Finally, we show that the following problem is decidable: given a schema mapping specified by an SO tgd and a GLAV mapping, are they CQ-equivalent? In contrast, as shown in [FPSS11] by building on results from [APR09], the following problem is undecidable: given a schema mapping specified by an SO tgd and a GLAV mapping, are they logically equivalent?

2. Preliminaries

A *schema* $\mathbf{R}$ is a finite sequence $\langle R_1, \ldots, R_k \rangle$ of relation symbols, where each R_i has a fixed arity. An *instance* I over $\mathbf{R}$, or an $\mathbf{R}$-*instance*, is a sequence $(R_1^I, \ldots, R_k^I)$, where each R_i^I is a finite relation of the same arity as R_i. We shall often use R_i to denote both the relation symbol and the relation R_i^I that instantiates it. A *fact* of an instance I (over $\mathbf{R}$) is an expression $R_i^I(v_1, \ldots, v_m)$ (or simply $R_i(v_1, \ldots, v_m)$), where R_i is a relation symbol of $\mathbf{R}$ and $(v_1, \ldots, v_m) \in R_i^I$. The expression $(v_1, \ldots, v_m)$ is also sometimes referred to as a *tuple* of R_i. An instance is often identified with its set of facts. An entry in a tuple of an instance I is an *element* or *value* from I, and the set of elements from I is the *active domain* of I.

Next, we define the concepts of *homomorphism* and *homomorphic equivalence*. Let I_1 and I_2 be instances over a schema $\mathbf{R}$. A function h is a *homomorphism* from I_1 to I_2 if for every relation symbol R in $\mathbf{R}$ and every tuple $(a_1, \ldots, a_n) \in R^{I_1}$, we have that $(h(a_1), \ldots, h(a_n)) \in R^{I_2}$. In data exchange, it is often convenient to assume the presence of two kinds of values, namely *constants* and *(labeled) nulls*, and to assume as part of the definition of a homomorphism h that $h(c) = c$ for every constant c; however, we do not make that assumption in this paper. We use the notation $I_1 \rightarrow I_2$ to denote that there is a homomorphism from I_1 to I_2. Since we do not assume that a homomorphism necessarily maps each constant into itself, it is sometimes important to specify that a homomorphism h *respects* I for some instance I, which means that $h(x) = x$ for every element x of I. If there is a homomorphism from I_1 to I_2 that respects I, then we may write $I_1 \xrightarrow{I} I_2$. We say that I_1 is *homomorphically equivalent* to I_2, written $I_1 \leftrightarrow I_2$, if $I_1 \rightarrow I_2$ and $I_2 \rightarrow I_1$. The *core* of an instance K is the smallest subinstance of K that is homomorphically equivalent to K. If there are multiple cores of K, then they are all isomorphic [HN92].

Schema mappings A *schema mapping* is a triple $\mathbf{M} = (\mathbf{S}, \mathbf{T}, \Sigma)$, where $\mathbf{S}$ and $\mathbf{T}$ are schemas with no relation symbols in common, and Σ is a set of constraints (typically, formulas in some logic) that describe the relationship between $\mathbf{S}$ and $\mathbf{T}$. We say that $\mathbf{M}$ is *specified by* Σ. We refer to $\mathbf{S}$ as the *source schema*, and $\mathbf{T}$ as the *target schema*. Similarly, we refer to $\mathbf{S}$-instances as *source instances*, and $\mathbf{T}$-instances as *target instances*. We say that schema mappings $\mathbf{M}_1$ and $\mathbf{M}_2$ are *logically equivalent* if the constraints that specify $\mathbf{M}_1$ are logically equivalent to the constraints that specify $\mathbf{M}_2$.

If I is a source instance and J is a target instance such that the pair (I, J) satisfies Σ (written $(I, J) \models \Sigma$), then we say that J is a *solution* of I w.r.t. $\mathbf{M}$. We say that J is a *universal solution for I* w.r.t. $\mathbf{M}$ [FKMP05] if J is a solution for I and for every solution J' for I, we have $J \xrightarrow{I} J'$.

An *atom* is an expression $R(x_1, ..., x_n)$, where R is a relation symbol and $x_1, \ldots, x_n$ are variables that are not necessarily distinct. A *source-to-target tuple-generating dependency (s-t tgd)* is a first-order sentence of the form $\forall \mathbf{x}(\varphi(\mathbf{x}) \rightarrow \exists \mathbf{y} \psi(\mathbf{x}, \mathbf{y}))$, where $\varphi(\mathbf{x})$ is a conjunction of atoms over $\mathbf{S}$, each variable in $\mathbf{x}$ occurs in at least one atom in $\varphi(\mathbf{x})$, and $\psi(\mathbf{x}, \mathbf{y})$ is a conjunction of atoms over $\mathbf{T}$ with variables in $\mathbf{x}$ and $\mathbf{y}$. For simplicity, we will often suppress writing the universal quantifiers $\forall \mathbf{x}$ in the above formula. We refer to $\varphi(\mathbf{x})$ as the *left-hand side*, or *premise*, and $\exists \mathbf{y} \psi(\mathbf{x}, \mathbf{y})$ as the *right-hand side*, or *conclusion*. Another name for s-t tgds is *global-and-local-as-view* (GLAV) constraints (see [Len02]). They contain several important special cases, which we now define.

A GAV *(global-as-view)* constraint is an s-t tgd in which the conclusion is a single atom with no existentially quantified variables, that is, it is of the form $\forall \mathbf{x}(\varphi(\mathbf{x}) \rightarrow P(\mathbf{x}))$, where $P(\mathbf{x})$ is an atom over the target schema.

There are several competing notions of a LAV *(local-as-view)* constraint. The definition we shall use is that a LAV constraint is an s-t tgd of the form $\forall \mathbf{x}(Q(\mathbf{x}) \rightarrow \exists \mathbf{y} \psi(\mathbf{x}, \mathbf{y}))$, where $Q(\mathbf{x})$ is a single atom over the source schema and no repeated variables in $Q(\mathbf{x})$ are allowed. This is the notion of LAV used by Arocena, Fuxman, and Miller [AFM10], for their result that the composition of LAV mappings is logically equivalent to a LAV mapping. Another notion of LAV is obtained by dropping the restriction that there are no repeated variables in the premise $Q(\mathbf{x})$. We shall refer to such constraints as *extended LAV*. In a number of papers, including [ABFL04, FKMP05, Fag07, FKPT11], our notion of "extended LAV" is called simply "LAV", and in [FKPT11], our notion of "LAV" is called "strict LAV". Note also that there is yet another notion of "LAV" in the literature, which is defined even more strictly than our definition, by requiring that all variables in $\mathbf{x}$ appear in the conclusion.

We refer to a schema mapping specified entirely by a finite set of GLAV (respectively, GAV, LAV, extended LAV) constraints as a GLAV (respectively, GAV, LAV, extended LAV) mapping.

On occasion, we will also consider schema mappings whose specification also includes target constraints. A target *equality generating dependency (egd)* is a first-order sentence that is of the form $\forall \mathbf{x}(\varphi(\mathbf{x}) \rightarrow (x_i = x_j))$, where $\varphi(\mathbf{x})$ is a conjunction of atoms over $\mathbf{T}$, each variable in $\mathbf{x}$ occurs in at least one atom in $\varphi(\mathbf{x})$, and x_i, x_j are among the variables in $\mathbf{x}$. A target *tuple-generating dependency (tgd)* is a first-order sentence of the form $\forall \mathbf{x}(\varphi(\mathbf{x}) \rightarrow \exists \mathbf{y} \psi(\mathbf{x}, \mathbf{y}))$, where both $\varphi(\mathbf{x})$ and $\psi(\mathbf{x}, \mathbf{y})$ are conjunctions of atoms over $\mathbf{T}$, and each variable in $\mathbf{x}$ occurs in at least one atom in $\varphi(\mathbf{x})$. A target *full tgd* is a target tgd whose conclusion has no existential quantifiers.

We shall also make use of *second-order tgds*, or *SO tgds*. These were introduced in [FKPT05], where it was shown that SO tgds are exactly what is needed to specify the composition of an arbitrary number of GLAV mappings. Before we formally define SO tgds, we need to define *terms*.

Given collections $\mathbf{x}$ of variables and $\mathbf{f}$ of function symbols, a *term (based on $\mathbf{x}$ and $\mathbf{f}$)* is defined recursively as follows:

1. Every variable in $\mathbf{x}$ is a term.

2. If f is a k-ary function symbol in $\mathbf{f}$ and $t_1, \ldots, t_k$ are terms, then $f(t_1, \ldots, t_k)$ is a term.

DEFINITION 2.1. Let $\mathbf{S}$ be a source schema and $\mathbf{T}$ a target

schema. A *second-order tuple-generating dependency (SO tgd)* is a formula of the form:

$$\exists \mathbf{f}((\forall \mathbf{x_1}(\phi_1 \rightarrow \psi_1)) \wedge ... \wedge (\forall \mathbf{x_n}(\phi_n \rightarrow \psi_n))),$$

where

1. Each member of $\mathbf{f}$ is a function symbol.

2. Each ϕ_i is a conjunction of
   - atoms $S(y_1, ..., y_k)$, where S is a k-ary relation symbol of schema $\mathbf{S}$ and $y_1, \ldots, y_k$ are variables in $\mathbf{x_i}$, not necessarily distinct, and
   - equalities of the form $t = t'$ where t and t' are terms based on $\mathbf{x_i}$ and $\mathbf{f}$.

3. Each ψ_i is a conjunction of atoms $T(t_1, ..., t_l)$, where T is an l-ary relation symbol of schema $\mathbf{T}$ and $t_1, \ldots, t_l$ are terms based on $\mathbf{x_i}$ and $\mathbf{f}$.

4. Each variable in $\mathbf{x_i}$ appears in some atomic formula of ϕ_i.

Each subformula $\forall \mathbf{x_i}(\phi_i \rightarrow \psi_i)$ is a *tgd part* of the SO tgd. $\square$

As an example, in a personnel database, where $\text{Emp}(e)$ means that e is an employee, $\text{Mgr}(e, e')$ means that e' is the manager of e, and $\text{SelfMgr}(e)$ means that e is his own manager, we might have the following SO tgd, where, intuitively $f(e)$ is the manager of e:

$$\exists f(\forall e(\text{Emp}(e) \rightarrow \text{Mgr}(e, f(e))) \wedge \qquad (1)$$
$$\forall e(\text{Emp}(e) \wedge (e = f(e)) \rightarrow \text{SelfMgr}(e)).$$

We now give the definition (from [FKPT05]) of the composition of schema mappings. Let $\mathbf{M}_{12} = (\mathbf{S}_1, \mathbf{S}_2, \Sigma_{12})$ and let $\mathbf{M}_{23} = (\mathbf{S}_2, \mathbf{S}_3, \Sigma_{23})$ be two schema mappings such that the schemas $\mathbf{S}_1, \mathbf{S}_2, \mathbf{S}_3$ have no relation symbol in common pairwise. A schema mapping $\mathbf{M}_{13} = (\mathbf{S}_1, \mathbf{S}_3, \Sigma_{13})$ is a *composition of $\mathbf{M}_{12}$ and $\mathbf{M}_{23}$* if for every $\mathbf{S}_1$-instance I_1 and every $\mathbf{S}_3$-instance I_3 we have that $(I_1, I_3) \models \Sigma_{13}$ if and only if there is an $\mathbf{S}_2$-instance I_2 such that $(I_1, I_2) \models \Sigma_{12}$ and $(I_2, I_3) \models \Sigma_{23}$. We may then write $\mathbf{M}_{13} = \mathbf{M}_{12} \circ \mathbf{M}_{23}$, and $\Sigma_{13} = \Sigma_{12} \circ \Sigma_{23}$.

Chase The *chase procedure* [ABU79, MMS79] has been used in a number of settings over the years, and several variants of the chase procedure have been considered. In this paper, we use the variant described in [FKNP08], which is sometimes called the *naive chase* or the *parallel chase*.. The basic idea of the naive chase procedure on a source instance I with a GLAV mapping $\mathbf{M} = (\mathbf{S}, \mathbf{T}, \Sigma)$ is that for every s-t tgd $\forall \mathbf{x}(\varphi(\mathbf{x}) \rightarrow \exists \mathbf{y} \psi(\mathbf{x}, \mathbf{y}))$ in Σ and for every tuple $\mathbf{a}$ of values from the active domain of I, such that $I \models \varphi(\mathbf{a})$, we add all facts in $\psi(\mathbf{a}, \mathbf{N})$ to the output of the chase procedure, where $\mathbf{N}$ is a tuple of new, distinct values (usually called labeled nulls) interpreting the existential quantified variables $\mathbf{y}$. Note that in the naive chase, we add these facts whether or not there is already a tuple $\mathbf{b}$ of values such that $\psi(\mathbf{a}, \mathbf{b})$ is in the current output of the chase procedure. From now on, we refer to the naive chase procedure as simply the *chase procedure* or the *chase*, and we write $chase_{\mathcal{M}}(I)$ or $chase_{\Sigma}(I)$ to denote the result of applying the chase procedure on the instance I. It is shown in [FKMP05] that $chase_{\mathcal{M}}(I)$ is a universal solution of I w.r.t. $\mathbf{M}$.

Note that all of our results hold no matter which variant of the chase procedure is used, because for a fixed GLAV mapping, the results of all variants are homomorphically equivalent,

A *conjunctive query* over a schema $\mathbf{R}$ is a formula of the form $\exists \mathbf{y} \phi(\mathbf{x}, \mathbf{y})$ where $\phi(\mathbf{x}, \mathbf{y})$ is a conjunction of atoms over $\mathbf{R}$. If $\mathbf{x}$ is empty (that is, if every variable is existentially quantified) then we call the conjunctive query *Boolean*.

Let $\mathbf{M}$ be a schema mapping, q a k-ary query, for $k \geq 0$, over the target schema $\mathbf{T}$, and I a source instance. The *certain answers of q with respect to* I, denoted by $certain_M(q, I)$, is the set of all k-tuples t of elements from I such that for every solution J for I with respect to $\mathbf{M}$, we have that $t \in q(J)$. In symbols,

$$certain_M(q, I) = \bigcap \{q(J) : J \text{ is a solution for } I \text{ w.r.t. } \mathbf{M}\}.$$

If q is a Boolean query, then $certain_M(q, I) = true$ precisely when $q(J) = true$, for every solution J for I w.r.t. $\mathbf{M}$. If $\mathbf{M}$ is specified by Σ, then we may write $certain_\Sigma(q, I)$ instead of $certain_M(q, I)$.

We shall make use of the following theorem from [FKMP05].

THEOREM 2.2 ([FKMP05]). *Let* $\mathbf{M}$ *be an arbitrary schema mapping and* I *an arbitrary source instance such that* I *has a universal solution* U *with respect to* $\mathbf{M}$. *Let* q *be a conjunctive query.*[1] *Then* $certain_M(q, I) = q(U)_{\downarrow}$, *which is the result of evaluating* q *on* U *and then keeping only those tuples formed entirely of values from* I.

3. Local Transformations

We begin by introducing a unifying notion of a *local transformation*.

DEFINITION 3.1. Let $D = \{D_n : n \geq 1\}$ be a family of binary relations between instances such that for each n, we have that $D_{n+1} \subseteq D_n$, and for each I_1, I_2, if $D_n(I_1, I_2)$, then I_1 and I_2 are instances over the same schema.

Let $\mathbf{S}$ and $\mathbf{T}$ be schemas. If $\mathcal{F}$ is a function "preserv from the class of $\mathbf{S}$-instances to the class of $\mathbf{T}$-instances, then we say that $\mathcal{F}$ is a *D-local transformation* if for every positive integer n, there is a positive integer N such that for all $\mathbf{S}$-instances I_1 and I_2 with $D_N(I_1, I_2)$, we have that $D_n(\mathcal{F}(I_1), \mathcal{F}(I_2))$. $\square$

If $\mathcal{F}$ is D-local, then for every positive integer n, there is a positive integer N such that for all $m \geq N$ and for all $\mathbf{S}$-instances I_1 and I_2 with $D_m(I_1, I_2)$, we have that $D_n(\mathcal{F}(I_1), \mathcal{F}(I_2))$. This is so because it follows from Definition 3.1 that $D_m \subseteq D_N$ when $m \geq N$. Before we give our case of greatest interest, we need another definition.

DEFINITION 3.2. Assume that I_1 and I_2 are $\mathbf{S}$-instances over a schema $\mathbf{S}$, and let n be a positive integer. We say that I_1 and I_2 are CQ_n-*equivalent*, and write $I_1 \equiv_n^{cq} I_2$, if I_1 and I_2 satisfy the same Boolean conjunctive queries with at most n variables. $\square$

The binary relations $\equiv_n^{cq}$, $n \geq 1$, give rise to the family

$$\mathrm{CQ} = \{\equiv_n^{cq}: n \geq 1\}.$$

Our case of greatest interest for D-locality in Definition 3.1 is when $D = \mathrm{CQ}$. Thus, a transformation $\mathcal{F}$ is CQ-local if for every positive integer n, there is a positive integer N such that for all instances I_1 and I_2, if $I_1 \equiv_N^{cq} I_2$, then $\mathcal{F}(I_1) \equiv_n^{cq} \mathcal{F}(I_2)$.

We shall make use of the following simple lemma, which follows easily from the fact that the $\equiv_n^{cq}$ relationship between two instances depends only on their homomorphism equivalence classes.

LEMMA 3.3. *Assume that* $I_1 \leftrightarrow I_1'$, $I_2 \leftrightarrow I_2'$, *and* $I_1 \equiv_n^{cq} I_2$. *Then* $I_1' \equiv_n^{cq} I_2'$.

We now point out that CQ-locality can be viewed as a type of uniform continuity with respect to a natural metric that has been studied in graph theory. We begin with a measure of *similarity* between two instances.

DEFINITION 3.4. If I_1 and I_2 are $\mathbf{S}$-instances for some schema $\mathbf{S}$, and n is a positive integer, then

$$sim(I_1, I_2) = \min\{|C| : ((C \rightarrow I_1) \text{ and } (C \not\rightarrow I_2)) \text{ or } \\ ((C \not\rightarrow I_1) \text{ and } (C \rightarrow I_2))\},$$

where $|C|$ is size of the active domain of C. $\square$

We have the following simple proposition.

PROPOSITION 3.5. *Assume that* I_1 *and* I_2 *are* $\mathbf{S}$-*instances over a schema* $\mathbf{S}$, *and* n *is a positive integer. Then* $I_1 \equiv_n^{cq} I_2$ *if and only if* $sim(I_1, I_2) > n$.

This proposition is an immediate consequence of the Chandra-Merlin Theorem [CM77]. Indeed, for every positive integer n and for all instances I_1 and I_2, the following are equivalent:

- I_1 and I_2 satisfy the same conjunctive queries with at most n variables.
- For every instance C with at most n elements, we have that $C \rightarrow I_1$ if and only if $C \rightarrow I_2$.

EXAMPLE 3.6. For every positive integer m, let C_m be the undirected cycle with m elements and let K_m be the clique with m elements. It is easy to verify that the following are true:

1. $sim(C_{2i+1}, C_{2j+1}) = 2i + 1$, for $1 \leq i < j$.
2. $sim(K_2, C_{2j+1}) = 2j + 1$, for $j \geq 1$
3. $sim(K_i, K_j) = i + 1$, for $i < j$. In particular, we have that $sim(K_2, K_j) = 3$, for $j \geq 3$. $\square$

Define a distance measure d between $\mathbf{S}$-instances by letting

$$d(I_1, I_2) = \frac{1}{sim(I_1, I_2)}.$$

In particular, $d(I_1, I_2) = 0$ if and only if $sim(I_1, I_2) = \infty$, which holds if and only if I_1 and I_2 are homomorphically equivalent. Moreover, if $I_1 \leftrightarrow I_1'$ and $I_2 \leftrightarrow I_2'$, then $d(I_1, I_2) = d(I_1', I_2')$. Therefore, d can be viewed as a distance between $\leftrightarrow$-equivalence classes of $\mathbf{S}$-instances, where two $\mathbf{S}$-instances are in the same equivalence class precisely if they are homomorphically equivalent. We then have the first required property for a metric, namely, that the distance between two equivalence classes is 0 if and only if they are the same equivalence class. We now discuss the other three properties: nonnegativity, symmetry and triangle inequality. Clearly, d is nonnegative and symmetric. As for the triangle inequality, it is easy to see that d in fact satisfies the following strengthened version of the triangle inequality: $d(I_1, I_3) \leq \max\{d(I_1, I_2), d(I_2, I_3)\}$ (this makes d not just a metric, but an *ultrametric*). This metric d has been studied extensively in graph theory, where it has been used to characterize *restricted dualities* (see [NdM09] for a survey).

Returning to Example 3.6, the first statement implies that C_{2i+1}, $i \geq 1$, is a *Cauchy* sequence, that is, for every $\epsilon > 0$, there is a positive integer n such that if $i, j \geq n$, then $d(C_{2i+1}, C_{2j+1}) < \epsilon$. The second statement shows that $\lim_{i \to \infty} C_{2i+1} = K_2$ (this fact has been pointed out in [NdM09]). It is easy to see that a limit, when it exists, is unique up to homomorphic equivalence. The third statement implies that K_i, $i \geq 1$, is also a Cauchy sequence. However, there is *no* finite graph H such that $\lim_{i \to \infty} K_i = H$. This is so because if m is the size of the biggest clique contained in some finite graph H, then for all $i > |H|$, we have that $sim(K_i, H) \leq m + 1$, hence $d(K_i, H) \geq 1/(m + 1)$. This shows that d is not a *complete* metric space. The completion of d (obtained by adding limits of all Cauchy sequences–the same way that the real numbers are obtained from the rational numbers) plays an important role in the characterization of restricted dualities [NdM09].

---

[1] This theorem is shown in [FKMP05] to hold a little more generally: not just for conjunctive queries, but also for unions of conjunctive queries.

A function $\mathcal{F}$ is *uniformly continuous* if for every $\epsilon > 0$, there is $\delta > 0$ such that if $d(I_1, I_2) < \delta$, then $d(\mathcal{F}(I_1), \mathcal{F}(I_2)) < \epsilon$.[2] It is easy to see that under our definitions, a function $\mathcal{F}$ from the class of **S**-instances to the class of **T**-instances is CQ-local if and only if it is uniformly continuous. This helps demonstrate the naturalness of the notion of CQ-locality.

We shall show that for GLAV mappings, the chase is CQ-local. We shall show this result by two different proofs. The first proof makes use of earlier results in the literature, but gives very large bounds on the size of N (a stack of exponentials in n) The second proof is direct, and gives a bound on N that is polynomial in n.

We now consider D-locality for another choice of D. We first give another definition.

DEFINITION 3.7. Assume that I_1 and I_2 are **S**-instances over a schema **S**, and let n be a positive integer. We say that I_1 and I_2 are FO_n-*equivalent*, and write $I_1 \equiv_n I_2$, if I_1 and I_2 satisfy the same first-order formulas of quantifier depth at most n. $\square$

The binary relations $\equiv_n$, $n \geq 1$, give rise to the family

$$\text{FO} = \{\equiv_n : n \geq 1\}.$$

Thus, $\mathcal{F}$ is FO-local if for every positive integer n, there is a positive integer N such that if $I_1 \equiv_N I_2$, then $\mathcal{F}(I_1) \equiv_n \mathcal{F}(I_2)$.

This notion of FO-locality was used, but not named, in the full, unpublished version of [ABFL04], to help prove non-rewritability of queries in data exchange. FO-locality is somewhat similar to the notion in [ABFL04] of "local consistency under FO-equivalence".

3.1 CQ-Local vs. FO-Local

In what follows, we will explore the relationship between CQ-local transformations and FO-local transformations. In doing so, we shall make use of the following theorem, which follows from the proof of Theorem 1.9 of Rossman [Ros08], and which is the main technical tool in proving his deep theorem on preservation under homomorphisms in the finite.

THEOREM 3.8 ([Ros08]). *Assume that* **S** *is a schema. For every positive integer* n, *there is a positive integer* N *and a function* f_n *such that for all* **S**-*instances* I_1 *and* I_2, *the following hold:*

1. $I_1 \leftrightarrow f_n(I_1)$ *and* $I_2 \leftrightarrow f_n(I_2)$.
2. *If* $I_1 \equiv_N^{cq} I_2$, *then* $f_n(I_1) \equiv_n f_n(I_2)$.

We say that $\mathcal{F}$ *preserves homomorphic equivalence* if whenever $I_1 \leftrightarrow I_2$, then $\mathcal{F}(I_1) \leftrightarrow \mathcal{F}(I_2)$. Note that this is yet another notion of D-locality; indeed, $\mathcal{F}$ preserves homomorphism equivalence precisely when $\mathcal{F}$ is H-local, where H $= \{H_n : n \geq 1\}$ and $H_n = \leftrightarrow$, for every $n \geq 1$.

For example, if **M** is a GLAV mapping, then the chase procedure w.r.t. **M** preserves homomorphic equivalence; that is, if $I_1 \leftrightarrow I_2$, then $chase_\mathbf{M}(I_1) \leftrightarrow chase_\mathbf{M}(I_2)$ This is so because, as shown in [FKMP05], if $I_1 \rightarrow I_2$, then $chase_\mathbf{M}(I_1) \rightarrow chase_\mathbf{M}(I_2)$. In fact, the same holds true for schema mappings specified by SO tgds, as well as for schema mappings specified by a finite set of s-t tgds and a finite set of full target tgds. Note, however, that if target egds or arbitrary target tgds are allowed in the specification of a schema mapping **M**, then the chase procedure need not be a total function, that is, $chase_\mathbf{M}(I)$ may not exist for some source instance I.

PROPOSITION 3.9. *If* $\mathcal{F}$ *is* CQ-*local, then* $\mathcal{F}$ *preserves homomorphic equivalence.*

PROOF. Assume that $\mathcal{F}$ is CQ-local, and that $I_1 \leftrightarrow I_2$; we must show that $\mathcal{F}(I_1) \leftrightarrow \mathcal{F}(I_2)$. Let n be the maximum of the number of members of the active domains of $\mathcal{F}(I_1)$ and $\mathcal{F}(I_2)$. It is easy to see that $\mathcal{F}(I_1) \equiv_n^{cq} \mathcal{F}(I_2)$ if and only if $\mathcal{F}(I_1) \leftrightarrow \mathcal{F}(I_2)$. Since $\mathcal{F}$ is CQ-local, there is N such that if $I_1 \equiv_N^{cq} I_2$, then $\mathcal{F}(I_1) \equiv_n^{cq} \mathcal{F}(I_2)$. Since $I_1 \leftrightarrow I_2$, we have $I_1 \equiv_N^{cq} I_2$, and so $\mathcal{F}(I_1) \equiv_n^{cq} \mathcal{F}(I_2)$, hence $\mathcal{F}(I_1) \leftrightarrow \mathcal{F}(I_2)$, as desired. $\square$

As we shall see in Fact 3.11, the converse of Proposition 3.9 fails. We now make use of Rossman's Theorem (Theorem 3.8) to prove the next result.

THEOREM 3.10. *If* $\mathcal{F}$ *preserves homomorphic equivalence and is* FO-*local, then* $\mathcal{F}$ *is* CQ-*local.*

PROOF. Assume that $\mathcal{F}$ is FO-local. Given the positive integer n, let n' be the positive integer guaranteed by FO-locality of $\mathcal{F}$, such that whenever $I_1 \equiv_{n'} I_2$, then $\mathcal{F}(I_1) \equiv_n \mathcal{F}(I_2)$. Let N be the positive integer guaranteed by Theorem 3.8 when the role of n is played by n'.

Assume now that $I_1 \equiv_N^{cq} I_2$; we must show that $\mathcal{F}(I_1) \equiv_n^{cq} \mathcal{F}(I_2)$. Let $f_{n'}$ be as in Theorem 3.8 when the role of n is played by n'. Since $I_1 \equiv_N^{cq} I_2$, it follows from Theorem 3.8 that $f_{n'}(I_1) \equiv_{n'} f_{n'}(I_2)$. It therefore follows from our choice of n' and by FO-locality that $\mathcal{F}(f_{n'}(I_1)) \equiv_n \mathcal{F}(f_{n'}(I_2))$. Since Boolean conjunctive queries with at most n variables are a special case of first-order formulas with quantifier depth at most n, it follows that

$$\mathcal{F}(f_{n'}(I_1)) \equiv_n^{cq} \mathcal{F}(f_{n'}(I_2)). \tag{2}$$

Now $I_1 \leftrightarrow f_{n'}(I_1)$ by Theorem 3.8 when the role of n is played by n'. Since $\mathcal{F}$ preserves homomorphic equivalence, it follows that

$$\mathcal{F}(I_1) \leftrightarrow \mathcal{F}(f_{n'}(I_1)). \tag{3}$$

Similarly,

$$\mathcal{F}(I_2) \leftrightarrow \mathcal{F}(f_{n'}(I_2)). \tag{4}$$

By Lemma 3.3, it follows from (2), (3), and (4) that $\mathcal{F}(I_1) \equiv_n^{cq} \mathcal{F}(I_2)$, as desired. $\square$

FACT 3.11. As we now discuss, neither assumption in Theorem 3.10 can be dropped. First, the assumption that $\mathcal{F}$ is FO-local is needed. That is, there is $\mathcal{F}$ that preserves homomorphic equivalence, but is not CQ-local (so the converse of Proposition 3.9 fails). Here is the reason. If **M** is a schema mapping specified by a finite set of s-t tgds and full target tgds, then as we noted, the chase with **M** preserves homomorphic equivalence. However, such a chase need not be CQ-local, as we shall show in Theorem 3.20.

We now show that the assumption in Theorem 3.10 that $\mathcal{F}$ preserves homomorphic equivalence is needed. That is, there is $\mathcal{F}$ that is FO-local, but is not CQ-local. Let $\mathcal{F}$ be a function that maps every graph with at least two nodes (where a *node* is a member of the active domain) to a triangle (a cycle of length 3), and every graph with one node to a single edge. It is easy to see that $\mathcal{F}$ is FO-local – in fact, we can always take $N = 2$, since if $I_1 \equiv_2 I_2$, then I_1 has at least two nodes if and only if I_2 has at least two nodes, and so if $I_1 \equiv_2 I_2$, then $\mathcal{F}(I_1)$ and $\mathcal{F}(I_2)$ are isomorphic.

To show that $\mathcal{F}$ is not CQ-local, we need only show (by Proposition 3.9) that $\mathcal{F}$ does not preserve homomorphic equivalence. Let I_1 consist of a single node with a self-loop, and let I_2 consist of two nodes, each with a self-loop. It is easy to see that $I_1 \leftrightarrow I_2$. However, $\mathcal{F}(I_1)$ is a single edge, and $\mathcal{F}(I_2)$ is a triangle, and so $\mathcal{F}(I_1) \not\leftrightarrow \mathcal{F}(I_2)$.

The next proposition states what we have just shown.

---

[2]This is *uniform* continuity, since δ does not depend on the choice of I_1 or I_2. If the choice of δ depended on I_1, then we would have continuity of $\mathcal{F}$ at I_1, rather than uniform continuity of $\mathcal{F}$.

PROPOSITION 3.12. *There is a transformation $\mathcal{F}$ that is FO-local but not CQ-local.*

We now show that the converse of Theorem 3.10 fails. While it is true that CQ-locality implies preservation of homomorphic equivalence (Proposition 3.9), the next proposition says that CQ-locality does not imply FO-locality.

PROPOSITION 3.13. *There is a transformation $\mathcal{F}$ that is CQ-local but not FO-local.*

PROOF. Define $\mathcal{F}_{\text{core}}$ by letting $\mathcal{F}_{\text{core}}(I)$ be the core of I. We now show that $\mathcal{F}_{\text{core}}$ is CQ-local, where we let $N = n$. Thus, assume that $I_1 \equiv_n^{cq} I_2$; we must show that $\mathcal{F}_{\text{core}}(I_1) \equiv_n^{cq} \mathcal{F}_{\text{core}}(I_2)$. Now $\mathcal{F}_{\text{core}}(I_1) \leftrightarrow I_1$, and $\mathcal{F}_{\text{core}}(I_2) \leftrightarrow I_2$. Since also $I_1 \equiv_n^{cq} I_2$, it follows from Lemma 3.3 that $\mathcal{F}_{\text{core}}(I_1) \equiv_n^{cq} \mathcal{F}_{\text{core}}(I_2)$.

We now show that $\mathcal{F}_{\text{core}}$ is not FO-local. Assume that it is; we shall derive a contradiction. Since by assumption $\mathcal{F}_{\text{core}}$ is FO-local, there is N such that if $I_1 \equiv_N I_2$, then $\mathcal{F}_{\text{core}}(I_1) \equiv_2 \mathcal{F}_{\text{core}}(I_2)$ (thus, we are taking $n = 2$, and finding N corresponding to n). It is well known that given N, there is N' such that if I_1 and I_2 are each undirected cycles with at least N' nodes, then $I_1 \equiv_N I_2$ (this follows, for example, from Theorem 4.3 of [FSV95]). Take I_1 to be an odd undirected cycle with at least N' nodes, and I_2 to be an even undirected cycle with at least N' nodes, It is straightforward to verify that $\mathcal{F}_{\text{core}}(I_1) = I_1$, and $\mathcal{F}_{\text{core}}(I_2)$ consists of a single edge of I_2. It follows easily that $\mathcal{F}_{\text{core}}(I_1) \not\equiv_2 \mathcal{F}_{\text{core}}(I_2)$. This is our desired contradiction. □

We feel that Propositions 3.12 and 3.13, along with Theorem 3.10, show an interesting relationship between two notions of locality: FO-locality and CQ-locality. We proved Theorem 3.10 using Rossman's Theorem. We do not know whether there is a proof of Theorem 3.10 that does not require the depth of Rossman's Theorem.

3.2 CQ-Locality of the Chase Procedure for GLAV Mappings

To give our first proof of the CQ-locality of the chase for GLAV mappings, we make use of the following theorem, which is a special case of a result in the full, unpublished version of [ABFL04].

THEOREM 3.14. *Let $\mathbf{M}$ be a GLAV mapping. Then the chase with respect to $\mathbf{M}$ is FO-local.*

Our first proof that the chase with respect to GLAV mappings is CQ-local follows immediately by combining Theorem 3.10 with Proposition 3.9 and Theorem 3.14.

THEOREM 3.15. *Let $\mathbf{M}$ be a GLAV mapping. Then the chase with respect to $\mathbf{M}$ is CQ-local.*

We now show that Theorem 3.15 generalizes from schema mappings specified by a finite set of s-t tgds to schema mappings specified by a second-order tgd (SO tgd). It is shown in [FKPT05] that SO tgds have a chase procedure, that produces a universal solution.

COROLLARY 3.16. *If $\mathbf{M}$ is a schema mapping specified by an SO tgd, then the chase with respect to $\mathbf{M}$ is CQ-local.*

PROOF. We first show that the composition of CQ-local transformations is CQ-local. Assume that $\mathcal{F}_1$ and $\mathcal{F}_2$ are CQ-local, and let n be a positive integer. Since $\mathcal{F}_1$ is CQ-local, we know that there is n' such that if $\mathcal{F}_2(I_1) \equiv_{n'}^{cq} \mathcal{F}_2(I_2)$, then $\mathcal{F}_1(\mathcal{F}_2(I_1)) \equiv_n^{cq} \mathcal{F}_1(\mathcal{F}_2(I_2))$. Since $\mathcal{F}_2$ is CQ-local, there is N such that if $I_1 \equiv_N^{cq} I_2$, then $\mathcal{F}_2(I_1) \equiv_{n'}^{cq} \mathcal{F}_2(I_2)$. Therefore, if $I_1 \equiv_N^{cq} I_2$, then we have $\mathcal{F}_1(\mathcal{F}_2(I_1)) \equiv_n^{cq} \mathcal{F}_1(\mathcal{F}_2(I_2))$, and so $\mathcal{F}_1 \circ \mathcal{F}_2$ is CQ-local.

Since the schema mapping $\mathbf{M}$ is specified by an SO tgd, it follows from [AFN11] that there are GLAV mappings $\mathbf{M}_1$ and $\mathbf{M}_2$ such that $\mathbf{M} = \mathbf{M}_1 \circ \mathbf{M}_2$.[3] It is shown in [Fag07, Proposition 7.2] that $chase_{\mathbf{M}_2}(chase_{\mathbf{M}_1}(I))$ is a universal solution for I with respect to $\mathbf{M}_1 \circ \mathbf{M}_2$. Further, it is shown in [FKPT05, Theorem 6.8] that $chase_{\mathbf{M}}(I)$ is universal for I with respect to $\mathbf{M}$. Since $\mathbf{M} = \mathbf{M}_1 \circ \mathbf{M}_2$, and since all universal solutions are homomorphically equivalent, it follows that $chase_{\mathbf{M}}(I) \leftrightarrow chase_{\mathbf{M}_2}(chase_{\mathbf{M}_1}(I))$.

Since (1) the chase with respect to $\mathbf{M}_1$ and the chase with respect to $\mathbf{M}_2$ are each CQ-local (by Theorem 3.15), (2) the composition of CQ-local transformations is CQ-local, and (3) $chase_{\mathbf{M}}(I) \leftrightarrow chase_{\mathbf{M}_2}(chase_{\mathbf{M}_1}(I))$, it follows that the chase with respect to $\mathbf{M}$ is CQ-local, which was to be shown. □

Theorem 3.15 tells us that for every positive integer n, there is a positive integer $N(n)$ (that, in general, depends on n) such that if $I_1 \equiv_{N(n)}^{cq} I_2$, then $chase_{\mathbf{M}}(I_1) \equiv_n^{cq} chase_{\mathbf{M}}(I_2)$. The proof of Theorem 3.15 yields an $N(n)$ that is a stack of exponentials in n, because this blow-up occurs in the proof of Rossman's Theorem (Theorem 3.8) and, to date, no smaller bounds are known. In what follows, we give a direct proof of Theorem 3.15 with much improved bounds that does not make use of Rossman's Theorem. In fact, our direct proof gives $N(n)$ as a polynomial in n whose degree is equal to the maximum arity of the relation symbols in the target schema.

We begin by introducing a new family of binary relations between instances.

DEFINITION 3.17. Assume that I_1 and I_2 are $\mathbf{S}$-instances over a schema $\mathbf{S}$, and let n be a positive integer. We write $I_1 \rightarrow_n^{cq} I_2$ to denote that every Boolean conjunctive query with at most n variables that is true on I_1 is also true on I_2. □

Intuitively, $\rightarrow_n^{cq}$ is about preservation of conjunctive queries with at most n variables. As such, $\rightarrow_n^{cq}$ is a relaxation of $\equiv_n^{cq}$, since $I_1 \equiv_n^{cq} I_2$ if and only if $I_1 \rightarrow_n^{cq} I_2$ and $I_2 \rightarrow_n^{cq} I_1$. The binary relations $\rightarrow_n^{cq}$, $n \geq 1$, give rise to the family

$$\text{PCQ} = \{\rightarrow_n^{cq} : n \geq 1\},$$

where PCQ stands for "preservation of conjunctive queries".

The next theorem, which is the key step in our direct proof of Theorem 3.15, tells us that for GLAV mappings, the chase is PCQ-local, and also gives a polynomial bound on N.

THEOREM 3.18. *Assume that $\mathbf{M} = (\mathbf{S}, \mathbf{T}, \Sigma)$ is a GLAV mapping specified by a finite set Σ of s-t tgds.*

- *The chase with respect to $\mathbf{M}$ is PCQ-local.*
- *Let k be the number of relation symbols in the target schema $\mathbf{T}$, let r be the maximum arity of the relation symbols in $\mathbf{T}$, and let m be the maximum number of universally quantified variables in the s-t tgds in Σ. For every natural number n, let $N(n) = mkn^r$. If I_1, I_2 are source instances such that $I_1 \rightarrow_{N(n)}^{cq} I_2$, then $chase_{\mathbf{M}}(I_1) \rightarrow_n^{cq} chase_{\mathbf{M}}(I_2)$.*

PROOF. Let I_1 and I_2 be $\mathbf{S}$-instances such that $I_1 \rightarrow_{N(n)}^{cq} I_2$. Put $J_1 = chase_{\mathbf{M}}(I_1)$ and $J_2 = chase_{\mathbf{M}}(I_2)$. We have to show that $J_1 \rightarrow_n^{cq} J_2$. In order to show this, it suffices to show that if $\exists z_1 \cdots \exists z_n \theta(z_1, \ldots, z_n)$ is a Boolean conjunctive query such that $J_1 \models \exists z_1 \cdots \exists z_n \theta(z_1, \ldots, z_n)$, then we also have that $J_2 \models$

---

[3] Our proof of Corollary 3.16 could simply make use of the weaker fact, proved in [FKPT05], that a schema mapping $\mathbf{M}$ specified by an SO tgd is the composition of a finite number m of GLAV mappings, but we may as well use the stronger fact that we can take $m = 2$.

$\exists z_1 \cdots \exists z_n \theta(z_1, \ldots, z_n)$. Let $a_1, \ldots, a_n$ be (not necessarily distinct) elements from J_1 such that $J_1 \models \theta(a_1, \ldots, a_n)$. Note that $\theta(a_1, \ldots, a_n)$ can be viewed as a collection of facts from the **T**-instance J_1. Since **T** has k relation symbols, each of which is of arity at most r, it follows that $\theta(a_1, \ldots, a_n)$ consists of at most kn^r distinct facts $f_1, \ldots, f_{kn^r}$ from J_1. Since $J_1 = chase_{\mathbf{M}}(I_1)$, it follows that for each such fact f_j, where $1 \leq j \leq kn^r$, there are an s-t tgd $\forall \mathbf{x}_j(\varphi_j(\mathbf{x}_j) \rightarrow \exists \mathbf{y}_j \psi_j(\mathbf{x}_j, \mathbf{y}_j))$ in Σ, a tuple $\mathbf{c}_j$ of elements from I_1, and a tuple $\mathbf{d}_j$ of elements from J_1 such that

- $I_1 \models \varphi_j(\mathbf{c}_j)$;
- $J_1 \models \psi_j(\mathbf{c}_j, \mathbf{d}_j)$;
- f_j is one of the facts occurring in $\psi_j(\mathbf{c}_j, \mathbf{d}_j)$.

By renaming variables as needed, we may assume that the tuples $\mathbf{x}_j$ and $\mathbf{x}_{j'}$ have no variables in common if $j \neq j'$ (for $1 \leq j \leq kn^r$ and $1 \leq j' \leq kn^r$). Since every s-t tgd in Σ has at most m universally quantified variables, it follows that the total number of variables in $\mathbf{x}_1, \ldots, \mathbf{x}_{kn^r}$ is at most mkn^r. Note that each a_i is either a null in J_1 that is not in I_1 or it is equal to an element occurring in at least one tuple $\mathbf{c}_j$. Furthermore, if it is a null in J_1 that is not in I_1, then a_i is the witness to one and only one existentially quantified variable in one of the above s-t tgds from Σ. Note also that two tuples $\mathbf{c}_j$ and $\mathbf{c}_l$ may have elements in common. Let $\chi(\mathbf{x}_1, \ldots, \mathbf{x}_{kn^r})$ be a conjunction of equalities such that $\chi(\mathbf{c}_1, \ldots, \mathbf{c}_{kn^r})$ is a complete list of all equalities that hold between the elements from I_1 that occur in the tuples $\mathbf{c}_1, \ldots, \mathbf{c}_{kn^r}$. Consequently,

$$I_1 \models \exists \mathbf{x}_1 \cdots \exists \mathbf{x}_{kn^r}((\bigwedge_{j=1}^{kn^r} \varphi_j(\mathbf{x}_j)) \wedge \chi(\mathbf{x}_1, \ldots, \mathbf{x}_{kn^r})).$$

Note that the formula in the preceding expression is logically equivalent to a conjunctive query with (at most) $N(n) = mkn^r$ variables. Since $I_1 \rightarrow_{N(n)}^{cq} I_2$, we have that

$$I_2 \models \exists \mathbf{x}_1 \cdots \exists \mathbf{x}_{kn^r}((\bigwedge_{j=1}^{kn^r} \varphi_j(\mathbf{x}_j)) \wedge \chi(\mathbf{x}_1, \ldots, \mathbf{x}_{kn^r})).$$

Let $\mathbf{c}'_1, \ldots, \mathbf{c}'_{kn^r}$ be tuples of elements from I_2 such that $I_2 \models (\bigwedge_{j=1}^{kn^r} \varphi_j(\mathbf{c}'_j)) \wedge \chi(\mathbf{c}'_1, \ldots, \mathbf{c}'_{kn^r})$. As a result of the chase procedure, there are tuples $\mathbf{d}'_1, \ldots, \mathbf{d}'_{kn^r}$ from J_2 such that $J_2 \models \bigwedge_{j=1}^{kn^r} \psi_j(\mathbf{c}'_j, \mathbf{d}'_j)$.

We will show that $J_2 \models \exists z_1 \cdots \exists z_n \theta(z_1, \ldots, z_n)$. In fact, we will show that the existential quantifiers $\exists z_i$, $1 \leq i \leq n$, in this conjunctive query can be witnessed by elements b_i, $1 \leq i \leq n$, chosen from the tuples $\mathbf{c}'_1, \ldots, \mathbf{c}'_{kn^r}, \mathbf{d}'_1, \ldots, \mathbf{d}'_{kn^r}$ in a way that we now describe. For $i \leq n$, let a_i be the element that witnessed the existential quantifier $\exists z_i$ in J_1. We distinguish two cases.

Case 1: The element a_i is a null in J_1 that is not in I_1. In this case, every occurrence of a_i in the facts $f_1, \ldots, f_{kn^r}$ arises from only one tuple $\mathbf{c}_j$ and from only one s-t tgd $\forall \mathbf{x}_j(\varphi_j(\mathbf{x}_j) \rightarrow \exists \mathbf{y}_j \psi_j(\mathbf{x}_j, \mathbf{y}_j))$ in Σ; moreover, a_i witnesses one and only one existential quantifier, say $\exists y$, in the tuple $\exists \mathbf{y}_j$. In this case, we take b_i to be the element from the tuple $\mathbf{d}'_j$ that witnesses $\exists y$ in J_2. Note that b_i is a null in J_2 that is not in I_2.

Case 2: The element a_i is in I_1. In this case, a_i may occur in several different tuples $\mathbf{c}_j$. Pick one of them, say $\mathbf{c}_r$. Let b_i be the element of I_2 that occurs in the tuple $\mathbf{c}'_r$ and in the same position as a_i does in $\mathbf{c}_r$. Note that b_i is an element of J_2. Moreover, if a tuple $\mathbf{c}_s$ different from $\mathbf{c}_r$ had been chosen where a_i occurs in $\mathbf{c}_s$, then the same element b_i would have been obtained.

Since J_1 satisfying $\bigwedge_{j=1}^{kn^r} \psi_j(\mathbf{c}_j, \mathbf{d}_j)$ has the effect that J_1 satisfies $\theta(a_1, \ldots, a_n)$, and since J_2 satisfies $\bigwedge_{j=1}^{kn^r} \psi_j(\mathbf{c}'_j, \mathbf{d}'_j)$, this tells us (from our mimicking construction, where b_i mimics a_i) that J_2 satisfies $\theta(b_1, \ldots, b_n)$. Hence, $J_2 \models \exists z_1 \cdots \exists z_n \theta(z_1, \ldots, z_n)$, as desired. $\square$

As an immediate consequence of Theorem 3.18, we obtain a significantly improved version of Theorem 3.15 in which N has a polynomial dependence on n. In fact, the degree of the polynomial is equal to the maximum arity of the target schema.

THEOREM 3.19. (Theorem 3.15 revisited) *Assume that* $\mathbf{M} = (\mathbf{S}, \mathbf{T}, \Sigma)$ *is a GLAV mapping specified by a finite set* Σ *of s-t tgds. Let* k *be the number of relation symbols in the target schema* $\mathbf{T}$, *let* r *be the maximum arity of the relation symbols in* $\mathbf{T}$, *and let* m *be the maximum number of universally quantified variables in the s-t tgds in* Σ. *For every natural number* n, *let* $N(n) = mkn^r$. *If* I_1 *and* I_2 *are source instances such that* $I_1 \equiv_{N(n)}^{cq} I_2$, *then* $chase_{\mathbf{M}}(I_1) \equiv_n^{cq} chase_{\mathbf{M}}(I_2)$.

3.3 Failures of CQ-Locality

The next theorem says that Theorem 3.15 cannot be extended to allow target dependencies.

THEOREM 3.20. *There is a schema mapping* $\mathbf{M}$ *specified by three s-t tgds and by a full target tgd such that the chase with respect to* $\mathbf{M}$ *is not CQ-local.*

PROOF. Define the schema mapping $\mathbf{M}$ as follows. The source schema consists of a binary relation symbol P, and unary relation symbols R and S. The target schema consist of a binary relation symbol P', and unary relation symbols R' and S'. The dependencies of $\mathbf{M}$ are:

$$P(x, y) \rightarrow P'(x, y), \quad R(x) \rightarrow R'(x), \quad S(x) \rightarrow S'(x),$$
$$P'(x, y) \wedge P'(y, z) \rightarrow P'(x, z).$$

In the full version of this paper, we show that $\mathbf{M}$ is not CQ-local. $\square$

In Corollary 3.16, we showed that if $\mathbf{M}$ is a schema mapping specified by an SO tgd, then the chase with respect to $\mathbf{M}$ is CQ-local. However, as a corollary of Theorem 3.20, we now show that this is not true when the schema mapping is specified by an st-SO dependency, as defined in [AFN11]. These st-SO dependencies are similar to SO tgds, but allow equalities in the conclusion. A notion of the chase for st-SO dependencies, which produces a universal solution, is defined in [AFN11].

COROLLARY 3.21. *There is a schema mapping* $\mathbf{M}$ *specified by an st-SO dependency such that the chase with respect to* $\mathbf{M}$ *is not CQ-local.*

PROOF. Let $\mathbf{M}$ be as in the proof of Theorem 3.20, where the chase with respect to $\mathbf{M}$ is not CQ-local. Let $\mathbf{M}'$ be the "copy" schema mapping specified by the s-t tgds $P'(x, y) \rightarrow P''(x, y)$, $R'(x) \rightarrow R''(x)$, and $S'(x) \rightarrow S''(x)$. Let $\mathbf{M}'' = \mathbf{M} \circ \mathbf{M}'$. Then $\mathbf{M}''$ is the same as $\mathbf{M}$, up to a renaming of relation symbols. It is shown in [AFN11] that if $\mathbf{M}_1$ is a schema mapping specified by s-t tgds, target egds, and a weakly acyclic [FKMP05] set of target tgds, and $\mathbf{M}_2$ is a schema mapping specified by s-t tgds, then $\mathbf{M}_1 \circ \mathbf{M}_2$ is a schema mapping specified by an st-SO dependency. Therefore, $\mathbf{M}''$ is specified by an st-SO dependency. The result of the chase using the st-SO dependency that specifies $\mathbf{M}''$ is a universal solution w.r.t. d$\mathbf{M}''$. But the universal solutions for $\mathbf{M}''$ are the same as the universal solutions for $\mathbf{M}$, up to a renaming of relation symbols, since $\mathbf{M}''$ is the same as $\mathbf{M}$, up to a renaming of relation symbols. Since the chase with respect to $\mathbf{M}$ is not CQ-local, it follows easily that the chase with respect to $\mathbf{M}''$ is not CQ-local. $\quad\square$

4. Degrees of Equivalence of Schema Mappings

Schema mappings $\mathbf{M}_1$ and $\mathbf{M}_2$ are CQ-*equivalent* [FKNP08] if $certain_{\mathbf{M}_1}(q, I) = certain_{\mathbf{M}_2}(q, I)$ for every (not necessarily Boolean) conjunctive query q and every source instance I. As mentioned in the Introduction, Madhavan and Halevy [MH03] based their notion of composition on CQ-equivalence. Later on, Fagin et al. [FKNP08] studied CQ-equivalence in the context of schema mapping optimization, while Arenas et al. [APRR09] studied CQ-equivalence in the context of inverting schema mappings.

The two main questions we will focus on in this section are:

- When is the composition of two GLAV mappings logically equivalent to a GLAV mapping?
- When is the composition of two GLAV mappings CQ-equivalent to a GLAV mapping?

The way we deal with these problems is to divide GLAV mappings into a small number of well-studied classes, namely GAV, LAV, extended LAV, and general GLAV (of course, these classes are not mutually exclusive), and see when the composition of schema mappings from these various classes can be guaranteed to be a GLAV mapping, and also to see when they can be guaranteed to be CQ-equivalent to a GLAV mapping. It turns out that up to now, there has been one gap in each of these scenarios, and we will fill both of these gaps, in order to obtain a complete picture.

We also consider a bounded form of CQ-equivalence. If n is a positive integer and $\mathbf{M}_1$, $\mathbf{M}_2$ are two schema mappings, then $\mathbf{M}_1$ and $\mathbf{M}_2$ are CQ_n-*equivalent* if $certain_{\mathbf{M}_1}(q, I) = certain_{\mathbf{M}_2}(q, I)$ for every (not necessarily Boolean) conjunctive query q with at most n variables and for every source instance I. It follows from [MH03, Proposition 3] that for every $n \geq 1$, the composition of two GLAV mappings is always CQ_n-equivalent to some GLAV mapping. We feel that it is useful to give a direct proof of this fact, which we do in Section 4.3.

4.1 Logical Equivalence

In the case of logical equivalence, the gap in our knowledge until now has been the question as to whether the composition of a GLAV mapping with a LAV mapping is necessarily logically equivalent to a GLAV mapping. Our next theorem answers this positively. This generalizes a result of Arocena, Fuxman, and Miller [AFM10], that the composition of LAV mappings is logically equivalent to a GLAV mapping (in fact, to a LAV mapping). Our proof also provides an alternative proof that the composition of LAV mappings is logically equivalent to a LAV mapping, since in our proof that a GLAV mapping composed with a LAV mapping is GLAV, it happens that if the first mapping is LAV, then the composition is actually specified by LAV constraints.

We begin with a lemma. Recall that an *element*, or *value*, is an entry of a tuple of a relation. If f is a function on the elements, and I is an instance, then we write $f(I)$ for the result of replacing every element x in every tuple of I by $f(x)$.

LEMMA 4.1. *Let* $\mathbf{M}$ *be a LAV mapping. If J is a solution for I with respect to $\mathbf{M}$, and f is an arbitrary function on the elements, then $f(J)$ is a solution for $f(I)$ with respect to $\mathbf{M}$.*

PROOF. This follows fairly easily from the viewpoint that f is simply a renaming of elements (not necessarily one-to-one), and

LAV tgds are indifferent to renamings (thus, they fire in the same way on tuples whether or not some entries of the tuple are equal). The feature of LAV tgds that we used in this argument is that no variable appears twice in a premise. $\quad\square$

We now define a *restriction* of a tgd $\alpha \to \exists \bar{y}\beta$. Let X be the set of variables that appear in α, let X' be a subset of X, and let F be a function from X to X' that maps every variable in X' into itself. Let $\alpha' \to \exists \bar{y}\beta'$ be the result of modifying $\alpha \to \exists \bar{y}\beta$ by replacing every variable x in X by $F(x)$. Then we call the tgd $\alpha' \to \exists \bar{y}\beta'$ a *restriction* of the tgd $\alpha \to \exists \bar{y}\beta$. For example, the tgd $R(x, x, z, x) \to \exists y Q(x, x, y)$ is a restriction of the tgd $R(w, x, z, w) \to \exists y Q(w, x, y)$, where w is mapped to x.

THEOREM 4.2. *If $\mathbf{M}_{12}$ is a GLAV mapping and $\mathbf{M}_{23}$ is a LAV mapping, then $\mathbf{M}_{12} \circ \mathbf{M}_{23}$ is logically equivalent to a GLAV mapping.*

PROOF. *(Sketch)* Let $\mathbf{M}_{12} = (\mathbf{S}_1, \mathbf{S}_2, \Sigma_{12})$ and $\mathbf{M}_{23} = (\mathbf{S}_2, \mathbf{S}_3, \Sigma_{23})$, where Σ_{12} is a finite set of s-t tgds, and Σ_{23} is a finite set of LAV s-t tgds. For convenience, we assume that Σ_{12} is closed under restriction (this is without loss of generality, since a tgd logically implies each of its restrictions). We now define Σ_{13}, and we shall show that for the schema mapping $\mathbf{M}_{13} = (\mathbf{S}_1, \mathbf{S}_3, \Sigma_{13})$, we have $\mathbf{M}_{13} = \mathbf{M}_{12} \circ \mathbf{M}_{23}$. Our definition of Σ_{13} is different from that given in [AFM10]. We describe our construction of Σ_{13} somewhat informally, by speaking about chasing formulas to get other formulas. For each tgd $\alpha \to \exists \bar{y}\beta$ in Σ_{12}, we chase β with Σ_{23}, call the result δ, and let $\alpha \to \exists \bar{q}\delta$ be a member of Σ_{13}, where $\bar{q}$ consists of the variables in δ but not α.

We now show that Σ_{13} specifies the composition. We first show that if $(I_1, I_2) \models \Sigma_{12}$ and $(I_2, I_3) \models \Sigma_{23}$, then $(I_1, I_3) \models \Sigma_{13}$. This is immediate, since the result of a chase is "forced". We conclude by showing that if $(I_1, I_3) \models \Sigma_{13}$, then there is I_2 such that $(I_1, I_2) \models \Sigma_{12}$ and $(I_2, I_3) \models \Sigma_{23}$. To simplify the discussion, assume without loss of generality that I_1 contains only constants.

Let us define a *restricted chase* of an instance I to be one where a tgd $\alpha \to \exists \bar{y}\beta$ is applied only when there is a *one-to-one* homomorphism of α into I. Since by assumption, Σ_{12} is closed under restriction, it follows easily that a restricted chase of I is a universal solution for I with respect to Σ. Let J_2 be the result of doing a restricted chase of I_1 with Σ_{12}. We shall discuss how to assign a value $f(n)$ (which may be a constant or a null) to each null n in J_2 to obtain I_2. Assume that the tgd $\alpha \to \exists \bar{y}\beta$ fires in the restricted chase of I_1 with Σ_{12}. Let J_2' be the subset of J_2 that is obtained by one firing of this tgd. We now define a function f that assigns values to the nulls of J_2'. The s-t tgd $\alpha \to \exists \bar{y}\beta$ yields J_2' in the restricted chase of I_1 with Σ_{12} because of a one-to-one homomorphism h from α to I_1. Since h is one-to-one, the relation corresponding to the formula β in our identification of formulas with instances is J_2', up to a one-to-one renaming of variables by values. Let $\alpha \to \exists \bar{q}\delta$ be the member of Σ_{13} that arises from the tgd $\alpha \to \exists \bar{y}\beta$ in our construction of Σ_{13}. Since $(I_1, I_3) \models \alpha \to \exists \bar{q}\delta$, it follows from our construction of $\alpha \to \exists \bar{q}\delta$ that there is a homomorphism h' from U, the result of chasing J_2' with Σ_{23}, into I_3, where h' respects I_1 (maps constants into themselves). Define f to agree with h' on the active domain of U, and to be the identity otherwise. Since U is a solution for J_2' with respect to Σ_{23}, it follows from Lemma 4.1 that $f(U)$ is a solution for $f(J_2')$ with respect to Σ_{23}. That is, $(f(J_2'), f(U)) \models \Sigma_{23}$. Since $f(U) = h'(U) \subseteq I_3$, it follows that $(f(J_2'), I_3) \models \Sigma_{23}$.

If a different J_2' (call it J_2'') arises from a different step of the restricted chase, then the active domains of J_2' and J_2'' have in common at most constants, on which f is the identity. So if we repeat this process to define $f(n)$ for every null n in J_2, we obtain a well-defined function f. Let $I_2 = f(J_2)$. Since (1) $(f(J_2'), I_3) \models \Sigma_{23}$ for each J_2' in our construction, (2) I_2 is the union of these instances $f(J_2')$, and (3) Σ_{23} is extended LAV (all we need for this argument is that the premises of the s-t tgds are singletons), it follows that $(I_2, I_3) \models \Sigma_{23}$. Furthermore, $(I_1, I_2) \models \Sigma_{12}$, since J_2 is a solution for I_1 (it is even universal), and I_2 is a homomorphic image of J_2 under a homomorphism (namely, f) that respects I_1 (and the solutions of I_1 w.r.t. Σ_{12} are closed under homomorphisms that respect I_1). Since we have shown that $(I_1, I_2) \models \Sigma_{12}$ and $(I_2, I_3) \models \Sigma_{23}$, this completes the proof. □

COROLLARY 4.3 ([AFM10]). *If both* $\mathbf{M}_{12}$ *and* $\mathbf{M}_{23}$ *are LAV mappings, then* $\mathbf{M}_{12} \circ \mathbf{M}_{23}$ *is logically equivalent to a LAV mapping.*

PROOF. In the construction of the composition formula Σ_{13} in the proof of Theorem 4.2, each premise of Σ_{13} is a premise of Σ_{12}. So if Σ_{12} is LAV, then so is Σ_{13}. □

Let us now consider Table 1, about the results of composition. When an entry under the "Logical Equivalence" column is GLAV, this means that the composition is guaranteed to be logically equivalent to a GLAV mapping. For example, the entry under "Logical Equivalence" for the row GAV ∘ GLAV says "GLAV", and this means that the composition of a GAV mapping with a GLAV mapping is always logically equivalent to a GLAV mapping. When an entry is "Not GLAV", this means that there is an example where that composition is not logically equivalent to any GLAV mapping. For example, the entry under "Logical Equivalence" for the row LAV ∘ ex. LAV says "Not GLAV", and this means that there is a LAV mapping $\mathbf{M}_{12}$ and an extended LAV mapping $\mathbf{M}_{23}$ such that $\mathbf{M}_{12} \circ \mathbf{M}_{23}$ is not logically equivalent to any GLAV mapping.

If we now look at the first two columns ("Composition" and "Logical Equivalence") of Table 1, it is straightforward to verify that we have covered all combinations of composing LAV, extended LAV, GAV, and GLAV up to logical equivalence (that is, they are easily inferred from what is in the table). For example, the case of GAV ∘ extended LAV is covered by the case of GAV ∘ GLAV, in the sense that because GAV ∘ GLAV is necessarily logically equivalent to a GLAV mapping, so is GAV ∘ extended LAV. As another example, the case of extended LAV ∘ extended LAV is covered by the case of LAV ∘ extended LAV, in the sense that because there is an example of LAV ∘ extended LAV where the result is not logically equivalent to any GLAV mapping, this negative example covers also extended LAV ∘ extended LAV.

4.2 CQ-equivalence

Let us consider an example from [FKPT05]. There are three schemas $\mathbf{S}_1$, $\mathbf{S}_2$ and $\mathbf{S}_3$. Schema $\mathbf{S}_1$ consists of a single unary relation symbol Emp of employees. Schema $\mathbf{S}_2$ consists of a single binary relation symbol Mgr_1, that associates each employee with a manager. Schema $\mathbf{S}_3$ consists of a similar binary relation symbol Mgr, that is intended to provide a copy of Mgr_1. and an additional unary relation symbol SelfMgr, that is intended to store employees who are their own manager. Consider now the schema mappings $\mathbf{M}_{12} = (\mathbf{S}_1, \mathbf{S}_2, \Sigma_{12})$ and $\mathbf{M}_{23} = (\mathbf{S}_2, \mathbf{S}_3, \Sigma_{23})$, where

$$\Sigma_{12} = \{ \forall e (\text{Emp}(e) \rightarrow \exists m \text{Mgr}_1(e, m)) \}$$

$$\Sigma_{23} = \{ \forall e \forall m (\text{Mgr}_1(e, m) \rightarrow \text{Mgr}(e, m)), \\ \forall e (\text{Mgr}_1(e, e) \rightarrow \text{SelfMgr}(e)) \}.$$

The SO tgd that specifies the composition $\mathbf{M}_{12} \circ \mathbf{M}_{23}$ is given in (1) in Section 2. It is shown in [FKPT05] that this SO tgd is not

logically equivalent to any finite (or even infinite) set of s-t tgds. Note that $\mathbf{M}_{12}$ is LAV, and $\mathbf{M}_{23}$ is extended LAV. Can we say anything positive about the composition of a LAV mapping with an extended LAV mapping? In Theorem 4.6, we show that such a composition (and even more, the composition of an arbitrary GLAV mapping with an extended LAV mapping) is always CQ-equivalent to a GLAV mapping. The proof of this theorem depends on a characterization in [FKNP08] about when a schema mapping specified by an SO tgd is CQ-equivalent to a GLAV mapping. We begin with some definitions from [FKNP08].

DEFINITION 4.4. Assume that $\mathbf{M} = (\mathbf{S}, \mathbf{T}, \Sigma)$ is a schema mapping, where Σ is either a finite set of s-t tgds or an SO tgd.

- Let I be a source instance and K a target instance.

  The *Gaifman graph of facts of K w.r.t. I* is a graph whose nodes are the facts of K, and with an edge between two facts if they have in common some element not in the active domain of I.[4]

  A *fact block* (or simply *f-block*) of K w.r.t. I is a connected component of the Gaifman graph of facts of K w.r.t. I.

  The *f-block size* of K w.r.t. I is the maximum size of the f-blocks of K w.r.t. I.

  When I is understood from the context, we simply refer to the Gaifman graph of facts of K, the f-blocks of K, and the f-block size of K.

- We say that $\mathbf{M}$ (or Σ) has *bounded f-block size* if there is a positive integer b such that for every source instance I, the f-block size of $\text{core}(chase_{\mathbf{M}}(I))$ w.r.t. I is at most b. We then refer to the minimal such b as the *f-block size of $\mathbf{M}$* (or *of Σ*). □

We have the following theorem from [FKNP08].

THEOREM 4.5 ([FKNP08]). *A schema mapping* $\mathbf{M}$ *specified by an SO tgd is CQ-equivalent to a schema mapping specified by a finite set of s-t tgds if and only if* $\mathbf{M}$ *has bounded f-block size.*

We can now prove that the composition of a GLAV mapping with an extended LAV mapping is CQ-equivalent to a GLAV mapping.

THEOREM 4.6. *If* $\mathbf{M}_{12}$ *is a GLAV mapping and* $\mathbf{M}_{23}$ *is an extended LAV mapping, then* $\mathbf{M}_{12} \circ \mathbf{M}_{23}$ *is CQ-equivalent to a GLAV mapping.*

PROOF. Let $\mathbf{M}_{12} = (\mathbf{S}_1, \mathbf{S}_2, \Sigma_{12})$ and $\mathbf{M}_{23} = (\mathbf{S}_2, \mathbf{S}_3, \Sigma_{23})$ be schema mappings, where Σ_{12} is a finite sets of s-t tgds, and Σ_{23} is a finite set of extended LAV constraints. Let $\mathbf{M}_{13} = \mathbf{M}_{12} \circ \mathbf{M}_{23}$. We must show that $\mathbf{M}_{13}$ is CQ-equivalent to a GLAV mapping.

By [FKPT05], we know that there is an SO tgd Σ_{13} such that $\mathbf{M}_{13} = (\mathbf{S}_1, \mathbf{S}_3, \Sigma_{13})$. It follows from Theorem 4.5 that to prove the theorem, it is sufficient to show that $\text{core}(chase_{\Sigma_{13}}(I))$ has bounded f-block size w.r.t. I. Since, as shown in the proof of Corollary 3.16, $chase_{\Sigma_{13}}(I)$ and $chase_{\Sigma_{23}}(chase_{\Sigma_{12}}(I))$ are homomorphically equivalent, and since homomorphically equivalent instances have the same core (up to isomorphism), it is sufficient for us to show that $\text{core}(chase_{\Sigma_{23}}(chase_{\Sigma_{12}}(I)))$ has bounded f-block size.w.r.t. I. So it suffices to show that the f-blocks of $chase_{\Sigma_{23}}(chase_{\Sigma_{12}}(I))$ have sizes bounded by a constant that depends only on Σ_{12} and Σ_{23} (this is so because the core of an instance K is a subinstance of K, hence a bound on the sizes of the f-blocks of K is inherited by the core of K).

---

[4]In [FKNP08], it was assumed that the source instance I consists only of constants, and so the Gaifman graph of K was defined not w.r.t. I, but instead by defining the Gaifman graph of facts of K to be a graph whose nodes are the facts of K, and with an edge between two facts if they have a null value in common,

Let n be the maximum number of atoms in the conclusions of the s-t tgds in Σ_{12}, let m be the maximum number of atoms in the conclusions of the s-t tgds in Σ_{23}, and let s be the number of s-t tgds in Σ_{23}. Let I be an $\mathbf{S}_1$-instance. We claim that every f-block of $chase_{\Sigma_{23}}(chase_{\Sigma_{12}}(I))$ is of size at most nms. To see this, first note that every f-block of $chase_{\Sigma_{12}}(I)$ is of size at most n. Fix now an s-t tgd, say τ, in Σ_{23}. Since τ is an extended LAV s-t tgd (that is, it has a singleton premise), when we chase $chase_{\Sigma_{12}}(I)$ with Σ_{23}, we produce f-blocks that have size at most nm. By going over all tgds in Σ_{23}, we have that the f-blocks of $chase_{\Sigma_{23}}(chase_{\Sigma_{12}}(I))$ are of size at most nms. $\square$

The preceding result enables us to complete the picture on CQ-equivalence, as given in the third column ("CQ-equivalence") of Table 1. For this CQ-equivalence column, just as for the Logical Equivalence column, it is straightforward to verify that we have covered all combinations of composing LAV, extended LAV, GAV, and GLAV up to CQ-equivalence (that is, they are easily inferred from what is in the table). The first three entries in the CQ-equivalence column of Table 1 (those with no citation) follow immediately from the corresponding entries in the Logical Equivalence column of the table. The fourth and fifth entries in the CQ-equivalence column of Table 1 follow from Theorem 4.6.

4.3 Bounded CQ-Equivalence

Again, let us begin with an example from [FKPT05]. Consider the following three schemas $\mathbf{S}_1$, $\mathbf{S}_2$ and $\mathbf{S}_3$. Schema $\mathbf{S}_1$ consists of a single binary relation symbol Takes, that associates student names with the courses they take. Schema $\mathbf{S}_2$ consists of a similar binary relation symbol Takes$_1$, that is intended to provide a copy of Takes, and of an additional binary relation symbol Student, that associates each student name with a student id. Schema $\mathbf{S}_3$ consists of one binary relation symbol Enrollment, that associates student ids with the courses the students take. Consider now the schema mappings $\mathbf{M}_{12} = (\mathbf{S}_1, \mathbf{S}_2, \Sigma_{12})$ and $\mathbf{M}_{23} = (\mathbf{S}_2, \mathbf{S}_3, \Sigma_{23})$, where

$$\Sigma_{12} = \{ \forall n \forall c(\text{Takes}(n,c) \rightarrow \text{Takes}_1(n,c)),$$
$$\forall n \forall c(\text{Takes}(n,c) \rightarrow \exists s \text{Student}(n,s)) \}$$
$$\Sigma_{23} = \{ \forall n \forall s \forall c(\text{Student}(n,s) \wedge \text{Takes}_1(n,c) \rightarrow$$
$$\text{Enrollment}(s,c)) \}$$

It is shown in [FKPT05] that the composition $\mathbf{M}_{12} \circ \mathbf{M}_{23}$ is not CQ-equivalent to any GLAV mapping. Note that $\mathbf{M}_{12}$ is LAV, and $\mathbf{M}_{23}$ is GAV. Can we say anything positive about the composition of a LAV mapping with a GAV mapping? The next proposition says that in fact the composition of any pair of GLAV mappings is always CQ$_n$-equivalent to a GLAV mapping. As we noted, this result follows from [MH03, Proposition 3]. We feel that it is useful to give a direct proof of this result, which we now do. In the fourth column ("CQ$_n$-equivalence) of Table 1, all entries are GLAV, which follows since the last entry is GLAV.

PROPOSITION 4.7. *Let n be a positive integer. The composition of GLAV mappings is CQ$_n$-equivalent to a GLAV mapping.*

PROOF. Let $\mathbf{M}_{12} = (\mathbf{S}_1, \mathbf{S}_2, \Sigma_{12})$ and $\mathbf{M}_{23} = (\mathbf{S}_2, \mathbf{S}_3, \Sigma_{23})$ be schema mappings, where Σ_{12} and Σ_{23} are finite sets of s-t tgds. By [FKPT05], we know that there is an SO tgd σ that specifies $\mathbf{M}_{12} \circ \mathbf{M}_{23}$. Let I be an $\mathbf{S}_1$-instance, and let J be a result of chasing I with σ. Let $c_1, \ldots, c_r$ be the distinct elements of I, and let $d_1, \ldots, d_m$ be the distinct remaining elements of J. Let ϕ_I be the formula that is the conjunction of all atoms over $x_1, \ldots, x_r$

that hold in I when x_i plays the role of c_i, for each i. For example, if $R(c_3, c_7)$ holds in I, then one conjunct is $R(x_3, x_7)$. Let ψ_I be the formula that is the conjunction of all atoms over $x_1, \ldots, x_r, y_1, \ldots, y_m$ that hold in J when x_i plays the role of c_i, and y_j plays the role of d_j, for each i, j. For example, if $S(c_3, d_9)$ holds in J, then one conjunct is $S(x_3, y_9)$. Let τ_I be the s-t tgd

$$\forall x_1 \cdots \forall x_r(\phi_I \rightarrow \exists y_1 \cdots \exists y_m \psi_I).$$

Intuitively, τ_I describes exactly a result of chasing I with σ.

Let n be as in the statement of the proposition, let d be the number of relation symbols in $\mathbf{S}_3$, let r be the maximum arity of a relation symbol of $\mathbf{S}_3$, and let $N = dn^r$. It is easy to see that each conjunctive query over $\mathbf{S}_3$ with at most n variables has at most N distinct atoms. Let k be the maximum number of atoms in a premise of a conjunct ("tgd part") of σ. Let Σ be the set of s-t tgds $\tau_{I'}$ where I' has at most Nk facts. Let q be an arbitrary conjunctive query over $\mathbf{S}_3$ with at most n variables, and let I be a source instance. By definition of CQ$_n$-equivalence, we need only show that $certain_\Sigma(q, I) = certain_\sigma(q, I)$. Now $certain_\Sigma(q, I) \subseteq certain_\sigma(q, I)$, since Σ is a logical consequence of σ. We now show the opposite inclusion. Assume that $\bar{e} \in certain_\sigma(q, I)$; we wish to show that $\bar{e} \in certain_\Sigma(q, I)$. Let J be a result of chasing I with σ. So $\bar{e} \in q(J)$. Since q has at most N atoms, there is J' with at most N facts such that $J' \subseteq J$ and $\bar{e} \in q(J')$. There is then I_0 with at most Nk facts such that J' is in the result of chasing I_0 with σ. Let J_0 be the result of chasing I_0 with σ. Since $J' \subseteq J_0$, it follows that $\bar{e} \in q(J_0)$. Let J_1 be the result of chasing I with Σ. So J_1 contains the result of chasing I_0 with Σ, which contains the result of chasing I_0 with τ_{I_0}, which contains J_0. We just showed that $J_0 \subseteq J_1$. Since $\bar{e} \in q(J_0)$, it then follows that $\bar{e} \in q(J_1)$. Hence, since J_1 is a universal solution for I with respect to Σ, it follows from Theorem 2.2 that $\bar{e} \in certain_\Sigma(q, I)$, as desired. $\square$

5. Deciding CQ-equivalence

Let $\mathbf{M}_1$ and $\mathbf{M}_2$ be two given schema mappings, each specified by either a finite set of s-t tgds or by an SO tgd. Assume that we wish to tell whether $\mathbf{M}_1$ and $\mathbf{M}_2$ are logically equivalent, and also whether they are CQ-equivalent. For each of these two decision problems, there are three cases to consider.

1. $\mathbf{M}_1$ *and* $\mathbf{M}_2$ *are both GLAV:* It follows from Proposition 3.14 of [FKNP08] that two such mappings are CQ-equivalent if and only if they are logically equivalent. Moreover, telling whether two given finite sets of s-t tgds are logically equivalent is a decidable problem, by using the chase [ABU79, MMS79].

2. $\mathbf{M}_1$ *and* $\mathbf{M}_2$ *are both specified by SO tgds:* Telling whether two given SO tgds are logically equivalent is an undecidable problem [FPSS11, Theorem 1]. The decidability status of telling whether two given SO tgds are CQ-equivalent is not known. However, as also shown in [FPSS11], this problem does become undecidable in the presence of additional source key constraints, that is, in the case where $\mathbf{M}_1$ and $\mathbf{M}_2$ are each specified by an SO tgd and a finite set of source key constraints.

3. *One of* $\mathbf{M}_1$ *or* $\mathbf{M}_2$ *is specified by an SO tgd, and the other is GLAV:* Telling whether a given SO tgd and a given finite set of s-t tgds are logically equivalent is an undecidable problem. This follows by examining the proof of Theorem 1 in [FPSS11], which actually is derived from an undecidability result in [APR09] about inverses of schema mappings. In contrast, here we show that telling whether a given SO tgd and a given finite set of s-t tgds are CQ-equivalent is a decidable problem.

Table 1: Results of composition

Composition	Logical Equivalence	CQ-Equivalence	CQ_n-Equivalence
GAV ∘ GAV	GLAV (even GAV) [FKPT05]	GLAV (even GAV)	GLAV (even GAV)
GAV ∘ GLAV	GLAV [FKPT05]	GLAV	GLAV
GLAV ∘ LAV	GLAV Theorem 4.2; [AFM10] for LAV ∘ LAV	GLAV	GLAV
LAV ∘ ex. LAV	Not GLAV [FKPT05]	GLAV Theorem 4.6	GLAV
GLAV ∘ ex. LAV	Not GLAV [FKPT05]	GLAV Theorem 4.6	GLAV
LAV ∘ GAV	Not GLAV [FKPT05]	Not GLAV [FKPT05]	GLAV
GLAV ∘ GLAV	Not GLAV [FKPT05]	Not GLAV [FKPT05]	GLAV [MH03]; Proposition 4.7

As the first step in showing our decidability result, we prove the next proposition. An f-block is defined in Definition 4.4.

PROPOSITION 5.1. *The following two decision problems are reducible to each other.*

- *Given an SO tgd σ and a finite set Σ of s-t tgds, is σ CQ-equivalent to Σ?*
- *Given an SO tgd σ and a positive integer b, is the f-block size of σ bounded by b?*

PROOF. The proof of Theorem 4.10 in [FKNP08] shows that, given an SO tgd σ and a positive integer b, we can construct a finite set $\Sigma_{\sigma,b}$ of s-t tgds with the following property: the f-block size of σ is bounded by b if and only if σ is CQ-equivalent to $\Sigma_{\sigma,b}$.[5]

We now show that the first problem is reducible to the second. Suppose we are given an SO tgd σ and a finite set Σ of s-t tgds, and we want to test whether or not σ is CQ-equivalent to Σ. Let b be the maximum number of atoms in the conclusions of the tgds in Σ; as pointed out in [FKNP08], the f-block size of Σ is bounded by b. We first test whether or not the f-block size of σ is bounded by b. If the answer is "no", then σ is not CQ-equivalent to Σ. This is because if σ and Σ were CQ-equivalent, then it follows from Theorem 3.5 of [FKNP08] that for each source instance I, necessarily $core(chase_\sigma(I))$ and $core(chase_\Sigma(I))$ would be isomorphic, and so the f-block sizes of σ and Σ would be the same. So assume that the answer is 'yes'. By our earlier comment, it follows that σ is CQ-equivalent to $\Sigma_{\sigma,b}$. So σ is CQ-equivalent to Σ if and only if Σ is CQ-equivalent to $\Sigma_{\sigma,b}$. As we noted earlier, it follows from Proposition 3.14 of [FKNP08] that for finite sets of s-t tgds, logical equivalence coincides with CQ-equivalence. So Σ is CQ-equivalent to $\Sigma_{\sigma,b}$ if and only if Σ is logically equivalent to $\Sigma_{\sigma,b}$. But it is decidable whether Σ is logically equivalent to $\Sigma_{\sigma,b}$, by using the chase [ABU79, MMS79].

Next we show that the second problem is reducible to the first. For this, given an SO tgd σ and a bound b, we first construct the set $\Sigma_{\sigma,b}$ and then test whether or not σ is CQ-equivalent to $\Sigma_{\sigma,b}$. As we noted, σ is CQ-equivalent to $\Sigma_{\sigma,b}$ if and only if the f-block size of σ is bounded by b. □

We now prove the decidability of the question in the second bullet of Proposition 5.1.

PROPOSITION 5.2. *There is an algorithm for the following problem: Given an SO tgd σ and a positive integer b, is the f-block size of σ bounded by b?*

PROOF. Let σ be an SO tgd, and let $r(\sigma)$ be the maximum number of atoms in any of the premises inside of σ. It is shown in the proof of Proposition 4.8 in [FKNP08] that $r(\sigma)$ witnesses that σ has *bounded support*, that is to say, for every source instance I and every target instance J, if $J \xrightarrow{I} core(chase_\sigma(I))$, then there is a subinstance I' of I such that $|I'| \leq r(\sigma)|J|$ and $J \xrightarrow{I'} core(chase_\sigma(I'))$.[6]

Consider the following algorithm: given an SO tgd σ and a positive integer b, go over all source instances I' such that $|I'| \leq r(\sigma)(b+1)$ (there are only finitely many such instances, and they can be computed from σ and b). For each such instance I', compute the f-block size of $core(chase_\sigma(I'))$. If one of these f-block sizes is bigger than b, report that the f-block size of σ is bigger than b; otherwise, report that the f-block size of σ is at most b.

For the correctness of the algorithm, it is clear that if one of the computed f-block sizes is bigger than b, then the f-block size of σ is greater than b. For the other direction, we will show that if the f-block size of σ is bigger than b, then there is an instance I' such that $|I'| \leq r(\sigma)(b+1)$ and the f-block size of $core(chase_\sigma(I'))$ is bigger than b. So, assume that the f-block size of σ is bigger than b. Then there is a source instance I such that the f-block size of $core(chase_\sigma(I))$ is at least $b+1$. Consider an f-block C of $core(chase_\sigma(I))$ of size at least $b+1$. Let J be a subset of C such that $|J| = b+1$ and J is a connected subgraph of the Gaifman graph of facts of $core(chase_\sigma(I))$ w.r.t. I. Since $J \subseteq core(chase_\sigma(I))$, we have $J \xrightarrow{I} core(chase_\sigma(I))$, and so by our earlier comments, there is a subinstance I' of I such that $|I'| \leq r(\sigma)|J| = r(\sigma)(b+1)$ and $J \xrightarrow{I} core(chase_\sigma(I'))$. Let h be the homomorphism from J to $core(chase_\sigma(I'))$ that respects I. Since $I' \subseteq I$, it follows that h is a homomorphism from J to $core(chase_\sigma(I))$. Therefore, since J is a part of an f-block in $core(chase_\sigma(I))$, it follows that h cannot map J into anything smaller than J, so h simply renames the nulls in a one-to-one manner. Moreover, the image of J under this homomorphism h is a connected subgraph of the Gaifman graph of facts

---

[5]This property of $\Sigma_{\sigma,b}$ is not stated explicitly in that proof, but it can be derived from that proof by in particular noting that the f-block size of $\Sigma_{\sigma,b}$ is bounded by b. We remark that $\Sigma_{\sigma,b}$ consists of s-t tgds of the form τ_I, as defined in Proposition 4.7.

[6]In [FKNP08] it was assumed that I consists only of constants, and that homomorphisms map each constant onto itself, and so $\rightarrow$ rather than $\xrightarrow{I}$ was used in the definition of bounded support.

of core($chase_\sigma(I')$), since the facts of J form a connected graph. Hence, core($chase_\sigma(I')$) contains a f-block of size at least $b+1$, which was to be shown. $\square$

By combining Proposition 5.1 with Proposition 5.2, we obtain the following result.

THEOREM 5.3. *There is an algorithm for the following decision problem: Given a schema mapping $\mathbf{M_1}$ specified by an SO tgd and a GLAV mapping $\mathbf{M_2}$, is $\mathbf{M_1}$ CQ-equivalent to $\mathbf{M_2}$?*

COROLLARY 5.4. *There is an algorithm for the following decision problem: Given three GLAV mappings $\mathbf{M_1}$, $\mathbf{M_2}$, and $\mathbf{M_3}$, is $\mathbf{M_1} \circ \mathbf{M_2}$ CQ-equivalent to $\mathbf{M_3}$?*

PROOF. In [FKPT05], there is algorithm for finding an SO tgd σ that is logically equivalent to $\mathbf{M_1} \circ \mathbf{M_2}$. We then check whether σ is CQ-equivalent to $\mathbf{M_3}$, by making use of the algorithm guaranteed by Theorem 5.3. $\square$

Madhavan and Halevy [MH03] claim without proof that the decision problem in Corollary 5.4 is in Π_2^p. This claim would imply Theorem 5.3, since it is shown in [AFN11] that given a schema mapping $\mathbf{M}$ specified by an SO tgd, there is a procedure for finding GLAV mappings $\mathbf{M_1}$ and $\mathbf{M_2}$ such that $\mathbf{M} = \mathbf{M_1} \circ \mathbf{M_2}$.

6. Concluding Remarks

We have introduced the notion of a CQ-local transformation. Intuitively, a CQ-local transformation has the property that if two instances are indistinguishable using conjunctive queries of a sufficiently large size N, then their images under the transformation are also indistinguishable using conjunctive queries of a given size n. We proved that for GLAV mappings, the chase is CQ-local, and showed that N can be taken to be polynomial in n. One way of looking at the CQ-locality of the chase is that the chase is "uniformly continuous". We showed that if target dependencies are allowed, then CQ-locality of the chase may fail.

We investigated several different notions of equivalence of schema mappings and completed the picture as to when the composition of schema mappings from various subclasses of GLAV mappings is guaranteed to be logically equivalent to a GLAV mapping, and when it is guaranteed to be CQ-equivalent to a GLAV mapping.

Finally, we proved that the following problem is decidable: given an SO tgd and a finite set of s-t tgds, are they CQ-equivalent? This result sheds light on the differences between CQ-equivalence and logical equivalence, since the following problem is known to be undecidable: given an SO tgd and a finite set of s-t tgds, are they logically equivalent?

There are several interesting issues to pursue. A concrete technical question is the decidability of the following problem: given an SO tgd, is it CQ-equivalent to *some* GLAV mapping? It follows from results in [AFN11] that this is equivalent to the decidability of the following problem: given two GLAV mappings, is their composition CQ-equivalent to *some* GLAV mapping? More broadly, we feel that the notion of CQ-locality (and its alternate interpretation as uniform continuity) is potentially a valuable tool, with much more to be explored.

7. References

[ABFL04] M. Arenas, P. Barceló, R. Fagin, and L. Libkin. Locally consistent transformations and query answering in data exchange. In *ACM Symp. on Principles of Database Systems*, pages 229–240, 2004.

[ABLM10] M. Arenas, P. Barceló, L. Libkin, and F. Murlak. *Relational and XML Data Exchange*. Synthesis Lectures on Data Management. Morgan & Claypool Publishers, 2010.

[ABU79] A. V. Aho, C. Beeri, and J. D. Ullman. The theory of joins in relational databases. *ACM Trans. on Database Systems*, 4(3):297–314, 1979.

[AFM10] P.C. Arocena, A. Fuxman, and R.J. Miller. Composing local-as-view mappings: closure and applications. In *Int. Conf. on Database Theory*, pages 209–218, 2010.

[AFN11] M. Arenas, R. Fagin, and A. Nash. Composition with target constraints. *Logical Methods in Computer Science*, 7(3:13):1–38, 2011.

[APR09] M. Arenas, J. Pérez, and C. Riveros. The recovery of a schema mapping: Bringing exchanged data back. *ACM Trans. on Database Systems*, 34(4), 2009.

[APRR09] M. Arenas, J. Pérez, J.L. Reutter, and C. Riveros. Inverting schema mappings: Bridging the gap between theory and practice. *PVLDB*, 2(1):1018–1029, 2009.

[CM77] A. K. Chandra and P. M. Merlin. Optimal implementation of conjunctive queries in relational data bases. In *ACM Symp. on Theory of Computing*, pages 77–90, 1977.

[Fag07] R. Fagin. Inverting schema mappings. *ACM Trans. on Database Systems*, 32(4), 2007.

[FKMP05] R. Fagin, P. G. Kolaitis, R. J. Miller, and L. Popa. Data exchange: Semantics and query answering. *Theoretical Computer Science*, 336(1):89–124, 2005.

[FKNP08] R. Fagin, P. G. Kolaitis, A. Nash, and L. Popa. Towards a theory of schema-mapping optimization. In *ACM Symp. on Principles of Database Systems*, pages 33–42, 2008.

[FKPT05] R. Fagin, P. G. Kolaitis, L. Popa, and W.-C. Tan. Composing schema mappings: Second-order dependencies to the rescue. *ACM Trans. on Database Systems*, 30(4):994–1055, 2005.

[FKPT11] R. Fagin, P.G. Kolaitis, L. Popa, and W-C. Tan. Schema mapping evolution through composition and inversion. In Z. Bellahsene, A. Bonifati, and E. Rahm, editors, *Schema Matching and Mapping*, pages 191–222. Springer, 2011.

[FPSS11] I. Feinerer, R. Pichler, E. Sallinger, and V. Savenkov. On the undecidability of the equivalence of second-order tuple generating dependencies. In *Alberto Mendelzon Workshop*, 2011.

[FSV95] R. Fagin, L. Stockmeyer, and M. Y. Vardi. On monadic NP vs. monadic co-NP. *Inf. and Computation*, 120(1):78–92, July 1995.

[HN92] P. Hell and J. Nešetřil. The core of a graph. *Discrete Mathematics*, 109:117–126, 1992.

[Kol05] P. G. Kolaitis. Schema mappings, data exchange, and metadata management. In *ACM Symp. on Principles of Database Systems*, pages 61–75, 2005.

[Len02] M. Lenzerini. Data integration: A theoretical perspective. In *ACM Symp. on Principles of Database Systems*, pages 233–246, 2002.

[MH03] J. Madhavan and A. Y. Halevy. Composing mappings among data sources. In *Int. Conf. on Very Large Data Bases*, pages 572–583, 2003.

[MMS79] D. Maier, A. O. Mendelzon, and Y. Sagiv. Testing implications of data dependencies. *ACM Trans. on Database Systems*, 4(4):455–469, 1979.

[NdM09] J. Nešetřil and P. Ossona de Mendez. From sparse graphs to nowhere dense structures: Decompositions, independence, dualities and limits. In *Proc. of the Fifth European Congress of Mathematics*, 2009.

[PSS11] R. Pichler, E. Sallinger, and V. Savenkov. Relaxed notions of schema mapping equivalence revisited. In *Int. Conf. on Database Theory*, pages 90–101, 2011.

[Ros08] B. Rossman. Homomorphism preservation theorems. *J. ACM*, 55(3), 2008.

A Dichotomy in the Complexity of Deletion Propagation with Functional Dependencies

Benny Kimelfeld

IBM Research–Almaden, San Jose, CA 95120, USA
kimelfeld@us.ibm.com

ABSTRACT

A classical variant of the view-update problem is deletion propagation, where tuples from the database are deleted in order to realize a desired deletion of a tuple from the view. This operation may cause a (sometimes necessary) side effect—deletion of additional tuples from the view, besides the intentionally deleted one. The goal is to propagate deletion so as to maximize the number of tuples that remain in the view. In this paper, a view is defined by a self-join-free conjunctive query (sjf-CQ) over a schema with functional dependencies. A condition is formulated on the schema and view definition at hand, and the following dichotomy in complexity is established. If the condition is met, then deletion propagation is solvable in polynomial time by an extremely simple algorithm (very similar to the one observed by Buneman et al.). If the condition is violated, then the problem is NP-hard, and it is even hard to realize an approximation ratio that is better than some constant; moreover, deciding whether there is a side-effect-free solution is NP-complete. This result generalizes a recent result by Kimelfeld et al., who ignore functional dependencies. For the class of sjf-CQs, it also generalizes a result by Cong et al., stating that deletion propagation is in polynomial time if keys are preserved by the view.

Categories and Subject Descriptors: H.2 [Database Management]: Systems, Database Administration, F.2 [Analysis of Algorithms and Problem Complexity]: Nonnumerical Algorithms and Problems

General Terms: Algorithms, Theory

Keywords: Deletion propagation, functional dependencies, complexity dichotomy

1. INTRODUCTION

A classical problem in database management is that of *view update* [1, 4–6, 10–12]: translate an update operation on the view to an update of the source database, so that the update on the view is properly realized. A special case of this problem is that of *deletion propagation* in relational databases: given an *undesired* tuple in the view (defined by some monotonic query), delete some tuples from the base relations (where such tuples are referred to as *facts*), so that the undesired tuple disappears from the view. The database resulting from this deletion of tuples is called a *solution*. The *side effect* is the set of deleted view tuples that are different from the undesired one. If *only* the undesired tuple gets to be deleted from the view, then the solution is *side-effect free*. A solution that is side-effect free does not necessarily exist, and therefore, the task is relaxed to that of *minimizing* the side effect [3–5, 14]. That is, the goal is to delete tuples from the base relations so that the undesired tuple disappears from the view, but as many as possible other tuples remain.

Following is a simple example by Cui and Widom [7] (also referenced and used later by Buneman et al. [3] and Kimelfeld et al. [14]). Suppose that we have two relations, GroupUser(group, user) and GroupFile(group, file), representing memberships of users in groups and access permissions of groups to files, respectively. A user u can access the file f if u belongs to a group that can access f; that is, there is some g, such that GroupUser(g, u) and GroupFile(g, f). Suppose that we want to restrict the access of a specific user to a specific file, by eliminating some user-group or group-file pairings. Furthermore, we would like to do so in a way that a maximum number of user-file access permissions remain. This is exactly the deletion-propagation problem, where the view is defined by the following conjunctive query (CQ):

$$\text{Access}(u, f) :- \text{GroupUser}(g, u), \text{GroupFile}(g, f) \quad (1)$$

Formally, for a CQ Q (the view definition), the input for the deletion-propagation problem consists of a database instance I and a tuple $\mathbf{a} \in Q(I)$. A *solution* is a subinstance J of I (i.e., J is obtained from I by deleting facts) such that $\mathbf{a} \notin Q(J)$, and an *optimal solution* maximizes the number of tuples in $Q(J)$. The *side effect* is the set $(Q(I) \setminus \{\mathbf{a}\}) \setminus Q(J)$. Buneman et al. [3] identify some classes of CQs (e.g., projection-free CQs) for which a straightforward algorithm produces an optimal solution in polynomial time. But those tractable classes are restricted, as Buneman et al. show that even for a CQ as simple as the above Access(u, f), testing whether there is a solution that is side-effect free is NP-complete. Therefore, finding an *optimal solution* minimizing the side effect is NP-hard for Access(u, f). More recently, Kimelfeld et al. [14] considered views that are defined by a self-join-free CQ (sjf-CQ), and proved a dichotomy theorem implying that the views for which the straightforward algorithm is suboptimal are *exactly* those for which deletion propagation is NP-hard. Later, we discuss that dichotomy theorem in more detail.

Still discussing the view Access(u, f) of (1), suppose that now we have the restrictions that each user belongs to at most one group, and each file is associated with at most one group. It is easy to show that then, deletion propagation is in polynomial time, since to delete a tuple (`user`,`file`) from the view, it is enough to consider (and select the best out of) two possible solutions: one obtained by deleting the single fact of the form GroupUser$(g, $`user`$)$, and the other by deleting the single fact of the form GroupFile$(g, $`file`$)$. Actually, this example is a special case of the result of Cong et al. [4], stating that when the view (defined by a CQ) preserves keys, deletion propagation is in polynomial time. Now what if each file is associated with one group, but a user may belong to any number of groups (as commonly practiced by operating systems)? It is not difficult to show that, here also, the problem is in polynomial time. Actually, it turns out that *every* nontrivial key constraint suffices for the tractability of deletion propagation in the special case of Access(u, f); moreover, there is one very simple algorithm, which we later refer to as the *unirelation* algorithm, that realizes the polynomial time for each of these key constraints.

The above example illustrates the fact that *functional dependencies* (e.g., key constraints, {conference, year} →chair, etc.), abbreviated *fds*, have an immediate and direct effect on the complexity of deletion propagation. Moreover, this effect is on one direction: if for a certain view definition the problem is in polynomial time when disregarding the fds, it continues to be in polynomial time when fds are taken into account; however, if the problem is hard without the fds, it may no longer be hard when fds are accounted for. Therefore, the class of views that are known to be tractable for deletion propagation would expand as a result of the investigation of the problem in the presence of functional dependencies. This is what we do in this paper.

The formal setting is as follows. The view is defined by an sjf-CQ Q over a schema **S** that may have functional dependencies. (Exact definitions of sjf-CQs and schemas are in Section 2.) In the problem MAXDP$\langle \mathbf{S}, Q \rangle$ (where "DP" stands for "Deletion Propagation"), the input consists of a database instance I over **S** and a tuple $\mathbf{a} \in Q(I)$. A *solution* is a subinstance J of I (i.e., J is obtained from I by deleting facts) such that $\mathbf{a} \notin Q(J)$. The goal is to find an *optimal solution*, which is a solution that maximizes the number of tuples in $Q(J)$. The decision problem FREEDP$\langle \mathbf{S}, Q \rangle$ has the same input (i.e., I and $\mathbf{a}$), and the goal is to decide whether there is a solution that is side-effect free, that is, a subinstance J of I with $Q(J) = Q(I) \setminus \{\mathbf{a}\}$.

The main result of this paper is a generalization of the dichotomy theorem of Kimelfeld et al. [14] to accommodate functional dependencies. More precisely, in Section 3 we phrase a syntactic condition on (the fds of) the schema **S** and the sjf-CQ Q at hand. We call this condition the *tractability condition*. Then, the following is proved (Theorem 6.1).

- If the tractability condition is met, then MAXDP$\langle \mathbf{S}, Q \rangle$ (as well as FREEDP$\langle \mathbf{S}, Q \rangle$) is solvable in polynomial time by a straightforward algorithm. (Section 3.)
- Otherwise, MAXDP$\langle \mathbf{S}, Q \rangle$ is NP-hard, even to approximate better than some constant smaller than one; moreover, FREEDP$\langle \mathbf{S}, Q \rangle$ is NP-complete. (Section 5.)

The straightforward algorithm in the positive side of the dichotomy is called the *unirelation* algorithm, and is described in Section 3. This algorithm is very similar to the "trivial" algorithm used by Kimelfeld et al. [14] and originally observed by Buneman et al. [3]. The notion of approximation used in the negative side of the dichotomy is that of Kimelfeld et al. [14], which differs from that of Buneman et al. [3]. In particular, here the goal is to *maximize* the number of tuples that remain in the view, rather than to *minimize* the side effect [3]. (See [14] for a discussion on the difference between the two notions of approximation.)

To give the flavor of our tractability condition, we illustrate it on the CQ Access(u, f) defined in (1). (More involved examples are in the body of the paper.) In this CQ, u and f are *head variables* while g is an *existential variable*. Suppose first that the underlying schema **S** has no fds. In the *existential-connectivity graph* of Q, denoted $\mathcal{G}_\exists(Q)$, each atom is a node, and two atoms are connected by an edge whenever they share at least one existential variable. The tractability condition in the dichotomy of Kimelfeld et al. [14] says that for each connected component P of $\mathcal{G}_\exists(Q)$ there is an atom that contains all head variables of P. For $Q = $ Access(u, f), the graph $\mathcal{G}_\exists(Q)$ has only one connected component (containing the two atoms). Since no atom contains both u and f, the tractability condition of Kimelfeld et al. [14] is violated, thus MAXDP$\langle \mathbf{S}, Q \rangle$ is NP-hard. Now suppose that **S** has the fd file → group (i.e., every file belongs to one group). Then the existential variable g is *functionally determined* by the head variables; that is, in a mapping from Q to the database, if we know what the head variables are mapped to, then we also know what g is mapped to. So, we treat g as if it were a head variable. But now, the edge of $\mathcal{G}_\exists(Q)$ disappears (as the two atoms no longer share an existential variable), and we get two connected components, each with one node. Then, the tractability condition of Kimelfeld et al. [14] trivially holds, and so, MAXDP$\langle \mathbf{S}, Q \rangle$ is now in polynomial time. Lastly, suppose that instead of file → group, the schema **S** contains the fd group → user (i.e., every group has at most one user). Although the atom GroupFile(g, f) does not contain both head variables (u and f), it functionally determines both of them. This implies that the tractability condition of this paper is satisfied, and hence, MAXDP$\langle \mathbf{S}, Q \rangle$ is again in polynomial time.

Proving the tractable part of the dichotomy is fairly simple. However, the proof of the hardness part is nontrivial, and entails a fairly intricate construction and case analysis. A central concept in the proof is that of *graph separation*. In Section 5, we review the proof, which is restricted to the NP-completeness of FREEDP$\langle \mathbf{S}, Q \rangle$. In Section 6 we discuss the adaptation of the proof to hardness of approximation for MAXDP$\langle \mathbf{S}, Q \rangle$; the discussion is brief, as this adaptation uses ideas similar to the ones used by Kimelfeld et al. [14].

The work reported here is restricted to a special setting within view update: deletion propagation for sjf-CQs in the presence of fds, with the goal of preserving as many tuples of the view as possible. Other aspects of deletion propagation, and view update in general, have been studied in the literature. For example, deletion propagation was studied with the goal of minimizing the *source side effect* [3–5], namely, finding a solution with a minimal number of missing facts. A significant research effort has been invested on defining the semantics of (and notions of correctness for) general view-update operations (e.g., deletion and insertion of tuples) [1, 6, 10, 12]. For example, Cosmadakis and Papadimitriou [6] introduced a requirement for a view to keep intact a *complement view*.

Several dichotomies in the complexity of operations involving CQs (and sjf-CQs) were proved in the literature. For example, Dalvi and Suciu [9] considered query evaluation over probabilistic databases with independent tuples, and classified the sjf-CQs into those that can be evaluated in polynomial time and those that are #P-hard. Later, Dalvi et al. [8] extended this result to the class of unions of conjunctive queries (allowing self joins). More recently, Meliou et al. [18] showed a dichotomy (polynomial time vs. NP-completeness) in the complexity of computing the *degree of responsibility* of a database tuple for an answer in the result of an sjf-CQ. Examples of dichotomy theorems that involve CQs and key constraints are within the topic of *consistent query answering*. Kolaitis and Pema [15] proved a dichotomy (polynomial time vs. coNP-hardness) in the complexity of computing the consistent answers of a Boolean sjf-CQ with exactly two atoms. Finally, Maslowski and Wijsen [16] showed a dichotomy (polynomial vs. #P-hardness) in the complexity of counting the database repairs that satisfy a Boolean sjf-CQ. We are not aware of any dichotomy theorem that applies to sjf-CQs and general functional dependencies like the main theorem in this paper (Theorem 6.1).

The classical use case for deletion propagation is database administration: actual translation of a deletion in the view to deletions in the base relations. Kimelfeld et al. [14] discuss further motivation (e.g., information extraction) in the context of database debugging: the undesired answer is a detected error (false positive), and the facts deleted in an (approximately) optimal solution serve as a possible *cause* of the error. That cause is meaningful in the sense that it is focused on the erroneous answer and has a small (if any) effect on the other results. This notion of causality is different from that of Meliou et al. [17], which actually corresponds to deletion propagation with a minimal source side effect.

Due to a lack of space, the proofs are omitted, and presented in the extended version of this paper [13].

2. SETTING AND BACKGROUND

This section describes the formal setting for this paper, and provides some needed background.

2.1 Schemas and Functional Dependencies

In this paper, a *schema* $\mathbf{S}$ is a pair $(\mathcal{R}, \Delta)$, where $\mathcal{R} = \{R_1, \ldots, R_n\}$ is a finite set of *relation symbols* and Δ is a set of *functional dependencies*. We abbreviate *functional dependency* as fd. Each relation symbol $R_i \in \mathcal{R}$ has an *arity*, denoted $\mathrm{arity}(R_i)$, which is a natural (nonzero) number. An fd $\delta \in \Delta$ has the form $R_i : A \to B$, where $R_i \in \mathcal{R}$ and A and B are subsets of $\{1, \ldots, \mathrm{arity}(R_i)\}$. We use $R_i : A \to j$ and $R_i : j' \to j$ as shorthand notations of $R_i : A \to \{j\}$ and $R_i : \{j'\} \to \{j\}$, respectively.

We assume an infinite set Const of *constants*. A database over a schema $\mathbf{S}$ is called an *instance* (*over $\mathbf{S}$*), and its values are taken from Const. Formally, an instance I over a schema $\mathbf{S} = (\mathcal{R}, \Delta)$ consists of a finite relation $R_i^I \subseteq \mathsf{Const}^{\mathrm{arity}(R_i)}$ for each relation symbol $R_i \in \mathcal{R}$, such that all the fds of $\mathbf{S}$ are satisfied; that is, for each fd $R_i : A \to B$ in Δ and tuples $\mathbf{t}$ and $\mathbf{u}$ in R_i^I, if $\mathbf{t}$ and $\mathbf{u}$ agree on (i.e., have the same values for) the indices of A, then they also agree on the indices of

B. If I is an instance over $\mathbf{S}$ and $\mathbf{t}$ is a tuple in R_i^I, then we say that $R_i(\mathbf{t})$ is a *fact of I*. Notationally, we view an instance I as the set of its facts. As an example, $J \subseteq I$ means that $R_i^J \subseteq R_i^I$ for all $R_i \in \mathcal{R}$, in which case we say that J is *subinstance* of I. (Note that if I satisfies Δ, then every subinstance of I satisfies Δ as well.)

2.2 Conjunctive Queries

We fix an infinite set Var of *variables*, disjoint from Const. We usually denote variables by lowercase letters from the end of the Latin alphabet (e.g., x, y and z). We use the Datalog style for denoting a conjunctive query (abbrev. CQ); that is, a CQ over a schema $\mathbf{S}$ is an expression of the form $Q(\mathbf{y}) :\!-\, \varphi(\mathbf{x}, \mathbf{y}, \mathbf{c})$, where $\mathbf{x}$ and $\mathbf{y}$ are disjoint tuples of variables (from Var), $\mathbf{c}$ is a tuple of constants (from Const), and $\varphi(\mathbf{x}, \mathbf{y}, \mathbf{c})$ is a conjunction of atomic formulas $\phi_i(\mathbf{x}, \mathbf{y}, \mathbf{c})$ over $\mathbf{S}$; an atomic formula is also called an *atom*. We may write just $Q(\mathbf{y})$, or even just Q, if $\varphi(\mathbf{x}, \mathbf{y}, \mathbf{c})$ is irrelevant. We denote by atoms(Q) the set of atoms of Q. We usually write $\varphi(\mathbf{x}, \mathbf{y}, \mathbf{c})$ by simply listing the atoms of Q. We require every variable of $\mathbf{y}$ to occur (at least once) in $\varphi(\mathbf{x}, \mathbf{y}, \mathbf{c})$. The *arity of Q*, denoted arity(Q), is the length of the tuple $\mathbf{y}$.

Let $Q(\mathbf{y}) :\!-\, \varphi(\mathbf{x}, \mathbf{y}, \mathbf{c})$ be a CQ. A variable in $\mathbf{x}$ is called an *existential* variable, and a variable in $\mathbf{y}$ is called a *head* variable. We use $\mathsf{Var}_\exists(Q)$ and $\mathsf{Var}_\mathsf{h}(Q)$ to denote the sets of existential variables and head variables of Q, respectively. Similarly, if ϕ is an atom of Q, then $\mathsf{Var}_\exists(\phi)$ and $\mathsf{Var}_\mathsf{h}(\phi)$ denote the sets of existential and head variables, respectively, that occur in ϕ. We denote by $\mathsf{Var}(Q)$ and $\mathsf{Var}(\phi)$ the unions $\mathsf{Var}_\exists(Q) \cup \mathsf{Var}_\mathsf{h}(Q)$ and $\mathsf{Var}_\exists(\phi) \cup \mathsf{Var}_\mathsf{h}(\phi)$, respectively.

This paper mostly considers CQs that are *self-join free*, which means that each relation symbol occurs at most once in the CQ. We use *sjf-CQ* as an abbreviation of *self-join-free CQ*. If R is a relation symbol that occurs in the sjf-CQ $Q(\mathbf{y}) :\!-\, \varphi(\mathbf{x}, \mathbf{y}, \mathbf{c})$, then the unique atom over R is denoted by $\phi_R(\mathbf{x}, \mathbf{y}, \mathbf{c})$ or just ϕ_R. Similarly, R_ϕ denotes the relation symbol of the atom ϕ.

EXAMPLE 2.1. An important CQ in this work is the sjf-CQ $Q^\star$ which is the same as the CQ Access(u, f) defined in (1), up to renaming of relation symbols and variables. The schema is $\mathbf{S}^\star$, and it has two binary relation symbols R_1 and R_2 and no functional dependencies. The sjf-CQ $Q^\star$ over $\mathbf{S}^\star$ is the following.

$$Q^\star(y_1, y_2) :\!-\, R_1(x, y_1), R_2(x, y_2) \tag{2}$$

The atoms of $Q^\star$ are $\phi_{R_1} = R_1(x, y_1)$ and $\phi_{R_2} = R_2(x, y_2)$. In the examples of this paper, R_i and R_j are assumed to be different symbols whenever $i \neq j$. In particular, $R_1 \neq R_2$, so $Q^\star$ is indeed an sjf-CQ. There is only one existential variable in $Q^\star$, namely x, and the two head variables are y_1 and y_2. Hence $\mathsf{Var}_\exists(Q) = \{x\}$ and $\mathsf{Var}_\mathsf{h}(Q) = \{y_1, y_2\}$. Furthermore, $\mathsf{Var}_\exists(\phi_{R_1}) = \{x\}$ and $\mathsf{Var}_\mathsf{h}(\phi_{R_1}) = \{y_1\}$. □

Let $\mathbf{S}$ be a schema and let $Q(\mathbf{y})$ be a CQ over $\mathbf{S}$. An *assignment* for Q is a mapping $\mu : \mathsf{Var}(Q) \to \mathsf{Const}$. For an assignment μ for Q, the tuple $\mu(\mathbf{y})$ is the one obtained from $\mathbf{y}$ by replacing every head variable y with the constant $\mu(y)$. Similarly, for an atom ϕ of Q, the fact $\mu(\phi)$ is the one obtained from ϕ by replacing every variable z with the constant $\mu(z)$. Let I be an instance over $\mathbf{S}$. A *match for Q in I* is an assignment μ for Q, such that $\mu(\phi)$ is a fact of I for all $\phi \in \mathrm{atoms}(Q)$. We denote by $\mathcal{M}(Q, I)$ the set of all matches for Q in I. If $\mu \in \mathcal{M}(Q, I)$, then $\mu(\mathbf{y})$ is called an *answer* (*for Q in I*). The *result* of evaluating Q over I, denoted $Q(I)$, is the set of all the answers for Q in I; that is, $Q(I)$ is the set $\{\mu(\mathbf{y}) \mid \mu \in \mathcal{M}(Q,I)\}$.

Over a given schema, let $Q(\mathbf{y})$ be a CQ, let I be an instance, and let $\mathbf{b}$ be an answer. A fact $f \in I$ is $(Q, \mathbf{b})$-*useful* (*in I*) if for some $\mu \in \mathcal{M}(Q,I)$ and $\phi \in \text{atoms}(Q)$ we have $\mu(\mathbf{y}) = \mathbf{b}$ and $\mu(\phi) = f$. A fact $f \in I$ is Q-*useful* (*in I*) if f is $(Q, \mathbf{b})$-useful for some answer $\mathbf{b}$.

EXAMPLE 2.2. Take the schema $\mathbf{S}^\star$ and the CQ $Q^\star$ of Example 2.1. Let $I^\star$ be the instance with the following facts:

$$R_1(0, \triangleleft) \quad R_1(0, \mathsf{a}) \quad R_1(1, \triangleleft) \quad R_1(1, \mathsf{c})$$
$$R_2(0, \triangleright) \quad R_2(0, \mathsf{b}) \quad R_2(1, \triangleright)$$

The top six cells in the leftmost column of the table in Figure 4 show the matches in $\mathcal{M}(Q^\star, I^\star)$ (the rest of the table will be discussed in Section 5). As a shorthand notation, we use the triple c, b_1, b_2 (e.g., $0, \triangleleft, \mathsf{b}$) to specify the match that maps $x^\star$, $y_1^\star$ and $y_2^\star$ to c, b_1 and b_2, respectively. Note that $Q^\star(I^\star) = \{(\triangleleft, \triangleright), (\triangleleft, \mathsf{b}), (\mathsf{a}, \triangleright), (\mathsf{a}, \mathsf{b}), (\mathsf{c}, \triangleright)\}$. For the answer $\mathbf{a}^\star = (\triangleleft, \triangleright)$, the $(Q^\star, \mathbf{a}^\star)$-useful facts are $R_1(0, \triangleleft)$, $R_1(1, \triangleleft)$, $R_2(0, \triangleright)$ and $R_2(1, \triangleright)$. Finally, note that every fact of $I^\star$ is $Q^\star$-useful; but if we added the fact $R_1(3, \mathsf{a})$, it would not be $Q^\star$-useful (since it would have no fact of R_2 to join with). $\square$

2.2.1 CQs and Functional Dependencies

Let $\mathbf{S} = (\mathcal{R}, \Delta)$ be a schema, and let Q be a CQ over $\mathbf{S}$. If μ is an assignment for Q and Z is a subset of $\text{Var}(Q)$, then $\mu[Z]$ denotes the restriction of μ to the variables in Z (i.e., Z is the domain of $\mu[Z]$, and $\mu[Z](z) = \mu(z)$ for all $z \in Z$). Let Z_1 and Z_2 be subsets of $\text{Var}(Q)$. We denote by $Q : Z_1 \to Z_2$ the functional dependency stating that for every instance I over $\mathbf{S}$ and matches $\mu, \mu' \in \mathcal{M}(Q,I)$ we have:

$$\mu[Z_1] = \mu'[Z_1] \Rightarrow \mu[Z_2] = \mu'[Z_2]$$

Note that when Δ is empty (e.g., as in the setting of [3,14]), $Q : Z_1 \to Z_2$ is equivalent to $Z_1 \supseteq Z_2$. We may write $Q : Z \to z$ instead of $Q : Z \to \{z\}$. The *image* of Z, denoted $img(Z)$, is the set of all the variables $z \in \text{Var}(Q)$ with $Q : Z \to z$. Note that $Z \subseteq img(Z)$. For $\phi \in \text{atoms}(Q)$, we use $img(\phi)$ as a shorthand notation of $img(\text{Var}(\phi))$.

EXAMPLE 2.3. Let $\mathbf{S} = (\mathcal{R}, \Delta)$ be such that $\mathcal{R}$ contains two binary relation symbols R_1, R_2 and two ternary relation symbols S and T. Suppose that Δ has the following fds:

$$R_1 : 1 \to 2 \quad R_2 : 1 \to 2 \quad S : \{1, 2\} \to 3$$

Let Q be the following CQ.

$$Q(y_1, y_2, y_3) :- $$
$$R_1(x_1, y_1), R_2(x_2, y_2), S(y_1, y_3, x), T(x, x_1, x_2)$$

We have $img(\{x_1\}) = \{x_1, y_1\}$ due to the fd $R_1 : 1 \to 2$, $img(\{x_2\}) = \{x_2, y_2\}$ due to $R_2 : 1 \to 2$, and $img(\{y_1, y_3\}) = \{y_1, y_3, x\}$ due to $S : \{1, 2\} \to 3$. Finally, we have $img(\phi_T) = \{x, x_1, x_2, y_1, y_2\}$ due to the fds $R_1 : 1 \to 2$ and $R_2 : 1 \to 2$. (Recall that ϕ_T is the atom $T(x, x_1, x_2)$.) $\square$

2.3 Deletion Propagation

Let $\mathbf{S}$ be a schema, and let Q be a CQ. The problem of maximizing the view in deletion propagation, with Q as the view definition, is denoted by $\text{MAXDP}\langle \mathbf{S}, Q \rangle$ and is defined

as follows. The input consists of an instance I over $\mathbf{S}$, and a tuple $\mathbf{a} \in Q(I)$. A *solution* (*for I and $\mathbf{a}$*) is a subinstance $J \subseteq I$, such that $\mathbf{a} \notin Q(J)$. The goal is to find an *optimal* solution, which is a solution J that maximizes $|Q(J)|$; that is, J is such that $|Q(J)| \geq |Q(J')|$ for all solutions J'. The problem of determining whether there is a *side-effect-free* solution, denoted $\text{FREEDP}\langle \mathbf{S}, Q \rangle$, is that of deciding whether there is a solution in which we lose exactly $\mathbf{a}$; that is, given the input I and $\mathbf{a}$, decide whether there is a subinstance $J \subseteq I$ with $Q(J) = Q(I) \setminus \{\mathbf{a}\}$.

For example, take the schema $\mathbf{S}^\star$ and the CQ $Q^\star$ of Example 2.1. The input for $\text{MAXDP}\langle \mathbf{S}^\star, Q^\star \rangle$, as well as for $\text{FREEDP}\langle \mathbf{S}^\star, Q^\star \rangle$, consists of an instance $I^\star$ over $\mathbf{S}^\star$ and an answer $\mathbf{a}^\star = (a_1, a_2)$. To obtain a solution, we need to delete from $I^\star$ facts, so that for all constants c where both $R_1(c, a_1)$ and $R_2(c, a_2)$ are in $I^\star$, at least one of the two is deleted. In $\text{MAXDP}\langle \mathbf{S}^\star, Q^\star \rangle$, the goal is to have as many as possible pairs remaining in $Q^\star(I^\star)$ after the deletion. In $\text{FREEDP}\langle \mathbf{S}^\star, Q^\star \rangle$, the goal is to determine whether there is a solution that preserves every original answer except for $\mathbf{a}^\star$.

As follows from the presentation, we analyze the complexity of $\text{MAXDP}\langle \mathbf{S}, Q \rangle$ and $\text{FREEDP}\langle \mathbf{S}, Q \rangle$ under the yardstick of *data complexity*: the schema $\mathbf{S}$ and the CQ Q (that parameterize the problems) are fixed, and the input consists of the instance I and the answer $\mathbf{a}$. Buneman et al. [3] proved the following.

THEOREM 2.4. [3] $\text{FREEDP}\langle \mathbf{S}^\star, Q^\star \rangle$ *is NP-complete (and hence, $\text{MAXDP}\langle \mathbf{S}^\star, Q^\star \rangle$ is NP-hard).*

Kimelfeld et al. [14] generalized Theorem 2.4 to a complexity dichotomy over the class of all sjf-CQs Q; we discuss that in the next section.

Another problem that falls in our setting is that of deletion propagation for *key-preserving views* [4], which is described as follows. Let $\mathbf{S} = (\mathcal{R}, \Delta)$ be a schema. For a relation symbol $R \in \mathcal{R}$, a *primary key* for R is a set K of indices in $\{1, \ldots, \text{arity}(R)\}$, such that Δ contains the fd $K \to \{1, \ldots, \text{arity}(R)\}$. We say that a CQ Q over $\mathbf{S}$ is *key preserving* if for every $\phi \in \text{atoms}(Q)$ there is a key K_ϕ for R_ϕ, such that ϕ has no existential variables in the positions of K_ϕ. Cong et al. [4] proved the following.

THEOREM 2.5. [4] *Let $\mathbf{S}$ be a schema and let Q be a CQ over $\mathbf{S}$, such that Q is key preserving. Then $\text{MAXDP}\langle \mathbf{S}, Q \rangle$ (as well as $\text{FREEDP}\langle \mathbf{S}, Q \rangle$) is solvable in polynomial time.*

In Section 3, we will show how Theorem 2.5 is a special case of the main result of this paper in the case where Q is self-join free.

2.4 Head Domination and Dichotomy

Let $\mathbf{S}$ be a schema, and let Q be a CQ over a $\mathbf{S}$. The *existential-connectivity graph* of Q, denoted $\mathcal{G}_\exists(Q)$, is the undirected graph that has atoms(Q) as the set of nodes, and that has an edge $\{\phi_1, \phi_2\}$ whenever ϕ_1 and ϕ_2 have at least one existential variable in common (in notation, $\text{Var}_\exists(\phi_1) \cap \text{Var}_\exists(\phi_2) \neq \emptyset$). Let P be a subset of atoms(Q). We denote by $\text{Var}(P)$ the set of all the variables that occur in P, by $\text{Var}_\text{h}(P)$ the set $\text{Var}(P) \cap \text{Var}_\text{h}(Q)$, and by $\text{Var}_\exists(P)$ the set $\text{Var}(P) \cap \text{Var}_\exists(Q)$.

EXAMPLE 2.6. The left side of Figure 1 shows the graph $\mathcal{G}_\exists(Q)$ for the CQ Q of Example 2.3. Observe that there is no

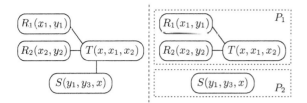

Figure 1: The graphs $\mathcal{G}_\exists(Q)$ (left) and $\mathcal{G}_\exists(Q^+)$ (right) for the CQ Q of Example 2.3

edge between $R_1(x_1, y_1)$ and $S(y_1, y_3, x)$ since the two atoms do not share an existential variable (they share y_1, which is a head variable). The graph $\mathcal{G}_\exists(Q)$ is connected, and its single connected component P satisfies $\mathsf{Var_h}(P) = \{y_1, y_2, y_3\}$ and $\mathsf{Var_\exists}(P) = \{x, x_1, x_2\}$. $\quad\square$

Kimelfeld et al. [14] defined the *head-domination* property of a CQ.

DEFINITION 2.7. (**Head Domination [14]**) A CQ Q over a schema $\mathbf{S}$ has the *head-domination* property if for every connected component P of $\mathcal{G}_\exists(Q)$ there is an atom ϕ of Q such that $\mathsf{Var_h}(P) \subseteq \mathsf{Var}(\phi)$. $\quad\square$

Note that in the definition, the atom ϕ satisfying $\mathsf{Var_h}(P) \subseteq \mathsf{Var}(\phi)$ is not necessarily in P.

EXAMPLE 2.8. A CQ that has head domination is the following:

$$Q'(y_1, y_2, y_3) :\!- R_1(x, y_1), R_2(x, y_2), S(y_1, y_2), T(y_2, y_3)$$

Note that $\mathcal{G}_\exists(Q')$ has three connected components: $P_1 = \{\phi_{R_1}, \phi_{R_2}\}$, $P_2 = \{\phi_S\}$, $P_3 = \{\phi_T\}$. Since $\mathsf{Var_h}(P_1) \subseteq \mathsf{Var}(\phi_S)$, $\mathsf{Var_h}(P_2) \subseteq \mathsf{Var}(\phi_S)$ and $\mathsf{Var_h}(P_3) \subseteq \mathsf{Var}(\phi_T)$, we get that, indeed, Q' has head domination.

As a negative example, consider again the CQ Q of Example 2.3. As shown in Example 2.6 (through Figure 1), $\mathcal{G}_\exists(Q)$ has only one connected component. Since no atom contains all the head variables of Q, we get that Q does not have head domination. $\quad\square$

Kimelfeld et al. [14] proved the following theorem, which states a dichotomy in the complexities of $\text{MAxDP}\langle \mathbf{S}, Q\rangle$ and $\text{FREEDP}\langle \mathbf{S}, Q\rangle$ in the absence of fds.

THEOREM 2.9. [14] *Let $\mathbf{S} = (\mathcal{R}, \Delta)$ be a schema and let Q be an sjf-CQ over $\mathbf{S}$.*

1. *If Q has head domination, then $\text{MAxDP}\langle \mathbf{S}, Q\rangle$ can be solved in polynomial time.*

2. *If $\Delta = \emptyset$ and Q does not have head domination, then $\text{FREEDP}\langle \mathbf{S}, Q\rangle$ is NP-complete.*

In this paper, we extend the complexity dichotomy of Theorem 2.9 to account for fds (Theorem 6.1). Specifically, in the next section we define a *tractability condition*, which is a syntactic condition on the schema $\mathbf{S}$ and the CQ Q at hand, such that fds are taken into account to weaken the property of head domination. We will show that the tractability condition gives a dichotomy similar to that of Theorem 2.9, that is, its satisfaction implies tractability of $\text{MAxDP}\langle \mathbf{S}, Q\rangle$ and its violation implies NP-completeness of $\text{FREEDP}\langle \mathbf{S}, Q\rangle$. (Of course, the tractability condition is equivalent to head

domination in the absence of fds.) As we will show, this extension of Theorem 2.9 requires arguments, concepts and constructions that are significantly different from those used for proving Theorem 2.9.

Actually, the result of Kimelfeld et al. [14] is stronger than Theorem 2.9. In the tractable part (item 1), the problem $\text{MAxDP}\langle \mathbf{S}, Q\rangle$ is solved by an extremely simple algorithm that has been observed already by Buneman et al. [3]. We will show that the tractable side in the current paper is solved by essentially the same algorithm, with a slight modification. In the intractable part of Theorem 2.9 (item 2), Kimelfeld et al. further show some hardness of approximation for $\text{MAxDP}\langle \mathbf{S}, Q\rangle$. To simplify the presentation, we ignore approximation through most of the paper, except for Section 6; there, we will show that a similar hardness of approximation is in the intractable side of this paper's dichotomy as well.

3. TRACTABILITY

In this section, we define and discuss the tractability condition on a schema $\mathbf{S}$ and an sjf-CQ Q over $\mathbf{S}$. Also in this section we will state that the condition is indeed sufficient for $\text{MAxDP}\langle \mathbf{S}, Q\rangle$ to be solvable in polynomial time. In Section 5, we will state that the condition is also necessary for this tractability (under standard complexity assumptions). We begin by describing the *unirelation algorithm*, which is a very simple algorithm that produces a (not-necessarily optimal) solution given the input I and $\mathbf{a}$ for $\text{MAxDP}\langle \mathbf{S}, Q\rangle$.

3.1 The Unirelation Algorithm

Let $\mathbf{S}$ be a schema, and let Q be a CQ over $\mathbf{S}$. Buneman et al. [3] observed the following simple algorithm (also called *the trivial algorithm* [14]) for producing a solution, given the input I and $\mathbf{a}$ for $\text{MAxDP}\langle \mathbf{S}, Q\rangle$. For each $\phi \in \text{atoms}(Q)$, construct the candidate solution J_ϕ by deleting from I every fact that can be obtained from ϕ by an assignment that agrees with $\mathbf{a}$ on the head variables; then, select the J_ϕ with the maximal $|Q(J_\phi)|$. The *unirelation algorithm*, denoted $\text{UniRel}\langle \mathbf{S}, Q\rangle$ and depicted in Figure 2, is essentially the same algorithm, except that we delete only facts that are $(Q, \mathbf{a})$-useful (that is, the facts we delete are always of the form $\mu(\phi)$ where $\mu \in \mathcal{M}(Q, I)$ is such that $\mu(\mathbf{y}) = \mathbf{a}$). The following straightforward proposition states that the unirelation algorithm is correct and terminates in polynomial time.

PROPOSITION 3.1. $\text{UniRel}\langle \mathbf{S}, Q\rangle(I, \mathbf{a})$ *returns a solution in polynomial time.*

It follows immediately from the results of Kimelfeld et al. [14] that if Q is an sjf-CQ with head domination, then $\text{UniRel}\langle \mathbf{S}, Q\rangle$ produces an optimal solution. It also follows immediately that in the absence of fds, head domination is a necessary condition for the optimality of $\text{UniRel}\langle \mathbf{S}, Q\rangle$; but this is no longer true when fds are present, as the following example shows.

EXAMPLE 3.2. Consider again the CQ $Q^\star$ over $\mathbf{S}^\star$ (Example 2.1), but now let us use the schema $\mathbf{S}_0^\star$, which is the same as $\mathbf{S}^\star$ except that it has the fd $R_1 : 1 \to 2$. We claim that, given input $I^\star$ and $\mathbf{a}^\star = (a_1, a_2)$, the execution of $\text{UniRel}\langle \mathbf{S}_0^\star, Q^\star\rangle(I^\star, \mathbf{a}^\star)$ returns an optimal solution. As proof, we will show that for $\phi = R_2(x, y_2)$ the solution J_ϕ, constructed by the algorithm, is optimal. Let J_{opt} be

---

Algorithm UniRel$\langle \mathbf{S}, Q \rangle(I, \mathbf{a})$

1: $J \leftarrow \emptyset$
2: **for all** $\phi \in \text{atoms}(Q)$ **do**
3:    $J_\phi \leftarrow I$
4:    Remove from J_ϕ every fact over R_ϕ that is $(Q, \mathbf{a})$-useful in I
5:    **if** $|Q(J_\phi)| > |Q(J)|$ **then**
6:       $J \leftarrow J_\phi$
7: **return** J

Figure 2: The unirelation algorithm

an optimal solution. It is enough to show that every fact $R_2(c, a_2)$ that is $(Q^\star, \mathbf{a}^\star)$-useful in $I^\star$ is not Q-useful in J_{opt} (hence, $Q(J_{\text{opt}}) \subseteq Q(J_\phi)$). Indeed, if J_{opt} contains both $R_1(c, b_1)$ and $R_2(c, a_2)$, then the fd implies that $b_1 = a_1$, since $I^\star$ contains also $R_1(c, a_1)$ (or otherwise $R_2(c, a_2)$ is not $(Q^\star, \mathbf{a}^\star)$-useful in $I^\star$). This means that $Q(J_{\text{opt}})$ contains $\mathbf{a}^\star$, which contradicts the fact that J_{opt} is a solution. $\quad\square$

3.2 Functional Head Domination

The idea that is used in Example 3.2 to show the optimality of UniRel$\langle \mathbf{S}_0^\star, Q^\star \rangle$ is the following. The head variables of the single connected component of $\mathcal{G}_\exists(Q^\star)$ are y_1 and y_2. The atom ϕ_{R_2} does not contain both y_1 and y_2, but $img(\phi_{R_2})$ does. So, intuitively, we can treat ϕ_{R_2} as if it contains both y_1 and y_2. This idea is formalized next.

DEFINITION 3.3. (**Functional Head Domination**) A CQ Q over a schema $\mathbf{S}$ has the *functional head-domination* property if for every connected component P of $\mathcal{G}_\exists(Q)$ there is an atom ϕ of Q such that $\text{Var}_h(P) \subseteq img(\phi)$. $\quad\square$

For example, the CQ $Q^\star$ over $\mathbf{S}_0^\star$ in Example 3.2 has functional head domination, since $img(\phi_{R_2})$ contains both y_1 and y_2 (as previously explained). Another example follows.

EXAMPLE 3.4. Consider the schema $\mathbf{S}$ and CQ Q of Example 2.3. Recall that the left side of Figure 1 shows the graph $\mathcal{G}_\exists(Q)$. Since $\mathcal{G}_\exists(Q)$ is connected and no atom ϕ of Q is such that $img(\phi)$ contains all the head variables, Q does not have functional head domination.

Now, let Q' be obtained from Q by adding x to the head (so the head variables of Q' are x and the y_i). The right side of Figure 1 shows $\mathcal{G}_\exists(Q')$. For the connected component P_1 we have $\text{Var}_h(P_1) = \{x, y_1, y_2\} \subseteq img(\phi_T)$, and $\text{Var}_h(P_2) = \{x, y_1, y_3\} \subseteq img(\phi_S)$. Thus, Q' has functional head domination. $\quad\square$

The following theorem generalizes the idea illustrated in Example 3.2: in the absence of self joins, functional head domination is sufficient for MAXDP$\langle \mathbf{S}, Q \rangle$ to be solvable in polynomial time. This theorem follows from Theorems 3.10 and 3.11 given later in this section.

THEOREM 3.5. *Let $\mathbf{S}$ be a schema, and let Q be an sjf-CQ over $\mathbf{S}$. If Q has functional head domination, then* UniRel$\langle \mathbf{S}, Q \rangle$ *optimally solves* MAXDP$\langle \mathbf{S}, Q \rangle$.

Nevertheless, functional head domination is still not a necessary condition for the optimality of the unirelation algorithm, as the following example shows.

EXAMPLE 3.6. Consider again the CQ $Q^\star$ over $\mathbf{S}^\star$ (Example 2.1), but now let us use the schema $\mathbf{S}_1^\star$, which is the same as $\mathbf{S}^\star$ except that it has the fd $R_1 : 2 \rightarrow 1$ (recall that in Example 3.2 we used the fd $R_1 : 1 \rightarrow 2$). We again claim that, given input $I^\star$ and $\mathbf{a}^\star = (a_1, a_2)$, the execution of UniRel$\langle \mathbf{S}_0^\star, Q^\star \rangle(I^\star, \mathbf{a}^\star)$ returns an optimal solution. To see that, let J_{opt} be an optimal solution. If none of the facts $R_2(c, a_2)$ that are $(Q^\star, \mathbf{a}^\star)$-useful in $I^\star$ are Q-useful in J_{opt}, we are done as in Example 3.2. Otherwise, take such a fact $R_2(c, a_2)$, and we will show that none of the facts $R_1(c', a_1)$ that are $(Q^\star, \mathbf{a}^\star)$-useful in $I^\star$ are Q-useful in J_{opt} (which means that $Q(J_{\text{opt}}) \subseteq Q(J_\phi)$ for $\phi = R_1(x, y_1)$). Indeed, if $R_1(c', a_1)$ is a counterexample, then $R_1 : 2 \rightarrow 1$ implies $c' = c$, since we know that $I^\star$ contains $R_1(c, a_1)$ (or otherwise $R_2(c, a_2)$ is not $(Q^\star, \mathbf{a}^\star)$-useful in $I^\star$), and then $\mathbf{a}^\star \in Q^\star(J_{\text{opt}})$, which is of course a contradiction. $\quad\square$

The optimality of the unirelation algorithm in Example 3.6 is due to the fact that the existential variable x is functionally dependent on the head variables (i.e., $x \in img(\{y_1, y_2\})$), which means that given an answer in $Q(I^\star)$, every realizing assignment maps x to the same value. In effect, this means that x can be treated as a head (rather than existential) variable, which may change the structure of $\mathcal{G}_\exists(Q)$ and can potentially lead to functional head domination. Indeed, if x becomes a head variable in $Q^\star$, then no existential variables remain in $Q^\star$, and then (functional) head domination trivially holds. Next, we formalize this intuition.

For a CQ Q over a schema $\mathbf{S}$, we denote by Q^+ the CQ that is obtained by appending (in some order) all the existential variables in $\text{Var}_\exists(Q) \cap img(\text{Var}_h(Q))$ to the head of Q. As an example, for the CQ $Q = Q^\star$ over the schema $\mathbf{S}_1^\star$ of Example 3.6, the CQ Q^+ is:

$$Q^+(y_1, y_2, x) :- R_1(x, y_1), R_2(x, y_2)$$

The following lemma is straightforward.

LEMMA 3.7. *Let $\mathbf{S}$ be a schema, and let Q be a CQ over $\mathbf{S}$. Given an instance I over $\mathbf{S}$, there is a function $\beta : Q(I) \rightarrow Q^+(I)$, such that β is a bijection from $Q(J)$ to $Q^+(J)$ for every $J \subseteq I$; moreover, β is computable in polynomial time in the size of I.*

As a conclusion of Lemma 3.7, we get the following.

LEMMA 3.8. *Let Q be a CQ over a schema $\mathbf{S}$.*

- *There is a polynomial-time reduction from the problem* FREEDP$\langle \mathbf{S}, Q \rangle$ *to the problem* FREEDP$\langle \mathbf{S}, Q^+ \rangle$ *and vice versa.*
- *There is a polynomial-time, approximation-preserving reduction from* MAXDP$\langle \mathbf{S}, Q \rangle$ *to* MAXDP$\langle \mathbf{S}, Q^+ \rangle$ *and vice versa.*

3.3 Tractability Condition

We can now define our tractability condition.

DEFINITION 3.9. (**Tractability Condition**) For an sjf-CQ Q over a schema $\mathbf{S}$, the *tractability condition* is that Q^+ has functional head domination. $\quad\square$

Later on, we show that the tractability condition indeed implies tractability. But first, the following theorem states that this condition is weaker than functional head domination, which in turn is weaker than head domination. The proof uses Theorem 4.2 (specifically, Part 3) that we present and discuss in the next section.

THEOREM 3.10. *Let Q be a CQ over a schema $\mathbf{S}$.*
1. *If Q has head domination, then Q has functional head domination.*
2. *If Q has functional head domination, then Q^+ has functional head domination.*

Furthermore, none of the two reverse implications hold.

Following is the main result for this section, and it says that when the tractability condition is satisfied (and in the absence of self joins), the unirelation algorithm is optimal.

THEOREM 3.11. *Let Q be an sjf-CQ over a schema $\mathbf{S}$. If Q^+ has functional head domination, then $\mathsf{UniRel}\langle \mathbf{S}, Q \rangle$ optimally solves $\mathrm{MAXDP}\langle \mathbf{S}, Q \rangle$ (in polynomial time).*

Next, we illustrate applications of Theorem 3.11.

EXAMPLE 3.12. Consider again the schema $\mathbf{S}$ and CQ Q of Example 2.3, where it is stated that the existential variable x is in $img(\{y_1, y_2\})$. So $x \in img(\mathsf{Var_h}(Q))$. The reader can verify that none of x_1 and x_2 are in $img(\mathsf{Var_h}(Q))$. Therefore, the CQ Q^+ is the following:

$$Q^+(y_1, y_2, y_3, x) :-$$
$$R_1(x_1, y_1), R_2(x_2, y_2), S(y_1, y_3, x), T(x, x_1, x_2)$$

Hence, Q^+ is actually the CQ Q' of Example 3.4, where it is shown to have functional head domination. Therefore, the tractability condition is satisfied, and hence, Theorem 3.11 says that $\mathrm{MAXDP}\langle \mathbf{S}, Q \rangle$ is optimally solvable in polynomial time by the unirelation algorithm. □

As another example, we will show how Theorem 2.5 (by Cong et al. [4]) follows from Theorem 3.11 for the class of sjf-CQs. Let $\mathbf{S}$ be a schema and let Q be an sjf-CQ over $\mathbf{S}$, such that Q is key preserving. It is straightforward to show that Q being key preserving implies that Q^+ has no existential variables. Hence, $\mathcal{G}_\exists(Q)$ has no edges, and so Q^+ has (functional) head domination. Then, Theorem 3.11 says that $\mathrm{MAXDP}\langle \mathbf{S}, Q \rangle$ is in polynomial time.

4. FD-SEPARATION

Before we proceed to proving the hardness side of our complexity dichotomy, we introduce the concept of *fd-separation*, which plays an important role in our proofs.

Let Q be a CQ over a schema $\mathbf{S}$. The *variable co-occurrence graph* of Q, denoted $\mathcal{G}_v(Q)$, is the graph that has $\mathsf{Var}(Q)$ as the set of nodes, and an edge $\{z_1, z_2\}$ whenever z_1 and z_2 co-occur in the same atom of Q (i.e., $\{z_1, z_2\} \subseteq \mathsf{Var}(\phi)$ for some $\phi \in atoms(Q)$). Consider two variables $z_1, z_2 \in \mathsf{Var}(Q)$ and a subset Z of $\mathsf{Var}(Q)$. We say that Z *separates* z_1 from z_2 if every path of $\mathcal{G}_v(Q)$ connecting z_1 and z_2 visits one or more nodes in Z. Observe that as a special case, if $z_1 \in Z$ then Z separates z_1 from every other variable z_2. Moreover, if Z separates z_1 from itself then z_1 is necessarily in Z.

Let Z be a subset of $\mathsf{Var}(Q)$, and let $z_1, z_2 \in \mathsf{Var}(Q)$ be two variables. We say that Z *fd-separates* z_1 *from* z_2 if $img(Z)$ separates z_1 from z_2. We also say that an atom ϕ of Q *fd-separates* z_1 *from* z_2 if $\mathsf{Var}(\phi)$ fd-separates z_1 from z_2. We denote by $fdSep(Z, z)$ (respectively, $fdSep(\phi, z)$) the set of all the variables z' of Q that Z (respectively, ϕ) fd-separates z from z'.

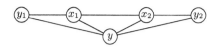

Figure 3: $\mathcal{G}_v(Q)$ **in Example 4.1**

EXAMPLE 4.1. Let $\mathbf{S}$ be a schema with three ternary relation symbols R_1, R_2 and S, and the fd $S : \{1, 3\} \to 2$. Consider the following CQ over $\mathbf{S}$:

$$Q(y_1, y_2, y) :- R_1(y_1, y, x_1), S(x_1, y, x_2), R_2(x_2, y, y_2)$$

The graph $\mathcal{G}_v(Q)$ is depicted in Figure 3. The singleton $\{x_1\}$ does not fd-separate y_1 from y_2, since the path $y_1 - y - y_2$ does not contain any node in $img(\{x_1\}) = \{x_1\}$. Similarly, $\{x_2\}$ does not fd-separate y_1 from y_2. However, $\{x_1, x_2\}$ fd-separates y_1 from y_2, since every path between y_1 and y_2 visits a node in $img(\{x_1, x_2\}) = \{x_1, x_2, y\}$. This also shows that ϕ_S fd-separates y_1 from y_2, or in other words, $y_2 \in fdSep(\phi_S, y_1)$. □

The following theorem states some facts on fd-separation. This theorem is important for this work, as it is used repeatedly in the proofs for the other results in this paper.

THEOREM 4.2. *Let Q be a CQ over a schema $\mathbf{S}$, let $Z \subseteq \mathsf{Var}(Q)$ be a set of variables, and let $z \in \mathsf{Var}(Q)$ be a variable. The following hold.*

1. *$fdSep(Z, z)$ is closed under fds; that is:*

$$img(fdSep(Z, z)) = fdSep(Z, z)$$

2. *$fdSep(Z, z)$ is closed under fd-separation by subsets; that is, for all $Z' \subseteq \mathsf{Var}(Q)$ we have:*

$$Z' \subseteq fdSep(Z, z) \Rightarrow fdSep(Z', z) \subseteq fdSep(Z, z)$$

3. *Z determines z whenever Z separates from z a set that determines z; that is, for all $Z' \subseteq \mathsf{Var}(Q)$ we have:*

$$(Q : Z' \to z \wedge Z' \subseteq fdSep(Z, z)) \Rightarrow Q : Z \to z$$

5. HARDNESS

In this section, we discuss the proof of the hardness side of our complexity dichotomy: for an sjf-CQ Q over a schema $\mathbf{S}$, if the tractability condition is violated, then $\mathrm{FREEDP}\langle \mathbf{S}, Q \rangle$ is NP-complete. In Section 6 we discuss hardness of approximation for $\mathrm{MAXDP}\langle \mathbf{S}, Q \rangle$. We will explain the main steps involved in the proof; actual proofs and intermediate steps are in the extended version of the paper [13].

Similarly to the proof of Theorem 2.9 by Kimelfeld et al. [14], the proof of hardness here is by a reduction from $\mathrm{FREEDP}\langle \mathbf{S}^\star, Q^\star \rangle$; recall that $\mathbf{S}^\star$ and $Q^\star$ are defined in Example 2.1. But the reduction here is quite different from that of Theorem 2.9, due to the accommodation of functional dependencies. We first set some notation and assumptions that we will hold for the remainder of this section.

5.1 Notation and Assumptions

Throughout this section, we fix a schema $\mathbf{S} = (\mathcal{R}, \Delta)$ and an sjf-CQ Q over $\mathbf{S}$, such that the tractability condition is violated: Q^+ does not have functional head domination. Membership of $\mathrm{FREEDP}\langle \mathbf{S}, Q \rangle$ in NP is straightforward (nondeterministically choose a subinstance and test whether it is a side-effect-free solution). The goal is to prove that $\mathrm{FREEDP}\langle \mathbf{S}, Q \rangle$ is NP-hard. By Lemma 3.8, it suffices to prove that $\textsc{FreeDP}\langle \mathbf{S}, Q^+\rangle$ is NP-hard. Therefore, to avoid carrying the plus superscript, we will simply assume that $Q = Q^+$. We fix a component P of $\mathcal{G}_\exists(Q)$, such that none of the atoms ϕ of Q satisfy $\mathsf{Var_h}(P) \subseteq img(\phi)$; such P exists, since Q does not have functional head domination.

For the sake of presentation, we rephrase $\mathbf{S}^\star$ and $Q^\star$ for a clear distinction from $\mathbf{S}$ and Q. Specifically, we will assume that the two relation symbols of $\mathbf{S}^\star$ are $R_1^\star$ and $R_2^\star$ (rather than R_1 and R_2 as in Example 2.1), and that the CQ $Q^\star$ over $\mathbf{S}^\star$ is the following sjf-CQ:

$$Q^\star(y_1^\star, y_2^\star) :\!- R_1^\star(x^\star, y_1^\star), R_2^\star(x^\star, y_2^\star)$$

It is known that $\textsc{FreeDP}\langle \mathbf{S}^\star, Q^\star\rangle$ is NP-complete [3]. Recall that $\mathbf{S}^\star$ has no fds. We will reduce $\textsc{FreeDP}\langle \mathbf{S}^\star, Q^\star\rangle$ to $\textsc{FreeDP}\langle \mathbf{S}, Q\rangle$. For the remainder of this section we fix the input $I^\star$ and $\mathbf{a}^\star$ for $\textsc{FreeDP}\langle \mathbf{S}^\star, Q^\star\rangle$. We assume that $\mathbf{a}^\star$ is the pair $(\lhd, \rhd)$. Our reduction will construct the input I and $\mathbf{a}$ for the problem $\textsc{FreeDP}\langle \mathbf{S}, Q\rangle$.

EXAMPLE 5.1. A running example in this section is over the following CQ.

$$Q(y_1, y_2, y_3) :\!- S_1(y_1, x_1), R_1(x_1, x), R_2(x, x_2), S_2(x_2, y_2),$$
$$T(x_1, x', x_2), U(x, x'', y_3), V(x_3, y_2, y_3)$$

The schema $\mathbf{S}$ has the relation symbols of Q (with the corresponding arities). In addition, $\mathbf{S}$ has the following fds.

$$S_1 : 2 \to 1 \qquad S_2 : 1 \to 2 \qquad U : 1 \to 3$$

Observe that $Q = Q^+$ since no existential variable belongs to $img(\{y_1, y_2, y_3\})$. The graph $\mathcal{G}_\exists(Q)$ has two connected components, where one consists of just $V(x_3, y_2, y_3)$ and the other, which we fix here as P, consists of all remaining atoms. It is easy to verify that no atom ϕ of Q is such that $img(\phi)$ contains all of y_1, y_2 and y_3 (i.e., the head variables of P); hence, the tractability condition is violated.

As example input for $\textsc{FreeDP}\langle \mathbf{S}^\star, Q^\star\rangle$, we use the instance $I^\star$ of Example 2.2. Recall that $\mathcal{M}(Q^\star, I^\star)$ is shown in the leftmost column of the table in Figure 4. For later use, the matches that produce $\mathbf{a}^\star = (\lhd, \rhd)$ are repeated in the bottom of the column. The reader can verify that there is no side-effect-free solution for $I^\star$ and $\mathbf{a}^\star$. □

5.2 Template Construction

To reduce $\textsc{FreeDP}\langle \mathbf{S}^\star, Q^\star\rangle$ to $\textsc{FreeDP}\langle \mathbf{S}, Q\rangle$, we first define a *template construction*, which produces an instance I_Θ over $\mathbf{S}$. Intuitively, I_Θ *simulates* $I^\star$ in the sense that there is a direct correspondence between $Q^\star(I^\star)$ and $Q(I_\Theta)$, and between $\mathcal{M}(Q^\star, I^\star)$ and $\mathcal{M}(Q, I_\Theta)$. The challenge is to assure that *(1)* I_Θ satisfies the fds of $\mathbf{S}$ (Lemma 5.4), *and (2)* correspondence is achieved (Lemma 5.5). Next, we show how it is done. Still, I_Θ will not be the final I of the reduction, since $\textsc{FreeDP}\langle \mathbf{S}, Q\rangle$ may be "too easy" on I. But I_Θ is a crucial step in the construction of I, and in fact, I_Θ will be a subinstance of I.

Recall that we are given the input $I^\star$ and $\mathbf{a}^\star = (\lhd, \rhd)$ for $\textsc{FreeDP}\langle \mathbf{S}^\star, Q^\star\rangle$. Also recall that $Q^\star$ uses three variables: $x^\star$, $y_1^\star$, $y_2^\star$. We fix a constant $\diamond$ that does not appear in $I^\star$. We first define a *template assignment* Θ, which maps every variable $z \in \mathsf{Var}(Q)$ to a triple $\Theta(z) = \langle w, w_1, w_2\rangle$, where w is either the variable $x^\star$ or the constant $\diamond$, w_1 is either the variable $y_1^\star$ or the constant $\lhd$, and w_2 is either the variable $y_2^\star$ or the constant $\rhd$.

The template construction is parameterized by two variables $y_1, y_2 \in \mathsf{Var_h}(P)$ and two atoms $\phi_1, \phi_2 \in P$. Intuitively, each y_i simulates $y_i^\star$, and the existential variables of P simulate $x^\star$. Roughly speaking, ϕ_i "guards" y_i from functional dependency on the variables that simulate the other two variables of $Q^\star$. In the next section, we discuss in detail the way these parameters are chosen (which is critical for the correctness of the reduction); for now, assume that they are already present. Given the parameters y_1, y_2, ϕ_1 and ϕ_2, the triple $\Theta(z)$, where $z \in \mathsf{Var}(Q)$, is constructed as follows.

- Begin with $\Theta(z) = \langle x^\star, y_1^\star, y_2^\star\rangle$.
- If $z \notin \mathsf{Var}_\exists(P)$, then replace $x^\star$ with $\diamond$.
- If $z \in fdSep(\phi_2, y_1)$, then replace $y_1^\star$ with $\lhd$.
- If $z \in fdSep(\phi_1, y_2)$, then replace $y_2^\star$ with $\rhd$.

Recall from Section 4 that $fdSep(\phi, y)$ is the set of all variables $z \in \mathsf{Var}(Q)$, such that ϕ fd-separates y from z (i.e., $img(\phi)$ separates y from z in the graph $\mathcal{G}_\mathsf{v}(Q)$).

EXAMPLE 5.2. We continue with our running example, which is introduced in Example 5.1. Figure 5 shows the graph $\mathcal{G}_\mathsf{v}(Q)$. The grey shadow should be ignored for now; we discuss it later in this section. Recall that P consists of all the atoms of Q, except for $V(x_3, y_2, y_3)$.

Suppose that the parameters of the template construction are y_1, y_2, $\phi_1 = R_1(x_1, x)$ and $\phi_2 = R_2(x, x_2)$. (Later, we discuss the manner in which these specific parameters are chosen.) The sets $img(\phi_1)$ and $img(\phi_2)$ are surrounded by boxes with dotted edges. For each variable z of Q, the corresponding node contains $\Theta(z)$ below z. As an example, consider the variable x'. As shown in the figure, $\Theta(x') = \langle x^\star, y_1^\star, y_2^\star\rangle$. The occurrence of $x^\star$ is due to the fact that x' is an existential variable in P; that of $y_1^\star$ is due to the fact that ϕ_2 does not fd-separate x' from y_1, as evidenced by the path $x' - x_1 - y_1$, and similar is the explanation for $y_2^\star$.

As another example, note that $\Theta(x'') = \langle x^\star, \lhd, \rhd\rangle$, since ϕ_2 (resp., ϕ_1) fd-separates x'' from y_1 (resp., y_2), as the edges that are incident to x'' connect x'' to variables in the intersection $img(\phi_1) \cap img(\phi_2)$. Finally, for x_3 we have $\Theta(x_3) = \langle \diamond, \lhd, y_2^\star\rangle$, where the reason for the occurrence of $\diamond$ is that x_3 is not in $\mathsf{Var}_\exists(P)$; besides that, the explanations for $\lhd$ and $y_2^\star$ are like those for x'' and x', respectively. □

Let μ be a match in $\mathcal{M}(Q^\star, I^\star)$. The assignment Θ_μ is the same as Θ, except that in the image, every occurrence of $x^\star$, $y_1^\star$ and $y_2^\star$ is replaced with $\mu(x^\star)$, $\mu(y_1^\star)$ and $\mu(y_2^\star)$, respectively. We call Θ_μ an *instantiation* of Θ. The *template construction* builds the instance I_Θ that comprises of all the $\Theta_\mu(\phi)$ over all $\mu \in \mathcal{M}(Q^\star, I^\star)$ and $\phi \in \text{atoms}(Q)$.

EXAMPLE 5.3. We continue with our running example. For presentation sake, in our examples we may write just cb_1b_2 instead of $\langle c, b_1, b_2\rangle$ (e.g., $\diamond\lhd\rhd$ instead of $\langle \diamond, \lhd, \rhd\rangle$).

Recall that Figure 5 shows the values that Θ assigns the variables to. Each of the top six rows in the table of Figure 4 corresponds to one of the six matches $\mu \in \mathcal{M}(Q^\star, I^\star)$. (We later discuss the bottom two rows.) The leftmost element (under "$\mathcal{M}(Q^\star, I^\star)$") is μ, as explained in Example 5.1. The cells under the atom ϕ represent the facts $\Theta_\mu(\phi)$. As an example, if μ is the match represented by $0, \lhd, \mathsf{b}$ and ϕ is $S_1(y_1, x_1)$, then $\Theta_\mu(\phi) = S(\diamond\lhd\mathsf{b}, 0\lhd\mathsf{b})$. So, the top six rows in the table depict I_Θ (with some facts repeated). □

Next, we discuss some basic properties of the template construction, which hold regardless of the choice of the parameters ϕ_i and y_i. The following lemma states that I_Θ is

$\mathcal{M}(Q^\star,I^\star)$	$S_1(y_1,x_1)$	$R_1(x_1,x)$	$R_2(x,x_2)$	$S_2(x_2,y_2)$	$T(x_1,x',x_2)$	$U(x,x'',y_3)$	$V(x_3,y_2,y_3)$	$Q(I)$
$0,\triangleleft,\triangleright$	$\diamond\triangleleft\triangleright,0\triangleleft\triangleright$	$0\triangleleft\triangleright,0\triangleleft\triangleright$	$0\triangleleft\triangleright,0\triangleleft\triangleright$	$0\triangleleft\triangleright,\diamond\triangleleft\triangleright$	$0\triangleleft\triangleright,0\triangleleft\triangleright,0\triangleleft\triangleright$	$0\triangleleft\triangleright,0\triangleleft\triangleright,\diamond\triangleleft\triangleright$	$\diamond\triangleleft\triangleright,\diamond\triangleleft\triangleright,\diamond\triangleleft\triangleright$	$\diamond\triangleleft\triangleright,\diamond\triangleleft\triangleright,\diamond\triangleleft\triangleright$
$0,\triangleleft,b$	$\diamond\triangleleft\triangleright,0\triangleleft\triangleright$	$0\triangleleft\triangleright,0\triangleleft\triangleright$	$0\triangleleft\triangleright,0\triangleleft b$	$0\triangleleft b,\diamond\triangleleft b$	$0\triangleleft\triangleright,0\triangleleft b,0\triangleleft b$	$0\triangleleft\triangleright,0\triangleleft\triangleright,\diamond\triangleleft\triangleright$	$\diamond\triangleleft b,\diamond\triangleleft b,\diamond\triangleleft\triangleright$	$\diamond\triangleleft\triangleright,\diamond\triangleleft b,\diamond\triangleleft\triangleright$
$0,a,\triangleright$	$\diamond a\triangleright,0 a\triangleright$	$0 a\triangleright,0\triangleleft\triangleright$	$0\triangleleft\triangleright,0\triangleleft\triangleright$	$0\triangleleft\triangleright,\diamond\triangleleft\triangleright$	$0 a\triangleright,0 a\triangleright,0\triangleleft\triangleright$	$0\triangleleft\triangleright,0\triangleleft\triangleright,\diamond\triangleleft\triangleright$	$\diamond\triangleleft\triangleright,\diamond\triangleleft\triangleright,\diamond\triangleleft\triangleright$	$\diamond a\triangleright,\diamond\triangleleft\triangleright,\diamond\triangleleft\triangleright$
$0,a,b$	$\diamond a\triangleright,0 a\triangleright$	$0 a\triangleright,0\triangleleft\triangleright$	$0\triangleleft\triangleright,0\triangleleft b$	$0\triangleleft b,\diamond\triangleleft b$	$0 a\triangleright,0 a\triangleright,0\triangleleft b$	$0\triangleleft\triangleright,0\triangleleft\triangleright,\diamond\triangleleft h$	$\diamond\triangleleft b,\diamond\triangleleft b,\diamond\triangleleft\triangleright$	$\diamond a\triangleright,\diamond\triangleleft b,\diamond\triangleleft\triangleright$
$1,\triangleleft,\triangleright$	$\diamond\triangleleft\triangleright,1\triangleleft\triangleright$	$1\triangleleft\triangleright,1\triangleleft\triangleright$	$1\triangleleft\triangleright,1\triangleleft\triangleright$	$1\triangleleft\triangleright,\diamond\triangleleft\triangleright$	$1\triangleleft\triangleright,1\triangleleft\triangleright,1\triangleleft\triangleright$	$1\triangleleft\triangleright,1\triangleleft\triangleright,\diamond\triangleleft\triangleright$	$\diamond\triangleleft\triangleright,\diamond\triangleleft\triangleright,\diamond\triangleleft\triangleright$	$\diamond\triangleleft\triangleright,\diamond\triangleleft\triangleright,\diamond\triangleleft\triangleright$
$1,c,\triangleright$	$\diamond c\triangleright,1 c\triangleright$	$1 c\triangleright,1\triangleleft\triangleright$	$1\triangleleft\triangleright,1\triangleleft\triangleright$	$1\triangleleft\triangleright,\diamond\triangleleft\triangleright$	$1 c\triangleright,1 c\triangleright,1\triangleleft\triangleright$	$1\triangleleft\triangleright,1\triangleleft\triangleright,\diamond\triangleleft\triangleright$	$\diamond\triangleleft\triangleright,\diamond\triangleleft\triangleright,\diamond\triangleleft\triangleright$	$\diamond c\triangleright,\diamond\triangleleft\triangleright,\diamond\triangleleft\triangleright$
$0,\triangleleft,\triangleright$	$\diamond\triangleleft\triangleright,0\triangleleft\triangleright$	$0\triangleleft\triangleright,\heartsuit_0^{\phi_T}$	$\heartsuit_0^{\phi_T},0\triangleleft\triangleright$	$0\triangleleft\triangleright,\diamond\triangleleft\triangleright$	$0\triangleleft\triangleright,0\triangleleft\triangleright,0\triangleleft\triangleright$	$\heartsuit_0^{\phi_T},\heartsuit_0^{\phi_T},\heartsuit_0^{\phi_T}$	$\heartsuit_0^{\phi_T},\diamond\triangleleft\triangleright,\heartsuit_0^{\phi_T}$	$\diamond\triangleleft\triangleright,\diamond\triangleleft\triangleright,\heartsuit_0^{\phi_T}$
$1,\triangleleft,\triangleright$	$\diamond\triangleleft\triangleright,1\triangleleft\triangleright$	$1\triangleleft\triangleright,\heartsuit_1^{\phi_T}$	$\heartsuit_1^{\phi_T},1\triangleleft\triangleright$	$1\triangleleft\triangleright,\diamond\triangleleft\triangleright$	$1\triangleleft\triangleright,1\triangleleft\triangleright,1\triangleleft\triangleright$	$\heartsuit_1^{\phi_T},\heartsuit_1^{\phi_T},\heartsuit_1^{\phi_T}$	$\heartsuit_1^{\phi_T},\diamond\triangleleft\triangleright,\heartsuit_1^{\phi_T}$	$\diamond\triangleleft\triangleright,\diamond\triangleleft\triangleright,\heartsuit_1^{\phi_T}$

Figure 4: **The instance I constructed in the running example (introduced in Example 5.1)**

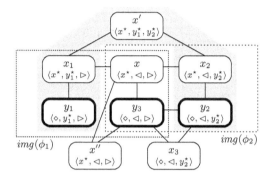

Figure 5: $\mathcal{G}_\vee(Q)$ **in the running example (introduced in Example 5.1)**

an instance of **S** (i.e., all fds are satisfied). The proof uses Part 1 of Theorem 4.2.

LEMMA 5.4. *I_Θ satisfies every fd of Δ.*

The next lemma, which is central to the correctness of our construction, states that there are no matches for Q in I_Θ except for the instantiations of Θ (used for constructing I_Θ).

LEMMA 5.5. *$\mathcal{M}(Q,I_\Theta) = \{\Theta_\mu \mid \mu \in \mathcal{M}(Q^\star,I^\star)\}$.*

The tuple **a** (in the input for $\text{FREEDP}\langle \mathbf{S},Q\rangle$) is the one obtained from **y** by replacing each variable y with the triple $\langle \diamond, \triangleleft, \triangleright \rangle$. As as example, with our shorthand notation the tuple **a** in our running example is $(\diamond\triangleleft\triangleright, \diamond\triangleleft\triangleright, \diamond\triangleleft\triangleright)$.

Up to now, we showed how to construct I_Θ and **a** from the input $I^\star$ and $\mathbf{a}^\star$ for $\text{FREEDP}\langle \mathbf{S}^\star,Q^\star\rangle$, given parameters for the template construction. For our reduction, can we can use I_Θ and **a** directly as input for $\text{FREEDP}\langle \mathbf{S},Q\rangle$? As stated later in Lemma 5.7, the existence of a side-effect-free solution for $I^\star$ and $\mathbf{a}^\star$ implies the existence of a side-effect-free solution for I_Θ and **a**. But the other direction is not necessarily true: there may be a side-effect-free solution for I_Θ and **a** even if no such a solution exists for $I^\star$ and $\mathbf{a}^\star$.

EXAMPLE 5.6. Consider again the instances $I^\star$ and I_Θ, and the tuples $\mathbf{a}^\star$ and **a**, constructed in our running example. Recall that I_Θ is depicted in the top part of the table in Figure 4. Recall from Example 5.1 that there is no side-effect-free solution for $I^\star$ and $\mathbf{a}^\star$. But *there is* a side-effect-free solution for I and **a**. To see that, observe (in Figure 4) that the facts $f_0 = T(0\triangleleft\triangleright, 0\triangleleft\triangleright, 0\triangleleft\triangleright)$ and $f_1 = T(1\triangleleft\triangleright, 1\triangleleft\triangleright, 1\triangleleft\triangleright)$ are used exactly in those matches that produce **a**. Lemma 5.5 implies that Figure 4 has all the answers for Q in I_Θ. So, by removing f_1 and f_2 from I_Θ we get a solution that is side-effect free. $\square$

The "problem" illustrated in Example 5.6 is that one of the atoms ϕ, specifically $T(x_1,x',x_2)$, is such that $\Theta(\phi)$ contains both $y_1^\star$ and $y_2^\star$. Indeed, in the example both of $y_1^\star$ and $y_2^\star$ appear in $\Theta(x')$. An atom ϕ of Q such that $\Theta(\phi)$ contains both $y_1^\star$ and $y_2^\star$ (not necessarily in the image of a single variable) is called an *encounter*. Following is a key lemma that will later guide us in the further definition of the reduction. This lemma shows that, under some condition, the reduction thus far is "correct" up to the issue of Example 5.6. That is, the existence of a side-effect-free solution for $I^\star$ and $\mathbf{a}^\star$ implies the existence of a side-effect-free solution for I_Θ and **a**, and on the other direction, the existence of a side-effect-free solution J_Θ for I_Θ and **a** implies the existence of a side-effect-free solution for $I^\star$ and $\mathbf{a}^\star$ *provided that J_Θ does not miss any of the facts over the encounters.*

LEMMA 5.7. *Suppose that P has two non-encounters γ_1 and γ_2, such that $\Theta(\gamma_1)$ contains $y_1^\star$ and $\Theta(\gamma_2)$ contains $y_2^\star$. Then, the following are equivalent.*
1. *There is a side-effect-free solution for $I^\star$ and $\mathbf{a}^\star$.*
2. *There is a side-effect-free solution J_Θ for I_Θ and **a**, such that $R_\phi^{J_\Theta} = R_\phi^{I_\Theta}$ for all encounters ϕ.*

In the next section, we branch into cases, based on properties of **S** and Q, and show how we build on Lemma 5.7 to complete the reduction in each of these cases.

5.3 Cases

We proceed by considering different cases, where in each case we specify the parameters for the template construction. We use the following terminology. A set Z of variables is *simultaneously determined* if there is an atom ϕ of Q, such that $Z \subseteq img(\phi)$. Two variables z_1 and z_2 are *fd-separable* if there is an atom ϕ of Q with the following properties:
- $img(\phi)$ contains neither z_1 nor z_2.
- ϕ fd-separates z_1 from z_2.

Case 1: *P has two head variables y_1 and y_2 that are not simultaneously determined.*

The variables y_1 and y_2 will act as parameters for the template construction. With y_1 and y_2 chosen, we branch into two sub-cases, where in each sub-case we choose the parameters ϕ_1 and ϕ_2 differently.

Case 1.a: *y_1 and y_2 are fd-separable.*

In Case 1.a, we choose an atom ϕ, such that ϕ fd-separates y_1 from y_2 and $img(\phi)$ contains neither y_1 nor y_2.

LEMMA 5.8. *In Case 1.a, $\phi \in P$.*

Now, both parameters ϕ_1 and ϕ_2 are chosen to be ϕ. Recall that ϕ_1 and ϕ_2 are required to be in P, so this choice is justified by Lemma 5.8.

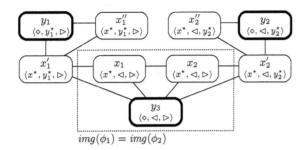

$$img(\phi_1) = img(\phi_2)$$

Figure 6: Case 1.a—$\mathcal{G}_v(Q)$ in Example 5.9

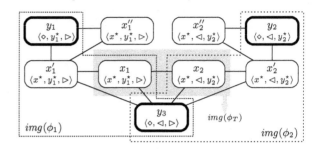

Figure 7: Case 1.b—$\mathcal{G}_v(Q)$ in Example 5.12

EXAMPLE 5.9. Consider the following CQ.

$$Q(y_1, y_2, y_3) :- S_1(x''_1, y_1, x'_1), R_1(x'_1, y_3, x_1),$$
$$T(x_1, x_2), R_2(x_2, y_3, x'_2), S_2(x'_2, y_2, x''_2)$$

The schema **S** has the relation symbols of Q (with the corresponding arities). In addition, **S** has the following fds.

$$R_1 : 3 \to 2 \qquad S_1 : 3 \to 2 \qquad S_2 : 1 \to 2$$

It is easy to verify that $\mathcal{G}_\exists(Q)$ is connected (i.e., has just one connected component), and that no atom ϕ satisfies $\{y_1, y_2\} \subseteq img(\phi)$. Therefore, y_1 and y_2 are not simultaneously determined, and we are in Case 1. Figure 6 shows the graph $\mathcal{G}_v(Q)$. Surrounded by a rectangle (with dotted edges) is the set $img(\phi_T)$, where ϕ_T is the atom $T(x_1, x_2)$. As can be seen in the figure, neither y_1 nor y_2 appears in $img(\phi_T)$, and $img(\phi_T)$ separates y_1 from y_2. Therefore, y_1 and y_2 are fd-separable, and we are in Case 1.a. As ϕ_1 and ϕ_2 we select the atom ϕ_T (actually, ϕ_T is the only possible choice). Finally, having chosen all the parameters of the template construction, the box of each variable z in Figure 6 contains the triple $\Theta(z)$. □

Observe the following for the CQ Q over the schema **S** in Example 5.9 (with $\mathcal{G}_v(Q)$ depicted in Figure 6). First, none of the atoms are encounters. Second, $\Theta(y_1)$ contains $y_1^\star$ and $\Theta(y_2)$ contains $y_2^\star$. The following lemma shows that these observations always hold in Case 1.a. This lemma is useful, since it suffices for completing the reduction in Case 1.a.

LEMMA 5.10. *In Case 1.a, $\Theta(y_i)$ contains $y_i^\star$ for $i = 1, 2$, and there are no encounters.*

So, for the instance I of our reduction from the problem FREEDP$\langle \mathbf{S}^\star, Q^\star \rangle$ to FREEDP$\langle \mathbf{S}, Q \rangle$ we simply choose $I = I_\Theta$. Based on Lemma 5.10, we can now apply Lemma 5.7 with γ_1 and γ_2 being any atoms in P that contain y_1 and y_2, respectively.

COROLLARY 5.11. *In Case 1.a, there is a side-effect-free solution for $I^\star$ and $\mathbf{a}^\star$ if and only if there is a side-effect-free solution for I and $\mathbf{a}$.*

Still within Case 1, the next case we consider is the complement of Case 1.a.

Case 1.b: y_1 and y_2 are not fd-separable.

In Case 1.b, we choose the atoms $\phi_1, \phi_2 \in P$ (used as parameters of the template construction) as follows. The atom ϕ_1 is such that $y_1 \in img(\phi_1)$ (hence, $y_2 \notin img(\phi_1)$)

since we are in Case 1) and $fdSep(\phi_1, y_2)$ has the maximal number of elements among the atoms $\phi \in P$ that satisfy $y_1 \in img(\phi)$. (Actually, it is enough for $fdSep(\phi_1, y_2)$ not to be strictly contained in any $fdSep(\phi, y_2)$ for those atoms ϕ.) The atom ϕ_2 is selected similarly, except that y_1 and y_2 swap roles. This manner of selecting ϕ_1 and ϕ_2 is crucial for the correctness of our reduction.

EXAMPLE 5.12. Consider again the CQ Q and schema **S** of Example 5.9, except that now we assume that the fds of **S** are the following.

$$R_1 : \{3, 2\} \to 1 \quad R_2 : \{1, 2\} \to 3 \quad S_1 : 3 \to 2 \quad S_2 : 1 \to 2$$

Like in Example 5.9, y_1 and y_2 are not simultaneously determined, which means that we are in Case 1. Figure 7 shows the graph $\mathcal{G}_v(Q)$. Unlike Example 5.9, now the set $img(\phi_T)$ contains just x_1 and x_2, and as can be seen in Figure 7 the atom ϕ_T no longer fd-separates y_1 from y_2. Actually, it is easy to see that for each atom ϕ of Q it holds that $img(\phi)$ either contains one of y_1 and y_2 or does not separate y_1 from y_2. We are therefore in Case 1.b.

The atoms ϕ with $y_1 \in img(\phi)$ are ϕ_{R_1} and ϕ_{S_1}, namely, $R_1(x'_1, y_3, x_1)$ and $S_1(x''_1, y_1, x'_1)$, respectively. We have:

$$fdSep(\phi_{R_1}, y_2) = \{x''_1, y_1, x'_1, x_1, y_3\}$$
$$fdSep(\phi_{S_1}, y_2) = \{x''_1, y_1, x'_1\}$$

Since $|fdSep(\phi_{R_1}, y_2)| > |fdSep(\phi_{S_1}, y_2)|$, we choose $\phi_1 = \phi_{R_1}$. We similarly choose $\phi_2 = \phi_{R_2}$. In Figure 7, the sets $img(\phi_1)$ and $img(\phi_2)$ are surrounded by polygons with dotted edges. Finally, with all parameters chosen, the box of each variable z in Figure 7 contains the triple $\Theta(z)$. □

Note that in Example 5.12, the atom ϕ_T (i.e., $T(x_1, x_2)$) is an encounter, since $\Theta(x_1)$ contains $y_1^\star$ and $\Theta(x_2)$ contains $y_2^\star$. In particular, we cannot just set $I = I_\Theta$ as in Case 1.a: similarly to Example 5.6 it can be shown that there is always a side-effect-free solution for I_Θ and $\mathbf{a}$, no matter what $I^\star$ and $\mathbf{a}^\star$ are. In the following section, we deal with encounters for both this case and Case 2, which we discuss next.

Case 2: *Every two head variables of P are simultaneously determined.*

In Case 2, the selection of the parameters for the template construction is more intricate than in the previous cases. For lack of space, here we do not provide the justification for this selection, and refer the reader to the full proof [13]. We first look at the sets $Z \subseteq \mathsf{Var_h}(P)$ that are simultaneously determined by an atom of P, and among those we select a Z_1 with a maximal cardinality. Note that Z_1 is a strict subset of $\mathsf{Var_h}(P)$, due to our assumption that P violates the tractability condition. Also note that Z_1 may be a strict subset of $\mathsf{Var_h}(\phi)$ for some atom $\phi \notin P$. Next, among those sets Z that are *not* contained in Z_1, we again select a set Z_2 with a maximal cardinality. Note that neither $Z_1 \subseteq Z_2$ nor $Z_2 \subseteq Z_1$ holds. So, as y_1 we select an element of $Z_1 \setminus Z_2$, and as y_2 we select an element of $Z_2 \setminus Z_1$. Finally, we consider the atoms $\phi \in P$ with $img(\phi) \cap \mathsf{Var_h}(P) = Z_1$ and select ϕ_1 to be a ϕ with a maximal $|fdSep(\phi, y_2)|$. Similarly, we consider the atoms $\phi \in P$ with $img(\phi) \cap \mathsf{Var_h}(P) = Z_2$, and select ϕ_2 to be a ϕ with a maximal $|fdSep(\phi, y_1)|$. We now have all four parameters needed for the template construction.

EXAMPLE 5.13. An example of Case 2 is the CQ Q over the schema $\mathbf{S}$ in our running example (introduced in Example 5.1). Indeed, y_1 and y_2 are simultaneously determined (by ϕ_T), and so are y_1 and y_3 (by ϕ_{R_1}) as well as y_2 and y_3 (by ϕ_{R_2}). In a possible parameter setting, Z_1 is $\{y_1, y_3\}$, Z_2 is $\{y_2, y_3\}$, and the parameters are y_1, y_2, ϕ_{R_1} and ϕ_{R_2}. Recall that Figure 5 shows $\mathcal{G}_v(Q)$ along with $\Theta(z)$ for each $z \in \mathsf{Var}(Q)$. The sets $img(\phi_1)$ and $img(\phi_2)$ are surrounded by boxes with dotted edges. Observe that $T(x_1, x', x_2)$ is an encounter (since $\Theta(x')$ contains both $y_1^\star$ and $y_2^\star$). $\quad\square$

As shown in Example 5.13 (and previously in Example 5.6), in Case 2 there may be encounters, and we deal with those in the next section. Still, the following lemma states that for this case, as well as Case 1.b, we can use ϕ_1 and ϕ_2 as γ_1 and γ_2, respectively, in Lemma 5.7. Again, Part 1 of Theorem 4.2 is used in the proof.

LEMMA 5.14. *In Cases 1.b and 2, each ϕ_i ($i = 1, 2$) is a non-encounter, and $\Theta(\phi_i)$ contains $y_i^\star$.*

5.4 Handling Encounters

Our approach to handling encounters (in Cases 1.b and 2) is as follows. Let ϕ is an encounter. Denote by $\mathcal{M}_{\mathbf{a}^\star}(Q^\star, I^\star)$ the set of all matches $\mu \in \mathcal{M}(Q^\star, I^\star)$ with $\mu(y_1^\star, y_2^\star) = \mathbf{a}^\star$. As illustrated in Example 5.6, we can always obtain a side-effect-free solution for I_Θ and $\mathbf{a}$ by deleting from I_Θ all the facts of the form $\Theta_\mu(\phi)$ where $\mu \in \mathcal{M}_{\mathbf{a}^\star}(Q^\star, I^\star)$. The idea is to make each such $\Theta_\mu(\phi)$ necessary for a side-effect-free solution. This is done by adding to I_Θ facts so that in the resulting instance I, there are new answers for which every $\Theta_\mu(\phi)$ is needed. An idea in this spirit was used by Kimelfeld et al. [14], but details greatly differ as they did not handle fds. The addition of facts is such that if there is a side-effect-free solution for $I^\star$ and $\mathbf{a}^\star$ then there is still a side-effect-free solution for I and $\mathbf{a}$. Moreover, if J is a side-effect-free solution for I and $\mathbf{a}$, then J necessarily contains all the facts $\Theta_\mu(\phi)$ where $\mu \in \mathcal{M}_{\mathbf{a}^\star}(Q^\star, I^\star)$; we will then be able to assume that $J_\Theta = J \cap I_\Theta$ contains $R_\phi^{I_\Theta}$, and finally apply Lemma 5.7 to conclude the existence of a side-effect-free solution for $I^\star$ and $\mathbf{a}^\star$. Next, we give the details.

Let ϕ be an encounter, and let $\mu_c \in \mathcal{M}_{\mathbf{a}^\star}(Q^\star, I^\star)$ be a match with $\mu_c(x^\star) = c$. We define the assignment ν_c^ϕ for Q, as follows. In Case 1.b:

$$\nu_c^\phi(z) \stackrel{\text{def}}{=} \begin{cases} \Theta_{\mu_c}(z) & \text{if } z \in fdSep(\phi, y_1) \cap fdSep(\phi, y_2); \\ \heartsuit_c^\phi & \text{otherwise.} \end{cases}$$

And in Case 2:

$$\nu_c^\phi(z) \stackrel{\text{def}}{=} \begin{cases} \Theta_{\mu_c}(z) & \text{if } z \in \bigcap_{y \in \mathsf{Var_h}(P)} fdSep(\phi, y); \\ \heartsuit_c^\phi & \text{otherwise.} \end{cases}$$

Here, $\heartsuit_c^\phi$ is a fresh new constant that is unique to ϕ and c. Note that $z \in \bigcap_{y \in \mathsf{Var_h}(p)} fdSep(\phi, y)$ means that in $\mathcal{G}_v(Q)$, the set $img(\phi)$ separates z from every head variable y of P.

As an example, consider Q and $\mathbf{S}$ from Example 5.12, which fall in Case 1.b. There is a single encounter, namely $\phi_T = T(x_1, x_2)$. In Figure 7, the set $img(\phi_T)$ is shaded by a grey rectangle. Since every variable $z \notin \{x_1, x_2\}$ is reachable from y_1 (and y_2) by a path that does not visit $img(\phi_T)$, we have $\nu_c^{\phi_T}(z) = \heartsuit_c^{\phi_T}$ for $z \notin \{x_1, x_2\}$, while $\nu_c^{\phi_T}(z) = \Theta_{\mu_c}(z)$ for $z \in \{x_1, x_2\}$. Example 5.16 will discuss Case 2.

Finally, to construct I we start with $I = I_\Theta$, and for each encounter ϕ, assignment ν_c^ϕ and atom γ of Q, we add to I the fact $\nu_c^\phi(\gamma)$ (unless it is already in I). The following lemma states that I is a legal instance over $\mathbf{S}$. Again, the proof uses Part 1 of Theorem 4.2.

LEMMA 5.15. *In Cases 1.b and 2, I satisfies each fd of $\mathbf{S}$.*

EXAMPLE 5.16. We continue with our running example, which falls in Case 2. There is a single encounter: $\phi_T = T(x_1, x', x_2)$. As shown in Figure 4, there are two matches in $\mathcal{M}_{\mathbf{a}^\star}(Q^\star, I^\star)$: the one of the first row maps $x^\star$ to 0, and the one of the fifth row maps $x^\star$ to 1; let us call these matches μ_0 and μ_1, respectively. In Figure 5, the set $img(\phi_T)$ is shaded by a grey polytope. Since $img(\phi_T)$ does not separate any node from y_3, except for the nodes in $img(\phi_T)$ itself, we have $\nu_0^{\phi_T}(z) = \heartsuit_0^{\phi_T}$ and $\nu_1^{\phi_T}(z) = \heartsuit_1^{\phi_T}$ for $z \notin img(\phi_T)$, and $\nu_0^{\phi_T}(z) = \Theta_{\mu_0}(z)$ and $\nu_1^{\phi_T}(z) = \Theta_{\mu_1}(z)$ for $z \in img(\phi_T)$. The facts that are added to construct I are in the bottom two rows of Figure 4. $\quad\square$

For proving the correctness of the reduction, we show that for all encounters ϕ and matches $\mu_c \in \mathcal{M}_{\mathbf{a}^\star}(Q^\star, I^\star)$, the mapping ν_c^ϕ maps ϕ to $\Theta_{\mu_c}(\phi)$, and moreover, gives rise to a unique new answer that contains at least one occurrence of $\heartsuit_c^\phi$. (See Figure 4 for illustration.) In particular, $\Theta_{\mu_c}(\phi)$ is necessary for a side-effect-free solution. Based on that, we prove the following.

LEMMA 5.17. *In Cases 1.b and 2, these are equivalent:*
1. *There is a side-effect-free solution for I and $\mathbf{a}$.*
2. *There is a side-effect-free solution J_Θ for I_Θ and $\mathbf{a}$, such that $R_\phi^{J_\Theta} = R_\phi^{I_\Theta}$ for all encounters ϕ.*

The proof of Lemma 5.17 is fairly involved; moreover, Theorem 4.2 is used here again, now Parts 1 and 2. Finally, we get the correctness of the reduction (in Cases 1.b and 2) by combining Lemmas 5.7, 5.14, 5.15 and 5.17.

COROLLARY 5.18. *In Cases 1.b and 2, there is a side-effect-free solution for $I^\star$ and $\mathbf{a}^\star$ if and only if there is a side-effect-free solution for I and $\mathbf{a}$.*

5.5 Summary and Conclusion

To summarize this section, we fixed $\mathbf{S}$ and Q that violate the tractability condition, and showed a reduction from FREEDP$\langle \mathbf{S}^\star, Q^\star \rangle$ to FREEDP$\langle \mathbf{S}, Q \rangle$, taking the input $I^\star$ and $\mathbf{a}^\star$ for FREEDP$\langle \mathbf{S}^\star, Q^\star \rangle$ and constructing the input I and $\mathbf{a}$ for FREEDP$\langle \mathbf{S}, Q \rangle$. We started with $I = I_\Theta$, which we built by means of the assignments Θ_μ, using the template assignment Θ. To handle encounters, we added tuples to I using the assignments ν_c^ϕ. The correctness of the reduction was stated in Corollaries 5.11 and 5.18. Combined with the observation that the construction of I and $\mathbf{a}$ takes polynomial time, we get the main result of this section.

THEOREM 5.19. *If Q^+ does not have functional head domination, then* FREEDP$\langle \mathbf{S}, Q \rangle$ *is NP-complete.*

6. MAIN RESULT

In this section, we state the complexity dichotomy established in the previous sections, and further strengthen it by considering (hardness of) approximation.

6.1 Dichotomy

Combining Theorems 3.11 and 5.19, we get the main result of this paper, stating that for an sjf-CQ Q over a schema $\mathbf{S}$ the complexities of MAXDP$\langle \mathbf{S}, Q \rangle$ and FREEDP$\langle \mathbf{S}, Q \rangle$ are precisely determined by the satisfaction of the tractability condition (i.e., Q^+ has functional head domination).

THEOREM 6.1. *Let Q be an sjf-CQ over a schema $\mathbf{S}$.*

- *If Q^+ has functional head domination, then* UniRel$\langle \mathbf{S}, Q \rangle$ *optimally solves* MAXDP$\langle \mathbf{S}, Q \rangle$ *(in polynomial-time).*

- *If Q^+ does not have functional head domination, then* FREEDP$\langle \mathbf{S}, Q \rangle$ *is NP-complete.*

6.2 Hardness of Approximation

For a number $\alpha \in [0,1]$, a solution J is α-*optimal* if $|Q(J)| \geq \alpha \cdot |Q(K)|$ for all solutions K. Kimelfeld et al. [14] showed that for an sjf-CQ Q over a schema $\mathbf{S}$ without fds, when MAXDP$\langle \mathbf{S}, Q \rangle$ is NP-hard, it cannot be approximated better than some constant $\alpha_Q \in (0,1)$ unless P = NP. For that, they showed a PTAS reduction from MAXDP$\langle \mathbf{S}^\star, Q^\star \rangle$ to MAXDP$\langle \mathbf{S}, Q \rangle$ (i.e., the reduction is such that for all α there is α_Q, such that an α_Q-approximation for the generated MAXDP$\langle \mathbf{S}, Q \rangle$ instance gives an α-approximation for the original MAXDP$\langle \mathbf{S}^\star, Q^\star \rangle$ instance), rather than a reduction from FREEDP$\langle \mathbf{S}^\star, Q^\star \rangle$ to FREEDP$\langle \mathbf{S}, Q \rangle$ as given here. Nevertheless, using ideas very similar to those in the construction of Kimelfeld et al. [14] (specifically, using multiple copies of the constant $\heartsuit_c^\phi$), we can adjust the reduction of Section 5 to a PTAS reduction.[1] As a result, we get the following addition to the hardness part of Theorem 6.1.

THEOREM 6.2. *Let Q be an sjf-CQ over a schema $\mathbf{S}$. If Q^+ does not have functional head domination, then there is a constant α_Q such that it is NP-hard to α_Q-approximate* MAXDP$\langle \mathbf{S}, Q \rangle$.

Combining Theorems 6.1 and 6.2, we conclude the following about MAXDP$\langle \mathbf{S}, Q \rangle$ for an sjf-CQ Q over a schema $\mathbf{S}$. Either the problem is straightforward, or our ability to even approximate it is limited.

The dependency of the constant α_Q on Q is already known to be unavoidable [14]: for each constant $\alpha \in (0,1)$ there is an sjf-CQ Q_α over a schema $\mathbf{S}$ without fds, such that Q_α does not have (functional) head domination, and yet, MAXDP$\langle \mathbf{S}, Q \rangle$ is α-approximable in polynomial time (and by the unirelation algorithm). In other words, there is no global α that can replace all the α_Q in Theorem 6.2.

---

[1]We gave a reduction from FREEDP$\langle \mathbf{S}^\star, Q^\star \rangle$ to FREEDP$\langle \mathbf{S}, Q \rangle$, rather than a PTAS one from MAXDP$\langle \mathbf{S}^\star, Q^\star \rangle$ to MAXDP$\langle \mathbf{S}, Q \rangle$, since it greatly simplifies the presentation, yet still, entails essentially all of the novelty.

7. CONCLUSIONS

The complexity dichotomy established in this paper shows how exactly functional dependencies extend the class of sjf-CQs where maximum deletion propagation is in polynomial time. On the negative side, it shows that if optimal solutions (or arbitrarily good approximations, e.g., PTAS) are sought, then even with functional dependencies there are no tractable sjf-CQs beyond those that the straightforward unirelation algorithm handles. Many natural directions are left for future work. Among them are exploring CQs with self joins (with or without fds), utilizing fds to generalize and improve upon approximation algorithms [14], handling additional constraints (like general equality-generating dependencies [2] and foreign keys), and extending our results to deletion of multiple tuples (a.k.a. group deletion [4]).

Acknowledgments

The author is grateful to Jan Vondrák for helpful and insightful discussions, and to Phokion G. Kolaitis for being a source of education and inspiration for this work.

8. REFERENCES

[1] F. Bancilhon and N. Spyratos. Update semantics of relational views. *ACM Trans. Database Syst.*, 6(4):557–575, 1981.

[2] C. Beeri and M. Y. Vardi. A proof procedure for data dependencies. *J. ACM*, 31(4):718–741, 1984.

[3] P. Buneman, S. Khanna, and W. C. Tan. On propagation of deletions and annotations through views. In *PODS*, pages 150–158, 2002.

[4] G. Cong, W. Fan, and F. Geerts. Annotation propagation revisited for key preserving views. In *CIKM*, pages 632–641, 2006.

[5] G. Cong, W. Fan, F. Geerts, J. Li, and J. Luo. On the complexity of view update analysis and its application to annotation propagation. *IEEE Trans. Knowl. Data Eng.*, 24(3):506–519, 2012.

[6] S. S. Cosmadakis and C. H. Papadimitriou. Updates of relational views. *J. ACM*, 31(4):742–760, 1984.

[7] Y. Cui and J. Widom. Run-time translation of view tuple deletions using data lineage. Technical report, Stanford University, 2001. http://dbpubs.stanford.edu:8090/pub/2001-24.

[8] N. N. Dalvi, K. Schnaitter, and D. Suciu. Computing query probability with incidence algebras. In *PODS*, pages 203–214, 2010.

[9] N. N. Dalvi and D. Suciu. Efficient query evaluation on probabilistic databases. *VLDB J.*, 16(4):523–544, 2007.

[10] U. Dayal and P. A. Bernstein. On the correct translation of update operations on relational views. *ACM Trans. Database Syst.*, 7(3):381–416, 1982.

[11] R. Fagin, J. D. Ullman, and M. Y. Vardi. On the semantics of updates in databases. In *PODS*, pages 352–365. ACM, 1983.

[12] A. M. Keller. Algorithms for translating view updates to database updates for views involving selections, projections, and joins. In *PODS*, pages 154–163. ACM, 1985.

[13] B. Kimelfeld. A dichotomy in the complexity of deletion propagation with functional dependencies (extended version). Accessible from the author's home page, 2012.

[14] B. Kimelfeld, J. Vondrák, and R. Williams. Maximizing conjunctive views in deletion propagation. In *PODS*, pages 187–198, 2011.

[15] P. G. Kolaitis and E. Pema. A dichotomy in the complexity of consistent query answering for queries with two atoms. In press, 2011.

[16] D. Maslowski and J. Wijsen. On counting database repairs. In *LID*, pages 15–22, 2011.

[17] A. Meliou, W. Gatterbauer, J. Y. Halpern, C. Koch, K. F. Moore, and D. Suciu. Causality in databases. *IEEE Data Eng. Bull.*, 33(3):59–67, 2010.

[18] A. Meliou, W. Gatterbauer, K. F. Moore, and D. Suciu. The complexity of causality and responsibility for query answers and non-answers. *PVLDB*, 4(1):34–45, 2010.

The Wavelet Trie: Maintaining an
Indexed Sequence of Strings in Compressed Space[*]

Roberto Grossi
Dipartimento di Informatica
Università di Pisa, Italy
grossi@di.unipi.it

Giuseppe Ottaviano[†]
Dipartimento di Informatica
Università di Pisa, Italy
ottavian@di.unipi.it

ABSTRACT

An *indexed sequence of strings* is a data structure for storing a *string sequence* that supports random access, searching, range counting and analytics operations, both for exact matches and prefix search. String sequences lie at the core of column-oriented databases, log processing, and other storage and query tasks. In these applications each string can appear several times and the order of the strings in the sequence is relevant. The prefix structure of the strings is relevant as well: common prefixes are sought in strings to extract interesting features from the sequence. Moreover, space-efficiency is highly desirable as it translates directly into higher performance, since more data can fit in fast memory.

We introduce and study the problem of *compressed indexed sequence of strings*, representing indexed sequences of strings in nearly-optimal compressed space, both in the static and dynamic settings, while preserving provably good performance for the supported operations.

We present a new data structure for this problem, the *Wavelet Trie*, which combines the classical Patricia Trie with the Wavelet Tree, a succinct data structure for storing a compressed sequence. The resulting Wavelet Trie smoothly adapts to a sequence of strings that changes over time. It improves on the state-of-the-art compressed data structures by supporting a dynamic alphabet (i.e. the set of distinct strings) and prefix queries, both crucial requirements in the aforementioned applications, and on traditional indexes by reducing space occupancy to close to the entropy of the sequence.

Categories and Subject Descriptors

E.1 [**Data**]: Data Structures—*Trees*; E.4 [**Data**]: Coding and Information Theory—*Data compaction and compression*

[†]Part of the work done while the author was an intern at Microsoft Research, Cambridge.

[*]Work partially supported by MIUR of Italy under project AlgoDEEP prot. 2008TFBWL4.

General Terms

Algorithms, Theory

Keywords

Wavelet Trie, Wavelet Tree, Compressed sequences, Indexing

1. INTRODUCTION

Many problems in databases and information retrieval ultimately reduce to storing and indexing sequences of strings. Column-oriented databases represent relations by storing individually each column as a sequence; if each column is indexed, efficient operations on the relations are possible. XML databases, taxonomies, and word tries are represented as labeled trees, and each tree can be mapped to the sequence of its labels in a specific order; indexed operations on the sequence enable fast tree navigation. In data analytics query logs and access logs are simply sequences of strings; aggregate queries and counting queries can be performed efficiently with specific indexes. Textual document search is essentially the problem of representing a text as the sequence of its words, and queries locate the occurrences of given words in the text. Even the storage of non-string (for example, numeric) data can be often reduced to the storage of strings, as usually the values can be binarized in a natural way.

Indexed sequence of strings. An *indexed sequence of strings* is a data structure for storing a *string sequence* that supports random access, searching, range counting and analytics operations, both for exact matches and prefix search. Each string can appear several times and the order of the strings in the sequence is relevant. For a sequence $S \equiv \langle s_0, \ldots, s_{n-1} \rangle$ of strings, the primitive operations are:

- Access(pos): retrieve string s_{pos}, where $0 \leq \text{pos} < n$.

- Rank(s, pos): count the number of occurrences of string s in $\langle s_0, \ldots, s_{\text{pos}-1} \rangle$.

- Select(s, idx): find the position of the idx-th occurrence of s in $\langle s_0, \ldots, s_{n-1} \rangle$.

By composing these three primitives it is possible to implement other powerful index operations. For example, functionality similar to inverted lists can be easily formulated in terms of Select. These primitives can be extended to prefixes.

- RankPrefix(p, pos): count the number of strings in $\langle s_0, \ldots, s_{\text{pos}-1} \rangle$ that have prefix p.

- SelectPrefix(p, idx): find the position of the idx-th string in $\langle s_0, \ldots, s_{n-1} \rangle$ that has prefix p.

Prefix search operations can be easily formulated in terms of SelectPrefix. Other useful operations are range counting and analytics operations, where the above primitives are generalized to a range $[\text{pos}', \text{pos})$ of positions, hence to $\langle s_{\text{pos}'}, \ldots, s_{\text{pos}-1} \rangle$. In this way statistically interesting (e.g. frequent) strings in the given range $[\text{pos}', \text{pos})$ and having a given prefix p can be quickly discovered (see Section 5 for further operations).

The sequence S can change over time by defining the following operations, for any arbitrary string s (which could be *previously unseen*).

- Insert(s, pos): update the sequence S as
  $S' \equiv \langle s_0, \ldots, s_{\text{pos}-1}, s, s_{\text{pos}}, \ldots, s_{n-1} \rangle$ by inserting s immediately before s_{pos}.

- Append(s): update the sequence S as
  $S' \equiv \langle s_0, \ldots, s_{n-1}, s \rangle$ by appending s at the end.

- Delete(pos): update the sequence S as
  $S' \equiv \langle s_0, \ldots, s_{\text{pos}-1}, s_{\text{pos}+1}, \ldots, s_{n-1} \rangle$ by deleting s_{pos}.

Motivation. String sequences lie at the core of column-oriented databases, log processing, and other storage and query tasks. The prefix operations supported by an indexed sequence of strings arise in many contexts. Here we give a few examples to show that the proposed problem is quite natural. In data analytics for query logs and access logs, the sequence order is the *time* order, so that a range of positions $[\text{pos}', \text{pos})$ corresponds to a given time frame. The accessed URLs, paths (filesystem, network, . . .) or any kind of hierarchical references are chronologically stored as a sequence $\langle s_0, \ldots, s_{n-1} \rangle$ of strings, and a common prefix denotes a common domain or a common folder for the given time frame: we can retrieve access statistics using RankPrefix and report the corresponding items by iterating SelectPrefix (e.g. "what has been the most accessed domain during winter vacation?"). This has a wide array of applications, from intrusion detection and website optimization to database storage of telephone calls. Another interesting example arises in web graphs and social networks, where a *binary relation* is stored as a graph among the entities, so that each edge is conceptually a pair of URLs or hierarchical references (URIs). Edges can change over time, so we can report what changed in the adjacency list of a given vertex in a given time frame, allowing us to produce snapshots on the fly (e.g. "how did friendship links change in that social network during winter vacation?"). In the above applications the many strings involved require a suitable compressed format. Space-efficiency is highly desirable as it translates directly into higher performance, since more data can fit in fast memory.

Compressed indexed sequence of strings. We introduce and study the problem of *compressed indexed sequence of strings* representing indexed sequences of strings in nearly-optimal compressed space, both in the static and dynamic settings, while preserving provably good performance for the supported operations.

Traditionally, indexed sequences are stored by representing the sequence explicitly and indexing it using auxiliary data structures, such as B-Trees, Hash Indexes, Bitmap Indexes. These data structures have excellent performance and both external and cache-oblivious variants are well studied [23]. Space efficiency is however sacrificed: the total occupancy is

several times the space of the sequence alone. In a latency constrained world where more and more data have to be kept in internal memory, this is not feasible anymore.

The field of succinct and compressed data structures comes to aid: there is a vast literature about compressed storage of sequences, under the name of Rank/Select sequences [15]. The existing Rank/Select data structures, however, assume that the alphabet from which the sequences are drawn is *integer* and *contiguous*, i.e. each element of the sequence is just a symbol in $\{1, \ldots, \sigma\}$. Non-integer or non-contiguous alphabets need to be mapped first to an integer range. Letting S_{set} denote the set of distinct strings in the sequence $S \equiv \langle s_0, \ldots, s_{n-1} \rangle$, the representation of S as a sequence of n integers in $\{1, \ldots, |S_{\text{set}}|\}$ requires to map each s_i to its corresponding integer, thus introducing at least two issues: (a) once the mapping is computed, it cannot be changed, which means that in dynamic operations the alphabet must be known in advance; (b) for string data the string structure is lost, hence no prefix operations can be supported. Issue (a) in particular rules out applications in database storage, as the set of values of a column (or even its cardinality) is very rarely known in advance; similarly in text indexing a new document can contain unseen words; in URL sequences, new URLs can be created at any moment.

Wavelet Trie. We introduce a new data structure, the *Wavelet Trie*, that overcomes the previously mentioned issues. The Wavelet Trie is a generalization for string sequences S of the Wavelet Tree [13], a compressed data structure for sequences, where the shape of the tree is induced from the structure of the string set S_{set} as in the Patricia Trie [19]. This enables efficient prefix operations and the ability to grow or shrink the alphabet as values are inserted or removed. We first present a static version of the Wavelet Trie in Section 3. We then give an append-only dynamic version of the Wavelet Trie, meaning that elements can be inserted only at the end—the typical scenario of query logs and access logs—and a fully dynamic version that is useful for database applications (see Section 4).

Our time bounds are reported in Table 1, and some comments are in order. Recall that S denotes the input sequence of strings stored in the Wavelet Trie, and S_{set} is the set of distinct strings in S. For a string s to be queried, let h_s denote the number of nodes traversed in the binary Patricia Tree storing S_{set} when s is searched for. Observe that $h_s \leq |s| \log |\Sigma|$, where Σ is the alphabet of symbols from which s is drawn, and $|s| \log |\Sigma|$ is the length in bits of s (while $|s|$ denotes its number of symbols as usual). The cost for the queries on the static and append-only versions of the Wavelet Trie is $O(|s| + h_s)$ time, which is the *same* cost as searching in the binary Patricia Trie. Surprisingly, the cost of appending s to S is still $O(|s| + h_s)$ time, which means that compressing and indexing a sequential log on the fly is very efficient. The cost of the operations for the fully dynamic version are also competitive, without the need of knowing the alphabet in advance. This answers positively a question posed in [12] and [18].

All versions are nearly optimal in space as shown in Table 1. In particular, the lower bound $\text{LB}(S)$ for storing an indexed sequence of strings can be derived from the lower bound $\text{LT}(S_{\text{set}})$ for storing S_{set} given in [7] plus Shannon classical zero-order entropy bound $nH_0(S)$ for storing S as a sequence of symbols. The static version uses an additional number of bits that is just a lower order term $o(\bar{h}n)$, where

	Query	Append	Insert	Delete	Space (in bits)
Static	$O(|s| + h_s)$	–	–	–	LB $+o(\tilde{h}n)$
Append-only	$O(|s| + h_s)$	$O(|s| + h_s)$	–	–	LB $+$ PT $+o(\tilde{h}n)$
Fully-dynamic	$O(|s| + h_s \log n)$	$O(|s| + h_s \log n)$	$O(|s| + h_s \log n)$	$O(|s| + h_s \log n)^\dagger$	LB $+$ PT $+O(nH_0)$

Table 1: **Bounds for the Wavelet Trie.** *Query* is the cost of Access, Rank(Prefix), Select(Prefix), LB is the information theoretic lower bound LT $+nH_0$ (Sect. 3), and PT the space taken by the dynamic Patricia Trie (Sect. 4). †Note that deletion may take $O(\hat{\ell} + h_s \log n)$ time when deleting the last occurrence of a string, where $\hat{\ell}$ is the length of the longest string in S_{set}.

$\tilde{h}$ is the average height of the Wavelet Tree (Definition 3.4). The append-only version only adds $\text{PT}(S_{\text{set}}) = O(|S_{\text{set}}| \log n)$ bits for keeping $O(|S_{\text{set}}|)$ pointers to the dynamically allocated memory (assuming that we do not have control on the memory allocator on the machine). The fully dynamic version has a redundancy of $O(nH_0(S))$ bits.

Results. Summing up the above contributions: we address a new problem on sequences of strings that is meaningful in real-life applications; we introduce a new compressed data structure, the Wavelet Trie, and analyze its nearly optimal space; we show that the supported operations are competitive with those of uncompressed data structures, both in the static and dynamic setting. We have further findings in this paper. In case the prefix operations are not needed (for example when the values are numeric), we show in Section 6 how to use a Wavelet Trie to maintain a probabilistically balanced Wavelet Tree, hence guaranteeing access times logarithmic in the alphabet size. Again, the alphabet does not need to be known in advance. We also present an append-only compressed bitvector that supports constant-time Rank, Select, and Append in nearly optimal space. We use this bitvector in the append-only Wavelet Trie.

Related work. While there has been extensive work on compressed representations for *sets* of strings, to the best of our knowledge the problem of representing *sequences* of strings has not been studied. Indexed sequences of strings are usually stored in the following ways: *(1)* by mapping the strings to integers through a dictionary, the problem is reduced to the storage of a sequence of integers; *(2)* by concatenating the strings with a separator, and compressing and full-text indexing the obtained string; *(3)* by storing the concatenation (s_i, i) in a string dictionary such as a B-Tree.

The approach in *(1)*, used implicitly in [3, 8] and most literature about Rank/Select sequences, sacrifices the ability to perform prefix queries. If the mapping preserves the lexicographic ordering, prefixes are mapped to contiguous ranges; this enables some prefix operations, by exploiting the two-dimensional nature of the Wavelet Tree: RankPrefix can be reduced to the RangeCount operation described in [17]. To the best of our knowledge, however, even with a lexicographic mapping there is no way to support efficiently SelectPrefix. More importantly, in the dynamic setting it is not possible to change the alphabet (the underlying string set S_{set}) without rebuilding the tree, as previously discussed.

The approach in *(2)*, called *Dynamic Text Collection* in [18], although it allows for potentially more powerful operations, is both slower, because it needs a search in the compressed text index, and less space-efficient, as it only compresses according to the k-order entropy of the string, failing to exploit the redundancy given by repeated strings.

The approach in *(3)*, used often in databases to implement indexes, only supports Select, while another copy of the sequence is still needed to support Access, and it does not support Rank. Furthermore, it offers little or no guaranteed compression ratio.

2. PRELIMINARIES

Information-theoretic lower bounds. We assume that all the logarithms are in base 2, and that the word size is $w \geq \log n$ bits. Let $s = c_1 \ldots c_n \in \Sigma^*$ be a sequence of length $|s| = n$, drawn from an alphabet Σ. The *binary representation* of s is a binary sequence of $n\lceil \log |\Sigma| \rceil$ bits, where each symbol c_i is replaced by the $\lceil \log |\Sigma| \rceil$ bits encoding it. The *zero-order empirical entropy* of s is defined as $H_0(s) = -\sum_{c \in \Sigma} \frac{n_c}{n} \log \frac{n_c}{n}$, where n_c is the number of occurrences of symbol c in s. Note that $nH_0(s) \leq n \log |\Sigma|$ is a lower bound on the bits needed to represent s with an encoder that does not exploit context information. If s is a binary sequence with $\Sigma = \{0, 1\}$ and p is the fraction of 1s in s, we can rewrite the entropy as $H_0(s) = -p \log p - (1 - p) \log(1 - p)$, which we also denote by $H(p)$. We use $\mathcal{B}(m, n)$ as a shorthand for $\lceil \log \binom{n}{m} \rceil$, the information-theoretic lower bound in bits for storing a set of m elements drawn from an universe of size n. We implicitly make extensive use of the bounds $\mathcal{B}(m, n) \leq nH(\frac{m}{n}) + O(1)$, and $\mathcal{B}(m, n) \leq m \log(\frac{n}{m}) + O(m)$.

Bitvectors and FIDs. Binary sequences, i.e. $\Sigma = \{0, 1\}$, are also called *bitvectors*, and data structures that encode a bitvector while supporting Access/Rank/Select are also called *Fully Indexed Dictionaries*, or *FIDs* [22]. The representation of [22], referred to as RRR, can encode a bitvector with n bits, of which m 1s, in $\mathcal{B}(m, n) + O((n \log \log n)/ \log n)$ bits, while supporting all the operations in constant time.

Wavelet Trees. The Wavelet Tree, introduced in [13], is the first data structure to extend Rank/Select operations from bitvectors to sequences on an arbitrary alphabet Σ, while keeping the sequence compressed. Wavelet Trees reduce the problem to the storage of a set of $|\Sigma| - 1$ bitvectors organized in a tree structure.

The alphabet is recursively partitioned in two subsets, until each subset is a singleton (hence the leaves are in one-to-one correspondence with the symbols of Σ). The bitvector β at the root has one bit for each element of the sequence, where β_i is $0/1$ if the i-th element belongs to the left/right subset of the alphabet. The sequence is then projected on the two subsets, obtaining two subsequences, and the process is repeated on the left and right subtrees. An example is shown in Figure 1.

Note that the 0s of one node are in one-to-one correspondence with the bits of the left node, while the 1s are in correspondence with the bits of the right node, and the correspondence is given downwards by Rank and upwards by

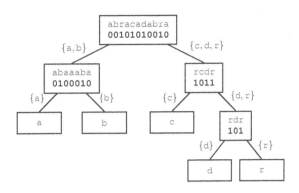

Figure 1: A Wavelet Tree for the input sequence abracadabra from the alphabet $\{a, b, c, d, r\}$.

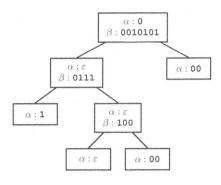

Figure 2: The Wavelet Trie of the sequence of strings $\langle 0001, 0011, 0100, 00100, 0100, 00100, 0100 \rangle$.

Select. Thanks to this mapping, it is possible to perform Access and Rank by traversing the tree top-down, and Select by traversing it bottom-up.

By using RRR bitvectors, the space is $nH_0(S) + o(n \log |\Sigma|)$ bits, while operations take $O(\log |\Sigma|)$ time.

Patricia Tries. The *Patricia Trie* [19] (or *compacted binary trie*) of a non-empty prefix-free set of binary strings is a binary tree built recursively as follows. (*i*) The Patricia Trie of a single string is a node labeled with the string. (*ii*) For a nonempty string set $\mathcal{S}$, let α be the longest common prefix of $\mathcal{S}$ (possibly the empty string). Let $\mathcal{S}_b = \{\gamma | \alpha b \gamma \in \mathcal{S}\}$ for $b \in \{0, 1\}$. Then the Patricia trie of $\mathcal{S}$ is the tree whose root is labeled with α and whose children (respectively labeled with **0** and **1**) are the Patricia Tries of the sets $\mathcal{S}_0$ and $\mathcal{S}_1$. Unless otherwise specified, we use *trie* to indicate a *Patricia Trie*, and we focus on binary strings.

3. THE WAVELET TRIE

We informally define the *Wavelet Trie* of a sequence of binary strings S as a Wavelet Tree on S (seen as a sequence on the alphabet $\Sigma = S_{\text{set}}$) whose tree structure is given by the Patricia Trie of S_{set}. We focus on binary strings without loss of generality, since strings from larger alphabets can be binarized as described in Section 2. Likewise, we can assume that S_{set} is prefix-free, as any set of strings can be made prefix-free by appending a terminator symbol to each string.

A formal definition of the Wavelet Trie can be given along the lines of the Patricia Trie definition of Section 2.

DEFINITION 3.1. *Let S be a non-empty sequence of binary strings, $S \equiv \langle s_0, \ldots, s_{n-1} \rangle$, $s_i \in \{0, 1\}^*$, whose underlying string set S_{set} is prefix-free. The* Wavelet Trie *of S, denoted $WT(S)$, is built recursively as follows:*

(i) If the sequence is constant, i.e. $s_i = \alpha$ for all i, the Wavelet Trie is a node labeled with α.

*(ii) Otherwise, let α be the longest common prefix of S. For any $0 \le i < n$ we can write $s_i = \alpha b_i \gamma_i$, where b_i is a single bit. For $b \in \{0, 1\}$ we can then define two sequences $S_b = \langle \gamma_i | b_i = b \rangle$, and the bitvector $\beta = \langle b_i \rangle$; in other words, S is partitioned in the two subsequences depending on whether the string begins with $\alpha 0$ or $\alpha 1$, the remaining suffixes form the two sequences S_0 and S_1, and the bitvector β discriminates whether the suffix γ_i is in S_0 or S_1. Then the Wavelet Trie of S is the tree whose root is labeled with α and β, and whose children (respectively labeled with **0** and **1**) are the Wavelet Tries of the sequences S_0 and S_1.*

An example is shown in Fig. 2. Note that leaves are labeled only with the common prefix α while internal nodes are labeled both with α and the bitvector β. The Wavelet Trie is a generalization of the Wavelet Tree on S: each node splits the underlying string set S_{set} in two subsets and a bitvector is used to tell which elements of the sequence belong to which subset. Using the same algorithms in [13] we obtain the following.

LEMMA 3.2. *The Wavelet Trie supports Access, Rank, and Select operations. In particular, if h_s is the number of internal nodes in the root-to-node path representing s in $WT(S)$, Access(pos) performs $O(h_s)$ Rank operations on the bitvectors, where s is the resulting string; Rank(s, pos) performs $O(h_s)$ Rank operations on the bitvectors; Select(s, idx) performs $O(h_s)$ Select operations on the bitvectors.*

It is interesting to note that any Wavelet Tree can be seen as a Wavelet Trie through a specific mapping of the alphabet to binary strings. For example the classic balanced Wavelet Tree can be obtained by mapping each element of the alphabet to a distinct string of $\lceil \log \sigma \rceil$ bits; another popular variant is the Huffman-tree shaped Wavelet Tree, which can be obtained as a Wavelet Trie by mapping each symbol to its Huffman code.

Prefix operations. It follows immediately from Definition 3.1 that for any prefix p occurring in at least one element of the sequence, the subsequence of strings starting with p is represented by a subtree of $WT(S)$.

This simple property allows us to support two new operations, RankPrefix and SelectPrefix, as defined in the introduction. The implementation is identical to Rank and Select, with the following modifications: if n_p is the node obtained by prefix-searching p in the trie, for RankPrefix the top-down traversal stops at n_p; for SelectPrefix the bottom-up traversal starts at n_p. This proves the following lemma.

LEMMA 3.3. *Let p be a prefix occurring in the sequence S. Then RankPrefix(p, pos) performs $O(h_p)$ Rank operations on the bitvectors, and SelectPrefix(p, idx) performs $O(h_p)$ Select operations on the bitvectors.*

Note that, since S_{set} is prefix-free, Rank and Select on any string in S_{set} are equivalent to RankPrefix and SelectPrefix, hence it is sufficient to implement these two operations.

Average height. To analyze the space occupied by the Wavelet Trie, we define the *average height*.

DEFINITION 3.4. *The average height $\tilde{h}$ of a WT(S) is defined as $\tilde{h} = \frac{1}{n}\sum_{i=0}^{n-1} h_{s_i}$.*

Note that the average is taken on the *sequence*, not on the set of distinct values. Hence we have $\tilde{h}n \leq \sum_{i=0}^{n-1}|s_i|$ (i.e. the total input size), but we expect $\tilde{h}n \ll \sum_{i=0}^{n-1}|s_i|$ in real situations, for example if short strings are more frequent than long strings, or they have long prefixes in common (exploiting the path compression of the Patricia Trie). The quantity $\tilde{h}n$ is equal to the sum of the lengths of all the bitvectors β, since each string s_i contributes exactly one bit to all the internal nodes in its root-to-leaf path. Also, the root-to-leaf paths form a prefix-free encoding for S_{set}, and their concatenation for each element of S is an order-zero encoding for S, thus it cannot be smaller than the zero-order entropy of S, as summarized in the following lemma.

LEMMA 3.5. *Let $\tilde{h}$ be the average height of $WT(S)$. Then $H_0(S) \leq \tilde{h} \leq \frac{1}{n}\sum_{i=0}^{n-1}|s_i|$.*

Static succinct representation. Our first representation of the Wavelet Trie is static. We show how by using suitable succinct data structures the space can be made very close to the information theoretic lower bound.

To store the Wavelet Trie we need to store its two components: the underlying Patricia Trie and the bitvectors in the internal nodes.

We represent the trie using a DFUDS [2] encoding, which encodes a tree with k nodes in $2k + o(k)$ bits, while supporting navigational operations in constant time. Since the internal nodes in the tree underlying the Patricia Trie have exactly two children, we compute the corresponding tree in the first-child/next-sibling representation. This brings down the number of nodes from $2|S_{set}| - 1$ to $|S_{set}|$, while preserving the operations. Hence we can encode the tree structure in $2|S_{set}| + o(|S_{set}|)$ bits. If we denote the number of trie edges as $e = 2(|S_{set}| - 1)$, the space can be written as $e + o(|S_{set}|)$.

The e labels α of the nodes are concatenated in depth-first order in a single bitvector L. We use the partial sum data structure of [22] to delimit the labels in L. This adds $\mathcal{B}(e, |L| + e) + o(|S_{set}|)$ bits. The total space (in bits) occupied by the trie structure is hence $|L| + e + \mathcal{B}(e, |L| + e) + o(|S_{set}|)$.

We now recast the lower bound in [7] using our notation, specializing it for the case of binary strings.

THEOREM 3.6 ([7]). *For a prefix-free string set S_{set}, the information-theoretic lower bound $LT(S_{set})$ for encoding S_{set} is given by $LT(S_{set}) = |L| + e + \mathcal{B}(e, |L| + e)$, where L is the bitvector containing the e labels α of the nodes concatenated in depth-first order.*

It follows immediately that the trie space is just the lower bound LT plus a negligible overhead.

It remains to encode the bitvectors β. We use the RRR encoding, which takes $|\beta|H_0(\beta) + o(|\beta|)$ to compress the bitvector β and supports constant-time Rank/Select operations. In [13] it is shown that, regardless of the shape of the tree, the sum of the entropies of the bitvectors β's add up to the total entropy of the sequence, $nH_0(S)$, plus negligible terms.

With respect to the redundancy beyond $nH_0(S)$, however, we cannot assume that $|S_{set}| = o(n)$ and that the tree is balanced, as in [13] and most Wavelet Tree literature; in our applications, it is well possible that $|S_{set}| = \Theta(n)$, so a

more careful analysis is needed. In Appendix A, Lemma A.4 we show that in the general case the redundancy add up to $o(\tilde{h}n)$ bits.

We concatenate the RRR encodings of the bitvectors, and use again the partial sum structure of [22] to delimit the encodings, with an additional space occupancy of $o(\tilde{h}n)$. The bound is proven in Appendix A, Lemma A.5. Overall, the set of bitvectors occupies $nH_0(S) + o(\tilde{h}n)$ bits.

All the operations can be supported with a trie traversal, which takes $O(|s|)$ time, and $O(h_s)$ Rank/Select operations on the bitvectors. Since the bitvector operations are constant time, all the operations take $O(|s| + h_s)$ time. Putting together these observations, we obtain the following theorem.

THEOREM 3.7. *The Wavelet Trie $WT(S)$ of a sequence of binary strings S can be encoded in $LT(S_{set}) + nH_0(S) + o(\tilde{h}n)$ bits, while supporting the operations Access, Rank, Select, RankPrefix, and SelectPrefix on a string s in $O(|s| + h_s)$ time.*

Note that when the tree is balanced both time and space bounds are basically equivalent to those of the standard Wavelet Tree. We remark that the space upper bound in Theorem 3.7 is just the information theoretic lower bound $LB(S) \equiv LT(S_{set}) + nH_0(S)$ plus an overhead negligible in the input size.

4. DYNAMIC WAVELET TRIES

In this section we show how to implement dynamic updates to the Wavelet Trie, resulting in the first compressed dynamic sequence with dynamic alphabet. This is the main contribution of the paper.

Dynamic variants of Wavelet Trees have been presented recently [16, 12, 18]. They all assume that the alphabet is known a priori, hence the tree structure is static. Under this assumption it is sufficient to replace the bitvectors in the nodes with *dynamic bitvectors with indels*, bitvectors that support the insertion of deletion of bits at arbitrary points. Insertion at position pos can be performed by inserting 0 or 1 at position pos of the root, whether the leaf corresponding to the value to be inserted is on the left or right subtree. A Rank operation is used to find the new position pos' in the corresponding child. The algorithm proceeds recursively until a leaf is reached. Deletion is symmetric.

The same operations can be implemented on a Wavelet Trie. The novelty consists in the ability of inserting strings that do not already occur in the sequence, and of deleting the last occurrence of a string, in both cases changing the alphabet S_{set} and thus the shape of the tree. To do so we represent the underlying tree structure of the Wavelet Trie with a dynamic Patricia Trie. We summarize the properties of a dynamic Patricia Trie in the following lemma. The operations are standard, but we describe them in Appendix B for completeness.

LEMMA 4.1. *A dynamic Patricia Trie on k binary strings occupies $O(kw) + |L|$ bits, where L is defined as in Theorem 3.6. Besides the standard traversal operations in constant time, insertion of a new string s takes $O(|s|)$ time. Deletion of a string s takes $O(\hat{\ell})$ time, where $\hat{\ell}$ is the length of the longest string in the trie.*

Updating the bitvectors. Each internal node of the trie is augmented with a bitvector β, as in the static Wavelet

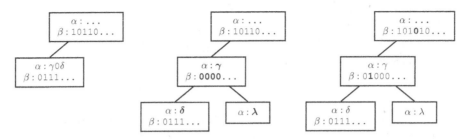

Figure 3: Insertion of the new string $s = \ldots \gamma 1 \lambda$ at position 3. An existing node is split by adding a new internal node with a constant bitvector and a new leaf. The corresponding bits are then inserted in the root-to-leaf path nodes.

Trie. Inserting and deleting a string induce the following changes on the bitvectors βs.

Insert(s, pos): If the string is not present, we insert it into the Patricia Trie, causing the split of an existing node: a new internal node and a new leaf are added. We initialize the bitvector in the new internal node as a constant sequence of bits b if the split node is a b-labeled child of the new node; the length of the new bitvector is equal to the length of the sequence represented by the split node (i.e. the number of b bits in the parent node if the split node is a b-labeled child). The algorithm then follows as if the string was in the trie. This operation is shown in Figure 3. Now we can assume the string is in the trie. Let prefix α and bitvector β be the labels in the root. Since the string is in the trie, it must be in the form $\alpha b \gamma$, where b is a bit. We insert b at position pos in β and compute pos$' = $ Rank(b, pos) in β, and insert recursively γ in the b-labeled subtree of the root at position pos$'$. We proceed until we reach a leaf.

Delete(pos): Let β be the bitvector in the root. We first find the bit corresponding to position pos in the bitvector, $b = $ Access(pos) in β. Then we compute pos$' = $ Rank(b, pos) in β, and delete recursively the string at position pos$'$ from the b-labeled subtree. We then delete the bit at position pos from β. We then check if the parent of the leaf node representing the string has a constant bitvector; in this case the string deleted was the last occurrence in the sequence. We can then delete the string from the Patricia Trie, thus deleting an internal node (whose bitvector is now constant) and a leaf.

In both cases the number of operations (Rank, Insert, Delete) on the bitvectors is bounded by $O(h_s)$. The operations we need to perform on the bitvectors are the standard insertion/deletion, with one important exception: when a node is split, we need to create a new constant bitvector of arbitrary length. We call this operation Init(b, n), which fills an empty bitvector with n copies of the bit b. The following remark rules out for our purposes most existing dynamic bitvector constructions.

REMARK 4.2. *If the encoding of a constant (i.e. $\mathbf{0}^n$ or $\mathbf{1}^n$) bitvector uses $\omega(f(n))$ memory words (of size w), Init(b, n) cannot be supported in $O(f(n))$ time.*

Uncompressed bitvectors use $\Omega(n/w)$ words; the compressed bitvectors of [18, 12], although they have a desirable occupancy of $|\beta| H_0(\beta) + o(|\beta|)$, have $\Omega(n \log \log n/(w \log n))$ words of redundancy. Since we aim for polylog operations, these constructions cannot be considered *as is*.

Main results. We first consider the case of append-only sequences. We remark that, in the Insert operation described above, when appending a string at the end of the sequence the bits inserted in the bitvectors are appended at the end, so it is sufficient that the bitvectors support an Append operation in place of a general Insert. Furthermore, Init can be implemented simply by adding a left offset in each bitvector, which increments each bitvector space by $O(\log n)$ and can be checked in constant time. Using the append-only bitvectors described in Section 4.1, and observing that the redundancy is as in Section 3, we can state the following theorem.

THEOREM 4.3. *The append-only Wavelet Trie on a dynamic sequence S supports the operations* Access, Rank, Select, RankPrefix, SelectPrefix, *and* Append *in $O(|s| + h_s)$ time. The total space occupancy is $O(|S_{set}|w) + |L| + nH_0(S) + o(\tilde{h}n)$ bits, where L is defined as in Theorem 3.6.*

Using instead the fully-dynamic bitvectors in Section 4.2, we can state the following theorem.

THEOREM 4.4. *The dynamic Wavelet Trie on a dynamic sequence S supports the operations* Access, Rank, Select, RankPrefix, SelectPrefix, *and* Insert *in $O(|s| + h_s \log n)$ time.* Delete *is supported in $O(|s| + h_s \log n)$ time if s occurs more than once, otherwise time is $O(\hat{\ell} + h_s \log n)$, where $\hat{\ell}$ is the length of the longest string. The total space occupancy is $O(nH_0(S) + |S_{set}|w) + L$ bits, where L is defined as in Theorem 3.6.*

Note that, using the compact notation defined in the introduction, the space bound in Theorem 4.3 can be written as $\text{LB}(S) + \text{PT}(S_{set}) + o(\tilde{h}n)$, while the one in Theorem 4.4 can be written as $\text{LB}(S) + \text{PT}(S_{set}) + O(nH_0)$.

4.1 Append-only bitvectors

In this section we describe an append-only bitvector with constant-time Rank/Select/Append operations and nearly-optimal space occupancy. The data structure uses RRR as a black-box data structure, assuming only its query time and space guarantees. We require the following *decomposable* property on RRR: given an input bitvector of n bits packed into $O(n/w)$ words of size $w \geq \log n$, RRR can be built in $O(n'/\log n)$ time for any chunk of $n' \geq \log n$ consecutive bits of the input bitvector, using table lookups and the Four-Russians trick; moreover, this $O(n'/\log n)$-time work can be spread over $O(n'/\log n)$ steps, each of $O(1)$ time, that can be interleaved with other operations not involving the chunk at hand. This a quite mild requirement and, for this reason, it is a general technique that can be applied to other static compressed bitvectors other than RRR with the same guarantees. Hence we believe that the following approach is of independent interest.

THEOREM 4.5. *The append-only bitvector supports* Access, Rank, Select, *and* Append *on a bitvector* β *in* $O(1)$ *time. The total space is* $nH_0(\beta) + o(n)$ *bits, where* $n = |\beta|$.

Before describing the data structure and proving Theorem 4.5 we need to introduce some auxiliary lemmas.

LEMMA 4.6 (SMALL BITVECTORS). *Let* β' *be a bitvector of bounded size* $n' = O(\text{polylog}(n))$. *Then there is a data structure that supports* Access, Rank, Select, *and* Append *on* β' *in* $O(1)$ *time, while occupying* $O(\text{polylog}(n))$ *bits.*

PROOF. It is sufficient to store explicitly all the answers to the queries Rank and Select in arrays of n' elements, thus taking $O(n' \log n') = O(\text{polylog}(n))$. Append can be supported in constant time by keeping a running count of the **1**s in the bitvector and the position of the last **0** and **1**, which are sufficient to compute the answers to the Rank and Select queries for the appended bit. $\square$

LEMMA 4.7 (AMORTIZED CONSTANT-TIME). *There is a data structure that supports* Access, Rank, *and* Select *in* $O(1)$ *time and* Append *in amortized* $O(1)$ *time on a bitvector* β *of* n *bits. The total space occupancy is* $nH_0(\beta) + o(n)$ *bits.*

PROOF. We split the input bitvector β into t smaller bitvectors $V_t, V_{t-1}, \ldots, V_1$, such that β is equal to the concatenation $V_t \cdot V_{t-1} \cdots V_1$ at any time. Let $n_i = |V_i| \geq 0$ be the length of V_i, and m_i be the number of **1**s in it, so that $\sum_{i=1}^{t} m_i = m$ and $\sum_{i=1}^{t} n_i = n$. Following Overmars's logarithmic method [21], we maintain a collection of static data structures on $V_t, V_{t-1}, \ldots, V_1$ that are periodically rebuilt.

(a) A data structure F_1 as described in Lemma 4.6 to store $\beta' = V_1$. Space is $O(\text{polylog}(n))$ bits.

(b) A collection of static data structures $F_t, F_{t-1}, \ldots, F_2$, where each F_i stores V_i using RRR. Space occupancy is $nH_0(\beta) + o(n)$ bits.

(c) Fusion Trees [10] of constant height storing the partial sums on the number of **1**s, $s_i^1 = \sum_{j=t}^{i+1} m_j$, where $s_t^1 = 0$, and symmetrically the partial sums on the number of **0**s, $s_i^0 = \sum_{j=t}^{i+1} (n_j - m_j)$, setting $s_t^1 = 0$. Predecessor takes $O(1)$ time and construction is $O(t)$ time. Space occupancy is $O(t \log n) = o(n)$ bits.

We fix $r = c \log n_0$ for a suitable constant $c > 1$, where n_0 is the length $n > 2$ of the initial input bitvector β. We keep this choice of r until F_t is reconstructed: at that point, we set n_0 to the current length of β and we update r consistently. Based on this choice of r, we guarantee that $r = \Theta(\log n)$ at any time and introduce the following constraints: $n_1 \leq r$ and, for every $i > 1$, n_i is either 0 or $2^{i-2}r$. It follows immediately that $t = \Theta(\log n)$, and hence the Fusion Trees in (c) contain $O(\log n)$ entries, thus guaranteeing constant height.

We now discuss the query operations. $\text{Rank}(b, \text{pos})$ and $\text{Select}(b, \text{idx})$ are performed as follows for a bit $b \in \{\mathbf{0}, \mathbf{1}\}$. Using the data structure in (c), we identify the corresponding bitvector V_i along with the number s_i^b of occurrences of

bit b in the preceding ones, $V_t, \ldots, V_{i+1}$. The returned value corresponds to the index i of F_i, which we query and combine the result with s_i^b: we output the sum of s_i^b with the result of $\text{Rank}(b, \text{pos} - \sum_{j=t}^{i+1} n_i)$ query on F_i in the former case; we output $\text{Select}(b, \text{idx} - s_i^b)$ query on F_i in the latter. Hence, the cost is $O(1)$ time.

It remains to show how to perform $\text{Append}(b)$ operation. While $n_1 < r$ we just append the bit b to F_1, which takes constant time by Lemma 4.6. When n_1 reaches r, let j be the smallest index such that $n_j = 0$. Then $\sum_{i=1}^{j-1} n_i = 2^{j-2}r$, so we concatenate $V_{j-1} \cdots V_1$ and rename this concatenation V_j (no collision since it was $n_j = 0$). We then rebuild F_j on V_j and set F_i for $i < j$ to empty (updating $n_j, \ldots, n_1$). We also rebuild the Fusion Trees of (c), which takes an additional $O(\log n)$ time. When F_t is rebuilt, we have that the new V_t corresponds to the whole current bitvector β, since $V_{t-1}, \ldots, V_1$ are empty. We thus set $n_0 := |\beta|$ and update r consequently. By observing that each F_j is rebuilt every $O(n_j)$ Append operations and that RRR construction time is $O(n_j / \log n)$, it follows that each Append is charged $O(1/\log n)$ time on each F_j, thus totaling $O(t/\log n) = O(1)$ time. $\square$

We now show how to de-amortize the data structure in Lemma 4.7. In the de-amortization we have to keep copies of some bitvectors, so the nH_0 term becomes $O(nH_0)$.

LEMMA 4.8 (REDUNDANCY). *There is a data structure that supports* Access, Rank, Select, *and* Append *in* $O(1)$ *time on a bitvector* β *of* n *bits. The total space occupancy is* $O(nH_0(\beta)) + o(n)$.

PROOF. To de-amortize the structure we follow Overmars's classical method of partial rebuilding [21]. The idea is to spread the construction of the RRR's F_j over the next $O(n_j)$ Append operations, charging extra $O(1)$ time each. We already saw in Lemma 4.7 that this suffices to cover all the costs. Moreover, we need to increase the speed of construction of F_j by a suitable constant factor with respect to the speed of arrival of the Append operations, so we are guaranteed that the construction of F_j is completed before the next construction of F_j is required by the argument shown in the proof of Lemma 4.7. We refer the reader to [21] for a thorough discussion of the technical details of this general technique.

While V_1 reaches its bound of r bits, we have a budget of $\Theta(r) = \Theta(\log n)$ operations that we can use to prepare the next version of the data structure. We use this budget to perform the following operations.

(1) Identify the smallest j such that $n_j = 0$ and start the construction of F_j by creating a *proxy bitvector* $\tilde{F}_j$ which references the existing $F_{j-1}, \ldots, F_1$ and Fusion Trees in (c), so that it can answer queries in $O(1)$ time as if it was the fully built F_j. When we switch to this version of the data structure, these $F_{j-1}, \ldots, F_1$ become accessible only inside $\tilde{F}_j$.

(2) Build the Fusion Trees in (c) for the next reconstruction of the data structure. Note that this would require to know the final values of the n_is and m_is when V_1 is full and the reconstruction starts. Instead, we use the current values of n_i and m_i: only the values for the last non-empty segment will be wrong. We can *correct* the

Fusion Trees by adding an additional *correction* value to the last non-empty segment; applying the correction at query time has constant-time overhead.

(3) Build a new version of the data structure which references the new Fusion Trees, the existing bitvectors $F_t, \ldots, F_{j+1}$, the proxy bitvector $\tilde{F}_j$ and new empty bitvectors $F_{j-1}, \ldots, F_1$ (hence, $n_j = 2^{j-2}r$ and $n_{j-1} = \cdots = n_1 = 0$).

When n_1 reaches r, we can replace in constant time the data structure with the one that we just finished rebuilding.

At each Append operation, we use an additional $O(1)$ budget to advance the construction of the F_js from the proxies $\tilde{F}_j$s in a round-robin fashion. When the construction of one F_j is done, the proxy $\tilde{F}_j$ is discarded and replaced by F_j. Since, by the amortization argument in the proof of Lemma 4.7, each F_j is completely rebuilt by the time it has to be set to empty (and thus used for the next reconstruction), at most one copy of each bitvector has to be kept, thus the total space occupancy grows from $nH_0(\beta) + o(n)$ to $O(nH_0(\beta)) + o(n)$. Moreover, when r has to increase (and thus the n_i's should be updated), we proceed as in [21]. □

We can now use the de-amortized bitvector to bootstrap a constant-time append-only bitvector with space occupancy $nH_0(\beta) + o(n)$, thus proving Theorem 4.5.

PROOF OF THEOREM 4.5. Let β be the input bitvector, and $L = \Theta(\mathrm{polylog}(n))$ be a power of two. We split β into $n_L \equiv \lfloor n/L \rfloor$ smaller bitvectors B_i's, each of length L and with $\hat{m}_i$ **1**s ($0 \le \hat{m}_i \le L$), plus a residual bitvector B' of length $0 \le |B'| < L$: at any time $\beta = B_1 \cdot B_2 \cdots B_{n_L} \cdot B'$. Using this partition, we maintain the following data structures:

(1) A collection $\hat{F}_1, \hat{F}_2, \ldots, \hat{F}_{n_L}$ of static data structures, where each $\hat{F}_i$ stores B_i using RRR.

(2) The data structure in Lemma 4.6 to store B'.

(3) The data structure in Lemma 4.8 to store the partial sums $\hat{s}_i^1 = \sum_{j=1}^{i-1} \hat{m}_j$, setting $\hat{s}_1^1 = 0$. This is implemented by maintaining a bitvector that has a **1** for each position $\hat{s}_i^1$, and **0** elsewhere. Predecessor queries can be implemented by composing Rank and Select. The bitvector has length $n_L + m$ and contains n_L **1**s. The partial sums $\hat{s}_i^0 = \sum_{j=1}^{i-1} (L - \hat{m}_j)$ are kept symmetrically in another bitvector.

Rank(b, pos) and Select(b, idx) are implemented as follows for a bit $b \in \{\mathbf{0}, \mathbf{1}\}$. Using the data structure in (3), we identify the corresponding bitvector B_i in (1) or B' in (2) along with the number $\hat{s}_i^b$ of occurrences of bit b in the preceding segments. In both cases, we query the corresponding dictionary and combine the result with $\hat{s}_i^b$. These operations take $O(1)$ time.

Now we focus on Append(b). At every Append operation, we append a **0** to the one of the bitvectors in (3) depending on whether b is **0** or **1**, thus maintaining the partial sums invariant. This takes constant time. We guarantee that $|B'| \le L$ bits: whenever $|B'| = L$, we conceptually create $B_{n_L+1} := B'$, still keeping its data structure in (2); reset B' to be empty, creating the corresponding data structure in (2); append a **1** to the bitvectors in (3). We start building a new static compressed data structure $\hat{F}_{n_L+1}$ for B_{n_L+1}

using RRR in $O(L/\log n)$ steps of $O(1)$ time each. During the construction of $\hat{F}_{n_L+1}$ the old B' is still valid, so it can be used to answer the queries. As soon as the construction is completed, in $O(L/\log n)$ time, the old B' can be discarded and queries can be now handled by $\hat{F}_{n_L+1}$. Meanwhile the new appended bits are handled in the new B', in $O(1)$ time each, using its new instance of (2). By suitably tuning the speed of the operations, we can guarantee that by the time the new reset B' has reached $L/2$ (appended) bits, the above $O(L)$ steps have been completed for $\hat{F}_{n_L+1}$. Hence, the total cost of Append is just $O(1)$ time in the worst case.

To complete our proof, we have to discuss what happens when we have to double $L := 2 \times L$. This is a standard task known as global rebuilding [21]. We rebuild RRR for the concatenation of B_1 and B_2, and deallocate the latter two after the construction; we then continue with RRR on the concatenation of B_3 and B_4, and deallocate them after the construction, and so on. Meanwhile, we build a copy (3') of the data structure in (3) for the new parameter $2 \times L$, following an incremental approach. At any time, we only have (3') and $\hat{F}_{2i-1}, \hat{F}_{2i}$ duplicated. The implementation of Rank and Select needs a minor modification to deal with the already rebuilt segments. The global rebuilding is completed before we need again to double the value of L.

We now perform the space analysis. As for (1), we have to add up the space taken by $\hat{F}_1, \ldots, \hat{F}_{n_L}$ plus that taken by the one being rebuilt using $\hat{F}_{2i-1}, \hat{F}_{2i}$. This sum can be upper bounded by $\sum_{i=1}^{n_L} (\mathcal{B}(m_i, L) + o(L)) + O(L) = H_0(\beta) + o(n)$. The space for (2) is $O(\mathrm{polylog}(n)) = o(n)$. Finally, the occupancy of the s_i^1 partial sums in (3) is $\mathcal{B}(n_L, n_L + m) + o(n_L + m) = O(n_L \log(1 + m/n_L)) = O(n \log n/L) = o(n)$ bits, since the bitvector has length $n_L + m$ and contains n_L **1**s. The analysis is symmetric for the s_i^0 partial sums, and for the copies in (3'). □

4.2 Fully dynamic bitvectors

We introduce a new dynamic bitvector construction which, although the entropy term has a constant greater than 1, supports logarithmic-time Init and Insert/Delete.

To support both insertion/deletion and initialization in logarithmic time we adapt the dynamic bitvector presented in Section 3.4 of [18]; in the paper, the bitvector is compressed using Gap Encoding, i.e. the bitvector $\mathbf{0}^{g_0}\mathbf{1}\mathbf{0}^{g_1}\mathbf{1}\ldots$ is encoded as the sequence of *gaps* $g_0, g_1, \ldots$, and the gaps are encoded using Elias delta code [5]. The resulting bit stream is split in chunks of $\Theta(\log n)$ (without breaking the codes) and a self-balancing binary search tree is built on the chunks, with partial counts in all the nodes. Chunks are split and merged upon insertions and deletions to maintain the chunk size invariant, and the tree rebalanced.

Because of gap encoding, the space has a linear dependence on the number of **1**s, hence by Remark 4.2 it is not suitable for our purposes. We make a simple modification that enables an efficient Init: in place of gap encoding and delta codes we use RLE and Elias gamma codes [5], as the authors of [9] do in their *practical dictionaries*. RLE encodes the bitvector $\mathbf{0}^{r_0}\mathbf{1}^{r_1}\mathbf{0}^{r_2}\mathbf{1}^{r_3}\ldots$ with the sequence of *runs* $r_0, r_1, r_2, r_3, \ldots$. The runs are encoded with Elias gamma codes. Init(b, n) can be trivially supported by creating a tree with a single leaf node, and encoding a run of n bits b in the node, which can be done in time $O(\log n)$. In [6] it is proven the space of this encoding is bounded by $O(nH_0)$, but even if the coefficient of the entropy term is not 1 as in RRR bitvectors, the experimental analysis performed in [9] shows that RLE bitvectors perform extremely well in practice. The rest of the data structure is left unchanged; we refer to [18] for the details.

THEOREM 4.9. *The dynamic RLE+γ bitvector supports* Access, Rank, Select, Insert, Delete, *and* Init *on a bitvector* β *in* $O(\log n)$ *time. The total space occupancy is* $O(nH_0(\beta) + \log n)$ *bits.*

5. OTHER QUERY ALGORITHMS

In this section we describe range query algorithms on the Wavelet Trie that can be useful in particular in database applications and analytics. We note that the algorithms for *distinct values in range* and *range majority element* are similar to the *report* and *range quantile* algorithms presented in [11]; we restate them here for completeness, extending them to prefix operations. In the following we denote with $\mathcal{C}_{\mathrm{op}}$ the cost of Access/Rank/Select on the bitvectors; $\mathcal{C}_{\mathrm{op}}$ is $O(1)$ for static and append-only bitvectors, and $O(\log n)$ for fully dynamic bitvectors.

Sequential access. Suppose we want to enumerate all the strings in the range $[l, r)$, i.e. $S^{[l,r)} = S_l, \ldots, S_{r-1}$. We could do it with $r - l$ calls to Access, but accessing each string s_i would cost $O(|s_i| + h_{s_i}\mathcal{C}_{\mathrm{op}})$. We show instead how to enumerate the values of a range by enumerating the bits of each bitvector: suppose we have an iterator on root bitvector for the range $[l, r)$. Then if the current bit is 0, the next value is the next value given by the left subtree, while if it is 1 the next value is the next value of the right subtree. We proceed recursively by keeping an iterator on all the bitvectors of the internal nodes we traverse during the enumeration.

When we traverse an internal node for the first time, we perform a Rank to find the initial point, and create an iterator. Next time we traverse it, we just advance the iterator. Note that both RRR bitvectors and RLE bitvectors can support iterators with $O(1)$ advance to the next bit.

By using iterators instead of performing a Rank each time we traverse a node, a single Rank is needed for each traversed node, hence to extract the i-th string it takes $O(|s_i| + \frac{1}{r-l}\sum_{s \in S^{[l,r)}_{\mathrm{set}}} h_s\mathcal{C}_{\mathrm{op}})$ amortized time.

Note that if $S^{[l,r)}_{\mathrm{set}}$ (the set of distinct strings occurring in $S^{[l,r)}$) is large, the actual time is smaller due to shared nodes in the paths. In fact, in the extreme case when the whole string set occurs in the range, we can give a better bound, $O(|s_i| + \frac{1}{r-l}|S_{\mathrm{set}}|\mathcal{C}_{\mathrm{op}})$ amortized time.

Distinct values in range. Another useful query is the enumeration of the distinct values in the range $[l, r)$, which we called $S^{[l,r)}_{\mathrm{set}}$. Note that for each node the distinct values of the subsequence represented by the node are just the distinct values of the left subtree plus the distinct values of the right subtree in the corresponding ranges. Hence, starting at the root, we compute the number of **0**s in the range $[l, r)$ with two calls to Rank. If there are no **0**s we just enumerate the distinct elements of the right child in the range $[\mathrm{Rank}(\mathbf{1}, l), \mathrm{Rank}(\mathbf{1}, r))$. If there are no **1**s, we proceed symmetrically. If there are both **0**s and **1**s, the distinct values are the union of the distinct values of the left child in the range $[\mathrm{Rank}(\mathbf{0}, l), \mathrm{Rank}(\mathbf{0}, r))$ and those of the right child in the range $[\mathrm{Rank}(\mathbf{1}, l), \mathrm{Rank}(\mathbf{1}, r))$. Since we only traverse nodes that lead to values that are in the range, the total

running time is $O(\sum_{s \in S^{[l,r)}_{\mathrm{set}}} |s| + h_s\mathcal{C}_{\mathrm{op}})$, which is the same time as accessing the values, if we knew their positions. As a byproduct, we also get the number of occurrences of each value in the range.

We can stop early in the traversal, hence enumerating the distinct *prefixes* that satisfy some property. For example in an URL access log we can find efficiently the distinct hostnames in a given time range.

Range majority element. The previous algorithm can be modified to check if there is a majority element in the range (i.e. one element that occurs more than $\frac{r-l}{2}$ times in $[l, r)$), and, if there is such an element, find it. Start at the root, and count the number of **0**s and **1**s in the range. If a bit b occurs more than $\frac{r-l}{2}$ times (note that there can be at most one) proceed recursively on the b-labeled subtree, otherwise there is no majority element in the range.

The total running time is $O(h\mathcal{C}_{\mathrm{op}})$, where h is the height of the Wavelet Trie. In case of success, if the string found is s, the running time is just $O(h_s\mathcal{C}_{\mathrm{op}})$. As for the distinct values, this can be applied to prefixes as well by stopping the traversal when the prefix we found until that point satisfies some property.

A similar algorithm can be used as an heuristic to find all the values that occur in the range at least t times, by proceeding as in the enumeration of distinct elements but discarding the branches whose bit has less than t occurrences in the parent. While no theoretical guarantees can be given, this heuristic should perform very well with power-law distributions and high values of t, which are the cases of interest in most data analytics applications.

6. PROBABILISTICALLY-BALANCED DYNAMIC WAVELET TREES

In this section we show how to use the Wavelet Trie to maintain a dynamic Wavelet Tree on a sequence from a bounded alphabet with operations that with high probability do not depend on the universe size.

A compelling example is given by numeric data: a sequence of integers, say in $\{0, \ldots, 2^{64} - 1\}$, cannot be represented with existing dynamic Wavelet Trees unless the tree is built on the whole universe, even if the sequence only contains integers from a much smaller subset. Similarly, a text sequence in Unicode typically contains few hundreds of distinct characters, far fewer than the $\approx 2^{17}$ (and growing) defined in the standard.

Formally, we wish to maintain a sequence of symbols $S = \langle s_0, \ldots, s_{n-1} \rangle$ drawn from an alphabet $\Sigma \subseteq U = \{0, \ldots, u - 1\}$, where we call U the *universe* and Σ the *working alphabet*, with Σ typically much smaller than U and not known a priori. We want to support the standard Access, Rank, Select, Insert, and Delete but we are willing to give up RankPrefix and SelectPrefix, which would not make sense anyway for non-string data.

We can immediately use the Wavelet Trie on S, by mapping injectively the values of U to strings of length $\lceil \log u \rceil$. This supports all the required operations with a space bound that depends only logarithmically in u, but the height of the resulting trie could be as much as $\log u$, while a balanced tree would require only $\log |\Sigma|$.

To obtain a balanced tree without having to deal with complex rotations we employ a simple randomized technique that will yield a balanced tree with high probability. The main idea is to randomly permute the universe U with an easy to compute permutation, such that the probability that the alphabet Σ will produce an unbalanced trie is negligibly small.

To do so we use the hashing technique described in [4]. We map the universe U onto itself by the function $h_a(x) = ax \pmod{2^{\lceil \log u \rceil}}$ where a is chosen at random among the odd integers in $[1, 2^{\lceil \log u \rceil} - 1]$ when the data structure is initialized. Note that h_a is a bijection, with the inverse given by $h^{-1}(x) = a^{-1}x \pmod{2^{\lceil \log u \rceil}}$. The result of the hash function is considered as a binary string of $\lceil \log u \rceil$ bits written LSB-to-MSB, and operations on the Wavelet Tree are defined by composition of the hash function with operations on the Wavelet Trie; in other words, the values are hashed and inserted in a Wavelet Trie, and when retrieved the hash inverse is applied.

To prove that the resulting trie is balanced we use the following lemma from [4].

LEMMA 6.1 ([4]). *Let $\Sigma \subseteq U$ be any subset of the universe, and $\ell = \lceil (\alpha + 2) \log |\Sigma| \rceil$ so that $\ell \leq \lceil \log u \rceil$. Then the following holds*

$$\text{Prob}\left(\forall x, y \in \Sigma \quad h_a(x) \not\equiv h_a(y) \pmod{2^\ell}\right) \geq 1 - |\Sigma|^{-\alpha}$$

where the probability is on the choice of a.

In our case, the lemma implies that with very high probability the hashes of the values in Σ are distinguished by the first ℓ bits, where ℓ is logarithmic in the $|\Sigma|$. The trie on the hashes cannot be higher than ℓ, hence it is balanced. The space occupancy is that of the Wavelet Trie built on the hashes. We can bound L, the sum of trie labels in Theorem 3.6, by the total sum of the hashes length, hence proving the following theorem.

THEOREM 6.2. *The randomized Wavelet Tree on a dynamic sequence $S = \langle s_0, \ldots, s_{n-1} \rangle$ where $s_i \in \Sigma \subseteq U = \{0, \ldots, u-1\}$ supports the operations Access, Rank, Select, Insert, and Delete in time $O(\log u + h \log n)$, where $h \leq (\alpha + 2) \log |\Sigma|$ with probability $1 - |\Sigma|^{-\alpha}$ (and $h \leq \lceil \log u \rceil$ in the worst case).*

The total space occupancy is $O(nH_0(S) + |\Sigma|w) + |\Sigma| \log u$ bits.

7. CONCLUSION AND FUTURE WORK

We have presented the Wavelet Trie, a new data structure for maintaining compressed sequences of strings with provable time and compression bounds. We believe that the Wavelet Trie will find application in real-world storage problems where space-efficiency is crucial. To this end, we plan to evaluate the practicality of the data structure with an experimental analysis on real-world data, evaluating several performance/space/functionality trade-offs. We are confident that a properly engineered implementation can perform well, as other algorithm engineered succinct data structures have proven very practical ([20, 1, 14]).

It would be also interesting to *balance* the Wavelet Trie, even for pathological sets of strings. In [14] it was shown that in practice the cost of unbalancedness can be high. Lastly, it is an open question how the Wavelet Trie would perform in external or cache-oblivious models. A starting point would be a fanout larger than 2 in the trie, but internal nodes would

require vectors with non-binary alphabet. The existing non-binary dynamic sequences do not directly support Init, hence they are not suitable for the Wavelet Trie.

Acknowledgments

We would like to thank Ralf Herbrich for suggesting the problem of compressing relations, and Rossano Venturini for numerous insightful discussions. We would also like to thank the anonymous reviewers for several helpful comments and suggestions which helped improving the presentation.

8. REFERENCES

[1] D. Arroyuelo, R. Cánovas, G. Navarro, and K. Sadakane. Succinct trees in practice. In *ALENEX*, pages 84–97, 2010.

[2] D. Benoit, E. D. Demaine, J. I. Munro, R. Raman, V. Raman, and S. S. Rao. Representing trees of higher degree. *Algorithmica*, 43(4):275–292, 2005.

[3] F. Claude and G. Navarro. Practical rank/select queries over arbitrary sequences. In *Proc. 15th International Symposium on String Processing and Information Retrieval (SPIRE)*, LNCS 5280, pages 176–187. Springer, 2008.

[4] M. Dietzfelbinger, T. Hagerup, J. Katajainen, and M. Penttonen. A reliable randomized algorithm for the closest-pair problem. *J. Algorithms*, 25(1):19–51, 1997.

[5] P. Elias. Universal codeword sets and representations of the integers. *IEEE Transactions on Information Theory*, 21(2):194–203, 1975.

[6] P. Ferragina, R. Giancarlo, and G. Manzini. The myriad virtues of wavelet trees. *Inf. Comput.*, 207(8):849–866, 2009.

[7] P. Ferragina, R. Grossi, A. Gupta, R. Shah, and J. S. Vitter. On searching compressed string collections cache-obliviously. In *PODS*, pages 181–190, 2008.

[8] P. Ferragina, F. Luccio, G. Manzini, and S. Muthukrishnan. Compressing and indexing labeled trees, with applications. *J. ACM*, 57(1), 2009.

[9] L. Foschini, R. Grossi, A. Gupta, and J. S. Vitter. When indexing equals compression: Experiments with compressing suffix arrays and applications. *ACM Trans. on Algorithms*, 2(4):611–639, 2006.

[10] M. L. Fredman and D. E. Willard. Surpassing the information theoretic bound with fusion trees. *Journal of Computer and System Sciences*, 47(3):424–436, Dec. 1993.

[11] T. Gagie, G. Navarro, and S. J. Puglisi. New algorithms on wavelet trees and applications to information retrieval. *Theoretical Computer Science*, to appear.

[12] R. González and G. Navarro. Rank/Select on dynamic compressed sequences and applications. *Theor. Comput. Sci.*, 410(43):4414–4422, 2009.

[13] R. Grossi, A. Gupta, and J. S. Vitter. High-order entropy-compressed text indexes. In *SODA*, pages 841–850, 2003.

[14] R. Grossi and G. Ottaviano. Fast compressed tries through path decompositions. In *ALENEX*, 2012.

[15] G. Jacobson. Space-efficient static trees and graphs. In *FOCS*, pages 549–554, 1989.

[16] S. Lee and K. Park. Dynamic compressed

representation of texts with rank/select. *JCSE*, 3(1):15–26, 2009.

[17] V. Mäkinen and G. Navarro. Position-restricted substring searching. In *LATIN*, pages 703–714, 2006.

[18] V. Mäkinen and G. Navarro. Dynamic entropy-compressed sequences and full-text indexes. *ACM Transactions on Algorithms*, 4(3), 2008.

[19] D. R. Morrison. Patricia - practical algorithm to retrieve information coded in alphanumeric. *J. ACM*, 15(4):514–534, 1968.

[20] D. Okanohara and K. Sadakane. Practical entropy-compressed rank/select dictionary. In *ALENEX*, 2007.

[21] M. H. Overmars. *The design of dynamic data structures*, volume 156 of *Lecture Notes in Computer Science*. Springer-Verlag, 1983.

[22] R. Raman, V. Raman, and S. S. Rao. Succinct indexable dictionaries with applications to encoding n-ary trees, prefix sums and multisets. *ACM Transactions on Algorithms*, 3(4), 2007.

[23] J. S. Vitter. *Algorithms and Data Structures for External Memory*. Foundations and trends in theoretical computer science. Now Publishers, 2008.

APPENDIX

A. MULTIPLE STATIC BITVECTORS

LEMMA A.1. *Let S be a sequence of length n on an alphabet of cardinality σ, with each symbol of the alphabet occurring at least once. Then the following holds:*

$$nH_0(S) \geq (\sigma - 1)\log n.$$

PROOF. The inequality is trivial when $\sigma = 1$. When there are at least two symbols, the minimum entropy is attained when $\sigma - 1$ symbols occur once and one symbol occurs the remaining $n - \sigma + 1$ times. To show this, suppose by contradiction that the minimum entropy is attained by a string where two symbols occur more than once, occurring respectively a and b times. Their contribution to the entropy term is $a\log\frac{n}{a} + b\log\frac{n}{b}$. This contribution can be written as $f(a)$ where

$$f(t) = t\log\frac{n}{t} + (b + a - t)\log\frac{n}{b + a - t},$$

but $f(t)$ has two strict minima in 1 and $b + a - 1$ among the positive integers, so the entropy term can be lowered by making one of the symbol absorb all but one the occurrences of the other, yielding a contradiction.

To prove the lemma, it is sufficient to see that the contribution to the entropy term of the $\sigma - 1$ singleton symbols is $(\sigma - 1)\log n$. □

LEMMA A.2. $O(|S_{set}|)$ *is bounded by* $o(\tilde{h}n)$.

PROOF. It suffices to prove that

$$\frac{|S_{\text{set}}|}{\tilde{h}n}$$

is asymptotic to 0 as n grows. By Lemma 3.5 and Lemma A.1, and assuming $|S_{\text{set}}| \geq 2$,

$$\frac{|S_{\text{set}}|}{\tilde{h}n} \leq \frac{|S_{\text{set}}|}{nH_0(S)} \leq \frac{|S_{\text{set}}|}{(|S_{\text{set}}| - 1)\log n} \leq \frac{2}{\log n},$$

which completes the proof. □

LEMMA A.3. *The sum of the redundancy of σ RRR bitvectors of $m_1, \ldots, m_\sigma$ bits respectively, where $\sum_i m_i = m$, can be bounded by*

$$O\left(m\frac{\log\log\frac{m}{\sigma}}{\log\frac{m}{\sigma}} + \sigma\right).$$

PROOF. The redundancy of a single bitvector can be bounded by $c_1\frac{m_i\log\log m_i}{\log m_i} + c_2$. Since $f(x) = \frac{x\log\log x}{\log x}$ is concave, we can apply the Jensen inequality:

$$\frac{1}{\sigma}\sum_i\left(c_1\frac{m_i\log\log m_i}{\log m_i} + c_2\right) \leq c_1\frac{\frac{m}{\sigma}\log\log\frac{m}{\sigma}}{\log\frac{m}{\sigma}} + c_2.$$

The result follows by multiplying both sides by σ. □

LEMMA A.4. *The redundancy of the RRR bitvectors in $WT(S)$ can be bounded by $o(\tilde{h}n)$.*

PROOF. Since the bitvector lengths add up to $\tilde{h}n$, we can apply Lemma A.3 and obtain that the redundancy are bounded by

$$O\left(\tilde{h}n\frac{\log\log\frac{\tilde{h}n}{|S_{\text{set}}|}}{\log\frac{\tilde{h}n}{|S_{\text{set}}|}} + |S_{\text{set}}|\right).$$

The term in $|S_{\text{set}}|$ is already taken care of by Lemma A.2. It suffices then to prove that

$$\frac{\log\log\frac{\tilde{h}n}{|S_{\text{set}}|}}{\log\frac{\tilde{h}n}{|S_{\text{set}}|}}$$

is negligible as n grows, and because $f(x) = \frac{\log\log x}{\log x}$ is asymptotic to 0, we just need to prove that $\frac{\tilde{h}n}{|S_{\text{set}}|}$ grows to infinity as n does. Using again Lemma 3.5 and Lemma A.1 we obtain that

$$\frac{\tilde{h}n}{|S_{\text{set}}|} \geq \frac{nH_0(S)}{|S_{\text{set}}|} \geq \frac{(|S_{\text{set}}| - 1)\log n}{|S_{\text{set}}|} \geq \frac{\log n}{2}$$

thus proving the lemma. □

LEMMA A.5. *The partial sum data structure used to delimit the RRR bitvectors in $WT(S)$ occupies $o(\tilde{h}n)$ bits.*

PROOF. By Lemma A.4 the sum of the RRR encodings is $nH_0(S) + o(\tilde{h}n)$. To encode the $|S_{\text{set}}|$ delimiters, the partial sum structure of [22] takes

$$|S_{\text{set}}|\log\left(\frac{nH_0(S) + o(\tilde{h}n) + |S_{\text{set}}|}{|S_{\text{set}}|}\right) + O(|S_{\text{set}}|)$$

$$\leq |S_{\text{set}}|\log\left(\frac{nH_0(S)}{|S_{\text{set}}|}\right) + |S_{\text{set}}|\log\left(\frac{o(\tilde{h}n)}{|S_{\text{set}}|}\right) + O(|S_{\text{set}}|).$$

The third term is negligible by Lemma A.2. The second just by dividing by $\tilde{h}n$ and noting that $f(x) = \frac{\log x}{x}$ is asymptotic to 0. It remains to show that the first term is $o(\tilde{h}n)$. Dividing by $\tilde{h}n$ and using again Lemma 3.5 we obtain

$$\frac{|S_{\text{set}}|\log\left(\frac{nH_0(S)}{|S_{\text{set}}|}\right)}{\tilde{h}n} \leq \frac{|S_{\text{set}}|\log\left(\frac{nH_0(S)}{|S_{\text{set}}|}\right)}{nH_0(S)} = \frac{\log\left(\frac{nH_0(S)}{|S_{\text{set}}|}\right)}{\frac{nH_0(S)}{|S_{\text{set}}|}}$$

By using again that $f(x) = \frac{\log x}{x}$ is asymptotic to 0 and proving as in Lemma A.4 that $\frac{nH_0(S)}{|S_{\text{set}}|}$ grows to infinity as n does, the result follows. □

B. DYNAMIC PATRICIA TRIE

For the dynamic Wavelet Trie we use a straightforward Patricia Trie data structure. Each node contains two pointers to the children, one pointer to the label and one integer for its length. For k strings, this amounts to $O(kw)$ space. Given this representation, all navigational operations are trivial. The total space is $O(kw) + |L|$, where L is the concatenation of the labels in the compacted trie as defined in Theorem 3.6

Insertion of a new string s *splits* an existing node, where the mismatch occurs, and adds a leaf. The label of the new internal node is set to point to the label of the split node, with the new label length (corresponding to the mismatch of s in the split node). The split node is modified accordingly. A new label is allocated with the suffix of s starting from the mismatch, and assigned to the new leaf node. This operation takes $O(|s|)$ time and the space grows by $O(w)$ plus the length of the new suffix, hence maintaining the space invariant.

When a new string is deleted, its leaf is deleted and the parent node and the other child of the parent need to be merged. The highest node that shares the label with the deleted leaf is found, and the label is deleted and replaced with a new string that is the concatenation of the labels from that node up to the merged node. The pointers in the path from the found node and the merged node are replaced accordingly. This operation takes $O(\hat{\ell})$ where $\hat{\ell}$ is the length of the longest string in the trie, and the space invariant is maintained.

On the Optimality of Clustering Properties of Space Filling Curves

Pan Xu
Iowa State University
panxu@iastate.edu

Srikanta Tirthapura [*]
Iowa State University
snt@iastate.edu

ABSTRACT

Space filling curves have for long been used in the design of data structures for multidimensional data. A fundamental quality metric of a space filling curve is its "clustering number" with respect to a class of queries, which is the average number of contiguous segments on the space filling curve that a query region can be partitioned into. We present a characterization of the clustering number of a general class of space filling curves, as well as the first non-trivial lower bounds on the clustering number for any space filling curve. Our results also answer an open problem that was posed by Jagadish in 1997.

Categories and Subject Descriptors

H.3.1 [**Content Analysis and Indexing**]: Indexing Methods

General Terms

Algorithms, Performance, Theory

Keywords

space filling curves, clustering, Hilbert curve, lower bound

1. INTRODUCTION

Many query processing techniques for multidimensional data are based on a *space filling curve* (SFC), which is a bijection from points in a discrete multidimensional universe to a one dimensional universe of the same cardinality. For example, Orenstein and Merrett [10] proposed the use of SFCs for answering range queries on multidimensional data: *Preprocess (index) a set of input points P such that when presented with a query box Q, it is possible to quickly compute a function of the set of all points in P that fall in Q.* The advantage of an SFC is that conventional data structures that were used to organize one dimensional data can

be directly used on higher dimensional data. The simplicity and elegance of this idea has caused it to become very popular, and now there are numerous databases that use SFCs to organize multidimensional data, including Oracle Spatial [9].

When data is ordered according to an SFC, a query region in multidimensional space will be partitioned into some number of segments on the SFC, and all such segments need to be retrieved and examined in order to process the query. It is desirable that a query region be partitioned into a small number of "clusters" such that each cluster consists of points that are contiguously ordered by the SFC. This leads us to define the "clustering number" of an SFC π with respect to a given query region q as the *smallest number of clusters into which q can be partitioned such that the points within a cluster are ordered consecutively by the SFC.* When processing a query on data stored on the disk, the clustering number is a measure of the number of disk "seeks" that need to be performed in order to process the query. Since a disk seek is an expensive operation, this is a significant and useful metric to have. The smaller the clustering number of a query, the better is the performance of the index.

In an influential work, Moon *et al.* [7] presented an analysis of the clustering number of the Hilbert SFC. They showed that the average number of clusters on the Hilbert curve due to a "rectilinear polyhedron" query was equal to the surface area of the polyhedron divided by two times the number of dimensions. Since the publication of this work, it has received more than 300 citations. But even after a decade since this work, and more than two decades of interest in the clustering number of an SFC, many basic questions remain unanswered. In particular:

1. **Lower Bound:** Are there any lower bounds on the clustering number of an SFC? This question has been raised before by Jagadish [6] in the context of a 2×2 square query region, but no non-trivial lower bounds were known so far.

2. **Optimality:** It is a widely held belief that the Hilbert curve achieves the best possible clustering, on average. For what classes of queries is the Hilbert curve optimal? For what classes of queries is it sub-optimal?

3. Are there any general methods for analyzing the clustering number of a curve? Given a query class, which is the best SFC for this class?

*Supported in part by NSF grants 0834743, 0831903.

1.1 Contributions

In this work, we present substantial progress towards answering the above questions. We consider two basic query types, a multidimensional *rectangular* query, formed by the intersection of halfplanes, and a *rectilinear* query, which is formed by the union of multidimensional rectangles. For both query classes, it assumed that the size of the bounding box of the query (the smallest rectangle that contains the query) is a constant that does not grow with the size of the universe. We consider the average clustering number on a set of queries formed by applying all possible *translations* and one or more *rotations* on a single query.

- **Lower Bound.** We present a lower bound on the clustering number of *any* SFC for the class of rectangular queries, for any set of rotations. This answers a more general version of the question raised by Jagadish [6]. Prior to our work, only upper bounds on the clustering number of specific SFCs, such as the Hilbert SFC were known.

- **Exact Characterization of Continuous SFCs.** We consider a class of SFCs that we call "continuous SFCs", which have the property that neighbors along the SFC are also nearest neighbors in the high-dimensional grid. For any rectilinear query g, and any set of rotations, we show that the clustering number of any SFC can be expressed as a simple formula involving the scalar product of two vectors, one derived from the query shape and the set of rotations, and the other derived from the space filling curve itself.

  When all possible rotations are considered, surprisingly, *every continuous SFC is optimal for rectangular queries*. The result of Moon *et al.* [7] on the analysis of the Hilbert curve follows as a special case of our result on continuous SFCs.

- **Non-Continuous SFCs.** For the class of SFCs that are not continuous, we show the surprising result that on certain queries a non-continuous SFC may have a much smaller clustering number (i.e. perform much better) than any continuous SFC. This is to be contrasted with the case of rectangular queries, for which there always exists a continuous SFC that is optimal.

1.2 Related Work

The work of Moon *et al.* [7] considered an analysis of the Hilbert curve in d dimensions. Similar to our model, they also considered the query class of all translations of any rectilinear query g, and showed the elegant result that as n, the size of the universe, approaches ∞, the clustering number of the Hilbert curve approaches the surface area of the query g, divided by twice the number of dimensions. Since the Hilbert curve is a continuous curve, our analysis of a continuous curve applies here. In particular, Corollary 1 implies the result of [7].

Jagadish [6] considered the clustering performance of the two-dimensional Hilbert curve on a $\sqrt{n} \times \sqrt{n}$ universe when the query region was a $m \times m$ square. For 2×2 queries, he derived that the average clustering number approaches 2 as n approaches ∞. He says "We conjecture that this number 2 is an asymptotic optimum. $\cdots$. Proving this conjecture is a subject for future research". Our results show that the optimum clustering number for a 2×2 square over any SFC

is indeed equal to 2. Our analysis considers lower bounds for a more general problem, where the SFC is over a general multidimensional universe, and the query is any rectangle.

Asano *et al.* [2] present an analysis of the clustering properties of SFCs in two dimensions in a model that is different from ours, and is more "relaxed" in the following respect. For a query q consisting of $|q|$ cells, the query processor is allowed to return a set of $C|q|$ cells which is a *superset* of q, and can be divided into a small number of clusters, where C is a constant greater than 1. In contrast, in our model, we require the query processor to return the set of exactly the cells present in the query q, and consider the number of clusters thus created. In our model the number of clusters is always greater than or equal to the number of clusters in the model of [2]. Alber and Niedermeier [1] present a precise characterization of Hilbert curves in dimensions $d \geq 3$. There is a large literature on SFCs that we will not attempt to cite here, but to our knowledge, no previous work has considered lower bounds and a general analysis of clustering properties of SFC as we do here.

Organization of Paper: The rest of this paper is organized as follows. We define the model and the problem in Section 2. In Section 3, we present a general technique for computing the clustering number of an SFC for a class of queries, which forms the basis for further analysis. We present the results for a continuous SFC in Section 4, the lower bound on any SFC in Section 5, and we consider non-continuous SFCs and extensions in Section 6.

2. MODEL AND PROBLEM DEFINITION

Let U denote the d dimensional $\sqrt[d]{n} \times \cdots \times \sqrt[d]{n}$ grid of n cells. We assume $\sqrt[d]{n} = 2^k$ for some positive integer k. Each point in U is a d-tuple $(x_1, x_2, \ldots, x_d)$ where for each $i = 1 \ldots d$, $0 \leq x_i < \sqrt[d]{n}$. For $x = (x_1, x_2, \ldots, x_d)$ and $y = (y_1, y_2, \ldots, y_d)$, the Manhattan distance between them is defined to be $\sum_{i=1}^{d} |x_i - y_i|$.

DEFINITION 1. *An SFC π on U is a bijective mapping $\pi : U \to \{0, 1, \cdots, n-1\}$.*

Some popularly used space filling curves are the Z-curve [10, 8] (also known as the Morton ordering), the Hilbert curve [5], and the Gray code curve [3, 4]. Figures 1, 2, and 3 show the Hilbert curve, the row-major curve, and the Z curve, respectively.

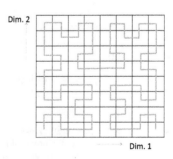

Figure 1: The Hilbert SFC in two dimensions

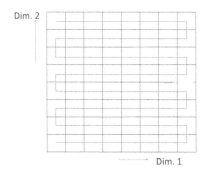

Figure 2: The row-major SFC

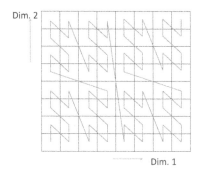

Figure 3: The Z-SFC

DEFINITION 2. *An SFC π is said to be a continuous SFC if it has the property that for every $0 \le i \le n-2$, the Manhattan distance between $\pi^{-1}(i)$ and $\pi^{-1}(i+1)$ is 1.*

In other words, a continuous SFC always travels from one cell on the grid to another cell that is at a Manhattan distance of 1. According to Definition 2, the row-major curve (Figure 2) and the Hilbert curve are both continuous SFCs while the Z-curve is not.

DEFINITION 3. *A set of cells $C \subseteq U$ is said to be a "cluster" of an SFC π if the cells of C are numbered consecutively by π.*

For instance, the universe U is a cluster for any SFC.

Queries: A query q is any subset of U. The volume of query q, denoted $|q|$, is the number of cells in it. A rectangular query is a set of cells of the form $\{(x_1, x_2, \ldots, x_d) | \ell_i \le x_i \le \hbar_i, \text{ for each } i = 1 \ldots d\}$. For a query q which may not be a rectangle, the *bounding box* of q denoted $B(q)$, is the smallest rectangle that contains all cells in q. In particular, if q is a rectangle then $B(q)$ is equal to q. We say that a query $g \subset U$ is of a *fixed size* if the volume of $B(g)$ is independent of n, the size of the universe.

DEFINITION 4. *The clustering number of an SFC π for a query q, denoted $c(q, \pi)$, is defined as the minimum number of clusters of π that q can be partitioned into.*

See Figure 4 for an example of the above definition.

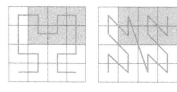

Hilbert Curve   Z Curve

Figure 4: For the same query region shown, the Hilbert curve has a clustering number of 1, and the Z curve has a clustering number of 2.

It is not very interesting to consider the clustering number of an SFC with respect to a single query, for the following reasons. First, it is rarely the case that there is only one query of interest we need to optimize for. Second, it is easy to come up with an SFC that yields the optimal clustering (one cluster) for a specific query. Thus, we always consider the average clustering number of an SFC with respect to a set of queries.

DEFINITION 5. *The average clustering number of an SFC π for a non-empty set of queries Q, denoted by $c(Q, \pi)$, is defined as:*

$$c(Q, \pi) = \frac{\sum_{q \in Q} c(q, \pi)}{|Q|}$$

Query Sets. The set of queries that we consider is constructed as follows. We first consider a basic query, for example, a two dimensional rectangle r consisting of the cells $\{(2+i, 3+j) | 1 \le i \le 2, 1 \le j \le 3\}$. Then we consider all possible *translations* of this shape r combined with a set of one or more *rotations* along the different axes, to arrive at a set of queries.

We handle rotation by treating it as a permutation of the coordinates along different dimensions. Other definitions of rotation are also possible, and they essentially lead to the same results as we get here. For example, in two dimensions, a 2×3 rectangle can be rotated to a 3×2 rectangle by interchanging dimensions 1 and 2. More precisely, let Λ^* be the set of all possible permutations of $(1, 2, \cdots, d)$. For $\lambda \in \Lambda^*$, and $1 \le i \le d$, let $\lambda(i)$ denote the image of i under λ. For any $\lambda \in \Lambda^*$, we define the rotation of a cell $x \in U$ under λ as:

$$\mathcal{P}(x = (x_1, \ldots, x_d), \lambda) = (x_{\lambda(1)}, x_{\lambda(2)}, \ldots, x_{\lambda(d)})$$

The rotation of any query $g \subseteq U$ with λ is defined as:

$$\mathcal{P}(g, \lambda) = \{\mathcal{P}(v, \lambda) | v \in g\}$$

For a query $g \subseteq U$, given a d dimensional vector $\delta = (\delta_1, \delta_2, \ldots, \delta_d)$, the translation of g subject to δ yields a new query defined as follows (note that "+" denotes vector addition):

$$\mathcal{L}(g, \delta) = \{v + \delta | v \in g\}$$

Given a query g, the set of all possible translations of the query is defined as the set of all possible queries that can be obtained by a translation of g (see Figure 5):

$$\mathcal{T}(g) = \{h \subseteq U | \exists \delta, h = \mathcal{L}(g, \delta)\}$$

DEFINITION 6. *For a query g and a non-empty set of rotations $\Lambda \subseteq \Lambda^*$, the query set $Q(g, \Lambda)$ is defined as*

$$\mathcal{Q}(g, \Lambda) = \bigcup_{\lambda \in \Lambda} \mathcal{T}(\mathcal{P}(g, \lambda))$$

For simplicity, we interpret the above to be a multiset, where we consider the queries in $\mathcal{T}(\mathcal{P}(g, \lambda_1))$ and $\mathcal{T}(\mathcal{P}(g, \lambda_2))$ to be distinct as long as $\lambda_1 \neq \lambda_2$. Note that it is possible that $\lambda_1 \neq \lambda_2$, but $\mathcal{T}(\mathcal{P}(g, \lambda_1))$ and $\mathcal{T}(\mathcal{P}(g, \lambda_2))$ are the same set of queries. For example, g may be a single cell whose coordinates are the same along all dimensions, so that any rotation λ makes no difference. Our results for rectangular queries can be extended in a straightforward manner to the case when we do not consider the multiset union above, but a regular set union, as we detail in Section 6.2.

For example, suppose $d = 2$ and r is a 2×3 rectangle, with length 2 along dimension 1 and 3 along dimension 2. Then $\Lambda^* = \{(1, 2), (2, 1)\}$, and $\mathcal{Q}(r, \Lambda^*)$ is equal to the set of all possible 2×3 or 3×2 rectangles. It is easy to verify that in this case $|\mathcal{Q}(r, \Lambda^*)| = 2(\sqrt{n} - 1)(\sqrt{n} - 2)$. Suppose that $\Lambda = \{(1, 2)\}$. Then, $\mathcal{Q}(r, \Lambda)$ is the set of all 2×3 rectangles, and $|\mathcal{Q}(r, \Lambda)| = (\sqrt{n} - 1)(\sqrt{n} - 2)$. The following observations follows from the definition of $\mathcal{Q}(\cdot, \cdot)$.

LEMMA 1. *Let r be a d-dimensional rectangle and for $1 \leq i \leq d$, let r_i denote the size of r along dimension i. Let $\Lambda \subseteq \Lambda^*$.*

$$|\mathcal{Q}(r, \Lambda)| = |\Lambda| \prod_{i=1}^{d} (\sqrt[d]{n} - r_i + 1)$$

Sketch of proof: First, we note that for any $\lambda \in \Lambda$, the set of cells $\mathcal{P}(r, \lambda)$ is still a rectangle, whose side length along dimension i is $r_{\lambda(i)}$. Second, we show that $|\mathcal{T}(r)| = \prod_{i=1}^{d}(\sqrt[d]{n} - r_i + 1)$. To see this, note that along each dimension i, r has $(\sqrt[d]{n} - r_i + 1)$ different translations. Since r can be translated along each dimension independently, the total number of translations should be $\prod_{i=1}^{d}(\sqrt[d]{n} - r_i + 1)$. Finally, we note that for any λ, the number of translations of $\mathcal{P}(r, \lambda)$ is the same as the number of translations of r. $\square$

LEMMA 2. *Let g be a query that is not necessarily a rectangle and for $1 \leq i \leq d$, let b_i denote the length of the bounding box $B(g)$ along dimension i. Let $\Lambda \subseteq \Lambda^*$.*

$$|\mathcal{Q}(g, \Lambda)| = |\Lambda| \prod_{i=1}^{d} (\sqrt[d]{n} - b_i + 1)$$

Sketch of proof: Recall $|\mathcal{Q}(g, \Lambda)| = \sum_{\lambda \in \Lambda} |\mathcal{T}(\mathcal{P}(g, \lambda))|$. It is possible to show that for any query g, $|\mathcal{T}(g)| = |\mathcal{T}(B(g))|$, so we have $|\mathcal{Q}(g, \Lambda)| = \sum_{\lambda \in \Lambda} |\mathcal{T}(B(\mathcal{P}(g, \lambda)))|$. Next we note that for $\lambda \in \Lambda$, the size of $B(\mathcal{P}(g, \lambda))$ is $b_{\lambda(i)}$ along dimension i, and the rest of this proof proceeds similar to the proof of Lemma 1. $\square$

3. GENERAL TECHNIQUES

Consider an arbitrary SFC π. For any two cells $\alpha, \beta \in U$ and query $q \subseteq U$, we define the function $I(q, \alpha, \beta)$ as:

$$\begin{aligned} I(q, \alpha, \beta) &= 1 && \text{if } \alpha \in q \text{ and } \beta \in q \\ &= 0 && \text{otherwise.} \end{aligned}$$

The SFC can be thought of as a set of directed edges that go from one cell to another, visiting each cell exactly once. Let $N(\pi)$ be the set of all such edges in SFC π, where each edge goes from a cell numbered i to a cell numbered $(i + 1)$, for some $0 \leq i \leq (n - 2)$.

$$N(\pi) = \{(\pi^{-1}(i), \pi^{-1}(i+1)) | 0 \leq i \leq n - 2\}$$

The following lemma applies to any SFC combined with any query, and gives us a powerful framework to compute the clustering number.

LEMMA 3. *For any query q and any SFC π,*

$$c(q, \pi) = |q| - \sum_{(\alpha, \beta) \in N(\pi)} I(q, \alpha, \beta)$$

PROOF. We use proof by induction on $\sum_{(\alpha, \beta) \in N(\pi)} I(q, \alpha, \beta)$. Let $\pi(q) = \{\pi(v) | v \in q\}$. For the base case, note that the clustering number of π for q is equal to $|q|$ when no two elements in $\pi(q)$ are consecutive, since in such a case, no two elements of q can belong to the same cluster. It can be seen that the cluster number will decrease by one for each pair of elements in $\pi(q)$ that are consecutive, thus forming the inductive step. $\square$

Example: Consider the two dimensional 4×4 grid and SFC π as shown in Figure 5(a). The linear order imposed by the SFC is determined by the integer assigned to each cell, shown in the upper left corner of the cell. Let q be the query shown by the shaded region. Note $|q| = 3$, and $I(q, \alpha, \beta)$ is non-zero for only one pair from $N(\pi)$, which is $(\pi^{-1}(1), \pi^{-1}(2))$. Thus, we have from Lemma 3 that the clustering number is $c(q, \pi) = 3 - 1 = 2$, which can be verified to be correct.

For any query q and a non-empty set of rotations Λ, let query set $Q = \mathcal{Q}(q, \Lambda)$. For a pair of vertices $\alpha, \beta \in U$ (perhaps non-neighboring), let $P_Q(\alpha, \beta)$ be defined as: $P_Q(\alpha, \beta) = \{r \in Q | I(r, \alpha, \beta) = 1\}$.

LEMMA 4.

$$c(Q, \pi) = |q| - \frac{\sum_{i=0}^{n-2} |P_Q(\pi^{-1}(i), \pi^{-1}(i+1))|}{|Q|}$$

PROOF. Applying Lemma 3 to Definition 5, we have:

$$\begin{aligned} c(Q, \pi) &= \frac{\sum_{q \in Q} c(q, \pi)}{|Q|} \\ &= \frac{1}{|Q|} \sum_{q \in Q} \left(|q| - \sum_{(\alpha, \beta) \in N(\pi)} I(q, \alpha, \beta) \right) \\ &= |q| - \frac{1}{|Q|} \sum_{(\alpha, \beta) \in N(\pi)} \sum_{q \in Q} I(q, \alpha, \beta) \\ &= |q| - \frac{1}{|Q|} \sum_{(\alpha, \beta) \in N(\pi)} |P_Q(\alpha, \beta)| \\ &= |q| - \frac{\sum_{i=0}^{n-2} |P_Q(\pi^{-1}(i), \pi^{-1}(i+1))|}{|Q|} \end{aligned}$$

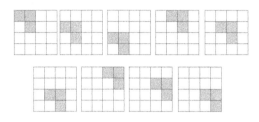

(a) The line represents the SFC while the shaded region represents a possible query q.

(b) The different query regions formed by translation of q.

Figure 5: An Example Set of Query Regions for an SFC

□

The above formula relates the clustering number $c(Q, \pi)$ to structural properties of Q and π, and provides a basis for the computation of lower and upper bounds.

4. ANALYSIS OF A CONTINUOUS SFC FOR A RECTILINEAR QUERY

In this section, we present an exact analysis of a continuous SFC π for any rectilinear query g of a fixed size. A rectilinear query is the union of multiple disjoint d-dimensional rectangles. Since each cell is trivially a d-dimensional rectangle, and an arbitrary query can be written as the union of its constituent cells, an arbitrary query is also a rectilinear query.

From the universe U, we derive an undirected graph $G(U) = (U, E(U))$, whose vertex set is U and where there is an edge between two vertices v_1 and v_2 in U whenever v_1 and v_2 are at a Manhattan distance of 1. For an edge $e = (v_1, v_2) \in E(U)$, we say "e lies along dimension i" iff the coordinates of v_1 and v_2 differ along dimension i (and are equal along the other dimensions). For $i = 1 \ldots d$, let $E_i(U)$ denote the subset of $E(U)$ consisting of all edges that lie along dimension i.

For any rectilinear query g, we associate a graph $G(g) = (g, E(g))$, defined as the induced subgraph of $G(U)$ with the vertex set g. For $i = 1 \ldots d$, let $E_i(g)$ denote the set $E(g) \cap E_i(U)$, i.e. all edges in $E(g)$ that lie along dimension i. Note that $G(g)$ and $E_i(g)$ depend only on the query g, and are independent of the SFC.

For any SFC π, and dimension i, $1 \le i \le d$, let $N^i(\pi)$ be the set of pairs $(\alpha, \beta) \in U \times U$ such that (1) $\pi(\beta) = \pi(\alpha) + 1$, and (2) $(\alpha, \beta) \in E_i(U)$. Informally, the set $N^i(\pi)$ is the set of all edges of π that connect points in U that are at a Manhattan distance of 1, and lie along dimension i.

4.1 Statement of Results

DEFINITION 7. *For an SFC π, vector $\mu(\pi)$ of length d is defined as:* $\mu(\pi) = (\mu_1(\pi), \mu_2(\pi), \ldots, \mu_d(\pi))$, *where for* $i = 1 \ldots d$

$$\mu_i(\pi) = \lim_{n \to \infty} \frac{|N^i(\pi)|}{n - 1}$$

It is assumed that the above limits exist for all the SFCs that we consider.

DEFINITION 8. *Given a query g, vector $\nu(g)$ of length d is defined as:* $\nu(g) = (\nu_1(g), \ldots, \nu_d(g))$ *where for* $1 \le i \le d$, $\nu_i(g) = |E_i(g)|$.

The main theorem for the clustering number of a continuous SFC with respect to translations is given below.

THEOREM 1. **Continuous SFC, Translations Only:** *For any continuous SFC π, any query g of fixed size, the average clustering number of π for query set $\mathcal{T}(g)$ is given as:*

$$\lim_{n \to \infty} c(\mathcal{T}(g), \pi) = |g| - \mu(\pi) \cdot \nu(g)$$

where $\cdot$ denotes the vector dot product.

We next present the theorem when a subset of possible rotations are considered along with translations. We first introduce a new parameter for a query g subject to a set of rotations Λ.

DEFINITION 9. *Given a query g, and a non-empty set of rotations $\Lambda \subseteq \Lambda^*$ we define a vector $\nu(g, \Lambda)$ of length d as:* $\nu(g, \Lambda) = (\nu_1(g, \Lambda), \ldots, \nu_d(g, \Lambda))$ *where for* $1 \le i \le d$,

$$\nu_i(g, \Lambda) = \frac{\sum_{\lambda \in \Lambda} \nu_i(\mathcal{P}(g, \lambda))}{|\Lambda|}$$

THEOREM 2. **Continuous SFC, Translations and Rotations:** *For any continuous SFC π, any query g of a fixed size, the average clustering number of π for query set $\mathcal{Q}(g, \Lambda)$ is given as:*

$$\lim_{n \to \infty} c(\mathcal{Q}(g, \Lambda), \pi) = |g| - \mu(\pi) \cdot \nu(g, \Lambda)$$

For example, consider an SFC π_1 shown on the left in Figure 6. Though the picture shows an 8×8 grid, the idea for a $m \times m$ grid is that the SFC goes horizontally (mostly) for the top $5m/8$ rows, and then vertically (mostly) for the bottom $3m/8$ rows. On the right are two queries A and B, and the induced graphs $G(A)$ and $G(B)$ are shown within the queries.

By the above definitions, it can be calculated that $\mu(\pi_1) = [5/8, 3/8]$. On the right side of the figure are shown two queries A and B. We have $\nu(A) = [2, 2]$, since $E(A)$ has

Dimension 2

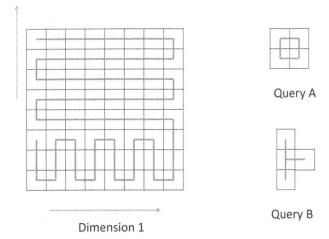

Query A

Query B

Dimension 1

Figure 6: On the left is an SFC π_1 and on the right are two queries A and B.

4 edges, two of them horizontal and two vertical. From Theorem 1, we have the clustering number $c(\mathcal{T}(A), \pi_1) = 4 - (5/8)(2) - (3/8)(2) = 2$. Similarly, $\nu(B) = [1, 2]$. From Theorem 1, we have the clustering number $c(\mathcal{T}(B), \pi_1) = 4 - (5/8)(1) - (3/8)(2) = 21/8$.

4.2 Proofs of Theorems 1 and 2

The first part of this proof applies to a query set Q constructed from a basic query g. It does not matter whether we construct Q from translations of g only, or through translations and rotations. Hence, this part will apply to proofs of both Theorems 1 and 2.

From Lemma 4, we have

$$c(Q, \pi) = |g| - \frac{\sum_{j=0}^{n-2} |P_Q(\pi^{-1}(j), \pi^{-1}(j+1))|}{|Q|} \quad (1)$$

Let $S(\cdot, \cdot)$ be defined as:

$$S(Q, \pi) = \sum_{j=0}^{n-2} |P_Q(\pi^{-1}(j), \pi^{-1}(j+1))| \quad (2)$$

Since π is continuous, for each $j, 0 \leq j \leq (n-2)$, we have the pair $(\pi^{-1}(j), \pi^{-1}(j+1)) \in N^i(\pi)$ for some $i, 1 \leq i \leq d$. We can get the following.

$$\bigcup_{j=0}^{n-2} \{(\pi^{-1}(j), \pi^{-1}(j+1))\} = \bigcup_{i=1}^{d} N^i(\pi)$$

From the above, S can be rewritten as:

$$S(Q, \pi) = \sum_{i=1}^{d} \sum_{(\alpha, \beta) \in N^i(\pi)} |P_Q(\alpha, \beta)| \quad (3)$$

We will need the following lemmas to prove Theorem 1. For a query set Q and dimension $i, 1 \leq i \leq d$, let ρ_Q^i be

defined as:

$$\rho_Q^i = \max_{(\alpha, \beta) \in N^i(\pi)} |P_Q(\alpha, \beta)| \quad (4)$$

LEMMA 5. *For any $i, 1 \leq i \leq d$ and any query g,*
$$\rho_{\mathcal{T}(g)}^i \leq \nu_i(g)$$

PROOF. Consider any edge (α, β) from $E_i(U)$. From the definition of P, we have that if query r is in $P_{\mathcal{T}(g)}(\alpha, \beta)$, then $\alpha \in r$ and $\beta \in r$. Since edge (α, β) is parallel to the ith axis, we have the number of translations of g which can include (α, β) should be no more than the number of edges in $E(g)$ which lie along dimension i. Thus we have:

$$|P_{\mathcal{T}(g)}(\alpha, \beta)| \leq |E_i(g)| = \nu_i(g)$$

Since the above is true for any edge $(\alpha, \beta) \in E_i(U)$, we get $\rho_{\mathcal{T}(g)}^i \leq \nu_i(g)$. $\square$

For dimension $i, 1 \leq i \leq d$, let $N_i(\pi)$ be a subset of $N^i(\pi)$ defined as:

$$N_i(\pi) = \left\{ (\alpha, \beta) \in N^i(\pi) \,\middle|\, |P_{\mathcal{T}(g)}(\alpha, \beta)| = \nu_i(g) \right\}$$

LEMMA 6. *For any dimension $i, 1 \leq i \leq d$, and any query g of a fixed size, $\lim_{n \to \infty} \frac{|N^i(\pi)|}{|\mathcal{T}(g)|} = \lim_{n \to \infty} \frac{|N_i(\pi)|}{|\mathcal{T}(g)|} = \mu_i(\pi)$*

PROOF. Let $b_i, 1 \leq i \leq d$ be the length of $B(g)$ along dimension i. From Lemma 2, we have $\mathcal{T}(g) = \prod_{i=1}^{d}(\sqrt[d]{n} - b_i + 1)$. So from definition of $\mu_i(\pi)$, we get:

$$\lim_{n \to \infty} \frac{|N^i(\pi)|}{|\mathcal{T}(g)|} = \mu_i(\pi)$$

Now we show the second equality. Let $b^* = \max_{1 \leq i \leq d} b_i$. Let $U' \subset U$ be the set of all cells $(x_1, \ldots, x_d)$ such that for each dimension $i, b^* - 1 \leq x_i \leq \sqrt[d]{n} - b^*$.

For any $(\alpha, \beta) \in N^i(\pi)$, if $\alpha, \beta \in U'$, then it can be seen that $|P_{\mathcal{T}(g)}(\alpha, \beta)| = |\nu_i(g)|$. The total number of pairs (α, β) such that α or β lies outside of U' is bounded by $n - (\sqrt[d]{n} - 2b^*)^d$. So we have:

$$|N^i(\pi)| - (n - (\sqrt[d]{n} - 2b^*)^d) \leq |N_i(\pi)| \leq |N^i(\pi)|$$

Note that

$$\lim_{n \to \infty} \frac{n - (\sqrt[d]{n} - 2b^*)^d}{\mathcal{T}(g)} = 0$$

So we have:

$$\lim_{n \to \infty} \frac{|N^i(\pi)|}{|\mathcal{T}(g)|} = \lim_{n \to \infty} \frac{|N_i(\pi)|}{|\mathcal{T}(g)|}$$
$$= \mu_i(\pi)$$

$\square$

PROOF OF THEOREM 1. We start from Equations 3 and 4. Setting $Q = \mathcal{T}(g)$ in Equation 3,

$$
\begin{aligned}
S(\mathcal{T}(g), \pi) &= \sum_{i=1}^{d} \sum_{(\alpha, \beta) \in N^i(\pi)} |P_{\mathcal{T}(g)}(\alpha, \beta)| \\
&\leq \sum_{i=1}^{d} |N^i(\pi)| \rho_{\mathcal{T}(g)}^i \quad \text{From Defn. of } \rho \\
&\leq \sum_{i=1}^{d} |N^i(\pi)| \nu_i(g) \quad \text{Using Lemma 5}
\end{aligned}
$$

Using this back in Equation 1

$$c(\mathcal{T}(g), \pi) \geq |g| - \frac{\sum_{i=1}^{d} |N^i(\pi)| \nu_i(g)}{|\mathcal{T}(g)|} \qquad (5)$$

Taking limits on the right side and applying Lemma 6:

$$
\begin{aligned}
\lim_{n \to \infty} c(\mathcal{T}(g), \pi) &\geq |g| - \lim_{n \to \infty} \sum_{i=1}^{d} \frac{|N^i(\pi)|}{|\mathcal{T}(g)|} \nu_i(g) \\
&= |g| - \sum_{i=1}^{d} \mu_i(\pi) \nu_i(g)
\end{aligned}
$$

We now consider the upper bound on $c(\mathcal{T}(g), \pi)$. The starting point for this is Equations 3 and 4. Using Equation 3

$$S(\mathcal{T}(g), \pi) \geq \sum_{i=1}^{d} |N_i(\pi)| \nu_i(g)$$

Proceeding as above,

$$c(\mathcal{T}(g), \pi) \leq |g| - \frac{\sum_{i=1}^{d} |N_i(\pi)| \nu_i(g)}{|\mathcal{T}(g)|} \qquad (6)$$

Taking limits on both sides and applying Lemma 6

$$\lim_{n \to \infty} c(\mathcal{T}(g), \pi) \leq |g| - \sum_{i=1}^{d} \mu_i(\pi) \nu_i(g)$$

This upper bound on the clustering number, when combined with the lower bound, completes the proof. $\square$

PROOF OF THEOREM 2.

$$P_Q(\pi^{-1}(j), \pi^{-1}(j+1)) = \bigcup_{\lambda \in \Lambda} P_{Q(\lambda)}(\pi^{-1}(j), \pi^{-1}(j+1))$$

Since the different $P_Q(\lambda)$s are disjoint for different λ

$$
\begin{aligned}
S(Q, \pi) &= \sum_{j=0}^{n-2} |P_Q(\pi^{-1}(j), \pi^{-1}(j+1))| \\
&= \sum_{j=0}^{n-2} \sum_{\lambda \in \Lambda} |P_{Q(\lambda)}(\pi^{-1}(j), \pi^{-1}(j+1))| \\
&= \sum_{\lambda \in \Lambda} \sum_{j=0}^{n-2} |P_{Q(\lambda)}(\pi^{-1}(j), \pi^{-1}(j+1))|
\end{aligned}
$$

From Equation 1, we have:

$$c(\mathcal{Q}(g, \Lambda), \pi) = |g| - \frac{S(\mathcal{Q}(g, \Lambda), \pi)}{|\mathcal{Q}(g, \Lambda)|}$$

$$= |g| - \frac{1}{|\Lambda| |Q(\lambda)|} \sum_{\lambda \in \Lambda} \sum_{j=0}^{n-2} |P_{Q(\lambda)}(\pi^{-1}(j), \pi^{-1}(j+1))|$$

$$= \frac{1}{|\Lambda|} \sum_{\lambda \in \Lambda} \left[|g| - \frac{\sum_{j=0}^{n-2} |P_{Q(\lambda)}(\pi^{-1}(j), \pi^{-1}(j+1))|}{|Q(\lambda)|} \right]$$

Applying Theorem 1:

$$\lim_{n \to \infty} c(\mathcal{Q}(g, \Lambda), \pi) = \frac{1}{|\Lambda|} \sum_{\lambda \in \Lambda} (|g| - \mu(\pi) \cdot \nu(\mathcal{P}(g, \lambda)))$$

After simplification, we have:

$$\lim_{n \to \infty} c(\mathcal{Q}(g, \Lambda), \pi) = |g| - \mu(\pi) \cdot \nu(g, \Lambda)$$

$\square$

4.3 All Possible Rotations

When $\Lambda = \Lambda^*$, the set of all possible rotations, we get a much simpler form for the clustering number of a continuous SFC, as follows. For any query $q \subset U$ such that q does not contain a cell adjacent to the boundary of U (i.e. q does not have any cell with a coordinate equal to 0 or $\sqrt[d]{n} - 1$) the surface area of q is defined to be the number of cells $\beta \in U$ such that $\beta \notin q$, and β is at a Manhattan distance of 1 from some cell α in q. For a query q that has at least one cell on the boundary of U, we add for each such cell, the number of its coordinates that are equal to 0, or $\sqrt[d]{n} - 1$.

LEMMA 7. *The surface area of g is $S_g = 2d|g| - 2|E(g)|$.*

PROOF. For $\alpha \in g$, let $\omega(\alpha)$ denote the degree of α in $G(g)$. The contribution of α to the surface area is $2d - \omega(\alpha)$. Thus, the total surface area of g is: $\sum_{\alpha \in g} [2d - \omega(\alpha)] = 2d|g| - \sum_{\alpha \in g} \omega(\alpha)$. The lemma follows by noting that for a graph the sum of degrees is twice the number of edges. $\square$

THEOREM 3. *For any continuous SFC π, and any query g of a fixed size,*

$$\lim_{n \to \infty} c(\mathcal{Q}(g, \Lambda^*), \pi) = \frac{S_g}{2d}$$

PROOF. From Theorem 2, we have

$$\lim_{n \to \infty} c(\mathcal{Q}(g, \Lambda^*), \pi) = |g| - \mu(\pi) \cdot \nu(g, \Lambda^*)$$

Note that for $1 \leq i \leq d$,

$$\nu_i(g, \Lambda^*) = \frac{\sum_{\lambda \in \Lambda^*} |E_i(\mathcal{P}(g, \lambda))|}{|\Lambda^*|}$$

Let $e_i = \sum_{\lambda \in \Lambda^*} |E_i(\mathcal{P}(g, \lambda))|$. When all the $d!$ possible rotations are considered, by symmetry we have $e_1 = e_2 = \ldots = e_d$. Further, $\sum_{i=1}^{d} e_i = |E(g)| d!$. Thus, we have $e_i = \frac{|E(g)| d!}{d}$ for each $i, 1 \leq i \leq d$. $\nu_i(g, \Lambda^*) = \frac{|E(g)|}{d}$

$$
\begin{aligned}
A &= |g| - \mu(\pi) \left[\frac{|E(g)|}{d}, \frac{|E(g)|}{d}, \ldots, \frac{|E(g)|}{d} \right] \\
&= |g| - \frac{|E(g)|}{d} \text{ since } \sum_{i=1}^{d} \mu_i(\pi) = 1 \\
&= \frac{S_g}{2d} \text{ using Lemma 7}
\end{aligned}
$$

$\square$

Since the Hilbert curve is a continuous curve, the result of Moon *et al.* [7] follows from the above theorem.

4.4 Symmetric SFCs

We say that a continuous SFC π is *symmetric* if it has (nearly) the same number of edges along each dimension i. More precisely, we need that for each $i = 1 \ldots d$, $\mu_i(\pi)$ exists and is equal to $\frac{1}{d}$.

COROLLARY 1. *For any symmetric SFC π, for any query g of a fixed size, for any non-empty set of rotations $\Lambda \subseteq \Lambda^*$*

$$\lim_{n \to \infty} c(\mathcal{Q}(g, \Lambda), \pi) = \frac{S_g}{2d}$$

PROOF. The proof follows from Theorem 2, and then using a similar technique used in the proof of Theorem 3. The difference being that in Theorem 3 the vector $\nu(g, \Lambda)$ had all elements equal, while in this case the vector $\mu(\pi)$ has all elements equal. $\square$

It is known that the d-dimensional Hilbert curve $\mathcal{H}_d$ is symmetric (see [7], Section 3). From the above corollary, it follows that Hilbert curve yields the same performance for a query irrespective of the set of rotations considered.

5. RECTANGULAR QUERIES: LOWER BOUND FOR ANY SFC

In this section, we present a lower bound on the clustering number of any SFC, for rectangular queries. Further, we show that *for a query set formed by translation and/or rotations of a rectangular query, there exists a continuous SFC that is optimal.*

5.1 Statement of Results

Consider the query set $\mathcal{Q}(r, \Lambda)$, where r is a rectangular query, and $\Lambda \subseteq \Lambda^*$ is a non-empty set of rotations. Let $\nu^{max} = \nu^{max}(r, \Lambda) = \max_{1 \leq i \leq d} \nu_i(r, \Lambda)$. The main results in this section are stated in Theorems 4 and 5.

THEOREM 4. *Given a rectangular query r of a fixed size and a non-empty set of rotations $\Lambda \subseteq \Lambda^*$, for any SFC π (not necessarily continuous), if $\lim_{n \to \infty} c(\mathcal{Q}(r, \Lambda), \pi)$ exists, then*

$$\lim_{n \to \infty} c(\mathcal{Q}(r, \Lambda), \pi) \geq |r| - \nu^{max}$$

THEOREM 5. *For a rectangular query r of a fixed size and $\Lambda \subseteq \Lambda^*$, there exists a continuous SFC π whose clustering number is optimal, i.e.:*

$$\lim_{n \to \infty} c(\mathcal{Q}(r, \Lambda), \pi) = |r| - \nu^{max}$$

We also have the following surprising fact, that when the set of all rotations are considered for a rectangular query, every continuous SFC π is optimal.

COROLLARY 2. *For a rectangular query r of a fixed size, if all possible rotations are considered, then* any *continuous SFC π is optimal.*

5.2 Proofs of Theorems 4 and 5

To prove Theorem 4, we need the following lemma.

LEMMA 8. *For any SFC π and any pair $(\alpha, \beta) \in N(\pi)$, query set $Q = \mathcal{Q}(r, \Lambda)$, we have:*

$$|P_Q(\alpha, \beta)| \leq |\Lambda| \nu^{max}$$

PROOF. Recall that $P_Q(\alpha, \beta) = \{q \in Q | I(q, \alpha, \beta) = 1\}$. Let $\gamma = \{\alpha, \beta\}$. For each $t \in P_Q(\alpha, \beta)$, we have $\gamma \subseteq t$. Since t is a rectangle it must also be true that the bounding box of γ, $B(\gamma)$ is contained in t. Since $B(\gamma)$ is a rectangle, there is at least one neighbor of α, say α' such that $\alpha' \in B(\gamma)$, and hence $\alpha' \in t$. Note that it is possible $\alpha' = \beta$, if β is at a Manhattan distance of 1 from α.

Let $\gamma' = \{\alpha, \alpha'\}$. Since $\gamma' \subseteq t$, we have $t \in P_Q(\gamma')$. Thus we have that $P_Q(\gamma) \subseteq P_Q(\gamma')$.

$$|P_Q(\gamma)| \leq |P_Q(\gamma')| \tag{7}$$

For $\lambda \in \Lambda$, let $Q(\lambda) = \mathcal{T}(\mathcal{P}(r, \lambda))$. Note that:

$$|P_Q(\gamma')| = \sum_{\lambda \in \Lambda} |P_{Q(\lambda)}(\gamma')| \tag{8}$$

Assume γ' is parallel to the ith axis. For any $\lambda \in \Lambda$, we have the following:

$$|P_{Q(\lambda)}(\gamma')| \leq \nu_i(\mathcal{P}(r, \lambda)) \tag{9}$$

The above can be proved using an argument identical to the one used in Lemma 5. In Lemma 5, this was used to bound the size of $P_Q(\alpha'', \beta'')$ where α'' and β'' are neighbors in a continuous SFC, but this exact argument can be used here too since α and α' are at a Manhattan distance of 1.

Combining Equations 7, 8, and 9,

$$|P_Q(\gamma)| \leq \sum_{\lambda \in \Lambda} \nu_i(\mathcal{P}(r, \lambda)) = |\Lambda| \nu_i(r, \Lambda) \leq |\Lambda| \nu^{max}$$

$\square$

PROOF OF THEOREM 4. From Lemma 4, we have:

$$c(Q, \pi) = |r| - \frac{1}{|Q|} \sum_{(\alpha, \beta) \in N(\pi)} |P_Q(\alpha, \beta)|$$

Let $r_i, 1 \leq i \leq d$ denote the length of r along dimension i. Applying Lemma 1, we have:

$$c(\mathcal{Q}(r, \Lambda), \pi) = |r| - \frac{1}{|\Lambda| \prod_{i=1}^d (\sqrt[d]{n} - r_i + 1)} \sum_{(\alpha, \beta) \in N(\pi)} |P_Q(\alpha, \beta)|$$

Applying Lemma 8:

$$\begin{aligned} c(\mathcal{Q}(r, \Lambda), \pi) &\geq |r| - \frac{1}{|\Lambda| \prod_{i=1}^d (\sqrt[d]{n} - r_i + 1)} (n-1)|\Lambda| \nu^{max} \\ &= |r| - \nu^{max} - o(1) \end{aligned}$$

In the above, we use $o(1)$ to denote a function of n that approaches 0 as $n \to \infty$. The proof depends on the fact $\lim_{n \to \infty} \frac{n-1}{\prod_{i=1}^d (\sqrt[d]{n} - r_i + 1)} = 1$ which is true since r_i and d are constants independent of n. $\square$

PROOF OF THEOREM 5. We construct a continuous SFC whose performance meets the above bound.
Let $j = \text{argmax}_{1 \leq i \leq d} \nu_i(r, \lambda)$, so that $\nu_j = \nu^{max}$. Consider SFC S^j defined as follows:

$$S^j((x_1, \ldots, x_d)) = \sum_{i=1}^{j-1} x_i (\sqrt[d]{n})^i + x_j + \sum_{i=j+1}^d x_i (\sqrt[d]{n})^{i-1}$$

We can check that:

$$\mu_j(S^j) = 1, \quad \mu_i(S^j) = 0, \forall i \neq j$$

From Theorem 2, we get that for any rectilinear query r and rotation set Λ,

$$\lim_{n \to \infty} c(\mathcal{Q}(r, \Lambda), S^j) = |r| - \nu^{max}$$

So from Theorem 4, we conclude that for any rectangle query r and any nonempty set of rotations $\Lambda \subseteq \Lambda^*$, S^j is optimal among all SFCs. $\square$

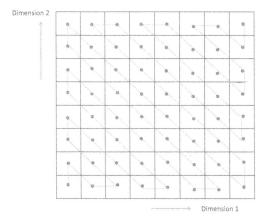

(a) A non-continuous SFC π

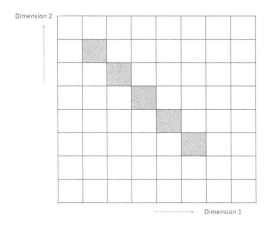

(b) An example query q

Figure 7: The performance of a non-continuous SFC can dominate the performance of any continuous SFC for the above query.

PROOF OF COROLLARY 2. Consider a continuous SFC π. Using Theorem 3,

$$c(\mathcal{Q}(r, \Lambda^*), \pi) = \frac{S_r}{2d}$$

where S_r denotes the surface area of r. If $\Lambda = \Lambda^*$, then for $i = 1 \ldots d$, $\nu^{max} = \nu_i(r, \Lambda^*)$, and thus $\nu^{max} = \frac{|E(r)|}{d}$.

The lower bound from Theorem 4 is $|r| - \nu^{max} = |r| - \frac{|E(r)|}{d}$. Proceeding similarly to the proof of Theorem 3, we get the above expression to be $\frac{S_r}{2d}$. Thus, the performance of π meets the lower bound, showing that it is optimal. $\square$

6. EXTENSIONS

6.1 Noncontinuous SFCs

We now consider the performance of SFCs that are not continuous. For rectangular queries of a fixed size, Theorem 5 shows that a non-continuous SFC cannot outperform the best possible continuous SFC. It is natural to ask if the class of continuous SFCs contains an optimal SFC for a general query.

We show that this is not true in general. *There exist query classes where the performance of a non-continuous SFC can be much better than that of the best continuous SFC for that query.* In Figure 7(a), we show a specific noncontinuous SFC π and in Figure 7(b), we show a query q. It is clear that $c(q, \pi) = 1$. It is also clear that $\lim_{n \to \infty} c(\mathcal{T}(q), \pi)$ is 1. Though the picture shows a specific noncontinuous SFC for an 8×8 grid, the same SFC can be extended to a $\sqrt{n} \times \sqrt{n}$ grid for an arbitrary n, and the clustering number for $\mathcal{T}(q)$ is still 1.

However, the clustering number of any continuous SFC for $\mathcal{T}(q)$ must be 5, since no two cells of the query can belong to the same cluster of a continuous SFC. The performance of the best continuous SFC is 5 times as bad as that of a non-continuous SFC. Clearly, by constructing queries that are the same shape with $|q|$ cells, the performance of a continuous SFC can be $|q|$ times as bad as that of a noncontinuous SFC.

6.2 Query Models

Given a rectangle r, and set of rotations Λ^* we note that in Definition 6, we have defined $\mathcal{Q}(r, \Lambda^*)$ as the multiset union of the collection of sets $\{\mathcal{T}(\mathcal{P}(g, \lambda)) | \lambda \in \Lambda^*\}$.

Suppose we constructed a set of queries $\mathcal{Q}'(r, \Lambda^*)$ not through a multiset union of the above collection of sets, but through a simple union. Then queries that belong to both $\mathcal{T}(\mathcal{P}(g, \lambda_1))$ and $\mathcal{T}(\mathcal{P}(g, \lambda_2))$ for distinct $\lambda_1, \lambda_2 \in \Lambda^*$ are included only once in $\mathcal{Q}'(r, \Lambda^*)$, but multiple times in $\mathcal{Q}(r, \Lambda^*)$. The following lemma holds.

LEMMA 9. *For any SFC π, whether continuous or not:*

$$c(\mathcal{Q}'(r, \Lambda^*), \pi) = c(\mathcal{Q}(r, \Lambda^*), \pi)$$

PROOF. First, we note that for distinct $\lambda_1, \lambda_2 \in \Lambda^*$, the query sets $\mathcal{T}(r, \lambda_1)$ and $\mathcal{T}(r, \lambda_2)$ are either equal to each other, or completely disjoint from each other. For each $\lambda \in \Lambda^*$, let $Q(\lambda) = \mathcal{T}(\mathcal{P}(r, \lambda))$. Let $\Lambda' \subseteq \Lambda^*$ be the largest subset such that the sets $\{Q(\lambda) | \lambda \in \Lambda'\}$ are all distinct. From the above, we have:

$$c(\mathcal{Q}'(r, \Lambda^*), \pi) = c(\mathcal{Q}(r, \Lambda'), \pi) \qquad (10)$$

For each $\lambda \in \Lambda^*$, let $G_\lambda = \{\lambda_1 \in \Lambda^* | Q(\lambda_1) = Q(\lambda)\}$. The main tool for us here is Lemma 10.

From the definition, it follows

$$c(\mathcal{Q}(r, \Lambda^*), \pi) = \frac{\sum_{q \in \mathcal{Q}(r, \Lambda^*)} c(q, \pi)}{|\mathcal{Q}(r, \Lambda^*)|}$$

Using Lemma 10, we get $|\mathcal{Q}(r, \Lambda^*)| = |\mathcal{Q}(r, \Lambda')||G_\lambda|$, for some $\lambda \in \Lambda'$. Also, using Lemma 10 the numerator of the above reduces to $|G_\lambda| \sum_{q \in \mathcal{Q}(r, \Lambda')} c(q, \pi)$.

$$
\begin{aligned}
c(\mathcal{Q}(r, \Lambda^*), \pi) &= \frac{|G_\lambda| \sum_{q \in \mathcal{Q}(r, \Lambda')} c(q, \pi)}{|\mathcal{Q}(r, \Lambda')||G_\lambda|} \\
&= \frac{\sum_{q \in \mathcal{Q}(r, \Lambda')} c(q, \pi)}{|\mathcal{Q}(r, \Lambda')|} \\
&= c(\mathcal{Q}(r, \Lambda'), \pi) \\
&= c(\mathcal{Q}'(r, \Lambda^*), \pi) \quad \text{using Equation 10}
\end{aligned}
$$

which yields the desired result. $\square$

LEMMA 10. *For any rectangle r and distinct $\lambda_1, \lambda_2 \in \Lambda'$*

$$|G_{\lambda_1}| = |G_{\lambda_2}|$$

PROOF. Let $r_i, 1 \leq i \leq d$ be the length of r along dimension i. From Lemma 1, we know for each $\lambda \in \Lambda^*$, the length of $\mathcal{P}(r, \lambda)$ along dimension i is $r_{\lambda(i)}$.

For two rectangles, the sets formed by all translations of the rectangles are equal if and only if the lengths of the two rectangles along each dimension are equal. In other words, $Q(\lambda_1) = Q(\lambda_2)$ iff for each $i = 1 \ldots d$, $r_{\lambda_1(i)} = r_{\lambda_2(i)}$ So we can rewrite the definition of G_λ as
$G_\lambda = \{\lambda_1 \in \Lambda^* | r_{\lambda_1(i)} = r_{\lambda(i)}, \forall 1 \leq i \leq d\}$.

Assume $\{r_i | 1 \leq i \leq d\}$ has K distinct numbers. Without loss of generality, we assume $r_i \neq r_j$ for all $1 \leq i, j \leq K$, and $i \neq j$. For $1 \leq i \leq K$, let $I_i \subseteq \{1, 2, \ldots d\}$ be the set of numbers such that for each $j \in I_i, r_j = r_i$. It can be seen that for each $\lambda \in \Lambda^*$,

$$|G_\lambda| = \prod_{i=1}^{K} (|I_i|!)$$

That is because for any fixed $\lambda \in \Lambda^*$, $r_{\lambda_1(i)} = r_{\lambda(i)}$ for all $1 \leq i \leq d$ iff and only of λ_1 can be equal to λ after some permutations in $I_i, 1 \leq i \leq K$. $\square$

7. CONCLUSION

We presented results that characterize the clustering properties of space filling curves over query sets that are formed by translations and rotations of a basic query shape. When the basic shape is a rectangle of a fixed size, our analysis presents a near-complete picture in the sense that we obtain matching upper and lower bounds on the clustering number.

One consequence of our work is that any continuous SFC is optimal for rectangular queries of a fixed size, when all rotations are considered. This shows that while the Hilbert curve works well for such queries, since it is a continuous SFC, there is nothing that sets the Hilbert curve apart from say, the row-major curve. In fact, when only a subset of rotations are considered for a rectangular query that is not a cube, the optimal SFC, which can be derived from our analysis, may be strictly better than the Hilbert curve.

When the basic query shape is a more general rectilinear region, we present an analysis of the clustering number for the class of continuous SFCs. An interesting question is to generalize our results to the case an arbitrary SFC, for a general query shape.

References

[1] J. Alber and R. Niedermeier. On Multidimensional Curves with Hilbert Property. *Theory Comput. Syst.*, 33(4):295–312, 2000.

[2] T. Asano, D. Ranjan, T. Roos, E. Welzl, and P. Widmayer. Space-filling curves and their use in the design of geometric data structures. *Theor. Comput. Sci.*, 181(1):3–15, 1997.

[3] C. Faloutsos. Multiattribute hashing using gray codes. *SIGMOD Record*, 15:227–238, June 1986.

[4] C. Faloutsos. Gray codes for partial match and range queries. *IEEE Trans. Software Engg.*, 14:1381–1393, 1988.

[5] D. Hilbert. Uber die stetige Abbildung einer Linie auf ein Flachenstuck. *Math. Ann.*, 38:459–460, 1891.

[6] H. V. Jagadish. Analysis of the Hilbert curve for representing two-dimensional space. *Information Processing Letters*, 62:17–22, 1997.

[7] B. Moon, H. V. Jagadish, C. Faloutsos, and J. H. Saltz. Analysis of the clustering properties of the Hilbert space-filling curve. *IEEE Trans. Knowledge and Data Engineering*, 13(1):124–141, 2001.

[8] G.M. Morton. A computer oriented geodetic data base; and a new technique in file sequencing. Technical report, IBM, 1966.

[9] Oracle. Oracle spatial and oracle locator. `http://www.oracle.com/technetwork/database/options/spatial/overview/introduction/index.html`.

[10] J. A. Orenstein and T. H. Merrett. A class of data structures for associative searching. In *Proceedings of the 3rd ACM SIGACT-SIGMOD symposium on Principles of database systems*, PODS '84, pages 181–190, 1984.

Nearest-Neighbor Searching Under Uncertainty[*]

Pankaj K. Agarwal
Department of Computer
Science
Duke University
pankaj@cs.duke.edu

Alon Efrat
Department of Computer
Science
The University of Arizona
alon@cs.arizona.edu

Swaminathan
Sankararaman[*]
Department of Computer
Science
Duke University
swami@cs.duke.edu

Wuzhou Zhang
Department of Computer
Science
Duke University
wuzhou@cs.duke.edu

ABSTRACT

Nearest-neighbor queries, which ask for returning the nearest neighbor of a query point in a set of points, are important and widely studied in many fields because of a wide range of applications. In many of these applications, such as sensor databases, location based services, face recognition, and mobile data, the location of data is imprecise. We therefore study nearest neighbor queries in a probabilistic framework in which the location of each input point and/or query point is specified as a probability density function and the goal is to return the point that minimizes the expected distance, which we refer to as the expected nearest neighbor (ENN). We present methods for computing an exact ENN or an ε-approximate ENN, for a given error parameter $0 < \varepsilon < 1$, under different distance functions. These methods build an index of near-linear size and answer ENN queries in polylogarithmic or sublinear time, depending on the underlying function. As far as we know, these are the first nontrivial methods for answering exact or ε-approximate ENN queries with provable performance guarantees.

Categories and Subject Descriptors

F.2 [**Analysis of algorithms and problem complexity**]: Nonnumerical algorithms and problems; H.3.1 [**Information**

storage and retrieval]: Content analysis and indexing—*indexing methods*

General Terms

Theory

Keywords

Indexing uncertain data, nearest-neighbor queries, expected nearest neighbor (ENN), approximate nearest neighbor

1. INTRODUCTION

Motivated by a wide range of applications, nearest neighbor searching has been studied in many different fields including computational geometry, database systems and information retrieval; see [7, 14] for surveys on this topic. In its simplest form, it asks for preprocessing a set S of n points in $\mathbb{R}^d$ into an index so that the nearest neighbor (NN) in S of a query point can be reported quickly. The earlier methods for answering NN queries assumed that the input points and the query points were precise. In many applications, such as sensor databases, location based services, face recognition, and mobile data, the location of data is imprecise. This has led to a flurry of activity on query processing over uncertain data, and algorithms for answering range query, top-k queries, skyline queries and NN queries have been proposed, among numerous results. See e.g. [4, 15] for recent work.

In this paper we are interested in answering NN queries over uncertain data —the location of input points or the query point is not precisely known, and we assume that it is given as a probability density function. The existing methods for answering NN queries on precise data cannot be applied directly to this setting and new methods are needed.

Our model. An *uncertain* point P in $\mathbb{R}^d$ is represented as a probability density function (pdf) $f_P : \mathbb{R}^d \to \mathbb{R}_{\geq 0}$[1]. We assume f_P to be a simple pdf such as Gaussian distribution, inverse distance function, or a histogram; we make this notion more precise later. We also consider *discrete pdfs*, in which P is represented as a finite set $P = \{p_1, \cdots, p_k\} \subset \mathbb{R}^d$ along with a set $\{w_1, \cdots, w_k\} \subset [0, 1]$ where $w_i = \Pr\{P \text{ is } p_i\}$ and

[*]P.A. and W.Z. are supported by NSF under grants CNS-05-40347, CCF-06 -35000, IIS-07-13498, and CCF-09-40671, by ARO grants W911NF-07-1-0376 and W911NF-08-1-0452, by an NIH grant 1P50-GM-08183-01, and by a grant from the U.S.–Israel Binational Science Foundation. A.E. and S.S. are supported by NSF CAREER Grant 0348000.

[*]This work was partly undertaken while S.S. was at the University of Arizona.

---

[1]If the location of data is precise, we refer to it as *certain*.

$\sum_{i=1}^{k} w_i = 1$. Discrete pdfs arise in a wide range of applications [19, 23], e.g., because of multiple observations, and continuous pdfs can be approximated as discrete pdfs.

Let $d(\cdot, \cdot)$ denote a distance function in $\mathbb{R}^d$; we consider L_1, L_2, L_∞-metrics or squared Euclidean distance[2]. For a given $d(\cdot, \cdot)$, the *expected distance* between two independent uncertain points P and Q is defined as

$$\mathsf{Ed}(P, Q) = \iint f_P(x) f_Q(y) d(x, y) dx dy.$$

If f_P and f_Q are discrete pdfs of size k each, then

$$\mathsf{Ed}(P, Q) = \sum_{i=1}^{k} \sum_{j=1}^{k} w_i w'_j d(p_i, q_j),$$

where w_i, w'_j are the probabilities of P and Q being at p_i and q_j respectively. If Q is a (certain) point in $\mathbb{R}^d$, i.e., $Q = \{q\}$, then

$$\mathsf{Ed}(P, q) = \sum_{i=1}^{k} w_i d(p_i, q).$$

We say that the *description complexity* of f_P is k if it can be represented using $O(k)$ parameters and certain basic primitive operations on f_P can be performed in $O(k)$ time. In particular, $\mathsf{Ed}(P, x)$, for any $x \in \mathbb{R}^2$, can be computed in $O(k)$ time, and the expected location $\int x f_P(x) dx$ of P, also called the *centroid* of P, can be computed in $O(k)$ time. Examples include a discrete pdf consisting of at most k points, and piecewise-constant or piecewise-linear pdf consisting of at most k pieces. Gaussian (under certain distance functions) and inverse-distance distributions have constant description complexity.

Let $\mathcal{P} = \{P_1, \cdots, P_n\}$ be a set of n uncertain points in $\mathbb{R}^d$, each of which is independently chosen. For simplicity, let f_i denote f_{P_i}, the pdf of P_i. For an uncertain point Q, its *expected nearest neighbor* (ENN), denoted by $\varphi(\mathcal{P}, Q)$, is

$$\varphi(\mathcal{P}, Q) = \operatorname*{argmin}_{P \in \mathcal{P}} \mathsf{Ed}(P, Q).$$

For a parameter $0 < \varepsilon < 1$, we call a point $P \in \mathcal{P}$ an ε-*approximate* ENN (or ε-ENN, for brevity) of Q if

$$\mathsf{Ed}(P, Q) \leq (1 + \varepsilon) \mathsf{Ed}(\varphi(\mathcal{P}, Q), Q).$$

Next, we introduce the notion of the *expected Voronoi diagram* of $\mathcal{P}$. For $1 \leq i \leq n$, we define the *expected Voronoi cell* $\mathrm{EVor}(P_i)$ as

$$\mathrm{EVor}(P_i) = \{x \in \mathbb{R}^d \mid \mathsf{Ed}(P_i, x) \leq \mathsf{Ed}(P_j, x), \forall j\}.$$

The decomposition of $\mathbb{R}^d$ into maximal connected regions induced by $\mathrm{EVor}(P_i)$, $1 \leq i \leq n$, is called the expected Voronoi diagram, $\mathrm{EVD}(\mathcal{P})$ of $\mathcal{P}$. See Figure 2 for an example of an EVD in $\mathbb{R}^2$ where $d(\cdot, \cdot)$ is the L_1 metric. A decomposition of $\mathbb{R}^d$ into connected cells, each cell τ labeled with $\lambda(\tau) \in \mathcal{P}$, is called an ε-*approximate* EVD of $\mathcal{P}$ (ε-$\mathrm{EVD}(\mathcal{P})$, for brevity), if for all $x \in \tau$, $\lambda(\tau)$ is an ε-ENN of x.

In this paper, we study the problem of answering exact or approximate ENN queries when input points are uncertain or the query is an uncertain point. We also study the problem of computing $\mathrm{EVD}(\mathcal{P})$ and ε-$\mathrm{EVD}(\mathcal{P})$.

---

[2]the squared Euclidean distance between two points $p, q \in \mathbb{R}^d$ is $||p - q||^2$ where $|| \cdot ||$ is the L_2 metric.

Previous results. In the exact setting, Voronoi diagrams may be used to perform nearest neighbor searching among a set of n input data points in $\mathbb{R}^2$ with $O(n \log n)$ preprocessing time, $O(n)$ space and $O(\log n)$ query time. Unfortunately, the size of the Voronoi diagram is $\Theta(n^{\lceil d/2 \rceil})$ in $\mathbb{R}^d$. The best known method for answering an NN query, requires $O((n/m^{1/\lceil d/2 \rceil})$ polylog $n)$ query time for an $O(m)$-space structure, where $n < m < n^{\lceil d/2 \rceil}$ [3]. To obtain better performance, many researchers turned to approximate nearest neighbor searching: Given any $\varepsilon > 0$, a point p is an ε-approximate nearest neighbor of q if $d(q, p) \leq (1+\varepsilon) d(q, p^*)$, where p^* is the actual nearest neighbor. Arya *et al.* [6] generalized space-time trade-offs for approximate nearest neighbor searching: Given a tradeoff parameter γ, where $2 \leq \gamma \leq 1/\varepsilon$, there exists an index of space $O(n \gamma^{d-1} \log(1/\varepsilon))$ that can answer queries in time $O(\log(n\gamma) + 1/(\varepsilon \gamma)^{(d-1)/2})$. There is also extensive work on answering approximate nearest neighbor queries using locality sensitive hashing, when d is not a constant and the goal is to have an algorithm whose query time is polynomial in d; see e.g. [5, 18, 20].

Different models have been proposed for geometric computing on *uncertain* data: mainly classified into *deterministic models* and *probabilistic models*. In deterministic models, each point is assumed to be inside a given region (see e.g. [9, 10, 29, 37]). Probabilistic models can be further classified into the *existential model* and the *locational model*. In the existential model, each point is assumed to appear with certain probability. Suri *et al.* [22] proposed a linear-space index with $O(\log n)$ query time to compute an ε-approximate value of the expected distance from a query point to its nearest neighbor when the dimension d is a constant.

In the locational model, the coordinates of each point are assumed to be chosen from a known probability distribution. In this paper, we focus on the locational model of uncertainty to study the problem of nearest neighbor searching. When the data is uncertain but the query is exact, researchers have studied top-k probable nearest neighbor, ranking queries, probabilistic nearest neighbor, and superseding nearest neighbor [8, 11, 12, 19, 23, 28, 36, 39]. Ljosa *et al.* [28] investigated the expected k-NN under L_1 metric using and obtained ε-approximation. Cheng *et al.* [11] studied the probabilistic nearest neighbor query that returns those uncertain points whose probabilities of being the nearest neighbor are higher than some threshold, allowing some given error in the answers. All of these methods were based on heuristics and did not provide any guarantee on the query time in the worst case. Moreover, recent results that rely on Voronoi diagram for supporting nearest neighbor queries under uncertainty cannot be adapted to answer ENN (see [13, 21, 33]). We are not aware of any index that uses near-linear space and returns in sublinear time the expected nearest neighbor or a point that is the most likely nearest neighbor.

The problem of computing the expected nearest neighbor when the queries are uncertain but the input is exact is closely related to the *aggregate nearest neighbors* (ANN) problem. Given a set of points $\mathcal{P}$ in a metric space X with a distance function d, the aggregate nearest neighbor to a set of query points Q is defined as $\mathrm{ANN}(Q, \mathcal{P}) = \arg \min_{p \in \mathcal{P}} g(p, Q)$, where $g(p, Q)$ is some aggregation function of the distances from points of Q to p. The aggregation functions commonly considered are SUM, corresponding to a summation of the individual distances and MAX, corresponding to the minimization of the maximum distance.

If the pdf is a uniform distribution, the ENN problem is the same as the ANN problem under the SUM aggregation function. Several heuristics are known for answering ANN queries [17, 25, 27, 30, 31, 34, 38]. Li *et al.* [24] provided a polynomial-time approximation scheme for ANN queries under the MAX aggregation function. Li *et al.* [26] presented approximation schemes under MAX and SUM functions for any metric space as long as an efficient nearest-neighbor algorithm is provided. For the SUM function, they provide a 3-approximation which, to the best of our knowledge, is the best approximation-factor known previously. See also [27].

Our results. We present efficient algorithms for answering ENN queries under various distance functions. For simplicity, we state the results in $\mathbb{R}^2$, i.e., $\mathcal{P} = \{P_1, \cdots, P_n\}$ is a set of n uncertain points in $\mathbb{R}^2$. We assume that the description complexity of the pdf of each P_i is at most k.

Squared Euclidean distance. If $d(\cdot, \cdot)$ is the squared Euclidean distance, then we show that a set $\mathcal{P}$ of n uncertain points can be replaced by a set $\overline{\mathcal{P}}$ of n weighted points such that the weighted Voronoi diagram of $\overline{\mathcal{P}}$ under $d(\cdot, \cdot)$ (also called the *power diagram* of $\overline{\mathcal{P}}$ [7]) is the same as EVD($\mathcal{P}$). In particular, EVD($\mathcal{P}$) has linear size and can be computed in $O(n \log n + nk)$ time if the pdf of each P_i has description complexity at most k. Furthermore, EVD($\mathcal{P}$) can be preprocessed in $O(n \log n)$ time into a linear size index so that an ENN query for a (certain) point can be answered in $O(\log n)$ time. If the query is also an uncertain point Q, then we show that $\varphi(\mathcal{P}, Q)$ is the same as $\varphi(\mathcal{P}, \bar{q})$, where $\bar{q} = \int x f_Q(x) dx$ is the centroid of Q.

Rectilinear distance. We assume that each pdf f_i is a discrete pdf consisting of k points. We show that EVD($\mathcal{P}$) has $O(n^2 k^2 \alpha(n))$ complexity and it can be computed in the same time. We also show that there exists a set $\mathcal{P}$ of n uncertain points with $k = 2$ such that EVD($\mathcal{P}$) has $\Omega(n^2)$ vertices. We then describe an index of size $O(k^2 n \log^2 n)$ that can answer an ENN query in $O(\log^3(kn))$ time. The index can be built in $O(k^2 n \log^3 n)$ time. Next, we show that a set $\mathcal{P}$ of n (certain) points in $\mathbb{R}^2$ can be stored in an index of size $O(n \log^2 n)$ so that for an uncertain point with discrete pdf consisting of at most k points, an ENN query can be answered in $O(k^2 \log^3 n)$ time. The index can be built in $O(n \log^2 n)$ time. We note that L_1 and L_∞ metrics are closely related, so these results also hold for the L_∞ metric.

Euclidean distance. Since the expected distance function under Euclidean distance is algebraically quite complex even for discrete pdfs, we focus on answering ε-ENN queries. First, we show that the expected distance to an uncertain point P can be approximated by a piecewise-constant function, consisting of $O(1/\varepsilon^2 \log(1/\varepsilon))$ pieces, plus the distance to the centroid of P. Using this result, we construct, in $O((n/\varepsilon^2) \log^2 n \log(n/\varepsilon) \log(1/\varepsilon))$ time, an ε-EVD of $\mathcal{P}$ of size $O((n/\varepsilon^2) \log(1/\varepsilon))$; each face of the subdivision is the region lying between two nested squares —it can be partitioned into at most four rectangles, so that the ε-EVD is a rectangular subdivision. Moreover, for any query point, we can return its ϵ-ENN in $O(\log(n/\varepsilon))$ time.

Finally, we show that a set $\mathcal{P}$ of n (certain) points in $\mathbb{R}^2$ can be stored in an index of linear size so that, for an uncertain point with pdf of k description complexity, an ENN query can be answered in $O((k/\varepsilon^2) \log(1/\varepsilon) \log n)$ time. The index can be built in $O(n \log n)$ time. These results can be extended to any L_p metric.

We remark that most of our algorithms extend to higher dimensions, but the query time increases exponentially with d; we mention specific results in the appropriate sections.

Outline of the paper. We begin in Section 2 by describing a few geometric concepts that will be useful. Section 3 describes our algorithms for the squared Euclidean distance function, Section 4 for the L_1 and L_∞ metrics, and Section 5 for the Euclidean distance. We conclude by making a few final remarks in Section 6.

2. PRELIMINARIES

In this section, we describe a few geometric concepts and data structures that we need.

Lower envelopes and Voronoi diagrams. Let $F = \{f_1, \cdots, f_n\}$ be a set of n bivariate functions. The lower envelope of F is defined as

$$\mathbb{L}_F(x) = \min_{1 \le i \le n} f_i(x),$$

and the *minimization diagram* of F, denoted by $\mathbb{M}(F)$, is the projection of the graph of $\mathbb{L}_F$. $\mathbb{M}(F)$ is a planar subdivision in which the same function appears on the lower envelope for all points inside a cell. The (combinatorial) complexity of $\mathbb{L}_F$ and $\mathbb{M}(F)$ is the number of vertices, edges, and faces in $\mathbb{M}(F)$. If we define $f_i(x)$ to be $\mathsf{Ed}(P_i, x)$, then EVD($\mathcal{P}$) is the minimization diagram of the resulting functions. Figure 1 shows the Voronoi diagram of a set of exact points as the minimization diagram of its distance functions.

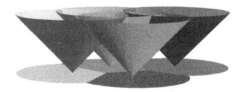

Figure 1. Euclidean Voronoi diagram of (certain) points as the minimization diagram of their distance functions.

The notion of lower envelope and minimization diagram can be extended to partially defined functions: f_i is defined over a region $V_i \subseteq \mathbb{R}^2$, then $\mathbb{L}_F(x)$ is the minimum over all functions f_i of F that are defined at x, i.e., $x \in V_i$. Let $\mathcal{R}$ be a set of polygons, each consisting of a constant number of vertices (e.g., triangles, rectangles) in $\mathbb{R}^3$. By viewing each of them as the graph of a partially-defined linear function, we can define the lower envelope $\mathbb{L}_\mathcal{R}$ and minimization diagram $\mathbb{M}(\mathcal{R})$ of $\mathcal{R}$. It is known that the complexity of $\mathbb{M}(\mathcal{R})$ is $\Theta(n^2 \alpha(n))$ and that it can be computed in $O(n^2 \alpha(n))$ time [35], where $\alpha(n)$ is the inverse Ackermann function.

Compressed quadtree. A square is called *canonical* if its side length is 2^l for an integer l and its bottom-left corner is $(2^l a, 2^l b)$ for some integers a, b. Note that two canonical squares are either disjoint or one of them is contained in the other.

A *quadtree* on a canonical square H is a 4-way tree T, each of whose nodes v is associated with a canonical square $\square_v \subseteq H$. The root of T is associated with H itself. The squares associated with the children of a node v are obtained by dividing each side of $\square_v$ into two halves, thereby dividing $\square_v$ into four congruent canonical squares. If the side length of H is 2^L, then the nodes of T at depth δ induce a $2^\delta \times 2^\delta$ uniform grid inside H; each grid cell has side length $2^{L-\delta}$.

Let $\mathcal{B} = \{B_1, \cdots, B_m\}$ be a set of m canonical squares inside H. We construct a *compressed quadtree* $\mathbb{T}$ on $(\mathcal{B}, H)$ as follows: Let T be the quadtree on H as described above. A square $B \in \mathcal{B}$ is stored at a node v if $\square_v = B$. The leaves of $\mathbb{T}$ are the lowest nodes that store a square of $\mathcal{B}$. They induce a subdivision of H into canonical squares, none of them contains any square of $\mathcal{B}$ in its interior. If a node $v \in T$ does not store a square of $\mathcal{B}$ and both v and $p(v)$, the parent of v, have degree one, we delete v and the child of v becomes the child of $p(v)$. We repeat this step until no such node is left. The size of $\mathbb{T}$ is $O(m)$, and it can be constructed directly, without constructing T, in $O(m \log m)$ time [18].

We call a node v of $\mathbb{T}$ *exposed* if its degree is at most one. We associate a region R_v with each exposed node v. If v is a leaf, then $R_v = \square_v$. Otherwise, v has one child w and we set $R_v = \square_v \setminus \square_w$. For a point $x \in R_v$, v is the lowest node such that $x \in \square_v$. The regions R_v of the exposed nodes induce a partition $\mathbb{M}(\mathcal{B}, H)$ of H of size $O(m)$. Each face of $\mathbb{M}(\mathcal{B}, H)$ is a canonical square or the difference between two canonical squares, and none of the faces contains a square of $\mathcal{B}$ in its interior. The depth of $\mathbb{T}$ is $\Theta(m)$ in the worst case. Nevertheless, using standard tree-decomposition schemes, for a point $x \in H$, the lowest node of $\mathbb{T}$ such that $x \in \square_v$ can be computed in $O(\log m)$ time [18].

$\mathbb{T}$ can also be used to store a set $S = \{p_1, \cdots, p_m\}$ of points in H. We again build a quadtree T on H. A node $v \in T$ is a leaf if $|S \cap \square_v| \leq 1$. We compress the nodes as above and define the partition $\mathbb{M}(S, H)$ as earlier. Again, using tree-decomposition schemes, we can now determine in $O(\log m)$ time whether $\sigma \cap S \neq \emptyset$ for a canonical square σ. If the answer is yes, we can also return a point of $S \cap \sigma$. We thus have the following:

LEMMA 2.1. *Let H be a canonical square, let $\mathcal{B}$ be a set of m canonical squares in H, and let S be a set of n points in H.*

(i) *A compressed quadtree $\mathbb{T}$ on $(\mathcal{B}, H)$ of size $O(m)$ can be constructed in $O(m \log m)$ time. Furthermore, it can be processed in $O(m \log m)$ time into a linear-size index, so that for a point $q \in H$, the lowest node v of $\mathbb{T}$ such that $q \in \square_v$ can be reported in $O(\log m)$ time.*

(ii) *A compressed quadtree $\mathbb{T}$ on (S, H) of size $O(n)$ can be constructed in $O(n \log n)$ time. Furthermore, it can be processed in $O(n \log n)$ time into a linear-size index, so that for a canonical square σ, a point of $S \cap \sigma$ can be returned in $O(\log n)$ time if $S \cap \sigma \neq \emptyset$.*

3. SQUARED EUCLIDEAN DISTANCE

In this section, for two points $a, b \in \mathbb{R}^d$, $\mathsf{d}(a, b) = \|a - b\|^2$. We first show how to compute the EVD of a set of uncertain points, and then show how to answer an ENN query with an uncertain point.

3.1 Uncertain data

Let $\mathcal{P} = \{P_1, \ldots, P_n\}$ be a set of n uncertain points in $\mathbb{R}^2$. The following lemma, well known in mathematics, suggests how to replace $\mathcal{P}$ with a set of weighted points. We state the lemma in $\mathbb{R}^d$ and provide a proof for the sake of completeness.

LEMMA 3.1. *Let P be an uncertain point in $\mathbb{R}^d$, let f be its pdf, let $\overline{p}$ be its centroid, and let $\sigma^2 = \int_{\mathbb{R}^d} \|x - \overline{p}\|^2 f(x) dx$. Then for any point $q \in \mathbb{R}^d$,*

$$\mathsf{Ed}(P, q) = \|q - \overline{p}\|^2 + \sigma^2.$$

PROOF. Let $\langle p, q \rangle$ denote the inner product of p and q, and $\| \cdot \|$ denote the Euclidean metric. Using the fact that $\int_{\mathbb{R}^d} f(x) dx = 1$, we obtain

$$
\begin{aligned}
\mathsf{Ed}(P, q) &= \int_{\mathbb{R}^d} \|q - x\|^2 f(x) dx \\
&= \|q\|^2 - 2\langle q, \int_{\mathbb{R}^d} x f(x) dx \rangle + \int_{\mathbb{R}^d} \|x\|^2 f(x) dx \\
&= \|q - \overline{p}\|^2 - \|\overline{p}\|^2 + \int_{\mathbb{R}^d} \|x\|^2 f(x) dx \\
&= \|q - \overline{p}\|^2 - 2\|\overline{p}\|^2 \\
&\quad + \int_{\mathbb{R}^d} \Big(\|x - \overline{p}\|^2 + 2\langle x, \overline{p} \rangle \Big) f(x) dx \\
&= \|q - \overline{p}\|^2 - 2\|\overline{p}\|^2 + \sigma^2 + 2\langle \overline{p}, \overline{p} \rangle \\
&= \|q - \overline{p}\|^2 + \sigma^2.
\end{aligned}
$$

$\square$

Let p be a weighted point in $\mathbb{R}^d$ with weight w_p. For a point $q \in \mathbb{R}^d$, we define the (weighted) distance from q to p as

$$\delta(q, p) = \|q - p\|^2 + w_p.$$

If we replace each point in $P_i \in \mathcal{P}$ by a weighted point $\overline{p}_i$ whose weight is $\sigma_i^2 = \int_{\mathbb{R}^d} \|x - \overline{p}_i\|^2 f_i(x) dx$, then by the above lemma $\delta(q, \overline{p}_i) = \mathsf{Ed}(P_i, q)$. Set $\overline{\mathcal{P}} = \{\overline{p}_1, \ldots, \overline{p}_n\}$. EVD$(\mathcal{P})$ is the same as the Voronoi diagram of $\overline{\mathcal{P}}$ under the distance function $\delta(\cdot, \cdot)$. We now show how to compute the Voronoi diagram of $\overline{\mathcal{P}}$.

For each $1 \leq i \leq n$, we define a linear function $h_i : \mathbb{R}^2 \to \mathbb{R}$ as

$$h_i(x) = 2\langle \overline{p}_i, x \rangle - \|\overline{p}_i\|^2 - \sigma_i^2.$$

The proof of the following lemma is straightforward.

LEMMA 3.2. *For any $q \in \mathbb{R}^2$,*

$$\arg \min_{1 \leq i \leq n} \delta_i(q, \overline{p}_i) = \arg \max_{1 \leq i \leq n} h_i(q).$$

Let $h_i^+ = \{x \in \mathbb{R}^3 \mid h_i(x) \geq 0\}$ be the halfspace lying above the plane h_i. Set $H^+ = \{h_i^+ \mid 1 \leq i \leq n\}$. By Lemma 3.2, the minimization diagram of functions $\{\delta(x, \overline{p}_i)\}$ is the same as the xy-projection of $\bigcap_{h^+ \in H^+} h^+$. Since the intersection of n halfspaces in $\mathbb{R}^3$ has linear size and can be computed in $O(n \log n)$ time [16], we conclude that the Voronoi diagram of $\overline{\mathcal{P}}$, under $\delta(\cdot, \cdot)$ as the distance function, can be computed in $O(n \log n)$ time, and thus EVD$(\mathcal{P})$ can be computed in $O(n \log n + nk)$ time, where the extra $O(nk)$ time is for computing $\overline{\mathcal{P}}$. Furthermore, by preprocessing EVD$(\mathcal{P})$ into a linear-size index for point-location queries, an ENN query for a point $q \in \mathbb{R}^2$ can be answered in $O(\log n)$ time. We thus obtain the following.

THEOREM 3.3. *Let $\mathcal{P}$ be a set of n uncertain points in $\mathbb{R}^2$. EVD$(\mathcal{P})$ under the squared Euclidean distance has $O(n)$ size. If the description complexity of the pdf of every point in $\mathcal{P}$ is k, then EVD$(\mathcal{P})$ can be computed in $O(n \log n + nk)$ time. Furthermore, EVD$(\mathcal{P})$ can be preprocessed in a linear-size index so that for a point $q \in \mathbb{R}^2$, an ENN query can be answered in $O(\log n)$ time.*

3.2 Uncertain query

Let Q be an uncertain query point in $\mathbb{R}^2$ represented as a pdf f_Q.

LEMMA 3.4. *For an uncertain point Q with a pdf f_Q,*

$$\varphi(\mathcal{P}, Q) = \arg\min_{p \in \mathcal{P}} ||\bar{q} - p||^2,$$

where $\bar{q}$ is the centroid of Q.

PROOF. For a point $p \in \mathcal{P}$, we have

$$\mathsf{Ed}(p, Q) = \int_{\mathbb{R}^d} ||p - x||^2 f_Q(x) dx$$

$$= ||p||^2 + \int_{\mathbb{R}^d} ||x||^2 f_Q(x) dx - 2\langle p, \bar{q} \rangle. \quad (1)$$

Observing that the second term in RHS of (1) is independent of p, we obtain

$$\arg\min_{p \in \mathcal{P}} \mathsf{Ed}(p, Q) = \arg\min_{p \in \mathcal{P}} ||p||^2 - 2\langle p, \bar{q} \rangle$$

$$= \arg\min_{p \in \mathcal{P}} ||p - \bar{q}||^2,$$

as claimed. □

The preprocessing step is to compute the Voronoi diagram $\mathrm{VD}(\mathcal{P})$ of the points $\mathcal{P}$ in time $O(n \log n)$. Once a query Q with a pdf of description complexity k is given, we compute its centroid $\bar{q}$ in $O(k)$ time and find the nearest neighbor $\mathrm{NN}(\mathcal{P}, \bar{q}) = \arg\min_{p \in \mathcal{P}} ||\bar{q} - p||^2$ in $O(\log n)$ time by querying $\mathrm{VD}(\mathcal{P})$ with q.

THEOREM 3.5. *Let $\mathcal{P}$ be a set of n exact points in $\mathbb{R}^2$. We can preprocess $\mathcal{P}$ into an index of size $O(n)$ in $O(n \log n)$ time so that, for a query point Q with a pdf of description complexity k, $\varphi(\mathcal{P}, Q)$, under the squared Euclidean distance, can be computed in $O(k + \log n)$ time.*

Remarks. The algorithm extends to higher dimensions but the query time becomes roughly $O(n^{1-1/\lceil d/2 \rceil})$.

4. RECTILINEAR METRIC

In this section we assume the distance function to be the L_1 metric. That is, for any two points $p = (p_x, p_y)$ and $q = (q_x, q_y)$,

$$\mathrm{d}(p, q) = |p_x - q_x| + |p_y - q_y|.$$

The results in this section also hold for the L_∞ metric, i.e., when $\mathrm{d}(p, q) = \max\{|p_x - q_x|, |p_y - q_y|\}$. We first consider the case when the input is a set of n uncertain points in $\mathbb{R}^2$, each with a discrete pdf, and the query is a certain point and then consider the case when the input is a set of certain points and the query is a uncertain point with a discrete pdf.

4.1 Uncertain data

Let $\mathcal{P} = \{P_1, \cdots, P_n\}$ be a set of n uncertain points in $\mathbb{R}^2$, each with a discrete pdf of size k as described above. We first prove a lower bound on the complexity of $\mathrm{EVD}(\mathcal{P})$ and then present a near-linear-size index to answer ENN queries.

Expected Voronoi diagram. Fix a point $P_i = \{p_{i,1}, p_{i,2}, \cdots, p_{i,k}\}$ of $\mathcal{P}$. Let H_i^- (resp. $H_i^|$) be the set of k horizontal (resp. vertical) lines in $\mathbb{R}^2$ passing through the points of P_i. Let $\mathcal{B}_i$ be the set of $O(k^2)$ rectangles in the grid induced

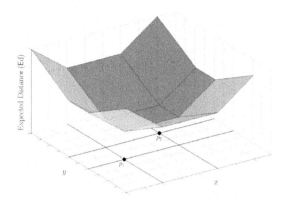

Figure 3. $\mathsf{Ed}(P_i, q)$ when the uncertain point P_i is composed of two points p_1 and p_2 with probabilities 0.5 each. The grid induced by H_i^- and $H_i^|$ is shown below and $\mathsf{Ed}(P_i, q)$ is linear within each rectangle of $\mathcal{B}_i$.

by the lines in $H_i^- \cup H_i^|$. It can be checked that $\mathsf{Ed}(P_i, q)$ is a linear function $f_\square$ within each rectangle $\square$ of $\mathcal{B}_i$; see Figure 3. For each $\square \in \mathcal{B}_i$, let $\square^\uparrow$ be the rectangle in $\mathbb{R}^3$ formed by restricting the graph of $f_\square$ with $\square$, i.e.,

$$\square^\uparrow = \{(x, y, f_\square(x, y)) \mid (x, y) \in \square\}.$$

Let $\mathcal{B}_i^\uparrow = \{\square^\uparrow \mid \square \in \mathcal{B}_i\}$. By definition, the rectangles in $\mathcal{B}_i^\uparrow$ form the graph of the function $\mathsf{Ed}(P_i, q)$. Set $\mathcal{B} = \bigcup_{i=1}^n \mathcal{B}_i$ and $\mathcal{B}^\uparrow = \bigcup_{i=1}^n \mathcal{B}_i^\uparrow$. By construction and the discussion in Section 2, $\mathrm{EVD}(\mathcal{P})$ is the minimization diagram $\mathbb{M}(\mathcal{B}^\uparrow)$ of $\mathcal{B}^\uparrow$. We prove an almost tight bound on the complexity of $\mathrm{EVD}(\mathcal{P})$.

THEOREM 4.1. *Let $\mathcal{P}$ be a set of n uncertain points in $\mathbb{R}^2$, each with a discrete pdf consisting of k points, and let $\mathrm{d}(\cdot, \cdot)$ be the L_1 metric. Then the complexity of $\mathrm{EVD}(\mathcal{P})$ is $O(k^2 n^2 \alpha(n))$, where $\alpha(n)$ is the inverse Ackermann function. Moreover, there is a set $\mathcal{P}$ of n uncertain points with $k = 2$ such that $\mathrm{EVD}(\mathcal{P})$ has $\Omega(n^2)$ size.*

PROOF. We first prove the upper bound. Set $H^- = \bigcup_{i=1}^n H_i^-$ and $H^| = \bigcup_{i=1}^n H_i^|$; $|H^-| = |H^|| = nk$. We sort the lines in H^- by their y values and choose a subset G^- of n lines by selecting every kth line. Let $G^|$ be a similar subset of $H^|$. Let $\mathcal{R}$ be the set of rectangles in the non-uniform grid formed by the lines in $G^- \cup G^|$. For each rectangle $R \in \mathcal{R}$, let $\mathcal{B}_R \subseteq \mathcal{B}$ be the set of rectangles whose boundaries intersect R, and let $\overline{\mathcal{B}}_R \subseteq \mathcal{B}$ be the set of rectangles that contain R. Since R lies between two adjacent lines of G^- and $G^|$, at most $2n$ lines of $H^- \cup H^|$ intersect R, implying that $|\mathcal{B}_R| \leq 2n$. $|\overline{\mathcal{B}}_R| \leq n$ because at most one rectangle of $\mathcal{B}_i$ can contain R for any $1 \leq i \leq n$. Set $\mathcal{B}_R^\uparrow = \{\square^\uparrow \mid \square \in \mathcal{B}_R\}$ and $\overline{\mathcal{B}}_R^\uparrow = \{\square^\uparrow \mid \square \in \overline{\mathcal{B}}_R\}$. We note that $\mathbb{M}(\mathcal{B}^\uparrow) \cap R = \mathbb{M}(\mathcal{B}_R^\uparrow \cup \overline{\mathcal{B}}_R^\uparrow) \cap R$. Since $|\mathcal{B}_R| + |\overline{\mathcal{B}}_R| \leq 3n$, the complexity of $\mathbb{M}(\mathcal{B}_R^\uparrow \cup \overline{\mathcal{B}}_R^\uparrow)$ is $O(n^2 \alpha(n))$. The $O(k^2)$ rectangles in $\mathcal{R}$ tile the entire plane, therefore the complexity of $\mathbb{M}(\mathcal{B}^\uparrow)$, and thus of $\mathrm{EVD}(\mathcal{P})$, is $O(k^2 n^2 \alpha(n))$.

Next, we show that there exists a set $\mathcal{P}$ of n uncertain points in $\mathbb{R}^2$ with $k = 2$ such that $\mathrm{EVD}(\mathcal{P})$ has $\Omega(n^2)$ size. Assume that $n = 2m$ for some positive integer m. Each point $P_i \in \mathcal{P}$ has two possible locations p_{i1} and p_{i2}, each with

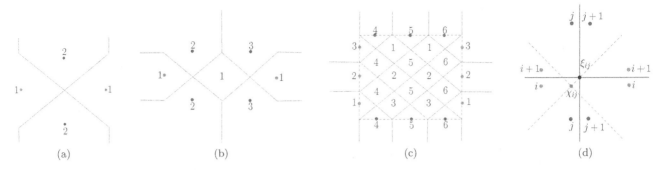

Figure 2. Lower bound construction for EVD. EVD of (a) 2 points, (b) 3 points, (c) 6 points on the boundary of a square σ. (d) Bisectors of (P_i, P_j), (P_i, P_{i+1}), and (P_j, P_{j+1}).

probability 0.5. All the points lie on the boundary of the square $\sigma = [0, 2m]^2$ (see Figure 2). More specifically, for $1 \leq i \leq m$, the two possible locations of P_i are $p_{i1} = (0, 2i - 1)$ and $p_{i2} = (2m, 2i - 1)$. For $1 \leq j \leq m$, the two possible locations of P_{m+j} are $p_{m+j,1} = (2j - 1, 0)$ and $p_{m+j,2} = (2j - 1, 2m)$. We claim that EVD($\mathcal{P}$) has $\Omega(n^2)$ size. Notice that for any pair $1 \leq i \leq m < j \leq 2m$, the bisector of P_i and P_j inside the square σ consists of two lines: $y = x + 2(m+i-j)$ and $y = -x + 2(i+j-m-1)$ (see Figure 2(d), dashed lines). Let χ_{ij} be the intersection point of these two lines. We observe that $\mathsf{Ed}(P_i, \chi_{ij}) = \mathsf{Ed}(P_j, \chi_{ij}) = m$ and $\mathsf{Ed}(P_k, \chi_{ij}) > m$ for all $k \notin \{i, j\}$. Hence χ_{ij} is a vertex of EVD($\mathcal{P}$). Similarly, for all $1 \leq i < m$, the bisector of P_i and P_{i+1} is the line $y = 2i$, and for all $m < j < 2m$, the bisector of P_j and P_{j+1} is the line $x = 2j - 2m$ (see Figure 2(d), solid lines). The intersection point of these two bisectors, $\xi_{ij} = (2j - 2m, 2i)$, is also a vertex of EVD($\mathcal{P}$): $\mathsf{Ed}(P_i, \xi_{ij}) = \mathsf{Ed}(P_{i+1}, \xi_{ij}) = \mathsf{Ed}(P_j, \xi_{ij}) = \mathsf{Ed}(P_{j+1}, \xi_{ij}) = m + 0.5 < \mathsf{Ed}(P_k, \xi_{ij})$, for all $k \notin \{i, i+1, j, j+1\}$. Hence EVD($\mathcal{P}$) has $\Omega(n^2)$ vertices inside σ. $\square$

Remark. By preprocessing EVD($\mathcal{P}$) for point-location queries [32, 16], an ENN query can be answered in $O(\log n)$ time using $O(k^2 n^2 \alpha(n))$ space. For higher dimensions, the complexity of EVD($\mathcal{P}$) is $O(k^d n^d \alpha(n))$.

Near-linear size index. Next we show that despite the size of EVD($\mathcal{P}$) being $\Omega(n^2)$, we can build an index of size $O(k^2 n \log^2 n)$ so that an ENN query can be answered in $O(\log^3(kn))$ time.

For a query point $q \in \mathbb{R}^2$, let l_q be the line parallel to the z-axis passing through q, and oriented in the $(+z)$-direction. Then $\varphi(\mathcal{P}, q)$ is P_i if the first rectangle of $\mathcal{B}^\uparrow$ that l_q intersects belongs to $\mathcal{B}_i$. We label each rectangle $\square^\uparrow$ in $\mathcal{B}_i^\uparrow$ with i and build an index on $\mathcal{B}^\uparrow$ so that the first rectangle intersected by a line parallel to the z-axis can be reported quickly. The index works in two stages. In the first stage, it builds a family $\mathcal{F} = \{C_1, C_2, \cdots, C_u\}$ of *canonical subsets* of $\mathcal{B}$, i.e., each $C_i \subseteq \mathcal{B}$, so that for a query point $q \in \mathbb{R}^2$, the subset $\mathcal{B}_q \subseteq \mathcal{B}$ of rectangles containing q can be represented as the union of $O(\log^2(kn))$ canonical subsets of $\mathcal{F}$. That is, there exists a subset $\mathcal{F}_q \subseteq \mathcal{F}$ of size $O(\log^2 n)$ such that $\mathcal{B}_q = \bigcup \mathcal{F}_q$. Furthermore, $\sum_{i \geq 1} |C_i| = O(k^2 n \log^2 n)$. Next, for a rectangle $\square \in \mathcal{B}$, let $\gamma_\square$ be the plane containing the rectangle $\square^\uparrow$, i.e., the graph of the linear function $f_\square$. For

each $1 \leq i \leq u$, set $T_i = \{\gamma_\square \mid \square \in C_i\}$. We build an index of linear size on T_i that can report the first plane of T_i intersected by a vertical line l_q in $O(\log n)$ time [16]. This index is similar to one described by Agarwal *et al.* [1], so we omit the details from here and conclude the following.

THEOREM 4.2. *Let $\mathcal{P}$ be a set of n uncertain points in $\mathbb{R}^2$, each with a discrete pdf consisting of k points, and let $d(\cdot, \cdot)$ be the L_1 or L_∞ metric. $\mathcal{P}$ can be stored in an index of size $O(k^2 n \log^2 n)$, so that an ENN query can be answered in $O(\log^3(kn))$ time. The index can be built in $O(k^2 n \log^3 n)$ time.*

Remarks. The algorithm extends to higher dimension. For $d \geq 3$, the size of the index will be $O(k^d n \log^d n)$ and the query time will be $O(n^{1 - 1/\lceil d/2 \rceil} \log^{O(d)} n)$ [3].

4.2 Uncertain query

Let $\mathcal{P} = \{p_1, p_2 \ldots, p_n\}$ be a set of n certain input data points in $\mathbb{R}^2$. We first build an index such that the ENN of an uncertain query point Q, which is represented as a discrete pdf of k points, can be found quickly.

Given an uncertain query Q, which has a discrete pdf of k points $\{q_1, \ldots, q_k\}$ with associated probabilities $\{w_1, \ldots, w_k\}$, let H^- (resp. $H^|$) be the set of k horizontal (resp. vertical) lines in $\mathbb{R}^2$ passing through the points of Q. Let $\mathcal{B}$ be the set of $O(k^2)$ rectangles in the grid induced by the lines in $H^- \cup H^|$ (see Figure 4(a)). For every rectangle $\square \in \mathcal{B}$, let $\mathcal{P}_\square = \mathcal{P} \cap \square$. Let k_{nw} denote the number of points of Q which are above and to the right of $\square$. We similarly define $k_{\mathrm{ne}}, k_{\mathrm{sw}}, k_{\mathrm{se}}$ for points of Q which are at top-right, bottom-left and bottom-right of $\square$. We call these regions the quadrants of $\square$; see Figure 4(b).

LEMMA 4.3. *For every point $p = (x_p, y_p) \in \square$,*
$$\mathsf{Ed}(p, Q) = k_x x_p + k_y y_p + c,$$
where $k_x = k_{\mathrm{nw}} + k_{\mathrm{sw}} - k_{\mathrm{ne}} - k_{\mathrm{se}}$, $k_y = k_{\mathrm{sw}} + k_{\mathrm{se}} - k_{\mathrm{nw}} - k_{\mathrm{ne}}$ and c is independent of p.

PROOF. Note that no point of Q lies vertically above or below, or horizontally to the left or right of $\square$. Let $v_{\mathrm{nw}} = (x_{\mathrm{nw}}, y_{\mathrm{nw}})$ (resp. $v_{\mathrm{ne}}, v_{\mathrm{sw}}, v_{\mathrm{se}}$) denote the top-left (resp. top-right, bottom-left, bottom-right) corner of $\square$. Let $Q_{\mathrm{nw}}, Q_{\mathrm{ne}}, Q_{\mathrm{sw}}$ and Q_{se} denote the points of Q that lie in the top-left, top-right, bottom-left and bottom-right quadrants of $\square$

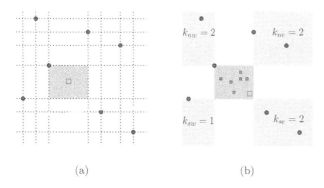

(a)   (b)

Figure 4. (a) The set of rectangles $\mathcal{B}$ induced by horizontal lines H^- and vertical lines $H^|$ through the points of Q. A single rectangle $\square$ is also shown. (b) The four quadrants of $\square$ are shown along with the number of points of Q in each. The points $\mathcal{P}_\square$ in $\square$ are shown as red squares.

respectively, and let $q \in Q_{\text{nw}}$. Then $\text{d}(p,q) = \text{d}(p,v_{\text{nw}}) + \text{d}(v_{\text{nw}},q)$. Thus the total contributions of points of Q in this quadrant to $\text{Ed}(p,Q)$ is

$$\sum_{q \in Q_{\text{nw}}} \text{d}(q,v_{\text{nw}}) + k_{\text{nw}}\text{d}(v_{\text{nw}},q)$$

$$= \sum_{q \in Q_{\text{nw}}} \text{d}(q,v_{\text{nw}}) + k_{\text{nw}}(x_p - x_{\text{nw}}) + k_{\text{nw}}(y_{\text{nw}} - y_p).$$

Similar expressions holds for the remaining quadrants. Thus, summing over all quadrants, the lemma follows. $\square$

LEMMA 4.4. *The point p^* such that*

$$p^* = \arg\min_{p \in P_\square} \text{Ed}(p,Q)$$

is a vertex of the convex hull $\text{conv}(\mathcal{P}_\square)$ of $\mathcal{P}_\square$.

PROOF. By Lemma 4.3, p^* is an extreme point of $\mathcal{P}_\square$ minimizing a linear function of $p \in \mathcal{P}_\square$. Thus, without loss of generality, it realizes its minimum when p^* is a vertex of $\text{conv}(\mathcal{P}_\square)$. $\square$

Preprocessing step. Our index is simply a two dimensional range-tree on the points in $\mathcal{P}$ [16] with a single modification to enable efficient ENN queries. The range-tree consists of two levels. We first construct a balanced binary tree $\mathcal{T}$ on the x-coordinates of the points of $\mathcal{P}$. We call this the *primary tree*. Its leaves store the points of $\mathcal{P}$ in sorted x-order from left to right, and internal nodes store splitting values to guide the search. Each node v in this tree corresponds to a subset of the points of $\mathcal{P}$ whose x-coordinates lie in the interval corresponding to the node. For each node v in the tree, a similar balanced binary tree $\mathcal{T}_v$ is constructed on the y-coordinates of the points of $\mathcal{P}$ in the subtree of $\mathcal{T}$ rooted at v. We call these *secondary trees*. For a node u in a secondary tree $\mathcal{T}_v$ corresponding to a node v in $\mathcal{T}$, we have an associated subset of the points of $\mathcal{P}$. All such subsets are termed as *canonical subsets*. Given a query rectangle, the points of $\mathcal{P}$ in the rectangle are reported as the disjoint union of $O(\log^2 n)$ canonical subsets. See [16] for more details on range-trees.

We make the following modification to the range-tree structure. For any canonical subset $\mathcal{P}_u$ corresponding to a node u in a secondary tree $\mathcal{T}_v$, we store the convex hull $\text{conv}(\mathcal{P}_u)$

of the points of $\mathcal{P}_u$. For any secondary tree $\mathcal{T}_v$, the convex hull of the canonical subsets may be computed by performing a bottom-up traversal while merging the convex hulls of the children at any internal node. Thus, if there are m nodes in $\mathcal{T}_v$, the total time for constructing the convex hulls is $O(m \log m)$. This, in turn, implies that the total preprocessing time is $O(n \log^2 n)$ and the space required for the index is $O(n \log^2 n)$ as well.

Query step. When a query Q is given, we construct $\mathcal{B}$ as above, and compute, for each rectangle $\square \in \mathcal{B}$, the values $k_{\text{ne}}, k_{\text{nw}}, k_{\text{se}}$ and k_{sw}. Next, we perform a range query in $\mathcal{T}$, to find the points of $\mathcal{P}_\square$ as the union of $O(\log^2 n)$ canonical subsets of $\mathcal{P}$. We find the point p^* by performing a binary search on the points on the convex hulls of each subset and picking the minimum over all subsets. By Lemma 4.4, the point p^* must be among these points. Hence, the total time is $O(k^2 \log^3 n)$.

THEOREM 4.5. *Let $\mathcal{P}$ be a set of n exact points in $\mathbb{R}^2$ and let $\text{d}(\cdot,\cdot)$ be the L_1 or L_∞ metric. $\mathcal{P}$ can be stored in an index of size $O(n \log^2 n)$, which can be constructed in $O(n \log^2 n)$ time, such that for an uncertain query Q as a discrete pdf with k points, its ENN can be reported in $O(k^2 \log^3 n)$ time.*

Remark. If we know an upper bound on k in advance of the query, we may perform further preprocessing to obtain a query time of $O(k^2 \log^2 n \log k)$ since the linear function from Lemma 4.3 can have at most $O(k^2)$ orientations, corresponding to the possible coefficients of x_p and y_p. Thus, we may find the minimum of this function for all the $O(k^2)$ possible orientations in advance.

5. EUCLIDEAN DISTANCE

We now consider the case when $\text{d}(\cdot,\cdot)$ is the Euclidean distance. For any two points $a,b \in \mathbb{R}^2$, we use $||a - b||$ to denote the Euclidean distance $\text{d}(a,b)$. Since the expected distance under the Euclidean distance is algebraically quite complex, we focus on answering ε-ENN queries in this section. We first describe an algorithm for computing a function that approximates the expected distance from a fixed uncertain point to any (certain) point in $\mathbb{R}^2$. The construction is similar to the one given in [2]. We use this algorithm to answer ε-ENN queries, first when the input is a set of uncertain points but the query is a certain point and next, when the input data points are certain but the query point is uncertain. In the former case, we construct an approximate expected Voronoi diagram of $\mathcal{P}$.

5.1 Approximation of the expected Euclidean distance

Let P be an uncertain point in $\mathbb{R}^2$, and let $f_P : \mathbb{R}^2 \to \mathbb{R}_{\geq 0}$ be its pdf. Let the description complexity of f_P be k. We construct a function $g_P : \mathbb{R}^2 \to \mathbb{R}_{\geq 0}$ of description complexity $O((1/\varepsilon^2)\log(1/\varepsilon))$ such that for any $x \in \mathbb{R}^2$,

$$\text{Ed}(P,x) \leq g_P(x) \leq (1 + \varepsilon)\text{Ed}(P,x).$$

Let $\bar{p}$ be the centroid of P. The following two lemmas follow from the triangle inequality.

LEMMA 5.1. *For any two points $a,b \in \mathbb{R}^2$,*

$$|\text{Ed}(P,a) - \text{Ed}(P,b)| \leq ||a - b||.$$

231

PROOF.

$$|\mathsf{Ed}(P,a) - \mathsf{Ed}(P,b)| = \int_{\mathbb{R}^2} f_P(x)\big|\|x-a\| - \|x-b\|\big|dx$$

$$\leq \int_{\mathbb{R}^2} f_P(x)\|a-b\|dx$$

$$= \|a-b\|.$$

$\square$

LEMMA 5.2. $\mathsf{Ed}(P,\bar{p}) \leq 2\min_{x \in \mathbb{R}^2}\mathsf{Ed}(P,x).$

PROOF. Let $p_{\min} = \arg\min_{x \in \mathbb{R}^2}\mathsf{Ed}(P,x)$. By Lemma 5.1,

$$|\mathsf{Ed}(P,\bar{p}) - \mathsf{Ed}(P,p_{\min})| \leq \|\bar{p} - p_{\min}\|$$

$$= \|p_{\min} - \int_{\mathbb{R}^2} x f_P(x)dx\|$$

$$= \|\int_{\mathbb{R}^2} f_P(x)(x-p_{\min})dx\|$$

$$\leq \int_{\mathbb{R}^2} f_P(x)\|x - p_{\min}\|dx$$

$$= \mathsf{Ed}(P,p_{\min}).$$

The lemma now follows. $\square$

LEMMA 5.3. *Let $0 < \varepsilon < 1$ be a parameter, let $\bar{\rho} = \mathsf{Ed}(P,\bar{p})$, and for any $x \in \mathbb{R}^2$, let*

$$g(x) = \|x - \bar{p}\| + \bar{\rho}.$$

Then for any point $q \in \mathbb{R}^2$ such that $\|q - \bar{p}\| > 8\bar{\rho}/\varepsilon$, we have

$$\mathsf{Ed}(P,q) \leq g(q) \leq (1+\varepsilon)\mathsf{Ed}(P,q).$$

PROOF. Let $q \in \mathbb{R}^2$ be a point with $\|q - \bar{p}\| > 8\bar{\rho}/\varepsilon$. By Lemma 5.1,

$$\mathsf{Ed}(P,q) \leq \mathsf{Ed}(P,\bar{p}) + \|q - \bar{p}\| = \bar{\rho} + \|q - \bar{p}\| \leq g(q).$$

Similarly,

$$\mathsf{Ed}(P,q) \geq \|q - \bar{p}\| - \mathsf{Ed}(P,\bar{p}) = \|q - \bar{p}\| - \bar{\rho}.$$

Therefore

$$g(q) = \|q - \bar{p}\| + \bar{\rho} \leq \mathsf{Ed}(P,q) + 2\bar{\rho}. \qquad (2)$$

Let D be the disk of radius $4\bar{\rho}/\varepsilon$ centered at $\bar{p}$. For any point $x \notin D$, $\|x - \bar{p}\| > 4\bar{\rho}/\varepsilon$. Hence,

$$\bar{\rho} = \int_{\mathbb{R}^2} \|x - \bar{p}\|f_P(x)dx \geq \int_{\mathbb{R}^2 \setminus D} \|x - \bar{p}\|f_P(x)dx$$

$$\geq \frac{4\bar{\rho}}{\varepsilon}\int_{\mathbb{R}^2 \setminus D} f_P(x)dx,$$

implying that

$$\int_{\mathbb{R}^2 \setminus D} f_P(x)dx \leq \varepsilon/4 \quad \text{and} \quad \int_D f_P(x)dx \geq 1 - \varepsilon/4.$$

On the other hand, for any point $x \in D$, $\|x - q\| > 4\bar{\rho}/\varepsilon$. Therefore

$$\mathsf{Ed}(P,q) = \int_{\mathbb{R}^2} \|x - q\|f_P(x)dx \geq \int_D \|x - q\|f_P(x)dx$$

$$\geq \frac{4\bar{\rho}}{\varepsilon}\int_D f_P(x)dx \geq \frac{4\bar{\rho}}{\varepsilon}(1 - \varepsilon/4) \geq \frac{2\bar{\rho}}{\varepsilon},$$

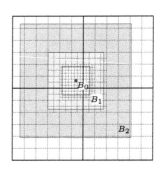

Figure 5. Covering B_l with four canonical squares and drawing an exponential grid composed of canonical squares.

which implies that $\bar{\rho} \leq \varepsilon\mathsf{Ed}(P,q)/2$. Substituting this in (2),

$$g(q) \leq (1+\varepsilon)\mathsf{Ed}(P,q).$$

$\square$

Set $\bar{\rho} = \mathsf{Ed}(P,\bar{p})$. For a point $x \in \mathbb{R}^2$ and a value $r \geq 0$, let $B(x,r)$ denote the square of side length $2r$ centered at x. Let $l = \lceil\log_2(8/\varepsilon)\rceil$. For $0 \leq i \leq l$, set $B_i = B(\bar{p},\bar{\rho}2^i)$; set $B_{-1} = \emptyset$. Finally, set $\rho_i = \varepsilon 2^i\bar{\rho}/8$.

We cover B_l by at most four congruent canonical squares $C_1,\ldots,C_4$ of side length at most $2\rho_l = \bar{\rho}2^{l+1}$. The union of $C_1,\ldots,C_4$ is also a square C; see Figure 5. We set

$$g_P(x) = \|x - \bar{p}\| + \bar{\rho}, \quad \forall x \notin C.$$

For $1 \leq j \leq 4$ and $0 \leq i \leq l$, we cover $C_j \cap (B_i \setminus B_{i-1})$ with canonical squares of size 2^{Δ_i} where $\Delta_i = \lfloor\log_2\rho_i\rfloor$; see Figure 5. For each such square $\square$, let $a_\square$ be its center and set

$$\delta_\square = \mathsf{Ed}(P,a_\square) + 4 \cdot 2^{\Delta_i}.$$

Finally, we also cover $C \setminus B_l$ with canonical squares of size 2^{Δ_l} and set $\delta_\square$ as above. Let $\mathcal{B}$ be the resulting set of $O((1/\varepsilon^2)\log(1/\varepsilon))$ canonical squares. We construct a compressed quadtree $\mathcal{T}$ on $(\mathcal{B},C)$ as described in Section 2. It can be checked that each exposed node on $\mathcal{T}$ is a leaf and therefore the rectilinear subdivision of C induced by $\mathbb{M} = \mathbb{M}(\mathcal{B},C)$ is a hierarchical grid composed of canonical squares. If a square σ in $\mathbb{M}$ lies in multiple squares of $\mathcal{B}$, we set $\delta_\sigma = \delta_\square$ where $\square$ is the smallest square of $\mathcal{B}$ containing σ. Finally, for every $\sigma \in \mathbb{M}$, we set

$$g_P(x) = \delta_\sigma, \quad \forall x \in \sigma.$$

LEMMA 5.4. *Let P be an uncertain point in $\mathbb{R}^2$ with a pdf of description complexity k, and let $0 < \varepsilon < 1$ be a parameter. A function $g_P : \mathbb{R}^2 \to \mathbb{R}_{\geq 0}$ can be constructed in $O((k/\varepsilon^2)\log(1/\varepsilon))$ time such that*

(i) g_P is piecewise constant inside a square C, which is the union of four canonical squares.

(ii) Each piece of g_P is defined over a canonical square, and the number of pieces is $O((1/\varepsilon^2)\log(1/\varepsilon))$.

(iii) $C \supseteq B[\bar{p}, 8\mathsf{Ed}(P,\bar{p})/\varepsilon]$ and $g_P(x) = \|x - \bar{p}\| + \mathsf{Ed}(P,\bar{p})$ for $x \notin C$.

(iv) $\mathsf{Ed}(P,x) \leq g_P(x) \leq (1+\varepsilon)\mathsf{Ed}(P,x)$ for all $x \in \mathbb{R}^2$.

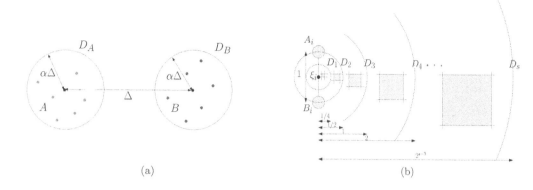

(a) (b)

Figure 6. (a) A single pair (A, B) in an α-WSPD. (b) The $D_1, \ldots, D_s$ for a suitable $s = O(\log(1/\varepsilon))$ constructed for a pair (A_i, B_i) in a $(1/8)$-WSPD. D_j has radius 2^{j-3} and is covered by canonical squares of side length γ_j.

PROOF. (i) and (ii) follow from the construction, and (iii) follows from Lemma 5.3, so we only need to prove (iv). We describe the proof for the case when $x \in B_0$, a similar argument holds when $x \in B_i \setminus B_{i-1}$, for $i \geq 1$. Suppose x lies in a grid cell τ of B_0. Then, using Lemma 5.1,

$$\begin{aligned}
g_P(x) &= \mathsf{Ed}(P, a_\tau) + 4 \cdot 2^{\Delta_0} \\
&\geq \mathsf{Ed}(P, x) - \|x - a_\tau\| + 2\rho_0 \\
&\geq \mathsf{Ed}(P, x).
\end{aligned}$$

On the other hand,

$$\begin{aligned}
g_P(x) &\leq \mathsf{Ed}(P, x) + \|x - a_\tau\| + 4 \cdot 2^{\Delta_0} \\
&\leq \mathsf{Ed}(P, x) + 2\rho_0 + 4\rho_0 \\
&\leq \mathsf{Ed}(P, x) + \frac{3\varepsilon}{4}\overline{\rho} \\
&\leq (1 + \varepsilon)\mathsf{Ed}(P, x).
\end{aligned}$$

$\square$

Remark. We remark that a similar function can be constructed that approximates $\mathsf{Ed}(P, x)$ even when $\mathrm{d}(\cdot, \cdot)$ is any L_p metric.

5.2 Uncertain data

Let $\mathcal{P} = \{P_1, \cdots, P_n\}$ be a set of n uncertain points in $\mathbb{R}^2$, each with a pdf of description complexity k. We describe a method for computing an ε-ENN of a query point $q \in \mathbb{R}^2$ in $\mathcal{P}$. For each $1 \leq i \leq n$, we construct the function $g_i : \mathbb{R}^2 \to \mathbb{R}_{\geq 0}$, using Lemma 5.4, such that $g_i(q) \leq (1+\varepsilon/3)\mathsf{Ed}(P_i, q)$, for all $q \in \mathbb{R}^2$. Let C_i be the canonical square inside which g_i is a piecewise-constant function. Let $G = \{g_1, \ldots, g_n\}$. By definition, the minimization diagram $\mathbb{M}(G)$ of G is an ε-EVD($\mathcal{P}$). Hence, it suffices to construct $\mathbb{M}(G)$ and build an index on $\mathbb{M}(G)$ for point-location queries. The difficulty with this approach is that we do not have a near-linear upper bound on the complexity of $\mathbb{M}(G)$ even in $\mathbb{R}^2$. Moreover, the complexity of $\mathbb{M}(G)$ is $\Omega(n^{\lceil d/2 \rceil})$ in higher dimensions, so this approach will not be practical for $d \geq 3$. We circumvent this problem by using the ideas from Arya *et al.* [6] and constructing a different ε-EVD($\mathcal{P}$) of near-linear size.

Here is the outline of the algorithm. We construct two sets $\mathcal{B}_{\mathrm{in}}$ and $\mathcal{B}_{\mathrm{out}}$ of canonical squares. Set $\mathcal{B} = \mathcal{B}_{\mathrm{in}} \cup \mathcal{B}_{\mathrm{out}}$. The size of $\mathcal{B}$, denoted by m, will be $O((n/\varepsilon^2)\log(1/\varepsilon))$, and we construct $\mathcal{B}$ in $O(n \log n + (n/\varepsilon^2)\log(1/\varepsilon))$ time. We

build, in $O(m \log m)$ time, a compressed quad tree $\mathbb{T}$ of size $O(m)$ on $\mathcal{B}$, and preprocess it in additional $O(m)$ time so that for a point $q \in \mathbb{R}^2$, the exposed node of $\mathbb{T}$ containing q can be computed in $O(\log m)$ time. Let $\mathbb{M}$ be the planar subdivision induced by the exposed nodes of $\mathbb{T}$. We refine each cell of $\mathbb{M}$ into $O(1)$ faces to construct an ε-EVD of $\mathcal{P}$. More precisely, for a point $x \in \mathbb{R}^2$, let $\mathcal{P}_{\mathrm{in}}[x] = \{P_i \mid x \in C_i\}$ and $\mathcal{P}_{\mathrm{out}}[x] = \{P_i \mid x \notin C_i\}$. $\mathbb{T}$ has the property that for every exposed node v, $\mathcal{P}_{\mathrm{in}}[x]$ and $\mathcal{P}_{\mathrm{out}}[x]$ are the same for all points in the region R_v. We denote these sets by $\mathcal{P}_{\mathrm{in}}[v]$ and $\mathcal{P}_{\mathrm{out}}[v]$. We associate two presentative points $P_v^{\mathrm{in}} \in \mathcal{P}_{\mathrm{in}}[v]$, $P_v^{\mathrm{out}} \in \mathcal{P}_{\mathrm{out}}[v]$ such that P_v^{in} is an ε-ENN of any point of R_v in $\mathcal{P}_{\mathrm{in}}[v]$ and P_v^{out} is an ε-ENN of any point of R_v in $\mathcal{P}_{\mathrm{out}}[v]$. If $P_v^{\mathrm{in}} = P_i$, we store the canonical square $\square_v$ of the function g_i that contains R_v, and if $P_v^{\mathrm{out}} = P_j$, we also store the centroid $\overline{p}_j$ of P_j at v.

For all $x \in R_v$, $g_i(x)$ is constant and $g_j(x) = \|x - \overline{p}_j\| + \mathsf{Ed}(P_j, \overline{p}_j)$. The minimization diagram of g_i and g_j within R_v, denoted by Σ_v, has $O(1)$ size; see Figure 7(a). We compute Σ_v for all exposed nodes of $\mathbb{T}$ and show that the planar subdivision induced by the Σ_v's is the desired ε-EVD of $\mathcal{P}$; Figure 7(b) shows a section of such a planar subdivision.

We first describe the computation of $\mathcal{B}_{\mathrm{in}}$ and $\mathcal{B}_{\mathrm{out}}$ followed by the computation of the representative points P_v^{in} and P_v^{out} for each exposed node v in $\mathbb{T}$. Finally, we describe how to construct an ε-EVD using the representative points.

Constructing $\mathcal{B}_{\mathrm{in}}$. For $1 \leq i \leq n$, let $\mathcal{B}_i$ be the set of canonical squares that define the pieces of the piecewise-constant portion of g_i. Set $\mathcal{B}_{\mathrm{in}} = \bigcup_{i=1}^n \mathcal{B}_i$. For each $\square \in \mathcal{B}_i$, we associate a value $\delta_\square$ with $\square$, which is $g_i(x)$ for any $x \in \square$. If a square $\square$ appears in multiple $\mathcal{B}_i$'s, we keep only one copy of $\square$ in $\mathcal{B}_{\mathrm{in}}$ and $\delta_\square$ is the minimum of the values associated with the different copies of $\square$. For each square $\square \in \mathcal{B}_i$, we set $P_\square = P_i$.

Constructing $\mathcal{B}_{\mathrm{out}}$. $\mathcal{B}_{\mathrm{out}}$ is constructed using the algorithm by Arya *et al.* [6] for computing an ε-VD of a set S of N (certain) points. We therefore sketch their algorithm in $\mathbb{R}^2$. Two point sets $A, B \subset \mathbb{R}^2$ are called α-*well-separated* if A and B can be contained in disks D_A and D_B respectively, whose centers are at distance Δ and whose radii are at most $\alpha\Delta$; see Figure 6(a). A partition of $S \times S$ into a family $Z = \{(A_1, B_1), \ldots, (A_M, B_M)\}$ of α-well-separated pairs is called an α-*well-separated pair decomposition* (α-WSPD) of S. It is well known that an α-WSPD of S with $O(N/\varepsilon^2)$

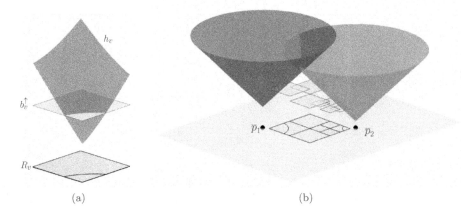

(a)   (b)

Figure 7. (a) The minimization diagram, Σ_v (shown below) of $b_v^\uparrow$ and h_v for an exposed node v of $\mathbb{T}$. The complexity of Σ_v is $O(1)$. (b) A portion of the ε-EVD (shown below) obtained by replacing each cell of $\mathbb{M}$ by Σ_v. The corresponding $b_v^\uparrow$'s (raised squares) and h_v's (cones) are also shown.

pairs can be computed in $O((N/\varepsilon^2)\log N)$ time [18]. Arya et al. [6] first compute a $(1/8)$-WSPD Z of S. Let (A_i, B_i) be a pair in Z. Without loss of generality, assume that A_i and B_i are contained in disks of radii $1/8$ and the centers of these disks are at distance 1. Let ξ_i be the midpoint of these centers. They construct a family of $s = O(\log_2(1/\varepsilon))$ disks $D_1, \ldots, D_s$ centered at ξ_i where the radius of D_j is 2^{j-3}. Let $\gamma_j = 2^{j-c-\lceil\log_2(1/\varepsilon)\rceil}$ where $c \geq 3$ is a constant. Let $\mathcal{C}_j$ be the set of canonical squares of side length γ_j that intersect D_j; $|\mathcal{C}_j| = O(1/\varepsilon^2)$; see Figure 6(b). Set $\tilde{\mathcal{B}}_i = \bigcup_{1 \leq j \leq s} \mathcal{C}_j$. They repeat the above procedure for each pair in Z. Let $\tilde{\mathcal{B}}$ be the overall set of canonical squares constructed; $|\tilde{\mathcal{B}}| = O((N/\varepsilon^2)\log(1/\varepsilon^2))$. $\tilde{\mathcal{B}}$ can be constructed in $O((N/\varepsilon^2)\log(1/\varepsilon) + N\log N)$ time. Next, they store $\tilde{\mathcal{B}}$ into a compressed quadtree to construct an ε-VD of S.

We adapt their procedure as follows. For $1 \leq i \leq n$, as before, let $\overline{p}_i$ be the centroid of P_i and C_i the square outside which $g_i(x) = \|x - \overline{p}_i\| + \mathsf{Ed}(P_i, \overline{p}_i)$. Set $\overline{P} = \{\overline{p}_i \mid 1 \leq i \leq n\}$. We execute the procedure of Arya et al. [6] on $\overline{P}$ and generate a set $\mathcal{B}_{\text{out}}$ of $O((n/\varepsilon^2)\log(1/\varepsilon))$ canonical squares.

Computing the representative points. For a point $x \in \mathbb{R}^2$, let $\overline{P}_{\text{out}}[x] = \{\overline{p}_i \mid P_i \in \mathcal{P}_{\text{out}}[x]\}$. Similar to the index in Section 4.1, we construct an index for answering stabbing queries which can find, for a query point q, which rectangles in C_i do not contain q and thus, find $\overline{P}_{\text{out}}[q]$. This index stores a family of canonical subsets of $\overline{P}$ such that for any query point q, $\overline{P}_{\text{out}}[q]$ can be represented as the union of $O(\log^2 n)$ canonical subsets. For each of the canonical subsets, we also store an $(\varepsilon/12)$-VD from Arya et al. [6] of this subset. The total space required for the index is $O((n/\varepsilon^2)\log^2 n\log(1/\varepsilon))$ and it takes the same time to construct. For a query point q, we can now compute an $(\varepsilon/12)$-NN of q in $\overline{P}_{\text{out}}[q]$ in $O(\log^2 n\log(n/\varepsilon))$ time. This index is only needed for preprocessing and removed after representative points have been computed.

We build a compressed quadtree $\mathbb{T}$ on $\mathcal{B} = \mathcal{B}_{\text{in}} \cup \mathcal{B}_{\text{out}}$ as mentioned above. Let v be an exposed node of $\mathbb{T}$. If none of the ancestors of v (including v itself) stores a square of $\mathcal{B}_{\text{in}}$, P_v^{in} is undefined. Otherwise, among the squares $\square$ of

$\mathcal{B}_{\text{in}}$ stored at the ancestors of v, let $\overline{\square}$ be the one with the smallest value of $\delta_\square$. We set $P_v^{\text{in}} = P_{\overline{\square}}$, $b_v = \overline{\square}$, and $b_v^\uparrow$ to the square in $\mathbb{R}^3$ obtained by lifting $\overline{\square}$ to the height $\delta_{\overline{\square}}$.

Next, we pick a point $x \in R_v$ and compute an $(\varepsilon/12)$-NN of x in $\overline{P}_{\text{out}}[x]$, say $\overline{p}_i$. We set $P_v^{\text{out}} = P_i$ and $\overline{p}_v = \overline{p}_i$. Let $h_v(x) = \|x - \overline{p}_i\| + \mathsf{Ed}(P_i, \overline{p}_i)$.

Finally, we compute the minimization diagram Σ_v of $b_v^\uparrow$ and h_v within R_v; see Figure 7(a). By replacing each cell R_v of $\mathbb{M}$ with Σ_v, we obtain the desired ε-EVD of $\mathcal{P}$, whose size is $O(m) = O((n/\varepsilon^2)\log(1/\varepsilon))$; Figure 7(b) shows a portion of such an ε-EVD. The total time spent in constructing this ε-EVD is $O((n/\varepsilon^2)\log^2 n\log(n/\varepsilon)\log(1/\varepsilon))$.

The correctness of the algorithm follows from the following lemma.

Lemma 5.5. *Let q be a point lying in R_v for an exposed node v of $\mathbb{T}$. Let P_q^{out} and P_q^{in} be the expected nearest neighbor of q in $\mathcal{P}_{\text{out}}[q]$ and $\mathcal{P}_{\text{in}}[q]$ respectively. Then,*

(i) $\mathsf{Ed}(P_v^{\text{in}}, q) \leq (1+\varepsilon)\mathsf{Ed}(P_q^{\text{in}}, q)$.

(ii) $\mathsf{Ed}(P_v^{\text{out}}, q) \leq (1+\varepsilon)\mathsf{Ed}(P_q^{\text{out}}, q)$.

Proof. (i) Let $\mathcal{B}_q = \{\square \in \mathcal{B}_{\text{in}} \mid P_i \in \mathcal{P}_{\text{in}}[q] \wedge q \in \square\}$. By construction, each square in $\mathcal{B}_q$ is stored at an ancestor of v in $\mathbb{T}$. Hence, $P_v^{\text{in}} = \arg\min_{P_i \in \mathcal{P}_{\text{in}}[q]} g_i(q)$. Now, (i) follows from Lemma 5.4.

(ii) By construction, the set $\{C_i \mid x \notin C_i\}$ is the same for all $x \in R_v$. Therefore, $\mathcal{P}_{\text{out}}[q] = \mathcal{P}_{\text{out}}[v]$ and $P_v^{\text{out}} \in \mathcal{P}_{\text{out}}[q]$. Let $\overline{p}_v$ and $\overline{p}_q$ be the centroids of P_v^{out} and P_q^{out} respectively. The argument in Arya et al. [6] implies that $\|\overline{p}_v - q\| \leq (1 + \varepsilon/3)\|\overline{p}_q - q\|$. Hence,

$$\mathsf{Ed}(P_v^{\text{out}}, q) \leq (1+\varepsilon/3)\|\overline{p}_q - q\| + \mathsf{Ed}(P_v^{\text{out}}, \overline{p}_v)$$
$$\leq (1+\varepsilon/3)\|\overline{p}_q - q\| + \varepsilon/24\|\overline{p}_v - q\|$$
$$\leq (1+\varepsilon/3)(1+\varepsilon/24)(\|\overline{p}_q - q\| + \mathsf{Ed}(P_q^{\text{out}}, \overline{p}_q)).$$

Since $P_v \in \mathcal{P}_{\text{out}}[q]$, $\|\overline{p}_v - q\| \geq 24\mathsf{Ed}(P_v, \overline{p}_v)/\varepsilon$. Thus,

$$\mathsf{Ed}(P_v^{\text{out}}, q) \leq (1+\varepsilon/2)(1+\varepsilon/3)\mathsf{Ed}(P_q^{\text{out}}, q) \leq (1+\varepsilon)\mathsf{Ed}(P_q^{\text{out}}, q),$$

proving part (ii). $\qquad\qquad\square$

Putting everything together, we conclude the following.

THEOREM 5.6. *Let $\mathcal{P}$ be a set of n uncertain points in $\mathbb{R}^2$, each with a pdf of description complexity k, let $0 < \varepsilon < 1$ be a parameter and let $\mathrm{d}(\cdot, \cdot)$ be the Euclidean distance. An ε-EVD of $\mathcal{P}$ of size $O((n/\varepsilon^2)\log(1/\varepsilon))$ can be constructed in $O((n/\varepsilon^2)\log^2 n \log(n/\varepsilon)\log(1/\varepsilon))$ time. It can be processed in additional $O((n/\varepsilon^2)\log(1/\varepsilon)))$ time into an index of $O((n/\varepsilon^2)\log(1/\varepsilon))$ size so that an ε-ENN of a query point can be constructed in $O(\log(n/\varepsilon))$ time.*

Noting that for an uncertain point P, the function g_P that approximates $\mathsf{Ed}(P, x)$ under any L_p metric can be constructed in the same time, we also obtain the following.

THEOREM 5.7. *Let $\mathcal{P}$ be a set of n uncertain points in $\mathbb{R}^2$, each with a pdf of description complexity k, let $0 < \varepsilon < 1$ be a parameter. For any L_p metric, an ε-EVD of $\mathcal{P}$ of size $O((n/\varepsilon^2)\log(1/\varepsilon))$ can be constructed in $O((n/\varepsilon^2)\log^2 n \log(n/\varepsilon)\log(1/\varepsilon))$ time. It can be processed in $O((n/\varepsilon^2)\log(1/\varepsilon))$ additional time into an index of $O((n/\varepsilon^2)\log(1/\varepsilon))$ size so that an ε-ENN of a query point under the L_p metric can be constructed in $O(\log(n/\varepsilon))$ time.*

Remarks. (i) Note that we do not have to construct the minimization diagram Σ_v for each exposed node $v \in \mathbb{T}$. We can simply use $P_v^{\mathrm{in}}, P_v^{\mathrm{out}}, b_v^{\uparrow}$ and h_v stored at v to compute an ε-ENN of a query point.

(ii) The algorithm can be extended to higher dimensions. The size of the index becomes $O((n/\varepsilon^d)\log(1/\varepsilon))$, the preprocessing time become $O((n/\varepsilon^d)\log^d n \log(1/\varepsilon))$, and the query time remains the same.

5.3 Uncertain query

Let $\mathcal{P} = \{p_1, \cdots, p_n\}$ be a set of (certain) points in $\mathbb{R}^2$. For an uncertain query point Q of description complexity k and a parameter $0 < \varepsilon < 1$, we wish to compute its ε-ENN in $\mathcal{P}$. We preprocess $\mathcal{P}$ into a compressed quadtree $\mathbb{T}$ as described in Section 2. We also preprocess $\mathcal{P}$ for answering NN queries, by constructing its Voronoi diagram and preprocessing it for point-location queries. The size of the index is $O(n)$ and it can be built in $O(n\log n)$ time [16].

To answer a given query Q, we construct the function $g_Q : \mathbb{R}^2 \to \mathbb{R}_{\geq 0}$ using Lemma 5.4. Let $\mathcal{B}$ be the set of canonical squares defining g_Q. For each $\square \in \mathcal{B}$, we query $\mathbb{T}$ and report a point $p_\square \in \square \cap \mathcal{P}$ if there exists one. Among all the points reported, we return the point $p^* = \arg\min_{p_\square} g_Q(p_\square)$. If no point is reported, then we return the point of $\mathcal{P}$ that is closest to $\bar{q}$, the centroid of Q. The correctness of the algorithm follows from the Lemma 5.4. Querying each $\square \in \mathcal{B}$ takes $O(\log n)$ time, by Lemma 2.1, and the NN of $\bar{q}$ can be computed in $O(\log n)$ time, so we conclude the following:

THEOREM 5.8. *Let $\mathcal{P}$ be a set of n (certain) points in $\mathbb{R}^2$. An index of $O(n)$ size can be built on $\mathcal{P}$ in $O(n\log n)$ time so that for an uncertain query point Q with a pdf of description complexity k and for a parameter $0 < \varepsilon < 1$, an ε-ENN of Q can be computed in $O((k/\varepsilon^2)\log(1/\varepsilon)\log n)$ time.*

Remarks. (i) The algorithm can be extended to higher dimensions. The size and the preprocessing time remain the same, but the query time in $\mathbb{R}^d$ increases to $O((k/\varepsilon^d)\log(1/\varepsilon)\log n)$.

(ii) All pieces of the function g_Q need not be computed in the beginning itself. They can be constructed hierarchically

while querying the compressed quadtree on $\mathcal{P}$. This does not affect the worst-case running time but it is more efficient in practice.

6. CONCLUSION

In this paper we considered the problem of answering NN queries under uncertainty. We used a probabilistic framework to model the uncertainty in the location of input data or query point, and presented indexing schemes of linear or near-linear size that answer exact or ε-approximate ENN queries in $\mathbb{R}^2$ in polylog(n) time under squared Euclidean, L_1, L_2, and L_∞ distance functions. As far as we know, these are the first methods to obtain such bounds. We conclude by mentioning a few open problems:

(i) What is the combinatorial complexity of EVD$(\mathcal{P})$ when $d(\cdot, \cdot)$ is the Euclidean distance? Can a quadratic upper bound be proved? Although the algebraic complexity of a bisector is large, the combinatorial complexity, i.e., the number of vertices, can be small.

(ii) The expected distance is not a reliable indicator when the variance of the pdfs is not small. In this case, one is interested in computing a point that is the nearest neighbor with highest probability or the points that are the nearest neighbors with probability higher than a given threshold. Is there a linear-size index to answer these queries in sublinear time in the worst case? This problem seems hard even for very simple pdfs such as Gaussians.

7. REFERENCES

[1] P. K. Agarwal, S.-W. Cheng, Y. Tao, and K. Yi, Indexing uncertain data, *Proc. ACM Symposium on Principles of Database Systems*, 2009, pp. 137–146.

[2] P. K. Agarwal, S. Har-Peled, M. Sharir, and Y. Wang, Hausdorff distance under translation for points and balls, *ACM Transactions on Algorithms*, 6 (2010), 71:1–71:26.

[3] P. K. Agarwal and J. Matousek, Ray shooting and parametric search, *SIAM Journal on Computing*, 22 (1993), 794–806.

[4] C. C. Aggarwal, *Managing and Mining Uncertain Data*, Springer, 2009.

[5] A. Andoni and P. Indyk, Near-optimal hashing algorithms for approximate nearest neighbor in high dimensions, *Communications of the ACM*, 51 (2008), 117–122.

[6] S. Arya, T. Malamatos, and D. M. Mount, Space-time tradeoffs for approximate nearest neighbor searching, *Journal of the ACM*, 57 (2009), 1:1–1:54.

[7] F. Aurenhammer and R. Klein, Voronoi diagrams, in: *Handbook of Computational Geometry* (J. E. Goodman and J. O'Rourke, eds.), Elsevier Science Publishers, Amsterdam, 2000, pp. 201–290.

[8] G. Beskales, M. A. Soliman, and I. F. Ilyas, Efficient search for the top-k probable nearest neighbors in uncertain databases, *Proc. International Conference on Very Large Databases*, 1 (2008), 326–339.

[9] S. Cabello, Approximation algorithms for spreading points, *Journal of Algorithmss*, 62 (2007), 49–73.

[10] S. Cabello and M. J. van Kreveld, Approximation algorithms for aligning points, *Proc. 19th ACM Symposium on Computational Geometry*, 2003, pp. 20–28.

[11] R. Cheng, J. Chen, M. Mokbel, and C.-Y. Chow, Probabilistic verifiers: Evaluating constrained nearest-neighbor queries over uncertain data, *Proc. IEEE International Conference on Data Engineering*, 2008, pp. 973–982.

[12] R. Cheng, L. Chen, J. Chen, and X. Xie, Evaluating probability threshold k-nearest-neighbor queries over uncertain data, *Proc. 12th International Conference on Extending Database Technology: Advances in Database Technology*, 2009, pp. 672–683.

[13] R. Cheng, X. Xie, M. L. Yiu, J. Chen, and L. Sun, Uv-diagram: A voronoi diagram for uncertain data, *Proc. IEEE International Conference on Data Engineering*, 2010, pp. 796–807.

[14] K. L. Clarkson, Nearest-neighbor searching and metric space dimensions, *Nearest-Neighbor Methods for Learning and Vision: Theory and Practice*, (2006), 15–59.

[15] N. N. Dalvi, C. Ré, and D. Suciu, Probabilistic databases: diamonds in the dirt, *Communications of the ACM*, 52 (2009), 86–94.

[16] M. de Berg, M. van Kreveld, M. Overmars, and O. Schwarzkopf, *Computational Geometry: Algorithms and Applications*, Springer-Verlag, 2000.

[17] A. Guttman, R-trees: a dynamic index structure for spatial searching, *Proc. ACM SIGMOD International Conference on Management of Data*, 1984, pp. 47–57.

[18] S. Har-Peled, *Geometric Approximation Algorithms*, American Mathematical Society, 2011.

[19] M. Hua, J. Pei, W. Zhang, and X. Lin, Ranking queries on uncertain data: a probabilistic threshold approach, *Proc. ACM SIGMOD International Conference on Management of Data*, 2008, pp. 673–686.

[20] P. Indyk, Nearest neighbors in high-dimensional spaces, in: *Handbook of Discrete and Computational Geometry* (J. E. Goodman and J. O'Rourke, eds.), CRC Press LLC, 2004.

[21] M. Jooyandeh, A. Mohades, and M. Mirzakhah, Uncertain voronoi diagram, *Information Processing Letters*, 109 (2009), 709–712.

[22] P. Kamousi, T. M. Chan, and S. Suri, Closest pair and the post office problem for stochastic points, *Proc. 12th International Conference on Algorithms and Data Structures*, 2011, pp. 548–559.

[23] H.-P. Kriegel, P. Kunath, and M. Renz, Probabilistic nearest-neighbor query on uncertain objects, *Proc. 12th International Conference on Database Systems for Advanced Applications*, 2007, pp. 337–348.

[24] F. Li, B. Yao, and P. Kumar, Group enclosing queries, *IEEE Transactions on Knowledge and Data Engineering*, 23 (2011), 1526 –1540.

[25] H. Li, H. Lu, B. Huang, and Z. Huang, Two ellipse-based pruning methods for group nearest neighbor queries, *Proc. 13th Annual ACM International Workshop on Geographic Information Systems*, 2005, pp. 192–199.

[26] Y. Li, F. Li, K. Yi, B. Yao, and M. Wang, Flexible aggregate similarity search, *Proc. ACM SIGMOD International Conference on Management of Data*, 2011, pp. 1009–1020.

[27] X. Lian and L. Chen, Probabilistic group nearest neighbor queries in uncertain databases, *IEEE Transactions on Knowledge and Data Engineering*, 20 (2008), 809–824.

[28] V. Ljosa and A. Singh, Apla: Indexing arbitrary probability distributions, *Proc. IEEE International Conference on Data Engineering*, 2007, pp. 946 –955.

[29] M. Löffler and M. J. van Kreveld, Largest bounding box, smallest diameter, and related problems on imprecise points, *Computational Geometry*, 43 (2010), 419–433.

[30] Y. Luo, H. Chen, K. Furuse, and N. Ohbo, Efficient methods in finding aggregate nearest neighbor by projection-based filtering, *Proc. 12th International Conference on Computational Science and Its Applications*, 2007, pp. 821–833.

[31] D. Papadias, Q. Shen, Y. Tao, and K. Mouratidis, Group nearest neighbor queries, *Proc. IEEE International Conference on Data Engineering*, 2004, pp. 301 – 312.

[32] N. Sarnak and R. E. Tarjan, Planar point location using persistent search trees, *Communications of the ACM*, 29 (1986), 669–679.

[33] J. Sember and W. Evans, Guaranteed voronoi diagrams of uncertain sites, *Proc. 20th Canadian Conference on Computational Geometry*, 2008.

[34] M. Sharifzadeh and C. Shahabi, Vor-tree: R-trees with voronoi diagrams for efficient processing of spatial nearest neighbor queries, *Proc. International Conference on Very Large Databases*, 3 (2010), 1231–1242.

[35] M. Sharir and P. K. Agarwal, *Davenport-Schinzel Sequences and Their Geometric Applications*, Cambridge University Press, New York, 1995.

[36] G. Trajcevski, R. Tamassia, H. Ding, P. Scheuermann, and I. F. Cruz, Continuous probabilistic nearest-neighbor queries for uncertain trajectories, *Proc. 12th International Conference on Extending Database Technology: Advances in Database Technology*, 2009, pp. 874–885.

[37] M. J. van Kreveld, M. Löffler, and J. S. B. Mitchell, Preprocessing imprecise points and splitting triangulations, *SIAM Journal on Computing*, 39 (2010), 2990–3000.

[38] M. Yiu, N. Mamoulis, and D. Papadias, Aggregate nearest neighbor queries in road networks, *IEEE Transactions on, Knowledge and Data Engineering*, 17 (2005), 820 – 833.

[39] S. M. Yuen, Y. Tao, X. Xiao, J. Pei, and D. Zhang, Superseding nearest neighbor search on uncertain spatial databases, *IEEE Transactions on Knowledge and Data Engineering*, 22 (2010), 1041 –1055.

Classification of Annotation Semirings over Query Containment

Egor V. Kostylev
University of Edinburgh
ekostyle@inf.ed.ac.uk

Juan L. Reutter
University of Edinburgh
juan.reutter@ed.ac.uk

András Z. Salamon
University of Edinburgh
andras.salamon@ed.ac.uk

ABSTRACT

We study the problem of query containment of (unions of) conjunctive queries over annotated databases. Annotations are typically attached to tuples and represent metadata such as probability, multiplicity, comments, or provenance. It is usually assumed that annotations are drawn from a commutative semiring. Such databases pose new challenges in query optimization, since many related fundamental tasks, such as query containment, have to be reconsidered in the presence of propagation of annotations.

We axiomatize several classes of semirings for each of which containment of conjunctive queries is equivalent to existence of a particular type of homomorphism. For each of these types we also specify all semirings for which existence of a corresponding homomorphism is a sufficient (or necessary) condition for the containment. We exploit these techniques to develop new decision procedures for containment of unions of conjunctive queries and axiomatize corresponding classes of semirings. This generalizes previous approaches and allows us to improve known complexity bounds.

Categories and Subject Descriptors

H.2.4 [**Database Management**]: Systems—*query processing*; H.2.1 [**Database Management**]: Data Models

Keywords

Annotation, Provenance, Query Optimization

1. INTRODUCTION

Relational database annotation is rapidly coming to market. The expressive power of curated [2] and probabilistic databases [12, 21], various forms of provenance [9, 3, 15], and even bag semantics as a way to model standard SQL [6], derives from an annotation attribute with special behaviour. In [15] it was observed that in all of these cases annotations propagate through queries as we expect if the domain of annotations has the structure of a *commutative semiring*.

Every application that supports annotations should be able to compare queries to perform standard tasks such as query rewriting and query optimization. However, as noted in [17, 6] for the particular case of bag semantics and quite generally in [14], the introduction of annotations requires a complete rethinking of these kinds of tasks: a pair of queries may behave differently when posed over ordinary relations or over annotated relations; the behaviour can be different even for different semirings. Hence a general theory is needed to explain how queries behave over annotated relations, and to provide query optimization and query rewriting techniques, regardless of the semiring chosen for annotations.

In this paper, we study the problem of *containment* of queries, specifically for the classes of *conjunctive queries* (CQs) and *unions of conjunctive queries* (UCQs). For this purpose we formally generalize the standard notion of containment for relational databases so that it subsumes previously studied containments for bag semantics [17, 6] and several naturally ordered semirings [14]. We study in our view the most general reasonable notion of containment, based on a few intuitive axioms which any containment should satisfy.

The ideal would be to obtain a decision procedure to decide containment of CQs or UCQs, for an arbitrary annotation semiring. However, there is evidence that obtaining such a procedure for all semirings is a truly challenging, if not impossible, task. Indeed, this would require solving containment for bag semantics, which is undecidable for UCQs [17] (and even for CQs with inequalities [18]), and is a long-standing open problem for CQs [6, 17, 1, 7]. With these observations in mind, we instead ask the following, narrower question: are there reasonable classes of semirings for which we can prove that containment of CQs or UCQs is decidable? In this paper we answer this question positively, by finding several such classes. Our main results generalize and extend previous work [14, 13] unifying how semantic properties of query containment link to syntactic properties of different types of *homomorphisms* between queries. We also show that these classes are of importance in practice, as they contain the majority of the annotation semirings that have been proposed.

In Sec. 3 we begin our study with containment of CQs. For standard relational databases (which can be modelled by a set semantics semiring consisting of just two elements **true** and **false**), query containment corresponds precisely to the NP-complete problem of deciding whether there exists a homomorphism between these queries [5]. Thus, the natural starting point of our search for decidable classes is to ask for which semirings the CQ containment problem coincides with CQ containment for the usual set semantics. This question was partially answered in [17], where for semirings which are so called type A systems, containment was shown to be equivalent to the existence of a homomorphism. We show that it is possible to describe the class $\mathbf{C}_{\text{hom}}$ of *all* such semirings by two simple axioms: idempotence of multiplication and annihilation of the multiplicative identity. Interestingly, this class corresponds precisely to the class of type A′ systems [17], for which such a characterization was open.

Continuing our search for decidable classes, in Sec. 4 we consider those classes obtained by relaxing the axioms for $\mathbf{C}_{\text{hom}}$. In Sec. 4.1 to 4.4 we show that for each of these classes there exists a well-known natural type of homomorphism that characterizes the class, but only as a *sufficient condition* for containment of CQs. As an example, consider the class of semirings that satisfy only the annihilation axiom. In Sec. 4.2 we demonstrate that this class contains precisely all the semirings for which the existence of an *injective homomorphism* is a sufficient condition for containment of two CQs. A sufficient condition does not guarantee the decidability of the containment problem; one needs a necessary condition as well. For this purpose, we describe the *largest* class for which an injective homomorphism is necessary for containment of CQs. Thereby, we have that for all semirings in the intersection of these two classes, the existence of an injective homomorphism is both a necessary and sufficient condition for the containment of two CQs, resulting in a class of semirings for which containment is decidable.

We establish similar results for several other classes of semirings obtained by relaxing the axioms that define the class $\mathbf{C}_{\text{hom}}$, and show how these classes are characterized by other well known types of homomorphism. This gives us decision procedures for the corresponding classes of semirings. We provide tight complexity bounds for these procedures: all of them are NP-complete, just as for the class $\mathbf{C}_{\text{hom}}$ [5].

To describe some of these classes, we introduce the notion of CQ-*admissible polynomials*. A polynomial is CQ-admissible if it can be obtained by evaluating a CQ over a database annotated with variables. In Sec. 4.5 we give a syntactic characterization of these polynomials, which allows us to axiomatize several classes of semirings. This novel concept is of independent interest; e.g. in [19] the properties of such polynomials were used implicitly for effectively storing and manipulating the provenance of CQ results.

Moving beyond homomorphisms, in Sec. 4.6 we also find several semirings for which containment can be solved via a *small model property*, by looking for a small enough database witness for absence of containment. This results in new decision procedures to solve containment of CQs, for a wide range of semirings that had not been previously addressed.

In Sec. 5 we develop decision procedures to solve the containment of UCQs, which naturally extend the procedures we used for the case of CQs. In this respect, most of the existing positive results correspond to semirings for which one can decide containment of UCQs by checking their elements locally, one by one [14]. We identify the relationship of this property with idempotence of the semiring's addition, which gives us a decision procedure for containment of UCQs for several classes of semirings, including $\mathbf{C}_{\text{hom}}$. However, for other classes this simple local method does not work. To overcome its limitations, we introduce the notion of a *complete description* of a UCQ (inspired by [11] and [8]), which is a union of special CQs with inequalities, equivalent to the

original UCQ. This allows us to identify classes of semirings for which a modified local method works, though applied not to UCQs themselves but to their complete descriptions.

Complete descriptions open up new possibilities for deciding containment of UCQs over different semantics. Our machinery allows us to devise in Sec. 5.2 a syntactic condition for checking containment of UCQs for the important semiring of provenance polynomials [15], for which only a small model property based approach was known [14]; and based on this, to improve the complexity upper bound. Also, complete descriptions allow us to improve the existing sufficient and necessary conditions for containment of UCQs over bag semantics.

2. PRELIMINARIES

Commutative semirings An algebraic structure $\mathcal{K} = \langle K, \oplus, \otimes, \mathbb{0}, \mathbb{1} \rangle$ with binary operations *sum* $\oplus$ and *product* $\otimes$ and constants $\mathbb{0}$ and $\mathbb{1}$ is a (*commutative*) *semiring* iff $\langle K, \oplus, \mathbb{0} \rangle$ and $\langle K, \otimes, \mathbb{1} \rangle$ are commutative monoids[1] with identities $\mathbb{0}$ and $\mathbb{1}$ respectively, $\otimes$ is distributive over $\oplus$, and $a \otimes \mathbb{0} = \mathbb{0}$ holds for each $a \in K$. It will be convenient for us to consider only *nontrivial* semirings, i.e. semirings such that $\mathbb{0} \neq \mathbb{1}$. We use the symbols $\sum$ and $\prod$ to denote sum and product of sets of semiring elements in the usual way.

$\mathcal{K}$-relations A *schema* $\mathbb{S}$ is a finite set of *relational symbols*, each of which is assigned a non-negative *arity*. For a semiring $\mathcal{K} = \langle K, \oplus, \otimes, \mathbb{0}, \mathbb{1} \rangle$ and an infinite domain $\mathbb{D}$ of constants, a $\mathcal{K}$-*instance* I over a schema $\mathbb{S}$ assigns to each relational symbol R from $\mathbb{S}$ of arity m a $\mathcal{K}$-*relation* R^I, which is a (total) function from the set of *tuples* $\mathbb{D}^m$ to K such that its *support*, i.e. the set $\{ \mathbf{t} \mid \mathbf{t} \in \mathbb{D}^m, R^I(\mathbf{t}) \neq \mathbb{0} \}$, is finite. We call $R^I(\mathbf{t})$ the *annotation* of the tuple $\mathbf{t}$ in R^I.

Queries A *conjunctive query* (*CQ*) Q over a schema $\mathbb{S}$ is an expression of the form $\exists \mathbf{v} \, \phi(\mathbf{u}, \mathbf{v})$, where $\mathbf{u}$ is a list of *free* variables, $\mathbf{v}$ is a list of *existential* variables and $\phi(\mathbf{u}, \mathbf{v})$ is a multiset of relational atoms over $\mathbb{S}$ using variables $\mathbf{u} \cup \mathbf{v}$. As usual we write $\phi(\mathbf{u}, \mathbf{v}) = R_1(\mathbf{u}_1, \mathbf{v}_1), \ldots, R_n(\mathbf{u}_n, \mathbf{v}_n)$, where $\mathbf{u}_1 \cup \ldots \cup \mathbf{u}_n = \mathbf{u}$ and $\mathbf{v}_1 \cup \ldots \cup \mathbf{v}_n = \mathbf{v}$, keeping in mind that R_i and R_j in this expression can be the same symbol. A *union* of conjunctive queries (*UCQ*) $\mathbf{Q}$ is a multiset of CQs over the same schema and the same set of free variables.

Evaluations For CQ $Q = \exists \mathbf{v} \, R_1(\mathbf{u}_1, \mathbf{v}_1), \ldots, R_n(\mathbf{u}_n, \mathbf{v}_n)$ and a tuple $\mathbf{t}$, denote by $\mathcal{V}(Q, \mathbf{t})$ the set of all mappings f from $\mathbf{u} \cup \mathbf{v}$ to the domain $\mathbb{D}$ such that $f(\mathbf{u}) = \mathbf{t}$. Given a $\mathcal{K}$-instance I, the *evaluation* of Q on I for $\mathbf{t}$ is the value

$$Q^I(\mathbf{t}) = \sum_{f \in \mathcal{V}(Q,\mathbf{t})} \prod_{1 \leq i \leq n} R_i^I(f(\mathbf{u}_i, \mathbf{v}_i)).$$

Similarly, the *evaluation* of a UCQ $\mathbf{Q}$ on I for $\mathbf{t}$ is

$$\mathbf{Q}^I(\mathbf{t}) = \sum_{Q \in \mathbf{Q}} Q^I(\mathbf{t}).$$

From this definition it follows that if $\mathbf{Q} = \emptyset$ then $\mathbf{Q}^I(\mathbf{t}) = \mathbb{0}$.

3. GENERAL FRAMEWORK

3.1 $\mathcal{K}$-containment and positive semirings

As noted in [15], the introduction of annotations on relations requires a complete rethinking of the notions of query

---

[1]A commutative monoid is a set with an associative and commutative binary operation and an identity element.

optimization and query rewriting. In particular, it was first discovered in [6] that two queries that are equivalent when posed over ordinary relations may not be equivalent when evaluated on $\mathcal{K}$-relations. Furthermore, for two different semirings $\mathcal{K}_1$ and $\mathcal{K}_2$, two queries may be equivalent under $\mathcal{K}_1$-relations, but not equivalent under $\mathcal{K}_2$-relations.

Our main aim is to explore the problem of query containment over different $\mathcal{K}$-relations. First we need to formally specify what we mean by "equivalence" and "containment" of queries. The notion of equivalence is naturally formalised as follows: given a semiring $\mathcal{K}$, UCQs $\mathbf{Q}_1$ and $\mathbf{Q}_2$ over the same schema are $\mathcal{K}$-equivalent (denoted $\mathbf{Q}_1 \equiv_\mathcal{K} \mathbf{Q}_2$) iff for every $\mathcal{K}$-instance I and tuple $\mathbf{t}$ it holds that $\mathbf{Q}_1^I(\mathbf{t}) = \mathbf{Q}_2^I(\mathbf{t})$. However, to study containment of queries over some semiring $\mathcal{K}$, we should be able to compare elements of $\mathcal{K}$ not only for equality. Therefore, we assume that the semiring $\mathcal{K}$ is equipped with a *partial order*[2] $\preceq_\mathcal{K}$. This allows us to define when a UCQ $\mathbf{Q}_1$ is $\mathcal{K}$-contained in a UCQ $\mathbf{Q}_2$, which we denote by $\mathbf{Q}_1 \subseteq_\mathcal{K} \mathbf{Q}_2$:

$$\mathbf{Q}_1 \subseteq_\mathcal{K} \mathbf{Q}_2 \Longleftrightarrow \forall I \; \forall \mathbf{t} \; \mathbf{Q}_1^I(\mathbf{t}) \preceq_\mathcal{K} \mathbf{Q}_2^I(\mathbf{t}).$$

We always assume that $\preceq_\mathcal{K}$ is *minimal* with respect to $\subseteq_\mathcal{K}$, i.e. there is no subrelation of $\preceq_\mathcal{K}$ that produces the same $\mathcal{K}$-containment. However, for some partial orders the above definition results in a rather spartan notion of $\mathcal{K}$-containment. For example, by considering the usual order $\leq$ on the semiring $\mathbb{Z}$ of *integers*, one can easily verify that the empty UCQ is not $\mathbb{Z}$-contained in any non-empty UCQ.

Thus, we need to restrict the class of partially ordered semirings that we consider for our study. In order to do so, we list four intuitive requirements that, in our view, any definition of $\mathcal{K}$-containment should satisfy, and then identify all the semirings $\mathcal{K}$ equipped with partial orders $\preceq_\mathcal{K}$ for which the definition of $\mathcal{K}$-containment is guaranteed to satisfy our requirements. These requirements are as follows:

(C1) $\subseteq_\mathcal{K}$ is a *preorder*, i.e. reflexive and transitive;
(C2) $\mathbf{Q}_1 \equiv_\mathcal{K} \mathbf{Q}_2$ iff $\mathbf{Q}_1 \subseteq_\mathcal{K} \mathbf{Q}_2$ and $\mathbf{Q}_2 \subseteq_\mathcal{K} \mathbf{Q}_1$;
(C3) $\emptyset \subseteq_\mathcal{K} \mathbf{Q}$ holds for all $\mathbf{Q}$;
(C4) if $\mathbf{Q}_1 \subseteq_\mathcal{K} \mathbf{Q}_2$ then $\mathbf{Q}_1 \cup \mathbf{Q}_3 \subseteq_\mathcal{K} \mathbf{Q}_2 \cup \mathbf{Q}_3$ for any $\mathbf{Q}_3$.

Note that requirement (C3) rules out the example with $\mathbb{Z}$ and $\leq$. It turns out that we can easily axiomatize the class of semirings with partial orders that have $\mathcal{K}$-containments satisfying (C1) – (C4). The following proposition says that this class consists of all *positive* semirings, i.e. semirings $\mathcal{K} = \langle K, \oplus, \otimes, \mathbb{0}, \mathbb{1} \rangle$ equipped with a partial order $\preceq_\mathcal{K}$, such that

- $\mathbb{0} \preceq_\mathcal{K} a$ for all $a \in K$, and
- $a \preceq_\mathcal{K} b \Rightarrow a \oplus c \preceq_\mathcal{K} b \oplus c$ for all $a, b, c \in K$.

PROPOSITION 3.1 *A semiring $\mathcal{K}$ equipped with a partial order $\preceq_\mathcal{K}$ is positive iff the corresponding $\mathcal{K}$-containment $\subseteq_\mathcal{K}$ satisfies requirements* (C1) – (C4).

We assume for the rest of the paper that all semirings are positive and denote the class of such semirings by $\mathbf{S}$.

We focus in this work on the following decision problems:

CQ $\mathcal{K}$-CONTAINMENT	
Input:	CQs Q_1, Q_2
Question:	Is $Q_1 \subseteq_\mathcal{K} Q_2$?

UCQ $\mathcal{K}$-CONTAINMENT	
Input:	UCQs $\mathbf{Q}_1$, $\mathbf{Q}_2$
Question:	Is $\mathbf{Q}_1 \subseteq_\mathcal{K} \mathbf{Q}_2$?

[2]A partial order is a transitive, reflexive and antisymmetric binary relation.

In particular, we are interested in classifying the semirings in $\mathbf{S}$ for which different conditions on CQs (and UCQs) are sufficient for $\mathcal{K}$-containment, and also for which semirings they are necessary. If for a semiring $\mathcal{K}$ such a condition is both sufficient and necessary, and it is possible to check the condition algorithmically, then we have a decision procedure for $\mathcal{K}$-containment.

3.2 Naturally ordered semirings and provenance polynomials

In [14] it was noted that in most semantics considered so far, including set and bag semantics, the notion of containment is based on natural orders of the semirings. A semiring $\mathcal{K} = \langle K, \oplus, \otimes, \mathbb{0}, \mathbb{1} \rangle$ is *naturally ordered* iff the preorder $\preceq_\mathcal{K}^{\mathrm{nat}}$, defined as $a \preceq_\mathcal{K}^{\mathrm{nat}} b \Longleftrightarrow \exists c \; a \oplus c = b$, is a partial order. In principle, this condition appears to be too restrictive, and for this reason we have opted for the more general approach based on positive semirings. It is straightforward to show that any naturally ordered semiring is a positive semiring. Thus, our approach is general enough to include all previous work, as far as we are aware.

In [14] the problem of $\mathcal{K}$-containment of CQs and UCQs was considered for several naturally ordered semirings, including the one known as the semiring of *provenance polynomials*, $\mathcal{N}[X] = \langle \mathbb{N}[X], +, \times, 0, 1 \rangle$. This is the set $\mathbb{N}[X]$ of polynomials over a set of variables X, with natural number coefficients, equipped with the usual operations $+$ and $\times$. In [15] it was pointed out that this semiring (without any order) is special among such semirings since it is "most general", i.e. possesses the *universal property*: for any (unordered) semiring $\mathcal{K} = \langle K, \oplus, \otimes, \mathbb{0}, \mathbb{1} \rangle$ any function $\nu \colon X \to K$ can be uniquely extended to a *morphism* $\mathsf{Eval}_\nu \colon \mathbb{N}[X] \to K$, i.e. a mapping between semirings which preserves all the operations and relations (including constants 0 and 1). In [14] it was shown that $\mathcal{N}[X]$, now with its natural order, is universal for all naturally ordered semirings. It turns out that this is also true for all (positive) semirings.

PROPOSITION 3.2 *Given a set of variables X, $\mathcal{N}[X]$ is universal for the set $\mathbf{S}$ of all (positive) semirings.*

Based on this property, we can formulate different universal axioms on semirings, involving the order $\preceq_\mathcal{K}$, in terms of $\mathcal{N}[X]$. Given a semiring $\mathcal{K} = \langle K, \oplus, \otimes, \mathbb{0}, \mathbb{1} \rangle$ from $\mathbf{S}$, a set X of n variables, and polynomials P_1 and P_2 from $\mathbb{N}[X]$, we write $\mathsf{P}_1 \preceq_\mathcal{K} \mathsf{P}_2$ iff *for all* values $a_1, \ldots, a_n$ from K, the inequality $\mathsf{P}_1(a_1, \ldots, a_n) \preceq_\mathcal{K} \mathsf{P}_2(a_1, \ldots, a_n)$ holds. Here $\mathsf{P}_1(a_1, \ldots, a_n)$ and $\mathsf{P}_2(a_1, \ldots, a_n)$ denote the valuations of P_1 and P_2 over values $a_1, \ldots, a_n$. Since $\preceq_\mathcal{K}$ is a partial order, we can also write $\mathsf{P}_1 =_\mathcal{K} \mathsf{P}_2$ for $\mathsf{P}_1 \preceq_\mathcal{K} \mathsf{P}_2 \wedge \mathsf{P}_2 \preceq_\mathcal{K} \mathsf{P}_1$. We will use such polynomial notation throughout the paper.

3.3 Containment by homomorphisms

The study of query containment in the context of query optimization had begun for relational databases by the 1970s [5]. These databases can be naturally modelled by $\mathcal{B}$-relations, where $\mathcal{B} = \langle \{\mathbf{false}, \mathbf{true}\}, \vee, \wedge, \mathbf{false}, \mathbf{true} \rangle$ is the *set semantics* semiring. Here a tuple is annotated with $\mathbf{true}$ iff it is in the relation and $\mathbf{false}$ otherwise. For $\mathcal{B}$-containment the natural order $\preceq_\mathcal{B}$ is assumed, which is defined as $\mathbf{false} \preceq_\mathcal{B} \mathbf{true}$. A CQ Q_1 is $\mathcal{B}$-contained in a CQ Q_2 iff one can find a homomorphism from Q_2 to Q_1, by the classical result of [5]. Given CQs $Q_1 = \exists \mathbf{v}_1 \, \phi_1(\mathbf{u}_1, \mathbf{v}_1)$ and $Q_2 = \exists \mathbf{v}_2 \, \phi_2(\mathbf{u}_2, \mathbf{v}_2)$, a *homomorphism* (also known as *containment mapping*) from

Q_2 to Q_1 is a function $h: \mathbf{u}_2 \cup \mathbf{v}_2 \rightarrow \mathbf{u}_1 \cup \mathbf{v}_1$ such that $h(\mathbf{u}_2) = \mathbf{u}_1$ and for each atom $R(\mathbf{u}, \mathbf{v})$ from $\phi_2(\mathbf{u}_2, \mathbf{v}_2)$, the atom $R(h(\mathbf{u}, \mathbf{v}))$ is in $\phi_1(\mathbf{u}_1, \mathbf{v}_1)$. A homomorphism extends to atoms and sets of atoms in the usual way. We write $Q_2 \rightarrow Q_1$ iff there exists a homomorphism from Q_2 to Q_1.

Based on the results of [14] or [17] it is straightforward to show that the existence of a homomorphism between CQs is necessary for their $\mathcal{K}$-containment over any semiring $\mathcal{K}$ from $\mathbf{S}$. Thus, a first natural question to ask is: which semirings behave the same as $\mathcal{B}$ with respect to containment of CQs, i.e. for which semirings $\mathcal{K}$ is it the case that $Q_2 \rightarrow Q_1$ is sufficient for $Q_1 \subseteq_{\mathcal{K}} Q_2$? This question was answered partially in [15, 14, 17]. In [13] it was shown that this correspondence holds if $\mathcal{K}$ is a distributive bilattice. As the main result of this section we show that it is possible to axiomatize the class of all semirings for which $\mathcal{K}$-containment of CQs coincides with the usual set semantics containment.

Denote by $\mathbf{C}_{\text{hom}}$ the class of semirings $\mathcal{K}$ that satisfy the following axioms (using the convenient polynomial notation introduced at the end of Sec. 3.2, i.e. assuming that all variables are universally quantified):

1. ($\otimes$-idempotence) $x \times x =_{\mathcal{K}} x$;
2. ($\mathbb{1}$-annihilation) $1 + x =_{\mathcal{K}} 1$.

Next we will see that $\mathbf{C}_{\text{hom}}$ contains exactly all semirings that behave like set semantics, w.r.t. $\mathcal{K}$-containment of CQs.

THEOREM 3.3 *The following are equivalent:*

- *semiring $\mathcal{K}$ belongs to $\mathbf{C}_{\text{hom}}$;*
- *$Q_1 \subseteq_{\mathcal{K}} Q_2$ iff $Q_2 \rightarrow Q_1$, for all CQs Q_1 and Q_2.*

Deciding the existence of a homomorphism between CQs is well known to be NP-complete [5]. We therefore obtain the following corollary.

COROLLARY 3.4 *If $\mathcal{K} \in \mathbf{C}_{\text{hom}}$ then CQ $\mathcal{K}$-CONTAINMENT is NP-complete.*

Many semirings used for annotations are distributive lattices, and hence belong to $\mathbf{C}_{\text{hom}}$. Besides the set semantics $\mathcal{B}$, they include the semiring of positive boolean expressions PosBool$[X]$ described in [15], which is used in incomplete databases [16], and the probabilistic semiring $\mathcal{P}(\Omega)$ used in event tables [12, 21]. Also, the class $\mathbf{C}_{\text{hom}}$ corresponds precisely to the class of *type* A$'$ *systems* introduced in [17]; in fact, Thm. 3.3 answers the question from this paper, of what the decision procedure is for CQ containment over such systems. However, many annotation semirings do not belong to $\mathbf{C}_{\text{hom}}$, including provenance polynomials $\mathcal{N}[X]$, the why-provenance semiring Why$[X]$ from [3], or bag semantics $\mathcal{N}$ [6]. In the next section, we study what happens when we relax the conditions for $\mathbf{C}_{\text{hom}}$.

4. $\mathcal{K}$-CONTAINMENT OF CQS

From a practical point of view, it would be useful to have a decision procedure for $\mathcal{K}$-containment of CQs for an arbitrary semiring $\mathcal{K}$. However, there is evidence that obtaining such a procedure for all semirings not in $\mathbf{C}_{\text{hom}}$ is a truly challenging, if not impossible, task. The semiring $\mathcal{N} = \langle \mathbb{N}_0, +, \times, 0, 1 \rangle$ of natural numbers with zero, with the usual arithmetic operations and the natural order, is used to model bag semantics [15]. A universal decision procedure for CQ $\mathcal{K}$-CONTAINMENT would thus require being able to solve this problem for the special case of bag semantics $\mathcal{N}$,

which is a long-standing open problem [6, 17]. It is also not difficult to show that there are infinitely many semirings $\mathcal{K}$ for which the $\mathcal{K}$-containment of CQs is at least as hard as for bag semantics.

With these observations in mind, we instead ask the following, narrower question: are there any reasonable classes of semirings for which we can prove that $\mathcal{K}$-containment of CQs is decidable? We have already pointed out that this is the case for the class $\mathbf{C}_{\text{hom}}$, since for all semirings $\mathcal{K}$ in $\mathbf{C}_{\text{hom}}$ the problem of $\mathcal{K}$-containment can be solved by deciding the existence of a homomorphism. A natural starting point for our search is therefore to relax the axioms of the class $\mathbf{C}_{\text{hom}}$. We thus obtain the class of semirings that satisfy the $\otimes$-idempotence axiom, that we denote by $\mathbf{S}_{\text{hcov}}$; the class of semirings that satisfy the $\mathbb{1}$-annihilation axiom, denoted by $\mathbf{S}_{\text{in}}$; and, if we relax both axioms, the class $\mathbf{S}$ of all (positive) semirings.

We show that for each of these classes there exists a natural type of homomorphism that characterizes the class, but only as a *sufficient condition* for $\mathcal{K}$-containment of CQs. In the search for classes similar to $\mathbf{C}_{\text{hom}}$, we then provide the *largest* class of semirings for which each of these conditions is *necessary* for $\mathcal{K}$-containment, resulting in analogues of Thm. 3.3 for different classes of semirings and different types of homomorphisms.

After $\mathbf{S}_{\text{hcov}}$, $\mathbf{S}_{\text{in}}$, and $\mathbf{S}$ we look at one more class, that we denote by $\mathbf{S}_{\text{sur}}$. This class lies "between" $\mathbf{S}_{\text{hcov}}$ and $\mathbf{S}$, in the sense that it can be obtained from $\mathbf{S}_{\text{hcov}}$ by a partial, instead of complete, relaxation of the $\otimes$-idempotence axiom. The class $\mathbf{S}_{\text{sur}}$ is interesting in its own right, since it can be characterized by the well studied notion of *surjective* homomorphism ([6, 17]) as yielding a sufficient condition for CQ $\mathcal{N}$-containment. In the same fashion, we identify the largest class of semirings for which this condition is also necessary.

Notice that, up to this point, we have only considered solving the $\mathcal{K}$-containment problem by means of finding different types of homomorphism between CQs. Thus, it is natural to ask whether there exists a different approach for solving this problem. We address this question at the end of this section, and show that there exists a large class of semirings which possesses a *small model property*: if a CQ Q_1 is not $\mathcal{K}$-contained in a CQ Q_2, then this is witnessed by a small enough $\mathcal{K}$-instance.

4.1 Containment by homomorphic covering

We begin with the class $\mathbf{S}_{\text{hcov}}$ of semirings satisfying the $\otimes$-idempotence axiom. For these semirings, we exploit the notion of homomorphic covering: given CQs Q_1 and Q_2, we say that Q_2 *homomorphically covers* Q_1, and write $Q_2 \rightrightarrows Q_1$, if for every atom $R(\mathbf{u}, \mathbf{v})$ in Q_1 there exists a homomorphism h from Q_2 to Q_1 with $R(\mathbf{u}, \mathbf{v})$ in the image of h.

This type of homomorphism arose in the context of query optimization as a necessary condition for $\mathcal{N}$-containment of CQs over bag semantics $\mathcal{N}$ [6]. It was also noted that existence of a homomorphic covering is not sufficient to guarantee $\mathcal{N}$-containment. Homomorphic coverings were also used in [14] to show that $Q_2 \rightrightarrows Q_1$ is both necessary and sufficient for $Q_1 \subseteq_{\text{Lin}[X]} Q_2$, where Lin$[X]$ is the lineage semiring [9].

Next we establish axiomatic bounds for semirings to have homomorphic covering as both a sufficient and necessary condition for $\mathcal{K}$-containment of CQs. Our next result shows that the class $\mathbf{S}_{\text{hcov}}$ captures precisely all semirings for which $Q_2 \rightrightarrows Q_1$ is a sufficient condition.

PROPOSITION 4.1 *The following are equivalent:*

- *semiring $\mathcal{K}$ belongs to $\mathbf{S}_{\mathrm{hcov}}$;*
- $Q_2 \rightrightarrows Q_1$ *implies* $Q_1 \subseteq_{\mathcal{K}} Q_2$, *for all CQs* Q_1, Q_2.

Of course, a sufficient condition itself does not guarantee the decidability of the $\mathcal{K}$-containment problem; one needs such a condition to be necessary as well. Since one can easily find semirings in $\mathbf{S}_{\mathrm{hcov}}$ for which the existence of a homomorphic covering is not a necessary condition (for example, any semiring in $\mathbf{C}_{\mathrm{hom}}$), our only hope is to describe the *largest* class for which a homomorphic covering is necessary for $\mathcal{K}$-containment of CQs. Denote by $\mathbf{N}_{\mathrm{hcov}}$ the class of semirings $\mathcal{K}$ such that for every $n, k \geq 1$ it holds that

$$x_1 \times \ldots \times x_n \times y \not\preceq_{\mathcal{K}} (x_1 + \ldots + x_n)^k$$

(again, assuming all variables to be universally quantified).

PROPOSITION 4.2 *The following are equivalent:*

- *semiring $\mathcal{K}$ belongs to $\mathbf{N}_{\mathrm{hcov}}$;*
- $Q_1 \subseteq_{\mathcal{K}} Q_2$ *implies* $Q_2 \rightrightarrows Q_1$, *for all CQs* Q_1, Q_2.

Therefore, bag semantics $\mathcal{N}$ is in $\mathbf{N}_{\mathrm{hcov}}$, but not in $\mathbf{S}_{\mathrm{hcov}}$. However, $\mathtt{Lin}[X]$ is in both, and we have the following result for the class $\mathbf{C}_{\mathrm{hcov}} = \mathbf{S}_{\mathrm{hcov}} \cap \mathbf{N}_{\mathrm{hcov}}{}^3$ of all semirings which behave the same as $\mathtt{Lin}[X]$ w.r.t. $\mathcal{K}$-containment of CQs.

THEOREM 4.3 *The following are equivalent:*

- *semiring $\mathcal{K}$ belongs to $\mathbf{C}_{\mathrm{hcov}}$;*
- $Q_1 \subseteq_{\mathcal{K}} Q_2$ *iff* $Q_2 \rightrightarrows Q_1$, *for all CQs* Q_1 *and* Q_2.

We also know that checking for homomorphic covering between CQs is an NP-complete problem [14]. This gives us the following result.

COROLLARY 4.4 *If* $\mathcal{K} \in \mathbf{C}_{\mathrm{hcov}}$ *then CQ $\mathcal{K}$-CONTAINMENT is NP-complete.*

4.2 Containment by injective homomorphism

In this section we consider the class $\mathbf{S}_{\mathrm{in}}$ of semirings which satisfy the $\mathbb{1}$-annihilation axiom. This class was considered implicitly in previous studies of containment on $\mathcal{K}$-relations [15, 14, 17], and has notable applications. In the context of the Semantic Web it was shown in [4] that $\mathbf{S}_{\mathrm{in}}$ is the class of all semirings which can be safely used as annotation domains for RDF data while respecting the inference system of RDFS. An extension of the SPARQL query language for querying annotated RDF data then followed in [22], entailing a need to solve optimization problems for this class of semirings. As an example of a semiring which is in $\mathbf{S}_{\mathrm{in}}$, but not in $\mathbf{C}_{\mathrm{hom}}$, we give the *tropical* semiring $\mathcal{T}^+ = \langle \mathbb{N}_0 \cup \{\infty\}, \min, +, \infty, 0 \rangle$ (with its natural order).

To study the class $\mathbf{S}_{\mathrm{in}}$, we introduce the notion of injective homomorphism: given CQs $Q_1 = \exists \mathbf{v}_1 \ \phi_1(\mathbf{u}_1, \mathbf{v}_1)$ and $Q_2 = \exists \mathbf{v}_2 \ \phi_2(\mathbf{u}_2, \mathbf{v}_2)$, a homomorphism h from Q_2 to Q_1 is *injective* (or *one-to-one*) if h is injective on atoms, i.e. the multiset of atoms $h(\phi_2(\mathbf{u}_2, \mathbf{v}_2))$ is contained in the multiset of atoms $\phi_1(\mathbf{u}_1, \mathbf{v}_1)$. We write $Q_2 \hookrightarrow Q_1$ iff there exists an injective homomorphism from Q_2 to Q_1. Similar to the case of $\mathbf{S}_{\mathrm{hcov}}$, the following proposition shows that the class $\mathbf{S}_{\mathrm{in}}$ is precisely the class of semirings for which the existence of an injective homomorphism is a sufficient condition for $\mathcal{K}$-containment of CQs.

---

[3]Since $\otimes$-idempotence defines $\mathbf{S}_{\mathrm{hcov}}$, the exponent k may be omitted from the necessary condition of $\mathbf{C}_{\mathrm{hcov}}$.

PROPOSITION 4.5 *The following are equivalent:*

- *semiring $\mathcal{K}$ belongs to $\mathbf{S}_{\mathrm{in}}$;*
- $Q_2 \hookrightarrow Q_1$ *implies* $Q_1 \subseteq_{\mathcal{K}} Q_2$, *for all CQs* Q_1, Q_2.

Unfortunately, as shown in the following example, $Q_2 \hookrightarrow Q_1$ is just a sufficient, but not always necessary condition for CQ $\mathcal{K}$-containment for a semiring $\mathcal{K}$ from $\mathbf{S}_{\mathrm{in}} \setminus \mathbf{C}_{\mathrm{hom}}$.

EXAMPLE 4.6 Consider the conjunctive queries

$$Q_1 = \exists u, v, w \ R(u, v), R(u, w), \quad Q_2 = \exists u, v \ R(u, v), R(u, v).$$

We will see in Sec. 4.6 that Q_1 is $\mathcal{T}^+$-contained in Q_2. However, there is no injective homomorphism from Q_2 to Q_1.

To identify the largest class for which the existence of an injective homomorphism is a necessary condition for CQ $\mathcal{K}$-containment, we need the following definition.

DEFINITION 4.7 *A polynomial P from $\mathbb{N}[X]$ is CQ-admissible iff there exists a CQ Q, an $\mathcal{N}[X]$-instance I each tuple of which is annotated with either a unique variable from X or 0, and a tuple $\mathbf{t}$, such that $Q^I(\mathbf{t}) = \mathsf{P}$.*

Essentially, a polynomial is CQ-admissible if it is possible to obtain it by a CQ on an *abstractly tagged* instance ([15]).

We write $\mathbb{N}^{cq}[X]$ for the set of all CQ-admissible polynomials with variables X. We will use this notion intensively in the rest of this paper; for now, we have opted to give a non-constructive definition, but we will give an algebraic characterization of $\mathbb{N}^{cq}[X]$ in Sec. 4.5. Next we exploit the connection between CQ $\mathcal{K}$-containment and comparison of polynomials from $\mathbb{N}^{cq}[X]$ to define precisely the class of semirings for which an injective homomorphism is a corresponding necessary condition.

Denote by $\mathbf{N}_{\mathrm{in}}$ the class of semirings $\mathcal{K}$ for which for every polynomial P from $\mathbb{N}^{cq}[X]$ and any set of variables $x_1, \ldots, x_n$, the inequality

$$x_1 \times \ldots \times x_n \preceq_{\mathcal{K}} \mathsf{P}$$

implies that there exists a subset $x_{i_1}, \ldots, x_{i_m}$ of the variables $x_1, \ldots, x_n$ such that P contains the monomial $x_{i_1} \times \ldots \times x_{i_m}$.

PROPOSITION 4.8 *The following are equivalent:*

- *semiring $\mathcal{K}$ belongs to $\mathbf{N}_{\mathrm{in}}$;*
- $Q_1 \subseteq_{\mathcal{K}} Q_2$ *implies* $Q_2 \hookrightarrow Q_1$, *for all CQs* Q_1, Q_2.

Thus, Prop. 4.5 and 4.8 give us decidability of CQ $\mathcal{K}$-CONTAINMENT for all semirings $\mathcal{K}$ from $\mathbf{C}_{\mathrm{in}} = \mathbf{S}_{\mathrm{in}} \cap \mathbf{N}_{\mathrm{in}}$. Moreover, by showing that deciding the existence of an injective homomorphism between queries is NP-complete, we can say the same about $\mathcal{K}$-containment of CQs for any $\mathcal{K} \in \mathbf{C}_{\mathrm{in}}$.

THEOREM 4.9
(1) The following are equivalent:

- *semiring $\mathcal{K}$ belongs to $\mathbf{C}_{\mathrm{in}}$;*
- $Q_1 \subseteq_{\mathcal{K}} Q_2$ *iff* $Q_2 \hookrightarrow Q_1$, *for all CQs* Q_1 *and* Q_2.

(2) If $\mathcal{K} \in \mathbf{C}_{\mathrm{in}}$ then CQ $\mathcal{K}$-CONTAINMENT is NP-complete.

Having this result, we however note that there are interesting semirings (including the tropical semiring $\mathcal{T}^+$), which lie in $\mathbf{S}_{\mathrm{in}}$, but neither in $\mathbf{C}_{\mathrm{hom}}$ nor in $\mathbf{C}_{\mathrm{in}}$. In Sec. 4.6 we will see how to obtain decidability for some semirings in $\mathbf{S}_{\mathrm{in}}$, but at the cost of higher complexity.

4.3 Containment by bijective homomorphism

We continue with the class obtained from $\mathbf{C}_{\mathrm{hom}}$ by relaxing both of its axioms. This is just the class of all (positive) semirings $\mathbf{S}$. For this class we use the notion of bijective homomorphism. Given CQs $Q = \exists \mathbf{v}_1 \, \phi_1(\mathbf{u}_1, \mathbf{v}_1)$ and $Q_2 = \exists \mathbf{v}_2 \, \phi_2(\mathbf{u}_2, \mathbf{v}_2)$, we say that a homomorphism h from Q_2 to Q_1 is *bijective* (or *exact*) if it is a bijection on atoms, i.e. the multiset of atoms $h(\phi_2(\mathbf{u}_2, \mathbf{v}_2))$ is the same as the multiset of atoms $\phi_1(\mathbf{u}_1, \mathbf{v}_1)$. We write $Q_2 \hookrightarrow Q_1$ if there exists a bijective homomorphism from Q_2 to Q_1.

As shown in [14], the condition $Q_2 \hookrightarrow Q_1$ is both sufficient and necessary for $\mathcal{N}[X]$-containment of CQs over the provenance polynomials semiring $\mathcal{N}[X]$. Since $\mathcal{N}[X]$ is universal for $\mathbf{S}$ by Prop. 3.2, we can conclude that this condition is sufficient for CQ $\mathcal{K}$-containment for an arbitrary semiring $\mathcal{K}$, i.e. $Q_2 \hookrightarrow Q_1$ always implies $Q_1 \subseteq_{\mathcal{K}} Q_2$.

From [14] we also know that existence of a bijective homomorphism is necessary for $\mathcal{B}[X]$-containment of CQs, where $\mathcal{B}[X] = \langle \mathbb{B}[X], +, \times, 0, 1 \rangle$ is the semiring of *boolean provenance polynomials*, i.e. polynomials over X with boolean coefficients from $\mathbb{B} = \{\mathbf{false}, \mathbf{true}\}$. This means that $\mathcal{B}[X]$ behaves the same as $\mathcal{N}[X]$ w.r.t. $\mathcal{K}$-containment of CQs. As we have seen in previous sections, this is not the case for all semirings. Also, one can easily show that the existence of a bijective homomorphism is not necessary for bag semantics $\mathcal{N}$, or even for the semiring $\mathcal{R}^+$ of non-negative reals with the usual operations and order.

Our next aim is to identify all semirings which behave as $\mathcal{N}[X]$. To do so we again exploit the notion of CQ-admissible polynomials. Denote by $\mathbf{C}_{\mathrm{bi}}$ the class of all semirings $\mathcal{K}$ for which for every polynomial P from $\mathbb{N}^{cq}[X]$ and any set of variables $x_1, \ldots, x_n$, the inequality

$$x_1 \times \ldots \times x_n \preceq_{\mathcal{K}} \mathsf{P}$$

implies that P contains the monomial $x_1 \times \ldots \times x_n$.

THEOREM 4.10 *The following are equivalent:*

- *semiring $\mathcal{K}$ belongs to $\mathbf{C}_{\mathrm{bi}}$;*
- $Q_1 \subseteq_{\mathcal{K}} Q_2$ *iff* $Q_2 \hookrightarrow Q_1$, *for all CQs Q_1 and Q_2.*

In particular, notice that both $\mathcal{B}[X]$ and $\mathcal{N}[X]$ belong to $\mathbf{C}_{\mathrm{bi}}$. Thus, this theorem can be seen as a generalization of the results of [14]. There it was also shown that $\mathcal{N}[X]$-containment of CQs is an NP-complete problem. We can now extend this result to the entire class $\mathbf{C}_{\mathrm{bi}}$.

COROLLARY 4.11 *If $\mathcal{K} \in \mathbf{C}_{\mathrm{bi}}$ then CQ $\mathcal{K}$-CONTAINMENT is NP-complete.*

This corollary completes our study of $\mathcal{K}$-containment of CQs for the classes of semirings obtained from $\mathbf{C}_{\mathrm{hom}}$ by relaxing its axioms. Next we will look at another class, which corresponds to one more well-known type of homomorphism.

4.4 Containment by surjective homomorphism

Looking back to the bag semantics semiring $\mathcal{N}$, we know that it lies in the class $\mathbf{N}_{\mathrm{hcov}}$ for which homomorphic covering is necessary, but neither in $\mathbf{C}_{\mathrm{hcov}}$ nor in $\mathbf{C}_{\mathrm{bi}}$. However, there does exist a well-known sufficient condition for $\mathcal{N}$-containment, other than just a bijective homomorphism. This condition is the existence of a surjective homomorphism ([6, 17]): given CQs $Q_1 = \exists \mathbf{v}_1 \, \phi_1(\mathbf{u}_1, \mathbf{v}_1)$ and $Q_2 = \exists \mathbf{v}_2 \, \phi_2(\mathbf{u}_2, \mathbf{v}_2)$ a homomorphism h from Q_2 to Q_1 is *surjective* (or *onto*) if h is a surjection on atoms, i.e. the multiset

of atoms $\phi_1(\mathbf{u}_1, \mathbf{v}_1)$ is contained in the multiset of atoms $h(\phi_2(\mathbf{u}_2, \mathbf{v}_2))$. We write $Q_2 \twoheadrightarrow Q_1$ iff there exists a surjective homomorphism from Q_2 to Q_1.

It is therefore natural to ask for which semirings $Q_2 \twoheadrightarrow Q_1$ is sufficient for $\mathcal{K}$-containment of CQs, and for which this is necessary. Besides $\mathcal{N}$, this condition is sufficient for a larger class of semirings denoted *type B systems* [17]. From [14] it is known that $Q_2 \twoheadrightarrow Q_1$ is equivalent to $\mathtt{Why}[X]$- and $\mathtt{Trio}[X]$-containment of CQs, where $\mathtt{Why}[X]$ is a semiring capturing *why provenance* of [3], and $\mathtt{Trio}[X]$ is a semiring for the provenance model used in the Trio project [10]. However, the exact axiomatic bounds for these classes of semirings were not previously known.

As usual, we start by axiomatizing semirings which have $Q_2 \twoheadrightarrow Q_1$ as a sufficient condition. Denote by $\mathbf{S}_{\mathrm{sur}}$ the class of semirings that satisfy the axiom:

$1'$. ($\otimes$-*semi-idempotence*) $x \times y \preceq_{\mathcal{K}} x \times x \times y$.

This class can be obtained by relaxing the $\otimes$-idempotence axiom of $\mathbf{S}_{\mathrm{hcov}}$, but only partially, i.e. $\mathbf{S}_{\mathrm{hcov}} \subset \mathbf{S}_{\mathrm{sur}}$. Other than the semirings already mentioned as belonging to $\mathbf{S}_{\mathrm{hcov}}$, it contains the semiring $\mathcal{T}^- = \langle \mathbb{N}_0 \cup \{-\infty\}, \max, +, -\infty, 0 \rangle$ known as the *schedule* (or *max-plus*) *algebra* (with its natural order). As desired, the class $\mathbf{S}_{\mathrm{sur}}$ corresponds to all the semirings for which the existence of a surjective homomorphism is a sufficient condition for $\mathcal{K}$-containment of CQs.

PROPOSITION 4.12 *The following are equivalent:*

- *semiring $\mathcal{K}$ belongs to $\mathbf{S}_{\mathrm{sur}}$;*
- $Q_2 \twoheadrightarrow Q_1$ *implies $Q_1 \subseteq_{\mathcal{K}} Q_2$, for all CQs Q_1, Q_2.*

As we saw for the bag semantics semiring $\mathcal{N}$, the existence of a surjective homomorphism is not necessary for $\mathcal{N}$-containment, but homomorphic covering is. The same can be said about $\mathcal{T}^-$, but not $\mathtt{Why}[X]$ or $\mathtt{Trio}[X]$. Hence, again we need to axiomatize the class of semirings for which $Q_2 \twoheadrightarrow Q_1$ is necessary for $\mathcal{K}$-containment of CQs. For this we exploit once more the notion of CQ-admissible polynomials. Denote by $\mathbf{N}_{\mathrm{sur}}$ the class of semirings $\mathcal{K}$ for which for every polynomial P from $\mathbb{N}^{cq}[X]$ and any set of variables $x_1, \ldots, x_n$, the inequality

$$x_1 \times \ldots \times x_n \preceq_{\mathcal{K}} \mathsf{P}$$

implies that there exist exponents $m_1, \ldots, m_n \geq 1$ such that P contains the monomial $x_1^{m_1} \times \ldots \times x_n^{m_n}$.

PROPOSITION 4.13 *The following are equivalent:*

- *semiring $\mathcal{K}$ belongs to $\mathbf{N}_{\mathrm{sur}}$;*
- $Q_1 \subseteq_{\mathcal{K}} Q_2$ *implies $Q_2 \twoheadrightarrow Q_1$, for all CQs Q_1, Q_2.*

For those semirings $\mathcal{K}$ that do belong to $\mathbf{C}_{\mathrm{sur}} = \mathbf{S}_{\mathrm{sur}} \cap \mathbf{N}_{\mathrm{sur}}$ (like $\mathtt{Why}[X]$ and $\mathtt{Trio}[X]$), we have once again a decision procedure for $\mathcal{K}$-containment of CQs. This is summarized by the following theorem.

THEOREM 4.14 *The following are equivalent:*

- *semiring $\mathcal{K}$ belongs to $\mathbf{C}_{\mathrm{sur}}$;*
- $Q_1 \subseteq_{\mathcal{K}} Q_2$ *iff* $Q_2 \twoheadrightarrow Q_1$, *for all CQs Q_1 and Q_2.*

The complexity follows from the fact that checking a surjective homomorphism between CQs is NP-complete ([6]).

COROLLARY 4.15 *If $\mathcal{K} \in \mathbf{C}_{\mathrm{sur}}$ then CQ $\mathcal{K}$-CONTAINMENT is NP-complete.*

As mentioned in the introduction, we leave open the problem of finding decision procedures for all semirings that belong to $\mathbf{S}_{\mathrm{sur}}$, but not to $\mathbf{N}_{\mathrm{sur}}$, such as $\mathcal{N}$ or $\mathcal{T}^-$. In Sec. 4.6 we show that for some of these semirings, such as $\mathcal{T}^-$, the problem of $\mathcal{K}$-containment of CQs can be solved using a different approach, albeit with higher computational complexity.

We finish this section with a remark that a homomorphism is bijective iff it is both injective and surjective. Thus, we obtain that $\mathbf{C}_{\mathrm{bi}} = \mathbf{N}_{\mathrm{in}} \cap \mathbf{N}_{\mathrm{sur}}$.

4.5 CQ-admissible polynomials

We defined the *evaluation* of a CQ $Q = \exists \mathbf{v}\ R_1(\mathbf{u}_1, \mathbf{v}_1), \ldots,$ $R_n(\mathbf{u}_n, \mathbf{v}_n)$ on a $\mathcal{K}$-instance I for a tuple $\mathbf{t}$ as

$$Q^I(\mathbf{t}) = \sum_{f \in \mathcal{V}(Q, \mathbf{t})} \prod_{1 \leq i \leq n} R_i^I(f(\mathbf{u}_i, \mathbf{v}_i)).$$

Thus, the evaluation of a CQ on a $\mathcal{N}[X]$-instance with unique variables from the set X as annotations is a polynomial over X. In Def. 4.7 we called such polynomials *CQ-admissible*. We heavily used this notion in the definitions of the classes $\mathbf{N}_{\mathrm{in}}$, $\mathbf{N}_{\mathrm{bi}}$, and $\mathbf{N}_{\mathrm{sur}}$. The goal of this section is to give a constructive algebraic characterization of the set $\mathbb{N}^{cq}[X]$ of all CQ-admissible polynomials. As we mentioned in the introduction, this notion is of independent interest: for instance, it was implicitly used in [19].

From the definition of evaluation we immediately obtain that every CQ-admissible polynomial must be homogeneous. Moreover, let Q be a CQ consisting of k atoms, and I be an $\mathcal{N}[X]$-instance with tuples annotated with variables $X = \{x_1, \ldots, x_n\}$, such that the mappings in the set $\mathcal{V}(Q, \mathbf{t})$ allow us to obtain any possible combination of images of the atoms of Q to non-zero annotated tuples of I. Then $Q^I(\mathbf{t}) = (x_1 + \ldots + x_n)^k$. Therefore, every P from $\mathbb{N}^{cq}[X]$ of degree k satisfies $\mathsf{P} \preceq_{\mathcal{N}[X]} (x_1 + \ldots + x_n)^k$. (This property allowed us to formulate the axiom for the class $\mathbf{N}_{\mathrm{hcov}}$ in Sec. 4.1 without reference to CQ-admissible polynomials.) Hence polynomials such as $2x$ and $x^2 + y$ are not in $\mathbb{N}^{cq}[X]$.

The polynomials x^2, $2xy$ and $x + y$ satisfy the requirements above, and it is not difficult to construct CQs which admit them. Unfortunately, these are not the only requirements: the polynomial $x^2 + xy + y^2$ satisfies them, but can be proved not to be in $\mathbb{N}^{cq}[X]$. In order to present the precise characterization, we need an auxiliary notion: for a set of variables X an *ordered monomial of degree n* (or *o-monomial*) is a string from X^n. For an o-monomial $\vec{\mathsf{M}}$ we denote by $\vec{\mathsf{M}}[i]$ the variable appearing in its i-th position.

PROPOSITION 4.16 *A polynomial P is in $\mathbb{N}^{cq}[X]$ iff it can be represented in a form*

$$\vec{\mathsf{P}} = \sum_{1 \leq \ell \leq m} \vec{\mathsf{M}}_\ell, \text{ such that}$$

1. $\vec{\mathsf{M}}_\ell$, $1 \leq \ell \leq m$, are pairwise distinct o-monomials over X of the same degree n (here concatenation in $\vec{\mathsf{M}}_\ell$ as a string is interpreted as product in P), and

2. if for an o-monomial $\vec{\mathsf{M}}$ of degree n, and for each i, j with $1 \leq i < j \leq n$, the representation $\vec{\mathsf{P}}$ contains o-monomials (each of degree n) $\vec{\mathsf{M}}_1, \ldots, \vec{\mathsf{M}}_{2k+1}$, $k \geq 0$, such that

- $\vec{\mathsf{M}}_1[i] = \vec{\mathsf{M}}[i]$, $\vec{\mathsf{M}}_{2k+1}[j] = \vec{\mathsf{M}}[j]$ and
- $\vec{\mathsf{M}}_{2\ell-1}[j] = \vec{\mathsf{M}}_{2\ell}[j]$, $\vec{\mathsf{M}}_{2\ell}[i] = \vec{\mathsf{M}}_{2\ell+1}[i]$ for all $1 \leq \ell \leq k$,

then $\vec{\mathsf{M}}$ is contained in $\vec{\mathsf{P}}$.

4.6 Containment via small models

Up to now we have studied how to decide $\mathcal{K}$-containment of CQs by analyzing their structure, resulting in several classes of semirings for which the existence of a homomorphism of a corresponding type between the CQs is equivalent to their $\mathcal{K}$-containment. It is natural to ask whether the problem of decidability of CQ $\mathcal{K}$-CONTAINMENT can be solved by different techniques for some semirings which are not in any of these classes. Indeed, several other approaches have appeared in the literature. In [14] a PSPACE algorithm was suggested for checking $\mathcal{N}[X]$-containment of UCQs, based on the fact that if a UCQ Q_1 is not $\mathcal{N}[X]$-contained in a UCQ Q_2, then there exists a witnessing $\mathcal{N}[X]$-instance, with its size bounded by the size of Q_1 and Q_2. Another approach is to cast the problem of decidability of $\mathcal{K}$-containment as the problem of checking the corresponding order $\preceq_{\mathcal{K}}$ on polynomials, as done in [17] to show undecidability of UCQ $\mathcal{N}$-CONTAINMENT over bag semantics.

The main result of this section is that by combining these ideas one can obtain new decidability results for $\mathcal{K}$-containment of CQs over different semirings $\mathcal{K}$. In contrast with the rest of the paper, we identify several individual semirings for which our approach works, but leave a comprehensive description of such semirings for future research. In order to describe our algorithm we introduce some terminology.

A *CQ with inequalities* is a CQ with a set of inequalities $\neq$ on its existential variables. It is *complete* (a *CCQ*) if each pair of distinct variables is bounded by an inequality. A *complete description*[4] $\langle Q \rangle$ of a CQ Q with existential variables $\mathbf{v}$ is the multiset of CCQs such that for every partition π of $\mathbf{v}$ it contains a CCQ obtained from Q by identifying all the variables from each equivalence class induced by π, and attaching an inequality for every pair of variables that remain different.

EXAMPLE 4.6 (CONTINUED) For CQ $Q_1 = \exists u, v, w\ R(u, v),$ $R(u, w)$ we have $\langle Q_1 \rangle = \{Q_{11}, Q_{12}, Q_{13}, Q_{14}, Q_{15}\}$, where

$$
\begin{aligned}
Q_{11} &= \exists u, v, w\ R(u, v), R(u, w), u \neq v, u \neq w, v \neq w; \\
Q_{12} &= \exists u, v\ R(u, v), R(u, v), u \neq v; \\
Q_{13} &= \exists u, v\ R(u, v), R(u, u), u \neq v; \\
Q_{14} &= \exists u, w\ R(u, u), R(u, w), u \neq w; \text{ and} \\
Q_{15} &= \exists u\ R(u, u), R(u, u).
\end{aligned}
$$

We will heavily use complete descriptions in Sec. 5, but for now we are interested in CCQs from $\langle Q \rangle$ as a way of describing all possible images of a mapping from Q to a $\mathcal{K}$-instance. Formally, given a set of variables X, a *canonical instance* ([15]) $[\![Q]\!]$ of a CQ (or CCQ) Q is an $\mathcal{N}[X]$-instance with the same schema as Q and with the set of variables of Q as its domain, such that for every $\mathcal{N}[X]$-relation $R^{[\![Q]\!]}$ and for every tuple $\mathbf{u}, \mathbf{v}$ it holds that $R^{[\![Q]\!]}(\mathbf{u}, \mathbf{v}) = x_1 + \ldots + x_n$, where $n \geq 0$ is the number of atoms in Q of the form $R(\mathbf{u}, \mathbf{v})$, and $x_1, \ldots, x_n$ are unique (over all $[\![Q]\!]$) variables from X.

EXAMPLE 4.6 (CONTINUED) For Q_{11} and Q_{12} we have

$$
\begin{aligned}
R^{[\![Q_{11}]\!]}(u, v) = x_1, \quad & R^{[\![Q_{11}]\!]}(u, w) = x_2, \\
R^{[\![Q_{12}]\!]}(u, v) &= x_1 + x_2,
\end{aligned}
$$

and all other tuples in $[\![Q_{11}]\!]$ and $[\![Q_{12}]\!]$ are annotated by 0.

Denote by $\mathbf{S}^1$ the set of $\oplus$-*idempotent* semirings, i.e. the semirings where $x =_{\mathcal{K}} x + x$ holds (this notation will be explained and generalized in Sec. 5). We have the following.

---

[4]This is similar to the one from [11] and linearization of [8].

THEOREM 4.17 *Given a semiring $\mathcal{K}$ from $\mathbf{S}^1$ and CQs Q_1 and Q_2, we have that $Q_1 \subseteq_{\mathcal{K}} Q_2$ iff $Q_1^{[\![Q]\!]}(\mathbf{t}) \preceq_{\mathcal{K}} Q_2^{[\![Q]\!]}(\mathbf{t})$ for every CCQ $Q \in \langle\!\langle Q_1 \rangle\!\rangle$ and every tuple $\mathbf{t}$ of variables of Q_1.*

This theorem shows that for $\mathcal{K} \in \mathbf{S}^1$, CQ $\mathcal{K}$-CONTAINMENT can be reduced to a small number of problems of checking the order $\preceq_{\mathcal{K}}$ between CQ-admissible polynomials.

COROLLARY 4.18 *If $\mathcal{K} \in \mathbf{S}^1$ and it is decidable to check if $\mathsf{P}_1 \preceq_{\mathcal{K}} \mathsf{P}_2$ for any pair of polynomials $\mathsf{P}_1, \mathsf{P}_2$ from $\mathbb{N}^{cq}[X]$, then CQ $\mathcal{K}$-CONTAINMENT is decidable.*

We do not investigate the decidability of $\mathsf{P}_1 \preceq_{\mathcal{K}} \mathsf{P}_2$ for the entire class $\mathbf{S}^1$, but do so for some of its most important members that do not have any corresponding type of homomorphism – the tropical semiring $\mathcal{T}^+$ and the schedule algebra $\mathcal{T}^-$. Since we can decide in PSPACE whether $\mathsf{P}_1 \preceq_{\mathcal{T}^+} \mathsf{P}_2$ and $\mathsf{P}_1 \preceq_{\mathcal{T}^-} \mathsf{P}_2$, we have the following result.

PROPOSITION 4.19 *CQ $\mathcal{T}^+$- and $\mathcal{T}^-$-CONTAINMENT are in PSPACE.*

We illustrate this proposition by an extension of Ex. 4.6.

EXAMPLE 4.6 (CONTINUED) We know that $\langle\!\langle Q_1 \rangle\!\rangle = \{Q_{11}, Q_{12}, Q_{13}, Q_{14}, Q_{15}\}$. Hence

$$Q_1^{[\![Q_{11}]\!]}() = x_1^2 + 2x_1x_2 + x_2^2, \text{ and } Q_2^{[\![Q_{11}]\!]}() = x_1^2 + x_2^2.$$

It is straightforward to see that

$$x_1^2 + 2x_1x_2 + x_2^2 =_{\mathcal{T}^+} x_1^2 + x_2^2.$$

The same can be shown for the $\mathcal{T}^+$-instances $[\![Q_{12}]\!]$, $[\![Q_{13}]\!]$, $[\![Q_{14}]\!]$, and $[\![Q_{15}]\!]$. By Thm. 4.17 we have that $Q_1 \subseteq_{\mathcal{T}^+} Q_2$.

5. $\mathcal{K}$-CONTAINMENT OF UCQS

In this section we look at $\mathcal{K}$-containment of UCQs, which generalizes the problem for CQs considered in Sec. 4. We examine both existing algorithms for deciding containment of UCQs and new ones developed here. All of these exploit the procedures used for CQs. Similarly to before, we identify classes of semirings corresponding to these algorithms, refining the classes from the previous sections.

Started for set semantics in [20], the study of $\mathcal{K}$-containment for UCQs continued for some particular semirings [17, 14], as well as classes of semirings such as type A systems [17] and distributive bilattices [13]. Generally, semirings from $\mathbf{S}^1$ (i.e. $\oplus$-idempotent semirings) were identified as *well behaved* w.r.t. containment of UCQs. Prior works show NP-completeness of checking $\mathcal{K}$-containment for some particular semirings $\mathcal{K}$ from $\mathbf{S}^1$, essentially relying on the following fact.

PROPOSITION 5.1 *The following are equivalent:*

- *semiring $\mathcal{K}$ belongs to $\mathbf{S}^1$;*
- *if for UCQs $\mathbf{Q}_1$, $\mathbf{Q}_2$ it holds that for each $Q_1 \in \mathbf{Q}_1$ there exists $Q_2 \in \mathbf{Q}_2$ with $Q_1 \subseteq_{\mathcal{K}} Q_2$, then $\mathbf{Q}_1 \subseteq_{\mathcal{K}} \mathbf{Q}_2$.*

This proposition says that $\mathcal{K}$ is $\oplus$-idempotent iff for $\mathcal{K}$-containment of UCQs it is sufficient to check CQs in $\mathbf{Q}_1$ locally, one at a time. Hence, if we have a sufficient condition for containment of CQs for some class inside $\mathbf{S}^1$, then we have one also for UCQs. Since $\mathbb{1}$-annihilation implies $\oplus$-idempotence, we have that $\mathbf{S}_{in} \subseteq \mathbf{S}^1$. Thus, next we study UCQ $\mathcal{K}$-containment for semirings in $\mathbf{S}_{in}$ and its subclasses.

5.1 Containment by homomorphism and injective homomorphism

We start with the classes $\mathbf{C}_{hom}$ and $\mathbf{C}_{in}$ from Sec. 4 and investigate for which semirings from these classes Prop. 5.1 can be used in decision procedures for UCQ $\mathcal{K}$-containment.

Recall that we write $Q_2 \to Q_1$ (and $Q_2 \hookrightarrow Q_1$) if there is a homomorphism (resp., injective homomorphism) from a CQ Q_2 to a CQ Q_1. We generalize these notions to unions as follows: given UCQs $\mathbf{Q}_1$ and $\mathbf{Q}_2$ we write $\mathbf{Q}_2 \to \mathbf{Q}_1$ (and $\mathbf{Q}_2 \hookrightarrow \mathbf{Q}_1$) iff for each $Q_1 \in \mathbf{Q}_1$ there exists $Q_2 \in \mathbf{Q}_2$ such that $Q_2 \to Q_1$ (resp., $Q_2 \hookrightarrow Q_1$).

For the class $\mathbf{C}_{hom}$, we know that the existence of a homomorphism is a sufficient condition for containment of CQs, and thus by Prop. 5.1 we can conclude that $\mathbf{Q}_2 \to \mathbf{Q}_1$ implies $\mathbf{Q}_1 \subseteq_{\mathcal{K}} \mathbf{Q}_2$. It turns out, that for this class of semirings the "only if" direction of the second item of Prop. 5.1 holds as well, so this condition is also necessary. Hence, we can extend Prop. 5.1, and present the following theorem.

THEOREM 5.2 *The following are equivalent:*

- *semiring $\mathcal{K}$ belongs to $\mathbf{C}_{hom}$;*
- *$\mathbf{Q}_1 \subseteq_{\mathcal{K}} \mathbf{Q}_2$ iff $\mathbf{Q}_2 \to \mathbf{Q}_1$, for all UCQs $\mathbf{Q}_1$ and $\mathbf{Q}_2$.*

Thus, we have a decision procedure for $\mathcal{K}$-containment of UCQs, for all semirings $\mathcal{K}$ in $\mathbf{C}_{hom}$. The NP-completeness of this procedure was first obtained for the set semantics semiring $\mathcal{B}$ in [20], which we know to be in this class.

COROLLARY 5.3 *If $\mathcal{K} \in \mathbf{C}_{hom}$ then deciding $\mathcal{K}$-containment for UCQs is NP-complete.*

Unfortunately, once we move away from $\mathbf{C}_{hom}$, we cannot guarantee a similar result, since the "only if" direction of the second item of Prop. 5.1 does not hold for an arbitrary semiring in $\mathbf{S}^1$. This can be seen from the following example.

EXAMPLE 5.4 Consider again the tropical semiring $\mathcal{T}^+ = \langle \mathbb{N}_0 \cup \{\infty\}, \min, +, \infty, 0 \rangle$, and UCQs $\mathbf{Q}_1 = \{Q_{11}\}$ and $\mathbf{Q}_2 = \{Q_{21}, Q_{22}\}$ over a schema with unary relations R, S, where

$$Q_{11} = \exists v\; R(v), S(v);$$
$$Q_{21} = \exists v\; R(v), R(v); \quad Q_{22} = \exists v\; S(v), S(v).$$

It is possible to show that $\mathbf{Q}_1 \subseteq_{\mathcal{T}^+} \mathbf{Q}_2$, but neither of the containments $Q_{11} \subseteq_{\mathcal{T}^+} Q_{21}$ nor $Q_{11} \subseteq_{\mathcal{T}^+} Q_{22}$ holds.

From Prop. 5.1 and 4.5 we know that $\mathbf{Q}_2 \hookrightarrow \mathbf{Q}_1$ is a sufficient condition for $\mathcal{K}$-containment of UCQs, for all semirings in $\mathbf{S}_{in}$. However, the example above shows that this condition may not be necessary for all semirings from $\mathbf{S}_{in}$. Next we identify the semirings for which it is. Denote by $\mathbf{N}_{in}^1$ the class of semirings $\mathcal{K}$ for which for every polynomial $\mathsf{P} \in \mathbb{N}[X]$ without a constant term and any set of variables $x_1, \ldots, x_n$ from X, the inequality

$$x_1 \times \ldots \times x_n \preceq_{\mathcal{K}} \mathsf{P}$$

implies that there exists a subset $x_{i_1}, \ldots, x_{i_m}$ of variables $x_1, \ldots, x_n$ such that P contains the monomial $x_{i_1} \times \ldots \times x_{i_m}$. Note that this is the same condition as the one for $\mathbf{N}_{in}$, but it is required to hold not only for CQ-admissible, but for all polynomials without a constant term. This definition is justified by the fact that any such polynomial can be obtained on an $\mathcal{N}[X]$-instance with tuples annotated with unique variables. For $\mathbf{N}_{in}^1$ we have the desired proposition.

PROPOSITION 5.5 *The following two statements are equivalent:*

- semiring $\mathcal{K}$ belongs to $\mathbf{N}_{\mathrm{in}}^1$;
- $\mathbf{Q}_1 \subseteq_{\mathcal{K}} \mathbf{Q}_2$ implies $\mathbf{Q}_2 \hookrightarrow \mathbf{Q}_1$, for all UCQs $\mathbf{Q}_1$ and $\mathbf{Q}_2$.

For the class $\mathbf{C}_{\mathrm{in}}^1 = \mathbf{S}_{\mathrm{in}} \cap \mathbf{N}_{\mathrm{in}}^1$ we have the following result.

THEOREM 5.6
(1) The following are equivalent:
- semiring $\mathcal{K}$ belongs to $\mathbf{C}_{\mathrm{in}}^1$;
- $\mathbf{Q}_1 \subseteq_{\mathcal{K}} \mathbf{Q}_2$ iff $\mathbf{Q}_2 \hookrightarrow \mathbf{Q}_1$, for all UCQs $\mathbf{Q}_1$ and $\mathbf{Q}_2$.
(2) If $\mathcal{K} \in \mathbf{C}_{\mathrm{in}}^1$ then UCQ $\mathcal{K}$-CONTAINMENT is NP-complete.

In the following sections we will see that the classes $\mathbf{C}_{\mathrm{bi}}$, $\mathbf{C}_{\mathrm{sur}}$, and $\mathbf{C}_{\mathrm{hcov}}$, for which we have decision procedures for containment of CQs, do not lie inside $\mathbf{S}^1$ but have non-empty intersections with it. For these intersections, Prop. 5.1 gives a sufficient condition for $\mathcal{K}$-containment of UCQs. However, new techniques will have to be developed to handle semirings outside these intersections.

5.2 Containment by bijective homomorphism

In Sec. 4.3 we argued that the existence of a bijective homomorphism is a sufficient condition for $\mathcal{K}$-containment of two CQs, for any semiring $\mathcal{K}$. Thus, Prop. 5.1 gives us a sufficient condition for $\mathcal{K}$-containment of *UCQs* for any semiring $\mathcal{K}$ in $\mathbf{S}^1$: to affirm that $\mathbf{Q}_1 \subseteq_{\mathcal{K}} \mathbf{Q}_2$ it suffices for every CQ from $\mathbf{Q}_1$ to find a bijective homomorphism to it from some CQ of $\mathbf{Q}_2$. In [14] it was shown that this condition is also necessary for the semiring of boolean provenance polynomials $\mathcal{B}[X]$ (which is universal for $\mathbf{S}^1$). At the end of this section we will find a subclass $\mathbf{C}_{\mathrm{bi}}^1$ of $\mathbf{S}^1$ consisting of all semirings which behave the same as $\mathcal{B}[X]$ w.r.t. UCQs.

However, not much is known about decision procedures and complexity for containment of UCQs for semirings outside $\mathbf{S}^1$, other than the classic result that this problem is undecidable under bag semantics $\mathcal{N}$ [17]. As was observed in [14], if for UCQs $\mathbf{Q}_1$ and $\mathbf{Q}_2$ it holds that for every $Q_1 \in \mathbf{Q}_1$ there exists a *unique* $Q_2 \in \mathbf{Q}_2$ such that $Q_1 \subseteq_{\mathcal{K}} Q_2$, then $\mathbf{Q}_1 \subseteq_{\mathcal{K}} \mathbf{Q}_2$ for any semiring $\mathcal{K}$, i.e. this condition is sufficient for containment of UCQs for any semantics. However, it was also shown that this condition is not necessary for provenance polynomials $\mathcal{N}[X]$, and therefore for any semiring. This is shown in the following example.

EXAMPLE 5.7 Consider a schema with a binary relation R, and UCQs $\mathbf{Q}_1 = \{Q_{11}, Q_{12}\}$, $\mathbf{Q}_2 = \{Q_{21}, Q_{22}\}$, where

$Q_{11} = \exists u, v\ R(u,v), R(u,u);\quad Q_{12} = \exists u, v\ R(u,v), R(v,v);$
$Q_{21} = \exists u, v, w\ R(u,v), R(w,w);\ Q_{22} = \exists u\ R(u,u), R(u,u).$

We cannot find for every CQ Q in $\mathbf{Q}_1$ a unique CQ in $\mathbf{Q}_2$ containing Q. Later we will demonstrate that $\mathbf{Q}_1 \subseteq_{\mathcal{N}[X]} \mathbf{Q}_2$.

A PSPACE algorithm was suggested in [14] for deciding $\mathcal{N}[X]$-containment of UCQs. This algorithm involves *guessing* a small enough $\mathcal{N}[X]$-instance as a counterexample, and then posing the queries over it. However, the possibility of solving it using some type of homomorphism was left open.

In what follows, we use the techniques developed in Sec. 4.3 to devise a syntactic criterion to decide $\mathcal{N}[X]$-containment of unions of conjunctive queries. We also give a procedure for checking this criterion which allows us to improve the PSPACE upper bound given in [14]. Afterwards we shall see which semirings behave just as $\mathcal{N}[X]$ w.r.t. containment of UCQs (clearly, all such semirings lie in $\mathbf{C}_{\mathrm{bi}}$). But first, in order to study these problems, we revisit the notion of complete description from Sec. 4.6 and extend it to UCQs.

A *complete description* $\wr\mathbf{Q}\wr$ of a UCQ $\mathbf{Q}$ is a union of complete descriptions of its elements.[5] The semantics of a CCQ Q is the same as that of a CQ (given in the preliminaries), except that $\mathcal{V}(Q, \mathbf{t})$ for any $\mathbf{t}$ contains only mappings preserving the inequalities. Similarly, homomorphisms of all types considered in Sec. 4 between CCQs should preserve the inequalities. Hence, for any UCQ $\mathbf{Q}$ and semiring $\mathcal{K}$ we have that $\mathbf{Q} \equiv_{\mathcal{K}} \wr\mathbf{Q}\wr$, i.e. complete descriptions are just explicit representations of UCQs.

All endomorphisms of CCQs are automorphisms. This key property allows us to use CCQs in the condition for $\mathcal{N}[X]$-containment of UCQs. Further, for CCQs Q_1 and Q_2, this property implies that $Q_2 \hookrightarrow Q_1$ iff Q_1 and Q_2 are *isomorphic*, i.e. coincide up to renaming of existential variables. Given a UCQ $\mathbf{Q}$ and a CQ Q we write $\mathbf{Q}[Q^{\simeq}]$ for the number of CQs in $\mathbf{Q}$ that are isomorphic to Q.

DEFINITION 5.8 *Given UCQs $\mathbf{Q}_1$, $\mathbf{Q}_2$, we write $\wr\mathbf{Q}_2\wr \hookrightarrow_\infty \wr\mathbf{Q}_1\wr$ iff for each CCQ Q it holds that*

$$\wr\mathbf{Q}_1\wr[Q^{\simeq}] \leq \wr\mathbf{Q}_2\wr[Q^{\simeq}].$$

If $\mathbf{Q}_1 = \{Q_1\}$ and $\mathbf{Q}_2 = \{Q_2\}$ consist of single CQs then $\wr\mathbf{Q}_2\wr \hookrightarrow_\infty \wr\mathbf{Q}_1\wr$ is equivalent to $Q_2 \hookrightarrow Q_1$, so the definition above extends bijective homomorphisms. We are ready to state the decision procedure for $\mathcal{N}[X]$-containment of UCQs.

PROPOSITION 5.9 *For any UCQs $\mathbf{Q}_1$ and $\mathbf{Q}_2$ it holds that $\mathbf{Q}_1 \subseteq_{\mathcal{N}[X]} \mathbf{Q}_2$ iff $\wr\mathbf{Q}_2\wr \hookrightarrow_\infty \wr\mathbf{Q}_1\wr$.*

Next we continue Ex. 5.7 and show that $\mathbf{Q}_1 \subseteq_{\mathcal{N}[X]} \mathbf{Q}_2$.

EXAMPLE 5.7 (CONTINUED) Having that $\wr\mathbf{Q}_1\wr = \{Q'_{11}, Q'_{12}, Q'_{22}, Q'_{22}\}$ and $\wr\mathbf{Q}_2\wr = \{Q'_{21}, Q'_{11}, Q'_{12}, Q'_{22}, Q'_{22}\}$, where

$\begin{aligned}
Q'_{11} &= \exists u, v\ R(u,v), R(u,u), u \neq v; \\
Q'_{12} &= \exists u, v\ R(u,v), R(v,v), u \neq v; \\
Q'_{21} &= \exists u, v, w\ R(u,v), R(w,w), u \neq v, v \neq w, w \neq u; \\
Q'_{22} &= \exists u\ R(u,u), R(u,u),
\end{aligned}$

we conclude that $\wr\mathbf{Q}_2\wr \hookrightarrow_\infty \wr\mathbf{Q}_1\wr$, and hence $\mathbf{Q}_1 \subseteq_{\mathcal{N}[X]} \mathbf{Q}_2$.

Therefore, the condition $\wr\mathbf{Q}_2\wr \hookrightarrow_\infty \wr\mathbf{Q}_1\wr$ on UCQs $\mathbf{Q}_1$ and $\mathbf{Q}_2$ is equivalent to their $\mathcal{N}[X]$-containment. Using Prop. 3.2, we conclude that it is sufficient for $\mathcal{K}$-containment over any semiring $\mathcal{K}$. We leave the question of the complexity of checking this condition to the end of this section, but look now at semirings which behave the same as $\mathcal{N}[X]$, i.e. for which the condition is also necessary. Again we exploit the relationship between queries and polynomials.

Denote by $\mathbf{C}_{\mathrm{bi}}^\infty$ the class of all semirings $\mathcal{K}$ such that for every coefficient $\ell > 0$, polynomial $\mathsf{P} \in \mathbb{N}[X]$ without a constant term and monomial M over X, the inequality

$$\ell\,\mathsf{M} \preceq_{\mathcal{K}} \mathsf{P}$$

implies that M has a coefficient at least ℓ in P.

Notice that $\mathbf{C}_{\mathrm{bi}}^\infty$ is a subclass of $\mathbf{C}_{\mathrm{bi}}$. Also, as desired, $\mathcal{N}[X]$ is in $\mathbf{C}_{\mathrm{bi}}^\infty$, i.e. this class contains semirings $\mathcal{K}$ which behave the same as $\mathcal{N}[X]$ w.r.t. $\mathcal{K}$-containment of UCQs. It turns out that it contains all such semirings.

PROPOSITION 5.10 *The following are equivalent:*
- *semiring $\mathcal{K}$ belongs to $\mathbf{C}_{\mathrm{bi}}^\infty$;*
- *$\mathbf{Q}_1 \subseteq_{\mathcal{K}} \mathbf{Q}_2$ iff $\wr\mathbf{Q}_2\wr \hookrightarrow_\infty \wr\mathbf{Q}_1\wr$, for all UCQs $\mathbf{Q}_1$, $\mathbf{Q}_2$.*

---

[5]Recall here, that we assume that CCQs are multisets, i.e. this union is always disjoint.

The above proposition gives us a decision procedure for $\mathcal{K}$-containment of UCQs, for all semirings $\mathcal{K}$ in $\mathbf{C}_{\mathrm{bi}}^{\infty}$. For these semirings the equality $kx =_{\mathcal{K}} \ell x$ holds only when $k = \ell$. Coming back to $\oplus$-idempotent semirings $\mathcal{K}$ from the class $\mathbf{S}^1$, we have that $kx =_{\mathcal{K}} \ell x$ holds for all $k, \ell \in \mathbb{N}$. What happens for those semirings that lie "in between" these classes? Such semirings satisfy $kx =_{\mathcal{K}} \ell x$ not for all, but just for some $k \neq \ell$. In what follows, we will classify them and parameterize Prop. 5.10 over this classification.

A semiring $\mathcal{K}$ has *offset* k iff for all $\ell \geq k$ it holds that $kx =_{\mathcal{K}} \ell x$. In particular, $\oplus$-idempotent semirings from $\mathbf{S}^1$ have offset 1. The following proposition says that the smallest offset of a semiring $\mathcal{K}$ identifies all its axioms $kx =_{\mathcal{K}} \ell x$.

PROPOSITION 5.11 *Suppose $\mathcal{K}$ is a (positive) semiring. If $kx =_{\mathcal{K}} \ell x$ holds for some $1 \leq k < \ell$, then $\mathcal{K}$ has offset k.*

Based on this fact, we consider the classes $\mathbf{S}^k$, $k \in \mathbb{N}$, of semirings with offset k. We have already seen one such class, $\mathbf{S}^1$. Note, that for all $k \geq 1$ we have $\mathbf{S}^k \subset \mathbf{S}^{k+1}$. Our aim is to obtain a sufficient condition for containment of UCQs for each $\mathbf{S}^k$. The following example gives an idea how to do it.

EXAMPLE 5.7 (CONTINUED) Coming back to UCQs $\mathbf{Q}_1$ and $\mathbf{Q}_2$, we know that $\mathbf{Q}_1 \subseteq_{\mathcal{K}} \mathbf{Q}_2$ for any semiring $\mathcal{K}$. However, if we take $\mathbf{Q}_1' = \mathbf{Q}_1 \cup \{Q_{22}\}$ we have that now $\wr\mathbf{Q}_1'\wr = \wr\mathbf{Q}_1\wr \cup \{Q_{22}'\}$ has not two, but three CCQs isomorphic to Q_{22}'. Since $\wr\mathbf{Q}_2\wr$ has only two of them, we have that $\wr\mathbf{Q}_2\wr \not\hookrightarrow_\infty \wr\mathbf{Q}_1'\wr$ and thereby $\mathbf{Q}_1' \not\subseteq_{\mathcal{N}[X]} \mathbf{Q}_2$. At the same time, we see that $\mathbf{Q}_1' \subseteq_{\mathcal{K}} \mathbf{Q}_2$ for any semiring $\mathcal{K}$ with offset 2. The reason is that we can dismiss the third copy of Q_{22}' in $\wr\mathbf{Q}_1'\wr$, since it is made *redundant* by the offset 2 of $\mathcal{K}$, i.e. by removing it we do not alter the result of the query over any $\mathcal{K}$-instance.

The above example illustrates the intuition that to obtain a "tight" sufficient condition for some semiring $\mathcal{K}$, one should take into account its smallest offset and, if it is greater than 1, split UCQs to their complete descriptions. Hence, the desired sufficient condition for such semirings is likely to resemble $\wr\mathbf{Q}_2\wr \hookrightarrow_\infty \wr\mathbf{Q}_1\wr$. For the sake of uniformity we extend the notion of offset and say that any semiring has offset ∞; that is, $\mathbf{S}^\infty = \mathbf{S}$, and write $\mathbb{N}_\infty$ for $\mathbb{N} \cup \{\infty\}$. Using the ideas above, we can extend the condition stated in Def. 5.8 to each $k \in \mathbb{N}_\infty$, so that the criterion $\wr\mathbf{Q}_2\wr \hookrightarrow_k \wr\mathbf{Q}_1\wr$ also generalizes Prop. 5.1 for values of k other than 1. The definition is rather technical (it needs to take into account *automorphisms* of CCQs), and for space reasons is deferred to the full version. Using this criterion we state the following fact.

PROPOSITION 5.12 *For each $k \in \mathbb{N}_\infty$ the following are equivalent:*

- *semiring $\mathcal{K}$ belongs to $\mathbf{S}^k$;*
- $\wr\mathbf{Q}_2\wr \hookrightarrow_k \wr\mathbf{Q}_1\wr$ *implies $\mathbf{Q}_1 \subseteq_{\mathcal{K}} \mathbf{Q}_2$, for all UCQs $\mathbf{Q}_1, \mathbf{Q}_2$.*

Similarly to the homomorphism types from Sec. 4, for every $k \in \mathbb{N}$ we can axiomatize a class $\mathbf{N}_{\mathrm{bi}}^k$ for which $\wr\mathbf{Q}_2\wr \hookrightarrow_k \wr\mathbf{Q}_1\wr$ is necessary for containment of UCQs. All the axioms are similar to the one for $\mathbf{C}_{\mathrm{bi}}^\infty$ and are omitted. The semirings from each intersection $\mathbf{C}_{\mathrm{bi}}^k = \mathbf{S}^k \cap \mathbf{N}_{\mathrm{bi}}^k$ have the same smallest offset k. For these classes we have $\mathbf{C}_{\mathrm{bi}}^k \subset \mathbf{C}_{\mathrm{bi}}$, $k \geq 1$. The following theorem extends Prop. 5.10 to the classes $\mathbf{C}_{\mathrm{bi}}^k$ and uniformly establishes complexity bounds for all the procedures from this section.

THEOREM 5.13 *Let $k \in \mathbb{N}_\infty$.*
(1) The following are equivalent:

- *semiring $\mathcal{K}$ belongs to $\mathbf{C}_{\mathrm{bi}}^k$;*
- $\mathbf{Q}_1 \subseteq_{\mathcal{K}} \mathbf{Q}_2$ *iff $\wr\mathbf{Q}_2\wr \hookrightarrow_k \wr\mathbf{Q}_1\wr$, for all UCQs $\mathbf{Q}_1$ and $\mathbf{Q}_2$.*

(2) If $\mathcal{K} \in \mathbf{C}_{\mathrm{bi}}^k$ then UCQ $\mathcal{K}$-CONTAINMENT is NP-complete if $k = 1$, in Π_2^p if $2 \leq k < \infty$, and in $\mathrm{coNP}^{\#P}$ if $k = \infty$.

The complexity for $\mathbf{C}_{\mathrm{bi}}^1$ is lower, since the counterpart of Prop. 5.1 holds and splitting UCQs to complete descriptions is redundant. This agrees with the result of [14] for $\mathcal{B}[X]$. For the case of $k = \infty$ the $\mathrm{coNP}^{\#P}$ upper bound improves the result given there for $\mathcal{N}[X]$.[6] For the intermediate cases of $2 \leq k < \infty$, the complexity drops since the number of CCQs in the search space is bounded by k.

5.3 Containment by surjective homomorphism

In this section we look at the problem of containment of UCQs over semirings from the class $\mathbf{S}_{\mathrm{sur}}$, for which the existence of a surjective homomorphism is sufficient for containment of CQs. We develop a syntactic condition similar to the condition $\hookrightarrow_\infty$ from Sec. 5.2, which is sufficient for UCQ $\mathcal{K}$-containment for all semirings $\mathcal{K}$ from $\mathbf{S}_{\mathrm{sur}}$, and necessary for some of them, including the universal semirings of $\mathbf{S}_{\mathrm{sur}}$.

The naive approach is to state such a condition by requiring for every Q_1 in $\mathbf{Q}_1$ the existence of a unique CQ Q_2 in $\mathbf{Q}_2$ such that $Q_2 \twoheadrightarrow Q_1$. However, this condition suffers from the same problem as the similar condition for the class $\mathbf{S}$: it is sufficient for $\mathcal{K}$-containment of $\mathbf{Q}_1$ in $\mathbf{Q}_2$ over every $\mathcal{K}$ from $\mathbf{S}_{\mathrm{sur}}$, but modifying Ex. 5.7 it is possible to show that it is not necessary for any such semiring. Thus, such a condition doesn't suit our purposes, because it doesn't aid in our search for decision procedures for containment of UCQs. This leaves open the possibility of finding a stricter criterion, which is still sufficient for all semirings in $\mathbf{S}_{\mathrm{sur}}$. Using the power of complete descriptions, we devise such a criterion.

DEFINITION 5.14 *Given two UCQs $\mathbf{Q}_1$ and $\mathbf{Q}_2$ we write $\wr\mathbf{Q}_2\wr \twoheadrightarrow_\infty \wr\mathbf{Q}_1\wr$ iff for every CCQ Q_1 from $\wr\mathbf{Q}_1\wr$ there exists a unique CCQ Q_2 in $\wr\mathbf{Q}_2\wr$ such that $Q_2 \twoheadrightarrow Q_1$.*

With this condition in hand we can state the proposition.

PROPOSITION 5.15 *The following are equivalent:*

- *semiring $\mathcal{K}$ belongs to $\mathbf{S}_{\mathrm{sur}}$;*
- $\wr\mathbf{Q}_2\wr \twoheadrightarrow_\infty \wr\mathbf{Q}_1\wr$ *implies $\mathbf{Q}_1 \subseteq_{\mathcal{K}} \mathbf{Q}_2$, for all UCQs $\mathbf{Q}_1, \mathbf{Q}_2$.*

Notice that since bag semantics $\mathcal{N}$ is in $\mathbf{S}_{\mathrm{sur}}$, this proposition gives us a new sufficient condition for $\mathcal{N}$-containment of UCQs, which improves previous results of [6, 17].

COROLLARY 5.16 *If $\wr\mathbf{Q}_2\wr \twoheadrightarrow_\infty \wr\mathbf{Q}_1\wr$ then $\mathbf{Q}_1 \subseteq_{\mathcal{N}} \mathbf{Q}_2$.*

While it is possible to axiomatize the class $\mathbf{N}_{\mathrm{sur}}^\infty$ of semirings for which the condition $\wr\mathbf{Q}_2\wr \twoheadrightarrow_\infty \wr\mathbf{Q}_1\wr$ is necessary for a UCQ $\mathbf{Q}_1$ to be $\mathcal{K}$-contained in a UCQ $\mathbf{Q}_2$, the definition is somewhat technical, and we defer the reader to the full version. By the results of Sec. 4.4, this condition is not necessary for any semiring that is not in $\mathbf{N}_{\mathrm{sur}}$, like the bag semantics semiring ($\mathcal{N}$-containment of UCQs is in general undecidable [17]). One can also show that it is not necessary for any semiring from $\mathbf{N}_{\mathrm{sur}}$ with finite smallest offset.

As intended, $\wr\mathbf{Q}_2\wr \twoheadrightarrow_\infty \wr\mathbf{Q}_1\wr$ leads to a decision procedure for UCQ $\mathcal{K}$-containment for the class $\mathbf{C}_{\mathrm{sur}}^\infty = \mathbf{S}_{\mathrm{sur}} \cap \mathbf{N}_{\mathrm{sur}}^\infty$.

THEOREM 5.17 *The following two statements are equivalent:*

---

[6]This bound coincides with the best known bound for deciding bag-equivalence of CQs with inequalities $<$ (see [8]).

- *semiring $\mathcal{K}$ belongs to $\mathbf{C}_{\text{sur}}^\infty$;*
- $\mathbf{Q}_1 \subseteq_\mathcal{K} \mathbf{Q}_2$ *iff* $\wr\mathbf{Q}_2\wr \twoheadrightarrow_\infty \wr\mathbf{Q}_1\wr$, *for all UCQs $\mathbf{Q}_1$ and $\mathbf{Q}_2$.*

The proof exploits Hall's marriage theorem and the fact that, for CCQs Q_1 and Q_2 we have $Q_2 \twoheadrightarrow Q_1$ iff Q_2 is isomorphic to a CCQ which contains exactly the same atoms as Q_1 but with greater or equal multiplicities. Checking $\wr\mathbf{Q}_2\wr \twoheadrightarrow_\infty \wr\mathbf{Q}_1\wr$ can clearly be done in EXPTIME. We leave the issue of exact complexity open.

Finally, we analyze necessary conditions for the classes $\mathbf{S}_{\text{sur}}^k = \mathbf{S}_{\text{sur}} \cap \mathbf{S}^k$ of semirings having finite offsets. For semirings with minimal offsets $k \geq 2$ the straightforward extension on the base of complete descriptions does not work, and in order to find such a criterion one needs to use even more elaborate representations of UCQs. Formulating this criterion is possible, but extremely technical, and thus it appears unlikely that it would have any practical applicability.

Instead, we concentrate on the case $k = 1$, i.e. $\oplus$-idempotent semirings. Given UCQs $\mathbf{Q}_1$, $\mathbf{Q}_2$ we write $\mathbf{Q}_2 \twoheadrightarrow_1 \mathbf{Q}_1$ if for each $Q_1 \in \mathbf{Q}_1$ there exists $Q_2 \in \mathbf{Q}_2$ such that $Q_2 \twoheadrightarrow Q_1$.

It immediately follows from Prop. 5.1 and 4.12 that the condition $\mathbf{Q}_2 \twoheadrightarrow_1 \mathbf{Q}_1$ implies that $\mathbf{Q}_1 \subseteq_\mathcal{K} \mathbf{Q}_2$. Moreover, it was noted in [14] that this condition is also necessary for $\texttt{Why}[X]$-containment of $\mathbf{Q}_1$ and $\mathbf{Q}_2$. Next we identify all the semirings that behave just as $\texttt{Why}[X]$.

Denote by $\mathbf{N}_{\text{sur}}^1$ the class of semirings $\mathcal{K}$ for which for every polynomial $\mathsf{P} \in \mathbb{N}[X]$ without a constant term and any set of variables $x_1, \ldots, x_n$, the inequality

$$x_1 \times \ldots \times x_n \preceq_\mathcal{K} \mathsf{P}$$

implies that there exist exponents $m_1, \ldots, m_n \geq 1$ such that P contains the monomial $x_1^{m_1} \times \ldots \times x_n^{m_n}$. Similarly to the class $\mathbf{N}_{\text{in}}^1$, this condition is the same as the condition for $\mathbf{N}_{\text{sur}}$, but should hold not only for CQ-admissible, but for all polynomials without constant terms. Given that this is a stronger requirement, one expects that $\mathbf{N}_{\text{sur}}^1 \subset \mathbf{N}_{\text{sur}}$. This is indeed the case, since for example the semiring $\texttt{Trio}[X]$ is not in $\mathbf{N}_{\text{sur}}^1$, but is in $\mathbf{N}_{\text{sur}}$.

The class $\mathbf{N}_{\text{sur}}^1$ corresponds precisely to the class of semirings $\mathcal{K}$ for which $\mathbf{Q}_2 \twoheadrightarrow_1 \mathbf{Q}_1$ is necessary for $\mathcal{K}$-containment of UCQs. For the intersection $\mathbf{C}_{\text{sur}}^1 = \mathbf{S}_{\text{sur}} \cap \mathbf{N}_{\text{sur}}^1$ the following corollary holds. The complexity was first shown for the $\texttt{Why}[X]$ semiring in [14].

COROLLARY 5.18
(1) The following are equivalent:
- *semiring $\mathcal{K}$ belongs to $\mathbf{C}_{\text{sur}}^1$;*
- $\mathbf{Q}_1 \subseteq_\mathcal{K} \mathbf{Q}_2$ *iff $\mathbf{Q}_2 \twoheadrightarrow_1 \mathbf{Q}_1$, for all UCQs $\mathbf{Q}_1$ and $\mathbf{Q}_2$.*
(2) If $\mathcal{K} \in \mathbf{C}_{\text{sur}}^1$ then UCQ $\mathcal{K}$-CONTAINMENT is NP-complete.

5.4 Containment by homomorphic covering

So far we have generalized to UCQs all the types of homomorphisms from Sec. 4, except homomorphic covering. This section closes the remaining gap. We have left it to the end of the paper, since, when compared to the previous results, the case of $\mathbf{S}_{\text{hcov}}$ is rather specific. Nevertheless, we identify a sufficient condition for UCQ containment for the class $\mathbf{S}_{\text{hcov}}$ and show that for some semirings it is also necessary. It again is based on the concept of complete descriptions. It is important that all semirings in $\mathbf{S}_{\text{hcov}}$ have offset 2.

PROPOSITION 5.19 *The following holds: $\mathbf{S}_{\text{hcov}} \subseteq \mathbf{S}^2$.*

For the $\oplus$-idempotent semirings from $\mathbf{S}_{\text{hcov}}^1 = \mathbf{S}^1 \cap \mathbf{S}_{\text{hcov}}$ Prop. 5.1 holds, as usual. This time, however, the condition

requiring checking CQs in UCQs $\mathbf{Q}_1$ and $\mathbf{Q}_2$ only pairwise is never necessary, as shown in the following example.

EXAMPLE 5.20 Consider UCQs $\mathbf{Q}_1 = \{Q_{11}\}$ and $\mathbf{Q}_2 = \{Q_{21}, Q_{22}\}$ over a schema with unary relations R, S, where

$$Q_{11} = \exists v\, R(v), S(v); \qquad Q_{21} = \exists v\, R(v); \quad Q_{22} = \exists v\, S(v).$$

It is not difficult to show that $\mathbf{Q}_1 \subseteq_\mathcal{K} \mathbf{Q}_2$, over any semiring $\mathcal{K} \in \mathbf{S}_{\text{hcov}}$. However, neither $Q_{21} \rightrightarrows Q_{11}$ nor $Q_{22} \rightrightarrows Q_{11}$.

The above example captures the intuition that both Q_{21} and Q_{22} should be used *at the same time* to produce a covering for Q_{11}. Next we define a condition, that generalizes this intuition. Given UCQs $\mathbf{Q}_1$, $\mathbf{Q}_2$, we write $\mathbf{Q}_2 \rightrightarrows_1 \mathbf{Q}_1$ if for each $Q_1 \in \mathbf{Q}_1$ and every atom $R(\mathbf{u}, \mathbf{v})$ in Q_1 there is a homomorphism h from some $Q_2 \in \mathbf{Q}_2$ to Q_1 with $R(\mathbf{u}, \mathbf{v})$ in the image of h.

We shall see below that this condition is only adequate for those semirings in $\mathbf{S}_{\text{hcov}}$ which have offset 1. To define a general condition we need to use complete descriptions. First we extend the definition of $\rightrightarrows_1$ to complete descriptions, in the expected way: the homomorphisms from CCQs of $\wr\mathbf{Q}_2\wr$ covering all atoms of all CCQs in $\wr\mathbf{Q}_1\wr$ should preserve inequalities. Notice that $\mathbf{Q}_2 \rightrightarrows_1 \mathbf{Q}_1$ iff $\wr\mathbf{Q}_2\wr \rightrightarrows_1 \wr\mathbf{Q}_1\wr$.

In the condition $\wr\mathbf{Q}_2\wr \rightrightarrows_2 \wr\mathbf{Q}_1\wr$ for semirings with offset 2, we also require that every CCQ without automorphisms having multiplicity more than one in $\wr\mathbf{Q}_1\wr$ has to be covered by two CCQs in $\wr\mathbf{Q}_2\wr$. Formally, we have that $\wr\mathbf{Q}_2\wr \rightrightarrows_2 \wr\mathbf{Q}_1\wr$, if (1) $\wr\mathbf{Q}_2\wr \rightrightarrows_1 \wr\mathbf{Q}_1\wr$, and (2) for every CCQ Q_1 in $\wr\mathbf{Q}_1\wr$ without nontrivial automorphisms (preserving inequalities)
- either there exist two CCQs[7] $Q_2', Q_2'' \in \wr\mathbf{Q}_2\wr$ such that $Q_2' \rightarrow Q_1$ and $Q_2'' \rightarrow Q_1$,
- or $\min(\wr\mathbf{Q}_1\wr[Q_1^{\simeq}], 2) \leq \wr\mathbf{Q}_2\wr[Q_1^{\simeq}]$.

Finally, we can present the desired characterization.

PROPOSITION 5.21 *For $k = 1, 2$ the following are equivalent:*
- *semiring $\mathcal{K}$ belongs to $\mathbf{S}_{\text{hcov}}^k$;*
- $\wr\mathbf{Q}_2\wr \rightrightarrows_k \wr\mathbf{Q}_1\wr$ *implies $\mathbf{Q}_1 \subseteq_\mathcal{K} \mathbf{Q}_2$, for all UCQs $\mathbf{Q}_1$, $\mathbf{Q}_2$.*

Similarly to the previous conditions, it is possible to identify classes for which $\rightrightarrows_k$ is necessary for containment of UCQs. For $k = 1, 2$ denote by $\mathbf{N}_{\text{hcov}}^k$ the class of all semirings $\mathcal{K}$ such that for every coefficient ℓ and polynomial $\mathsf{P} \in \mathbb{N}[X]$ without a constant term, the inequality

$$\ell(x_1 \times \ldots \times x_n) \preceq_\mathcal{K} \mathsf{P}$$

implies that P uses all the variables $x_1, \ldots, x_n$ and has no less than $\min(\ell, k)$ monomials.

PROPOSITION 5.22 *For every $k = 1, 2$ the following are equivalent:*
- *semiring $\mathcal{K}$ belongs to $\mathbf{N}_{\text{hcov}}^k$;*
- $\mathbf{Q}_1 \subseteq_\mathcal{K} \mathbf{Q}_2$ *implies $\wr\mathbf{Q}_2\wr \rightrightarrows_k \wr\mathbf{Q}_1\wr$, for all UCQs $\mathbf{Q}_1$, $\mathbf{Q}_2$.*

Notice that the bag semantics semiring $\mathcal{N}$ belongs to $\mathbf{N}_{\text{hcov}}^2$. Thus the condition $\wr\mathbf{Q}_2\wr \rightrightarrows_2 \wr\mathbf{Q}_1\wr$ is of particular interest, since it is a new necessary condition for $\mathcal{N}$-containment of UCQs. This improves on conditions known previously [6].

COROLLARY 5.23 *If $\mathbf{Q}_1 \subseteq_\mathcal{N} \mathbf{Q}_2$ then $\wr\mathbf{Q}_2\wr \rightrightarrows_2 \wr\mathbf{Q}_1\wr$.*

As usual, for the intersections $\mathbf{C}_{\text{hcov}}^k = \mathbf{S}_{\text{hcov}}^k \cap \mathbf{N}_{\text{hcov}}^k$ we have the following theorem. The NP-completeness of UCQ

---

[7] CQs Q_2' and Q_2'' still may be isomorphic or even coincide.

K-containment of CQs				K-containment of UCQs			
class	key axioms	homomorphism type	compl.	sub-class	extra axiom	homomorphism type	compl.
$\mathbf{C}_{hom}$	$\otimes$-idempotence, $\mathbb{1}$-annihilation	$Q_2 \to Q_1$ (usual)	NP-c[†]	$\mathbf{C}_{hom}$	—	$\mathbf{Q}_2 \to \mathbf{Q}_1$	NP-c[†]
$\mathbf{C}_{hcov}$	$\otimes$-idempotence	$Q_2 \rightrightarrows Q_1$ (hom. cov.)	NP-c[†]	$\mathbf{C}_{hcov}^1$ $\mathbf{C}_{hcov}^2$	offset 1 —	$\mathbf{Q}_2 \rightrightarrows_1 \mathbf{Q}_1$ $\langle \mathbf{Q}_2 \rangle \rightrightarrows_2 \langle \mathbf{Q}_1 \rangle$	NP-c[†] in Π_2^p
$\mathbf{C}_{in}$	$\mathbb{1}$-annihilation	$Q_2 \hookrightarrow Q_1$ (injective)	NP-c	$\mathbf{C}_{in}^1$	—	$\mathbf{Q}_2 \hookrightarrow \mathbf{Q}_1$	NP-c
$\mathbf{C}_{sur}$	$\otimes$-semi-idempotence	$Q_2 \twoheadrightarrow Q_1$ (surjective)	NP-c[†]	$\mathbf{C}_{sur}^1$ $\mathbf{C}_{sur}^\infty$	offset 1 —	$\mathbf{Q}_2 \twoheadrightarrow_1 \mathbf{Q}_1$ $\langle \mathbf{Q}_2 \rangle \twoheadrightarrow_\infty \langle \mathbf{Q}_1 \rangle$	NP-c[†] in EXPTIME
$\mathbf{C}_{bi}$	—	$Q_2 \hookrightarrow\!\!\!\twoheadrightarrow Q_1$ (bijective)	NP-c[†]	$\mathbf{C}_{bi}^1$ $\mathbf{C}_{bi}^{k>1}$ $\mathbf{C}_{bi}^\infty$	offset 1 offset k —	$\mathbf{Q}_2 \hookrightarrow\!\!\!\twoheadrightarrow_1 \mathbf{Q}_1$ $\langle \mathbf{Q}_2 \rangle \hookrightarrow\!\!\!\twoheadrightarrow_k \langle \mathbf{Q}_1 \rangle$ $\langle \mathbf{Q}_2 \rangle \hookrightarrow\!\!\!\twoheadrightarrow_\infty \langle \mathbf{Q}_1 \rangle$	NP-c[†] in Π_2^p in coNP$^{\#P}$

Table 1: **Summary of semiring classes and complexity (results known before are marked by †). Key axioms define the corresponding sufficient classes; the axioms for the necessary classes are omitted for clarity.**

$\mathcal{K}$-containment for semirings from $\mathbf{C}_{hcov}^1$ was first provided in [14] for the case of the lineage semiring $\mathrm{Lin}[X]$.

THEOREM 5.24
(1) Given a number $k = 1, 2$, the following are equivalent:
- semiring $\mathcal{K}$ belongs to $\mathbf{C}_{hcov}^k$;
- $\mathbf{Q}_1 \subseteq_{\mathcal{K}} \mathbf{Q}_2$ iff $\langle \mathbf{Q}_2 \rangle \rightrightarrows_k \langle \mathbf{Q}_1 \rangle$, for all UCQs $\mathbf{Q}_1$ and $\mathbf{Q}_2$.
(2) UCQ $\mathcal{K}$-CONTAINMENT is NP-complete if $\mathcal{K} \in \mathbf{C}_{hcov}^1$, and in Π_2^p if $\mathcal{K} \in \mathbf{C}_{hcov}^2$.

6. CONCLUSION

We have studied containment of CQs and UCQs over annotated relations. We have established several interesting classes of semirings for which these problems are decidable by means of different syntactic criteria, developed by modifying and extending the well-known notion of homomorphism between CQs. Our work extends previous results on the subject and should have practical implications, since most semirings used for annotations in the literature fall into one of these well-behaved classes. Tab. 1 provides a summary, with complexity bounds for checking the associated criteria. For semirings that do not fall into these classes, we have extended the range of available machinery for query optimization problems, by providing generalized or improved necessary and sufficient conditions. For some of these semirings we also suggest new decision procedures based on small model properties.

Many problems remain open. In particular, we would like to continue studying the *small model property* approach, either proving or disproving that such methods can work for semirings with non-idempotent addition. It is also interesting to study *CQ-admissible polynomials* on their own, and in particular how to decide containment over them. We believe that this study may have consequences for solving some of the fundamental open problems in the area of query optimization. Finally, we anticipate that the concept of *complete descriptions* opens new possibilities to solve containment and equivalence problems over different semantics for not only CQs and UCQs, but for a much wider range of queries.

Acknowledgements We thank Peter Buneman, Jeff Egger, Diego Figueira and Tony Tan for useful discussions, and Todd J. Green for comments on previous results. Support provided by FET-Open Project FoX, grant agreement 233599; and EPSRC grants F028288/1 and G049165.

7. REFERENCES

[1] F.N. Afrati, M. Damigos, M. Gergatsoulis. Query containment under bag and bag-set semantics. *IPL* **110**(10), 2010.

[2] P. Buneman, J. Cheney, W.C. Tan, S. Vansummeren. Curated databases. *PODS* 2008, 1–12.

[3] P. Buneman, S. Khanna, W.C. Tan. Why and Where: a characterization of data provenance. *ICDT* 2001, 316–330.

[4] P. Buneman, E.V. Kostylev. Annotation Algebras for RDFS. *SWPM* 2010. CEUR Workshop Proc.

[5] A.K. Chandra, P.M. Merlin. Optimal implementation of conjunctive queries in relational data bases. *STOC* 1977.

[6] S. Chaudhuri, M.Y. Vardi. Optimization of *real* conjunctive queries. *PODS* 1993, 59–70.

[7] R. Chirkova. Equivalence and minimization of conjunctive queries under combined semantics. *ICDT* 2012.

[8] S. Cohen, W. Nutt, Y. Sagiv. Deciding equivalences among conjunctive aggregate queries. *JACM* **54**(2), 2007.

[9] Y. Cui, J. Widom, J.L. Wiener. Tracing the lineage of view data in a warehousing environment. *ACM ToDS* **25**(2), 179–227, 2000.

[10] A. Das Sarma, M. Theobald, J. Widom. Exploiting lineage for confidence computation in uncertain and probabilistic databases. *ICDE* 2008, 1023–1032.

[11] R. Fagin, P.G. Kolaitis, L. Popa, W.C. Tan. Quasi-inverses of schema mappings. *ACM ToDS* **33**(2), 2008.

[12] N. Fuhr, T. Rölleke. A probabilistic relational algebra for the integration of information retrieval and database systems. *ACM ToIS* **15**(1), 32–66, 1997.

[13] G. Grahne, N. Spyratos, D. Stamate. Semantics and containment of queries with internal and external conjunctions. *ICDT* 1997, *LNCS* 1186, 71–82.

[14] T.J. Green. Containment of conjunctive queries on annotated relations. *Th. Comp. Syst.* **49**(2), 429–459, 2011.

[15] T.J. Green, G. Karvounarakis, V. Tannen. Provenance semirings. *PODS* 2007, 31–40.

[16] T. Imieliński, W. Lipski, Jr. Incomplete information in relational databases. *JACM* **31**(4), 761–791, 1984.

[17] Y.E. Ioannidis, R. Ramakrishnan. Containment of conjunctive queries: beyond relations as sets. *ACM ToDS* **20**(3), 1995.

[18] T.S. Jayram, P.G. Kolaitis, E. Vee. The containment problem for *real* conjunctive queries with inequalities. *PODS* 2006.

[19] D. Olteanu, J. Závodný. Factorised representations of query results: size bounds and readability. *ICDT* 2012.

[20] Y. Sagiv, M. Yannakakis. Equivalences among relational expressions with the union and difference operators. *JACM* **27**(4), 633–655, 1980.

[21] E. Zimányi. Query evaluation in probabilistic relational databases. *TCS* **171**(1–2), 179–219, 1997.

[22] A. Zimmermann, N. Lopes, A. Polleres, U. Straccia. A general framework for representing, reasoning and querying with annotated Semantic Web data. *Web Semantics*. In press.

Efficient Approximations of Conjunctive Queries

Pablo Barceló
Department of Computer
Science, Universidad de Chile
pbarcelo@dcc.uchile.cl

Leonid Libkin
School of Informatics,
University of Edinburgh
libkin@inf.ed.ac.uk

Miguel Romero
Department of Computer
Science, Universidad de Chile
miromero@ing.uchile.cl

ABSTRACT

When finding exact answers to a query over a large database is infeasible, it is natural to approximate the query by a more efficient one that comes from a class with good bounds on the complexity of query evaluation. In this paper we study such approximations for conjunctive queries. These queries are of special importance in databases, and we have a very good understanding of the classes that admit fast query evaluation, such as acyclic, or bounded (hyper)treewidth queries.

We define approximations of a given query Q as queries from one of those classes that disagree with Q as little as possible. We mostly concentrate on approximations that are guaranteed to return correct answers. We prove that for the above classes of tractable conjunctive queries, approximations always exist, and are at most polynomial in the size of the original query. This follows from general results we establish that relate closure properties of classes of conjunctive queries to the existence of approximations. We also show that in many cases, the size of approximations is bounded by the size of the query they approximate. We establish a number of results showing how combinatorial properties of queries affect properties of their approximations, study bounds on the number of approximations, as well as the complexity of finding and identifying approximations. We also look at approximations that return all correct answers and study their properties.

Categories and Subject Descriptors. H.2.3 [**Database Management**]: Languages—*Query Languages*; G.2.2 [**Discrete Mathematics**]: *Graph algorithms*

Keywords. Conjunctive queries, query evaluation, query approximation, tractability, acyclic queries, treewidth, hypertree width, graphs, homomorphisms.

1. INTRODUCTION

The idea of finding approximate solutions to problems for which computing exact solutions is impossible or infeasible is ubiquitous in computer science. It is common in databases too: approximate query answering techniques help evaluate queries over extremely large databases or queries with very high inherent complexity, see, e.g., [10, 11, 14, 23, 28]. By analyzing the structure of both the database and the query one often finds a reasonable approximation of the answer, sometimes with performance guarantees. Approximate techniques are relevant even for problems whose complexity is viewed as acceptable for regular-size databases, since finding precise answers may become impossible for large data sets we often deal with these days.

To approximate a query, we must have a good understanding of the complexity of query evaluation, in order to find an approximation that is guaranteed to be efficient. For one very common class of queries – *conjunctive*, or select-project-join queries – we do have a very good understanding of their complexity. In fact, we know which classes of conjunctive queries (CQs from now on) are easy to evaluate [8, 15, 16, 19, 24, 34]. Given the importance of conjunctive queries, and our good understanding of them, we would like to initiate a study of their approximations. We do it from the *static analysis* point of view, i.e., independently of the input database: for a query Q, we want to find another query Q' that will be much faster than Q, and whose output would be close to the output of Q on *all* databases. Such analysis is essential when a query is repeatedly evaluated on a very large database (say, in response to frequent updates), and when producing approximations based on both data and queries may be infeasible.

The complexity of checking whether a tuple $\bar{a}$ belongs to the output of a CQ Q on a database D is of the order $|D|^{O(|Q|)}$, where $|\cdot|$ measures the size (of a database or a query) [3, 33]. In fact, the problem is known to be NP-complete, when its input consists of D as well as Q (even for Boolean CQs). In other words, the *combined complexity* of CQs is intractable [7]. Of course the *data complexity* of CQs is low, but having $O(|Q|)$ as the exponent may be prohibitively high for very large datasets. This observation led to an extensive study of classes of

CQs for which the combined complexity is tractable. The first result of this kind by Yannakakis [34] showed tractability for *acyclic* CQs. That was later extended to queries of *bounded treewidth* [8, 12, 24]; this notion captures tractability for classes of CQs defined in terms of their graphs [19]. For classes of CQs defined in terms of their hypergraphs, the corresponding notion guaranteeing tractability is *bounded hypertree width* [16], which includes acyclicity as a special case. All these conditions can be tested in polynomial time [5, 13, 16].

The question we address is whether we can approximate a CQ Q by a CQ Q' from one of such classes so that Q and Q' would disagree as little as possible. Assume, for example, that we manage to find an approximation of Q by an *acyclic* CQ Q', for which checking whether $\bar{a} \in Q'(D)$ is done in time $O(|D| \cdot |Q'|)$ [34]. Then we replaced the original problem of complexity $|D|^{O(|Q|)}$ with that of complexity

$$O\big(f(|Q|) + |D| \cdot s(|Q|)\big)$$

where $s(\cdot)$ measures the size of the resulting approximation, and $f(\cdot)$ is the complexity of finding one.

Thus, assuming that the complexity measures f and s are acceptable, the combined complexity of running Q' is much better than for Q. Hence, if the quality of the approximation Q is good too, then we may prefer to run the much faster query Q' instead of Q, especially in the case of very large databases. Thus, we need to answer the following questions:

- What are the acceptable bounds for constructing approximations, i.e., the functions f and s above?
- What types of guarantees do we expect from approximations?

For the first question, if Q' is of the same size as Q, or even if it polynomially increases the size, this is completely acceptable, as the exponent $O(|Q|)$ is now replaced by the factor $s(|Q|)$. For the complexity f of static computation (i.e., transforming Q to Q'), a single exponential is typically acceptable. Indeed, this is the norm in many static analysis and verification questions [29, 32], and small exponents (like $2^{O(|Q|)}$ or $2^{O(|Q| \log |Q|)}$ we shall mainly encounter) are significantly smaller than $|D|^{|Q|}$ if $|D|$ is large. Thus, in terms of their complexity, our desiderata for approximations are:

1. the approximating query should be at most polynomially larger than Q – and ideally, bounded by the size of Q; and
2. the complexity of finding an approximating query should not exceed single-exponential.

As for the guarantees we expect from approximations, in general they can be formulated in two different ways. By doing it qualitatively we state that an approximation is a query that cannot be improved in terms of how much it disagrees with the query it approximates. Alternatively, to do it quantitatively, we define a measure of disagreement between two queries, and look for approximations whose measure of disagreement with the query they approximate is below a certain threshold.

Here we develop the qualitative approach to approximating CQs. For a given Q, we compare queries from some good (tractable) class $\mathcal{C}$ by how much they disagree with Q: to do so, we define an ordering $Q_1 \sqsubseteq_Q Q_2$ saying, intuitively, that Q_2 disagrees with Q less often than Q_1 does. Then the best queries with respect to the ordering are our approximations from the class $\mathcal{C}$.

Furthermore, we require the approximations to return correct results. This approach is standard in databases (for instance, the standard approximation of query results in the settings of query answering using views and data integration is the notion of maximally contained rewriting [2, 20, 26]).

Our goal is to explore approximations of arbitrary CQs by tractable CQs. We shall see that approximations are guaranteed to exist for all the tractable classes of CQs mentioned earlier, which makes the notion worth studying.

We first explore CQs on graphs. Even though graph vocabularies often lack enough structure to exhibit interesting approximations, the essential machinery needs to be developed for them first. In addition, most lower bounds for complexity results are witnessed already in this simple case. Then we show how to extend results to queries over arbitrary databases.

The structure of approximations depends heavily on combinatorial properties of the (tableau of the) query Q we approximate. Consider, for instance, a Boolean query $Q_1():\!-E(x,y), E(y,z), E(z,x)$ over graphs. Its best acyclic approximation is $Q_1'():\!-E(x,x)$, which is contained in every Boolean graph query and thus provides us with little information. It turns out that this will be the case whenever the tableau of the query is not a bipartite graph. Let $P_m(x_0, \ldots, x_m)$ be the CQ stating that $x_0, \ldots, x_m$ form a path of length m, i.e., $E(x_0, x_1), \ldots, E(x_{m-1}, x_m)$. If we now look at $Q_2() :\!- P_3(x, y, z, u), P_3(x', y', z', u'), E(x, z'), E(y, u')$ (which has a cycle with variables x, y, z', u'), then it has a nontrivial acyclic approximation $Q_2'():\!-P_4(x', x, y, z, u)$. What changed is that the tableau of Q_2 is bipartite, guaranteeing the existence of nontrivial approximations for queries over graphs.

Going beyond graph vocabularies lets us find more approximations. Consider again Q_1 above, replace binary relation E with a ternary relation R, and introduce fresh variables in the middle positions, i.e., look at the query $Q():\!-R(x, u, y), R(y, v, z), R(z, w, x)$. This query does have several nontrivial acyclic approximations: for instance, $Q'():\!-R(x, u, y), R(y, v, u), R(u, z, x)$ is one.

These examples provides a flavor of the results we establish. We now provide a quick summary of the results of

Class of queries	Type of approximation	Existence of approximation	Size of approximation	Time to compute approximation
Graph queries	Acyclic		at most	
	Treewidth k	always exists	$|Q|$	single-exponential
Arbitrary queries	Acyclic		polynomial in $|Q|$	
	Hypertreewidth k			

Figure 1: Summary of results on approximations for conjunctive queries Q

the paper. As mentioned earlier, we first study queries over graphs and then lift results to arbitrary queries.

Results for graph queries For a query Q, we are interested in approximations Q' from a good class $\mathcal{C}$. The classes we consider are acyclic queries [34] and queries of fixed treewidth k, which capture the notion of tractability of CQs over graphs [19]. The first two rows in Figure 1 summarize some of our results: within both classes, approximations exist for all queries (this will follow from a general existence result that relates closure properties of classes of graphs to the existence of approximations), they do not increase the complexity of the query, and can be constructed in single-exponential time, thus satisfying all our desiderata for approximating queries.

In addition, we study the structure of approximations. We show a close relationship between $(k+1)$-colorability of the tableau and the existence of interesting treewidth-k approximations. For Boolean queries, we prove a finer trichotomy result for acyclic approximations, which also shows that such approximations are guaranteed to reduce the number of joins. We show that there are at most exponentially many non-equivalent approximations, and that the exponential number of approximations can be witnessed.

We provide further complexity analysis, showing that the problem of checking whether Q' is an acyclic (or treewidth-k) approximation of Q is complete for the class DP (this class, defined formally later, is "slightly" above both NP and coNP [31]). DP-completeness results appeared in the database literature in connection with computing cores of structures [9]; our result is of a very different nature because it holds even when both Q and Q' are minimized (i.e., their tableaux are cores).

Finally, we briefly consider approximations that drop the 'no false positives' requirement.

Results for arbitrary queries There are two ways of getting tractable classes of CQs over arbitrary databases, depending on whether one formulates conditions in terms of the *graph* of a query Q, or its *hypergraph*. For graph-based notions, it is known that bounded treewidth characterizes tractability [19]. For them, results for graph queries extend to arbitrary queries.

For hypergraph-based notions, we have the original notion of acyclicity from [34] and its more recent extension to the notion of bounded *hypertree width* [16]; it is known that hypertree width 1 coincides with acyclicity.

We again prove a general existence result for approximations. However, the closure conditions imposed on classes of hypergraphs are becoming more involved, and it actually requires an effort to prove that they hold for classes of bounded hypertree width. We show that it is still possible to find approximations in single exponential time. As for their sizes, they need not be bounded by $|Q|$, but they remain polynomial in $|Q|$, with polynomial depending only on the vocabulary (schema). Thus, as the summary table in Figure 1 shows, in this case too, our desiderata for approximations are met.

Regarding techniques required to prove these results, we mainly work with tableaux of queries, and characterize approximations via preorders based on the existence of homomorphisms. Thus, we make a heavy use of techniques from the theory of graph homomorphisms [21]. Besides graph theory and combinatorics, these are commonly used in constraint satisfaction [25], but recently they were applied in database theory as well [6, 27].

Organization Basic notations are given in Section 2. In Section 3 we define the notion of approximations. Section 4 studies queries over graphs, concentrating on acyclic and bounded treewidth approximations. In Section 5 we look at arbitrary databases, concentrating on acyclic and bounded hypertree width approximations. Overapproximations are studied in Section 6, and conclusions are given in Section 7. Due to space limitations, we only give a couple of sample (short) proofs here.

2. NOTATIONS

Graphs and digraphs Both graphs and digraphs are defined as pairs $G = \langle V, E \rangle$, where V is a set of nodes (vertices) and E is a set of edges. For graphs, an edge is a set $\{u, v\}$, where $u, v \in V$; for digraphs, an edge is a pair (u, v), i.e., it has an orientation from u to v. If $u = v$, we have a (undirected or directed) loop.

If $G = \langle V, E \rangle$ is a directed graph, then G^{u} is the underlying undirected graph: $G^{\mathrm{u}} = \langle V, \{\{u, v\} \mid (u, v) \in E\} \rangle$. We denote by K_m the complete graph on m vertices: $K_m = \langle \{u_1, \ldots, u_m\}, \{\{u_i, u_j\} \mid i \neq j, \ i, j \leq m\} \rangle$, and by $K_m^{\rightleftarrows}$ the complete digraph on m vertices, i.e., $K_m^{\rightleftarrows} = \langle \{u_1, \ldots, u_m\}, \{(u_i, u_j) \mid i \neq j, \ i, j \leq m\} \rangle$, so that edges go in both directions. Note that $(K_m^{\rightleftarrows})^{\mathrm{u}} = K_m$.

Graph homomorphisms and cores Given two graphs (directed or undirected) $G_1 = \langle V_1, E_1 \rangle$ and $G_2 = \langle V_2, E_2 \rangle$, a *homomorphism* between them is a map $h : V_1 \rightarrow V_2$ such that $h(e)$ is in E_2 for every edge $e \in E_1$. Of course by $h(e)$ we mean $\{h(u), h(v)\}$ if $e = \{u, v\}$ and $(h(u), h(v))$ if $e = (u, v)$. The image of h is the (di)graph $\mathrm{Im}(h) = \langle h(V_1), \{h(e) \mid e \in E_1\}\rangle$. If there is a homomorphism h from G_1 to G_2, we write $G_1 \rightarrow G_2$ or $G_1 \xrightarrow{h} G_2$.

A graph G is a *core* if there is no homomorphism $G \rightarrow G'$ into a proper subgraph G' of G. A subgraph G' of G is a *core of* G if G' is a core and $G \rightarrow G'$. It is well known that all cores of a graph are isomorphic and hence we can speak of the core of a graph, denoted by $\mathrm{core}(G)$. We say that two graphs G and G' are *homomorphically equivalent* if both $G \rightarrow G'$ and $G' \rightarrow G$ hold. Homomorphically equivalent graphs have the same core, i.e., $\mathrm{core}(G)$ and $\mathrm{core}(G')$ are isomorphic.

We shall also deal with graphs with distinguished vertices. Let G, G' be (di)graphs and $\bar{u}, \bar{u}'$ tuples of vertices in G and G', respectively, of the same length. Then we write $(G, \bar{u}) \rightarrow (G', \bar{u}')$ if there is a homomorphism $h : G \rightarrow G'$ such that $h(\bar{u}) = \bar{u}'$. With this definition, the notion of core naturally extends to graphs with distinguished vertices.

We write $G \rightleftarrows G'$ if $G \rightarrow G'$, but $G' \rightarrow G$ does not hold.

Databases (relational structures) While the case of graphs is crucial for understanding the main concepts, we shall also state results for conjunctive queries over arbitrary relational structures. A *vocabulary* (often called a *schema* in the database context) is a set σ of relation names $R_1, \ldots, R_l$, each relation R_i having an arity n_i. A *relational structure*, or a *database*, of vocabulary σ is $\mathcal{D} = \langle U, R_1^{\mathcal{D}}, \ldots, R_l^{\mathcal{D}}\rangle$, where U is a finite set, and each $R_i^{\mathcal{D}}$ is an n_i-ary relation over U, i.e., a subset of U^{n_i}. We usually omit the superscript $\mathcal{D}$ if it clear from the context. We also assume (as is normal in database theory) that U is the active domain of $\mathcal{D}$, i.e., the set of all elements that occur in relations $R_i^{\mathcal{D}}$'s.

Both directed and undirected graphs, for example, are relational structures of the vocabulary that contains a single binary relation E. For digraphs, it is the edge relation; for graphs, it contains pairs (u, v) and (v, u) for each edge $\{u, v\}$.

We often deal with databases together with a tuple of distinguished elements, i.e., $(\mathcal{D}, \bar{a})$, where $\bar{a}$ is a k-tuple of elements of the active domain, for some $k > 0$. Technically, these are structures of vocabulary σ expanded with k extra constant symbols, interpreted as $\bar{a}$.

Homomorphisms of structures are defined in the same way as for graphs: for $\mathcal{D}_1 = \langle U_1, (R_i^{\mathcal{D}_1})_{i \leq l}\rangle$ and $\mathcal{D}_2 = \langle U_2, (R_i^{\mathcal{D}_2})_{i \leq l}\rangle$, a homomorphism $h : \mathcal{D}_1 \rightarrow \mathcal{D}_2$ is a map from U_1 to U_2 so that $h(\bar{t}) \in R_i^{\mathcal{D}_2}$ for every n_i-ary tuple $\bar{t} \in R_i^{\mathcal{D}_1}$, for all $i \leq l$. As before, we write $\mathcal{D}_1 \rightarrow \mathcal{D}_2$ in this case. For databases with tuples of distinguished elements we have $(\mathcal{D}_1, \bar{a}_1) \rightarrow (\mathcal{D}_2, \bar{a}_2)$ if the homomorphism h in addition satisfies $h(\bar{a}_1) = \bar{a}_2$.

The notion of a core for relational structures (with distinguished elements) is defined just as for graphs, using homomorphisms of structures.

Conjunctive queries and tableaux A conjunctive query (CQ) over a relational vocabulary σ is a logical formula in the $\exists, \wedge$-fragment of first-order logic, i.e., a formula of the form $Q(\bar{x}) = \exists \bar{y} \bigwedge_{j=1}^{m} R_{i_j}(\bar{x}_{i_j})$, where each R_{i_j} is a symbol from σ, and $\bar{x}_{i_j}$ a tuple of variables among $\bar{x}, \bar{y}$ whose length is the arity of R_{i_j}. These are often written in a rule-based notation

$$Q(\bar{x}) :\!- R_{i_1}(\bar{x}_{i_1}), \ldots, R_{i_m}(\bar{x}_{i_m}). \tag{1}$$

The *number of joins* in the CQ (1) is $m - 1$. Given a database $\mathcal{D}$, the answer $Q(\mathcal{D})$ to Q is $\{\bar{a} \mid \mathcal{D} \models Q(\bar{a})\}$. If Q is a Boolean query (a sentence), the answer *true* is, as usual, modeled by the set containing the empty tuple, and the answer *false* by the empty set.

A CQ Q is *contained* in a CQ Q', written as $Q \subseteq Q'$, if $Q(\mathcal{D}) \subseteq Q'(\mathcal{D})$ for every database $\mathcal{D}$.

With each CQ $Q(\bar{x})$ of the form (1) we associate its *tableau* $(T_Q, \bar{x})$, where T_Q is the body of Q viewed as a σ-database; i.e., it contains tuples $\bar{x}_{i_j}$'s in relations R_{i_j}'s, for $j \leq m$. If Q is a Boolean CQ, then its tableau is just the σ-structure T_Q.

Many key properties of CQs can be stated in terms of homomorphisms of tableaux. For example, $\bar{a} \in Q(\mathcal{D})$ iff $(T_Q, \bar{x}) \rightarrow (\mathcal{D}, \bar{a})$. For CQs $Q(\bar{x})$ and $Q'(\bar{x}')$ with the same number of free variables, $Q \subseteq Q'$ iff $(T_{Q'}, \bar{x}') \rightarrow (T_Q, \bar{x})$. Hence, the combined complexity of CQ evaluation and the complexity of CQ containment are in NP (in fact, both are NP-complete [7]).

3. THE NOTION OF APPROXIMATION

We now explain the main idea of approximations. Suppose $\mathcal{C}$ is a class of conjunctive queries (e.g., acyclic, or of bounded treewidth). We are given a query Q not in this class, and we want to approximate it within $\mathcal{C}$. For that, we define an ordering $\sqsubseteq_Q$ on queries in $\mathcal{C}$: the meaning of $Q_1 \sqsubseteq_Q Q_2$ is that "Q_2 approximates Q better than Q_1 does", i.e., Q_2 agrees with Q more often than Q_1. Then we look for maximal elements with respect to $\sqsubseteq_Q$ as good approximations of Q. As explained earlier, we typically are interested in queries that are guaranteed to return correct results.

We now formalize this. For queries $Q(\bar{x})$ and $Q'(\bar{x}')$, a database $\mathcal{D}$ and a tuple $\bar{a}$, we say that Q *agrees with* Q' on $(\mathcal{D}, \bar{a})$ if either $\bar{a}$ belongs to both $Q(\mathcal{D})$ and $Q'(\mathcal{D})$, or to none of them. Then, for CQs $Q(\bar{x}), Q_1(\bar{x}_1), Q_2(\bar{x}_2)$, with $\bar{x}, \bar{x}_1, \bar{x}_2$ of the same length, we define

$$Q_1 \sqsubseteq_Q Q_2 \stackrel{\text{def}}{=} \forall (\mathcal{D}, \bar{a}) \left(\begin{array}{c} Q_1 \text{ agrees with } Q \text{ on } (\mathcal{D}, \bar{a}) \\ \Downarrow \\ Q_2 \text{ agrees with } Q \text{ on } (\mathcal{D}, \bar{a}) \end{array} \right)$$

That is, Q_2 approximates Q at least as well as Q_1

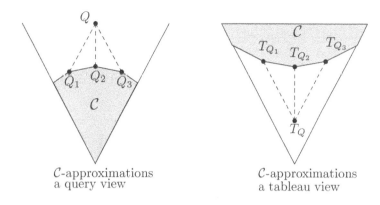

$\mathcal{C}$-approximations $\mathcal{C}$-approximations
a query view   a tableau view

Figure 2: $\mathcal{C}$**-approximations: an illustration**

does. Then Q_2 approximates Q better than Q_1 does if $Q_1 \sqsubset_Q Q_2$, i.e., $Q_1 \sqsubseteq_Q Q_2$ and $Q_2 \not\sqsubseteq_Q Q_1$.

Definition 3.1. (Approximations) *Given a class $\mathcal{C}$ of CQs and a query Q, a query $Q' \in \mathcal{C}$ such that $Q' \subseteq Q$ is a $\mathcal{C}$-approximation of Q if there is no query $Q'' \in \mathcal{C}$ with $Q'' \subseteq Q$ such that $Q' \sqsubset_Q Q''$.*

In other words, Q' is an approximation of Q if it is guaranteed to return correct results and no other query approximates Q better than Q'.

We next show that the use of the ordering $\sqsubseteq_Q$ in the definition can be replaced by a containment test:

Proposition 3.2. *Given a CQ $Q(\bar{x})$ and a CQ $Q'(\bar{x}') \in \mathcal{C}$ with the same number of free variables, the following are equivalent:*

1. *Q' is a $\mathcal{C}$-approximation of Q;*

2. *$Q' \subseteq Q$, and there is no $Q'' \in \mathcal{C}$ such that $Q' \subset Q'' \subseteq Q$;*

3. *$(T_Q, \bar{x}) \to (T_{Q'}, \bar{x}')$, and there is no $Q''(\bar{x}'') \in \mathcal{C}$ such that $(T_Q, \bar{x}) \to (T_{Q''}, \bar{x}'') \rightleftarrows (T_{Q'}, \bar{x}')$.*

Before describing the classes in which we shall try to approximate CQs, we present a useful view of approximations via orderings on queries and tableaux.

Approximations via ordering Both CQs and their tableaux come naturally equipped with two preorders: containment of CQs, and the existence of homomorphisms between tableaux. These preorders are dual to each other [7]: $Q \subseteq Q' \Leftrightarrow T_{Q'} \to T_Q$. These relations are reflexive and transitive but not antisymmetric (as we may have different equivalent queries), hence they are preorders. They become partial orders when restricted to cores, or minimized CQs. Indeed, if both $T_{Q'} \to T_Q$ and $T_Q \to T_{Q'}$ hold, then $T_{Q'}$ and T_Q are homomorphically equivalent and thus have the same core (which happens to be the tableau of the minimized version of Q). The preorder $\to$ and its restriction to cores have been actively studied over graphs, digraphs, and relational structures [21], and we shall heavily use their properties in our proofs.

With this view, we can visualize the result of Proposition 3.2 as shown in Fig. 2. The $\mathcal{C}$-approximations of Q are the "closest" elements of class $\mathcal{C}$ that are below Q in the $\subseteq$ ordering. If we switch to the tableau view, then approximations are the closest elements of $\mathcal{C}$ which are above the tableau of Q in the $\to$ ordering.

Good classes of queries We look for approximations within tractable classes of CQs, which include acyclic queries, as well as queries of bounded treewidth and hypertree width [8, 12, 16, 19, 24, 34]. We now define the first two (hypertree width is defined in Section 5).

We first need the notion of tree decompositions of hypergraphs of queries. Recall that a hypergraph $\mathcal{H} = \langle V, \mathcal{E} \rangle$ has a set of vertices V and a set of hyperedges $\mathcal{E}$; each hyperedge is a subset of V. For a CQ Q, its hypergraph $\mathcal{H}(Q)$ has all the variables used in Q as vertices; the hyperedges are sets of variables that appear in the same atom. For example, for the query with the body $R(x, y, z), R(x, v, v), E(v, z)$, the hyperedges are $\{x, y, z\}$, $\{x, v\}$, and $\{v, z\}$.

A *tree decomposition* of a hypergraph $\mathcal{H} = \langle V, \mathcal{E} \rangle$ is a tree T together with a map $f : T \to 2^V$ that associates a set of vertices in V with each node of T such that

1. each hyperedge from $\mathcal{E}$ is contained in one of the sets $f(u)$ for $u \in T$; and

2. for every $v \in V$, the set $\{u \in T \mid v \in f(u)\}$ is a connected subset of T.

The *width* of a decomposition is $\max_{u \in T} |f(u)| - 1$, and the *treewidth* of $\mathcal{H}$ is the minimum width of its tree decompositions. If $\mathcal{H}$ is a tree (or a forest) to start with, then its treewidth is 1. We refer to the classes of hypergraphs of treewidth at most k as $\mathsf{TW}(k)$, and, slightly abusing notation, we use $\mathsf{TW}(k)$ to also denote the classes of CQs (and their tableaux) whose hypergraphs have treewidth at most k.

A hypergraph is *acyclic* if there is a tree decomposition (T, f) of it such that every $f(u)$ is a hyperedge. A CQ is acyclic if its hypergraph is acyclic. We use

AC to denote the class of acyclic hypergraphs (and also acyclic CQs, and their tableaux). For queries over graphs, we have $\mathsf{AC} = \mathsf{TW}(1)$. In general the notions of bounded treewidth and acyclicity are incompatible (see, e.g., [12]).

Remark The notion of approximation is based on the semantics of queries, while the good classes are defined purely by syntactic means. It may happen that a query Q not from a good class $\mathcal{C}$ is equivalent to some query Q' from $\mathcal{C}$. In that case, $\mathcal{C}$-approximations of Q are simply equivalent to Q.

4. APPROXIMATING QUERIES OVER GRAPHS

In this section we look at queries over graphs. That is, the vocabulary σ has a single binary relation $E(\cdot, \cdot)$, interpreted as a directed graph. Given a CQ $Q(\bar{x})$, its tableau $(T_Q, \bar{x})$ is a digraph as well, with a distinguished tuple of elements $\bar{x}$. Thus, we shall define classes of queries in terms of classes $\mathcal{C}$ of graphs: a CQ Q is a $\mathcal{C}$-query iff the graph T_Q is in $\mathcal{C}$.

The standard tractable classes of acyclic CQs and treewidth-k CQs do arise in this way (we shall explain this shortly). But first we prove a very general result on the existence of approximations, which shows good behavior of those for many classes of queries.

Theorem 4.1. *Let $\mathcal{C}$ be a class of graphs closed under taking subgraphs. Then every CQ Q that has at least one $\mathcal{C}$-query contained in it also has a $\mathcal{C}$-approximation.*

Moreover, the number of non-equivalent $\mathcal{C}$-approximations of Q is at most exponential in the size of Q, and every $\mathcal{C}$-approximation of Q is equivalent to one which has at most as many joins as Q.

We give a simple proof to illustrate why techniques based on the homomorphism orderings are useful to us.

Proof. Given $Q(\bar{x})$ which is not a $\mathcal{C}$-query, let $H^{\mathcal{C}}(Q)$ be the set of all $\mathcal{C}$-queries whose tableaux are of the form $(\mathrm{Im}(h), h(\bar{x}))$, where h is a homomorphism defined on $(T_Q, \bar{x})$. All such queries are contained in Q. Up to equivalence (renaming of variables) there are finitely many elements in $H^{\mathcal{C}}(Q)$. Moreover, it is nonempty. Indeed, there is a $\mathcal{C}$-query $Q'(\bar{x}')$ with $Q' \subseteq Q$ and hence $(T_Q, \bar{x}) \xrightarrow{h} (T'_Q, \bar{x}')$ for some h (thus $h(\bar{x}) = \bar{x}'$). By the closure under subgraphs we know that $(\mathrm{Im}(h), \bar{x}')$ is a tableau of a $\mathcal{C}$-query. Now consider minimal elements, with respect to the preorder $\rightarrow$, in the set $H^{\mathcal{C}}(Q)$. We claim that they are $\mathcal{C}$-approximations of Q. Indeed let $(\mathrm{Im}(h_0), \bar{x}')$ be one such element, with $\bar{x}' = h_0(\bar{x})$. If it is not a $\mathcal{C}$-approximation, then we have $(T_Q, \bar{x}) \xrightarrow{g} (T, \bar{x}'') \xrightarrow{g_1} (\mathrm{Im}(h_0), \bar{x}')$ for some homomorphisms g and g_1 such that $(\mathrm{Im}(h_0), \bar{x}') \not\rightarrow (T, \bar{x}'')$, with $T \in \mathcal{C}$. Hence we have $(T_Q, \bar{x}) \xrightarrow{g} (\mathrm{Im}(g), \bar{x}'') \xrightarrow{g_1} (\mathrm{Im}(h_0), \bar{x}')$, as well as

$(\mathrm{Im}(h_0), \bar{x}') \not\rightarrow (\mathrm{Im}(g), \bar{x}'')$, and $\mathrm{Im}(g)$ is in $\mathcal{C}$ since $\mathcal{C}$ is closed under taking subgraphs. Hence $(\mathrm{Im}(g), \bar{x}'')$ is in $H^{\mathcal{C}}(Q)$, and by the minimality of $(\mathrm{Im}(h_0), \bar{x}')$ we conclude that it is equivalent to $(\mathrm{Im}(g), \bar{x}'')$, and thus is a $\mathcal{C}$-approximation.

If $Q'(\bar{x}')$ is a $\mathcal{C}$-approximation, then $(T_Q, \bar{x}) \xrightarrow{h} (T_{Q'}, \bar{x}')$ and thus $(T_Q, \bar{x}) \xrightarrow{h} (\mathrm{Im}(h), \bar{x}')$, with $\mathrm{Im}(h)$ being a subgraph of $T_{Q'}$, and thus in $\mathcal{C}$. By Proposition 3.2 this implies that $(\mathrm{Im}(h), \bar{x}')$ and $(T_{Q'}, \bar{x}')$ are homomorphically equivalent, and $(\mathrm{Im}(h), \bar{x}')$ is a $\mathcal{C}$-approximation equivalent to Q'. Hence, all $\mathcal{C}$-approximations can be chosen to be of the form $(\mathrm{Im}(h), \bar{x}')$, which shows that there are at most exponentially many of them, and that they need not have more joins than Q. □

Approximations for acyclic and treewidth-k queries We now explain how acyclic graph queries and treewidth-k graph queries appear as $\mathcal{C}$-queries for appropriately chosen classes $\mathcal{C}$. An undirected graph can be viewed as a hypergraph (in which all hyperedges are of cardinality 1 or 2), and thus a graph query Q is acyclic, or of treewidth-k, if T_Q^{u}, the underlying graph of its tableau, is acyclic (as a hypergraph), or has treewidth at most k. We still refer to these as AC and $\mathsf{TW}(k)$. Notice that acyclicity is not the graph acyclicity since loops are allowed: for instance, the undirected graph with an edge between nodes x and y and a loop on x is acyclic, since the hypergraph with hyperedges $\{x, y\}$ and $\{x\}$ is acyclic. Also we formulate these conditions in terms of undirected graphs: for instance, the query $Q() \colon\!- E(x, y), E(y, x)$ is acyclic, since T_Q^{u} contains a single edge between x and y. Basically, acyclicity disallows cycles of length 3 or more.

There is a *trivial* query that belongs to AC and all $\mathsf{TW}(k)$'s that every other CQ Q contains. Indeed, let $K_1^{\circlearrowleft}$ be a single-element loop, i.e., a graph with a single node x and a loop (x, x) on that node. Then, for each query $Q(\bar{x})$ with m free variables, we have, via a constant homomorphism: $(T_Q, \bar{x}) \rightarrow (K_1^{\circlearrowleft}, (x, \ldots, x))$, and thus $Q'(x, \ldots, x) \colon\!- E(x, x)$ is contained in Q.

This, together with the closure of AC and $\mathsf{TW}(k)$ under taking subgraphs, gives us:

Corollary 4.2. *Every CQ Q over graphs has an acyclic approximation, as well as a treewidth-k approximation, for each $k > 0$.*

Size and number of approximations Let $\mathcal{C}$-APPR(Q) be the set of all $\mathcal{C}$-approximations of Q. For example, AC-APPR(Q) is the class of acyclic approximations of Q. These sets are nonempty when $\mathcal{C}$ is AC or $\mathsf{TW}(k)$. They are infinite, but for a simple reason: each CQ has infinitely many equivalent CQs.

It is well known though [7] that each CQ $Q(\bar{x})$ has a unique (up to renaming of variables) equivalent minimal query: in fact, this is the query whose tableau is $\mathrm{core}(T_Q, \bar{x})$. It is obtained by the standard process of minimization of CQs. We thus denote by $\mathcal{C}\text{-APPR}_{\min}(Q)$ the set of all minimizations of $\mathcal{C}$-approximations of Q.

From Corollary 4.2 and Theorem 4.1 we obtain:

Corollary 4.3. *For every CQ Q, both $\text{AC-APPR}_{\min}(Q)$ and $\text{TW}(k)\text{-APPR}_{\min}(Q)$ are finite nonempty sets of queries. The number of queries in those sets is at most exponential in the size of Q, and each one has at most as many joins as Q. Moreover, a query from $\text{AC-APPR}_{\min}(Q)$ or $\text{TW}(k)\text{-APPR}_{\min}(Q)$ can be constructed in single-exponential time in $|Q|$.*

Hence, acyclic and treewidth-k approximations fulfill the criteria from the introduction: they always exist, they are not more complex than the original query, and they can be found with reasonable complexity.

Note that the exponential bound in Corollary 4.3 is not due to the minimization procedure which actually happens to be polynomial for queries of fixed treewidth. In general, there is a simple algorithm for finding approximations that just checks homomorphisms on T_Q and selects one whose image is minimal with respect to $\to$; it runs in time $2^{O(n \cdot \log n)}$, where n is the number of variables in Q. We shall discuss the complexity in more detail in Subsection 4.1.1.

As for the number of elements of $\mathcal{C}\text{-APPR}_{\min}(Q)$, a simple upper bound is $2^{n \cdot \log n}$ (a better bound is the nth Bell number [4]). This raises the question whether the exponential number of approximating queries can be witnessed. We prove that this is the case.

Proposition 4.4. *There is a family $(Q_n)_{n>0}$ of Boolean CQs over graphs such that the number of variables and joins in Q_n's grows linearly with n, and $|\text{AC-APPR}_{\min}(Q_n)| \geq 2^n$ for all $n > 0$.*

4.1 Acyclic approximations

We now study acyclic approximations in more detail. We begin with the case of Boolean queries, when the tableau of a query is just a graph, and show a trichotomy theorem for them, classifying approximations based on graph-theoretic properties of the tableau. Then we extend results to arbitrary queries. After that we study the complexity of acyclic approximations.

Boolean queries These queries are of the form $Q():\text{--} \ldots$ and thus produce yes/no answers; their tableaux are simply directed graphs T_Q. We already talked about them in the introduction, and mentioned that for nontrivial approximations, the tableau must be *bipartite*. Recall that a digraph G is bipartite if $G \to K_2^{\rightleftarrows}$, i.e., G is 2-colorable: its nodes can be split into two disjoint subsets A and B so that all edges have endpoints in different subsets.

Recall the example from the introduction: the cyclic query $Q_1():\text{--}E(x,y), E(y,z), E(z,x)$ had a *trivial*

acyclic approximation $Q^{\text{triv}}():\text{--}E(x,x)$ (which is contained in every Boolean graph query). The reason for that was T_{Q_1} was not bipartite. In the introduction, we saw an example of a query with a bipartite tableaux that had a nontrivial approximation stating the existence of a path of length 4. Note that every query whose tableau is bipartite will contain the *trivial bipartite* query $Q_2^{\text{triv}}():\text{--}E(x,y), E(y,x)$, whose tableau is $K_2^{\rightleftarrows}$. For some cyclic queries, e.g., $Q_3():\text{--}E(x,y), E(y,z), E(z,u), E(x,u)$, this trivial query is the only acyclic approximation. This behavior is caused by the cycle being unbalanced. We next define this concept [21], and then state the trichotomy result.

An *oriented cycle* is a digraph with vertices $u_1, \ldots, u_n$ and n edges such that either (u_i, u_{i+1}) or (u_{i+1}, u_i) is an edge, for each $i < n$, and either (u_1, u_n) or (u_n, u_1) is an edge. We shall refer to edges (u_i, u_{i+1}) and (u_n, u_1) as *forward edges* and to edges (u_{i+1}, u_i) and (u_1, u_n) as *backward edges*. An oriented cycle is *balanced* if the number of forward edges equals the number of backward edges, and a digraph is balanced if every oriented cycle in it is balanced.

Theorem 4.5. *Let Q be a Boolean CQ over graphs. Then, if its tableau T_Q:*

- *is not bipartite, then Q has only the trivial acyclic approximation Q^{triv};*

- *is bipartite but not balanced, then Q's only acyclic approximation is the trivial bipartite query Q_2^{triv};*

- *is bipartite and balanced, then none of Q's acyclic approximations is trivial, and none contains two subgoals of the form $E(x,y), E(y,x)$.*

Of course when we talk about the only approximation, we mean it up to query equivalence. Note that the conditions used in the theorem – being bipartite and balanced – can be checked in polynomial time [21, 35].

Proof sketch. Suppose the tableau T_Q is not bipartite and let Q' be an acyclic approximation of Q. If $T_{Q'}$ has no loops then, by acyclicity, it is bipartite; hence $T_Q \to T_{Q'} \to K_2^{\rightleftarrows}$, which contradicts bipartiteness of T_Q. Hence $T_{Q'}$ has a loop, and Q' is equivalent to Q^{triv}.

Let T_Q be bipartite and not balanced, and let Q' be an acyclic approximation of Q. We prove that $T_{Q'}$ is homomorphically equivalent to $K_2^{\rightleftarrows}$. Note that $T_{Q'}$ has no loops: otherwise $T_Q \to K_2^{\rightleftarrows} \rightleftarrows T_{Q'}$, and Q' is not an approximation. Thus, $T_{Q'}$ is bipartite and $T_{Q'} \to K_2^{\rightleftarrows}$. For the converse, assume $K_2^{\rightleftarrows} \not\to T_{Q'}$. Then $K_2^{\rightleftarrows}$ is not subgraph of $T_{Q'}$. Since Q' is acyclic, this implies that $T_{Q'}$ is balanced, and it is easy to see that $T_Q \to T_{Q'}$ implies that T_Q is balanced too, which is a contradiction.

Finally, let T_Q be balanced (and hence bipartite), and let Q' be an acyclic approximation of Q. As above, we see that Q' is not equivalent to the trivial CQ. We now prove that $K_2^{\rightleftarrows}$ is not a subgraph of $T_{Q'}$, implying the result. Assume otherwise; since T_Q is balanced, we can easily show that $T_Q \to \vec{P}_k$ (a path of length k) for some k. Since $\vec{P}_k \rightleftarrows K_2^{\rightleftarrows}$, we have $T_Q \to \vec{P}_k \rightleftarrows T_{Q'}$, which contradicts the minimality of $T_{Q'}$. □

Corollary 4.6. *Let Q be a Boolean cyclic CQ over graphs. Then all minimized acyclic approximations of Q have strictly fewer joins than Q.*

Theorem 4.5 says that the most interesting case, for graph queries, is when the tableau is bipartite and balanced (as we already mentioned in the introduction, for relations of higher arity, such restrictions need not be imposed). A natural question is whether CQs with such tableaux are still intractable (i.e., whether it still makes sense to approximate them). We prove that this is the case.

Proposition 4.7. *The combined complexity of evaluating Boolean CQs over graphs whose tableaux are bipartite and balanced is NP-complete.*

We conclude our investigation of Boolean CQs with a remark on a subclass of acyclic approximations with special properties. A query Q' is a *tight $\mathcal{C}$-approximation* of Q if it is a $\mathcal{C}$-approximation of Q and there is no query Q'' such that $Q' \subset Q'' \subset Q$. It is not clear a priori whether, and for which classes $\mathcal{C}$, such approximations exist. The results of [30] (reformulated in terms of tableaux of queries) imply that if a tight $\mathcal{C}$-approximation Q' of a query Q is minimized and connected, then Q' is acyclic. Hence, tightness forces the approximating query to be acyclic. The next question is whether acyclic tight approximations exist. We can show that this is the case.

Proposition 4.8. *There is an infinite family of nonequivalent Boolean CQs Q_n, Q'_n, for $n > 0$, so that Q'_n is a tight acyclic approximation of Q_n.*

Example 4.9. Consider a Boolean query Q whose tableau is the graph below, in which number k above an edge represents a path of length k:

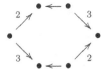

This graph is bipartite and balanced, so Theorem 4.5 tells us that is has nontrivial acyclic approximations. In fact it can be shown that Q has a unique (up to equivalence) acyclic approximation Q', whose tableau is the path of length 4 (i.e., the query $Q'():-P_4(x, y, u, z, v)$ mentioned in the Introduction).

The same Q' serves as a tight acyclic approximation to the query whose tableau is:

This is exactly the query Q_2 from the Introduction, for which, as stated there, Q' is an acyclic approximation.

Non-Boolean queries For CQs with free variables, it is still true that those whose tableaux are bipartite have nontrivial acyclic approximations. However, now some queries with non-bipartite tableaux may have approximations whose bodies do not trivialize to just $E(x, x)$. For example, consider a query $Q(x, y):-E(x, y), E(y, z), E(z, x)$. It can be shown easily that $Q'(x, y):-E(x, y), E(y, x), E(x, x)$ is an acyclic approximation of it; the tableau of Q' is $K_2^{\rightleftarrows}$ with a loop on one of the nodes (recall that the definition of query acyclicity refers to tree decompositions of the query hypergraphs, so Q' is indeed acyclic).

What distinguishes the case of bipartite tableaux now when we look at queries with free variables is that they do not have subgoals of the form $E(x, x)$ in approximations. That is, we have the following dichotomy:

Theorem 4.10. *Let $Q(\bar{x})$ be a cyclic CQ over graphs. If its tableau T_Q*

- *is not bipartite, then all of Q's acyclic approximations have a subgoal of the form $E(x, x)$.*

- *is bipartite, then Q has an acyclic approximation without a subgoal of the form $E(x, x)$.*

The reason we do not have a trichotomy here (as in Theorem 4.5) is that there are examples of non-Boolean queries $Q(\bar{x})$ such that T_Q is bipartite but not balanced, and tableaux of all its acyclic approximations Q' are different from $K_2^{\rightleftarrows}$.

For Boolean queries we saw that acyclic approximations also have strictly fewer joins than Q. With free variables, the number of joins may sometimes be the same as for Q itself.

Proposition 4.11. *There is a non-Boolean cyclic CQ over graphs such that all of its minimized acyclic approximations have exactly as many joins as Q.*

4.1.1 Complexity

We have seen that a (minimized) acyclic approximation can be found in single-exponential time. Of course this is expected given NP-hardness of most static analysis tasks related to CQs. To do a more detailed analysis of complexity, we formulate it as the following decision problem:

PROBLEM:	ACYCLIC APPROXIMATION
INPUT:	a cyclic CQ Q, an acyclic CQ Q'.
QUESTION:	Is Q' an acyclic approximation of Q?

To solve ACYCLIC APPROXIMATION, we need to check two things:

1. $Q' \subseteq Q$; and

2. there is no acyclic Q'' such that $Q' \subset Q'' \subseteq Q$.

The first subproblem is solvable in NP. Checking whether there is an acyclic query Q'' not equivalent to Q' with $Q' \subseteq Q'' \subseteq Q$ is solvable in NP too. This means $T_Q \to T_{Q''} \not\rightleftarrows T_{Q'}$ and hence such Q'', if it exists can always be chosen not to exceed the size of Q. Therefore, one can guess $T_{Q''}$ and all homomorphisms in NP. Furthermore, since both $T_{Q''}$ and $T_{Q'}$ are acyclic, checking that $T_{Q'} \not\to T_{Q''}$ can be done in polynomial time. Thus, the second subproblem is solvable in coNP.

Hence, to solve ACYCLIC APPROXIMATION, we need to solve an NP subproblem and a coNP subproblem. This means that the problem is in complexity class DP: this is the class of problems (languages) which are intersections of an NP language and a coNP language [31]. It turns out that the problem is also hard for the class.

Theorem 4.12. *The problem* ACYCLIC APPROXIMATION *is* DP-*complete. It remains* DP-*complete even if Q' is fixed and both Q and Q' are Boolean and minimized (i.e., their tableaux are cores).*

DP-completeness appeared in database literature in connections with cores: checking whether $G' = \mathrm{core}(G)$, for two graphs G and G', is known to be DP-complete [9]. The source of DP-completeness in our case is completely different, as hardness applies even if the tableaux of queries are cores to start with, and the proof, which is quite involved, uses techniques different from those in [9].

4.2 Bounded treewidth queries

We have already seen that treewidth-k approximations of a CQ Q always exist, that they cannot exceed the size of Q, and can be constructed in single-exponential time. There is an analog of the dichotomy for acyclic queries, in which bipartiteness (i.e., being 2-colorable) is replaced by $(k+1)$-colorability for $\mathsf{TW}(k)$.

Theorem 4.13. *Let Q be a CQ over graphs. If its tableau T_Q*

- *is not $(k+1)$-colorable, then all of its $\mathsf{TW}(k)$-approximations have a subgoal of the form $E(x,x)$;*
- *is $(k+1)$-colorable, then Q has a $\mathsf{TW}(k)$-approximation without a subgoal of the form $E(x,x)$.*

Recall that a Boolean CQ $Q^{\mathrm{triv}}():-E(x,x)$ is a trivial (acyclic, or treewidth-k) approximation of every Boolean CQ. In the acyclic case, 2-colorability (or bipartiteness) of T_Q was equivalent to the existence of nontrivial approximations. This result extends to treewidth-k.

Corollary 4.14. *A Boolean CQ Q over graphs has a nontrivial $\mathsf{TW}(k)$-approximation iff its tableau T_Q is $(k+1)$-colorable.*

Note the big difference in the complexity of testing for the existence of nontrivial approximations: while it is in PTIME in the acyclic case, the problem is already NP-complete for $\mathsf{TW}(2)$.

If a Boolean CQ Q has a nontrivial $\mathsf{TW}(k)$-approximation, then the query Q_{k+1}^{triv} with the tableau $K_{k+1}^{\rightleftarrows}$ is contained in Q. For $k=1$, we had a necessary and sufficient condition for such a query to be an approximation (it was the PTIME-testable condition of not being balanced, see Theorem 4.5). For $\mathsf{TW}(k)$, we do not have such a characterization, but we do know that even for $\mathsf{TW}(2)$, the criterion will be much harder than for the acyclic case due to the following.

Proposition 4.15. *For every $k > 1$, testing, for a Boolean CQ Q over graphs, whether Q_{k+1}^{triv} is a $\mathsf{TW}(k)$-approximation of Q is NP-hard.*

Thus, while the behavior of acyclic and treewidth-k approximations for $k > 1$ is in general similar, testing conditions that guarantee certain properties of approximations is harder even for treewidth-2, compared to the acyclic case.

Finally, we note that the analog of the ACYCLIC APPROXIMATION problem for treewidth k (i.e., checking if Q' is a $\mathsf{TW}(k)$-approximation of Q) remains DP-complete for all $k \geq 1$. Indeed, the proof of the upper bound for the acyclic case applies to bounded treewidth, and the lower bound is already established for $k=1$.

5. APPROXIMATING ARBITRARY QUERIES

We now switch to queries over arbitrary vocabularies. For them, tractability restrictions could be either *graph-based* and *hypergraph-based*. For the graph-based notions, one deals with the graph of query Q, denoted by $G(Q)$. The nodes of $G(Q)$ are variables used in Q. If there is an atom $R(x_1, \ldots, x_n)$ in Q, then $G(Q)$ has undirected edges $\{x_i, x_j\}$ for all $1 \leq i < j \leq n$. Note that for graph queries, we have $G(Q) = T_Q^{\mathrm{u}}$.

For hypergraph-based notions, we put restrictions on the hypergraph $\mathcal{H}(Q)$ of Q. Recall that its nodes again are variables used in Q, and its hyperedges correspond to the atoms of Q, i.e., for each atom $R(x_1, \ldots, x_n)$ in Q, we have a hyperedge $\{x_1, \ldots, x_n\}$.

Restrictions on queries are imposed as follows. If $\mathcal{C}$ is a class of graphs, or hypergraphs, then a query Q is

- a *graph-based $\mathcal{C}$-query* if $G(Q) \in \mathcal{C}$, and
- a *hypergraph-based $\mathcal{C}$-query* if $\mathcal{H}(Q) \in \mathcal{C}$.

In general, these are incompatible: there are graph-based classes that are not hypergraph-based, and vice versa [12].

5.1 Graph-based classes

For graph-based queries, it is easy to transfer results from queries over graphs to queries over arbitrary schemas. We state the result below only for the classes of tractable graph-based queries, but a general existence theorem, extending Theorem 4.1, is true as well.

Tractability of CQ answering with respect to graph-based classes of queries was fully characterized in [19] (under a certain complexity-theoretic assumption): given a class $\mathcal{C}$, query answering for graph-based $\mathcal{C}$-queries is tractable iff $\mathcal{C} \subseteq \mathsf{TW}(k)$ for some k.

We call a CQ Q' a *graph-based $\mathcal{C}$-approximation* of Q if it is an approximation of Q in the class of graph-based $\mathcal{C}$-queries. Then we have an analog of the existence of approximation results from Section 4.

Theorem 5.1. *Every CQ Q has a graph-based $\mathsf{TW}(k)$-approximation, for every $k \geq 1$, with at most as many joins as Q. Moreover, such an approximation can be found in single-exponential time.*

5.2 Hypergraph-based classes

We now look at *hypergraph-based $\mathcal{C}$-approximations*, i.e., approximations in the class of hypergraph-based $\mathcal{C}$ queries.

The oldest tractability criterion for CQs, acyclicity [34], is a hypergraph-based notion (see the definition in Section 3). An analog of bounded treewidth for hypergraphs was defined in [16]; that notion of bounded *hypertree width* properly extended acyclicity and led to tractable classes of CQs over arbitrary vocabularies.

Our first goal, therefore, is to have a general result about the existence of approximations that will apply to both acyclicity and bounded hypertree width (to be defined formally shortly).

Note we cannot trivially lift the closure condition used in Theorem 4.1 for hypergraphs, since even acyclic hypergraphs are not closed under taking subhypergraphs. Indeed, take a hypergraph $\mathcal{H}$ with hyperedges $\{a, b, c\}, \{a, b\}, \{b, c\}, \{a, c\}$. It is acyclic: the decomposition has $\{a, b, c\}$ associated with the root of the tree, and two-element edges with the children of the root. However, it has cyclic subhypergraphs, for instance, one that contains its two-element edges.

The closure conditions we use instead are:

- *Closure under induced subhypergraphs.* If $\mathcal{H} = \langle V, \mathcal{E} \rangle$ is in $\mathcal{C}$ and $\mathcal{H}'$ is an induced subhypergraph, then $\mathcal{H}' \in \mathcal{C}$. Recall that an induced subhypergraph is one of the form $\langle V', \{e \cap V' \mid e \in \mathcal{E}\}\rangle$.

- *Closure under edge extensions:* if $\mathcal{H} = \langle V, \mathcal{E} \rangle$ is in $\mathcal{C}$ and $\mathcal{H}'$ is obtained by adding new vertices V' to one hyperedge $e \in \mathcal{E}$, where V' is disjoint from V, then $\mathcal{H}' \in \mathcal{C}$.

We shall see that these will be satisfied by the classes of hypergraphs of interest to us. The analog of the previous existence results can now be stated as follows.

Theorem 5.2. *Let $\mathcal{C}$ be a class of hypergraphs closed under induced subhypergraphs and edge extensions. Then every CQ Q that has at least one hypergraph-based $\mathcal{C}$-query contained in it, has a hypergraph-based $\mathcal{C}$-approximation.*

Moreover, the number of non-equivalent hypergraph based $\mathcal{C}$-approximations of Q is at most exponential in the size of Q, and every such approximation is equivalent to one which has at most $O(n^{m-1})$ variables and at most $O(n^m)$ joins, where n is the number of variables in Q, and m is the maximum arity of a relation in the vocabulary.

It is straightforward to check that the class of acyclic hypergraphs satisfies both closure conditions, and that any constant homomorphism on a query Q produces an acyclic query. Thus,

Corollary 5.3. *For every vocabulary σ, there exist two polynomials p_σ and r_σ such that every CQ Q over σ has a hypergraph-based acyclic approximation of size at most $p_\sigma(|Q|)$ that can be found in time $2^{r_\sigma(|Q|)}$.*

Next, we extend these results to hypertree width. First we recall the definitions [16]. A *hypertree decomposition* of a hypergraph $\mathcal{H} = \langle V, \mathcal{E} \rangle$ is a triple $\langle T, f, c \rangle$, where T is a rooted tree, f is a map from T to 2^V and c is a map from T to $2^{\mathcal{E}}$, such that

- (T, f) is a tree decomposition of $\mathcal{H}$.
- $f(u) \subseteq \bigcup c(u)$ holds for every $u \in T$.
- $\bigcup c(u) \cap \bigcup\{f(t) \mid t \in T_u\} \subseteq f(u)$ holds for every $u \in T$, where T_u refers to the subtree of T rooted at u.

The *width* of a hypertree decomposition $\langle T, f, c \rangle$ is $\max_{u \in T} |c(u)|$. The *hypertree width* $hw(\mathcal{H})$ of $\mathcal{H}$ is the minimum width over all its hypertree decompositions. We denote by $\mathsf{HTW}(k)$ the class of hypergraphs with hypertree width at most k, and slightly abusing notation, the class of CQ's or tableaux whose hypergraphs have hypertree width at most k.

The key result of [16] is that for each fixed k, CQs from $\mathsf{HTW}(k)$ can be evaluated in polynomial time with respect to combined complexity. It is also shown in [16] that a hypergraph $\mathcal{H}$ is acyclic iff its hypertree width is 1. That is, $\mathsf{AC} = \mathsf{HTW}(1)$.

To apply the existence result, we need to check the closure conditions for hypergraphs of fixed hypertree width. It turns out they are satisfied.

Lemma 5.4. *For each k, the class $\mathsf{HTW}(k)$ is closed under induced subhypergraphs and edge extensions.*

This gives us the desired result about the existence of approximations within $\mathsf{HTW}(k)$ for every k.

Corollary 5.5. *For every vocabulary σ, there exist two polynomials p_σ and r_σ such that every CQ Q over σ has a hypergraph-based $\mathsf{HTW}(k)$-approximation of size at most $p_\sigma(|Q|)$ that can be found in time $2^{r_\sigma(|Q|)}$, for every $k \geq 1$.*

Example 5.6. Consider a Boolean query

$$Q() :- R(x_1, x_2, x_3), R(x_3, x_4, x_5), R(x_5, x_6, x_1)$$

over a schema with one ternary relation. If we had a binary relation instead and omitted the middle attribute, we would obtain a query whose tableau is a cycle of length 3, thus having only trivial approximations. However, going beyond graphs lets us find nontrivial acyclic approximations. In fact this query has 3 non-equivalent acyclic approximations (all queries below are minimized):

- With fewer joins than Q:
$$Q_1'() :- R(x, y, x).$$

- With as many joins as Q:
$$Q_2'() :- R(x_1, x_2, x_3), R(x_3, x_4, x_2), R(x_2, x_5, x_1).$$

- With more joins than Q:
$$Q_3'() :- \begin{aligned}& R(x_1, x_2, x_3), R(x_3, x_4, x_5), \\ & R(x_5, x_6, x_1), R(x_1, x_3, x_5).\end{aligned}$$

6. EXTENSIONS

So far approximations were required to produce only correct answers, i.e., no false positives. In general, one can drop this assumption, or replace it by a different one. We now take a quick look at what happens in those cases, leaving more detailed investigation to further work.

Our first result concerns the ordering $\sqsubseteq_Q$ we used to define approximations. Recall that $Q_1 \sqsubseteq_Q Q_2$ means that Q_2 approximates Q as well as Q_1 does: that is, whenever Q and Q_1 agree on a database, then Q and Q_2 agree on it too. We now provide the exact complexity of testing this ordering.

Note that even the upper bound on the complexity of $Q_1 \sqsubseteq_Q Q_2$ is not straightforward. Indeed, the definition of $\sqsubseteq_Q$ involves universal quantification over databases, and then checking whether CQs evaluate to true or false over them. To start with, given universal quantification over all databases, a priori it is not clear if $Q_1 \sqsubseteq_Q Q_2$ is decidable. Assuming, however, that we manage to prove that it suffices to check only databases of polynomial size (in terms of the sizes of Q, Q_1, and Q_2), then parsing the definition of $\sqsubseteq_Q$, would give us a Π_2^p upper bound. However, we can lower the complexity (and, somewhat surprisingly, to a class that only permits existential guessing).

Proposition 6.1. *The following problem is NP-complete: given three CQs Q, Q_1, Q_2, is $Q_1 \sqsubseteq_Q Q_2$?*

It remains NP-complete if Q_1, Q_2 are restricted to be from the class AC of acyclic queries, or from $\mathsf{TW}(k)$ for $k \geq 1$.

The proof establishes structural properties of $\sqsubseteq_Q$ based on the properties of the $\rightarrow$ ordering; those in turn lead to an NP algorithm.

We finish the paper by looking at the assumption that is opposite to the one we have considered so far: instead of insisting that approximating queries return no false positives (i.e., only correct answers), we now look at approximations that produce all correct answers, and perhaps something else, i.e., no false negatives. We refer to them as *overapproximations*.

Formally, for a CQ Q not in a class $\mathcal{C}$ of CQs, a query $Q' \in \mathcal{C}$ such that $Q \subseteq Q'$ is a $\mathcal{C}$-*overapproximation* of Q if there is no query $Q'' \in \mathcal{C}$ with $Q \subseteq Q''$ such that $Q' \sqsubset_Q Q''$. In other words, Q' is an overapproximation of Q if it is guaranteed to return all results of Q and no other such query approximates Q better than Q'.

As for approximations we have studied, the use of the ordering $\sqsubseteq_Q$ can be replaced by containment tests.

Proposition 6.2. *Given a CQ Q, a CQ $Q' \in \mathcal{C}$ satisfying $Q \subseteq Q'$ is a $\mathcal{C}$-overapproximation of Q iff there is no $Q'' \in \mathcal{C}$ such that $Q \subseteq Q'' \subset Q'$.*

We now look at overapproximations of graph queries. Recall that for acyclic approximations of Boolean graph queries, we had two cases which resulted in trivial approximations Q^{triv} and Q_2^{triv}, whose tableaux are the single-element loop $K_1^\circlearrowleft$ and the graph $K_2^{\rightleftarrows}$. These may serve as acyclic overapproximations as well, but in general we have both existence and nonexistence results.

Proposition 6.3. *Let Q be a cyclic Boolean CQ over graphs. Then:*

- *If T_Q contains $K_1^\circlearrowleft$ as a subgraph, then Q^{triv} is the unique, up to equivalence, acyclic overapproximation of Q.*

- *If T_Q contains $K_2^{\rightleftarrows}$ as a subgraph, but does not contain $K_1^\circlearrowleft$, then Q_2^{triv} is the unique, up to equivalence, acyclic overapproximation of Q.*

- *If T_Q contains neither $K_1^\circlearrowleft$ nor $K_2^{\rightleftarrows}$ as a subgraph, then:*

  1. *When T_Q is not a balanced graph, Q has no acyclic overapproximations.*

  2. *When T_Q is a balanced graph, Q may or may not have acyclic overapproximations.*

Specifically, the proof shows that if T_Q is a balanced cycle, then Q has no acyclic overapproximations; it also exhibits a class of queries with balanced tableaux that do possess acyclic approximations.

7. CONCLUSIONS

We have primarily concentrated on approximations of conjunctive queries that are guaranteed to return correct answers. Given the importance of acyclic CQs and very good complexity bounds for them, we have focused on acyclic approximations, but we also provided results on approximations within classes of bounded treewidth and bounded hypertree width. We have proved the existence of approximations, and showed they can be found with an acceptable computational overhead, and that their sizes are at most polynomial in the size of the original query, and sometimes are bounded by the size of the original query.

Several technical problems remain open: for instance, we do not know whether there exist queries without tight acyclic approximations, and our understanding of overapproximations is still very limited. Another possible line for future work is to see whether using the notion of generalized hypertree width [17] makes it easier to construct approximations; even though computing decompositions is harder [18], this will be subsumed by the single-exponential overall complexity of finding approximations.

Here we dealt with the qualitative approach to approximations; in the future we would like to study quantitative guarantees as well, by defining measures showing how different from the original query approximations are. One approach is to find probabilistic guarantees for approximations. Note that such guarantees have been studied for queries from expressive languages (e.g., with fixed points or infinitary connectives) [1, 22], with typical results showing that queries are equivalent to those from simpler logics (e.g, FO) almost everywhere. One possibility is to specialize these results to much weaker logics, e.g., to CQs and their tractable subclasses.

Acknowledgments We thank Wenfei Fan, Claudio Gutierrez, and the referees for their comments. Partial support provided by Fondecyt grant 1110171, EPSRC grants G049165 and F028288, and FET-Open Project FoX, grant agreement 233599. Part of this work was done when the first and the third authors visited Edinburgh, and the second author visited Santiago.

8. References

[1] S. Abiteboul, K. Compton, and V. Vianu. Queries are easier than you thought (probably). In *ACM Symp. on Principles of Database Systems*, 1992, ACM Press, pages 23–32.

[2] S. Abiteboul, O. Duschka. Complexity of answering queries using materialized views. In *PODS 1998*, pages 254–263.

[3] S. Abiteboul, R. Hull, and V. Vianu. *Foundations of Databases*. Addison-Wesley, 1995.

[4] M. Aigner. *Combinatorial Theory*. Springer, 1997.

[5] H. Bodlaender. A linear-time algorithm for finding tree-decompositions of small treewidth. *SIAM Journal on Computing*, 25 (1996), 1305–1317.

[6] B. ten Cate, Ph. Kolaitis, W.-C. Tan. Database constraints and homomorphism dualities. In *CP 2010*, pages 475–490.

[7] A. Chandra and P. Merlin. Optimal implementation of conjunctive queries in relational data bases. In *ACM Symp. on Theory of Computing*, 1977, pages 77–90.

[8] C. Chekuri, A. Rajaraman. Conjunctive query containment revisited. *Theor. Comput. Sci.* 239(2): 211-229 (2000).

[9] R. Fagin, Ph. Kolaitis, L. Popa. Data exchange: getting to the core. *ACM TODS* 30 (2005), 90–101.

[10] W. Fan, J. Li, S. Ma, N. Tang, Y. Wu. Graph pattern matching: from intractable to polynomial time. *PVLDB* 3(1): 264-275 (2010).

[11] R. Fink, D. Olteanu. On the optimal approximation of queries using tractable propositional languages. In *ICDT 2011*, pages 174–185.

[12] J. Flum, M. Frick, and M. Grohe. Query evaluation via tree-decompositions. *J. ACM*, 49 (2002), 716–752.

[13] J. Flum and M. Grohe. *Parameterized Complexity Theory*. Springer, 2006.

[14] M. Garofalakis and P. Gibbons. Approximate query processing: taming the terabytes. In *VLDB'01*.

[15] G. Gottlob, N. Leone, and F. Scarcello. The complexity of acyclic conjunctive queries. *J. ACM*, 48 (2001), 431–498.

[16] G. Gottlob, N. Leone, and F. Scarcello. Hypertree decompositions and tractable queries. *JCSS*, 64 (2002), 579–627.

[17] G. Gottlob, N. Leone, and F. Scarcello. Robbers, marshals, and guards: game theoretic and logical characterizations of hypertree width. *JCSS*, 66 (2003), 775–808.

[18] G. Gottlob, Z. Miklos, and T. Schwentick. Generalized hypertree decompositions: NP-hardness and tractable variants. *J. ACM*, 56(6): (2009).

[19] M. Grohe, T. Schwentick, and L. Segoufin. When is the evaluation of conjunctive queries tractable? In *ACM Symp. on Theory of Computing*, 2001, pages 657–666.

[20] A. Halevy. Answering queries using views: A survey. *VLDB J.* 10(4):270-294 (2001).

[21] P. Hell and J. Nešetřil. *Graphs and Homomorphisms*. Oxford University Press, 2004.

[22] L. Hella, Ph. Kolaitis, and K. Luosto. Almost everywhere equivalence of logics in finite model theory. *Bull. of Symbolic Logic*, 2 (1996), 422–443.

[23] Y. Ioannidis. Approximations in database systems. In *ICDT'03*, pages 16–30.

[24] Ph. Kolaitis and M. Vardi. Conjunctive-query containment and constraint satisfaction. *JCSS* 61(2):302-332 (2000).

[25] Ph. Kolaitis and M. Vardi. A logical approach to constraint satisfaction. In *Finite Model Theory and Its Applications*, Springer 2007, pages 339–370.

[26] M. Lenzerini. Data integration: a theoretical perspective. In *PODS'02*, pages 233–246.

[27] L. Libkin. Incomplete information and certain answers in general data models. In *PODS 2011*, pages 59–70.

[28] Q. Liu. Approximate query processing. *Encyclopedia of Database Systems*, 2009, pages 113–119.

[29] S. Malik and L. Zhang. Boolean satisfiability: from theoretical hardness to practical success. *CACM* **52**(8), 76–82, 2009.

[30] J. Nešetřil, C. Tardif. Duality theorems for finite structures (Characterising gaps and good characterisations). *J. Combin. Theory, Ser. B* 80(1):80-97 (2000).

[31] C. H. Papadimitriou and M. Yannakakis. The complexity of facets (and some facets of complexity). *JCSS*, 28 (1986), 244–259.

[32] A. Robinson, A. Voronkov, eds. *Handbook of Automated Reasoning*. The MIT Press, 2001.

[33] M. Vardi. On the complexity of bounded-variable queries. In *PODS'95*, pages 266–276.

[34] M. Yannakakis. Algorithms for acyclic database schemes. In *Proc. Conf. on Very Large Databases*, 1981, pages 82–94.

[35] D. West. *Introduction to Graph Theory*. Prentice Hall, 2001.

On the Complexity of Package Recommendation Problems

Ting Deng
School of Computer Science
and Engineering
Beihang University
Beijing, China
dengting@act.buaa.edu.cn

Wenfei Fan
Lab. for Foundations of
Computer Science
School of Informatics
University of Edinburgh, UK
wenfei@inf.ed.ac.uk

Floris Geerts
Dept. of Mathematics &
Computer Science
University of Antwerp
Antwerp, Belgium
floris.geerts@ua.ac.be

ABSTRACT

Recommendation systems aim to recommend items that are likely to be of interest to users. This paper investigates several issues fundamental to such systems.

(1) We model recommendation systems for packages of items. We use queries to specify multi-criteria for item selections and express compatibility constraints on items in a package, and use functions to compute the cost and usefulness of items to a user.

(2) We study recommendations of points of interest, to suggest top-k packages. We also investigate recommendations of top-k items, as a special case. In addition, when sensible suggestions cannot be found, we propose query relaxation recommendations to help users revise their selection criteria, or adjustment recommendations to guide vendors to modify their item collections.

(3) We identify several problems, to decide whether a set of packages makes a top-k recommendation, whether a rating bound is maximum for selecting top-k packages, whether we can relax the selection query to find packages that users want, and whether we can update a bounded number of items such that the users' requirements can be satisfied. We also study function problems for computing top-k packages, and counting problems to find how many packages meet the user's criteria.

(4) We establish the upper and lower bounds of these problems, *all matching*, for combined and data complexity. These results reveal the impact of variable sizes of packages, the presence of compatibility constraints, as well as a variety of query languages for specifying selection criteria and compatibility constraints, on the analyses of these problems.

Categories and Subject Descriptors: H.3.5 [**Information Systems**]: Online Information Services – *Web-based services*; F.2.0 [**Theory of Computation**]: Analysis of Algorithms and Problem Complexity – *General*

Keywords: Recommendation problems, Complexity, Query relaxation.

1. INTRODUCTION

Recommendation systems, *a.k.a.* recommender systems, recommendation engines or platforms, aim to identify and suggest information items or social elements that are likely to be of interest to users. Traditional recommendation systems are to select top-k items from a collection of items, *e.g.*, books, music, news, Web sites and research papers [3], which satisfy certain criteria identified for a user, and are ranked by ratings with a utility function. More recently recommendation systems are often used to find top-k packages, *i.e.*, *sets of items*, such as travel plans [34], teams of players [22] and various course combinations [19, 26, 27]. The items in a package are required not only to meet multi-criteria for selecting individual items, but also to satisfy compatibility constraints defined on all the items in a package taken together, such as team formation [22] and course prerequisites [26]. Packages may have variable sizes subject to a cost budget, and are ranked by overall ratings of their items [34].

Recommendation systems are increasingly becoming an integral part of Web services [34], Web search [4], social networks [4], education software [27] and commerce services [3]. A number of systems have been developed for recommending items or packages, known as *points of interest (POI)* [34] (see [3, 4] for surveys). These systems use relational queries to specify selection criteria and compatibility constraints [2, 7, 19, 27, 34]. There has also been work on the complexity of computing POI recommendations [22, 26, 27, 34].

However, to understand central issues associated with recommendation systems, there is much more to be done. (1) The previous complexity results were developed for individual applications with specific selection criteria and compatibility constraints. They may not carry over to other settings. This highlights the need for studying recommendation problems in a *uniform model*. (2) In most cases only lower bounds were given (NP-hard by *e.g.*, [26, 27]). Worse still, among the few upper bounds claimed, some are not quite correct. It is necessary to set the record straight by establishing *matching* upper and lower bounds. (3) No previous work has studied where high complexity arises. Is it from variable sizes of packages, compatibility constraints or from complex selection criteria? The need for understanding this is evident when developing practical recommendation systems. (4) In practice one often gets no sensible recommendations. When this happens, a system should be able to come up with recommendations for the users to *revise selection criteria*, or for vendors to *adjust their item collections*. However, no matter how important these issues are, no previous work has studied recommendations beyond POI.

Example 1.1: Consider a recommendation system for travel plans, which maintains two relations specified by:

flight(f#, From, To, DT, DD, AT, AD, Pr),
POI(name, city, type, ticket, time).

Here a flight tuple specifies flight f# from From to To that departs at time DT on date DD and arrives at time AT on date AD, with airfare Pr. A POI tuple specifies a place name to visit in the city, its ticket price, type (*e.g.*, museum, theater), and the amount of time needed for the visit.

(1) Recommendations of items. A user wants to find top-3 flights from EDI to NYC with at most one stop, departing on 1/1/2012, with lowest possible airfare and duration time. This can be stated as item recommendation: (a) flights are items; (b) the selection criteria are expressed as a union $Q_1 \cup Q_2$ of conjunctive queries, where Q_1 and Q_2 select direct and one-stop flights from EDI to NYC leaving on 1/1/2012, respectively; and (c) the items selected are ranked by a utility function $f()$: given an item s, $f(s)$ is a real number computed from the airfare Pr and the duration Dur of s such that the higher the Pr and Dur are, the lower the rating of s is. Here Dur can be derived from DT, DD, AT and AD, and $f()$ may associate different weights with Pr and Dur.

(2) Recommendations of packages. One is planing a 5-day holiday, by taking a direct flight from EDI to NYC departing on 1/1/2012 and visiting as many places in NYC as possible. In addition, she does not want to have more than 2 museums in a package, which is a compatibility constraint [34]. Moreover, she wants the plans to have the lowest overall price. This is an example of package recommendations: (a) the selection criteria are expressed as the following conjunctive query (CQ) Q, which finds pairs of flights and POI as items:

$Q(\text{f\#, Pr, name, type, ticket, time}) = \exists\, \text{DT}, \text{AT}, \text{AD}, x_{\text{To}}$
$(\text{flight}(\text{f\#, EDI}, x_{\text{To}}, \text{DT}, 1/1/2012, \text{AT, AD, Pr}) \wedge$
$\text{POI}(\text{name}, x_{\text{To}}, \text{type, ticket, time}) \wedge x_{\text{To}} = \text{NYC});$

(b) a package N consists of some items that have the same f# (and hence Pr); (c) the rating of N, denoted by val(N), is a real number such that the higher the sum of the Pr and ticket prices of the items in N is, the lower val(N) is; (d) the compatibility constraint can be expressed as a CQ query Q_c such that $Q_c(N) = \emptyset$ iff the requirement is satisfied (see Section 2); and (e) the cost of N, denoted by cost(N), is the total time taken on visiting all POI in N. Note that the number of items in N is *not* fixed: N may contain as many POI as possible, as long as cost(N) does not exceed the total time allocated for sightseeing in 5 days. Putting these together, the travel planning is to find top-k such packages ranked by val(N), for a constant k chosen by the user.

(3) Computational complexity. To develop a recommendation system, one naturally wants to know the complexity for computing top-k packages or top-k items. The complexity may depend on what query language we use to specify selection criteria and compatibility constraints. For instance, in the package recommendation example given above, the criteria and constraints are expressed as CQ queries. Suppose that the user can bear with indirect flights with an unlimited number of stops. Then we need to express the selection criteria in, *e.g.*, DATALOG, which is more costly to evaluate than the CQ queries. What is the complexity of package recommendations when criteria and constraints are expressed in various languages? Will the complexity be lower if compatibility constraints are absent? Will it make

our lives easier if we fix the size of each package? To the best of our knowledge, these questions have not been answered.

(4) Query relaxation recommendations. One may not get any direct flight from EDI to NYC. Nevertheless, if we relax the CQ Q given above by, *e.g.*, allowing To to be a city within 15 miles of NYC, then direct flights are available, *e.g.*, from EDI to EWR. This suggests that we help the user revise her selection criteria by recommending query relaxations.

(5) Adjustment recommendations. The collection of POI in the system may consist of museums only, which users may not want to see too many, as indicated by the compatibility constraint Q_c above. This motivates us to study adjustment recommendations, by recommending the vendor of the system to include, *e.g.*, theaters, in their POI collection. □

These highlight the need for a full treatment of recommendation problems, to study them in a generic model, establish their matching upper and lower bounds, and identify where the complexity arises. Moreover, analogous to POI recommendations, query relaxation recommendations and adjustment recommendations should logically be part of a practical system, and hence, deserve to be investigated.

A model for package recommendations. Following [2, 7, 19, 26, 27, 34] we consider a database D that includes items in a recommendation system. We specify (a) multicriteria for selecting items as a relational query Q; (b) compatibility constraints on the items in a package N as another query Q_c such that $Q_c(N, D) = \emptyset$ iff N satisfies the constraints; (c) a rating function val() from packages to real numbers $\mathbb{R}$ such that val(N) assesses the usefulness of a package N to a user; and (d) a cost budget C and a function cost() from packages to $\mathbb{R}$ such that a package N is a "valid" choice iff cost(N) $\leq C$. Given a constant k, package recommendation is to find top-k packages based on val() such that each package consists of items selected by Q and satisfies the constraints Q_c. As shown in Example 1.1, packages may have *variable sizes*: we want to maximize val(N) as long as cost(N) does not exceed the budget C.

Traditional item recommendations are a special case. We use a utility function $f()$ that gives a rating in $\mathbb{R}$ to each tuple in $Q(D)$. For a given k, it is to find top-k items that meet the criteria specified by Q, ranked by the function $f()$.

This yields a model for top-k package querying that subsumes previous models studied for, *e.g.*, travel and course recommendations. We study recommendation problems in a generic setting when selection criteria and compatibility constraints are expressed as queries, and when cost(), val() and $f()$ are only assumed to be computable in PTIME.

Recommendation problems. We identify several problems for POI recommendations. (a) Decision problems: Is a set of packages a top-k recommendation? Is a constant B the largest bound such that there exists a top-k recommendation in which each package is rated above B? (b) Function problem: find a top-k recommendation if there exists one. (c) Counting problem: how many valid packages are there that have ratings above a bound B?

Beyond POI recommendations, we propose to study the following features that future recommendater systems could support. (a) Query relaxation recommendations: Can we find a "minimum" relaxation of the users' selection criteria Q to allow a top-k recommendation? (b) Adjustment recommendations: Can we update a bounded number of items in D such that the users' requirements can be satisfied? We parameterize each of these problems with various query languages $\mathcal{L}_Q$ in which selection criteria Q and compatibility constraints Q_c are expressed. We consider the following $\mathcal{L}_Q$, all with built-in predicates $-, \neq, <, \leq, >, \geq$:

- conjunctive queries (CQ),
- union of conjunctive queries (UCQ),
- positive existential FO queries ($\exists\text{FO}^+$),
- nonrecursive datalog queries (DATALOG_{nr}),
- first-order queries (FO), and
- datalog (DATALOG).

Complexity results. For all these problems, we establish its combined complexity and data complexity. We also study special cases of package recommendations, such as when compatibility constraints are absent, when packages have a fixed size, and when both conditions are imposed (item recommendations). We provide their upper and lower bounds, *all matching*, for all the query languages given above.

These results give a complete characterization of the complexity in this model, from decision problems to function and counting problems. They tell us where complexity arises, complementing previously stated results.

(a) Query languages dominate the complexity of recommendation problems, *e.g.*, the problem for deciding the maximum bound for top-k package recommendations ranges from D_2^p-complete for CQ, PSPACE-complete for FO and DATALOG_{nr}, to EXPTIME-complete for DATALOG.

(b) Variable package sizes do not make our lives harder when combined complexity is concerned for all the languages given above. Indeed, when packages may have variable sizes, all these problems have the same combined complexity as their counterparts when packages are restricted to be singleton sets. In fact, variable sizes of packages have impact only on data complexity, or when $\mathcal{L}_Q$ is a simple language with a PTIME complexity for its membership problem. These clarify the impact of package sizes studied in, *e.g.*, [34].

(c) The presence of compatibility constraints does not increase the complexity when the query language $\mathcal{L}_Q$ is FO, DATALOG_{nr} or DATALOG. Indeed, for these languages, all the problems for package recommendations and their counterparts for item recommendations have the same complexity. Moreover, these constraints do *not* complicate the data complexity analyses. However, compatibility constraints increase combined complexity when $\mathcal{L}_Q$ is contained in $\exists\text{FO}^+$.

(d) In the absence of compatibility constraints, the decision problem for top-k package recommendations is DP-complete and its function problem is FP^{NP}-complete when $\mathcal{L}_Q$ is CQ. They are coNP-hard and FP^{NP}-hard, respectively, even when selection criteria are given by an identity query. These give precise bounds for the problems studied in, *e.g.*, [34].

These results are also of interest to the study of top-k query answering, among other things. A variety of techniques are used to prove the results, including a wide range of reductions, and constructive proofs with algorithms (*e.g.*, for the function problems). In particular, the proofs demonstrate that the complexity of these problems for CQ, UCQ and $\exists\text{FO}^+$ is inherent to top-k package querying itself, rather than a consequence of the complexity of the query languages.

Related work. Traditional recommendation systems aim to find, for each user, items that maximize the user's utility (see, *e.g.*, [3] for a survey). Selection criteria are decided by content-based, collaborative and hybrid approaches, which consider preferences of each user in isolation, or preferences of similar users [3]. The prior work has mostly focused on how to choose appropriate utility functions, and how to extrapolate such functions when they are not defined on the entire item space, by deriving unknown values from known ones. Our model supports content-based, collaborative and hybrid criteria in terms of various queries. We *assume a given utility function* that is total, and focus on the computational complexity of recommendation problems.

Recently recommendation systems have been extended to finding packages, which are presented to the user in a ranked order based on some rating function [6, 22, 26, 27, 34]. A number of algorithms have been developed for recommending packages of a fixed size [6, 22] or variable sizes [26, 27, 34]. Compatibility constraints [22, 26, 27, 34] and budget restrictions [34] on packages have also been studied. Instead of considering domain-specific applications, we model recommendations of both items and packages (fixed size or polynomial size) by specifying general selection criteria and compatibility constraints as queries, and supporting aggregate constraints defined with cost budgets and rating bounds.

Several decision problems for course package recommendations have been shown NP-hard [26, 27]. It was claimed that problems of forming a team with compatibility constraints [22] and the problem of finding packages that satisfy some budget restrictions (without compatibility constraints) [34] are NP-complete. In contrast, we establish the precise complexity of a variety of problems associated with POI recommendations (Table 1, Section 7). Moreover, we provide the complexity of query relaxation and adjustment recommendations, which have not been studied by prior work.

There has also been a host of work on recommending items and packages taken from views of the data [2, 7, 19, 23, 34]. Such views are expressed as relational queries, representing preferences or points of interest [2, 7, 19]. Here recommendations often correspond to top-k query answers. Indeed, top-k query answering retrieves the k-items (tuples) from a query result that are top-ranked by some scoring function [16]. Such queries either simply select tuples, or join and aggregate multiple inputs to find the top-k tuples, by possibly incorporating user preference information [19, 29]. A number of top-k query evaluation algorithms have been developed (*e.g.*, [12, 23, 28]; see [16] for a survey), as well as algorithms for incremental computation of ranked query results [10, 14, 24] that retrieve the top-k query answers one at a time. A central issue there concerns how to combine different ratings of the same item based on multiple criteria. Our work also retrieves tuples from the result of a query. It differs from the previous work in the following. (1) In contrast to top-k query answering, we are to find items and sets of items (packages) provided that a utility or rating function is given. (2) We focus on the complexity of recommendations problems rather than the efficiency or optimization of query evaluation. (3) Beyond recommendations of POI, we also study query relaxation and adjustment recommendations.

Query relaxations have been studied in, *e.g.*, [8, 13, 17, 18]. Several query generalization rules are introduced in [8], assuming that query acceptance conditions are monotonic. Heuristic query relaxation algorithms are developed in [13,

17]. The topic is also studied for top-k query answering [18]. We focus on the main idea of query relaxation recommendations, and borrow query generalization rules from [8]. We consider acceptance conditions (*i.e.*, rating functions, compatibility constraints and aggregate constraints) that are not necessarily monotonic. Moreover, none of the previous work supports queries beyond CQ, while we consider more powerful languages such as FO and DATALOG. In addition, the prior work focuses on the design of efficient relaxation algorithms, but does not study computational complexity.

Organization. Section 2 introduces the model for package recommendations. Section 3 formulates and studies fundamental problems in connection with POI recommendations, followed by special cases in Section 4. Query relaxation recommendations are studied in Section 5, followed by adjustment recommendations in Section 6. Section 7 summarizes the main results of the paper and identifies open issues.

2. MODELING RECOMMENDATIONS

We first specify recommendations of packages and items. We then review query languages considered in this work.

Item collections. Following [2, 7, 19, 26, 27, 34], we assume a database D consisting of items for selection. The database is specified with a relational schema $\mathcal{R}$, with a collection of relation schemas $(R_1, \ldots, R_n)$. Each schema R_i is defined over a fixed set of attributes. For each attribute A in R_i, its domain is specified in R_i, denoted as $\mathsf{dom}(R_i.A)$.

Package recommendations. As remarked earlier, in practice one often wants packages of items, *e.g.*, combinations of courses to be taken to satisfy the requirements for a degree [27], travel plans including multiple POI [34], and teams of experts [22]. Package recommendation is to find top-k packages such that the items in each package (a) meet the selection criteria, (b) satisfy some compatibility constraints, *i.e.*, they have no conflicts, and moreover, (c) their ratings and costs satisfy certain aggregate constraints. To specify these, we extend the models proposed in [27, 34] as follows.

Selection criteria. We use a query Q in a query language $\mathcal{L}_Q$ to specify multi-criteria for selecting items from D. For instance, as shown in Example 1.1, we use a query to specify what flights and sites a user wants to find.

Compatibility constraints. To specify the compatibility constraints for a package N, we use a query Q_c such that N satisfies Q_c iff $Q_c(N, D) = \emptyset$. That is, Q_c identifies inconsistencies among items in N. In Example 1.1, to assert "no more than 2 museums" in a travel package N [34], we use the following Q_c that selects 3 distinct museums from N:

$$Q_c() = \exists~ \mathsf{f\#}, \mathsf{Pr}, n_1, t_1, p_1, n_2, t_2, p_2, n_3, t_3, p_3$$
$$\big(R_Q(\mathsf{f\#}, \mathsf{Pr}, n_1, museum, p_1, t_1) \land$$
$$R_Q(\mathsf{f\#}, \mathsf{Pr}, n_2, museum, p_2, t_2) \land$$
$$R_Q(\mathsf{f\#}, \mathsf{Pr}, n_3, museum, p_3, t_3) \land$$
$$n_1 \neq n_2 \land n_1 \neq n_3 \land n_2 \neq n_3 \big),$$

where R_Q denotes the schema of the query answer $Q(D)$. As another example, for a course package N, we use a query Q_c to assure that for each course in N, its prerequisites are also included in N [26]. This query needs to access not only courses in N but also the prerequisite relation stored in D.

To simplify the discussion, we assume that query Q_c for specifying compatibility constraints and query Q for specifying selection criteria are in the same language $\mathcal{L}_Q$. If a system supports compatibility constraints in $\mathcal{L}_Q$, there is no reason for not supporting queries in the same language for selecting items. We defer to future work the study in the setting when Q_c and Q are expressed in different languages. Note that queries in various query languages are capable of expressing compatibility constraints commonly found in practice, including those studied in [19, 22, 26, 27, 34].

Aggregate constraints. To specify aggregate constraints, we define a cost function and a rating function over packages, following [34]: (1) $\mathsf{cost}(N)$ computes a value in $\mathbb{R}$ as the cost of package N; and (2) $\mathsf{val}(N)$ computes a value in $\mathbb{R}$ as the overall rating of N. For instance, $\mathsf{cost}(N)$ in Example 1.1 is computed from the total time taken for visiting POI, while $\mathsf{val}(N)$ is defined in terms of airfare and total ticket prices.

We just assume that $\mathsf{cost}()$ and $\mathsf{val}()$ are PTIME computable aggregate functions, defined in terms of *e.g.*, max, min, sum, avg, as commonly found in practice.

We also assume a cost budget C, and specify an aggregate constraint $\mathsf{cost}(N) \leq C$. For instance, the cost budget C in Example 1.1 is the total time allowed for visiting POI in 5 days, and the aggregate constraint $\mathsf{cost}(N) \leq C$ imposes a bound on the number of POI in a package N.

Top-k package selections. For a database D, queries Q and Q_c in $\mathcal{L}_Q$, a natural number $k \geq 1$, a cost budget C, and functions $\mathsf{cost}()$ and $\mathsf{val}()$, a *top-k package selection* is a set $\mathcal{N} = \{ N_i \mid i \in [1, k] \}$ of packages such that for each $i \in [1, k]$,

(1) $N_i \subseteq Q(D)$, *i.e.*, its items meet the criteria given in Q;

(2) $Q_c(N_i, D) = \emptyset$, *i.e.*, the items in the package satisfy the compatibility constraints specified by query Q_c;

(3) $\mathsf{cost}(N_i) \leq C$, *i.e.*, its cost is below the budget;

(4) the number $|N_i|$ of items in N_i is no larger than $p(|D|)$, where p is a predefined polynomial and $|D|$ is the size of D; indeed, it is not of much practical use to find a package with exponentially many items; as will be seen in Section 4, we shall also consider a constant bound B_p for $|N_i|$;

(5) for all packages $N' \notin \mathcal{N}$ that satisfies conditions (1–4) given above, $\mathsf{val}(N') \leq \mathsf{val}(N_i)$, *i.e.*, packages in $\mathcal{N}$ have the k highest overall ratings among all feasible packages; and

(6) $N_i \neq N_j$ if $i \neq j$, *i.e.*, the packages are pairwise distinct.

Note that packages in $\mathcal{N}$ may have *variable* sizes. That is, the number of items in each package is not bounded by a constant. We just require that N_i satisfies the constraint $\mathsf{cost}(N_i) \leq C$ and $|N_i|$ does not exceed a polynomial in $|D|$.

Package recommendation is to find a *top-k package selection* for $(Q, D, Q_c, \mathsf{cost}(), \mathsf{val}(), C)$, if there exists one.

As shown in Example 1.1, users may want to find, *e.g.*, a top-k travel-plan selection with the minimum price.

Item recommendations. To rank items, we use a *utility function* $f()$ to measure the usefulness of items selected by $Q(D)$ to a user [3]. It is a PTIME-computable function that takes a tuple s from $Q(D)$ and returns a real number $f(s)$ as the rating of item s. The functions may incorporate users' preference [29], and may be *different for different users*.

Given a constant $k \geq 1$, a *top-k selection for* (Q, D, f) is a set $S = \{ s_i \mid i \in [1, k] \}$ such that (a) $S \subseteq Q(D)$, *i.e.*, items in S satisfy the criteria specified by Q; (b) for all $s \in Q(D) \setminus S$ and $i \in [1, k]$, $f(s) \leq f(s_i)$, *i.e.*, items in S have the highest ratings; and (c) $s_i \neq s_j$ if $i \neq j$, *i.e.*, items in S are *distinct*.

Given D, Q, f and k, *item recommendation* is to find a top-k selection for (Q, D, f) if there exists one.

For instance, a top-3 item selection is described in Example 1.1, where items are flights and the utility function $f()$ is defined in terms of the airfare and duration of each flight.

The connection between item and package selections. Item selections are a special case of package selections. Indeed, a top-k selection $S = \{s_i \mid i \in [1,k]\}$ for (Q,D,f) is a top-k package selection $\mathcal{N}$ for $(Q,D,Q_c,\mathsf{cost}(),\mathsf{val}(),C)$, where $\mathcal{N} = \{N_i \mid i \in [1,k]\}$, and for each $i \in [1,k]$, (a) $N_i = \{s_i\}$, (b) Q_c is a constant query that returns $\emptyset$ on any input, referred to as the *empty query*; (c) $\mathsf{cost}(N_i) = |N_i|$ if $N_i \neq \emptyset$, and $\mathsf{cost}(\emptyset) = \infty$; that is, $\mathsf{cost}(N_i)$ counts the number of items in N_i if $N_i \neq \emptyset$, and the empty set is not taken as a recommendation; (d) the cost budget $C = 1$, and hence, N_i consists of a single item by $\mathsf{cost}(N_i) \leq C$; and (e) $\mathsf{val}(N_i) = f(s_i)$.

In the sequel, we use top-k package selection *specified in terms of* (Q,D,f) to refer to a top-k selection S for (Q,D,f), *i.e.*, a top-k package selection for $(Q,D,Q_c,\mathsf{cost}(),\mathsf{val}(),C)$ in which $Q_c, \mathsf{cost}(), \mathsf{val}()$ and C are defined as above.

We say that compatibility constraints are *absent* if Q_c is the empty query; *e.g.*, Q_c is absent in item selections.

One might want to consider general **PTIME** compatibility constraints Q_c. As will be seen in Section 4, the complexity when Q_c is in **PTIME** remains the same as its counterpart when Q_c is absent for all the problems studied in this paper.

Query languages. We consider Q, Q_c in a query language $\mathcal{L}_Q$, ranging over the following (see *e.g.*, [1] for details):

(a) conjunctive queries (CQ), built up from atomic formulas with constants and variables, *i.e.*, relation atoms in database schema $\mathcal{R}$ and built-in predicates $(=, \neq, <, \leq, >, \geq)$, by closing under conjunction $\wedge$ and existential quantification $\exists$;

(b) union of conjunctive queries (UCQ) of the form $Q_1 \cup \cdots \cup Q_r$, where for each $i \in [1,r]$, Q_i is in CQ;

(c) positive existential FO queries ($\exists \mathsf{FO}^+$), built from atomic formulas by closing under $\wedge$, *disjunction* $\vee$ and $\exists$;

(d) nonrecursive datalog queries (DATALOG$_{\mathsf{nr}}$), defined as a collection of rules of the form $p(\bar{x}) \leftarrow p_1(\bar{x}_1), \ldots, p_n(\bar{x}_n)$, where the head p is an IDB predicate and each p_i is either an atomic formula or an IDB predicate, such that its dependency graph is acyclic; the *dependency graph* of a DATALOG query Q is a directed graph $G_Q = (V,E)$, where V includes all the predicates of Q, and (p',p) is an edge in E iff p' is a predicate that appears in a rule with p as its head [9];

(e) first-order logic queries (FO) built from atomic formulas using $\wedge, \vee$, *negation* $\neg, \exists$ and universal quantification $\forall$; and

(f) datalog queries (DATALOG), defined as a collection of rules $p(\bar{x}) \leftarrow p_1(\bar{x}_1), \ldots, p_n(\bar{x}_n)$, for which the dependency graph may possibly be cyclic, *i.e.*, DATALOG is an extension of DATALOG$_{\mathsf{nr}}$ with an inflational fixpoint operator.

These languages specify both multi-criteria for item selections and compatibility constraints for package selections.

3. RECOMMENDATIONS OF POI'S

In this section we investigate POI recommendations. We identify four problems for package recommendations (Section 3.1), and establish their complexity (Section 3.2).

3.1 Recommendation Problems

We investigate four problems, stated as follows, which are fundamental to computing package recommendations. We start with a decision problem for package selections. Con-

sider a database D, queries Q and Q_c in a query language $\mathcal{L}_Q$, functions $\mathsf{val}()$ and $\mathsf{cost}()$, a cost budget C, and a natural number $k \geq 1$. Given a set $\mathcal{N}$ consisting of k packages, it is to decide whether $\mathcal{N}$ makes a top-k package selection. That is, each package N in $\mathcal{N}$ satisfies the selection criteria Q, compatibility constraint Q_c, and aggregate constraints $\mathsf{cost}(N) \leq C$ and $\mathsf{val}(N) \geq \mathsf{val}(N')$ for all $N' \notin \mathcal{N}$. As remarked earlier, we assume a predefined polynomial such that $|N| \leq p(|D|)$ (omitted from the problem statement below for simplicity). Intuitively, this problem is to decide whether a set $\mathcal{N}$ of packages should be recommended.

RPP($\mathcal{L}_Q$):	*The recommendation problem (package).*
INPUT:	A database D, two queries Q and Q_c in $\mathcal{L}_Q$, two functions $\mathsf{cost}()$ and $\mathsf{val}()$, natural numbers C and $k \geq 1$, and a set $\mathcal{N} = \{N_i \mid i \in [1,k]\}$.
QUESTION:	Is $\mathcal{N}$ a top-k package selection for $(Q,D,Q_c,\mathsf{cost}(),\mathsf{val}(),C)$?

After all, recommendation systems have to compute top-k packages, rather than expecting that candidate selections are already in place. This highlights the need for studying the function problem below, to compute top-k packages.

FRP($\mathcal{L}_Q$):	*The function rec. problem (packages).*
INPUT:	$D,Q,Q_c,\mathsf{cost}(),\mathsf{val}(),C,k$ as in RPP.
OUTPUT:	A top-k package selection for $(Q,D,Q_c,\mathsf{cost}(),\mathsf{val}(),C)$ if it exists.

The next question concerns how to find a maximum rating bound for computing top-k packages. We say that a constant B is a *rating bound* for $(Q,D,Q_c,\mathsf{cost}(),\mathsf{val}(),C,k)$ if (a) there exists a top-k package selection $\mathcal{N} = \{N_i \mid i \in [1,k]\}$ for $(Q,D,Q_c,\mathsf{cost}(),\mathsf{val}(),C)$ and moreover, (b) $\mathsf{val}(N_i) \geq B$ for each $i \in [1,k]$. That is, B allows a top-k package selection. We say that B is *the maximum bound for packages* with $(Q,D,Q_c,\mathsf{cost}(),\mathsf{val}(),C,k)$ if for all bounds B', $B \geq B'$. Obviously B is unique if it exists. Intuitively, when B is identified, we can capitalize on B to compute top-rated packages. Furthermore, vendors could decide, *e.g.*, price for certain items on sale with such a bound, for risk assessment.

MBP($\mathcal{L}_Q$):	*The maximum bound problem (packages).*
INPUT:	$D,Q,Q_c,\mathsf{cost}(),\mathsf{val}(),C,k$ as in RPP, and a natural number B.
QUESTION:	Is B the maximum bound for packages with $(Q,D,Q_c,\mathsf{cost}(),\mathsf{val}(),C,k)$?

A package N is *valid* for $(Q,D,Q_c,\mathsf{cost}(),\mathsf{val}(),C,B)$ if (a) $N \subseteq Q(D)$, (b) $Q_c(N,D) = \emptyset$, (c) $\mathsf{cost}(N) \leq C$, and (d) $\mathsf{val}(N) \geq B$, where $|N|$ is bounded by a polynomial in $|D|$. Given B, one naturally wants to know how many valid packages are out there, and hence, can be selected. This suggests that we study the following counting problem.

CPP($\mathcal{L}_Q$):	*The counting problem (packages).*
INPUT:	$D,Q,Q_c,\mathsf{cost}(),\mathsf{val}(),C,B$ as in MBP.
OUTPUT:	The number of packages that are valid for $(Q,D,Q_c,\mathsf{cost}(),\mathsf{val}(),C,B)$.

3.2 Deciding, Finding and Counting Top-k Packages

We now establish the complexity of RPP($\mathcal{L}_Q$), FRP($\mathcal{L}_Q$), MBP($\mathcal{L}_Q$) and CPP($\mathcal{L}_Q$), including their (1) combined complexity, when the query Q, compatibility constraint Q_c and database D may vary, and (2) data complexity, when only D varies, while Q and Q_c are predefined and fixed. We study these problems for all the query languages $\mathcal{L}_Q$ of Section 2.

Deciding package selections. We start with RPP($\mathcal{L}_Q$). The result below tells us that the combined complexity of the problem is mostly determined by what query language $\mathcal{L}_Q$ we use to specify selection criteria and compatibility constraints. Indeed, it is Π_2^p-complete when $\mathcal{L}_Q$ is CQ, PSPACE-complete for DATALOG$_{nr}$ and FO, and it becomes EXPTIME-complete when $\mathcal{L}_Q$ is DATALOG. The data complexity is coNP-complete for all the languages considered.

Theorem 3.1: For RPP($\mathcal{L}_Q$), the combined complexity is

- Π_2^p-complete when $\mathcal{L}_Q$ is CQ, UCQ, or $\exists$FO$^+$;
- PSPACE-complete when $\mathcal{L}_Q$ is DATALOG$_{nr}$ or FO; and
- EXPTIME-complete when $\mathcal{L}_Q$ is DATALOG.

The data complexity is coNP-complete for all the languages presented in Section 2, *i.e.*, when $\mathcal{L}_Q$ is CQ, UCQ, $\exists$FO$^+$, DATALOG$_{nr}$, FO or DATALOG. □

Proof sketch: (1) We show that RPP is Π_2^p-hard for CQ by reduction from the complement of *the compatibility problem*. The latter is to decide whether there exists a valid package N with $\mathrm{val}(N) > B$ for some bound B. We show that the compatibility problem is Σ_2^p-complete for CQ by reduction from the $\exists^*\forall^*$3DNF problem, which is Σ_2^p-complete [30].

For RPP($\exists$FO$^+$), we give a Π_2^p algorithm that first tests whether a given set $\mathcal{N}$ of packages satisfies the criteria and constraints, in DP; it then checks whether there exists *no* package with a higher rating than some $N \in \mathcal{N}$, in Π_2^p.

(2) We show that RPP is PSPACE-hard for DATALOG$_{nr}$ by reduction from Q3SAT (cf. [25]), and for FO by reduction from the membership problem for FO ("given a query Q, a database D and a tuple t, whether $t \in Q(D)$") [32], which are PSPACE-complete. We provide an NPSPACE (= PSPACE) algorithm to check RPP for these two languages.

(3) For DATALOG, we show that RPP is EXPTIME-hard by reduction from the membership problem for DATALOG, which is EXPTIME-complete [32]. For the upper bound, we give an EXPTIME algorithm to check RPP(DATALOG).

(4) For the data complexity, we first show that the compatibility problem is NP-complete when Q and Q_c are fixed CQ queries, by reduction from 3SAT, an NP-complete problem (cf. [25]). From this it follows that RPP(CQ) is already coNP-hard. We also give a coNP algorithm for RPP when Q and Q_c are fixed queries in either FO or DATALOG. □

One might think that the absence of compatibility constraints Q_c would make our lives easier. Indeed, RPP(CQ) becomes DP-complete in the absence of Q_c, as opposed to Π_2^p-complete in the presence of Q_c. However, when $\mathcal{L}_Q$ is powerful enough to express FO or DATALOG$_{nr}$ queries, dropping Q_c does not help: RPP($\mathcal{L}_Q$) in this case has the same complexity as its counterpart when Q_c is present.

Theorem 3.2: In the absence of Q_c, RPP($\mathcal{L}_Q$) is

- DP-complete when $\mathcal{L}_Q$ is CQ, UCQ, or $\exists$FO$^+$;
- PSPACE-complete when $\mathcal{L}_Q$ is DATALOG$_{nr}$ or FO; and

- EXPTIME-complete when $\mathcal{L}_Q$ is DATALOG.

Its data complexity remains coNP-complete for all the query languages given in Section 2. □

Proof sketch: (1) We show that RPP(CQ) is DP-hard by reduction from SAT-UNSAT. The latter is to decide, given a pair (φ_1, φ_2) of 3SAT instances, whether φ_1 is satisfiable and φ_2 is not satisfiable. It is DP-complete (cf. [25]).

In the absence of Q_c, the algorithm given earlier for RPP($\exists$FO$^+$) is in DP, and hence so is RPP($\exists$FO$^+$).

(2-4) The lower bound proofs (2-4) of Theorem 3.1 do not use compatibility constraints and hence remain intact. The upper bounds obviously carry over to this special case. □

Computing top-k packages. We give the complexity of the function problem FRP($\mathcal{L}_Q$) as follows:

Theorem 3.3: For FRP($\mathcal{L}_Q$), the combined complexity is

- FP$^{\Sigma_2^p}$-complete when $\mathcal{L}_Q$ is CQ, UCQ or $\exists$FO$^+$;
- FPSPACE(poly)-complete if $\mathcal{L}_Q$ is DATALOG$_{nr}$ or FO;
- FEXPTIME(poly)-complete when $\mathcal{L}_Q$ is DATALOG.

In the absence of compatibility constraints, its combined complexity remains unchanged for DATALOG$_{nr}$, FO and DATALOG, but it is FP^{NP}-complete for CQ, UCQ and $\exists$FO$^+$.

Its data complexity is FP^{NP}-complete for all the languages, in the presence or absence of compatibility constraints. □

Here FP^{NP} is the class of all functions from strings to strings that can be computed by a PTIME Turing machine with an NP oracle (cf. [25]), and FP$^{\Sigma_2^p}$ is the class of all functions computable by a PTIME 2-alternating max-min Turing machine [20]. By FPSPACE(poly) (resp. FEXPTIME(poly)) we mean the class of all functions associated with a two-argument predicate R_L that satisfies the following conditions: (a) R_L is *polynomially balanced*, *i.e.*, there is a polynomial q such that for all strings x and y, if $R_L(x, y)$ then $|y| \leq q(|x|)$, and (b) the decision problem "given x and y, whether $R_L(x, y)$" is in PSPACE (resp. EXPTIME) [21]. Given a string x, the function associated with R_L is to find a string y such that $R_L(x, y)$ if such a string exists.

These results tell us that it is nontrivial to find top-k packages. Indeed, to express compatibility constraints on travel plans given in [34], we need at least CQ; for course combination constraints of [19, 26, 27], we need FO; and for connectivity of flights we need DATALOG. These place FRP in FP$^{\Sigma_2^p}$, FPSPACE(poly) and FEXPTIME(poly), respectively.

It was claimed in several earlier papers that when $k = 1$, it is NP-complete to find a top-1 package. Unfortunately, it is not the case. Indeed, the proofs of Theorems 3.1, 3.2 and 3.3 tell us that when $k = 1$, the function problem FRP($\mathcal{L}_Q$) remains FP$^{\Sigma_2^p}$-complete and the decision problem RPP($\mathcal{L}_Q$) is Π_2^p-complete even when $\mathcal{L}_Q$ is CQ, not to mention more expressive $\mathcal{L}_Q$. Even when Q and Q_c are both fixed, FRP is FP^{NP}-complete and RPP is coNP-complete when $k = 1$.

In the absence of compatibility constraints, only the analyses of the combined complexity of FRP for CQ, UCQ and $\exists$FO$^+$ are simplified. This is consistent with Theorem 3.2.

Proof sketch: (1) We show that FRP(CQ) is FP$^{\Sigma_2^p}$-hard by reduction from the MAXIMUM Σ_2^p problem, which is FP$^{\Sigma_2^p}$-complete [20]. The latter is to find, given a formula $\varphi(X) = \forall Y \psi(X, Y)$, the truth assignment μ_X^{last} of X that satisfies φ and comes last in the lexicographical ordering if it exists,

where ψ is a 3SAT instance. We give an $\mathsf{FP}^{\Sigma_2^p}$ algorithm for $\mathsf{FRP}(\exists\mathsf{FO}^+)$ to compute a top-k package selection if it exists.
(2) We show that $\mathsf{FRP}(\mathcal{L}_Q)$ is $\mathsf{FPSPACE}(\mathsf{poly})$-hard by reducing to it all functions computable by a PSPACE Turing machine in which the output on the working tape is bounded by a polynomial, when $\mathcal{L}_Q$ is $\mathsf{DATALOG}_{\mathsf{nr}}$ or FO; similarly for $\mathsf{FRP}(\mathsf{DATALOG})$. For the upper bounds, we give an algorithm in $\mathsf{FPSPACE}(\mathsf{poly})$ (resp. $\mathsf{FEXPTIME}(\mathsf{poly})$) for $\mathsf{FRP}(\mathcal{L}_Q)$ when $\mathcal{L}_Q$ is $\mathsf{DATALOG}_{\mathsf{nr}}$ or FO (resp. $\mathsf{DATALOG}$).
(3) When Q and Q_c are fixed, we show that $\mathsf{FRP}(\mathsf{CQ})$ in the absence of Q_c is $\mathsf{FP}^{\mathsf{NP}}$-hard by reduction from MAX-WEIGHT SAT, which is $\mathsf{FP}^{\mathsf{NP}}$-complete (cf. [25]). Given a set $\mathcal{C}$ of clauses with weights, MAX-WEIGHT SAT is to find a truth assignment that satisfies a set of clauses in $\mathcal{C}$ with the most total weight. For the upper bound, we give an $\mathsf{FP}^{\mathsf{NP}}$ algorithm for $\mathsf{FRP}(\mathcal{L}_Q)$ when $\mathcal{L}_Q$ is FO or $\mathsf{DATALOG}$.
(4) When Q_c is absent, $\mathsf{FRP}(\mathsf{CQ})$ is $\mathsf{FP}^{\mathsf{NP}}$-hard by proof (3) given above, and the algorithm for $\mathsf{FRP}(\exists\mathsf{FO}^+)$ given in proof (1) is now in $\mathsf{FP}^{\mathsf{NP}}$. The proofs for $\mathsf{DATALOG}_{\mathsf{nr}}$, FO and $\mathsf{DATALOG}$ given in (2) still work in this special case, as no Q_c is used there when verifying the lower bounds. □

Deciding the maximum bound. We show that $\mathsf{MBP}(\mathsf{CQ})$ is D_2^p-complete. Here D_2^p is the class of languages recognized by oracle machines that make a query to a Σ_2^p oracle and a query to a Π_2^p oracle. That is, L is in D_2^p if there exist languages $L_1 \in \Sigma_2^p$ and $L_2 \in \Pi_2^p$ such that $L = L_1 \cap L_2$ [33], analogous to how DP is defined with NP and coNP [25].

When $\mathcal{L}_Q$ is FO, $\mathsf{DATALOG}_{\mathsf{nr}}$ or $\mathsf{DATALOG}$, $\mathsf{MBP}(\mathcal{L}_Q)$ and $\mathsf{RPP}(\mathcal{L}_Q)$ have the same complexity. Moreover, the absence of Q_c has the same impact on $\mathsf{MBP}(\mathcal{L}_Q)$ as on $\mathsf{RPP}(\mathcal{L}_Q)$.

Theorem 3.4: For $\mathsf{MBP}(\mathcal{L}_Q)$, the combined complexity is
- D_2^p-complete when $\mathcal{L}_Q$ is CQ, UCQ or $\exists\mathsf{FO}^+$;
- PSPACE-complete when $\mathcal{L}_Q$ is $\mathsf{DATALOG}_{\mathsf{nr}}$ or FO; and
- $\mathsf{EXPTIME}$-complete when $\mathcal{L}_Q$ is $\mathsf{DATALOG}$.

When compatibility constraints are absent, its combined complexity remains unchanged for $\mathsf{DATALOG}_{\mathsf{nr}}$, FO and $\mathsf{DATALOG}$, but it is DP-complete for CQ, UCQ and $\exists\mathsf{FO}^+$.

Its data complexity is DP-complete for all the languages, in the presence or absence of compatibility constraints. □

Proof sketch: (1) We show that $\mathsf{MBP}(\mathsf{CQ})$ is D_2^p-hard by reduction from $\exists^*\forall^*3\mathsf{DNF}$-$\forall^*\exists^*3\mathsf{CNF}$. Given a pair (φ_1, φ_2) of $\exists^*\forall^*3\mathsf{DNF}$ instances, the latter is to decide whether φ_1 is true and φ_2 is false, and is D_2^p-complete [33]. We show that $\mathsf{MBP}(\exists\mathsf{FO}^+)$ is in D_2^p by giving an algorithm that makes a query to a Σ_2^p oracle and a query to a Π_2^p oracle.
(2) For $\mathsf{DATALOG}_{\mathsf{nr}}$, FO and $\mathsf{DATALOG}$, the proof for MBP extends its counterpart in the proofs (2-3) of Theorem 3.1.
(3) When Q and Q_c are fixed, we show that $\mathsf{MBP}(\mathsf{CQ})$ is DP-hard by reduction from SAT-UNSAT, and give a DP algorithm for $\mathsf{MBP}(\mathcal{L}_Q)$ when $\mathcal{L}_Q$ is FO or $\mathsf{DATALOG}$.
(4) In the absence of Q_c, the lower bound proofs given in (3) for CQ and in (2) for the others remain intact, since no Q_c is used there. The upper bounds given in (2-3) still hold. □

Counting valid packages. When it comes to the counting problem $\mathsf{CPP}(\mathcal{L}_Q)$, we provide its complexity as follows.

Theorem 3.5: For $\mathsf{CPP}(\mathcal{L}_Q)$, the combined complexity is
- $\#\cdot\mathsf{coNP}$-complete when $\mathcal{L}_Q$ is CQ, UCQ or $\exists\mathsf{FO}^+$;
- $\#\cdot\mathsf{PSPACE}$-complete when $\mathcal{L}_Q$ is $\mathsf{DATALOG}_{\mathsf{nr}}$ or FO;
- $\#\cdot\mathsf{EXPTIME}$-complete when $\mathcal{L}_Q$ is $\mathsf{DATALOG}$.

In the absence of compatibility constraints, its combined complexity remains unchanged for $\mathsf{DATALOG}_{\mathsf{nr}}$, FO and $\mathsf{DATALOG}$, but it is $\#\cdot\mathsf{NP}$-complete for CQ, UCQ and $\exists\mathsf{FO}^+$.

Its data complexity is $\#\cdot\mathsf{P}$-complete for all the languages in the presence or absence of compatibility constraints. □

Here we use the framework of predicate-based counting classes introduced in [15]. For a complexity class C of decision problems, $\#\cdot\mathsf{C}$ is the class of all counting problems associated with a predicate R_L that satisfies the following conditions: (a) R_L is polynomially balanced (see its definition above); and (b) the decision problem "given x and y, whether $R_L(x, y)$" is in C. A counting problem is to compute the cardinality of the set $\{y \mid R_L(x, y)\}$, i.e., it is to find how many y there are such that $R_L(x, y)$ is satisfied.

It is known that $\#\cdot\mathsf{P} = \#\mathsf{P}$, $\#\cdot\mathsf{NP} \subseteq \#\mathsf{NP} = \#\cdot\mathsf{P}^{\mathsf{NP}} = \#\cdot\mathsf{coNP}$, but $\#\cdot\mathsf{NP} = \#\cdot\mathsf{coNP}$ iff $\mathsf{NP} = \mathsf{coNP}$, where $\#\mathsf{P}$ and $\#\mathsf{NP}$ are counting classes in the machine-based framework of [31]. From these we know that the combined complexity of $\mathsf{CPP}(\mathsf{CQ})$ is $\#\cdot\mathsf{NP}$-complete, and the data complexity of $\mathsf{CPP}(\mathcal{L}_Q)$ is $\#\cdot\mathsf{P}$-complete for all the languages considered.

Proof sketch: (1) We show that $\mathsf{CPP}(\mathsf{CQ})$ is $\#\cdot\mathsf{coNP}$-hard by reduction from $\#\Pi_1\mathsf{SAT}$. Given $\varphi(X, Y) = \forall X\, \psi(X, Y)$, where ψ is a 3DNF, $\#\Pi_1\mathsf{SAT}$ is to count the number of truth assignments of Y that satisfy φ, and is $\#\cdot\mathsf{coNP}$-complete [11]. The reduction is an 1-1 mapping from the solutions to $\mathsf{CPP}(\mathsf{CQ})$ to the truth assignments for $\varphi(X, Y)$, and hence is *parsimonious*. We also show that $\mathsf{CPP}(\exists\mathsf{FO}^+)$ is in $\#\cdot\mathsf{coNP}$.
(2) We show that CPP is $\#\cdot\mathsf{PSPACE}$-hard for $\mathsf{DATALOG}_{\mathsf{nr}}$ and FO by parsimonious reductions from $\#\mathsf{QBF}$, which is $\#\cdot\mathsf{PSPACE}$-complete [21]. Given $\varphi = \exists X \forall y_1 P_2 y_2 \cdots P_n y_n\, \psi$, where ψ is a 3SAT instance over X and $\{y_i \mid i \in [1, n]\}$, and P_i is $\forall$ or $\exists$, $\#\mathsf{QBF}$ is to count the number of truth assignments of X that satisfy φ. For $\mathsf{DATALOG}$, we verify that CPP is $\#\cdot\mathsf{EXPTIME}$-hard by parsimonious reduction from all counting problems in $\#\cdot\mathsf{EXPTIME}$. We also show that CPP is in $\#\cdot\mathsf{PSPACE}$ (resp. $\#\cdot\mathsf{EXPTIME}$) for $\mathsf{DATALOG}_{\mathsf{nr}}$ and FO (resp. $\mathsf{DATALOG}$) by the definition of $\#\cdot\mathsf{C}$ classes.
(3) When Q and Q_c are fixed, we show that $\mathsf{CPP}(\mathsf{CQ})$ is $\#\cdot\mathsf{P}$-complete by parsimonious reduction from $\#\mathsf{SAT}$, which is $\#\cdot\mathsf{P}$-complete (cf. [25], by $\#\mathsf{P} = \#\cdot\mathsf{P}$). Given an instance ψ of 3SAT, $\#\mathsf{SAT}$ is to count truth assignments that satisfy ψ. We also show that CPP is in $\#\cdot\mathsf{P}$ for all the languages.
(4) When Q_c is absent, we show that $\mathsf{CPP}(\mathsf{CQ})$ is $\#\cdot\mathsf{NP}$-hard by parsimonious reduction from $\#\Sigma_1\mathsf{SAT}$, which is $\#\cdot\mathsf{NP}$-complete [11]. Given $\varphi(X, Y) = \exists X\, \psi(X, Y)$, $\#\Sigma_1\mathsf{SAT}$ is to count truth assignments of Y that satisfy φ, where ψ is a 3DNF. We also show that $\mathsf{CPP}(\exists\mathsf{FO}^+)$ is in $\#\cdot\mathsf{NP}$. When $\mathcal{L}_Q$ is $\mathsf{DATALOG}_{\mathsf{nr}}$, FO or $\mathsf{DATALOG}$, the proofs of (2) given above carry over (its lower bound proofs do not use Q_c). □

4. SPECIAL CASES OF POI RECOMMENDATIONS

The results of Section 3 tell us that RPP, FRP, MBP and CPP have rather high complexity. In this section we revisit these problems for special cases of package recommendations, to explore the impact of various parameters of these problems on their complexity. We consider the settings when packages are bounded by a constant instead of a polynomial, when $\mathcal{L}_Q$ is a language for which the membership problem is in PTIME, and when compatibility constraints are simply PTIME functions. We also study item recommendations, for which each package has a single item, and compatibility constraints are absent. Our main conclusion of this section is that the complexity of these problem is rather *robust*: these restrictions simplify the analyses, but not much.

Packages with a fixed bound. One might be tempted to think that fixing package size would simplify the analyses. Below we study the impact of fixing package sizes on package selections, in the presence of compatibility constraints Q_c, by considering packages N such that $|N| \leq B_p$, where B_p is a predefined *constant* rather than a polynomial.

We show that fixing package sizes does not make our lives easier when combined complexity is concerned. In contrast, this does simplify the analyses of data complexity.

Corollary 4.1: For packages with a constant bound B_p, the combined complexity bounds of RPP, FRP, MBP and CPP are the same as given in Theorems 3.1, 3.3, 3.4 and 3.5, respectively; and the data complexity is

- in PTIME for RPP,
- in FP for FRP,
- in PTIME for MBP, and
- in FP for CPP,

for all the languages of Section 2. The complexity remains unchanged even when B_p is fixed to be 1. □

Proof sketch: (1) The lower bounds of RPP, FRP, MBP and CPP in the presence of Q_c hold here, since their proofs (Theorems 3.1, 3.3, 3.4 and 3.5) use only top-1 package with one item, and all the upper bounds carry over here. (2) For fixed Q and Q_c, we give algorithms in PTIME, FP, PTIME and FP for RPP, FRP, MBP and CPP, respectively. □

SP queries. In contrast, for queries that have a PTIME complexity for their membership problem, variable package sizes lead to higher complexity of RPP, FRP, MBP and CPP than their counterparts for packages with a fixed bound.

To illustrate this, we consider SP queries, a simple fragment of CQ queries that support projection and selection operators only. An SP query is of the form

$$Q(\vec{x}) = \exists \vec{x} \vec{y} \, (R(\vec{x}, \vec{y}) \wedge \psi(\vec{x}, \vec{y})),$$

where ψ is a conjunction of predicates $=, \neq, <, \leq, >$ and $\geq$.

The result below holds for all query languages with a PTIME membership problem, including but not limited to SP. In fact the lower bounds remain intact even when the selection criteria are specified by an *identity query*, when $|\vec{y}| = 0$ and ψ is a tautology in an SP query.

Corollary 4.2: For SP queries, the combined complexity and data complexity are

- coNP-complete for RPP, but in PTIME for packages with a fixed (constant) bound B_p;
- FP^{NP}-complete for FRP, but in FP for fixed B_p;
- DP-complete for MBP, but in PTIME for fixed B_p; and
- #·P-complete for CPP, but in FP for fixed B_p.

when compatibility constraints are present or absent. □

Proof sketch: (1) For packages of variable sizes, the lower bounds of RPP, FRP, MBP and CPP with fixed Q in CQ hold for SP. Indeed, their proofs of Theorems 3.1, 3.3, 3.4 and 3.5 use an identity query as Q, which is in SP. For the upper bounds, the algorithms given there for RPP, FRP, MBP and CPP with a fixed Q apply to arbitrary SP queries.

(2) For packages with a constant bound, the algorithms for fixed Q of Corollary 4.1 apply to SP queries, fixed or not. □

PTIME compatibility constraints. One might also think that we would get lower complexity with PTIME compatibility constraints. That is, we simply treat compatibility constraints as PTIME functions rather than queries in $\mathcal{L}_Q$. In this setting, the complexity remains the same as its counterpart when Q_c is absent, no better and no worse.

Corollary 4.3: With PTIME compatibility constraints Q_c, the combined complexity and data complexity of RPP, FRP MBP and CPP remain the same as their counterparts in the absence of Q_c, as given in Theorems 3.2, 3.3, 3.4 and 3.5, respectively, for all the languages of Section 2. □

Proof sketch: The lower bounds of RPP, FRP, MBP and CPP in the absence of Q_c obviously carry over to this setting, since when Q_c is empty (see Section 2), Q_c is in PTIME. The upper bound proofs for Theorems 3.2, 3.3, 3.4 and 3.5 in the absence of Q_c also remain intact here. Indeed, adding an extra PTIME step for checking $Q_c(N, D) = \emptyset$ does not increase the complexity of the algorithms given there. □

Item recommendations. As remarked in Section 2, item recommendations are a special case of package recommendations when (a) compatibility constraints Q_c are *absent*, and (b) each package consists of a single item, *i.e.*, with *a fixed size* 1. Given a database D, a query $Q \in \mathcal{L}_Q$, a utility function $f()$ and a natural number $k \geq 1$, a top-k item selection is a top-k package selection specified in terms of (Q, D, f).

When Q_c is absent and packages have a fixed size 1, one might expect that the recommendation analyses would become much simpler. Unfortunately, this is not the case.

Theorem 4.4: For items, RPP, FRP, MBP and CPP have

- the same combined complexity as their counterparts in the absence of Q_c (Theorems 3.2, 3.3, 3.4, 3.5), and
- the same data complexity as their counterparts for packages with a constant bound (Corollary 4.1),

for all the query languages given in Section 2. □

Proof sketch: (1) Combined complexity. The upper bounds of these problems in the absence of Q_c (Theorems 3.2, 3.3, 3.4, 3.5) obviously remain intact here. The lower bound proofs for RPP and CPP given there are still valid for item recommendations, since they require only top-1 packages with a single item. For FRP and MBP, however, new lower bound proofs are required for item recommendations.

More specifically, we show that FRP(CQ) is FP^{NP}-hard by reduction from MAX-WEIGHT SAT, and that MBP(CQ) is DP-hard by reduction from SAT-UNSAT, for item recommendations. For other languages $\mathcal{L}_Q$, the proofs for FRP($\mathcal{L}_Q$) and MBP($\mathcal{L}_Q$) are given along the same lines as their counterparts for Theorems 3.3 and 3.4, respectively.

(2) Data complexity. The algorithms developed for Corollary 4.1 suffice for item selections when Q is fixed. □

Summary. From these results we find the following.

Variable sizes of packages. (1) For simple queries that have a PTIME membership problem, such as SP, the problems with variable package sizes have higher combined *and* data complexity than their counterparts with a fixed (constant) package size. This is in line with the claim of [34]. (2) In contrast, for any query language that subsumes CQ, variable sizes of packages have no impact on the *combined complexity* of these problems. This is consistent with the observation of [26]. (3) When it comes to *the data complexity*, however, variable (polynomially) package sizes make our lives harder: RPP, FRP, MBP and CPP in this setting have a higher data complexity than their counterparts with a fixed package size.

Compatibility constraints. (1) For CQ, UCQ and $\exists \text{FO}^+$, the presence of Q_c increases the combined complexity of the analyses. (2) In contrast, for more powerful languages such as DATALOG$_{nr}$, FO and DATALOG, neither Q_c nor variable sizes make any difference. Indeed, RPP, FRP, MBP and CPP have exactly the same combined complexity as their counterparts for item recommendations, in the presence or absence of Q_c. (3) For data complexity, the presence of Q_c has no impact. Indeed, when Q_c is fixed, it is in PTIME to check $Q_c(N, D) = \emptyset$ for all $\mathcal{L}_Q$ in which Q_c is expressed; hence Q_c can be encoded in the cost() function, and no longer needs to be treated separately. (4) To simplify the discussion we use $\mathcal{L}_Q$ to specify Q_c. Nonetheless, all the complexity results remain intact for any class $\mathcal{C}$ of Q_c whose satisfiability problem has the same complexity as the membership problem for $\mathcal{L}_Q$. In particular, when $\mathcal{C}$ is a class of PTIME functions, the presence of Q_c has no impact on the complexity.

The number k of packages. All the lower bounds of RPP, FRP and MBP remain intact *when $k = 1$* (k is irrelevant to CPP), *i.e.*, they carry over to top-1 package selections.

5. RECOMMENDATIONS OF QUERY RELAXATIONS

We next study query relaxation recommendations. In practice a selection query Q often finds no sensible packages. When this happens, the users naturally want the recommendation system to suggests how to revise their selection criteria by relaxing the query Q. We are not aware of any recommendation systems that support this functionality.

Below we first present query relaxations (Section 5.1). We then identify two query relaxation recommendation problems, and establish their complexity bounds (Section 5.2).

5.1 Query Relaxations

Consider a query Q, in which a set X of variables (free or bound) and a set E of constants are parameters that can be modified, *e.g.*, variables or constants indicating departure time and date of flights. Following [8], we relax Q by replacing constants in E with variables, and replacing repeated variables in X with distinct variables, as follows.

(1) For each constant $c \in E$, we associate a variable w_c with c. We denote the tuple consisting of all such variables as $\vec{w}$.

(2) For each variable $x \in X$ that appears at least twice in atoms of Q, we introduce a new variable u_x and substitute u_x for one of the occurrences of x. For instance, an equijoin $Q_1(\vec{v}, y) \wedge Q_2(y, \vec{v}')$ is converted to $Q_1(\vec{v}, y) \wedge Q_2(u_y, \vec{v}')$, a Cartesian product. This is repeated until no variable has multiple occurrences. Let $\vec{u}$ be the tuple of all such variables.

We denote the domain of w_c (resp. u_x) as dom$(R.A)$ if c (resp. x) appears in Q as an A-attribute value in relation R.

To prevent relaxations that are too general, we constrain variables in $\vec{w}$ and $\vec{u}$ with certain ranges, by means of techniques developed for query relaxations [8, 18] and preference queries [29]. To simplify the discussion, we assume that for each attribute A in a relation R, a distance function

dist$_{R.A}(a, b)$ is defined. Intuitively, if dist$_{R.A}(a, b)$ is within a bound, then b is close enough to a, and we can relax Q by replacing a with its "neighbor" b. For instance, DB can be generalized to CS if dist(DB, CS) is small enough [8]. We denote by Γ the set of all such distance functions.

Given Γ, we define a *relaxed query* Q_Γ of $Q(\vec{x})$ as:

$$Q_\Gamma(\vec{x}) = \exists \vec{w} \exists \vec{u} \, (Q'(\vec{x}, \vec{w}, \vec{u}) \wedge \psi_w(\vec{w}) \wedge \psi_u(\vec{u})),$$

where Q' is obtained from Q by substituting w_c for constant c, and u_x for a repeated occurrence of x. Here $\psi_w(\vec{w})$ is a conjunction of predicates of either (a) dist$_{R.A}(w_c, c) \leq d$, where the domain of w_c is dom$(R.A)$, and d is a constant, or (b) $w_c = c$, *i.e.*, the constant c is unchanged. Query $\psi_w(\vec{w})$ includes such a conjunct for each $w_c \in \vec{w}$; similarly for $\psi_u(\vec{u})$.

We define *the level* gap(γ) *of relaxation of a predicate* γ in $\psi_w(\vec{w})$ as follows: gap$(\gamma) = d$ if γ is dist$_{R.A}(w_c, c) \leq d$, and gap$(\gamma) = 0$ if γ is $w_c = c$; similarly for a predicate in $\psi_u(\vec{u})$.

We define *the level of relaxation of query* Q_Γ, denoted by gap(Q_Γ), to be sum$_{\gamma \in (\psi_w(\vec{w}) \cup \psi_u(\vec{u}))}gap(\gamma)$.

Example 5.1: Recall query Q defined on flight and POI in Example 1.1. The query finds no items, as there is no direct flight from EDI to NYC. Suppose that E has constants EDI, NYC, 1/1/2012 and $X = \{x_{\text{To}}\}$, and that the user accepts a city within 15 miles of the original departure city (resp. destination) as From (resp. To), where dist( ) measures the distances between cities. Then we can relax Q as:

$Q_1(\text{f\#}, \text{Pr}, \text{nm}, \text{tp}, \text{tkt}, \text{tm}) = \exists \text{DT}, \text{AT}, \text{AD}, u_{\text{To}}, w_{\text{Edi}}, w_{\text{NYC}}, w_{\text{DD}}$
$(\text{flight}(\text{f\#}, w_{\text{Edi}}, x_{\text{To}}, \text{DT}, w_{\text{DD}}, \text{AT}, \text{AD}, \text{Pr}) \wedge x_{\text{To}} = w_{\text{NYC}}$
$\wedge \text{POI}(\text{nm}, u_{\text{To}}, \text{tp}, \text{tkt}, \text{tm}) \wedge w_{\text{DD}} = 1/1/2012$
$\wedge \text{dist}(w_{\text{NYC}}, \text{NYC}) \leq 15 \wedge \text{dist}(w_{\text{Edi}}, \text{EDI}) \leq 15 \wedge x_{\text{To}} = u_{\text{To}}).$

The relaxed Q_1 finds direct flights from EDI to EWR, since the distance between NYC to EWR is within 15 miles.

We can relax Q_1 by allowing w_{DD} to be within 3 days of 1/12/11, where the distance function for dates is dist$_d()$:

$Q_2(\text{f\#}, \text{Pr}, \text{nm}, \text{tp}, \text{tkt}, \text{tm}) = \exists \text{DT}, \text{AT}, \text{AD}, u_{\text{To}}, w_{\text{Edi}}, w_{\text{NYC}}, w_{\text{DD}}$
$(\text{flight}(\text{f\#}, w_{\text{Edi}}, x_{\text{To}}, \text{DT}, w_{\text{DD}}, \text{AT}, \text{AD}, \text{Pr}) \wedge x_{\text{To}} = w_{\text{NYC}}$
$\wedge \text{POI}(\text{nm}, u_{\text{To}}, \text{tp}, \text{tkt}, \text{tm}) \wedge \text{dist}_d(w_{\text{DD}}, 1/1/2012) \leq 3$
$\wedge \text{dist}(w_{\text{NYC}}, \text{NYC}) \leq 15 \wedge \text{dist}(w_{\text{Edi}}, \text{EDI}) \leq 15 \wedge x_{\text{To}} = u_{\text{To}}).$

Then Q_2 may find more available direct flights than Q_1, with possibly cheaper airfare. One can further relax Q_2 by allowing u_{To} and x_{To} to match different cities nearby, *i.e.*, we convert the equijoin to a Cartesian product. □

We consider simple query relaxation rules here just to illustrate the main idea of query relaxation recommendations, and defer a full treatment of this issue to future work.

5.2 Query Relaxation Recommendations

We now study recommendation problems for query relaxations, for package selections and for item selections.

The query relaxation problem for packages. Consider a database D, queries Q and Q_c in $\mathcal{L}_Q$, functions cost() and val(), a cost budget C, a rating bound B, and a natural number $k \geq 1$. When there exists no top-k package selection for $(Q, D, Q_c, \text{cost}(), \text{val}(), C)$, we need to relax Q to find more packages for the users. More specifically, let Γ be a collection of distance functions, and X and E be sets of variables and constants in Q, respectively, which are parameters that can be modified. We want to find a relaxed query Q_Γ of Q such that there exists a set $\mathcal{N}$ of k valid packages for $(Q_\Gamma, D, Q_c, \text{cost}(), \text{val}(), C, B)$, *i.e.*, for each $N \in \mathcal{N}$, $N \subseteq Q_\Gamma(D)$, $Q_c(N, D) = \emptyset$, cost$(N) \leq C$, val$(N) \geq B$, and $|N|$

is bounded by a polynomial in $|D|$. Moreover, we want Q_Γ to *minimally differ* from the original Q, stated as follows.

For a constant g, a relaxed query Q_Γ of Q is called *a relaxation of Q for* $(Q, D, Q_c, \mathsf{cost}(), \mathsf{val}(), C, B, k, g)$ if (a) there exists a set $\mathcal{N}$ of k distinct valid packages for $(Q_\Gamma, D, Q_c, \mathsf{cost}(), \mathsf{val}(), C, B)$, and (b) $\mathsf{gap}(Q_\Gamma) \leq g$.

QRPP($\mathcal{L}_Q$): *The query relaxation rec. problem (packages)*
INPUT: A database D, a query $Q \in \mathcal{L}_Q$ with sets X and E identified, a query $Q_c \in \mathcal{L}_Q$, two functions $\mathsf{cost}()$ and $\mathsf{val}()$, natural numbers C, B, g and $k \geq 1$, and a collection Γ of distance functions.
QUESTION: Does there exist a relaxation Q_Γ of Q for $(Q, D, Q_c, \mathsf{cost}(), \mathsf{val}(), C, B, k, g)$?

No matter how important, QRPP is nontrivial: it is Σ_2^p-complete for CQ, PSPACE-complete for DATALOG$_{nr}$ and FO, and EXPTIME-complete for DATALOG. It is NP-complete when selection criteria Q and compatibility constraints Q_c are both fixed. Fixing Q_c alone reduces the combined complexity of QRPP($\mathcal{L}_Q$) when $\mathcal{L}_Q$ is CQ, UCQ or $\exists$FO$^+$, but it does not help when it comes to DATALOG$_{nr}$, FO and DATALOG, or when the data complexity is concerned.

Theorem 5.1: For QRPP($\mathcal{L}_Q$), the combined complexity is

- Σ_2^p-complete when $\mathcal{L}_Q$ is CQ, UCQ or $\exists$FO$^+$;
- PSPACE-complete when $\mathcal{L}_Q$ is DATALOG$_{nr}$ or FO; and
- EXPTIME-complete when $\mathcal{L}_Q$ is DATALOG.

In the absence of compatibility constraints, its combined complexity remains unchanged for DATALOG$_{nr}$, FO and DATALOG, and it is NP-complete for CQ, UCQ and $\exists$FO$^+$.

Its data complexity is NP-complete for all the languages, in the presence or absence of compatibility constraints. □

Proof sketch: (1) We verify that QRPP(CQ) is Σ_2^p-hard by reduction from the $\exists^*\forall^*$3DNF problem, by using relaxed queries. We show that QRPP($\exists$FO$^+$) is in Σ_2^p by giving a nondeterministic PTIME algorithm that calls an NP oracle.

(2) For DATALOG$_{nr}$ and FO, we show that QRPP is PSPACE-hard by reductions from Q3SAT and the membership problem for FO, respectively, by using relaxed queries. We give a PSPACE algorithm to check QRPP. Along the same lines we show that QRPP(DATALOG) is EXPTIME-complete.

(3) When Q is fixed, we show that QRPP(CQ) is already NP-hard in the absence of Q_c, by reduction from 3SAT. We show the upper bound by giving an NP algorithm to check QRPP($\mathcal{L}_Q$) for fixed queries Q and Q_c in FO or DATALOG.

(4) In the absence of Q_c, it has been shown that QRPP(CQ) is NP-hard by the proof of (3) above, and the algorithm for QRPP($\exists$FO$^+$) given in (1) is now in NP. For DATALOG$_{nr}$, FO and DATALOG, the proofs given in (2) above can be applied here, since their lower bound proofs do not use Q_c, and their upper bounds still hold in this special case. □

The query relaxation problem for items. We also study a special case of QRPP, for item selections. Given D, Q, Γ, B, k, and a utility function $f()$, QRPP *for items* is to decide whether there exist a relaxation Q_Γ of Q for $(Q, D, Q_c, \mathsf{cost}(), \mathsf{val}(), C, B, k, g)$, when Q_c is empty, and $\mathsf{cost}()$, $\mathsf{val}()$ and C are derived from $f()$ as given in Section 2.

Compared to its package counterpart, item selections simplify the data complexity analyses of query relaxation rec-

ommendations. However, it gets no better than QRPP in the absence of Q_c when the combined complexity is concerned.

Corollary 5.2: For all the query languages $\mathcal{L}_Q$ given in Section 2, QRPP($\mathcal{L}_Q$) for items (1) has the same combined complexity as QRPP($\mathcal{L}_Q$) in the absence of compatibility constraints; and (2) its data complexity is in PTIME. □

Proof sketch: For items, (1) we show that QRPP(CQ) is NP-hard by reduction from 3SAT. To check QRPP($\exists$FO$^+$) we give an NP algorithm. For DATALOG$_{nr}$, FO or DATALOG, the lower bounds of Theorem 5.1 hold here since their proofs use top-1 items only. The upper bounds of the combined complexity also carry over. (2) We give a PTIME algorithm to check QRPP for fixed Q in FO or DATALOG. □

Remarks. (1) All the lower bounds of this section remains intact when $k = 1$, *i.e.*, for top-1 package or item selections. (2) The proofs of Theorem 5.1 and Corollary 5.2 also tell us that for packages with a constant bound, QRPP($\mathcal{L}_Q$) has the same combined complexity as its counterpart for packages with variable sizes, and it has the same data complexity as its counterpart for items. (3) In addition, when Q_c is a PTIME function, QRPP($\mathcal{L}_Q$) has the same combined and data complexity as its counterpart in the absence of Q_c. These are consistent with Corollaries 4.1 and 4.3.

6. ADJUSTMENT RECOMMENDATIONS

We next study adjustment recommendations. In practice the collection D of items maintained by a recommendation system may fail to provide items that most users want. When this happens, the vendors of the system would want the system to recommend how to "minimally" modify D such that users' requests could be satisfied. Below we first present adjustments to D (Section 6.1). We then study adjustment recommendations problems (Section 6.2).

6.1 Adjustments to Item Collections

Consider a database D consisting of items provided by a system, and a collection D' of additional items. We use $\Delta(D, D')$ to denote *adjustments to D*, which is a set consisting of (a) tuples to be deleted from D, and (b) tuples from D' to be inserted into D. We use $D \oplus \Delta(D, D')$ to denote the database obtained by modifying D with $\Delta(D, D')$.

Consider queries Q, Q_c in $\mathcal{L}_Q$, functions $\mathsf{cost}()$ and $\mathsf{val}()$, a cost budget C, a rating bound B, and a natural number $k \geq 1$, such that there exists no top-k package selection for $(Q, D, Q_c, \mathsf{cost}(), \mathsf{val}(), C)$. We want to find a set $\Delta(D, D')$ of adjustments to D such that there exists a set $\mathcal{N}$ of k valid packages for $(Q, D \oplus \Delta(D, D'), Q_c, \mathsf{cost}(), \mathsf{val}(), C, B)$, *i.e.*, $D \oplus \Delta(D, D')$ yields k packages N that are rated above B, and satisfy the selection criteria Q, compatibility constraints Q_c as well as aggregate constraints $\mathsf{cost}(N) \leq C$.

One naturally wants to find a "minimum" $\Delta(D, D')$ to adjust D. For a constant $k' \geq 1$, we call $\Delta(D, D')$ a *package adjustment* for $(Q, D, Q_c, \mathsf{cost}(), \mathsf{val}(), C, B, k, k')$ if (a) $|\Delta(D, D')| \leq k'$, and (b) there exist k distinct valid packages for $(Q, D \oplus \Delta(D, D'), Q_c, \mathsf{cost}(), \mathsf{val}(), C, B)$.

6.2 Deciding Adjustment Recommendations

These suggest that we study the following problem.

The adjustment recommendation problem. Given D, D', Q, Q_c, $\mathsf{cost}()$, $\mathsf{val}()$, k and k', the *adjustment recommendation problem for packages*, ARPP, is to decide whether there is a package adjustment $\Delta(D, D')$ for

$(Q, D, Q_c, \mathsf{cost}(), \mathsf{val}(), C, B, k, k')$. This problem is no easier than the analyses of query relaxation recommendations. Indeed, ARPP($\mathcal{L}_Q$) has the same combined and data complexity as QRPP($\mathcal{L}_Q$), although their proofs are quite different.

Theorem 6.1: The combined complexity of ARPP($\mathcal{L}_Q$) is

- Σ_2^p-complete when $\mathcal{L}_Q$ is CQ, UCQ or $\exists\mathrm{FO}^+$;
- PSPACE-complete when $\mathcal{L}_Q$ is DATALOG$_{\mathsf{nr}}$ or FO; and
- EXPTIME-complete when $\mathcal{L}_Q$ is DATALOG.

In the absence of compatibility constraints, its combined complexity remains unchanged for DATALOG$_{\mathsf{nr}}$, FO and DATALOG, and it is NP-complete for CQ, UCQ and $\exists\mathrm{FO}^+$.

Its data complexity is NP-complete for all the languages, in the presence or absence of compatibility constraints. □

Proof sketch: (1) We show that ARPP(CQ) is Σ_2^p-hard by reduction from the $\exists^*\forall^*3$DNF problem. The reduction here makes use of updates $\Delta(D, D')$, and is different from the one for QRPP(CQ). To verify the upper bound, we give an NP algorithm that uses an NP oracle to check ARPP($\exists\mathrm{FO}^+$).

(2) For DATALOG$_{\mathsf{nr}}$ and FO, we show that ARPP is PSPACE-hard by reductions from Q3SAT and the membership problem for FO, respectively, which again use $\Delta(D, D')$ and are different from the ones used earlier. We give a PSPACE algorithm to check ARPP for DATALOG$_{\mathsf{nr}}$ and FO. Similarly we show that ARPP(DATALOG) is EXPTIME-complete.

(3) When Q and Q_c are fixed, we show that ARPP(CQ) is NP-hard without Q_c by reduction from 3SAT. We also provide an NP algorithm to check ARPP for FO and DATALOG.

(4) When Q_c is absent, ARPP(CQ) is NP-hard even when Q is fixed by the proof of (3), and the algorithm for $\exists\mathrm{FO}^+$ given in (1) is now in NP. For the languages considered in (2), their lower bound proofs do not use Q_c, and their upper bound proofs cover this special case. Moreover, the algorithm developed in (3) and the lower bound of ARPP(CQ) verify that the data complexity is NP-complete. □

The adjustment recommendation problem for items. Given D, D', Q, B, k, k' and a utility function $f()$, ARPP *for items* is to decide whether there is an adjustment $\Delta(D, D')$ for $(Q, D, Q_c, \mathsf{cost}(), \mathsf{val}(), C, B, k, k')$, where Q_c is empty, and $\mathsf{cost}(), \mathsf{val}(), C$ are derived from $f()$ (see Section 2).

One might expect that fixing package sizes in item selections would simplify the analyses of adjustment recommendations. Recall that all the problems we have studied so far have a lower data complexity for item selections than their counterparts for packages. For instance, the data complexity of QRPP for items is in PTIME while it is NP-complete for packages; similarly for RPP, FRP, MBP and CPP. In contrast, we show below that the data complexity of ARPP for packages is *robust*: it remains intact for items. In other words, fixing package sizes does not help here.

Corollary 6.2: For all the languages $\mathcal{L}_Q$ given in Section 2, ARPP in the absence of compatibility constraints and ARPP for items have the same combined and data complexity. □

Proof sketch: All the lower bound proofs for ARPP($\mathcal{L}_Q$) in the absence of Q_c use top-k item selections, and ARPP(CQ) is NP-hard for fixed Q. Hence for all $\mathcal{L}_Q$, ARPP without Q_c has the same combined complexity as ARPP for items, and the data complexity of ARPP carries over to item selections. Note that when proving ARPP(CQ) is NP-hard for fixed Q, we do not use $k = 1$, the only case in the entire paper. □

Remarks. One can find the following from the proofs of Theorem 6.1 and Corollary 6.2. (1) For packages with a constant bound, ARPP($\mathcal{L}_Q$) has the same combined complexity as ARPP($\mathcal{L}_Q$) for packages with variable sizes, and it has the same data complexity as ARPP($\mathcal{L}_Q$) for items. (3) When Q_c is in PTIME, ARPP($\mathcal{L}_Q$) has the same combined and data complexity as ARPP($\mathcal{L}_Q$) in the absence of Q_c.

7. CONCLUSIONS

We have studied a general model for recommendation systems, and investigated several fundamental problems in the model, from decision problems RPP, MBP to function problem FRP and counting problem CPP. Beyond POI recommendations, we have proposed and studied QRPP for query relaxation recommendations, and ARPP for adjustment recommendations. We have also investigated special cases of these problems, when compatibility constraints Q_c are absent or in PTIME, when all packages are bounded by a constant B_p, and when both Q_c is absent and B_p is fixed to be 1 for item selections. We have provided a complete picture of the lower and upper bounds of these problems, *all matching*, for both their data complexity and combined complexity, when $\mathcal{L}_Q$ ranges over a variety of query languages. These results tell us where complexity of these problems arises.

The main complexity results are summarized in Table 1, annotated with their corresponding theorems (the results for SP (Corollary 4.2) are excluded). As remarked earlier, (1) the data complexity is *independent of* query languages, and remains *unchanged* in the presence of compatibility constraints Q_c or not. However, it *varies* when packages have variable sizes or a constant bound, as shown in Table 1. (2) The complexity bounds of these problems for CQ, UCQ and $\exists\mathrm{FO}^+$ *vary* when Q_c is present or not, and when packages have a constant bound or not. In contrast, the bounds for FO, DATALOG$_{\mathsf{nr}}$ and DATALOG are *robust, regardless of* the presence of Q_c and package sizes. (3) When Q_c is a PTIME function, these problems have the same complexity as their counterparts in the absence of Q_c. (4) Item selections do not come with Q_c and have a fixed package size (see Table 1).

The study of recommendation problems is still preliminary. First, we have only considered simple rules for query relaxations and adjustment recommendations, to focus on the main ideas. These issues deserve a full investigation. Second, this work aims to study a general model that subsumes previous models developed for various applications, and hence adopts generic functions $\mathsf{cost}()$, $\mathsf{val}()$ and $f()$. These need to be fine tuned by incorporating information about users, collaborative filtering and specific aggregate functions. Third, to simplify the discussion we assume that selection criteria Q and compatibility constraints Q_c are expressed in the same language (albeit PTIME Q_c). It is worth studying different languages for Q and Q_c. Fourth, the recommendation problems are mostly intractable. An interesting topic is to identify practical and tractable cases. Another issue to consider are group recommendations [5], to a group of users instead of a single user.

Acknowledgments. Fan and Geerts are supported in part by an IBM scalable data analytics award, and the RSE-NSFC Joint Project Scheme. Fan is also supported in part by the 973 Program 2012CB316200 and NSFC 61133002 of China. Deng is supported in part by 863 2012AA011203, NSFC 61103031 and CPSF 2011M500208 of China.

Problems	Languages	Combined complexity		Data complexity	
		With Q_c	Without Q_c	Poly-bounded	Constant bound
RPP	CQ, UCQ, $\exists FO^+$ DATALOG$_{nr}$, FO DATALOG	Π_2^p-complete$^{(\S)}$ PSPACE-complete$^{(\S)}$ EXPTIME-complete$^{(\S)}$ (Th. 3.1)	DP-complete$^{(\star,\dagger)}$ PSPACE-complete$^{(\star,\dagger)}$ EXPTIME-complete$^{(\star,\dagger)}$ (Th. 3.2)	coNP-complete$^{(\dagger)}$ coNP-complete$^{(\dagger)}$ coNP-complete$^{(\dagger)}$ (Th. 3.1)	PTIME $^{(\star)}$ PTIME $^{(\star)}$ PTIME $^{(\star)}$ (Cor. 4.1)
FRP	CQ, UCQ, $\exists FO^+$ DATALOG$_{nr}$, FO DATALOG	$FP^{\Sigma_2^p}$-complete$^{(\S)}$ FPSPACE(poly)-complete$^{(\S)}$ FEXPTIME(poly)-complete$^{(\S)}$ (Th. 3.3)	FP^{NP}-complete$^{(\star,\dagger)}$ FPSPACE(poly)-complete$^{(\star,\dagger)}$ FEXPTIME(poly)-complete$^{(\star,\dagger)}$ (Th. 3.3)	FP^{NP}-complete$^{(\dagger)}$ FP^{NP}-complete$^{(\dagger)}$ FP^{NP}-complete$^{(\dagger)}$ (Th. 3.3)	FP $^{(\star)}$ FP $^{(\star)}$ FP $^{(\star)}$ (Cor. 4.1)
MBP	CQ, UCQ, $\exists FO^+$ DATALOG$_{nr}$, FO DATALOG	D_2^p-complete PSPACE-complete$^{(\S)}$ EXPTIME-complete (Th. 3.4)	DP-complete$^{(\star,\dagger)}$ PSPACE-complete$^{(\star,\dagger)}$ EXPTIME-complete$^{(\star,\dagger)}$ (Th. 3.4)	DP-complete$^{(\dagger)}$ DP-complete$^{(\dagger)}$ DP-complete$^{(\dagger)}$ (Th. 3.4)	PTIME $^{(\star)}$ PTIME $^{(\star)}$ PTIME $^{(\star)}$ (Cor. 4.1)
CPP	CQ, UCQ, $\exists FO^+$ DATALOG$_{nr}$, FO DATALOG	#·coNP-complete$^{(\S)}$ #·PSPACE-complete$^{(\S)}$ #·EXPTIME-complete$^{(\S)}$ (Th. 3.5)	#·NP-complete$^{(\star,\dagger)}$ #·PSPACE-complete$^{(\star,\dagger)}$ #·EXPTIME-complete$^{(\star,\dagger)}$ (Th. 3.5)	#·P-complete$^{(\dagger)}$ #·P-complete$^{(\dagger)}$ #·P-complete$^{(\dagger)}$ (Th. 3.5)	FP $^{(\star)}$ FP $^{(\star)}$ FP $^{(\star)}$ (Cor. 4.1)
QRPP	CQ, UCQ, $\exists FO^+$ DATALOG$_{nr}$, FO DATALOG	Σ_2^p-complete$^{(\S)}$ PSPACE-complete$^{(\S)}$ EXPTIME-complete$^{(\S)}$ (Th. 5.1)	NP-complete$^{(\star,\dagger)}$ PSPACE-complete$^{(\star,\dagger)}$ EXPTIME-complete$^{(\star,\dagger)}$ (Th. 5.1)	NP-complete$^{(\dagger)}$ NP-complete$^{(\dagger)}$ NP-complete$^{(\dagger)}$ (Th. 5.1)	PTIME $^{(\star)}$ PTIME $^{(\star)}$ PTIME $^{(\star)}$ (Cor. 5.2)
ARPP	CQ, UCQ, $\exists FO^+$ DATALOG$_{nr}$, FO DATALOG	Σ_2^p-complete$^{(\S)}$ PSPACE-complete$^{(\S)}$ EXPTIME-complete$^{(\S)}$ (Th. 6.1)	NP-complete$^{(\star,\dagger)}$ PSPACE-complete$^{(\star,\dagger)}$ EXPTIME-complete$^{(\star,\dagger)}$ (Th. 6.1)	NP-complete$^{(\dagger)}$ NP-complete$^{(\dagger)}$ NP-complete$^{(\dagger)}$ (Th. 6.1)	NP-complete$^{(\star)}$ NP-complete$^{(\star)}$ NP-complete$^{(\star)}$ (Cor. 6.2)

Table 1: Complexity results ($^{(\star)}$: items (Th. 4.4); $^{(\S)}$: constant bound (Cor. 4.1); $^{(\dagger)}$: PTIME Q_c (Cor. 4.3))

8. REFERENCES

[1] S. Abiteboul, R. Hull, and V. Vianu. *Foundations of Databases*. Addison-Wesley, 1995.

[2] G. Adomavicius and A. Tuzhilin. Multidimensional recommender systems: A data warehousing approach. In *WELCOM*, 2001.

[3] G. Adomavicius and A. Tuzhilin. Toward the next generation of recommender systems: A survey of the state-of-the-art and possible extensions. *TKDE*, 17(6):734–749, 2005.

[4] S. Amer-Yahia. Recommendation projects at Yahoo! *IEEE Data Eng. Bull.*, 34(2):69–77, 2011.

[5] S. Amer-Yahia, S. B. Roy, A. Chawla, G. Das, and C. Yu. Group recommendation: Semantics and efficiency. *PVLDB*, 2(1):754–765, 2009.

[6] A. Angel, S. Chaudhuri, G. Das, and N. Koudas. Ranking objects based on relationships and fixed associations. In *EDBT*, 2009.

[7] A. Brodsky, S. Henshaw, and J. Whittle. CARD: A decision-guidance framework and application for recommending composite alternatives. In *RecSys*, 2008.

[8] S. Chaudhuri. Generalization and a framework for query modification. In *ICDE*, 1990.

[9] S. Chaudhuri and M. Y. Vardi. On the equivalence of recursive and nonrecursive Datalog programs. *JCSS*, 54(1):61–78, 1997.

[10] S. Cohen and Y. Sagiv. An incremental algorithm for computing ranked full disjunctions. *JCSS*, 73(4):648–668, 2007.

[11] A. Durand, M. Hermann, and P. G. Kolaitis. Subtractive reductions and complete problems for counting complexity classes. *TCS*, 340(3):496–513, 2005.

[12] R. Fagin, A. Lotem, and M. Naor. Optimal aggregation algorithms for middleware. *JCSS*, 66(4):614–656, 2003.

[13] T. Gaasterland and J. Lobo. Qualifying answers according to user needs and preferences. *Fundam. Inform.*, 32(2):121–137, 1997.

[14] K. Golenberg, B. Kimelfeld, and Y. Sagiv. Optimizing and parallelizing ranked enumeration. *PVLDB*, 4(11):1028–1039, 2011.

[15] L. A. Hemaspaandra and H. Vollmer. The satanic notations: counting classes beyond #P and other definitional adventures. *SIGACT News*, 26(1):2–13, 1995.

[16] I. F. Ilyas, G. Beskales, and M. A. Soliman. A survey of top-k query processing techniques in relational database systems. *ACM Comput. Surv.*, 40(4):11:1–11:58, 2008.

[17] A. Kadlag, A. V. Wanjari, J. Freire, and J. R. Haritsa. Supporting exploratory queries in databases. In *DASFAA*, 2004.

[18] N. Koudas, C. Li, A. K. H. Tung, and R. Vernica. Relaxing join and selection queries. In *VLDB*, 2006.

[19] G. Koutrika, B. Bercovitz, and H. Garcia-Molina. FlexRecs: expressing and combining flexible recommendations. In *SIGMOD*, 2009.

[20] M. W. Krentel. Generalizations of Opt P to the polynomial hierarchy. *TCS*, 97(2):183–198, 1992.

[21] R. E. Ladner. Polynomial space counting problems. *SIAM J. Comput.*, 18(6):1087–1097, 1989.

[22] T. Lappas, K. Liu, and E. Terzi. Finding a team of experts in social networks. In *KDD*, 2009.

[23] C. Li, M. A. Soliman, K. C.-C. Chang, and I. F. Ilyas. RankSQL: supporting ranking queries in relational database management systems. In *VLDB*, 2005.

[24] A. Natsev, Y.-C. Chang, J. R. Smith, C.-S. Li, and J. S. Vitter. Supporting incremental join queries on ranked inputs. In *VLDB*, 2001.

[25] C. H. Papadimitriou. *Computational Complexity*. AW, 1994.

[26] A. G. Parameswaran, H. Garcia-Molina, and J. D. Ullman. Evaluating, combining and generalizing recommendations with prerequisites. In *CIKM*, 2010.

[27] A. G. Parameswaran, P. Venetis, and H. Garcia-Molina. Recommendation systems with complex constraints: A course recommendation perspective. *TOIS*, 29(4), 2011.

[28] K. Schnaitter and N. Polyzotis. Evaluating rank joins with optimal cost. In *PODS*, 2008.

[29] K. Stefanidis, G. Koutrika, and E. Pitoura. A survey on representation, composition and application of preferences in database systems. *TODS*, 36(3), 2011.

[30] L. J. Stockmeyer. The polynomial-time hierarchy. *TCS*, 3(1):1–22, 1976.

[31] L. Valiant. The complexity of computing the permanent. *TCS*, 8(2):189 – 201, 1979.

[32] M. Y. Vardi. The complexity of relational query languages. In *STOC*, 1982.

[33] M. Wooldridge and P. E. Dunne. On the computational complexity of qualitative coalitional games. *Artif. Intell.*, 158(1):27–73, 2004.

[34] M. Xie, L. V. S. Lakshmanan, and P. T. Wood. Breaking out of the box of recommendations: from items to packages. In *RecSys*, 2010.

Space-Efficient Estimation of Statistics over Sub-Sampled Streams

Andrew McGregor[*]
University of Massachusetts
mcgregor@cs.umass.edu

A. Pavan[†]
Iowa State University
pavan@cs.iastate.edu

Srikanta Tirthapura[‡]
Iowa State University
snt@iastate.edu

David P. Woodruff
IBM Almaden
dpwoodru@us.ibm.com

ABSTRACT

In many stream monitoring situations, the data arrival rate is so high that it is not even possible to observe each element of the stream. The most common solution is to sample a small fraction of the data stream and use the sample to infer properties and estimate aggregates of the original stream. However, the quantities that need to be computed on the sampled stream are often different from the original quantities of interest and their estimation requires new algorithms. We present upper and lower bounds (often matching) for estimating frequency moments, support size, entropy, and heavy hitters of the original stream from the data observed in the sampled stream.

Categories and Subject Descriptors

F.2 [**Analysis of Algorithms & Problem Complexity**]

General Terms

Algorithms, Theory

Keywords

data streams, frequency moments, sub-sampling

1. INTRODUCTION

In many stream monitoring situations, the data arrival rate is so high that it is possible to observe each element in the stream. The most common solution is to sample a small fraction of the data stream and use the sample to infer properties of the original stream. For example, in an IP router, aggregated statistics of the packet stream are maintained through a protocol such as Netflow [6]. In

[*]Supported by NSF CAREER Award CCF-0953754.

[†]Supported in part by NSF CCF-0916797.

[‡]Supported in part by NSF CNS-0834743, CNS-0831903.

high-end routers, the load due to statistics maintenance can be so high that a variant of Netflow called *sampled Netflow* has been developed. In randomly sampled netflow, the monitor gets to view only a random sample of the packet stream, and must maintain statistics on the original stream, using this view.

In such scenarios of extreme data deluge, we are faced with two constraints on data processing. First, the entire data set is not seen by the monitor; only a random sample is seen. Second, even the random sample of the input is too large to be stored in main memory (or in secondary memory), and must be processed in a single pass through the data, as in the usual data stream model.

While there has been a large body of work that has dealt with data processing using a random sample (see for example, [2, 3]), and extensive work on the one-pass data stream model (see for example, [1, 15, 17]), there has been little work so far on data processing in the presence of both constraints, where only a random sample of the data set must be processed in a streaming fashion. We note that the estimation of frequency moments over a sampled stream is one of the open problems from [16], posed as Question 13, "Effects of Subsampling".

1.1 Problem Setting

We assume the setting of *Bernoulli sampling*, described as follows. Consider an input stream $P = \langle a_1, a_2, \ldots, a_n \rangle$ where $a_i \in \{1, 2, \ldots, m\}$. For a parameter p, $0 < p \leq 1$, a sub-stream of P, denoted L is constructed as follows. For $1 \leq i \leq n$, a_i is included in L with probability p. The stream processor is only allowed to see L, and cannot see P. The goal is to estimate properties of P through processing stream L. In the following discussion, L is called the *sampled stream*, and P is called the *original stream*.

1.2 Our Results

We present algorithms and lower bounds for estimating key aggregates of a data stream by processing a randomly sampled substream. We consider the basic frequency related aggregates, including the number of distinct elements, the kth frequency moments (F_k for $k \geq 1$), the empirical entropy of the frequency distribution, and the heavy hitters.

1. **Frequency Moments:** For the frequency moments $F_k, k \geq 2$, we present $(1+\varepsilon, \delta)$-approximation algorithms with space complexity[1] $\tilde{O}(p^{-1}m^{1-2/k})$. We show a matching lower

[1]Where $\tilde{O}$ notation suppresses factors polynomial in $1/\varepsilon$ and $1/\delta$ and factors logarithmic in m and n.

bound of $\Omega(p^{-1}m^{1-2/k})$, showing that the above algorithm is space optimal. This result yields an interesting tradeoff between the sampling probability and the space used by the algorithm. The smaller the sampling probability (up to a certain minimum probability), the greater is the streaming space complexity of F_k. The algorithms and lower bounds for F_k are presented in Section 3.

2. **Distinct Elements:** For the number of distinct elements, F_0, we show that the current best offline methods for estimating F_0 from a random sample can be implemented in a streaming fashion using very small space. While it is known that random sampling can significantly reduce the accuracy of an estimate for F_0 [5], we show that the need to process this stream using small space does not. The upper and lower bounds are presented in Section 4.

3. **Entropy:** For estimating entropy we first show that no multiplicative approximation is possible in general even when p is constant. However, we show that estimating the empirical entropy on the sampled stream yields a constant factor approximation to the entropy of the original stream given that the entropy is larger than some vanishingly small function of p and n. These results are presented in Section 5.

4. **Heavy Hitters:** We show tight bounds for identifying a set of $O(1/\alpha)$ elements whose frequency exceeds $\alpha F_k^{1/k}$ for $k \in \{1, 2\}$. In the case of $k = 1$, we show that existing heavy hitter algorithms can be used if the stream is sufficiently long compared with p. In the case of $k = 2$, we show how to adapt ideas used in Section 3 to prove matching $\tilde{\Theta}(1/p)$ upper and lower bounds. These results are presented in Section 6.

Another way of interpreting our results is in terms of time-space tradeoffs for data stream problems. Almost every streaming algorithm has a time complexity of at least n, since the algorithm reads and processes each stream update. We show that for estimating F_k (and other problems) it is unnecessary to process each update; instead, it suffices for the algorithm to read each item independently with probability p, and maintain a data structure of size $\tilde{O}(p^{-1} \cdot m^{1-2/k})$. Interestingly, the time to update the data structure per sampled stream item is still only $\tilde{O}(1)$. The time to output an estimate at the end of observation is $\tilde{O}(p^{-1} \cdot m^{1-2/k})$, i.e., roughly linear in the size of the data structure. As an example of the type of tradeoffs that are achievable, for estimating F_2 if $n = \Theta(m)$ we can set $p = \tilde{\Theta}(1/\sqrt{n})$ and obtain an algorithm using $\tilde{O}(\sqrt{n})$ time and $\tilde{O}(\sqrt{n})$ space.

1.3 Related Work

Duffield et al. [9] study issues in Internet traffic measurement using a sampled packet stream, and consider the estimation of the sizes of IP flows and the number of IP flows in a packet stream through observing the sampled stream. In a follow up work [10], they provide methods for estimating the distribution of the sizes of the input flows by observing samples of the original stream; this can be viewed as constructing an approximate histogram. This work is focused on Internet traffic estimation. The techniques used here are maximum likelihood estimation, as well as protocol level detail at the IP and TCP level. While this work deals with inference from a random sample in detail, it does not consider the streaming aspect of the computation, as we do here. Further, the aggregates that we consider (frequency moments, entropy) are not considered there.

Rusu and Dobra [18] consider the estimation of the second frequency moment of a stream, equivalently, the size of the self-join,

through processing the sampled stream. Our work differs from theirs in the following ways. First, their algorithm for the second frequency moment does not yield an $(1 + \epsilon, \delta)$ approximation of the second frequency moment, while ours does. Next, we consider higher frequency moments F_k, for $k > 2$, as well as the entropy, while they do not. Finally, our technique for estimating F_2 is different from theirs; ours relies on counting the number of collisions in the sampled stream, while theirs relies on estimating the second frequency moment of the sampled stream; this way we are able to get the theoretically optimal dependence of space on the sampling probability p. Rusu and Dobra have not explicitly mentioned the space bound of their algorithm; when we derived an $(1 + \epsilon, \delta)$ estimator for F_2 based on their algorithm, we found that the estimator took $\tilde{O}(1/p^2)$ space. We improve the dependency on the sampling probability and obtain an algorithm that only requires $\tilde{O}(1/p)$ space.

Bhattacharya et al. [4] consider stream processing in the model where the stream processor can adaptively "skip" past stream elements, and look at only a fraction of the input stream, thus speeding up stream computation. In their model, the stream processor has the power to decide which elements to see and which to skip past, hence it is "adaptive"; in our model, the stream processor does not have such power, and must deal with the randomly sampled stream that is presented to it. Our model reflects the setup in current network monitoring equipment, such as Randomly Sampled Netflow [6]. They present a constant factor approximation for F_2, while we present $(1 + \epsilon, \delta)$ approximations for all frequency moments $F_k, k \geq 2$.

There is work on *probabilistic data streams* [7, 14], where the data stream itself consists of "probabilistic" data, and each element of the stream is a probability distribution over a set of possible events. In contrast with our model, in this model the stream processor gets to see the entire input.

2. NOTATION AND PRELIMINARIES

Throughout this paper, we will denote the original length-n stream by $P = \langle a_1, a_2, \ldots, a_n \rangle$ and will assume that each element $a_i \in \{1, 2, \ldots, m\}$. We denote the sampling probability with p. The sampled stream L is constructed by including each a_i, $1 \leq i \leq n$, with probability p. It is assumed that the sampling probability p is fixed in advance and is known to the algorithm.

Throughout let f_i be the frequency of item i in the original stream P. Let g_i be the frequency in the sub-sampled stream and note that $g_i \sim \text{Bin}(f_i, p)$. Thus the stream P can be thought of as a frequency vector $\mathbf{f} = (f_1, f_2, \ldots, f_m)$. Similarly L can be represented by frequency vector $\mathbf{g} = (g_1, g_2, \ldots, g_m)$.

When considering a function F on a stream (e.g., a frequency moment or the entropy) we will denote $F(P)$ and $F(L)$ to indicate that value of the function on the original and sampled stream respectively. When the context is clear, we will also abuse notation and use F to indicate $F(P)$.

We will primarily be interested in (randomized) multiplicative approximations.

DEFINITION 2.1. *For $\alpha > 1$ and $\delta \in [0, 1]$, we say $\tilde{X}$ is an an (α, δ)-estimator for X if* $\Pr\left[\alpha^{-1} \leq X/\tilde{X} \leq \alpha\right] \geq 1 - \delta$.

3. FREQUENCY MOMENTS

We first present our algorithm for estimating the kth frequency moment F_k, and then in Section 3.3, we present lower bounds on space for estimating F_k. We assume k is constant throughout. The guarantee provided by our algorithm is as follows.

THEOREM 3.1. *There is a one pass streaming algorithm which observes L and outputs a $(1+\epsilon,\delta)$-estimator to $F_k(P)$ using $\tilde{O}(p^{-1}m^{1-2/k})$ space, assuming $p = \tilde{\Omega}(\min(m,n)^{-1/k})$.*

For $p = \tilde{O}(\min(m,n)^{-1/k})$ there is not enough information to obtain an $(1+\varepsilon,\delta)$ approximation to $F_k(P)$ with any amount of space, see Theorem 4.33 of [2].

DEFINITION 3.1. *The number of ℓ-wise collisions in P is $C_\ell(P) = \sum_{i=1}^{m}\binom{f_i}{\ell}$. Similarly $C_\ell(L) = \sum_{i=1}^{m}\binom{g_i}{\ell}$.*

Our algorithm is based on the following connection between the ℓth frequency moment of a stream and the ℓ-wise collisions in the stream.

$$F_\ell(P) = \ell! \cdot C_\ell(P) + \sum_{i=1}^{\ell-1}\beta_i^\ell F_i(P) \qquad (1)$$

where

$$\beta_i^\ell = (-1)^{\ell-i+1} \sum_{1 \le j_1 \le \dots \le j_{\ell-i} \le \ell-1} j_1 \cdot j_2 \cdots j_{\ell-i}$$

The following lemma relates the expectation of $C_\ell(L)$ to $C_\ell(P)$ and bounds the variance.

LEMMA 3.1.

$$\mathbb{E}\left[C_\ell(L)\right] = p^\ell C_\ell(P)$$
$$\mathbb{V}\left[C_\ell(L)\right] = O(p^{2\ell-1} F_\ell^{2-1/\ell}).$$

PROOF. Let C denote $C_\ell(L)$. Since each ℓ-way collision in P appears in L with probability p^ℓ, we have $\mathbb{E}\left[C\right] = p^\ell C_\ell(P)$. For each $i \in [m]$, let C_i be the number of ℓ-wise collisions in L among items that equal i. Then $C = \sum_{i \in [m]} C_i$. By independence of the C_i,

$$\mathbb{V}\left[C\right] = \sum_{i \in [m]} \mathbb{V}\left[C_i\right].$$

Fix an $i \in [m]$. Let S_i be the set of indices in the original stream equal to i. For each $J \subseteq S_i$ with $|J| = k$, let X_J be an indicator random variable if each of the stream elements in J appears in the sampled stream. Then $C_i = \sum_J X_J$. Hence,

$$
\begin{aligned}
\mathbb{V}\left[C_i\right] &= \sum_{J,J'} \mathbb{E}\left[X_J X_{J'}\right] - \mathbb{E}\left[X_J\right]\mathbb{E}\left[X_{J'}\right] \\
&= \sum_{J,J'} p^{|J \cup J'|} - p^{2\ell} \\
&= \sum_{j=1}^{\ell} \binom{f_i}{j}\binom{f_i-j}{2\ell-2j}\binom{2\ell-2j}{\ell-j} \cdot (p^{2\ell-j} - p^{2\ell}) \\
&= \sum_{j=1}^{\ell} O(f_i^{2\ell-j} p^{2\ell-j}).
\end{aligned}
$$

Since $F_{2\ell-j}^{1/(2\ell-j)} \le F_\ell^{1/\ell}$ for all $j = 1,\dots,\ell$, we have

$$\mathbb{V}\left[C\right] = O(1) \cdot \sum_{j=1}^{\ell} F_{2\ell-j} \cdot p^{2\ell-j} = O(1) \cdot \sum_{j=1}^{\ell} F_\ell^{2-j/\ell} \cdot p^{2\ell-j}.$$

If we can show that the first term of this sum dominates, the desired variance bound follows. This is the case if $p \cdot F_\ell^{1/\ell} \ge 1$,

---

Algorithm 1: $F_k(P)$

1 Compute $F_1(L)$ exactly and set $\tilde{\phi}_1 = F_1(L)/p$.
2 for $\ell = 2$ *to* k **do**
3 $\quad$ Let $\tilde{C}_\ell(L)$ be an estimate for $C_\ell(L)$, computed as described in the text.
4 $\quad$ Compute

$$\tilde{\phi}_\ell = \frac{\tilde{C}_\ell(L)\ell!}{p^\ell} + \sum_{i=1}^{\ell-1}\beta_i^\ell\tilde{\phi}_i$$

5 end
6 Return $\tilde{\phi}_k$.

---

since this is the ratio of two consecutive summands. Note that F_ℓ is minimized when there are F_0 frequencies each of value F_1/F_0. In this case,

$$F_\ell^{1/\ell} = (F_0 \cdot (F_1/F_0)^\ell)^{1/\ell} = F_1/F_0^{1-1/\ell}.$$

Hence, $p \ge 1/F_\ell^{1/\ell}$ if $p \ge F_0^{1-1/\ell}/F_1$, which holds by assumption. $\square$

We will first describe the intuition behind our algorithm. To estimate $F_k(P)$, by Eq. 1, it suffices to obtain estimates for $F_1(P)$, $F_2(P),\dots,F_{k-1}(P)$ and $C_k(P)$. Our algorithm attempts to estimate $F_\ell(P)$ for $\ell = 1, 2,\dots$ inductively. Since, by Chernoff bounds, $F_1(P)$ is very close to $F_1(L)/p$, $F_1(P)$ can be estimated easily. Thus our problem reduces to estimating $C_k(P)$ by observing the sub-sampled stream L. Since the expected number of collisions in L equals $p^k C_k(P)$, our algorithm will attempt to estimate $C_k(L)$, the number of k-wise collisions in the sub-sampled stream. However, it is not possible to find a good relative approximation of $C_k(L)$ in small space if $C_k(L)$ is small. However, when $C_k(L)$ is small, it does not contribute significantly to the final answer and we do not need a good relative error approximation! We only need that our estimator does not grossly over estimate $C_k(L)$. Our algorithm to estimate $C_k(L)$ will have the following property: If $C_k(L)$ is large, then it outputs a good relative error approximation, and if $C_k(L)$ is small the it outputs a value that is at most $3C_k(L)$.

3.1 The Algorithm

Define a sequence of random variables ϕ_ℓ:

$$\phi_1 = \frac{F_1(L)}{p}, \quad \text{and} \quad \phi_\ell = \frac{C_\ell(L)\ell!}{p^\ell} + \sum_{i=1}^{\ell-1}\beta_i^\ell\phi_i \quad \text{for } \ell > 1.$$

Algorithm 1 inductively computes an estimate $\tilde{\phi}_i$ for each ϕ_i. Note that if $C_\ell(L)/p^\ell$ takes its expected value of $C_\ell(P)$ and we could compute $C_\ell(L)$ exactly, then Eq. 1 implies that the algorithm would return $F_k(P)$ exactly. While this is excessively optimistic we will show that $C_\ell(L)/p^\ell$ is sufficiently close to $C_\ell(P)$ with high probability and that we can construct an estimate for $\tilde{C}_\ell(L)$ for $C_\ell(L)$ such that the final result returned is still a $(1+\epsilon)$ approximation for $F_k(P)$ with probability at least $1-\delta$.

We compute our estimate of $\tilde{C}_\ell(L)$ via an algorithm by Indyk and Woodruff [13]. This algorithm attempts to obtain a $1 + \epsilon_{\ell-1}$ approximation of $C_\ell(L)$ for some value of $\epsilon_{\ell-1}$ to be determined. The estimator is as follows. For $i = 0, 1, 2,\dots$ define

$$S_i = \{j \in [m] : \eta(1+\epsilon')^i \le g_j \le \eta(1+\epsilon')^{i+1}\}$$

where η is randomly chosen between 0 and 1 and $\epsilon' = \epsilon_{\ell-1}/4$. The algorithm of Indyk and Woodruff [13] returns an estimate $\tilde{s}_i$

for $|S_i|$ and our estimate for $C_\ell(L)$ is defined as

$$\tilde{C}_\ell(L) := \sum_i \tilde{s}_i \binom{\eta(1+\epsilon')^i}{k}$$

The space used by the algorithm is $\tilde{O}(p^{-1}m^{1-2/\ell})$. We defer the details to Section 3.2.

We next define an event $\mathcal{E}$ that corresponds to our collision estimates being sufficiently accurate and the sampled stream being "well-behaved." The next lemma establishes that $\Pr[\mathcal{E}] \geq 1 - \delta$. We will defer the proof until Section 3.2.

LEMMA 3.2. *Define the event $\mathcal{E} = \mathcal{E}_1 \cap \mathcal{E}_2 \cap \ldots \cap \mathcal{E}_k$ where*

$\mathcal{E}_1 \; : \; \tilde{\phi}_1 \in (1 \pm \epsilon_1) F_1(P)$

$\mathcal{E}_\ell \; : \; |\tilde{C}_\ell(L)/p^\ell - C_\ell(P)| \leq \epsilon_{\ell-1} F_\ell(P)/\ell!$ *for* $\ell \geq 2$

where $\epsilon_k = \epsilon$, $\epsilon_\ell = (A_\ell + 1)\epsilon_{\ell-1}$, and $A_\ell = \sum_{i=1}^\ell |\beta_i^\ell|$. Then

$$\Pr[\mathcal{E}] \geq 1 - \delta \; .$$

The next theorem establishes that, conditioned on the event $\mathcal{E}$, the algorithm returns a $(1\pm\epsilon)$ approximation of $F_k(P)$ as required.

LEMMA 3.3. *Conditioned on $\mathcal{E}$, we have $\tilde{\phi}_\ell \in (1 \pm \epsilon_\ell) F_\ell(P)$ for all $\ell \in [k]$ and specifically $\tilde{\phi}_k \in (1 \pm \epsilon) F_k(P)$.*

PROOF. The proof is by induction on ℓ. By our assumption $\tilde{\phi}_1$ is an $(1 \pm \epsilon_1)$ approximation of $F_1(P)$. If $i \leq j$, $\epsilon_i \leq \epsilon_j$. Thus the induction hypothesis ensures that $\tilde{\phi}_1, \tilde{\phi}_2, \ldots, \tilde{\phi}_{\ell-1}$ are each $(1 \pm \epsilon_{\ell-1})$ approximations for $F_1(P), \ldots, F_{\ell-1}(P)$ respectively. Now consider $\tilde{\phi}_\ell$:

$$
\begin{aligned}
\tilde{\phi}_\ell &= \frac{\tilde{C}_\ell(L)\ell!}{p^\ell} + \sum_{i=1}^{\ell-1} \beta_i^\ell \tilde{\phi}_i \\
&\in \frac{\tilde{C}_\ell(L)\ell!}{p^\ell} + \sum_{i=1}^{\ell-1} \beta_i^\ell (1 \pm \epsilon_{\ell-1}) F_i(P) \\
&\subset \ell! C_\ell(P) \pm \epsilon_{\ell-1} F_\ell(P) + \sum_{i=1}^{\ell-1} \beta_i^\ell (1 \pm \epsilon_{\ell-1}) F_i(P) \\
&\subset [\ell! C_\ell(P) + \sum_{i=1}^{\ell-1} \beta_i^\ell F_i(P)] \pm [\epsilon_{\ell-1} F_\ell(P) \\
&\quad + \sum_{i=1}^{\ell-1} \beta_i^\ell \epsilon_{\ell-1} F_\ell(P)] \\
&\subset F_\ell(P) \pm (A_l + 1)\epsilon_{\ell-1} F_\ell(P) \\
&\subset (1 \pm \epsilon_\ell) F_\ell(P) \; .
\end{aligned}
$$

$\square$

3.2 Proof of Lemma 3.2.

Our goal is to show that $\Pr[\mathcal{E}_1 \cap \mathcal{E}_2 \cap \ldots \cap \mathcal{E}_k] \geq 1 - \delta$. To do this it will suffice to show that for each $\ell \in [k]$, $\Pr[\mathcal{E}_\ell] \geq 1 - \delta/k$ and appeal to the union bound. It is easy to see that, by Chernoff bounds, the event $\mathcal{E}_1$ happens with probability at least $1 - \delta/k$. To analyze $\Pr[\mathcal{E}_\ell]$ for $2 \leq \ell \leq k$ we consider the events:

$\mathcal{E}_\ell^1 \; : \; \left|C_\ell(L)/p^\ell - C_\ell(P)\right| \leq \frac{\epsilon_{\ell-1} F_\ell(P)}{2\ell!}$

$\mathcal{E}_\ell^2 \; : \; \left|\tilde{C}_\ell(L) - C_\ell(L)\right| \leq \frac{\epsilon_{\ell-1} F_\ell(P)}{2\ell!} \; .$

By the triangle inequality it is easy to see that $\Pr[\mathcal{E}_\ell^1 \cap \mathcal{E}_\ell^2] \leq \Pr[\mathcal{E}_\ell]$ and hence it suffices to show that $\Pr[\mathcal{E}_\ell^1] \geq 1 - \delta/(2k)$ and $\Pr[\mathcal{E}_\ell^2] \geq 1 - \delta/(2k)$. The first part follows easily from the variance bound in Lemma 3.1.

LEMMA 3.4. $\Pr[\mathcal{E}_\ell^1] \geq 1 - \frac{\delta}{4k}$.

PROOF. There are two cases depending on the size of $\mathbb{E}[C_\ell(L)]$.

Case I: First assume $\mathbb{E}[C_\ell(L)] \leq \frac{\delta\epsilon_{\ell-1}p^\ell F_\ell}{8k\ell!}$. Therefore, by Lemma 3.1, we also know that

$$C_\ell(P) \leq \frac{\delta\epsilon_{\ell-1} F_\ell}{8k\ell!} \; . \tag{2}$$

By Markov's bound

$$\Pr\left[C_\ell(L) \leq \frac{\epsilon_{\ell-1}p^\ell F_\ell}{2\ell!}\right] \geq 1 - \frac{\delta}{4k} \; . \tag{3}$$

Eq. 2 and Eq. 3 together imply that with probability at least $1 - \frac{\delta}{4k}$

$$\left|C_\ell(L)/p^\ell - C_\ell(P)\right| \leq \max\left(C_\ell(L)/p^\ell, C_\ell(P)\right) \leq \frac{\epsilon_{\ell-1} F_\ell}{2\ell!}$$

Case II: Next assume $\mathbb{E}[C_\ell(L)] > \frac{\delta\epsilon_{\ell-1}p^\ell F_\ell}{8k\ell!}$. By Chebyshev's bound, and using Lemma 3.1, we get:

$$
\begin{aligned}
&\Pr\left[|C_\ell(L) - \mathbb{E}[C_\ell(L)]| \geq \frac{\epsilon_{\ell-1}\mathbb{E}[C_\ell(L)]}{2}\right] \\
&\leq \frac{4\mathbb{V}[C_\ell(L)]}{\epsilon_{\ell-1}^2(\mathbb{E}[C_\ell(L)])^2} \leq \frac{Dk^2(\ell!)^2}{\delta^2\epsilon_{\ell-1}^4 pF_\ell^{1/\ell}} \leq \frac{\delta}{4k}
\end{aligned}
$$

where D is a sufficiently large constant. The last inequality follows because $F_\ell^{1/\ell} \geq F_1/F_0^{1-1/\ell}$ and our assumption on p.

Since $\mathbb{E}[C_\ell(L)] = p^\ell C_\ell(P)$ and $C_\ell(P) \leq F_\ell(P)/\ell!$, we have that

$$\Pr\left[\left|C_\ell(L)/p^\ell - C_\ell(P)\right| \leq \frac{\epsilon_{\ell-1} F_\ell(P)}{2\ell!}\right] \geq 1 - \frac{\delta}{4k}$$

as required. $\square$

We will now show that $\mathcal{E}_\ell^2$ happens with high probability by analyzing the algorithm that computes $\tilde{C}_\ell(L)$. We need the following result due to Indyk and Woodruff [13]. Recall that $\epsilon' = \epsilon_{\ell-1}/4$.

THEOREM 3.2 (INDYK AND WOODRUFF [13]). *Let G be the set of indices i for which*

$$|S_i|(1+\epsilon')^{2i} \geq \frac{\gamma F_2(L)}{\text{poly}(\epsilon'^{-1}\log n)}, \tag{4}$$

then

$$\Pr\left[\forall i \in G, \tilde{s}_i \in (1 \pm \epsilon')|S_i|\right] \geq 1 - \frac{\delta}{8k}.$$

For every i (whether it is in G or not) $\tilde{s}_i \leq 3|S_i|$. Moreover, the algorithm runs in space $\tilde{O}(1/\gamma)$.

We say that a set S_i contributes if

$$|S_i| \cdot \binom{(1+\epsilon')^i}{k} > \frac{C_\ell(L)}{B}.$$

where $B = \text{poly}(\epsilon'^{-1}\log n)$. We will first show that for every S_i that contributes, Eq. (4) holds with high probability with $\gamma = pm^{-1+2/\ell}$.

276

LEMMA 3.5. *Suppose that* $C_\ell(L) > \frac{\epsilon_{\ell-1}p^\ell F_\ell(P)}{4\ell!}$. *If S_i contributes then*

$$\Pr\left[|S_i|(1+\epsilon')^{2i} \geq \frac{\delta p F_2(L)}{m^{1-2/\ell}\operatorname{poly}(\epsilon'^{-1}\log n)}\right] \geq 1-\frac{\delta}{8k}.$$

PROOF. Consider a set S_i that contributes. Note that the probability that number $\eta < 1/\operatorname{poly}(\delta^{-1}\epsilon'^{-1}\log n)$ with is at most $1/\operatorname{poly}(\delta^{-1}\epsilon'^{-1}\log n)$. Without loss of generality we can take this probability to be less than $\delta/16k$. By our assumption on $C_\ell(L)$,

$$|S_i|(1+\epsilon')^{\ell i} \geq \frac{\epsilon' p^\ell F_\ell(P)}{B\ell!}$$

holds with probability at least $1-\delta/8k$. Thus

$$|S_i|(1+\epsilon')^{2i} \geq \frac{\epsilon'^{2/\ell}p^2 F_\ell^{2/\ell}(P)}{(B\ell!)^{2/\ell}} \geq \frac{p^2 F_2(P)}{m^{1-2/\ell}\operatorname{poly}(\epsilon'^{-1}\log n)}$$

where the second inequality is an application of Hölder's inequality.

Note that

$$\mathbb{E}\left[F_2(L)\right] = p^2 F_2(P) + p(1-p)F_1(P) \leq 2p F_2(P).$$

Thus, an application of the Markov bound,

$$\Pr\left[F_2(L) \leq \frac{32kp F_2(P)}{\delta}\right] \geq 1-\frac{\delta}{16k}.$$

Thus

$$|S_i|(1+\epsilon')^{2i} \geq \frac{\delta p F_2(L)}{m^{1-2/\ell}\operatorname{poly}(\epsilon'^{-1}\log n)}$$

with probability at least $1-\delta/8k$. $\square$

Now we are ready to prove that the event $\mathcal{E}_\ell^2$ holds with high probability.

LEMMA 3.6. $\Pr\left[\mathcal{E}_\ell^2\right] \geq 1-\frac{\delta}{2k}$

PROOF. There are two cases depending on the size of $C_\ell(L)$.

Case I: Assume $C_\ell(L) \leq \frac{\epsilon_{\ell-1}p^\ell F_\ell(P)}{4\ell!}$. By Theorem 3.2, it follows that $\tilde{C}_\ell(L) \leq 3C_\ell(L)$. Thus

$$\left|\tilde{C}_\ell(L)-C_\ell(L)\right| \leq 2C_\ell(L) \leq \frac{\epsilon_{\ell-1}p^\ell F_\ell(P)}{2\ell!}.$$

Case 2: Assume $C_\ell(L) > \frac{\epsilon_{\ell-1}p^\ell F_\ell}{4\ell!}$. By Lemma 3.5, for every S_i that contributes,

$$\Pr\left[|S_i|(1+\epsilon')^{2i} \geq \frac{\delta p F_2(L)}{m^{1-2/\ell}\operatorname{poly}(\epsilon'^{-1}\log n)}\right] \geq 1-\frac{\delta}{8k}.$$

Now by Theorem 3.2 for each S_i that contributes $\tilde{s}_i \in (1\pm\epsilon')|S_i|$, with probability at least $1-\frac{\delta}{8k}$. Therefore,

$$\Pr\left[\left|\tilde{C}_\ell(L)-C_\ell(L)\right| \leq \epsilon' C_\ell(L)\right] \geq 1-\frac{\delta}{4k}.$$

If $\mathcal{E}_\ell^1$ is true, then:

$$C_\ell(L) \in C_\ell(P)p^\ell \pm \frac{\epsilon_{\ell-1}F_\ell(P)p^\ell}{2\ell!}.$$

Since $\mathcal{E}_\ell^1$ holds with probability at least $1-\frac{\delta}{4k}$, the following inequalities hold with probability at least $1-\frac{\delta}{2k}$.

$$
\begin{aligned}
\left|\tilde{C}_\ell(L)-C_\ell(L)\right| &\leq \epsilon' C_\ell(L) \leq \epsilon' C_\ell(P)p^\ell + \frac{\epsilon_{\ell-1}\epsilon' F_\ell(P)p^\ell}{2\ell!} \\
&\leq \frac{\epsilon' F_\ell(P)p^\ell}{\ell!} + \frac{\epsilon_{\ell-1}\epsilon' F_\ell(P)p^\ell}{2\ell!} \\
&\leq \frac{F_\ell(P)p^\ell}{4\ell!}(\epsilon_{\ell-1}+\epsilon_{\ell-1}\epsilon_{\ell-1}) \\
&\leq \frac{F_\ell(P)p^\ell\epsilon_{\ell-1}}{2\ell!}
\end{aligned}
$$

$\square$

3.3 Lower Bounds

In this section we prove that $\Omega(n^{1-2/k}/p)$ bits of space are necessary for estimating F_k in the Bernoulli sampling model for $n = \Theta(m)$. Henceforth we assume $p < 1/2$ since for any constant $p > 0$, an $\Omega(n^{1-2/k})$ bound follows immediately from existing bounds when there is no subsampling [11]. The bound will also apply if the original stream P is not ordered adversarially but has been permuted at random.

3.3.1 Intuition

The intuition behind the result is as follows. Existing data stream research establishes that $\Omega(nt^{-2})$ bits of space are required to distinguish between the cases a) all n elements in a stream are unique and b) there exists a high frequency element with multiplicity t. If $t \geq n^{1/k}$, then a good constant approximation of F_k distinguishes these cases. However, if every element of the stream is only observed with probability p, then the length of the new stream is roughly $n' = np$ and any high frequency element now only has frequency roughly $t' = pt$. Hence, distinguishing the two cases now requires $\Omega(n't'^{-2}) = \Omega(nt^{-2}/p) = \Omega(n^{1-2/k}/p)$ bits of space.

3.3.2 Details

Consider the following distribution $\mu(n,p,t)$ over data streams:

- With probability $1/2$: for each of n items, include it in the stream once with probability p, otherwise do not include it. Output a random ordering.

- With probability $1/2$: choose a random special item i, include i in the stream t times, and for each $j \in [n] \setminus \{i\}$, include j in the stream once with probability p, otherwise do not include it. Output a random ordering.

Guha and Huang [11] show that any $1/3$-error, 1-pass streaming algorithm that determines whether there is a special item in a stream stream distributed according to $\mu(n,1/2,t)$, requires $\Omega(n/t^2)$ bits of space. Furthermore, and importantly for our application, they show this even if the streaming algorithm is given an arbitrarily large read-only random tape. This follows from the fact that the lower bound in Theorem 2 of their paper is for a multi-party communication game with public coins. In the reduction from the streaming algorithm to a communication game, the first player runs the streaming algorithm on his input, who passes the state of the algorithm to the second player, etc. Therefore, we can assume the public-coin encodes an arbitrarily large read-only random tape that the streaming algorithm can access.

We need to generalize the lower bound of [11] to hold for streams distributed according to $\mu(n,p,t)$. We assume, w.l.o.g., that $n\cdot(2p)$ and n are powers of 2.

LEMMA 3.7. *There is a constant $\delta_0 > 0$ for which any constant-pass streaming algorithm which with probability at least $1 - \delta_0$ decides whether there is a special item in the stream, when the stream is distributed according to $\mu(n, p, t)$, requires $\Omega(np/t^2)$ bits of space.*

PROOF. Suppose we had a constant-pass streaming algorithm A for $\mu(n, p, t)$ which succeeds with sufficiently large constant probability $1 - \delta_0$. We claim that A also succeeds with probability at least $2/3$ on $\mu(n \cdot (2p), 1/2, t)$. The reduction is as follows.

Given a stream S from $\mu(n \cdot (2p), 1/2, t)$, we use the algorithm's random tape to specify a uniformly random injection $h : [n \cdot (2p)] \to [n]$. This can be done using $O(\log n)$ bits of space (not counting that for the random tape), since given an $i \in [n \cdot (2p)]$, specified with $O(\log n)$ bits, the streaming algorithm sets $h(i)$ to equal the i-th chunk of $\log n$ bits in the random tape. The algorithm replaces each item $i \in [n \cdot (2p)]$ in S with the item $h(i)$, obtaining a stream S'. Observe that there is a special item in S' if and only if there is a special item in S.

It is clear that S' is randomly ordered since S is randomly ordered, so we just need to compare the induced distribution on frequency vectors of S' and of those from a stream drawn from $\mu(n, p, t)$. The latter corresponds to n i.i.d. Bernoulli(p) variables. For the former, we choose a random subset of $[n]$ of size $n \cdot (2p)$, then include each element in our subset in the stream independently with probability $1/2$.

We argue that the variation distance of these two distributions on frequency vectors is sufficiently small. To make this argument, it suffices to consider the number of non-zero frequencies in both distributions, since conditioned on this number any set is equally likely in both distributions.

In one case the number of non-zero frequencies is distributed as $\text{Bin}(n, p)$, and in the other case it is distributed as $\text{Bin}(2pn, 1/2)$. We use the following well-known fact about binomial distributions.

FACT 3.1 (FOLKLORE). *Consider a $\text{Bin}(m, q)$ distribution μ, where $q \geq (\log m)/m$. There are absolute constants $C_{m,q}^U \geq C_{m,q}^L > 0$ so that for any $i \in [qm - \sqrt{qm}, qm + \sqrt{qm}]$,*

$$\frac{C_{m,q}^L}{\sqrt{qm}} \leq \mu(i) \leq \frac{C_{m,q}^U}{\sqrt{qm}}.$$

Let μ_1 be the $\text{Bin}(n, p)$ distribution, and μ_2 the $\text{Bin}(2pn, 1/2)$ distribution. Applying Fact 3.1, there are positive constants $D^L \leq D^U$ so that for any $i \in [pn - \sqrt{pn}, pn + \sqrt{pn}]$ and $\mu \in \{\mu_1, \mu_2\}$,

$$\frac{D^L}{\sqrt{pn}} \leq \mu(i) \leq \frac{D^U}{\sqrt{pn}}.$$

If $\Delta(\mu_1, \mu_2)$ denotes the variation distance, it follows that

$$\Delta(\mu_1, \mu_2) = \frac{1}{2}\|\mu_1 - \mu_2\|_1 \leq \frac{1}{2} \cdot (2 - 2D^L) = 1 - D^L < 1.$$

Hence, if A succeeds with sufficiently high success probability on $\mu(n, p, t)$, then it succeeds with probability at least $2/3$ on $\mu(n \cdot (2p), 1/2, t)$. By the lower bound of [11], A requires $\Omega(np/t^2)$ bits of space. $\square$

In our Bernoulli sampling with probability p model, parameterized by s, we have the following distribution:

- With probability $1/2$, the frequency vector is $(1, 1, ..., 1)$.

- With probability $1/2$, the frequency vector is $(s, 1, ..., 1)$.

In each case we randomly permute the multiset of items (in the first case there are n, while in the second case there are $n + s$), then the stream is formed by walking through the permutation and including each item independently with probability p.

The claim is that if we had a streaming algorithm A for distinguishing these two cases with sufficiently large probability $1 - \delta_1$, then we could design a streaming algorithm for deciding whether there is a special item in the stream when the stream is distributed according to $\mu(n, p, t)$ for a value $t \in [ps - \sqrt{ps}, ps + \sqrt{ps}]$. Indeed, by Fact 3.1 and averaging, there must be a value t in this range so that A succeeds with probability at least $2/3$ conditioned on the number of samples of the special item equaling t. The resulting distribution is equal to $\mu(n, p, t)$, and so by Lemma 3.7, A must use $\Omega(np/(p^2s^2)) = \Omega(n/(ps^2))$ bits of space.

To get a lower bound for F_k, we set $s = n^{1/k}$ to obtain a constant factor gap in the F_k-value of the streams. Hence, we have the following theorem.

THEOREM 3.3. *Any constant-pass streaming algorithm which $(1+\varepsilon, \delta_1)$-approximates F_k, for sufficiently small constants $\varepsilon, \delta_1 > 0$, in the Bernoulli sampling model, requires $\Omega(m^{1-2/k}/p)$ bits of space.*

4. DISTINCT ELEMENTS

There are strong lower bounds for the accuracy of estimates for the number of distinct values through random sampling. The following theorem is from Charikar et al. [5], which we have restated slightly to fit our notation (the original theorem is about database tables). Let F_0 be the number of elements in a data set T of total size n. Note that T maybe a stored data set, and need not be processed in a one-pass manner.

THEOREM 4.1 (CHARIKAR ET AL. [5]). *Consider any (randomized) estimator $\hat{F}_0$ for the number of distinct values F_0 of T, that examines at most r out of the n elements in T. For any $\gamma > e^{-r}$, there exists a choice of the input T such that with probability at least γ, the multiplicative error is at least $\sqrt{(n - r)/(2r) \ln \gamma^{-1}}$.*

The above theorem implies that if we observe $o(n)$ elements of P, then it is not possible to get even an estimate with a constant multiplicative error. This lower bound for the non-streaming model leads to the following lower bound for sampled streams.

THEOREM 4.2 (F_0 LOWER BOUND). *For sampling probability $p \in (0, 1/12]$, any algorithm that estimates F_0 by observing L, there is an input stream such that the algorithm will have a multiplicative error of $\Omega\left(1/\sqrt{p}\right)$ with probability at least $(1 - e^{-np})/2$.*

PROOF. Let $\mathcal{E}_1$ denote the event $|L| \leq 6np$. Let β denote the multiplicative error of any algorithm (perhaps non-streaming) that estimates $F_0(P)$ by observing L. Let $\alpha = \sqrt{\frac{\ln 2}{12p}}$. Let $\mathcal{E}_2$ denote the event $\beta \geq \alpha$.

Note that $|L|$ is a binomial random variable. The expected size of the sampled stream is $\mathbb{E}[|L|] = np$. By using a Chernoff bound:

$$\Pr[\mathcal{E}_1] = 1 - \Pr[|L| > 6\mathbb{E}[|L|]] \geq 1 - 2^{-6\mathbb{E}[|L|]} > 1 - e^{-np}$$

If $\mathcal{E}_1$ is true, then the number of elements in the sampled stream is no more than $6np$. Substituting $r = 6np$ and $\gamma = 1/2$ in Theorem 4.1, we get:

$$\Pr[\mathcal{E}_2|\mathcal{E}_1] \geq \Pr\left[\beta > \sqrt{\left(\frac{n - 6np}{12np}\right) \ln 2} \,\middle|\, \mathcal{E}_1\right] \geq \frac{1}{2}$$

Simplifying, and using $p \leq 1/12$, we get:

$$\Pr[\mathcal{E}_2] \geq \Pr[\mathcal{E}_1 \wedge \mathcal{E}_2] = \Pr[\mathcal{E}_1] \cdot \Pr[\mathcal{E}_2 | \mathcal{E}_1] \geq \frac{1}{2}(1 - e^{-np})$$

$\square$

We now describe a simple streaming algorithm for estimating $F_0(P)$ by observing $L(P, p)$, which has an error of $O(1/\sqrt{p})$ with high probability.

Algorithm 2: $F_0(P)$

---

1 Let X denote a $(1/2, \delta)$-estimate of $F_0(L)$, derived using any streaming algorithm for F_0 (such as [15]).

2 Return $X/\sqrt{p}$

LEMMA 4.1 (F_0 UPPER BOUND). *Algorithm 2 returns an estimate Y for $F_0(P)$ such that the multiplicative error of Y is no more than $4/\sqrt{p}$ with probability at least $1 - (\delta + e^{-pF_0(P)/8})$.*

PROOF. Let $D = F_0(P)$, and $D_L = F_0(L)$. Let $\mathcal{E}_1$ denote the event $(D_L \geq pD/2)$, $\mathcal{E}_2$ denote $(X \geq D_L/2)$, and $\mathcal{E}_3$ denote the event $(X \leq 3D_L/2)$. Let $\mathcal{E} = \cap_{i=1}^3 \mathcal{E}_i$.

Without loss of generality, let $1, 2, \ldots, D$ denote the items that occurred in stream P. Define $X_i = 1$ if at least one copy of item i appeared in L, and 0 otherwise. The different X_is are all independent. Thus $D_L = \sum_{i=1}^D X_i$ is a the sum of independent Bernoulli random variables and

$$\mathbb{E}[D_L] = \sum_{i=1}^D \Pr[X_i = 1] .$$

Since each copy of item i is included in D_L with probability p, we have $\Pr[X_i = 1] \geq p$. Thus, $\mathbb{E}[D_L] \geq pD$. Applying a Chernoff bound,

$$\Pr[\overline{\mathcal{E}_1}] = \Pr\left[D_L < \frac{pD}{2}\right] \leq \Pr\left[D_L < \frac{\mathbb{E}[D_L]}{2}\right]$$
$$\leq e^{-\mathbb{E}[D_L]/8} \leq e^{-pD/8}$$

Suppose $\mathcal{E}$ is true. Then we have the following:

$$\frac{pD}{4} \leq \frac{D_L}{2} \leq X \leq \frac{3D_L}{2} \leq \frac{3D}{2}$$

and therefore X has a multiplicative error of no more than $4/\sqrt{p}$. We now bound the probability that $\mathcal{E}$ is false.

$$\Pr[\overline{\mathcal{E}}] \leq \sum_{i=1}^4 \Pr[\overline{\mathcal{E}_i}] \leq \delta + e^{-pD/8}$$

where we have used the union bound, Eq. (5), and the fact that X is a $(1/2, \delta)$-estimator of D_L. $\square$

5. ENTROPY

In this section we consider approximating the entropy of a stream.

DEFINITION 5.1. *The* entropy *of a frequency vector*

$$\mathbf{f} = (f_1, f_2, \ldots, f_m)$$

is defined as $H(\mathbf{f}) = \sum_{i=1}^m \frac{f_i}{n} \lg \frac{n}{f_i}$ *where* $n = \sum_{i=1}^m f_i$.

Unfortunately, in contrast to F_0 and F_k, it is not possible to multiplicatively approximate $H(\mathbf{f})$ even if p is constant.

LEMMA 5.1. *No multiplicative error approximation is possible with probability* 9/10 *even with* $p > 1/2$. *Furthermore,*

1. *There exists* $\mathbf{f}$ *such that* $H(\mathbf{f}) = \Theta(\log n/pn)$ *but* $H(\mathbf{g}) = 0$ *with probability at least* 9/10.

2. *There exists* $\mathbf{f}$ *such that* $|H(\mathbf{f}) - H(\mathbf{g})| \geq |\lg(2p)|$ *with probability at least* 9/10.

PROOF. First consider the following two scenarios for the contents of the stream. In Scenario 1, $f_1 = n$ and in Scenario 2, $f_1 = n - k$ and $f_2 = f_3 = \ldots = f_{k+1} = 1$. In the first case the entropy $H(\mathbf{f}) = 0$ whereas in the second,

$$H(\mathbf{f}) = \frac{n-k}{n}(\lg e)\ln\frac{n}{n-k} + \frac{k}{n}\lg n$$
$$= \frac{n-k}{n}\Theta(k/(n-k)) + \frac{k}{n}\lg n$$
$$= (\Theta(1) + \lg n)\frac{k}{n} .$$

Distinguishing these streams requires that at least one value other that 1 is present in the subsampled stream. This happens with probability $(1-p)^k > 1 - pk$ and hence with $k = p^{-1}/10$ this probability is less than 9/10.

For the second part of the lemma consider the stream with $f_1 = f_2 = \ldots = f_m = 1$ and hence $H(\mathbf{f}) = \lg m$. But $H(\mathbf{g}) = \lg|L|$ where $|L|$ is the number of elements in the sampled stream. By an application of the Chernoff bound $|L|$ is at most $2pm$ with probability at least 9/10 and the result follows. $\square$

Instead we will show that it is possible to approximate $H(\mathbf{f})$ up to a constant factor with an additive error term that tends to zero if $p = \omega(n^{-1/3})$. It will also be convenient to consider the following quantity:

$$H_{pn}(\mathbf{g}) = \sum_{i=1}^m \frac{g_i}{pn}\lg\frac{pn}{g_i} .$$

The following propositions establishes that $H_{pn}(\mathbf{g})$ is a very good approximation to $H(\mathbf{g})$.

PROPOSITION 5.1. *With probability* 199/200,

$$|H_{pn}(\mathbf{g}) - H(\mathbf{g})| = O(\log m/\sqrt{pn}) .$$

PROOF. By an application of the Chernoff bound, with probability 199/200

$$\left|pn - \sum_{i=1}^m g_i\right| \leq c\sqrt{pn}$$

for some constant $c > 0$. Hence, if $n' = \sum_{i=1}^m g_i$ and $\gamma = n'/pn$ it follows that $\gamma = 1 \pm O(1/\sqrt{pn})$. Then

$$H_{pn}(\mathbf{g}) = \sum_{i=1}^m \frac{g_i}{pn}\lg\frac{pn}{g_i}$$
$$= \sum_{i=1}^m \frac{\gamma g_i}{n'}\lg\frac{n'}{\gamma g_i}$$
$$= H(\mathbf{g}) + O(1/\sqrt{pn}) + O(H(\mathbf{g})/\sqrt{pn}) .$$

$\square$

The next lemma establishes that the entropy of $\mathbf{g}$ is within a constant factor of the entropy of $\mathbf{f}$ plus a small additive term.

279

LEMMA 5.2. *With probability 99/100, if $p = \omega(n^{-1/3})$,*

1. $H_{pn}(\mathbf{g}) \leq O(H(\mathbf{f}))$.

2. $H_{pn}(\mathbf{g}) \geq H(\mathbf{f})/2 - O\left(\frac{1}{p^{1/2}n^{1/6}}\right)$

PROOF. For the first part of the lemma, first note that

$$
\begin{aligned}
\mathbb{E}\left[H_{pn}(\mathbf{g})\right] &= \sum_{i=1}^{m} \mathbb{E}\left[\frac{g_i}{pn}\lg\frac{pn}{g_i}\right] \\
&\leq \sum_{i=1}^{m} \frac{\mathbb{E}\left[g_i\right]}{pn}\lg\frac{pn}{\mathbb{E}\left[g_i\right]} \\
&= \sum_{i=1}^{m} \frac{pf_i}{pn}\lg\frac{pn}{pf_i} \\
&= H(\mathbf{f})
\end{aligned}
$$

where the inequality follows from Jensen's inequality since the function $x\lg x^{-1}$ is concave. Hence, by Markov's inequality

$$\Pr\left[H_{pn}(\mathbf{g}) \leq 100H(\mathbf{f})\right] \geq 99/100 .$$

To prove the second part of the lemma, define $f^* = cp^{-1}\epsilon^{-2}\log n$ for some sufficiently large constant c and $\epsilon \in (0,1)$. We then partition $[m]$ into $A = \{i : f_i < f^*\}$ and $B = \{i : f_i \geq f^*\}$ and consider $H(\mathbf{f}) = H^A(\mathbf{f}) + H^B(\mathbf{f})$ where

$$H^A(\mathbf{f}) = \sum_{i \in A} \frac{f_i}{n}\lg\frac{n}{f_i} \quad \text{and} \quad H^B(\mathbf{f}) = \sum_{i \in B} \frac{f_i}{n}\lg\frac{n}{f_i} .$$

By applications of the Chernoff and union bounds, with probability at least $299/300$,

$$
|g_i - pf_i| \leq \begin{cases} \epsilon p f^* & \text{if } i \in A \\ \epsilon p f_i & \text{if } i \in B \end{cases} .
$$

Hence,

$$
\begin{aligned}
H^B_{pn}(\mathbf{g}) &= \sum_{i \in B} \frac{g_i}{pn}\lg\frac{pn}{g_i} \\
&= \sum_{i \in B} \frac{f_i(1 \pm \epsilon)}{n}\lg\frac{n}{(1 \pm \epsilon)f_i} \\
&= (1 \pm \epsilon)H^B(\mathbf{f}) + O(\epsilon) .
\end{aligned}
$$

For $H^A_{pn}(\mathbf{g})$ we have two cases depending on whether $\sum_{i \in A} f_i$ is smaller or larger than $\theta := cp^{-1}\epsilon^{-2}$. If $\sum_{i \in A} f_i \leq \theta$ then

$$H^A(\mathbf{f}) = \sum_{i \in A} \frac{f_i}{n}\lg\frac{n}{f_i} \leq \frac{\theta\lg n}{n} .$$

On the other hand if $\sum_{i \in A} f_i \geq \theta$ then by an application of the Chernoff bound,

$$\left|\sum_{i \in A} g_i - p\sum_{i \in A} f_i\right| \leq \epsilon p\sum_{i \in A} f_i$$

and hence

$$
\begin{aligned}
H^A_{pn}(\mathbf{g}) &= \sum_{i \in A} \frac{g_i}{pn}\lg\frac{pn}{g_i} \\
&\geq \lg\frac{n}{(1+\epsilon)f^*}\sum_{i \in A} \frac{g_i}{pn} \\
&\geq (1-\epsilon)\lg\frac{n}{(1+\epsilon)f^*}\sum_{i \in A} \frac{f_i}{n} \\
&\geq \left(1 - \epsilon - \frac{\lg(1+\epsilon)f^*}{\lg n}\right)H^A(\mathbf{f}) .
\end{aligned}
$$

Combining the above cases we deduce that

$$H_{pn}(\mathbf{g}) \geq (1 - \epsilon - \frac{\lg(p^{-1}\epsilon^{-2}\log n)}{\lg n})H(\mathbf{f}) - O(\epsilon) - \frac{\epsilon^{-2}\ln n}{pn} .$$

Setting $\epsilon = p^{-1/2}n^{-1/6}$ we get

$$
\begin{aligned}
H_{pn}(\mathbf{g}) &\geq (1 - p^{-1/2}n^{-1/6} - \frac{\lg(n^{1/3}\log n)}{\lg n})H(\mathbf{f}) \\
&\quad -O(p^{-1/2}n^{-1/6}) - O\left(\frac{\log n}{n^{2/3}}\right) \\
&\geq H(\mathbf{f})/2 - O(p^{-1/2}n^{-1/6}) .
\end{aligned}
$$

$\square$

Therefore, by using an existing entropy estimation algorithm (e.g., [12]) to multiplicatively estimate $H(\mathbf{g})$ we have a constant factor approximation to $H(\mathbf{f})$ if $H(\mathbf{f}) = \omega(p^{-1/2}n^{-1/6})$. The next theorem follows directly from Proposition 5.1 and Lemma 5.2.

THEOREM 5.1. *It is possible to approximate $H(\mathbf{f})$ up to a constant factor in $O(\text{polylog}(m, n))$ space if $H(\mathbf{f}) = \omega(p^{-1/2}n^{-1/6})$.*

6. HEAVY HITTERS

There are two common notions for finding heavy hitters in a stream: the F_1-heavy hitters, and the F_2-heavy hitters.

DEFINITION 6.1. *In the F_k-heavy hitters problem, $k \in \{1, 2\}$ we are given a stream of updates to an underlying frequency vector f and parameters $\alpha > \varepsilon$, and δ. The algorithm is required to output a set S of $O(1/\alpha)$ items such that: (1) every item i for which $f_i \geq \alpha(F_k)^{1/k}$ is included in S, and (2) no item i for which $f_i < (1 - \varepsilon)\alpha(F_k)^{1/k}$ is included in S. The algorithm is additionally required to output approximations f'_i with*

$$\forall i \in S, \quad f'_i \in [(1 - \varepsilon)f_i, (1 + \varepsilon)f_i] .$$

The overall success probability should be at least $1 - \delta$.

The intuition behind the algorithm for heavy hitters is as follows. Suppose an item i was an F_k heavy hitter in the original stream P, i.e. $f_i \geq \alpha(F_k)^{1/k}$. Then, by a Chernoff bound, it can be argued that with high probability, g_i the frequency of i in the sampled stream is also close to pf_i. In such a case, it can be shown that i is also a heavy hitter in the sampled stream and will be detected by an algorithm that identifies heavy hitters on the sampled stream (with the right choice of parameters). Similarly, it can be argued that an item i such that $f_i < (1 - \varepsilon)\alpha(F_k)^{1/k}$ cannot reach the required frequency threshold on the sampled stream, and will not be returned by the algorithm. We present the analysis below assuming that the heavy hitter algorithm on the sampled stream is the CountMin sketch. Other algorithms for heavy hitters can be used too, such as the Misra-Gries algorithm [17]; note that the Misra-Gries algorithm works on insert-only streams, while the CountMin sketch works on general update streams, with additions as well as deletions.

THEOREM 6.1. *Suppose that*

$$F_1(P) \geq Cp^{-1}\alpha^{-1}\varepsilon^{-2}\log(n/\delta)$$

for a sufficiently large constant $C > 0$. There is a one pass streaming algorithm which observes the sampled stream L and computes the F_1 heavy hitters of the original stream P with probability at least $1 - \delta$. This algorithm uses $O(\varepsilon^{-1}\log^2(n/(\alpha\delta)))$ bits of space.

PROOF. The algorithm is to run the $\mathsf{CountMin}(\alpha', \varepsilon', \delta')$ algorithm of [8] for finding the F_1-heavy hitters problem on the sampled stream, for $\alpha' = (1 - 2\varepsilon/5) \cdot \alpha$, $\varepsilon' = \varepsilon/10$, and $\delta' = \delta/4$. We return the set S of items i found by $\mathsf{CountMin}$, and we scale each of the f_i' by $1/p$.

Recall that g_i the frequency of item i in the sampled stream L. Then for sufficiently large $C > 0$ given in the theorem statement, by a Chernoff bound,

$$\Pr\left[g_i > \max\left\{p\left(1 + \frac{\varepsilon}{5}\right)f_i, \frac{C}{2\varepsilon^2}\log\left(\frac{n}{\delta}\right)\right\}\right] \leq \frac{\delta}{4n}.$$

By a union bound, with probability at least $1 - \delta/4$, for all $i \in [n]$,

$$g_i \leq \max\left\{p\left(1 + \frac{\varepsilon}{5}\right)f_i, \frac{C}{2\varepsilon^2}\log\left(\frac{n}{\delta}\right)\right\}. \tag{5}$$

We also need the property that if $f_i \geq (1 - \varepsilon)\alpha F_1(P)$, then $g_i \geq p(1 - \varepsilon/5)f_i$. For such i, by the premise of the theorem we have

$$\mathbb{E}[g_i] \geq p(1 - \varepsilon)\alpha F_1(P) \geq C(1 - \varepsilon)\varepsilon^{-2}\log(n/\delta).$$

Hence, for sufficiently large C, applying a Chernoff and a union bound is enough to conclude that with probability at least $1 - \delta/4$, for all such i, $g_i \geq p(1 - \varepsilon/5)f_i$.

We set the parameter δ' of $\mathsf{CountMin}$ to equal $\delta/4$, and so $\mathsf{CountMin}$ succeeds with probability at least $1 - \delta/4$.

Also, $\mathbb{E}[[F_1(L)] = pF_1(P) \geq C\alpha^{-1}\varepsilon^{-2}(\log n/\delta)$, the inequality following from the premise of the theorem. By a Chernoff bound,

$$\Pr\left[\left(1 - \frac{\varepsilon}{5}\right)pF_1(P) \leq F_1(L) \leq \left(1 + \frac{\varepsilon}{5}\right)pF_1(P)\right] \geq 1 - \frac{\delta}{4}.$$

By a union bound, all events discussed thus far jointly occur with probability at least $1 - \delta$, and we condition on their joint occurrence in the remainder of the proof.

LEMMA 6.1. *If $f_i \geq \alpha F_1(P)$, then*

$$g_i \geq (1 - 2\epsilon/5) \cdot \alpha F_1(L).$$

If $f_i < (1 - \epsilon)\alpha F_1(P)$, then

$$g_i \leq (1 - \epsilon/2)\alpha F_1(L).$$

PROOF. Since $g_i \geq p(1 - \varepsilon/5)f_i$ and also $F_1(L) \leq p(1 + \varepsilon/5)F_1(P)$. Hence,

$$g_i \geq \frac{1 - \varepsilon/5}{1 + \varepsilon/5} \cdot \alpha F_1(L) \geq (1 - 2\varepsilon/5) \cdot \alpha F_1(L).$$

Next consider any i for which $f_i < (1 - \varepsilon)\alpha F_1(P)$. Then

$$\begin{aligned}
g_i &\leq \max\left\{p\left(1 + \frac{\varepsilon}{5}\right)(1 - \varepsilon)\alpha F_1(P), \frac{C}{2\varepsilon^2}\log\left(\frac{n}{\delta}\right)\right\} \\
&\leq \max\left\{\left(1 - \frac{3\varepsilon}{5}\right)\alpha F_1(L), \frac{C}{2\varepsilon^2}\log\left(\frac{n}{\delta}\right)\right\} \\
&\leq \max\left\{\left(1 - \frac{\varepsilon}{2}\right)\alpha F_1(L), \frac{\alpha}{2} \cdot \mathbb{E}[F_1(L)]\right\} \\
&\leq \max\left\{\left(1 - \frac{\varepsilon}{2}\right)\alpha F_1(L), \left(1 + \frac{\varepsilon}{5}\right)\frac{\alpha}{2}F_1(L)\right\} \\
&\leq \left(1 - \frac{\varepsilon}{2}\right)\alpha F_1(L).
\end{aligned}$$

$\square$

It follows that by setting $\alpha' = (1 - 2\varepsilon/5) \cdot \alpha$ and $\varepsilon' = \varepsilon/10$, $\mathsf{CountMin}(\alpha', \varepsilon', \delta')$ does not return any $i \in S$ for which $f_i < (1 - \varepsilon)\alpha F_1(P)$, since for such i we have $g_i \leq (1 - \varepsilon/2)\alpha F_1(L)$, and so $g_i < (1 - \varepsilon/10)\alpha' F_1(L)$. On the other hand, for every $i \in S$ for which $f_i \geq \alpha F_1(P)$, we have $i \in S$, since for such i we have $g_i \geq \alpha' F_1(L)$.

It remains to show that for every $i \in S$, we have $f_i' \in [(1 - \varepsilon)f_i, (1 + \varepsilon)f_i]$. By the previous paragraph, for such i we have $f_i \geq (1 - \varepsilon)\alpha F_1(P)$. By the above conditioning, this means that $g_i \geq p(1 - \varepsilon/5)f_i$. We will also have $g_i \leq p(1 + \varepsilon/5)f_i$ if $p\left(1 + \frac{\varepsilon}{5}\right)f_i \geq \frac{C}{2\varepsilon^2}\log\left(\frac{n}{\delta}\right)$. Since $f_i \geq (1 - \varepsilon)\alpha F_1(P)$, this in turn holds if

$$F_1(P) \geq \frac{1}{2(1 - \varepsilon)(1 + \varepsilon/5)} \cdot Cp^{-1}\alpha^{-1}\varepsilon^{-2}\log\left(\frac{n}{\delta}\right),$$

which holds by the theorem premise provided ε is less than a sufficiently small constant. This completes the proof.

The proof of the next theorem follows from the proofs of Theorem 3.1 for $k = 2$ and Theorem 6.1 We omit the details.

THEOREM 6.2. *Suppose that $p = \tilde{\Omega}(m^{-1/2})$. There is a one pass streaming algorithm which observes the sampled stream L and computes the F_2 heavy hitters of the original stream P with probability at least $1 - \delta$. This algorithm uses $\tilde{O}(p^{-1})$ bits of space.*

THEOREM 6.3. *Any algorithm for solving the F_2-heavy hitters problem with probability at least $2/3$ in the Bernoulli sampling with probability p model must use $\Omega(p^{-1})$ bits of space.*

PROOF. This follows from our lower bound in Section 3.3 for estimating F_2 in this model. Indeed, there we show that any algorithm which distinguishes between the case when the frequency vector is $(1, 1, \ldots, 1)$ and the case when the frequency vector is $(s, 1, \ldots, 1)$ requires $\Omega(m/(ps^2))$ bits of space. If we set $s = m^{1/2}$, then in the first case the heavy hitters algorithm is required to return an empty list, while in the second case the heavy hitters algorithm must return a list of size 1. Hence the algorithm can distinguish the two cases and requires $\Omega(1/p)$ bits of space. $\square$

7. CONCLUSION

In this paper we presented small-space stream algorithms and space lower bounds for estimating functions of interest when observing a random sample of the original stream.

The are numerous directions for future work. As we have seen, our results imply time/space tradeoffs for several natural streaming problems. What other data stream problems have interesting time/space tradeoffs? Also, we have so far assumed that the sampling probability p is fixed, and that the algorithm has no control over it. Suppose this was not the case, and the algorithm can change the sampling probability in an adaptive manner, depending on the current state of the stream. Is it possible to get algorithms that can observe fewer elements overall and get the same accuracy as our algorithms? For which precise models and problems is adaptivity useful?

8. REFERENCES

[1] N. Alon, Y. Matias, and M. Szegedy. The Space Complexity of Approximating the Frequency Moments. *J. Comput. Syst. Sci.*, 58(1):137–147, 1999.

[2] Z. Bar-Yossef. *The complexity of massive dataset computations*. PhD thesis, UC Berkeley, 2002.

[3] Z. Bar-Yossef. Sampling lower bounds via information theory. In *STOC*, pages 335–344, 2003.

[4] S. Bhattacharyya, A. Madeira, S. Muthukrishnan, and T. Ye. How to scalably and accurately skip past streams. In *ICDE Workshops*, pages 654–663, 2007.

[5] M. Charikar, S. Chaudhuri, R. Motwani, and V. R. Narasayya. Towards estimation error guarantees for distinct values. In *PODS*, 2000.

[6] Cisco Systems. *Random Sampled NetFlow*. http://www.cisco.com/en/US/docs/ios/12_0s/feature/guide/nfstatsa.html.

[7] G. Cormode and M. Garofalakis. Sketching probabilistic data streams. In *Proceedings of the 2007 ACM SIGMOD international conference on Management of data*, SIGMOD '07, pages 281–292, 2007.

[8] G. Cormode and S. Muthukrishnan. An improved data stream summary: the count-min sketch and its applications. *J. Algorithms*, 55(1):58–75, 2005.

[9] N. G. Duffield, C. Lund, and M. Thorup. Properties and prediction of flow statistics from sampled packet streams. In *Internet Measurement Workshop*, pages 159–171, 2002.

[10] N. G. Duffield, C. Lund, and M. Thorup. Estimating flow distributions from sampled flow statistics. In *SIGCOMM*, pages 325–336, 2003.

[11] S. Guha and Z. Huang. Revisiting the direct sum theorem and space lower bounds in random order streams. In *ICALP (1)*, pages 513–524, 2009.

[12] N. J. A. Harvey, J. Nelson, and K. Onak. Sketching and streaming entropy via approximation theory. In *FOCS*, pages 489–498, 2008.

[13] P. Indyk and D. P. Woodruff. Optimal approximations of the frequency moments of data streams. In *Proceedings of the 37th Annual ACM Symposium on Theory of Computing (STOC)*, pages 202–208, 2005.

[14] T. S. Jayram, A. McGregor, S. Muthukrishnan, and E. Vee. Estimating statistical aggregates on probabilistic data streams. *ACM Trans. Database Syst.*, 33:26:1–26:30, December 2008.

[15] D. M. Kane, J. Nelson, and D. P. Woodruff. On the exact space complexity of sketching and streaming small norms. In *SODA*, pages 1161–1178, 2010.

[16] A. McGregor, editor. *Open Problems in Data Streams and Related Topics*, 2007. http://www.cse.iitk.ac.in/users/sganguly/data-stream-probs.pdf.

[17] J. Misra and D. Gries. Finding repeated elements. *Science of Computer Programming*, 2(2):143–152, 1982.

[18] F. Rusu and A. Dobra. Sketching sampled data streams. In *ICDE*, pages 381–392, 2009.

Rectangle-Efficient Aggregation in Spatial Data Streams

Srikanta Tirthapura [*]
Iowa State University
snt@iastate.edu

David P. Woodruff
IBM Research-Almaden
dpwoodru@us.ibm.com

ABSTRACT

We consider the estimation of aggregates over a data stream of multidimensional axis-aligned rectangles. Rectangles are a basic primitive object in spatial databases, and efficient aggregation of rectangles is a fundamental task. The data stream model has emerged as a de facto model for processing massive databases in which the data resides in external memory or the cloud and is streamed through main memory. For a point p, let $n(p)$ denote the sum of the weights of all rectangles in the stream that contain p. We give near-optimal solutions for basic problems, including (1) the k-th frequency moment $F_k = \sum_{\text{points } p} |n(p)|^k$, (2) the counting version of stabbing queries, which seeks an estimate of $n(p)$ given p, and (3) identification of heavy-hitters, i.e., points p for which $n(p)$ is large. An important special case of F_k is F_0, which corresponds to the volume of the union of the rectangles. This is a celebrated problem in computational geometry known as "Klee's measure problem", and our work yields the first solution in the streaming model for dimensions greater than one.

Categories and Subject Descriptors

F.2.0 [**Analysis of Algorithms and Problem Complexity**]: General

General Terms

Algorithms, Theory

Keywords

rectangle efficiency, distinct elements, frequency moments, streaming, spatial databases, data mining

1. INTRODUCTION

Spatial and temporal data arise in diverse domains such as geographic information systems, astronomy, VLSI design,

---

[*]Supported in part by NSF grants 0834743, 0831903.

and animation. Quoting Guting [28], a spatial database such as OpenGIS [1] "needs to deal with large collections of relatively simple geometric objects". Perhaps the most basic type of object in spatial and spatiotemporal databases is the multidimensional rectangle. For instance, [11] proposes modeling of coordinates of objects in space and time through "parametric rectangles", which are multi-dimensional axis-aligned rectangles, formed through a cross product of intervals. In the constraint database model [34] each object is itself formed by the intersection of constraints and is often an axis-aligned rectangle, and query processing in a constraint database can be viewed as a computation over this set of geometric objects; for example, as studied in [6, 46]. Aggregation of axis-aligned rectangles is also considered in the context of Online Analytical Processing (OLAP) [35, 42, 48, 51].

We consider aggregation of multi dimensional rectangles in the standard one-pass data stream model using limited workspace. In addition to online aggregation of a massive stream that cannot be physically stored, a data stream algorithm is useful for processing queries on a large database stored in external memory because it can be implemented using a memory-efficient sequential scan through the data. When new items arrive, the algorithm can update its state without having to rescan the entire dataset. While the data stream model has been widely studied over the past decade or so, there has been little work on aggregating high dimensional geometric objects.

1.1 Problem Definition

We consider a discrete d-dimensional universe $[\Delta]^d = \{1, 2, \ldots, \Delta\}^d$, where Δ is the maximum coordinate along any dimension. While assuming the universe is discrete is not very common in computational geometry, where typically the coordinates are assumed to be real, finite precision is a common assumption in the data stream literature. Without such an assumption, storage is not well-defined, since, e.g., many real numbers can be encoded into a single real number. Geometric problems in the data stream literature are thus often studied with finite precision, see [30]. Also, by imposing a sufficiently fine grid and snapping the input points to grid points, it is easy to adapt our algorithms to the case when the minimum inter-point distance is 1 and the diameter is bounded by Δ.

The input is a stream Υ of m items, where each item is a rectangle and an integer (positive or negative) weight associated with it:

$$\Upsilon = \{(r_1, w_1), (r_2, w_2), \cdots, (r_m, w_m)\},$$

where $r_i \subseteq [\Delta]^d$ and $w_i \in \mathbb{Z}$. For a point p, its frequency $n(p)$ is defined as the sum of the weights $\sum_{(r_i, w_i) \in \Upsilon, p \in r_i} w_i$ of all rectangles that contain p.

We consider the problem of estimating the kth frequency moment $F_k(\Upsilon)$, defined as $F_k(\Upsilon) = \sum_{\text{points } p} |n(p)|^k$. When each input rectangle is a single point, this definition reduces to the classical definition of the kth frequency moment of a stream, which has been very well studied in the literature starting from the work of Alon, Matias, and Szegedy [2] [1] (see for example the references in the recent papers [3, 9]). As shown by Braverman and Ostrovsky [10], techniques for understanding the frequency moments were used to characterize the class of all sketchable functions. Note that $F_0(\Upsilon)$ is the volume of the union of all rectangles in the input stream, and is a celebrated problem in computational geometry, known as Klee's measure problem [33].

We also consider one of the most famous problems in spatial databases - the stabbing problem (see, e.g., [46]). Given a point p and an aggregation function F, a query reports the aggregate of the weights of the rectangles in Υ containing p. Typically F is MAX or SUM. See [35, 42, 48, 51] for numerous applications of such queries in spatial databases. Note that a data structure for stabbing queries when F is SUM can also be used to compute the maximum depth $\max_p n(p)$. The points p for which $n(p)$ is large are often called "heavy hitters" or "iceberg queries".

Despite the large body of work on streaming algorithms, the streaming complexity of aggregates on spatial data is not well understood. Classical streaming algorithms can be used to process rectangles by considering the points in the rectangle one at a time. Such solutions, while space-efficient, have prohibitively high time complexity since the time taken to process a rectangle is proportional to its volume. The first works to try to overcome this were for 1-dimensional rectangles, i.e., line segments. The notion of a *range-efficient* sketch was introduced in [5] for F_k-estimation, and further refined for F_0 estimation in [43, 47], allowing one to process a segment in time only logarithmic in its length. Many other problems have been reduced to range-efficient F_k-estimation, for $k \geq 0$, such as distinct summation problem [18, 43], duplicate insensitive sketches [38], maximum-dominance norm [19], self-join size of the symmetric difference of relations [44], and counting triangles in graphs [5]. Attempts at generalizing this to larger dimensions fall short of what is desired. One generalization is in [5], where statistics of d-dimensional points were estimated by designing *range-efficient algorithms in every coordinate*. However, this is still essentially a one-dimensional object, since the coordinates in the object are allowed to have a range of values along one dimension, but fixed along the other dimensions. If we were to use a range-efficient algorithm to process a two dimensional rectangle, the time taken would still be proportional to the length of the smaller side.

1.2 Our Results

We give the first *rectangle-efficient* algorithms for computing frequency moments and identifying heavy hitters in the data stream model. By rectangle-efficient, we mean that our algorithms process each rectangle in the stream in time significantly sublinear in the volume of the rectangle.

---

[1] See Google Scholar for a list of the 900+ citations of their paper on frequency moments.

We say that a random variable x is an (ε, δ)-approximation to a number y if $\Pr[|x - y| \leq \varepsilon y] \geq 1 - \delta$. We let $O^*(f)$ denote a function of the form $f \cdot (\varepsilon^{-1} d \log(m\Delta/\delta))^{O(1)}$.

1.2.1 Frequency Moments

We present the following results for $F_k, k \geq 0$.

- For F_0, i.e., the Klee's measure problem, we give an algorithm that returns an (ε, δ)-approximation to the volume of the union of rectangles in Υ using space as well as update time $O^*(1)$. This is the first efficient solution to Klee's measure problem in the streaming model for $d \geq 2$. In the turnstile model (which allows negatively-weighted rectangles [37]), this is the first algorithm for F_0 even for $d = 1$.

- For $F_k, 0 < k \leq 2$, we give (ϵ, δ)-approximation algorithms using space and time $O^*(1)$ in the turnstile model. This is most interesting for F_1 with deletions, which, e.g., can be used to measure variation distance of distributions on multi-dimensional data approximated by box histograms [49]. We note that in the special case of $d = 1$ and $k = 2$, a range-efficient algorithm for F_2 was previously known [25].

- For $F_k, k > 2$, our space bound is polynomial in Δ^d, namely, it is $O^*(\Delta^{d(1-2/k)})$, while our update time is also $O^*(\Delta^{d(1-2/k)})$. The dependence on Δ in the space complexity is the best possible, due to known lower bounds even when the input consists only of points [4]. That is, a special case of our problem is when all of the input rectangles are points. Given a universe of m possible items, the known space lower bound [4] is $\Omega(m^{1-2/k})$, and plugging in $m = \Delta^d$ establishes an $\Omega(\Delta^{d(1-2/k)})$ bound. We note this is first algorithm to achieve optimal space (up to $O^*(1)$ factors) with less than the trivial Δ^d running time, even for $d = 1$.

  For the insertion only model, we present an alternate algorithm for $F_k, k > 2$ that uses $O^*(\Delta^{d(1-1/k)}) \cdot O(\log \Delta)^d$ space, which is slightly more (for small d) but still sublinear, but reduces the time per rectangle to $O^*(1) \cdot O(\log \Delta)^d$.

  Rectangle-efficient algorithms were not known for any $F_k, k > 2$, for $d > 1$. Even for $d = 1$ algorithms for $F_k, k > 2$ were known only in the insertion only model [5], and used space and time $O^*(\Delta^{1-1/k})$. Our algorithms improve space or time, work in the general turnstile model, and handle $d > 1$.

1.2.2 Stabbing Queries, Maximum Depth, and Heavy Hitters

We present a data structure that uses $O^*(1)$ space and $O^*(1)$ time to process each rectangle, and can return for any $p \in [\Delta]^d$, an estimator of $n'(p)$ of $n(p)$ (the "stabbing number" of p) such that with high probability $n'(p) \in \left[n(p) \pm O\left(\varepsilon \sqrt{\sum_{q \neq p} n(q)^2} \right) \right]$. It is well-known that in general it is impossible to get a better additive approximation to $n(p)$ in $O^*(1)$ streaming space (see, e.g., [4]).

- **Maximum Depth.** Clearly such a data structure gives an additive $O(\varepsilon \sqrt{\sum_{q \neq p} n(q)^2})$ approximation to

$\max_p n(p)$, also known the *maximum depth* [14] of a set of axis-aligned rectangles.

- **Heavy Hitters.** The heavy-hitters problem asks to return all points p for which $n(p)$ is at least $\alpha\sqrt{\sum_q n(q)^2}$, but not return any point p for which $n(p)$ is less than $(\alpha-\varepsilon)\sqrt{\sum_q n(q)^2}$ (note that this is a stronger guarantee than returning those p for which $n(p) \geq \alpha\sqrt{\sum_q n(q)^2}$). Given any algorithm for estimating $n(p)$, there is a generic procedure which, with an additional $O^*(1)$ factor in space and time, converts it into an algorithm for finding the heavy hitters. The idea is to build a quadtree of the input grid, obtaining $\log \Delta$ levels, and in each region in each level, the weight of all points in the region is aggregated into a single "meta-point". In each level we estimate $n(q)$ with additive error, where q is a meta-point, and we recurse on those q for which $n(q)$ is large. See, e.g., section 5.2 "Turnstile Case" in [20]. We thus find all heavy hitters in space and time $O^*(\varepsilon^{-1})$.

We note that many of our results have space and time complexity polynomial in the dimension d. While many of our applications are for constant d, this is an important feature for large values of d.

Extensions: As mentioned, many of our results allow for arbitrary positive or negative weights on the input rectangles, and thus allow us to estimate F_k of the difference of two data streams. Thus, for example, we can rectangle-efficiently approximate the volume of the difference of two collections of rectangles, and find the heavy hitters in the presence of negative weights. The main application of negative weights is to analyzing the difference of two streams. This cannot be done using random sampling, for example. Our method can be applied to streams of other objects that can be approximated by a union of $O^*(1)$ axis-aligned rectangles. Rectangles are commonly used as bounding boxes for approximating other objects. See, e.g, [22] for ways of approximating a convex polygon this way.

1.3 Our Techniques

Many problems in the data stream literature can be solved by a combination of three techniques: (1) sub-sampling the items into a logarithmic number ϕ of levels, where in the j-th level, roughly a 2^{-j} fraction of items are included, (2) multiplying item weights by random signs, and (3) for each level of sub-sampling, hashing the included items into buckets and maintaining the sum of item weights in each bucket. Let us associate the points x in the input grid $[\Delta]^d$ with vectors in the vector space $\{GF(\Delta)\}^d$, where we assume Δ is a power of 2, and $GF(\Delta)$ denotes the finite field containing Δ elements. In the rest of this paper, we use $GF(\Delta)^d$ to denote $\{GF(\Delta)\}^d$. Each of these three operations can be thought of as applying a hash function to x. For (1), x is included in the j-th substream if $g(x) \leq \Delta^d/2^{j-1}$ for a random function $g : GF(\Delta)^d \to GF(\Delta^d)$, and an arbitrary mapping from $GF(\Delta)^d$ to the integers $\{1, 2, \ldots, \Delta^d\}$. For (2), the sign of x is equal to $s(x)$, where $s : GF(\Delta)^d \to \{-1, 1\}$ is a random function. For (3), the bucket x is assigned to is $f(x)$ for a random function $f : GF(\Delta)^d \to GF(B)$, where B is the total number of buckets (w.l.o.g., B is a power of 2).

Our first insight is that if we were lucky enough that each of g, s, and f could be implemented by a pairwise-independent hash function for the problem we are trying to solve, then we would be in great shape. Indeed, it is well-known that the function mapping x to $Ax+b$, for a random matrix A and vector b with entries in $GF(\Delta)$ is pairwise-independent. Hence, the set of input points x which map to the j-th level of sub-sampling, have a positive sign, and map to a particular bucket $k \in GF(B)$ is just the intersection of three equations: $A^1 x + b^1 = 0$, $A^2 x + b^2 = 0$, and $A^3 x + b^3 = k$, for appropriately chosen A^1, A^2, A^3, b^1, b^2, and b^3. By using Gaussian elimination, which is efficient for d-dimensional x, we can equivalently describe such x as the solutions to a single equation $Cx = d$ for a certain matrix C and vector x. We thus obtain $\phi \cdot 2 \cdot B$ systems of equations, one for each combination of level of subsampling, positive or negative sign, and bucket k. Typically ϕ and B are $O^*(1)$, and so we can afford to spend time solving each such system.

To solve each system given an input rectangle, there are several approaches possible. One is to decompose the rectangle into dyadic intervals along each dimension, and note that the cross product of dyadic intervals over the d dimensions forms a partition of the input rectangle into smaller rectangles of a special kind. Importantly, for each such smaller rectangle, it corresponds to a set of vectors x for which some number of coordinates take on fixed values, while the remaining coordinates range over all possible bitstrings as x ranges over the rectangle. This property allows us to count the number of solutions x using Gaussian elimination, and since the number of rectangles in the partition is not too large (for small d), we can sum up the number of solutions over the rectangles in the partition.

While multi-dimensional dyadic decomposition is possible, it leads to bounds that are exponential in d. Although many of the applications are for constant d, it is still useful to have bounds which are polynomial in d. To achieve this, one can use a technique of Pagh [41] instead of multidimensional dyadic decomposition. In this case, s and f must have a special form, namely if $x = (x_1, \ldots, x_d) \in GF(\Delta)^d$ then $s(x) = s_1(x_1) \cdots s_d(x_d)$ and $f(x) = f(x_1) + \cdots + f(x_d)$ mod B, for independent functions $s_i : GF(\Delta) \to \{-1, 1\}$ and $f_i : GF(\Delta) \to GF(B)$, with an arbitrary mapping of elements of $GF(B)$ to elements of $\{0, 1, 2, \ldots, B-1\}$. Here each s_i and f_i is drawn from a pairwise-independent family of functions. Then, if the rectangle R has the form $[a_1, b_1] \times [a_2, b_2] \times \cdots \times [a_d, b_d]$, then using the Fast Fourier Transform we can efficiently compute for each $k \in GF(\Delta)$, the quantity $\sum_{x \in R \mid f(x) = k} s(x)$, given only $\sum_{x_j \in [a_j, b_j] \mid f_j(x_j) = k} s_j(x_j)$ for each $j \in [d]$. The latter d quantities can be found using 1-dimensional dyadic decomposition and solving systems of linear equations, as described above.

One problem with this overall approach is that while it was recently discovered that g and f can be implemented with pairwise-independent hash functions [3, 9] for estimating F_k, it was not known that s can also be implemented with a pairwise-independent hash function. For example, the seminal work of Alon, Matias, and Szegedy [2] requires 4-wise independence for estimating F_2 to within a constant factor. Intuitively, this is because the algorithm takes the sum of squares of counters as its expectation, which requires 2-wise independence for sign-cancellation, and then takes the square of this to bound the variance, which requires 4-wise independence for sign-cancellation. The previous algorithm for F_k with the smallest independence known which followed this three-step process (sub-sampling, random signs, bucketing) was 4-wise independence [9], and this is because their algorithm effectively estimates F_2 inside of a routine for estimating the heavy hitters (the so-called CountSketch algorithm) so as to make sure that all heavy hitters returned have relative-error estimates. We observe that if we relax the guarantee of the estimates to the heavy hitters to give total additive error, rather than a per heavy hitter relative error guarantee, then we can slightly tweak the analysis of [9] to show that correctness is maintained. Now we do not need to implicitly estimate F_2, and since CountSketch only requires pairwise independence, there is an algorithm for estimating F_k using this three step process, for any $k \geq 0$, with only pairwise independence.

It is also likely to be possible to use our ideas to rectangle-efficiently implement a recent F_k-estimation algorithm of [3], which achieves pairwise-independence (they do not achieve range or rectangle-efficiency). There the authors skip the sub-sampling phase by multiplying the items by appropriate weights (so-called "precisions"). We would need to discretize their weights and enumerate them (as we are enumerating levels of sub-sampling above) and apply our procedure for counting the number of items in an input rectangle with a given weight. This may be less efficient, depending on the discretization required. We choose to follow the exposition of [9] both for simplicity and due to its extreme generality: as we shall see in Section 3.1, we can obtain a rectangle-efficient algorithm for any problem for which there is a rectangle-efficient heavy hitters algorithm.

1.4 Other Approaches

One could ask why 4-wise independence for s would not suffice for our purposes. The difficulty is that it does not seem easy to compose with the 2-wise independent functions f and g. An example 4-wise independent function would be $s(x) = x^T A x + B x + c$ for certain random matrices A, B, and c from a special family of second-order Reed-Muller codes [26]. We do not know how to quickly count the number of solutions x to the equation $s(x) = d$ for general matrices A, B and vector c, while we can count such x for heavily-structured A, B, and c coming from a special family based on Reed-Muller codes. This is problematic when composing it with the linear constraints imposed by f and g, since the new matrices obtained after substitution no longer correspond to a function s in the special family. There is some work on range-summable functions for higher-order Reed-Muller codes [12], but as far as we are aware the problem for order three and above is #P-complete [36].

Another completely different approach, often used in computational geometry, would be to treat multidimensional rectangles as points in a higher dimension (typically twice the original dimension), and to convert operations on rectangles to corresponding operations on higher dimensional points. This works for certain types of operations on rectangles. For example, given a collection $\mathcal{R}$ of line segments (i.e. one dimensional rectangles) and a query segment r^*, suppose we want to find all segments $r \in \mathcal{R}$ such that r completely contains r^*. For segment $[a, b]$ the function $\mathcal{P}()$ yields a point in two dimensions, defined as $\mathcal{P}([a, b]) = (-a, b)$. It is easy to see that segment r_1 contains segment r_2 iff $\mathcal{P}(r_1)$ dominates $\mathcal{P}(r_2)$, i.e., each coordinate of $\mathcal{P}(r_1)$ is greater than or equal to the corresponding coordinate of $\mathcal{P}(r_2)$. Thus, the problem of finding all 1-dimensional rectangles that contain a query (1-dimensional) rectangle can be posed as the problem of finding all 2-dimensional points that dominate a given 2-dimensional point. This reduction can be easily generalized to higher dimensions. While the above reduction works for certain relationships among a pair of rectangles, it does not seem to work for the aggregate functions that we consider. For example, it is not clear how the computation of the size of the union of rectangles can be reduced to a computation over a set of higher dimensional points, and if such a reduction can be easily used.

1.5 Related Work

Das, Gehrke, and Riedewald [21] consider approximation techniques for spatial data streams, and present algorithms for estimating aggregates on data, using an extension of the linear AMS sketches (Alon, Matias, Szegedy [2]) for F_2. Their algorithm is for rectangle intersection, and does not give sublinear space guarantees in the worst case. Hershberger, Shrivastava, and Suri [29] consider the sketching of a stream of points in 2 dimensions, to maintain its geometric shapes through a collection of convex hulls. Note that their input is a stream of (multidimensional) points, while our input is a stream of rectangles. There has been a long line of work on Klee's measure problem [33, 23, 7, 40, 13, 16, 17, 24, 50], but none of these works seem relevant for computation in the streaming model. There is a previous attempt at a solution to Klee's measure problem on a data stream [45]. This was found to have an error, and was withdrawn from arXiv. This work uses a different technique than was used in [45]. The algorithm in [45] was based on sampling, along the lines of [43], while our algorithm is based on sub-sampling and linear sketches with special properties.

Klee [33] introduced the one-dimensional version of the problem now known as Klee's measure problem (KMP) in the RAM model, and gave an $O(m \log m)$ time algorithm for computing the size of the union of m line segments in one dimension. This was shown to be time-optimal (for a class of algorithms) by Fredman and Weide [23]. Bentley [7] presented an $O(m \log m)$ time and $O(m)$ space solution for KMP on m two dimensional rectangles. Bentley's algorithm can be extended to d dimensions, but takes time $O(m^{d-1} \log m)$ time. Overmars and Yap [40] gave an algorithm that improved the time for d dimensions to $O(m^{d/2} \log m)$. More recent work includes [13, 16, 17, 24, 50]. Recent work has focused on the space complexity of the algorithm. Chen and Chan [16] gave an algorithm for KMP in two dimensions that uses $O(m^{3/2} \log m)$ time with $O(\sqrt{m})$ extra space, which is in addition to the space needed for representing the input rectangles (so this does not apply to the data stream model). Note that the time taken by this algorithm is worse than the optimal time achieved by Bentley, but the (additional) space required is small. Vahrenhold [50] improved the (additional) space to $O(1)$, while maintaining the same running time. In the model used by [16, 50], there was no constraint on the number of passes of the processor.

Paper Overview: We present our main primitive data structure RectangleCountSketch in Section 2. We show how to use this to estimate F_k rectangle-efficiently for any $k \geq 0$ in Section 3. In Section 4, we present the rectangle-efficient algorithm for F_k for insertion-only streams.

2. RECTANGLE-COUNTSKETCH

We define RectangleCountSketch(γ) for an input parameter $\gamma \in (0, 1)$. We assume all points in the input grid $[\Delta]^d$ are identified with the vector space $GF(\Delta)^d$, where $GF(\Delta)$ denotes the finite field with Δ elements, where we assume Δ is a power of 2,

Notice that since Δ is a power of 2, we can also think of elements of $GF(\Delta)$ as length-$(\log \Delta)$ bitstrings where addition of $x, y \in GF(\Delta)$ corresponds to component-wise XOR of the corresponding bitstrings. Similarly, we can think of elements in the vector space $GF(\Delta)^d$ as length-$(d \log \Delta)$ bitstrings where addition of $x, y \in GF(\Delta)^d$ corresponds to component-wise XOR of the corresponding bitstrings.

The goal of the algorithm is to provide an estimate $\Phi(x)$ to v_x for each $x \in GF(\Delta)^d$, where v_x is the current sum of the weights of the rectangles in the input stream which contain x. Our estimate $\Phi(x)$ will be correct up to an additive error that can be reduced by increasing the memory requirements of the scheme.

The algorithm is the same as CountSketch [15] except that it is also rectangle-efficient. Let $B > 3\gamma^{-2}$ be a power of 2. We assume $B \leq \Delta$.

FACT 1. *([27]) Let $f : GF(2)^k \to GF(2)^r$ be defined as $f(x) = Ax + b$, where A is a uniformly random $k \times r$ matrix and b is a uniformly random column vector of length r. Then f is a pairwise-independent function, that is, for any $x \neq x' \in GF(2)^k$ and $y, y' \in GF(2)^r$,*

$$\Pr[f(x) = y \wedge f(x') = y'] = \frac{1}{2^{2r}}.$$

Notice that pairwise-independence also implies that for any fixed $x \in GF(2)^k$, $f(x)$ is uniformly random over the choice of f.

In fact, it is known that f is pairwise independent even if A is chosen to be a uniformly random Toeplitz matrix and b is a uniformly random vector. This latter property can be used to reduce the time complexity of computing Ax by using the Fast Fourier Transform (FFT) to perform the matrix-vector multiplication. Moreover, the memory required to represent A is smaller since a random Toeplitz matrix requires less randomness to specify. Since these optimizations are relatively minor in our setting, as k and r will be quite small, we omit them in our analysis.

PROOF. See page 8 of [27] for the construction with Toeplitz matrices. See Appendix 2 of [27] for the proof for both random matrices A and Toeplitz matrices A. ■

REMARK 2. The fact that A can be a uniformly random Toeplitz matrix and b a uniformly random vector can be used to reduce the time complexity of computing Ax by using the Fast Fourier Transform (FFT) to perform the matrix-vector multiplication. It can also be used to reduce the space complexity since a random Toeplitz matrix requires less randomness to generate. Since we will use matrices A with only a logarithmic number of rows and columns, such improvements are relatively minor and we omit them in our algorithm and analysis below.

Define pairwise-independent functions:

- For each $j \in [d]$, independently choose $f_j : GF(\Delta) \to GF(B)$, $f_j(x) = A_j \cdot x + b_j$ for a random $(\log \Delta) \times (\log B)$ matrix A_j with entries in $GF(2)$, and random

$b_j \in GF(B)$. Here x is interpreted as a length-$(\log \Delta)$ bitstring and b_j is interpreted as a length-$(\log B)$ bitstring.

- For each $j \in [d]$, independently choose $s_j : GF(\Delta) \to \{-1, 1\}$, $s_j(x) = (-1)^{\langle \sigma_j, x \rangle + \tau_j}$, for random vector $\sigma_j \in GF(\Delta)$ and $\tau_j \in GF(2)$. Here x and σ_j are interpreted as length-$(\log \Delta)$ bitstrings, and $\langle \sigma_j, x \rangle$ denotes their inner product.

Now let $x = (x_1, \ldots, x_d) \in GF(\Delta)^d$ and define the following functions:

- $f(x) = f_1(x_1) + f_2(x_2) + \cdots + f_d(x_d) \mod B$.

- $s(x) = s_1(x_1) \cdot s_2(x_2) \cdots s_d(x_d)$.

It is easy to verify that $f : GF(\Delta)^d \to GF(B)$ and $s : GF(\Delta)^d \to \{-1, 1\}$ are pairwise independent functions since $f_1, \ldots, f_d, s_1, \ldots, s_d$ are each pairwise independent, and independent of each other.

The basic data structure maps an input vector $v \in \mathbb{Z}^{[\Delta]^d}$ to a vector $c \in \mathbb{Z}^{\{0,1,2,\ldots,B-1\}}$ of "counters", where for each "bucket" $k \in \{0, 1, 2, \ldots, B-1\}$, we have counter

$$c_k = \sum_{\{x \mid f(x) = k\}} s(x) \cdot v_x.$$

Here and throughout, we often arbitrarily associate the buckets, indexed by elements of $GF(B)$, with the integers $0, 1, 2, \ldots, B-1$. Observe that this data structure maintains a linear function of v, which allows us to process updates to the coordinates of v. We will show how to process updates to rectangles of coordinates of v very efficiently.

For each $x \in GF(\Delta)^d$, we estimate v_x as:

$$\Phi(x) = s(x) \cdot c_{f(x)}$$

LEMMA 3. *For any $\eta > 0$,*

$$\Pr[|\Phi(x) - v_x| > \eta \|v\|_2] \leq \frac{1}{\eta^2 B}$$

PROOF. For the expectation, we use pairwise-independence of s and that $\mathbf{E}[s(y)] = 0$ for any vector y:

$$
\begin{aligned}
\mathbf{E}[\Phi(x)] &= \mathbf{E}\left[s(x) \sum_{y \mid f(x) = f(y)} s(y) v_y \right] \\
&= v_x + \sum_{y \mid f(x) = f(y), \ x \neq y} \mathbf{E}[s(x)s(y)] \cdot v_y \\
&= v_x
\end{aligned}
$$

For the second moment, we additionally use the pairwise-independence of f:

$$
\begin{aligned}
\mathbf{E}[\Phi(x)^2] &= \mathbf{E}[c_{f(x)}^2] = \sum_{y, y' \mid f(x) = f(y) = f(y')} \mathbf{E}[s(y)s(y')] v_y v_{y'} \\
&= \sum_{y \mid f(x) = f(y)} v_y^2 \leq v_x^2 + \frac{1}{B} \sum_{x \neq y} v_y^2 \\
&\leq v_x^2 + \frac{\|v\|_2^2}{B}
\end{aligned}
$$

Hence, $\mathbf{Var}[\Phi(x)] \leq \frac{\|v\|_2^2}{B}$. By Chebyshev's inequality,

$$\Pr[|\Phi(x) - v_x| > \eta \|v\|_2] \leq \frac{\mathbf{Var}[\Phi(x)]}{\eta^2 \|v\|_2^2} \leq \frac{\|v\|_2^2}{\eta^2 B \|v\|_2^2} = \frac{1}{\eta^2 B}.$$

By Lemma 3, for $B > \frac{3}{\gamma^2}$, we have $\Pr[|\Phi(x) - v_x| \leq \gamma\|v\|_2] \geq \frac{2}{3}$. Hence, if we take $r = O(d\log(\Delta/\delta))$ independent copies of the basic data structure, obtaining $\Phi^1(x), \ldots, \Phi^r(x)$ for each $x \in GF(\Delta)^d$, and set $\hat{\Phi}(x) = \text{median}_{\ell=1}^r \Phi^\ell(x)$, then by a Chernoff and union bound, with probability at least $1 - \delta$, for all $x \in GF(\Delta)^d$, $|\hat{\Phi}(x) - v_x| \leq \gamma\|v\|_2$. The total space complexity of the scheme for $B = O(\gamma^{-2})$, ignoring the cost to represent the hash functions, is $O(\gamma^{-2} \cdot d\log(\Delta/\delta))$ words, since this is the number of counters maintained. Notice that each f_j and s_j requires only $O(\log\Delta \cdot \log B)$ bits to store in each of the $O(d\log(\Delta/\delta))$ basic data structures, giving a space bound of $O(d^2\log(\Delta/\delta)\log\Delta\log B)$ to represent all of the hash functions.

Rectangle-Efficiency: Given a rectangle $R = [a_1, b_1] \times [a_2, b_2] \times \cdots \times [a_d, b_d]$, we show how to efficiently update our data structure. We show how to do this independently for each basic data structure, and multiply the time by $O(d\log(\Delta/\delta))$. To implement our basic data structure, we show how to update our counters given R.

Since our data structure is linear, it suffices to show how to perform updates of the form $(R, 1)$, i.e., a rectangle update with weight 1. Indeed, if we show how to compute a vector c_{change} of changes to the counters, i.e., a vector for which $c \leftarrow c + c_{change}$ to process an update of the form $(R, 1)$, then to process an update of the form (R, w) for a general weight w, it suffices to set $c \leftarrow c + w \cdot c_{change}$.

For each $j \in [d]$, we recursively partition $[a_j, b_j]$ into $t_j = O(\log\Delta)$ intervals:

$$[a_{j,1}, b_{j,1}], [a_{j,2}, b_{j,2}], \ldots, [a_{j,t_j}, b_{j,t_j}].$$

We first find the largest integer q so that there is an integer u with $[u2^q, (u+1)2^q) \subseteq [a_j, b_j]$. The important property of an interval of the form $[u2^q, (u+1)2^q)$ is that all $i \in [a_j, b_j]$ have the same length-$(N - q)$ prefix α in their binary representation, while the suffix ranges over all 2^q possible bit strings. We then recursively divide $[a_j, u2^q - 1]$ and $[(u+1)2^q, b_j]$. This is a standard decomposition into dyadic intervals (see, e.g., [5]), and the recursion produces $t_j = O(\log\Delta)$ disjoint intervals.

For each $j \in [d]$, each dyadic interval $[a_{j,\ell}, b_{j,\ell}]$ for an $\ell \in [t_j]$, and each bucket $k \in \{0, 1, \ldots, B-1\}$, we show how to find the number of $x \in [a_{j,\ell}, b_{j,\ell}]$ for which $f_j(x) = k$ and $s_j(x) = 1$, and the number of $x \in [a_{j,\ell}, b_{j,\ell}]$ for which $f_j(x) = k$ and $s_j(x) = -1$.

If $x \in [a_{j,\ell}, b_{j,\ell}]$ satisfies $f_j(x) = k$ and $s_j(x) = 1$, then $A_j x + b_j = k$ and $\langle \sigma_j, x\rangle + \tau_j = 0$. For $x \in GF(\Delta)$, we break each x into the concatenation of x^{pre} and x^{suf} as follows. Suppose $[a_{j,\ell_j}, b_{j,\ell_j}]$ is a dyadic interval of the form $[u2^q, (u+1)2^q)$ for integers u and q. We let x^{pre} be the common length $(\log\Delta) - q$ prefix of all $x \in [a_{j,\ell_j}, b_{j,\ell_j}]$, and we let x^{suf} be the suffix of x, which ranges over all 2^q bitstrings as x ranges over the interval $[a_{j,\ell_j}, b_{j,\ell_j}]$. We append q 0s to x^{pre} and we prepend $(\log\Delta) - q$ 0s to x^{suf}, and so we have $x = x^{pre} + x^{suf}$.

We break the matrix A_j into two contiguous groups A_j^{pre} and A_j^{suf} of its columns, so that

$$A_j x = A_j^{pre} x^{pre} + A_j^{suf} x^{suf},$$

and similarly break σ into two contiguous groups

σ^{pre} and σ^{suf} of its columns so that

$$\langle \sigma_j, x\rangle = \langle \sigma_j^{pre}, x^{pre}\rangle + \langle \sigma_j^{suf}, x^{suf}\rangle$$

Using that x^{pre} is a fixed vector, we can write the constraint $A_j x + b_j = k$ as

$$A_j^{suf} x^{suf} = -A_j^{pre} x^{pre} - b_j + k,$$

where the right hand side is a fixed vector, and the vector x^{suf} is unconstrained. Similarly, we can write the constraint $\langle \sigma_j, x\rangle = \tau_j$ as

$$\langle \sigma_j^{suf}, x^{suf}\rangle = -\langle \sigma_j^{pre}, x^{pre}\rangle + \tau_j,$$

where the right hand side is a fixed bit, and the vector x^{suf} is unconstrained.

We can thus write the conjunction of these linear systems as another linear system, and use Gaussian elimination to diagonalize the system to count the number of solutions x^{suf} to the conjunction of these linear systems in $O^*(d^3) = O^*(1)$ time. We solve such a linear system for each $\ell \in [t_j]$, each $k \in \{0, 1, \ldots, B-1\}$, and for both $s_j(x) = 1$ and $s_j(x) = -1$. Since the $[a_{j,\ell}, b_{j,\ell}]$ partition $[a_j, b_j]$, we have thus found, for each $k \in \{0, 1, \ldots, B-1\}$, the total number $e_{j,k,1}$ of $x \in [a_j, b_j]$ for which $f_j(x) = k$ and $s_j(x) = 1$, as well as the total number $e_{j,k,-1}$ of $x \in [a_j, b_j]$ for which $f_j(x) = k$ and $s_j(x) = -1$. We do this for each $j \in [d]$. The total time spent is therefore $B \cdot \text{poly}(d) = \gamma^{-2} \cdot O^*(1)$.

We now leverage a technique due to Pagh [41]. Pagh shows how to efficiently combine a 1-dimensional CountSketch applied to a set S_1 with a 1-dimensional CountSketch applied to a set S_2, to obtain a 2-dimensional CountSketch applied to the set $S_1 \times S_2$. We can this technique with our technique of computing a 1-dimensional CountSketch, described above.

Pagh's idea is to associate the B counters of CountSketch with the coefficients of a univariate polynomial with formal variable z. If the current state of the counters is $c_0, c_1, \ldots, c_{B-1}$, then a polynomial that represents this state is $\sum_{k=0}^{B-1} c_k z^k$. Given the counters, this polynomial can be constructed in $O(k)$ time, and given this polynomial, all of the counters can be extracted in $O(k)$ time.

In our setting, for each $j \in [d]$ we create a corresponding univariate degree-$(B-1)$ polynomial $p_j(z)$. The coefficient of z^k is equal to $e_{j,k,1} - e_{j,k,-1}$. That is,

$$p_j(z) = \sum_{k=0}^{B-1} \sum_{x \in [a_j, b_j] \text{ such that } f_j(x) = k} s_j(x) \cdot z^k.$$

We would like to compute the following polynomial $q(z)$:

$$
\begin{aligned}
q(z) &= \sum_{\substack{k \in \{0, \ldots, B-1\} \\ x \in R \mid f(x) = k}} s(x) \cdot z^k \\
&= \sum_{\substack{k \in \{0, \ldots, B-1\} \\ x \in R \mid f(x) = k}} s(x_1) \cdots s(x_d) \cdot z^{f(x_1) + \cdots + f(x_d) \bmod B} \\
&= \sum_{\substack{k \in \{0, \ldots, B-1\} \\ x \in R \mid f(x) = k}} s(x_1) \cdots s(x_d) \cdot z^{f(x_1)} \cdots z^{f(x_d)} \\
&\qquad \bmod (z^B - 1) \\
&= \prod_{j=1}^{d} \sum_{x_j \in [a_j, b_j]} s(x_j) z^{f(x_j)} \bmod (z^B - 1) \\
&= \prod_{j=1}^{d} p_j(z) \bmod (z^B - 1),
\end{aligned}
$$

where for univariate polynomials $p(z)$ and $q(z)$ with rational coefficients, the notation $p(z) \bmod q(z)$ indicates the unique polynomial (the "remainder") $r(z)$ for which $p(z) = m(z) \cdot q(z) + r(z)$, where $r(z)$ has degree strictly less than that of $q(z)$.

LEMMA 4. *For any two polynomials $p_1(z)$ and $p_2(z)$, we have $(p_1(z) \cdot p_2(z)) \bmod (z^B - 1) = ((p_1(z) \bmod (z^B - 1)) \cdot (p_2(z) \bmod (z^B - 1))) \bmod (z^B - 1)$.*

PROOF. Let $r(z)$ be the remainder of division of $p_1(z) \cdot p_2(z)$ by $z^B - 1$, so that $p_1(z)p_2(z) = m(z)(z^B - 1) + r(z)$ with the degree of $r(z)$ less than B, for some polynomial $m(z)$. Let $r_1(z)$ be the remainder of division of $p_1(z)$ by $z^B - 1$, so $p_1(z) = m_1(z)(z^B - 1) + r_1(z)$ with the degree of $r_1(z)$ less than B, for some polynomial $m_1(z)$. Similarly define $r_2(z)$ and $m_2(z)$. Then $p_1(z)p_2(z) \bmod (z^B - 1) = (m_1(z)m_2(z)(z^B - 1)^2 + m_1(z)(z^B - 1)r_2(z) + m_2(z)(z^B - 1)r_1(z) + r_1(z)r_2(z)) \bmod (z^B - 1) = r_1(z) \cdot r_2(z) \bmod (z^B - 1)$, which completes the proof. ∎

It follows by Lemma 4 that to compute $q(z)$ we can first compute $p_1(z) \cdot p_2(z) \bmod (z^B - 1)$, then compute the product of this polynomial with $p_3(z)$, and then take this modulo $z^B - 1$, etc. In this way, the computation of $q(z)$ is that of d multiplications of polynomials of degree $B - 1$. Each polynomial multiplication can be done in $O(B \log B)$ time using the FFT, provided that B is a power of 2. It is also trivial to reduce the polynomial modulo $z^B - 1$, since this just involves replacing a monomial z^k with $z^{k \bmod B}$. Hence, the total time to compute $q(z)$ given $p_1(z), \ldots, p_d(z)$ is $O(dB \log B)$.

Given $q(z)$, we can read off its coefficients to update each of the counters c_k in $O(B)$ time. Hence, the total update time is $\gamma^{-2} \cdot O^*(1)$. We summarize our findings in the following theorem.

THEOREM 5. *The data structure RectangleCountSketch(γ) can be updated rectangle-efficiently in time $\gamma^{-2} \cdot O^*(1)$. The total space is $\gamma^{-2} \cdot O^*(1)$ words. The data structure can be used to answer any query $x \in GF(\Delta)^d$, returning a number $\Phi(x)$ with $|\Phi(x) - v_x| \leq \gamma \|v\|_2$. The algorithm succeeds on all queries simultaneously with probability $\geq 1 - \delta$.*

3. RECTANGLE-EFFICIENT F_K

In this section we consider rectangle-efficient estimation of F_k, for constant $k \geq 0$. Here, F_k of a vector $v \in [\Delta]^d$ is defined as $\sum_{j \in [\Delta]^d} v_j^k = \|v\|_k^k$, which is equal to the k-th power of the k-norm [2]. Note that 0^0 is interpreted as 0 in case of F_0. On page 8 of [9], Braverman and Ostrovsky provide an algorithm RecursiveSum[0](D, ε) which takes in a stream D, an error parameter ε, and provides an $(\varepsilon, 3/10)$-approximation to the k-th frequency moment F_k, for constant $k \geq 2$. The success probability can be amplified to $1 - \delta$ by independent repetition. We will build on this work in several ways. Their algorithm is in turn a simplification of earlier work [8, 32].

We choose to follow [9] since it provides a simpler exposition and has several properties we will exploit. First, we will show that it works for any constant real $k \geq 0$ instead of just $k \geq 2$. This first part is a simple, yet very useful observation. Indeed, most algorithms in the literature for estimating F_k, $k \leq 2$, rely on k-stable random variables [31], and we do not know how to make them rectangle-efficient. Next, and importantly, we relax a requirement of their analysis in Lemma 6 below, which is needed in order for us to combine their algorithm with our RectangleCountSketch algorithm.

Let $\phi = O(d \log \Delta)$. The algorithm of Braverman and Ostrovsky (in our language) chooses a pairwise-independent hash function $g : GF(\Delta)^d \to GF(\Delta^d)$ and defines ϕ substreams $D_1, \ldots, D_\phi$, where the j-th substream D_j consists of the input stream D restricted to those items $i \in GF(\Delta)^d$ for which $g(i) \leq \Delta^d / 2^{j-1}$, where we arbitrarily map the elements of $GF(\Delta^d)$ to the elements of the set $\{1, 2, \ldots, \Delta^d\}$. For each substream, the algorithm runs the CountSketch algorithm of Charikar, Chen, and Farach-Colton [15]. The CountSketch algorithm of [15] is identical to our RectangleCountSketch algorithm when all stream updates are single points, rather than rectangles, and additionally requires that $d = 1$. From this data structure, at the end of the stream Braverman and Ostrovsky produce an estimate to F_k, $k \geq 2$. This is described in more detail in Figure 1 in the next subsection.

In our implementation we simply replace CountSketch with RectangleCountSketch. This completely specifies the algorithm up to the parameter γ we choose in RectangleCountSketch, and how we process the data structure to output an estimate to F_k after seeing the data stream.

The following lemma is a relaxed version of Corollary 5.3 in [9], and yields a procedure to return the heavy hitters in a specific substream D_j from our RectangleCountSketch data structure after processing the stream. We return a set P of items together with approximations to their frequencies. The difference between this Lemma and [9] is that we bound the total additive error of the approximations while [9] guarantees that the frequency of each item in P has a small relative error. The reason for this is that we do not know how to achieve a small relative error for each item by using only pairwise independence, which is in turn crucial for making our algorithm rectangle-efficient.

LEMMA 6. *Fix a value $j \in [\phi]$. Let $v \in \mathbb{Z}^{[\Delta]^d}$ be the frequency vector of items $i \in [\Delta]^d$ in substream D_j, that is $v(i)$ is the number of occurrences of i in D if $g(i) \leq \Delta^d / 2^{j-1}$*

---

[2] Technically, for $k < 1$, $\|v\|_k$ is not a norm since it doesn't satisfy the triangle inequality, but it is still a well-defined quantity.

(under an arbitrary mapping of $GF(\Delta)^d$ to $\{1, 2, \ldots, \Delta^d\}$), and is 0 otherwise. For any constant real number $k \in (0, \infty)$, there is an algorithm which uses RectangleCountSketch(γ) with $\gamma = \Theta(\varepsilon^{1+1/k}\alpha^{1/k})$ if $k \in (0, 2]$, and $\gamma = \Theta(\varepsilon^{1+1/k}\alpha^{1/k}/\Delta^{d/2-d/k})$ for $k > 2$, so that with probability at least $1 - \delta$, it outputs a set P of $O(1/\alpha)$ pairs (i, v_i') for which $\sum_{(i,v_i') \in P} ||v_i'|^k - |v_i|^k| \leq \varepsilon\|v\|_k^k$, and such that all elements i with $|v_i|^k \geq \alpha\|v\|_k^k$ appear as the first element of some pair in P. The algorithm uses $O^*(\gamma^{-2})$ words of space.

PROOF. By Theorem 5, with probability at least $1 - \delta$, for all i we have $|\Phi(i) - v_i| \leq \gamma\|v\|_2$ if we use $O(\gamma^{-2} \cdot d \log(\Delta/\delta))$ words of space in RectangleCountSketch. We assume this event occurs and add δ to the error probability. Our algorithm uses the output of RectangleCountSketch(γ) to find the set P of the pairs $(i, \Phi(i))$ corresponding to the i with the largest $2/\alpha$ values $\Phi(i)$.

We will call an i for which $|v_i| \geq (\varepsilon\alpha/4)^{1/k}\|v\|_k$ heavy. Otherwise, we will say i is light.

The following fact is well-known and follows from basic inequalities on norms.

FACT 7. If $k \geq 2$, then $\|v\|_2 \leq \Delta^{d/2-d/k}\|v\|_k$, while if $k < 2$, then $\|v\|_k \geq \|v\|_2$.

Since k is an absolute constant, for any $(i, \Phi(i)) \in P$ for which $|v_i| \geq (\varepsilon\alpha/4)^{1/k}\|v\|_k$ we have that (for appropriately chosen constants in the $\Theta(\cdot)$ notation defining γ above):

$$
\begin{aligned}
\left(1 - \frac{\varepsilon}{10k}\right)|v_i| &\leq |v_i| - \frac{\gamma \cdot \max(1, \Delta^{d/2-d/k})}{(\varepsilon\alpha/4)^{1/k}}|v_i| \\
&\leq |v_i| - \gamma \cdot \max(1, \Delta^{d/2-d/k})\|v\|_k \\
&\leq |v_i| - \gamma\|v\|_2 \leq |\Phi(i)|,
\end{aligned}
$$

where we have used Fact 7. We also have that, using Fact 7,

$$
\begin{aligned}
|\Phi(i)| &\leq |v_i| + \gamma\|v\|_2 \\
&\leq |v_i| + \gamma \cdot \max(1, \Delta^{d/2-d/k})\|v\|_k \\
&\leq |v_i|(1 + \gamma \cdot \max(1, \Delta^{d/2-d/k})/(\varepsilon\alpha/4)^{1/k}) \\
&\leq (1 + \varepsilon/(10k))|v_i|.
\end{aligned}
$$

Hence, for such i, we have

$$(1 - \varepsilon/3)|v_i|^k \leq |\Phi(i)|^k \leq (1 + \varepsilon/3)|v_i|^k.$$

Next, for any $(i, \Phi(i)) \in P$ for which $|v_i| < (\varepsilon\alpha/4)^{1/k}\|v\|_k$, we have, using Fact 7,

$$
\begin{aligned}
0 &\leq |\Phi(i)|^k \leq (|v_i| + \gamma\|v\|_2)^k \\
&\leq \|v\|_k^k((\varepsilon\alpha/4)^{1/k} + \gamma\|v\|_2/\|v\|_k)^k \\
&\leq \|v\|_k^k((\varepsilon\alpha/4)^{1/k} + \Theta(\varepsilon^{1+1/k}\alpha^{1/k}))^k \\
&\leq \|v\|_k^k \cdot \varepsilon\alpha/3.
\end{aligned}
$$

Hence,

$$
\begin{aligned}
&\sum_{(i,\Phi(i)) \in P} ||\Phi(i)|^k - |v_i|^k| \\
&= \sum_{\text{heavy } i} ||\Phi(i)|^k - |v_i|^k| + \sum_{\text{light } i} ||\Phi(i)|^k - |v_i|^k| \\
&\leq \frac{\varepsilon}{3}\sum_{\text{heavy } i} |v_i|^k + \frac{2}{\alpha} \cdot \max\left\{\frac{\varepsilon\alpha\|v\|_k^k}{4}, \frac{\varepsilon\alpha\|v\|_k^k}{3}\right\} \leq \varepsilon\|v\|_k^k.
\end{aligned}
$$

Finally, let T be the set of i for which $|v_i|^k \geq \alpha\|v\|_k^k$. It remains to show each $i \in T$ occurs in some pair in P. As shown above, for such i, we have $|\Phi(i)|^k \geq (1 - \varepsilon/3)|v_i|^k$. If i is not in a pair in P, then there are at least $2/\alpha$ different j for which

$$|\Phi(j)|^k \geq |\Phi(i)|^k \geq (1 - \varepsilon/3)|v_i|^k \geq (1 - \varepsilon/3)\alpha\|v\|_k^k.$$

It follows that j cannot be light, since for such j we have $|\Phi(j)|^k \leq (\varepsilon\alpha/3)\|v\|_k^k$. On the other hand, for a heavy j, we have $|\Phi(j)|^k \leq (1 + \varepsilon/3)|v_j|^k$, and so there would need to be at least $2/\alpha$ different heavy j for which $|v_j|^k \geq \frac{1}{1+\varepsilon/3} \cdot (1 - \varepsilon)\alpha\|v\|_k^k$, which is a contradiction, as the sum of v_j^k over such j would be larger than $\|v\|_k^k$. ∎

We next prove the analogue of Lemma 6 in the case that $k = 0$.

LEMMA 8. Fix a value $j \in [\phi]$. Let $v \in \mathbb{Z}^{[\Delta]^d}$ be the frequency vector of items $i \in [\Delta]^d$ in substream D_j, that is v_i is the number of occurrences of i in D if $g(i) \leq \Delta^d/2^{j-1}$ (under an arbitrary mapping of $GF(\Delta)^d$ to $\{1, 2, \ldots, \Delta^d\}$), and is 0 otherwise. There is an algorithm which uses RectangleCountSketch(γ) with $\gamma = \Theta(\alpha\varepsilon)$ so that with probability at least $1 - \delta$, it outputs a set P of $O(1/\alpha)$ items i for which $\sum_{i \in P} |1 - |v_i|^0| \leq \varepsilon\|v\|_0$, and such that all elements i with $|v_i| \geq \alpha\|v\|_0$ occur in P. The algorithm uses $O^*(\gamma^{-2})$ words of space.

PROOF. The algorithm is to run RectangleCountSketch with parameter $\gamma = \alpha\varepsilon/3$. Then, find the set P of items i for which $\Phi(i) \geq 2/3$. If $|P| \leq 1/\alpha$, then output P. Otherwise, output $\emptyset$.

First suppose that $|v|_0 \leq 1/(\varepsilon\alpha)$. Then by Theorem 5, with probability at least $1 - \delta$, for $\gamma = \alpha\varepsilon/3$ and for all i, we have $|\Phi(i) - v_i| \leq 1/3$. This implies that the output of RectangleCountSketch(γ) can be used to find the set of at most $1/(\varepsilon\alpha)$ non-zero values v_i. Hence, it can output this set as P if $|P| \leq 1/\alpha$ and incur zero additive error. If the set $|P|$ it finds satisfies $|P| > 1/\alpha$, then it outputs $\emptyset$, and incurs zero additive error. In both cases, all i with $|v_i| \geq \alpha\|v\|_0$ are output, as desired.

Now suppose that $\|v\|_0 > 1/(\varepsilon\alpha)$. Since $|P| \leq 1/\alpha$ and $\varepsilon\|v\|_0 > 1/\alpha$, and since there is no i with $|v_i| \geq \alpha\|v\|_0$, the lemma is trivially satisfied. ∎

The key is that our Lemma 6 and Lemma 8 can be used instead of Corollary 5.3 of [9] in the remaining analysis of [9], replacing various steps that require that each $|v_i'| = (1 \pm \varepsilon)|v_i|$ for i occurring as a first coordinate of a pair in P with the weaker condition of Lemma 6 that instead bounds the total additive error (and similarly for Lemma 8). We give the details of the tweaked analysis in Section 3.1.

Rectangle-Efficiency: Given a rectangle $R = [a_1, b_1] \times [a_2, b_2] \times \cdots \times [a_d, b_d]$, we show how to efficiently update the data structure used in RecursiveSum[0](D, ε).

The idea is the same as in our RectangleCountSketch algorithm. Namely, for each substream D_j, for each bucket $k \in [B]$ in a basic data structure of RectangleCountSketch, we need to find the number of $i \in R$ which are placed in bucket k with a sign of -1, and the number of i with a sign of $+1$. Since g is a pairwise-independent hash function, it can be expressed as $Ai + b$, where $A \in GF(\Delta)^d \times GF(\Delta)^d$ and b is a vector of length Δ^d. Then an element i is in D_j if and only if $Ai + b$ has a prefix of at least $j - 1$ zeros. Equivalently, by removing all but $j - 1$ rows of A and b, obtaining matrix A' and vector b', we require that $A'i + b' = 0$. As in the RectangleCountSketch algorithm, we can count the number of solutions to the intersection of this linear equation and the linear equations imposed by the pairwise-independent hash functions h and s used in RectangleCountSketch in the previous section. We thus obtain the following theorem, whose proof is given in Subsection 3.1.

THEOREM 9. *For constant $k \in [0, \infty)$, there is a rectangle-efficient single-pass streaming algorithm which we call* RecursiveSum[0](D, ε) *which outputs an (ε, δ)-approximation to F_k. For $k \in [0, 2]$, it uses $O^*(1)$ words of space and $O^*(1)$ time to process each rectangle in the stream. For $k > 2$, it uses $O^*(\Delta^{d-2d/k})$ words of space and $O^*(\Delta^{d-2d/k})$ time to process each rectangle in the stream.*

3.1 Finishing the Analysis for F_k-Estimation

We show how to use our Lemma 6 and Lemma 8 in place of Corollary 5 in the analysis of [9] to produce an estimate to F_k, $k \geq 0$, thereby filling in the details of the proof of Theorem 9. We point out where our relaxation to total additive error is used. The analysis closely follows that of [9].

We recall the following definitions of [9]. Let V be an N-dimensional vector of non-negative values V_j (we note our notation is slightly different than that of [9], who use lower-case v_j to denote the coordinate values) and $\|V\|_1 = \sum_{j=1}^n V_j$ be its 1-norm. An element V_i is α-major with respect to V if $V_i \geq \alpha \|V\|_1$. A set $S \subseteq [N]$ is an α-core with respect to V if $i \in S$ for any α-major V_i.

Here we relax the definition of (α, ε)-cover in [9]. The first bullet below is where we incorporate our total additive error guarantee. In [9], the first bullet below instead states that for all $j \in [t]$, $(1 - \varepsilon)V_{i_j} \leq w_j \leq (1 + \varepsilon)V_{i_j}$.

A non-empty set Q of the form $\{(i_1, w_1), \ldots, (i_t, w_t)\}$ for some $t \in [n]$ and distinct $i_1, \ldots, i_t$ is a **relaxed** (α, ε)-cover with respect to V if the following hold:

1. $\sum_{j \in [t]} |V_{i_j} - w_j| \leq \varepsilon \|V\|_1$.

2. $\forall i \in [n]$, if V_i is α-major then there exists a $j \in [t]$ such that $i_j = i$.

For a distribution $\mathcal{D}$ on sets Q of the form $\{(i_1, w_1), \ldots, (i_t, w_t)\}$, we say that $\mathcal{D}$ is δ-good if

$$\Pr_{Q \sim \Delta}[Q \text{ is a relaxed } (\alpha, \varepsilon) - \text{cover}] \geq 1 - \delta.$$

We sometimes define a randomized mapping g from vectors V to sets Q and say that g is δ-good with respect to V if its output distribution is δ-good. For a set $Q = \{(i_1, w_1), \ldots, (i_t, w_t)\}$ of the above form, let

$$Ind(Q) = \{i_1, \ldots, i_t\}.$$

For $i \in Ind(Q)$, let $w_Q(i)$ be such that $(i, w_Q(i)) \in Q$.

LEMMA 10. *(Corollary 3.6 of [9]) Let g be a δ-good mapping for a vector V and let $Q \sim g(V)$. Let H be a random N-dimensional vector independent of V and Q with pairwise-independent zero-one entries H_i. Define*

$$X' = \sum_{i \in Ind(Q)} V_i + 2 \sum_{i \notin Ind(Q)} H_i V_i.$$

Then $\Pr[|X' - \|V\|_1| \geq \varepsilon \|V\|_1] \leq \frac{\alpha}{\varepsilon^2}$. (we note there is a typo in their paper, they write $\frac{\varepsilon}{\alpha^2}$ instead of the correct $\frac{\alpha}{\varepsilon^2}$.)

Let $H^1, \ldots, H^\phi$ be i.i.d. random vectors with pairwise-independent zero-one entries. For two vectors U and V of dimension N, let $Had(V, U)$ be a vector of dimension N with entries $U_i \cdot V_i$. Define: $V^0 = V$ and $V^j = Had(V^{j-1}, H^j)$ for $j \in [\phi]$ (again, our notation is slightly different than that of [10], who use V_j to indicate what we are calling V^j). Let $Q^0 \sim V^0, Q^1 \sim V^1, \ldots, Q^\phi \sim V^\phi$. Define $w_j(i) = w_{Q^j}(i)$. Define the sequence:

$$X'_j = \sum_{i \in Ind(Q^j)} V_i^j + 2 \sum_{i \notin Ind(Q^j)} H_i^{j+1} V_i^j,$$

for $j = 0, 1, 2, \ldots, \phi - 1$, and $X'_\phi = \|V^\phi\|_1$.

FACT 11. *(Fact 3.7 of [9].) $\Pr[\cup_{j=0}^\phi |X'_j - \|V^j\|| \geq \varepsilon \|V^j\|_1] \leq (\phi + 1)\left(\frac{\alpha}{\varepsilon^2} + \delta\right)$.*

Define Y'_ϕ to be any random variable depending on V^ϕ for which $\Pr[|Y'_\phi - \|V^\phi\|_1| \geq \varepsilon \|V^\phi\|_1] \leq \delta$. For $j = 0, 1, 2, \ldots, \phi - 1$, define

$$Y'_j = 2Y'_{j+1} + \sum_{i \in Ind(Q^j)} (1 - 2H_i^{j+1})w_i^j.$$

In the next lemma we use our relaxed (α, ε)-covers instead of the (α, ε)-covers in [9].

LEMMA 12. *For any ϕ, γ, and V, for $\alpha = \Theta(\gamma^2/\phi^3)$ and $\delta = \Theta(1/\phi)$, $\Pr[|Y'_0 - \|V\|_1| \geq \gamma \|V\|_1] \leq 1/5$.*

PROOF. The proof is almost identical to that of Lemma 3.8 of [9]. The only difference is that our Q^j are relaxed (α, ε)-covers, while their Q^j are (α, ε)-covers. The only place that changes is that in the end of the proof they argue $\Pr[\cup_{j=0}^\phi(|\overline{Err}_j^3| \geq \varepsilon \|V^j\|_1)] \leq (\phi + 1)\delta$, using that $Err_j^3 = \sum_{i \in Ind(Q^j)} |w_j(i) - V_i^j|$ and their Q^j is an (α, ε)-cover. However, this bound also holds by definition for Q^j a relaxed (α, ε)-cover, and so their proof remains unchanged. ∎

The next theorem follows from Lemma 12.

THEOREM 13. *(Theorem 4.2 of [9]) Algorithm* RecursiveSum *computes a $(1 \pm \varepsilon)$-approximation of $\|V\|_1$ and errs with probability at most $3/10$. The space complexity is $O(\log n)$ times that of finding a relaxed (α, ε)-cover with error probability $O(1/\log n)$, where α is set to $\varepsilon^2/\log^3 n$.*

To conclude the analysis, we simply plug in our Lemma 6 and Lemma 8 for computing a relaxed (α, ε)-cover for $k > 0$ and $k = 0$, respectively, into step 2 of RecursiveSum.

Proof (: of Theorem 9) We set the dimension N in the vectors V^j in RecursiveSum to equal Δ^d, and identify the coordinates with elements of $GF(\Delta)^d$. We define the vector V^0 as follows: $V_x^0 = |v_x|^k$, where v is the input vector and we are trying to estimate $\|v\|_k^k$. We need to show how to efficiently obtain a relaxed (α, ε)-cover for each V^j, where $\alpha = \varepsilon^2/\log n$. This is exactly what is given by Lemma 6 and Lemma 8. The time and space bounds follow by these lemmas, and the correctness follows from Theorem 13. ∎

1. Generate $\phi = O(\log n)$ pairwise-independent zero one-vectors $H^1, \ldots, H^\phi$, and let D_j be the substream restricted to those inputs i with $H_i^1 \cdot H_i^2 \cdots H_i^j = 1$.
2. Let Q^j be a relaxed (α, ε)-cover for the vector V^j underlying D_j.
3. If $F_0(V^\phi) > 10^{10}$, then output 0 and stop. Otherwise compute $Y_\phi = \|V^\phi\|_1$.
4. For each $j = \phi - 1, \ldots, 0$, compute $Y_j = 2Y_{j+1} - \sum_{i \in Ind(Q^j)} (1 - 2H_i^j) w_i^j$.
5. Output Y_0.

Figure 1: The RecursiveSum[0](D, ε) algorithm of [9], with our relaxation in step 2 to relaxed (α, ε)-covers.

4. RECTANGLE-EFFICIENT $F_K, K > 2$, IN POLYLOGARITHMIC TIME IN THE INSERTION-ONLY MODEL

In [5] it was shown how to range-efficiently implement the algorithm of [2] in one dimension in the insertion-only model, retaining $O^*(\Delta^{1-1/k})$ bits of space, but reducing the time per range from $O^*(\Delta)$ to $O^*(\Delta^{1-1/k})$. Here we will considerably strengthen this for small values of d, improving the time per range from $O^*(\Delta^{1-1/k})$ to $O^*(1) \cdot O(\log \Delta)^d$, while retaining $O^*(\Delta^{1-1/k}) \cdot O(\log \Delta)^d$ bits of space. Also, our algorithm generalizes to yield a rectangle-efficient algorithm for $d > 1$:

THEOREM 14. *There is a rectangle-efficient algorithm for positively-weighted input rectangles which (ε, δ)-approximates F_k, $k \geq 2$, using $O^*(\Delta^{d(1-1/k)}) \cdot O(\log \Delta)^d$ bits of space and $O^*(1) \cdot O(\log \Delta)^d$ time to process each rectangle.*

PROOF. We use the F_k-estimation algorithm of [2]. On a stream of points, the algorithm of [2] works by sampling $r = O^*(\Delta^{d(1-1/k)})$ random positions $i_1, \ldots, i_r$ in the data stream, obtaining a list of points $p_{i_1}, \ldots, p_{i_r}$ occurring at these positions in the stream. Then for $j = 1, 2, \ldots, r$, the algorithm counts the number $f(p_{i_j})$ of occurrences of point p_{i_j} in the stream after position i_j. Note that if the points are weighted (positively) instead of just occurring with weight 1, and if W is the sum of their weights, then $i_1, \ldots, i_r$ would be chosen randomly from the set $\{1, 2, 3, \ldots, W\}$, and p_{i_j} would equal the point in the stream for which the sum of weights of points seen so far is equal to i_j. A natural implementation of this algorithm would be, for each input rectangle, to check how many points $p_{i_1}, \ldots, p_{i_r}$ occur in the rectangle, and update the counts $f(p_{i_j})$. This takes $O(r)$ time, and corresponds to the algorithm of [5].

We first show how to achieve amortized $O^*(1) \cdot O(\log \Delta)^d$ time. The idea is to batch updates of r rectangles together and build a data structure for the d-dimensional stabbing counting query problem on these r rectangles. More precisely, we partition the input stream into contiguous blocks of r rectangles, except for the last block which may contain fewer than r rectangles. To process a rectangle which does not occur at the end of a block, we simply store the endpoints of the rectangle. At the end of each block, we need to update the $f(p_{i_j})$ values (some of these may previously be 0). The naïve implementation would take $O^*(r^2)$ time. Instead, we use the following, which boils down to computing segment trees inside internal nodes of segment trees, nested d levels deep.

THEOREM 15. *(See Theorem 4.2 in [39] for the result for $d = 1$. The extension to $d > 1$ is implied by the first two paragraphs of Section 4.2 of [39].) Given a set of n rectangles in $[\Delta]^d$, they can be stored in a multi-dimensional segment tree using $O(n \log^d n)$ words of space, which can be constructed in $O(n \log^d n)$ time, and such that for any point $p \in [\Delta]^d$, we can determine the sum of the weights of rectangles containing point p in $O(\log^d n)$ time.*

Using Theorem 15, we can build a multi-dimensional segment tree in $O(r \log^d r)$ time. Then, for each of the at most r points $p_{i_1}, \ldots, p_{i_r}$, we can determine its weight with a query which takes only $O(\log^d r)$ time, giving total time $O(r \log^d r)$ time for updating the $f(p_{i_j})$ values. The total space complexity of the scheme is $O^*(r \log^d r)$.

Finally, the algorithm can be de-amortized in the following way. Namely, since we spend $O(r \log^d r)$ time at the end of each block, we can instead spread the work required of one block over the updates of the next block. Hence, the time we take per input rectangle is $O^*(1) \cdot O(\log \Delta)^d$ in the worst-case. At the end of the stream, to return an answer we take $O^*(r \log^d r)$ time, both to combine the estimates $f(p_{i_j})$ for $j = 1, \ldots, r$, and to process the second to last and last blocks, whose work has been pushed to the end of the stream. ■

Acknowledgment: We would like to thank the anonymous referees for many helpful comments, especially those that helped us to reduce the dependence on d in our update times.

5. REFERENCES

[1] http://www.opengeospatial.org/.

[2] Noga Alon, Yossi Matias, and Mario Szegedy. The Space Complexity of Approximating the Frequency Moments. *J. Comput. Syst. Sci.*, 58(1):137–147, 1999.

[3] Alexandr Andoni, Robert Krauthgamer, and Krzysztof Onak. Streaming algorithms via precision sampling. In *FOCS*, pages 363–372, 2011.

[4] Ziv Bar-Yossef, T. S. Jayram, Ravi Kumar, and D. Sivakumar. An information statistics approach to data stream and communication complexity. *J. Comput. Syst. Sci.*, 68(4):702–732, 2004.

[5] Ziv Bar-Yossef, Ravi Kumar, and D. Sivakumar. Reductions in streaming algorithms, with an application to counting triangles in graphs. In *SODA*, pages 623–632, 2002.

[6] Michael Benedikt and Leonid Libkin. Exact and approximate aggregation in constraint query languages. In *PODS*, pages 102–113, 1999.

[7] J.L. Bentley. Algorithms for Klee's rectangle problem. Unpublished notes, Computer Science Department, Carnegie Mellon University, 1978.

[8] Lakshminath Bhuvanagiri, Sumit Ganguly, Deepanjan Kesh, and Chandan Saha. Simpler algorithm for estimating frequency moments of data streams. In *SODA*, pages 708–713, 2006.

[9] Vladimir Braverman and Rafail Ostrovsky. Recursive sketching for frequency moments. *CoRR*, abs/1011.2571, 2010.

[10] Vladimir Braverman and Rafail Ostrovsky. Zero-one frequency laws. In *STOC*, pages 281–290, 2010.

[11] Mengchu Cai, Dinesh Keshwani, and Peter Z. Revesz. Parametric rectangles: A model for querying and animation of spatiotemporal databases. In *EDBT*, pages 430–444, 2000.

[12] A. Robert Calderbank, Anna C. Gilbert, Kirill Levchenko, S. Muthukrishnan, and Martin Strauss. Improved range-summable random variable construction algorithms. In *SODA*, pages 840–849, 2005.

[13] Timothy M. Chan. A (slightly) faster algorithm for Klee's measure problem. In *SoCG*, pages 94–100, 2008.

[14] Timothy M. Chan and Mihai Patrascu. Counting inversions, offline orthogonal range counting, and related problems. In *SODA*, pages 161–173, 2010.

[15] Moses Charikar, Kevin Chen, and Martin Farach-Colton. Finding frequent items in data streams. In *ICALP*, pages 693–703, 2002.

[16] Eric Y. Chen and Timothy M. Chan. Space-efficient algorithms for Klee's measure problem. In *CCCG*, pages 27–30, 2005.

[17] Bogdan S. Chlebus. On the Klee's measure problem in small dimensions. In *SOFSEM '98: Proceedings of the 25th Conference on Current Trends in Theory and Practice of Informatics*, pages 304–311, London, UK, 1998. Springer-Verlag.

[18] Jeffrey Considine, Feifei Li, George Kollios, and John Byers. Approximate aggregation techniques for sensor databases. In *ICDE*, page 449, 2004.

[19] Graham Cormode and S. Muthukrishnan. Estimating dominance norms of multiple data streams. In *ESA*, pages 148–160, 2003.

[20] Graham Cormode and S. Muthukrishnan. An improved data stream summary: the count-min sketch and its applications. *J. Algorithms*, 55(1):58–75, 2005.

[21] Abhinandan Das, Johannes Gehrke, and Mirek Riedewald. Approximation techniques for spatial data. In *SIGMOD*, pages 695–706, 2004.

[22] Paul Fischer and Klaus-Uwe Hãüffgen. Computing a maximum axis-aligned rectangle in a convex polygon. *Inf. Process. Lett.*, 51(4):189–193, 1994.

[23] Michael L. Fredman and Bruce Weide. On the complexity of computing the measure of $\cup[a_i, b_i]$. *CACM*, 21(7):540–544, 1978.

[24] Hillel Gazit. New upper bounds in Klee's measure problem. *SIAM Journal on Computing*, 20(6):1034–1045, 1991.

[25] Anna C. Gilbert, Yannis Kotidis, S. Muthukrishnan, and Martin Strauss. Surfing wavelets on streams: One-pass summaries for approximate aggregate queries. In *VLDB*, pages 79–88, 2001.

[26] Anna C. Gilbert, Yannis Kotidis, S. Muthukrishnan, and Martin Strauss. One-pass wavelet decompositions of data streams. *IEEE Trans. Knowl. Data Eng.*, 15(3):541–554, 2003.

[27] Oded Goldreich. A sample of samplers: A computational perspective on sampling. In *Studies in Complexity and Cryptography*, pages 302–332. 2011.

[28] Ralf Hartmut Güting. An introduction to spatial database systems. *VLDB J.*, 3(4):357–399, 1994.

[29] John Hershberger, Nisheeth Shrivastava, and Subhash Suri. Cluster hull: A technique for summarizing spatial data streams. In *ICDE*, page 138, 2006.

[30] Piotr Indyk. Algorithms for dynamic geometric problems over data streams. In *Proceedings of the 36th Annual ACM Symposium on Theory of Computing (STOC)*, pages 373–380, 2004.

[31] Piotr Indyk. Stable distributions, pseudorandom generators, embeddings, and data stream computation. *J. ACM*, 53(3):307–323, 2006.

[32] Piotr Indyk and David P. Woodruff. Optimal approximations of the frequency moments of data streams. In *STOC*, pages 202–208, 2005.

[33] V. Klee. Can the measure of $\cup[a_i, b_i]$ be computed in less than $O(n \log n)$ steps? In *American Mathematical Monthly*, volume 84, pages 284–285, 1977.

[34] Gabriel M. Kuper, Leonid Libkin, and Jan Paredaens, editors. *Constraint Databases*. Springer, 2000.

[35] Iosif Lazaridis and Sharad Mehrotra. Progressive approximate aggregate queries with a multi-resolution tree structure. In *SIGMOD*, pages 401–412, 2001.

[36] K. Levchenko and Y.-K Liu. Counting solutions of polynomial equations, 2005. Manuscript.

[37] S. Muthukrishnan. Data Streams: Algorithms and Applications. *Foundations and Trends in Theoretical Computer Science*, 1(2):117–236, 2005.

[38] Suman Nath, Phillip B. Gibbons, Srinivasan Seshan, and Zachary R. Anderson. Synopsis diffusion for robust aggregation in sensor networks. In *SENSYS*, pages 250–262, 2004.

[39] Mark Overmars. Geometric data structures for computer graphics: an overview. In *Theoretical Foundations of Computer Graphics and CAD*, pages 21–49, 1988.

[40] Mark H. Overmars and Chee-Keng Yap. New upper bounds in Klee's measure problem. *SICOMP*, 20(6):1034–1045, 1991.

[41] Rasmus Pagh. Compressed matrix multiplication. In *ICTS*, pages 442–451, 2012.

[42] Dimitris Papadias, Panos Kalnis, Jun Zhang, and Yufei Tao. Efficient OLAP operations in spatial data warehouses. In *SSTD*, pages 443–459, 2001.

[43] A. Pavan and Srikanta Tirthapura. Range-efficient counting of distinct elements in a massive data stream. *SIAM J. Comput.*, 37(2):359–379, 2007.

[44] Florin Rusu and Alin Dobra. Fast range-summable random variables for efficient aggregate estimation. In *SIGMOD*, pages 193–204, 2006.

[45] Gokarna Sharma, Costas Busch, and Srikanta Tirthapura. A streaming approximation algorithm for Klee's measure problem. *CoRR*, abs/1004.1569, 2010.

[46] Cheng Sheng and Yufei Tao. New results on two-dimensional orthogonal range aggregation in external memory. In *PODS*, pages 129–139, 2011.

[47] He Sun and Chung Keung Poon. Two improved range-efficient algorithms for F_0 estimation. *Theor. Comput. Sci.*, 410(11):1073–1080, 2009.

[48] Yufei Tao and Dimitris Papadias. Range aggregate processing in spatial databases. *IEEE TKDE*, 16(12):1555–1570, 2004.

[49] Nitin Thaper, Sudipto Guha, Piotr Indyk, and Nick Koudas. Dynamic multidimensional histograms. In *SIGMOD*, pages 428–429, 2002.

[50] Jan Vahrenhold. An in-place algorithm for Klee's measure problem in two dimensions. *IPL*, 102(4):169–174, 2007.

[51] Donghui Zhang, Alexander Markowetz, Vassilis J. Tsotras, Dimitrios Gunopulos, and Bernhard Seeger. On computing temporal aggregates with range predicates. *ACM Trans. Database Syst.*, 33(2), 2008.

Randomized Algorithms for Tracking Distributed Count, Frequencies, and Ranks[*]

Zengfeng Huang
Department of CSE, HKUST
huangzf@cse.ust.hk

Ke Yi
Department of CSE, HKUST
yike@cse.ust.hk

Qin Zhang
MADALGO, University of Aarhus
qinzhang@cs.au.dk

ABSTRACT

We show that randomization can lead to significant improvements for a few fundamental problems in distributed tracking. Our basis is the *count-tracking* problem, where there are k players, each holding a counter n_i that gets incremented over time, and the goal is to track an ε-approximation of their sum $n = \sum_i n_i$ continuously at all times, using minimum communication. While the deterministic communication complexity of the problem is $\Theta(k/\varepsilon \cdot \log N)$, where N is the final value of n when the tracking finishes, we show that with randomization, the communication cost can be reduced to $\Theta(\sqrt{k}/\varepsilon \cdot \log N)$. Our algorithm is simple and uses only $O(1)$ space at each player, while the lower bound holds even assuming each player has infinite computing power. Then, we extend our techniques to two related distributed tracking problems: *frequency-tracking* and *rank-tracking*, and obtain similar improvements over previous deterministic algorithms. Both problems are of central importance in large data monitoring and analysis, and have been extensively studied in the literature.

Categories and Subject Descriptors

F.2 [**Analysis of Algorithms and Problem Complexity**]: Nonnumerical Algorithms and Problems

General Terms

Algorithms, theory

Keywords

Distributed tracking

1. INTRODUCTION

We start with a very basic problem in distributed tracking, what we call *count-tracking*. There are k players each

[*]This work is supported by a DAG and an RPC grant from HKUST and a Google Faculty Research Award.

holding a counter n_i that is initially 0. Over time, the counters get incremented and we denote by $n_i(t)$ the value of the counter n_i at time t. The goal is to track an ε-approximation of the total count $n(t) = \sum_i n_i(t)$, i.e., an $\hat{n}(t)$ such that $(1-\varepsilon)n(t) \leq \hat{n}(t) \leq (1+\varepsilon)n(t)$,[1] continuously at all times. There is a coordinator whose job is to maintain such an $\hat{n}(t)$, and will try to do so using minimum communication with the k players (the formal model of computation will be defined shortly).

There is a trivial solution to the count-tracking problem: Every time a counter n_i has increased by a $1+\varepsilon$ factor, the player informs the coordinator of the change. Thus, the coordinator always has an ε-approximation of every n_i, hence an ε-approximation of their sum n. Letting N denote the final value of n, simple analysis shows that the communication cost of this algorithm is $O(k/\varepsilon \cdot \log N)$.[2] This algorithm was actually used in [15] for solving essentially the same problem, which also provided many practical motivations for studying this problem. Note that this algorithm is deterministic and only uses one-way communication (from the players to the coordinator), and yet it turns out this simple algorithm is already optimal for deterministic algorithms, even if two-way communication is allowed [28]. Thus the immediate questions are: What about randomized algorithms that are allowed to fail with a small probability? Is two-way communication not useful at all? In this paper, we set out to address these questions, and then move on to consider other related distributed tracking problems.

1.1 The distributed tracking model

We first give a more formal definition of the computation model that we will work with, which is essentially the same as those used in prior work on distributed tracking [2, 3, 5, 6, 8, 9, 15, 28]. There are k distributed *sites* $S_1, \ldots, S_k$, each receiving a stream of elements over time, possibly at varying rates. Let N be the total number of elements in all k streams. We denote by $A_i(t)$ the multiset (bag) of elements received by S_i up until time t, and let $A(t) = \biguplus_{i=1}^k A_i(t)$ be the combined data set, where $\uplus$ denotes multiset addition. There is a coordinator whose job is to maintain (an approximation of) $f(A(t))$ continuously at all times, for a given function f (e.g., $f(A(t)) = |A(t)|$ for the count-tracking problem above). The coordinator has a direct two-way communication channel with each of the sites; note that broad-

---

[1]We sometimes omit "(t)" when the context is clear.

[2]A more careful analysis leads to a slightly better bound of $O(k/\varepsilon \cdot \log(\varepsilon N/k))$, but we will assume that N is sufficiently large, compared to k and $1/\varepsilon$, to simplify the bounds.

casting a message costs k times the communication for a single message. The sites do not communicate with each other directly, but this is not a limitation since they can always pass messages via the coordinator. We assume that communication is instant, i.e., no element will arrive until all parties have decided not to send more messages. As in prior work, our measures of complexity will be the communication cost and the space used to process each stream. Unless otherwise specified, the unit of both measures is a *word*, and we assume that any integer less than N, as well as an element from the stream, can fit in one word.

This model was initially abstracted from many applied settings, ranging from distributed data monitoring, wireless sensor networks, to network traffic analysis, and has been extensively studied in the database community. From 2008 [8], the model has started to attract interests from the theory community as well, as it naturally combines two well-studied models: the data stream model and multi-party communication complexity. When there is only $k = 1$ site who also plays the role of the coordinator, the model degenerates to the standard streaming model; when $k \geq 2$ and our goal is to do a one-shot computation of $f(A(\infty))$, then the model degenerates to the (number-in-hand) k-party communication model. Thus, distributed tracking is more general than both models. Meanwhile, it also appears to be significantly different from either, with the above count-tracking problem being the best example. This problem is trivial in both the streaming and the communication model (even computing the exact count is trivial), whereas it becomes nontrivial in the distributed tracking model and requires new techniques, especially when randomization is allowed, as illustrated by our results in this paper.

Note that there is some work on *distributed streaming* (see e.g. [11, 16]) that adopts a model very similar to ours, but with a fundamental difference. In their model there are k streams, each of which runs a streaming algorithm on its local data. But the function f on the combined streams is computed only at the end or upon requests by the user. As one can see that the count-tracking problem is also trivial in this model. The crucial difference is that, in this model, the sites wait passively to get polled. If we want to track f continuously, we have to poll the sites all the time. Whereas in our model, the sites actively participate in the tracking protocol to make sure that f is always up-to-date.

1.2 Problem statements, previous and new results

In this paper, we first study the count-tracking problem. Then we extend our approach to two related, more general problems: *frequency-tracking* and *rank-tracking*. Both problems are of central importance in large data monitoring and analysis, and have been extensively studied in the literature. In all the communication upper bounds, we will assume $k \leq 1/\varepsilon^2$; otherwise all of them will carry an extra additive $O(k \log N)$ term. All our results are summarized in Table 1; below we discuss each of them separately.

As mentioned earlier, the deterministic communication complexity for the count-tracking problem has been settled at $\Theta(k/\varepsilon \cdot \log N)$ [28][3], with or without two-way communication. In this paper, we show that with randomization *and*

two-way communication, this is reduced to $\Theta(\sqrt{k}/\varepsilon \cdot \log N)$. We first in Section 2.1 present a randomized algorithm with this communication cost that, at *any one* given time instance, maintains an ε-approximation of the current n with a constant probability. The algorithm is very simple and uses $O(1)$ space at each site. It is easy to make the algorithm correct for *all* time instances and boost the probability to $1 - \delta$: Since we can use the same approximate value $\hat{n}$ of n until n grows by a $1 + \varepsilon$ factor, it suffices to make the algorithm correct for $O(\log_{1+\varepsilon} N) = O(1/\varepsilon \cdot \log N)$ time instances. Then running $O(\log(\frac{\log N}{\delta \varepsilon}))$ independent copies of the algorithm and taking the median will achieve the goal of tracking n continuously at all times, with probability at least $1 - \delta$. The $\Omega(\sqrt{k}/\varepsilon \cdot \log N)$ lower bound (Section 2.2) actually holds on the number of messages that have to be exchanged, regardless of the message size, and holds even assuming the sites have unlimited space and computing power. That randomization is necessary to achieve this $\sqrt{k}$-factor improvement follows from the previous deterministic lower bound [28]; here in Section 2.2 we give a proof that two-way communication is also required. More precisely, we show that any randomized algorithm with one-way communication has to use $\Omega(k/\varepsilon \cdot \log N)$ communication, i.e., the same as that for deterministic algorithms.

In the *frequency-tracking* (a.k.a. *heavy hitters tracking*) problem, $A(t)$ is a multiset of cardinality $n(t)$ at time t. Let $f_j(t)$ be the frequency of element j in $A(t)$. The goal is to maintain a data structure from which $f_j(t)$, for any given j, can be estimated with absolute error at most $\varepsilon n(t)$, with probability at least 0.9 (say). Note that this problem degenerates to count-tracking when there is only one element. It is reasonable to ask for an error in terms of $n(t)$: if the error were $\varepsilon f_j(t)$, then every element would have to be reported if they were all distinct. In fact, this error requirement is the widely accepted definition for the heavy hitters problem, which has been extensively studied in the streaming literature [7]. Several algorithms with the optimal $O(1/\varepsilon)$ space exist [17–19]. In the distributed tracking model, we previously [28] gave a deterministic algorithm with $O(k/\varepsilon \cdot \log N)$ communication, which is the best possible for deterministic algorithms. In this paper, by generalizing our count-tracking algorithm, we reduce the cost to $O(\sqrt{k}/\varepsilon \cdot \log N)$, with randomization (Section 3). Since this problem is more general than count-tracking, by the count-tracking lower bound, this is also optimal. Our algorithm uses $O(1/(\varepsilon \sqrt{k}))$ space to process the stream at each site, which is actually smaller than the $\Omega(1/\varepsilon)$ space lower bound for this problem in the streaming model. This should not come as a surprise: Due to the fact that the site is allowed to communicate to the coordinator *during* the streaming process, the streaming lower bounds do not apply in our model. To this end, we prove a new space lower bound of $\Omega(1/(\varepsilon \sqrt{k}))$ bits for our model, showing that our algorithm also uses near-optimal space. This space lower bound is conditioned upon the requirement that the communication cost should be $O(\sqrt{k}/\varepsilon \cdot \log N)$ bits. Note that it is not possible to prove a space lower bound unconditional of communication: A site can send every element to the coordinator and thus only needs $O(1)$ space. In fact, what we prove is a space-communication trade-off; please see Section 3.2 for the precise statement.

For the *rank-tracking* problem, it will be convenient to assume that the elements are drawn from a totally ordered universe and $A(t)$ contains no duplicates. The *rank* of an

---

[3]The lower bound in [28] was stated for the heavy hitters tracking problem, but essentially the same proof works for count-tracking.

		space (per site)	communication
count-tracking	trivial	$O(1)$	$\Theta(k/\varepsilon \cdot \log N)$
	new	$O(1)$	$O(\sqrt{k}/\varepsilon \cdot \log N)$ $\Omega(\sqrt{k}/\varepsilon \cdot \log N)$ messages
frequency-tracking	[28]	$O(1/\varepsilon)$	$\Theta(k/\varepsilon \cdot \log N)$
	new	$O(1/(\varepsilon\sqrt{k}))$ $\Omega(1/(\varepsilon\sqrt{k}))$ bits*	$O(\sqrt{k}/\varepsilon \cdot \log N)$ $\Omega(\sqrt{k}/\varepsilon \cdot \log N)$ messages
rank-tracking	[28]	$O(1/\varepsilon \cdot \log n)$	$O(k/\varepsilon \cdot \log N \log^2(1/\varepsilon))$
	new	$O\left(1/(\varepsilon\sqrt{k}) \cdot \log^{1.5}\frac{1}{\varepsilon} \log^{0.5}\frac{1}{\varepsilon\sqrt{k}}\right)$ $\Omega(1/(\varepsilon\sqrt{k}))$ bits*	$O\left(\sqrt{k}/\varepsilon \cdot \log N \log^{1.5}\frac{1}{\varepsilon\sqrt{k}}\right)$ $\Omega(\sqrt{k}/\varepsilon \cdot \log N)$ messages
sampling	[9]	$O(1)$	$O(1/\varepsilon^2 \cdot \log N)$

Table 1: **Space and communication costs of previous and new algorithms. We assume $k \leq 1/\varepsilon^2$. All upper bounds are in terms of words.** *This is conditioned upon the communication cost being $O(\sqrt{k}/\varepsilon \cdot \log N)$ bits.

element x in $A(t)$ (x need not be in $A(t)$) is the number of elements in $A(t)$ smaller than x, and our goal is to compute a data structure from which the rank of any given x can be estimated with error at most $\varepsilon n(t)$, with constant probability. Note that a rank-tracking algorithm also solves the frequency-tracking problem (but not vice versa), by turning each element x into a pair (x, y) to break all ties (by comparing the pairs lexicographically) and maintaining such a rank-tracking data structure. When the frequency of x is desired, we ask for the ranks of $(x, 0)$ and (x, ∞) and take the difference. We previously [28] gave a deterministic algorithm for the rank-tracking problem with communication $O(k/\varepsilon \cdot \log N \log^2(1/\varepsilon))$. In this paper, we show in Section 4 how randomization can bring this down to $O(\sqrt{k}/\varepsilon \cdot \log N \log^{1.5}(1/\varepsilon\sqrt{k}))$, which is again optimal ignoring polylog$(1/\varepsilon, k)$ factors. Since rank-tracking is more general than frequency-tracking, the previous lower bounds also hold here. Our algorithm uses space that is also close to the $\Omega(1/(\varepsilon\sqrt{k}))$ lower bound.

Since we are talking about randomized algorithms with a constant success probability, we should also compare with random sampling. It is well known [24] that this probabilistic guarantee can be achieved for all the problems above by taking a random sample of size $O(1/\varepsilon^2)$. A random sample can be maintained continuously over distributed streams [9, 23], solving these distributed tracking problems, with a communication cost of $O(1/\varepsilon^2 \cdot \log N)$. This is worse than our algorithms when $k = o(1/\varepsilon^2)$. As noted earlier, all the upper bounds we have mentioned above have a hidden additive $O(k \log N)$ term. Thus when $k = \Omega(1/\varepsilon^2)$, all of them boil down to $O(k \log N)$,[4] so our results are more interesting for the $k \leq 1/\varepsilon^2$ case, which we will assume in all the upper bounds throughout the paper. In the lower bound statements, however, we do distinguish between the two cases. The lower bounds in Table 1 assume $k \leq 1/\varepsilon^2$, and they all match the upper bounds (except for the rank-tracking problem); for the $k = \Omega(1/\varepsilon^2)$ case, the lower bound is $\Omega(k)$ (Theorem 2.3), which leaves a gap of $\Theta(\log N)$ from the upper bound.

The idea behind all our algorithms is very simple. Instead of deterministic algorithms, we use randomized algorithms that produce unbiased estimators for n_i, the frequencies, and ranks with variance $(\varepsilon n)^2/k$, leading to an overall variance

of $(\varepsilon n)^2$, which is sufficient to produce an estimate within error εn with constant probability. This means we can afford an error of $\varepsilon n/\sqrt{k}$ from each site, as opposed to $\varepsilon n/k$ for deterministic algorithms. This is essentially where we obtain the $\sqrt{k}$-factor improvement by randomization. Our algorithms are simple and extremely lightweight, in particular the count-tracking and frequency-tracking algorithms, thus can be easily implemented in power-limited distributed systems like wireless sensor networks.

1.3 Other related work

As distributed tracking is closely related to the streaming and the k-party communication model, it could be enlightening to compare with the known results of the above problems in these models. As mentioned earlier, the count-tracking problem is trivial in both models, requiring $O(1)$ space in the streaming model and $O(k)$ communication in the k-party communication model.

Both the frequency-tracking and rank-tracking problems have been extensively studied in the streaming model with a long history. The former was first resolved by the MG algorithm [19] with the optimal space $O(1/\varepsilon)$, though several other algorithms with the same space bound have been proposed later on [17, 18]. The rank problem is also one of the earliest problems studied in the streaming model [20]. The best deterministic algorithm to date is the one by Greenwald and Khanna [12]. It uses $O(1/\varepsilon \cdot \log n)$ working space to maintain a structure of size $O(1/\varepsilon)$, from which any rank can be estimated with error εn. Note that the rank problem is often studied as the *quantiles* problem in the literature. Recall that for any $0 \leq \phi \leq 1$, the ϕ-quantile of D is the element in $A(t)$ that ranks at $\lfloor \phi n \rfloor$, while an ε-approximate ϕ-quantile is any element that ranks between $(\phi - \varepsilon)n$ and $(\phi + \varepsilon)n$. Clearly, if we have the data structure for one problem, we can do a binary search to solve the other. Thus the two problems are equivalent, for deterministic algorithms. For algorithms with probabilistic guarantees, we need all $O(\log(1/\varepsilon))$ decisions in the binary search to succeed, which requires the failure probability to be lowered by an $O(\log(1/\varepsilon))$ factor. By running $O(\log \log(1/\varepsilon))$ independent copies of the algorithm, this is not a problem. So the two problems differ by at most a factor of $O(\log \log(1/\varepsilon))$.

The existing streaming algorithms for the frequency and rank problems can be used to solve the one-shot version of the problem in the k-party communication model easily. More precisely, we use a streaming algorithm to sum-

---

[4]The bound of the random sampling algorithm [9, 23] is actually slightly better, which is $O(k \log N / \log(k\varepsilon^2))$.

marize the data set at each site with a structure of size $O(1/\varepsilon)$, and then send the these summary structures to the coordinator, resulting in a communication cost of $O(k/\varepsilon)$. Recently, we designed randomized algorithms for these two problems with $O(\sqrt{k}/\varepsilon)$ communication [13, 14], which have just been shown to be near-optimal [26]. Here we have extended the one-shot algorithms of [13, 14] to the continuous tracking setting. The results have demonstrated that, the seemingly more challenging tracking problem, which requires us to solve the one-shot problem continuously at all times, is only harder by an $\Theta(\log N)$ factor than the one-shot version (except for the count-tracking problem, which is much harder than its one-shot version).

Finally, we should mention that all these distributed tracking problems have been studied in the database community previously, but mostly using heuristics. Keralapura et al. [15] approached the count-tracking problem using prediction models, which do not work under adversarial inputs. Babcock and Olston [3] studied the top-k tracking problem, a variant of the frequency (heavy hitters) tracking problem, but did not offer a theoretical analysis. The rank-tracking problem was first studied by Cormode et al. [6]; their algorithm has a communication cost of $O(k/\varepsilon^2 \cdot \log N)$ under certain inputs.

2. TRACKING DISTRIBUTED COUNT

2.1 The algorithm

The algorithm with a fixed p.

Let p be a parameter to be determined later. For now we will assume that p is fixed. The algorithm is very simple: Whenever site S_i receives an element (hence n_i gets incremented by one), it sends the latest value of n_i to the coordinator with probability p. Let $\bar{n}_i$ be the last updated value of n_i received by the coordinator. We first estimate each n_i by

$$\hat{n}_i = \begin{cases} \bar{n}_i - 1 + 1/p, & \text{if } \bar{n}_i \text{ exists}; \\ 0, & \text{else}. \end{cases} \quad (1)$$

Then we estimate n as $\hat{n} = \sum_i \hat{n}_i$.

Analysis.

As mentioned in the introduction, our analysis will hold for any given one time instance. It is also important to note that this given time instance shall not depend on the randomization internal to the algorithm.

We show that each $\hat{n}_i$ is an unbiased estimator of n_i with variance at most $1/p^2$. This is very intuitive, since $n_i - \bar{n}_i$ is the number of failed trials until the site decides to send an update to the coordinator, when we look backward from the current time instance. This follows a geometric distribution with parameter p, but not quite, as it is bounded by n_i. This is why we need to separate the two cases in (1). The following calculation appeared in [13]; we include it here for completeness.

LEMMA 2.1. $\mathsf{E}[\hat{n}_i] = n_i$; $\mathsf{Var}[\hat{n}_i] \leq 1/p^2$.

Proof. Define the random variable

$$X = \begin{cases} n_i - \bar{n}_i + 1, & \text{if } \bar{n}_i \text{ exists}; \\ n_i + 1/p, & \text{else}. \end{cases}$$

Now we can rewrite $\hat{n}_i$ as $\hat{n}_i = n_i - X + 1/p$. Thus it suffices to show that $\mathsf{E}[X] = 1/p$ and $\mathsf{Var}[X] \leq 1/p^2$. Letting $t = n_i - \bar{n}_i + 1$, we have

$$\mathsf{E}[X] = \sum_{t=1}^{n_i} (t(1-p)^{t-1}p) + (n_i + 1/p)(1-p)^{n_i} = \frac{1}{p}.$$

$$\mathsf{Var}[X] = \sum_{t=1}^{n_i} ((t - 1/p)^2 (1-p)^{t-1}p) + (n_i + 1/p - 1/p)^2 (1-p)^{n_i}$$

$$= \frac{(1-p)(1-(1-p)^{n_i})}{p^2} \leq \frac{1}{p^2}.$$

$\square$

By Lemma 2.1, we know that $\hat{n}$ is an unbiased estimator of n with variance $\leq k/p^2$. Thus, if $p = \sqrt{k}/\varepsilon n$, the variance of $\hat{n}$ will be $(\varepsilon n)^2$, which means that $\hat{n}$ has error at most $2\varepsilon n$ with probability at least $3/4$, by Chebyshev inequality. Rescaling ε and p by a constant will reduce the error to εn and improves the success probability to 0.9, as desired.

Previously, we used similar ideas to solve the *one-shot* quantile problem over distributed data [13]. Here, we essentially treat the numerical values of the items in the quantile problem as the timestamps in the count-tracking problem, and simulate the one-shot sampling algorithm of [13] in the continuous setting.

Dealing with a decreasing p.

It is not possible and necessary to set p exactly to $\sqrt{k}/\varepsilon n$. From the analysis above, it should be clear that keeping $p = \Theta(\sqrt{k}/\varepsilon n)$ will suffice. To do so, we first track n within a constant factor. This can be done efficiently as follows. Each site S_i keeps track of its own counter n_i. Whenever n_i doubles, it sends an update to the coordinator. The coordinator sets $n' = \sum_{i=1}^{k} n_i'$, where n_i' is the last update of n_i. When n' doubles (more precisely, when n' changes by a factor between 2 and 4), the coordinator broadcasts n' to all the sites. Let $\bar{n}$ be the last broadcast value of n'. It is clear that $\bar{n}$ is always a constant-factor approximation of n. The communication cost is $O(k \log N)$, since each site sends $O(\log N)$ updates to the coordinator and the coordinator broadcasts $O(\log N)$ times, each of which costs k messages. These broadcasts divide the whole tracking period into $O(\log N)$ rounds, and within each round, n stays within a constant factor of $\bar{n}$, the broadcast value at the beginning of the round.

Now, when $\bar{n} \leq \sqrt{k}/\varepsilon$, all the sites set $p = 1$. This causes all the first $O(\sqrt{k}/\varepsilon)$ elements to be sent to the coordinator. When $\bar{n} > \sqrt{k}/\varepsilon$, the sites use $p = 1/\lfloor \varepsilon \bar{n}/\sqrt{k} \rfloor_2$, where $\lfloor x \rfloor_2$ denotes the largest power of 2 smaller than x. Since $\bar{n}$ is monotonically increasing, p gets halved over the rounds. At the beginning of a round, if the new p is half[5] of that in the previous round, each site S_i adjusts its $\bar{n}_i$ appropriately, as follows. First with probability $1/2$, the site decides if $\bar{n}_i$ remains the same. If so, nothing changes; otherwise, it repeatedly flips a coin with probability $1/p$ (with the new p). Every failed coin flip decrements $\bar{n}_i$ by one. It does so until a successful coin flip, or $\bar{n}_i = 0$. Finally, the site informs the coordinator of the new value of $\bar{n}_i$; if $\bar{n}_i = 0$, the coordinator will treat it as if $\bar{n}_i$ does not exist. It should be clear that

---
[5]To be more precise, the new p might also be a quarter of the previous p, but it can be handled similarly.

after this adjustment, the whole system looks as if it had always been running with the new p.

It is easy to see that the communication cost in each round is $O(k + pn) = O(k + \sqrt{k}/\varepsilon) = O(\sqrt{k}/\varepsilon)$, thus the total cost is $O(\sqrt{k}/\varepsilon \cdot \log N)$.

THEOREM 2.1. *There is an algorithm for the count-tracking problem that, at any time, estimates $n = \sum_i n_i$ within error εn with probability at least 0.9. It uses $O(1)$ space at each site and $O(\sqrt{k}/\varepsilon \cdot \log N)$ total communication.*

2.2 The lower bound

Before proving the lower bounds, we first state our lower bound model formally, in the context of the count-tracking problem. The N elements arrive at the k sites in an online fashion at arbitrary time instances. We do not allow spontaneous communication. More precisely, it means that a site is allowed to send out a message only if it has just received an element or a message from the coordinator. Likewise, the coordinator is allowed to send out messages only if it has just received messages from one or more sites. When a site S_j is allowed to send out a message, it decides whether it will indeed send a message, and the content of the message if so, based only on its local counter n_j and the message history between S_j and the coordinator, possibly using some random source. We assume that the site does not look at the current clock. We argue that the clock conveys no information since the elements arrive at arbitrary and unpredictable time instances. (If the elements arrive in a predictable fashion, say, one per time step, the problem can be solved without communication at all.) Similarly, when the coordinator is allowed to send out messages, it makes the decision on where and what to send based only on its message history and some random source. We will lower bound the communication cost only by the number of messages, regardless of the message size.

2.2.1 One-way communication lower bound

In this section we show that two-way communication is necessary to achieve the upper bound in Theorem 2.1, by proving the following lower bound. Remember that we assume N is sufficiently larger than k and $1/\varepsilon$.

THEOREM 2.2. *If only the sites can send messages to the coordinator but not vice versa, then any randomized algorithm for the count-tracking problem that, at any time, estimates n within error εn with probability at least 0.9 must send $\Omega(k/\varepsilon \cdot \log N)$ messages.*

Proof. We first define the hard input distribution μ.

(a) With probability $1/2$, all elements arrive at one site that is uniformly picked at random.

(b) Otherwise, the N elements arrive at the k sites in a round-robin fashion, each site receiving N/k elements in the end.

By Yao's Minimax principle [27], we only need to argue that any deterministic algorithm with success probability at least 0.8 under μ has expected cost $\Omega(k/\varepsilon \cdot \log N)$.

Note that when only one-way communication is allowed, a site decides whether to send messages to the coordinator only based on its local counter n_j. Thus the communication pattern can be essentially described as follows. Each site S_j

has a series of thresholds $t_j^1, t_j^2, \ldots$ such that when $n_j = t_j^i$, the site sends the i-th message to the coordinator. These thresholds should be fixed at the beginning.

We lower bound the communication cost by rounds. Let W_i be the number of elements that have arrived up until round i. We divide the rounds by setting $W_1 = k/\varepsilon$, and $W_{i+1} = \lceil (1+\varepsilon)W_i \rceil$ for $i \geq 1$. Thus there are $1/\varepsilon \cdot \log(\varepsilon N/k)$ rounds, which is $\Omega(1/\varepsilon \cdot \log N)$ for sufficiently large N.

At the beginning of round $i+1$, suppose that $S_1, S_2, \ldots, S_k$ have already sent $z_1^i, z_2^i, \ldots, z_k^i$ messages to the coordinator, respectively. Let $t_{\max}^{i+1} = (1+\varepsilon) \cdot \max\{t_j^{z_j^i} \mid j = 1, 2, \ldots, k\}$. We first observe that there must be at least $k/2$ sites with their next threshold $t_j^{z_j^i+1} \leq t_{\max}^{i+1}$. Otherwise, suppose there are less than $k/2$ sites with such next thresholds, then with probability at least $1/4$ case (a) happens and the random site S_j chosen to receive all elements has $t_j^{z_j^i+1} > t_{\max}^{i+1} \geq (1+\varepsilon)t_j^{z_j^i}$. Thus, with probability at least $1/4$ the algorithm fails when the $t_{\max}^{i+1}$-th element arrives, contradicting the success guarantee.

On the other hand, with probability $1/2$ case (b) happens. In this case all $t_j^{z_j^i}$ $(j = 1, 2, \ldots, k)$ are no more than W_i/k, since in case (b), elements arrive at all k sites in turn. In the next εW_i elements, each site S_j receives $\varepsilon W_i/k$ elements. If the site S_j has $t_j^{z_j^i+1} \leq t_{\max}^{i+1}$, then it must send a message in this round, since $W_i/k + \varepsilon W_i/k \geq t_{\max}^{i+1} \geq t_j^{z_j^i+1}$, that is, its $(z_j^i + 1)$-th threshold is triggered. As argued, there are $\geq k/2$ sites with $t_j^{z_j^i+1} \leq t_{\max}^{i+1}$, so the communication cost in this round is at least $k/2$.

Summing up all rounds, the total communication is at least $\Omega(k/\varepsilon \cdot \log N)$. $\square$

2.2.2 Two-way communication lower bound

Below we prove two randomized lower bounds when two-way communication is allowed. The first one justifies the assumption $k \leq 1/\varepsilon^2$, since otherwise, random sampling will be near-optimal.

THEOREM 2.3. *Any randomized algorithm for the count-tracking problem that, at any time, estimates n within error $0.1n$ with probability at least 0.9 must exchange $\Omega(k)$ messages.*

Proof. The hard input distribution is the same as that in the proof of Theorem 2.2. To prove this lower bound we are only interested in the number of sites that communicate with the coordinator at least once. Before any element arrives, we can still assume that each site keeps a triggering threshold. The thresholds of S_j shall remain the same unless it communicates with the coordinator at least once. We argue that there must be at least $k/2$ sites whose triggering threshold is no more than 1, since otherwise if case (a) happens and the randomly chosen site is one with a triggering threshold larger than 1, the algorithm will fail, which would happen with probability at least $1/4$. On the other hand, if case (b) happens, then all the sites with threshold 1 will have to communicate with the coordinator at least once: either their thresholds are triggered by the round-robin arrival of elements, or they receive a message from the coordinator, which can possibly change their threshold. $\square$

Finally, we show that the upper bound in Theorem 2.1 is tight. We first introduce the following primitive problem.

DEFINITION 2.1 (1-BIT). *Let s be either $k/2 + \sqrt{k}$ or $k/2 - \sqrt{k}$, each with probability $1/2$. From the k sites, a subset of s sites picked uniformly at random each have bit 1, while the other $k - s$ sites have bit 0. The goal of the communication problem is for the coordinator to find out the value of s with probability at least 0.8.*

We will show the following lower bound for the 1-BIT problem.

LEMMA 2.2. *Any deterministic algorithm that solves 1-bit has distributional communication complexity $\Omega(k)$.*

Lemma 2.2 immediately implies the following theorem:

THEOREM 2.4. *Any randomized algorithm for the count-tracking problem that, at any time, estimates n within error εn with probability at least 0.9 must exchange $\Omega(\sqrt{k}/\varepsilon \cdot \log N)$ messages, when $k < 1/\varepsilon^2$.*

Proof. We will again fix a hard input distribution first and then focus on the distributional communication complexity of deterministic algorithms with success probability at most 0.8. Let $[m] = \{0, 1, \ldots, m - 1\}$. The adversarial input consists of $\ell = \log \frac{\varepsilon N}{k} = \Omega(\log N)$ rounds. We further divide each round $i \in [\ell]$ into $r = 1/(2\varepsilon\sqrt{k})$ subrounds.

The input at round $i \in [\ell]$ is constructed as follows, at each subround $j \in [r]$, we first choose s to be $k/2 + \sqrt{k}$ or $k/2 - \sqrt{k}$ with equal probability. Then we choose s sites out of the k sites uniformly at random and send 2^i elements to each of them (the order does not matter).

It is easy to see that at the end of in each subround in round i, the total number of items is no more than $\tau_i = \sqrt{k}/\varepsilon \cdot 2^i$. Thus after $s \cdot 2^i$ elements have arrived in a subround, the algorithm has to correctly identify the value of s with probability at least 0.8, since otherwise with probability at least 0.2 the estimation of the algorithm will deviate from the true value by at least $\sqrt{k} \cdot 2^i > \varepsilon\tau_i$, violating the success guarantee of the algorithm. This is exactly the 1-bit problem defined above. By Lemma 2.2, the communication cost of each subround is $\Omega(k)$. Summing over all r subrounds and then all ℓ rounds, we have that the total communication is at least $\ell \cdot r \cdot \Omega(k) \geq \Omega(\sqrt{k}/\varepsilon \cdot \log N)$. $\square$

Now we prove Lemma 2.2.
Proof. (of Lemma 2.2) First of all, observe that whenever the coordinator communicates with a site, the site can send its whole input (i.e., its only bit) to the coordinator. After that, the coordinator knows all the information about that site and does not need to communicate with it further. Therefore all that we need to investigate is the number of sites the coordinator needs to communicate with.

There can be two types of actions in the protocol.

(a) A site initiates a communication with the coordinator based on the bit it has.

(b) The coordinator, based on all the information it has gathered so far, asks some site to send its bit.

Note that if a type (b) communication takes place before a type (a) communication, we can always swap the two,

since this only gives the coordinator more information at an earlier stage. Thus we can assume that all the type (a) communications happen before type (b) ones.

In the first phase where all the type (a) communications happen, let x be the number of sites that send bit 0 to the coordinator, and y be the number of sites that send bit 1 to the coordinator. If $\mathsf{E}[x + y] = \Omega(k)$, then we are done. So let us assume that $\mathsf{E}[x + y] = o(k)$. By Markov inequality we have that, with probability at least 0.9, $x + y = o(k)$. After the first phase, the problem becomes that there are $s' = s - y = s - o(k)$ sites having bit 1, out of a total $k' = k - x - y = k - o(k)$ sites. The coordinator needs to figure out the exact value of s' with probability at least $0.8 - (1 - 0.9) = 0.7$.

In the second phase where all type (b) communication happens, from the coordinator's perspective, all the remaining sites are still symmetric (by the random input we choose), therefore the best it can do is to probe an arbitrary site among those that it has not communicated with. This is still true even after the coordinator has probed some of the remaining sites. Therefore, the problem boils down to the following: The coordinator picks z sites out of the remaining k' sites to communicate and then decides the value of s' with success probability at least 0.7. We call this problem the *sampling* problem. We can show that to achieve the success guarantee, z should be at least $\Omega(k)$. This result is perhaps folklore; proofs to more general versions of this problem can be found in [4] (Chapter 4), and also [21, 25]. We include a simpler proof in the appendix for completeness. With this we conclude the proof of Lemma 2.2. $\square$

3. TRACKING DISTRIBUTED FREQUENCIES

In the frequency-tracking problem, A (we omit "(t)" when the context is clear) is a multiset and the goal is to track the frequency of any item j within error εn. Let f_{ij} denote the local frequency of element j in A_i, and let $f_j = \sum_{i=1}^k f_{ij}$.

3.1 The algorithm

The algorithm with a fixed p.

As in Section 2.1 we first describe the algorithm with a fixed parameter p. If each site tracks the local frequencies f_{ij} exactly, we can essentially use the count-tracking algorithm to track the f_j's. To achieve small space, we make use of the following algorithm due to Manku and Motwani [17] at each site S_i: The site maintains a list L_i of counters. When an element j arrives at S_i, the site first checks if there is a counter c_{ij} for j in L_i. If yes, it increases c_{ij} by 1. Otherwise, the site samples this element with probability p. If it is sampled, the site inserts a counter c_{ij}, initialized to 1, into L_i. It is easy to see that the expected size of L_i is $O(pn_i)$.

Next, we follow a similar strategy as in the count-tracking algorithm: The site reports the counter c_{ij} to the coordinator when it is first added to the counter list with an initial value of 1. Afterward, for every j that is arriving, the site always increments c_{ij} as before, but only sends the updated counter to the coordinator with probability p. We use $\bar{c}_{ij}$ to denote the last updated value of c_{ij}.

The tricky part is how the coordinator estimates f_{ij}, hence f_j. Fix any time instance. The difference between f_{ij} and

$\hat{c}_{ij}$ comes from two sources: one is the number of j's missed before a copy is sampled, and the other is the number of j's that arrive after the last update of c_{ij}. It is easy to see that both errors follow the same distribution as $n_i - \bar{n}_i$ in the count-tracking algorithm. Thus it is tempting to modify (1) as

$$\hat{f}_{ij} = \begin{cases} \bar{c}_{ij} & 2 + 2/p, & \text{if } \bar{c}_{ij} \text{ exists;} \\ 0, & \text{else.} \end{cases} \quad (2)$$

However, this estimator is biased and its bias might be as large as $\Theta(\varepsilon n/\sqrt{k})$. Summing over k streams, this would exceed our error guarantee. To see this, consider the f_{ij} copies of j. Effectively, the site samples every copy with probability p, while $\bar{c}_{ij} - 2$ is exactly the number of copies between the first and the last sampled copy (excluding both). We define X_1 as before

$$X_1 = \begin{cases} t_1, & \text{if the } t_1\text{th copy is the first one sampled;} \\ f_{ij} + 1/p, & \text{if none is sampled.} \end{cases}$$

We define X_2 in exactly the same way, except that we examine these f_{ij} copies backward:

$$X_2 = \begin{cases} t_2, & \text{if the } t_2\text{th copy is the first one sampled} \\ & \text{in the reverse order;} \\ f_{ij} + 1/p, & \text{if none is sampled.} \end{cases}$$

It is clear that X_1 and X_2 have the same distribution with $\mathsf{E}[X_1] = \mathsf{E}[X_2] = 1/p$ (by Lemma 2.1), so $\hat{f}_{ij} = f_{ij} - (X_1 + X_2) + 2/p$ is unbiased. Since $\bar{c}_{ij} - 2 = f_{ij} - t_1 - t_2$, the correct unbiased estimator should be

$$\hat{f}_{ij} = \begin{cases} \bar{c}_{ij} - 2 + 2/p, & \text{if } \bar{c}_{ij} \text{ exists;} \\ -f_{ij}, & \text{else.} \end{cases} \quad (3)$$

Compared with the previous wrong estimator (2), the main difference is how the estimation is done when no copy of j is sampled. When $f_{ij} = \Theta(\varepsilon n/\sqrt{k})$ and $p = \Theta(1/f_{ij})$, this happens with constant probability, which would result in a bias of $\Theta(f_{ij}) = \Theta(\varepsilon n/\sqrt{k})$.

However, the correct estimator (3) depends on f_{ij}, the quantity we want to estimate in the first place. The workaround is to use another unbiased estimator for f_{ij} when $\bar{c}_{ij}$ is not yet available. It turns out that we can just use simple random sampling: The site samples every element with probability p (this is independent of the sampling process that maintains the list L_i), and sends the sampled elements to the coordinator. Let d_{ij} be the number of sampled copies of j received by the coordinator from site i, the final estimator for f_{ij} is

$$\hat{f}'_{ij} = \begin{cases} \bar{c}_{ij} - 2 + 2/p, & \text{if } \bar{c}_{ij} \text{ exists;} \\ -d_{ij}/p, & \text{else.} \end{cases} \quad (4)$$

Since d_{ij} is independent of $\bar{c}_{ij}$, the estimator is still unbiased. Below we analyze its variance.

Analysis.

Intuitively, the variance is not affected by using the simple random sampling estimator d_{ij}/p, because it is only used when $\bar{c}_{ij}$ is not available, which means that f_{ij} is likely to be small, and when f_{ij} is small, d_{ij}/p actually has a small variance. When f_{ij} is large, d_{ij}/p has a large variance, but we will use it only with small probability. Below we give a formal proof.

LEMMA 3.1. $\mathsf{E}[\hat{f}'_{ij}] = f_{ij}$; $\mathsf{Var}[\hat{f}'_{ij}] = O(1/p^2)$.

Proof. We first analyze the estimator $\hat{f}_{ij}$ of (3). That $\mathsf{E}[\hat{f}_{ij}] = f_{ij}$ follows from the discussion above. Its variance is $\mathsf{Var}[\hat{f}_{ij}] = \mathsf{Var}[X_1 + X_2]$. Note that X_1 and X_2 are not independent, but they both have expectation $1/p$ and variance $\le 1/p^2$. We first rewrite

$$\begin{aligned} \mathsf{Var}[X_1 + X_2] &= \mathsf{E}[X_1^2 + X_2^2 + 2X_1X_2] - \mathsf{E}[X_1 + X_2]^2 \\ &= \mathsf{Var}[X_1] + \mathsf{E}[X_1]^2 + \mathsf{Var}[X_2] + \mathsf{E}[X_2]^2 \\ &\quad + 2\mathsf{E}[X_1X_2] - (\mathsf{E}[X_1] + \mathsf{E}[X_2])^2 \\ &\le 4/p^2 + 2\mathsf{E}[X_1X_2] - 4/p^2 \le 2\mathsf{E}[X_1X_2]. \end{aligned}$$

Let $\mathcal{E}_t$ be the event that the tth copy of j is the first being sampled. We have

$$\begin{aligned} &\mathsf{E}[X_1X_2] \\ &= \sum_{t=1}^{f_{ij}} (1-p)^{t-1} pt \mathsf{E}[X_2 \mid \mathcal{E}_t] + (1-p)^{f_{ij}}(f_{ij} + 1/p)^2 \\ &= \sum_{t=1}^{f_{ij}} (1-p)^{t-1} pt \left((1-p)^{f_{ij}-t}(f_{ij} - t + 1) \right. \\ &\quad \left. + \sum_{l=1}^{f_{ij}-t} (1-p)^{l-1} pl \right) + (1-p)^{f_{ij}}(f_{ij} + 1/p)^2 \\ &\le \frac{1}{p^2} + (1-p)^{f_{ij}} f_{ij}^2 + \frac{(1-p)^{f_{ij}} f_{ij}}{p}. \end{aligned}$$

Let $c = f_{ij}p$. If $c \le 2$, $f_{ij} \le 2/p$, and the variance is $O(1/p^2)$. Otherwise

$$\mathsf{E}[X_1X_2] \le \frac{1}{p^2} + \frac{c^2}{p^2 e^c} + \frac{c}{p^2 e^c} = O(1/p^2),$$

since $c^2 \le e^c$ when $c > 2$.

Next we analyze the final estimator $\hat{f}'_{ij}$ of (4). First, d_{ij} is the sum of f_{ij} Bernoulli random variables with probability p, so $\mathsf{E}[d_{ij}/p] = f_{ij}$ and $\mathsf{Var}[d_{ij}/p] \le f_{ij}p/p^2 = f_{ij}/p$. Let $\mathcal{E}_*$ be the event that $\hat{c}_{ij}$ is available, i.e., at least one copy of j is sampled, and $\mathcal{E}_0 = \overline{\mathcal{E}_*}$, then

$$\begin{aligned} \mathsf{E}[\hat{f}'_{ij}] &= \mathsf{E}[\hat{f}_{ij} \mid \mathcal{E}_*]\mathsf{Pr}[\mathcal{E}_*] + \mathsf{E}[-d_{ij}/p \mid \mathcal{E}_0]\mathsf{Pr}[\mathcal{E}_0] \\ &= \mathsf{E}[\hat{f}_{ij} \mid \mathcal{E}_*]\mathsf{Pr}[\mathcal{E}_*] + (-f_{ij})\mathsf{Pr}[\mathcal{E}_0] \\ &= \mathsf{E}[\hat{f}_{ij}] = f_{ij}. \end{aligned}$$

The variance is

$$\begin{aligned} \mathsf{Var}[\hat{f}'_{ij}] &= \mathsf{E}[\hat{f}'^2_{ij}] - \mathsf{E}[\hat{f}'_{ij}]^2 \\ &= \mathsf{E}[\hat{f}^2_{ij} \mid \mathcal{E}_*]\mathsf{Pr}[\mathcal{E}_*] + \mathsf{E}[(d_{ij}/p)^2 \mid \mathcal{E}_0]\mathsf{Pr}[\mathcal{E}_0] - f_{ij}^2 \\ &= \mathsf{E}[\hat{f}^2_{ij} \mid \mathcal{E}_*]\mathsf{Pr}[\mathcal{E}_*] - f_{ij}^2 + \mathsf{E}[(d_{ij}/p)^2]\mathsf{Pr}[\mathcal{E}_0] \\ &= \mathsf{E}[\hat{f}^2_{ij} \mid \mathcal{E}_*]\mathsf{Pr}[\mathcal{E}_*] - f_{ij}^2 + (\mathsf{Var}[d_{ij}/p] + f_{ij}^2)\mathsf{Pr}[\mathcal{E}_0] \end{aligned}$$

Note that

$$\begin{aligned} \mathsf{Var}[\hat{f}_{ij}] &= \mathsf{E}[\hat{f}^2_{ij}] - f_{ij}^2 \\ &= \mathsf{E}[\hat{f}^2_{ij} \mid \mathcal{E}_*]\mathsf{Pr}[\mathcal{E}_*] + \mathsf{E}[\hat{f}^2_{ij} \mid \mathcal{E}_0]\mathsf{Pr}[\mathcal{E}_0] - f_{ij}^2 \\ &= \mathsf{E}[\hat{f}^2_{ij} \mid \mathcal{E}_*]\mathsf{Pr}[\mathcal{E}_*] + f_{ij}^2 \mathsf{Pr}[\mathcal{E}_0] - f_{ij}^2, \end{aligned}$$

so

$$\begin{aligned} \mathsf{Var}[\hat{f}'_{ij}] &= \mathsf{Var}[\hat{f}_{ij}] + \mathsf{Var}[d_{ij}/p]\mathsf{Pr}[\mathcal{E}_0] \\ &\le \mathsf{Var}[\hat{f}_{ij}] + \frac{f_{ij}}{p} \cdot (1-p)^{f_{ij}}. \end{aligned}$$

Due to the same reason as above, the second term is $O(1/p^2)$, and the proof completes. ◻

Dealing with a decreasing p.

As in the count-tracking algorithm, we divide the whole tracking period into $O(\log N)$ rounds. Within each round, n stays within a constant factor of $\bar{n}$, while $\bar{n}$ remains fixed for the whole round.

Within a round, we set the parameter p for all sites to be $p = 1/\lfloor \varepsilon\bar{n}/\sqrt{k}\rfloor_2$. When we proceed to a new round, all sites clear their memory and start a new copy of the algorithm from scratch with the new p. Given an item j, the coordinator estimates its frequency from each round separately, and add them up. Since the variance in a round is $O(k/p^2)$ and p increases geometrically over the rounds, the total variance is asymptotically bounded by the variance of the last round, i.e., $O(1/\varepsilon^2)$, as desired.

The space used at some site could still be large, since the site may receive too many elements in a round. If all the $O(n)$ elements in a round have gone to the same site, the site will need to use space $O(pn) = O(\sqrt{k}/\varepsilon)$. To bound the space, we restrict the amount of space used by each site. More precisely, when a site receives more than $\bar{n}/k$ elements, it sends a message to the coordinator for notification, clears its memory, and starts a new copy of the algorithm from scratch. The coordinator will treat the new copy as if it were a new site, while the original site no longer receives more elements. Now the space used at each site is at most $p\bar{n}/k = O(1/(\varepsilon\sqrt{k}))$. Since there are at most $O(k)$ such new "virtual" sites ever created in a round, this does not affect the variance by more than a constant factor.

It remains to show that the total communication cost is $O(\sqrt{k}/\varepsilon \cdot \log N)$. From earlier we know that there are $O(\log N)$ rounds; within each round, $\bar{n}$ is the same and n stays within $\Theta(\bar{n})$. Focus on one round. For each arriving element, the site S_i updates $\bar{c}_{ij}$ with probability p and also independently samples it with probability p to maintain d_{ij}. This costs $O(n \cdot p) = O(\sqrt{k}/\varepsilon)$ communication.

THEOREM 3.1. *There is an algorithm for the frequency-tracking problem that, at any time, estimates the frequency of any element within error εn with probability at least 0.9. It uses $O(1/(\varepsilon\sqrt{k}))$ space at each site and $O(\sqrt{k}/\varepsilon \cdot \log N)$ communication.*

3.2 Space lower bound

It is easy to see that the communication lower bounds for the count-tracking problem also hold for the frequency-tracking problem. In this section, we prove the following space-communication trade-off.

THEOREM 3.2. *Consider any randomized algorithm for the frequency-tracking problem that, at any time, estimates the frequency of any element within error εn with probability at least 0.9. If the algorithm uses C bits of communication and uses M bits of space per site, then we must have $C \cdot M = \Omega(\log N/\varepsilon^2)$, assuming $k \leq 1/\varepsilon^2$.*

Thus, if the communication cost is $C = O(\sqrt{k}/\varepsilon \cdot \log N)$ bits, the space required per site is at least $\Omega(1/(\varepsilon\sqrt{k}))$ bits, as claimed in Table 1. If we ignore the word/bit difference, the space bounds are also tight. Interestingly, this lower bound also shows that the random sampling algorithm [9] (see Table 1) actually attains the other end of this space-communication trade-off.

Proof. (of Theorem 3.2) We will use a result in [26] which states that, under the k-party communication model, there is an input distribution μ_k such that, any algorithm that solves the one-shot version of the problem under μ_k with error $2\varepsilon n$ with probability 0.9 needs at least $c\sqrt{k}/\varepsilon$ bits of communication for some constant c, assuming $k \leq 1/\varepsilon^2$. Moreover, any algorithm that solves ℓ independent copies of the one-shot version of the problem needs at least $\ell \cdot c\sqrt{k}/\varepsilon$ bits of communication.

We will consider the problem over ρk sites, for some integer $\rho \geq 1$ to be determined later. We divide the whole tracking period into $\log N$ rounds. In each round $i = 1, \ldots, \log N$, we generate an input independently chosen from distribution $\mu_{\rho k}$ to the sites. We pick elements from a different domain for every round so that we have $\log N$ independent instances of the problem. In round i, for every element e picked from $\mu_{\rho k}$ for any site, we replace it with 2^{i-1} copies of e. We arrange the element arrivals in a round so that site S_1 gets all its elements first, then S_2 gets all its elements, and so on so forth. We will only require the continuous tracking algorithm to solve the frequency estimation problem at the end of each round. Since the last round always contains half of all the elements that have arrived so far, the algorithm must solve the problem for the elements in each round, namely, $\log N$ independent instances of the one-shot problem. By the result in [26], the communication cost to solve all these instances of the problem is at least $c\sqrt{\rho k}/\varepsilon \cdot \log N$.

Let $\mathcal{A}_k$ be a continuous tracking algorithm over k sites that communicates C bits in total and uses M bits of space per site. Below we show how to solve the problem over the ρk sites in each round, by simulating the k-site algorithm $\mathcal{A}_k$. In each round, we start the simulation with sites $S_1, \ldots, S_k$. Whenever $\mathcal{A}_k$ exchanges a message, we do the same. When S_1 has received all its elements, it sends its memory content to S_{k+1}, which then takes the role of S_1 in the simulation and continues. Similarly, when S_2 has received all its elements, it sends its memory content to S_{k+2} which replaces S_2 in the simulation. In general, when S_j is done with all its elements, it passes its role to S_{j+k}. When $S_{\rho k}$ is done, the simulation finishes for this round. $S_{\rho k}$ then sends a broadcast message and we proceed to the next round.

Let us analyze the communication cost of the simulation. First, we exchange exactly the same messages as $\mathcal{A}_k$ does, which costs C. We also communicate $\rho(k-1)$ memory snapshots and a broadcast message in each round, which costs $\leq \rho k M \log N$ over all rounds. Thus, we have

$$C + \rho k M \log N \geq c\sqrt{\rho k}/\varepsilon \cdot \log N.$$

Rearranging,

$$M \geq \frac{c}{\varepsilon\sqrt{\rho k}} - \frac{C}{\rho k \log N} = \frac{1}{\sqrt{\rho k}}\left(\frac{c}{\varepsilon} - \frac{C}{\sqrt{\rho k}\log N}\right).$$

Thus, if we set $\sqrt{\rho} = \left\lceil \frac{2C\varepsilon}{c\sqrt{k}\log N} \right\rceil$, then

$$M \geq \frac{c}{2\varepsilon\sqrt{\rho k}} = \Omega\left(\frac{\log N}{C\varepsilon^2}\right),$$

as claimed. ◻

4. TRACKING DISTRIBUTED RANKS

On a stream of n elements, an algorithm that produces an unbiased estimator for any rank with variance $O((\varepsilon n)^2)$ was presented in [22], which has been very recently improved and made to work in a stronger model [1]. It uses $O(1/\varepsilon \cdot \log^{1.5}(1/\varepsilon))$ working space to maintain a rank estimation summary structure of size $O(1/\varepsilon)$. We call this algorithm $\mathcal{A}$ and will use it as a black box in our distributed tracking algorithm.

The overall algorithm.

As before, with $O(k \log N)$ communication, we first track $\bar{n}$, a constant factor approximation of the current n. This also divides the tracking period into $O(\log N)$ rounds. The $\Theta(n)$ elements arriving in a round are divided into chunks of size at most $\bar{n}/k$, each processed by an instance of algorithm $\mathcal{C}$, described below. A site may receive more than $\bar{n}/k$ elements. When the $(\bar{n}/k + 1)$th element arrives, the site finishes the current instance of $\mathcal{C}$, and starts a new one, which will process the next $\bar{n}/k$ elements, and so on so forth.

Algorithm $\mathcal{C}$.

Algorithm $\mathcal{C}$ reads at most $\bar{n}/k$ elements, and divides them into blocks of size $b = \varepsilon \bar{n}/\sqrt{k}$, so there are at most $\frac{1}{\varepsilon \sqrt{k}}$ blocks. The algorithm builds a balanced binary tree on the blocks in the arrival order, and the height of the tree is $h \le \log \frac{1}{\varepsilon \sqrt{k}}$. For each node v in the tree, let $D(v)$ be all the elements contained in the leaves in the subtree rooted at v. For each $D(v)$, the site starts an instance of $\mathcal{A}$, denoted as $\mathcal{A}_v$, to process its elements as they arrive. We say that v is *active* if $\mathcal{A}_v$ is still accepting elements. For a node v at level ℓ (the leaves are said to be on level 0), the error parameter of $\mathcal{A}_v$ is set to $2^{-\ell}/\sqrt{h}$. We say v is *full* if all the elements in $D(v)$ have arrived. When v is full, the site sends the summary computed by $\mathcal{A}_v$ to the coordinator, and free the space used by $\mathcal{A}_v$. Furthermore, for each element that is arriving, the site samples it with probability $p = \frac{\sqrt{k}}{\varepsilon \bar{n}}$, and if it is sampled, the site sends it to the coordinator.

Analysis of costs.

We first analyze the various costs of $\mathcal{C}$. At any time there are at most h active nodes, one at each level, so the space used by $\mathcal{C}$ is at most

$$\sum_{\ell=0}^{h} \sqrt{h} 2^\ell \log^{1.5} \frac{1}{\varepsilon} = O\left(\frac{\sqrt{h}}{\varepsilon \sqrt{k}} \log^{1.5} \frac{1}{\varepsilon}\right).$$

The communication for $\mathcal{C}$ includes all the summaries computed, and the elements sampled. For each ℓ, the total size of the summaries on level ℓ is

$$O\left(\frac{1}{\varepsilon \sqrt{k}} 2^{-\ell} \cdot 2^\ell \sqrt{h}\right) = O\left(\frac{\sqrt{h}}{\varepsilon \sqrt{k}}\right).$$

Summing over all h levels, it is $\frac{h^{1.5}}{\varepsilon \sqrt{k}}$. There are at most $2k$ instances of $\mathcal{C}$ in a round, therefore the total communication cost in a round is $O(h^{1.5}\sqrt{k}/\varepsilon)$. The number of sampled elements in a round is $O(np) = O(\sqrt{k}/\varepsilon)$. Thus, over all $O(\log N)$ rounds, the total communication cost is $O(h^{1.5}\sqrt{k}/\varepsilon \cdot \log N)$.

Estimation.

It remains to show how the coordinator estimates the rank of any given element x at any time with variance $O((\varepsilon n)^2)$. We decompose all n elements that have arrived so far into smaller subsets, and estimate the rank of x in each of the subsets. Since all estimators are unbiased, the overall estimator is also unbiased; the variance will be the sum of all the variances.

We will focus on the current round; all previous rounds can be handled similarly. Recall that there are $O(\bar{n})$ elements arriving in this round and $\bar{n} = \Theta(n)$. Every chunk of $\bar{n}/k$ elements are processed by one instance of $\mathcal{C}$. Consider any such chunk. Suppose up to now, n' elements in this chunk have arrived for some $n' \le \bar{n}/k$. We write n' as $n' = q \cdot b + r$ for some $r < b$, and decompose these n' elements into at most $h+1$ subsets. The first qb elements are decomposed into at most h subsets, each of which corresponds to a full node in the binary tree of $\mathcal{C}$. The node has already sent its summary to the coordinator, which we can use to estimate the rank. For a node at level ℓ, the variance is $((2^{-l}/\sqrt{h}) \cdot 2^l b)^2 = b^2/h$, so the total variance from all h nodes is b^2.

For the last r elements of the chunk that are still being processed by an active node, the coordinator does not have any summary for them. But recall that the site always samples each element with probability $p = \sqrt{k}/(\varepsilon \bar{n})$ and sends it to the coordinator if it is sampled. Thus, the rank of x in these r elements can be estimated by simply counting the number c of elements sampled that are smaller than x, and the estimator is c/p. The variance of this estimator is $r/p \le b/p = b^2$. Thus, the variance from any chunk is $O(b^2)$. Since there are at most $2k$ chunks in the round, the total variance is $O(b^2 k) = O((\varepsilon \bar{n})^2) = O((\varepsilon n)^2)$. As the variances of the previous rounds are geometrically decreasing, the total variance from all the rounds is still bounded by $O((\varepsilon n)^2)$, as desired.

THEOREM 4.1. *There is an algorithm for the rank-tracking problem that, at any time, estimate the rank of any element within error εn with probability at least 0.9. It uses $O\left(\frac{1}{\varepsilon \sqrt{k}} \log^{1.5} \frac{1}{\varepsilon} \log^{0.5} \frac{1}{\varepsilon \sqrt{k}}\right)$ space at each site with communication cost $O\left(\frac{\sqrt{k}}{\varepsilon} \log N \log^{1.5} \frac{1}{\varepsilon \sqrt{k}}\right).$*

5. REFERENCES

[1] P. K. Agarwal, G. Cormode, Z. Huang, J. M. Phillips, Z. Wei, and K. Yi. Mergeable summaries. In *Proc. ACM Symposium on Principles of Database Systems*, 2012.

[2] C. Arackaparambil, J. Brody, and A. Chakrabarti. Functional monitoring without monotonicity. In *Proc. International Colloquium on Automata, Languages, and Programming*, 2009.

[3] B. Babcock and C. Olston. Distributed top-k monitoring. In *Proc. ACM SIGMOD International Conference on Management of Data*, 2003.

[4] Z. Bar-Yossef. *The complexity of massive data set computations*. PhD thesis, University of California at Berkeley, 2002.

[5] H.-L. Chan, T. W. Lam, L.-K. Lee, and H.-F. Ting. Continuous monitoring of distributed data streams over a time-based sliding window. *Algorithmica*, 62(3–4):1088–1111, 2011.

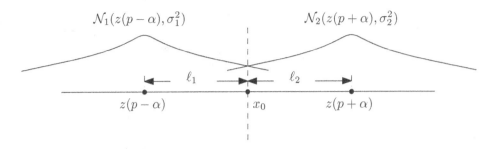

$\mathcal{N}_1(z(p-\alpha), \sigma_1^2)$ $\mathcal{N}_2(z(p+\alpha), \sigma_2^2)$

ℓ_1 ℓ_2

$z(p-\alpha)$ x_0 $z(p+\alpha)$

Figure 1: Differentiating two distributions

[6] G. Cormode, M. Garofalakis, S. Muthukrishnan, and R. Rastogi. Holistic aggregates in a networked world: Distributed tracking of approximate quantiles. In *Proc. ACM SIGMOD International Conference on Management of Data*, 2005.

[7] G. Cormode and M. Hadjieleftheriou. Finding frequent items in data streams. In *Proc. International Conference on Very Large Data Bases*, 2008.

[8] G. Cormode, S. Muthukrishnan, and K. Yi. Algorithms for distributed functional monitoring. *ACM Transactions on Algorithms*, 7(2), Article 21, 2011. Preliminary version in SODA'08.

[9] G. Cormode, S. Muthukrishnan, K. Yi, and Q. Zhang. Continuous sampling from distributed streams. *Journal of the ACM*, 59(2), 2012. Preliminary version in PODS'10.

[10] W. Feller. *An introduction to probability theory and its applications*. Wiley, New York, 1968.

[11] P. B. Gibbons and S. Tirthapura. Estimating simple functions on the union of data streams. In *Proc. ACM Symposium on Parallelism in Algorithms and Architectures*, 2001.

[12] M. Greenwald and S. Khanna. Space-efficient online computation of quantile summaries. In *Proc. ACM SIGMOD International Conference on Management of Data*, 2001.

[13] Z. Huang, L. Wang, K. Yi, and Y. Liu. Sampling based algorithms for quantile computation in sensor networks. In *Proc. ACM SIGMOD International Conference on Management of Data*, 2011.

[14] Z. Huang, K. Yi, Y. Liu, and G. Chen. Optimal sampling algorithms for frequency estimation in distributed data. In *IEEE INFOCOM*, 2011.

[15] R. Keralapura, G. Cormode, and J. Ramamirtham. Communication-efficient distributed monitoring of thresholded counts. In *Proc. ACM SIGMOD International Conference on Management of Data*, 2006.

[16] A. Manjhi, V. Shkapenyuk, K. Dhamdhere, and C. Olston. Finding (recently) frequent items in distributed data streams. In *Proc. IEEE International Conference on Data Engineering*, 2005.

[17] G. Manku and R. Motwani. Approximate frequency counts over data streams. In *Proc. International Conference on Very Large Data Bases*, 2002.

[18] A. Metwally, D. Agrawal, and A. Abbadi. An integrated efficient solution for computing frequent and top-k elements in data streams. *ACM Transactions on Database Systems*, 31(3):1095–1133, 2006.

[19] J. Misra and D. Gries. Finding repeated elements. *Science of Computer Programming*, 2:143–152, 1982.

[20] J. I. Munro and M. S. Paterson. Selection and sorting with limited storage. *Theoretical Computer Science*, 12:315–323, 1980.

[21] B. Patt-Shamir and A. Shafrir. Approximate distributed top-k queries. *Distributed Computing*, 21(1):1–22, 2008.

[22] S. Suri, C. Toth, and Y. Zhou. Range counting over multidimensional data streams. *Discrete and Computational Geometry*, 2006.

[23] S. Tirthapura and D. P. Woodruff. Optimal random sampling from distributed streams revisited. In *Proc. International Symposium on Distributed Computing*, 2011.

[24] V. N. Vapnik and A. Y. Chervonenkis. On the uniform convergence of relative frequencies of events to their probabilities. *Theory of Probability and its Applications*, 16:264–280, 1971.

[25] D. P. Woodruff. *Efficient and Private Distance Approximation in the Communication and Streaming Models*. PhD thesis, Massachusetts Institute of Technology, 2007.

[26] D. P. Woodruff and Q. Zhang. Tight bounds for distributed functional monitoring. In *Proc. ACM Symposium on Theory of Computing*, 2012.

[27] A. C. Yao. Probabilistic computations: Towards a unified measure of complexity. In *Proc. IEEE Symposium on Foundations of Computer Science*, 1977.

[28] K. Yi and Q. Zhang. Optimal tracking of distributed heavy hitters and quantiles. In *Proc. ACM Symposium on Principles of Database Systems*, 2009.

APPENDIX

A. LOWER BOUND FOR THE SAMPLING PROBLEM

CLAIM A.1. *To solve the sampling problem we need to probe at least $\Omega(k)$ sites.*

Proof. Suppose that the coordinator only samples $z = o(k)$ sites. Let X be the number of sites that are sampled with bit 1. Then X is chosen from the hypergeometric distribution with probability density function (pdf) $\Pr[X =$

304

$x] = \binom{s'}{x}\binom{k'-s'}{z-x}/\binom{k'}{z}$. The expected value of X is $\frac{z}{k'} \cdot s'$, which is $\frac{z}{k'}\left(\frac{k}{2} - y + \sqrt{k}\right)$ or $\frac{z}{k'}\left(\frac{k}{2} - y - \sqrt{k}\right)$, depending on the value of s'. Let $p = \left(\frac{k}{2} - y\right)/k' = \frac{1}{2} \pm o(1)$ and $\alpha = \sqrt{k}/k' = 1/\sqrt{k} \pm o(1/\sqrt{k})$. To avoid tedious calculation, we assume that X is picked randomly from one of the two normal distributions $\mathcal{N}_1(\mu_1, \sigma_1^2)$ and $\mathcal{N}_2(\mu_2, \sigma_2^2)$ with equal probability, where $\mu_1 = z(p - \alpha), \mu_2 = z(p + \alpha), \sigma_1, \sigma_2 = \Theta(\sqrt{zp(1-p)}) = \Theta(\sqrt{z})$. In Feller [10] it is shown that the normal distribution approximates the hypergeometric distribution very well when z is large and $p \pm \alpha$ are constants in $(0, 1)$ [6]. Now our task is to decide from which of the two distributions X is drawn based on the value of X with success probability at least 0.7.

Let $f_1(x; \mu_1, \sigma_1^2)$ and $f_2(x; \mu_2, \sigma_2^2)$ be the pdf of the two normal distributions $\mathcal{N}_1, \mathcal{N}_2$, respectively. It is easy to see that the best deterministic algorithm of differentiating the two distributions based on the value of a sample X will do the following.

- If $X > x_0$, then X is chosen from $\mathcal{N}_2$, otherwise X is chosen from $\mathcal{N}_1$, where x_0 is the value such that $f_1(x_0; \mu_1, \sigma_1^2) = f_2(x_0; \mu_2, \sigma_2^2)$ (thus $\mu_1 < x_0 < \mu_2$).

Indeed, if $X > x_0$ and the algorithm decides that "X is chosen from $\mathcal{N}_1$", we can always flip this decision and improve the success probability of the algorithm.

The error comes from two sources: (1) $X > x_0$ but X is actually drawn from $\mathcal{N}_2$; (2) $X \leq x_0$ but X is actually drawn from $\mathcal{N}_1$. The total error is

$$1/2 \cdot (\Phi(-\ell_1/\sigma_1) + \Phi(-\ell_2/\sigma_2)),$$

where $\ell_1 = x_0 - \mu_1$ and $\ell_2 = \mu_2 - x_0$. (Thus $\ell_1 + \ell_2 = \mu_2 - \mu_1 = 2\alpha z$). $\Phi(\cdot)$ is the cumulative distribution function (cdf) of the normal distribution. See Figure 1.

Finally note that $\ell_1/\sigma_1 = O(\alpha z/\sqrt{z}) = O(\sqrt{z/k}) = o(1)$ and $\ell_2/\sigma_2 = O(\alpha z/\sqrt{z}) = o(1)$, so $\Phi(-\ell_1/\sigma_1) + \Phi(-\ell_2/\sigma_2) > 0.99$. Therefore, the failure probability is at least 0.49, contradicting our success probability guarantee. Thus we must have $z = \Omega(k)$. $\square$

---

[6] In Feller's book [10] the following is proved. Let $p \in (0, 1)$ be some constant and $q = 1 - p$. The population size is N and the sample size is n, so that $n < N$ and Np, Nq are both integers. The hypergeometric distribution is $P(k; n, N) = \binom{Np}{k}\binom{Nq}{n-k}/\binom{N}{n}$ for $0 \leq k \leq n$.

THEOREM A.1. [10] If $N \to \infty, n \to \infty$ so that $n/N \to t \in (0, 1)$ and $x_k := (k - np)/\sqrt{npq} \to x$, then

$$p(k; n, N) \sim \frac{e^{-x^2/2(1-t)}}{\sqrt{2\pi npq(1-t)}}$$

Continuous Distributed Counting
for Non-monotonic Streams

Zhenming Liu*
zhliu@eecs.harvard.edu
Harvard School of Engineering
and Applied Sciences

Božidar Radunović
bozidar@microsoft.com
Microsoft Research
Cambridge

Milan Vojnović
milanv@microsoft.com
Microsoft Research
Cambridge

ABSTRACT

We consider the continual count tracking problem in a distributed environment where the input is an aggregate stream that originates from k distinct sites and the updates are allowed to be non-monotonic, i.e. both increments and decrements are allowed. The goal is to continually track the count within a prescribed relative accuracy ϵ at the lowest possible communication cost. Specifically, we consider an adversarial setting where the input values are selected and assigned to sites by an adversary but the order is according to a random permutation or is a random i.i.d process. The input stream of values is allowed to be non-monotonic with an unknown drift $-1 \leq \mu \leq 1$ where the case $\mu = 1$ corresponds to the special case of a monotonic stream of only non-negative updates. We show that a randomized algorithm guarantees to track the count accurately with high probability and has the expected communication cost $\tilde{O}(\min\{\sqrt{k}/(|\mu|\epsilon), \sqrt{kn}/\epsilon, n\})$, for an input stream of length n, and establish matching lower bounds. This improves upon previously best known algorithm whose expected communication cost is $\tilde{\Theta}(\min\{\sqrt{k}/\epsilon, n\})$ that applies only to an important but more restrictive class of monotonic input streams, and our results are substantially more positive than the communication complexity of $\Omega(n)$ under fully adversarial input. We also show how our framework can also accommodate other types of random input streams, including fractional Brownian motion that has been widely used to model temporal long-range dependencies observed in many natural phenomena. Last but not least, we show how our non-monotonic counter can be applied to track the second frequency moment and to a Bayesian linear regression problem.

Categories and Subject Descriptors

F.2.2 [**Analysis of algorithms and problem complexity**]: Nonnumerical algorithms and problems; H.2.4 [**Database management**]: Systems-distributed databases

---

*Work performed while an intern with Microsoft Research Cambridge.

General Terms

Algorithms, theory

Keywords

Distributed counting, non-monotonic streams

1. INTRODUCTION

A continuous distributed tracking model was introduced in [7] to address the challenges of designing an effective strategy to constantly track statistics in a dynamic, distributed environment. In this model, data arrive in multiple streams to a number of sites. All the sites are connected to a coordinator, and the goal of the coordinator is to continuously track some function of the aggregate data, and update it as new data arrives. An exact tracking would require each data sample to be communicated to the coordinator, which would incur a prohibitively large communication cost - linear in the size of the input stream. Similarly, space and time processing requirements may be very large. However, for most applications it is satisfactory to provide an approximate tracking. Thus, a general formulation of a continuous distributed tracking problem is to design an algorithm that will minimize the space, time and/or communication complexity while providing approximation guarantees on the tracking accuracy. Continuous distributed tracking problems have recently gained much interest in the research community [23, 8, 1, 22].

One of the basic building blocks for many of the existing algorithms is a counter. The goal of the counter is to report, with a given relative accuracy, the sum of values of all elements that have arrived across the aggregate stream arriving from distributed sites. The main assumption in almost all the previous works is that the input stream being counted is monotonic non-decreasing and, surprisingly, there is very little work on continuous distributed non-monotonic counters. Similarly, most of the previous algorithms using counters are not guaranteed to work correctly under non-monotonic input stream.

However, many data streams do not satisfy the monotonicity property. A simple motivating example is a voting/ranking application. Suppose users' votes come in a distributed stream. The goal is to keep a continuous track of which of the two options has a higher number of votes, and approximately by which voting margin. Here, the votes for each option can essentially be seen as two separate data streams, but we are interested in continuously monitoring the *difference* of the two streams, which is clearly non-monotonic. The naive approach of estimating the count of each option separately and then taking the difference will not provide a relative error guarantee for the difference.

Non-monotonic streams are common in many situations when

dealing with instantaneous instead of cumulative phenomena, e.g. tracking a difference. One example we analyze in more detail is monitoring a process that exhibits long-range dependency, a phenomena that has been found to be prevalent in nature, e.g. network traffic [14]. Also, non-monotonic counters are useful as building blocks in more complex algorithms whose inputs are not necessarily monotonic. A source of non-monotonicity could be the use of random projections that transform an input data stream into a non-monotonic stream. Another example that we discuss is a streaming implementation of a Bayesian linear regression problem (c.f. [2]), which is useful in the context of machine learning platforms for processing of large-scale data (e.g. [16]).

In this work we are interested in designing a continuous non-monotonic distributed counter with optimal communication complexity. We will also discuss its applications in different scenarios. In the next section, we define the problem in more detail.

1.1 Problem Definition

Consider a standard distributed streaming model where k sites are connected to a coordinator. Each site is allowed to communicate with the coordinator but they cannot communicate with each other directly (and a broadcast message counts as k messages). Data items $a_1, \ldots, a_n$ arrive at sites $\psi(1), \ldots, \psi(n)$ respectively, at time instants $\tau_1 < \cdots < \tau_n$. We shall refer to the item a_t as the t-th update. In a general continuous distributed monitoring problem, the coordinator is responsible to maintain a value of a function $f(a_1, \ldots, a_t)$ at each time τ_t with a relative accuracy ϵ. We are interested in the *counter* problem, where the goal is to track a sum $S_t = \sum_{i \leq t} a_i$ of all the items that have arrived until time τ_t. The coordinator then needs to maintain an estimate that is between $(1-\epsilon)S_t$ and $(1+\epsilon)S_t$. Note that, by definition, the counter problem has low space and time complexity, and thus we focus on minimizing communication complexity.

A monotonic counter only allows for positive increments. In particular, a canonical example of a monotonic counter [12] implies $a_t = 1$ for all t, meaning that a counter is incremented by one whenever an update arrives. We relax the assumption that a_t is positive, and we call this a *non-monotonic counting* problem. In the streaming literature, this input model is usually called a general (non-strict) turnstile model [17].

To the best of our knowledge, the only research so far dealing with non-monotonic input streams is Arackaparambil et al. [1], who studied the tracking of frequency moments F_p, where deletion operations are allowed ($a_t = 1$ denotes an insertion and $a_t = -1$ denotes a deletion). There, a strong negative result is established for the adversary input case for both tracking counts and tracking F_p when deletion is allowed: the worst-case communication complexity is $\Omega(n)$ messages for an input stream of n elements. It is straightforward to construct a worst-case input for the counter problem: consider the case where there is only one site and the updates consist of alternations between an insertion and a deletion. In this case, the true global counter evolves as the sequence $0, 1, 0, 1, \ldots$. When one update is missed from the site, then the multiplicative error from the server becomes unbounded. Therefore, upon the arrival of each update, the site has to send a message to the server, which implies a communication lower bound of $\Omega(n)$ messages. While there is no way to circumvent this linear lower bound barrier for the worst-case input, it is natural to ask what the communication complexity is when the input is not fully adversarial and consider the following question:

Can we design a continuous, distributed tracking protocols for counter for non-monotonic updates that has a sublinear communication complexity when the input is randomized?

In particular, we are interested in a random permutation model. In this model, an adversary first decides the entire sequence of updates $a'_1, \ldots, a'_n$ for all sites. We only assume that the sequence is bounded. Then, the "nature" decides a random permutation π. The final input to the sites is $a_1 = a'_{\pi(1)}, a_2 = a'_{\pi(2)}, \ldots, a_n = a'_{\pi(n)}$. This model is very natural in large-scale settings (such as Internet scale, for example), where data is collected from a large number of individuals (e.g. Twitter or Facebook users). In such a model, a large amount of data is generated in short time intervals, and it is reasonable to assume that the order in which the individuals enter their inputs in the system is random, but the input itself can be arbitrary.

We are also interested if sublinear algorithms can be obtained for other types of random inputs that are well motivated by applications. For example, the use of random projections for computing sketches motivates to consider random i.i.d. updates. Another example is found in nature where many real-world phenomena exhibit self-similarity and long-range dependence (e.g. network traffic [14]) which where traditionally modeled by random processes such as fractional Brownian motion and found to be in good conformance with empirical data.

In all these data models, we shall assume that an adversary chooses the function $\psi(t)$ which defines how the stream is partitioned among the sites (an example is a load-balancing algorithm that can arbitrarily scatter inputs across sites). The adversary can only decide the function $\psi(t)$ based on the information observed up to a point in time. This means that when the input is a random permutation, $\psi(t)$ can depend on the content of the updates decided by the adversary, the prefix of the permutation observed so far, and the values $\psi(1), \ldots, \psi(t-1)$; while when the input is random, the function $\psi(t)$ can only depend on the values of $a_1, \ldots, a_{t-1}$ and the values of $\psi(1), \ldots, \psi(t-1)$; . We will also assume that the times $\tau_1, \ldots, \tau_n$ at which the inputs arrive are decided by an adversary. This essentially implies that the coordinator and the other sites have no knowledge of the time instants at which an input arrives to its corresponding site, and any communication can only be initiated by a site that has received an update.

Note that our model is a strict generalization of the standard monotonic stream model for counting (c.f. Huang et al. [12]), where the updates are fixed to $a_t = 1$, and the arrival times and sites are adversarial. In our case, we relax the assumption on the value of updates and allow for randomly permuted adversarial or entirely random values of updates, while still keeping the adversarial data partitioning and arrival times.

1.2 Our Contributions

Our main results in this paper are matching upper and lower bounds on the communication complexity for a continuous, distributed, non-monotonic counter (up to a poly-logarithmic factor), which are sublinear in the size of the input. While these bounds hold for different types of inputs, we give a single algorithm that is optimal for all the types of inputs considered, and whose communication cost also matches the corresponding lower bounds. The algorithm is lightweight in having only $\tilde{O}(1)$ space and update time complexity[1].

We first provide results for the case of Bernoulli i.i.d. input (Section 3) where we develop basic techniques that will be used in subsequent analysis. In the Bernoulli i.i.d. model, we assume that each update a_t is a Bernoulli random variable, with $\Pr[a_t = 1] =$

---

[1]We use $\tilde{O}(x) = x \log^{O(1)}(nk/\epsilon)$ notation to ignore log factors.

$1 - \Pr[a_t = -1] = p$, for some unknown parameter $p \in [0, 1]$. The counter value S_t is then a Bernoulli random walk with a drift $\mu = 2p - 1$. In the case of a Bernoulli i.i.d. input without a drift ($\mu = 0$), we show that a count can be tracked with $\tilde{O}(\sqrt{kn}/\epsilon)$ communication cost. In case of a Bernoulli i.i.d. input with an unknown drift $\mu \in [-1, 1]$, the achievable communication cost is $\tilde{O}(\min\{\sqrt{kn}, \sqrt{k}/|\mu|\}/\epsilon)$. In both cases, our algorithm does not need to know the drift. We also give matching lower bounds for most important cases (Section 4), showing the optimality of our algorithm.

This result should be compared with the communication cost $\tilde{\Theta}(\sqrt{k}/\epsilon)$ for a monotonic counter (with $a_t = 1$) that was recently established in [12]. We show that the same bound holds for a more general choice of updates (any i.i.d. Bernoulli input), as long as the drift is a positive constant. This is perhaps not entirely surprising, as for the constant drift case we use the algorithm from [12] as one of the building blocks for our algorithm. The key novel insight is that the communication cost increases to $\tilde{O}(\sqrt{kn}/\epsilon)$ when the drift is $|\mu| = O(1/\sqrt{n})$. Thus, we demonstrate that we are still able to track the count with a sublinear communication cost, and we describe the parameter ranges in which the cost is polynomial vs. polylog in the input size.

We next turn to our main results for the permutation model. Here we show that tracking is achievable with $\tilde{O}(\sqrt{kn}/\epsilon)$ communication cost and we give a matching lower bound (Section 4). This is to be contrasted with $\Theta(n)$ lower bound for a non-monotonic counter in a fully adversarial setting [1]. We show that, in a setting where all other parameters are chosen by an adversary, randomly permuting an arbitrary non-monotonic input is enough to permit a tracking algorithm with a sublinear communication cost. This shows that a sublinear tracking of non-monotonic input is still possible in a large number of real-world scenarios.

We further show that our algorithm can track a fractional Brownian motion with Hurst parameter $H \in [1/2, 1)$, where $1 < \delta \leq 1/H$ is an arbitrary parameter (Section 3.4) with total expected communication cost of $\tilde{O}(k^{\frac{3-\delta}{2}} n^{1-H}/\epsilon)$ messages. For the case of independent increments ($H = 1/2$), we get the same bound as before. For the case of positively correlated increments ($1/2 < H < 1$), which is of most interest in applications, we get a smaller communication cost. This is intuitive in view of the facts that increments are positively correlated which makes the process more predictable and the variance is larger. This in turn implies smaller expected residence of the count in the region of small values where there is a higher sensitivity to relative errors. Interestingly, the algorithm does not require to know the exact value of the parameter H, but only needs to have an estimate $1/\delta$ such that $H \leq 1/\delta$.

Finally, we show how our counter can be used as a building block for some instances of distributed tracking problems (Section 5). First, we construct an algorithm to track the second frequency moment (F_2 tracking) with $\tilde{O}(\sqrt{kn}/\epsilon^2)$ communication complexity (Section 5.1) and then provide a $\Omega(\min\{\sqrt{kn}/\epsilon, n\})$ lower bound that is matching in both n and k. We also show how to use the non-monotonic counter as a building block for a Bayesian linear regression problem (Section 5.2), and show that the Bayesian linear regression can also be tracked with sublinear communication cost.

It is noteworthy that while the communication cost for non-monotonic random streams with subconstant drift is sublinear in the input size, this is significantly larger than for monotonic streams ($\tilde{O}(\sqrt{n})$ vs $\tilde{O}(1)$), which is because the problem is intrinsically more difficult. However, the fact that the communication cost is sublinear in the input size would still make the algorithm of ap-

peal for practical applications. For example, Twitter users generate more than 10^8 tweets a day [21]. In this scenario, the communication cost of our algorithm for tracking a single counter would only be in the order of 10^4 messages per day, which is a significant reduction of the traffic load. Furthermore, our bounds are matching with the bounds for the monotonic counters in k and ϵ parameters.

Finally, we briefly discuss the main techniques used in this paper. As we are designing algorithms for random streams in a distributed environment, our solution naturally calls for an integration of different techniques from sampling theory, analysis of stochastic processes, classical streaming algorithms, and distributed algorithm design. The main ingredient in our algorithm to tackle an otherwise intractable problem in the adversarial setting is to make an optimal prediction on the evolution of the counter process using a scarce communication resource and adaptively changing the tracking strategy as we continuously update our predictions. Making the prediction requires us to understand the volatility structure of the counter process; in our specific case, this boils down to the analysis of first passage time of random walks and random permutations. Designing a communication efficient tracking algorithm requires us to construct a sampling based protocol that can judiciously cope with the volatile structure of the process. To prove our matching lower bounds, we needed to carefully decompose the entire tracking process into disjoint segments so that we can apply results from the communication complexity and sampling theory separately on each segment and reach a strong lower bound that is polynomial in n.

Due to space constraints, we omit some of the proofs. All the proofs can be found in the technical report [15].

1.3 Related Work

The research on functional monitoring in distributed systems has considered a variety of problems (e.g. [9, 10, 3, 6, 18]) including one-shot and continuous tracking query problems. To the best of our knowledge, Cormode et al. [7] is the first work that articulated the distributed computation model that we consider in the present paper. Substantial progress has recently been made on understanding various problems under this model, including drawing a sample with or without replacement (e.g. [8, 22]) and answering holistic queries such as tracking the rank of an item or computing a quantile (e.g. [12, 5, 23]).

The most closely related work to ours is the recent work of Huang et al. [12] and Arackaparambil et al. [1]. The work of Huang et al. examines the same counter problem as ours but assuming an important but more restrictive class of monotonic streams, where only positive increments are allowed. Our work relaxes this assumption on the input by allowing for non-monotonic streams where decrements are allowed (either i.i.d. or random permutation). Specifically, we assume that the rate of positive increments is $(1 + \mu)/2$, for some unknown drift parameter $-1 \leq \mu \leq 1$. For the special case of the drift parameter $\mu = 1$, our counter algorithm would solve the same counter problem as in [12] with the matching performance.

The work of Arackaparambil et al. considered non-monotonic functional monitoring in the adversarial setting, including the problem of continuously tracking F_2 that we study here. They established an $\Omega(n)$ lower bound for the 1-site case and an $\Omega(n/k)$ lower bound for the k-site case. For the random input stream that we study here, we establish a tight lower bound that is sublinear in n and grows with k, suggesting that our problem under random input may have a different structure than the one under fully adversarial input.

2. ALGORITHMS AND NOTATIONS

We now present our algorithm for continuous distributed counting for non-monotonic streams. The algorithm is applicable to all input models, subject to choosing appropriate constants. In the subsequent sections we will show how to choose the constants for each input model under consideration.

In what follows, we shall write X_i be the i-th input (because the input is stochastic) and let $\mu = \mathrm{E}[X_i]$ be the *drift rate* of the counter process, $\hat{S}_t$ be the coordinator's estimate of S_t. When the context is clear, we refer to a_t as both the t-th update and the item arrived at time t interchangeably though we shall be clear that the actual physical time is irrelevant in our algorithm. Also, we shall assume that each site always keeps track of the total number of updates arrived locally and maintain a local sum counter. Let us start with introducing the basic constructs we need for the design of our distributed algorithm.

2.1 Building Blocks

The key novel building block in our scheme is:

Sampling and Broadcasting (SBC). In this protocol, the coordinator broadcasts its current estimate $\hat{S}_t$ to all the sites at the beginning. Each site maintains a common sampling rate $\approx 1/(\epsilon^2 \hat{S}_t^2)$ that depends only on the global estimate $\hat{S}_t$. Whenever a site receives a new update, it samples a Bernoulli random variable R_t with the above rate. If $R_t = 1$, the following actions will be carried out sequentially (invoking $\tilde{\Theta}(k)$ message exchanges):

1. The site signals the coordinator to sync all data.

2. The coordinator broadcasts a message to all the sites to collect their local counters.

3. Each site reports its local counter to the coordinator. The coordinator computes the new exact count and broadcasts this new count to all sites.

Upon receiving the new count $\hat{S}_t$, each site adjusts the sampling rate of the Bernoulli random variable to

$$\text{Sample-Prob}(\hat{S}_t, t) = \min \left\{ \frac{\alpha \log^\beta n}{\epsilon^2 \hat{S}_t^2}, 1 \right\} \quad (1)$$

where α and β are some appropriately chosen positive constants.

We will also use the following building blocks:

HYZ counter. In [12], a distributed counter is developed to track monotonic updates with a relative accuracy ϵ and error probability δ using $\tilde{O}(\frac{\sqrt{k}}{\epsilon} \log(1/\delta))$ communication when $k = O(1/\epsilon^2)$ and $\tilde{O}(k \log(1/\delta))$ communication when $k = \omega(1/\epsilon^2)$ (here, $\tilde{O}(\cdot)$ hides the poly-logarithmic dependencies on n). We shall refer this protocol as HYZ(ϵ, δ).

Geometric Progression Search for μ (GPSearch). The goal of this building block is to produce a reliable estimator of μ. It will report an estimate $\hat{\mu}$ only when sure w.h.p. that $\hat{\mu} \in [(1-\epsilon)\mu, (1+\epsilon)\mu]$, where ϵ is a given constant. It also guarantees that $\hat{\mu}$ is found before time $\Theta(\log n/\mu^2)$. We describe the GPSearch protocol in more details in [15].

Straightforward Synchronization (StraightSync). In this protocol, the coordinator pulls out the exact values of t and S_t from the sites in the beginning of the protocol. When a local site receives an update, it contacts the coordinator and executes the following steps sequentially:

1. The site sends both the total number of local updates and the local counter to the coordinator.

2. The coordinator updates the global count and the global number of updates.

3. The coordinator sends the updated global count and global number of updates to the site.

2.2 Algorithm Overview

Our algorithm, called **Non-monotonic Counter**, consists of two phases.

Phase 1: The first phase covers updates from $t = 0$ to $t = \tau$, where $\tau = c \log n/(\mu^2 \epsilon)$ for some sufficiently large constant $c > 0$. During this phase, we have two communication patterns:

- When $(\epsilon \hat{S}_t)^2 \geq k$, we use the SBC protocol.

- When $(\epsilon \hat{S}_t)^2 < k$, we use the StraightSync protocol.

The coordinator shall make a broadcast when the algorithm makes a switch between SBC and StraightSync protocol.

Phase 2: The second phase covers from $t = \tau$ to $t = n$ (the second phase could be empty when $\tau \geq n$). In the second phase, the algorithm maintains a HYZ$(\Theta(\epsilon\mu), \Theta(1/n^2))$ to track the total number of positive updates and another HYZ$(\Theta(\epsilon\mu), \Theta(1/n^2))$ to track the total number of negative updates. The difference between the positive updates and the negative updates is the estimator maintained by the coordinator.

In addition, our GPSearch procedure is executed in the background, and it will be able to tell us a good estimate of μ, and decide when Phase 1 ends. When the algorithm changes from the first phase to the second phase, the coordinator shall make a broadcast to inform different sites of the phase change.

3. UPPER BOUNDS

In this section, we analyze *Non-monotonic Counter* for i.i.d. input, randomly ordered streams, and fractional Brownian motion. Because the input is of stochastic nature, we shall write the updates as $X_1, X_2, \ldots, X_n$ instead of $a_1, \ldots, a_n$ to emphasize the randomness. Our analysis starts with the simplest case, where $k = 1$ and the input is i.i.d. with $\mu = 0$. Then we move to the more complex scenarios, in which there are multiple sites and unknown μ. Finally, we generalize our algorithms and analysis to the randomly ordered stream and fractional Brownian motion case, where the updates are no longer independent. Along the way, we shall explain the reasons why we design the algorithm in such a way and gradually unfold the key techniques used in the analysis.

3.1 I.I.D. Input with Zero Drift

Recall the algorithm Non-monotonic Counter that is described in Section 2. To analyze the behavior of our algorithm we start by giving an upper bound for the single-site case ($k = 1$), and we then turn to the multi-site case. In the single-site case, we need to introduce a small modification to the algorithm. Since the site is aware of the exact counter value $\hat{S}_t = S_t$, there is no need for the straightforward stage and we assume that the algorithm is always in the broadcast stage. Also, there is no need for the coordinator to send messages back to the site.

We will use the sampling probability as defined earlier in (1) with $\alpha > 9/2$ and $\beta = 2$. The parameter α controls the tradeoff between communication complexity and the success probability. The choice of p_t is intuitive because the smaller S_t is, the more likely that a small change of S_t will cause large multiplicative change; therefore, the site should report the value to the coordinator with higher probability.

We have the following theorem:

THEOREM 3.1. *For the single-site case, the randomized algorithm Non-monotonic Counter with the sampling probability as in (1), with $\alpha > 9/2$ and $\beta = 2$, guarantees to track the count within the relative accuracy $\epsilon > 0$ with probability $1 - O(1/n)$ and uses the total expected communication of $O(\min\{\sqrt{n}/\epsilon \cdot \log n, n\})$ messages.*

Proof is provided in [15]. Here, we comment on the intuition of using a sampling based algorithm and setting the sampling probability as specified in (1). We want the site to send messages to the coordinator as infrequently as possible. Suppose that at time t, we have $S_t = s$ and a message is sent to the server. We need to understand what the next appropriate time would be to send another message. Ideally, this shall happen at the time where S_t first passes through either $s/(1 + \epsilon)$ or $s/(1 - \epsilon)$. Implementing this strategy is feasible when there is only one site but it is unclear how it can scale up to k site case (because the challenge of distributed tracking algorithms exactly lies in the difficulties of *exactly* tracing the aggregate statistics and thus it is hard to spot the exact first passage time). It is therefore desirable to use a "smooth" strategy by a site, i.e. the algorithm does not critically rely on the knowledge on the time when S_t first passes through some pre-specified points. The sampling based algorithm possesses such a property. We also need to estimate the sampling rate of the algorithm. Intuitively, it takes an unbiased random walk approximately $(\epsilon s)^2$ time to travel for a distance of about length ϵs (to hit either $s/(1 - \epsilon)$ or $s/(1 + \epsilon)$). When ϵs becomes sufficiently large, we even have a concentration result, i.e. with high probability, the time it takes to hit either $s/(1 - \epsilon)$ or $s/(1 + \epsilon)$ is $\tilde{\Theta}((\epsilon s)^2)$. Therefore, sampling at rate $\tilde{\Theta}(1/(\epsilon s)^2)$ is not only sufficient to maintain high accuracy but also optimal.

We now extend to the multiple site case. Let us first go through the intuition why we want to distinguish the two stages of the algorithm, the straightforward (StraightSync) stage and the broadcast (SBC) stage, described in Section 2. The main idea of our distributed algorithm is to simulate the behavior of the sampling algorithm for the single site case (Theorem 3.1). For that we require that each site has a good estimate $\hat{S}_t$ of the global count S_t. As $\hat{S}_t$ gets updated, the copies of the counter at all sites need to be updated, in order to maintain the correct local sampling rate. The only way to achieve so is to broadcast the counter, which would result in $\tilde{\Theta}(k)$ messages exchanged. The crucial observation here is that when $\hat{S}_t$ gets updated frequently (i.e., when S_t is sufficiently small), broadcasting messages after each update could be wasteful. It may be even worse than the trivial approach where a site synchronizes only with the coordinator whenever it receives an update (resulting in $\tilde{\Theta}(1)$ messages). This "trivial" approach is captured in our straightforward strategy, and we switch to it whenever it is less expensive. Note that we can use the estimator $\hat{S}_t$ instead of the actual value S_t to decide whether the broadcasting or the straightforward strategy has the smaller communication cost, because we guarantee a sufficiently high accuracy of the estimator.

We have the following theorem.

THEOREM 3.2. *The randomized algorithm Non-monotonic Counter with the sampling probability as in (1), with α large enough positive constant and $\beta = 2$, guarantees to track the count within the relative accuracy $\epsilon > 0$ with probability $1 - O(1/n)$ and uses the total expected communication of $O(\min\{\sqrt{kn}/\epsilon \cdot \log n, n\})$ messages.*

Proof is provided in [15]. It is based on a coupling argument that enables us to reuse the result of Theorem 3.1.

3.2 I.I.D. Input with Unknown Drift

In the previous section we have seen that the communication complexity in the case with no drift is $\tilde{O}(\sqrt{n})$. However, the monotonic counter from [12] is a special case of our model with $\mu = 1$, and its communication complexity is $\tilde{O}(1)$. Clearly, we conclude that a positive drift might help. The natural question then is whether this observation holds for an arbitrary drift $\mu \neq 0$, and how can we exploit it when the drift is unknown.

To gain an intuition on the input's behavior for an arbitrary drift, it is helpful to re-parameterize each input X_t as $X_t = \mu + Z_t$, where μ is the drift term and Z_t is a random variable representing the "noise" term, We shall intuitively view Z_t as noise that behaves similar to Gaussian noise. We want to identify which term contributes more to the estimation error. Suppose $S_t = s$. It takes the drifting term ϵt time units to reach $\pm \epsilon s$ while it takes the noise term $(\epsilon s)^2$ to do so. When $\epsilon t < (\epsilon s)^2$, the drifting term dominates the process, otherwise, the noise term dominates the process. Approximating s by its mean $s \approx t\mu$ and solving the equation, $\epsilon t < (\epsilon s)^2$, we get $t \approx 1/(\mu^2 \epsilon)$. Therefore, the random walk S_t qualitatively behaves as follows: up to time $t = \Theta(1/(\epsilon \mu^2))$, the "noise" sum term dominates the process; after time $\Theta(1/(\epsilon \mu^2))$, the drifting term dominates the process. Therefore, intuitively, for $t \leq 1/(\epsilon \mu^2)$ we should use the algorithm that deals with the non-drift case, and for $t \geq 1/(\epsilon \mu^2)$ we might be able to use the monotonic counter HYZ.

Note that the algorithm does not know the actual value of the drift μ. We use an online estimator (the GPSearch algorithm, described in Section 2) to obtain an estimate $\hat{\mu}$. Our estimator is conservative in the sense that it does not report $\hat{\mu}$ until confident that it is within $[(1 - \epsilon')\mu, (1 + \epsilon')\mu]$ (the performance of the GPSearch estimator is discussed in [15]). Once the estimator $\hat{\mu}$ is reported, we can safely switch to the monotonic counter HYZ.

However, we need to guarantee correctness of the algorithm even before we have an estimate of $\hat{\mu}$. The monotonic counter HYZ essentially samples with sampling probability $\Theta(1/(\epsilon t))$. So to guarantee the correctness before we know whether we are in the no-drift phase or in the drift phase, we need to sample with the maximum of the sampling rate $\Theta(1/(\epsilon^2 s^2))$ of the no-drift phase and the sampling rate $\Theta(1/(\epsilon t))$ of the monotonic counter. We shall choose a slightly more conservative rate by tuning the constants in the sampling probability (1) so that Sample-Prob$(S_t, t) \geq \tilde{\Theta}(1/\epsilon^2 s^2 + 1/\epsilon t)$ for all $t < 1/(\mu^2 \epsilon)$.

The crucial observation here is that this conservative way of sampling will not result in substantial increase in communication resource. Indeed, we have two types of unnecessary communication costs:

- Type 1: when $t \leq 1/(\epsilon \mu^2)$, the term $\tilde{\Theta}(1/\epsilon t)$ in the sampling rate is wasteful.

- Type 2: when $t > 1/(\epsilon \mu^2)$, the term $\tilde{\Theta}(1/(\epsilon s)^2)$ in the sampling rate is wasteful.

The total expected communication cost of type 1 is $O(\sum_{t \leq n}(1/t)) = O(\log n)$, which is acceptable. Computing the waste of type 2 is a bit more tedious, but we would be able to see that in expectation $\sum_{t \leq 1/(\epsilon \mu^2)} 1/(\epsilon^2 S_t^2) = \Omega\left(\sum_{t \leq n} 1/(\epsilon^2 S_t^2)\right)$. In other words, $\sum_{1/(\epsilon \mu^2) < t \leq n} 1/(\epsilon^2 S_t^2) = O\left(\sum_{t \leq 1/(\epsilon \mu^2)} 1/(\epsilon^2 S_t^2)\right)$, i.e the total wasted communication from the term $\tilde{\Theta}(1/(\epsilon s)^2)$ is bounded by the total "useful" communication from the same term. Therefore, the conservative sampling strategy is also optimal.

Finally, we can also split the no-drift phase into the the straightforward (StraightSync) stage and the broadcast (SBC) stage, as discussed in the previous section. We then have the following theorem.

THEOREM 3.3. *There exists a choice of constants α and $\beta > 0$ for the randomized algorithm Non-monotonic Counter, for the k-site count problem with unknown drift, to guarantee the continuous tracking within a prescribed relative accuracy ϵ with high probability and the following communication cost in expectation:*

- $\tilde{O}\left(\min\left\{\frac{\sqrt{k}}{|\mu|\epsilon}, \frac{\sqrt{kn}}{\epsilon}, n\right\} + \frac{\sqrt{k}}{\epsilon}\right)$, *if $k = O(1/(\mu\epsilon)^2)$, and*

- $\tilde{O}\left(\min\left\{\frac{\sqrt{k}}{|\mu|\epsilon}, \frac{\sqrt{kn}}{\epsilon}, n\right\} + k\right)$, *if $k = \omega(1/(\mu\epsilon)^2)$.*

Notice that our algorithm's communication cost has two types of asymptotic behaviors for different k because the HYZ counter uses different strategies for different k. Proof of Theorem 3.3 is provided in [15].

3.3 Randomly Ordered Data Streams

We now move to the random permutation case. We use the same tracking algorithm described in Section 2 to solve this problem by using the sampling rate defined in (1) with $\beta = 2$ and sufficiently large $\alpha > 0$.

THEOREM 3.4. *Let $a_1, \ldots, a_n$ be an arbitrary, randomly permuted, sequence of bounded real values. The randomized algorithm Non-monotonic Counter with the sampling probability in (1) for $\beta = 2$ and sufficiently large constant $\alpha > 0$ guarantees to track the count within the relative accuracy ϵ with probability $1 - O(1/n)$ and uses the total expected communication of $O(\sqrt{kn}/\epsilon \cdot \log n + \log^3 n)$ messages.*

Note that here, because of the adversarial choice of the input sequence, we cannot exploit the drift. We remark that when the update is a fractional number from $[-1, 1]$ rather than $\{-1, 1\}$, our Non-monotonic Counter algorithm still holds. The key difference between the analysis for Theorem 3.4 and the one for i.i.d. input is that the updates are correlated when the content of the stream is decided in advance. This difference boils down to a modified analysis for the first passage time of the partial sums. In the Bernoulli i.i.d. case, a straightforward application of Hoeffding's inequality suffices to give a bound on the first passage time. While here Hoeffding's inequality is no longer applicable, we are able to use tail inequalities for sampling without replacement [11, 20] to circumvent this problem. Technical report [15] gives a detailed analysis.

3.4 Fractional Brownian Motion

In this section we consider the counting process S_t evolving as a fractional Brownian motion with parameters $\sigma > 0$ and $0 < H < 1$ where we extend the counting process to continuous time in a natural manner. We briefly discuss some of the basic properties of fractional Brownian motion (more details can be found, e.g. in [19]). Fractional Brownian motion is a process with stationary increments whose finite dimensional distributions are Gaussian. Specifically, for a fractional Brownian motion S_t, we have $\mathrm{E}[S_t] = 0$, for every $t \geq 0$ and the covariance of the process is defined as

$$\mathrm{E}[S_t S_u] = \frac{\sigma^2}{2}\left(|t|^{2H} + |u|^{2H} - |u - t|^{2H}\right).$$

Thus, the variance of the process is $\mathrm{E}[S_t^2] = \sigma^2 |t|^{2H}$, for every $t \geq 0$. The parameter H is known as the Hurst parameter. For $H = 1/2$, the process corresponds to a Brownian motion whose increments are independent. For $0 < H < 1/2$, the variance of S_t grows sublinearly with t and the process has a negative auto-correlation while for $1/2 < H < 1$, the variance of S_t grows superlinearly with t. The process is self-similar, meaning that random variables S_{at} and $a^H S_t$ have the same distribution. To simplify notation, in the remainder, we will assume $\sigma^2 = 1$. Notice that this is without loss of generality as it amounts only to rescaling of the time units. It is noteworthy that the fractional Brownian motion is one of standard statistical models that captures some of the salient properties of temporal statistical dependencies that were observed in many natural phenomena, including self-similarity and long-range dependency (see, e.g. [19]).

We present an algorithm that requires only an upper bound on the Hurst parameter H and guarantees continual tracking within prescribed relative accuracy with high probability for the range $H \in [1/2, 1)$. Note that this is the range of particular interest in practice since typical values of the Hurst parameter observed in nature fall precisely in this region. For the purpose of deriving an upper bound on the communication complexity, we will write the sampling probability in the following form, for $1 < \delta \leq 2$,

$$\text{Sample-Prob}(S_t, t) = \min\left\{\frac{\alpha_\delta \log^{1+\delta/2} n}{(\epsilon|S_t|)^\delta}, 1\right\} \quad (2)$$

where $\alpha_\delta = c(2(c+1))^{\delta/2}$, for any $c > 3/2$.

As before, we start with the single site ($k=1$) case. We have the following theorem (proof in Technical report [15]).

THEOREM 3.5. *For the single site ($k = 1$) case, the randomized algorithm Non-monotonic Counter with the sampling probability as in (2) guarantees to track the count within the relative accuracy $\epsilon > 0$ with probability $1 - 1/n$ for every $1/2 \leq H \leq 1/\delta$, where $1 < \delta \leq 2$, with the total expected communication of $O(n^{1-H}/\epsilon \cdot \log^{1/2+1/\delta} n)$ messages.*

We observe that for standard Brownian motion, which we may interpret as a continuous-time analog of a random walk, we have $H = 1/\delta = 1/2$, and in this case, the sampling probability and the result of the last theorem matches that of Theorem 3.1. For values of the Hurst parameter H in $(1/2, 1)$, the communication complexity of the algorithm is sublinear in n, with the upper bound increasing with n as a polynomial with the exponent decreasing with H as $1 - H$ (up to a poly-logarithmic factor). Note that this is inline with the intuition as a larger value of the parameter H means a larger variance and thus less of a concentration around value zero where the relative error tolerance is the most stringent.

Multiple sites. Finally, we look at the case with multiple sites. Let the sampling probability be as in (2) but with constant $\gamma_{\alpha,\delta}$ redefined as follows $\alpha_\delta = 9 \cdot 2^{\delta/2}(c+1)^{1+\delta/2}$, for any $c > 3/2$. Using the same coupling argument as in Theorem 3.3, we have the following corollary (proof in [15].)

COROLLARY 3.6. *The randomized algorithm Non-monotonic Counter, with the sampling probability given in (1), guarantees to track the count across k sites within the relative accuracy $\epsilon > 0$ with probability $1 - O(1/n)$ for every $1/2 \leq H \leq 1/\delta$, where $1 < \delta \leq 2$, with the total expected communication of $\tilde{O}(n^{1-H} k^{\frac{3-\delta}{2}}/\epsilon)$ messages*

4. LOWER BOUNDS

In this section, we establish matching lower bounds for the two cases of inputs: i.i.d. Bernoulli and random permutation. Recall that we denote with M_n the number of messages exchanged over an input of size n. We are interested in the lower bounds on the expected number of messages $E[M_n]$ that is necessary to track the value over an interval of n updates within ϵ relative accuracy with high probability. We use sample-path arguments to prove the results.

We start by presenting lower bounds for the single site case, first without and then with a drift. We then provide our main results that provides a lower bound parameterized with the number of sites k for the case without drift. We conclude by giving a lower bound for the case with random permutation input stream.

THEOREM 4.1. *Consider the single site ($k = 1$) continual count-tracking problem for an input of n random i.i.d. updates without a drift ($\Pr[X_i = 1] = \Pr[X_i = -1] = 1/2$) within relative accuracy $\epsilon > 0$ with probability at least $1 - O(1/n)$. Then the expected number of messages exchanged is $\Omega(\min\{\sqrt{n}/\epsilon, n\})$.*

Proof is provided in Technical report [15] . The key idea of the proof is the observation that whenever the value of the counter is in $\mathcal{E} = \{s \in \mathbb{Z} : |s| \le 1/\epsilon\}$, the site must report the value to the coordinator as otherwise an error would occur with a constant probability. The proof then follows by noting that $\sum_{t \le n} \Pr[S_t \in \mathcal{E}] = \Omega(\sqrt{n}/\epsilon)$.

The lower bound in Theorem 4.1 is established by counting the average number of visits to the set $\mathcal{E}$, and we can use the same argument to establish a lower bound for the general case of Bernoulli updates with with an arbitrary drift $-1 < \mu < 1$ (that is $0 < p < 1$). Intuitively, the no drift case should be the worst case with respect to communication complexity as observed in Section 3. Also, for any constant $\mu > 0$ we expect to have the lower bound similar to the bound from [12] for a monotonic counter $E[M_n] = \Omega(1/\epsilon)$. It is thus of interest to ask what the lower bound would be for small but non-zero drift $\mu = o(1)$. We have the following result (proof in Technical report [15]).

THEOREM 4.2. *Consider the single site ($k = 1$) continual count-tracking with Bernoulli random walk updates with drift $\mu = o(1)$ and relative accuracy parameter $\epsilon > 0$. Suppose $\epsilon = \omega(1/\sqrt{n})$ and $|\mu| = O(\epsilon)$. Then, for the tracking to succeed with probability at least $1 - O(1/n)$, the expected number of messages is $\Omega\left(\min\left\{\sqrt{n}, \frac{1}{|\mu|}\right\} \cdot \frac{1}{\epsilon}\right)$.*

The result is in line with the intuition that any non-zero drift may only reduce the communication complexity, and it matches the bound in [12] for large enough μ. Our lower bound matches the corresponding upper bound result (presented in Technical report [15]) up to poly-logarithmic factors.

We now move to the main result of this section which provides a lower bound that is parameterized with the number of sites k. We consider only the non-drift case, as this is used to establish the lower bound for the permutation model. While the proof for $k = 1$ case essentially only needs to exploit the structure of a simple random walk, here we need to carefully integrate techniques from communication complexity theory with the structure of random walks. The main step is a reduction to a query problem (Lemma 4.4) that at a time instance asks whether the sum of updates over all k sites is larger than or equal to a $\Theta(\sqrt{k})$ threshold, which requires $\Omega(k)$ communication to guarantee a sufficiently low probability of error; otherwise, the overall error probability does not satisfy the requirements.

We start our analysis by introducing a building block for communication complexity.

DEFINITION 4.3 (TRACKING k INPUTS). *Let c be a constant. Consider the following functional monitoring problem: let X_1, X_2,*

..., X_k *be i.i.d. variables from $\{-1, 1\}$ such that $\Pr[X_i = -1] = \Pr[X_i = 1] = 1/2$ that arrive uniformly to each of the sites (i.e. each site receives exactly one update). Upon the arrival of the last update, we require the coordinator to*

- *be able to tell whether the sum is positive or negative if $|\sum_{i \le k} X_i| \ge c\sqrt{k}$.*

- *do anything (i.e. no requirement) when $|\sum_{i \le k} X_i| < c\sqrt{k}$.*

We have the following lemma.

LEMMA 4.4. *Solving the tracking k inputs problem with probability $1 - c_0$ (w.r.t. both the protocol and the input) for some constant c_0 requires $\Theta(k)$ communication.*

We provide a proof in Technical report [15] that is based on the same main ideas as in the proof of Lemma 2.2 in [12] with some minor technical differences to account for particularities of our setting.

We are now ready to present our main lower bound theorem for the k-site case.

THEOREM 4.5. *For the case of $k < n$ sites, the expected amount of communicated messages to guarantee relative accuracy $\epsilon > 0$ with probability at least $1 - O(1/n)$ is $\Omega(\min\{\sqrt{kn}/\epsilon, n\})$.*

Proof is provided in Technical report [15] . Here, again our lower bound matches the corresponding upper bound presented in Theorem 3.3. The intuition behind the result is as follows. We chop the stream into phases of k updates each, where each site gets exactly one update per phase. If the counter value S_t is in between $-\sqrt{k}/\epsilon$ and $\sqrt{k}/\epsilon$, we show that our problem is equivalent to the tracking of k input problems, and $\Theta(k)$ messages need to be sent to guarantee correctness. Summing the expected number of visits of the counter to these states, we obtain the lower bound.

Random Permutation. Finally, we have the following corollary providing a lower bound on the communication complexity for randomly permuted input stream (proof in [15]).

COROLLARY 4.6. *The expected total communication in presence of a randomly permuted adversarial input, with $-1 \le a_t \le 1$ for all $1 \le t \le n$, is at least $\Omega(\sqrt{kn}/\epsilon)$ messages.*

5. APPLICATIONS

5.1 Tracking the Second Frequency Moment

We now apply our distributed counter algorithms for continuously tracking second frequency moment of the randomly ordered stream. Let us recall the F_2 problem. The input stream consists of $a_1, a_2, ..., a_n$, where $a_t = (\alpha_t, z_t)$, α_t are all items from the universe $[m]$, and $z_t \in \{-1, 1\}$ for all $t \le n$. Denote with $m_i(t) = \sum_{s \le t : \alpha_s = i} z_s$ the sum of elements of type i in the stream at time t. Here, we allow the count $m_i(t)$ to be non-monotonic in t (i.e. allow decrements of the counts). Our goal is to continuously track the second moment of the stream, i.e. $F_2(t) = \sum_{i \le m} m_i^2(t)$, at the coordinator. We shall refer to this problem as *monitoring $F_2(t)$ with decrements*.

Next, we review the fast AMS sketching algorithm for this problem (see [4] and references therein). Consider a set of counters $(S_{i,j})_{i \le I, j \le J}$ whose values at the t-th update are $S_{ij}(t)$, and set $S_{ij}(0) = 0$. Let $g_j : [m] \to \{-1, 1\}$ and $h_j : [m] \to J$ (for $j \le I$) be two sets of 4-wise independent hash functions. Upon receiving the t-th item (α_t, z_t), we add $z_t \cdot g_j(\alpha_t)$ to all

$(S_{j,h_j(\alpha_t)}(t))_{j \le I}$. When $I = O(\log 1/\delta)$ and $J = O(1/\epsilon^2)$, we are able to recover F_2 with ϵ-relative guarantee with prob. $1 - \delta$ for a specific t. We can then execute $\log n$ copies of the fast AMS sketches in parallel to make sure our estimator is correct for all updates.

An important property of fast AMS sketching is that it updates only $O(\log(1/\delta) + \log n) = \tilde{O}(1)$ counters after each update. Let $n_i = \sum_{s \le n} \mathrm{II}\{\alpha_s = i\}$ be the number of occurencies of item i in the stream until time t. Clearly, $\sum_{i \in [m]} n_i = n$. Further, let $\tilde{N}_{ij} = \{k \in [m] : h_j(k) = i\}$ be the set of items that map to the counter S_{ij}. Tracking counter S_{ij} in randomly ordered stream takes $\tilde{O}(\sqrt{k \sum_{k \in \tilde{N}_{ij}} n_k}/\epsilon)$ communication. Summing over all counter, and using Jensen inequality, we get that the expected total number of communicated messages is $\tilde{O}(\sqrt{kn}/\epsilon^2)$. We also remark that the lower bound $\Omega(\sqrt{kn}/\epsilon)$ for counter in randomly ordered stream is also a lower bound for $F_2(\cdot)$ for randomly ordered streams. We may summarize the upper bound and the lower bound results in the following corollary.

COROLLARY 5.1. *The communication lower bound for tracking the frequency moment $F_2(t)$ with decrements in randomly ordered stream is $\Omega(\min\{\sqrt{kn}/\epsilon, n\})$. There exists a randomized algorithm for tracking $F_2(t)$ using the total expected communication of $\tilde{O}(\sqrt{kn}/\epsilon^2)$ messages.*

5.2 Bayesian Linear Regression

We next describe another application of a distributed non-monotonic counter in tracking the posterior of the coefficients in a *Bayesian linear regression*. Recall the Bayesian linear regression problem (c.f. [2]): assume we are given a set of training data $(\mathbf{x}_1, y_1), (\mathbf{x}_2, y_2), \ldots, (\mathbf{x}_n, y_n)$, where $\mathbf{x}_i$ is a row-vector $\mathbf{x}_i \in \mathbb{R}^d$ and $y_i \in \mathbb{R}$. We are interested in carrying out a linear regression over this data, i.e. finding a $\mathbf{w} \in \mathbb{R}^d$ such that $y = \mathbf{w}^T \cdot \mathbf{x}$ best fits the training data $\{(\mathbf{x}_t, y_t)\}_{t \le n}$. Furthermore, we impose an initial prior knowledge over the vector $\mathbf{w}_0$, and in particular we assume that it follows a multivariate Gaussian distribution $\mathbf{w}_0 \sim \mathcal{N}(\mathbf{m}_0, S_0)$. Our goal is to maintain a posterior belief over $\mathbf{w}_t$, as the training data $\{(\mathbf{x}_t, y_t)\}_{t \le n}$ arrives.

In the distributed functional monitoring setting, the training data $\{(\mathbf{x}_t, y_t)\}_{t \le n}$ arrives at different sites in a streaming fashion and the coordinator has to continuously track an approximate estimate of the mean $\mathbf{m}_t$ and the variance S_t of $\mathbf{w}_t$. We assume that the training data is an arbitrary bounded sequence selected by an adversary, and randomly permuted, as in the random permutation model.

We next describe how we may use $O(d^2)$ counters to track the posterior belief. Let A_t be an $t \times d$ matrix so that the i-th column of A_t is $\mathbf{x}_i$. Also, denote with $\mathbf{y}_t \in \mathbb{R}^t$ a vector whose i-th component is y_i. Furthermore, let β be the inverse of the variance of the noise variable in the model, i.e., $y_t = \mathbf{w}^T \cdot A_t + \mathcal{N}(0, \beta^{-1})$. The value of β is usually assumed to be a known parameter (see Bishop [2] for a detailed description of the model). It turns out that the posterior of $\mathbf{w}$ is also a Gaussian distribution with mean $\mathbf{m}_t$ and variance S_t, where

$$\begin{aligned} \mathbf{m}_t &= S_t(S_0^{-1}\mathbf{m}_0 + \beta A_t^T \mathbf{y}_t) \\ S_t^{-1} &= S_0^{-1} + \beta A_t^T A_t. \end{aligned} \quad (3)$$

The inverse of S_t^{-1} at time t is also referred as the *precision matrix*. Observe that tracking the precision matrix S_t^{-1} as well as the vector $A_t^T \mathbf{y}$ suffices to recover the posterior structure of $\mathbf{w}$. Our specific goal here is to continuously track S_t^{-1} and $A_t^T \mathbf{y}_t$ by using our counter algorithm.

Upon the arrival of the $t + 1$-st update, we have

$$S_{t+1}^{-1} = S_t^{-1} + \beta \underbrace{x_{t+1}^T x_{t+1}}_{\text{outer product of } x_{t+1}}$$

and $A_{t+1}^T \mathbf{y}_{t+1} = A_t^T \mathbf{y}_t + (y_{t+1} \times (x_{t+1})_1, y_{t+1} \times (x_{t+1})_2, \ldots, y_{t+1} \times (x_{t+1})_d)^T$.

Therefore, to track $S_t^{-1} \in \mathbb{R}^{d \times d}$, it suffices to keep d^2 counters $\{C_{i,j}\}_{i,j \le d}$ such that upon the arrival of the t-th training data, $C_{i,j} \leftarrow C_{i,j} + \beta(x_t)_i(x_t)_j$. Similarly, we may keep another d copies of counters $\{D_i\}_{i \le d}$ to track $A_t^T \mathbf{y}_t$, where $D_i \leftarrow D_i + y_t \times (x_t)_i$ at the t-th update. Notice that here our algorithm can guarantee each entry in S_t^{-1} and $A_t^T \mathbf{y}$ has at most ϵ-relative error. The actual error of our estimate for $\mathbf{m}_t$, however, also depends on how sensitive of the precision matrix's inverse is when it is perturbed.

The total communication complexity using this algorithm thus is $\tilde{O}(\sqrt{kn}d^2/\epsilon)$, being sublinear in the size of training data for a wide range of parameters.

Acknowledgments

We thank Zengfeng Huang, Ke Yi and Qin Zhang for useful discussions regarding the relation of Lemma 2.2 in [12] and the lower bound for the sampling problem in Lemma 4.4. We thank Graham Cormode for pointing out how to improve the bound for F_2 tracking using the fast AMS sketching.

6. REFERENCES

[1] C. Arackaparambil, J. Brody, and A. Chakrabarti. Functional monitoring without monotonicity. In *Proc. of ICALP*, 2009.

[2] C. Bishop. *Pattern Recognition and Machine Learning*. Springer, 2006.

[3] G. Cormode and M. Garofalakis. Sketching streams through the net: Distributed approximate query tracking. In *Proc. of International Conference on Very Large Databases*, 2005.

[4] G. Cormode, M. Garofalakis, P. J. Haas, and C. Jermaine. Synopses for massive data: Samples, histograms, wavelets, sketches. *Foundations and Trends in Databases*, 2011.

[5] G. Cormode, M. Garofalakis, S. Muthukrishnan, and R. Rastogi. Holistic aggregates in a networked world: Distributed tracking of approximate quantiles. In *Proc. of SIGMOD*, June 2005.

[6] G. Cormode, S. Muthhukrishnan, and W. Zhuang. What's different: Distributed, continuous monitoring of duplicate-resilient aggregates on data streams. In *Proc. IEEE International Conference on Data Engineering*, 2006.

[7] G. Cormode, S. Muthukrishnan, and K. Yi. Algorithms for distributed functional monitoring. In *Proc. of SODA*, 2008.

[8] G. Cormode, S. Muthukrishnan, K. Yi, and Q. Zhang. Optimal sampling from distributed streams. In *Proc. of PODS*, June 2010.

[9] M. B. Greenwald and S. Khanna. Space-efficient online computation of quantile summaries. In *Proc. of SIGMOD*, pages 58–66, 2001.

[10] M. B. Greenwald and S. Khanna. Power-conserving computation of order-statistics over sensor networks. In *Proc. of PODS*, 2004.

[11] W. Hoeffding. Probability inequalities for sums of bounded random variables. *American Statistical Association Journal*, pages 13–30, March 1963.

[12] Z. Huang, K. Yi, and Q. Zhang. Randomized algorithms for tracking distributed count, frequencies, and ranks. In *arXiv:1108.3413v1*, Aug 2011.

[13] T. Konstantopoulos. *Markov Chains and Random Walks*. Lecture notes, 2009.

[14] W. Leland, M. Taqqu, W. Willinger, and D. Wilson. On the self-similar nature of ethernet traffic. *IEEE/ACM Transactions on Networking*, 2(1):1–15, 1994.

[15] Z. Liu, B. Radunović, and R. Vojnović. Continuous distributed counting for non-monotonic streams. In *Technical Report MSR-TR-2011-128*, 2011.

[16] Y. Low, J. Gonzalez, A. Kyrola, D. Bickson, C. Guestrin, and J. Hellerstein. Graphlab: A new framework for parallel machine learning. In *Proc. of the 26th Conference on Uncertainty in Artificial Intelligence (UAI)*, 2010.

[17] S. Muthukrishnan. Data streams: Algorithms and applications. *Foundations and Trends in Computer Science*, 2005.

[18] C. Olston, J. Jiang, and J. Widom. Adaptive filters for continuous queries over distributed data streams. In *Proc. ACM SIGMOD International Conference on Management of Data*, 2003.

[19] G. Samorodnitsky and M. S. Taqqu. *Stable non-Gaussian random processes*. Chapman & Hall, 1994.

[20] R. J. Serfling. Probability inequalities for the sum in sampling without replacement. *Ann. Statist*, 2(1):39–48, 1974.

[21] T. S. Team. The engineering behind twitter's new search experience, 2011.

[22] S. Trithapura and D. P. Woodruff. Optimal random sampling from distributed streams revisited. In *Proc. of DISC*, Roma, Italy, Sep 2011.

[23] K. Yi and Q. Zhang. Optimal tracking of distributed heavy hitters and quantiles. In *Proc. of PODS*, June 2009.

APPENDIX

A.   ADDITIONAL NOTATIONS

We will repeatedly use some notation in the rest of the appendices which we summarize in the following. We will denote the sampling probability in SBC for the t-th update with $p_t = $ Sample-Prob$(\hat{S}_t, t)$. For an algorithm, we define E_n to be the number of errors observed over an input of size n. We will be interested in algorithms such that $\Pr[E_n > 0] = O(1/n)$. We define M_n to be the number of messages transmitted over an input of size n. We note that it is sufficient to limit the size of a message to $O(\log n)$ bits to convey any possible counter value. Thus the number of bits transmitted over an input of size n is $\tilde{\Theta}(M_n)$. We define R_t to be 1 if a message is sent to the coordinator and otherwise $R_t = 0$. We further denote with U_t the time until next message is sent to the coordinator as observed at time t. Similarly, we define V_t to be the time until the count process exits the ball $\mathbf{B}_\epsilon(S_t) = \{s \in \mathbb{Z} : |x - S_t| \le \epsilon S_t\}$.

For the purpose of exposition, we will first start with the most fundamental case with Bernoulli i.i.d. increments. Recall that in this case $\Pr[X_t = 1] = p$ and $\Pr[X_t = -1] = 1 - p$. The expected increment in each step is then $\mu \triangleq p - (1 - p) = 2p - 1$. We shall refer to μ as the *drift* of the problem. We will first treat the case without drift ($\mu = 0$ and $p = 1/2$) and then the general case with an unknown drift. The analysis for other distributions heavily utilizes the idea developed for these simple cases.

B.   ANALYSIS FOR I.I.D. INPUT WITH ZERO DRIFT

B.1   Single Site Case

In this subsection, we prove Theorem 3.1.

Communication cost. We first show that the expected number of communicated messages is bounded as asserted. Let $\vartheta = \sqrt{\alpha}/\epsilon \cdot \log n$ and note

$$\mathrm{E}[R_t] = \Pr[|S_t| \le \vartheta] + \vartheta^2 \mathrm{E}[\frac{1}{S_t^2} I(|S_t| > \vartheta)].$$

Since $\Pr[|S_t| \le \vartheta] = \Theta(\vartheta/\sqrt{t})$ and $\mathrm{E}[\frac{1}{S_t^2} I(|S_t| > \vartheta)] = \Theta(1/(\vartheta\sqrt{t}))$, it follows

$$\mathrm{E}[R_t] = \Theta(\vartheta/\sqrt{t}).$$

Hence, the expected number of transmitted messages is

$$\sum_{t \le n} \mathrm{E}[R_t] = O(\vartheta\sqrt{n}) = O(\sqrt{n}/\epsilon \cdot \log n).$$

Correctness. We next establish the asserted bound on the probability of error. Let us write $\mathcal{F}_t$ to be the σ-algebra generated by $X_1, \ldots, X_t$ and $R_1, \ldots, R_t$, i.e. all the information available up to the t-th update is measurable by $\mathcal{F}_t$. Define the indicator variable R_t that sets to 1 if and only if at the t-th update the site sends a message to the coordinator. Notice that our algorithm guarantees that $R_1 = 1$. Let U_t be the number of updates until the next report is sent to the coordinator as observed at the t-th update, i.e. $U_t = \min\{\tau > 0 : R_{t+\tau} = 1\}$. We remark that U_t depends on a future event and thus, it is not measurable by $\mathcal{F}_t$. Next, let $V_t = \min\{\tau > 0 : S_{t+\tau} \notin \mathbf{B}_\epsilon(S_t)\}$ be the number of updates until the first instance at which the coordinator fails to track the counter within the relative accuracy ϵ, and let E_n be the number of such update instances. Notice that a necessary and sufficient condition that at least one error happens is that there exists at least one $t \le n$ such that $R_t = 1$ and $V_t < U_t$. We thus have

$$\Pr[E_n > 0] = \Pr[R_t = 1 \text{ and } V_t < U_t, \text{ for some } 1 \le t \le n],$$

where $I(\cdot)$ is an indicator function that sets to 1 if and only if its parameter is true. By using the union bound, we have

$$\Pr[E_n > 0] \le \sum_{t \le n} \mathrm{E}[R_t \cdot I(V_t < U_t)]. \tag{4}$$

Using the fact that R_t is measurable by $\mathcal{F}_t$, we have

$$
\begin{aligned}
\mathrm{E}[R_t \cdot I(V_t < U_t)] &= \mathrm{E}_{\mathcal{F}_t}[\mathrm{E}[R_t I(V_t < U_t) \mid \mathcal{F}_t]] \\
&= \mathrm{E}_{\mathcal{F}_t}[R_t \mathrm{E}[I(V_t < U_t) \mid \mathcal{F}_t]] \\
&= \mathrm{E}_{\mathcal{F}_t}[R_t \Pr[V_t < U_t \mid S_t]] \\
&\le \mathrm{E}_{\mathcal{F}_t}\left[R_t \cdot \max_s \Pr[V_t < U_t \mid S_t = s]\right] \\
&= \mathrm{E}_{\mathcal{F}_t}[R_t] \cdot \max_s \Pr[V_t < U_t \mid S_t = s].
\end{aligned}
$$

We next proceed to give an upper bound for $\Pr[V_t < U_t \mid S_t = s]$. Note that for every $r \ge 0$, it holds

$$
\begin{aligned}
&\Pr[V_t < U_t \mid S_t = s] \\
={}& \Pr[V_t < U_t, V_t > r \mid S_t = s] \\
&+ \Pr[V_t < U_t, V_t \le r \mid S_t = s] \\
\le{}& \Pr[r < U_t \mid S_t = s, V_t > r] + \Pr[V_t \le r \mid S_t = s] \quad (5)
\end{aligned}
$$

We start by giving a bound on $\Pr[V_t \le r \mid S_t = s]$. Notice that under $S_t = s$ the distribution of V_t is equal to the distribution of the first passage time of either value $\lceil s/(1-\epsilon)\rceil - s$ or value $\lfloor s/(1+\epsilon)\rfloor - s$ for a symmetric random walk started at the origin. The following lemma follows by standard results from the theory of random walks (c.f. [13]) and the Hoeffding bound:

LEMMA B.1. *For every $r \geq 0$, it holds*

$$\Pr[V_t \leq r \mid S_t = s] \leq 2\exp(-\frac{(\frac{\epsilon}{1-\epsilon})^2 s^2}{2r}). \quad (6)$$

PROOF. Let V_t^+ denote the number of steps until the random walk up-crosses the value $\lceil\frac{s}{1-\epsilon}\rceil$, starting from value s. Similarly, we define V_t^- to be the number of steps until the random walk down-crosses the value $\lfloor\frac{s}{1+\epsilon}\rfloor$ starting from value s. Then,

$$\Pr[V_t \leq r|S_t = s] \leq \Pr[V_t^+ \leq r|S_t = s] + \Pr[V_t^- \leq r|S_t = s]$$
$$\leq 2\Pr[V_t^+ \leq r|S_t = s].$$

Now, let $b = \lceil\frac{s}{1-\epsilon}\rceil - s$ and note that by the reflection principle of random walks, we have

$$\Pr[V_t^+ \leq r|S_t = s] = \Pr[X_1 + X_2 + \cdots + X_r = b]$$
$$+ 2\Pr[X_1 + X_2 + \cdots + X_r > b]$$
$$\leq 2\Pr[X_1 + X_2 + \cdots + X_r \geq b].$$

By applying the Hoeffding's inequality, we bound the the probability in the right-hand side with $\exp(-\frac{b^2}{2r})$ which yields the asserted result. $\square$

From (6), we observe that $\Pr[V_t \leq r \mid S_t = s] \leq 2/n^c$ for given $c > 0$, iff it holds

$$\text{(C1):} \quad r \leq \frac{1}{2c\log n}\left(\frac{\epsilon}{1-\epsilon}\right)^2 s^2.$$

We next note

$$\Pr[r < U_t|S_t = s, V_t > r] \leq (1 - \rho_\epsilon(s))^r \quad (7)$$

where $\rho_\epsilon(s) = \text{Sample-Prob}(s/(1-\epsilon), t)$. Requiring that the right-hand side in the above inequality is less than or equal to $1/n^c$, we obtain

$$\text{(C2):} \quad \rho_\epsilon(s) \geq 1 - \exp(-\frac{c\log n}{(1-\epsilon)^2 r}).$$

Indeed, both conditions (C1) and (C2) hold true by taking $r = \frac{1}{2c\log n}\left(\frac{\epsilon}{1-\epsilon}\right)^2 s^2$ and $\rho_\epsilon(s) = \min\{\frac{2c^2\log^2 n}{(\epsilon s)^2}, 1\}$. The latter choice is a sufficient condition for (C2) in view of the fact that $\min\{x, 1\} \geq 1 - e^{-x}$, for $x \geq 0$. Therefore, we showed that for $\Pr[V_t < U_t|S_t = s] \leq 3/n^c$ to hold, it suffices that the sampling probability satisfies

$$p_t \geq \min\{\frac{2c^2\log n}{\epsilon^2 S_t^2}, 1\}. \quad (8)$$

Combining with (4), we have

$$\Pr[E_n > 0] \leq \sum_{t \leq n} \mathrm{E}[R_t] \cdot O(1/n^c)$$
$$= \Theta(\vartheta n^{1/2-c}) = \Theta(n^{1/2-c}\log n).$$

From the last inequality, we note that no error occurs with high probability provided that $c > 3/2$. Hence, in view of the inequality (8), it suffices to to choose the sampling probability as in (1) with $\alpha = 2c^2 > 9/2$ and $\beta = 2$. This completes the proof.

B.2 Multiple Sites

In this subsection, we prove Theorem 3.2. We need again to show that the algorithm is correct and the communication complexity is as described. We start with showing the correctness part.

Correctness. We will invoke a coupling argument that will allow us to reuse the results of Theorem 3.1. We couple the proposed multiple sites algorithm with the single site sampling algorithm with a different set of error parameters over the same set of input. Specifically, we also execute a single site algorithm with relative accuracy $\epsilon/3$ and success rate $1 - O(1/n^2)^2$, in parallel to the multiple sites algorithm over the same input sequence. We shall couple the random tosses in these two algorithms and show that when the single site algorithm makes no error, our multiple sites algorithm will also make no error.

We need a few more notations. Let $p_{s,i}$ be the sampling rate for the single site algorithm and $R_{s,i}$ be its corresponding Bernoulli random variable. Let $p_{m,i}$ be the sampling rate for the multiple sites algorithm and $R_{m,i}$ be its corresponding Bernoulli random variable. When we are in the straightforward stage, we shall assume $p_{m,i} = 1$. Finally, let $\hat{S}_{s,t}$ be the estimator of the single site algorithm at time t and $\hat{S}_{m,t}$ be the estimator for the multiple sites algorithm.

We couple the Bernoulli random variable in the following way.

- When $p_{s,i} > p_{m,i}$: the two Bernoulli variables are sampled independently.

- When $p_{s,i} \leq p_{m,i}$: if $R_{s,i} = 1$, then we set $R_{m,i} = 1$; otherwise, we set $R_{m,i} = 1$ with probability $(p_{m,i} - p_{s,i})/(1 - p_{s,i})$ and $R_{m,i} = 0$ otherwise. One may see that we still have $\Pr[R_{m,i} = 1] = p_{m,i}$.

Now using the above coupling rules, we show that when the single site makes no error, our multiple sites algorithm also makes no error. Suppose on the contrary that at time t the multiple sites algorithm makes the first error. Then our algorithm ensures that for every $\tau < t$, it holds $p_{m,\tau} \geq p_{s,\tau}$ (by our choice of sampling probabilities), i.e. the multiple sites algorithm samples more frequently than the single site algorithm. Therefore, our coupling rule gives us $\hat{S}_{m,t} = S_{t_1}$ and $\hat{S}_{s,t} = S_{t_2}$, where $t_1 > t_2$, i.e. the multiple sites algorithm is holding a more recent value of the count. We can now get a contradiction using the following arguments,

1. At time t_2, the single site algorithm's estimator is S_{t_1} and is correct. Therefore, $S_{t_1} \in \mathbf{B}_{\epsilon_3}(S_{t_2})$, i.e.

$$|S_{t_2} - S_{t_1}| \leq \frac{\epsilon}{3}|S_{t_2}|. \quad (9)$$

2. At time t, the multiple site algorithm is wrong. Therefore, $S_{t_1} \notin \mathbf{B}_\epsilon(S_t)$, i.e.

$$|S_{t_1} - S_t| > \epsilon|S_t|. \quad (10)$$

3. At time t, the single site algorithm is correct, i.e. $S_{t_2} \in \mathbf{B}_\epsilon(S_t)$. We have $|S_{t_2} - S_t| \leq \epsilon|S_t|$. We can use $\epsilon \leq 1$ to relax this inequality and get

$$|S_{t_2}| \leq 2|S_t|. \quad (11)$$

Using (9) and (10) and a triangle inequality, we have

$$|S_{t_2} - S_t| > \epsilon|S_t| - \frac{\epsilon}{3}|S_{t_2}| \geq \epsilon|S_t| - \frac{2\epsilon}{3}|S_t| \geq \frac{\epsilon}{3}|S_t|. \quad (12)$$

---

[2]To boost the success rate, we need to use a larger constant in the sampling parameter, i.e. Sample-Prob$(\hat{S}_t, t) = \min\left\{\frac{2(1+c)^2\log^2 n}{\epsilon^2 \hat{S}_t^2}, 1\right\}$, any $c > 3/2$

The second inequality holds because of (11). (12) implies that the single site algorithm errs at time t, which contradicts with our assumption.

Communication cost. We have the following types of communications,

1. At the straightforward stage, whenever there is an update, $O(1)$ messages are exchanged.

2. At the broadcast stage, whenever there is an update, $O(k)$ messages are exchanged.

3. At the beginning and the end of the broadcasting stage, the coordinator needs to make a broadcast to signal the stage change, which takes $\Theta(k)$ messages.

Notice that in order to change from the broadcast stage to straightforward stage, type 2 messages are sent for at least once. Therefore, the total complexity of the type 3 messages is asymptotically smaller than type 2 messages. We need to only focus on the communication complexity for the first two type of messages.

Let C_t be the communication cost associated with the t-th update and let $R_{m,t}$ indicates the event that a message is sent to the communicator after the t-th update ($R_{m,t}$ shall correspond with R_t in Theorem 3.1). Therefore, when $(\epsilon \hat{S}_t)^2 < k$, $C_t = 1$; otherwise, $\mathrm{E}[C_t] = k\mathrm{E}[R_{m,t}]$. We estimate C_t using the following rule:

- If $(1 - \epsilon)(\epsilon S_t)^2 \leq k$, we set $C_t = 1$;
- If $(1 + \epsilon)(\epsilon S_t)^2 > k$, we set $C_t = k\mathrm{E}[R_{m,t}]$.

This rule intuitively gives a conservative guess on which stage we are in (conditioned on the estimator being correct). Notice that when $(1 - \epsilon)(\epsilon S_t)^2 < k < (1 + \epsilon)(\epsilon S_t)^2$, in this case, we can set $C_t = 1 + k\mathrm{E}[R_{m,t}]$ without impacting the asymptotic behavior. The case where our estimator makes an error (and thus the above rules may not give an overestimate of C_t) is an asymptotically smaller term.

We next proceed with computing the expectation of C_t using our overestimation rule,

$$
\begin{aligned}
\mathrm{E}[C_t] \leq &\underbrace{\Pr[S_t \leq \frac{\sqrt{k}}{\epsilon\sqrt{1-\epsilon}}]}_{\text{straightforward stage}} \\
&+ \underbrace{k\mathrm{E}[R_{m,t}I(S_t \geq \frac{\sqrt{k}}{\epsilon\sqrt{1+\epsilon}})]}_{\text{broadcast stage}} \quad (13)\\
&+ \underbrace{O(1/n^2)}_{\text{estimator fails}} \\
= &\; O(\frac{\sqrt{k}\cdot\log n}{\epsilon\sqrt{t}}).
\end{aligned}
$$

We can compute the above terms using Theorem 3.1. Thus, the total communication cost in expectation is $O(\sqrt{nk}/\epsilon \cdot \log^2 n)$.

C. COMMUNICATION COMPLEXITY LOWER BOUNDS

In this section we provide proofs for our results on lower bounds on the communication complexity of the continuous distributed counting problem with non-monotonic input stream.

C.1 Proof of Theorem 4.1

Let $\mathcal{E} = \{s \in \mathbb{Z} : |s| \leq 1/\epsilon\}$. Our crucial observation here is that whenever S_t walks inside the region $\mathcal{E}$ we have $\epsilon|S_t| < 1$ and no errors are allowed. Specifically, let I_t be the indicator random variable that sets to 1 if and only if $S_t \in \mathcal{E}$. Notice

that $\mathrm{E}[I_t] = \Pr[S_t \in \mathcal{E}] = \Omega(|\mathcal{E}|/\sqrt{t}) = \Omega(1/(\sqrt{t}\epsilon))$ and $\mathrm{E}[\sum_{t\leq n} I_t] = \Theta(\min\{\sqrt{n}/\epsilon, n\})$. On the other hand, our error requirement gives us $\Pr[M_n \geq \sum_{t\leq n} I_t] \geq 1 - 1/n$. We can then derive $\mathrm{E}[M_n]$ from $\mathrm{E}[\sum_{t\leq n} I_t]$ using the following argument. Let $\mathcal{A}$ be the subset of the probability space where $M_n \geq \sum_{t\leq n} I_t$ and let $\neg\mathcal{A}$ be the subset where this does not hold. We have

$$
\begin{aligned}
\mathrm{E}[M_n] &\geq \int_{\mathcal{A}} M_n dF \geq \int_{\mathcal{A}} \sum_{t\leq n} I_t dF \\
&= \mathrm{E}[\sum_{t\leq n} I_t] - \int_{\neg\mathcal{A}} \sum_{t\leq n} I_t dF \geq \mathrm{E}[\sum_{t\leq n} I_t] - 1
\end{aligned}
$$

where the last equality follows from the facts that $\sum_{t\leq n} I_t \leq n$ by construction, and that $\int_{\neg\mathcal{A}} dF \leq 1/n$.

C.2 Proof of Theorem 4.2

The proof is by direct analysis of the probability of event $S_t \in \mathcal{E} = \{s \in \mathbb{Z} : |s| \leq 1/\epsilon\}$, where the distribution of S_t is given by

$$
\Pr[S_t = s] = \binom{t}{\frac{t+s}{2}} p^{\frac{t+s}{2}} (1-p)^{\frac{t-s}{2}}.
$$

We remark that in the proof it is implicitly assumed that p, μ and ϵ are sequences indexed with n, but we omit to make this explicit in the notation for simplicity of presentation.

For convenience, we introduce the notation $\sigma^2 = \mathrm{Var}[X_1] = 4p(1-p)$ and let $\rho = \sqrt{\frac{p}{1-p}}$. We then have

$$
\Pr[S_t = s] = \sigma^t \frac{1}{2^t} \binom{t}{\frac{t+s}{2}} \rho^s.
$$

Since $\frac{1}{2^t}\binom{t}{\frac{t}{2}} = \sqrt{\frac{2}{\pi}}\frac{1}{\sqrt{t}}$ for $s = o(\sqrt{t})$, we have

$$
\Pr[S_t = s] = \sqrt{\frac{2}{\pi}}\frac{1}{\sqrt{t}}\sigma^t \rho^s \cdot [1 + o(1)], \text{ for } s = o(\sqrt{t}).
$$

In order to simplify the notation and with a slight abuse in the remainder of the proof we omit to write the factor $[1 + o(1)]$.

Let $\theta_0 \geq 0$ and $\theta_1 \geq 0$ be such that $|\theta_0| = o(\sqrt{t})$ and $\theta_1 = o(\sqrt{t})$ and consider $\Pr[S_t \in [-\theta_0, \theta_1]]$, for $t = 1, 2, \ldots, n$. For $1/2 < p < 1$ and $s = o(\sqrt{t})$, we have

$$
\begin{aligned}
\Pr[S_t \in [-\theta_0, \theta_1]] &= \sqrt{\frac{2}{\pi}}\frac{1}{\sqrt{t}}\sigma^t \sum_{s=-\theta_0}^{\theta_1} \rho^s \\
&= \sqrt{\frac{2}{\pi}}\frac{1}{\sqrt{t}}\sigma^t \left(\frac{\rho^{\theta_1+1} - 1 + \rho^{\theta_0+1} - 1}{\rho - 1} - 1\right).
\end{aligned}
$$

Let $E_n[-\theta_0, \theta_1]$ denote the number of visits of the set $[-\theta_0, \theta_1]$ by the counter S_t and let $\tau_n = \omega(\max\{\theta_0, \theta_1\})$. Then, note

$$
\begin{aligned}
\mathrm{E}[E_n[-\theta_0, \theta_1]] &\geq \sum_{t=\tau_n}^{n} \Pr[S_t \in [-\theta_0, \theta_1]] \\
&= \left(\frac{\rho^{\theta_1+1} - 1 + \rho^{\theta_0+1} - 1}{\rho - 1} - 1\right) \cdot \sqrt{\frac{2}{\pi}} \sum_{t=\tau_n}^{n} \frac{1}{\sqrt{t}}\sigma^t.
\end{aligned}
$$

Notice that for every $c > 0$,

$$
\begin{aligned}
\sum_{t=\tau_n}^{n} \frac{1}{\sqrt{t}}e^{-ct} &= \int_{\tau_n}^{n} \frac{1}{\sqrt{t}}e^{-ct} dt \geq \int_{2\sqrt{\tau_n}}^{2\sqrt{n}} e^{-\frac{c}{4}u^2} du \\
&= 2\sqrt{\frac{\pi}{c}}[\Phi(\sqrt{2cn}) - \Phi(\sqrt{2c\tau_n})]
\end{aligned}
$$

where Φ is the distribution of a standard normal random variable.

Therefore,

$$E[E_n[-\theta_0, \theta_1]] \geq \frac{4a_n b_n}{\log^{1/2}(\frac{1}{\sigma^2})} \tag{14}$$

where

$$a_n = \frac{\rho^{\theta_1+1} - 1 + \rho^{\theta_0+1} - 1}{\rho - 1} - 1$$

$$b_n = \Phi(\log^{1/2}(\frac{1}{\sigma^2})\sqrt{n}) - \Phi(\log^{1/2}(\frac{1}{\sigma^2})\sqrt{\tau_n}).$$

Now, we consider the case of a small but non-zero drift $\mu = p - (1 - p) = o(1)$ and $\theta_0 = \theta_1 = 1/\epsilon$ where $1/\epsilon$ is a positive integer. We will assume that $\tau_n = o(n)$ and $\tau_n = \omega(1/\epsilon^2)$, thus $\epsilon = \omega(1/\sqrt{n})$.

It is straightforward to show that the following asymptotes hold:

$$\rho = 1 + \mu + O(\mu^2)$$
$$\rho - 1 = \mu + O(\mu^2)$$
$$\sigma^2 = 1 - \mu^2$$
$$\log(\frac{1}{\sigma^2}) = \mu^2 + O(\mu^3)$$

For the term a_n, it holds

$$a_n = 2\frac{\rho^{\frac{1}{\epsilon}+1} - 1}{\rho - 1} - 1 = \frac{2}{\mu}(e^{\frac{\mu}{\epsilon}} - 1) \cdot [1 + o(1)].$$

Hence, $a_n = \Theta(1/\mu)$, for $\mu = O(\epsilon)$. Notice that for the case $\epsilon = o(\mu)$, a_n grows as $\Omega(e^{\mu/\epsilon})$.

For the term b_n, we observe

$$b_n = \Phi(\log^{1/2}(\frac{1}{\sigma^2})\sqrt{n}) - \Phi(\log^{1/2}(\frac{1}{\sigma^2})\sqrt{\tau_n})$$
$$= [\Phi(\mu\sqrt{n}) - \Phi(\mu\sqrt{\tau_n})] \cdot [1 + o(1)]$$

and is easy to derive that $b_n = \Theta(1)$, for $\mu = O(1/\sqrt{n})$ and $b_n = \Theta(\mu\sqrt{n})$ for $\mu = o(1/\sqrt{n})$. Indeed, these are easy to derive from the above asymptotes and the facts $\Phi(\mu\sqrt{n}) - \Phi(\mu\sqrt{\tau_n}) = 1 - 1/2 = 1/2$ for $\mu = \omega(1/\sqrt{n})$ and $\Phi(\mu\sqrt{n}) - \Phi(\mu\sqrt{\tau_n}) \geq \frac{1}{\sqrt{2\pi}}e^{-\frac{\mu^2 n}{2}}\mu(\sqrt{n} - \sqrt{\tau_n})$.

The assertion of the theorem follows by plugging the derived asymptotes for a_n, b_n and $\log^{1/2}(1/\sigma^2)) = \mu[1 + o(1)]$ into (14).

C.3 Proof of Lemma 4.4

The proof in this section follows that of Lemma 2.2 in [12]. Here, we only need to argue that the communication lower bound still holds for a two round *deterministic* protocol such that

- in the first round, a subset of sites report their individual values to the coordinator;

- in the second round, the coordinator probes a subset of sites to make the decision.

The lemma follows in view of the fact that a randomized protocol can be seen as a distribution over a set of deterministic algorithms. It suffices to consider the case where $o(k)$ messages are sent in the first round, as otherwise we are done with the proof. This essentially reduces the communication complexity problem to a known sampling complexity problem [12]. The only remaining obstacle here is that the input distribution under our consideration is not exactly the same as the one studied in [12]. Therefore, we need to re-establish the sampling lower bound in our setting, which is provided in the remainder of this section.

Let $k' = \Theta(k)$ be the number of sites that have not sent any messages in the first round, and without loss of generality, assume that these sites are $1, 2, \ldots, k'$. Since the number of messages sent in the first round is $o(k)$, in the second round, we need to solve a problem that is at least as hard as the following one:

- answer whether the sum $\sum_{i \leq k} X_i$ is positive or negative, if $|\sum_{i \leq k'} X_i| \geq c\sqrt{k'}$;

- do anything (i.e. no requirement) when $|\sum_{i \leq k'} X_i| < c\sqrt{k'}$

where c is a positive constant.

Let us denote with z the number of sites that are sampled by the coordinator in the second round, and without loss of generality, let us assume that these sites are $1, 2, \ldots, z$. To contradict, let us suppose $z = o(k')$. Let $N = \sum_{i \leq z} X_i$ be the cumulative update value of the sampled sites and $U = \sum_{z < i \leq k'} X_i$ be the cumulative update value of the unsampled sites. Clearly, the optimal detection algorithm for the sampling problem is to declare $\sum_{i \leq k'} X_i > c\sqrt{k'}$ if $N > 0$, to declare $\sum_{i \leq k'} X_i < -c\sqrt{k'}$ if $N < 0$ and to declare either (with probability $1/2$) if $N = 0$. The probability of error is then

$$\Pr[\text{error}] \geq \Pr[N < 0, N + U \geq c\sqrt{k'}]$$
$$\geq \Pr[-c\sqrt{z} \leq N < 0]\Pr[U \geq c(\sqrt{k'} + \sqrt{z})].$$

Since N is a sum of independent and identically distributed random variables of mean zero and variance 1, we have $E[N] = 0$ and $\text{Var}[N] = z$, and thus $\Pr[-c\sqrt{z} \leq N < 0] = \Theta(1)$. Similarly, since U is a sum of independent and identically random variables of mean zero and variance 1, we have $E[U] = 0$ and $\text{Var}[U] = k' - z$, and under our assumption $z = o(k')$, it holds $c(\sqrt{k'} + \sqrt{z}) = c\sqrt{k' - z} \cdot [1 + o(1)] = c\text{Var}[U] \cdot [1 + o(1)]$, and thus $\Pr[U \geq c(\sqrt{k'} + \sqrt{z})] = \Theta(1)$. Therefore, the probability of error is $\Omega(1)$ which contradicts the error requirement, for sufficiently small constant c_0 in the statement of the lemma.

C.4 Proof of Theorem 4.5

We partition the updates into n/k phases, each of which consists of k updates. In each phase, the k updates are randomly matched to k sites (so that each site receives exactly one update). Let I_j be an indicator random variable that sets to 1 when, at the beginning of the jth phase, the sum is in the interval $[-a_{j,k,\epsilon}, a_{j,k,\epsilon}]$ where $a_{j,k,\epsilon} \triangleq \min\{\sqrt{k}/\epsilon, \sqrt{jk}\}$. Notice that when the sum is in the interval $[-a_{j,k,\epsilon}, a_{j,k,\epsilon}]$, the additive error we can tolerate is at most $\epsilon\sqrt{k}/\epsilon = \sqrt{k}$. Therefore, at the end of the jth stage, the tracking algorithm has to be able to tell whether the absolute value of j-th phase's sum is below $-\sqrt{k}$, above $\sqrt{k}$, or in between the two. This is at least as difficult as the *tracking k inputs* problem we studied above, with $\Theta(k)$ communication lower bound.

Let M_n be the total number of messages exchanged between the coordinator and the sites. Our correctness requirement gives us $\Pr[M_n \geq \Omega(k\sum_{i \leq n/k} I_i)] \geq 1 - 1/n$. Using the fact that $E[\sum_i I_i] = \min\{\sqrt{n/(\epsilon k)}, n/k\}$, and following similar arguments as in the proof of Theorem 4.1, we get $\Omega(\min\{\sqrt{kn}/\epsilon, n\})$.

C.5 Proof of Corollary 4.6

Consider an adversary that select each input a'_t randomly such that $\Pr[a'_t = 1] = \Pr[a'_t = -1] = 1/2$. Then the process (a_t) obtained by randomly permuting (a'_t) is also a sequence of Bernoulli variables, and from Theorem 4.5 we know that $E[M_n] \geq \Omega(\sqrt{kn}/\epsilon)$. Clearly, using an averaging argument, there is at least one deterministic sequence a'_t that, randomly permuted, requires on average $\Omega(\sqrt{kn}/\epsilon)$ messages. This proves the claim.

Author Index